CASES *and* CONCEPTS

in Comparative Politics

AN INTEGRATED APPROACH

CASES *and* CONCEPTS

in Comparative Politics

AN INTEGRATED APPROACH

PATRICK H. O'NEIL | **KARL FIELDS** | **DON SHARE**

W. W. NORTON & COMPANY

NEW YORK • LONDON

W. W. Norton & Company has been independent since its founding in 1923, when William Warder Norton and Mary D. Herter Norton first published lectures delivered at the People's Institute, the adult education division of New York City's Cooper Union. The firm soon expanded its program beyond the Institute, publishing books by celebrated academics from America and abroad. By midcentury, the two major pillars of Norton's publishing program—trade books and college texts—were firmly established. In the 1950s, the Norton family transferred control of the company to its employees, and today—with a staff of four hundred and a comparable number of trade, college, and professional titles published each year—W. W. Norton & Company stands as the largest and oldest publishing house owned wholly by its employees.

Editor: Peter Lesser
Project Editor: Linda Feldman
Associate Editor: Samantha Held
Managing Editor, College: Marian Johnson
Managing Editor, College Digital Media: Kim Yi
Production Manager: Elizabeth Marotta
Media Editor: Spencer Richardson-Jones
Media Associate Editor: Michael Jaoui
Media Editorial Assistant: Ariel Eaton
Marketing Manager, Political Science: Erin Brown
Design Director: Hope Miller Goodell
Text Design: Lisa Buckley Design
Map Design: Mapping Specialists
Photo Editor: Catherine Abelman
Permissions Manager: Megan Schindel
Composition: Six Red Marbles
Manufacturing: TC–Transcontinental Printing

Permission to use copyrighted material is included on p. A-111

ISBN 978-0-393-63130-2 (pbk.)

W. W. Norton & Company, Inc., 500 Fifth Avenue, New York, NY 10110-0017
wwnorton.com

W. W. Norton & Company Ltd., Castle House, 15 Carlisle Street, London W1D 3BS

1 2 3 4 5 6 7 8 9 0

Brief Contents

Contents

4   POLITICAL ECONOMY   82

UNITED STATES   232

FRANCE   260

GERMANY   292

● JAPAN   322

RUSSIA   416

CHINA 444

10 DEVELOPING COUNTRIES 480

INDIA   510

BRAZIL   600

SOUTH AFRICA   628

About the Authors

PATRICK H. O'NEIL is Distinguished Professor of politics and government at the University of Puget Sound in Tacoma, Washington. He received his Ph.D. in political science from Indiana University. Professor O'Neil's teaching and research interests are in the areas of authoritarianism and democratization. His past research focused on Eastern Europe, and his current research deals with the Middle East, particularly Iran. His publications include the books *Revolution from Within: The Hungarian Socialist Workers' Party and the Collapse of Communism* and *Communicating Democracy: The Media and Political Transitions* (editor).

KARL FIELDS is Distinguished Professor of politics and government and former Director of Asian Studies at the University of Puget Sound in Tacoma, Washington. He has a Ph.D. in political science from the University of California, Berkeley. Professor Fields' teaching and research interests focus on various topics of East Asian political economy, including government-business relations, economic reform, and regional integration. His publications include *Enterprise and the State in Korea and Taiwan*.

DON SHARE is Professor Emeritus of politics and government at the University of Puget Sound in Tacoma, Washington. He has a Ph.D. in political science from Stanford University. He has taught comparative politics and Latin American politics, and has published widely on democratization and Spanish politics. His published books include *The Making of Spanish Democracy* and *Dilemmas of Social Democracy*.

Preface

The past three decades have seen the dramatic transformation of comparative politics: the end of the Cold War and the collapse of the Soviet Union, the spread of democracy around the world, the rise of new economic powers in Asia, the emergence of globalization. For a time, many looked upon these changes as unmitigated progress that would bring about a decline in global conflict and produce widespread prosperity. Recently, however, there has been growing doubt, as the uncertainties of the future seem to portend more risk than reward, more conflict than peace. One can no longer suggest that a country and its citizens can function well without a good understanding of the billions of people who live outside of its borders. Consider the Arab Spring and conflict across the Middle East: Will the region face violence and repression for the foreseeable future, or could the current turmoil eventually pave way for greater stability and democracy? Clearly we ignore such questions at our peril.

This textbook is meant to contribute to our understanding of comparative politics (the study of domestic politics around the world) by investigating the central ideas and questions that make up this field. It begins with the most basic struggle in politics—the battle between freedom and equality and the task of reconciling or balancing these ideals. How this struggle has unfolded across place and time represents the core of comparative politics. The text continues by emphasizing the importance of institutions. Human action is fundamentally guided by the institutions that people construct, such as culture, constitutions, and property rights. Once established, these institutions are both influential and persistent—not easily overcome, changed, or removed. How these institutions emerge, and how they affect politics, is central to this work.

With these ideas in place, we tackle the basic institutions of power—states, markets, societies, democracies, and nondemocratic regimes. What are states, how do they emerge, and how can we measure their capacity, autonomy, and efficacy? How do markets function, and what kinds of relationships exist between states and markets? How do societal components like nationalism, ethnicity, and ideology shape political values? And what are the main differences between democratic and nondemocratic regimes, and what explains why one or the other predominates in various parts of the world? These are a few of the questions we will attempt to answer.

Alongside an in-depth exploration of these concepts and questions, we will apply them directly to thirteen political systems (we call them *cases*)—developed democracies, communist and postcommunist countries, and developing countries. Selecting only thirteen cases is, of course, fraught with drawbacks. Nevertheless, we believe that this collection represents countries that are both important in their own right and representative of a broad range of political systems. Each of the 13 cases has special importance in the context of the study of comparative politics. Five of our cases (France, Germany, Japan, the United States, and the United Kingdom) are advanced industrial democracies, but they represent a wide range of institutions, societies, political-economic models, and relationships with the world. Japan is an important example of a non-Western industrialized democracy and an instructive case of democratization imposed by foreign occupiers. Though the United Kingdom and the United States have been known for political stability, France and Germany have fascinating histories of political turmoil and regime change.

Two of our cases, China and Russia, share a past of Marxist-Leninist totalitarianism. Communism thrived in these two large and culturally distinct nations. Both suffered from the dangerous concentration of power in the hands of communist parties and, at times, despotic leaders. The Soviet Communist regime imploded and led to a troubled transition to an authoritarian regime with a capitalist political economy. China has retained its communist authoritarian political system but has experimented with a remarkable transition to a largely capitalist political economy.

The remaining six cases illustrate the diversity of the developing world. Of the six, India has had the longest history of stable democratic rule, but like most countries in the developing world, it has nevertheless struggled with massive poverty and inequality. The remaining five have experienced various forms of authoritarianism. Brazil and Nigeria endured long periods of military rule. Mexico's history of military rule was ended by an authoritarian political party that ruled for much of the twentieth century through a variety of nonmilitary means. South Africa experienced decades of racially based authoritarianism that excluded the vast majority of its population. Iran experienced a modernizing authoritarian monarchy followed by its current authoritarian regime, a theocracy ruled by Islamic clerics.

Cases and Concepts in Comparative Politics: An Integrated Approach can be traced to a decades-long experiment undertaken by the three comparative political scientists in the Department of Politics and Government at the University of Puget Sound. Over the years we spent much time discussing the challenges of teaching our introductory course in comparative politics. In those discussions we came to realize that each of us taught the course so differently that students completing our different sections of the course did not really share a common conceptual vocabulary. Over several years we fashioned a unified curriculum for Introduction to Comparative Politics, drawing on the strengths of each of our particular approaches.

All three of us now equip our students with a common conceptual vocabulary. All of our students now learn about states, nations, and different models of political economy. All students learn the basics about nondemocratic and democratic regimes, and they become familiar with characteristics of communist systems and advanced democracies. In developing our common curriculum, we became frustrated trying to find country studies that were concise, uniformly organized, sophisticated, and written to address the major concepts of comparative politics.

We also began to introduce students to country studies using pairs of cases (over the years we have varied the pairs) as a way to get students to think comparatively and to hone their understanding of key concepts. We found that teaching Japan and the United Kingdom, for example, was a wonderful way to study the main features and dilemmas of advanced democracies, while teaching students that such systems can thrive in very different political, economic, and cultural settings. Because we almost always assign reading that covers two countries at once, we have produced country studies that are organized identically and written with a common depth and style. Instructors can therefore easily assign the sections on the historical development of the state (to take one example) from any of the 13 case studies, and have students draw meaningful comparisons.

STRUCTURE OF THE BOOK

The three of us have logged over 70 combined years teaching Introduction to Comparative Politics, and we are well aware that there are many ways to approach this challenging course. With that in mind, we have created this first edition of *Cases and Concepts in Comparative Politics: An Integrated Approach* for instructors who prefer a single text containing both conceptual chapters and country studies. While the conceptual chapters reproduce much of the material contained in Patrick O'Neil's *Essentials of Comparative Politics*, they have been enhanced by the inclusion of comparative examples drawn from our 13 country studies. In Chapter 5, Political Violence, for instance, we include a section that considers whether recent acts of political violence in the United States might be designated as terrorism or as hate crimes. To take another example, in Chapter 8, Nondemocratic Regimes, a special section compares the relative successes and failures of military rule in Brazil and Nigeria. Unlike other texts that ask students to navigate back and forth across the book, we hope that these integrated examples show students more easily how comparative politics concepts apply to real-world situations and institutions. Likewise, although the country studies are based on those found in our co-authored *Cases in Comparative Politics*, we've significantly streamlined those chapters, so as to be able to include them with the conceptual chapters in a single volume. Country studies are placed throughout the book after the most relevant conceptual chapters. The Russia and China cases, for example, immediately follow Chapter 8, Nondemocratic Regimes, and Chapter 9, Communism and Postcommunism.

ACKNOWLEDGMENTS

As we have developd this approach over the years we have incurred numerous debts. First, and foremost, we wish to thank our wonderful colleagues in the Department of Politics and Government at the University of Puget Sound. By encouraging us to develop a common curriculum for our Introduction to Comparative Politics offering, and by allowing us to team-teach the course in different combinations, they allowed us to learn from each other. These cases are much stronger as a result. The university has also been extremely supportive in recognizing that writing for the classroom is as valuable as writing scholarly publications, and in providing course releases and summer stipends toward that end. Student assistants Brett Venn, Jess Box, Liz Kaster, Céad Nardi-Warner, and Tullan Baird proved extremely helpful in conducting research for our various cases; Irene Lim has, as always, supported us with her amazing technical and organizational skills. Our colleagues Bill Haltom, Robin Jacobsen, and David Sousa provided very helpful input throughout the project.

We very much appreciate the many helpful comments we have received from fellow instructors of comparative politics and area experts, including Emily Acevedo (California State University, Los Angeles), James Allan (Wittenberg University), Michelle Allendoerfer (George Washington University), Josephine Andrews (University of California, Davis), David C. Andrus, (College of the Canyons), Oana Armeanu, (University of Southern Indiana), Jason Arnold (Virginia Commonwealth University), Alan Arwine, (University of Kansas), Alex Avila (Mesa Community College), Gregory Baldi (Western Illinois University), Caroline Beer (University of Vermont), Marni Berg (Colorado State University), Prosper Bernard Jr. (College of Staten Island), Jeremy Busacca (Whittier College), Anthony Butler (University of Cape Town), Roderic Camp (Claremont McKenna College), Ryan Carlin (Georgia State University), Matthew Carnes (Georgetown University), Robert Compton

(SUNY Oneonta), Isabelle Côté (Memorial University of Newfoundland), Lukas K. Danner (Florida International University), Suheir Daoud (Coastal Carolina University), Helma de Vries-Jordan (University of Pittsburgh at Bradford), Bruce Dickson (George Washington University), Emily Edmonds-Poli (University of San Diego), Kenly Fenio (Virginia Tech), Bonnie Field, (Bentley University), Nathan W. Freeman (University of Georgia), John French (Depaul University/University of Illinois at Chicago), John Froitzheim (College of William & Mary), John Gaffney (Aston Centre for Europe), Sumit Ganguly (Indiana University), Julia George (Queens College, CUNY), Sarah Goodman (University of California at Irvine), Anna Gregg, (Austin Peay State University), Ivy Hamerly (Baylor University), Rongbin Han (University of Georgia), Kikue Hamayotsu (Northern Illinois University), Holley Hansen (Oklahoma State University), Cole Harvey (University of North Carolina, Chapel Hill), William Heller (Binghamton University), Yoshiko Herrera (University of Wisconsin at Madison), Robert Jackson (University of Redlands), Maiah Jaskoski (Northern Arizona University), John Jaworsky (University of Waterloo), Alexandra Hennessy (Seton Hall University), Jeffrey Hernden (State College of Florida), Yoshiko Herrera (University of Wisconsin at Madison), Robert Hinckley (SUNY Potsdam), Matthew Hoddie (Towson University), Maiah Jaskoski (Northern Arizona University), John Jaworsky (University of Waterloo), Aleisha Karjala (University of Science and Arts of Oklahoma), Arang Keshavarzian (New York University), Joon S. Kil, (Irvine Valley College), Tamara Kotar (University of Ottawa), Peter Kingstone (King's College), Tamara Kotar (University of Ottawa), Brian Kupfer (Tallahassee Community College), Ahmet Kuru (San Diego State University), Ricardo Larémont (Binghamton University), Lisa Laverty (Eastern Michigan University), Jeffrey Lewis (Cleveland State University), Peter H. Loedel (West Chester University), Gregory Love, (University of Mississippi), Mona Lyne (University of Missouri, Kansas City), Mary Malone (University of New Hampshire), Pamela Martin (Coastal Carolina University), Audrey Mattòon (Washington State University), Rahsaan Maxwell (University of North Carolina, Chapel Hill), Mark Milewicz (Gordon College), Michael Mitchell (Arizona State Univerity), Joseph H. Moskowitz (New Jersey City University), Christopher Muste (University of Montana), John Occhipinti (Canisius College), Omobolaji Olarinmoye (Hamilton College), Anthony O'Regan (Los Angeles Valley College), T. J. Pempel (University of California, Berkeley), Sharon Rivera, (Hamilton College), David Rossbach (Chatham University), Paul Rousseau (University of Windsor), Jennifer Rutledge, (John Jay College of Criminal Justice), Stephanie Sapiie (SUNY Nassau Community College), Hootan Shambayati, (Florida Gulf Coast University), Steve Sharp (Utah State University, Logan), Jennifer Smith (University of Wisconsin, Milwaukee), Thomas Sowers (Lamar University), Richard Stahler-Sholk, (Eastern Michigan University), Boyka Stefanova (University of Texas at San Antonio), Aaron Stuvland (George Mason University), Sandra L. Suarez (Temple University), Emmanuel J. Teitelbaum (George Washington University), Markus Thiel (Florida International University), John Tirman (Massachusetts Institute of Technology), Hubert Tworzecki (Emory University), José Vadi (Cal Poly, Pomona), Sydney Van Morgan (Cornell University), Steven Vogel (University of California, Berkeley), Brian Wampler (Boise State University), Syed A. Wasif (Montgomery College, Takoma Park), Shawn H. Williams (Campbellsville University), Mark A. Wolfgram (Oklahoma State University), Dwayne Woods (Purdue University), Kathleen Woodward (University of North Georgia), Stacey Philbrick Yadav (Hobart & William Smith Colleges), Jeremy Youde (University of Minnesota, Duluth), and Lyubov Zhyznomirska (Saint Mary's University).

Many thanks to all the folks at Norton—Peter Lesser, Ann Shin, Roby Harrington, Aaron Javsicas, and Jake Schindel among others—who have contributed to the success of this project over many years. For this inaugural edition of *Cases and Concepts in Comparative Politics* we want to give Samantha Held our special thanks for her extraordinary hard work and attention to detail. Finally, we thank our students at the University of Puget Sound who inspired us to write these cases and provided valuable feedback throughout the entire process.

Patrick H. O'Neil
Karl Fields
Don Share
Tacoma, WA
2017

A note about the data: *The data that are presented throughout the text in numerous tables, charts, and other figures are drawn from the* CIA World Factbook *unless otherwise noted.*

	UNITED KINGDOM	UNITED STATES	FRANCE	GERMANY	JAPAN	RUSSIA
Geographic Size Ranking	80	3	43	63	62	1
Population Size Ranking	22	3	21	18	10	9
GDP per Capita at PPP, $	$42,600	$57,500	$41,500	$48,700	$41,500	$23,200
GDP per Capita at PPP, Ranking (Estimated)	38	20	39	30	43	71
UN Human Development Index Ranking	16	10	21	4	17	49
Freedom House Rating	Free	Free	Free	Free	Free	Not free
Transparency International Corruption Score Ranking	10	18	23	10	20	131
Capital City	London	Washington, D.C.	Paris	Berlin	Tokyo	Moscow
Head of State	Queen Elizabeth II	Donald Trump	Emmanuel Macron	Joachim Gauck	Akihito	Vladimir Putin
Head of Government	Theresa May	Donald Trump	Édouard Philippe	Angela Merkel	Shinzō Abe	Dmitry Medvedev
Legislative–executive System	Parliamentary	Presidential	Semi-Presidential	Parliamentary	Parliamentary	Semi-Presidential
Unitary or Federal?	Unitary	Federal	Unitary	Federal	Unitary	Federal
Electoral System for Lower House of Legislature	Single-member districts with plurality	Single-member districts with plurality	Single-member districts with two rounds of voting	Mixed proportional representation and single-member districts with plurality	Mixed proportional representation and single-member districts with plurality	Proportional representation
Political-economic System	Liberal	Liberal	Social democratic	Social democratic	Mercantilist	Mercantilist

CHINA	INDIA	IRAN	MEXICO	BRAZIL	SOUTH AFRICA	NIGERIA
4	7	18	14	5	25	32
1	2	16	11	5	25	7
$15,500	$6,600	$17,000	$17,900	$15,100	$13,200	$5,900
111	157	91	89	110	117	162
90	131	69	77	79	119	152
Not free	Free	Not free	Partly free	Free	Free	Partly free
79	79	131	123	79	64	136
Beijing	New Delhi	Tehran	Mexico City	Brasília	Pretoria, Cape Town, Bloemfontein	Abuja
Xi Jinping	Ram Nath Kovind	Ali Khamenei	Enrique Peña Nieto	Michel Temer	Jacob Zuma	Muhammadu Buhari
Li Keqiang	Narendra Modi	Hassan Rouhani	Enrique Peña Nieto	Michel Temer	Jacob Zuma	Muhammadu Buhari
Communist party authoritarian regime	Parliamentary	Semi-presidential theocracy	Presidential	Presidential	Parliamentary	Presidential
Unitary	Federal	Unitary	Federal	Federal	Unitary	Federal
Not applicable	Single-member districts with plurality	Single- and multimember districts	Mixed proportional representation and single-member districts with plurality	Proportional representation	Proportional representation	Single-member districts with plurality
Mercantilist	Liberal	Mercantilist	Liberal	Liberal	Liberal	Liberal

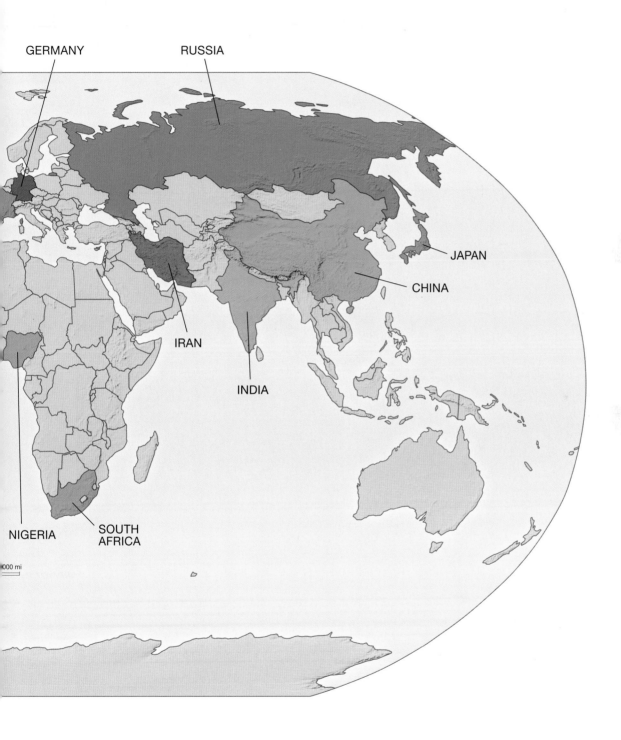

GERMANY

RUSSIA

JAPAN

CHINA

IRAN

INDIA

NIGERIA

SOUTH
AFRICA

000 mi

CASES *and* CONCEPTS
in Comparative Politics

AN INTEGRATED APPROACH

Protesters in Yemen attend a rally to commemorate the anniversary of Mohamed Bouazizi's death. In December 2010, the Tunisian street vendor set himself on fire to protest corruption in his home country, inspiring the Arab Spring that ignited the region in the following year. Members of the crowd hold a banner that reads, "We are all Bouazizi."

Introduction

What can political science tell us that we don't already know?

WHO WOULD HAVE PREDICTED 10 years ago that the Middle East would change so much in such a short period of time? Dramatic historical events often take scholars, politicians, and even participants by surprise. For example, in the 1980s few people expected that communism would come to a dramatic end in Eastern Europe—if anything, modest reforms in the Soviet Union were expected to give communist institutions a new lease on life. Following the collapse of communism and increased democratization in parts of Asia and Latin America, many scholars expected that regimes in the Middle East would be next. But by the turn of the century, these expectations appeared unfounded; authoritarianism in the region seemed immune to change. Scholars chalked this up to a number of things—the role of oil, Western economic and military aid, lack of civic institutions, or the supposedly undemocratic nature of Islam.

Yet again, history took us by surprise. The opening events of the Arab Spring were disarmingly simple. In December 2010, a young Tunisian man, Mohamed Bouazizi, set himself on fire to protest police corruption and government indifference. Angry protests broke out shortly thereafter, and the long-standing government was overthrown within weeks. New protests then broke out across the region in January and February 2011. In Egypt, President Hosni Mubarak was forced to resign after 30 years in office. In Libya, protests turned to widespread armed conflict and led to the killing of Muammar Gaddafi after more than 40 years of rule. In Syria, Bashar al-Assad clung to power as peaceful protests eventually turned into a civil war that has devastated the country, killed over 400,000 people, and triggered a migration crisis.

The immediate political future of these and other countries in the region is uncertain. Tunisia has transitioned into a fragile democracy, while Egypt has returned to dictatorship; Libya is plagued by regional and tribal conflict, while Syria has drawn in foreign forces, some bent on establishing an Islamist political system across the region. At the same time, an entire range of countries in the region have faced down public protests or not faced them at all. This is especially true among the monarchies of the Persian Gulf, where one might have imagined that these anachronistic forms of rule would have been the first to fall.

We are thus left with a series of puzzles. Why did the Arab Spring take place? What was the source of these tumultuous changes—revolution, civil war, and one of the largest refugee crises in recent history? Why did these uprisings take different forms and differ in the level of violence from place to place? Finally, why did some countries not see significant public protest to begin with? The hopeful nature of an Arab Spring has since been replaced by a much darker sense of the future politics of the region. Democracy, even political stability, seems further away than ever, and there are serious repercussions for the Middle East and beyond. Can political science help us answer these questions? Can it provide us with the tools to shape our own country's policies in this regard? Or are dramatic political changes, especially regional ones, simply too complex?

LEARNING OBJECTIVES

- Explain the methods political scientists use to understand politics around the world.
- Discuss whether comparative politics can be more scientific and predict political outcomes.
- Define the role and importance of institutions in political life.
- Compare freedom and equality and consider how politics reconciles the two across countries.

DURING THE PAST 25 YEARS, the world has seen an astonishing number of changes: the rise of new economic powers in Asia, the collapse of communism, revolutions across the Middle East, the return of religion to politics, the spread of information technology and social media, and the shifting effects of globalization. Many of the traditional assumptions and beliefs held by scholars, policy makers, and citizens have been overturned. New centers of wealth may reduce poverty, but they may also increase domestic inequality. Democracy, often seen as an inexorable force, can founder on such obstacles as religious or economic conflict. Technological change may create new, shared identities and sources of cooperation, but it can destabilize and fragment communities.

One pertinent example, which we have seen emerge in the civil wars in Syria and Iraq, is the role of ethnic and religious conflict. Why does this form of political violence occur? Is it a response to inequality or political disenfranchisement? Is it a function of cultural differences, a "clash of civilizations"? Is it fostered or tempered by globalization? Perhaps the explanation lies somewhere else entirely, beyond our purview or comprehension. How can we know what is correct? How do we scrutinize a range of explanations and evaluate their merits? Competing assumptions and explanations are at the heart of political debates and policy decisions, yet we are often asked to choose in the absence of reliable evidence or a good understanding of cause and effect. To be better citizens, we should be better students of political science and **comparative politics**—the study and comparison of domestic politics across countries. Comparative politics can be contrasted with another related field in political science, **international relations**. While comparative politics looks at the politics inside countries (such as elections, political parties, revolutions, and judicial systems), international relations concentrates on relations between countries (such as foreign policy, war, trade, and foreign aid). Of course the two overlap in many places, such as in ethnic or religious conflict, which often spills over borders, or political change, which can be shaped by international organizations or military force. For now, however, our discussion will concentrate on political structures and actions within countries.

> **comparative politics** The study and comparison of domestic politics across countries
>
> **international relations** A field in political science that concentrates on relations between countries, such as foreign policy, war, trade, and foreign aid

This chapter lays out some of the most basic vocabulary and structures of political science and comparative politics. These will fall under three basic categories: *analytical concepts* (assumptions and theories that guide our research), *methods* (ways to study and test those theories), and *ideals* (beliefs and values about preferred outcomes). Analytical concepts help us ask questions about cause and effect, methods provide tools to seek out explanations, and ideals help us compare existing politics with what we might prefer.

Our survey will consider some of the most basic questions: What is politics? How does one compare different political systems around the world? We will spend some time on the methods of comparative politics and how scholars have approached its study. Over the past century, political scientists have struggled with the challenge of analyzing politics and have asked whether such analysis can actually be considered a science. Exploring these issues will give us a better sense of the limitations and possibilities in the study of comparative politics. We will consider comparative politics through the concept of **institutions**—organizations or activities that are self-perpetuating and valued for their own sake. Institutions play an important role in defining and shaping what is possible and probable in political life by laying out the rules, norms, and structures in which we live. Finally, in addition to institutions, we will take up the ideals of freedom and equality. If institutions shape how the game of politics is played, then the goal of the game is the right mix of freedom and equality. Which ideal is more important? Must one come at the expense of the other? Perhaps some other ideal is preferable to both? With the knowledge gained by exploring these questions, we will be ready to take on complex politics around the world.

> **institution** An organization or activity that is self-perpetuating and valued for its own sake

What Is Comparative Politics?

politics The struggle in any group for power that will give one or more persons the ability to make decisions for the larger group

First, we must identify what comparative politics is. **Politics** is the struggle in any group for power that will give one or more persons the ability to make decisions for the larger group. This group may range from a small organization to the entire world. Politics occurs wherever there are people and organizations. For example, we may speak of "office politics" when we are talking about power relationships in a business. Political scientists in particular concentrate on the struggle for leadership and power in a political community—a political party, an elected office, a city, a region, or a country. It is therefore hard to separate the idea of politics from the idea of **power**, which is the ability to influence others or impose one's will on them. Politics is the competition for public power, and power is the ability to extend one's will.

power The ability to influence others or impose one's will on them

In political science, comparative politics is a subfield that compares this pursuit of power across countries. The method of comparing countries can help us make arguments about cause and effect by drawing evidence from across space and time. For example, one important puzzle we will return to frequently is why some countries are democratic, while others are not. Why have politics in some countries resulted in power being dispersed among more people, while in others power is concentrated in the hands of a few? Why is South Korea democratic, while North Korea is not? Looking at North Korea alone won't necessarily help us understand why South Korea went down a different path, or vice versa. A comparison of the two, perhaps alongside similar cases in Asia, may better yield explanations. As should be clear from our discussion of the Arab Spring, these are not simply academic questions. Democratic countries and pro-democracy organizations actively support the spread of like-minded regimes around the world, but if it is unclear how or why this comes about, democracy becomes difficult or even dangerous to promote. It is therefore important to separate ideals from our concepts and methods and not let the former obscure our use of the latter. Comparative politics can inform and even challenge our ideals, providing alternatives and questioning our assumption that there is one right way to organize political life.

THE COMPARATIVE METHOD

If comparison is an important way to test our assumptions and shape our ideals, how we compare cases is important. If there is no criterion or guide by which we gather information or draw conclusions, our studies become little more than a collection of details. Researchers thus often seek out puzzles—questions about politics with no obvious answer—as a way to guide their research. From there, they rely on some **comparative method**—a way to compare cases and draw conclusions. By comparing countries or subsets within them, scholars seek out conclusions and generalizations that could be valid in other cases.

comparative method The means by which social scientists make comparisons across cases

To return to our earlier question, let us say that we are interested in why democracy has failed to develop in some countries. This question was central to debates in the West over the future of the Middle East and elsewhere. We might approach the puzzle of democracy by looking at North Korea. Why has the North Korean government remained communist and highly repressive even as similar regimes around the world have collapsed?

A convincing answer to this puzzle could tell scholars and policy makers a great deal and even guide our tense relations with North Korea in the future. Examining one country closely may lead us to form hypotheses about why a country operates as it does. We call this approach **inductive reasoning**—the means by which we go from studying a case to generating a hypothesis. But while a study of one country can generate interesting hypotheses, it does not provide enough evidence to test them. Thus we might study North Korea and perhaps conclude that the use of nationalism by those in power has been central to the persistence of nondemocratic rule. In so concluding, we might then suggest that future studies look at the relationship between nationalism and authoritarianism in other countries. Inductive reasoning can therefore be a foundation on which we build greater theories in comparative politics.

Comparative politics can also rely on **deductive reasoning**—starting with a puzzle and from there generating some hypothesis about cause and effect to test against a number of cases. Whereas inductive reasoning starts with the evidence as a way to uncover a hypothesis, deductive reasoning starts with the hypothesis and then seeks out the evidence. In our example of inductive reasoning, we started with a case study of North Korea and ended with some testable generalization about nationalism; in deductive reasoning, we would start with our hypothesis about nationalism and then test that hypothesis by looking at a number of countries. By carrying out such studies, we may find a **correlation**, or apparent association, between certain factors or variables. If we were particularly ambitious, we might claim to have found cause and effect, or a **causal relationship**.[1] Inductive and deductive reasoning can help us to better understand and explain political outcomes and, ideally, could help us predict them.

Unfortunately, inductive and deductive reasoning, or finding correlation and causation, is not easy. Comparativists face seven major challenges in trying to examine political features across countries. Let's move through each of these challenges and show how they complicate the comparative method and comparative politics in general. First, political scientists have difficulty controlling the variables in the cases they study. In other words, in our search for correlations or causal relationships, we are unable to make true comparisons because each of our cases is different. By way of illustration, suppose a researcher wants to determine whether increased exercise by college students leads to higher grades. In studying the students who are her subjects, the researcher can control for a number of variables that might also affect grades, such as the students' diet, the amount of sleep they get, or any factor that might influence the results. By controlling for these differences and making certain that many of these variables are the same across the subjects with the exception of exercise, the researcher can carry out her study with greater confidence.

But political science offers few opportunities to control the variables because the variables are a function of real-world politics. As will become clear, economies, cultures, geography, resources, and political structures are amazingly diverse, and it is difficult to control for these differences. Even in a single case study, variables change over time. At best, we can control as much as possible for variables that might otherwise distort our conclusions. If, for example, we want to understand why gun ownership laws are so much less restrictive in the United States than in most other industrialized countries, we are well served to compare the United States with countries that have similar historical, economic, political, and social experiences, such as Canada and Australia, rather than Japan or South Africa. This approach allows us to

inductive reasoning Research that works from case studies in order to generate hypotheses

deductive reasoning Research that works from a hypothesis that is then tested against data

correlation An apparent relationship between two or more variables

causal relationship Cause and effect; when a change in one variable causes a change in another variable

control our variables more effectively, but it still leaves many variables uncontrolled and unaccounted for.

A second, related problem concerns the interactions between the variables themselves. Even if we can control our variables in making our comparisons, there is the problem that many of these variables are interconnected and interact. In other words, many variables interact to produce particular outcomes, in what is known as **multicausality**. A single variable like a country's electoral system or the strength of its judicial system is unlikely to explain the variation in countries' gun control laws. The problem of multicausality also reminds us that in the real world there are often no single, easy answers to political problems.

A third problem involves the limits to our information and information gathering. Although the cases we study have many uncontrolled and interconnected variables, we often have too few cases to work with. In the natural sciences, researchers often conduct studies with a huge number of cases—hundreds of stars or thousands of individuals, often studied across time. This breadth allows researchers to select their cases in such a way as to control their variables, and the large number of cases prevents any single unusual case from distorting the findings. But in comparative politics, we are typically limited by the number of countries in the world—fewer than 200 at present, most of which did not exist a few centuries ago. Even if we study some subset of comparative politics (like political parties or acts of terrorism), our total number of cases will remain relatively small. And if we attempt to control for differences by trying to find a number of similar cases (for example, wealthy democracies), our total body of cases will shrink even further.

A fourth problem in comparative politics concerns how we access the few cases we do have. Research is often further hindered by the very factors that make countries interesting to study. Much information that political scientists seek is not easy to acquire, necessitating work in the field—that is, conducting interviews or studying government archives abroad. International travel requires time and money, and researchers may spend months or even years in the field. Interviewees may be unwilling to speak on sensitive issues or may distort information. Libraries and archives may be incomplete, or access to them restricted. Governments may bar research on politically sensitive questions. Confronting these obstacles in more than one country is even more challenging. A researcher may be able to read Russian and travel to Russia frequently, but if he wants to compare authoritarianism in Russia and China, it would be ideal to be able to read Chinese and conduct research in China as well. Few comparativists have the language skills, time, or resources to conduct field research in many countries. There are almost no comparativists in North America or Europe who speak both Russian and Chinese. As a result, comparativists often master knowledge of a single country or language and rely on deductive reasoning. Single-case study can be extremely valuable—it gives the researcher a great deal of case depth and the ability to tease out novel observations that may come only from close observation. However, such narrow focus can also make it unclear to researchers whether the politics they see in their case study has important similarities to the politics in other cases. In the worst-case scenario, scholars come to believe that the country they study is somehow unique and fail to recognize its similarities with other cases.

Fifth, even where comparativists do widen their range of cases, their focus tends to be limited to a single geographic region. The specialist on communist Cuba is

multicausality When variables are interconnected and interact together to produce particular outcomes

more likely to study other Latin American countries than to consider China or North Korea, and the specialist on China is more likely to study South Korea than Russia. This isn't necessarily a concern, given our earlier discussion of the need to control variables—it may make more sense to study parts of the world where similar variables are clustered rather than compare countries from different parts of the world. This regional focus, however—often referred to as **area studies**—is distributed unevenly around the world. For decades, the largest share of research tended to focus on Western Europe, despite the increasing role of Asia in the international system.[2] Why? As mentioned earlier, some of this is a function of language; many scholars in the West are exposed to European languages in primary or secondary school, and in many European countries the use of English is widespread, thus facilitating research. English is also widespread in South Asia, yet scholarship has lagged behind. For example, we find that over the past 50 years one of the top journals in comparative politics published as many articles on Sweden as on India. To be fair, much of this is changing thanks to a new generation of scholars. Yet overall, comparative politics remains slow to redirect its attention when new issues and questions arise.

Sixth, the problem of bias makes it even harder to control for variables and to select the right cases. This is a question not of political bias, though that can sometimes be a problem, but of how we select our cases. In the natural sciences, investigators randomize case selection as much as possible to avoid choosing cases that support one hypothesis or another. But for the reasons mentioned earlier, such randomization is not possible in political science. Single-case studies are already influenced by the fact that comparativists study a country because they know its language or find it interesting. Yet even if we rely instead on deductive reasoning—beginning with a hypothesis and then seeking out our cases—we can easily fall into the trap of **selection bias**.

For example, say we want to understand revolutions, and we hypothesize that the main cause is a rapid growth in inequality. How should we select our cases? Most of us would respond by saying that we should find as many cases of revolution as possible and then see whether an increase in inequality preceded the revolutions. We might focus on revolutions in France, Mexico, Russia, China, and Iran. But this is a mistake—by looking only at cases of revolution, we miss all the cases where inequality grew but revolution did *not* take place. For example, we would overlook Brazil, South Africa, India, and Nigeria, four of the world's most unequal countries that never experienced a revolution. Indeed, there may be many more cases of unequal growth without revolution than with it, disproving our hypothesis. So, we would do better to concentrate on what we think is the cause (growth in inequality) rather than on what we think is the effect. While this may seem the obvious choice, it is a frequent mistake among scholars who are often so drawn to particular outcomes that they start there and then work backward.

A seventh and final concern deals with the heart of political science—the search for cause and effect. Let us for the sake of argument assume that the half-dozen problems we have laid out can be overcome through careful case selection, information gathering, and control of variables. Let us further imagine that with these problems in hand, research finds, for example, that countries with a low rate of female literacy are less likely to be democratic than countries where female literacy is high. Even if we are confident enough to claim that there is a causal relationship between female literacy and democracy—a bold statement indeed—a final and perhaps intractable problem looms. Which variable is cause and which is effect? Do low rates of female literacy

area studies A regional focus when studying political science, rather than studying parts of the world where similar variables are clustered

selection bias A focus on effects rather than causes, which can lead to inaccurate conclusions about correlation or causation

- Controlling a large number of variables.
- Controlling for the interaction of variables (multicausality).
- Limited number of cases to research.
- Limited access to information from cases.
- Uneven research across cases and regions.
- Cases selected on the basis of effect and not cause (selection bias).
- Variables may be either cause or effect (endogeneity).

endogeneity The issue that cause and effect are not often clear, in that variables may be both cause and effect in relationship to one another

limit public participation, empowering nondemocratic actors, or do authoritarian leaders (largely men) take little interest in promoting gender equality? This problem of distinguishing cause and effect, known as **endogeneity**, is a major obstacle in any comparative research. Even if we are confident that we have found cause and effect, we can't easily ascertain which is which. On reflection, this is to be expected; one political scientist has called endogeneity "the motor of history," for causes and effects tend to evolve together, each transforming the other over time. Thus early forms of democracy, literacy, and women's rights may well have gone hand in hand, each reinforcing and changing the others. In short, many things matter, and these many things affect each other. This makes an elegant claim about cause and effect problematic, to say the least.[3]

CAN WE MAKE A SCIENCE OF COMPARATIVE POLITICS?

theory An integrated set of hypotheses, assumptions, and facts

We have so far elaborated many of the ways in which comparative politics—and political science in general—makes for difficult study. Variables are hard to control and can be interconnected, while actual cases may be few. Getting access to information may be difficult, and comparisons may be limited by regional knowledge and interests. What questions are asked may be affected by selection bias and endogeneity. All these concerns make it difficult to generate any kind of political science **theory**, which we can define as an integrated set of hypotheses, assumptions, and facts. At this point, you may well have concluded that a science of politics is hopeless. But it is precisely these kinds of concerns that have driven political science, and comparative politics within it, toward a more scientific approach. Whether this has yielded or will yield significant benefits, and at what cost, is something we will consider next.

Political science and comparative politics have a long pedigree. In almost every major society, there are masterworks of politics, prescribing rules or, less often, analyzing political behavior. In the West, the work of the philosopher Aristotle (384–322 B.C.E.) departed from the traditional emphasis on political ideals to conduct comparative research on existing political systems (what we will call *regimes*), eventually gathering and analyzing the constitutions of 158 Greek city-states. Aristotle's objective was to delineate between what he took to be "proper" and "deviant," or despotic political regimes. He also framed this discussion in terms of a puzzle—why were some regimes despotic and others not? With this approach, Aristotle conceived of an empirical (that is, observable and verifiable) science of politics with a practical purpose: statecraft, or how to govern. Aristotle was perhaps the first Westerner to separate the study of politics from that of philosophy.[4]

Aristotle's early approach did not immediately lead to any systematic study of politics. For the next 1,800 years, discussions of politics remained embedded in the realm of philosophy, with the emphasis placed on how politics should be rather than on how politics was actually conducted. Ideals, rather than conclusions drawn from evidence, were the norm. Only with the works of the Italian Niccolò Machiavelli (1469–1527) did a comparative approach to politics truly emerge. Like Aristotle, he sought to analyze different political systems—those that existed around him as well as those that had preceded him, such as the Roman Empire—and even tried to make generalizations about success and failure. These findings, he believed, could then be applied by statesmen to avoid their predecessors' mistakes. Machiavelli's work reflects this pragmatism, dealing with the mechanics of government, diplomacy, military strategy, and power.[5]

Because of his emphasis on statecraft and empirical knowledge, Machiavelli is often cited as the first modern political scientist, paving the way for other scholars. His writings came at a time when the medieval order was giving way to the Renaissance, with its emphasis on science, rationalism, secularism, and real-world knowledge over abstract ideals. The resulting work over the next four centuries reinforced the idea that politics, like any other area of knowledge, could be developed as a logical, rigorous, and predictable science.

During those centuries, a number of major thinkers took up the comparative approach to the study of politics, which slowly retreated from moral, philosophical, or religious foundations. In the seventeenth century, authors like Thomas Hobbes and John Locke followed in Machiavelli's footsteps, advocating particular political systems on the basis of empirical observation and analysis. They were followed in the eighteenth century by such scholars as Jean-Jacques Rousseau and the Baron de Montesquieu, whose studies of the separation of power and civil liberties would directly influence the writing of the American Constitution and other constitutions to follow. The work of Karl Marx and Max Weber in the nineteenth and early twentieth centuries would further add to political science, with analyses of the nature of political and economic organization and power. All these developments reflected widespread changes in scholarly inquiry and often blended political ideals with analytical concepts and some attempt at a systematic method of study.

Thus, by the turn of the twentieth century, political science formally existed as a field of study, but it still looked much different from the way it does now. The study of comparative politics, while less focused on ideals or philosophy, resembled a kind of political journalism: largely descriptive, atheoretical, and concentrated on Europe, which still dominated world politics through its empires. Little in this work resembled a comparative method.

The two world wars and the rise of the Cold War would mark a turning point in political science and comparative politics, particularly in the United States. There were several reasons for this. First, a growing movement surfaced among universities toward applying more rigorous methods to studying human behavior, whether in sociology, economics, or politics. Second, the world wars raised serious questions about the ability of scholars to meaningfully contribute to an understanding of world affairs. The creation of new countries, the rise of fascism, and the failure of democracy throughout much of interwar Europe were vital concerns, but political scholarship

Major Thinkers in Comparative Politics

Aristotle (384–322 B.C.E.)	First separated the study of politics from that of philosophy; used the comparative method to study Greek city-states; in *The Politics*, conceived of an empirical study of politics with a practical purpose.
Niccolò Machiavelli (1469–1527)	Often cited as the first modern political scientist due to his emphasis on statecraft and empirical knowledge; analyzed different political systems, believing the findings could be applied by statesmen; discussed his theories in *The Prince*.
Thomas Hobbes (1588–1679)	Developed the notion of a "social contract," whereby people surrender certain liberties in favor of order; advocated a powerful state in *Leviathan*.
John Locke (1632–1704)	Argued that private property is essential to individual freedom and prosperity; advocated a weak state in *Two Treatises of Government*.
Charles-Louis de Secondat, Baron de Montesquieu (1689–1755)	Studied government systems; advocated the separation of powers within government in *The Spirit of Laws*.
Jean-Jacques Rousseau (1712–78)	Argued that citizens' rights are inalienable and cannot be taken away by the state; influenced the development of civil rights; discussed these ideas in *The Social Contract*.
Karl Marx (1818–83)	Elaborated a theory of economic development and inequality in *Das Kapital*; predicted the eventual collapse of capitalism and democracy.
Max Weber (1864–1920)	Wrote widely on such topics as bureaucracy, forms of authority, and the impact of culture on economic and political development; developed many of these themes in *Economy and Society*.

did not seem to shed enough light on these issues and what they meant for international stability. Third, the Cold War with a rival Soviet Union, armed with nuclear weapons and revolutionary ideology, made understanding comparative politics seem a matter of survival. Finally, the postwar period ushered in a wave of technological innovation, such as early computers. This development generated a widespread belief that through technological innovation, many social problems could be recast as technical concerns, finally to be resolved through science. The fear of another war was thus married with a belief that science was an unmitigated good that had the answers to almost all problems. The question was how to make the science work.

Although these changes dramatically transformed the study of politics, the field itself remained a largely conservative discipline, taking capitalism and democracy as the ideal. In comparative politics, these views were codified in what was known as **modernization theory**, which held that as societies developed, they would become capitalist democracies, converging around a set of shared values and characteristics. The United States and other Western countries were furthest ahead on this path, and the theory assumed that all countries would eventually catch up unless "diverted" by alternative systems such as communism (as fascism had done in the past).

During the 1950s and 1960s, comparativists influenced by modernization theory expanded their research to include more cases. Field research, supported

modernization theory
A theory asserting that as societies developed, they would take on a set of common characteristics, including democracy and capitalism

by government and private grants, became the normal means by which political scientists gathered data. New computer technologies combined with statistical methods were also applied to this expanding wealth of data. Finally, the subject of investigation shifted away from political institutions (such as legislatures and constitutions) and toward individual political behavior. This trend came to be known as the **behavioral revolution**. Behavioralism hoped to generate theories and generalizations that could help explain and even predict political activity. Ideally, this work would eventually lead to a "grand theory" of political behavior and modernization that would be valid across countries.

behavioral revolution
A movement within political science during the 1950s and 1960s to develop general theories about individual political behavior that could be applied across all countries

Behavioralism and modernization theory were two different things—modernization theory was a set of hypotheses about how countries develop, and behavioralism was a set of methods with which to approach politics. However, both were attempts to study politics more scientifically to achieve certain policy outcomes.[6] Behavioralism also promoted deductive, large-scale research over the single-case study common in inductive reasoning. It seemed clear to many that political science, and comparative politics within it, would soon be a "real" science.

By the late 1970s, however, this enthusiasm began to meet with resistance. New theories and sophisticated methods of analysis increased scholars' knowledge about politics around the world, but this knowledge in itself did not lead to the expected breakthroughs. The theories that had been developed, such as modernization theory, increasingly failed to match politics on the ground; instead of becoming more capitalist and more democratic, many newly independent countries collapsed in the face of violent conflict and revolution, to be replaced by authoritarianism that in no way reflected Western expectations or ideals. What had gone wrong?

Some critics charged that the behavioral revolution's obsession with appearing scientific had led the discipline astray by emphasizing methodology over knowledge and technical jargon over clarity. Others criticized the field for its ideological bias, arguing that comparativists were interested not in understanding the world but in prescribing the Western model of modernization. At worst, their work could be viewed as simply serving the foreign policy interests of the United States. Since that time, comparative politics, like all of political science, has grown increasingly fragmented. While few still believe in the old descriptive approach that dominated the earlier part of the century, there is no consensus about where scholarship is going and what research methods or analytical concepts are most fruitful. This lack of consensus has led to several main divisions and lines of conflict.

IN FOCUS   Trends in Comparative Politics

TRADITIONAL APPROACH	Emphasis on describing political systems and their various institutions.
BEHAVIORAL REVOLUTION	The shift from a descriptive study of politics to one that emphasizes causality, explanation, and prediction; emphasizes the political behavior of individuals more than larger political structures and quantitative more than qualitative methodology; modernization theory predominates.

RESEARCH METHODS One area of conflict is over methodology—how best to gather and analyze data. We have already spoken about the problems of comparative methodology, involving selecting cases and controlling variables. Within these concerns are further questions of how one gathers and interprets the data to compare these cases and measure these variables. Some comparative political scientists rely on **qualitative methods**, evidence, and methodology, such as interviews, observations, and archival and other forms of documentary research. Qualitative approaches are often narrowly focused, deep investigations of one or a few cases drawing from scholarly expertise. However, some qualitative studies (such as work on modernization or revolution) do involve numerous cases spread out across the globe and spanning centuries. Either way, qualitative approaches are typically inductive, beginning with case studies to generate theory.

For some political scientists, a qualitative approach is of dubious value. Variables are not rigorously defined or measured, they argue, and hypotheses are not tested by using a large sample of cases. Asserting that qualitative work fails to contribute to the accumulation of knowledge and is little better than the approach that dominated the field a century ago, these critics advocate **quantitative methods** instead. They favor a wider use of cases unbound by area specialization, greater use of statistical analysis, and mathematical models often drawn from economics. This quantitative methodology is more likely to use deductive reasoning, starting with a theory that political scientists can test with an array of data. Many advocates of qualitative research question whether quantitative approaches measure and test variables that are of any particular value or simply focus on the (often mundane) things that can be expressed numerically. Overdependence on quantifiable measures can lead scholars to avoid the important questions that often cannot be addressed using such strict scientific methods.

THEORY A second, related debate concerns the theoretical assumptions of human behavior. Are human beings rational, in the sense that their behavior conforms to some generally understandable behavior? Some say yes. These scholars use what is known as **rational choice** or **game theory** to study the rules and games by which politics is played and how human beings act on their preferences (like voting, choosing a party, or supporting a revolution). Such models can, ideally, lead not only to explanation but also to prediction—a basic element of science. As you might guess, rational choice theory is closely associated with quantitative methods. And like the critics of quantitative methods in general, those who reject rational choice theory assert that the emphasis on individual rationality discounts the importance of things like historical complexity, unintended outcomes, or cultural factors. In fact, some consider

qualitative method Study through an in-depth investigation of a limited number of cases

quantitative method Study through statistical data from many cases

rational choice Approach that assumes that individuals weigh the costs and benefits and make choices to maximize their benefits

game theory An approach that emphasizes how actors or organizations behave in their goal to influence others; built upon assumptions of rational choice

INFOCUS	Quantitative Method versus Qualitative Method
QUANTITATIVE METHOD	Gathering of statistical data across many countries to look for correlations and test hypotheses about cause and effect. Emphasis on breadth over depth.
QUALITATIVE METHOD	Mastery of a few cases through the detailed study of their history, language, and culture. Emphasis on depth over breadth.

rational choice theories, as they do behavioralism, to be Western (or specifically American) assumptions about self-interest, markets, and individual autonomy that do not easily describe the world.

As these debates have persisted, the world around us continues to change. Just as the wrenching political changes in the Middle East were not anticipated, neither was the end of the Cold War some twenty years earlier. Few scholars, regardless of methodology or theoretical focus, anticipated or even considered either dramatic set of events. Similarly, religion has reemerged as an important component in politics around the globe—a force that modernization theory (and research focused on Europe) told us was on the wane. New economic powers have emerged in Asia, coinciding with democracy in some cases but not in others. Terrorism, once the tactic of secular revolutionary groups in the 1970s, has also resurfaced, albeit in the hands of different actors. It seems that many political scientists, whatever their persuasion, have had little to contribute to many of these issues—time and again, scholars have been caught off guard.

Where does this leave us now? In recent years, some signs of conciliation are emerging. Scholars recognize that careful (and sloppy) scholarship and theorizing are possible with both qualitative and quantitative methods. Inductive and deductive reasoning can both generate valuable theories in comparative politics. Rational choice and historical or cultural approaches can contribute to and be integrated into each other. One finds more mixed-method approaches that use both quantitative and qualitative research. As a result, some scholars have spoken optimistically of an integration of mathematics, "narrative" (case studies), and rational choice models, each contributing to the other. For example, large-scale quantitative studies of political activity can be further elucidated by turning to individual cases that investigate the question in greater detail. Such mixed-method research is growing, though skeptics remain who argue that simply expanding the number and kinds of methods does not lead to more reliable outcomes.[7] These ongoing problems are not limited to comparative politics, political science, or the social sciences. It is worth noting that even in such fields as biology, much research suffers from design flaws, leading to results that cannot be reproduced.

A final observation is in order as we bring this discussion to a close. Irrespective of methodology or theory, many have observed that political science as a whole has lost touch with real-world concerns, has become inaccessible to laypersons, and has failed to speak to those who make decisions about policy—whether voters or elected leaders. Following the surprise of the Arab Spring, commentators resurrected the long-standing criticism that political science has created "a culture that glorifies arcane unintelligibility while disdaining impact and audience."[8] This is somewhat unfair—for some years, there has been an increasing emphasis on reconnecting political science to central policy questions and also on reengaging political ideals, something in the past discarded as "unscientific."

This new emphasis is not a call for comparativists' research to be biased in favor of a particular ideal—rather, comparative politics should not simply be about what we can study or what we want to study but also about how our research can reach people, empower them, and help them be better citizens and leaders. After decades of asserting that political science should have an objective and scientifically neutral approach, this call for greater relevance and contribution to the ideals of civic life represents a change for many scholars, but relevance and rigor are not at odds. They are in fact central to a meaningful political science and comparative politics.

A Guiding Concept: Political Institutions

A goal of this textbook is to provide a way to compare and analyze politics around the world in the aftermath of recent changes and uncertainties. Given the long-standing debates within comparative politics, how can we organize our ideas and information? One way is through a guiding concept, a way of looking at the world that highlights some important features while deemphasizing others. There is certainly no one right way of doing this; any guide, like a lens, will sharpen some features while distorting others. With that said, our guiding concept is institutions, defined at the beginning of this chapter as organizations or patterns of activity that are self-perpetuating and valued for their own sake. In other words, an institution is something so embedded in people's lives as a norm or value that it is not easily dislodged or changed. People see an institution as central to their lives, and, as a result, the institution commands and generates legitimacy. Institutions embody the rules, norms, and values that give meaning to human activity.

Consider an example from outside politics. We often hear in the United States that baseball is an American institution. What exactly does this mean? In short, Americans view baseball not simply as a game but as something valued for its own sake, a game that helps define society. Yet few Americans would say that soccer is a national institution. The reason is probably clear: we do not perceive soccer as indispensable in the way that baseball is. Whereas soccer is simply a game, baseball is part of what defines America and Americans. Even Americans who don't like baseball would probably say that America wouldn't be the same without it. Indeed, even at the local level, teams command such legitimacy that when they merely threaten to move to another city, their fans raise a hue and cry. The Brooklyn Dodgers moved to Los Angeles in 1958, yet many in New York still consider them "their" team half a century later. For many Canadians, while baseball is important, hockey is a national institution, thought of as "Canada's Game" and an inextricable part of Canadian identity and history. In Europe and much of the world, soccer reigns as a premier social institution, and teams provoke such fervent loyalty that fan violence is quite common. Because of their legitimacy and apparent indispensability, institutions command authority and can influence human behavior; we accept and conform to institutions and support rather than challenge them. Woe betide the American, Canadian, or European who derides the national sport!

Another example connects directly to politics. In many countries, democracy is an institution: it is not merely a means to compete over political power but a vital element in people's lives, bound up in the very way they define themselves. Democracy is part and parcel of collective identity, and some democratic countries and their people would not be the same without it. Even if they are cynical about democracy in practice, citizens of democracies will defend and even die for the institution when it is under threat. In many other countries, this is not the case: democracy is absent, poorly understood, or weakly institutionalized and unstable. People in such countries do not define themselves by democracy's presence or absence, and so democracy's future there is more insecure. However, these same people might owe a similar allegiance to a different set of institutions, such as their ethnic group or religion. Clearly, no single, uniform set of institutions holds power over people all around the world, and understanding the differences among institutions is central to the study of comparative politics.

What about a physical object or place? Can that, too, be an institution? Many would argue that the World Trade Center was an American institution—not just a set of office buildings, but structures representing American values. The same can be said about the Pentagon. When terrorists attacked these buildings on September 11, 2001, they did so not simply to cause a great loss of life but also to show that their hostility was directed against America itself—its institutions, as they shape and represent the American way of life, and its relation to the outside world. Like the World Trade Center and the Pentagon, the city of Jerusalem is a powerful cultural and national institution, in this case reflecting the identity and ideals of two peoples: Israelis and Palestinians. Both groups claim it as their capital, and for both the city holds key historical, political, and religious significance.

The examples just described raise the distinction between formal and informal institutions. When we think of **formal institutions**, we assume they are based on officially sanctioned rules that are relatively clear. Yet there are also **informal institutions**—unwritten and unofficial, but no less powerful as a result. And of course, institutions can be a combination of both.

Because institutions are embedded in each of us, in how we see the world and what we think is valuable and important, it is difficult to change or eliminate them. When institutions are threatened, people will rush to their defense and even re-create them when they are shattered. This bond is the glue of society. However, one problem that institutions pose is this very "stickiness," in that people may come to resist even necessary change because they have difficulty accepting the idea that certain institutions have outlived their value. Thus, while institutions can and do change, they are by nature persistent. This, however, is not to say that institutions are eternal. Such structures can decline in power in the face of alternative norms, or be swept away when people find them too constraining or outmoded. The rise and institutionalization of soccer in the United States may mirror the decline of baseball, which is viewed by many young Americans as an outdated sport.

Politics is full of institutions. The basic political structures of any country are composed of institutions: the army, the police, the legislature, and the courts, to name a few. We obey them not only because we think it is in our self-interest to do so but also because we see them as legitimate ways to conduct politics. Taxation is a good example. In many Western democracies, income taxes are an institution; we may not like them, but we pay them nonetheless. Is this because we are afraid of going to jail if we fail to do so? Perhaps. But research indicates that a major source of tax compliance is people's belief that taxation is a legitimate way to fund the programs that society needs. We pay, in other words, when we believe that it is the right thing to do, a norm. By contrast, in societies where taxes are not institutionalized, tax evasion tends to be rampant; people view taxes as illegitimate and those who pay as suckers. Similarly, where electoral politics is weakly institutionalized, people support elections only when their preferred candidate wins, and they cry foul, take to the streets, and even threaten or use violence when the opposition gains power. Institutions can thus be stronger or weaker, and rise or decline in power, over time.

Institutions are a useful way to approach the study of politics because they set the stage for political behavior. Because institutions generate norms and values (good and bad), they favor and allow certain kinds of political activity and not

formal institutions Institutions usually based on officially sanctioned rules that are relatively clear

informal institutions Institutions with unwritten and unofficial rules

Institutions

- Organizations or patterns of activity that are self-perpetuating and valued for their own sake.
- Embody norms or values that are considered central to people's lives and thus are not easily dislodged or changed.
- Set the stage for political behavior by influencing how politics is conducted.
- Vary from country to country.
- Exemplified by the army, taxation, elections, and the state.

others, making a more likely "path" for political activity (what is known as *path dependence*). As a result, political institutions are critical because they influence politics; and how political institutions are constructed, intentionally or unintentionally, will profoundly affect how politics is conducted.

In many ways, our institutional approach takes us back to the study of comparative politics as it existed before the 1950s. Prior to the behavioral revolution, political scientists spent much of their time documenting and describing the institutions of politics, often without asking how those institutions actually shaped politics. The behavioral revolution that followed emphasized cause and effect but turned its attention toward political actors and their calculations, resources, or strategies. The actual institutions were seen as less important. The return to the study of institutions in many ways combines these two traditions. From behavioralism, institutional approaches take their emphasis on cause-and-effect relationships, something that will be prevalent throughout this book. However, institutions are not simply the product of individual political behavior; they powerfully affect how politics functions. In other words, institutions are not merely the result of politics; they can also be an important cause. Their emergence—and disappearance—can have a profound impact on politics.

As recent events have shown us, there is still a tremendous amount of institutional variation around the world that needs to be recognized and understood. This textbook will map some of the basic institutional differences between countries, acknowledging the diversity of institutions while pointing to some features that allow us to compare and evaluate them. By studying political institutions, we can hope to gain a better sense of the political landscape across countries.

A Guiding Ideal: Reconciling Freedom and Equality

At the start of this chapter, we spoke about analytical concepts (such as institutions), methods (such as inductive or deductive, quantitative or qualitative), and political ideals. We defined politics as the struggle for power people engage in to make decisions for society. The concept of institutions gives us a way to organize our study by investigating the different ways that struggle can be shaped. Yet this raises an important question: People may struggle for political power, but what are they fighting for? What do they seek to achieve once they have gained power? This is where ideals come in, and we will concentrate on one core debate that lies at the heart of all politics: the struggle between freedom and equality. This struggle has existed as long as human beings have lived in organized communities, and it may be that these are more than ideals—they are a part of our evolutionary history as we transitioned from small, nomadic bands to larger, settled communities.

Politics is bound up in the struggle between individual freedom and collective equality and in how these ideals are to be reconciled. Since *freedom* and *equality* can mean different things to different people, it is important to define each term. When we speak of **freedom**, we are talking about an individual's ability to act independently, without fear of restriction or punishment by the state or other individuals or groups in society. At a basic level, freedom connotes autonomy; in the modern world, it encompasses such concepts as free speech, free assembly, freedom of religion, and other civil liberties. **Equality** refers to a material standard of living shared by individuals within a community, society, or country. The relation between equality and freedom is typically viewed in terms of justice or injustice—a measurement of whether our ideals have been met.

Freedom and equality are tightly interconnected, and the relation between the two shapes politics, power, and debates over justice. It is unclear, however, whether one must come at the expense of the other. Greater personal freedom, for example, may imply a smaller role for the state and limits on its powers to do such things as redistribute income through welfare and taxes. As a result, inequality may increase as individual freedom trumps the desire for greater collective equality. This growing inequality can in turn undermine freedom if too many people feel as though the political system no longer cares about their material needs. Even if this discontent is not a danger, there remains the question of whether society as a whole has an obligation to help the poor—an issue of justice. The United States, as we shall see, has one of the highest degrees of economic inequality among developed democracies. Is this inequality undermining democratic institutions, as some suggest?

Alternatively, a focus on equality may erode freedom. Demands for greater material equality may lead a government to take greater control of private property and personal wealth, all in the name of redistribution for the "greater good." Yet when economic and political powers are concentrated in one place, they may threaten individual freedom since people control fewer private resources of their own. In the Soviet Union, under communism, for example, the state held all economic power, giving it the ability to control people's lives—where they lived, the education they received, the jobs they held, the money they earned. Levels of inequality were in turn quite low.

Is the balance between freedom and equality a zero-sum game, in which the gain of one represents the loss of the other? Not necessarily. Some would assert that freedom and equality can also reinforce each other: material security can help to secure certain political rights, and vice versa. In addition, while a high degree of state power may weaken individual freedom, the state also plays an important role in helping to define individual freedom and protect it from infringement by other individuals. Finally, the meaning of freedom and equality may change over time as the material world and our values change. For some, managing freedom and equality necessitates centralized political power. Others view such power as the very impediment to freedom or equality. We will look at these debates more closely when we consider political ideologies in subsequent chapters.

freedom The ability of an individual to act independently, without fear of restriction or punishment by the state or other individuals or groups in society

equality A shared material standard of individuals within a community, society, or country

Can We Make a Science of Politics?

In much of our discussion, there is a sense that political science remains hindered by problems of data and theory that could prevent explanation, or even prediction, of political behavior. To use a metaphor coined by the philosopher Karl Popper: Do humans function in a regular, clocklike way, such that we can find out "what makes us tick" and predict how we will act? Or are humans more like clouds, shifting and complex? Some people do believe that humans are more clocklike, and that science can produce better explanations and perhaps even predictions of human behavior. In this view, the main problem has been a lack of the necessary tools. However, certain scientific advances are under way that some believe will transform the social sciences. Researchers are at work in two interesting areas, both focusing on human nature in different but complementary ways.

The first we can call a macro-level approach to human nature. In this approach, the future of the discipline lies in the integration of life sciences, such as genetics, neuroscience, and related fields. Politics can be investigated by starting with these biological factors as the foundation of political actions and institutions. For example, biological studies of politics increasingly suggest that many key aspects of politics, such as ideological orientation, levels of social trust, and propensity toward political participation, may be as much inherited as learned. This does not suggest that people have a gene for such things as democracy or authoritarianism, conservatism or liberalism. But the macro-level approach does argue that biology can partially shape people's view of some issues and that political orientation is not simply a function of individual preference or existing social structures.

To return to our discussion of the wave of revolutions and civil conflict across the Middle East, macro-level research might focus on demographics, such as the large population under age 30, and the intersection of particular forms of youth behavior (such as risk taking) and institutionalized barriers to opportunity (such as corruption). It might also consider the interaction between culture and biology in levels and sources of shame and humiliation. Mohamed Bouazizi did not set himself on fire because he was crazy, or because he thought it would touch off a revolution. In our understanding, his act was irrational. But if we reconsider it as an explicable psychological response based on his particular environment, we gain a different insight. This of course does not provide any prediction of why a revolution would happen in the first place, or why in Tunisia as opposed to Algeria, which escaped the Arab Spring.

This is where micro-level approaches come into play. If macro-level studies look at how biological forces can interact with the social environment, micro-level research focuses on the science of cognition—how our tools for judgment frequently lead to a range of involuntary cognitive errors, including overconfidence, a misunderstanding of statistics and probability, mental "shortcuts" that lead to biases and stereotypes, and the tendency to discern cause-and-effect relationships where none exist. In this scholarship, the very notion of human rationality is deeply problematic. This understanding can help explain why political scientists were surprised by

Egyptian demonstrators face off against the army in 2011, eventually leading to the downfall of President Hosni Mubarak.

the Arab Spring or the collapse of communism. The human tendency to construct narratives that explain the past and downplay the role of chance typically leads humans to mistakenly project the present into the future. This behavior discounts the possibility for dramatic political change.[a]

While this discussion has gone some way to bringing more science into political science, these explanations don't seem to give us more in terms of prediction. Yet there is hope. Political psychologist Philip Tetlock's Good Judgment Project asked several thousand volunteers to regularly make predictions about a range of world events up to one year out. Among them emerged a group of "superforecasters" whose predictions even beat those of intelligence analysts with access to classified information. What made these superforecasters so good? Tetlock noted that forecasters can be divided into two basic categories, borrowed from the late philosopher Isaiah Berlin: hedgehogs and foxes.

Hedgehogs know one big thing; they tend to look for a single overarching explanation that can explain many different political events and are more likely to reject information that runs counter to their beliefs. Foxes are less confident in their views, which consist of many small ideas cobbled together and subject to frequent revision. As you might suspect, hedgehogs are much worse predictors of world events and are more interested in trying to fit the world into their preconceptions than revising their beliefs on the basis of new information.

Which approach one uses may simply be inherited, like a particularly open-minded and self-critical mode of thinking. But Tetlock also found that good prediction can be taught, reducing biases and increasing clarity in forecasts. No one believes that superforecasters will be able to predict the next Arab Spring. In fact, the majority of forecasters incorrectly predicted that the United Kingdom's 2016 referendum to leave the European Union would fail (see Chapter 7), nor did they predict President Trump's victory. But there is clear evidence that we can approach politics more systematically and draw better conclusions about what might happen in the near future.[b]

In short, politics is driven by the ideal of reconciling individual freedom and collective equality. This inevitably leads to questions of power and of the people's role in political life. How much should any individual or group be allowed to influence others or impose their will on them? Who should be empowered to make decisions about freedom and equality? Should power be centralized or decentralized, public or private? When does power become a danger to others, and how can we manage this threat? Each political system must address these questions and in so doing determine where political power shall reside and how much shall be given to whom. Each political system creates a unique set of institutions to structure political power, shaping the role people play in politics.

In Sum: Looking Ahead and Thinking Carefully

Politics is the pursuit of power in any organization, and comparative politics is the study of this struggle around the world. Over the past centuries, the study of politics has evolved from philosophy to a field that emphasizes empirical research and the quest to explain politics and even predict political change. This approach has limitations: despite the earlier desire to emulate the natural sciences, comparative politics, like political science as a whole, has been unable to generate any grand or even smaller theories of political behavior. Yet the need to study politics remains as important as ever; dramatic changes over the past quarter-century have called on comparativists to shed light on these developments and concerns.

Political institutions can help us organize this task. Since institutions generate norms and values, and different configurations of institutions lead to different forms of political activity, they can help us map the political landscape. Specifically, they can show how political activity attempts to reconcile the competing values of individual freedom and collective equality. All political groups, including countries, must reconcile these two forces, determining where power should reside. In the chapters to come, we will return to this question of freedom and equality and to the way in which these values influence, and are influenced by, institutions.

A final thought before we conclude on how to use all this information. Much of our discussion in this chapter has been about the controversies over how best to study politics—What method? What concepts? What role for ideals? In all of this, it may seem that we have gained little understanding of how to "do" political science well. If scholars can't agree on the best way to analyze politics, what hope do we have of making sense of the world?

Our "Institutions in Action" box provides some insight. We note that Philip Tetlock's study of political predictions found that participants can be divided into hedgehogs and foxes; the former look for an overarching explanation that may reject information that challenges their view, while the latter are less confident of their explanations and more willing to change their views in the face of evidence to the contrary. The flexibility and even humility of foxes leads to a better track record in forecasting future events.

An important lesson we can take away from these findings is that the most fruitful approach to comparative politics is to be skeptical, not simply of others—that's the easy part—but also of what we believe and take for granted. We should be ready to reconsider our beliefs in the face of new evidence and arguments and to remember that every explanation in this book is conjecture, subject to revision if we can find new or contradictory evidence. With this approach, by the end of this course you will be able to draw your own conclusions about the contours of politics and what combination of values might construct a better political order. So, drop your assumptions about how the world works, and let's begin.

Key Terms

area studies (p. 9)
behavioral revolution (p. 13)
causal relationship (p. 7)
comparative method (p. 6)
comparative politics (p. 5)
correlation (p. 7)
deductive reasoning (p. 7)
endogeneity (p. 10)
equality (p. 19)
formal institutions (p. 17)
freedom (p. 19)
game theory (p. 14)
inductive reasoning (p. 7)

informal institutions (p. 17)
institution (p. 5)
international relations (p. 5)
modernization theory (p. 12)
multicausality (p. 8)
politics (p. 6)
power (p. 6)
qualitative method (p. 14)
quantitative method (p. 14)
rational choice (p. 14)
selection bias (p. 9)
theory (p. 10)

A woman holds an electric bulb in her mouth as part of a protest against electricity shortages in Pakistan. Millions endure electricity cuts for up to 12 hours a day, calling into question the effectiveness of the Pakistani state.

2

States
How do countries create and maintain political power?

THE YEAR 2013 REPRESENTED a political milestone for Pakistan. For the first time since the country's establishment in 1947, one democratically elected government handed power over to another. Parliamentary elections led to the sweeping victory of the Pakistan Muslim League, and its leader, Nawaz Sharif, became prime minister. Up to this point, the democratic alternation of power had been interrupted by martial law or a military coup. For many, this election represented a major step forward in this unstable country, perhaps toward the institutionalization of democracy. But while Pakistan may have made progress in the transfer of political power, there is another power challenge, one that was at the heart of the elections: electricity.

For such a large country (at around 180 million, it is nearly two-thirds the population of the United States), Pakistan suffers from an acute shortage of energy. Many wealthier countries in Europe, such as France and Germany, consume around 7,000 kilowatts of electricity per capita per year. Pakistan consumes less than a tenth of that. We might think that this is simply a function of the fact that Pakistan is a poorer country, where people would have fewer uses for electricity (such as consumer goods) or would be unable to afford it. Yet countries with a comparable level of development often show much higher levels of consumption. Although Pakistan has been actively developing nuclear technology for military purposes (something we will turn to at the end of this chapter), it has been much less successful in meeting the energy needs of its citizens, providing only around half of what is required. Pakistan is a country that literally cannot keep the lights on. Why?

Pakistan's energy problems are an excellent example of many of the points we will cover in this chapter. Part of the problem is a function of a rapidly growing population that is outstripping supply. But the country's inability to keep up with demand has been exacerbated by bureaucratic infighting and poor management, including the inability to collect payments. Power theft is widespread—by some estimates accounting for nearly half of all electricity produced. This in turn means less revenue for investment, and less energy for industrial production. By 2008, Pakistan began to suffer from rolling blackouts, sometimes lasting for more than twelve hours. The result has been increasing political protests and riots, especially in summer, as the lights go out and fans and air conditioners go silent. Solving the country's energy crisis became a critical issue in the 2013 elections and contributed to the incumbent government's loss at the polls. The electricity shortages are emblematic of a much deeper national problem. While security in Pakistan is often viewed by outsiders in terms of terrorism or other forms of political violence, this ignores basic state institutions, like laws, roads, or education, that generate political legitimacy. Where weak states are unable to build and maintain these institutions, legitimacy erodes. And where legitimacy is low, a weakly institutionalized democracy can easily collapse and give way to such alternatives as military rule. This has been the history of Pakistan, and quite possibly its future as well, unless progress is made in such areas as energy supply.

Since the elections, the Sharif government has made a number of promises to deal with the energy crisis. An obvious problem is undercapacity, as there are not enough plants to produce energy. However, another major problem is the inability of the state to meter and bill electricity. While this might sound far easier than building power plants, it is no small feat when a huge part of the public relies on illegal electrical lines, and when state institutions like the national railway, the military, and even parliament fail to pay for the energy they consume. The lack of power supplies in the face of growing demands is one of the greatest obstacles to Pakistan's development and stability. To date, modest improvements in capacity have not kept up with increasing demand. Promises notwithstanding, it appears unlikely that Sharif will be able to meet his campaign promises by the next elections in 2018. Indeed, the situation may only be worse.

- Understand the concept of the state as a central institution in comparative politics.
- Explain how regimes serve as the fundamental rules and norms of politics.
- Distinguish the concept of government as the leadership in charge of running the state.
- Compare different forms of political legitimacy: charismatic, traditional, and rational-legal.
- Analyze how states can vary in autonomy and capacity, and how this can shape their power.

WE BEGIN OUR STUDY OF the basic institutions of politics by looking at the state. This discussion is often difficult for North Americans, who are not used to thinking about politics in terms of centralized political power. Indeed, for Americans the word *state* typically conjures up the idea of local, not centralized, politics. But for most people around the world, *state* refers to centralized authority, the locus of power.[1] In this chapter, we will break down the basic institutions that make up states and discuss how states manage freedom and equality and distribute power toward achieving their authority. The chapter will define what states are and what they comprise, distinguishing a state from a government and a regime. We will also consider their origins. For most of human history, politics was built on organizations other than states, and myriad forms of authority existed around the world. Yet now only states remain. What caused them to come into existence?

Once we have discussed the nature and origins of the state, we will look at some different ways in which states can be compared. This discussion will analyze the different forms of legitimacy that give states their power and the varying degrees of this power. Can we speak of states as weak or strong? If so, how would we measure their strength or weakness? To answer this question, we will make a distinction between state capacity and state autonomy and examine how this might differ across cases and policy areas. Here, we consider states as a cause, a force that can shape other institutions. With these ideas more clearly in hand, we will return to our theme of individual freedom and collective equality and consider the future of the state.

Defining the State

What exactly do we mean by *state*? Political scientists, drawing on the work of the German scholar Max Weber, typically define the **state** as the organization that maintains a monopoly of violence over a territory.[2] This definition of what a state is and does may seem severe, but a bit of explanation should help flesh out this concept. One of the most important elements of a state is what we call **sovereignty**, the ability to carry out actions and policies within a territory independent of external actors and internal rivals. In other words, a state needs to be able to act as the primary authority over its territory and the people who live there, passing and enforcing

state (1) The organization that maintains a monopoly of force over a given territory; (2) a set of political institutions to generate and execute policy regarding freedom and equality

sovereignty The ability of a state to carry out actions or policies within a territory independently from external actors or internal rivals

laws, defining and protecting rights, resolving disputes between people and organizations, and generating domestic security.

To achieve this, a state needs power, typically (but not only) physical power. If a state cannot defend its territory from outside actors such as other states, then it runs the risk that those rivals will interfere with its authority, inflicting damage, taking its territory, or destroying the state outright. Similarly, if the state faces powerful opponents within its own territory, such as organized crime or rebel movements, its rules and policies may be undermined. Thus, to secure control, a state must be armed. To protect against international rivals, states need armies. And in response to domestic rivals, states need a police force. In fact, the word *police* comes from an old French word meaning "to govern."

A state is thus a set of institutions that seeks to wield the most force within a territory, establishing order and deterring challengers from inside and out. In so doing, it provides security for its subjects by limiting the danger of external attack and internal crime and disorder—both of which threaten the state and its citizens. In some ways, a state (especially a nondemocratic one) is a kind of protection racket—demanding money in return for security and order, staking out turf, defending those it protects from rivals, settling internal disputes, and punishing those who do not pay.[3]

But most states are far more complex than mere entities that apply force. Unlike criminal rackets, the state is made up of a large number of institutions that are engaged in the process of turning political ideas into policy. Laws and regulations, property rights, health and labor, the environment, and transportation are but a few policy areas that typically fall under the responsibility of the state. Because of these responsibilities, the state serves as a set of institutions (ministries, offices, army, police) that society deems necessary to achieve basic goals. When there is a lack of agreement on these goals, the state must attempt to reconcile different views and seek (or impose) consensus.

The public views the state as legitimate, vital, and appropriate. States are thus strongly institutionalized and not easily changed. Leaders and policies may come and go, but the state remains, even in the face of crisis, turmoil, or revolution. Although destruction through war or civil conflict can eliminate states altogether, even this outcome is unusual and states are soon re-created. Thus, the state is defined as a monopoly of force over a given territory, but it is also the set of political institutions that helps create and implement policies and resolve conflict. It is, if you will, the machinery of politics, establishing order and turning politics into

---

IN FOCUS   **The State Is . . .**

- The monopoly of force over a given territory.
- A set of political institutions that generate and carry out policy.
- Typically highly institutionalized.
- Sovereign.
- Characterized by such institutions as an army, a police force, taxation, a judiciary, and a social welfare system.

policy. Thus, many social scientists argue that the state, as a bundle of institutions, is an important driver of economic development, the rise of democracy, and other processes.

Beyond *state*, a few other terms need to be defined. First, we should make a distinction between a state and a **regime**, which is defined as the fundamental rules and norms of politics. More specifically, a regime embodies long-term goals that guide the state with regard to individual freedom and collective equality, where power should reside, and how power should be used. At the most basic level, we can speak of a democratic regime or a nondemocratic one. In a democratic regime, the rules and norms of politics give the public a large role in governance, as well as certain individual rights and liberties. A nondemocratic regime, in contrast, limits public participation and favors those in power. Both types of regimes can vary in the extent to which power is centralized and in the relationship between freedom and equality. The democratic regime of the United States is not the same as that of Canada; China's nondemocratic regime is not the same as Cuba's or Syria's. Some of these regime differences can be found in basic documents such as constitutions, but often the rules and norms that distinguish one regime from another are informal, unwritten, and implicit, requiring careful study. Finally, we should also note that in some nondemocratic countries where politics is dominated by a single individual, observers may use *regime* to refer to that leader, emphasizing the view that all decisions flow from that one person. As King Louis XIV of France famously put it, *L'état, c'est moi* ("I am the state"). However, the term *regime* is not inherently negative any more than are *rules* or *norms*.

In summary, if the state is a monopoly of force and a set of political institutions that secure the population and generate policy, then the regime is defined as the norms and rules that establish the proper relation between freedom and equality and the use of power toward that end. If the state is the machinery of politics, like a computer, one can think of a regime as its software, the programming that defines its capabilities. Each computer runs differently, and more or less productively, depending on the software installed. Over time, software becomes outdated and unstable, and machines become less efficient or even crash. However, countries and regimes are not like consumer electronics that we can simply throw away or upgrade. In fact, as we know all too well, it can be disastrous to upgrade from one operating system to another. No matter how hard we try to erase old political institutions, many aspects of them tend to persist. This is a particularly big obstacle to reforming or transforming states and regimes—building democracy, reducing corruption, or ameliorating ethnic conflict all involve changing existing, deeply embedded institutions. We cannot simply reformat or reboot existing institutions.

regime The fundamental rules and norms of politics, embodying long-term goals regarding individual freedom and collective equality, where power should reside, and the use of that power

---

| **IN FOCUS** | A Regime Is . . . |

- Norms and rules regarding individual freedom and collective equality, the locus of power, and the use of that power.
- Institutionalized, but can be changed by dramatic social events such as a revolution.
- Categorized at the most basic level as either democratic or authoritarian.
- Often embodied in a constitution.

FRANCE

SOUTH AFRICA

RUSSIA

COMPARING REGIME CHANGE IN FRANCE, SOUTH AFRICA, AND RUSSIA

Regimes are an important component of the larger state framework. Regimes do not easily or quickly change, although they can be transformed or altered, usually by dramatic social events such as revolutions and national crises. Most revolutions, in fact, can be seen as revolts not against the state or even the leadership but against the current regime—to overthrow the old rules and norms and replace them with new ones.

One good example can be seen in France. In 1789, the French Revolution overthrew the monarchy and established what is known as the First Republic, whose constitution for the first time placed power in the hands of the people and the legislature. Since then a number of important political events—the rise and fall of Napoleon, the Franco-Prussian War, and World War II—triggered the subsequent collapse of existing political institutions and thus necessitated the construction of a new set of rules and political norms. Some of these regimes were more strongly institutionalized than others. The Fourth Republic, which lasted between 1946 and 1958, was notably unstable, with power vested in the legislature and divided among a number of polarized political parties. As the country struggled with decolonization in the late 1950s, France teetered on the verge of a military coup. Former General Charles De Gaulle, noted for his role as leader of the wartime resistance, was brought out of retirement to prevent violence, and the legislature suspended the constitution. In 1958, the Fifth Republic introduced a directly elected presidency and a new electoral system meant to limit the number of parties (we shall discuss both of these in Chapter 6 and in the France case). These institutional changes were meant to address past political instability by concentrating greater power in the hands of the executive.

In another example, during most of the twentieth century South Africa functioned under a racist regime that institutionalized discrimination against the majority nonwhite population, severely limiting its political and economic rights. After many decades of domestic and international opposition, the government agreed to free elections that paved the way for a political transition. The end of white apartheid rule led to the drafting of an entirely new constitution in 1996 that extended a range of civil rights to all South Africans. One of these new rights was the official recognition of eleven national languages, meant to address the substantial ethnic diversity repressed under the previous regime.

But changes in constitutions do not always mean that there has been an immediate or a complete change in the regime. For example, South Africa's media still faces government pressure and censorship in spite of democratization, in part as a result of national security laws retained from the apartheid era. A failed coup in the Soviet Union in 1991 led to the end of the communist regime and the breakup of the Soviet Union into fifteen new states, including Russia. However, even this dramatic change did not lead to the institutionalization of democracy, and many communist-era political values and norms have persisted. Most notable is the continued centralization of power around the president and a narrow ruling elite, known as the *siloviki*, or "men of power." These individuals largely hail from the communist-era security services. Certainly most would regard the cases of South Africa and Russia as regime changes, based on their profound political transformations. However, our broader point is that even in the case of regime change a much wider range of institutions, formal and informal, do not disappear, and in some cases may subvert new political rules. The United States learned this, tragically, in the case of Iraq, where there was a widespread belief that the elimination of Saddam Hussein would lead to a relatively straightforward transition to democracy.

Our third term related to the concepts of state and regime is the most familiar one: *government*. **Government** can be defined as the leadership that runs the state. If the state is the machinery of politics, and the regime its programming, then the government operates the machinery. The government may consist of democratically elected legislators, presidents, and prime ministers, or it may be made up of leaders who gained office through force or other nondemocratic means. Whatever their path to power, governments all hold particular ideas regarding freedom and equality, and they all attempt to use the state to realize those ideas. But few governments are able to act with complete autonomy in this regard. Democratic and nondemocratic governments must confront the existing regime that has built up over time. Push too hard against an existing regime, and resistance, rebellion, or collapse may occur. For example, Mikhail Gorbachev's attempt to transform the Soviet Union's regime in the 1980s contributed to that country's dissolution. Today, the Chinese government fears similar chaos if political reforms allow for greater participation or political competition against the Communist Party.

In part because of the power of regimes, governments tend to be weakly institutionalized—that is, the public does not typically view those in power as irreplaceable or believe that the country would collapse without them (Figure 2.1). In democratic regimes, governments are replaced fairly frequently, and even in nondemocratic settings rulers are continuously threatened by rivals and by their own mortality. Governments come and go, whereas regimes and states may live on for decades or centuries.

Finally, the term **country** can be taken as shorthand for the combined political entities defined so far—state, regime, government—as well as for the people who live within that political system. We will often speak about various countries in this textbook, and when we do, we are referring to the entire political entity and its citizens.

government The leadership or elite in charge of running the state

country Term used to refer to state, government, regime, and the people who live within that political system

---

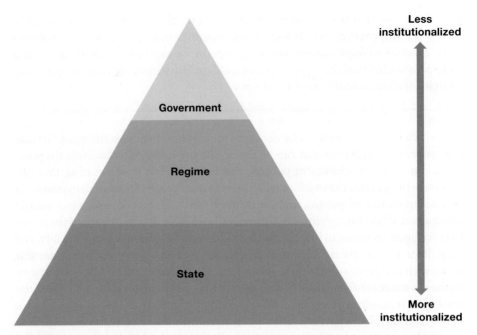

FIGURE 2.1 State, Regime, and Government

Governments are relatively less institutionalized than regimes and states. Governments may come and go, while regimes and states usually have more staying power.

The Origins of Political Organization

So far, we have noted that modern politics is defined by states, which monopolize force and generate and realize policy. This political machinery is directed by a particular regime and by the government in power. Governments generate short-term goals regarding freedom and equality, which are in part based on an existing regime that provides an institutionalized set of political norms and values. This combination, linking state, regime, and government, is relatively new in human history, though, to be clear, as long as there have been human beings (around 200,000 years), there has been some form of human organization. In our earliest stages, we were likely organized by families and tribes. Genetic research suggests that the modern human population outside Africa derives largely from a group of people who rapidly migrated outward less than 100,000 years ago, displacing other archaic human populations around the world as they went. Groups descended from these bands also traveled by sea (at least 60,000 years ago, and perhaps much earlier). These developments suggest organization, some technological sophistication, and the ability to pass knowledge from generation to generation.

By 8000 B.C.E., agriculture, animal domestication, and sedentary communities emerged in the Middle East, allowing more complex political systems to form. From about 4000 B.C.E., if not earlier, cities of several thousand people emerged. Technological sophistication led to specialization, consumer goods, and trade; agricultural surplus helped increase population density; and from these developments came issues of inequality and personal freedom. Those with economic surpluses sought to protect their riches from theft. Those without surpluses sought a greater share of the group's resources. And both feared attack by outside groups or internal competitors that might covet their lands, crops, and homes. It was human innovations like technology, trade, and agriculture that probably first led to the conflict between the individual and the collective. Who gets what? Who has the right to do what? And how should these decisions be made and enforced? Having to reconcile freedom and equality in turn raises questions about where power should reside and toward what end. Alongside the city, the state emerged to answer these questions.

There are several things in this account that remain unclear. What was the sequence of urbanization and state building? Our earlier discussion suggests that communities formed, settled, and then built political institutions, but we could also imagine early forms of political leadership that helped establish sedentary communities. An endogenous explanation—that both were institutionalized simultaneously—may make the most sense. Further questions concern the role of centralization, consensus, and coercion. Did loose communities form and slowly centralize because of the economic opportunities this provided? Did communities perhaps develop for primarily defensive reasons? Were these systems constructed through consensus or coercion?

In the absence of evidence, philosophers have long debated these questions. Some, like the philosopher Thomas Hobbes, believed that human beings voluntarily submitted to political authority to overcome anarchy, which ensures neither freedom nor equality. In return for giving up many of their rights, people gained security and a foundation upon which to build a civilization. In contrast, Jean-Jacques Rousseau believed that human beings were in essence "noble savages" who were instinctively compassionate and egalitarian. It was civilization and the rise of the state that corrupted them by institutionalizing a system of inequality. These competing visions provide different interpretations of civilization and political organization, but both emphasize that sovereignty emerged through a "social contract" between rulers and ruled.

For a long time, scholars have debated whether Rousseau or Hobbes provided a more accurate view of early state development. Recent research, however, indicates that neither was correct. Many scholars assumed that humans lived relatively solitary lives—what one calls "primordial individualism"—before modern forms of political organization took hold, but we now know that family and tribal organization has a much older past. In addition, while warfare was possibly a driver of political organization, it may have broken out less between individuals, as was often assumed, than between rival groups. As human populations expanded, tribes battled one another for resources and territory. Pre-state societies were probably much more violent than states are now. By some estimates, anywhere from a quarter to over half of the male population died at the hands of others, and the expansion of pre-state societies coincided with the extermination of many large species around the world that were apparently hunted to extinction. The widespread taking of life appears to have begun with the emergence of modern humans, long before the rise of the state.

States, then, appear to have emerged out of this history of violence. As one group conquered others, political organizations brought new peoples and territories under control. Such organizations also allowed for more effective defense, especially in urbanized communities that could build city walls and stockpile weapons. In short, where the inherent conflict between people intersected with agricultural technology, population density, and urbanization, state building followed. Whereas we once speculated that technological innovation, civilization, and human political organization were the sources of violence, the opposite now appears to be true.[4]

Complex organizations began to emerge about 8,000 years ago in the Middle East, bearing the hallmarks of politics that exist to this day, such as taxation, bureaucracy, laws, military force, and leadership. Some of these political units were relatively small, such as the city-states that emerged in ancient Greece some 2,700 years ago. In other cases, large and highly sophisticated empires emerged, as in China, South America, the Middle East, and Africa. Many of these developments occurred at relatively the same time, between the ninth and thirteenth centuries. Across these political systems, economic relations were based on agricultural production, while specialized goods and trade were secondary activities. Unlike modern countries, these early political systems often did not have defined borders, though many experienced increasing forms of political centralization.

The Rise of the Modern State

The diversity of early political systems eventually gave way to the modern state, which first took shape in Europe. Why the modern state emerged in Europe and came to dominate the world is uncertain, but it may in part be due to historical chance and the curious advantage of backwardness. Two thousand years ago, Europe, like other parts of the world, was dominated by a single, large empire—in this case, the Roman Empire. Spanning thousands of miles across western Europe, North Africa, and Egypt, the Roman Empire developed a complex political system that tied together millions of people and generated an advanced infrastructure of cities, laws, trade, knowledge, and roads. After a thousand years, however, the Roman Empire eventually declined, succumbing to the pressures of overexpansion and increased attacks by rival forces. In the fifth century C.E., Rome itself was sacked by invaders.

As the Roman Empire collapsed, the complex political institutions and the other benefits that had extended across its territory largely disappeared, particularly in western Europe. The security generated by imperial control evaporated, replaced by roving bands of marauders. Roads and the other basic forms of infrastructure that people depended on eroded. Rules and regulations fragmented and lost their power. The knowledge and technology accumulated under the empire were lost or forgotten, and the advanced system of trade and travel between communities came to an end. Much of Europe reverted to anarchy, entering the period commonly known as the Dark Ages, from about 500 C.E. to about 1000 C.E. Europe's rise to power was thus not preordained; around 1000 C.E., Europe's total wealth was less than half that of China or India, and it would not begin to close this gap until the nineteenth century. It may be hard to believe, but during the first half of this millennium, virtually every part of the globe experienced a period of growth and innovation—except Europe.[5]

Yet, paradoxically, this period of dramatic decline and anarchy appears to have set the stage for the creation of the modern state. As the sociologist Charles Tilly has noted, in Europe's fragmented, unstable, and violent environment, new political organizations began to develop, in constant competition with their rivals.[6] In some cases, these were formed by marauders who realized that they could earn a better living by controlling and taxing one group of people than by pillaging one place and moving on to the next. Warlords staked out small areas of land that they could easily defend and consolidated control over these regions, fighting off rival groups. In other cases, the people banded together to defend themselves. As Tilly and others have concluded, the modern state emerged from and in reaction to what was essentially organized crime: armed groups staking out turf, offering protection, and demanding payment in return. The constant warfare among these numerous rivals, which created a competitive and fluid environment, seems to have generated a kind of rapid organizational evolution. Groups that could quickly adapt in response to new challenges and challengers survived, while less successful groups were conquered and disappeared.

Not only history but also geography has played a role in the rise of the modern state. Europe's rapid political evolution probably also owed something to the continent's proximity to Asia and the Middle East, which gave it access to new plants, animals, and technological innovations that were unavailable to peoples in the Americas or Africa. China, which also benefited from its ability to import a range of foreign goods and technologies, had by the third century B.C.E. developed one of the most sophisticated political organizations of the time, at least a thousand years before Europe. Why then did China not come to rule the world instead of Europe, and why did "Europe" come to mean a collection of rival states while "China" came to mean a single enormous country? One explanation may involve the centralization of the Chinese Empire, which was facilitated by the absence of significant internal geographic boundaries, the related ethnic and cultural homogenization of the population, and the absence of major neighboring political rivals. This led to an early and highly developed state—though its lack of major competitors eventually limited its organizational evolution. In contrast, Europe's weaknesses—ethnic and linguistic fragmentation, numerous rival actors, and geographic boundaries—hindered the creation of a single European state. That said, we should not be too deterministic in explaining these outcomes. For example, the preceding discussion largely discounts the role of ideas. It may be that Europe's political development was driven by the rise of Christianity and the impact of religious values and/or the struggle between the Catholic Church and various states. But China also faced numerous upheavals, warfare, and religious changes across its history. At various points, these struggles could have led to the permanent fragmentation of China into a collection of states similar to Europe—albeit with a thousand-year head start in technology, bureaucracy, and education.[7]

TIMELINE Political Organization

8th–7th CENTURIES B.C.E.	Beginning of Greek city-states; centralization of political power in Europe
6th–5th CENTURIES B.C.E.	Establishment of Roman republic; first development of democracy in Athens
5th–3rd CENTURIES B.C.E.	Unification of China under Qin dynasty
2nd–1st CENTURIES B.C.E.	Roman conquest of Greece
1st–2nd CENTURIES C.E.	Roman Empire expands across Europe and into the Middle East; zenith of centralized imperial power in Europe
3rd–4th CENTURIES C.E.	Internal decline of Roman Empire; beginning of European Dark Ages; development stagnates
5th–6th CENTURIES C.E.	Rome sacked by the Visigoths; widespread strife among competing European warlords
7th–8th CENTURIES C.E.	Rise of Islamic Empire from Southern Europe to Central Asia
9th–10th CENTURIES C.E.	Viking raids across Europe
11th–12th CENTURIES C.E.	European crusades into Middle East; beginning of consolidation of Europe into distinct political units through warfare
12th–13th CENTURIES C.E.	Period of rapid innovation and development: invention of mechanical clock; adoption of paper and compass from Asia and the Middle East
13th CENTURY C.E.	Rise of Ottoman Empire in Southern Europe, North Africa, and the Middle East
14th–15th CENTURIES C.E.	Voyages of exploration and early imperialism; centralization of early European states
16th–17th CENTURIES C.E.	Scientific revolution; development of modern states; development of modern identities of nationalism and patriotism

Out of the constant warfare of the European Dark Ages emerged the first modern states, which possessed three important advantages over alternative forms of political organization. First, states encouraged economic development. Before and during the Dark Ages, most Europeans lived under an economic system based on subsistence agriculture. Property such as land tended to be monopolized by those in power rather than owned by those who worked it. Warlords could tie the people to the land (through serfdom), extract their labor, and levy heavy taxes on those who produced nonagricultural goods. However, such economic conditions were counterproductive for society as a whole: individuals had little incentive to produce if the fruits of their labor were simply taken by others. Rulers who created laws, regulations, and infrastructure that permitted and respected private property and individual profit found that production grew, giving the ruler more resources to tax or borrow (and with which to make war). Property rights thus became a hallmark of state development.[8]

Second, states encouraged technological innovation. Some rulers who pursued such innovation to increase their economic and military power recognized that, like private commerce and trade, new technologies would stimulate economic development by providing new goods and services. When technological innovation was harnessed to commerce, economic development grew dramatically. These rulers viewed technological change not as a threat to their power but as a means to expand it. Many of the technologies that made Europe powerful as it set off to conquer the world—gunpowder, advanced mathematics, modern mapmaking, paper, astronomy—originated in other parts of the world. But the Europeans absorbed these innovations and put them to new use. What mattered most was not who made the discoveries but how these discoveries were encouraged or used by the state. Whether this application of innovation was a function primarily of intense European competition or of cultural values is still a source of debate (see Chapter 3).[9] Whatever the reason, technological innovation, combined with state power, set the stage for modern politics.

A third advantage was domestic stability, which increased trade and commerce and permitted the development of infrastructure. Finally, and related to this, people's ability to travel more freely within the territory of their country encouraged interaction and the emergence of a shared identity. The state, through printed documents, education, and legal codes, also contributed to the standardization of language. People in Europe began to see themselves as having a common identity comprising shared values. Instead of defining themselves primarily by their trade, clan, religion, or town, people began to see themselves as, for example, English, French, or German. Ethnicity proved to be a powerful asset to the state, for it in turn fostered nationalism. This will be discussed in detail in the next chapter.

Although the modern state offered all these advantages, by around 1500, modern states covered only 20 percent of the globe—the rest was ruled by alternative forms of centralized organization or none at all. But this was soon to change. Well-organized and armed with advanced technologies, growing national identity, and economic resources, the states of Europe began to rapidly accrue power. As economic power grew, so did the ability of the state to manage ever-greater numbers of people and ever more territory. Increased finances and state organization also allowed for the development of major militaries. Able to conquer and control larger pieces of land, states began to defeat and absorb their European rivals. Spiritual rivals also lost political power. The Thirty Years' War (1618–48), in part a struggle between Roman Catholicism and Protestantism, culminated in the Treaty of Westphalia in 1648. Under this treaty, the authority of the pope over Europe's people was radically curtailed. Without this rival spiritual authority, states were free to direct religion within their own territory, subordinating the spiritual to the political. State sovereignty as we understand it today is often dated from the Treaty of Westphalia.

European states now began to expand their economic, technological, and military powers beyond their own shores. During the seventeenth and eighteenth centuries, Spain and Portugal took control of large parts of the Americas, while the Dutch, French, and British expanded state power into Asia. By the nineteenth century, nearly all of Africa had similarly been divided up among European states and incorporated into their respective empires.

The organizational structure of the state was thus imposed around the world by force. Yet as European control receded in the twentieth century, the structure of the state remained—indeed, states grew in number as the lands and peoples subjugated by Europe gained sovereignty. Although peoples all around the world resisted and eventually threw off European domination, they viewed the state as a superior—or at least inevitable—form of political evolution, and they adopted it for their own purposes. The world thus became a world of states. States established international boundaries and rules and were the primary actors in domestic and international politics around the world. Countries like Mexico or Nigeria threw off colonial rule, but they retained and expanded the state institutions originally imposed by imperialism.

The rapid spread of states may be viewed as the triumph of a form of organization that allowed groups of people to destroy political rivals, no matter how sophisticated. But this has not come without cost. Whereas Europe took several hundred years to create the modern state, much of the world has been forced to take up this form of organization and its institutions more quickly. And the historical paths of Africa, Asia, and South America were radically different from that of Europe. Many of the new states on these continents have lacked the resources, infrastructure, shared national identities, and capital that much older states developed over a thousand years. Consequently, these newer states often face significant challenges, such as establishing sovereignty over territories where a multitude of peoples, languages, religions, and cultures may coexist—problems that most European states solved only over the course of centuries and at the cost of many lives lost in wars and revolutions.[10] For better or worse, although Europe no longer directly rules over much of the earth, it has left us with the legacy of the state.

CHINA

GERMANY

COMPARING THE CONSOLIDATION OF STATES

China and Germany illustrate how the timing of the consolidation of states can influence political development (and even contemporary politics). A centralized state in China can be traced back to the Qin dynasty (221–206 B.C.E.), well before the emergence of states in Europe. China's early centralization facilitated its rise to being a global leader in science, culture, and international trade. But the early development of a powerful and overbearing state bureaucracy, steeped in conservative Confucian ideas, stunted entrepreneurialism and may partly explain why China missed out on the Industrial Revolution that was taking place in Europe. China's resulting lack of industrialization, in turn, helps explain why it ultimately was unable to resist military incursions by European powers and the Japanese. Under attack by more economically advanced foreign powers, the Chinese state was eroded, and the last Chinese dynasty was displaced in 1911. After a period of decentralized warlord rule and civil war, the Chinese Communist Party, under the leadership of Mao Zedong, destroyed its rivals and recentralized the Chinese state, giving it control over important areas like the economy. In spite of economic reform over the past four decades, the Chinese state maintains a great deal of power in such areas as the development of infrastructure or censorship.

Germany, in contrast, lacked a centralized state until the nineteenth century, and lagged behind the more modern centralized and industrialized parts of Europe. The nineteenth-century rise and consolidation of the kingdom of Prussia (located in the eastern portion of contemporary Germany) led to the creation of an efficient bureaucracy and a powerful military, and became the core of the first centralized German state, established only in 1871. Late unification facilitated Germany's rapid industrialization, but its state was more powerful and militaristic than in most other industrialized countries of the time, and much less constrained by a middle class or democratic checks. Newly unified Germany pursued its impressive statist "modernization from above" within an authoritarian political system. Its efficient and overbearing state helped it to catch up with and surpass the industrialized European countries. But it also promoted German aggression against its European neighbors that culminated in Germany's disastrous defeat in two world wars. Germany's loss in World War II led to the German state being divided in two, and it was only reunified in 1990 after the end of the Cold War.

Contemporary China's authoritarian leadership benefits from a long and proud tradition of a strong state that is unquestioned by most of its citizens. In contrast, Germans today associate a strong state with fascism, consecutive defeats in the two world wars, and the division of the German state. After World War II, Germany adopted a political system that limits state power through federalism and a strong constitutional court. Most Germans today are uncomfortable showing pride in their state.

Comparing State Power

It is clear from the preceding discussion that political evolution has been a lengthy and somewhat arbitrary process. Where conditions allowed for human beings to settle permanently, complex forms of political organization emerged, with features that reflect the modern struggle over freedom, equality, and the allocation of power. But only over the past few centuries has the modern state taken shape, forging new political, economic, and social institutions that have made it so powerful. States quickly eradicated every other form of political organization and now lay claim to all corners of the earth.

Still, not all states are the same. As we have observed, some states are powerful, effective, prosperous, and stable; others are weak, disorganized, and largely incapable of effective action—even basic tasks we take for granted in countries with stronger states. Moreover, a single state can have a commanding presence in one area but be ineffectual in another—such as Pakistan, for example: able to build nuclear weapons, but unable to provide regular electricity. What explains this range? How do we understand differences in what we might call "stateness"— that is, in the power of states? To answer this question and make effective comparisons, we need a few more conceptual tools with which to work.

LEGITIMACY

The first concept, **legitimacy**, is a value whereby something or someone is recognized and accepted as right and proper. A legitimate institution or person, therefore, is widely accepted and recognized by the public. Legitimacy confers authority and power. In the case of states, we know that they wield a great deal of force. But is that the only reason that people recognize their authority? In the absence of legitimacy, states must rely largely on coercion to retain their power. However, where there is legitimacy, people obey the law even when the threat of punishment is slight. We may pay our taxes, stand at the crosswalk, or serve in the military not because we fear punishment or seek immediate reward but because we assume that the state has the authority to ask these things of us. As states provide security and other benefits, they

legitimacy A value whereby an institution is accepted by the public as right and proper, thus giving it authority and power

can engender a sense of reciprocal responsibility to the state. Legitimacy thus creates power that relies not on coercion but on consent. Without legitimacy, a state would have to use the continuous threat of force to maintain order—a difficult task—or expect that many of its rules and policies would go unheeded. As one scholar puts it, in the absence of legitimacy "the state can never be anything but a predatory imposition upon many or most citizens."[11]

Legitimacy is therefore a critical component of stateness. Legitimacy, however, does not depend on freedom or equality; a society may be largely unfree or unequal and still view its state as legitimate, no matter how difficult we might imagine that to be.

How then does a state become legitimate? Let us turn again to Max Weber, who argued that political legitimacy comes in three basic forms: traditional, charismatic, and rational-legal.[12] **Traditional legitimacy** rests on the idea that someone or something is valid because "it has always been that way." In other words, this legitimacy is built on the idea that certain aspects of politics are to be accepted because they have been built over a long period of time. They are viewed as part of the historical identity of the people themselves. Traditional legitimacy often embodies historical myths and legends as well as the continuity between past and present. Rituals and ceremonies all help to reinforce traditional legitimacy by providing actions and symbols that are ancient, unique, and dramatic. A long-standing monarchy, where one family retains power over generations, is a good example of a traditionally legitimate institution. However, *traditional* is not the same as outdated. Even a modern institution, like an elected office or a regime, can develop traditional legitimacy if it is in place long enough. In short, traditional legitimacy is built on history and continuity. Its legitimacy comes in part from the simple fact that it has the weight of history on its side. Change becomes difficult to imagine if an institution has existed "since time immemorial."

Charismatic legitimacy is in many ways the opposite of traditional legitimacy. When we use the word *charisma* in everyday conversation, we often mean someone who is good-looking or charming. But this is a much-reduced version of the term's original meaning, sometimes rendered as "the gift of grace," meaning the favor of God. Instead of relying on the weight of history and the continuity of certain roles or values, charismatic legitimacy is based on the power of ideas or beliefs. Charisma is typically embodied by individuals who can move and persuade the public through ideas and the manner in which they present them. Some individuals possess a certain magnetism that binds who they are to what they say. Jesus and Muhammad are perfect examples of charismatic figures who could gather huge followings through the power of their ideas, which they asserted were transmitted to them from God. Although in its origins *charisma* indicated this spiritual link, in modern politics charisma can encompass secular ideas as well. Adolf Hitler was clearly a charismatic figure who wielded ideas and language to articulate the need for war and genocide.

As you can imagine, charismatic legitimacy is not institutionalized and thus is fairly tenuous, since it commonly dies with the individual who possesses it. But charismatic legitimacy can be transformed into traditional legitimacy through the creation of rituals and values that are meant to capture the spirit and intent of the charismatic leader's power. Religions, monarchies, even constitutions and regimes can be examples of this. Weber called this kind of institutionalization "the routinization of charisma."

In contrast to the first two forms of legitimacy, **rational-legal legitimacy** is based not on history or rituals (traditional legitimacy) or on the force of ideas and those who present them (charismatic legitimacy) but rather on a system of laws and procedures

traditional legitimacy Legitimacy that accepts aspects of politics because they have been institutionalized over a long period of time

charismatic legitimacy Legitimacy built on the force of ideas embodied by an individual leader

rational-legal legitimacy Legitimacy based on a system of laws and procedures that are highly institutionalized

that are presumed to be neutral or rational. Leaders or political officials gain legitimacy through the rules by which they come to office. People abide by the decisions of those in power because those individuals are abiding by existing institutionalized rules. In this case, it is not the individual leaders who are important, or even their values or ideas, but the offices they hold. Once they leave office, they lose much of their authority. This can be contrasted with traditional or charismatic legitimacy, where authority tends to reside with individuals rather than a set of rules.

The world of modern states is built on a rational-legal foundation. States rely on bureaucracies, paperwork, and thousands of individuals to make daily decisions on a wide range of issues. Ideally, the public accepts these decisions as the proper way to get things done, and it presumes that these decisions are reasonably fair and predictable. For example, if there are elections, the people accept the outcome even if their preferred candidate loses, and they obey those who won. What's more, legitimacy is not confined to political actors within the state; our own individual legitimacy as citizens comes from a rational-legal foundation: our driver's licenses, identification numbers, passports, or voter registration cards all confer a certain form of authority and power—from the state to the citizen.

Although modern states are built on rational-legal legitimacy, traditional and charismatic legitimacy have not disappeared. In almost any country, one can see variations in the mix of traditional, charismatic, and rational-legal legitimacy. Political leaders in many countries throughout modern history have wielded a great deal of charismatic power and have sometimes become the centers of large "cults of personality," which we will explore further in Chapter 8. These cults portray the leader as the father (or, occasionally, the mother) of the nation and imbue him or her with almost superhuman powers. Charismatic leadership, and the power that it places in the hands of one individual, can corrupt, as we have seen in the case of North Korea's Kim Jong-Il and his son, Kim Jong-Un. But some charismatic figures, political leaders like Mohandas K. Gandhi, who fought for independence from British rule in India, or Nelson Mandela, who struggled to end apartheid in South Africa, have dramatically changed the course of politics for the better.

Traditional power can similarly be found in a wide variety of countries. The United Kingdom, Japan, Saudi Arabia, and more than forty other countries still have monarchs. The powers of most, though not all, of these monarchs are now quite limited, yet even constitutional monarchs remain important symbols and attract national

IN FOCUS   Three Types of Legitimacy

TYPE	CHARACTERISTICS	EXAMPLE
TRADITIONAL LEGITIMACY	Built by habit and custom over time, stressing history; strongly institutionalized	Monarch (Queen Elizabeth II)
CHARISMATIC LEGITIMACY	Built on the force of ideas and the presence of the leader; weakly institutionalized	Revolutionary hero (Vladimir Ilyich Lenin)
RATIONAL-LEGAL LEGITIMACY	Built on rules and procedures and the offices that create and enforce those rules; strongly institutionalized	Elected executive (Donald Trump)

and sometimes even international attention. Families can have a similar legitimacy in politics. In India, Indira Gandhi of the Congress Party (no relation to Mohandas) served as prime minister for 15 years, in the 1960s, 1970s, and 1980s. Upon her death, her son Rajiv became prime minister. After his death, his wife, Sonia, became head of Congress, and until recent elections her uncharismatic son, Rahul, was duly expected to become prime minister. Not just individuals and families but also rules and regulations can gain a kind of traditional legitimacy if they function for so long that people can't imagine doing things any other way. The U.S. Constitution, for example, is not only a set of rules for conducting politics; it is also considered a sacred symbol of what makes the United States unique and powerful. Is it difficult to modify the Constitution because of the procedures involved, or because a resistance has developed over time to tinkering with this "sacred" document? If the latter is true, then it is not simply rational-legal legitimacy but also traditional legitimacy that binds American politics together.

To summarize, legitimacy is a central component of stateness. Traditional legitimacy stresses ritual and continuity; charismatic legitimacy, the force of ideas as embodied in a leader; rational-legal legitimacy, laws and rules. Whatever its form, legitimacy makes it possible for the state to carry out its basic functions. Without it, states find it very difficult to function. If the public has little faith in the state, it will frequently ignore political responsibilities, such as paying taxes, abiding by regulations, or serving in the armed forces. Under these conditions, the state has only one tool left to maintain order: the threat of force. While we might assume that violent states are somehow inherently powerful, states that use the most coercion against their citizens are often the most weakly institutionalized, because without violence, they cannot get the public to willingly comply with the rules and duties set forth.

CENTRALIZATION OR DECENTRALIZATION

In addition to enjoying various kinds and levels of political legitimacy, states are defined by different distributions of power. As we noted in Chapter 1, individual freedom is typically associated with the decentralization of power, whereas collective equality usually accompanies a greater centralization of power.

federalism A system in which significant state powers, such as taxation, lawmaking, and security, are devolved to regional or local bodies

asymmetric federalism When power is divided unevenly between regional bodies—for example, some regions are given greater power over taxation or language rights than others—a more likely outcome in a country with significant ethnic divisions

unitary state A state in which most political power exists at the national level, with limited local authority

State power can be centralized or decentralized in a couple of different ways, the first of which is the dispersal of power within the state. Under federalism, powers such as taxation, lawmaking, and security are devolved to regional bodies (such as states in the United States and India, *Länder* in Germany, and provinces in Canada) and to local legislatures that control specific territories within the country. These powers are defined in the national constitution and therefore not easily constricted or eliminated by any government. Here the argument is that federalism helps represent local interests as well as check the growth of central power (which may be viewed as a threat to democracy). We should note that federalism need not be uniform; some countries, like Spain, Russia, and India, rely on asymmetric federalism, whereby power is divided unevenly between regional bodies. Some regions are given greater power over taxation or language rights than others, a more likely outcome in a country with significant ethnic divisions. In unitary states, by contrast, political power is concentrated at the national level, and local authority is limited. The central government is responsible for most areas of policy. Territorial divisions in unitary states like China, Japan, and France have less bearing on political power. If federalism reflects a view that overcentralization is unrepresentative or dangerous, the argument for a unitary state is that local interests can be represented without recourse to regional political institutions. Federalism may weaken state efficiency by dispersing power among too many competing authorities, and exacerbate, rather than weaken, ethnic or regional conflict.

In recent years, there has been a greater tendency toward decentralization in many states. This process, called **devolution**, has become popular for a number of reasons. In some cases, devolution has been viewed as a way to increase state legitimacy by moving political power closer to the people, a concern as states have grown larger and more complex over time. In other cases, devolution has been seen as a way to resolve problems like ethnic or religious differences by giving greater local powers to regions. This has sometimes meant the elimination of unitary government; in 2005, Iraq became a federal country for the first time in its history; Nepal abolished its monarchy in 2007 and in 2015 adopted a new federal constitution with seven states. Often devolution does not lead to outright federalism but nevertheless results in a significant movement of power downward from the central state, as in the United Kingdom. We will speak more about devolution in subsequent chapters.

devolution A process in which political power is "sent down" to lower levels of state and government

CENTRALIZATION AND DECENTRALIZATION IN THE UNITED KINGDOM, THE UNITED STATES, AND INDIA

The cases of the United Kingdom and two of its former colonies, the United States and India, illustrate the range of centralization and decentralization in the contemporary world. As a unitary state, all political authority in the UK is constitutionally centralized in the national government in London. UK governments have the power to overrule local or regional governments on virtually any matter, and can establish or abolish subnational governments with a simple vote of Parliament. In 1985, the Conservative government of Margaret Thatcher passed a law that abolished the Greater London Council (London's city government) and six other city governments that Thatcher believed were inefficient and bastions of the opposition Labour Party. These cities lost their governments and mayors until they were restored by Tony Blair's Labour governments in the late 1990s. Blair passed additional measures to establish regional legislatures and governments in Wales, Scotland, and Northern Ireland. Although a 2014 independence referendum was rejected by Scottish voters, its near passage secured the devolution of additional authority to Scotland's regional government. Nonetheless, future governments in London could, theoretically, take back this authority and abolish those institutions, as the British Parliament retains sovereignty over its devolved regional governments.

UK

USA

INDIA

The United States, in contrast, is a federal system in which the Constitution reserves some powers for the federal government (national commerce, foreign policy, and defense), leaving all other powers (over such matters as health, education, and welfare) to the states. U.S. states differ considerably in their levels and forms of taxation, in their provision of social services, and in their laws regarding everything from same-sex marriage to the legalization of marijuana. Since its foundation, the United States has experienced a built-in tension between states' rights and federal power. The federal government, with the backing of the federal judiciary, has often imposed its authority on states that are deemed to be violating principles of the Constitution (it has played a major role in ending racial segregation and enforcing voting rights). But the states have often challenged federal authorities as a way of dragging the federal government into the future. A recent example is the legalization of marijuana, which challenges the federal government's authority to regulate drugs.

India is also constitutionally a federal republic, with power divided between federal and state authorities. However, unlike the United States, Indian states and territories reflect linguistic or ethno-religious differences. At the same time, India's states and territories have unequal powers in such areas as the use of minority languages or the ability to collect taxes. This is more akin to the devolution seen in the United Kingdom, though, as we mentioned, the UK is not formally federal (that is, enshrined in a constitution). To date, India's asymmetric federalism has managed to keep the country unified, despite India's challenging diversity of linguistic and ethno-religious groups.

POWER, AUTONOMY, AND CAPACITY

strong state A state that is able to fulfill basic tasks, such as defending territory, making and enforcing rules, collecting taxes, and managing the economy

At the most basic level, we can make a distinction between **strong states** and **weak states**. Strong states are those that are able to fulfill basic tasks: defend their territory, make and enforce rules and rights, collect taxes, and manage the economy, to name a few. In contrast, weak states cannot execute such tasks very well. Rules are haphazardly applied, if at all; tax evasion and other forms of public noncompliance are widespread; armed rivals to the state, such as rebel movements, organized crime, or other states, may control large chunks of territory or the economy. State officials themselves, having little faith in their offices or responsibilities, may use their jobs simply to fill their own pockets through corruption and theft. Economic development is certain to be much lower as a result of this unstable political environment. In general, weak states are not well institutionalized and lack authority and legitimacy. At an extreme, the very structures of the state may become so weak that they break down. When this occurs, a country is commonly termed a fragile or, at a more severe level, a **failed state** (see Table 2.1).[13] Before 2001, Afghanistan was typically viewed as a failed state, and it remains one today, with only limited power that must be backed up by international force. But a failed state does not necessarily mean complete anarchy. Piracy off the coast of Somalia (considered one of the world's "most failed" states) is seen as a natural outgrowth of state failure, but one study suggests that piracy thrives when state power is weak but not wholly absent, allowing pirates to rely on functioning markets and infrastructure on land. As the authors put it, even criminals need some degree of law and order.[14] States can fail to different degrees, in different areas, and in different ways.

weak state A state that has difficulty fulfilling basic tasks, such as defending territory, making and enforcing rules, collecting taxes, and managing the economy

failed state A state so weak that its political structures collapse, leading to anarchy and violence

In short, speaking of states as merely weak or strong fails to capture the complexity of state power. In fact, we get stuck in a loop of circular logic if we simply argue that if a state can do something it must be strong and if it can't it must be weak. American elected officials can wage large-scale wars around the globe but can't ban handguns, whereas in Canada just the opposite is true. Which one, then, is weak or strong? Comparative politics builds on the categories of weak and strong states through the use of two other terms: *capacity* and *autonomy*. **Capacity** is the ability of the state to wield power in order to carry out the basic tasks of providing security and reconciling freedom and equality. A state with high capacity is able to formulate and enact fundamental policies and ensure stability and security for both itself and its citizens. A state with low capacity is unable to do these things effectively. High capacity requires not just money but also organization, legitimacy, and effective

capacity The ability of the state to wield power to carry out basic tasks, such as defending territory, making and enforcing rules, collecting taxes, and managing the economy

leadership. Roads get paved, schools get built, regulations are created and followed, and those who break the law are punished.

In contrast, **autonomy** is the ability of the state to wield its power independently of the public or international actors. This is closely related to the idea of sovereignty. In the case of sovereignty, we are speaking of a state's formal and legal independence. In the case of autonomy, we are speaking of the informal, practical ability to act on that independence. In other words, if an autonomous state wishes to carry out a policy or an action, it can do so without having to consult the public or worry about strong public or international opposition that might force it to reverse its decision. A state with a high degree of autonomy may act on behalf of the public, pursuing what it believes are the best interests of the country, irrespective of public opinion. A state with a low degree of autonomy will act largely at the behest of private individuals, groups, or other states and will be less able to disobey the public will or the demands of well-organized groups. Scholars sometimes describe states with low autonomy as "captured" by certain interests that control specific issues or policies.

The concepts of capacity and autonomy help us to evaluate differences in state power. Strong states with a high degree of capacity and autonomy may be able to execute major policies relatively easily. A case in point is China's infrastructure, including new roads, rails, and dams, which it has been able to construct despite technical challenges, enormous cost, and sometimes domestic opposition. High capacity and autonomy, however, may come at the expense of individual freedom (though this is not always the case). By contrast, states with high capacity but lower autonomy may have widespread powers but are more subject to public intervention. The United States and Canada are good examples of states with lower autonomy, facilitated by their federal structure. Individual freedom may be high, but this can constrain central authority and consequently hinder national policy making. States with high autonomy but low capacity, meanwhile, may have few limits on their decision making but lack the ability to realize those policies effectively. Russia falls into this category: during the last decade the state has become more centralized and autonomous, but it still does not have the capacity to successfully promulgate and enforce regulations. The Venezuelan state under Hugo Chávez similarly gained increased autonomy over the past decade even as its capacity declined.

Finally, states may lack both autonomy and capacity. This is true of many less-developed countries, such as those in Africa that have been "captured" by elites or certain ethnic or religious groups and are largely unable to fulfill some of the most important national tasks, like encouraging economic development and ensuring public education.

In short, speaking of state power in terms of autonomy and capacity can help us better understand stateness: what states are and are not able to do, and why. However, we should note that the degree of a state's autonomy and capacity may vary widely depending on the issue at hand. An observer of China may conclude that this state enjoys high autonomy and capacity. However, China's corruption and large numbers of public protests, some of them violent, indicate that its autonomy and capacity are in many areas circumscribed. Japan's state capacity was long seen as a model for successful development, but its ongoing economic difficulties and sluggish response to the 2011 earthquake raise questions in this regard. Brazil's Bolsa Família, a novel and ambitious social welfare program, has cut poverty nearly in half

autonomy The ability of the state to wield its power independently of the public

TABLE 2.1 Top Twenty Fragile States

FRAGILE STATE INDEX, 2017

RANK	COUNTRY	DEMOGRAPHIC PRESSURES	REFUGEES AND INTERNALLY DISPLACED PERSONS	GROUP GRIEVANCE	HUMAN FLIGHT AND BRAIN DRAIN	UNEVEN ECONOMIC DEVELOPMENT
1	**South Sudan**	9.9	10.0	9.7	6.4	8.9
2	**Somalia**	10.0	10.0	8.9	9.8	9.3
3	**Central African Republic**	9.0	10.0	9.1	7.5	10.0
4	**Yemen**	9.3	9.4	9.3	7.3	8.2
5	**Sudan**	9.3	9.8	10.0	8.9	7.4
5	**Syria**	8.2	9.8	9.8	8.4	7.7
7	**Congo (D.R.)**	9.4	10.0	10.0	6.6	8.4
8	**Chad**	10.0	9.6	8.0	8.8	9.1
9	**Afghanistan**	9.3	9.8	8.4	8.2	7.5
10	**Iraq**	8.6	7.9	9.6	7.7	7.3
11	**Haiti**	9.5	7.7	6.5	8.8	9.8
12	**Guinea**	8.7	8.2	8.6	7.4	7.7
13	**Nigeria**	9.1	7.5	9.2	7.2	8.6
13	**Zimbabwe**	9.1	8.5	7.3	7.9	8.5
15	**Ethiopia**	9.8	9.3	9.1	7.6	6.5
16	**Guinea Bissau**	8.6	7.3	5.2	8.1	9.1
17	**Burundi**	9.3	8.6	7.9	6.3	7.2
17	**Pakistan**	8.4	8.7	10.0	7.2	6.5
19	**Eritrea**	8.8	8.3	7.1	8.3	7.8
20	**Niger**	9.0	7.9	8.0	7.5	8.5

Note: Areas are ranked on a 10-point scale, where 10 represents the worst conditions. Countries may share rankings. Brief definitions for each indicator are as follows: Demographic Pressures: Impact of population or environmental pressures on state capacity; Refugees and Internally Displaced Persons: Impact of forced displacements of large communities; Group Grievance: Schisms between different groups in society over access to the state; Human Flight and Brain Drain: Human displacement for economic or political reasons; Uneven Economic Development: Levels of inequality;

Source: http://fundforpeace.org/fsi/data (accessed 5/16/17).

over the past decade. Yet at the same time, the country has been unable to tackle an organized crime system that virtually functions as a parallel state.[15] Autonomy and capacity, therefore, are useful concepts for comparing states, but the degree to which an individual state possesses them depends on the issue or task at hand.

Finally, we are left with some big questions: Why are some states more centralized or decentralized? Why do they have more or less capacity or autonomy? Some of the

ECONOMIC DECLINE AND POVERTY	STATE LEGITIMACY	PUBLIC SERVICES	HUMAN RIGHTS AND RULE OF LAW	SECURITY APPARATUS	FACTIONALIZED ELITES	EXTERNAL INTERVENTION
10.0	10.0	10.0	9.5	10.0	9.7	9.8
8.9	9.3	9.0	9.5	9.4	10.0	9.3
9.1	9.7	10.0	9.7	9.0	9.7	9.8
9.3	9.7	9.6	9.7	9.8	9.5	10.0
8.5	9.8	8.9	9.6	9.0	9.7	9.7
8.1	9.9	9.2	9.8	9.8	9.9	10.0
8.4	9.6	9.5	9.8	9.0	9.8	9.5
8.5	9.1	9.7	9.1	9.4	9.8	8.3
8.3	9.1	9.9	8.5	10.0	8.6	9.7
6.6	9.5	8.2	8.7	10.0	9.6	9.7
8.7	9.7	9.7	7.6	7.7	9.6	10.0
9.2	9.6	9.5	7.7	8.8	9.6	7.4
8.0	8.6	9.2	8.9	9.2	9.6	6.5
8.6	9.2	8.9	8.2	8.1	9.8	7.5
7.0	8.2	8.8	9.0	8.4	8.7	8.3
8.3	9.2	9.4	7.5	8.9	9.6	9.0
8.0	8.8	8.0	8.8	8.8	8.2	9.4
6.9	8.1	7.7	8.0	9.1	8.9	7.7
8.1	9.3	8.4	9.0	7.2	8.1	8.1
7.5	7.3	9.5	6.5	8.7	8.9	9.2

Economic Decline: Patterns of economic hardship; State Legitimacy: Representativeness and openness of government; Public Services: Presence of basic state functions and public goods; Human Rights and Rule of Law: Respect for fundamental freedoms; Security Apparatus: Security threats from inside and outside of the state; Factionalized Elites: Elite fragmentation along such divisions as ethnicity, class, or religion; External Intervention: Impact of external actors in functioning of state.

answers lie in history, particularly the nature of international threats and how they have affected the relation between taxation (needed to pay for wars) and representation (how much say people have in how the state conducts itself). Cultural norms regarding freedom and equality may also play a role. For more recently founded states, however, such idiosyncratic and historical explanations are not particularly useful. Can you develop policies for countries like Afghanistan or Nigeria that would lead

Why Has Pakistan Slid toward State Failure?

Pakistan displays many of the hallmarks of a typical failing state (see Table 2.1). It is not just a problem of electricity, as we spoke of in the chapter opener. Other public services, like education and health care, are also lacking. The level of corruption is extremely high. The judicial system is unresponsive to the public, and the military and intelligence institutions appear unaccountable to government officials. The country suffers from the world's fourth-largest number of terrorist deaths, and large swaths of the country's border with Afghanistan are not effectively under state control. The killing of Osama bin Laden, who had been living for several years in a home in Pakistan, raised serious questions inside and outside the country: were segments of the Pakistani military or intelligence involved in sheltering him, or were they unaware of his presence? Many of Pakistan's issues of state capacity and autonomy are not unique; however, they are of particular concern to the international community because Pakistan supports guerrilla and terrorist activity in Afghanistan and India and possesses nuclear weapons.

The broad problem, as numerous scholars have expressed, is that a failing Pakistani state may also be an "irrational" one. Many scholars assume that states are "rational" in the sense that they focus primarily on national security. However, this also assumes that governments are able to coordinate with and control their states. Without some centralized authority, rationality may give way as different segments of the state pursue contradictory and competing goals. Because central authority is weak, Pakistan lacks the ability to gain control over the violence that occurs within its borders. Terrorist attacks have been frequent, and in some regions the state has lost much of its territorial sovereignty. At the same time, the country's armed forces are fragmented and lack a clear chain of civilian or military authority. Such state fragmentation can breed risky behavior, as individual leaders or segments of the state vie for power or their own short-term interests. There is clear evidence that military and intelligence forces in Pakistan have supported terrorist attacks inside India, which have in the past brought the two countries to the brink of war. In addition, while the United States views Pakistan as a key ally in its war against the Taliban, it is evident that the Taliban finds support among elements inside the Pakistani state. Most worrisome, it is unclear who has effective control over Pakistan's nuclear weapons or how secure these weapons are. Although Pakistan has become one of the top recipients of U.S. foreign aid, there is little sign that this aid has done much to stop the erosion of Pakistan's state capacity.

How did Pakistan end up this way? This is quite puzzling, especially when we compare Pakistan with its neighbor, India. In 1947, as India gained independence from British rule, Muslim leaders demanded their own independent state of Pakistan, so that they would not be a perpetual minority under Hindu rule. Upon independence (known as *partition*), both countries faced similar kinds of opportunities and problems, including poverty, weak states, linguistic and regional differences, and democratic institutions inherited from the British. If anything, Pakistan would seem to have had more potential—it was built on a common religious identity and was wealthier than

Pakistan's Inter-Services Intelligence (ISI) agency is viewed by many observers as directly connected to the Taliban, Al Qaeda, and Pakistan's nuclear program.

First, while the Indian state attained independence with limited disruption, in the newly created Pakistan a state had to be constructed largely from scratch. Second, Pakistan's birth was almost immediately followed by a war with the much larger India over disputed territory. This subsequently led to an emphasis on building a new state with a strong military force, which ultimately became stronger than the government. Finally, the initial ruling party, the Muslim League, had been built around the struggle for Indian independence, and after this goal was accomplished with partition, it lacked a strong leadership or set of ideological values on which to institutionalize a new regime. This combination of a weak state, regime, and government left the military a powerful but largely unaccountable force, and it became the primary institution of sovereign power and national identity. In the absence of accountability, the Pakistani military has both grown and become fragmented, increasing its control over the state but remaining unable to solidify that control into effective state capacity. At its core, the state is a monopoly of violence, but without nonmilitary political institutions, this monopoly can be just as destabilizing as its absence.[a]

India. Yet now Pakistan's per capita GDP is lower than India's, with a weaker state that has been under military rule for most of its history. Perhaps we have constructed our puzzle in the wrong way: that Pakistan would succumb to military rule and state failure is not the mystery, as this has been the fate of many poor countries. Perhaps the puzzle is why India escaped this trap. We examine India's ascent in more detail in the next chapter.

There are some institutional factors, though, that scholars believe help explain Pakistan's trajectory.

State Autonomy and Capacity

	HIGH AUTONOMY	LOW AUTONOMY
HIGH CAPACITY	State is able to fulfill basic tasks with a minimum of public intervention; power highly centralized; strong state. Danger: Too high a level of capacity and autonomy may prevent or undermine democracy.	State is able to fulfill basic tasks, but public plays a direct role in determining policy and is able to limit state power and scope of activity. Danger: State may be unable to develop new policies or respond to new challenges owing to the power of organized opposition.
LOW CAPACITY	State is able to function with a minimum of public interference or direct control, but its capacity to fulfill basic tasks is limited. Danger: State is ineffectual, limiting development, and slow development may provoke public unrest.	State lacks the ability to fulfill basic tasks and is subject to direct public control and interference—power highly decentralized among state and nonstate actors; weak state. Danger: Too low a level of capacity and autonomy may lead to internal state failure.

to more viable and effective states? Is there an ideal mix of different forms of legitimacy, centralization, autonomy, and capacity? Where do you start? Scholars and policy makers are often at odds over these issues, which we will take up in subsequent chapters.

In Sum: Studying States

This chapter began by defining the state as a monopoly of force but also as the set of institutions charged with transforming freedom and equality from ideas into concrete action. The kinds of decisions made toward this end are shaped by regimes and governments. Regimes are the fundamental rules and norms of politics, providing long-term goals regarding individual freedom and collective equality and the location and use of power toward those goals. Governments, in contrast, are the political elites in charge of running the state. Influenced and constrained by the existing regime, they attempt to formulate policy that may then be executed by the state. These represent the most basic facets of states everywhere—and, indeed, states are everywhere. Although similar political organizations have existed for thousands of years, only within the past few centuries did modern states arise in Europe and quickly come to dominate the globe. States are the main political players in the world today.

The universal presence of states, and variations in their stateness, compels comparativists to find some way to study and evaluate them. One way is by assessing their legitimacy; different kinds of legitimacy—traditional, charismatic, and rational-legal—create their own kinds of authority and power. The other is by assessing the dispersal of power; states may be weaker or stronger, with more or less capacity and autonomy, depending on how power is distributed within the state and between the state and the public. Too much power in the hands of the state risks tyranny; too little power risks anarchy. Finding the right mix is not simply a technical question but one that shapes how states and societies reconcile freedom and equality. This debate over freedom and equality ranges far beyond the boundaries of the state itself. As we shall see in the chapters that follow, it is influenced by ethnic and national identity, by culture and ideology, by economic institutions and the interaction between states and markets, and by democratic and nondemocratic practices.

Since the dawn of humanity, people have relied on some form of political organization to construct a relationship between individual freedom and collective equality. For the past few centuries, modern states have been the dominant expression of that relation. We might thus conclude that states now represent an end point in human intellectual and organizational evolution. But why should this be so? It seems logical that in the future new forms of political organization will displace states, just as states displaced empires, city-states, and other institutions. Perhaps challenges to states—environmental, economic, or cultural—will overwhelm many of them and they will revert to earlier forms, such as empires and city-states. Some suggest we are already at the start of that process. Or perhaps technological innovation will make old forms of political centralization weak or irrelevant, binding humans in communities where sovereignty is virtual, not physical. Perhaps the core debate over freedom and equality that has stretched over millennia will be reconciled once and for all, changing the very nature of politics as we understand it. These questions may seem unanswerable, more amenable to fortune-telling than to research. But as we shall see, they lie at the heart of ideas and conflicts that have transformed the world in the past and may dominate our future.

Key Terms

asymmetric federalism (p. 42)
autonomy (p. 45)
capacity (p. 44)
charismatic legitimacy (p. 40)
country (p. 31)
devolution (p. 43)
failed state (p. 44)
federalism (p. 42)
government (p. 31)
legitimacy (p. 39)

rational-legal legitimacy (p. 40)
regime (p. 29)
sovereignty (p. 27)
state (p. 27)
strong state (p. 44)
traditional legitimacy (p. 40)
unitary state (p. 42)
weak state (p. 44)

Indian police march at celebrations for India's newest federal state, Telangana, which was created in 2014. The establishment of a new state is one example of how countries manage diverse cultural identities.

Nations and Society

How do people organize themselves into political communities?

INDIA'S 2014 PARLIAMENTARY ELECTIONS REPRESENTED a historic political shift. Since independence, politics in India has been dominated by the Indian National Congress, a party first established in 1885 to pursue the cause of a sovereign country. Built on an ideology of secularism and inclusive of all religious and ethnic groups, upon independence in 1947 it came to power in the first democratic elections and held power, almost unceasingly, since that time. However, after more than a half-century of rule voters finally dealt the party a decisive blow when Congress and its allied parties lost nearly 80 percent of their seats—dropping from 262 to 58—in the lower house of parliament, the Lok Sabha. Meanwhile, the Hindu nationalist Bharatiya Janata Party (BJP) shot from 116 to 282 seats, giving them a significant majority in parliament. Running on a campaign of economic growth, anticorruption, and an increased emphasis on Hindu religious and national identity, the BJP's victory allowed for the possibility of dramatic change that could pave the way for greater development. It also raises the danger of increased conflict between various ethnic and religious groups if the BJP aggressively pursues a policy of *Hindutva*, or Hindu nationalism.

India's parliamentary elections were not the only important political act in 2014. The country changed its federal structure as well as its government. In June, India went from 28 to 29 states by carving the new state of Telangana from the existing state of Andhra Pradesh. Why did India create a new state in a country that already had so many? The origins of Telangana can tell us a great deal about how India manages different identities within its democratic institutions, and some of the problems that come from this balancing act.

Located in the south, Andhra Pradesh is one of India's largest states in both size and population. The state was formed in 1956 from the areas of Andhra and Telangana to create a territory that shared a common Telugu culture and language. Yet while the creation of Andhra Pradesh was meant to consolidate ethnic and linguistic identity among people who had been separated before independence, this policy had the opposite effect. Rather than having a common identity, residents of the poorer Telangana region felt marginalized because elites from elsewhere in Andhra Pradesh monopolized economic and political power. This feeling led the people to resent what they viewed as a kind of "internal colonialism," and they began to call for separation.

Such sentiments first emerged in the 1960s, and by the early 2000s shifts in the political leadership in Andhra Pradesh allowed for the issues to gain traction. A new Telangana independence party, the Telangana Rashtra Samithi (TRS), grew in power, as did regular mass protests. This deepening crisis in turn became part of the political battle between Congress and the BJP for national power as each group vied to capture regional votes. Unable to find a compromise, in February 2014 the Lok Sabha voted behind closed doors on the creation of Telangana State. This event was marked by violent clashes, both inside the Lok Sabha and on the streets outside, between advocates and opponents of separation. Telangana was subsequently forged out of 10 districts from Andhra Pradesh—including, controversially, the wealthy state capital, Hyderabad, a center of India's information technology economy.

The long-term implications of this separation are unclear. For Telangana and Andhra Pradesh, there are issues of dividing assets (such as institutions of higher education). Tensions between the two states will continue into the immediate future, as the two states share Hyderabad as a common capital until 2025. For India as a whole, there is similar uncertainty. Some assert that the creation of Telangana opens the floodgate to various groups that will now demand their own states, often drawn on ethnic lines. Might this increase ethnic fragmentation in India and weaken the state? Others suggest that these fears are overblown and that such devolution can accommodate population growth across various religious, ethnic, and regional identities. The case of Telangana raises fascinating questions about how people organize themselves. What is a society? What is a nation? What do we mean by *political identity*?

LEARNING OBJECTIVES

- Understand the components of ethnic identity.
- Understand the ways that national identity binds people together.
- Distinguish citizenship and patriotism in their legal and emotional relationship to the state.
- Analyze the causes of ethnic and national conflict.
- Compare political ideologies and attitudes regarding political change and the goals of politics.
- Define political culture and analyze its influence in society.

SOCIETY IS A BROAD TERM that refers to complex human organization, a collection of people bound by shared institutions that define how human relations should be conducted. From country to country and place to place, societies differ in how individuals define themselves and their relationships to one another, to government, and to the state. Each relationship is unique; for all the surface similarities that may exist between societies, each country views itself and the wider world around it in a distinct way. These differences make comparative politics a rich field of study but also a frustrating one, as social scientists seek to find similarities that are often few and far between.

In this chapter, we look at the ways people identify themselves and are identified, both as individuals and as groups, and how these identifications relate to politics and the state. We will start with the concepts of ethnic and national identity, two of the most basic ways that individuals and groups define themselves. What does it mean to be part of an ethnic group? How is such a group defined? What is the difference between an ethnic group and a nation? We will also make distinctions between ethnicity, nationality, and citizenship. A related question arises in the distinction between nationalism and patriotism: What is the difference between being patriotic and being nationalist? We will answer these questions by looking at some examples and tracing their historical origins. Throughout recent history, the world has seen violent domestic and international conflicts connected to national and ethnic identities. Why do such conflicts occur? Are they a natural and inevitable part of human organization, or are such conflicts manufactured by political leaders to serve their own purposes? In this chapter, we will also look at some of the effects of conflict between different ethnic and nationalist identities.

From there, we will move on to a discussion of political attitudes and ideologies. Whereas ethnicity, nationality, and citizenship are group identities, political attitudes and ideologies are the values individuals hold and the positions they take with regard to freedom and equality. How should these values and positions be reconciled and to what end? One thing we will see is that although there are only a few basic political attitudes and ideologies, which can be broadly compared across countries or regions, their relative strength or influence differs dramatically from country to country. We'll discuss why this is the case.

Before moving ahead, we should ask whether identities like ethnicity, nationality, or ideology are a fixed part of our nature. Scholars have answered this question in different ways. At one end, many social scientists argue that identities exist

society Complex human organization; a collection of people bound by shared institutions that define how human relations should be conducted independent of any biological functions and are a set of "social constructions" that have emerged largely in the modern era. At the other end, many evolutionary psychologists emphasize the role that biological functions (such as kin recognition and genetic similarity) have played in building human identities for tens of thousands of years.[1] These views appear diametrically opposed, and their supporters are often dismissive of each other. But there clearly is room for integration—a view that recognizes an underlying human instinct to sort groups by preference and to elevate one over another, and that notes how modern politics has helped shape that instinct into particular political identities. Whatever their approach, social scientists have grown skeptical that ethnicity or nationalism will become a thing of the past or that collective identities will somehow no longer be a central part of defining who we are. Let us consider some of the most powerful societal institutions that shape comparative politics.

Ethnic Identity

People identify themselves in many ways. One way is by ethnicity, as when they speak of themselves as German or Irish, Kurdish or Zulu, Latino or Ukrainian Canadian. When we use the term **ethnic identity** or **ethnicity**, we emphasize a person's relation to other members of society. Ethnic identity is a set of institutions that bind people together through a common culture. These institutions can include language, religion, geographic location, customs, appearance, and history, among other things. As these distinct attributes are institutionalized, they provide members of a group with a shared identity. This process is called *ascription*—the assigning of a particular quality at birth. People do not choose their ethnicities; they are born into them, and their ethnic identity remains largely stable throughout life, though the borders between ethnic groups may be more blurry than we think, as we see in the case of Telangana. Ethnicity provides social solidarity and can generate greater equality as well. Groups with a high degree of ethnic solidarity may also be more willing to redistribute resources within the group and, conversely, less willing to share resources with groups that are ethnically different. Related research has focused on the relationship between trust, inequality, and ethnic diversity.[2]

Each ethnic group is characterized by a set of institutions that embody norms and standards of behavior, and a single society can be broken up into numerous ethnic groups. For example, Singaporean society is made up of ethnic Chinese, Malays, and Indians. Most countries in the world are not ethnically homogeneous; rarely are society and ethnicity one and the same. Societies are made up of various ethnic groups—in some cases only a few, in other cases tens or even hundreds—each with its own identity, as in the case of India. It is important to note that ethnicity is at its core a social, not a political, identity. People may identify themselves with an ethnic group without drawing any particular conclusions about politics on that basis. Ethnicity and the solidarity it provides are not inherently political, though they can become so.

Although we have looked at a number of attributes that often define ethnic differences, there is no master list of differences that automatically define one group as ethnically different from another. In Bosnia, for example, the main ethnic groups—Croats, Serbs, and Muslims—speak the same language and are similar in numerous other ways. What divides Bosnians is primarily religion: Croats are mostly Roman Catholic, Serbs are Eastern Orthodox Christian, and Muslims practice Islam. Yet we speak of Germans as a single ethnic group, even though some are Catholic and some are Protestant. Why are ethnic groups in Bosnia divided by religion, while in Germany such divisions don't produce different ethnic groups? In an even more confusing case, that of Rwanda, the Hutu and Tutsi ethnic groups cannot be easily distinguished by any of the factors we have discussed. Both groups speak the same language, practice the same religions, live in the same geographic regions, and share the same customs. To most outside observers, there is no real ethnic difference between the two, and even Hutus and Tutsis cannot easily distinguish between one another, since they rely on such vague distinctions as diet. But we cannot say that ethnicity is therefore a fiction because it has no single, neat origin. Ethnicity exists when people acknowledge and are acknowledged by outsiders as belonging to a distinct group. In Rwanda, even though ethnic distinctions between Hutu and Tutsi are unclear, ethnic conflict in the 1990s led to the deaths of several hundred thousand civilians. Rwanda shows us that though distinctions may be difficult to observe, these ascriptive identities can have powerful effects.

RACE IN BRAZIL AND SOUTH AFRICA

Brazil and South Africa illustrate the contentious nature of race and politics. If ethnicity is a complicated concept, the idea of race is even more problematic, because it often incorporates elements of ethnicity but also the dubious social construct that biological differences are socially meaningful. Both Brazil and South Africa share a legacy of rule by whites of European origin despite the fact that a majority of the population (90 percent in South Africa and about 51 percent in Brazil) self-identity as nonwhite. Brazil has a legacy of centuries of slavery (which was only outlawed in 1888), and South Africa experienced decades of racist apartheid rule (ending in 1994), during which nonwhites were entirely disenfranchised. In both places, nonwhites are far more likely to live in poverty, have worse access to health care, and have less education.

Despite these similarities, race is viewed quite differently in the two cases. In South Africa, the apartheid regime was obsessed with racial identity, and South Africans were meticulously sorted into four constructed racial categories (Black, White, Coloured, and Asian) and were identified accordingly on their identification cards. There was strict segregation of the four racial groups in housing, education, and

BRAZIL

SOUTH AFRICA

even personal relationships. With the end of apartheid, South Africa's new constitution called for a "rainbow nation," where all types of discrimination based on race or ethnic division would be outlawed.

But the legacy of state-enforced racial segregation did not disappear with the end of apartheid. Blacks have made some progress under black governments, but racism, and especially the endemic poverty of blacks, has persisted. Mixed-race South Africans, designated as "coloured" under apartheid (and who would be considered black in the United States), continue to view themselves as distinct from and in some ways in competition with blacks.

Brazilian intellectuals, in contrast, have long denied the importance of race or ethnicity and have portrayed Brazil as a racial democracy. As much as 80 percent of Brazilians have some African ancestry, and Brazilians employ a complex vocabulary to describe the spectrum of skin colors. As a result, it is less clear in Brazil who is of African or European origin, who is black and who is white. But the impact of race is felt in every aspect of Brazilian society. Brazil has never had a nonwhite president, and black Brazilians are grossly underrepresented in higher education and the more prestigious professions, and overrepresented in Brazil's notorious urban slums. Curiously, Brazil has never experienced the type of race-based social movements that were critical in ending apartheid in South Africa.

Both countries have struggled to deal with the persistence of discrimination and inequality. Since 1994, black governments in South Africa have cautiously imposed incentive systems that favor the promotion of blacks into leadership positions in private businesses, while avoiding the type of strict quotas many have advocated. Critics claim that the measures have created a small privileged black elite while ignoring the condition of most South African blacks. Brazil, in contrast, and despite the shockingly small presence of blacks in government, has enacted strict race-based quotas in its public universities, and as a result has doubled the percentage of black students attending those institutions. Critics of the policy, from both the left and right, have argued that the policy exacerbates racism by forcing Brazilians into strict apartheid-like racial categories that have never existed. In fact, Brazil was forced to employ inspectors to determine the race of university applicants (based on photos). In 2007, inspectors deemed one identical twin black and the other white, the kind of contradictory and troubling outcome that was commonplace in apartheid South Africa.

Examining race in South Africa and Brazil reminds us that identities are complex and are very much conditioned by the political, cultural, and economic contexts of each society.

National Identity

nation A group that desires self-government through an independent state

national identity A sense of belonging to a nation and a belief in its political aspirations

In contrast to ethnicity, which may be constructed in a unique manner from group to group and is not an inherently political concept, the idea of a **nation**—a group that desires self-government, often through an independent state—is largely consistent from case to case and is inherently political. If ethnic identity is a set of institutions that bind people together through a common culture, then **national identity** is an institution that binds people together through common political aspirations.

Among these, the most important are self-government and sovereignty. National identity implies a demand for greater freedom through sovereignty, as when a colony revolts against its colonial master. It also involves a demand for equality, as when a secessionist movement argues that sovereignty would eliminate unequal treatment of one group by another. Pakistan's secession from India in 1947, Kosovo's declaration of independence from Serbia in 2008, and independence movements in Xinjiang and Tibet in China reflect one group's aspiration toward greater freedom (from another, dominant group) and toward equality with others in the international system (through the creation of a sovereign state).

As you can see, national identity often—but not always—develops from ethnic identity. For example, an ethnic group may chafe against the existing political system because its members may feel that they lack certain rights or freedoms. As a result, some leaders may argue that the ethnic group should have greater political control and that the group's interests would be better served if it controlled its own political destiny. The interaction between ethnicity and national identity can be seen in past developments in Canada. There the French-speaking population of the province of Québec constitutes its own ethnic group, quite distinct from the English-speaking citizens of the rest of Canada (as well as from their own French ancestors). By the 1960s, this ethnicity began to develop into a sense of national identity as some in Québec argued for separation from Canada, where they saw themselves as a minority whose unique concerns were not being considered. Such arguments actually led to national referenda on the issue of secession in 1980 and 1995. In the latter case, the proposal that Québec secede failed by little more than 1 percent of the vote. Twenty years later, surveys suggest that a third of French-speaking Québecois consistently support independence.[3]

National identity can create **nationalism**, a pride in one's people and the belief in their own sovereign political destiny that is separate from those of others. In Québec, we find a people uncertain of whether they are just an ethnic group or also a nation—a group that desires self-government through an independent state. This lack of clarity between ethnicity and national identity is also evident in other groups, such as the Scots in the United Kingdom, who similarly held an unsuccessful referendum for independence in September 2014 (which may resurface in light of the United Kingdom's decision to leave the European Union). In other words, although ethnic identity often leads to a political identity built on nationalism, this is not always the case. Just as groups can vary in the strength of their ethnic identification, people may also vary in the degree of their nationalism. Peruvians and South Africans have strong ethnic identification across numerous groups but at the same time

nationalism Pride in one's people and the belief that they have a unique political destiny

---

INFOCUS National Identity Is . . .

- A sense of belonging to a nation (a group that desires self-government through an independent state) and a belief in its political aspirations.
- Often (but not always) derived from ethnic identity.
- Inherently political.
- The basis for nationalism: pride in one's people and belief that they have a unique political destiny.

a high degree of pride in their national identity; in the more homogeneous Germany and Japan, national pride is far lower, reflecting the disastrous results of extreme nationalism in both countries in the past.

If we can have ethnicity without leading to national identity, can we have national identity without ethnicity? Must ethnicity always be the source of nationalism? At first glance, it would seem logical that without ethnicity there is no foundation for national identity; people would lack a common source of solidarity and a set of institutions on which to build national pride. But like ethnicity, nationality lacks a "master list" of defining attributes. In the case of the United States, it is easy to conclude that there is no single American ethnic group. But is there an American nation? Some might say no, because nationalism is often assumed to require an ethnicity on which political aspirations can be built. Yet Americans are bound by certain common historical symbols, such as flags, anthems, a constitution, and common cultural values (recall our discussion of baseball in Chapter 1). Thus it could be argued that even in the face of great ethnic diversity, the United States is indeed a nation, whose people are bound together by, among other things, a sense of pride in certain democratic ideals. Some make this distinction by differing between "civic" and "ethnic" nationalism. Finally, we should recognize that nationalism is not inherently bad, as is often believed. Nationalism carries in it a tension with those who are outside the group, but it can also be seen as a vehicle for much of what we consider modern civilization.

Citizenship and Patriotism

Our final form of identification is citizenship. So far, we have noted that ethnicity is not inherently political, although it may develop a political aspect through nationalism. At the other end of this spectrum, citizenship is a political identity, developed not out of some unique set of circumstances or ascribed by birth but rather developed explicitly by states and accepted or rejected by individuals. Citizenship can be defined as an individual's or group's relation to the state; those who are citizens swear allegiance to that state, and that state in return is obligated to provide rights to those individuals or the members of that group. Citizenship can also convey certain obligations, such as the duty to serve in the armed forces or pay taxes. Citizens are therefore defined by their particular relation to one state rather than to one another. Although citizenship is often gained at birth, it has qualities quite separate from those of ethnic or national identity.

citizenship An individual's relationship to the state, wherein citizens swear allegiance to that state and the state in return is obligated to provide rights to those citizens

Citizenship is a potentially more inclusive or flexible concept than national or ethnic identity. Like those two identities, however, citizenship can vary in clarity and power. Citizenship may confer a host of benefits, such as education and health care, or relatively few, depending on the state. In addition, one state may not necessarily grant citizenship to all those born on its territory, while another may allow citizenship in more than one country. Matters can be further complicated if citizenship is founded on ethnic or national identity. In an extreme example, in the 1950s, South Africa's apartheid regime created internal "homelands" for blacks as a means of stripping them of their South African citizenship. Many Palestinians lack any citizenship, living in areas under Israeli occupation or as refugees in nearby countries. The boundaries between citizenship and ethnic identity can be murky if the former is conditional on the latter.

Citizenship, in turn, can give rise to **patriotism**, or pride in one's state. People are patriotic when they have pride in their political system and seek to defend and promote it. When we think of patriotism, some of the things that may come to mind are our flag, important historical events, wars, anthems—anything that people associate with politics and the state. It can be hard to separate the definitions of patriotism and nationalism. National identity is bound up in the quest for sovereignty, as is patriotism. As a result, the two can closely overlap. However, they can also be quite distinct: there may be a high degree of national identity without patriotism. Returning to the Palestinians, we can note that they have a strong sense of national identity but, for now, no state of their own—hence, the term *patriotism* is probably not a useful term in their case. An ethnic minority's sense of nationalism may be confined to the political aspirations of its own members, and as a result that group may have a low level of patriotism—that is, of pride in their state, which they do not see as their own. The United States (along with India and Canada) may be a case where there is not one clear sense of nationalism, as we argued earlier, but rather strong patriotism that emphasizes pride in the state. Since patriotism emphasizes the state, those states that are weak or illegitimate often have difficulty instilling patriotism in their citizens. This situation makes tasks like defending the state in times of war very difficult. Being a citizen does not automatically make you patriotic, nor does a strong ethnic or national identity.

To sum up, ethnicity, nationality, and citizenship are institutions that define groups in different ways and that carry different political implications. Ethnic identity is built on social attributes that are unique to a group of people, such as language or culture, whereas national identity implies political aspirations, specifically sovereignty. Although a dominant ethnic identity often leads to a national identity and nationalism, it does not always do so, nor does the absence of a dominant ethnicity necessarily prevent nationalism from developing. Finally, citizenship is an identity built on a relation to the state. As should be clear, none of these identities is exclusive; all of us possess different combinations of ethnicity, national identity, and citizenship, and each contributes to how we see the world and our role within it.

patriotism Pride in one's state

Ethnic Identity, National Identity, and Citizenship: Origins and Persistence

Now that we have distinguished among these three identities, it is worth considering their origins: Where did they come from and why do they exist? From our earlier discussion, we might assume that before the modern era people lacked clear identities.

In truth, for thousands of years communities defined themselves by culture, language, and gods, often contrasting themselves with "barbarians"—people who were different and therefore, in their view, uncivilized. Some communities in Asia and the Middle East—China, for example—similarly viewed themselves as distinct from other communities. However, the specific concepts of ethnic and national identity are relatively recent, having emerged in Europe toward the end of the eighteenth century. Citizenship, too, has relatively recent origins: although the concept can be traced back to ancient Athens and to the Roman Empire, it disappeared with the fall of Rome, only resurfacing centuries later.

The emergence (or reemergence, in the case of citizenship) of these identities had much to do with the formation of the modern state.[4] As states took form in Europe in the fifteenth and sixteenth centuries, asserting sovereign control over people and territory, people could travel greater distances, enjoying the security provided by the state. This mobility in turn increased commerce, which was often centered near the city where the state leadership was based. These fortified capitals served as centers for trade, information, and new social relations. Such interaction in turn fostered increased homogeneity. Languages and dialects began to merge into a common tongue, further standardized by the state through education and documentation. Common cultural and religious practices also developed, often created or supported by the state (as during the Protestant Reformation in the sixteenth century). Local identities were often forcibly eradicated. Social institutions began to take a shape that was meaningful to most of a country's population. People could now identify themselves not only by village or profession, clan or tribe but also, more abstractly, by the institutions they shared with many thousands of other people across space and time. These institutions formed the foundation for ethnic identity. People in turn slowly began to identify with each other primarily on the basis of broad cultural institutions—as, for instance, German or French or English.

Growing ethnic identity was thus tightly connected to state development. More-over, state leaders also saw this development as something that could serve their own interests. By encouraging the formation of a single ethnic identity, the state could in turn claim that it existed to defend and promote the unique interests and values of its people. The state came to be portrayed as the institution that embodied the people's collective identity.

In the linked development of ethnic identity and of the state, we can see the seeds of national identity, which became a potent force in the eighteenth century. National identity, when added to ethnic identity, powerfully asserts that the state is legitimate because it is the defender of national values. Further, national identity unites the people and the state in the quest to chart an independent political future. The development and fusion of ethnic and national identities radically transformed states. Based on the idea that the people and their state were bound together in common cause, states could mobilize the public in ways never before possible. Most important, countries with a strong sense of nationalism could raise mass armies and generate tax revenue because people would sacrifice their resources and very lives for the glory and destiny of their nation.

The thought that individuals would fight and die for an abstract political concept marked a radical change in human history. In Europe, Napoleonic France became the first country able to use such nationalist sentiment to its own advantage, raising a huge volunteer army that would conquer much of Europe. Both threatened and inspired by such nationalist fervor, other European peoples and states in turn forged their own national identities and aspired to independence and self-government. This transformation gave rise to the idea of a **nation-state**, a sovereign state encompassing one dominant nation that it claims to embody and represent. Within a hundred years, most of the multiethnic empires that dominated Europe would be destroyed, replaced by nation-states that were dominated by distinct ethnic groups and political identities.

Finally, the development of ethnic and national identities paved the way for the concept of citizenship. As societies viewed themselves first in ethnic and then in national terms, their relation to the state began to change. If the state was the instrument of national will, some extended this logic to conclude that state and people must be bound by mutual accountability and obligation in the form of a social contract, as we mentioned in Chapter 2. How far this citizenship should be extended and what rights it should entail have come to be central concerns for all societies and states.

With the rise of European imperial power, the institutions of ethnic and national identity and citizenship began to spread around the world. Just as states now lay claim to almost all the earth, so too have nearly all human beings become identified by some ethnicity, some nationality, some form of citizenship. In some cases, this has been the foundation for political stability, economic development, and democracy; at the other extreme, where identities are weakly held or come into conflict, the result can be civil strife. Why these conflicts emerge and how to prevent them from becoming violent can be a matter of life and death.

ETHNIC AND NATIONAL CONFLICT

Why are some countries able to forge consensus between different ethnic and national identities, whereas in other countries such differences lead to seemingly irreconcilable conflict? Why is it that different identities can coexist peacefully and then suddenly clash? Political scientists have a range of often-contending explanations for such forms of conflict, and the debate has intensified rapidly over the past two decades as ethnic and national conflicts have grown in number and intensity. Before discussing these debates, we should clarify our terms.

Ethnic conflict can be defined as conflict between ethnic groups that struggle to achieve certain political or economic goals at each other's expense. Each group may hope to increase its power by gaining greater control over existing political institutions like the state or government. By contrast, groups involved in **national conflict** seek to gain (or prevent the other from gaining) sovereignty, clashing with one another over issues of autonomy, such as the quest to form an independent state. In both of these cases, violence is a common tool for using, bypassing, or destroying the coercive powers of the state.

Around the world, we can find examples of ethnic and national conflict as well as cases where both are present. Afghanistan, for example, has seen frequent ethnic conflict, but this is not national; most Afghan groups are seeking not independence but greater power over each other. Ethnic conflict in Nigeria and South Sudan over the past decade has similarly pitted rival ethnic groups against one another over contested presidential elections. In contrast, the American Revolution can be seen as a national rather than an ethnic conflict. The American colonies broke away from

nation-state A state encompassing one dominant nation that it claims to embody and represent

ethnic conflict A conflict in which different ethnic groups struggle to achieve certain political or economic goals at each other's expense

national conflict A conflict in which one or more groups within a country develop clear aspirations for political independence, clashing with others as a result

Great Britain to form a separate country, but this separation was based more on conflicts over political rights and the desire for sovereignty than on a strong "American" identity that did not yet exist. And finally, conflicts can be both ethnic and national, such as in Yugoslavia and the Soviet Union in the 1990s, where various ethnic groups seceded to create their own nation-states.

Why do such conflicts break out in the first place? Scholars emphasize different factors, which we can group by where they place the primary cause: society, the economy, or politics. Societal explanations tend to emphasize such issues as ethnic heterogeneity—the number of ethnic groups and their degree of integration or polarization. Economic explanations concentrate on the struggle for resources (natural or otherwise) between groups, as well as the general level of poverty across a country as a whole. A political explanation emphasizes the state and regime, such as the relative capacity or autonomy of the state and the degree and form of democratic or nondemocratic regimes.

Of course, these three categories bleed into one another, and in the case of actual conflicts it can be hard to distinguish cause from effect. Still, we can see how each explanation can give us a way to think about ethnic and national conflict. For example, in Africa we see a great deal of ethnic heterogeneity, particularly across the central part of the continent, and these divisions correspond to several major conflicts, as in Nigeria, Kenya, and Sudan (see Figure 3.1). In a number of these cases, ethnic clashes are influenced by the presence of natural resources. Congo is a horrific example. Although ethnic divisions were less pronounced there than in other countries, when ethnic conflict spilled over from Rwanda in the 1990s it sparked battles over gold and diamonds in a war that left between 2 and 5 million people dead—the worst conflict since World War II. Finally, political difficulties abound in much of Africa: borders drawn by colonial powers that do not conform to major ethnic divisions; weak states that are often "captured" by one ruling ethnic group that benefits disproportionately from that control and dominates the military; authoritarian systems that prevent effective participation or conciliation. Any one of these three factors can contribute to ethnic conflict, and when all are present they can create a dangerous dynamic.[5]

How do we prevent ethnic and national conflicts or bring them to an end? In part, this effort depends on the nature of the conflict, and whether the struggle is based on demands for greater equality or on some territorial demand, like autonomy or secession. It may be possible to create institutions that make most of the players feel that the political system is fair and serves their needs. One example of power sharing can be devolution; as we saw in the case of Telangana, federal structures, asymmetric

---

IN FOCUS   Views of Ethnic and National Conflict

- Societal explanations emphasize such issues as ethnic heterogeneity.
- Economic explanations emphasize poverty and the struggle for natural or other resources.
- Political explanations emphasize state capacity or autonomy and the type of regime.

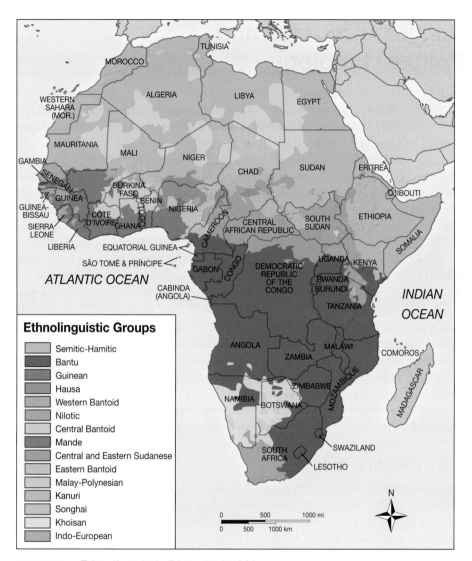

FIGURE 3.1 Ethnolinguistic Diversity in Africa

or otherwise, can provide groups with greater rights and autonomy. Representative structures (such as presidencies or legislatures) and electoral systems can make a difference as well, something we will address in detail in Chapter 6.

However, not all scholars are convinced that power-sharing institutions, even when carefully crafted, necessarily resolve these problems. One concern is that such structures may "freeze," or institutionalize, group divisions and conflicts. The challenge, then, is to build institutions that can meet existing group demands while remaining flexible enough to foster cooperation and integration across these divides.[6]

Political Attitudes and Political Ideology

We have spent some time discussing ways that people's identities are shaped by their membership in larger ethnic or national groups. But such groups do not completely define our political identity. We also hold individual views regarding the ideal relation between freedom and equality. In the rest of this chapter, we will divide these views into two categories: political attitudes and political ideology. Political attitudes are concerned with the speed of political change and the methods used to achieve it. Political ideology comprises the basic values an individual holds about the fundamental goals of politics regarding freedom and equality. Political attitudes focus on the specific context of political change in a given country. By contrast, political ideologies are more universal, since they assume there is one ideal way to balance freedom and equality.

Where do political attitudes and ideologies come from? These views are not defined by birth or by the state, although they may be influenced by either. Nor are the boundaries between such views as clear or evident as are those that define ethnicity, national identity, or citizenship. At the same time, these views do not simply materialize out of thin air. Ideologies are built over time out of a set of ideas, and attitudes are articulated in response to the institutional conditions around us. More fundamentally, it may be that attitudes and ideologies—our individual or group preferences regarding freedom, equality, and the degree of change needed to achieve them—stem from basic human traits that balance our need to establish order and our need to embrace change. While our own political views may not be inherited, having such views in the first place is central to what makes us human.

POLITICAL ATTITUDES

political attitude Description of one's views regarding the speed and methods with which political changes should take place in a given society

Political attitudes describe views regarding the necessary pace and scope of change in the balance between freedom and equality. The attitudes are typically broken up into the categories of radical, liberal, conservative, and reactionary and are often arrayed on a spectrum going from left to right.

radicals Those with a political attitude that favors dramatic, often revolutionary change

Radicals are placed on the extreme left. **Radicals** believe in dramatic, often revolutionary change of the existing political, social, or economic order. Radicals believe that the current system is broken and cannot simply be improved or repaired but must be scrapped in favor of a new order. As a result, most radicals do not believe in slow, evolutionary change. Politics will be improved, they believe, only when the entire political structure has been fundamentally transformed, remaking the political institutions of government, regime, and state. As a result, some radicals may be more inclined to favor violence as a necessary or unavoidable part of politics. The institutions of the old order, in some radicals' view, will not change willingly; they will have to be destroyed. Not all or even most radicals hold these views, however. Many may argue that radical change can be achieved through peaceful means, by raising public consciousness and mobilizing mass support for wide-ranging change.

liberals Those with a political attitude that favors evolutionary change and who believe that existing institutions can be instruments of positive change

Liberals, like radicals, believe that much can be improved in the current political, social, and economic institutions; and liberals, too, support widespread change. However, instead of a revolutionary transformation, **liberals** favor evolutionary change. In the liberal view, progressive change can happen through changes within the system; it does not require an overthrow of the system itself. Moreover, liberals part from radicals in their belief that existing institutions can be instruments of positive change. Liberals also believe that change can and sometimes must occur over a long period of time. They are skeptical that institutions can be replaced or transformed quickly and believe that only constant effort can create fundamental change.

Conservatives break with both radicals and liberals in this view of the necessity of change. Whereas radicals and liberals both advocate change, disagreeing on the degree of change and the tactics needed to achieve it, **conservatives** question whether any significant or profound change in existing institutions is necessary. Conservatives are skeptical of the view that change is good in itself and instead view it as disruptive and leading to unforeseen outcomes. They see existing institutions as key to providing basic order and continuity; should too much change take place, conservatives argue, it might undermine the very legitimacy of the system. Conservatives also question whether the problems that radicals and liberals point to can ever really be solved. At best, they believe, change will simply replace one set of problems with another, and, at worst, it will create more problems than it solves.

Reactionaries are similar to conservatives in their opposition to further evolutionary or revolutionary change. Yet, unlike conservatives and like radicals, they view the current order as fundamentally unacceptable. Rather than transforming the system into something new, however, **reactionaries** seek to restore political, social, and economic institutions. Reactionaries advocate restoring values, changing back to a previous regime or state that they believe was superior to the current order. Some reactionaries do not even look back to a specific period in history but instead seek to return to an envisioned past ideal that may never have existed. Reactionaries, like radicals, may in some cases be more willing to use violence to advance their cause.

This left–right continuum of political attitudes gives the impression that the farther one travels from the center, the more polarized politics becomes. By this logic, then, radicals and reactionaries are miles apart from one another and have nothing in common (Figure 3.2, top). But our preceding discussion indicates that in many ways this impression is incorrect. Viewing left and right as extending along a single continuum is misleading, for the closer one moves toward the extremes, the closer the attitudes become. In other words, the continuum of left and right is more aptly portrayed as a circle, bringing the two ends, radical and reactionary, close together (Figure 3.2, bottom). And in fact, radicals and reactionaries have much in common. Both believe in dramatic change, though in different directions, and both contemplate the use of violence to achieve this change. Although their ends may be quite different, the means of both groups can often be similar. Just as liberals sometimes become conservatives and vice versa, radicals and reactionaries often cross over into each other's camps. For example, many reactionary fascists in Europe became

conservatives Those with a political attitude that is skeptical of change and supports the current order

reactionaries Those who seek to restore the institutions of a real or an imagined earlier order

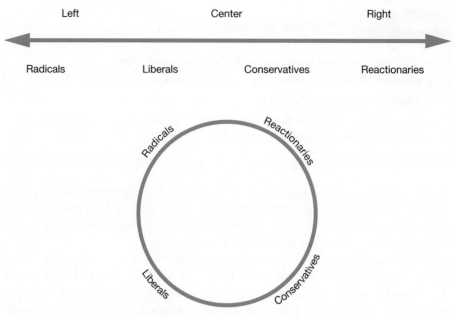

FIGURE 3.2 Two Views of Political Attitudes

supporters of radical communism after World War II. In Europe voters who may have gravitated in the past to more radical parties have embraced more reactionary politics that include xenophobia (the fear of foreigners). Similar forces are at work in the United States.

You may have noticed that our discussion of the spectrum of political attitudes has not provided any specific examples of political issues, such as welfare, civil liberties, immigration, or national defense—common sources of political division that separate right from left in most industrialized democracies. But these policy areas are the concern of political ideology, the basic beliefs about how politics should be constructed. It is important to emphasize again that ideology and political attitudes are not interchangeable. The attitudes of radicals, liberals, conservatives, and reactionaries often take on different ideological content in different societies, depending on the context. What might be considered radical in one country could be conservative in another.

Consider some examples. In the United States, Canada, and Western Europe, radicals are viewed as those who seek to fundamentally transform or overthrow the current capitalist democratic order, replacing it with a system of greater economic and social equality. Liberals in these countries are sympathetic to some of these ideas but believe in pursuing gradual changes within the current system, engaging democratic institutions. Conservatives believe that the current economic and social structures are as good as they are likely to be and that change is unlikely to improve the state of humanity and might make it worse. Reactionaries, meanwhile, would likely reject the radical and liberal critique of the status quo and favor a restoration of greater inequality or hierarchy between people. The foregoing is a simplified but accurate description of how political attitudes are manifested in North America and much of the West.

These same political attitudes would manifest themselves quite differently in a country such as China, however. Despite dramatic economic reforms, China still has a nondemocratic regime dominated by a communist party. A Chinese radical, defined as someone who seeks the destruction of the current system, would advocate the overthrow and replacement of communist rule, perhaps by a democracy like those found in the West. Students who were active in the Tiananmen Square protests for democracy in 1989 were frequently described or condemned by observers and the Chinese government as "radicals" because of their demands for sweeping political changes. Chinese liberals are also likely to support these changes, although they would favor a process of gradual change within the existing political system. Chinese conservatives, skeptical of institutional change, resist calls for democratic reform. They may support market reforms, but they do not view these steps as leading down an inevitable path to democracy. This might best describe those currently in power. Finally, Chinese reactionaries strongly oppose any reforms that might jeopardize communist rule. These neo-Maoists, as they are sometimes called, favor a return to earlier, "purer" communist values and policies, rolling back changes and restoring their communist ideal.

Clearly, American or Western European radicals would have little to say to Chinese radicals; they are united by their attitudes toward the scope and speed of political change, but their political values and goals—their ideologies—are dramatically different. Indeed, Chinese radicals might have more in common with American or European conservatives in terms of their ideological values, which we discuss next. Chinese reactionaries, on the other hand, might have more in common with American or Western European radicals. Context matters.

POLITICAL IDEOLOGY

The importance of context in understanding political attitudes might lead to the conclusion that comparing political attitudes in one country with those in another is impossible: what is radical in one country might be conservative in another. To move past these particularistic differences between countries, political scientists also speak about political ideologies.

Like much of modern politics, the concept of ideology is relatively recent: the term was first used during the French Revolution to speak of a "science of ideas."[7] This meaning reflects the fact that ideologies emerged with the construction of modern secular states as a means to guide politics. Ideologies were thus viewed as alternatives to traditional sets of values such as religion; they were seen as based on rational thought rather than spiritual notions of good and evil. For our purposes, **political ideologies** are defined as sets of political values held by individuals regarding the fundamental goals of politics. Instead of being concerned with the pace and scope of change in a given context, as political attitudes are, ideologies are concerned with the ideal relation between freedom and equality for all individuals and the proper role of political institutions in achieving or maintaining this relation. Supporters of each ideology work to ensure that their values become institutionalized as the basic regime. In the modern world, there are five primary ideologies.

Liberalism as an ideology (rather than as a political attitude) places a high priority on individual political and economic freedom. Adherents of a liberal ideology believe that politics should seek to create the maximum degree of liberty for all people, including free speech, the right of association, and other basic political rights. This goal requires a state with a low degree of autonomy and capacity, so that it can be

political ideology The basic values held by an individual about the fundamental goals of politics or the ideal balance of freedom and equality

liberalism (1) A political attitude that favors evolutionary transformation; (2) an ideology and political system that favors a limited state role in society and the economy and places a high priority on individual political and economic freedom

easily controlled or checked by the public should it begin encroaching on individual rights. For liberals, the lower the ability of the state to intervene in the public's affairs, the greater are the scope and promise of human activity and prosperity. As Thomas Jefferson said, "The legitimate powers of government extend to such acts only as are injurious to others. But it does me no injury for my neighbor to say there are twenty gods, or no God. It neither picks my pocket nor breaks my leg."[8]

From these ideas of liberalism, we take our current definition of democracy, which is often called **liberal democracy**—a system of political, social, and economic liberties, supported by competition, participation, and contestation (such as voting). To be sure, liberals do recognize that if everyone is left to their own devices not all individuals will succeed and great economic inequality inevitably will exist between the wealthiest and the poorest. Liberals argue that despite this shortcoming, a high degree of freedom will produce the greatest amount of general prosperity for the majority. As a final point, we should note that liberalism as an ideology and liberalism as a political attitude are very different things.

Communism differs greatly from liberalism in its view of freedom and equality. Whereas liberalism enshrines individual freedom over equality, communism rejects the idea that personal freedom will ensure prosperity for the majority. Rather, it holds that in the inevitable struggle over economic resources a small group will eventually come to dominate both the market and the state, using its wealth to control and exploit society as a whole. Prosperity will not be spread throughout society but will be monopolized by a few for their own benefit. The gap between rich and poor will widen, and poverty will increase. For communists, liberal democracy is "bourgeois democracy"—of the rich, by the rich, and for the rich. Such institutions as free speech and voting are meaningless when a few control the wealth of society.

To eliminate exploitation, communism advocates that the state control all economic resources and thus produce true economic equality for the community as a whole. This goal requires a powerful state in terms of both autonomy and capacity—a state able to restrict those individual rights (such as owning property or opposing the current regime) that would hinder the pursuit of economic equality. Individual liberties must give way to the needs of society as a whole, creating what communists would see as a true democracy. In the Soviet Union, from 1917 to 1991, this communist ideology was the political regime, as it has been in China since 1949 (though much less so since the 1980s).

Social democracy (sometimes called **socialism**) draws from ideas connected to both communism and liberalism to form its own distinct ideology. Social democracy accepts a strong role for private ownership and market forces while

liberal democracy A political system that promotes participation, competition, and liberty and emphasizes individual freedom and civil rights

communism (1) A political-economic system in which all wealth and property are shared so as to eliminate exploitation, oppression, and, ultimately, the need for political institutions such as the state; (2) a political ideology that advocates such a system

social democracy (socialism) (1) A political-economic system in which freedom and equality are balanced through the state's management of the economy and the provision of social expenditures; (2) a political ideology that advocates such a system

Different Meanings of the Term *Liberalism*

- As a political attitude: favoring slow, evolutionary change
- As a political ideology outside North America: favoring free markets and individualism, accepting greater inequality
- As a political ideology in North America: favoring a greater state role in limiting inequality; many outside the region would call this ideology "social democracy"
- As a political economy: favoring a limited state role in the economy

maintaining an emphasis on economic equality. A state with strong capacity and autonomy is considered important to social democrats to ensure greater economic equality through specific policies like job protection or social benefits like medical care, retirement, and higher education. This commitment to equality means that social democracy may limit freedom more than liberalism does, through such mechanisms as regulation or taxation. However, social democracy recognizes the importance of individual liberty as complementary to equality. In much of Europe, social democracy, rather than liberalism, is the guiding political regime. Many environmental parties, which seek to balance human and environmental needs, also have social democratic influences.

Fascism is hostile to the idea of individual freedom and also rejects the notion of equality. Instead, fascism rests on the idea that people and groups can be classified in terms of inferiority and superiority, justifying a hierarchy among them. Whereas liberals, social democrats, and communists all see inherent potential in every person (although they disagree on the best means to unleash this potential), fascists do not. Fascism conceives of society as an organic whole, a single living body, and the state as a vital instrument to express national will. State autonomy and capacity must therefore be high, and democracy, no matter how it is defined, is rejected as anathema, just as freedom and equality are rejected. No fascist regimes currently exist in the world, although fascism is well remembered from the Nazi regime that ruled Germany from 1933 to 1945. More recently, parties with a fascist orientation have resurfaced in Europe, such as Golden Dawn in Greece and Jobbik in Hungary, and have done surprisingly well in some elections.

fascism A political ideology that asserts the superiority and inferiority of different groups of people and stresses a low degree of both freedom and equality in order to achieve a powerful state

Anarchism departs from these other ideologies quite drastically. If liberalism, communism, and fascism differ over how powerful the state should be, anarchism rejects the notion of the state altogether. Anarchists share with communists the belief that private property leads to inequality, but they are opposed to the idea that the state can solve this problem. As the Russian anarchist Mikhail Bakunin (1814–76) once stated, "I am not a communist, because communism unites all the forces of society in the state and becomes absorbed in it . . . while I seek the complete elimination of the principles of authority and governmental guardianship, which under the pretense of making men moral and civilizing them, has up to now always enslaved, oppressed, exploited, and ruined them."[9]

anarchism A political ideology that stresses the elimination of the state and private property as a way to achieve both freedom and equality for all

Thus, like liberals, anarchists view the state as a threat to freedom and equality rather than as their champion, but they believe that both individual freedom and equality can be achieved only by eliminating the state entirely. Without a state to reinforce inequality or limit personal freedom, argue anarchists, people would be able to cooperate freely as true equals. Given that we live in a world of states, anarchism is the only one of the five primary ideologies that has never been realized. However, anarchist ideas played a role in the Russian Revolution (1917) and in the Spanish Civil War (1936–39). In North America, some versions of libertarianism come close to an anarchist view in their hostility to the state, though libertarians differ from anarchists in their emphasis on private property. The digital currency bitcoin is a good example of where libertarian and anarchist views overlap.

Political ideologies differ according to what they consider the proper balance between freedom and equality to be as well as what role the state should have in achieving that balance. Building on the preceding chapters' discussion of freedom and equality and state strength, Figure 3.3 shows how liberalism, social democracy, communism, fascism, and anarchism try to reconcile freedom and equality with state power. These values are not particularistic, like political attitudes, but are universal in their outlook. And although ethnic and national identities and citizenship may draw the lines of conflict between groups, ideologies and attitudes shape the arena of political conflict within groups. How much change should there be? How fast should it occur? Should it be achieved through peaceful or violent means? What end should it serve? This is the essence of political life, as ideologies rise and fall in

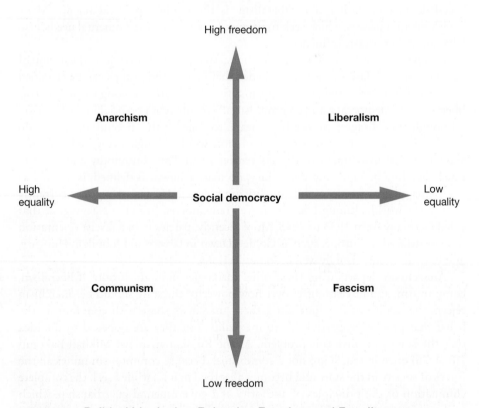

FIGURE 3.3 Political Ideologies: Balancing Freedom and Equality

Liberals and anarchists favor decentralized power and weaker (or nonexistent) states as well as high levels of individual freedom; communists and fascists favor the concentration of state power at the expense of individual freedom; social democrats prefer a balance between state power and individual freedom.

prominence, compete peacefully or violently, and pass from the scene as new ones take their place. In 200 years, such ideologies as liberalism and social democracy may make no more sense than monarchism does today.

WHY HAS THE UNITED STATES RESISTED SOCIAL DEMOCRACY?

USA

In our discussion earlier, we have noted that while political attitudes are particularistic—a function of the specific context—ideologies are universal. This means that ideologies are roughly comparable across time and space. A communist in one country, for example, should rely on essentially the same assumptions about freedom and equality as a communist regime elsewhere. But this may incorrectly suggest that all ideologies are present everywhere. As we know, communism has had a tremendous impact on states and regimes in the Soviet Union/Russia and China, but has had much less impact in Africa. Similarly, while liberalism is the dominant ideology across the former colonies of the British Empire, it has found much less traction in most of Europe. This makes for an interesting puzzle: why do some ideologies have greater power in some countries or regions as opposed to others?

In fact, there is one case where this is particularly puzzling: the United States. While the United States is typically cited as a case where liberal ideology is enshrined in the regime, social democratic values historically have had a much harder time influencing politics. Some might respond by saying that in fact there is a clear ideological distinction in the United States, with the Democratic Party favoring such things as health care, universal state-provided health care, or unemployment benefits. Although true, even Democrats fall far short of standard social democratic values found across Europe, like extensive maternity benefits or low-cost higher education. A simple explanation that the strength of liberalism has "crowded out" social democracy is unsatisfying. The United Kingdom, the birthplace of liberalism, has both strong liberal and social democratic parties.

What then explains the United States' peculiar ideological profile? For a century, political scientists and social democrats have struggled with this question, and there may be no single answer. One common argument focuses on the concept of political culture, which we will turn to shortly. In this view, the particular founding values of the American regime, emphasizing individual liberty over state power, generates skepticism toward social democracy's emphasis on state-supported equality. Another related argument is that the emphasis on individualism has weakened the kind of working-class solidarity needed to build a strong, labor-oriented social democratic party. The fact that most Americans view themselves as "middle class" and upwardly mobile limits support for an ideology ostensibly focused on lower classes. However, it is not necessarily the case that the weakness of social democracy was somehow predetermined. During the Great Depression, social democracy made significant inroads into politics, but American social democratic leaders failed to build bridges to labor unions that could have institutionalized their ideology. Accordingly, there is no reason why social democracy could not reemerge in the United States as a more powerful force. In the 2016 U.S. presidential campaign, candidate Bernie Sanders promoted a social democratic agenda that attracted considerable support. The ongoing rise of inequality could in fact pave the way in the future for a social democratic America. We'll speak more about economic inequality and its political implications in Chapter 4.

IDEOLOGY	TENETS	CORRESPONDING POLITICAL ATTITUDE IN NORTH AMERICA
LIBERALISM	Favors a limited state role in society and economic activity; emphasizes a high degree of personal freedom over social equality.	Conservative
COMMUNISM	Emphasizes limited personal freedom and a strong state in order to achieve social equality; property is wholly owned by the state and market forces are eliminated; state takes on task of production and other economic decisions.	Radical
SOCIAL DEMOCRACY	Supports private property and markets but believes the state has a strong role to play in regulating the economy and providing benefits to the public; seeks to balance freedom and equality.	Liberal
FASCISM	Stresses a low degree of both personal freedom and equality in order to achieve a powerful state.	Reactionary
ANARCHISM	Stresses the elimination of the state and private property as a way to achieve both freedom and equality for all; believes that a high degree of personal freedom and social equality is possible.	Radical

Religion, Fundamentalism, and the Crisis of Identity

Political identities like nationalism and ideology emerged alongside the modern secular state in many ways as an alternative or a rival to religion. If religion had helped describe the world and prescribe people's behavior in relation to freedom, equality, and power, then political identities were nonspiritual guides to those same ends. Accordingly, political identities and religions are similar in many ways: both make assertions about the fundamental nature of humans and society and about the keys to a good life and an ideal community, and both provide their adherents with core texts, prophets, and a promise of salvation.

For more than a century, secular political identities have increasingly replaced religion in public life. Whereas in the premodern world, religion was central to public affairs, including politics, the rise of political identities such as citizenship, nationalism, and ideology led to "the privatization of religion," which entailed removing faith from the public sphere and relegating it to private life. This change was never complete or uniform from country to country, but the emergence of ideology and modern states was central to the development of secularism and the retreat of religion. Max Weber described the process as "the disenchantment of the world"—that is, the replacement of faith in the mystical and spiritual by faith in the material world, in human institutions, and in the notion of progress. But in the past few decades, the claims and power of secular politics have themselves come under attack.

Among many of the most developed countries, ideological values such as liberalism and social democracy have been weakened by their inability to grapple with economic challenges and demographic and social changes. This has intensified disagreements about national identity and citizenship: Who are we? What are the core values of our political community, and who gets to belong to it? In other parts of the world where the political identities are much more weakly institutionalized, the challenge can be greater. The utopian claims associated with modernization theory—that economic growth, science, and rationalism would usher in a golden age—have been discredited. As a result, many people have sought to make religion a powerful force in their lives again. This can affect politics in a number of ways. When religions become most intensely political, fundamentalist ideas and organizations emerge within them.

We should be clear about the meaning of fundamentalism. As with many politically charged words like *fascism* or *terrorism*, we speak indiscriminately of fundamentalism, often using it to describe any strong view that repels us. Some scholars even think the term should be restricted to its original use—a description of a particular kind of movement among Protestant Christians in the nineteenth century. But despite these problems or concerns, the term is useful and can describe a similar pattern across many religions.

The scholar Bruce Lawrence has defined *fundamentalism* as "the affirmation of religious authority as holistic and absolute, admitting of neither criticism nor reduction; it is expressed through the collective demand that specific creedal and ethical dictates derived from scripture be publicly recognized and legally enforced."[10] Following from this, we can view **fundamentalism** as an ideology that seeks to unite religion with the state or, rather, to make faith the sovereign authority—that is, to create a theocracy. This definition implies several things. First, fundamentalism is not the same as religiosity, puritanism, or religious conservatism. For example, Orthodox Jews or the Amish are by definition not fundamentalists; any group that retreats from public life and is suspicious of politics hardly fits our definition. The belief that spirituality should maintain or increase its role in politics or society, such as religious parties or a state-established church, is also not fundamentalism. Second, fundamentalism is not a premodern view. As mentioned earlier, in the premodern world religion played a central role in public life. The rise of the modern state pushed faith into the private realm, replacing it in part with ideology. However, fundamentalism seeks not to return faith to a premodern role but rather to restructure religion as the central political identity—to make faith the sole foundation for a modern regime, a concrete and inerrant guide for politics in the contemporary world.

To that end, fundamentalists base their beliefs on the failures of ideology and the modern state. Through secular political identities, people sought to create heaven on earth, believing they could deny the authority of God and seize control of their own destinies. The result has been, in the fundamentalists' view, greater human misery as well as spiritual malaise. Fundamentalists would point to ongoing injustice and conflict within all societies. Even those who have benefited materially are still truly lost, spiritually empty, and morally adrift, forced to fill their lives with mindless distractions—consumption, entertainment, sex—to avoid confronting this terrible truth. Fundamentalism is thus a critique of modernity itself.[11]

As a political attitude, fundamentalism can appear reactionary, radical, or a combination of the two. Fundamentalists will often claim they want to return to a golden age of faith, but they also seek to solve the problems of the modern world, not simply turn back the clock. This mixture of reactionary and radical attitudes also explains

fundamentalism A view of religion as absolute and inerrant and that should be legally enforced by making faith the sovereign authority

why fundamentalism is often associated with violence. However, we should be clear that only a small number of fundamentalists embrace such an approach. We will delve into this issue in depth in Chapter 5 when we consider political violence. To reiterate, we should not confuse religiosity or piety with fundamentalism, or fundamentalism with violence.

How does fundamentalism approach the relation between freedom and equality? Even within fundamentalist trends in a single religion, there is a great diversity of ideas. Some fundamentalist views emphasize collective equality and reject individual freedom in favor of submission to God; others posit an expression of individual freedom made possible through a political system based on faith and are less concerned with specific economic or social inequalities between people. Other views reject both freedom and equality in favor of hierarchy and the domination of believers over nonbelievers, men over women, or the more faithful over the less so. Some forms of fundamentalism see the possibility of a religiously correct state; for others, that very notion of the state is incompatible with faith. It is thus a mistake to think of fundamentalism as a single bundle of common values; rather, it is a recurring pattern across many religions and has produced various ideological forms. In some cases, these forms remain nebulous and attract few adherents. In other cases, they are well defined and exercise significant political power. As the politics of fundamentalism continues to develop, this aspect of the "return of God" may prove to be one of the most important developments in comparative politics.[12]

Political Culture

Our final area of consideration in this chapter is political culture. First, we need to understand what is meant by *culture* in general. If a society is a group of people bound by shared institutions, as it was defined at the start of this chapter, then **culture** is the content of the institutions that help define a society. Culture acts as a kind of social road map, providing norms and priorities that guide people as they organize their lives. While ethnicity, nationality, and citizenship define which group an individual belongs to, culture is the repository for the activities and ideas that the group considers proper and normal. **Political culture**, in turn, refers to a society's norms for political activity.

The study of culture in political science has changed over time. In the past, the economic and political development of countries was often explained as a function of cultural or religious factors. For example, Weber famously argued that a "Protestant work ethic," linked to religious values, fostered the accumulation and invest-

culture Basic institutions that define a society

political culture The basic norms for political activity in a society

---

INFOCUS   **Political Culture Is . . .**

- The basic norms for political activity in a society.
- A determining factor in what ideologies will dominate a country's political regime.
- Unique to a given country or group.
- Distinct from political attitudes and ideologies.

---

ment of wealth that was critical in sparking the Industrial Revolution. A related argument has stressed that the emphasis by Protestantism on private property and individualism also contributed to the emergence of democracy in Europe—in contrast to Catholicism, whose religious values were more authoritarian and anticapitalist. However, over time these kinds of arguments lost favor for several reasons. First, as we noted in the previous section, from the beginning of the twentieth century religion lost much of its authority in the developed world as ideologies and secular regimes grew in power. Second, modernization theory argued that culture in general was undergoing a process of transformation, such that as states modernized they would develop shared secular values. Inasmuch as there were different cultures, they were, like faith in God in general, remnants of a premodern era that would be swept away by material and technological progress. Given enough time and money, every society would eventually wind up looking like Western Europe. Third, even for those who advocated cultural explanations for politics, there was the problem of how to measure and compare culture.

But if God has returned as a subject of study, so has culture. As in the past, culture and religion are often interlinked—political scientists and social psychologists who define major cultural differences still do so largely on the basis of religion and region. As you can imagine, this resurgent interest is not without controversy—the idea that culture strongly influences politics goes against decades of scholarship that emphasized modernization and secularization. The best example of this debate has been the work of Samuel P. Huntington, who caused a firestorm with his 1996 book, *The Clash of Civilizations and the Remaking of World Order*.[13] In it, he argued that with the end of the Cold War cultural differences were now the main fault lines defining international relations. Huntington has been praised and pilloried—for example, he wrote that Islam has "bloody borders," drawing scorn for the implication that there is something inherently violent about the faith. At the same time, his observations about Ukraine as a "cleft country," prone to violence due to cultural divides, seem prescient. If we can get past the controversy, there are important puzzles to explore. Why are some countries richer than others? Why are some more unequal? Why are some more democratic? Why are some more prone to political violence? Can culture explain these differences?

In short, the study of political culture has resurfaced in political science, but there is still a great deal of confusion about what conclusions we can draw from it. Some of the best research we have in this regard is the work of Ronald Inglehart, who for three decades has been conducting public-opinion research in nearly 80 countries around the world. His data, known as the World Values Survey, allows us to track differences in beliefs across countries, cultures, and time. In particular, Inglehart distinguishes differences between societies along two dimensions. The first distinguishes between traditional and secular-rational values. Traditional values emphasize religion, family values, deference to authority, and national pride. Secular-rational values place much less emphasis on these same values. The second distinguishes survival and self-expression values. Survival values emphasize economic and physical security and are associated with low levels of trust. Self-expression values are focused on higher levels of tolerance and demands for individual participation in politics.

As we see in Figure 3.4, very poor countries are associated with traditional and survival values, much as we would expect. However, once societies develop, they do not all move in a neat diagonal line toward higher degrees of secular-rational and self-expression values. Moreover, even as they move, they tend to move along a

How Has India Held Together?

In Chapter 2, we addressed the question of why Pakistan has been unable to institutionalize democracy and has slid toward state failure. In that discussion, we made some comparisons to India because they were both part of a single country under British rule until 1947. Both countries faced similar challenges, including poverty, ethnic diversity, a weak state, and linguistic and regional differences. In fact, in a number of these areas it can be argued that India was at a greater disadvantage.

Upon independence, India was forced to contend with several major religious divisions, including those between Hindus, Muslims, Christians, and Sikhs; at least 10 major languages; hundreds, if not thousands, of caste divisions (hereditary classes); and the sheer size of the country, the seventh largest in the world geographically and the second largest in population (then and now). In the course of partition, approximately 15 million people moved between India and Pakistan, a situation that led to hundreds of thousands of deaths from ethnic and religious violence.

Following partition, India continued to face internal threats to its stability and sovereignty. For example, ownership of the Indian state of Jammu and Kashmir was contested with Pakistan due to the state's overwhelmingly Muslim population. Many Indian Kashmiris have continued to seek greater autonomy within India, unification with Pakistan, or outright independence. Adherents of the Sikh religion (established in India in the fifteenth century) similarly agitated for greater rights and complained of discrimination in a Hindu-majority country. This revolt eventually culminated in a separatist movement for an independent Sikh state and a violent conflict between government forces and Sikh separatists in

the 1980s. After that uprising was crushed, India's Prime Minister Indira Gandhi was assassinated by her own Sikh bodyguards. Although Sikh separatism has abated, violent conflict from, and toward, the Muslim community has increased. In the past two decades, riots and acts of terrorism have left several thousand dead. Hindu nationalism has also increased, led by the Bharatiya Janata Party (BJP), which has been associated with anti-Muslim violence.

Given these difficulties, we can well wonder how this country has managed to stay intact, let alone democratic. Numerous scholars have tackled this question, and their answers reflect many of the points we have mentioned in the chapter about the role of identity in shaping and defining political institutions.

Instead of founding the newly independent India on a strong, unified national identity, the country's leaders attempted to accommodate as many religious, ethnic, and cultural differences as possible. Indian identity in the new constitution was built around citizenship rather than ethnicity. English, alongside Hindi, was established as a national language of government, allowing for greater integration while not giving any single Indian language political dominance. Religious holidays for all major groups were officially recognized. To meet local demands, a system of asymmetric federalism (see Chapter 2) devolved power differently across states, as discussed at the start of this chapter. Finally, central executive and legislative institutions that would give any one group a chance to dominate the government—such as a presidency—were avoided. As a result, some scholars have concluded that India has managed to create multiple and complementary identities that have strengthened, not weakened, democ-

Thousands attended inauguration ceremonies for India's new prime minister, Narendra Modi, in 2014.

Moreover, they have implications for the question of how homogeneous societies (like those in Europe) might deal with increasingly diverse populations.

However, we should not conclude that India's solution is perfect. As we noted earlier, regional, ethnic, and national conflicts continue in India, and it can be argued that religious conflict in particular between Hindus and Muslims has intensified over time. Many Muslims feel disenfranchised from Indian democracy because of growing Hindu nationalism and Muslims' continuing exclusion from economic and political power.

In addition, some have argued that devolving economic and political power, as we saw in the case of Telangana, may simply create a new layer of local officials who seek to siphon off resources and buy votes. Corruption is a major problem in India, and one frequently seen as an obstacle to growth. Local power is also a significant check on central state power. Though we might assume that this check is a positive component of democracy, it also can create a barrier to implementing national policies, something that in India is visibly lacking. One question raised about modern India's political history is whether stability in such a diverse country comes at a cost—a reduction in state autonomy and capacity. In a country with major ambitions and significant deficiencies, this is no small concern.

racy. Rather than a nation-state, India can be seen as a state-nation in which multiple nations are given varying degrees of autonomy under one central state.[a] This structure is quite the opposite of Pakistan, where the state has not succeeded in effectively drawing diverse groups into a functioning political system.

These explanations are valuable not only in answering the puzzle of India's national and democratic success but also in shedding light on our question of how to craft institutions to prevent or resolve ethnic and national conflict elsewhere in the world.

THINKING CRITICALLY

1. How do India's political institutions accommodate the country's profound ethnic diversity?
2. What is an example of an ethnic conflict in India? What is an example of a national conflict? How do they differ?
3. In what ways are state stability and state autonomy and capacity at odds in India?

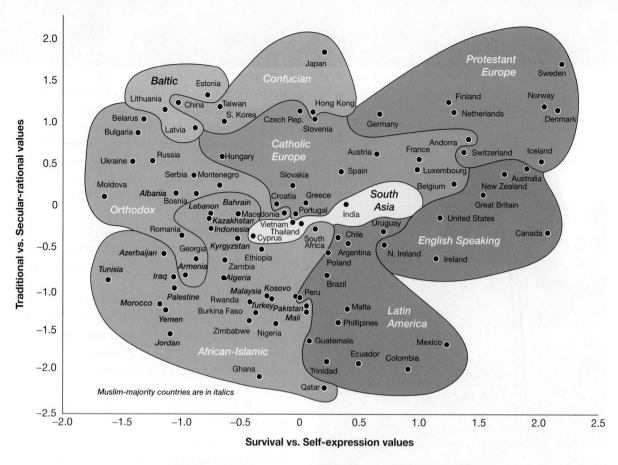

FIGURE 3.4 Inglehart Values Map

World Values Survey. www.worldvaluessurvey.org (accessed 12/20/16).

common path that reflects their shared cultural heritage. In other words, Scandinavian countries do not score highly in terms of secular-rational and self-expression values because they are wealthy but rather because of their Protestant heritage. Equally rich countries, such as the United States or Canada, show a lower level of secular-rational values for specific cultural reasons. Accordingly, as Islamic countries develop, they will move along a particular historical path. For example, these countries may develop a greater emphasis on self-expression even as they continue to maintain a stronger attachment to traditional values like family and religion. This path would be similar to the one taken by Latin America and some English-speaking countries. As Inglehart and his coauthor Christian Welzel assert, "a society's heritage—whether shaped by Protestantism, Catholicism, Islam, Confucianism, or communism—leaves a lasting imprint on a society's worldview."[14]

It is easy to fall into stereotypes and determinism when speaking about culture. But recall our discussion of multicausality and endogeneity, where we noted that it is often very difficult to identify cause and effect. Is it political culture that explains the weakness of social democracy in the United States? Moreover, in such important areas as democratization we have not seen that culture is a barrier to change—successful democracies have emerged across the map of political culture. We will speak more about this in Chapter 6. It is more helpful to observe that even as countries develop, their cultural heritage remains a distinct and powerful institution that shapes politics.

In Sum: Society and Politics

Societies are complex and often difficult to unravel. In looking at how societal organization shapes politics, we have found that people everywhere have a number of identities: ethnicity, national identity, citizenship, political attitude, ideology, and political culture. Ethnicity provides a group identity, binding individuals to a group, providing solidarity, and separating them from others. National identity provides a political aspiration for that group, a desire for freedom through self-government, and citizenship establishes a relation between that group and a state. Although each of these identities can be clearly defined, they are often strongly connected and in some cases blend into each other. Such identities may bind people together, but they can be the source of conflict when different groups see each other as threats to their freedom and equality.

Whereas group identities establish differences between groups as a whole, an individual is positioned within a group by political attitudes, ideologies, and culture. These three identities shape an individual's view of the ideal relation between freedom and equality in society and the scope and pace of political change.

Society's role in politics is clearly complicated, shaped by an array of factors that affect the ongoing debate over freedom and equality. Not long ago, many social scientists dismissed social identities such as nationalism and religion as outdated forms of identification that were giving way in the face of modernization and individualism. However, most now believe that collective identities are more resilient than was once thought and that they may in fact sharpen in the face of new societal challenges. Politics is not simply a sum of individual actions but the product of a rich array of institutions that overlap one another, giving our lives meaning and informing our ideas, viewpoints, and values. We will consider this idea further in the next chapter as we turn to a new set of institutions and ideas that shape the struggle over freedom and equality: those concerned with economic life.

Key Terms

anarchism (p. 71)

citizenship (p. 60)

communism (p. 70)

conservatives (p. 67)

culture (p. 76)

ethnic conflict (p. 63)

ethnic identity/ethnicity (p. 56)

fascism (p. 71)

fundamentalism (p. 75)

liberal democracy (p. 70)

liberalism (p. 69)

liberals (p. 66)

nation (p. 58)

national conflict (p. 63)

national identity (p. 58)

nationalism (p. 59)

nation-state (p. 63)

patriotism (p. 61)

political attitude (p. 66)

political culture (p. 76)

political ideology (p. 69)

radicals (p. 66)

reactionaries (p. 67)

social democracy (socialism) (p. 70)

society (p. 55)

People line up to buy toiletries in a supermarket in Caracas in June 2016. Despite Venezuela's massive oil reserves, consumers face shortages of food and consumer goods due to the policies of its leaders.

Political Economy

How do people use politics to create and distribute wealth?

IN MARCH 2013, VENEZUELA LOST ITS president, Hugo Chávez, who had been the country's leader since 1999. A highly charismatic and polarizing figure, Chávez had an enormous impact on the country and left behind a questionable legacy. Originally a military officer, Chávez embraced Marxist views early in his career. He concluded then that only radical change could solve the country's economic problems: Venezuela was blessed by natural resources such as oil and gas, but it was marked by extreme inequality and a high degree of poverty. In 1992, Chávez led an unsuccessful coup against the existing democratically elected government and was sentenced to two years in jail. His justification for the coup—to improve his country's social conditions—resonated with many Venezuelans, especially as the country underwent a period of wrenching economic reform. In the 1998 presidential elections, Chávez won over 50 percent of the vote and entered office with a call to transform the country.

Over the next 15 years, the country was indeed transformed, but not in ways that created greater democracy or economic stability. During his presidency, Chávez implemented a set of changes in the political-economic system. The new system, called "Bolivarian socialism," was meant both to improve the standard of living and increase political sovereignty (which Chávez and his supporters viewed as compromised by American imperialism). One major piece of Bolivarian socialism was Venezuela's oil reserves—the largest in the world. Although much of this industry was already under state control, the Chávez government carried out further nationalization, forcing out a number of international firms. The government also nationalized parts of the agricultural, industrial, telecommunications, and financial sectors.

Alongside these nationalizations, the government dramatically expanded its social welfare system. Medical clinics were built, staffed in part by over 30,000 Cuban medical personnel; primary and secondary education were extended to the population, with a particular focus on eliminating illiteracy; food and fuel prices were subsidized; and public housing was constructed. Venezuela enjoyed high rates of economic growth during the 2000s and an improved standard of living for many people. Inequality decreased, and poverty rates fell from 50 percent to 30 percent by 2012.

So was Bolivarian socialism a success? Current problems call this into question. First, nationalizations aside, Chávez's policies were financed by a nearly tenfold increase in the world price of oil, giving Chávez the means to implement his socialist policies. Despite calls for greater independence from global capitalism, the country became even more dependent on oil exports to the United States and elsewhere. Second, while improvements in the standard of living were evident, when placed in comparison with the rest of Latin America they were less impressive. During Chávez's rule, most other countries in Latin America had higher rates of economic growth, lower inflation, and better improvement in infant mortality rates. This was despite the unprecedented amounts of oil revenue Venezuela was dedicating to these goals. Finally, despite the economic improvements, homicide rates doubled, becoming the second highest in the world (after those of Honduras).

Venezuela entered the post-Chávez era in a politically unstable condition. The country's democratic institutions, which were concentrated in the hands of Chávez and his supporters, have been progressively weakened. This situation has in turn deepened the polarization between the poor and the middle and upper classes. Upon Chávez's death, a special presidential election in April 2013 pitted Vice President Nicolás Maduro against Henrique Capriles, the governor of Miranda State. The uncharismatic Maduro campaigned on a platform that he would uphold Chávez's Bolivarian socialism. Capriles drew his support from the middle and upper classes, promising an end to nationalization and a liberalization of the economy. The tightly fought election ended in a victory for Maduro, though by less than 2 percent.

Since that time, Maduro has attempted to sustain Chávez's policies. He faces increased opposition as more of the public grow concerned about the future. Protests, at times deadly, rally against shortages of basic goods like milk and flour, rising crime, and what is now the world's highest inflation rate, at over

700 percent. Meanwhile, weak investment in the oil industry, a result of nation-alization and the diversion of revenues toward other state expenditures, has led to a steady decline in output since Chávez first came to power. Because of the precipitous decline in world oil prices, there is less state revenue overall and more national debt, making it difficult for Maduro to maintain Bolivarian socialism. Venezuela is facing economic collapse, as much of the population has been pushed into poverty. Maduro's presidential term lasts until 2019, and it is difficult to see how this situation will be easily, or peacefully, resolved in the immediate future. The case of Venezuela shows that economics is not separate from politics, and that wealth may aggravate, rather than solve, issues of poverty and inequality.

LEARNING OBJECTIVES

- Understand how states are involved in the management of markets and property.
- Discuss how states provide public goods, which are shared by society to some collective benefit.
- Distinguish between political-economic systems in how they reconcile freedom and equality.
- Compare different political-economic systems through human development, wealth, and inequality.
- Analyze the future trends of political-economic systems.

LIKE POLITICS, ECONOMIES are made up of many different institutions—rules, norms, and values—that strongly influence how the economic system is constructed. People often think about economic systems as somehow "natural," with functions akin to the law of gravity. In reality, an economy relies on an array of institutions that enable individuals to exchange goods and resources with one another. Moreover, economic institutions, like political ones, are not easy to replace or change once they have been constructed. They become self-perpetuating, and people have a hard time imagining life without them.

Economic institutions directly influence politics, and vice versa. The economy is one of the major arenas of the struggle over freedom and equality. Some view the economy as the central means by which people can achieve individual freedom, whereas others view the economy as the central means by which people can achieve collective equality. Inevitably, this struggle involves the government, the state, and the regime. How the balance between freedom and equality is struck directly influences such things as the distribution of wealth, the kinds of economic activity and trade that citizens may conduct, and the overall degree of security and prosperity that people enjoy. In short, the interactions between political and economic institutions in any country will profoundly affect the prosperity of every citizen. The study of how politics and economics are related and how their relationship shapes the balance between freedom and equality is commonly known as **political economy**.

In this chapter, we address these issues by investigating the relationship between freedom and equality. We will start by asking what role states play in managing an

political economy The study of the interaction between states and markets

economy. States commonly involve themselves in economic life in several different areas; depending on such things as the dominant ideology and regime, the scope and impact of these actions can vary dramatically. Just as there are different ideologies concerning the ideal relationship between the state and society, as we saw in Chapter 3, there are different ideological views regarding the ideal relationship between the state and the market. And each ideology leads to a different political-economic system. Once we compare these differing views, we consider how we might measure and compare their relative outcomes. In the process, we will look at some of the most common standards of measuring wealth and its distribution. Finally, we will consider the future of the relationship between state and market and how their interaction shapes the balance between freedom and equality.

The Components of Political Economy

Before we compare the different types of relationships between states and economies around the world, we need to familiarize ourselves with the basic components of political economy. All modern states are strongly involved in the day-to-day affairs of their economies, at both the domestic and the global level. In shaping the economy to achieve their stated ideological goals, states and regimes use a variety of economic institutions.

MARKETS AND PROPERTY

The most fundamental components of political economy are markets and property. When people speak of markets, the first thing that may come to mind is a physical place where individuals buy and sell goods. For as long as human beings have lived in settled communities that were able to produce a surplus of goods, there have been markets. Markets are closely connected to the rise of cities and political institutions; people would settle around markets, and markets would often spring up around fortifications, where residents could engage in commerce with some sense of security provided by the state. Such markets are still common in much of the world.

When social scientists speak of markets, they mean the interaction of supply and demand, though without a specific location. **Markets** are the interactions between the forces of supply and demand, and they allocate resources through the process of those interactions. As these two forces interact, they create values for goods and services by arriving at specific prices. An amazing feature of markets is that they can be so decentralized. Who decides how many cars should be built this year? Or what colors they should be? Or the price of this textbook? These decisions are made not by any one person or government, but by millions of individuals making decisions about what they will buy and sell. If I produce a good and set its price at more than people are willing to pay, I will not be able to sell it and turn a profit. This result will force me to either lower my price or go out of business. Similarly, if I have a good that no one wants, I must change it or face economic ruin. Sellers seek to create products that people will desire or need, and buyers seek to buy the best or the most goods at the lowest price. Because more than one seller or producer typically exists for a product, this environment tends to generate competition and innovation. Sellers seek to dominate a market by offering their goods at the cheapest price or by offering a good that is innovative and therefore superior to any alternative.

market The interaction between the forces of supply and demand that allocates resources

Markets

- Sellers seek to create products that will be in demand.
- Buyers seek to buy the best or most goods at the lowest price.
- Markets are the medium through which buyers and sellers exchange goods.
- Markets emerge spontaneously and are not easily controlled by the state.

In short, markets are communities of buyers and sellers who are constantly interacting through the economic choices they make. At the same time, market forces typically require the state to enforce contracts, sanction activity, and regulate supply and demand where necessary. For example, by setting a minimum wage, a state is controlling to some extent the price of labor. By making certain drugs or prostitution illegal, the state is attempting to stamp out a part of the market altogether. Yet these goals are not always easily achieved. Minimum wages can be subverted by relying on illegal immigrants, and "black" or underground markets appear where drugs and prostitution are illegal. While markets typically rely on states, they also have a life of their own, and each state must decide in what way and to what extent it will sustain and control the market.

Property is a second element critical to any economy. **Property** refers to the ownership of the goods and services exchanged through markets. Property can refer to land, buildings, businesses, or personal items, to name some of its most common forms. In addition, a certain set of property rights can accompany ownership, such as the right to buy and sell property or the right not to have it taken away by the state or other citizens without a good reason (or what is known as "just cause") and compensation. As with market forces, property rights must be regulated by the state. Without state power functioning in a fair manner, property is insecure.

In many people's minds, property has a physical presence. I can see a car, buy it, own it, and sell it when I want a new one. However, property is not always tangible. *Intellectual property*, for example, refers to ownership of a specific type of knowledge or content—a song, a piece of software code, or a treatment for diabetes. As economic developments center more and more on such intangible forms of information and knowledge, the concept of property and property rights becomes as invisible as that of markets. We have no physical entity to make transactions clearer. Anyone who has downloaded a song or software from the Internet knows exactly what we are speaking of.

Like the role states play in regulating markets, the role they play in constructing and enforcing property rights, both between people and between the state and society, varies from state to state. States may fail to enforce the rights of individuals to protect their own property from other individuals—by neglecting to enact or uphold laws against counterfeiting or theft. States may also assume certain property rights for themselves, claiming ownership over property such as airwaves, oil, land, or businesses. It is important to understand that property rights do not automatically come into being. In fact, many less-developed countries enjoy a wealth of property but have a poverty of property rights, for these states are unable or unwilling to establish and enforce such rules. We will speak about this more in Chapter 10.

property Goods or services that are owned by an individual or a group, privately or publicly

PUBLIC GOODS

We have so far described property as goods that individuals acquire or use through the market for their own benefit. But there are limits to what property and the markets can achieve. In some cases, their interaction does not produce benefits that society desires. Take, for example, transportation. Forms of transportation infrastructure do exist in the private realm, such as toll roads or passenger ferries, and these private forms have a long history that predates the state. But most modern societies question the moral and practical implications of allowing these goods to belong only to a few. The privatization of such goods may limit economic development: a network of privately held roads might impede trade or fail to reach certain parts of the population. Because of such concerns, all states provide some level of public goods; indeed, the core definition of a state itself—a monopoly of violence—is the underlying public good on which all markets and property rest.

public goods Goods, provided or secured by the state, available to society, and which no private person or organization can own

Public goods can be defined as those goods, provided or secured by the state, that are available for society and indivisible, meaning that no one private person or organization can own them. Unlike private goods, with their inherent link to individual freedom, public goods can generate greater equality because the public is able to share broadly in their benefits.[1]

In many countries, roads, national defense, health care, and primary education are public goods, and everyone in the country may use them or benefit from their existence. But states do differ greatly in the extent of public goods they provide, largely due to the role of ideology in the relationship between states and markets. In the United States, health care is not a public good; it remains in private hands, and not everyone has equal access to it. In Canada, however, health care is a public good, provided by the state in the form of publicly owned hospitals and universal benefits for all citizens. In Cuba, the state owns most businesses, making them public goods as well. The goods and profits of these firms belong not to a private owner but to the state, to be distributed as the government sees fit.

NIGERIA

RUSSIA

IRAN

MEXICO

OIL AS A PUBLIC GOOD IN NIGERIA, RUSSIA, IRAN, MEXICO

Oil and gas are excellent examples of goods whose ownership varies from country to country, with significant political implications. In countries such as Brazil, Mexico, and Iran, oil and gas are viewed as a public good, and as a result their exploitation is under state control. In Nigeria and Russia, private companies have been allowed to control some of the oil industry, but the state still plays a crucial ownership role. In the United States and the United Kingdom, the oil industry is in private hands. While oil and gas deposits can provide an enormous wealth, as we see in the case of Venezuela this can create significant problems—what is commonly known as a "resource curse." There are several factors at work.

First, states that monopolize oil and gas through direct ownership may be more susceptible to authoritarian rule. The reasoning is simple, reflected in the American colonists' cry of "no taxation without representation." Where states have control over significant natural resources, the need to tax—and thus rely on—the public is much lower. In Russia and Iran, oil has helped support authoritarian governments by allowing them to buy off the public through such things as subsidies for gasoline. Political elites, too, remain loyal to those in power as a way to gain wealth, thus resisting pressures for political reform.

This leads us to a second concern. Natural resources can easily become a source of corruption. When oil or gas is in the hands of the state, those in power have easy access to profits that can be siphoned off for personal use. Authoritarian and democratic states alike may fall prey to this temptation. To take one example, Brazil's state-owned oil and gas company, Petrobras, has been engulfed in the biggest corruption scandal in the country's history. It announced in 2015 that it had lost $17 billion to corruption and mismanagement. Investigators uncovered a pattern of bribes and kickbacks that inflated costs of oil exploration and production, and that lined the pockets of politicians and executives of the national oil company. In Nigeria as much as $150 billion may have been stolen over the past decade.

Third, states that become dependent on the export of oil and gas to fund the national budget may wind up with unstable economies. Natural resources are highly vulnerable to price changes in international markets or a decline in the resource itself. This can be especially problematic if oil or gas revenues are used to fund the state budget, as is commonly the case. We can see this in the case of Russia. In that country, oil and gas revenues make up over half of total government revenue, and exports of oil and gas make up over two-thirds of Russia's total exports. The sudden plunge in world oil prices in 2014 created a major economic crisis in Russia. The value of Russia's currency declined by 46 percent in 2014, and the economy began to shrink. Oil production and revenues have also been in steady decline in Nigeria and Mexico, where the state has relied heavily on the oil sector for revenue.

Yet private ownership and production of oil may also pose threats to countries where the state lacks the capability to regulate and tax producers. Where oil production is controlled by foreign companies, weak states may find it difficult to capture a sizable percentage of the profits and direct them toward social spending, and often struggle to hold those companies to environmental standards. This is a problem in Nigeria, where private firms are responsible for oil extraction, and environmental damage is widespread. States with greater capacity, like the United States and the United Kingdom, have a much better record taxing and regulating their oil and gas producers.

SOCIAL EXPENDITURES: WHO BENEFITS?

This discussion of public goods leads us to the broader subject of **social expenditures**—the state's provision of public benefits, such as education, health care, and transportation, or what is commonly called *welfare* or the *welfare state*. For many Americans, the very word *welfare*, like *taxes*, has an inherently negative connotation; it calls up images of free riders living off the hard work of others. In many countries, redistribution of wealth in this manner can be controversial; its critics assert that social expenditures lead to counterproductive behavior. High unemployment benefits, they argue, may discourage people from seeking work. Moreover, alternative forms of social security that people have relied on in the past, such as the family, the community, or churches, could be weakened by too broad a welfare system. Issues of welfare are further complicated by immigration, given claims that immigrants rely on social expenditures more than the rest of the population. None of these arguments is necessarily true, or true for all countries. We'll talk more about this in a moment.

However valid these arguments may or may not be, one problem for many countries is that social expenditures can be very costly, especially where unemployment

social expenditures State provision of public benefits, such as education, health care, and transportation

is high or the population is aging. In recent years, many countries have sought to control the growth of social expenditures, but this effort is easier said than done. We will explore this issue further in Chapter 5 as we consider problems in advanced democracies.

Who benefits from social expenditures? Strictly defined, social expenditures are provided by the state to those who find themselves in circumstances where they require greater care: the unemployed or underemployed, children, the elderly, the poor, and the disabled. Such expenditures can include health care, job training, income replacement, and housing. However, many forms of social expenditures are public goods that are more widely used. For example, a national health care system treats employed and unemployed, wealthy and poor alike. Highways, public higher education, and cultural institutions such as museums may primarily benefit the well-off. In fact, if we look at social expenditures more broadly, we find that in many countries they mostly benefit the middle class, not the poor. In this sense, the modern welfare state is less a structure that taxes the middle class and the rich to benefit the poor than one that taxes the middle class and the rich for services that benefit themselves.

TAXATION

Over the past 50 years, states have become increasingly responsible for providing public goods and social expenditures. How do states pay for these expenses? One major source of funds is taxation. As with social expenditures, taxation generates passionate opinions: some view it as the means by which a greedy state takes the hard-earned revenues of its citizens, stunting economic growth, whereas others see it as a critical tool for generating a basic level of equality. Regardless of one's opinion of taxation, societies expect states to provide a number of public goods and services; and for most countries, taxation is the key source of revenue. The other option is to borrow money from domestic and international lenders.

How much tax is collected varies from country to country. Figure 4.1 illustrates this variation, showing that in some countries taxes consume a large portion of a country's **gross domestic product (GDP)**, defined as the total market value of goods and services produced by one country in a year. Many European countries with large social expenditures tend to have high overall tax rates to fund those expenses. In addition, countries differ in where this revenue comes from. Some countries rely on high personal taxation, while others rely on taxes on businesses or goods and services. All countries struggle with finding the right mix and level of taxation, aiming to extract needed funds and reinvest them in a way that will generate development and prosperity.

gross domestic product (GDP) The total market value of all goods and services produced by a country over a period of one year

MONEY, INFLATION, AND ECONOMIC GROWTH

It should be getting clearer that many political-economic processes are tightly interlinked. States must form a relationship with markets and property, deciding what goods and property should remain in private hands, what should be public, and what kinds of rights exist for each. They must also determine the level and forms of social expenditures needed to ensure a basic standard of living and security for all citizens. This distribution requires funds, and states must typically draw on the public's resources through taxation. But a successful and productive tax base needs

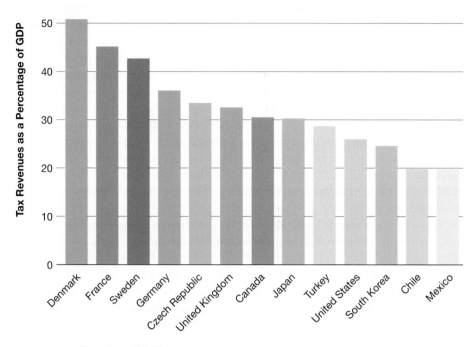

FIGURE 4.1 Taxation, 2017

Source: Heritage Foundation Index of Economic Freedom (accessed 8/23/17).

a dynamic and growing economy. So while the state is charged with managing markets, property, and public benefits, it also has a hand in fostering economic growth.

One basic way the state fosters growth is through the creation and management of money. Money is nothing more than a medium of exchange. Unlike wealth, which consists of property that has value, money is an instrument people use to conduct economic transactions. Money represents only a tiny fraction of the world's wealth, the rest of which is tied up in houses, factories, land, and other property. But without money, economic transactions are difficult. States thus play a critical role in providing money as a means to secure and stimulate economic transactions.

Long ago, money did not exist. As complex political systems began to take shape, however, they established some basic monetary relationships through a monetary system, which typically rested on metals that held some intrinsic value, like gold and silver. Within the past century, however, money has lost its intrinsic worth, and people have come to base their faith in a state's currency on their trust in that state. People accept payments in dollars or euros or yen because they know that others will accept them in turn. A society trusts its currency only so long as it trusts its state.

Because states control money, they have a great deal of influence over their domestic economies. Part of this power comes through what is known as a **central bank**, an institution that controls how much money is flowing through the economy as

central bank The state institution that controls how much money is flowing through the economy, as well as how much it costs to borrow money in that economy

well as how much it costs to borrow money in that economy. One of the main ways a central bank influences these two areas is by changing a national interest rate—the rate charged to private banks when they need to borrow funds from the central bank or one another. When the central bank lowers the interest rate charged to banks, those banks in turn typically lower their own interest rates for businesses and individuals. Loans become less expensive and saving becomes less lucrative, which can prompt people to borrow more and spend more. This activity in turn increases the amount of money active in the economy and stimulates economic growth. If the central bank raises interest rates, on the other hand, people are likely to borrow less and save more to take advantage of the higher interest their savings can earn. The money supply in the economy contracts as a result, and economic growth is likely to slow. Thus, during the first half of 2008, the U.S. Federal Reserve (the U.S. central bank) cut interest rates six times in an effort to stave off an economic downturn. As of 2016, the interest rate sat at one half of 1 percent (0.55%). In 1980, by contrast, it was 17 percent.

The actions the central bank takes are closely tied to two other important factors in any economy: inflation and deflation. **Inflation** is an increase in the overall prices in the economy when demand outstrips supply. Although small levels of inflation are not a problem, inflation can become problematic when it is too high. Wages and savings lose their value, and workers and those on fixed incomes, such as the retired, find that their money buys less and less. People press for higher wages or benefits to offset higher prices, further feeding inflation. Central banks can try to control inflation by raising interest rates, making credit more expensive and thereby reducing spending and lowering prices. However, the prices of many things, like oil or other imports, are beyond a state's control. States can also be the cause of inflation if the government, unable to cover its expenses, is forced to borrow money at ever-higher interest rates to attract lenders. This situation can lead to very high inflation.

In extreme cases, countries can experience **hyperinflation**: inflation that is higher than 50 percent a month for more than two months in a row. (The inflation rate in North America and Europe over the past decade ranged between 1 percent and 4 percent per year.) When governments find themselves lacking the tax revenues to cover basic expenditures and are unable to borrow from lenders, they may decide to print money to cover their debts, thus expanding the money supply. At the same time, such circumstances are often accompanied by a public belief that there is no longer a strong state to support the currency—a collapse of legitimacy. Under such conditions, normal economic processes fail. Zimbabwe is an extreme example. Starting around the turn of the century, its government, having largely disrupted its agricultural economy and thus its tax base, began to cover expenses by printing money. By 2008, inflation reached 231,000,000 percent. The largest banknotes issued were for 100 trillion Zimbabwean dollars—about 30 U.S. dollars. Hyperinflation typically leads to currency collapse because people increasingly refuse to accept the devalued currency as payment and switch to other means of transaction, from foreign currency to barter. This is what finally occurred in Zimbabwe and is developing in Venezuela.

The dangers of inflation might lead us to conclude that tight control over the money supply should be a government's first economic priority. But there are problems at the other end of the spectrum as well. Under some conditions, especially recently, states face the danger of **deflation**, when too many goods are chasing too little money. Dropping prices might sound like a good thing, but they can be dev-

inflation An outstripping of supply by demand, resulting in an increase in the general price level of goods and services and the resulting loss of value in a country's currency

hyperinflation Inflation of more than 50 percent a month for more than two months in a row

deflation A period of falling prices and values for goods, services, investments, and wages

astating if businesses are unable to make a profit. Lowering prices leads to unemployment, less spending, and even more deflation. This has been a serious problem in Japan, which has suffered deflation almost every year since 1998, and has been a concern in North America and Europe since 2008. Heavy levels of debt by banks, consumers, and states, as well as related unemployment, have led to a tightening in spending. Central banks have set their lending rates extremely low in the hope of stimulating borrowing, spending, and growth. However, they have had limited effect. States can certainly harm or hurt economies, but, as previously noted, markets also have a life of their own.[2]

REGULATION

So far, our discussion has dealt with the state's role in markets and property—what is to be provided, by whom, and at what cost. Yet states must concern themselves not only with economic output but also with the means by which that output is created. As with public goods, moral and technical issues often affect a state's approach in this area. Are some economic processes inherently counterproductive to creating goods and services? What about economic processes that can result in a detrimental impact on society, such as pollution? Whose rights are primary in these circumstances, those of citizens or businesses? These concerns draw states into the realm of economic regulation.

Regulations—rules or orders that set the boundaries of a given procedure—may take different forms. First, regulations may be fundamentally economic in nature. Such regulations may control prices for certain goods or services, such as food or energy. Economic regulations may also control what firms may operate in what markets. National rail systems, for example, have functioned in many countries as either a private or state monopoly—in other words, a market controlled by a single producer. A second set of regulations can be described as essentially social in nature. In contrast to economic regulations that focus on how businesses function in the market, social regulations deal more with managing risk, such as safety and environmental standards. Naturally, these kinds of regulations overlap—for example, environmental regulations can strongly affect what firms may enter the market and how they can operate.

regulation A rule or an order that sets the boundaries of a given procedure

monopoly A single producer that is able to dominate the market for a good or service without effective competition

TRADE

States must grapple with the challenge of regulating economic production not just within their country but between their citizens and the outside world. In most economies, markets are not only local—goods and services come from all over the world. States can influence the degree of competition and access to goods within their own country by determining what foreign goods and services may enter the domestic market.

tariff A tax on imported goods

quota A nontariff barrier that limits the quantity of a good that may be imported into a country

nontariff regulatory barriers Policies and regulations used to limit imports through methods other than taxation

The way that a state structures its trade can profoundly affect its own economic development. States have a number of tools to influence trade: **tariffs**, which are basically taxes on imported goods; **quotas**, which limit the quantity of a good coming into the country; and other **nontariff regulatory barriers**, which may create health, packaging, or other restrictions and whose purpose is to protect a state's citizens and make it difficult or expensive for foreign goods to be sold in the local market. For example, in Canada 35 percent of all music on AM and FM radio must be of Canadian origin, and for television programs, between 50 and 60 percent must be Canadian. Airlines that fly only within the United States must be American owned.

Why regulate trade? States may favor tariffs as a way to generate revenue, and they and local manufacturers may see such barriers as a way to stimulate or protect local industries and firms. Those who oppose trade barriers argue that trade leads to more competition, innovation, and **comparative advantage**—the ability to produce a particular good or service more efficiently than other countries.

comparative advantage The ability of one country to produce a particular good or service more efficiently relative to other countries' efficiency in producing the same good or service

We've covered a great deal in this section, so let's quickly review what we have discussed. The most basic building blocks of political economy are markets and property, and states are involved in creating and enforcing rules that govern both. States help fashion markets and define property, and they use taxation in part to provide public goods and services. States can influence the growth of an economy through interest rates and, through regulation and trade, what is produced and where. All these responsibilities are part of a complex web of cause and effect that can shape freedom, equality, and the generation of wealth. Which mixture of policies across these areas will result in economic prosperity and state power? States have taken radically different approaches to the ideal relationship between state and market, leading to a variety of distinct political-economic systems around the world—all of which are currently under challenge.

political-economic system The relationship between political and economic institutions in a particular country and the policies and outcomes they create

Political-Economic Systems

A **political-economic system** can be defined as the actual relationship between political and economic institutions in a particular country, as well as the policies and outcomes they create. Various types of political-economic systems view the ideal relationship between state and market, and between freedom and equality, in different ways. Political-economic systems are often classified as liberalism, social democracy, communism, or mercantilism. Three of these political-economic systems match the political ideologies we discussed in Chapter 3. This should not be too surprising: political-economic systems can be seen as the attempt to realize an abstract ideology in the form of real economic institutions and policies.

There is always a disjuncture, however, between theory and practice. For example, some subscribers to a liberal ideology would say that existing "liberal" political-economic systems around the world do not live up to liberal ideals. Many communists similarly condemned the communist political-economic system that was practiced in the Soviet Union as a betrayal of "true" communist thought. In addition, the ideologies of fascism and anarchism do not have a political-economic counterpart to speak of. The fascist political-economic systems that arose in the 1930s were destroyed by World War II, and anarchism has never been effectively realized.

These basic classifications simplify the complexity of political economy. In reality, of course, many different variations are found within these categories. Each of these categories strikes a different balance between state power and the economy, thereby shaping markets and property, public goods and social expenditures, taxation, regulation, and trade.

LIBERALISM

Recall from Chapter 3 that, as a political ideology, liberalism places a high priority on individual political and economic freedom and advocates limiting state power in order to foster and protect this freedom. Liberalism assumes that individuals are best suited to take responsibility for their own behavior and well-being. Liberal scholars such as Adam Smith put their faith in the market and in private property: if people are allowed to harness their own energies, sense of entrepreneurialism, and, yes, greed, they will generate more prosperity than any government could produce through "top-down" policy making and legislation.

For liberals, then, the best state is a weak one, constrained in its autonomy and capacity. Other than securing property rights, the state should have a limited involvement in the economy. Public goods should be located only in critical areas such as defense and education to prevent free riding (that is to say, benefiting from a good without paying for it) and to encourage individual responsibility. Unemployment should be accepted as an inevitable, even desirable part of market flexibility. Taxation should be kept to a minimum so that wealth remains in the hands of the public. Regulation should be light, and trade should be encouraged to stimulate competition and innovation. Overall, the state should act as a sort of night watchman, intervening to defend the public only when crises arise. These conditions describe the liberal tenet of **laissez-faire** (French for "let do"), which holds that the economy should be allowed to do what it wishes. This is what we typically think of as **capitalism**—a system of private property and free markets.

When the government's role is minimal, liberals believe, economic growth will be maximized. Moreover, under such conditions, people will enjoy the greatest amount of personal and political freedom. Liberals would in fact maintain that democracy requires a free market. If too much economic and political power is concentrated in the hands of the state, they believe, this monopoly would endanger democracy. Thus, weak states are best; as Smith, one of the fathers of liberal ideology, argued

laissez-faire The principle that the economy should be "allowed to do" what it wishes; a liberal system of minimal state interference in the economy

capitalism A system of production based on private property and free markets

in 1755, "Little else is requisite to carry a state to the highest degree of opulence from the lowest barbarism but peace, easy taxes, and a tolerable administration of justice: all the rest being brought about by the natural course of things."[3]

Liberalism as a political-economic system, then, is defined by its emphasis on individual freedoms over collective equality and on the power of markets over the state. As you might imagine, the United States is typically touted as a paragon of liberal values. Regulations are often weaker and social expenditures and taxation lower than in other industrialized democracies, and the American public is largely skeptical of state power and embraces capitalism. But the United States is not the only country in the liberal camp. The United Kingdom, the intellectual source of much of liberal thought, is also viewed as a liberal country, as are Canada, Australia, and New Zealand (all, like the United States, former British colonies). Many other countries around the world have over the past 20 years embraced the "neoliberal" economic model and are noted for their relatively low levels of government regulation, taxation, and social expenditures.

However, even though these countries can all be classified as liberal, they vary in a number of ways, such as the range of public goods they provide, like higher education and unemployment or retirement benefits. In addition, even though liberal ideology would argue that a free market and democracy are inseparable, we find countries with liberal political-economic systems that nevertheless restrict democratic rights. Singapore, Bahrain, and the United Arab Emirates are regularly noted for having some of the freest economic systems in the world, and yet they all restrict individual political and civil rights. In the 1980s, Chile, while suffering under military dictatorship, became a model of economic liberalism. Critics of liberalism often highlight this contradiction, pointing out that the free market can sit easily with political repression. We will discuss this contradiction further when we turn to authoritarianism in Chapter 8.

SOCIAL DEMOCRACY

In Chapter 3, we noted that social democracy draws from liberalism and communism in an attempt to temper the extremes of too much freedom and too much equality. Like liberalism, social democracy functions on a foundation of capitalism—private property and open markets—rejecting communists' call for revolution and the state appropriation of private property and wealth. Most notable among early social democratic thinkers was Eduard Bernstein (1850–1932). In his 1898 work *Evolutionary Socialism*, Bernstein rejected Karl Marx's belief in inevitable revolution, concluding instead that democracy could evolve into socialism through the ballot box rather than through the gun.[4]

Rejecting revolution and embracing democracy, social democracy accepts a role for private property and market forces, but it remains more cautious than liberalism about their ultimate benefits to society. Unchecked economic development produces great inequality, social democrats argue, by concentrating wealth in the hands of a very few. This in turn can polarize society, pitting owners against laborers, rich against poor, city against countryside. Proponents of this way of thinking see the state not as a threat to society or the economy but as a creator of social rights that are otherwise lost in the vicissitudes of the market.

State power can thus manifest itself in a number of ways. According to social democracy, the state should make available a wide array of public goods, such as

How Do Social Democracies Seek to Achieve Greater Equality?

- Through taxes, which make high levels of social expenditure possible while redistributing wealth from rich to poor
- Through trade, which is promoted but balanced with preserving domestic industry and jobs
- Through government regulation and even ownership of important sectors of the economy

health care, pensions, and higher education. The need for competition should not stand in the way of strong state regulation or even ownership of certain sectors of the economy, and trade should similarly be managed in such a way that it does not endanger domestic businesses and jobs. Finally, the goal of equality requires a higher level of social expenditures to ensure basic benefits for all. Taxes make these social expenditures possible while also redistributing wealth from the rich to the poor. Thus, taxes tend to be higher in a social democratic system and capitalism more constrained.

As with liberalism, social democracies are not all of one type. For example, social democratic systems can vary in labor flexibility. Jobs may be highly regulated in terms of hours worked and conditions of termination, or firms may be able to fire workers more easily and hire at full- or part-time. Unemployment benefits may be generous, or more limited and contingent on retraining or government work schemes. Tax rates and the redistribution of income can also be quite varied; taxes as a percentage of GDP are not significantly different in the liberal United Kingdom and social democratic Germany, though in general social democratic systems rely on higher taxes.[5]

Finally, social democratic systems may involve themselves in the economic system through partial or total state ownership of firms. The French state owns around 20 percent of Air France and the auto manufacturer Renault, a number that increased since 2015. Norway owns two-thirds of the firm Statoil, which controls oil and gas production in that country. Worldwide, state ownership has declined in recent decades, though economic difficulties have led some countries, like France, to in fact increase their ownership stakes. Social democratic systems are most common in Europe (particularly Scandinavia), where states have more autonomy and capacity to actively manage the economy.[6] Liberals criticize such systems as costly and a drag on innovation and competition. Social democrats respond that their system avoids the inequalities of liberalism while still encouraging entrepreneurial activity.

COMMUNISM

Whereas social democracy departs from liberalism in its attempt to balance individual freedom and collective equality, the political-economic system of communism chooses effectively to eliminate individual freedom to achieve equality. We will discuss communism in detail in Chapter 9, when we look at communist and postcommunist countries; for now, we will focus on its basic political-economic institutions. Communist thinkers such as Karl Marx began with the premise that capitalism, with its private property and free markets, cannot truly serve the needs of society as a whole. Communists view private property and markets as a form of power that inevitably leads to one person or group gaining control over others. Economic competition between people creates exploitation and the development of social classes in which a small group of the wealthy dominates and benefits from the labor of the poor majority. Both domestically and internationally, this exploitation opens an ever-wider gap between those who control the economy and those who merely labor in it. Such inequalities, Marx argued, will inevitably lead to a revolution, through which a single communist party will take control of the state on behalf of all people.

Communist systems use the state to transform markets and property. Private property is fully nationalized, placed in the hands of the state on behalf of the people. In other words, the entire economy becomes a public good, existing for the benefit of all. In addition, market forces are eliminated by the state; almost all private transactions take place illegally, on the black market. Under communism, economic decision making is entrusted entirely to the state, which is assumed to be the only institution that can rationally allocate resources fairly. This system requires a large bureaucracy to determine what needs to be made and how it should be distributed.

Because communist states centralize all economic decision making and ownership, many of the essential tasks of states in other political-economic systems are fundamentally different under communism. Taxation takes an indirect form through fixed prices and wages; any profit produced by a worker or a firm goes to the state for public expenditures. Labor is allocated by the state—in other words,

INFOCUS Political-Economic Systems

	LIBERALISM	SOCIAL DEMOCRACY	COMMUNISM	MERCANTILISM
ROLE OF THE STATE IN THE ECONOMY	Little; minimal welfare state	Some state ownership, regulation; large welfare state	Total state ownership; extensive welfare state	Much state ownership or direction; small welfare state
ROLE OF THE MARKET	Paramount	Important but not sacrosanct	None	Limited
STATE CAPACITY AND AUTONOMY	Low	Moderate	Very high	High
IMPORTANCE OF EQUALITY	Low	High	High	Low
POSSIBLE FLAWS	Inequality	Expense	Authoritarianism	Inefficiency
EXAMPLES	United States, UK, former British colonies	Europe (Germany, Sweden)	Cuba, Soviet Union, North Korea	Japan, South Korea

the state decides who will work and where. Competition is eliminated, and regulations, although present, may be much weaker since the state winds up regulating itself. Social expenditures are extensive: all basic services, including health care, education, retirement, and even leisure activities, are owned and provided by the state. Finally, trade is highly restricted; the only imports are those the state deems necessary because they cannot be produced domestically. State capacity and autonomy are extremely high; the state can operate without interference from either the public or private economic actors.[7]

As you would expect, supporters of private property and market forces argue that states with communist political-economic systems lack the ability to effectively centralize all the economic decisions that are the normal product of a decentralized market. Moreover, placing all economic power in the hands of the state would essentially make democracy impossible. If the people have no property rights and if the state makes all economic decisions, there is no separation between public and private. States wind up controlling people's fates—where they live and work, what they earn, what they may buy. In response, communists would say that what they offer is total equality for all; their system emphasizes equality over individual freedom, while liberalism does the opposite. And even if such a system is inefficient, its supporters might argue, better that economic resources are wasted in the attempt to provide for all than squandered on luxuries for a wealthy few, as seen in market economies.

MERCANTILISM

The final political-economic system, **mercantilism**, stands apart in the debate over freedom and equality that separates liberalism, social democracy, and communism. Whereas all three systems we have studied so far emphasize some mix of freedom and equality, mercantilism focuses on the needs of the state. National economic power is paramount, and the domestic economy is an instrument to generate that power. Mercantilist states focus in particular on their position in the international system, for they believe that economic weakness undermines national sovereignty.[8]

Although this system may seem a strange outlier in the debate over the proper balance between freedom and equality, since it seems to emphasize neither, mercantilism is the oldest of the four political-economic systems we have covered. Historically, most states engaged in mercantilist practices. The building of empires, in particular, was an outgrowth of mercantilism, a way that a state could use its political power to gain control over resources and markets and shut out its rivals. The British Empire's policy that its colonies trade only with the home country is a good example of mercantilist practices at work. In fact, Britain only embraced liberalism well after mercantilism had helped enrich the country. More recently, mercantilism has been used to great effect in Asia.

One way that mercantilist states attempt to achieve state economic power is through an active industrial policy. Economic ministries seek to direct the economy toward certain industries and away from others through such policies as taxation and subsidies. In some cases, they may rely on partial or full state ownership of specific industries (sometimes called **parastatals**), attempting to create or control businesses that are viewed as critical for international competitiveness.

mercantilism A political-economic system in which national economic power is paramount and the domestic economy is viewed as an instrument that exists primarily to serve the needs of the state

parastatal Industry partially owned by the state

Another complementary method is the use of tariffs, nontariff barriers, and other trade regulations. Here the rationale is that foreign goods drain away wealth and promote an increased dependence on foreign economies. High tariff barriers are a common way to shield and promote domestic industry. For example, after World War II, the Japanese government relied on its Ministry of International Trade and Industry to steer the economy toward exports such as electronics and automobiles. High tariff barriers kept foreign competition at bay, and subsidies were provided to certain industrial sectors, such as producers of semiconductors. South Korea and Brazil followed a similar set of policies.

In its emphasis on state power, mercantilism does not typically focus on social expenditures in the way that social democracy does. Welfare benefits tend to be much lower. Indeed, there is logic to this policy: a low level of benefits can encourage higher public savings, which can in turn be borrowed by the state or businesses. Lower levels of expenditure are also likely to translate into lower taxes. State capacity and autonomy tend to be higher in mercantilist political-economic systems, though markets and private property remain. This explains why many now use the somewhat vague term "state capitalism" to describe mercantilist systems.

Supporters of mercantilism cite its ability to direct an economy toward areas of industrial development and international competitiveness that the market, left on its own, might not pursue. For developing countries, such direction is particularly attractive, and Japan and South Korea are cited as exemplars of mercantilism's strengths. Critics of mercantilism observe that, as with communism, states are ill-suited to decide a country's industrial path, and the result is often inefficient industries that survive only because they are protected from outside competition. In addition, the tight relationship between private property and the state is a recipe for corruption, which may drag down development. In the past, mercantilism was often associated with nondemocratic and even fascist regimes. However, South Korea and postwar Japan are countries whose mercantilism did not preclude democracy. Recent global difficulties have made mercantilism more attractive. Many view President Donald Trump's economic policies, which emphasize higher tariff barriers and other trade restrictions, as a shift from America's long-standing liberal policies toward more mercantilist approaches.[9]

IN FOCUS   **How Do Mercantilist States Seek to Achieve Economic Power?**

- By directing the economy toward certain industries and away from others through the use of subsidies and taxation
- Through partial or full state ownership of industries that are considered critical (parastatals)
- With the strong use of tariffs, nontariff barriers, and other regulations
- By limiting social expenditures and thereby keeping taxation to a minimum
- With low interest rates set by the central bank to encourage borrowing and investment

THE TRADE-OFFS OF MERCANTILISM IN JAPAN AND CHINA

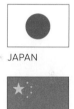

JAPAN

CHINA

As noted, several Asian countries have successfully pursued mercantilist policies to rapidly industrialize, increase national wealth, and enhance political power. If Japan offers the clearest illustration of a successful twentieth-century mercantilist political economy, China has become the prime example in the twenty-first century. Both cases reveal trade-offs associated with this political-economic system.

Both Japan in the 1870s and China a century later emerged from periods of international isolation fearing the consequences of their relative national weakness. Threatened by encroaching Western imperialism, Japan's authoritarian reformers destroyed the country's centuries-old feudal system, centralized state control, and launched a program of rapid modernization under the mercantilist slogan "rich country, strong military." Within decades, mercantilist Japan became a formidable imperial power, and, even after its military defeat in World War II, by the 1980s, the country had achieved industrial strength and economic prosperity surpassed only by the United States. Likewise, authoritarian reformers in China in the 1970s sought to reinvigorate an economy weakened by decades of inefficient communist state ownership and a pervasive welfare state with a similar mercantilist goal of achieving national "wealth and power." China is now the second largest economy in the world in terms of total GDP, behind the United States.

Both governments adopted industrial policies designed to promote national strategic industries and exclude foreign competitors, funding tax breaks and cheap loans for domestic companies willing to invest in important new industries and sponsoring research and development of key technologies. They promoted exports by devaluing national currencies and keeping factory workers' wages low. Foreign competitors were kept at bay through the imposition of tariff and nontariff barriers on imports.

The benefits of these mercantilist strategies are readily apparent. State-led development promoted unprecedented growth, raised consumption dramatically (China's modernization drive has lifted some 400 million Chinese out of poverty in four decades), and facilitated the rapid rise of each of these countries as economic superpowers. But the costs are also real. While state intervention can enhance relations between government and business, it also risks widespread corruption and collusion, as powerful policy makers interact with wealthy firms free from public discretion. Both Japan and China have struggled with the "crony capitalism" associated with mercantilism. Chinese leaders have recently launched a sweeping anticorruption campaign snaring hundreds of officials and executives, but critics argue the crackdown will accomplish little unless the underlying mercantilist system is changed. Moreover, wealth generated by rapid modernization in Japan and China has gone disproportionately to industry owners as opposed to consumers. Critics charge that Japan's mature mercantilist state has become a "corporate welfare state," propping up corporations at the expense of not just consumers but also national competiveness. Japan's twentieth-century economic juggernaut is now in its fourth decade of economic malaise. And wealth accruing in the hands of a well-connected economic elite in China may prove particularly disruptive in a society only a generation away from its communist welfare state (see Chapter 9).

Finally, having a "rich country" and a "strong military" can be a volatile combination in a rising power. Japan's rapid modernization gave its authoritarian leaders the military means to enhance national power at the expense of its neighbors—Japan became the dominant military power and lorded over the region. Today, China's neighbors worry about China's rapid military expansion and its growing territorial aspirations.

Political-Economic Systems and the State: Comparing Outcomes

Having gained an understanding of the different political-economic systems used around the world and the different ways they approach their tasks, we should next consider how to compare these systems. We can use various indicators; they are by no means the only way to make comparisons and draw conclusions, but they are useful tools for thinking about the real and ideal differences between economic outcomes.

MEASURING WEALTH

One basic criterion for comparison is a country's level of economic development. The most common tool that economists use to measure economic development is gross domestic product, or GDP, which we earlier defined as the total market value of all goods and services produced in a country over a period of one year. GDP provides a basic benchmark for the average per capita income in a country. However, GDP statistics can be quite misleading. For one, GDP is not the same as personal income, as it includes things like government expenditures, such as cleaning up natural disasters. Moreover, it does not assign a value to such things as leisure or innovation.

Another problem is how we compare this wealth across space and time. As we all know, a given amount of money will buy more in certain parts of a country than in others. A salary of $50,000 a year will go a lot further in Boise, Idaho, than it will in New York City, where by some estimates the cost of living is more than twice as much. The same problem arises when we compare countries: people may earn far more in some countries than they do in others, but those raw figures do not take into account the relative costs of living in those countries. Moreover, as exchange rates between national currencies rise or fall, countries can look richer or poorer than they are.

To address these difficulties, economists often calculate national GDP data on the basis of what is known as purchasing power parity. **Purchasing power parity (PPP)** attempts to estimate the buying power of income in each country by comparing similar costs, such as food and housing, by using prices in the United States as a benchmark. When these data are factored in, comparative incomes change dramatically, as shown in Table 4.1. For example, without PPP, Sweden's national income is

purchasing power parity (PPP) A statistical tool that attempts to estimate the buying power of income across different countries by using prices in the United States as a benchmark

TABLE 4.1 Economic Size and the Distribution of Wealth

COUNTRY	GDP PER CAPITA (IN U.S. $)	GDP PER CAPITA (PPP, IN U.S. $)	GINI INDEX AND YEAR (100 = COMPLETE INEQUALITY)
United States	57,500	57,500	41 (2013)
Sweden	51,600	49,200	25 (2013)
Canada	42,200	44,000	32 (2013)
Germany	41,900	48,700	30 (2011)
United Kingdom	39,900	42,600	33 (2012)
Japan	38,900	41,500	38 (2011)
France	36,600	41,500	29 (2015)
South Korea	27,500	35,800	30 (2014)
Russia	8,700	23,200	42 (2014)
Brazil	8,600	15,100	52 (2014)
Mexico	8,200	17,900	48 (2014)
China	8,100	15,500	47 (2014)
South Africa	5,300	13,200	63 (2013)
Iran	5,000	17,700	37 (2013)
Nigeria	2,200	5,900	49 (2013)
India	1,700	6,600	35 (2011)

Source: World Bank, United Nations Development Program, CIA World Factbook, Branko Milanovic.

much higher than Germany's; but when the cost of living in each country is factored in through PPP, their economies are revealed to be of similar size. Incomes in poorer countries such as China and India rise quite dramatically when PPP is taken into account.

Although GDP can be a useful way to measure wealth, it has limitations. One major problem is that it fails to capture much about the quality of life in a country, such as crime levels, mortality rates, and the health of the environment. Other elements of GDP provided by the state, such as health care or education, are hard to measure—meaning that social democratic countries, whose economies are greatly devalued using PPP, would appear to be much richer if these public goods were factored in. Many economists thus call for a revision if not the outright scrapping of GDP and its replacement with some other form of measurement.[10] Until that happens, we have other ways to determine the outcome of different political-economic systems.

MEASURING INEQUALITY AND POVERTY

Gini index A statistical formula that measures the amount of inequality in a society; its scale ranges from 0 to 100, where 0 corresponds to perfect equality and 100 to perfect inequality

Perhaps the most problematic aspect of GDP is that these data do not tell us how wealth is distributed among a population. One approach to this problem is the **Gini index**, a mathematical formula that measures the amount of economic inequality in a society. Complete equality is given a Gini ranking of zero, and complete inequality gets a ranking of 100. Thus the greater the Gini index number, the greater the inequality in a given economy. Some recent Gini coefficients are given in Table 4.1. If we look at these few cases, we note that the relationship between wealth and inequality is not automatic—more wealth does not make a country more or less equal. Second, political-economic systems do matter. Social democratic countries tend to have the lower Gini ratings, which is not surprising given their emphasis on equality. Liberal political-economic systems are more unequal, but levels of income disparity vary widely among them, from Canada at the low end of the spectrum to the United States at the high. Mercantilist and postcommunist countries show a similar range.

The most unequal countries in the world are very poor. However, inequality is not the same thing as poverty. Poverty tends to be measured in terms of absolute wealth. Organizations like the World Bank establish benchmarks for world poverty rates—typically less than $2 per person per day. In contrast, inequality is a measure of relative wealth. Thus, an entire society can become more materially wealthy and grow more unequal at the same time. Australia has become wealthier and more equal since the 1990s; South Africa has grown wealthier and more unequal.

What are the trends for poverty and inequality worldwide? First, people have grown wealthier overall. Perhaps contrary to expectations, extreme poverty has fallen dramatically. In 1981, over 40 percent of the world's population lived on less than $2 a day; in 2012, that number was 13 percent. This improvement has been driven by economic growth in Asia. This growth has in turn led to decreased inequality between countries like China and the United States as the former grows wealthier. Second, at the same time this economic development has been associated with increased inequality within many of these same countries, such as China and India. This result is not contradictory; a country often experiences rising standards of living across the board, while at the same time the wealthier increase their wealth faster than those who are poorer. This leads us to our third point regarding worldwide inequality between all people. It has been estimated that the Gini coefficient for the world—between all people, rather than just between individuals within a given country—is extremely high, at about 70. However, this may now be declining as economic growth expands around the world. In short, the conclusions you draw about inequality depend on how you compare the data: Do you focus on inequalities within nations, which have been growing, or inequality among all people, which has been decreasing?[11] We'll return to this in a moment when we examine shifts in global wealth and the implications for political-economic systems everywhere.

HUMAN DEVELOPMENT INDEX (HDI)

Poverty, inequality—how can we make sense of any of this if we simply want to know whether people are better off? Another kind of measurement might help. The **Human Development Index (HDI)**, created by the United Nations Development Program, not only looks at the total amount of wealth in a society and its distribution but also gives equal weight to income, health (life expectancy), and average years of schooling. By looking at such data, we can consider whether the wealth generated in a country is actually used in a way that provides a basic standard of living for all

Human Development Index (HDI) A statistical tool that attempts to evaluate the overall wealth, health, and knowledge of a country's people

TABLE 4.2 Measuring Wealth, Equality, and Prosperity

COUNTRY	UN HUMAN DEVELOPMENT RANKING	UN LIFE EXPECTANCY RANKING	UN EDUCATION RANKING	UN INCOME RANKING	UN GENDER EQUALITY RANKING
Germany	4	22	5	17	9
Canada	10	12	12	22	18
United States	10	36	8	11	43
Sweden	14	11	19	16	4
United Kingdom	16	27	10	26	28
Japan	17	2	22	29	21
South Korea	18	13	18	30	10
France	21	10	24	25	19
Russia	49	116	34	50	52
Iran	69	63	77	67	118
Mexico	77	48	101	68	73
Brazil	79	78	87	78	92
China	90	58	108	83	37
South Africa	119	176	75	90	90
India	131	133	131	127	125
Nigeria	152	183	147	129	n.a.

Source: United Nations Development Programme, http://hdr.undp.org/en/data (accessed 7/28/17).

GROSS DOMESTIC PRODUCT (GDP)	Measures total production within a country, regardless of who owns the products
PURCHASING POWER PARITY (PPP)	A way to calculate gross domestic product that takes the cost of living and buying power into account
GINI INDEX	Assesses inequality
HUMAN DEVELOPMENT INDEX (HDI)	Assesses health, education, and wealth of population

through public or private means. Nearly all countries in the world are ranked on the HDI. In 2016, Norway was ranked at number one and the Central African Republic came in at the very bottom.

The HDI does show a strong correlation between standard of living and a country's GDP, as shown in Table 4.2. The countries with the highest national incomes also show the highest levels of education and life expectancy in the world. Interestingly, among the top 20 ranked on the index, we find social democratic systems alongside more liberal countries such as the United States, Canada, and Australia and more mercantilist ones such as Japan and South Korea. But these findings are not quite as clear if we unpack their components of income, education, and health.

In Table 4.2, each of these indicators has been evaluated separately, showing very different sets of rankings. The United States does well in education and income, but its life expectancy lags far behind that of other wealthy countries. France's life expectancy ranks highly, but it does far less well in education given its overall HDI. Finally, we can add another important variable calculated by the United Nations but not included in the HDI: gender equality. If we look at all the relevant indicators (maternal mortality, female education, fertility rates, labor force participation, and share of seats in the legislature), our rankings are again quite different. The United States, the United Kingdom, and Canada do poorly, given their HDI. In contrast, social democracies show a stronger commitment to gender equality. China's communist commitment to equality is also reflected in its high gender equality ranking relative to its HDI.[12]

RUSSIA

POVERTY AND INEQUALITY IN THE SOVIET UNION AND RUSSIA

We will spend all of Chapter 9 looking at communism in theory and practice, but for now let us simply look at wealth, inequality, and poverty in the Soviet Union and how that has changed in post-communist Russia. Prior to the revolution in 1917, Russia was a poorly developed country, largely agrarian and highly unequal. Most economic wealth was consolidated in the hands of the monarchy and aristocracy and large landholders. After taking power, the Communist Party sought to reduce poverty and eliminate inequality by nationalizing private property and developing an expansive range of "cradle to grave" public goods, from higher education to vacation resorts. Similarly, prices and wages were set by central planners rather than the market. Professional jobs did not enjoy significantly higher wages than lower-class ones, and goods, though limited, were priced to be affordable to the public at large.

As a result, during the heyday of communist rule the Gini indexes for the Soviet Union and other European communist countries were somewhere in the upper 20 range, which were among the most equal on the continent. Moreover, the wide range of public goods, such as compulsory education and free health care, combined with rapid industrialization, helped lift millions out of poverty.

Why this system failed is something we shall turn to in Chapter 9; for now, it is enough to say that greater equality and reduced poverty came at the cost of innovation and entrepreneurialism, limiting economic growth. Yet even at their peak of economic growth, communist countries struggled with inequality and poverty. Why? One reason is that under the Soviet Union, public goods were distributed unevenly, with cities often favored over the countryside and with Russia favored over other Soviet republics (the Soviet Union was, at least on paper, a federal system). Some estimates are that by the 1980s, more than 10 percent of the Soviet population lived in poverty, and that levels of inequality between republics were as high as six to one. The Russian republic was six times richer than the republic of Tajikistan—as great as the current gap between Switzerland and Egypt. Equality between individuals was also complicated. Political leaders or those connected to them had access to benefits others did not: a better apartment, travel abroad, and goods that were imported or in limited supply. In the long run, this helped undermine communist legitimacy.

Since the end of the Soviet Union in 1991, inequality and poverty have taken a new course in Russia. In the first decade of transition, poverty soared as industry collapsed, prices skyrocketed, and many public goods declined in quality or disappeared. In the 2000s, the government of Vladimir Putin managed to reduce poverty by spending funds from oil exports (in part on expanding the number of jobs within the state), though poverty has begun to rise as oil prices have fallen. In the meantime, inequality has risen dramatically, as wealth has become concentrated in the hands of a few in and around the government. The richest 10 percent of Russians control nearly 90 percent of all wealth in the country. To date, oil has helped sustain the government's legitimacy. Will poverty and/or inequality undermine it?[13]

HAPPINESS

Given the rather technical nature of our discussions so far, it may seem strange to speak of happiness as an indicator that we can use to compare political-economic systems. But when we think about it, though it may be difficult to define, happiness is at the core of human activity. It is the result of the interaction between freedom and equality. From philosophers to evolutionary psychologists, a common argument holds that the pursuit of personal happiness is among the central motivations driving human behavior. If that is the case, happiness can be a useful indicator of political-economic development, and social scientists have recently paid more attention to it.

TABLE 4.3 Measuring Happiness, 2014–2016

COUNTRY/*REGION*	HAPPINESS (SCALE 0–10)	COUNTRY/*REGION*	HAPPINESS (SCALE 0–10)
Denmark	7.5	*East Asia (region)*	*5.4*
Canada	7.3	*World*	*5.3*
Australia	7.3	China	5.3
Costa Rica	7.1	Pakistan	5.3
North America, Australia, and New Zealand (region)	*7.0*	Indonesia	5.3
United States	7.0	*Middle East and North Africa (region)*	*5.1*
Germany	7.0	Nigeria	5.1
United Kingdom	6.7	South Africa	4.8
Brazil	6.6	Palestinian Territories	4.8
Mexico	6.6	Egypt	4.7
Western Europe (region)	*6.6*	Bulgaria	4.7
Saudi Arabia	6.3	Iran	4.7
Latin America and Caribbean (region)	*6.3*	*South Asia (region)*	*4.4*
Russia	5.9	India	4.3
Japan	5.9	*Sub-Saharan Africa (region)*	*4.3*
South Korea	5.8	Congo	4.3
Central and Eastern Europe (region)	*5.7*	Benin	3.7
Commonwealth of Independent States (region)	*5.5*	Togo	3.5
Southeast Asia (region)	*5.4*	Tanzania	3.3

Source: United Nations World Happiness Report, 2017. Regional scores are weighted by population.

At the most basic level, we can observe that richer countries generally are happier than poorer ones. This assumption is logical; people in extreme poverty have little security and few resources to advance their lives. Past that level of poverty, however, a long-standing debate continues over the sources and levels of happiness around the world. This debate can be seen in terms of absolute versus relative happiness. For example, in the case of extreme poverty, we can view happiness as an absolute good and little different from the idea of security—having enough money to eat regularly is quite likely to increase happiness. However, many psychologists have argued that beyond basic human needs, much happiness is neither sustained nor absolute. Similarly, according to the "Easterlin paradox," developed by the social scientist Richard A. Easterlin, when standards of living rise past a certain level (perhaps $10,000–15,000 per capita GDP), happiness stagnates. After that level, it is argued, people's relative income—our wealth relative to that of those around us—is a stronger predictor of happiness than our overall standard of living.[14]

However, not all scholars agree that people's level of happiness is a function of their relative wealth. While economic growth may generate greater "happiness returns" in poor countries, some studies indicate that richer countries, too, continue to see a modest growth in happiness. But is a country's happiness shaped only by its overall level of development?

If we look at Table 4.3, which calculates happiness based on positive emotions and life satisfaction, we see some interesting variations. First, wealth is not necessary to happiness. It is true that the unhappiest countries in the world are the most desperately poor and that most of the happiest countries in the world are wealthy states. But there are important exceptions. Mexico, Costa Rica, Argentina, and Brazil all rank within the top 25 happiest countries. These are all countries with modest levels of development (less than $15,000 per capita GDP at PPP) and high levels of economic inequality. If they have anything in common, it is culture and geography. In contrast, postcommunist countries have much lower levels of happiness, and some individual countries fall much further down the list than very poor countries—Bulgarians are less happy than Egyptians, even though their GDP per capita at PPP is twice as high. East Asian countries such as Japan and South Korea are less happy than we might expect if we assumed that GDP or HDI were the most important predictor of happiness. Other factors, such as corruption, social support, or individual freedom, go some way to explain these differences but still do not fully solve this puzzle. This imperfect fit between wealth, inequality, and happiness is important to consider alongside the Easterlin paradox. Extreme poverty produces misery, and many rich countries are happy. However, levels of wealth, inequality, and development do not correlate with happiness as neatly as we would expect.[15]

The Rise and Fall of Liberalism?

We've covered a lot of ground in this chapter, laying out variations in the relationships among property, markets, the state, and political-economic systems. From there, we laid out some different tools for making comparisons, such as GDP, the Gini index, the Human Development Index, and measurements of happiness. In this discussion, we've had glimpses of change in the international system but have not addressed this directly. Where do we seem to be heading?

For at least a century, our four major models of political economy have rivaled one another as they have sought to strike the ideal relationship between freedom and equality. At the dawn of modern capitalism, mercantilism was a dominant force, central to the establishment of empires and industries. At the same time, liberalism began to emerge as a challenge to mercantilism, particularly in the United Kingdom and its former colonies. But by the early twentieth century, liberalism was in turn threatened by fascist and communist regimes. Many believed that these regimes, coupled to powerful states, were superior to a liberalism faltering under global depression. Even when fascism was defeated, communism continued to spread worldwide, social democracy came to define much of Europe, and mercantilism drew adherents in many less-developed countries.

Yet as we stand at the beginning of the twenty-first century, the world is a quite different place. Communism has effectively vanished, even in places like China, where market forces now drive the economy, something we will discuss in Chapter 9. During the past 20 years, mercantilism, too, has been scaled back or dismantled in many developing countries, a trend we will consider in Chapter 10. For the past two decades, social democracy and liberalism have appeared to be the only viable political-economic systems, but even the countries using these systems have been undergoing further **economic liberalization**—cutting taxes, reducing regulation, privatizing state-owned businesses and public goods, and expanding property rights.

Table 4.4 compares the levels of economic change around the world consistent with liberalism, taking into account such factors as government expenditures, price controls, taxes, individual property rights, and trade. Changes in these areas that

economic liberalization
Changes consistent with liberalism that aim to limit the power of the state and increase the power of the market and private property in an economy

TABLE 4.4 Levels of Economic Liberalization, 2000–2014

COUNTRY	2000	2014
United States	8.7	7.8
New Zealand	8.5	8.4
United Kingdom	8.5	7.9
Canada	8.4	8.0
Japan	7.9	7.4
Germany	7.7	7.6
Sweden	7.6	7.5
Chile	7.3	7.8
France	7.3	7.3
South Africa	7.0	6.6
South Korea	6.8	7.4
World	*6.7*	*6.8*
Mexico	6.4	6.9
India	6.3	6.5
Brazil	5.9	6.3
Iran	5.9	5.3
China	5.8	6.5
Venezuela	5.6	3.3
Nigeria	5.3	6.5
Russia	5.2	6.7

Note: 10 = most liberal.
Source: Fraser Institute.

limit the state's power over private property and market forces are what we view as economic liberalization. The ratings in the table are given on a 10-point scale, where 10 is the most liberal and 1 is the least. The study concludes that since 1980 economic liberalization grew, in some cases dramatically, around the world.[16]

So is this the century of liberalism? Some qualifications are in order. First, despite the increasing liberalization of many economic systems, most industrialized democracies still largely adhere to extensive social expenditures that are often seen as contrary to liberalism. The United States is very much an outlier, though one could in fact argue that even it has a large welfare state, albeit one "hidden" in its complicated array of taxes and tax breaks. Second, despite increased liberalization, almost all of this occurred between 1980 and 2005. Since then there has been little overall change in total global levels, and in a number of important cases regulations and restrictions on trade have increased.

Third and most important, across richer countries in particular we have seen a growing resistance to liberalism perhaps unmatched since the 1930s. The immediate cause is the economic downturn of the last decade, but broader changes in global wealth, driven by globalization and technological change, have been developing for at least two decades. As Figure 4.2 shows, economic development around the world has

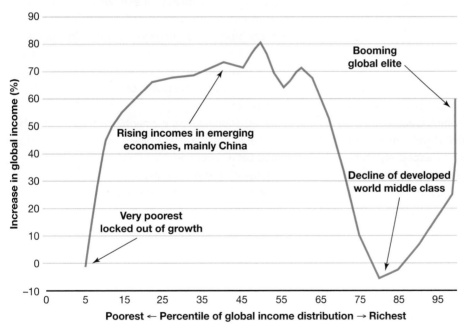

FIGURE 4.2 Winners and Losers in the Global Economy: Change in Real Income, 1988–2008 (%)

In the graph above, the vertical axis represents growth in incomes and the horizontal axis represents where people are distributed across global income. For example, individuals who rank approximately halfway between the world's richest and poorest have seen their incomes grow by up to 80 percent between 1988 and 2008. Those ranking at the bottom of global incomes have seen little growth in that same span of time, while those at the very top have seen growth of 60 percent. The middle class of the developed world, considered rich in comparison to most others around the world, have seen a decline in their income over time.

Source: Branko Milanovic, World Bank.

Why Have Poverty and Inequality Declined in Latin America?

At the start of this chapter, we discussed the economic and political fortunes of Venezuela and Hugo Chávez's attempt to use the state and natural resource revenues toward particular political-economic ends. As we noted, part of Chávez's public appeal was his call to address Venezuela's economic problems. Since the 1980s, the country's GDP per capita in PPP had been in steady decline, having lost in 1999 a third of its value by the time he came to power. But Venezuela is not unique in its problems.

For generations, Latin America has been marked by a high degree of poverty, inequality, and economic and political instability. Why? Some say this situation is a result of the particular forms of colonialism practiced by Spain and Portugal, which created a feudal agricultural system that stunted development and the rise of a middle class. Others, especially Marxists, point to more recent developments, laying the blame on unequal economic relations between Latin America and the United States and Europe during the twentieth century (see Chapter 10). Liberals have responded by critiquing Marxist and mercantilist political-economic ideas. Whatever the cause, the resulting economic difficulties seemed resistant to change, even as much poorer Asia surged ahead.

Yet, starting in the 1990s, poverty began to rapidly decline across the region, from over 40 percent in 1993 to under 25 percent in 2013. Equally surprising, during this same period inequality also declined, from an average Gini index of 53 to 49—the lowest since industrialization and the opposite of what has occurred in much of the rest of the world. Why this dramatic change? Why now?

Some have pointed to economic liberalization, which increased dramatically across the region (Venezuela is a notable exception) and created new opportunities for economic development by removing barriers to trade and job creation. Another factor has been an increase in economic globalization, in particular a growing global (particularly Chinese) demand for Latin American commodities such as copper and iron. However, these two explanations, while important, don't account for why growth has been coupled with a decrease in inequality. As the United Nations Development Programme has noted, development indicators in Latin America have performed better than the levels of economic growth would predict.

An additional factor we might overlook is one that is central to comparative politics: the state. Marxists viewed Latin American states as under the control of capitalism and American imperialism, favoring revolution along the lines of Cuba as a way to gain economic and political sovereignty. Mercantilists believed that only by developing domestic industries, shielded from international pressure, could the region develop (see Chapter 10). Meanwhile, liberals argued that Latin American states, bloated and inefficient, were the primary obstacle to economic growth. The argument turned into more of a discussion over whether the state was "good" or "bad" than a question of what *kind* of a state might alleviate economic misery.

In this regard, Latin America has been an innovator in the provision of public goods. Latin America has long suffered from a weak social safety net—a condition that exacerbates poverty and inequality. At

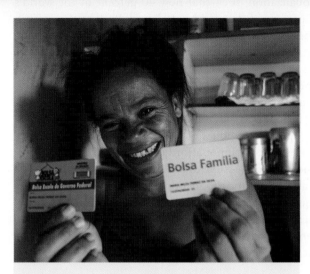

Brazilian Maria Nilza shows her "Bolsa Família" conditional cash transfer plan card.

the same time, weak capacity meant that developing new state institutions to improve social welfare was a challenge. As a result, a number of Latin American countries have embraced what are known as conditional cash transfers. These are essentially direct cash payments to the poor, contingent on meeting particular requirements. One of the most common conditions for cash transfers is that families keep their children in school, as opposed to using them for labor to supplement family income. Amounts are often relatively small but widespread. In Brazil and Mexico, around a quarter of the population benefits from such transfers. The success of these programs has in turn improved the level of education in Latin America, because more children stay in school, and resulted in a better-educated workforce. Social democratic policies, enacted alongside economic liberalization, are now viewed as a model for other parts of the world. Systems that rely overwhelmingly on state power, as in Venezuela, or largely on the free market

with little redistribution, as in liberal Chile, have been less successful in narrowing the gap between rich and poor.

It is easy to get carried away with these findings and assume that cash transfers are the silver bullet that can solve problems of inequality and poverty. Social welfare institutions are still very weak in Latin America. Keeping children in school is a major accomplishment, but educational systems across the region, from primary to higher education, are poor. This will be particularly important as the region requires more skilled labor for continued economic growth. Basic services, such as access to drinking water, electricity, and sanitation, are uneven, contributing to public health problems. Continued progress will require building state capacity, which, as we noted in Chapter 2, is no easy feat. The region may already be coming up against these barriers, as continued reduction in inequality has recently stagnated, and there are concerns that those on the margins may not see further gains. This may well be a function of the same kinds of economic challenges that richer countries are facing in the areas of employment and social expenditures. Nevertheless, we have found an important piece of this puzzle: issues like poverty and inequality are not simply economic problems that require economic solutions. The state is a critical institution in creating and redistributing wealth and prosperity.[a]

THINKING CRITICALLY

1. How has the state influenced Venezuela's economic growth, and why has it lagged behind that of other Latin American countries?
2. Do you think that direct cash transfers, which are effective in some countries, would work to alleviate poverty in all situations? Why or why not?

changed dramatically, affected by the rise of globalization. New economic opportunities in Asia have led to astounding economic growth, reducing poverty and creating a huge middle class in that part of the world. A much smaller global elite has equally benefited from economic globalization, such that now 40 percent of the world's wealth is held by less than 1 percent of the world population. Both of these developments have undermined the middle class in many richer countries, while the very poorest have seen little benefit overall. This represents a very real threat to liberalism: the traditional prescription of a small state, low regulations and taxes, and free trade is for many no longer convincing. As a result, in Europe and the United States we have seen parties and politicians who oppose free trade and other elements of globalization. In some cases, this is built upon illiberalism and authoritarianism, terms we will cover in the next chapter. Such critiques of liberalism may struggle to provide alternatives; many countries simply cannot afford the social expenditures they have enjoyed. At the same time, it is not possible to roll back technological changes, like computers, the Internet, and automatic production, that have eliminated many jobs altogether. Even if critiques of liberalism fail to articulate a viable alternative, we could still see the continued weakening of this ideology and political-economic institutions, with huge repercussions for capitalism and democracy around the globe. We will consider this at length in chapters to come.

In Sum: A New Economic Era?

As we have seen, states play a large role in both domestic and international economies. They must manage markets and property with an eye toward generating societal wealth and revenue so that basic political tasks can be funded. This is no small task, for it goes to the heart of freedom and equality: How should freedom and equality be reconciled through economic policy, and what mixture of the two will create the most wealth? Different political-economic systems give very different answers to those questions. Economic liberalism has weathered various challenges to emerge as the dominant system in much of the world. As we shall see in upcoming chapters, this "triumph" of liberalism has occurred alongside political liberalization as many nondemocratic regimes around the globe have given way to democracy.

At the same time, in the past few years serious questions about the limits of liberalism are being raised as various countries face sustained economic difficulties. A great deal of change is on the horizon, and we will spend much of the upcoming chapters trying to get a better glimpse of what may lie ahead.

Key Terms

capitalism (p. 95)

central bank (p. 91)

comparative advantage (p. 94)

deflation (p. 92)

economic liberalization (p. 110)

Gini index (p. 104)

gross domestic product (GDP) (p. 90)

Human Development Index (HDI) (p. 105)

hyperinflation (p. 92)

inflation (p. 92)

laissez-faire (p. 95)

market (p. 86)

mercantilism (p. 99)

monopoly (p. 93)

nontariff regulatory barriers (p. 94)

parastatal (p. 99)

political-economic system (p. 94)

political economy (p. 85)

property (p. 87)

public goods (p. 88)

purchasing power parity (PPP) (p. 103)

quota (p. 94)

regulation (p. 93)

social expenditures (p. 89)

tariff (p. 94)

The Arab Spring touched off political violence around the Middle East. Though political violence can take many forms, it sometimes turns deadly. Here, Syrians carry an injured man after a suicide car bomb attack in Damascus, Syria.

Political Violence

When does political conflict turn deadly?

HOW DID SYRIA END UP like this? Among the many calamities of the "Arab Spring," Syria has by far seen the most suffering—over 400,000 have died, and nearly 5 million are now refugees. A peaceful movement for change against the rule of President Bashar al-Assad eventually turned to calls for revolution, and this in turn fanned the flames of ethnic and religious conflict, guerrilla warfare, and terrorism. Now it is a challenge even to speak of Syria as a single state, because large swaths are no longer under sovereign control. Thinking about how Syria fell apart can help frame many of the concepts and questions we will deal with in this chapter.

Since its independence after World War II, Syria has been an authoritarian regime. It has also been highly patrimonial. As we will describe in Chapter 8, patrimonialism is a system that distributes political and economic power to a small group of regime supporters within the state while holding society in check by force. In Syria, power has been monopolized by the Assad family—first under Hafez al-Assad, who came to power in a military coup in 1970, and since his death in 2000 under his son Bashar al-Assad. The top ranks of the state and military are dominated by the Assad family's own Alawite Muslim sect, which makes up less than 15 percent of the population. Because of its patrimonialism, Syria has been more repressive than many other authoritarian regimes in the Middle East, relying more on coercion than co-optation.

The nature of patrimonialism in Syria helps us understand why the regime did not give way as it did in places like Tunisia or Egypt. Events in Syria began with a protest movement not unlike those occurring elsewhere in the region; it was catalyzed by the torture of several young men who were caught writing antigovernment graffiti in the city of Daraa. In response, in March 2011 protesters held a "day of dignity" protest in several Syrian cities, calling for a peaceful liberalization of the regime. Given the Assads' history of repression, it is not surprising that the regime opted to respond with deadly force. In response, citizens began to take up weapons to overthrow the regime.

Within this struggle, new factors began to emerge. First, the ongoing conflict radicalized some Syrians, who rejected the original call for secular democracy in favor of a theocratic regime. They were soon joined by fighters from outside the country (including Europe and North America) whose objectives were less about the Assad regime than creating a new Islamic state across the region. Such groups were more willing to embrace terrorism as a means to destroy both the Syrian state and rival guerrilla groups. The most extreme of these groups has been the Islamic State of Iraq and al-Sham (ISIS). First organized as a branch of Al Qaeda against the United States in Iraq, following the Arab Spring it began to expand into Syria through a mixture of guerrilla warfare (attacking the state) and terrorism (attacking civilians). Where ISIS has gained power, it has laid the groundwork for its own state, including a severe religious law. Though it is now in retreat, ISIS was able to build many of the elements of an independent state out of the wreckage of Syria and Iraq. And even if ISIS were defeated on the ground, it may well live on as a source of emulation for future terrorism around the globe. The revolutions of the Arab Spring, initially viewed as a step toward democracy, have led to consequences far from what most observers imagined.[1]

LEARNING OBJECTIVES

- Define political violence, and explain the factors that contribute to it.
- Compare revolution and terrorism as forms of political violence.
- Explain how religion and political violence sometimes become linked.
- Analyze the connections between state power and political violence.

IN PREVIOUS CHAPTERS, WE IDENTIFIED various institutions that define states, societies, and types of economic structures and regimes. We also saw how these institutions are constructed and function in different parts of the world. Power and legitimacy rest in these institutions, to varying degrees, but what happens when they lose power altogether or when people seek to take them down by force?

This chapter will shed some light on this complex question, providing ways to think about political violence and its implications. We begin by defining our terms: What do we mean by *political violence*, and how does it relate to the political institutions we have already covered? Next, we will look at some of the motivations of political violence, examining the different (and often conflicting) explanations for why such violence occurs. We will then concentrate on two important forms of political violence: revolution and terrorism. Each form is a phenomenon that can threaten governments, regimes, and states. Each form is also a loaded political term that stirs emotional responses, complicating analysis. We will look at some of the different ways revolution and terrorism can be defined and understood. In addition, we will explore the extent to which the two are related—how terrorism is often justified as a tool to achieve revolution. Once we have these concepts and arguments before us, we will look at them in the contemporary context of political violence motivated by religion. Finally, we will conclude with a discussion of how states and societies prevent or manage political violence and what this means for freedom and equality.

What Is Political Violence?

This textbook began with a focus on the state. This institution is the cornerstone of modern politics, one that we defined in its most basic terms as the monopoly of violence or force over a territory. Across human history, centralized political authority has been a part of this monopoly whereby states vanquish their domestic rivals, defend themselves from external threats, and establish order and security at home. This process has been described as the shift from "private war" to "public war," meaning that individuals lose the freedom to use violence against one another, turning that right over to the state. This right is exchanged for a greater sense of security for all.

Of course, the state's monopoly of violence is never perfect or complete. Other states always represent a potential threat, given their own capacity for violence. Even at the domestic level, violence persists in such forms as murder and armed robbery. In many countries, such problems, though persistent, are manageable and do not threaten the stability and security of the state, society, or economy. But under certain conditions, this may not be true. Public violence may grow so pervasive or destructive that the state loses its control. Governments, regimes, states, and individuals are subject to attack, and sovereignty is weakened or lost. We have already seen this in some detail in our discussion of ethnic and national conflict in Chapter 3.

Political violence, or politically motivated violence outside of state control, is the focus of this chapter. Some political scientists see much of this political violence as part of a larger category of "contentious politics," or collective political struggle. This can include such things as revolutions, civil war, riots, and strikes, but it also includes more peaceful protest movements, some of which we will consider at the end of this chapter. In the case of political violence, we are speaking of a phenomenon that operates beyond state sovereignty, neither war nor crime, and that seeks to achieve some political objective through the use of force. Such definitions are always cleaner in theory than in reality, of course. The lines between domestic and international and between war, crime, and contentious politics are often quite blurry.

political violence Violence outside of state control that is politically motivated

Why Political Violence?

Although defining political violence presents some challenges, a more controversial issue is why political violence occurs. What leads civilians to take up arms against a state or its citizens toward some political aim? Scholars have offered diverse reasons that have changed over time, but we can group them into three basic categories: institutional, ideational (based on ideas), and individual. These three explanations overlap to some degree; where one explanation ends and the other begins is not always clear. At the same time, such explanations are often debated by scholars or policy makers who tend to favor one explanation over others. We will examine each of these reasons generally before looking at how each one is used specifically in studies of revolution and terrorism. Each explanation seeks to answer the same questions: What motivates political violence, and toward what end is it perpetrated?

INSTITUTIONAL EXPLANATIONS

Because we have covered institutions at length, what we mean by this term should be relatively clear: we are referring to self-perpetuating organizations or patterns of activity that are valued for their own sake. Institutions define and shape human activity, and institutional explanations argue that their specific qualities or combination are essential to political violence. The emphasis can be on political institutions, such as states and regimes; economic institutions, such as capitalism; or societal institutions, such as culture and religion. Moreover, these explanations can be based on either a constraining or an enabling argument. It may be that institutions contain values or norms that implicitly or explicitly encourage political violence, or that they constrain human activity, thus provoking political violence. In Chapter 6 on democratic institutions, we will cover variations in executive structures and electoral systems; as some have argued, the variants that reduce the opportunity for power sharing—versions that produce "winner-take-all outcomes," like presidencies—increase the likelihood of marginalization, polarization, and conflict. Under these conditions, political violence can be a logical reaction when other forms of participation are blocked. Institutional explanations can be seen as a quest for a "root source" for violence, a necessary condition for violent actions to take place, and a presumption that changes in the institutional structure would eliminate the motivation for this violence.

IDEATIONAL EXPLANATIONS

ideational Having to do with ideas

If institutional explanations emphasize the impact of fixed organizations and patterns in fostering political violence, ideational explanations focus more on the rationale behind that violence. By **ideational**, we simply mean having to do with ideas. Ideas may be institutionalized—concepts rooted in some institution such as a political organization or a religion—but just as often they are uninstitutionalized, with no real organizational base. The argument here is that ideas play an important role in political violence in the way they set out a worldview, diagnose a set of problems, provide a resolution, and describe the means of getting there. Any or all of these elements can be bound up with a justification of violence. These ideational factors take us back to our discussion of political attitudes in Chapter 3. As we noted there, political violence is more likely to be associated with attitudes that are radical or reactionary, since

Explanations for Political Violence

EXPLANATION	REASONING	EXAMPLES
INSTITUTIONAL	Existing institutions may encourage violence or constrain human action, creating a violent backlash.	Presidentialism
IDEATIONAL	Ideas may justify or promote the use of violence.	Some forms of religious fundamentalism; nationalism
INDIVIDUAL	Psychological or strategic factors may lead people to carry out violence.	Humiliation; alienation

each attitude views the current institutional order as bankrupt and beyond reform. Hence, it is not only the content of the ideas that matters but also their relation to the domestic political status quo. Ideas seen as conservative in one context may become a source of radicalism or reaction, and perhaps violence, elsewhere.

INDIVIDUAL EXPLANATIONS

Finally, individual explanations center on those who carry out the violence. Here, the scholarship emphasizes the personal motivations that lead people to contemplate and carry out violence toward political ends. Scholars who study individual explanations of political violence usually follow one of two paths. One emphasizes psychological factors, conditions that draw individuals toward violence. Such factors can be a function of individual experiences, or they may be shaped by broader conditions in society, such as levels of economic development or gender roles. Such an approach tends to concentrate on how people may be driven to violence as an expression of desperation, the desire for liberation, or social solidarity. For example, some scholars of religious violence emphasize the role of humiliation as a motivating force, a sense that an individual's own beliefs are actively marginalized and denigrated by society. Individuals drawn to violence may be alienated from the society around them as well. Revolutionaries or terrorists, in this view, see violence as a way to give meaning to their lives and may be largely unconcerned with whether they are effectively achieving their goals—or even truly understand what their political goals are.

A contrary approach, however, rejects this view, seeing political violence as a rational act, carried out by those who believe it to be an effective political tool. Strategy, rather than despair, drives these actions. Political violence is in this view not an expression of deviance but a strategy that is carefully wielded by those who understand its costs and potential benefits.[2]

Comparing Explanations of Political Violence

One important element of comparison across these three explanations is how they approach free will—that is, to what extent people are the primary actors in political violence. Institutional explanations often are quite deterministic, seeing people as shaped and directed by larger structures that they do not control. An individual's recourse to violence is simply the final step in a much larger process. In contrast, individual explanations place their focus squarely on people; they are the primary makers of violence because they choose to be. Ideational explanations lie somewhere in between. Ideas are influenced by institutions but are also actively taken up and molded by individuals to justify political violence.

A second element of comparison concerns universal versus particularistic explanations. Institutional explanations tend to be more particularistic, stressing the unique combination and role of institutions in a given case that are not easily generalized and applied elsewhere. Individual explanations typically center on those personal or psychological attributes common to all humans that can lead to violence. Ideational explanations, again, lie somewhere in the middle, generalizing the importance of ideas while noting the distinct lessons that different ideas impart.

Which explanation is most convincing: institutional, ideational, or individual? These explanations are often placed in competition with one another, but they work well in conjunction. Institutional factors provide a context in which particular preconditions, problems, and conflicts may emerge. Ideational factors help describe and define those problems, ascribe blame, and provide solutions by calling for the transformation of the status quo. These ideas in turn influence and are shaped by individuals and groups that may already be prone to violent activity. Let's look at the case of the Basque independence group Euskadi Ta Askatasuna (ETA) in Spain, which used violence as a political tool for several decades until finally swearing off violence in 2011. If we examine ETA, we can see institutional factors that include a long period of repression under authoritarian rule and its effects on the Basque region. There are ideational factors as well, such as a belief among ETA members and supporters that the Basque people faced cultural extermination at the hands of the Spanish. Finally, individual factors include the role and motivations of many Basque youth in conducting *kale borroka* (urban struggle) in their support for an independent, revolutionary Basque state. We could do a similar analysis of ISIS, taking into consideration the role of authoritarianism in Iraq and Syria, the role of political Islam and anti-Americanism following the invasion of Iraq, and the appeal to many young foreigners to join the cause of building a new revolutionary religious state. These examples help illustrate the interconnection of these three factors and why political violence is relatively unpredictable and has emerged in a variety of contexts. We will consider these various explanations next as we look at revolution and terrorism.

Forms of Political Violence

So far, we have spoken of political violence in general terms, defining it as violence that is outside state control and politically motivated. This definition encompasses many forms of political violence: assassinations, riots, rebellions, military coups, civil war, and ethnic conflict, to name a few. We will concentrate on two forms of political violence: revolution and terrorism. Revolution is important to study because of its profound effects. Revolutions have ushered in sweeping changes in modern politics, overturning old institutions and dramatically transforming domestic and international relations. Terrorism, while less sweeping, holds our attention as a similar challenge to modern political institutions, one whose impact on domestic and international politics has spiked in recent years. Both are forces that seek dramatic change. Yet in many ways, revolution and terrorism are opposites. Revolution is an uprising of the masses, who take to the streets, seize control of the state, and depose the old regime. In contrast, terrorism is much more secret and hidden, a conspiratorial action carried out by a small group. But there are similarities in their sources and goals. As we analyze and compare the dynamics of revolution and terrorism, we will draw out some of these elements and show how these seemingly disparate forms of political violence can be linked.

REVOLUTION

The term *revolution* has many connotations. Although we speak of revolution as a form of political violence, the word is also used much more indiscriminately. Any kind of change that is dramatic is often described as revolutionary, whether the change is political or technological, and the term has a generally positive connotation, one that evokes progress. People speak of dramatic change as positive, so "counterrevolution" is seen as an attempt to turn back the clock to a darker time. None of this should be surprising; across much of the world, significant political change has been a result of revolution, and in countries where this is the case revolution is often associated with independence, sovereignty, and development. Thus *revolution* is a loaded term, albeit with mostly positive connotations.

For our purposes, we shall speak of revolution in a more limited manner. Revolution can be defined as a public seizure of the state in order to overturn the existing government and regime. Several factors are at work here. First, revolutions involve some element of public participation. To be certain, revolutions typically have leaders, organizers, and instigators who play a key role. But unlike a coup d'état, in which elites overthrow the government, in a revolution the public plays an important role in seizing power. Russia is an interesting example. While we typically speak of communism's triumph in 1917 as a revolution, some scholars call it a coup because Lenin and a handful of followers seized power rather than being part of some mass action toppling the government.

Another factor in our definition of revolutions is that the people involved are working to gain control of the state. This objective distinguishes these actions from such violence as ethnic conflict, through which groups may gain local control or even seek independence but do not or cannot take over the entire state. Finally, the objective of revolution is not simply removing those in power but removing the entire regime. Protests or uprisings and other forms of contentious politics intended to pressure a leader to leave office are not necessarily revolutionary. At their core, revolutions seek to fundamentally remake the institutions of politics and often economic and societal institutions as well. As a result, scholars sometimes speak of "social revolutions" to indicate that they are referring to events that completely reshape society.

Must revolutions be violent? This is a tricky question. Given the dramatic goals of revolution, violence is often difficult to avoid. Governments will resist overthrow, and such conflict can often lead to the fragmentation of the monopoly of violence as parts of the state (such as elements of the military) often side with revolutionaries. The aftermath of revolutions can also be very bloody—the losers may be killed or carry out a counterrevolutionary struggle against the new regime.

revolution Public seizure of the state in order to overturn the existing government and regime

However, not all revolutions are violent. In 1989, communist regimes in Eastern Europe collapsed in the face of public pressure, sweeping away institutions that many thought immovable. In most cases, violence was limited; only Romania experienced a violent struggle between the communist regime and revolutionaries that led to numerous deaths. Due to this absence of violence, many scholars would resist calling the collapse of communism in Eastern Europe revolutionary, preferring instead to speak of these changes as political transitions. Yet in most important ways, specifically in the overturning of the government and regime, these events did fulfill our definition of revolution. South Africa is another case of regime change, from apartheid to multiracial democracy, that most scholars are uncomfortable calling a revolution, because it was an elite-driven, largely nonviolent, and slowly negotiated process. One of the problems here is whether we believe that violence is a necessary component to revolutionary outcomes.

What causes revolution? There is no agreement on this question, and the consensus has changed over time. Scholars group studies of revolution into three phases. In the first phase, before World War II, scholars tended to describe rather than explain revolution. When causes were assigned, explanations were often unsystematic, blaming bad government policies or leaders. In the second phase, coinciding with the behavioral revolution of the 1950s and 1960s (see Chapter 1), social scientists sought more generalized explanations. Their new research efforts took on varied forms and areas of emphasis, but they shared a common view that dramatic economic and social change or disruption, such as modernization, was central in sparking revolutionary events. These views tended to focus on the role of individuals as potential revolutionaries and sought to understand what motivated them.

Among the main arguments emerging from this work was a psychological approach known as the **relative deprivation model**. According to this model, revolutions are less a function of specific conditions than of the gap between actual conditions and public expectations. Improving economic or political conditions might even help lead to revolution if, for example, such changes cause increased public demands that go unmet and thus foster discontent. It has been suggested that the 1979 Iranian Revolution and the 2011 Egyptian Revolution are examples of relative deprivation at work. As Iran experienced rapid modernization in the decades before the revolution, its progress only increased people's expectations for greater freedom and equality, especially among young adults. This is what is meant by relative deprivation: it is not absolute conditions that instigate revolution but rather how the public perceives them.

By the 1970s, these studies of revolution began to lose favor. In the third phase, critics argued that theories of revolution predicated on sudden change could not explain why some countries could undergo dramatic change without revolution (as in Japan during the early twentieth century) or what levels of change would be enough to trigger revolution. In the case of the relative deprivation model, there was little evidence that rising expectations or discontent preceded many past revolutions. Similarly, in many cases both expectations and discontent rose, but revolution did not result. New studies of revolution took a more institutional approach, moving away from a focus on public reactions to a focus on the target of revolutions: the state.

Most influential in this regard has been the work of Theda Skocpol and her landmark book *States and Social Revolutions*.[3] Focusing on France, China, and Russia,

relative deprivation model
Model that predicts revolution when public expectations outpace the rate of domestic change

INFOCUS Shifting Views of Revolution

PHASE	APPROACH	CRITICISMS
FIRST: PRE–WORLD WAR II	Studies of revolutionary events	Unsystematic and descriptive
SECOND: POST–WORLD WAR II BEHAVIORAL REVOLUTION	Studies of disruptive change, such as modernization, as driving revolutionary action	Not clear why change or rising discontent leads to revolution in some cases but not others
THIRD: 1970S–PRESENT	Studies of domestic and international state power as providing the opening for revolution	Too focused on institutions, to the neglect of ideas and individual actors

Skocpol argues that social revolutions require a very specific set of conditions. The first is competition between rival states as they vie for military and economic power in the international system through such things as trade and war. Such competition is costly and often betrays the weakness of states that cannot match their rivals. Second, as a result of this competition, weaker states often seek reform to increase their autonomy and capacity, hoping that changes to domestic institutions will boost their international power. These reforms can include greater state centralization and changes in agriculture, industry, education, and taxation. Such changes, however, can threaten the status quo, undermining the power of entrenched elites, sowing discord among the public, and creating resistance. The result is discontent, political paralysis, and an opening for revolution. In this view, it is not change per se that is central to revolution, but the power and actions of the state. Other actors are of relatively little importance.

The institutional approach to revolution became the dominant view during the 1980s, paralleling a wider interest in institutions and the power of the state. Yet institutional approaches themselves are subject to questions and criticism. Some argue that an overemphasis on institutions ignores the role played by leadership, civil society, or ideology in helping to catalyze and direct revolutionary action. Skocpol herself noted that the important example of Iran's revolution was a poor fit for her model.

These criticisms were underscored by the revolutions in Eastern Europe in 1989 and again in the Arab Spring revolutions of 2011. In the case of Eastern Europe, there can be no doubt that changes in the international system, specifically the Cold War and the Soviet Union's loosening of control over Eastern Europe, led to conflict and paralysis within these states. At the same time, however, public action was mobilized and shaped by opposition leaders who were strongly influenced by the ideas of liberalism, human rights, and nonviolent protest. In addition, mass protest appeared influenced by strategic calculation: successful public opposition in one country changed the calculations of actors elsewhere, increasing their mobilization and demands. Similar events have been at work in the Middle East (see "Institutions in Action," p. 138).

Drawing on these events, some scholars have reintegrated individual and ideational approaches. While state actions do matter, so do the motivations of opposition leaders, ruling elites, and the public as a whole; the views of all three groups regarding political change; and the resources available and used to mobilize the public. Small shifts in ideas and perceptions may have a cascading effect, bringing people into the streets when no one would have predicted it the day before—including the revolutionaries themselves.[4]

RUSSIA

CHINA

CAUSES OF REVOLUTION IN RUSSIA AND CHINA

Comparing and contrasting the two great social revolutions of the last century in Russia (1917–23) and China (1921–49) highlights some of the factors leading to revolutions and allows us to test the utility of approaches we have discussed.

Similarities between the two revolutions are perhaps most apparent. In the decades preceding the outbreak of revolutionary violence, relatively weak monarchies presided over peasant-based agrarian societies in both countries. Both the Romanov and Qing dynasties had ruled their respective empires for nearly three centuries and were facing marked decline even as neighboring countries rapidly modernized. In both cases, foreign conflict and domestic rebellion further weakened these states. The Japanese humiliated the Russians in the 1904–05 Russo-Japanese War, and Russia experienced even greater losses during World War I. In 1905, massive protests against the Russian monarchy spread among soldiers, peasants, ethnic nationalists, and workers. Similarly, Qing rulers quelled a series of peasant rebellions in late nineteenth-century China, even as they resisted efforts by Western imperialists to "carve up" the country. China also fought two wars with Japan, decisively losing the first (1894–95) and enduring horrific losses and Japanese occupation in the second (1937–45).

Facing wars on two fronts and recognizing their growing weakness relative to neighboring powers, emperors in both countries launched limited political reforms. Russian leaders introduced a multiparty electoral system and limited monarchy to Russia, and Chinese leaders promised to establish a constitutional monarchy. However, reactionary forces in both countries thwarted reforms and reasserted absolutist rule. But as the relative deprivation model predicts, these reforms awakened rising expectations within society, and urban intellectuals launched organized efforts of revolutionary resistance that in both cases ultimately succeeded. The collapse of monarchies produced revolutionary civil war between nationalist and communist contenders vying for power in both cases, further weakening state capacity and adding chaos to both societies. Charismatic communist leaders emerged in both Russia (Lenin) and China (Mao) who defeated their opponents and carried out sweeping political, economic, and social change.

But these revolutions were of course not identical. In Russia, successive military defeats weakened both the capacity and the legitimacy of a fairly robust imperial state, led to public disturbances, and ultimately fomented a military revolt that forced the tsar to step down. Continued public disorder and dissatisfaction with the provisional government permitted Lenin's small group of communist insurgents to carry out a successful coup d'état and launch the communist revolution. In China's case, an already weak and largely illegitimate monarchy simply collapsed, creating a vacuum in which both civil and foreign combatants struggled to obtain a monopoly of violence over Chinese territory. After decades of military conflict, Mao's communist forces emerged victorious. Thus, while both countries experienced civil war, in

Russia civil conflict followed the revolution and imposed even greater hardship on an already devastated society. For most Chinese, the revolution came after the civil war, establishing the Chinese Communists as heroes who defeated the Japanese, expelled Western imperialists, carried out land reform, and stabilized the economy. Finally, because China's revolution followed Russia's by several decades, Russia's successful example may be considered one of the causes of China's revolution.

So what causes revolutions? Weak states, distressed societies, foreign pressures, rising expectations, compelling ideologies, and charismatic leaders can all play a part, but predicting how or when the next one may occur is beyond our capacity.

Though revolutions may be instruments of progress, it is important to note what they do not achieve. Despite the call for greater freedom and equality that is a hallmark of revolution, the result is often the reverse. Revolutionary leaders who once condemned the state quickly come to see it as a necessary tool to consolidate their victory, and they often centralize power to an even greater extent than before. This is not necessarily bad if the centralization of power can facilitate the creation of a modern state with a necessary degree of autonomy and capacity. Revolutions are often the foundation of a modern state. However, revolutionary leaders may seek a high degree of state power, rejecting democracy as incompatible with the sweeping goals of the revolution. Egypt, Cuba, China, Russia, France, and Iran are all cases in which public demands for more rights ended with yet another dictatorship that uncannily echoed the previous authoritarian order.

Another impact is the high human cost that revolutionary change can incur. Revolutions are often destructive and bloody, especially if removing those in power is a protracted affair. Moreover, in the immediate aftermath revolutionary leaders and their opponents often use violence in their struggle over the new order. The Mexican Revolution led to the deaths of 1.5 million people; the Russian Revolution and subsequent civil war may have claimed the lives of well over 5 million. This violence can become an end in itself, as in the case of the Reign of Terror that followed the French Revolution of 1789. Enemies, supporters, and bystanders alike may all be consumed by an indiscriminate use of violence. It has been suggested that revolutionary states are also more likely to engage in interstate war, whether to promote their revolutionary ideology or because other countries feel threatened or see an opportunity to strike during this period of turmoil. Given the fragmentation of state power and the loss of the monopoly of force associated with revolution, the violence that follows in its wake is not surprising. One general observation we can make is that the greater the violence involved in bringing down the old regime, the more likely it is that violence will continue under the new one.

TERRORISM

The word *terrorism*, like *revolution*, is loaded with meaning and used rather indiscriminately. However, the conceptual difficulties surrounding the two terms are diametrically opposed. While *revolution*'s conceptual fuzziness comes in part from its inherently positive connotation (which can lead people to associate the term with all sorts of things), the word *terrorism* carries a stigma and is a term few willingly embrace. As a result, some confuse terrorism with a variety of other words, many of which are misleading, while others use the term indiscriminately to describe any kind of political force or policy they oppose. This situation has led some to conclude that terrorism is effectively impossible to define, and they fall back on an old cliché: "One man's terrorist is another man's freedom fighter." Such a conclusion undercuts the whole purpose of political science, which is to define our terms objectively. We should therefore seek out a definition as precise as possible and use it to distinguish terrorism from other forms of political violence. The continued rise of incidents of terrorism makes this particularly important (see Figure 5.1).

terrorism The use of violence by nonstate actors against civilians in order to achieve a political goal

Terrorism can be defined as the use of violence by nonstate actors against civilians to achieve a political goal. As with revolution, several components are at work in this definition, and we should take a moment to clarify each. First, there is the question of nonstate actors. Why should the term not be applied to states as well? Do they not also terrorize people? Indeed, as we shall discuss later, the concept of terrorism originally referred to state actions, not those of nonstate actors. Over time, the term came to be associated with nonstate actors who used terrorism in part because conventional military force was not available to them. This, however, does not mean that states cannot terrorize. Rather, other terms have come to describe such acts. When states use violence against civilian populations, we speak of war crimes or human rights violations, depending on the context. Both can include such acts as genocide and torture. *Terrorism* as a term is as much about the kind of political actor as it is about their actions and intent.

state-sponsored terrorism Terrorism supported directly by a state as an instrument of foreign policy

Finally, there is **state-sponsored terrorism**. States do sometimes sponsor nonstate terrorist groups as a means to extend their power by proxy, using terrorism as an instrument of foreign policy. For example, India has long faced terrorist groups fighting for control over Kashmir, a state with a majority Muslim population (unlike the rest of India, which is majority Hindu). These terrorists are widely believed to be trained and armed by the Pakistani military (see Chapter 2), which sees this as a way to influence Indian politics. In short, we speak of terrorism as a nonstate action not because states are somehow above such violence but rather because other terminology exists to describe forms of violence perpetrated by states.

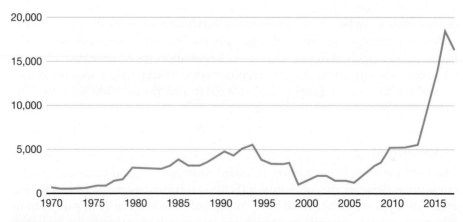

FIGURE 5.1 Incidents of Terrorism Worldwide, 1970–2015

Source: Global Terrorism Database.

Our definition of terrorism also emphasizes that the targets of violence are civilians. Here, the issue of intention is important. Violent conflicts often result in civilian casualties. But terrorists specifically target civilians, believing that this is a more effective way to achieve their political ends than attacking the state. This allows us to distinguish terrorism from **guerrilla war**, something that will come up in Chapter 8 when we compare South Africa and Zimbabwe. In contrast to terrorism, guerrilla war involves nonstate combatants who largely accept traditional rules of war and target the state rather than civilians. In the case of South Africa, during the military struggle against the regime the African National Congress considered, and then explicitly rejected, targeting civilians. In contrast, the Zimbabwean African National Union engaged in both guerrilla warfare and terrorism to achieve power. However, the line between these two can often be blurry: Is killing a policeman or a tax collector an act of terrorism or guerrilla warfare? Still, the central distinction remains, not only to observers but also, as suggested earlier, to those carrying out the violence. We will return to this point in a moment.

A further issue in defining terrorism centers on the political goal. It is important to recognize that terrorism has some political objective; as such, it is not simply a crime or a violent act without a larger purpose. Here, too, the lines can be less than clear: terrorists may engage in crime as a way to support their activities, and criminal gangs may engage in terrorism if they are under pressure from the state. Groups can also morph from one into the other. But in general, terrorism and other forms of violence can be sorted out by the primacy of political intent (Figure 5.2).

What are the causes of terrorism? As with revolution, scholars have proposed varied and conflicting hypotheses, and these have changed over time as the nature

> **guerrilla war** A conflict whereby nonstate combatants who largely abide by the rules of war target the state

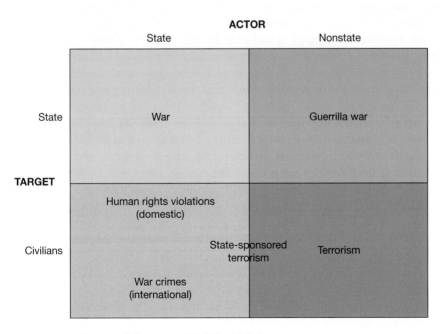

FIGURE 5.2 Forms of State and Political Violence

This chart distinguishes among forms of political violence, depending on who carries out the violence and who is the target of that violence. This includes both state and nonstate actors.

of terrorism has shifted. In addition, because terrorism is so amorphous and shadowy, we find few of the comprehensive theories we see in studies of revolution, though we can again group these in terms of institutional, ideational, and individual explanations.

One of the most common responses to terrorism is to cast it in institutional terms, often with the assertion that economic and educational background is critical to understanding terrorists' motivations. Poverty and lack of education are commonly cited in this regard, and terrorism is viewed as a tool of desperation when avenues for personal advancement (getting a job, starting a family) are absent or blocked. However, we know that terrorists are not necessarily impoverished—Osama bin Laden, for example, came from a wealthy background, and many European terrorists active in the 1970s were well-educated members of the middle class. It may be the case, however, that economic inequality helps foster terrorism by contributing to a sense of relative deprivation.[5] This may be compounded by political institutions. Where state capacity and autonomy are weak and mechanisms for public participation poorly institutionalized, terrorism may find both the rationale and opportunity to use force.

Ideational explanations are similarly useful and problematic. Terrorism is commonly blamed on some ideology, religion, or set of values. However, given how terrorism morphs over time, these explanations often cannot account for cause and effect particularly well. We cannot describe terrorism as a logical outcome of one particular ideology or religion if we can find terrorism associated across a range of values depending on the context. Still, ideas themselves are important because they can provide justification for terrorist acts; groups need a political goal to motivate them to commit such violence.

Some have asserted that for terrorists the crucial aspect of any set of ideas is its connection to nihilist views. By **nihilism**, we mean a belief that all institutions and values are essentially meaningless and that the only redeeming value a person can embrace is violence. In this view, violence is desirable for its own sake. Nihilism can also be combined with apocalyptic and utopian views, generating a conviction that violence can destroy and thus purify a corrupted world, ushering in a new order.

Finally, researchers have consistently turned to individual explanations in seeking to understand the personal motivations of terrorists. As mentioned earlier, one common explanation centers on feelings of injustice—that an individual's or community's self-worth has been denigrated by others—coupled with alienation or humiliation. Such feelings can generate frustration, anger, and, most important, a desire for vengeance. In addition, terrorist groups can provide a sense of identity and solidarity for alienated or humiliated individuals. Political violence can give a life meaning, a sense of greater purpose. In fact, it has been argued that terrorist groups, secular or otherwise, resemble religious cults, with their emphasis on community, the purity of their cause, faith in the rectitude of the group's own beliefs and actions, and the conviction that retribution paves the way toward some utopian outcome.

The effects of terrorism are harder to discern than the effects of revolutions. The first question to ask is whether terrorists are able to achieve their goals. In the case of revolution, the political violence is by definition successful—we study cases in which regimes have been successfully overthrown. In the case of terrorism, however, we focus on a tactic. Overall, evidence suggests that terrorism is mostly unsuccessful

nihilism A belief that all institutions and values are essentially meaningless and that the only redeeming value is violence

in achieving its goals, if we simply define success as getting states to change their policies to be more in line with what the terrorists want. The very nature of targeting civilians appears typically to signal to states that terrorists cannot be bargained with or satisfied; this stands in contrast to guerrilla fighters, who by targeting the state rather than civilians signal that they respect some fundamental political rules.[6]

However, this is not to say that terrorism has no impact. Economically, terrorism can be highly successful in depressing tourism, foreign direct investment, stock markets, and other sectors of the economy. Society can feel a similar impact, due not just to the effects of a weakened economy but also to increasing anxiety and insecurity that undermines people's sense of well-being.[7]

Terrorism can also distinctly affect politics. Countering terrorism can be a costly and frustrating process with little to show for itself, diverting national resources while failing to address public concerns. An eroded sense of confidence in the state can be the result. In the quest for greater security, governments and their citizens may favor increasing state power and curtailing civil liberties in the hope that such steps will limit terrorists' scope for action. However, this can lead to a weakening of democratic institutions and civil liberties. The result can be less trust in government and less public control over it. At an extreme, terrorism can help bring down a regime. In 1992, Alberto Fujimori, the president of Peru, dissolved the legislature and suspended the constitution, acts that he justified in part as necessary to battle two separate terrorist groups that had destabilized the country. Much of the public supported this action, seeing it as the only way to reestablish order. Terrorism in Russia by Chechen separatists similarly helped pave the way for Vladimir Putin to win the presidency in 2000, and Russia used subsequent attacks as justification for removing democratic institutions and limiting civil liberties. And as we well know from Afghanistan, terrorism can also be used as a tool to provoke international conflict.

This destruction of a regime is, of course, what most terrorists seek. Terrorism uses violence against civilians to undermine the institutional fabric of state, society, and economy, calling into question all those things we take for granted, including stability, security, and predictability. By disrupting these most basic elements of modern life and instilling fear, terrorists believe they will help pave the way for revolution.

Terrorism and Revolution: Means and Ends

What do terrorists want? That question leads us to consider terrorism and revolution as related forms of political violence. While we might think of these two as quite separate, it was not always this way. In modern politics, the concepts of terrorism and revolution were initially bound together as parts of a single process, having their origins in the French Revolution. For revolutionary leaders like Maximilien de Robespierre, terror was an essential part of revolution. Robespierre argued that "terror is nothing other than justice, prompt, severe, inflexible; it is therefore an emanation of virtue" in the service of revolutionary change.[8] Thus terror was not only a positive act but also a tool in the service of the revolutionary state.

Over time, this concept of the relation between terrorism and revolution began to shift. Revolutionaries who embraced the lessons of Robespierre concluded that terror is not needed to consolidate revolution after a regime has been overthrown but can instead be used as the means toward that revolutionary end. A small group could speak for and lead the masses, instigating violence as a way to spark revolution. These revolutionaries thus openly embraced the name *terrorist* as an expression of their desire to use violence to achieve their political goals. Although the label *terrorist* has become stigmatized over time, this relationship between terrorism and revolution remains in place.

Terrorism can therefore be understood not simply in terms of who is directing political violence toward whom but also in its revolutionary nature. Terrorists rarely seek limited goals, such as political or economic reform, since they see the entire political system as illegitimate. Rather, they believe that through their seemingly indiscriminate use of violence, all the dominant institutions can be shattered and remade. Consider, for example, this passage from an early manifesto of the Peruvian terrorist group the Shining Path:

> The people rise up, arm themselves and rebel, putting nooses on the necks of imperialism and reaction. The people take them by the throat, threaten their lives and will strangle them out of necessity. The reactionary meat will be trimmed of fat, they will be torn to tatters and rags, the scraps sunk into mire, and the remainders burned. The ashes will be thrown to the winds of the world so that only the sinister reminder of what must never return will remain.[9]

This link between terrorism and revolution also helps us to distinguish between terrorism and guerrilla war. We mentioned earlier that the line between these two forms of political violence is blurry but that we can distinguish between them in terms of their targets. Guerrilla war seeks to abide by traditional rules of war and avoids the targeting of civilians. This decision is driven by political goals. Guerrillas typically accept that their opponents are legitimate actors, and they themselves wish to be regarded as legitimate by their opponents and the international community. Their demands, while sometimes extensive (such as greater civil rights or independence for an ethnic group), do not deny the legitimacy of the other side, as is normally the case with terrorism. These distinctions matter, for such differences in means and ends will affect how extensively states can or will negotiate with such groups to bring an end to conflict.

For example, during the civil conflict in Algeria in the 1990s, two nonstate groups were operating: the Islamic Salvation Front (FIS) and the Armed Islamic Group (GIA). Both opposed the Algerian regime, which suppressed Islamic fundamentalist groups, but they fought it in very different ways. The FIS, which began as a nonviolent political movement, created an armed wing that targeted specific parts of the state seen as directly supporting the regime. The FIS declared that they could come to a compromise with the regime if certain demands were met, such as holding democratic elections. In contrast, the GIA rejected the entire regime and political process as un-Islamic and argued that anyone they viewed as having cooperated with the state in any manner, such as voting, deserved to be killed. The GIA's killing was thus much more indiscriminate and widespread, directed at state, society, and the FIS. Jihad (war), they argued, was the only means to an Islamic state.[10]

In short, revolution and terrorism have close connections. Revolution is often the ultimate goal of terrorists, who believe that using violence will help set the stage for revolution. More limited use of force, as in guerrilla war, reflects a desire to participate in or work with existing institutions rather than overthrow them. The issue, then, for nonstate wielders of violence is whether they desire a seat at the political table or seek to knock the table over.

Political Violence and Religion

Now that we have considered different ways to approach political violence, particularly revolution and terrorism, let us apply these ideas to the most pressing example in contemporary domestic and international politics: religious violence. In Chapter 3, we spoke about the rise of ideology and other secular identities, such as nationalism, as a challenge to religion in the modern world. Such identities appropriated for themselves many of the same claims and values that belonged to religion in the past, forcing religion out of the public and political sphere and into private life. However, the role of religion has reemerged in the public realm. This religious resurgence is accompanied by a particular element of fundamentalism: the desire to unite faith and the state, transforming religion into the ideological foundation for a political regime. While such fundamentalism may be uncompromising (as with many ideologies), it is not necessarily violent. Many fundamentalists believe that reestablishing God's sovereignty can be done through nonviolent engagement in politics or by withdrawing from politics and instead working to increase the societal power of religion. But, as in the case of secular ideologies, this form of religious fundamentalism contains a violent strain of thought.

What are the conditions under which religion becomes a source of political violence? As in our earlier discussion, they include institutional, ideational, and individual factors. First, one common factor is hostility to modernity. In this view, modern institutions, driven by states and nations, capitalism, ideology, secularism, individualism, and material prosperity, have stripped the world of greater meaning and driven people to alienation and despair. Indeed, political violence is often embraced by those who initially enjoyed modernity but at some point turned away from its "corrupt" lifestyle. This view has emerged in many different contexts but seems to be most powerful in societies where modern institutions are foreign in nature and poorly grafted onto traditional structures and values, and/or where modern institutions are under stress, often as a result of economic challenges. This can often be seen in developing countries, which we will turn to in Chapter 10. At this border between traditional and modern institutions, the tension can be the greatest, which may explain why proponents of religious violence are often urban and well-educated individuals: such persons are frequently most deeply immersed in modernity and may feel its contradictions most sharply.

A second factor is what the sociologist Mark Juergensmeyer calls "cosmic war."[11] In this view, the modern world not only actively marginalizes, humiliates, and denigrates the views of religious believers but also seeks to exterminate the believers outright. Those who hold this view see themselves as soldiers in a struggle between the righteousness of faith and its enemies (modernity), a war that transcends space and time. This perspective is often bound up in conspiracy theories that point to shadowy forces in league to exterminate the good. People holding these views can rationalize violence against civilians because they see the conflict not in terms of civilians versus combatants but in terms of the guilty versus the innocent: those who do not stand on the side of righteousness are by definition on the side of evil. Scholars note that this dehumanization of the enemy is an important component in justifying violence against civilians, since social or religious taboos against murder must be overcome.

Third, religion as a source of political violence is often connected to messianic, apocalyptic, and utopian beliefs. Although the forces of darkness (modernity) have gained the upper hand, the role of the righteous is to usher in or restore the sovereignty of God on earth. Violence is therefore not only acceptable but also a form of ritual, whether in the form of self-sacrifice (martyrdom) or the sacrifice of others. ISIS propaganda is frequently couched in these terms.

Religious groups or movements that resort to violence represent an extreme form of fundamentalism, since their path to violence requires them to reinterpret their faith in a way that divorces it from its conventional foundations. These groups or movements thus tend to break away from the mainstream faith and other fundamentalists, whom they accuse of having lost their way, by presenting their radical alternatives as restoration's of religious truth. Most Muslim, Christian, and other fundamentalists would thus find many of these radical views to be horrific and far removed from their views of faith.

To reiterate, it is a mistake to confuse fundamentalism with violence. Indeed, much of what we have noted earlier—hostility toward rival institutions, dehumanization, and utopian views—can be found in modern political ideologies. We can see this in the bloody revolutions that established communism in the Soviet Union and China. Even the French Revolution of 1789 that helped usher in the modern era was described by Alexis de Tocqueville in 1856 as akin to a religious revolution directed toward "the regeneration of the human race" that "roused passions such as the most violent political revolutions had been incapable of awakening . . . able, like Islamism, to cover the earth with its soldiers, its apostles, and its martyrs."[12] Bearing this in mind, we can consider some specific examples of how religion has intersected with politics to generate political violence.

Within Al Qaeda, ISIS, and similar jihadist groups, individuals like Osama bin Laden frequently have couched their violence in terms of a long global struggle against unbelievers. Hence, when bin Laden referred to the West as "Crusaders" in his 1996 manifesto he was reaching back to the battles between the Islamic and Christian worlds in the Middle Ages. In the modern world, bin Laden argued, this crusade against Islam and its followers continues, though the West's conspiracies are often cloaked by international organizations like the United Nations. In the September 11 attacks, we can see how the logic of cosmic war also fits into a greater narrative. Al Qaeda carried out these attacks not simply to weaken the United States but also to provoke a backlash that they believed would intensify the conflict between the Islamic and non-Islamic worlds and would in turn lead to the overthrow of "un-Islamic" regimes in the Middle East. Expanding on this idea, ISIS has argued that this violence would eventually culminate in a final apocalyptic battle with the West and the subsequent restoration of an Islamic empire and golden age.

In these circumstances, even Muslim civilians are fair targets, whether in the United States, Europe, or the Middle East. This position is justified because their "collaboration" with the forces of evil means that they are not true Muslims and therefore can be killed, sacrificed to the cause. Such justifications are commonly used by ISIS, which claims for itself the right to "excommunicate" other Muslims, thus making them fair targets.

Such views have strong parallels to certain violent strains drawn from Christianity. In the United States, some racist groups assert that Western Christianity has been corrupted and weakened by a global Jewish conspiracy, and they seek to rebuild Western society on the basis of a purified white race. One particularly important figure in this ideology was William Pierce, who died in 2002. Pierce, who held a Ph.D. in physics and was at one time a university professor, formed the National Alliance, a white supremacist organization, in 1974. Pierce departed from Christianity altogether as a faith tainted by its association with Judaism, offering instead a "cosmotheist" faith that viewed whites as belonging to a superior evolutionary track, on the road to unity with God. In his novel *The Turner Diaries*, Pierce describes the creation of a dedicated underground that would attack symbols of American authority, seize territory, and eventually launch a nuclear attack against the country itself. This apocalypse would destroy the state, allowing the revolutionaries to exterminate all nonwhites and those who do not accept the new order. This genocide would eventually extend worldwide. Timothy McVeigh's bombing of the federal courthouse in Oklahoma City in 1995, which killed 168 people, was directly inspired by *The Turner Diaries* and Pierce's argument that terrorism could trigger revolution. Pierce, while dissociating himself from McVeigh's act, nevertheless stated that McVeigh was

> a soldier, and what he did was based on principle. . . . He was at war against a government that is at war against his people. . . . In this war the rule is: Whatever is good for our people is good, and whatever harms our people is evil. That is the morality of survival.[13]

The Turner Diaries has been described as "arguably the most important single work of white nationalist propaganda in the English language" and continues to inform political violence in the United States and Europe.[14]

Violence extends also outside the monotheistic religions of the West. In Myanmar (Burma), a form of violent Buddhism has emerged in the 969 Movement, led by the monk Ashin Wirathu, which focuses its hostility on the country's Muslim minority. Although Muslims make up less than 5 percent of the population, Wirathu and the 969 Movement articulate a worldview that emphasizes the destruction of Buddhist communities in South and Southeast Asia by Islamic armies in the twelfth century as the beginning of an ongoing existential threat. Wirathu describes Muslims as an inherently violent "race" rather than followers of a religion, and followers of the movement have targeted Muslims in a series of deadly attacks, destroying mosques and displacing entire communities. The goal of the 969 Movement is to restore the role of Buddhism at the center of the nation and state as the country currently undergoes a tentative transition to democracy. However, one important question we should ask is whether the 969 Movement is better described as terrorism, ethnic conflict, or some combination of the two.[15]

In these three cases, we see important similarities. First, these groups radically reinterpreted an existing faith by arguing that it had lost its way. Osama bin Laden, William Pierce, and Ashin Wirathu each claimed for themselves the ability to recast the faith in an overtly ideological manner. Second, through this reinterpretation, they viewed the world in terms of an existential battle between good and evil, purity and corruption. Third, as the defenders of truth, they placed themselves in the role of warriors in the service of faith, able to mete out justice to all those who were seen as the enemy, whether state or society. And finally, they described this violence not as an unfortunate necessity but as a sacrifice to the cause that would bring forth or restore a higher order.

These kinds of religiously motivated political violence can parallel similar acts carried out by nonreligious groups. The failures and humiliations of modernity, the creation of a group of "true believers" who see the world in stark terms of good versus evil, and the idea of a transformation that will destroy the old order and usher in a new age can all be ascribed to many secular ideologies and similarly used to justify violence.

USA

TERRORISM OR HATE CRIME? POLITICAL VIOLENCE IN AMERICA

As we know, America is no stranger to political violence. The obvious example is that of September 11, but long before that there have been domestic actors willing and able to carry out acts of violence in the name of some greater political goal. In 1901, an anarchist assassinated President McKinley, and in 1919 a series of mail bombs were sent to political and economic elites across the country. In 1920, a wagon carrying several hundred pounds of explosives and shrapnel was detonated across from Wall Street, killing over 30 people. This wave of violence eventually subsided, but in the 1960s and 1970s a new generation of actors emerged, radicalized by such causes as opposition to the Vietnam War and Puerto Rican independence. During this time period, there were numerous bombing attacks on government institutions and university and civilian buildings, with several deaths. And as we already noted, over the past 30 years various American white supremacists have carried out violent attacks, with the most notable event being the 1995 Oklahoma City bombing that killed 168 people. More recently, in 2015, Dylann Roof attacked the Emanuel African Methodist Church in Charleston, South Carolina, killing nine. Roof believed that his attack would help trigger a race war.

Roof's actions and his motivations clearly fit the definition of political violence, and terrorism more specifically. Roof sought to carry out political change (indeed, he spoke of his disgust at the sight of the American flag), and believed that targeting civilians would help bring about a revolution. And yet in much of the discussion regarding this and similar attacks, the term "hate crime" is used instead. Why? Some of this is a function of existing laws that date back to the civil rights movement of the 1960s. A hate crime may be political, but in most cases we can assume that the attacker does not have regime change as a goal.

But are the terms we choose to use a function of existing laws? We have frequently returned to the point that conceptual clarity and consistency is important. Some argue that the use of the word "terrorism" in reference to political violence in the United States has everything to do with how Americans view domestic politics and political violence. For many Americans, terrorism is a concept associated with politics outside the United States. For example, in contrast to Roof, when Omar Mateen killed 49 individuals in Orlando in 2016, people quickly spoke of this as a terrorist attack, even though homophobia (rather than ISIS) seemed to be a primary motivation. If anything, Mateen's attack seems a better example of a hate crime while Roof's attack an example of terrorism. Dylann Roof and Timothy McVeigh demonstrate that a liberal democracy can produce home-grown terrorists who have no connections to a group or ideology based outside of the United States. This raises uncomfortable questions as to why such violence has emerged. Perhaps the reliance on the terminology of "hate crime" allows us to avoid the notion that we may confront a more intractable set of domestic political challenges.

Countering Political Violence

Our discussion indicates that political violence is a varied and constantly shifting force in the modern world. As long as states monopolize force, there will be actors who seek to wrest this power from the state so they can use it to pursue their own political objectives. Violence can be motivated by institutional, ideational, and individual factors—most likely some combination of the three. Though religious violence is a pressing concern, we see that in many ways the distinctions between secular and religious violence are not as great as we might have supposed.

Given the amorphous nature of political violence, what can states do to manage or prevent it? This is difficult to answer, since the response depends partly on the nature of the political violence itself. Although violence differs across time and from place to place, we can nevertheless make a few tentative observations, understanding that these are not ironclad answers.

One observation is that regime type appears to make a difference; terrorism and revolution are less likely in democratic societies. Why? The simplest answer is that democracies allow for a significant degree of participation among a wide enough number of citizens to make them feel that they have a stake in the system. While democracies produce their own share of cynicism and public unrest, including political violence, they also appear to co-opt and diffuse the motivations necessary for serious organized or mass violence against the state and civilians. Again, this is not to say that democracies are impervious to political violence, as we have seen in the United States and elsewhere. The observation is merely that democracies appear to be more effective at containing and limiting such groups by providing more options for political opposition.

Of course, one of the dangers is that terrorism and revolution sparked by one kind of regime can easily spill beyond its borders, particularly in such an interconnected world. While democracy may be an important factor in preventing violence carried out by its own citizens, it does not offer protection against political violence carried out by groups operating outside the state. Indeed, the paradox here is that open democratic societies may limit domestic conflict but make for a much more tempting target for globalized political violence.

What about states that are already liberal democracies and yet face political violence from domestic or international actors? In this case, the classic dilemma of freedom versus security raises its head. In the face of threats, democratic states and their citizens will often favor limiting certain civil liberties and increasing state autonomy and capacity in order to bring an end to political violence. In the United States, the 2001 PATRIOT Act is an example of such counterterrorism, with its increased powers to conduct public surveillance. Suspects in the United Kingdom can be detained up to 28 days without charge and under certain conditions can even be stripped of

Why Did the Arab Spring of 2011 Occur?

In Chapter 1, we began this book with a puzzle: Why did the Arab Spring take place, and why did these uprisings lead to such different results in different countries? Revolutions and transitions often seem to come out of the blue. Regimes that appeared impervious to change a year earlier are swept away before our eyes. No one expected that communism would collapse in Eastern Europe in the 1980s; at best, it seemed, reforms within the Soviet Union would lead to some modest liberalization, perhaps even reinvigorating the one-party regimes in the region. Just the opposite occurred.

In the recent case of the Arab Spring in North Africa and the Middle East, the signs were even less promising. Modernization in the region is often viewed as stunted. If we turn to the Human Development Index (see Chapter 4), we find development is especially lagging in levels of education and health care. This is true even in countries with significant natural resources, like Saudi Arabia, whose life expectancy trails that of much poorer China. Gender inequalities are also significant.

Oil, as well as foreign aid from the United States in particular, has helped support many of these states, creating systems built around a coterie of supporters who benefit directly from the state. These elite groups have relied on various means of repression—harassing, jailing, and killing opponents—to maintain their control over the state and the benefits they have drawn from it.

Civil society in much of the region is weak and fragmented, a result of state repression and low levels of development. Democratization and liber-alization are ideas tainted by their association with Western colonialism and U.S. foreign policy in the region, particularly after the invasion of Iraq. There is wariness of U.S. foreign policy, which for many years has supported nondemocratic regimes in the region.

How, then, in the face of all these challenges, did the Arab Spring burst forth? Why revolutions break out when they do is beyond the understanding of social scientists, much as geologists cannot simply tell us when an earthquake is going to occur. But to make some sense of these changes, we can turn to our institutional, ideational, and individual explanations. These explanations are not comprehensive but rather point to the complexity of revolutionary change.

Institutional explanations for the Arab Spring focus on the nature of authoritarian rule. For example, while Tunisia functioned as a highly repressive one-party system that sought to co-opt or control civil society, its regime also maintained just a small military force and a limited degree of patrimonialism. Thus, when protests intensified, the military refused to fire on the population, helping pave the way for revolution and democratization. In contrast, as we mentioned at the start of this chapter, Syria's highly patrimonial regime has relied largely on armed forces directly controlled by the ruling Assad family, giving those in power both the desire and the means to use violence against their opponents. Egypt seems to fall somewhere between the two, where the military first sided with revolutionaries but also had the capacity to seize power for itself, which it eventually did. Institutions like the military cannot fully account for why

Egyptian protesters gather at Tahrir Square, Cairo, at the start of the Egyptian Revolution in 2011.

revolution succeeded where it did, but they can be seen to have influenced the resources and strategies of political elites across the various cases.

Ideational explanations are similarly useful. In the case of Egypt, many point to the role young people played in shaping the message of the protests that brought down President Hosni Mubarak. Their "April 6 Youth Movement" studied how public protests brought down authoritarian regimes in Eastern Europe. To mobilize the public, activists relied on Facebook and YouTube, prompting the regime to cut off Internet access in a failed last-ditch effort to fend off the revolution. The role of Islam as a democratic or fundamentalist force across the region is also central to any understanding of political change. The rise to power of the Muslim Brotherhood in Egypt polarized the population, paving the way for a military coup in 2013, whereas in Tunisia the Islamist Ennahda Party supported a democratic and secular constitution, making that country the only one to successfully transition to democracy as a result of the Arab Spring.

Finally, we should not discount the role of individual action, which sparked these revolutions. Mohamed Bouazizi was a 26-year-old Tunisian man who had worked from a young age to support his family, selling produce as a street vendor. The police repeatedly harassed Bouazizi, ostensibly for lacking a business license but in reality because he failed to pay bribes. These repeated assaults took their toll; as his sister later noted, "those with no connections and no money for bribes are humiliated and insulted and not allowed to live."[a] After a final clash in December 2010, Bouazizi stood before the local governor's office, amid the traffic, where he doused himself in gasoline and set himself alight. Protests began soon thereafter and spread across the region, raising common demands: dignity and change. Large-scale, domestic and international, and state and societal forces were critical in explaining the Arab Spring (and all revolutions), but we should not forget the role of one apparently powerless person in shaping history.

THINKING CRITICALLY

1. What institutional factors help explain why Tunisia's revolution took such a different shape from Syria's?
2. How did institutional and ideational factors combine in the case of Egypt to spur its revolution?
3. Why did revolution overturning authoritarian regimes in the Middle East seem so unlikely in the first place?

REGIME TYPE	EFFECT ON TERRORISM	RESULT	RISK OF TERRORRISM
AUTHORITARIAN	Authoritarianism may foster terrorism, but the state can repress domestic terrorists; the state is unhindered by civil liberties.	Limited terrorism, but may be redirected outside of the country toward more vulnerable targets.	Lower
DEMOCRATIC	Participatory institutions and civil liberties are likely to undercut public support for terrorism.	Domestic terrorism less likely, but country may be a target of international terrorism generated in nondemocratic regimes.	Moderate
ILLIBERAL/ TRANSITIONAL	Weak state capacity, instability, and limited democratic institutions may generate both opportunities and motivations for terrorism.	Terrorism more likely due to domestic and/or international support.	Higher

their citizenship if suspected of terrorism. In France, state of emergency laws since the 2015 Paris terrorist attacks have allowed for raids and house arrests without judicial authorization.

There are dangers here. Focusing excessively on security over freedom may be dangerous to democracy. Placing too much power in the hands of the state to observe and control the public could seriously threaten to erode individual rights and with them democracy, creating what some have called a "surveillance state."[16] Such activities can in turn contribute to further political violence, since they confirm the idea that the state is conspiring to destroy its opponents, thus justifying violent resistance. Despite these dangers, people and politicians often seek dramatic and visible solutions because they provide a sense of security, although in reality they may have limited or even counterproductive effects. The old adage attributed to Benjamin Franklin is worth recalling: "Those who would give up essential liberty to purchase a little temporary safety deserve neither liberty nor safety."[17]

In Sum: Meeting the Challenge of Political Violence

Political violence is a complex issue for scholars, states, and societies. Often its objectives are cast in idealistic terms as part of necessary historical change. At the same time, this violence can come at a tremendous cost of human life, when violence becomes an end in itself. Because political violence is a response to existing institutions, the institutional context differs across time and space, making it hard to extrapolate general properties from specific instances. Like a virus, it may suddenly emerge in unexpected places, ravaging the population before disappearing again. Or it may lie dormant for many years, only to break out when certain conditions come together.

There is clearly no one way to stop or prevent political violence. Countries have to balance prevention, such as providing democratic institutions and opportunities for political contention, with treatment, such as military and legal methods to counter terrorism. Treatment carries its own risk, and even the most comprehensive forms of prevention cannot guarantee that political violence will never break out.

Key Terms

guerrilla war (p. 129)

ideational (p. 120)

nihilism (p. 130)

political violence (p. 119)

relative deprivation model (p. 124)

revolution (p. 123)

state-sponsored terrorism (p. 128)

terrorism (p. 128)

A voter casts her ballot at a polling station for the Indonesian presidential elections in 2014. Despite regular elections, is Indonesia a democracy?

Democratic Regimes

What makes democracy rise and prosper?

IS INDONESIA A DEMOCRACY? This question is not simply academic; Indonesia is the fourth largest country in the world by population and the fifteenth largest by size. It is also the largest Muslim country in the world. Why did Indonesia move away from authoritarianism? How institutionalized has its democracy become? What challenges does it still face? Looking at the 2014 presidential elections will provide some context.

Forged by Dutch imperialism, Indonesia gained its independence in 1945. The country then struggled to build a democratic system, though such attempts were short lived. In 1957, President Sukarno dismantled liberal democracy in favor of authoritarian rule. President Sukarno and then President Suharto (who overthrew Sukarno in 1966) would rule Indonesia for more than 40 years, tolerating few democratic rights or institutions while presiding over widespread corruption and nepotism. However, in the late 1990s an economic crisis in Asia devastated Indonesia's economy, weakened the regime's legitimacy, and prompted protests and calls for greater democracy. Suharto surrendered power in 1998, resulting in a period of political change known as *Reformasi*. This movement included the devolution of power to local governments, the creation of a strong constitutional court, and open elections.

How has *Reformasi* fared? How do we know when Indonesia—or any country—is a democracy? Elections are one obvious measure. Constitutional reforms in Indonesia guaranteed the direct election of the 560-seat legislature, and elections were held in 1999, 2004, and 2009. Regular elections to over 500 local assemblies have been held as well.

But elections are not the only way to evaluate democracy—they may in fact be quite misleading. If we expand our analysis, some concerns emerge. At the voter level, elections in Indonesia are marred by vote buying and electoral fraud, consistent with the high level of overall corruption that continues to plague the country. This situation has in turn undermined the legitimacy of the major political parties. The parties themselves are not clearly defined by their ideological differences as opposed to their association with powerful families or the previous regime. The lack of ideological clarity makes it difficult for the public to distinguish between the parties or hold them accountable to any political values. On the positive side, such frustrations have helped fuel civil society—activists have emerged to advance reforms, such as reducing corruption and increasing election transparency. Civic organization is often seen as critical to fostering public participation, and it is often the absence of such organizations that undermines new democracies.

Overall, a weak party system legislature alongside a strong civil society provides a very mixed picture of democratic progress in Indonesia. But there is a third institution that is crucial to the country's democratic institutionalization. As in the United States, Indonesia's executive takes the form of a directly elected president with a two-term limit. The first democratic elections for this office were held in 2004. The victor, Susilo Bambang Yudhoyono, was a former general under the Suharto regime. The 2014 presidential elections were thus considered critical in moving the country away from its authoritarian past and reducing the traditional role of the military in politics.

The elections came down to two very different candidates. Joko Widodo was a successful businessman and former mayor of the capital, Jakarta. Widodo campaigned on the need to reduce poverty and corruption, portraying himself as a hands-on leader with extensive political experience. Widodo's campaign contrasted starkly with that of his opponent, Prabowo Subianto. Subianto, previously a lieutenant general in the armed forces, had commanded the forces involved in the violent suppression of anti-Suharto protests in 1998. Whereas Widodo emphasized pragmatism and his record of good local governance, Subianto presented himself as a charismatic leader akin to a modern-day Sukarno. Early in the campaign, Subianto seemed a long shot for the presidency. However, he gained ground, relying in part on a message of nationalism and sectarianism that took aim at the small Christian and Hindu communities. In the end, this strategy did not work. In the July elections, Widodo gained 53 percent of the vote, and voter turnout was a remarkable 70 percent.

Widodo's election represents a clear break with the Suharto era and the long-standing role of the military in politics, though there remain questions about Indonesia's long-term democratic institutionalization. The government has been unable to bring the military firmly under its control, reminiscent of our discussion of Pakistan in Chapter 2. Moreover, the legal structure remains corrupt and ineffective, and the president has made little headway in establishing the rule of law. Surprisingly, in spite of the country's legal shortcomings President Widodo has lifted the country's moratorium on the death penalty, approved the execution of individuals for drug trafficking offences, and has proposed expanding the death penalty even further. Indonesia has made strides in the consolidation of its democratic institutions, but this progress in participation and competition may have been accompanied by an alarming decline of civil liberties.

LEARNING OBJECTIVES

- Define democracy and explain its components.
- Compare various explanations regarding why democracy has emerged in some cases and not in others.
- Compare executive, legislative, and judicial institutions in their construction and degree of power.
- Distinguish among parliamentary, presidential, and semi-presidential democracies.
- Evaluate the differences between and benefits of plurality, majority, and proportional electoral systems.

FOR MOST OF HUMAN HISTORY, societies have not been organized in a way that we would consider democratic. But in the last two centuries, revolution, war, and the destruction of rival ideologies have paved the way for democracy around the globe. From the perspective of those already living in a democratic society, the spread of this political system may appear natural or inevitable. But why would democracy be an attractive or effective form of government? How does democracy actually work? Does democracy by definition reconcile freedom and equality in a single way, or does it allow for different mixtures of the two?

This chapter will speak to these questions as we consider the origins, structures, strengths, and weaknesses of democracy. We will begin by defining democracy and then trace democracy's origins. Next we will consider the various institutions that represent the core "goods" of democracy: participation, competition, and liberty. As we shall see, there is no one relationship among these three. Various democracies construct them differently, shaping freedom, equality, and the locus of power. Finally, we will consider some of the challenges to democracy around the world as we move into the next set of chapters.

Defining Democracy

Before proceeding, we must nail down our terminology. The word *democracy* has an inherently positive connotation for many people: things that are "democratic" are good; things that are "undemocratic" are bad. Of course, in reality, this is far from the truth: a university is not a democratic institution, but that does not necessarily mean it is deficient. Because of the word's symbolism, however, many individuals and organizations describe themselves as democratic but define the term in very different ways. For example, in Chapter 3 we noted that for communists democracy means collective equality and not individual freedom. Countries such as China thus see themselves as "true" democracies, which they define as featuring, among other things, full employment, universal education, and the elimination of economic classes. These societies see democracy in the United States and Europe as little more than the struggle among members of a small elite group. Naturally, capitalist countries view communist systems, with their single-party control and lack of civil liberties, as anything but democratic. As you can see, each side uses different criteria to define democracy.

How can we make any comparisons if democracy is in the eye of the beholder? One way is to go back to the origin of the word. *Democracy* comes from the Greek words *demos*, meaning "the common people," and *kratia*, meaning "power" or "rule." Based on this origin, we can define democracy at its most fundamental as a system in which political power resides with the people. The people, in turn, may exercise that power either directly or indirectly. And the exercise of power typically takes three forms: participation, through means such as voting and elections; competition, such as that between political parties; and liberty, such as freedom of speech or of assembly. **Democracy**, then, can be fully defined as political power exercised either directly or indirectly by the people through participation, competition, and liberty.

This definition is subjective; it clearly emphasizes individual freedom and is in keeping with the ideology of liberalism. Indeed, many political scientists use the more specific term **liberal democracy** to indicate they are referring to a political system that promotes participation, competition, and liberty. Liberal democracies are rooted in the ideology of liberalism, with its emphasis on individual rights and freedoms.[1] But liberal democracy is not found only where a liberal ideology and a liberal political-economic system are predominant. Many liberal democracies have social democratic political-economic systems, which emphasize collective welfare much more than individual rights and so curtail individual freedoms in favor of greater equality. But social democracies nevertheless continue to respect the basic liberal democratic tenets of participation, competition, and liberty. Mercantilist political economies, too, emphasize a strong role for the state, resulting in fewer personal freedoms, but this has not prevented countries such as India, Japan, Taiwan, and South Korea from developing liberal democratic institutions. In each case, we find the basic rights of participation, competition, and liberty, though to different degrees. This variation in turn affects the degree of state autonomy and capacity.

Finally, it is important to remember what is not being said here about democracy. This book makes no claim that a particular kind of democracy, or even democracy itself, is the best way to organize politics. It is presenting democracy only as a particular system of institutions that have developed over time and out of liberal

democracy A political system in which political power is exercised either directly or indirectly by the people

liberal democracy A political system that promotes participation, competition, and liberty and emphasizes individual freedom and civil rights

thought. Each person must decide whether the particular goals enshrined in liberal democracy are the most important and whether society is best served by being organized in this manner.

Origins of Democracy

We now have an understanding of the most basic elements of democracy, but this still does not explain why it has come about and where it comes from. Some elements of democratic participation can be found in many societies around the world, dating back thousands of years. But liberal democratic institutions and practices have their roots in ancient Greece and Rome, where each country contributed to modern democracy in different ways.

Athenian and other early Greek democracies are important because they provide the foundation for the concept of public participation. Typically found in small communities, ancient Greek democracy allowed the public (excluding women, children, foreigners, and slaves) to participate directly in the affairs of government, choosing policies and making governing decisions. In this sense, the people were the state.[2] In contrast, the Roman Empire laid out the concept of **republicanism**, which emphasized the **separation of powers** within a state and the representation of the public through elected officials (as opposed to the unaccountable powers of a monarchy or the direct participation of the people). Thus, while Greece gives us the idea of popular sovereignty, it is from Rome that we derive the notion of legislative bodies like a senate. In their earliest forms, neither Greek democracy nor Roman republicanism would be defined as liberal democracies by today's standards. Both emphasized certain democratic elements but restricted them in fundamental ways. As political rights and institutions have expanded over the centuries, republicanism and democracy—Roman and Greek thought and practices—have become intertwined to produce the modern liberal democratic regime we know today.

The discussion so far may lead us to conclude that the development of democracy was a long, unbroken line from Greece to today. But that was not the case. Roman republicanism was quite different from Greek participatory democracy, and in time both collapsed. Yet democratic institutions and practices slowly reemerged, most notably in thirteenth-century England. At that time, English nobles forced King John to sign the Magna Carta, a document that curbed the rights of the king and laid the foundation for an early form of legislature, a key element of republicanism. In addition, the Magna Carta asserted that all freemen (at the time, only male members of the aristocracy) should enjoy due process before the law; this assertion set the stage for the idea of liberty. The Magna Carta states:

> No freeman shall be taken, imprisoned, . . . or in any other way destroyed . . . except by the lawful judgment of his peers, or by the law of the land. To no one will we sell, to none will we deny or delay, right or justice.

Although the Magna Carta was limited in its goals and application, it presented the idea that no individual, not even the king, was above the law. This concept thrived in England over the centuries as democratic practices expanded and an ever-greater proportion of the public was given political rights. The emergence of democracy in England was thus incremental, developing across centuries.

republicanism Indirect democracy that emphasizes the separation of powers within a state and the representation of the public through elected officials

separation of powers The clear division of power among different branches of government and the provision that specific branches may check the power of other branches

Was there something special about England that allowed democracy to flourish there in the first place? As noted in Chapter 2, European states emerged out of centuries of conflict as rival warlords slowly concentrated their holdings and extended their power. For various reasons, in England neither the state nor the feudal elite was able to get the upper hand, leading to a relative balance of power. This balance may have been facilitated by the defensive benefits of being an island; the need to maintain a large army to unify and defend the country was much lower for isolated England than for the many other European states. Ocean trade, too, provided revenue through port duties, which meant less need for a strong state to squeeze taxes from the public. The result was a relatively clear separation of power that facilitated individual freedom. This in turn would eventually give shape to the ideology of liberalism. It is no accident that an ideology emphasizing individual freedom and private property emerged in a country where the state capacity and autonomy were not excessive. The public, able to gain the upper hand against the state early on in England's political development, could check attempts by the state to increase its power. This public power paved the way for an expansion of rights over time, culminating in modern liberal democracy.[3]

Contemporary Democratization

Historical background helps us understand the emergence of democracy, but for scholars of contemporary politics it does not provide much guidance. Why is South Africa a democracy when neighboring Zimbabwe is not? What explains the wave of democratization across Latin America in the 1980s? Competing explanations for democratization and democratic institutionalization have fallen in and out of favor over time. Some of this may be a function of improved scholarship, but it may also be that explanations that were accurate at one time lose their explanatory power as the world changes.

MODERNIZATION AND DEMOCRATIZATION

One of the most prominent theories argues that democratization is correlated with, if not caused by, modernization. As we recall from Chapter 1, the behavioral revolution in political science was strongly connected to modernization theory, which posited that as societies became more modern, they would inevitably become more democratic. Why? Modernization is associated with better education, a weakening of older traditional institutions that stressed authority and hierarchy, greater gender equality, and the rise of a middle class. To sum up, modernization theory suggests that as societies become better educated and more economically

TIMELINE Milestones in the Rise of Democracy

18th CENTURY B.C.E.	Babylonian ruler Hammurabi establishes the earliest-known legal code.
6th CENTURY B.C.E.	Autocratic rule overthrown and first democracy established in Athens.
5th CENTURY B.C.E.	Democracy collapses in Athens as it is undermined by war and economic crisis.
1st CENTURY B.C.E.	Roman philosopher Cicero writes of *res publica*, or "affairs of the people," viewing the public as an important source of political power.
5th–10th CENTURIES C.E.	European Dark Ages: power in Europe is fragmented, fostering intense competition among rulers and setting the stage for the emergence of the nation-state.
1215	English Magna Carta establishes an early precedent for the rule of law.
1646	Treaty of Westphalia asserts the right of European states to choose their own religion, enforcing the notion of state sovereignty.
1689	Bill of Rights is passed in England, establishing parliamentary supremacy.
1690	English philosopher John Locke writes *Two Treatises of Government*, arguing that government's job is to protect "the right to life, liberty, and the ownership of property."
1762	Jean-Jacques Rousseau writes *The Social Contract*, arguing that if a government fails to serve its subjects the populace has the right to overthrow it.
1787	U.S. Constitution and Bill of Rights codify the separation of powers and civil rights.
1832–84	Reform Acts in the United Kingdom expand voting rights to much of the male population.
1893	New Zealand is the first country to grant women the right to vote.
1945	Defeat of the Axis powers eliminates fascism as a threat to democracy in Europe and Japan.
1948	United Nations approves the Universal Declaration of Human Rights, setting the stage for the internationalization of civil rights.
1989–91	Soviet Union disintegrates, leading to democratization in Eastern Europe.
1994	First democratic elections in South Africa, ending racial restrictions on voting.

sophisticated, they need and desire greater control over the state to achieve and defend their own interests.

In the 1970s, this theory fell out of favor. Democracy was failing in many countries in Latin America, while development in Asia leapt forward alongside nondemocratic regimes. It seemed that modernization at best was irrelevant to the development of democracy and at worst could destabilize existing institutions and lead to political violence (see Chapter 5) and democratic failure. Scholars no longer make sweeping claims that modernization inevitably leads to democracy. However, some note that while democracy can emerge in a variety of circumstances, wealth and ongoing economic development are critical to the institutionalization and long-term survival of any democracy.[4]

ELITES AND DEMOCRATIZATION

We noted earlier that modernization theory has risen, fallen, and risen again in prominence over time. In the past, modernization theory implied that democratization was almost automatic once a country developed a strong middle class and reached a certain standard of living. This argument, however, did not explain how the change would come about. We can also point to countries where standards of living have risen, such as the oil states of the Middle East, but democracy has not followed. What explains this?

One answer may lie in the role of those in power, the political elites. For the past several decades, many scholars who had turned away from modernization theory concentrated instead on the strategic motivations of those in power, and on what would lead them to hang on to or surrender power. Much of this work tended to describe rather than explain political change, but of late these arguments have gained new life by drawing on some earlier ideas of modernization theory.

Central to modernization theory is the idea that a middle class is essential for democratization—a significant segment of the population with the economic resources necessary to advance and demand their own rights. Similarly, overall poverty can be an obstacle to democracy—where people have little, they have little to fight for. But the distribution of wealth may be more important. Where economic assets are concentrated in the hands of those in power, political change is much less likely if they believe that it would divest them of their wealth. Think, for example, of countries like Nigeria or Saudi Arabia, where those in power control significant natural resources, such as oil. Those who control these assets may be loath to give them up. But sources of wealth are not fixed; natural resources may decline, and an economy may stagnate. Those in power may no longer see much value in clinging to power, especially if they believe they can take some wealth with them in exchange for stepping aside.[5] In short, economic development is important, but the nature of the resources that fuel it can determine the likelihood that democracy will emerge. We will speak of this in much greater detail in the next chapter, on nondemocratic regimes.

SOCIETY AND DEMOCRATIZATION

A somewhat different view of democratization emphasizes not the importance of political elites, but the political power of society itself. Elite-based theories can give us a sense of why leaders may be more or less willing to surrender power to the public, but not why the public would demand power in the first place. Likewise, modernization theory, though it explains how societies might change in a direction more in tune with democratic institutions, does not provide a clear sense of why society would want to move in this direction.

civil society Organizations outside of the state that help people define and advance their own interests

Scholars more interested in the role of society have in the past stressed the importance of public organization or, specifically, what is called **civil society**. Basically, civil society can be defined as organized life outside the state, or what the French scholar Alexis de Tocqueville called the "art of association."[6] Civil society is a fabric of organizations, not necessarily political, created by people to help define their own interests, whatever they may be: environmental groups, churches, sports teams, fraternal organizations, and the like. Under the right circumstances, these associations serve as a vehicle for democratization by allowing people to articulate, promote, and defend what is important to them.

Where civil society has been able to take root, it is argued, democratization is more likely because it provides the ideas and the tools of political action and mobilization that allow small-scale democratic practices to spread. Indeed, the term *civil society* gained currency in reference to movements in Eastern Europe in the 1970s that organized independent of communist rule.[7] Where civic association can emerge, it may create a powerful incentive for democratic change, even if that is not the original intent. Modernization may help foster civil society, and civil society in turn may pressure elites for change—and these elites may or may not acquiesce, depending on their incentives to do so.

INTERNATIONAL RELATIONS AND DEMOCRATIZATION

So far, our discussion of democratization has focused on variables inside the country in question. Can international factors also play a role? We can think of extreme cases, such as the occupation of Japan and Germany after World War II, or of Iraq and Afghanistan more recently. But scholars believe that the international community also plays a role in less overt ways. Modernization resulting from foreign investment, globalization, and trade may push democratization forward. In addition, international pressure or incentives may cause elites to favor democracy; some have suggested that the institutionalization of democracy in southern and Eastern Europe came about partly because democracy was a prerequisite for membership in the European Union. Civil society, too, can be strengthened by the transmission of ideas across borders by education, media, and nongovernmental organizations.

How influential the international community may be in each case probably depends on a number of factors, including how open to, and dependent on, the outside world that society is. North Korea's isolation means that little contact takes place between that society and those beyond its borders. The vast size of China's economic resources means that the international community has far fewer tools it can use to press for change within that country.

CULTURE AND DEMOCRATIZATION

Our last argument is a familiar one. In Chapter 3, we spoke of the idea of political culture, which is essentially the argument that the differences in societal institutions—norms and values—are shaping the landscape of political activity. Political culture may influence the preference for certain kinds of policies as well as the particular relationship between freedom and equality. Some scholars take this idea much further, arguing that democracy is basically a culture emerging from historical, religious, and philosophical foundations. In this view, for example, modernization does not lead to individualism and democracy; rather, Western democratic and individualist practice gave rise to modernity.

If this argument is true, then democratization is less likely to be found the farther we travel from the West, where historical developments forged strong national identities as well as a commitment to democracy in its own right. As we have discussed earlier, such arguments make many scholars uncomfortable, both because they are difficult to test and because they smack of stereotyping and determinism. They also have a questionable track record. Not long ago, countries such as Spain, Portugal, Italy, and many Latin American nations, whose cultures were dominated by hierarchical Roman Catholicism, were seen as unlikely to democratize—until they did. Similar arguments have been raised with regard to Asia, as we discussed in Chapter 3. However, we can certainly argue that political culture, while not necessarily determining democracy, can shape its particular character in each country. For example, in the case of Indonesia discussed earlier, in spite of democratization and a secular regime, civil liberties have come into tension with values held by some among the majority Muslim population. One example of this tension is the implementation of laws against blasphemy and discrimination against minority Islamic sects.

To summarize, there are numerous ways to explain why democratization takes place in some cases and not others. While scholars tend to favor one of these explanations over the others, we see that most, if not all, of these factors play some role in each case of democratization. Modernization can set the stage for political activity and awareness, which can find its organizational expression in civil society. Elites may be influenced by economic conditions at home and international inducements or sanctions. Even culture may encourage certain kinds of identities and ideas that catalyze democracy or get in its way. In the end, changing domestic and international conditions may mean that what leads to democracy now may be unrelated to how it comes about in the future. Politics is not a physical law, unchanging across time and space.

Institutions of the Democratic State

We now have an understanding of the basic definition of liberal democracy and some of the explanations for how it emerged in the past and present. Next, we should spend some time looking at how liberal democracies are constructed. As we shall see, liberal democratic institutions vary dramatically. Legislatures differ greatly from country to country, as do executives, and the legislative–executive relationship in each country is unique. Each judiciary, too, plays a distinct role in the democratic process. There is tremendous variation in the range and number of political parties, and this in part is shaped by the myriad electoral systems used around the world. Even what we consider basic civil rights and civil liberties differ from one liberal democracy to another. There is no one way—no right way—to build a liberal democracy. Let's look at some of the major ways in which each institution differs from country to country before we consider several of their most common combinations.

EXECUTIVES: HEAD OF STATE AND HEAD OF GOVERNMENT

executive The branch of government that carries out the laws and policies of a state

head of state The executive role that symbolizes and represents the people both nationally and internationally

head of government The executive role that deals with the everyday tasks of running the state, such as formulating and executing policy

We begin with what is the most prominent office in any country, the **executive**—the branch that carries out the laws and policies of a state. When we think of this office, what often comes to mind is a single person in charge of leading the country and setting a national agenda as well as leading foreign policy and serving as commander in chief in times of war. But in fact, the executive comprises two distinct roles. The first is **head of state**, a role that symbolizes and represents the people, both nationally and internationally, embodying and articulating the goals of the regime. Conducting foreign policy and waging war are also sometimes considered parts of the head of state's duties. In contrast, the **head of government** deals with the everyday tasks of running the state, such as formulating and executing domestic policy, alongside a cabinet of ministers who are charged with specific policy areas (such as education or agriculture). This distinction between direct policy management and international and symbolic functions is an old one that goes back to the days when monarchs reigned over their subjects, leaving ministers in charge of running the country.

Countries combine or separate these two roles to different degrees. Heads of government are usually referred to as prime ministers: they serve as the main executive over the other ministers in their cabinet. They may serve alongside a head of state, who may be a monarch or a president. A country may also combine the two roles, as in the United States, where the president is both head of state and head of government. The balance of power between the head of state and that of government differs from country to country, as you will learn shortly.

LEGISLATURES: UNICAMERAL AND BICAMERAL

The **legislature** is typically viewed as the body in which national politics is considered and debated. It is charged with making or at least passing legislation. As with executives, legislatures vary in their political powers and construction. The major distinction is between bicameral and unicameral systems. As you might guess from their names, **bicameral systems** are legislatures that contain two houses, whereas **unicameral systems** are those with one house. Small countries are more likely to have unicameral systems, though the majority of liberal democracies are bicameral.

Bicameral systems can be traced back to predemocratic England and other European states, where two or more chambers were created to serve the interests of different economic classes. Even as feudalism gave way to liberal democracy, the idea of bicameralism remained, for two major reasons. First, in some countries an upper chamber was retained as a check over the lower house, often reflecting a fear that a popularly elected lower house, too close to the people's current mood, would make rash decisions. Thus upper houses can often amend or veto legislation originating in the lower house. We can also see this concern in tenure: members of upper houses often serve for longer terms than members of lower houses.

A related element is federalism. Federal states typically rely on an upper house to represent local interests, so that members are able to oversee legislation particularly relevant to local policies. In some cases, local legislatures may even appoint or elect the members of that upper chamber, again reflecting a desire to check a directly elected lower house. In the United States, the Senate was indirectly elected by local legislatures until 1913. However, many unitary (nonfederal) liberal democratic systems also have bicameral legislatures. Legislatures may wield a great deal of power over the executive, serving as the prime engine of policy or legislation, or take a backseat to executive authority. Moreover, the balance of power between upper and lower houses differs from country to country and issue to issue, though upper houses generally are weaker than lower houses.

legislature The branch of government charged with making laws

bicameral system A political system in which the legislature comprises two houses

unicameral system A political system in which the legislature comprises one house

IN FOCUS	**Branches of Government**
BRANCH	FUNCTIONS, ATTRIBUTES, AND POWERS
EXECUTIVE	Head of state / head of government Parliamentary, presidential, and semi-presidential systems Term length may be fixed (president) or not (prime minister)
LEGISLATIVE	Lawmaking Unicameral or bicameral
CONSTITUTIONAL COURT	Determines the constitutionality of laws and acts Judicial review (abstract and concrete)

JUDICIARIES AND JUDICIAL REVIEW

The judiciary is the third major institution central to liberal democracies. All states rely on laws to prescribe behavior and lay out the rules of the political game. At the core of this body of laws lies a constitution, which is the fundamental expression of the regime and the justification for subsequent legislation and the powers of executives, legislatures, and other political actors. In nondemocratic systems, constitutions may count for little because the state acts as it sees fit. In liberal democracies, however, constitutional power is central to maintaining what we refer to as the **rule of law**—the sovereignty of law over the people and elected officials. As a result, judicial institutions are important components in upholding law and maintaining its adherence to the constitution.

As with executives and legislatures, judiciaries vary greatly across liberal democracies—not simply in their authority but also in how laws are interpreted and reviewed. Most (but not all) liberal democracies have some form of **constitutional court** charged with ensuring that legislation is compatible with the constitution. This is a relatively new development; in 1950, only a third of liberal democracies provided for **judicial review**, whereas now nearly 90 percent do. Alongside this rise in judicial review is the growth in the sheer number of rights that are protected under the constitution. This correlation makes sense; as constitutions define more rights, there is a greater need for judiciaries to rule on them.[8]

How these judiciaries function with regard to the constitution varies from country to country. In most countries, the right of judicial review is explicitly written into the constitution. However, in a few, such as the United States and Australia, this right is implicit and has become institutionalized in the absence of any specific provision in the constitution. Another variation is in the authority and division of high courts. Some countries, like the United States, Canada, Japan, and Australia, have a combined appellate and constitutional court. In other words, a single high court serves as a final court of appeals (to which lower court rulings can be appealed) and as a court of constitutional review. Because of this dual function, trials can be an important source of constitutional interpretation. Other countries, such as Brazil, have two separate high courts—a final court of appeals and a constitutional court. This structure greatly limits the influence of trials on constitutional interpretation.

Judicial systems also vary in their powers and how they can wield those powers. We might imagine that unified constitutional and appellate courts are by their nature more powerful than those whose two levels are separate. Yet other important variations can shape judicial authority as much, if not more. Judicial review can take different forms—most specifically, concrete or abstract. In **concrete review**, courts can consider the constitutionality of legislation only when a specific court case triggers this question—for example, in the case of separate appellate and constitutional courts, a case before a court of appeal may be forwarded to the constitutional court if the court of appeal believes there is a constitutional issue at stake. In **abstract review**, a constitutional court may rule on legislation without a specific court case. Such rulings are typically initiated upon request by one or more elected officials, such as members of the national or local legislatures. Courts can also differ in the timing of their review. In some countries, constitutional review may occur only after a piece of legislation is passed; in others, the constitutional court may give a ruling beforehand. Finally, courts differ in the appointment and tenure of their judges; these are typically fixed terms (the lifetime tenure of U.S. Supreme Court judges is

rule of law A system in which all individuals and groups, including those in government, are subject to the law, irrespective of their power or authority

constitutional court The highest judicial body in a political system that decides whether laws and policies violate the constitution

judicial review The mechanism by which courts can review the actions of government and overturn those that violate the constitution

concrete review Judicial review that allows the constitutional court to rule on the basis of actual legal disputes brought before it

abstract review Judicial review that allows the constitutional court to rule on questions that do not arise from actual legal disputes

an anomaly, and appears to be increasingly a source of polarization and deadlock). The combination of these factors can radically affect the power of the courts in the democratic process.

Models of Democracy: Parliamentary, Presidential, and Semi-Presidential Systems

With our overview of state institutions in hand, let's look at the main differences in how some of these institutions can be constructed in relation to one another. This section provides a generalized portrait of these systems; in reality, there are numerous variations within these basic categories.

PARLIAMENTARY SYSTEMS

Parliamentary systems can be found in most of the democracies around the world. Parliamentary systems comprise two basic elements: first, prime ministers and their cabinets (the other ministers who make up the government) come out of the legislature; and second, the legislature is also the instrument that elects and removes the prime minister from office. In these cases, political power and roles are divided between a head of government and a head of state. The overwhelming majority of power resides with the head of government (the prime minister). In contrast, the head of state may be a president who is either directly elected by the public or indirectly elected by the legislature, or a monarch who has inherited the office. The head of state's powers are typically little more than ceremonial, particularly in the case of monarchs. They may hold some reserve powers, such as the ability to reject legislation or forward it to a constitutional court if it is seen as undemocratic. Even in these cases, however, the powers of the president or monarch are rarely exercised.

The prime minister is elected from the legislature and therefore reflects the balance of power between parties in the legislature. Typically, he or she is the head of the party in the lower house that holds the largest number of seats. Indeed, in most parliamentary systems the prime minister continues to hold a seat in the lower house of the legislature, as do other members of her or his cabinet. This tight connection between the executive and the legislature means that although these two branches of government separate powers and responsibilities, they do not check and balance each other's power to the degree that they do in presidential systems. A party with a majority of seats in the legislature can choose its own prime minister and cabinet with little concern for other parties. However, when a party holds a plurality of seats—that is, more seats than any other party but fewer than 50 percent of them—it must commonly forge a coalition government with one or more other parties. In such a government, the prime minister will come from the largest party, while other members of the cabinet come from the coalition parties. When the largest party lacks a majority, it is also possible for a coalition of smaller parties to form a government and select the prime minister, in effect shutting out the largest party.

It is important to note that in these systems, the public does not directly elect its country's leader. That task is left to the parties. As a result, the length of time the prime minister serves in office is uncertain. Members of the legislature are voted in

parliamentary system A political system in which the roles of head of state and head of government are assigned to separate executive offices

and out of office in direct elections, but prime ministers usually serve in office for as long as they can command the support of their party and its allies. Prime ministers sometimes remain in office for many years—in Australia, Robert Menzies served from 1949 until 1966. Yet prime ministers can often be removed relatively easily through what is known as a **vote of no confidence**. Parliaments typically retain the right to dismiss a prime minister at any time simply by taking a vote of confidence. In such a vote, the absence of majority support for the prime minister will bring down the government. Depending on the constitution, this outcome may trigger a national parliamentary election or a search for a new government and prime minister from among the parties. Prime ministers also hold the right to call elections. While the constitution may specify that elections must be held within a specific time frame (such as every four or five years), prime ministers can often schedule these elections when they imagine it will serve their party best.

In parliamentary systems, legislatures and judiciaries often take a backseat to the prime minister, who along with the cabinet is the main driver of legislation and policy. Especially when the prime minister enjoys a majority in the parliament, the house's role may be limited to debating policy that comes down from the cabinet. Upper houses, too, typically have little say in the selection or removal of the prime minister, and what powers they may have in rejecting legislation can often be overturned by the lower house. Judicial systems are frequently much weaker under these conditions as well. In parliamentary systems, the idea of checks and balances is subordinated to a concentration of power that guarantees greater political autonomy. In addition, the fusion of the prime minister's power with that of the lower house, and the weakness of the upper house, means that fewer opportunities arise for real constitutional conflicts that would empower constitutional courts. Finally, in some cases heads of state and upper houses themselves have certain powers of constitutional review, further limiting the opportunity for independent judicial power.

PRESIDENTIAL SYSTEMS

Presidential systems make up a minority of democratic systems around the world. In this system, the president is directly elected by the public for a fixed term and has control over the cabinet and the legislative process. The positions of head of state and head of government are typically fused in the presidency. Here we see a significant difference between parliamentary and **presidential systems**. In the parliamentary systems, prime ministers and their cabinets come from the legislature and must command a majority of support to stay in office. In presidential systems, however, the president and legislature serve for fixed terms, typically between four and seven years. Election dates may not be altered easily. Nor can presidents or legislatures be removed by anything resembling a vote of no confidence. Only in the case of malfeasance can elected officials lose their seats.

This institutional relationship affects government profoundly. First, as a directly elected executive, the president is able to draw on a body of popular support in a way that no member of a legislature, or even a prime minister, can. Only a president can say that she or he has been elected by the whole of the people in a single national vote (even if the reality is more complicated than that). Second, as the head of the state and the government, the president serves as an important national symbol as well as the overseer of policy. Third, the president is able to choose a cabinet, many or perhaps all of whom are not members of the legislature. Unlike prime ministers, presidents need not be concerned that their cabinets are composed of party leaders. Since the

vote of no confidence Vote taken by a legislature as to whether its members continue to support the current prime minister; depending on the country, a vote of no confidence can force the resignation of the prime minister and/or lead to new parliamentary elections

presidential system A political system in which the roles of head of state and head of government are combined in one executive office

president is directly elected, minority parties lack the kind of influence over the executive that can be found in parliamentary systems, especially in coalition government. Fourth, the president's power is not directly beholden to the legislature, and vice versa. Neither branch has the ability to easily remove the other, creating a much stronger separation of powers between executive and legislature. This separation of powers is also more likely to lead to checks and balances and divided government. Presidents and legislative majorities can be from different parties, and even when they belong to the same party, the separation of these institutions means greater independence from each other. President and legislature can easily check each other's ability to pass legislation in a way unlikely to occur in a parliamentary system. Presidentialism can in fact weaken political parties, since their leaders are concerned with winning a single national and directly elected office. To become prime minister, by contrast, an individual must come up through the ranks of the party.

Finally, the conflict between an independent legislature and president may pave the way for a more active judiciary, drawing it into disputes between the president and legislature, as has often been the case in the United States. There are relatively few presidential democracies around the world. The United States is the most typically cited example, but presidentialism is also the norm in Latin America.

SEMI-PRESIDENTIAL SYSTEMS

Our final variant is an interesting hybrid between parliamentary and presidential systems that has become more widespread over the past 50 years (though it remains far less common than presidential and parliamentary systems). In this model, power is divided between the head of state and the head of government—a prime minister and a directly elected president both exercise power. Presidents enjoy fixed terms, while prime ministers remain subject to the confidence of the legislature and, in some cases, the confidence of the president as well.

How power is divided between these two offices depends on the country. In some cases, the prime minister is relatively independent from the president; the president exercises important powers but has limited control over the prime minister. In other

INFOCUS	Parliamentary, Presidential, and Semi-Presidential Systems: Basic Features
TYPE	EXECUTIVE POWERS AND RELATIONSHIPS
PARLIAMENTARY	Indirectly elected prime minister holds executive power as head of government; directs cabinet, formulates legislation and domestic and international policies. Serves for an unfixed term and may be removed by a vote of no confidence. Head of state (president or monarch) is largely ceremonial.
PRESIDENTIAL	Directly elected president holds majority of executive power as head of state and government. Directs cabinet and formulates legislation and international and domestic policies. Serves for a fixed term and cannot be easily removed from office.
SEMI-PRESIDENTIAL	Directly elected president and indirectly elected prime minister share power. President helps set policy, while prime minister executes it. President also manages foreign policy. Which office holds more power depends on the country.

cases, the prime minister is beholden to both the legislature and the president, thus giving the president greater authority over the selection, removal, and activity of the prime minister. In both cases, the president holds power independently of the legislature yet shares powers with a prime minister.

Semi-presidential systems tend to reflect the old distinction between "reign" and "rule" that existed under monarchies. Presidents will often set forth policy but expect the prime minister to translate those policy ideas into legislation and ensure that it is passed. Presidents will also take the lead in foreign policy and serve as commander in chief, representing the country in international relations. The most prominent semi-presidential systems, like the French one, place most of the power in the hands of the president while the prime minister plays a supporting role. In semi-presidential systems, the role of the judiciary varies. The independence of constitutional courts is often limited because they are appointed by the president. At the same time, however, conflicts between presidents and prime ministers, and a lack of clarity over which executive has what power, have on a few occasions created opportunities for more judicial authority. Since the collapse of communism, semi-presidentialism has spread into several former Soviet republics, most notably Russia, and it is also the form of government in a few countries in Asia and Africa, such as Taiwan, Sri Lanka, and Mali.

Parliamentary, Presidential, and Semi-Presidential Systems: Benefits and Drawbacks

Now that we have reviewed these three systems, it makes sense to ask which of them offers the best system of governance. Of course, that depends on how we define *best*; each system has certain advantages and drawbacks. Nevertheless, scholars have made some arguments about how effective, democratic, or stable these systems may be.

Advocates of parliamentary systems point out that the fusion of power between the executive and legislature promotes greater efficiency by reducing the chances of divided government and deadlock. The prime minister's office, even when beholden to several parties in a coalition government, can normally promulgate and pass legislation relatively quickly, without having to take into consideration the narrow interests of individual legislators or smaller parties. In fact, prime ministers can use the vote of no confidence to their own advantage, threatening, for example, to make a vote against individual pieces of legislation an effective vote of no confidence—should the legislature vote against the legislation, the prime minister will call for new elections. Critics assert that the efficiency made possible by parliamentary systems—the prime minister's ability to generate and quickly pass legislation—comes at the cost of a weaker separation of powers. Legislatures may have far fewer opportunities to influence the passage of legislation or effectively express the voters' specific interests, since legislation is more a top-down than a bottom-up process. The voters' distance from government decision making can apply to the executive as well, since that individual is directly accountable only to the legislature. Greater efficacy may thus mean weaker public oversight and control over elected officials.

Parliamentary, Presidential, and Semi-Presidential Systems: Benefits and Drawbacks

TYPE	BENEFITS AND DRAWBACKS
PARLIAMENTARY	Benefits: Prime minister can usually get legislation passed. Prime minister may also be more easily removed by the legislature through a vote of no confidence.
	Drawbacks: Public does not directly select prime minister and may feel that it has less control over the executive and the passing of legislation.
PRESIDENTIAL	Benefits: President is directly elected and can draw on a national mandate to create and enact legislation.
	Drawbacks: President and legislature may be controlled by different parties, leading to divided government. Office does not allow for power sharing, and president may not be easily removed from office except through elections.
SEMI-PRESIDENTIAL	Benefits: Directly elected president and indirectly elected prime minister share power and responsibilities, creating both a public mandate (presidency) and an indirectly elected office that may be supported by a coalition of parties (prime minister).
	Drawbacks: Conflict possible between prime minister and president over powers and responsibilities.

Presidentialism has its own problems. The chief benefit of this system is the public's ability to directly select its leader, who serves for a fixed term. But this situation can generate difficulties. Unlike prime ministers, who must keep the confidence of their party (or parties, in the case of coalition governments), presidents are not dependent on their parties in this way. Even if a president loses the public's confidence, he or she cannot be replaced except through new elections. Presidents also enjoy (or suffer from) the separation of power from the legislature, which can lead to divided government. Whether checks and balances are a benefit or a hindrance to democracy is open to debate. Several prominent scholars have asserted that presidentialism is a more unstable system, since it limits power sharing and also lacks the mechanism through which legislators and executives can be easily removed from office. The result can be more polarized, and therefore unstable, politics. This has been the concern with Indonesia's transition to democracy, as noted at the opening of this chapter, and is increasingly the case in the United States.

We might conclude, then, that semi-presidentialism would be the best of both worlds, but its track record is limited and mixed. In many cases, power still becomes concentrated in the presidential office, and, in some cases, like Russia, presidents can use their office to dismantle democracy.

PRESIDENTIALISM IN BRAZIL: A BLESSING OR A CURSE?

BRAZIL

Nowhere is the question of executive design more hotly debated than in Latin America, where almost every country adopted the U.S. model after independence in the early nineteenth century. Students of Latin American politics have vigorously debated whether Latin American presidentialism has contributed to the region's notorious political instability and authoritarianism. Latin American presidents, faced with weak and fragmented legislatures, have often used their authority to enhance their own power and to pack the judiciary, and have in some recent cases removed or modified limits on reelection. When combined with high levels of corruption, the spoils of the presidency are deemed so great that the stakes in presidential elections become dangerously high. Parties that fail to win the presidency are more likely to become disloyal opponents to the system, and often support regime change. Indeed, street protests have led to the resignation of quite a few Latin American presidents in the last two decades.

Brazil nicely illustrates some of the potential problems of presidentialism. Brazil's political party system has long been fragmented along both ideological and regional cleavages, and presidents almost always lack a majority in the legislature, which has at times led to political stalemate, and has occasionally led presidents to rule by decree. A period of political polarization between an elected leftist president (who was viewed by conservatives as seeking to enhance his own power) and a conservative legislature (that was unable to remove the president through legal means) culminated in a military dictatorship between 1964 and 1985. Those tasked with writing a new constitution after the return of democracy proposed a referendum to decide the legislative-executive system (presidential or parliamentary). Many intellectuals responsible for drafting the constitution favored a parliamentary system, but voters overwhelmingly preferred to keep the presidential model that had been the rule in Brazilian history. After two decades of being unable to directly select the head of government, Brazilians did not want to forfeit that right.

Did Brazilians make the right choice? Since the return of democracy, no Brazilian president's party has had a majority in the legislature. For example, when President Dilma Rousseff was elected in 2010, her party won less than 20 percent of the seats in the lower house of the legislature. Such divisions have required Brazilian presidents to either legislate by emergency decree (something that was commonplace in the 1990s) or bargain with legislators on virtually every piece of legislation. For the past 20 years, Brazilian presidents have cobbled together de facto legislative coalitions, offering opposition parties seats in the cabinet. This bargaining appears to have exacerbated Brazil's endemic corruption. In 2015, protests erupted in Brazil over a massive bribery scandal involving the state-owned oil firm Petrobras, which eventually culminated in the impeachment of President Rousseff a year later.

Some scholars discount such events as evidence of presidential instability. Corruption is not unique to presidencies, and horse-trading between presidents and the legislature and the creation of de facto coalitions makes Brazil work much like a parliamentary system. These scholars cite the earlier impeachments of presidents Collor de Mello (in 1992) and Rousseff (in 2016) as evidence that the legislature can hold the president accountable and limit the ability of the president to rule by decree. In fact, some suggest that it is the electoral system for the legislature in Brazil (an unusual form of proportional representation, which we will speak about in a moment) that is responsible for political conflict in Brazil. In spite of this critique, supporters of parliamentarism argue that this change would strengthen political parties, make political compromise and the formation of coalitions more routine and transparent, and would offer greater flexibility in times of political turmoil. Are there lessons here that we can use to consider the powers of the presidency in the United States?

Political Parties

James Madison, one of the founders of the U.S. political system and the country's fourth president, once wrote that "in every political society, parties are unavoidable."[9] Observers have offered several reasons for the forming of political parties. Parties are important organizations that bring together diverse groups of people and ideas under the umbrella of an ideological mandate. These organizations serve two functions. By bringing different people and ideas together, they help establish the means by which the majority can rule. Without political parties that provide candidates and agendas for politics, the political process would be too fragmented, and it would be impossible to enact policy or get much else done. But political parties remain relatively loose, containing various factions built around differing issues. This heterogeneity helps limit a "tyranny of the majority," since parties are often diverse enough that they are unable to fully dominate politics even when they hold a majority of power. Parties in liberal democracies are thus homogeneous enough to create majority rule but too weak to facilitate a tyranny of the majority, so long as open and regular elections create the opportunity to turn the ruling party out of power.

Political parties also create the means for the electorate and fellow political elites to hold politicians accountable. By articulating an ideology and a set of goals, parties ensure that their members work toward those goals. Voters are able to evaluate politicians on the basis of their fulfillment of a party's policy platform. A party can thus serve as a political symbol, a kind of shorthand for a set of ideas and objectives, and voters can distill a complex set of beliefs and preferences into the decision of whether to vote for party A or party B.

Countries exhibit a variety of party systems, shaped by a number of factors. Some countries have seen the virtual dominance of two or even one party over a long period of time—Sweden's Social Democratic Party and Japan's Liberal Democratic Party have been able to control government for much of the postwar era. In other countries, such as Italy, power has moved back and forth between a handful of parties on a frequent basis, creating greater instability. In some parliamentary systems, like Italy's, coalition governments are the norm, while in others coalition governments are rare. These

---

INFOCUS Competition in Democracy

- Political parties encourage democratic competition by gathering diverse groups under an ideological mandate while simultaneously preventing domination by any one group and create the means to hold government accountable.
- The separation of powers between different branches of government prevents abuses of power by any one branch.

differences involve so many reasons, specific to each case, that it is hard to make easy generalizations. One factor that accounts for the diversity in party politics, however, is the diversity in **electoral systems**.

Electoral Systems

We have discussed why political parties form, but we must look more closely at why certain countries have more parties than others and why each party exhibits its particular ideological content. These questions might have no simple answer—the fortunes of political parties rise and fall over time. But in looking around the world, we see tremendous diversity in the ways that members of the public cast their votes, how those votes are applied, and, as a result, how many and what kinds of parties enter the legislature.

All democracies divide their populations geographically into a number of electoral districts or **constituencies**—each a geographic area that an elected official represents. These constituencies are allocated a certain number of legislative seats. The total number of constituencies varies widely from country to country: Argentina is broken up into 24 constituencies that correspond to the country's 23 provinces plus Buenos Aires, whereas in Nigeria 360 constituencies elect members of the country's lower house. How these boundaries are drawn matters, too. For example, if an ethnic or a religious minority is concentrated in one constituency, it may have more political power (by winning a greater share of seats) than it would have if it were divided across a number of constituencies. Also, different districts may have very different population sizes but the same number of legislative seats, giving those in less populated districts more power. How governments draw electoral boundaries can thus have a huge impact on who gets elected, and these boundaries are often a source of great contention in new (and old) democracies.

A second distinction is how votes are cast and counted.[10] Essentially, two broad forms of electoral systems are being used in liberal democracies today. The first is made up of plurality and majority systems, often called **single-member district (SMD)** systems, and the second is **proportional representation (PR)** systems. Let us consider each one in turn.

A minority of democratic countries around the world, including the United Kingdom, Canada, the United States, India, Nigeria, and several other former British colonies, rely on plurality-based SMD systems, also called **first past the post** systems. In these systems, as in all SMD systems, electoral constituencies are single-member districts, which means that each constituency has only one representative. In plurality-based SMDs, the candidate who receives the most votes—whether a majority or plurality—wins the seat. In SMD systems, the votes cast for other candidates are effectively wasted—that is, if a

electoral system A set of rules that decide how votes are cast, counted, and translated into seats in a legislature

constituency A geographical area that an elected official represents

single-member district (SMD) An electoral district with one seat

proportional representation (PR) An electoral system in which political parties compete in multimember districts; voters choose between parties, and the seats in the district are awarded proportionally according to the results of the vote

first past the post An electoral system in which individual candidates compete in single-member districts; voters choose between candidates, and the candidate with the largest share of the vote wins the seat

---

IN FOCUS   Participation

- One of the most basic ways in which the public participates in politics is through voting and elections.

- Voters may also participate in political decision making through referenda and initiatives.

- The two main types of electoral systems are single-member district (SMD) and proportional representation (PR). Most of the democratic countries today use PR. Many use a mix of SMD and PR.

---

candidate for whom a vote is cast does not win, his or her votes do not count toward any other candidate's electoral bid. The SMD system's "winner take all" approach can amplify the political power of some parties while weakening the political power of others.

Political scientists have long argued that under SMD systems, most people are unwilling to vote for smaller parties. Since such parties are unlikely to win a plurality of the votes, voters feel that a vote cast for a small party will be wasted, so they are better off giving their vote to a stronger party that has a chance of coming in first.[11] As a result, an SMD system is much more likely to produce a legislature dominated by two parties, as in the United States, Canada, and the United Kingdom, and to marginalize or eliminate smaller parties.

To illustrate, let's look at the outcome of the 2017 elections for the House of Commons (the lower legislative house) in the United Kingdom. As Figure 6.1 shows, the Conservative Party won 42 percent of the vote and 49 percent of the seats; the Labour Party won 40 percent of the votes and 40 percent of the seats. The importance of this winner-take-all system, built around single-member districts, can also be seen in the case of smaller parties. Some parties with a small share of the vote—like Sinn Féin, Plaid Cymru, and the Democratic Unionist Party—gained between 4 and 10 seats. Why? These three regional parties in Wales and Northern Ireland have voters who are concentrated in local constituencies. The importance of supporters' geographic concentration

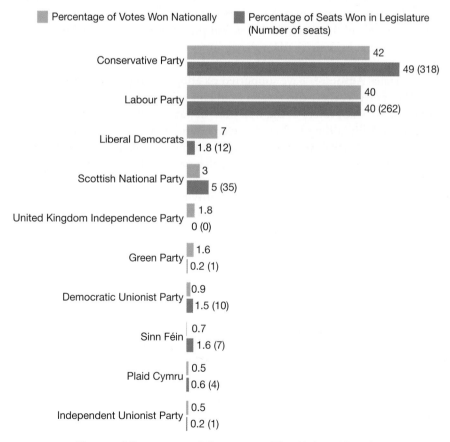

FIGURE 6.1 Electoral Systems and Outcomes: The United Kingdom
Plurality Single-Member District: United Kingdom, House of Commons, 2017

is particularly noticeable in the case of the Scottish National Party and the United Kingdom Independence Party, which we'll turn to in a moment.

In addition to determining the distribution of power across parties, SMD systems can affect power within the parties themselves. In SMD elections, voters are choosing between individual candidates within a constituency as much as they are choosing from among parties. Voters may be more interested in what a candidate has to say about their local needs than in party ideology, and individual candidates may therefore act more independently of their party if they believe that is what will get them elected. This approach to voting is especially likely under presidential systems. When the president is elected directly, voters do not have to worry about their party winning a majority of seats in the legislature so that it can choose the prime minister. National politics thus becomes more driven by local politics.

With a small modification in the electoral rules, a country can alter the impact of SMDs. Majority-based SMD systems, for instance, function in largely the same way plurality-based systems do, except they use certain mechanisms to ensure that the winner is elected by a majority of the voters in the district. The simplest way to do this is by having two electoral rounds: after the first round, the top two vote-getters go on to a runoff election. France uses this system.

In a more complicated variation, a majority can be generated by having voters rank candidates by preference. If no candidate wins an outright majority, the candidate with the lowest number of first preferences is eliminated, and her or his ballots are then reassigned on the basis of the second preferences on those ballots. Elimination of the lowest-ranking candidates continues until one candidate has a majority. This system, called alternative, preferential, or instant-runoff voting, is currently used in Australia. Advocates have supported its adoption in the United States and Canada.[12] Supporters believe this system would increase the chances for smaller parties to gain office, since voters would worry less about wasting their vote.

In 2011, the United Kingdom held a referendum on whether to switch to alternative voting. This move was strongly supported by the Liberal Democrats, who believed they would do much better under such a system. However, more than two-thirds of voters opposed the change.

Quite different from plurality- and majority-based SMD systems is proportional representation (PR), which is used in some form by a majority of democracies around the world. PR generally attempts to decrease the number of votes that are wasted, thus increasing the number of parties in the legislature. Instead of relying on SMDs, PR relies on **multimember districts (MMDs)**—in other words, more than one legislative seat is contested in each district.

multimember district (MMD)
An electoral district with more than one seat

In PR systems, voters cast their ballots for a party rather than for a candidate, and the percentage of votes a party receives in a district determines how many of that district's seats the party will gain. In a simple theoretical version, a party that won 17 percent of the vote in a district would receive 17 percent of that district's seats; if it won 100 percent of the vote in a district, it would receive all the seats. Votes are counted and applied in complex ways that can profoundly affect how seats are distributed among competing parties. Yet overall, in comparison with plurality and majority SMD systems, PR enables even a small percentage of the vote to win representation. The 2014 elections in South Africa, detailed in Figure 6.2, show how the number of votes under PR can correspond much more closely to the percentage of seats won in the legislature. Small parties that would not have won a single seat under plurality- or majority-based SMD systems are represented in the South African National Assembly.

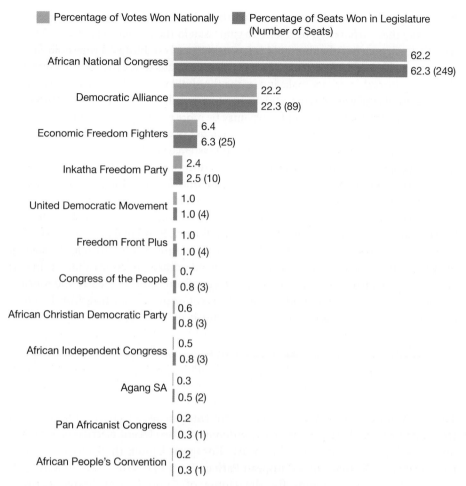

Legend:
- Percentage of Votes Won Nationally
- Percentage of Seats Won in Legislature (Number of Seats)

Party	Percentage of Votes Won Nationally	Percentage of Seats Won in Legislature (Number of Seats)
African National Congress	62.2	62.3 (249)
Democratic Alliance	22.2	22.3 (89)
Economic Freedom Fighters	6.4	6.3 (25)
Inkatha Freedom Party	2.4	2.5 (10)
United Democratic Movement	1.0	1.0 (4)
Freedom Front Plus	1.0	1.0 (4)
Congress of the People	0.7	0.8 (3)
African Christian Democratic Party	0.6	0.8 (3)
African Independent Congress	0.5	0.8 (3)
Agang SA	0.3	0.5 (2)
Pan Africanist Congress	0.2	0.3 (1)
African People's Convention	0.2	0.3 (1)

FIGURE 6.2 Electoral Systems and Outcomes: South Africa
Proportional Representation: South Africa, National Assembly, 2014

Because PR is based on multimember districts, elections are not centered on competitions between individuals, as in SMD systems. Instead, political parties draw up in advance a list of their candidates for each electoral district, often proposing as many candidates as there are seats. If a district has 10 seats and a party wins 50 percent of the vote in that district, the party will send the first five candidates on its party list to the legislature. Political parties themselves decide who will be placed on their party list and at what rank, and they list the most senior members at the top. A candidate would want to be listed as high on the list as possible to gain a seat even if the party gets a small share of the district vote.

Unlike voters in plurality or majority systems, who tend to support only parties with a chance of winning a large share of votes in a district, PR voters are more willing to vote for small parties, since they stand a better chance of winning at least some seats in the legislature. Even if a party wins less than 10 percent of the vote, it may well gain seats, as the 2014 South African elections showed. As a result, countries with PR systems are likely to have many more parties in the legislature. Israel's legislature, for example, has more than 15 parties, some of which are coalitions of several smaller parties. Some PR systems try to limit the number of small parties by establishing a minimum percentage of the vote that parties need to receive to gain seats in the legislature; in Germany and several other countries, the threshold is 5 percent; Israel established a threshold for the first time in 2015 of 3.25 percent. Of course, this also leads to wasted votes, since voters choosing parties that do not make it over the threshold will not have their votes count. Still, the number of wasted votes tends to be much smaller in PR than in SMD systems.

Finally, party discipline and ideology may be more pronounced in a PR system, for two reasons. First, the diversity of parties is related to their need to carve out distinct ideological spaces. This is different from SMD systems, in which parties want to reach as many people as possible in order to win a plurality or majority. Second, PR may lead to more internally disciplined parties, since those who do not follow the party rules can be dropped from the party lists in the next election. Where PR is combined with a parliamentary system, party discipline may be even greater because it can make the difference between stable government and a vote of no confidence. Brazil makes for an interesting contrast. In addition to a strong presidency, the legislature uses an "open-list" system of PR, where voters not only choose a party but also select their preferred candidate in that party. Seats are then allocated by the percentages of votes cast for a party and for each candidate in that party. This leads to candidates competing as much against their own party members as the opposing parties, which weakens party cohesion.

UK

DO ELECTORAL SYSTEMS MATTER? THE UNITED KINGDOM, UKIP, AND SNP

To further illustrate the impact of these different systems, let's return to the case of the United Kingdom and examine the outcomes of two recent elections conducted during a single year. As a member of the European Union, the United Kingdom participated in the May 2014 European Parliament (EP) elections and in May 2015 conducted national elections for the House of Commons. Although national parliamentary elections in the United Kingdom employ the SMD electoral system, the EP relies on a PR system to seat its members. The United Kingdom was allotted 73 seats for the EP elections divided into 12 constituency districts: nine English regions and one district each for Scotland, Wales, and Northern Ireland. All parties competing for seats generated lists of candidates for each district.

As our analysis predicts, this PR system offered incentives for a wide variety of parties to compete. Over 30 different parties received votes in the election, including the NO2EU and Animal Welfare parties, with 10 parties earning enough votes to seat at least one representative in the EP. Perhaps most surprising was the victory of the United Kingdom Independence Party (UKIP), which obtained both the most votes and therefore the most seats (24) of all parties. This was the first time in over a century that any party other than Labour or Conservatives had come first in a national election. Labour was a close second with 20 seats, and the Conservatives, though leading the United Kingdom's governing coalition, finished third with 19. The Green Party won three seats, the Scottish National Party (SNP) two, and five other parties earned one seat each. While some voters chose UKIP, a strong advocate for Britain's exit from the European Union, to express dissatisfaction with the European Union, UKIP also benefited from an electoral system not requiring it to be the first party past the post in local districts.

Contrast these results with those of the UK 2015 House of Commons election held almost exactly one year later. Predictably, this SMD election rewarded Britain's two largest parties, with Conservatives obtaining 37 percent of the vote and just over half of the seats and Labour gaining 31 percent of the votes and a little more than a third of the seats. Yet even though UKIP earned the next highest share of total votes (13 percent), because these voters were spread widely and thinly across a great many SMD constituencies, only one of UKIP's candidates came out on top and earned a seat in Parliament. UKIP candidates finished second in over 90 of the 650 electoral districts. At the same time, the SNP gained a record 56 seats (three shy of Scotland's total of 56 allotted seats) with only 5 percent of the total vote. The SNP benefited from the tight regional concentration of its supporters inside Scotland. In short, how votes are counted does matter and PR systems do generate more parties, but under the right circumstances, smaller regional parties can still thrive under SMD.

Which system is more representative, SMD or PR? Supporters of PR note that it wastes fewer votes and in so doing allows for a greater range of interests to be expressed politically. These can include the interests of groups defined by existing societal distinctions such as religion and ethnicity. One way to resolve ethnic conflict, we noted in Chapter 3, is to use institutions like PR to allow ethnic or religious groups to advance their causes, especially if these groups are not geographically concentrated and would fare poorly under SMD. PR can also encourage the sharpening and expansion of different ideological views, increasing the competition of ideas and providing a way for new issues to enter the system. Environmental parties, for example, were able to form and make an impact in many PR systems as early as the 1970s, but they remain marginal forces in SMD systems. In addition, when combined with the parliamentary form of government, PR often makes it necessary for parties to form coalitions to muster a majority of votes, thus building consensus across a range of views. Finally, PR's use of party lists can also make it easier for the parties themselves to expand the representation of underrepresented groups, such as women and minorities, by placing them high on their party lists.[13]

Those who favor SMD systems emphasize the benefits of single-member districts and winner-take-all elections. Under such systems, individuals can connect with their elected representatives more easily than they can under PR. As mentioned earlier, since SMD voters express their support or rejection of particular candidates, these candidates form ties to their constituents that are as close as those to their party, if not closer. Supporters also note that an SMD system allows for the creation of large parties that are able to muster the majorities needed to govern without being held hostage by smaller, often fringe parties. The flip side of party diversity under PR, critics argue, may be fragmentation and political instability.

Given that SMD and PR systems both have advantages and disadvantages, some countries have combined the two. For example, Germany, Hungary, Japan, and Mexico use what is known as a **mixed electoral system** that combines plurality or majority SMDs with PR. Voters are given two votes—one for a candidate and the other for a party (these two votes can be divided on one ballot paper itself, or voters may participate in two separate elections, one for the PR candidates and one for the SMD candidates). Candidates in the SMDs are elected on the basis of plurality or majority, while in the PR segment of the election votes are allocated proportionally. The percentage of seats allotted for each electoral method varies from country to country. For example, in Germany, the seats in the lower house of the legislature are divided evenly between SMDs and PR, whereas in Japan, the breakdown is 60 percent SMD and 40 percent PR. Under

mixed electoral system An electoral system that uses a combination of single-member districts and proportional representation

Electoral Systems

SINGLE-MEMBER DISTRICTS	Votes cast for individuals	Candidate with the largest share wins seat or majority	Fewer and larger parties
PROPORTIONAL REPRESENTATION (MULTIMEMBER DISTRICTS)	Votes cast for parties	Seats divided among parties on basis of share of vote	More smaller parties
MIXED SYSTEM	Votes cast both for parties and for individuals	Some seats filled by individual races, some by party outcome	Mixed outcome

this system, voters not only get two votes but also have the option to split their choice, voting for a candidate from one party with their SMD vote while choosing a different party with their PR vote. For example, in Germany an individual might vote for the large, left-wing Social Democratic Party on the plurality SMD portion of the ballot (since only a large party is likely to get the plurality of votes needed to win) while reserving the PR portion of the ballot for the smaller, environmentalist Green Party.

Finally, we should consider what bearing, if any, electoral systems have on executive–legislative relations. First, parliamentary systems that rely on SMDs are less likely to have coalition governments, since small parties are less likely to get into office and single parties are often able to command a majority of seats in the legislature. PR in parliamentary systems may make coalition governments more likely; this form of government can broaden the range of participation but also increase the likelihood for government instability inherent in managing so many contending interests. Second, the electoral system used for the legislature is unconnected to the form of executive–legislative relations. A presidential or parliamentary system may use PR or SMD for the legislature. A country could change its constitution so that the executive position changes from president to prime minister without changing its electoral system, or it could switch from PR to SMD (or vice versa) without having to modify its executive structure.

Referendum and Initiative

In addition to shaping how a voter's participation is counted, electoral systems can affect policy. Although voting is typically used to choose parties or candidates for office, many countries offer the public the option of voting directly on particular policy issues. Such a ballot is commonly known as a **referendum**. In contrast to the more indirect impact that elections have on politics, referenda allow the public to make direct decisions about policy.

referendum A national vote called by a government to address a specific proposal, often a change to the constitution

There is no constitutional provision for national referenda in the United States and Canada (although they exist in some local and state governments in those countries), but many other democracies use them. Italy and New Zealand have used national referenda to dramatically restructure their electoral and legislative systems. In Switzerland, where the political system comes closer to the idea of direct democracy than in any other country, many of the most important national decisions are regularly made by referenda. Constitutions and constitutional reforms are often put to referenda, and some European countries use referenda to approve changes in their relationship with the European Union. These referenda may be called by the government, and the formal power to do so often rests with the head of state.

In some countries, the citizens themselves may collect signatures to put a question to a national vote in what is known as an **initiative**. Such direct participation can help legitimize the democratic process, but some are concerned that national votes place too much power in the hands of an uninformed public, thus weakening representative democracy.

REFERENDA IN FRANCE AND THE EUROPEAN UNION

FRANCE

EUROPEAN UNION

France offers a good example of the ways in which referenda can be used or, perhaps, misused in the service of democracy. France was an early user of referenda going back to the French Revolution, and referenda were used sporadically at the national and local level during the nineteenth century in a binding or nonbinding form (the latter is sometimes referred to as a plebiscite). These public votes were often intended more to solidify authoritarian rule than to empower the public. For example, in 1802 Napoleon Bonaparte submitted a referendum to the public to grant him life tenure as head of state, bypassing the legislature in order to weaken its authority over him. In 1804, he turned again to a referendum to make himself emperor. Not surprisingly, by the twentieth century many French were skeptical of this form of voting.

However, as in previous cases, a domestic crisis and the power of charismatic leadership restored the referendum. When in 1958 the French government faced a coup d'état over the country's withdrawal from Algeria, former wartime leader Charles de Gaulle returned to power on the condition that the country create a new constitution that included a directly elected presidency with the power to call referenda on constitutional and nonconstitutional issues. De Gaulle believed that a directly elected president, combined with the power to call referenda, would concentrate executive power and provide stability. This eventually proved to be de Gaulle's downfall when a 1969 referendum on further constitutional changes failed, which de Gaulle took as a symbolic vote of no confidence. Since that time, the role of the referendum in France has shifted toward international concerns, specifically the expansion of the European Union. In 1972, voters approved new members into the body, and in 1992 approved (though barely) changes in the EU's powers under the Maastricht Treaty. In 2005, voters rejected a proposed constitution for the European Union, forcing the member states to adopt a less expansive treaty, which was then not put before the French public.

Since 2000, there have been more than 40 referenda dealing with international issues inside the European Union. In 2016, the United Kingdom voted to leave altogether (see Chapter 7), and parties in France and Germany have called for similar votes. This might strike us as a healthy exercise of direct democracy. However, at times it can also be seen as a ploy by parties, interest groups, and political leaders inside and outside government to push important decisions onto the voters. Those inside government may not want to take responsibility for difficult decisions, while those outside of government hope to bypass representative democracy and rely more on public passions. If overused, direct democracy can be devalued.[14]

What Explains Democratization in Asia?

Many scholars once regarded Asia as not amenable to democratization. Observers typically relied on cultural explanations, often referred to as the Asian Values argument. According to this view, Asian culture, strongly influenced by Confucianism, stresses deference to authority; an emphasis on community, hierarchy, and stability; and the importance of a strong leader who serves as the embodiment of the state. Democratic values with their emphasis on individual competition, participation, and liberty would run counter to this dominant culture. As we saw in Chapter 3, self-expression values are much lower in Asia than in Europe or North America. But this argument assumes that such values themselves are a barrier to democracy, rather than forces that would shape the actual practice of democracy in Asia.

In fact, over the past three decades several Asian countries have made the transition from authoritarianism to democratic regimes, while others made a partial transition to hybrid or illiberal regimes. The Philippines was one of the first to democratize in the late 1980s, followed shortly thereafter by South Korea. Taiwan began to democratize in the mid-1990s, and Indonesia began doing so at the turn of the millennium. Even in countries where complete democratization has not occurred—among them Singapore, Malaysia, Myanmar, and Bhutan—political rights and/or civil liberties have improved. Backsliding, as in the 2014 military coup in Thailand, has also taken place. In addition, communist regimes in China, Vietnam, and North Korea show little sign of increasing democratization. Yet overall, in the past decade Asia has made significant gains in democracy. Why?

The first and most common explanation for democratization focuses on the impact of modernization. Recall from Chapter 1 that modernization theory argues that economic growth is associated with a number of changes likely to push the public toward greater demands for democracy. Higher levels of education increase political awareness, fostering demands for greater participation in the state. Traditional forms of authority and hierarchy are also challenged. Finally, modernization means the emergence of a middle class, with an increased incentive for citizens to control the state. Such an explanation works particularly well in South Korea and Taiwan, whose democratization followed on the heels of their rapid industrialization. It is less helpful in cases like the Philippines, where GDP was and remains far lower. Nor does it account for the ongoing presence of authoritarianism in Singapore, which has the distinction of being both authoritarian and one of the wealthiest countries in the world. Nevertheless, as we noted in Chapter 4, we do see rising incomes and an emerging middle class across Asia that coincide roughly with democratization.

Societal explanations of democratization in Asia overlap with modernization theory. In our discussion, we looked at the important role played by civil society, defined as a fabric of organizations created by people to help define their interests. In fact, in a number of Asian countries, civil society drove democratization. In Taiwan and Indonesia, environmental groups played an important role; in South Korea, it was labor unions and student organizations; in the Philippines, the Catholic Church. Yet in other cases—Malaysia, for example—we have seen growing civil society while authoritarianism is still entrenched.

What about the role of elites? Recall that elite explanations focus on the distribution of power in society, both economic and political, and on how

Hyundai vehicles wait for shipment in Ulsan, South Korea. In 2015, Hyundai shipped its ten millionth vehicle to the United States.

this might affect the calculations of those in power. A more equal society means a political system where those in power do not monopolize wealth and therefore are less threatened by a loss of political power. South Korea and Taiwan's industrialization, for example, also created a political-economic system where inequality was relatively low and the Human Development Index score relatively high. On the other side, another elite role we have overlooked is that played by pro-democracy leaders. In several Asian cases, individuals like Kim Dae Jung in South Korea, Corazon Aquino in the Philippines, and Aung San Suu Kyi in Myanmar were critical in galvanizing and sustaining support for democracy, especially where dictators have been especially resistant to giving up power.

Finally, we should not overlook the role of international factors. Starting in the mid-1980s, the United States began putting pressure on authoritarian leaders in Asia. Democracy assistance by states and international nongovernmental organizations also expanded during the 1990s, supporting civil society in particular. We should also not underestimate the impact of demonstration effects. Once democratization began in the region, it increased expectations in neighboring states that such transitions were indeed possible. We saw similar kinds of regional waves in Latin America and Eastern Europe.

This discussion raises an interesting question about the big outlier in Asia: China. By some indicators, China seems primed for democratization. Levels of development and incomes have risen. We can see the emergence of civil society, such as new religious organizations and environmental groups. At the same time, growing inequality and the increasing concentration of wealth in the hands of party elites means they have a strong incentive to stay in power, as already evidenced by the 1989 crackdown against democracy. Some observers have already asserted that China could be a democracy within the next decade.[a] Skepticism is in order. Earlier some argued that China would democratize by 2015. But if the predictions come true, China's change in regime would represent a historic turning point: a world where the majority of people live under democratic rule.

Civil Rights and Civil Liberties

The last component of liberal democracy is liberty itself. To speak of liberty, we must go beyond democratic process and consider the substance of democracy: civil rights and civil liberties. **Civil rights** typically refers to the promotion of equality, whereas **civil liberties** refers to the promotion of freedom, though the two overlap. Civil rights and liberties include free speech and movement, the right to religious belief, the right of public assembly and organization, equal treatment under the law, the prevention of inhumane punishment, the right to a fair trial, the right to privacy, and the right of people to choose their own government. Rights and liberties depend on the rule of law—on legal institutions that all, rulers and ruled, are subject to and that uphold the laws supporting liberty.

Democratic constitutions around the world vary in the number of rights they articulate and the kinds of rights they emphasize. Despite these discrepancies, all can be characterized by their emphasis on one of two basic kinds of rights. In the first case, individuals are considered the primary vehicle of democratic rights, and their rights are defended from intrusion by the state and other individuals. The South African constitution goes quite far in this regard, asserting that "the state may not unfairly discriminate directly or indirectly against anyone on one or more grounds, including race, gender, pregnancy, marital status, ethnic or social origin, color, sexual orientation, age, disability, religion, conscience, belief, culture, language and birth." This was the first constitution to explicitly deal with rights associated with sexual orientation. At the same time, the constitution bans "advocacy of hatred that is based on race, ethnicity, gender or religion," which some would regard as a violation of individual free speech. Similarly, Germany's constitution has strong provisions for individual rights, but it also asserts, "Parties that, by reason of their aims or the behavior of their adherents, seek to undermine or abolish the free democratic basic order . . . shall be unconstitutional."

In the second case, democratic rights are seen as institutions created and defended by the state. Thus some democratic constitutions, particularly those of social democratic regimes, speak at length about social or economic institutions as rights, such as universal education, health care, and retirement benefits. For example, the Swedish constitution states that "the public institutions shall secure the right to employment, housing and education, and shall promote social care and social security, as well as favorable conditions for good health." The Brazilian constitution states that among its fundamental objectives are national development and the eradication of poverty, and it includes such provisions as a minimum wage, overtime, and annual vacations. Other constitutions enshrine state control over natural resources, or the obligation of the state to preserve the natural environment. What are the limits of individual rights and liberties, and what is the acceptable balance between individual rights and the role of the state in meeting society's needs? The concept of liberty will continue to evolve.

In the preceding discussion, we see that liberty is not simply the absence of controls over our scope of action—a negative freedom. Rather, liberty is also something that must be created, institutionalized, and defended—a positive freedom. The state, government, and regime are thus central to fostering and furthering liberty. But it would be a mistake to conclude that liberty flows only from the state as a gift to the people. Recall our opening discussion of democratization. Domestic and interna-

civil rights Individual rights regarding equality that are created by the constitution and the political regime

civil liberties Individual rights regarding freedom that are created by the constitution and the political regime

tional institutions, culture, civil society, modernization, committed leaders, and other factors can open the space for democratic change. The challenge becomes vesting that space with liberty—with the institutionalization of civil rights and civil liberties that fuels democratic participation and competition. Where liberty is weak or absent, the trappings of democracy may be in place, but repression will remain the norm. This will be the focus of our next chapter, as we turn to nondemocratic regimes.

In Sum: Future Challenges to Democracy

As we have seen, democracy is one way to maintain a balance between individual freedom and collective equality. It is a form of government whose origins this chapter has traced back thousands of years. In its modern, liberal form, democracy emphasizes individual freedom through participation, competition, and liberty. Participation, often through elections, helps provide the public a means of control over the state and the government; competition ensures an open arena of ideas and prevents too great a centralization of power; and liberty creates norms for human freedom and equality. When these elements are institutionalized—valued for their own sake, considered legitimate by the public—democracy is institutionalized and we can speak of the existence of a rule of law. No one can claim to stand above the democratic regime.

In the next chapter, we shall consider politics when this is not the case. In nondemocratic regimes, all those things we have taken for granted are weakly institutionalized or absent. Participation, competition, liberty, and the rule of law are circumscribed, with the preponderance of power resting in the hands of a few elites who are not accountable to the public. How do these systems come about? How do they differ? Are their days numbered, or will democracy continue to struggle against nondemocratic actors and institutions for the foreseeable future? We will discuss these questions further.

Key Terms

abstract review (p. 154)
bicameral system (p. 153)
civil liberties (p. 172)
civil rights (p. 172)
civil society (p. 150)
concrete review (p. 154)
constituency (p. 162)
constitutional court (p. 154)
democracy (p. 146)
electoral system (p. 162)
executive (p. 152)
first past the post (p. 162)
head of government (p. 152)
head of state (p. 152)
initiative (p. 169)
judicial review (p. 154)

legislature (p. 153)
liberal democracy (p. 146)
mixed electoral system (p. 167)
multimember district (MMD) (p. 164)
parliamentary system (p. 155)
presidential system (p. 156)
proportional representation (PR) (p. 162)
referendum (p. 168)
republicanism (p. 147)
rule of law (p. 154)
semi-presidential system (p. 158)
separation of powers (p. 147)
single-member district (SMD) (p. 162)
unicameral system (p. 153)
vote of no confidence (p. 156)

Then-leader of the United Kingdom Independence Party (UKIP) Nigel Farage shortly before the successful referendum to leave the European Union on June 23, 2016. UKIP and other supporters of leaving the EU relied in part on fears of immigration from inside and outside Europe.

Developed Democracies

Is democracy the key to peace and prosperity?

EVER SINCE THE EUROPEAN UNION (EU) was founded in 1951, some have been skeptical about its objectives and suspicious of its powers. The United Kingdom did not apply to join until 10 years later, and even then it was blocked by the French until 1973. Norway declined to join, as did Switzerland. Countries have also balked at new treaties that expanded the EU's powers, including adoption of the euro as a single currency in 2000. But in general, Euroskepticism has existed on the margins of the EU as it continued to expand in members and powers. By the mid-2000s, some even imagined—and wrote entire books about—how the European Union was on the road to becoming a "United States of Europe" and a superpower that would end American dominance.[1]

What a difference a decade makes. Even as pundits were lauding the emergence of this imagined superpower, hostility toward the EU among its citizens was growing. Rather than generating a common European identity, as its founders imagined, the EU began to generate a backlash across a number of nation-states. Economic recession led many to criticize the EU for being too bureaucratic, too economically liberal (or not liberal enough), and undemocratic. These concerns merged with fears of immigration and its impact on jobs, national identity, and political culture. Rising Euroskepticism began to shape domestic politics in a number of important states.

The United Kingdom Independence Party (UKIP) is one example of a Euroskeptic force. Founded in 1993, for years it was largely on the fringe of British politics. Yet in recent years, UKIP began to attract more supporters through its blunt party platform to leave the European Union. In the 2014 direct elections to the EU's European Parliament (EP), UKIP came in first place, winning 28 percent of the vote and 24 of the UK's 73 seats. As the UKIP leader, Nigel Farage, put it, European integration, once seemingly inevitable, was no longer so. Hoping to stem this rising Euroskepticism, the UK's ruling Conservative Party offered a referendum on continued membership in the European Union. UKIP and other backers of a British exit or "Brexit" argued that only by leaving the EU could the country control its borders, trade, and foreign policy, and retain British identity in the face of global challenges. Such populist arguments appealed to individuals across the political spectrum, but by and large they tended to appeal to older individuals and those with less education who believed that they had been hurt the most by globalization. While prediction markets (see Chapter 1) expected that the referendum would fail, on June 23, 2016, 52 percent of British voters chose Brexit. Article 50 of the Treaty on the European Union allows for any member state to withdraw, setting a two-year time limit to complete negotiations. However, this has never been put into practice, and it remains unclear how "hard" or "soft" the United Kingdom's exit will be in such areas as trade and common regulations.

Britain is not the only country where such parties have gained in power (though UKIP won no seats in the 2017 UK national elections). France, traditionally an engine for European integration alongside Germany, similarly has seen the rise of the Euroskeptic National Front. The Front has long tapped into a current of French nationalism that views the EU as a threat to national values, and Europe's economic recession provided a new opportunity for the party to make its case. Unlike UKIP, whose liberal orientation led its members to portray the EU as a regulatory monster that stifled British enterprise, the National Front took the opposite position by asserting that European integration was destroying the French economy through economic liberalization. Both parties, however, have in common a view that immigration from within and without the EU is a threat to jobs and national identity. As with UKIP, the Front came in first place in the 2014 EP elections in France, winning 25 percent of the votes and 24 of 74 available seats. The National Front's leader, Marine Le Pen, was a strong candidate in the 2017 presidential elections, coming in second place (albeit far behind the winner, Emmanuel Macron).

An optimistic interpretation could be that Euroskepticism and Brexit will open the doors for important reforms inside the EU and a deepening relationship between EU members. This may be more likely if Britain's economy declines as a result of Brexit, weakening other Euroskeptic groups. A less sanguine view is that Euroskepticism, fueled by fears of immigration and globalization, will expand across the

European Union, weakening it. Rather than a United States of Europe, a divided EU will be unable to meet the needs of its citizens or play an important role in the global community. Growing numbers of individuals across the developed democracies are now questioning economic and political integration, to a degree not seen since before World War II. What we had considered to be a relatively fixed set of institutions and values that represented developed democracies is now openly challenged.

LEARNING OBJECTIVES

- Describe the characteristics of developed democracies.
- Analyze how political, economic, and social institutions differ in the developed democracies.
- Compare how developed democracies have faced challenges to sovereignty.
- Analyze how developed democracies have seen a rise in postmodern values.
- Evaluate the challenges faced by the developed democracies' postindustrial economic institutions.

NOW THAT WE ARE FAMILIAR with various concepts that help us compare a range of political institutions, we can investigate how these institutions manifest themselves in the world. Instead of grouping countries by geographic location, we will look at countries whose political institutions resemble one another. Our first group of countries is commonly known as the **developed democracies**. This term is problematic since it is both value laden and teleological—that is, *developed democracies* connotes some "end stage" that other countries are heading toward. In recalling the hubris and disappointment of the behavioral movement and modernization theory, we should emphasize that the term can cover a diverse set of countries that may get only more diverse in the future. We use the term here to refer to countries that have institutionalized democracy and a high level of economic development and prosperity.

In this chapter, we look at the basic institutions and dynamics that characterize developed democracies, applying the concepts we have studied so far. What do developed democracies have in common with one another? What differences exist between them? This comparison will lead us to a discussion of the roles of individual freedom and collective equality in the developed democracies. How do these countries reconcile the two? Once we have a grasp of these ideas, we will move on to consider the challenges their institutions face in contemporary politics. The forces of integration and devolution—the transfer of power to international institutions or down to local ones—may challenge the notion of state sovereignty that has been at the core of modern politics. In economics, too, the emergence of postindustrial societies is transforming the very nature of wealth and labor. Similar changes can be seen in societal institutions as old and new social values come into conflict. All of these issues are compounded by demographic challenges as the populations of the developed democracies become older and more diverse.

> **developed democracy**
> A country with institutionalized democracy and a high level of economic development

Are the developed democracies on the brink of transformation, or are they approaching stagnation and decline? And what are the implications of either for comparative and international politics? This chapter lays out evidence that will allow us to consider possible scenarios.

Defining Developed Democracy

What, exactly, are developed democracies? In the past, scholars typically spoke of economically developed countries as belonging to the "First World." They were contrasted with the countries of the "Second World," or communist states, and those of the "Third World," the vast body of less-developed countries. Dividing countries into these three "worlds" was always somewhat problematic, since even within each category there was a great deal of institutional diversity. With the end of the Cold War and the collapse of communism, the three-worlds approach became even less useful.

Instead of using this problematic three-worlds approach, this book refers to "developed democracies," "communist and postcommunist countries," and "developing countries." These categories, too, have their limitations, and critics might say they differ from past approaches only in name. Indeed, in 2016 the World Bank began to phase out its classifications of developed and developing countries.[2] However, being able to make comparisons requires some control over variables, and as we discussed in Chapter 1, grouping countries by institutional similarities is a useful way to study politics. In Table 7.1, we list what we can consider developed democracies. At the same time, some of these countries will also appear in the subsequent chapters on postcommunist and developing countries, especially those that lie in an area of transition from one category to another.

How do we determine which countries are developed democracies? In the area of democracy, we can rely on the factors discussed in Chapter 6, looking at the degree and institutionalization of participation, competition, and liberty in each. In the area of economic development and prosperity, we can consider the issues raised in Chapter 4: the presence of private property, open markets, and the level of gross domestic product (GDP) at purchasing power parity (PPP). We might also consider the kind of economic output that countries produce. Developed democracies tend to derive a relatively small portion of their GDP from agriculture and industrial production. During and after the Industrial Revolution, industry displaced agriculture in many of today's developed democracies; today, industry itself is increasingly being displaced by the service sector, which includes jobs in retail sales, information technology, and education. Finally, we should also consider the output of wealth by looking at the overall well-being of society (as measured by the Human Development Index—HDI).

Table 7.2 provides measurements of some of these factors for several developed democracies as well as for a few nondeveloped democracies. The countries listed as developed democracies in Tables 7.1 and 7.2 have high levels of economic development (GDP per capita at PPP of over $13,000) and small agricultural sectors. They are also democratic regimes and are among the top third of countries on the HDI, classified by the United Nations as having very high or high levels of human development. As we noted earlier, within this category are several recently democratized and postcommunist countries that also exhibit the hallmarks of economic development and

TABLE 7.1 Developed Democracies, 2017

NORTH AND SOUTH AMERICA		EUROPE	
Antigua and Barbuda	Costa Rica	Andorra	Latvia
Argentina	Grenada	Austria	Lithuania
Bahamas	Mexico	Belgium	Luxembourg
Barbados	Palau	Bulgaria	Malta
Bermuda	Panama	Croatia	Netherlands
Brazil	Trinidad and Tobago	Cyprus	Poland
Canada	United States	Czech Republic	Portugal
Chile	Uruguay	Denmark	Romania
		Estonia	Slovakia
		Finland	Slovenia
		France	Spain
		Germany	Sweden
		Greece	United Kingdom
		Hungary	Iceland*
		Ireland	Norway*
		Italy	Switzerland*

ASIA/AUSTRALIA		MIDDLE EAST AND AFRICA	
Australia	South Korea	Israel	
Japan	Taiwan		
New Zealand			

*Non-EU members.

democracy. They contrast with countries that are poorer, have low HDI rankings, and lack a strong industrial and service sector and/or institutionalized liberal democracy.

Given our definition of developed democracies, the countries that we place in this category are diverse—and they have grown markedly more diverse over the past decade. For example, countries such as Poland and South Korea were historically categorized as part of the Second and Third Worlds, respectively. But with economic and political changes in both countries, it makes little sense to think of them in these terms. Postcommunist Poland now has much more in common economically and politically with countries like Germany and France than it has with neighboring countries that also were once part of the communist world; South Korea has more in common with Japan and the United States than it does with other, less-developed countries in Asia.

This group is not meant to be exhaustive or definitive—no doubt many readers would add or remove some countries on the basis of other criteria. In fact, a number of these countries will be discussed again in the chapters on postcommunist countries and developing countries. The central point for us to consider is that due to recent global economic and political changes, the camp of developed democracies has expanded well beyond its traditional provinces of Western Europe and North America.

TABLE 7.2 Developed Democracies in Comparative Perspective, 2016

COUNTRY	PERCENTAGE OF GDP CONTRIBUTED BY:			GDP PER CAPITA (PPP IN US $)	DEMOCRACY?	HDI RANK
	AGRICULTURE	INDUSTRY	SERVICES			
Germany	1	30	69	48,700	Y	4
United States	1	19	80	57,500	Y	10
Canada	2	28	70	44,000	Y	10
Sweden	2	34	64	49,200	Y	14
United Kingdom	1	19	80	42,600	Y	16
South Korea	2	38	60	35,800	Y	18
Japan	1	28	71	41,500	Y	17
France	2	19	79	41,500	Y	21
Poland	3	39	59	27,800	Y	36
Saudi Arabia	2	43	55	54,400	N	38
Iran	9	40	51	17,000	N	69
Mexico	4	33	63	17,900	Y*	77
Brazil	6	22	72	15,100	Y	79
China	9	41	51	15,500	N	90
South Africa	2	29	69	13,200	Y	119
India	17	30	45	6,600	Y	131
Nigeria	21	19	60	5,900	N*	152

*Freedom House categorizes Mexico and Nigeria as partly free.

Note: Countries in italics are *not* developed democracies.

Sources: CIA World Factbook, World Bank, United Nations Development Programme.

MEXICO

MEXICO'S TRANSITION TO A MIDDLE-CLASS SOCIETY

It might surprise readers to see Mexico included in our discussion of advanced democracies. After all, most of us are aware of the steady flow of Mexicans who attempt to enter the United States in search of economic opportunities and the drug war that continues to wreak havoc on Mexican society.

But Mexico has undergone a dramatic socioeconomic shift over the last two decades. For much of the twentieth century, Mexico had a one-party authoritarian regime. It had a highly protected economy that was heavily dependent on oil exports. The mercantilist economy was inefficient, produced very high domestic prices for consumer goods, and was wracked by corruption and clientelism.

Today, Mexico has become a democracy (though one facing serious challenges) and has become an icon of globalization. It has one of the world's most open economies that is heavily dependent on the trade of manufactured goods like appliances and automobiles, and oil no longer dominates Mexican trade. This economic change began during the 1980s, in the twilight of Mexican authoritarianism, when Mexico responded to a serious economic crisis by lowering trade barriers and privatizing state-owned enterprises. Mexico entered the North American Free Trade Agreement (NAFTA) with the United States and Canada, which created new competition within Mexico and gave Mexican exporters access to the prosperous U.S. market. As a result, Mexico experienced a surge in manufacturing and a boom in exports.

Since that time, and despite the much-reported violence associated with Mexico's drug cartels, Mexico has experienced an unprecedented period of political stability and economic growth. Mexicans benefited from a dramatic reduction in prices for consumer goods and gained access to new sources of credit to buy houses and start businesses. As a result, most Mexicans today have ascended to the middle class, and three-quarters of all Mexicans now live in urban areas. Many social changes commonly associated with middle-class societies have occurred in Mexico. There has been a significant increase of women in the workforce, a dramatic reduction of the average family size, and impressive increases in Mexicans' average educational level. Mexico's new affluence means that far more citizens own their homes and have gained access to modern appliances, cars, and computers.

If Mexico has become or is close to becoming a developed democracy, how can we explain Mexican immigration to the United States? As we have seen, the transformation of the Mexican economy that has come from its economic liberalization and globalization has made Mexico a middle-class society. But as is the case with most economic change, it also created a large number of individuals who have not benefited equally from that change. Millions of small farmers, especially those located in Mexico's poor and rural south, were driven out of business and off their land when faced with competition from more efficiently produced U.S. agricultural imports. Mexico's economic metamorphosis raised the standard of living of and created new opportunities for millions of Mexicans in the middle class, but the lives of many other Mexicans worsened as a result of the changes. Inequality is high, and Mexico's economic growth, hampered by the vestiges of decades of protectionism and authoritarianism (corruption, monopolies, poor infrastructure), has not been able to produce nearly enough jobs to accommodate those who have been displaced in the new economy. As a result, poor Mexicans continue to seek employment north of the border. However, in spite of what is heard in American political discourse, these numbers are now smaller than at any time since the 1990s, in part reflecting the growing economic opportunities in Mexico.[3]

Freedom and Equality in Developed Democracies

How do developed democracies achieve a balance between freedom and equality? All such countries share an institutionalized liberal democracy, private property, free markets, and a high level of economic development based on industry and services. However, developed democracies reconcile freedom and equality differently, particularly in the area of political economy. Countries with liberal political-economic systems are focused more on individual freedoms than on collective equality and so limit the role of the state in regulating the market and providing public goods, whereas social democratic political-economic systems normally do the opposite. Mercantilist systems, meanwhile, tend to focus more on development than either freedom or equality. Despite this wide variation, however, these countries are united by common democratic regimes and political-economic institutions.

First, consider the role of freedom: all developed democracies are institutionalized liberal democracies, sharing a belief in participation, competition, and liberty. Yet they define these terms differently. For example, civil rights or liberties may be expanded or restricted without calling into question the democratic nature of a country. Take the case of abortion. Some developed democracies, such as Sweden, Greece, and Canada, allow abortions during a pregnancy's first trimester with relatively few restrictions. In other countries, such as South Korea, Argentina, and Poland, abortions have significant limitations. And some developed democracies ban abortions altogether or allow them only under exceptional circumstances (Chile, Mexico, Brazil, and Ireland, for example). We can find similar discrepancies in the regulation of prostitution, drugs, or hate speech or in the degree to which privacy is protected from state or economic actors. The judicial systems of developed democracies interpret and defend their citizens' rights in various ways. Some of these countries rely on vigorous constitutional courts whose wide array of powers allows them to overturn legislation; other courts play a more conservative role, circumscribed by the existing forms of abstract and concrete review (see Chapter 6).

The public's level of political participation also varies among developed democracies. One or more of the electoral systems discussed in Chapter 6 can be found in all these countries. Their use of referenda and initiatives also differs greatly. Most developed democracies use them to some degree, although in a few countries (like the United States and Germany) such votes take place only at the local level, and in some others (like Japan) not at all. Nor is electoral competition uniform across the developed democracies. Its variations include the ways in which political parties and campaigns are funded: some countries limit the amount of money that private actors can contribute to any political party or candidate and require the disclosure of the source of private political contributions.

Politics are also shaped by the electoral systems in use. The majority of developed democracies rely on some form of proportional representation to elect their legislatures, but some developed democracies (the United States, France, the United Kingdom, Australia, and Canada) rely on some form of single-member district plurality or majority. Another group (including Mexico, Hungary, Italy, and Japan) uses mixed electoral systems that combine proportional representation and single-member districts. The role of the executive, too, differs. As we read in Chapter 6, prime ministers tend to be the dominant executive in most developed democracies, though we find purely presidential systems in the United States, Chile, Brazil, and Mexico and semi-presidential systems in France and South Korea. Some of these states have federal systems and others are unitary; their legislatures may be bicameral or unicameral. All these institutions manage liberal democracy in different ways.

In short, developed democracies are politically diverse. They all guarantee participation, competition, and liberty, but they differ in where the boundaries of these elements are drawn and how they are exercised. Freedom is a basic guarantee of the state to its citizens, but the form and content of freedom vary from case to case.

In addition to a commitment to freedom, developed democracies share a similar approach to equality that emphasizes capitalism—that is, private property and free markets. This approach appears to have generated a great deal of economic prosperity—basic standards of living are higher across the developed democracies than in other countries, and life expectancy is over 70 years (over 80 in some countries). But this prosperity coexists with varying degrees of inequality, and the wealth is sometimes concentrated disproportionately among certain ethnic groups. Recall from Chapter 4 that the Gini index, a measurement of inequality around the world, found a surprising amount of difference even among countries whose levels of economic development were roughly the same. For example, Germany, Canada, and the United States have comparable levels of economic development as measured by GDP but very different levels of inequality as measured by the Gini index.

This difference in equality is in part a function of the role of the state. Across the developed democracies, the economic functions of the state, including its role in the distribution of wealth, differ greatly. In the United States, Mexico, and Japan, the state expends relatively little on social welfare programs. Individuals or families have greater responsibility for funding basic needs, and the total tax burden on the public in these countries is typically lower as a result. In social democratic systems, such as those in much of Europe, taxation is often higher and the resulting revenues are used for income redistribution through an extensive system of social expenditures. Here, too, social democratic systems are not uniform; some have more job protection or high levels of unemployment insurance. All of these variations do not change the fact that in each developed democracy, private property and free markets are fundamental institutions (Table 7.3).

In sum, the developed democracies share a basic set of institutions through which they reconcile freedom and equality. These institutions include liberal democracy, with its emphasis on participation, competition, and liberty; and capitalism,

TABLE 7.3 Income Redistribution in Developed Democracies

COUNTRY	POLITICAL-ECONOMIC SYSTEM	TAXES AS A PERCENTAGE OF GDP, 2017	GINI INDEX
Sweden	Social democratic	43	25
Germany	Social democratic	36	30
France	Social democratic	45	29
Canada	Liberal	31	32
United Kingdom	Liberal	33	33
Japan	Mercantilist	30	38
United States	Liberal	26	41

Sources: CIA World Factbook, World Bank, Heritage Foundation.

INFOCUS Political Diversity in Developed Democracies

PARTICIPATION	COMPETITION	LIBERTIES
• Standards of voter eligibility differ.	• Different methods and levels of funding are used for political parties and campaigns.	• Distinctions exist in the regulation, allowance, or prohibition of activities such as abortion, prostitution, and hate speech.
• Referenda and initiatives are used in varying degrees.	• Separation of powers varies greatly and is based primarily on the relative strength of different branches of government.	• Different degrees of individual privacy are protected from state and corporate intrusion.
• Some, but not all, states automatically register all eligible voters.		
• Voting is compulsory in some nations but voluntary in most.		

with its emphasis on free markets and private property. Yet each of the developed democracies has constructed these institutions in a different way, resulting in quite significant variations among them.

Contemporary Challenges for Developed Democracies

modern Characterized as secular, rational, materialistic, technological, and bureaucratic, and placing a greater emphasis on individual freedom than in the past

The institutions that the developed democracies share are part of what makes these countries **modern**—that is, secular, rational, materialistic, technological, bureaucratic, and concerned more with individual freedom than with collective equality. But like any other group of countries, developed democracies are not only diverse but also dynamic; their institutions are subject to change under the influence of domestic and international forces. Indeed, for a number of years some scholars have argued that developed democracies are undergoing a significant shift away from modern social, political, and economic institutions. Those writing on this topic lack a proper word to describe this change, using instead the awkward term **postmodern**. Clearly, this word says more about what isn't than what is.

postmodern Characterized by a set of values that center on "quality of life" considerations and give less attention to material gain

We'll spend the remainder of this chapter considering the challenges to modernity in the developed democracies and whether these challenges are indicators of dramatic change. If so, are the developed democracies making a transition to postmodernity, and what would that mean? Or is change overstated or perhaps not in the direction we imagine? These are big questions that lie in the realm of speculation and rely on fragmentary evidence. We will look at them in the context of the categories that have defined our discussion up to this point: political, societal, and economic institutions.

Political Institutions: Sovereignty Transformed?

In Chapter 2, we discussed a number of ways to analyze and compare states. In particular, we spoke about state sovereignty and noted that state power can be viewed in terms of autonomy and capacity. Yet in recent decades, we have seen a movement toward greater integration between countries and greater devolution within countries.

Integration is a process by which states pool their sovereignty, surrendering some individual powers in exchange for political, economic, or societal benefits. Integration blurs the line between countries by forging tight connections, common policies, and shared rules that bind them together. In contrast, devolution is a process of devolving, or "sending down," political power to lower levels of government. This process is intended to increase local participation, efficiency, and flexibility by having local authorities manage tasks once handled at the national level. Although both integration and devolution can be found to varying degrees around the world, such processes have most profoundly changed the developed democracies.

Many have expected these twin processes of integration and devolution to effectively transform the modern state and sovereignty as we know it. However, countervailing processes may limit, or even end, these movements, as we already saw in our opening discussion.

THE EUROPEAN UNION: INTEGRATION, EXPANSION, AND RESISTANCE

The best-known example of integration, and one that we spoke of at the start of the chapter, is the European Union (EU). While the idea of a unified Europe may seem unexceptional today, it came on the heels of a devastating war between European countries that left millions dead.

In the aftermath of World War II, a number of European leaders argued that the repeated conflicts in the region were caused by a lack of interconnection between countries, which fostered insecurity, inequality, and nationalism. These leaders believed that if their countries could be bound together through economic, societal, and political institutions, they would reject war against one another as irrational. Moreover, they argued, a common political agenda would give European states greater international authority in a postwar environment that had become dominated by the Soviet Union and the United States. Some wanted integration to lead to a federal Europe; others had more limited expectations. With these motivations, a core of Western European countries began the process of integration in the early 1950s. This was a radical step away from sovereignty and not an easy one for any state or society to take. As a result, integration moved forward slowly and in piecemeal fashion.[4]

As the timeline on page 187 shows, the EU developed incrementally. It began among a handful of countries as a small agreement that dealt primarily with the production of steel and coal. The EU then expanded over time to become a body that included many more members and held vastly greater responsibilities. Out of this expansion, a basic set of institutions has developed that gave the EU increasingly sovereign power in many areas over the member states.

The European Council is charged with setting the "general political direction and priorities" of the EU and with helping member states resolve the complex or sensitive issues that arise between them.[5] The council comprises the heads of state or government of every EU member; the EU's own president is elected for 2.5-year terms by the council to help manage its affairs. The president is not directly elected by the EU public, nor does the office hold the kind of executive power that its title suggests.

The European Commission, in contrast, is a body made up of 28 members (one per member state), each responsible for some specific policy area, such as transport, environment, and energy. The commission, confusingly, has its own president, who is first chosen by the European Council but then must be approved by the European Parliament. He or she serves a 5-year term. The commission's president manages the work of the commission, which is to set policy objectives, propose legislation, as well as manage the EU budget.

A third body is the European Parliament. Unlike the council and commission, which are staffed, directed, or chosen by EU member governments, the European Parliament is a legislature whose 751 members are directly elected by the EU member states for 5-year terms. The parliament passes legislation proposed by the commission. It also passes the budget for the EU and approves members of the commission (and can call for their resignation). Each country's number of representatives is roughly proportional to the size of its population.

Finally, the EU Court of Justice, made up of one judge for each country, rules on EU laws and conflicts between EU laws and the laws of member states. Member countries, EU bodies, companies, and individuals all may appeal to the Court of Justice. EU laws supersede national laws.

intergovernmental system A system in which two or more countries cooperate on issues

supranational system An intergovernmental system with its own sovereign powers over member states

As these statelike institutions gained power over time, many people no longer saw the EU as an **intergovernmental system** like the United Nations, whose member countries cooperate on issues but may not be bound by the organization's resolutions. Instead, the EU looked more like a **supranational system**, where sovereignty is shared between the member states. In other words, the EU looked more like "an ever closer union," as the EU itself put it, on the road to becoming a federal state. However, state sovereignty would not so easily give way, eventually coming to threaten integration and unity.

One important point to make about European integration is that this was in many ways a technical project led by elites. Of course, most political projects are shaped by elites, who are able to provide the leadership and authority necessary to create institutions. However, successful institutions are not simply technical in nature; remember our discussion in Chapter 1, where we examined how institutions become valued for their own sake and take on a life of their own. For states and regimes, it is necessary to mobilize the public through ideas and identities, such as ideology, ethnicity, citizenship, and nationalism. Yet after World War II, these were seen as precisely the identities that had gotten Europe into trouble in the first place. Creating a European union was not simply a question of trying to forge a common European identity, or gaining the cooperation of leaders who had been at war only a few years before. It was also a question of whether Europe could transcend traditional political identities altogether—a postmodern view. As a result, European integration was conducted as a primarily technical project, and public participation was limited. The European Parliament became a directly elected body only in 1979,

TIMELINE European Integration

1951	European Coal and Steel Community (ECSC) founded by Belgium, France, Germany, Italy, Luxembourg, and the Netherlands.
1957	European Economic Community (EEC) created from ECSC.
1967	European Community (EC) created from EEC.
1973	Denmark, Ireland, and the United Kingdom join EC.
1979	Direct elections to the European Parliament.
1981	Greece joins EC.
1986	Spain and Portugal join EC.
1993	European Union (EU) created from EC.
1995	Sweden, Finland, and Austria join EU.
1999	Monetary union created among most EU member states.
2002	Euro currency enters circulation; most EU national currencies eliminated.
2004	EU accepts 10 new members, most former communist countries.
2007	Bulgaria and Romania join EU.
2009	Lisbon Treaty becomes new constitution of EU.
2013	Croatia joins EU.
2016	Referendum passes in the United Kingdom to leave EU.

and even now does not take on the important work of creating legislation. More fundamentally, it can be argued that the European Union lacks a democratic regime. While the EU is made up only of developed democracies, and enjoys a democratically elected institution like the Parliament, for many Europeans the EU itself is not seen as a source of democratic values. Indeed, over time many came to see the EU as running counter to democracy, driven by bureaucrats who were unaccountable to their citizens. An attempt to counter this lack of legitimacy with a formal constitution in 2001 resulted in a document nearly 500 pages long. Rejected by referenda in the Netherlands and France, a more limited treaty was eventually enacted in 2009.

The EU's inability to overcome its "democratic deficit," as some called it, was compounded by one of its achievements: monetary union. On January 1, 1999, the majority of EU member states linked their currencies to the euro, a single currency, under control of the European Central Bank. The logic of monetary union was that a single currency would allow for one measure of prices and values across the EU, increasing competition by stimulating trade and cross-border investment within the EU. Moreover, a single currency backed by some of the world's wealthiest countries would increase the EU's power in the international system by creating what could become a "reserve currency" for other countries—that is, a currency with global legitimacy that central banks would use as part of their monetary holdings. Finally, it was hoped that the euro could provide a shared sense of identity among EU citizens and their elected leaders.[6] Not all countries chose to join the euro: the United Kingdom, Denmark, and Sweden all opted out. However, all future members of the EU were expected to join the currency union in the future (as of 2017, six former communist countries had not yet joined the euro).

Why did monetary union undermine the EU? As a federal project, a single currency makes sense, as it does for the United States. However, creating a single currency across many different states, each with its own central bank, is much more problematic. Each euro member state now shared the same interest rate and exchange rate (see Chapter 4), in spite of significant economic differences. For poorer countries, interest rates under the euro dropped, encouraging rising private and government debt. This was particularly severe in Greece, where the government ran significant deficits and racked up debt as a result. When the global economic downturn occurred in 2008, the Greek state simply ran out of money and was no longer able to borrow enough to meet its public needs or cover what it already owed. Fearing economic collapse, other EU members were forced to loan money to Greece to keep it afloat (see "Institutions in Action," p. 198). This action exposed key fears within the EU—not only that problems affecting one member of the euro or EU would ripple across the whole institution but also that to ensure stability member states would need to take financial responsibility for one another. Needless to say, significant tensions have emerged between the EU countries over managing their levels of debt and determining whether some EU members must bail out other members in financial crisis.

A second achievement that has proved a source of conflict has been the ongoing expansion of the EU (Figure 7.1). From 1951 to 2004, the EU grew from 6 member states to 15, and with the collapse of communism in Eastern Europe a new wave of mostly postcommunist countries sought membership. Thirteen new countries were accepted between 2004 and 2013, adding over 100 million people to the EU. This brought the total population of the EU to a half billion (the U.S. population, by contrast, is approximately 320 million) and made the EU's total GDP close to that of the United States.

As with monetary union, the EU's enlargement has fueled Euroskepticism. Many former communist member states are poorer, and many Eastern Europeans have migrated westward looking for work, while many Western European firms have relocated to Eastern Europe to take advantage of lower wages. Both dynamics have raised tensions over immigration and jobs. Indeed, in the case of Britain's 2016 referendum to leave the European Union, a central concern was about immigrants from within the European Union, such as Poland, who are seen by some as competing for jobs. Free movement within the EU for its own citizens (19 million citizens of the European Union now live in a different state than the one in which they were born) has become entangled with discussions of non-European refugees and concerns about globalization. Far from the idea of a United States of Europe, it now seems unlikely that the European Union will undergo any significant enlargement in the near future—indeed, with the UK's exit the EU will actually shrink for the first time.

As we have noted, in some ways the EU has been a victim of its own success. One can make a strong argument that integration not only prevented conflict in Europe but also laid the foundation for economic development and prosperity across the

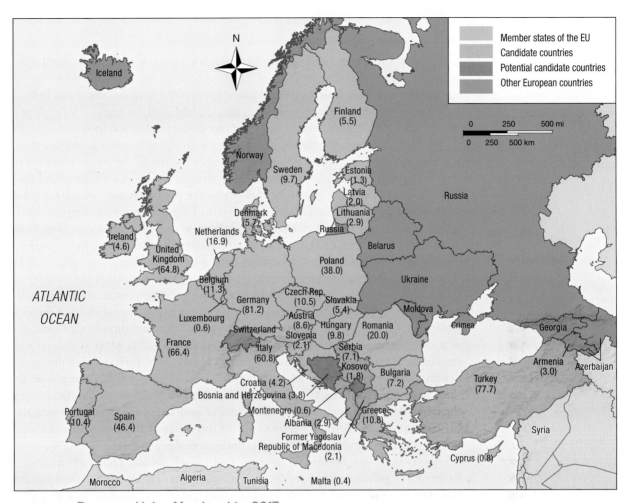

FIGURE 7.1 European Union Membership, 2017

Note: Numbers in parentheses indicate population size, in millions. The UK is currently in the process of negotiating its exit from the EU.

Source: http://ec.europa.eu/eurostat (accessed 7/14/16).

continent and institutionalized democracy in countries that had never experienced it. And yet in spite of these results, the perception among many is that the cost has been an unacceptable loss of sovereignty and weakening of national identity. The lessons here are not confined to Europe. Many have assumed that the European Union would serve as a template for other arrangements that would increase integration around the world, such as the North American Free Trade Agreement between the United States, Mexico, and Canada. But even when integration provides tangible benefits, they are not spread evenly, and many see the trade-offs as unacceptable. We will turn more to this dilemma in our final chapter on globalization.

DEVOLUTION AND DEMOCRACY

As the struggle over integration continues, a related force—devolution—is also shaping how developed democracies manage their sovereignty. As noted here and in Chapter 3, devolution is the process of transferring powers and resources away from central state institutions and vesting them at a lower level. In many ways, devolution reverses the historical development of the state, which is noteworthy for its centralization of power over time. Typically, power over institutions such as social welfare has increasingly moved from the local to the national level. Yet across the developed democracies, moves have been made to redirect power to the local level.

Why this apparent reversal? As we discussed with regard to Euroskepticism, there is widespread concern regarding growing public mistrust of the state, viewing it as too large, too distant, and too inflexible. Devolution is seen as a way to counteract this distrust by bringing government closer to the public, thereby increasing local control and participation. Devolution can also help give voice to marginal communities, such as ethnic minorities, by giving them greater control over their local affairs. Proponents of devolution believe that democracy can be reinvigorated by increasing the public's voice and capacity to shape politics.[7]

How does devolution take shape in reality? One way is through the transfer of responsibility and funds to local authorities, giving them a greater say in how policies are crafted and executed. When local institutions have more control and responsibility, they can craft policy to meet their own particular conditions. One example of such devolution occurred in the United States in the 1990s, when welfare reform created bulk transfers of funds to the states, which could then use this money to design and implement their own particular social welfare policies. More recently there has been a focus on a "new localism" in America and Europe that focuses on the rebirth of postindustrial cities as engines of political innovation.[8] And even the EU has encouraged devolution through its Committee of Regions that focuses on bringing local communities into the EU decision-making process.

Another way to effect devolution is by creating wholly new political institutions to provide a greater level of public participation. An example of such innovation was seen in 1999, when Canada created a new province, Nunavut, out of a portion of the Northwest Territories. By creating this new province, the government intended to give the native Inuit people self-government and control over the natural resources in the region where they lived. Similarly, in 1999 the United Kingdom created new, directly elected assemblies for the regions of Scotland, Wales, and Northern Ireland.

We have noted that of late there has been growing resistance to integration. Is this true of devolution as well? First, we should note that devolution and integration are not necessarily zero sum, where one gains only at the other's expense. As we see in the case of the EU, integration and devolution have been viewed as complementary projects, where greater powers at the EU level would require stronger connections to subnational institutions like regions and cities. Similarly, a new localism focus on cities

---

INFOCUS **Means of Devolution**

- Transfer of policy-making responsibility to lower levels of government.
- Creation of new political institutions at lower levels of government.
- Transfer of funds and powers to tax to lower levels of government, affording them more control over how resources are distributed.

can be an attempt to link urban areas more directly to international opportunities provided by globalization. But it is also true that devolution can emerge out of hostility to the state and integration, fueled by a populist demand for more local autonomy. This can weaken state capacity and autonomy. As we discussed in Chapter 3, when it is a response to ethnic conflict devolution may either help resolve the problem or only increase demands for sovereignty, depending on how the institutional reforms are structured. In the United Kingdom, devolution has gone a long way toward bringing religious conflict between Catholics and Protestants in Northern Ireland to an end. At the same time, it also increased the power of Scottish separatists, leading to an unsuccessful referendum for Scottish independence in September 2014. This issue is resurfacing following Britain's successful referendum to leave the EU, given the widespread support for EU membership in Scotland.

Finally, in the face of ongoing terrorist attacks across developed democracies a number of countries have moved away from devolution in important ways, centralizing and increasing capacity and autonomy as a way to fight the threat of terrorism and manage legal and illegal immigration. As with integration, devolution's pace and strength can be influenced by external and internal conditions. Not long ago, observers saw integration and devolution as inexorable processes that states and citizens could not stop. That no longer seems to be the case.

Societal Institutions: New Identities in Formation?

Just as advanced democratic states are facing a number of political challenges and changes in the new millennium, societies, too, are confronting change and are seemingly being pulled in two directions at once. Some political scientists point to a new set of shared norms and values emerging across the developed democracies that are not bound to traditional identities of nation and state; others emphasize the strengthening of local identities that are turning these same societies inward. These processes are strongly connected to the struggle over integration and devolution. The debate among political scientists is whether these social forces are complementary or contradictory and whether such developments are a sign of greater cooperation or conflict.

POSTMODERN VALUES AND ORGANIZATION

A number of political scientists track the emergence and development of what they see as postmodern values in the developed democracies.[9] In premodern societies, people were more focused on traditional forms of authority and on basic survival; this focus often led to authoritarian systems with clear standards of obedience and collectivism. Starting in the eighteenth century, the countries that would become the developed democracies began to embrace the notions of rationality and science, individualism and autonomy. The modern state, society, and economy promised a world of progress, development, and limitless possibilities, and they did enable unprecedented economic growth, material abundance, and improved standards of living for hundreds of millions of people.

Yet by the 1960s, modern values came under attack, just as they themselves had challenged premodern values more than two centuries earlier. These challenges took several forms. Questions were raised about the environmental cost of economic development. Modern values stressed the environment's utility for achieving material goals, but critics now argued that the environment should be valued for its own sake—a public good to be shared by all. Science, too, was viewed with greater skepticism. It was pointed out that technological innovation did not lead to unmitigated benefits but rather carried with it risks and uncertainty. Fears over nuclear power or pollution led many to believe that "progress" was a questionable goal. In politics, too, nationalism and patriotism were challenged and authority, hierarchy, and deference to the state were questioned. In general, these criticisms indicated the possible emergence of a new set of social norms and values.

Political scientists identify several key differences between modern and postmodern values. As already indicated, postmodern values are much less focused on the idea of progress as embodied by material goods, technological change, or scientific innovation. Instead, they center on what have been called "quality of life" or "postmaterialist" issues, which primarily involve concerns other than material gain, including the environment, health, and leisure as well as personal equality, identity, and diversity. Recall our discussion of the World Values Survey in Chapter 3, where we noted the shift from values focused on traditional survival to those based on self-expression and rationality. In many ways, these values, with their concern for tolerance among different kinds of people and their skepticism of centralized power, reflect both integrationist and devolutionary tendencies.

We must be careful not to overstate these findings, however. The central assumption among scholars has been that all developed democracies are converging toward a shared set of postmodern values, such as the recognition of same-sex marriage. Moreover, as the camp of developed democracies expands, its new members are also expected to trend in a postmodern direction. However, there are two important caveats. First, as we noted in our earlier discussion of political culture, research indicates that a society's religious heritage continues to shape societal values irrespective of the level of development. This may limit convergence in some important ways. Second, postmodernization suggests an inexorable progress tied to economic development. But as scholars of modernization themselves note, if economic development stagnates or is spread unequally, values may not change or even move back toward more traditional beliefs. These factors are in turn connected to questions about diversity and identity in developed democracies.

DIVERSITY, IDENTITY, AND THE CHALLENGE TO POSTMODERN VALUES

The twenty-first century has been marked by a wave of immigration to developed democracies unseen for a century. In 1960, around 4 percent of the population of the United States was foreign born; today, that number is 13 percent. In Canada, the figure is 20 percent, while in Australia over a quarter of the population is foreign born. In many larger countries of the EU (Germany, Spain, France, and the United Kingdom), over 10 percent of the population was born in other countries. There are over 30 million individuals living in the EU who were born outside of its borders. This rapid increase in immigration is changing the ethnic, religious, and racial compositions of these countries. For example, forecasters have concluded that by 2044, whites of European origin will comprise less than half of the U.S. population (down from 90 percent in 1960), and that by 2060, 20 percent of the population will be foreign born.[10]

Moreover, the makeup of the immigrant population is quite different across the advanced democratic countries. In the United States, the largest proportion of these immigrants comes from Latin America; in Canada, Australia, and New Zealand, the largest group comes from Asia; and in Europe, the largest group comes from North Africa and the Middle East. Thus, while many developed democracies are experiencing immigration, the nature of that immigration and the challenges or opportunities it brings are very different.

In many countries, growing numbers of immigrants have led to increased xenophobia—fear of foreigners—in the existing population. This xenophobia has economic, societal, and political dimensions. The economic dimension is perhaps most familiar to us. Although supporters of immigration note the benefits of new sources of labor and skills that can come from immigrants, critics view immigrants as a threat to existing workers, since they compete for scarce jobs and depress wages. Debates in Europe over the expansion and powers of the EU have turned in large part on fears of immigration. Immigration has been a similar sticking point in U.S.-Mexican relations, and Australians express concern over an influx of immigrants and refugees from Asia and beyond. Some countries, like Japan, have avoided this issue by strictly limiting immigration, though this tactic has its own problems, as we shall discuss shortly.

A more complicated issue is that of societal institutions. As more diverse groups of immigrants enter the developed democracies, they raise questions about what it means to be American, Canadian, French, or European. Developed democracies struggle with questions of assimilation and multiculturalism. How much leeway should new groups be given in deciding whether to participate in national institutions and take on national identities? At one end of the spectrum, arguments for multiculturalism assert that societies should help support these new groups, preserving what is distinct about them as a positive contribution to a diverse society. At the other end, arguments for assimilation hold that immigration implies an agreement to accept and adapt to the existing culture, values, and norms of a given society. For countries like the United States, Canada, and Australia, multiculturalism may be somewhat easier to embrace because the vast majority of citizens have come from somewhere else within the last two or three generations, so that the norm is for each person to bring a new contribution to society that can be incorporated into it. Yet even in these countries, people exhibit strong tendencies toward assimilation and fears that the sheer number of immigrants makes assimilation, even if desired, impossible. Openly xenophobic and racist arguments have grown in American political discourse, questioning how institutionalized postmodern values really are.

If multiculturalism is a source of controversy in traditionally immigrant countries, it is an explosive subject in countries where ethnic and national identities are much more tightly fused, as in much of Europe. There the influx of non-Europeans, especially Muslims from North Africa and the Middle East, has raised even greater fears. Racially, religiously, and ethnically homogeneous populations now confront people whose cultural, religious, and historical traditions are quite different. The paradox that has emerged is uniquely postmodern. In the past, many European states prided themselves on their high degree of secularism and tolerance for different lifestyles. But how do they tolerate immigrant groups that may be much more religiously and socially conservative? These are the kinds of concerns that have helped give rise to parties like UKIP and France's National Front, which themselves have drawn on more traditional values like family and nation to build support. The rise of such political parties suggests that postmodern values may be more contingent than we imagine. Under periods of material stress, postmaterialist views are also likely to come under duress, and xenophobia, nationalism, and illiberal political values can reemerge.

Finally, the new wave of immigrants may affect relations between the developed democracies. Although most of these countries, as we noted, face similar questions regarding immigration and its effects, the source of migration differs from country to country or region to region. This growing difference between the developed democracies may pull them apart by shaping different cultural values and external orientations. In North America, migration from Latin America and East Asia may reorient these countries south and east, away from Europe. In Europe, larger Muslim communities and EU expansion may draw these countries closer to the Middle East and South Asia. Faith may also come into play. As Hispanic immigrants moving into the United States are bringing with them Roman Catholic, Evangelical, or Pentecostal religious values, Islam is growing more central to European life. The developed democracies may see less and less of themselves in one another. This transformation need not be a source of conflict; democratic values and a commitment to prosperity link very different countries together as part of the community of developed democracies. But some speculate that a growing divergence of the developed democracies may eventually mean an end to the idea of a single set of secular, postmodern values that would define developed democracies.

Economic Institutions: A New Market?

Our discussion so far has asked to what extent postmodernity is changing state and societal institutions. Our last area of interest, economic development, is perhaps the most obvious. Dramatic changes have taken place in the economic structures of developed democracies over the past generation. Specifically, their reliance on traditional industries, such as manufacturing, has shifted to such an extent that it is no longer logical to refer to them as "industrial" at all. At the same time, long-standing assumptions about the role of the state in such areas as the redistribution of income and social expenditures have come into question, challenging the traditional functions of the welfare state. This situation may lead to an overturning of existing ideas and policies regarding the proper balance of freedom and equality in developed democracies.

POSTINDUSTRIALISM

So far, we have considered how postmodernity has affected advanced democratic states and societies. In both of these arenas, what is going on is open to interpretation. But in the economic realm, the data are clearer: developed democracies have experienced a dramatic shift during the last half-century from economies based primarily on industry and manufacturing to postindustrial economies.

In postindustrial countries, the bulk of profits are made and most of the people are employed in the service sector—work that involves not the creation of tangible goods, such as cars or computers, but industries such as finance, insurance, real estate, education, retail sales, transportation, communication, high technology, utilities, health care, and business and legal services. This shift has been occurring across developed democracies over the past several decades; on average, around three-quarters of the working population are now employed in the service sector (see Table 7.2, on p. 180). This shift has occurred for a number of reasons. Much industrial production has migrated outside developed democracies in search of lower labor and other costs. Globalization is accelerating this trend. Furthermore, technological innovation is changing the requirements of labor. Employees are expected to have higher levels of education than in the past; in the United States and Canada, over 40 percent of those between ages 25 and 34 have a college degree.[11] Automation is also reducing the need for much unskilled and even skilled labor.

Postindustrialism in some ways reflects and may reinforce the political and social trends discussed earlier. The emergence of an information-based economy, for example, may contribute to a greater devolution of power within the economy as firms become less hierarchical and more decentralized, less physical and more "virtual," less national and more international, and as they grant their employees greater autonomy and flexibility. However, for those who do not have specialized training and education—and even for many of those who do—postindustrialism may mean less freedom and equality. Technological changes may well marginalize many workers, creating an underclass whose prospects for upward mobility are limited. We can recall from Chapter 4 that inequality in the United States has risen over time. In the mid-1980s, the Gini index measurement for the United States was below 35; by 2013, it was 41. Increases in inequality have taken place across almost all developed democracies.[12]

Slow economic growth in most developed democracies over the past decade has raised significant questions about the long-term prospects of many postindustrial economies. Some have called for greater domestic and international economic regulation; a rethinking of how to invest public funds in education, infrastructure, and technology to meet the needs of the rapidly changing economic environment; and redesigned social safety nets that can protect the many individuals now on the margins of economic life. Others believe that the answer lies in rolling back globalization, limiting trade and immigration in favor of a more mercantilist political-economic system. These ideas share in common a major concern that the economic changes and disruptions of the last two decades will lead to an increasing concentration of opportunities and wealth into fewer and fewer hands, pushing even the well-educated into lower-paying jobs with fewer opportunities for advancement. This will in turn put pressure on the state to change how it approaches its social expenditures, which we will turn to next.

MAINTAINING THE WELFARE STATE

As our final aspect of economic transformation in the developed democracies, we will consider the future of the welfare state. As we discussed in Chapter 4, for the past half-century a defining element of developed democracies has been the development of social expenditures as a way to reduce inequality and provide public goods through such programs as national pension plans, public health care, education, and unemployment benefits. There can be no doubt that the welfare state has provided a wide array of benefits among developed democracies: extreme poverty has been reduced; infant mortality has declined, and life expectancy has increased; and literacy and education have improved dramatically. Social expenditures have played an important role in socializing risk—that is, making the uncertainties that come with work, health, and age a public rather than a private concern.

However, the welfare state has brought with it costs and controversies that have only been exacerbated by recent economic difficulties. First, although social expenditures have been lauded as an essential part of a humane society, they are increasingly expensive. During the early part of the twentieth century, social expenditures typically amounted to around 10 to 15 percent of developed democracies' GDPs. Currently, however, in most of these countries social expenditures (not including education) consume between a quarter and a third of GDP. This increased spending has required a choice. The first is to raise taxes, which among developed democracies consume nearly 35 percent of GDP (over 40 percent in several social democracies). Of course, if the public is willing to pay higher taxes in return for benefits this is not necessarily a problem, though the ideology of liberalism would assert that such large state expenditures reduce private income and profit and thus hinder growth. The second option is to borrow from the public or other states to cover budget deficits. Japan, whose public debt is now nearly 250 percent of its GDP, is the most extreme example, but the debts of many developed democracies, including the United States, Canada, the United Kingdom, and France, are over 100 percent of their GDP. As with individuals, paying interest on high levels of debt means fewer resources to spend elsewhere and less financial flexibility.

These trends will be magnified by important demographic changes within developed democracies. In 1900, residents of these countries had an average life expectancy of around 40 to 50 years; most now can expect to live more than 80 years. As life expectancies have risen, birthrates have declined. In most of the developed democracies, the birthrate is below the replacement level—more people die than are being born.[13] This is true even in some poorer democracies like Brazil. There are two results from these demographic changes. First, the populations of many developed democracies may eventually begin to shrink. Second, all developed democracies will see a growing elderly population. According to some estimates, by 2050 a third of the population in the developed democracies will be over 65 years old, compared with around 15 percent in 2000. As an ever-larger proportion of the population, this older segment of society will seek more welfare benefits, such as health care, but declining birthrates mean fewer working-age individuals are available to fill needed jobs and pay into these systems.

The solutions are not easy. Increased immigration is one obvious solution, especially given that the world population, most notably in Africa, will continue to grow. However, we've already noted the problems that accompany immigrants who are seen as competing for jobs. This dynamic becomes even more contentious when it involves social expenditures. Young immigrants may in fact be necessary to expand the labor force, but many instead view immigrants as the ones burdening the welfare system.[14] A second course is to cut back on benefits. However, politicians face well-organized opposition to welfare reform, and in many countries benefits have continued to increase even as revenues have shrunk, leading to deficits and debt. A third solution would be to reform the labor market. This could be done by raising the retirement age and making job markets more flexible, thus encouraging more part-time work among parents and younger or older workers. Although there is resistance, many European countries are now raising their retirement ages, which have typically been below 65. Some combination of increased immigration, reduced benefits, and later retirement will be necessary. Otherwise, developed democracies will borrow even more against the young and their future, cutting long-term investments in such areas as education and infrastructure in order to protect benefits directed toward older citizens. This lack of investment and high debt could result in further economic troubles down the road.

Japan provides an extreme example of the complexities involved in these demographic changes and policy responses. The population of Japan, around 127 million, has already peaked and is beginning to decline. By 2050, it is expected to have dropped to 100 million. Moreover, a third or more of the population will be over age 65. To prevent population decline, the country would need to accept several hundred thousand immigrants every year, which would dramatically transform the composition of a country that is ethnically very homogeneous. As can be imagined, people in Japan have little desire to follow such a course; in fact, during the recent economic downturns immigrants have been encouraged to leave, making it one of the few developed democracies where immigration has decreased over the last decade. The alternative is for the country to shrink significantly in population and wealth. If solutions are not found for Japan and the other developed democracies, many will find themselves unable to sustain some of the most basic elements of social security constructed over the past century, and they will face societal conflict that pits young against old and immigrant against native.

DEMOGRAPHIC CHANGE IN GERMANY, JAPAN, AND THE UNITED STATES

GERMANY

JAPAN

USA

If Japan faces the most dramatic demographic crisis, two other developed democracies—Germany and the United States—offer alternative solutions and circumstances. Germany shares many similarities with Japan, including an acute demographic challenge. It has both Europe's largest economy and its oldest population. Like Japan, its society is quite homogenous and has resisted immigration, though to a lesser extent. Similarly, life expectancy has risen sharply as birthrates have continued to decline in recent years from already low levels. By 2060, on par with Japan, over one-third of all Germans will be 65 or older.

But unlike Japan, Germans have proactively sought solutions to their demographic dilemma. The government has gradually raised the retirement age from 65 to 67, pushing employment rates for those in their early 60s from 25 percent a decade ago to now nearly half. Manufacturers have introduced more flexible and reduced work schedules to accommodate a more senior workforce. Efforts have also been made to bring more women into full-time employment while also encouraging them

What Explains the Greek Economic Crisis?

In 2008, a number of developed democracies underwent a profound economic crisis that by many measures was the worst since the Great Depression. These countries saw a sharp decline in housing prices and stocks, high unemployment, and negative or minimal growth. While many developed democracies have since slowly emerged from this crisis, profound effects remain, such as increased inequality. Of all the countries affected by the recession, the worst hit was a seemingly unlikely one—Greece. After 15 years of steady growth, between 2008 and 2012 Greece's GDP fell by an astounding 27 percent, which is roughly the same amount as in the United States during the Great Depression. Why did Greece fall so far?

Greece was a latecomer to both industrialization and liberal democracy. After World War II, the country experienced a devastating civil war that pitted communists against the monarchist government. During that war, both sides received support from their respective Cold War allies. The defeat of the communists and the end of the civil war did not create stability, however. Battles between leftist and rightist parties eventually resulted in a military coup and a dictatorship that lasted from 1967 to 1974. Following the end of military rule, the political parties that came to dominate politics—particularly the Panhellenic Socialist Movement, which ruled for much of the next 30 years—used clientelism to institutionalize their support. This strategy was reinforced by the relatively underdeveloped economy. In the absence of private economic opportunities, political parties could offer state benefits, such as jobs, to their backers.[a]

The result was a system that benefited those connected to the political parties but raised significant barriers to others. The Greek civil service grew large and offered some of the highest levels of compensation. The state created many regulatory barriers, making economic development difficult. Regulations emerged that limited such things as the number of pharmacies, lawyers, and long-haul truckers that were allowed to operate. These regulations have contributed to discrepancies in unemployment; the unemployment rate stood at 25 percent in 2016 (over double the rate across the European Union as a whole), and for those under 25 it was over 50 percent. This situation in turn has contributed to a brain drain as well-educated Greeks have moved elsewhere in the EU.

Finally, the deep connections created by clientelism between the state, economy, and political parties have led to widespread corruption. According to Transparency International, on its scale of corruption Greece ranks 69th out of 176 countries. That is a big improvement due to recent reforms, but remains one of the worst in Europe. Many businesses function in a "gray" or informal sector (see Chapter 10), where they are unlicensed and can therefore avoid state regulations and tax obligations. By some estimates, this group comprises over a quarter of the economy, functioning outside the law. Individuals and formal businesses similarly evade taxes, often by bribing tax officials or simply counting on the fact that an overburdened tax-collection system cannot catch them. This corruption points to a broader failure of state autonomy, capacity, and overall legitimacy; as we have noted earlier, tax compliance can be a function less of enforcement than of the public's general sense that taxation is acceptable and that most people are participating. In Greece, the *fakelaki*—a small envelope of cash, necessary to secure public services ranging from health care to building permits—has essentially replaced the tax system.

A woman walks past the Bank of Greece headquarters with a wall covered with graffiti that reads "Rob to Get Money" and "Bank of Berlin." This reflects the widespread view that the European Union, dominated by Germany, has forced unbearable economic cuts on the Greek state.

the condition that it would reduce its budget deficit. Instead, it fudged its books and continued to run high deficits, which as an EU member, it easily covered by borrowing money. As deficits continued to grow, so did debt.

What finally triggered the Greek crisis was the recession in the United States. Once the U.S. housing bubble popped, investors grew nervous about investments elsewhere in the world—including Greece, whose debt and deficits were becoming clearer. Investors were no longer confident that Greece could sustain its economic situation, or that the EU could or would bail the country out. Short of funds, the Greek government was forced into dramatic austerity measures: tax increases, a later retirement age, limits on pension benefits, and massive cuts to defense, health care, and education. Total household income dropped by a third and still remains below its level a decade ago. Not surprisingly, the economic crisis has led to political instability and polarization. Populist leaders associated with the left and right have gained supporters, including the fascist party Golden Dawn, which received 6 percent of the national vote in the 2015 Greek parliamentary elections and 9 percent of the Greek vote in the 2014 elections for the European Parliament.

The combination of these institutional factors explains the Greek crisis. In Greece, the weakness of the private economy combined with the state's corruption and outlays through clientelism have meant that the government has consistently faced a large budget deficit. Greece joined the EU in 2001, on

THINKING CRITICALLY

1. In what ways did the Greek government's use of clientelism hinder economic development?
2. What role did Greece's membership in the EU play in advancing its economic crisis? What concerns does this raise about the EU in general?
3. How has Greece's political and economic corruption affected the state's capacity and legitimacy?

to have more children. Policy makers have reduced tax breaks to married couples, investing instead in expanding day-care and after-school programs. German law now guarantees day care for all children over one year of age, lowered from the previous standard of three years of age. Finally, the state has taken steps to reverse population decline by relaxing immigration laws, targeting foreign skilled workers, expanding asylum for refugees, and seeking to soften public opinion regarding immigrants. These steps appear to be working.

Although demographic shifts are also putting pressure on the American welfare state, the country's "melting pot" culture has significantly offset these trends of shrinking and graying, and has provided the United States with a potential demographic dividend. As the baby boomer generation ages, the country's proportion of elderly is growing, with predictions that one-fifth of all Americans will be 65 or older by 2050. But at the same time, the overall population will continue to expand. Fertility rates are 50 percent higher in the United States than Japan or Germany, and the UN estimates that the United States will continue to accept a million immigrants each year. By 2050, the United States will have a population of over 400 million, an increase of 100 million in just four decades. And while more than a third of Japan and Germany's population will be older than 65 in 2050, in the United States it will be below 25 percent. But even these demographic changes will have profound consequences not just for the American welfare state but also for society more generally. By 2050, white Americans will be a minority.

In Sum: Developed Democracies in Transition

Developed democracies—their institutions and the challenges they face—are unlike other countries in many ways. Although there is variation among them, these countries are all characterized by liberal democracy and high levels of economic development. They represent what we consider modern social, economic, and political life. Yet their institutions are being directly challenged. State sovereignty is confronted by the twin dynamics of devolution and integration. Social norms are similarly in flux, as postmodern values challenge the status quo and are challenged in turn. Modern industrial structures have given way to a new, information-based economy that empowers some and dislocates others, and demographic changes will affect how countries provide public goods to their people. All these factors can affect general prosperity and shape the existing balance between freedom and equality.

In the coming chapters, we will turn to these same issues as they exist outside the developed democracies. Communist, postcommunist, and developing countries all confront issues of state sovereignty, social values, industrialization, and social welfare. The next two chapters will focus on the unique challenges these groups of countries face in these areas. Will these countries eventually join the ranks of the developed democracies in a convergence of political, economic, and social institutions around the globe? Will they face the same kinds of challenges on the paths to prosperity and democracy? These questions will follow us through our remaining discussion.

Key Terms

developed democracy (p. 177)

intergovernmental system (p. 186)

modern (p. 184)

postmodern (p. 184)

supranational system (p. 186)

British supporters of the United Kingdom's exit, or "Brexit," from the European Union celebrate their surprise victory in the June 2016 referendum.

United Kingdom

Why Study This Case?

For many reasons, most introductory works about comparative politics begin with a study of the United Kingdom. As the primogenitor of modern democracy, the UK political system is at once strikingly unique and a model for many other liberal democracies. The United Kingdom is the world's oldest democracy. Its transition to democracy was gradual, beginning with thirteenth-century limitations on absolute monarchs and continuing incrementally to the establishment of the rule of law in the seventeenth century and the extension of suffrage to women in the twentieth century. This democratization process persists today with reforms of the anachronistic upper house of the legislature, decentralization of power, and two recent popular referenda on Scottish independence in 2014 and British exit (Brexit) from the European Union (EU) in 2016. Unlike many other democracies, Britain cannot attach a specific date or event to the advent of its democracy. It is also unusual in that the main political rules of the game in that country have not been seriously interrupted or radically altered since the mid-seventeenth century.

The United Kingdom is one of only a handful of democracies without a written constitution. Its democracy's longevity and stability have thus depended largely on both traditional legitimacy and a unique political culture of accommodation and moderation. Although its constitution is unwritten, many aspects of its "Westminster system" of democracy have been adopted by a number of the world's other democracies, especially in areas of the globe once part of the far-flung British Empire.

Finally, the United Kingdom deserves careful study because it is the birthplace of the Industrial Revolution, which fueled British economic and political dominance during the nineteenth century. Some have attributed Britain's early industrialization to the emergence of its liberal political ideology. The United Kingdom was also the first major industrialized country to experience an extended economic decline after World War II, for reasons that have been much debated.

ATLANTIC
OCEAN

North
Sea

N

SCOTLAND

Glasgow   Edinburgh

NORTHERN
IRELAND
Belfast

ISLE
OF
MAN

Irish Sea

REPUBLIC
OF
IRELAND

Liverpool   Manchester

Sheffield

ENGLAND

Birmingham

WALES

Cardiff

Bristol

LONDON

Thames

Celtic Sea

English Channel

0   50   100 mi

0   50   100 km

CHANNEL
ISLANDS

FRANCE

The United Kingdom remains a fascinating case. In 1979, Margaret Thatcher of the Conservative Party was the first leader of an industrial democracy to experiment with neoliberal economic policies in an attempt to stem economic decline. These controversial policies were widely emulated in other democracies, including the United States. The Conservatives (Tories) remained in power until the 1997 election, when they were ousted by the Labour Party. Under the leadership of Tony Blair, the Labour Party sought to soften some of the harder edges of Thatcher's neoliberalism while still embracing many of her policies in what came to be known as the Third Way, a political compromise between the right and the left that also informed the improbable coalition that governed Britain from 2010 to 2015. Under David Cameron, the Conservatives won an outright majority in the 2015 election and pursued a more neoliberal platform, policies that Cameron's successor and current Conservative Prime Minister Theresa May has once again tempered. However, the capacity of May's government to carry out domestic reforms as well as its ability to negotiate Britain's departure from the European Union have been severely weakened by the Conservative Party's losses in a 2017 election that deprived the government of its majority in parliament.

Historical Development of the State

Since 1801, the United Kingdom of Great Britain and Northern Ireland has been the formal name of the United Kingdom. Great Britain itself consists of three nations (England, Scotland, and Wales). These three nations plus the northeastern part of the island of Ireland constitute the United Kingdom. All British citizens owe their allegiance to the Crown, the enduring symbol of the United Kingdom's state, rather than to a written constitution. The Crown symbolizes far more than just the monarchy or even Her Majesty's government. It represents the ceremonial and symbolic trappings of the British state. In addition, it represents the rules governing British political life (the regime) and the unhindered capacity (the sovereignty) to enforce and administer these rules and to secure the country's borders.

The evolutionary changes of the state over the past eight centuries have been thoroughgoing and not without violence. But in comparison with political change elsewhere in the world, the development of the modern British state has been gradual, piecemeal, and peaceful.

EARLY DEVELOPMENT

Although we commonly think of the United Kingdom as a stable and unified nation-state, the country experienced repeated invasions over a period of about 1,500 years. Celts, Romans, Angles, Saxons, Danes, and finally Normans invaded the British Isles, each leaving important legacies. For example, the Germanic Angles and Saxons left their language—except in Wales, Scotland, and other areas they could not conquer. Local languages remained dominant there until the eighteenth and nineteenth centuries. Today, we still refer to those areas on Britain's northern and western perimeter as the United Kingdom's Celtic fringe.

Another important legacy was the emergence of **common law**, a system based on local customs and precedent rather than formal legal codes. That system forms the basis of the contemporary legal systems of the United Kingdom (with the exception of Scotland), the United States, and many former British colonies.[1]

The last wave of invasions, by the Normans, occurred in 1066. Politically, their most important legacy was the institution of feudalism, which created a system of mutual obligation between lord and peasant on one level, and between monarch, lord, and vassal on another level. Indeed, some scholars have seen in these obligations the foundation for the eventual limits on royal power and the emergence of democracy. The most important initial document in this regard is the **Magna Carta**, which British nobles obliged King John to sign in 1215 and required the king to uphold feudal customs and the rights of England's barons, thereby subjecting British monarchs to the rule of law. As a result, the United Kingdom never experienced the type of royal absolutism common in other countries such as Russia, and this in turn helped pave the way for popular control over government and the state.

The United Kingdom was also fortunate to resolve relatively early in its historical development certain conflicts that other states would experience later in the modern era, such as religious divisions. During the reign of Henry VIII (1509–47), a major dispute between the British monarch and the Catholic Church led to unintended consequences. When the Catholic Church failed to grant Henry a divorce, he used **Parliament** to pass laws that effectively took England out of the Catholic Church and replaced Catholicism with a Protestant Church controlled by the English state instead of by Rome. This state-controlled Anglican Church was weaker and less autonomous than its counterparts in other European countries, and thus religion never plagued the United Kingdom as a polarizing force the way it did in so many other countries. Northern Ireland, where the split between Protestants and Catholics continues to create political division, is the bloody exception to the rule. A second unintended consequence was that Henry VIII's reliance on Parliament to sanction the changes strengthened and legitimized Parliament's power. As with the Magna Carta, piecemeal institutional changes helped pave the way for democratic control—even if that result was not foreseen at the time.

EMERGENCE OF THE MODERN BRITISH STATE

In addition to the early checks on monarchic rule, three major developments in the seventeenth and eighteenth centuries decisively undermined the power of British sovereigns and are crucial for our understanding of why the United Kingdom was one of the first nations to develop democracy.

First, the crowning of James I (a Scot) in 1603 united Scotland and England but created a political crisis. James was an absolutist at heart and resisted limits on his power imposed by Parliament, and his son Charles I continued this flaunting of royal power, eventually precipitating civil war. The **English Civil War** (1642–51) pitted the defenders of Charles against the supporters of Parliament, who won the bitter struggle and executed Charles I in 1649.

For the next decade, England had no monarch. It functioned as a republic led by Oliver Cromwell, whose rule soon became a military dictatorship. Parliament restored the monarchy in 1660 with the ascension of Charles II, but its power was forever weakened.

TIMELINE Political Development

1215	King John I forced to sign Magna Carta, thereby agreeing to a statement of the rights of English barons.
1295	Model Parliament of Edward I is convened, the first representative parliament.
1529	Reformation Parliament is summoned by Henry VIII, beginning process of cutting ties to the Roman Catholic Church.
1628	Charles I is forced to accept Petition of Right, Parliament's statement of civil rights, in return for funds.
1642–51	English Civil War is fought between Royalists and Parliamentarians.
1649	Charles I is tried and executed.
1689	Bill of Rights is issued by Parliament, establishing a constitutional monarchy in Britain.
1707	Act of Union is put into effect, uniting kingdoms of England and Scotland.
1721	Sir Robert Walpole is effectively made Britain's first prime minister.
1832, 1867	Reform Acts are passed, extending right to vote to virtually all urban males and some in the countryside.
1916–22	Anglo-Irish War is fought, culminating in establishment of independent Republic of Ireland; Northern Ireland remains part of the United Kingdom.
1973	United Kingdom is made a member of the European Economic Community (now the European Union).
1979–90	Margaret Thatcher serves as Conservative prime minister.
1982	Falklands War is fought with Argentina.
1997–2007	Tony Blair serves as Labour prime minister.
2007–10	Gordon Brown serves as Labour prime minister.
2010–16	David Cameron serves as Conservative prime minister.
2016	Referendum calling for Britain to leave the EU passes, and Theresa May replaces Cameron as Conservative prime minister.
2017	Theresa May's Conservatives suffer losses in a "snap" election, forcing the party to form a minority government.

Second, when James II, a brother of Charles II, inherited the throne in 1685, the monarchy and Parliament again faced off. James was openly Catholic, and Parliament feared a return to Catholicism and absolute rule. In 1688, it sent James II into exile and installed James's Protestant daughter Mary and her Dutch husband, William. A year later, Parliament enacted the Bill of Rights, institutionalizing its political supremacy. Since that time, monarchs have owed their position to Parliament. This so-called Glorious Revolution was a key turning point in the creation of the constitutional monarchy.

Third, in 1714, Parliament crowned George I (of German royalty), who spoke little English and was therefore forced to rely heavily on his **cabinet** (his top advisers, or ministers) and, specifically, his **prime minister**, who coordinated the work of the other ministers. From 1721 to 1742, Sir Robert Walpole fashioned the position of prime minister into much of what the office is today. By the late eighteenth century, largely in reaction to the loss of the colonies in America, prime ministers and their cabinets were no longer selected by monarchs but were instead appointed by Parliament. Monarchs never again had the power to select members of the government.[2]

EMPIRE AND INDUSTRIALIZATION

England began its overseas expansion in the sixteenth century, and by the early nineteenth century had vanquished its main European rivals to become the world's dominant military, commercial, and cultural power. Its navy helped open new overseas markets for its burgeoning domestic industry, and by the empire's zenith in 1870 the United Kingdom controlled about a quarter of all world trade, governed one-quarter of the world's population, directly ruled almost 50 countries, and dominated many more with its commercial muscle.

By the early twentieth century, however, the British Empire had begun to shrink. Following World War I, the United Kingdom granted independence to several of its former colonies, and by the conclusion of World War II, the tide had turned even more strongly against the empire. Local resistance in many colonies, international sentiment favoring self-determination for subject peoples, the cumulative costs of two World Wars, and the burden of maintaining far-flung colonies helped spell the end of the British Empire. Independence was willingly granted to most of the remaining colonial possessions throughout Southeast Asia, Africa, and the Caribbean.

The United Kingdom managed to retain control of a few small colonies, and in 1982 it fought a brief war with Argentina to retain possession of the remote Falkland Islands. One of the United Kingdom's last colonial possessions, Hong Kong, was returned to China in 1997. Today, the **Commonwealth** includes the United Kingdom and 54 of its former colonies and serves to maintain at least some of the economic and cultural ties established during its long imperial rule.

The United Kingdom can claim to be the first industrial nation, and this industrialization helped support the expansion of its empire. Beginning in the late eighteenth century, Britain gradually came to dominate textile, machinery, and iron production. By the mid-nineteenth century, most of the United Kingdom's workforce had moved away from the countryside to live in urban areas. While industrialization dramatically changed British politics and society, the process did not create the kind of political upheaval and instability seen in many late-developing nations, where industrialization occurred more rapidly. Because the British were the first to industrialize, the United Kingdom faced little initial competition and therefore amassed tremendous wealth. Moreover, the rise of a prosperous and propertied middle class demanding a stronger political voice also facilitated the country's first steps toward democracy.[3]

But the benefits of early industrialization were also factors in its economic decline. As a world leader, Britain spent lavishly on its empire and led the Allied forces in the two World Wars, which drained the United Kingdom economically. Moreover, as the first industrialized country, it was also one of the first nations to experience economic challenges inherent in "first-mover" industrialization. When British industries faced new competition and the obsolescence of some of their technologies after World War II, the country found it increasingly difficult to reform its economy, which began to decline.

GRADUAL DEMOCRATIZATION

We have seen how Parliament weakened the power of the British monarchs, but at the same time we should note that Parliament itself originally represented the interests of the British elite: only the wealthy could vote. The United Kingdom had an "upper" **House of Lords** representing the aristocracy, and a "lower" **House of Commons** representing the interests of the lower nobility and the merchant class. Two factors gradually democratized Parliament and further weakened monarchical power.

The first was the rise of political parties, which emerged in the eighteenth century as cliques of nobles but eventually reached out to broader sectors of society for support. The two largest cliques became the United Kingdom's first parties: the Conservatives (Tories) supported, while the **Liberals (Whigs)** opposed, the policies of the monarch. The Whigs were the first to cultivate support among members of Britain's burgeoning commercial class, many of whom were still excluded from the political system.

The second factor was the expansion of suffrage. In 1832, the Whigs were able to push through a Reform Act that doubled the size of the British electorate, though still excluding more than 90 percent of British adults. Over the next century, both parties gradually supported measures to expand suffrage, hoping in part to gain a political windfall. The process continued in 1928, when women over the age of 21 were granted the right to vote, and culminated in 1969 when the voting age was reduced to 18.

The gradual expansion of the vote to include all adult citizens forced the political parties to respond to demands for additional services. New voters called for improved working conditions, health care, education, and housing, and they looked to the state to provide these public goods. The Labour Party, formed in 1900 as an outgrowth of the trade union movement, had become by the end of World War I the main representative of the working class and the primary beneficiary of expanded suffrage. By the 1920s, Labour became the United Kingdom's largest center-left party and pushed for policies that would establish basic social services for all citizens, or what we commonly call the welfare state. The British workers who defended the United Kingdom so heroically during World War II returned from that conflict with a new sense of entitlement, electing Labour to power in 1945. Armed with a parliamentary majority, the Labour government quickly moved to implement a welfare state and to nationalize a number of industrial sectors, including coal, utilities, rail, and health care.

POSTWAR POLITICS, NATIONAL IDENTITY, AND STATE SOVEREIGNTY

The Labour Party initiated the welfare state, but British Conservatives generally supported it during much of the postwar period in what has been called the postwar **collectivist consensus**. By the 1970s, however, the British economy was in crisis, and a new breed of Tories (dubbed *neoliberals* due to their embrace of classical liberal values of limited state intervention) began to blame the United Kingdom's economic decline on the excesses of the welfare state. When Margaret Thatcher became prime minister in 1979, she broke with traditional Tory support for what she derided as Britain's "nanny" state and pledged to diminish government's role in the economy. Her government lowered taxes, cut state spending on costly social services, and replaced some state services (in areas as diverse as housing and mass transit) with private enterprise, marking the end of the postwar collectivist consensus.

Yet in some ways, a new consensus emerged around Thatcher's reforms.[4] Although the Labour Party's landslide victory over the Tories in 1997 can be seen as a rejection of some aspects of Thatcher's rollback of the state, the Labour Party returned to office that year under the banner of "New Labour." By adopting this new name, Prime Minister Tony Blair sought to rebrand the party and distinguish his government's "Third Way" centrist program from both Thatcher's hard-edged laissez-faire policies and Labour's more traditional platform as staunch defender of an elaborate welfare state. New Labour held government for 13 years, balancing popular progressive social reforms with policies of devolution and continued limits on social expenditures. The 2010 parliamentary election resulted in a **hung parliament** in which no party obtained a majority of seats. In what can be seen as a nod to both Thatcher and Blair, Prime Minister David Cameron and the Conservatives formed a coalition government with the center-left Liberal Democrats, calling for "fairness," but also "freedom" and "responsibility."

In the 2015 election, voters rewarded the Tories with an outright majority, signaling a conservative shift in the electorate on policies from government spending to immigration. Although his party won the election handily, Cameron struggled with controversial issues involving national identity and state sovereignty both at home and abroad. In 2014, Scotland held a referendum calling for independence from Britain, with Cameron leading the successful effort to reject independence and retain Scotland as a part of Great Britain. Two years later, the entire United Kingdom held a referendum on Britain's membership in the European Union, with Cameron once again leading the campaign for Britain to remain in the Union. In this case, those favoring an exit from the EU and greater sovereignty for Britain prevailed, leading to Cameron's resignation and triggering the process of Britain's departure from the Union after more than four decades of participation in the European project. Cameron was replaced by Theresa May in 2016 as leader of the Conservatives and as Britain's second female prime minister. In a failed effort to strengthen her government's Brexit bargaining position, May called an early "snap" election in 2017 in which her Conservatives ultimately lost seats. This returned the United Kingdom to a hung parliament and left the Conservatives with a minority government.

Early euphoria among the majority of British voters who supported Brexit soon gave way to the sober challenges of disentangling Britain from the European Union.

Political Regime

The political regime of the United Kingdom is notable among the world's democracies because of its highly **majoritarian** features. Under the rules of British politics, the majority in Parliament has virtually unchecked power. Unlike political parties in other democracies, even parliamentary democracies, the majority party in the United Kingdom can enact policies with few checks from other branches of government. Also unlike other democracies, Britain has no formal constitutional limits on its central government, few judicial restraints, and no constitutionally sanctioned local authorities to dilute the power of the central government. Only the historical traditions of democratic political culture and, while retaining membership in the European Union, restrictions imposed by that body have checked the possibility of the British government abusing its power.

POLITICAL INSTITUTIONS

THE CONSTITUTION No single document defines the rules of politics in the United Kingdom, but the constitution is generally understood to include a number of written documents and unwritten rules that most British citizens view as inviolable, including the Magna Carta, the 1689 Bill of Rights, and the 1707 Act of Union uniting Scotland and England.[5] What makes the United Kingdom's constitution particularly unusual is that it also consists of various acts of Parliament, judicial decisions, customs, and traditions. Since Parliament is sovereign, its democratically elected lower house can amend any aspect of the constitution by a simple majority vote. This power extends to the very existence of the monarchy, the powers of regions or local governments, and the powers of the houses of Parliament. Therefore, unlike most other democratic regimes, the United Kingdom has no constitutional court, because any law passed by Parliament is by definition constitutional.

The absence of written constitutional guarantees has consistently alarmed human rights advocates and has given rise to demands for written constitutional protections of basic rights. In 1998 the government incorporated into law the European Convention on Human Rights, a document that now serves as a basic set of constitutional liberties.

IN FOCUS   Essential Political Features

- **Legislative–executive system**: Parliamentary
- **Legislature**: Parliament
  - **Lower house**: House of Commons
  - **Upper house**: House of Lords
- **Unitary or federal division of power**: Unitary
- **Main geographic subunits**: England, Scotland, Wales, Northern Ireland
- **Electoral system for lower house**: Single-member districts with plurality
- **Chief judicial body**: Supreme Court of the United Kingdom

---

Although it is a source of concern to some political analysts, others have lauded the United Kingdom's unwritten constitution for its unparalleled flexibility and responsiveness to the majority. Admirers of the British constitution argue that it has delivered both political stability and flexibility since the late seventeenth century; in their view, a formal document does not necessarily make for a more democratic government.

THE CROWN We can think of the Crown, the legislature, the prime minister, the cabinet, and the judiciary as the United Kingdom's main branches of government. The Crown, embodied by the monarch, is the symbolic representative of the continuity of the British state. The monarch (currently Queen Elizabeth II) thus acts as head of state and a purely ceremonial figure. On matters of importance, she can act only at the behest of the cabinet even though the cabinet is referred to collectively as Her Majesty's government. The British monarchy is a continual source of popular fascination, in part because the institution and all its pomp and circumstance appear to be a relic in the twenty-first century. The reality, however, is less glamorous. The British monarch today is essentially a paid civil servant: the government allocates a budget to cover the royal family's expenses, and the queen spends much of her time signing papers, dedicating public works, and performing diplomatic functions.

The UK monarchy has survived for centuries precisely because it has agreed to act constitutionally, following the orders of elected representatives since the nineteenth century. For example, although the monarch always selects the head of government, the choice must always be the leader of the majority party in the lower house of Parliament. Likewise, the monarch is officially the commander of the British armed forces, but only the prime minister has the actual authority to declare wars and sign treaties.

The British monarchy is a hereditary institution that until recently followed the rule of primogeniture—the oldest son (or oldest daughter if there were no sons) inherited the throne. In an effort to modernize this most traditional of institutions, in 2011 the government passed a bill establishing that the eldest born of each generation, regardless of gender, is entitled to inherit the throne.

There have been occasional movements in the United Kingdom to eliminate the monarchy, but these have failed to garner much support. Despite scandals and the costs of royalty, public support for the institution remains strong. A 2016 poll, for example, placed confidence in the monarchy at an all-time high: three-fourths of Britons were in favor of retaining the monarchy, and only 17 percent preferred its elimination.[6]

THE BRANCHES OF GOVERNMENT

THE PRIME MINISTER Parliament is supreme in the United Kingdom's political system, but real power is concentrated in the prime minister and the cabinet, which together constitute the government. The prime minister is the head of government and, as in all parliamentary systems, must be an elected member of the legislature. She or he is the head of the largest party in the House of Commons (selection as party leader is handled in a party convention held before a general election). Once named prime minister by the monarch (a mere formality), this individual selects the cabinet.

British prime ministers are probably the most powerful heads of government of any contemporary democracy. Because they can expect their parliamentary majority to approve all legislation, because party discipline in the United Kingdom is very strong, and because there are few checks on the power of the central government, prime ministers usually get their way. They wield less power, though, when their parties hold a slim majority (Conservatives, 1990–97) or when they are forced to depend on a coalition of parties (Conservative–Liberal Democrat coalition, 2010–15). As with any other **Member of Parliament (MP)**, prime ministers in the United Kingdom are elected to a maximum term of five years. Before the passage of the 2011 Fixed-term Parliaments Act, the prime minister could choose to call elections at any time before that term had expired and would commonly do so to take advantage of favorable political conditions. The 2011 act fixed the date of subsequent elections for every five years beginning in 2015. The Conservative government's decision to call an early election in 2017 required a two-thirds parliamentary "supermajority" in order to override the Fixed-term Parliaments Act.

Of course, prime ministers are still subject to a legislative **vote of no confidence**, which can occur when the chamber rejects a measure deemed of high importance to the government. In such situations, either the entire cabinet must resign (and be replaced by a new one) or new elections must be called. Although such a check on the government exists, it is rarely used. Over the past century, only two governments have been toppled by a legislative vote of no confidence. In fact, the prime minister can use the threat of a no-confidence vote as a way to rally support. In 2003, Tony Blair submitted a motion to the House of Commons to support the use of force against Iraq even though a prime minister may take the country to war without parliamentary approval. Yet he chose to submit his decision to the House of Commons, threatening to resign if he failed to win support. The tactic worked: despite widespread opposition to the war among his Labour Party backbenchers (MPs holding no government office), a large majority in Parliament supported the war.

Prime ministers play a number of roles. As leaders of their party, they must maintain the support of their fellow MPs. They must appear in the legislature weekly for a televised question period, during which they must defend government policies and answer questions from MPs—and in so doing, display strong oratorical skills.[7] As head of government, the prime minister must direct the activity of the cabinet and smooth over differences among cabinet members. As a politician, she is expected to guide her party to victory in general elections and hold together a sometimes fractious party or even coalition of parties. Even though the monarch is head of state and the nation, the prime minister is expected to provide national leadership. British prime ministers are also diplomats and world leaders.

Prime ministers are always seasoned political veterans with, on average, more than two decades of experience in the House of Commons. As a result, British prime ministers are usually outstanding debaters, effective communicators, and skilled negotiators. In the British system, a political outsider has virtually no chance of becoming prime minister; those aspiring to this title must move up the ranks of the party before gaining the highest office.

THE CABINET Cabinets evolved out of the group of experts who originally advised Britain's monarchs. Contemporary British cabinets have about 20 members (called *ministers*), all of whom must be MPs. They are usually from the lower house but occasionally are members of the House of Lords. The prime minister generally appoints leading party officials to the top cabinet positions. Although the prime minister and the cabinet emerge from the Parliament, they stand apart from the legislature as a separate executive branch and have few checks on their powers.

As in most democracies, cabinet ministers in the United Kingdom preside over their individual government departments and are responsible for answering to

Parliament (during question time) about actions of the bureaucracies they oversee. The most important ministries are the Foreign Office (which conducts foreign policy), the Home Office (which oversees the judiciary), and the Exchequer (whose minister, called the chancellor, oversees financial policy).

One unwritten rule of cabinet behavior in the United Kingdom is **collective responsibility**—even when individual cabinet ministers oppose a given policy, the entire cabinet must appear unified and take responsibility for the policy. Unless given specific permission to dissent from the government's position (as Cameron authorized his cabinet in the lead-up to the Brexit referendum in 2016), cabinet ministers who cannot support a decision must resign and return to the legislature. (For example, three members of Blair's cabinet resigned over opposition to the war in Iraq, and a member of Cameron's cabinet resigned in 2016 in protest over government cuts to disability benefits.)

THE LEGISLATURE The British legislature, called Parliament, is perhaps the most powerful legislature on earth, due largely to the lack of constitutional constraints just discussed. The concentration of power is even more impressive when it is considered that of the two chambers of the legislature, the House of Commons and the House of Lords, only the former has any real power.

The House of Commons currently consists of 650 members representing individual districts in the United Kingdom. Members are elected for a maximum term of five years, though new elections may be called before the expiration of the term in the event of a successful vote of no confidence or a vote to override the Fixed-term Parliaments Act. Government and opposition parties face each other in a tiny rectangular chamber, where members of the government and leaders of the opposition sit in the front rows. The other MPs, called backbenchers, sit behind their leaders. A politically neutral Speaker of the House presides.

Despite the enormous power of the House of Commons, individual legislators are far less powerful than their counterparts in the United States. They receive relatively paltry salaries and have very small staffs and few resources. In parliamentary systems in general, the largest party elects the prime minister as head of government; as a result, political parties, not individual members, are what matter. Thus British legislators follow the lead of their party and, for fear of weakening party cohesion, generally do not undertake the type of individual initiative common to representatives in the United States. Moreover, parties designate certain members to serve as whips, who are charged with enforcing the party line. Nevertheless, MPs are typically more accessible than American legislators and offer frequent "clinics," or face-to-face meetings, with individual constituents to hear their concerns.

Even with these limitations, MPs do perform important tasks. They actively debate issues, participate in legislative committees (though these are less powerful than their U.S. counterparts), vote on legislation proposed by the government, and have the power to remove the prime minister through a vote of no confidence. Finally, although the government initiates the vast majority of legislation, individual members propose measures from time to time.

Thus, despite the doctrine of parliamentary supremacy, the legislature in the United Kingdom mostly deliberates, ratifies, and scrutinizes policies proposed by the executive. The government is usually able to impose its will on its majority in the House of Commons. MPs have traditionally voted with their parties more than 90 percent of the time, though both the coalition government (2010–15) and the current Conservative minority government have been predictably less disciplined.

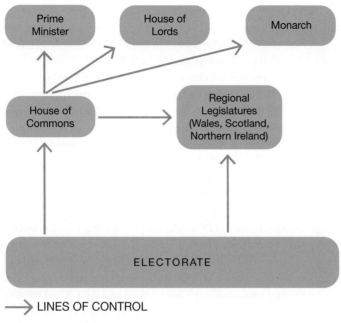

Structure of the Government

Weaker governments can embolden backbenchers in their own parties to defy party whips and vote against their own governments. Nevertheless, even governments with large majorities occasionally lose the vote in the lower house, which suggests that MPs sometimes act independently.

The House of Lords is another uniquely British institution. It was considered the *upper* house not only because it represented the aristocratic upper class but also because it was at the time considered the more powerful of the two chambers. As the United Kingdom democratized, however, it made sense for a chamber of appointed members of the aristocracy to lose most of its power, and today the House of Lords has gradually become nearly powerless. True to the British desire to accommodate tradition, it remains as yet another reminder of the United Kingdom's predemocratic past.

The House of Lords is composed of over 800 members, or peers, with most appointed for life by the Crown upon recommendation of the prime minister. The upper house has no actual veto power over legislation, but it can delay some legislation for up to one year and occasionally persuades governments to amend legislation.

Currently, there is considerable debate in the House of Commons and among the broader British citizenry about the future of the upper house and whether it should be directly elected and given greater powers. Advisory votes held in the House of Commons have been inconclusive but clearly seem to favor a directly elected upper house, perhaps with fixed terms of 12 to 15 years. Not surprisingly, the House of Lords has rejected any such reform, voting instead for a fully appointed chamber. Equally unsurprising may be the hesitance of the House of Commons to enact any actual reforms that would strengthen the legislative power of a second chamber at the expense of its own.[8]

THE JUDICIARY Compared with other parliamentary democracies, the judiciary in the United Kingdom plays a relatively minor role. Until recently, Britain had no tradition of judicial review (the right of courts to strike down legislation that contradicts the constitution) because any law passed by the legislature was, by definition, constitutional. Thus, the role of the courts in the United Kingdom has been mainly to ensure that parliamentary statutes have been followed.

Formerly the responsibility of law lords in the House of Lords, since 2009 a separate Supreme Court of the United Kingdom has served as the highest court of appeal on most legal matters. Reflecting their former jurisdiction, all current Supreme Court justices are also law lords from the House of Lords, selected from among distinguished jurists by the Lord Chancellor (the minister who heads the judiciary) and serving until retirement. Their replacements, however, will no longer be members of the House of Lords, but will be appointed by a commission.

Though politically weak, the courts have gradually become more politically involved over the past couple of decades. In part, this is because British governments have sought legal interpretations that would support their actions. A second factor has been the embrace of international laws, such as the adoption of the European Convention on Human Rights in 1998, which has given the courts new authority to strike down legislation as unconstitutional, though these powers have so far been used sparingly and may be further weakened with Brexit. Still, the days when we could speak of the United Kingdom as lacking judicial review may be slowly coming to an end.

The broader legal system, based on common law and developed in the twelfth century, contrasts starkly with the stricter code law practiced in the rest of Europe, which is less focused on precedent and interpretation. Like most democracies, the United Kingdom has an elaborate hierarchy of civil and criminal courts as well as a complex system of appeals.

THE ELECTORAL SYSTEM

The United Kingdom uses the single-member district (SMD) system based on plurality voting, or what is often known as "first past the post." Each of the 650 constituencies elects one MP, and that member needs to win only a plurality of votes (more than any other candidate), not a majority. Electoral constituencies are drawn according to population and are revised every five to seven years by a government commission.

The implications of this plurality SMD system are fairly clear. First, as shown in the table "Consequences of the British Electoral System, 2010–2017," the system favors and helps maintain the dominance of the two main political parties, Conservative and Labour. Second, and related, the system consistently penalizes smaller parties. The Liberal Democrats, with support spread relatively evenly across the country, regularly garner between one-fifth and one-quarter of votes in many districts, but rarely muster enough votes to edge out the larger parties. In fact, in 2015, support for the Liberal Democrats fell precipitously, matched by big vote gains for both the **United Kingdom Independence Party (UKIP)** and the **Scottish National Party (SNP)**. Like the Liberal Democrats, UKIP's nearly 13 percent of the popular vote was widely dispersed, yielding only one parliamentary seat. On the other hand, in the wake of the failed 2014 Scottish independence referendum, the regionally concentrated SNP swept 56 of Scotland's 59 seats in Parliament on less than 5 percent of the vote. In the 2017 election, however, the SMD system in turn punished both UKIP and the SNP, with the former party losing nearly all of its support and its single seat and the latter losing over a third of its seats.

Third, with the 2010 and 2017 elections as significant exceptions, the British electoral system has generally produced clear majorities in the House of Commons,

Consequences of the British Electoral System, 2010–2017

ELECTION YEAR	% OF VOTES	% OF SEATS	SEATS WON
Labour			
2010	29	40	258
2015	30	36	232
2017	40	40	262
Conservative			
2010	36	47	306
2015	37	51	331
2017	42	49	318
Liberal Democrat			
2010	23	9	57
2015	8	1	8
2017	7	2	12
Others			
2010	10	4	29
2015	25	12	79
2017	10	9	58

Note: Due to rounding, percentages do not always equal 100.

even when there was no clear majority in the electorate. In a system giving virtually unchecked power to the party with the majority of seats, an electoral process producing artificial majorities could be considered a serious distortion of democratic rule. It is no wonder that the parties most hurt by the electoral system, especially the Liberal Democrats, have long (and unsuccessfully) called for electoral reform.

Devolution has permitted greater electoral experimentation in regional legislatures. Scotland and Wales have adopted a mixed PR-SMD electoral system, and Northern Ireland uses a system known as *single-transferable vote*. Ironically, the governing Labour Party that authorized these regional parliaments in the 1990s—and benefited greatly from plurality SMD—favored a mixed system for the regional legislatures because it feared that plurality SMD would produce large majorities for the local nationalist parties.

LOCAL GOVERNMENT

Despite the devolution of some authority to regional bodies, the United Kingdom may be considered a unitary state in which no formal powers are constitutionally reserved for regional or local government. Indeed, Thatcher's Conservative government sharply curtailed the autonomy of municipal governments. The Labour government that followed devolved some political power to the United Kingdom's distinct nations as well as to local governments, and Conservative governments since 2010 have continued to grant more authority to local governments and communities. However, Parliament remains fully sovereign and can enact laws at any time to limit or even eliminate this devolved authority. In addition, unlike other federal systems, Britain's upper chamber is unelected and therefore not accountable to states or other regional bodies.

Although lacking constitutionally mandated local autonomy, British localities have enjoyed a long tradition of powerful local government. Concerned that local governments (or "councils" as they are known in the United Kingdom), especially left-leaning ones in large urban areas, were taxing and spending beyond their means, Thatcher's Conservative government passed a law sharply limiting the ability of these councils to raise revenue and abolished outright the Greater London council and mayor and several other metropolitan councils.

After 1997, Tony Blair restored considerable autonomy to municipal government, enacting reforms allowing Londoners to directly elect a mayor with significant powers and to choose representatives to a Greater London Assembly. Since restoring the office of mayor, Londoners have elected strong and colorful leaders, including Ken Livingstone (nicknamed "Red Ken" because of his identification with the radical left of the Labour Party) and Boris Johnson, an equally controversial and flamboyant Conservative. London's current leader, Sadiq Khan, is the city's first nonwhite mayor and the first Muslim mayor of any major Western capital.

Under the promise of creating a "big society," Conservative governments have sought to continue this process of devolution, requiring greater transparency in local government and giving local citizens more decision-making power regarding local taxation and public services.

As it did with local government, the Labour Party also promoted devolution to the United Kingdom's regions. In 1997, Scotland and Wales voted in referenda to create their own legislatures to address local issues, though their powers are not uniform: Scotland's Parliament is substantially more powerful and autonomous than Wales's Assembly, a reflection of the much stronger nationalist tendencies in Scotland as manifested in the 2014 vote for Scottish independence (see "Scotland's Bid for Independence," p. 228). Meanwhile, the 1998 **Good Friday Agreement** between Catholics and Protestants in Northern Ireland has allowed for the reestablishment of the Northern Ireland Assembly. Some observers view the development of these bodies as the first step toward a federal United Kingdom.[9] Ironically, England, which is the seat of British national government, is the only part of the United Kingdom without its own regional government.

Political Conflict and Competition

THE PARTY SYSTEM

In the United Kingdom's majoritarian parliamentary system, political parties are extremely important. The majority party controls government and can generally implement its policy goals, which are spelled out in the party manifesto.

From the end of World War II to 1970, the United Kingdom had a two-party system. The Conservative Party and the Labour Party together garnered more than 90 percent of the popular vote, with each party winning four elections. After 1974, a multiparty system emerged, which included the birth of a stronger centrist **Liberal Democratic Party** and more recently the UK Independence Party as well as a surge of support for nationalist parties in Scotland, Wales, and Northern Ireland. But since the Conservatives and Labour continue to prevail, the current system is often called a *two-and-a-half-party system*, in which smaller parties still trail far behind the other two parties.

The United Kingdom's party system differs regionally, even for national elections. In England, the three major parties (Labour, Conservative, and Liberal Democrat) compete with one another. In Scotland, Wales, and Northern Ireland, important regional parties compete with the three national political parties. Before turning to party politics today, let's look more closely at each of the United Kingdom's major parties.

THE LABOUR PARTY The Labour Party was formed in 1900 as an outgrowth of the trade union movement in an effort to give the British working class a voice in Parliament. The party championed a strong welfare state and some state ownership of industry, but its moderate politics never threatened to replace capitalism.

For most of its history, the Labour Party depended heavily on working-class votes, but by the mid-1970s, Britain's class structure began to change as fewer Britons engaged in blue-collar jobs. This badly divided the party between radical socialists who wanted the party to move to the left to shore up its working-class credentials and moderates who wanted it to move toward the political center. This internal bickering led to the defeat of Labour in every election from 1979 to 1997 and a gradual process of ideological moderation in the 1980s and 1990s.

Tony Blair, who became party leader in 1994, consolidated these changes and advocated moderate free-market policies with ambitious constitutional reform, policies eventually known as the Third Way.[10] Blair's landslide victory in the 1997 elections marked the beginning of a period of party unity and thirteen years of Labour government, first under Tony Blair and then Gordon Brown. After losing its majority of seats in the 2010 election, Brown stepped down as prime minister and resigned as leader of his party, replaced by Ed Miliband, who became leader of the party and leader of the opposition in Parliament for the next five years. Miliband took the blame for Labour's defeat in the 2015 election and was replaced by the left-leaning **Jeremy Corbyn**, a divisive figure well-loved by many of the party's rank and file but highly unpopular among Labour's more moderate leadership. Despite qualms among party leaders who feared he was taking Labour outside of the political mainstream, Corbyn led the party to a strong finish in the 2017 election, denying Conservatives the majority they had anticipated.

THE CONSERVATIVE PARTY If the Labour Party was never as leftist as some of its counterparts on the continent, the Conservatives (Tories) similarly have made for a rather moderate right. Because the Tories have usually been pragmatic conservatives, and because they have always embraced democratic rule, the party has garnered widespread respect and even electoral support among a wide range of voters.

But just as the Labour Party developed severe internal ideological divisions beginning in the 1970s, at about the same time, the Tories became divided between those advocating traditional conservative pragmatism and a limited welfare state and those promoting radical or neoliberal free-market reforms. Thatcher's rise to power in the late 1970s marked the dominance of the neoliberal faction and the Tories' abandonment of support for the postwar collectivist consensus. The party further split over policy regarding the European Union, with so-called Euroskeptics facing off against supporters of integration with Europe.[11]

Theresa May replaced David Cameron in 2016 as leader of the Conservative Party and prime minister.

The Tories struggled in opposition after their defeat in the 1997 elections. A series of ineffective leaders attempted unsuccessfully to lead the Conservative Party back to power. Following the 2005 elections, the Tories chose the young and charismatic David Cameron as party leader. Under Cameron's energetic leadership, and much like Labour under Blair, the Tories forged a more coherent and more centrist ideological position, captured in Cameron's call for a "big society" and more socially liberal policies regarding abortion and gay rights. In the 2010 elections, Conservatives obtained a solid plurality of seats in the House of Commons, but not the majority of seats necessary to govern alone. The Conservatives entered into a coalition government with the Liberal Democrats, forming an unlikely alliance that required ideological and political compromises from both parties.

The party won an outright majority of seats in the 2015 election and formed a single-party government with Cameron continuing as prime minister. Despite these gains, fault lines dividing the party since the 1970s continued to plague the party. In the wake of the 2008–2009 financial crisis, Cameron's push for austerity measures and a call for leaner government cheered some but angered others. Even more divisive has been the issue of the European Union. Faced with growing disenchantment and fears within his own party and among the broader British public about increased immigration and threats to British sovereignty, Cameron renegotiated some terms of Britain's EU membership and brought this new arrangement to the British people in 2016 in an "in" or "out" referendum. Although Cameron and EU advocates within the party hoped these efforts would both restore party unity and salvage Britain's membership in the Union, the measure failed on both counts. A number of Conservative MPs, including some party leaders, openly campaigned in favor of Brexit, and several Tory MPs even defected to the United Kingdom Independence Party. Likewise, British voters chose to exit the EU, leading Cameron to take responsibility for the vote and step down as prime minister. Cameron's successor Theresa May sought, like Cameron before her, to restore party unity and obtain a strong mandate to negotiate a favorable Brexit deal by calling a snap election in 2017. But like Cameron's Brexit referendum gamble, her effort backfired. Instead of gaining seats as polls had anticipated, the Tories lost seats and lost their parliamentary majority, forcing a weakened and divided Conservative party to lead a minority government.

THE LIBERAL DEMOCRATS A third-party refuge for voters embracing a range of values and political positions, the Liberal Democratic Party was formed in 1988 through the merger of the Liberal Party and defectors from the Labour Party.

The party's ideology is a mixture of classical liberalism's emphasis on both individual freedom and a weak state and social democracy's emphasis on collective equality. The Liberal Democrats have been consistent supporters of European integration, and though viewed as centrist, the party has often attacked Labour's policies as too timid and frequently called for increased taxation and social spending.

In the 2010 elections, the Liberal Democrats obtained the party's highest-ever share of the popular vote (23 percent) and found themselves for the first time in the position of deal-maker in Britain's 2010 hung parliament. They joined a coalition government as junior partners with the Conservatives, but many of the party's supporters felt that it got too few concessions from the Tories in terms of progressive policies and gave up too much (and particularly its leader and Deputy Prime Minister Nick Clegg) in an effort to keep the coalition together. What appeared in 2010 as a great opportunity for this third party to break the Labour/Conservative lock on government ultimately proved to be the party's weakening. In 2015 the party obtained less than 8 percent of the votes and captured only 8 seats in the House of Commons. Although the LibDems picked up four seats in the 2017 election, its percentage of the popular vote declined. Clegg stepped down as party leader after the 2015 election and his successor did the same following the 2017 poll.

OTHER PARTIES The apparent weakening of the Liberal Democrats as a third contender in British politics does not mean that smaller parties play no role in British politics. Other than the Liberal Democratic Party and the Green Party (which elected its first MP in 2010 after decades of political activity), historically regionally based parties—such as the Scottish National Party (SNP), the Welsh Plaid Cymru, and several Northern Irish parties (for example, Sinn Féin)—have been most successful in concentrating enough votes in some districts to win seats in the legislature. As noted earlier, the SNP fared particularly well in the 2015 election, securing all but 3 of the 59 seats representing Scotland in Parliament while winning less than 5 percent of the overall vote.

Finally, though it obtained only one seat in the 2015 election and lost that seat in the 2017 election, in recent years the United Kingdom Independence Party (UKIP) garnered significant support for its anti-EU, anti-immigration platform. Such support was particularly pronounced in local elections and, ironically, in elections to the European Parliament (even though the party firmly opposes the European Union).

How do we account for the UKIP's success? The party capitalized on growing "Europhobia" in Britain and rising unease with immigration in general. In addition, the party's outspoken populist leader (and member of the European Parliament), **Nigel Farage**, brought a great deal of publicity and popular support to the party. Although UKIP garnered nearly 13 percent of the popular vote in the 2015 House of Commons election, voters had little reason to remain loyal to this single-issue party following the successful Brexit referendum in 2016. UKIP obtained less than 2 percent of the popular vote in the 2017 election and lost its only MP.

PARTY POLITICS TODAY If British politics are supposed to be about staid traditions and predictable continuity, trends in the past two elections and disputes and divisions in all three major parties seem to be challenging these conventions. In the 2015 elections, voters ended the hung parliament by awarding a majority of seats to the Conservatives. However, the two leading parties together won only two-thirds of the vote, with the remaining third divided among a variety of parties. In total, 12 parties won seats in the House of Commons, up from 10 in 2010.[12] But just two years later, voters returned to the major parties, which together obtained over 90 percent of the vote. However, no party secured either a majority of votes or seats, giving Britain its second hung parliament in three elections. This forced the Conservatives to form a minority government with promised support on key votes from Northern Ireland's Democratic Unionist Party.

Moreover, since the 2015 election all three major parties have changed leaders: Labour is led by Jeremy Corbyn, a left-wing socialist loved by party loyalists but unsupported by many MPs from his own party. Theresa May now leads a Conservative

Seats in the House of Commons, 2017

PARTY	# SEATS
Conservative	318
Labour	262
Scottish National Party	35
Liberal Democrat	12
Democratic Unionist Party	10
Sinn Féin	7
Plaid Cymru	4
Green Party	1
Independent Unionist Party	1
Total Seats	650

Source: www.parliament.uk/mps-lords-and-offices/mps/current-state-of-the-parties (accessed 6/23/17).

Party and a minority government deeply divided by the issue of the UK's exit from the EU and as prime minister must now negotiate Britain's exit from the EU even though she campaigned for her country to remain a part of the body. Meanwhile, the Liberal Democrats, who also favored the losing side of the 2016 Brexit referendum, are licking their wounds from losses in the past two elections. Certainly party politics—and democracy—remain alive and well in contemporary Britain.

ELECTIONS

British voters select all 650 members of the House of Commons during a general election. With the passage of the Fixed-term Parliaments Act in 2011, the date for these elections was set on a five-year term beginning with the 2015 election (barring a vote of no confidence, a supermajority override—as happened to allow the 2017 election—or a change in this law). Usually about 60 to 70 percent of the electorate votes in British general elections, below the European average but far above the U.S. turnout.

British campaigns are short affairs, usually lasting less than a month. The voter has a relatively simple choice: which party should govern? British parties are for the most part well disciplined and have clear, published policy manifestos. Compared with voters in the United States, British voters are far more likely to know what each party stands for and how the parties differ. Candidates may not even reside in the district where they run for office. The notion of a candidate serving local (rather than party) interests first—that is, concentrating on bringing benefits (or pork) to local constituents to secure reelection—is of much less concern than it is in the United States.

CIVIL SOCIETY

As in virtually all democracies, the United Kingdom houses various groups articulating special interests. British interest groups influence public policy and public opinion, but interest-group lobbying of MPs is far less prevalent than such lobbying is in the U.S. Congress, because British parties are more highly disciplined. Interest groups must focus their attention on the party leadership (since parties, not individual MPs, make key policy decisions) and on the government bureaucracies, which often interpret and apply policies.

Perhaps the greatest influence of British interest groups comes through their participation in **quangos** (quasi-autonomous nongovernmental organizations). Quangos are policy advisory boards or other entities appointed or approved by the government that bring government officials and affected interest groups together to help develop policy. First established in the 1960s, quangos represent a move toward a neocorporatist model of public policy making, in which government and interest groups work together to develop policy. Although Conservative governments have attacked the quangos (seeing them as costly and empowering special interests and weakening government) and have trimmed their number, more than a thousand of these organizations remain, working in different policy areas.

In sheer numbers, the **Trades Union Congress (TUC)**, a confederation of the United Kingdom's largest trade unions, is the most important British interest group. For much of the postwar period, the TUC dominated the Labour Party and was thus extremely influential during periods of Labour government. Yet the TUC has seen its membership plummet as Britain's blue-collar work force has shrunk in recent years. In addition, Conservative governments passed laws restricting union activity in the 1980s, and the Labour Party carried out reforms in the 1990s that have sharply reduced the TUC's political power. The TUC is still an important source of funding and electoral support, but it can no longer dominate the selection of the Labour Party or exert its former influence on policy.

The most important business organization in the United Kingdom, and the main counterweight to the TUC, is the **Confederation of British Industry (CBI)**. Unlike the TUC, which has formal links to the Labour Party, the CBI has no direct link to the Tories. Britain's main industrial and financial interests usually favor Conservative policy, however, and top business leaders have exercised considerable influence in past Conservative governments. In recent decades, the Labour Party has also been careful to cultivate good relations with the CBI.

Society

The United Kingdom's social makeup is divided in many significant ways. The British state is both multinational and multiethnic; British society reveals class, religious, and even linguistic divisions. But while these divisions may appear rather sharp, compared with the social divisiveness in most other states, they have been relatively benign. Over the centuries, the United Kingdom has demonstrated remarkable national unity and enviable social and political stability.

CLASS IDENTITY

Class identity remains perhaps the most salient of all British social divisions and the one most noticed by outside observers. Historically, political parties and many key policy debates have reflected class differences, not differences of ethnicity, region, or religion. Twentieth-century social reforms did much to ease the huge income disparities and rigid occupation-based class lines of nineteenth-century England that preoccupied both Karl Marx and Charles Dickens. But increased social mobility has not yet erased the perception of a two-tier society divided between upper and working classes.

Chief among the legacies of the class system has been the education system, which has long channeled a minority of the British elite into so-called public schools (which are, in fact, private schools). Graduates of these elite schools go on to Oxford or Cambridge University before pursuing white-collar careers in government or industry, enhanced by elitist old-boy networks. Class differences are also perpetuated by continued self-identification with either the upper or working class, as manifested in preferred tastes and leisure activities—sherry versus warm beer, cricket versus football, opera versus pub—and variations in speech and accent. Regional disparities in income perpetuate this social division, with a more prosperous and vibrant white-collar southern England and a struggling blue-collar North.[13]

ETHNIC AND NATIONAL IDENTITY

Despite the UK's relative ethnic homogeneity, religious, linguistic, and cultural divisions do exist and in some cases are becoming more significant, even volatile. The 2005 London bombings by Islamic extremists and racially charged riots across England in 2011 offer evidence of continuing ethnic tensions. Nevertheless, the United Kingdom settled most of its religious differences early on, and its politics are more secular than those in the rest of Europe. Even today, however, Scots are mainly Catholic or Presbyterian, and the English mostly identify with the Church of England. Compared with the United States, however, religiously oriented social issues, such as gay rights and abortion, have generally not become politicized in the UK.[14]

Religion remains a significant source of conflict in **Northern Ireland**, though, where roughly half of the citizens are Protestant (of Scottish or English origin) and half are Irish Catholic. Northern Ireland, also known as Ulster, comprises the northeastern portion of the island of Ireland (about 17 percent of the island's territory) that remained part of the United Kingdom following the creation of an independent Republic of Ireland in 1921. This religious divide was compounded by both national and class differences, and Catholics were discriminated against in employment and education. Starting in the 1960s, members of the Irish Republican Army (IRA) turned to violence against British targets in the hope of unifying the region with the Republic of Ireland, and the British army and illegal Protestant paramilitary organizations fought back. Known as **The Troubles**, this three-decades-long period of conflict claimed nearly 4,000 casualties on both sides, many of them civilian.

Years of negotiation resulted in the 1998 Good Friday Agreement, in which the IRA agreed to renounce armed struggle in exchange for greater say in local government for Catholics. Both the British and the Irish governments supported the decision, as did important Northern Irish political groups, including Catholic republicans, who favor Northern Ireland's unification with the Republic of Ireland, and Protestant unionists, who favor maintaining Northern Ireland's inclusion in the United Kingdom. With this agreement, violence by both republican and unionist paramilitary organizations virtually came to an end, and self-rule was restored to Ulster in 2007.

Elsewhere, however, new divisions are emerging. Since the 1960s, former colonial subjects (primarily from Africa, the West Indies, India, and Pakistan) have immigrated to the United Kingdom in increasing numbers, giving British society a degree of racial diversity. For the most part, British society has not coped particularly well with this influx. Racial tension between the overwhelming majority of whites and the

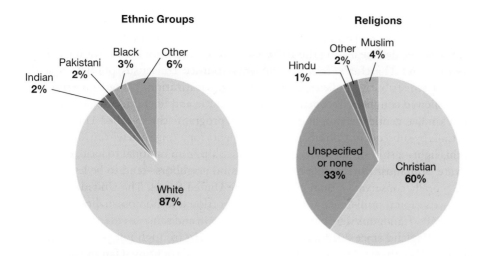

Ethnic Groups

Indian 2%
Pakistani 2%
Black 3%
Other 6%
White 87%

Religions

Hindu 1%
Other 2%
Muslim 4%
Unspecified or none 33%
Christian 60%

non-European minorities (totaling some 13 percent of the population) has sparked conflict and anti-immigrant sentiment, both of which nonetheless remain moderate by American and European standards. Parliament has sought to limit the nonwhite population by imposing immigration quotas. Even so, the country continues to face growing rates of immigration. Some predict that another 2 million immigrants will enter the United Kingdom over the next decade. This has already changed the social dynamics and increased xenophobic sentiment, strengthening parties such as the UKIP and bolstering the successful Brexit vote. Also, the integration (or lack thereof) of the United Kingdom's Muslim population has been a growing concern since the 2005 terrorist attacks on London's transit system.

In addition to ethnic groups, the United Kingdom also comprises a number of national groups, a fact outsiders tend to overlook. The United Kingdom's four nations—England, Scotland, Wales, and Northern Ireland—display substantial cultural and political differences. Most UK citizens first identify themselves not as British but as belonging to one of these four nationalities.[15]

Long-standing yearning for greater national autonomy has gained increasing political significance since the 1960s. Local nationalist parties successfully advocated for devolution with the establishment of local legislatures for Northern Ireland, Scotland, and Wales in 1999. Some feared that rather than pacify nationalist tendencies, devolution would contribute to the eventual breakup of the country, most notably with an independent Scotland (see the discussion "Scotland's Bid for Independence," p. 228).

While persistent regional loyalties and the localization of government have challenged British national identity, so, too, have the United Kingdom's growing economic and cultural integration with Europe over the past few decades. But at the same time, growing ambivalence about this dependence and British voters' decision to lessen those ties by exiting the EU have also complicated the British sense of identity. Although nearly half of British voters called for retaining membership in the European Union, it is safe to say that virtually all Britons remain very loyal to the Crown and to the notion of a sovereign British people (see "Brexit," p. 229).

IDEOLOGY AND POLITICAL CULTURE

British political values have been strongly influenced by classical liberalism and the conviction that government's influence over individuals ought to be limited. However, the postwar goals of full employment and the creation of a welfare state led to a new consensus as many Britons embraced the social-democratic values of increased state intervention and less individual freedom in exchange for increased social equality. Economic decline during the 1970s swung the pendulum back toward personal freedom, and Thatcher's Tory governments spurned consensus politics, rejected socialist redistributive policies, and advocated privatization. Labour governments that followed sought to reconcile social democratic and liberal ideologies, embracing a kindler, gentler version of this neoliberal program—the so-called Third Way.

Calls by subsequent Conservative governments for a "big society" can also be seen in this light—a shift of governance and stewardship from national to local, public to private. Still, most British—like their continental neighbors—tend to be less socially and morally conservative than citizens of the United States. The United Kingdom outlawed capital punishment and legalized abortion and homosexuality, all in the mid-1960s. Handguns were banned outright in 1998 and same-sex marriage has been legal in England since 2013 and Scotland since 2014 (though not yet in Northern Ireland). Also, there is far less emphasis on religion and traditional family values.

British political culture is typically described as pragmatic and tolerant. Compared with other societies, British society is thought to be less concerned with adhering to overarching ideological principles and more willing to tinker gradually with a particular political problem. Political radicalism, on either the left or the right, is rare. This pragmatism is bolstered by a classical liberal tolerance for opposing viewpoints, a strong sense of fair play, and a generally high level of consensus on the political rules of the game.

However, like any complex modern or postmodern society, British political culture examined more carefully comprises multiple subcultures. One can still see evidence of an aristocratic culture among the political elite, who share a sense of superiority and noblesse oblige toward those they deem less able to rule, as well as a mass or working-class culture of deference to those in authority. But in addition, policies of devolution, immigration, and multiculturalism, combined with the blurring of class lines, have challenged and complicated these dominant subcultures. And with economic recession, growing social inequality, and increased immigration over the past decade, simmering tensions within some of these groups have boiled over.

Political Economy

The United Kingdom is noteworthy for its contribution to the liberal economic model. Indeed, most political analysts would trace classical liberalism itself to Britain, where philosophers such as John Locke spoke of the inalienable rights of "life, liberty and estate," setting the stage for such political innovations as the U.S. Declaration of Independence.[16] Yet liberalism in the United Kingdom has undergone a number of shifts over the past decades, from the greater emphasis on social-democratic values after World War II to the neoliberalism under Margaret Thatcher, which has been softened but largely continued in subsequent governments.

If there is a common theme in the UK economy in the decades following the end of World War II, it is decline. As we recall, during the Industrial Revolution, the United Kingdom was "the workshop to the world," and the British Empire was led by the richest country on the planet. Yet over time, this position of dominance deteriorated. As of 2016, the country's per capita GDP at purchasing power parity (PPP) ranked 38th in the world, behind once far-poorer colonies such as Ireland and Australia (though the UK economy remains one of the 10 largest in the world). The financial drain of imperialism and wars, the waning competitiveness of obsolete technologies, the prioritization of social expenditures, and hesitation to pursue greater postwar economic integration with Europe all contributed to this decline.

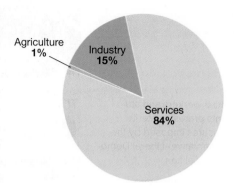

Labor Force by Occupation

Agriculture 1%

Industry 15%

Services 84%

Where does this leave the UK economy in the new century? Although such industries as steel, oil, and gas still play an important role, nearly three-quarters of post-industrial Britain's wealth is generated by the service sector, in particular financial services and tourism. Privatization has significantly shrunk the role of the state in the economy, and the welfare state has also undergone substantial changes, moving from a system that provided direct benefits to the unemployed to one that sponsors "welfare-to-work" programs emphasizing training to find employment. Even though Labour governments have tended to spend more on social welfare than do their Tory counterparts, even Labour has ended its traditional call for a greater role for the state in the economy—nationalization of industry was enshrined in the Labour Party constitution until 1995—and has distanced itself from its formerly close ties with organized labor.

To some observers, the Thatcher revolution, and its preservation under subsequent governments, helped the United Kingdom finally turn a corner. However, as in many other countries, neoliberal economic policies have increased financial inequality. Recognizing this growing inequality and sounding more like a Labour than a Conservative government, Prime Minister May has called for building an economy that works for all citizens, not just the wealthy. Her government has introduced programs designed to help the poor and disadvantaged, who have suffered disproportionately during the global financial crisis of the last decade and the more recent economic downturn caused by Brexit.

Moreover, this public spending has exacerbated the United Kingdom's growing gap between government revenues and government spending, a malady that Britain shares with most other industrialized countries. Britain's budget deficit became acute following the 2008 global financial crisis and was exacerbated by an inflated housing bubble and an economy largely dependent on financial services—the industry hardest hit by the financial crisis. In response, the Labour government partially nationalized a number of private banks, increased income taxes for the wealthy, and stepped up both public borrowing and public spending in an effort to stimulate the economy. After coming to office in 2010, the Conservative–Liberal Democrat coalition government shifted to a more liberal tack, cutting public spending and pursuing deregulation in an effort to reduce the government's growing deficit. The government faced great resistance from public-sector unions, university students, and others in pursuing these tough austerity measures, which have since been softened by the May government. The success or failure of these measures remains a subject of great debate.[17]

Finally, there is the issue of the United Kingdom's economic relationship with the outside world. Historic ties notwithstanding, over the past half century the country has become closely tied to the rest of Europe; half of its trade goes to EU member states. However, the United Kingdom never accepted the euro, the common currency of the European Union, and in 2016 elected to end its membership in the body. While the decision pleased Euroskeptics and relieved Britain of some of the

British workers and students protest austerity measures imposed by the Conservative–Liberal Democratic coalition.

political obligations of this decades-long association, it also proved economically costly in terms of investor confidence and concerns that the UK would suffer from the loss of full membership in Europe's single market. However, disentangling Britain from the EU has proven a slow and cautious process, and the May government has done all it can to retain the benefits of European integration while freeing itself from unwanted burdens (see "Brexit," p. 229).

Current Issues in the United Kingdom

SCOTLAND'S BID FOR INDEPENDENCE

Scotland was an independent state until the 1707 Act of Union—passed by the Scottish legislature despite widespread popular protest—fused it with England to form Great Britain. Scotland preserved its own legal system, its own church, and many of its own traditions. The Scottish National Party (SNP), formed in the 1930s, advocated Scottish independence but was relatively unsuccessful until fairly recently. Both the discovery of oil in the North Sea in the 1960s and dissatisfaction with Thatcher's neoliberal economic policies in the 1980s led to increasingly loud calls for devolution and bolstered the independence movement.

Coming to office on a mandate of devolution in 1997, Labour responded to the calls, granting Scotland its own legislature and broad powers over regional issues. The Labour government anticipated that its policy of devolution would satisfy Scottish demands for greater autonomy and weaken the movement for independence. The SNP won elections and formed regional governments in both 2007 and 2011, and with majority control of the Scottish parliament, the SNP scheduled a referendum on "home rule" in 2014.

Despite a strong surge in support for independence in the months leading up to the referendum, Scottish voters rejected the proposal by a clear margin of 56 percent to 44 percent. A majority of Scottish voters ultimately doubted whether Scotland could viably function as an independent state. Moreover, apparent growing support for independence in the weeks preceding the vote prompted the leaders of Britain's three largest parties to agree to hand over substantially more authority to Scotland's devolved government if voters elected to remain within the Union. Although at the time this compromise seemed to satisfy a significant majority of Scots, British voters' decision two years later to exit the European Union may turn the tables. While a majority of British voters elected to leave the EU, nearly two-thirds of Scots who went to the polls voted to remain. Many of these same voters, led by Scotland's devolved SNP government, subsequently proposed a new referendum on independence.

BREXIT

In recent years, many Scots have grumbled about their "democratic deficit" and other constraints imposed on them as Britons. During this same period, a growing number of British citizens complained that membership in the European Union threatened key aspects of British sovereignty, subjecting them to the dictates of distant Eurocrats.

Beginning in the 1950s, and progressing in fits and starts, a growing number of European countries have sought to forge ever-closer political, economic, and social ties among its members. The United Kingdom was late in warming to the idea and has remained less than enthusiastic about many aspects of the Union. This has been especially true with respect to the EU's ambitions for taking on more power and responsibilities, including monetary union and promoting a unified foreign policy.

To many Britons, the notion of participating in a stronger European Union has been simply unacceptable, fearing the regional economic union would become an unwieldy superstate, undermining national sovereignty, draining the domestic budget, and imposing continental values.[18] The United Kingdom's unwillingness to adopt the euro underlined this skepticism, which increased in the wake of the 2011 euro crisis and ongoing economic challenges facing the Continent. The European

---

INCOMPARISON | **European Union**

Do you think things are going in the right direction in the European Union? Percentage saying yes:

COUNTRY	PERCENTAGE
Germany	33
France	21
United Kingdom	20

Do you trust the European Union? Percentage saying yes:

COUNTRY	PERCENTAGE
France	31
Germany	28
United Kingdom	22

Source: "Europeans in 2014," *Special Eurobarometer 415* (July 2014), http://ec.europa.eu/public_opinion/archives/ebs/ebs_415_data_en.pdf (accessed 7/24/16).

migrant crisis beginning in 2015, combined with the EU policy of free movement of people throughout the single market, only compounded this sense of Europessimism among British citizens who felt Polish migrants were taking local jobs and migrants from Africa and the Middle East were destabilizing British society. On the other hand, proponents of the EU pointed to the huge trade and investment benefits of membership and the fears that the United Kingdom would lose even more economic and diplomatic power and marginalize itself, becoming a peripheral player in the emergence of a single European power.

In what came to be known as a "Brexit" vote, Cameron's conservative government held a simple "in-or-out" referendum on Britain's EU membership in 2016. Those campaigning for the "Leave" side, including several leading MPs and other members of Cameron's Conservative Party, argued that leaving the union would restore British sovereignty, protect British jobs, shield Britain from unmanageable levels of immigration, and free Britain from obligations to bail out struggling European economies. They argued that Britain would then be free to establish unilateral trade agreements with the United States and other countries and could still negotiate free-trade agreements with its European partners.[19] Those stumping for the "Remain" side, including Cameron, contended that the United Kingdom and its citizens were far wealthier as part of the European single market and that a seat at the European table gave Britain significant influence in Europe and beyond.[20] Most polls leading up to the vote gave the "Remain" side a bit of an edge, and most of these pollsters, as well as politicians and the British populace, were surprised by the outcome: nearly 52 percent of voters chose to leave while just over 48 percent elected to remain.

It is difficult to exaggerate the significance of this outcome. Prime Minister Cameron resigned, taking responsibility for the loss, and was replaced by Theresa May as leader of the Tories and as prime minister. All major political parties (other than the

A majority of Scottish voters rejected the 2014 referendum calling for independence. However, two years later two-thirds of these same voters unsuccessfully opposed the United Kingdom's exit from the European Union, raising the possibility of a new referendum on Scottish independence.

divided Tories) had joined Cameron in supporting the failed "Remain" campaign, most vocally the majority SNP in Scotland and Sinn Féin in Northern Ireland. Both parties called for referenda of their own that would permit continued membership in the EU: Scotland to again consider full independence and Northern Ireland to unite with the Republic of Ireland. Both Labour and the Liberal Democrats also favored the "Remain" side, but in many cases kept a low profile during the campaign in recognition that a growing number of their constituents were increasingly Euroskeptic. The United Kingdom Independence Party, long the most outspoken advocate of British withdrawal from the European Union, led the successful "Leave" campaign, and having achieved its long-held goal, seems to have outlived its usefulness. The torch passed to a weak and divided Conservative minority government to negotiate Britain's withdrawal from the European Union.

Key Terms

Blair, Tony (p. 205)
Brexit (p. 203)
cabinet (p. 207)
Cameron, David (p. 205)
Celtic fringe (p. 205)
collective responsibility (p. 214)
collectivist consensus (p. 209)
common law (p. 206)
Commonwealth (p. 208)
Confederation of British Industry (CBI) (p. 223)
Conservatives (Tories) (p. 205)
Corbyn, Jeremy (p. 219)
Crown (p. 212)
English Civil War (p. 206)
Farage, Nigel (p. 221)
Good Friday Agreement (p. 218)
House of Commons (p. 209)
House of Lords (p. 209)
hung parliament (p. 210)
Labour Party (p. 205)

Liberal Democratic Party (p. 218)
Liberals (Whigs) (p. 209)
Magna Carta (p. 206)
majoritarian (p. 211)
May, Theresa (p. 205)
Member of Parliament (MP) (p. 213)
neoliberal (p. 205)
Northern Ireland (p. 224)
Parliament (p. 206)
prime minister (p. 208)
quangos (p. 223)
Scottish National Party (SNP) (p. 216)
Thatcher, Margaret (p. 205)
The Troubles (p. 224)
Third Way (p. 205)
Trades Union Congress (TUC) (p. 223)
United Kingdom Independence Party (UKIP) (p. 216)
United Kingdom of Great Britain and Northern Ireland (p. 205)
vote of no confidence (p. 213)

U.S. citizens are generally patriotic but also skeptical of government. This combination is on display when the legislature or courts debate major policies. This rally, outside the U.S. Supreme Court, protests President Barack Obama's health care reform.

United States

Why Study This Case?

Some readers may believe that the United States is the standard to use in measuring advanced industrial democracies. After all, the United States is governed by the oldest written constitution still in effect, and it is the world's greatest military and economic power. Nevertheless, compared with other advanced capitalist democracies, the United States is best viewed as an anomaly filled with paradoxes. It is a large and wealthy nation with a relatively weak state. The United States has a highly legitimate political regime and enjoys widespread adherence to the rule of law despite having a political system deliberately designed to prevent decisive and coherent policy making. U.S. citizens are deeply proud of their state but distrust it and its bureaucracy in far greater numbers than the citizens of other industrialized democracies distrust theirs. Its political system has long been dominated by two political parties, but those parties are themselves relatively weak and at times undisciplined. It has a vibrant civil society but very low voter turnout. The United States is a secular democracy in which religion continues to play a comparatively large role in politics and society. It began as a society of immigrants, and national and regional identities are still in flux because of migration and geographic mobility. The United States has more wealth than any other democracy but is plagued by persistent inequality and the presence of an impoverished underclass more characteristic of developing countries. Americans cherish their freedom and individual liberty, yet 2.4 million American citizens are behind bars—an incarceration rate many times higher than in other advanced democracies. The United States leads the world in medical technology but has more citizens without medical insurance than any other advanced democracy. Blessed with peaceful borders and isolation from major world conflicts, the United States initially favored an isolationist foreign policy but has in recent decades intervened militarily in numerous global conflicts.

CANADA

Boston
New York
Baltimore
WASHINGTON, D.C.
Philadelphia
Charlotte

ATLANTIC
OCEAN

Detroit
Columbus
Indianapolis
Milwaukee
Chicago
Memphis
Atlanta
Jacksonville

Miami

THE
BAHAMAS

ATLANTIC OCEAN

Virgin Islands
(U.K.)

Virgin
Islands
(U.S.)

San Juan
Puerto Rico

Caribbean Sea

50 mi
0   25   50 km

St. Louis
Mississippi R.

Minneapolis
Missouri R.

Oklahoma
City
Dallas
Austin
Houston

New
Orleans

Gulf of Mexico

400 mi
0   200   400 km

N

San
Antonio

PACIFIC OCEAN

Agana   Guam

PACIFIC
OCEAN

50 mi
0   25   50 km

Denver

El Paso
Rio Grande

R O C K Y   M O U N T A I N S

MEXICO

PACIFIC OCEAN

Honolulu

200 mi
0   100   200 km

Phoenix

Seattle

Los
Angeles

San Diego

San
Francisco

San
Jose

PACIFIC
OCEAN

CANADA

Chukchi
Sea

RUSSIA

Bering
Sea

Yukon R.

Denali

Anchorage

Gulf of Alaska

400 mi
0   200   400 km

It is especially vital to understand the unusual workings of the U.S. political system given the country's tremendous power in today's world. The importance of U.S. technology, culture, military power, and economic might is undeniable, and the projection of those strengths is often a source of both admiration and resentment by citizens of other countries.

Despite these strengths, in the twenty-first century the United States has become an increasingly polarized and dysfunctional democracy. One prominent political scientist has argued that U.S. democracy is suffering political decay, calling it a "vetocracy," a system designed to stop government from acting.[1] Here is a central question for this case: Can the oldest constitutional democracy in the world, designed to prevent rapid change, deliver the necessary reforms to meet the challenges of the present and future?

Historical Development of the State

AMERICA AND THE ARRIVAL OF THE EUROPEAN COLONIZERS

The origins of the U.S. state can be found in the geographic expansion of European states in the early sixteenth century. A number of European countries began to explore and establish trading missions in the eastern part of the future United States. The French, the Dutch, the Spanish, and the English all attempted to form permanent settlements there.

By 1640, England had established 6 of the 13 colonies that would later form the United States. By the 1680s, the English had established 6 additional colonies, including New York, which was taken from the Dutch, and Pennsylvania. Though it is convenient to begin our discussion of the origins of the American political system with the establishment of the English colonies, more than 100 indigenous tribes inhabited what is now the United States, each with its own political regime. With the arrival of Europeans, many Native American societies collaborated with or tolerated the colonists, while others violently resisted. The chief cause of the declining indigenous population after the arrival of Europeans was disease, against which Native Americans lacked resistance. But Native American societies were also subject to military repression, murder, and forced relocation.

By the early eighteenth century, the British government had allowed elected legislatures to be established in the colonies, transplanting its own embryonic democratic institutions, and had imposed royally appointed colonial governors. And the colonies grew rapidly, fueled by a high birth rate, the importation of enslaved Africans, mostly to the southern colonies, and continued emigration from England and other European countries.

Between the 1680s and 1760s, the English colonists faced numerous foes. They fought indigenous tribes whose land they had taken. They also fought with the growing Spanish and French empires in America, who often allied themselves with Native American tribes and threatened to limit the English settlers' prospects for colonial expansion. In the French and Indian War (1754–63), the British effectively defeated the French Empire in North America and weakened the Spanish Empire

(Spain gave up claims to Florida in 1763). At the end of the French and Indian War, Britain inherited a vast empire in America that would prove both costly and difficult to control.

THE REVOLUTION AND THE BIRTH OF A NEW STATE

At its core, the American Revolution was caused by a conflict between two sovereignties: the sovereignty of the English king and Parliament, and the sovereignty of the colonial legislatures that had been established in America. Both believed that they had the exclusive right to raise the taxes paid by colonists. In the 1760s, the British Parliament unilaterally passed a number of taxes on colonists that sparked a spiral of colonial petitions, protests, boycotts, and acts of civil disobedience. The British responded by disbanding the colonial legislatures and repressing protest with military force. In the Boston Massacre (1770), British soldiers attacked a mob of colonists, further fueling the colonists' opposition to British intervention in colonial affairs. Colonial militias clashed with British military forces, a precursor to the impending revolution.

In 1774, in response to British repression, anti-British colonial elites convened in Philadelphia for the First Continental Congress. The assembly, composed of delegates from each of the 13 colonies, asserted the exclusive right of the colonial legislatures to raise taxes. The Second Continental Congress, meeting in 1775, created a Continental Army and named George Washington as its commander. In 1776, the Congress appointed a committee to draft a constitution and approve the Declaration of Independence.

The declaration of a new state and a new regime evoked an attack by a large and powerful British army. In the American Revolution (1775–83), the colonists were greatly outnumbered but were aided by their knowledge of the terrain and an alliance with France, an enemy of England. After its defeat at Yorktown, Virginia, in 1783, Britain granted independence to the 13 rebellious American colonies.

CONSOLIDATION OF A DEMOCRATIC REPUBLIC AND DEBATE OVER THE ROLE OF THE STATE

A unique theme of the American Revolution was its opposition to a British state perceived as overbearing. Fighting a war against the British required a central authority transcending the 13 colonial governments, each of which had begun functioning under new constitutions. The Articles of Confederation, approved in 1781, created a loose alliance of sovereign states. It featured a unicameral legislature with a single vote for each state. This weak central state made it difficult for the country to conduct foreign relations, ensure national security, control inflation, or carry out international trade.

In response to those problems, a Constitutional Convention of state delegates was held in 1787 to consider a stronger national state. The resulting constitutional document was a compromise between advocates of a strong federal state and supporters of sovereignty for the individual states. The states ratified the new constitution in 1788, effectively creating a new national state and a new political regime.

The first U.S. Congress met in 1789. It passed legislation that strengthened the state, built a federal judiciary, and imposed a tariff on imports to fund federal expenditures. It also attempted to address the concerns of those who feared the power of a

Political Development

1607	First permanent English settlement in America.
1754–63	French and Indian War ends the French Empire in America.
1775–83	American Revolution is fought.
1776	Declaration of Independence is signed.
1781	Articles of Confederation ratified.
1788	U.S. Constitution ratified.
1803	Louisiana Purchase expands the U.S. frontier westward.
1846–48	Mexican War is fought, further expanding U.S. territory.
1861–65	Civil War takes place.
1865	Thirteenth Amendment to the Constitution, abolishing slavery, is ratified.
1903–20	Progressive era.
1933–38	Era of the New Deal.
1955–65	Civil rights movement takes place.
2008	Barack Obama elected president.
2016	Donald Trump elected president.

strong central state by passing 12 amendments to the Constitution. The states ratified 10 of these amendments, which became known collectively as the **Bill of Rights**. The 10 constitutional amendments that compose the Bill of Rights aim largely to protect the rights of individuals against the federal government. Over time, most provisions of the Bill of Rights were gradually incorporated into state law, thus protecting individuals from state government as well.

THE MOVE WEST AND EXPANSION OF THE STATE

With the Louisiana Purchase in 1803, the acquisition of Florida from Spain in 1819, and the end of the War of 1812 with Britain in 1815, Americans were free to move westward. Like the original European settlements, this migration came at the expense of Native Americans. As Americans moved westward in search of land to be used for agriculture, the United States used legislation and military force to contain, relocate, or exterminate Native American populations.

The westward expansion continued with the 1845 annexation of Texas, which was a Mexican territory until non-Hispanic Americans led a successful separatist movement there. The United States declared war on Mexico in 1846 (the Mexican War, also known as the **Mexican-American War**) to protect its acquisition of Texas and lay claim to vast Mexican territories in present-day Arizona, California, Colorado, Nevada, New Mexico, Utah, and Wyoming. In all, the rapidly expanding United States gained one-third of Mexico's territory through military conquest, thus further encouraging the flood of migrants westward.

CIVIL WAR AND THE THREAT TO UNITY

The creation of a unified United States could not eliminate simmering regional differences that threatened to destroy the Union. These differences culminated in the **Civil War** (1861–65). At its roots were not just slavery but also the divergent paths of socioeconomic development in the southern and northern regions of the country. While the North experienced an industrial boom based on its prosperous cities, southern agriculture was still based on slave labor and export-oriented plantations.

To gain agreement on a federal constitution, the founders of the Republic had largely sidestepped the issue of slavery. Slavery had been abolished in the North after the Revolution, but the Constitution tolerated it. A number of factors brought the issue of slavery to center stage by the mid-nineteenth century. First, the westward expansion of the United States raised the contentious issue of whether new territories would be "slave" states or "free" states. Then, in the first half of the nineteenth century, slavery was banned by England and most of Latin America, and the northern states increasingly viewed the South as an anachronistic threat to free-market capitalism based on individual liberty and a free labor market. Finally, the early nineteenth century saw the emergence of a rapidly growing abolition movement, largely in the North, that viewed slavery as both undemocratic and anathema to Christian values.

The 1860 election of Abraham Lincoln and the rise to power of the new anti-slavery Republican Party provoked the secession of 11 southern states and the commencement of the Civil War. The southern states formed a rebel state, called the Confederate States of America, and enacted their own constitution, which guaranteed the institution of slavery.

The long and bloody conflict cost an estimated three-quarters of a million lives before the South was defeated in 1865 and the Union was preserved. Over the course of the next five years, three key constitutional amendments known as the **Civil War Amendments** were ratified in an effort to guarantee the freedom and civil rights of former slaves and all citizens. These included the Thirteenth Amendment (1865) abolishing slavery, the Fourteenth Amendment (1868) guaranteeing to all citizens due process and equal protection under the law, and the Fifteenth Amendment (1870) prohibiting voter discrimination on the basis of race (though not yet gender).

The importance of the Civil War in the development of the U.S. state was immense. The federal government had increased spending and built a huge army to subdue the South. It also gained enormous power through its role in reforming the South and reintegrating the southern states into the Union.

THE PROGRESSIVE ERA AND THE GROWTH OF STATE POWER

The three decades following the Civil War were marked by rapid industrialization, the growing wealth and influence of private business, and a large influx of immigrants. In response to these changes, the U.S. state employed its newfound clout to promote democratic reform during the **Progressive era** (1903–20). Progressives sought to use the federal state to restrict the power of big business, attack corruption, and address inequality.

Under President Theodore Roosevelt (1901–09), the federal government attacked monopolistic businesses and enhanced the ability of the Interstate Commerce Commission to regulate trade among the states. To protect public land from private development, Roosevelt created a vast system of national parks. Under President Woodrow Wilson (1913–21), laws were passed to curb further the power of large monopolies and to establish the centralized Federal Reserve System as a national lender of last resort. Perhaps the single greatest impetus for the growth of a centralized state was the adoption of the Sixteenth Amendment in 1913, which gave Congress authority to levy a national income tax. In addition, Wilson took the United States into World War I. Despite considerable popular opposition, it was an act that dramatically increased the size and power of the state.

THE GREAT DEPRESSION AND THE NEW DEAL

The stock market crash of 1929 and the ensuing Great Depression were pivotal factors in the 1932 election of Democratic Party candidate Franklin D. Roosevelt and the implementation of a set of social democratic welfare policies known collectively as the New Deal.

The New Deal policies were aimed at ameliorating the economic crisis and preserving the American capitalist system, but their long-term impact was to increase dramatically the power of the U.S. state. Roosevelt, with a Democratic majority in both houses of Congress, passed a series of unprecedented measures. Some of the most controversial pieces of legislation guaranteed workers the right to bargain collectively with employers, created state agencies to generate electric power, provided state subsidies to farmers who agreed to limit production, and heavily regulated the stock market. To carry out these policies, a massive extension of the state bureaucracy and the creation of numerous state agencies were needed. Many of those agencies still exist today. The Social Security Act (1935) established the foundation for the U.S. welfare state (though much later and much less comprehensively than in many northern European countries), creating unemployment insurance, retiree pensions, and other social welfare measures.

THE CIVIL RIGHTS MOVEMENT

Despite constitutional protections and the defeat of the South in the Civil War, U.S. democracy suffered from the legacy of slavery. Widespread discrimination against African Americans continued, most notably in the South but also in the North. After World War II (in which African Americans served and made valuable contributions), a growing civil rights movement, often backed by the federal government and the federal judiciary, advocated an end to all forms of racial discrimination.

The struggle for civil rights was only one of the popular reform movements that crystallized in the 1960s. During that decade, many U.S. citizens began to view economic inequality, gender discrimination, and environmental degradation by private business as impediments to democracy. In the mid-1960s, popular movements focused on those concerns combined with growing popular opposition to the Vietnam War, contributing to an atmosphere of unrest and rebellion.

In retrospect, it is clear that the United States was fortunate to build and consolidate its state under extremely favorable conditions. It did not have to contend with hostile neighbors and, after its founding, faced no appreciable external threats to its sovereignty. The development of the U.S. state during its first two centuries also coincided with the generally steady success of the economy and the steady expansion of U.S. power abroad.

Political Regime

Because of their fresh experience with, and deep distrust of, authoritarian colonial rule, the Founders of the United States established a democratic regime governed by the **rule of law**. This means that government can act and citizens can be punished only as authorized by legal statute, all citizens are equal before the law, and no one is above the law, not even political leaders. Those concepts were framed in a written constitution establishing a democratic regime grounded in rational-legal legitimacy. Inaugurated in 1789, the Constitution established a representative democratic regime governed by a presidential system. This section examines the institutional components of this regime, including its guiding principles of federalism and the separation of powers.

POLITICAL INSTITUTIONS

THE CONSTITUTION The Constitution of the United States of America was passed largely as a compromise between less and more populous states, between northern merchants and southern planters, between slaveholders and those not holding slaves, and between Federalists (who supported a strong central government) and Antifederalists (who advocated states' rights and preferred the decentralized confederal status quo). But the Constitution's framers and citizens on both sides of the debate shared two characteristics: fear of too much government in the form of an overbearing central authority, and recognition that the Articles of Confederation had provided too little government. The constitutional compromise was one of strengthened but nonetheless limited government checked by **federalism**, which divides governing authority between the national and state governments; the **separation of powers**, which prevents any one branch or office of government from

---

INFOCUS   **Essential Political Features**

- **Legislative–executive system**: Presidential
- **Legislature**: Congress
  - **Lower house**: House of Representatives
  - **Upper house**: Senate
- **Unitary or federal division of power**: Federal
- **Main geographic subunits**: States
- **Electoral system for lower house**: Single-member districts with plurality
- **Chief judicial body**: Supreme Court

dominating through a system of checks and balances; and the Bill of Rights, which protects the freedoms of individual citizens. In an unprecedented way, the U.S. Constitution created, tempered, and buffered three sovereign spheres—national, state, and individual—within a single political system.

THE BRANCHES OF GOVERNMENT

At the national level, the power of government is shared by three institutions: a president; a bicameral legislature (Congress); and a judiciary, led by the Supreme Court, that has the power to interpret the Constitution. The framers put in place several institutions designed to check and balance the powers of each respective branch of government. For example, the upper chamber of the legislature (the **Senate**) is given the authority to approve or disapprove executive appointments and to ratify or not ratify treaties. Both the Senate and the **House of Representatives** (the House) can refuse to pass legislation. The House can impeach, and the Senate can convict and remove from office, a president or a federal judge (for grievous offenses). The executive (the president) can veto legislation passed by the legislature and appoint judges to the federal judiciary. The judges, once appointed, have lifetime tenure and serve without political oversight. Most significantly, they have the power to interpret the Constitution and void any act of the other two branches or any of the individual states that they deem unconstitutional, if that act is brought before them in a court case. Ultimately, the framers sought to give Congress the upper hand, allowing it to override a presidential veto of legislation (with a two-thirds majority) and to overturn a constitutional decision of the Supreme Court by amending the Constitution (statutory interpretations can be overturned by a simple majority).

The Constitution's framers also intentionally gave each branch sources of legitimacy. Unlike a parliamentary system, which fuses executive authority and legislative authority and makes only members of parliament directly accountable to voters, the U.S. system seats its president and members of the legislative chambers in separate elections. Separate branches and separate elections can also allow a third possible check on power: divided government, in which different parties control the executive and legislative branches. Although a single party has often dominated both, the United States has experienced divided government over 40 percent of the time since 1830 and nearly 60 percent of the time since the end of World War II. Thus, what politicians and analysts often criticize as the tendency for American policy-making "gridlock" is an intended consequence of the system of checks and balances. It fosters a state with weak autonomy and a relatively fragmented policy-making process.

Historically, this formula has generally worked well; and at least until recently, there has been little evidence that divided governments in the United States have been any less able to produce major legislation than have unified party governments.[2] In recent years, increasingly polarized and unified parties (what might be called parliamentary-style party discipline in a divided government situation) have strained the constitutional order and created gridlock.

THE PRESIDENCY The U.S. president is both the head of state and the head of government. As a result, the presidency is invested with a great deal of formal authority, and key presidents have expanded the power and influence of the office over time, particularly in the past century. The president serves a fixed four-year term and can be elected only twice. Until the election of President **Barack Obama**, all U.S. presidents had been white men, and all but one have been Protestant Christians.

As the head of state and the only leader elected to represent the entire citizenry, the president has traditionally taken the lead role in U.S. foreign policy (although treaties are subject to approval of the Senate). The president is also commander in chief of the military. As head of government, the president—similar to a prime minister—is also responsible for managing the day-to-day affairs of the government and makes senior appointments to the executive and judicial branches (again, with Senate approval). Moreover, the president can initiate proposals for legislative action and veto legislative bills.

The president also manages an enormous bureaucracy, which has mushroomed over the years so that its civilian workforce now approaches 3 million employees. The workforce is overseen by a **cabinet** composed mostly of the heads of key departments, offices, and agencies. Although the degree to which a president comes to rely on cabinet officers and other key advisors has varied over time, all presidents have increasingly relied on a presidential bureaucracy to both manage and control this huge administrative staff of civil servants.

With a few exceptions (such as Andrew Jackson in the 1830s and Abraham Lincoln in the 1860s), presidents in office before the twentieth century were relatively weak leaders who exerted little political influence. The White House and the Executive Office of the President strengthened considerably over the course of the twentieth century.

THE LEGISLATURE   The framers of the Constitution intended Congress to be the dominant branch of the U.S. government. In many ways, despite the growing influence of the presidency and the substantial clout of the Supreme Court, this remains the case. The Constitution reserves the supreme power—the power to legislate—for Congress. It also gives Congress the power of the purse: sole authority to appropriate funds and thus to control the way its laws are implemented.

Another indication of the framers' appreciation for congressional power was their decision to divide the legislature against itself by making it bicameral. The House of Representatives consists of 435 members (a number unchanged since 1910), who are elected to two-year terms in single-member plurality districts. The number of seats and districts allotted to each state is determined by and distributed according to each state's population. Since 2010, each member of Congress has represented more than 700,000 citizens on average.

The Senate is composed of 100 members, each serving staggered terms of six years (one-third of the body is elected every two years). Senators are elected in statewide single-member plurality districts. Each state is allotted two seats regardless of its population, which in most cases gives each pair of senators a substantially larger constituency than their counterparts in the House of Representatives.

Given the differences in size, tenure, and assigned responsibilities, it is not surprising that the two chambers of Congress play different roles. The Senate is authorized to ratify treaties and approve presidential appointments, whereas the House is given exclusive power to originate tax and revenue bills. The Senate tends to be more deliberative, providing a forum for wide-ranging opinions and topics, and a minority of 41 senators can stop most business through delaying tactics known as filibusters. The House, on the other hand, is more centralized, places strict limits on debate, and conducts business on the basis of majority rules. Because senators serve a larger and more diverse constituency, they tend to be less specialized, less partisan,

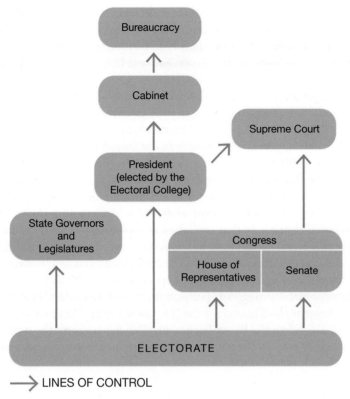

Structure of the Government

and more hesitant than representatives to take a position that might offend any major portion of their broad base of voters. House representatives, in contrast, stand for election every two years and are by necessity more attuned to the needs and interests of their more narrowly defined constituencies. House members tend to be more specialized in their expertise and less reliant on a staff. The House is generally more politicized and partisan. And whereas senators are more likely to cross the aisle to form an alliance or vote with members of the opposing party on an important issue, representatives are generally more likely to vote along partisan lines. However, since the election of Barack Obama in 2008, both houses have been extremely polarized.

THE JUDICIARY The third branch of the U.S. government, the judiciary, was the least defined by the Constitution and initially quite weak. But given the trust and legitimacy vested in the Constitution and the rule of law, it should not be surprising that the U.S. judiciary has come to play a prominent role in the American political system. Over time, the federal court system devised new tools of judicial authority and significantly broadened the scope of its jurisdiction. In 1789, Congress created the federal court system authorized by the Constitution, endowing it with the power to resolve conflicts between state and federal laws and between citizens of different states.

In the landmark decision of *Marbury v. Madison*, the Supreme Court in 1803 established its right of judicial review: the authority to judge unconstitutional or invalid an act of the legislative or executive branch or of a state court or legislature.

Although this power of judicial review can be exercised by federal and state courts, the Supreme Court is the court of last resort and has the final word on the interpretation of the U.S. Constitution. This kind of judicial power is uncommon but not exclusive to the United States; Australian and Canadian courts also have such authority.

Federal judges are given lifetime appointments, which afford them substantial autonomy from both partisan politics and the executive and legislative branches of government. But the Court's power is checked by its reliance on presidential nomination and Senate approval of nominees to the federal bench, and by legislative or executive enforcement of its decisions. Nonetheless, the federal courts have played an increasingly influential role, particularly since the second half of the twentieth century. They were involved in determining important policy outcomes in such areas as school desegregation and abortion, and even in determining the winner of the 2000 presidential election. In that case, the Court overturned the decision of a state supreme court (Florida's), and in so doing invalidated a partial recount of ballots in that hotly contested election. Currently, the Court is divided 5–4 between conservatives and liberals. It is little wonder that appointments to the Supreme Court have become bitter political struggles as partisan forces seek to project their influence on this now-prominent third branch of the U.S. government. This partisanship was in evidence in 2016, when the Republican-controlled Senate took the unprecedented step of refusing to vote on the confirmation of President Obama's nominee to fill a vacancy on the Supreme Court.

THE ELECTORAL SYSTEM

Nearly all elections in the United States are conducted according to a single-member district plurality system. There is one representative per district, and the seat is awarded to the candidate with the most votes (but not necessarily with a majority). This system has favored the emergence of two broadly defined parties and has effectively discouraged the survival of smaller and single-issue parties. Unlike a system of proportional representation, the plurality system in effect "wastes" votes for all but the dominant candidate, forcing coalitions to emerge to compete in the winner-take-all contests.

One process that parties have used to enhance their prospects for electoral success has been to establish electoral districts and thus determine constituencies for the House of Representatives and many state and local offices. States are required to adjust voting districts every 10 years to reflect changes in population, and the dominant party in the state legislature is often able to control the process. Parties seek to influence electoral outcomes by redrawing the districts in ways that will favor their candidates and voting blocs: a process known as gerrymandering.

Although members of both chambers of Congress are elected directly by a popular vote, the president and the vice president are elected indirectly by the electoral college. The Founders established the electoral college as a means of tempering the particular interests (and feared ignorance) of voters. In this system, voters technically do not vote for a presidential candidate; instead, each party from each state chooses or appoints a slate of electors. Each state receives a total of electoral votes equal to its combined number of senators and representatives. In addition, the federal District of Columbia has three votes, for a sum of 538 electoral votes (100 plus 435 plus 3). But unlike in a plurality system, in the electoral college, a candidate

National Election Results, 1992–2016

YEAR	HOUSE OF REPRESENTATIVES* TOTAL SEATS: 435†		SENATE* TOTAL SEATS: 100†		PRESIDENT* (PARTY)
	DEMOCRATS	REPUBLICANS	DEMOCRATS	REPUBLICANS	
2000	212	221	50	50	Bush (Republican)
2002	204	229	51	48	—
2004	202	232	44	55	Bush (Republican)
2006	233	202	49	49	—
2008	257	178	57	41	Obama (Democrat)
2010	193	242	51	47	—
2012	201	234	53	45	Obama (Democrat)
2014	188	247	44	54	—
2016	194	241	46	52	Trump (Republican)

*House terms of office are fixed at two years, and all seats are elected every two years. Senate terms are fixed at six years, and one-third of the seats are elected every two years. Presidential terms are fixed at four years, and elections are held every four years.

†When Democrats and Republicans together comprise less than the total number of seats, the independent representatives account for the difference.

requires a majority of votes (270) to claim victory. If no candidate obtains a majority, the contest is determined by the House of Representatives (this happened twice in the early nineteenth century).

Because all but two states use a winner-take-all formula for awarding electoral votes, winning a plurality of the popular vote in a state earns a candidate all of the state's electoral votes. Thus, winning many states by large margins but losing key electoral-rich battleground states by narrow margins can lead to a popular victory but a loss in the electoral college. This has happened five times in U.S. history, most recently in the controversial 2000 election between George W. Bush and Al Gore, and in 2016, when Donald Trump won a majority in the electoral college despite losing the popular vote by almost three million votes.

LOCAL GOVERNMENT

The United States has a federal political system dividing authority between self-governing states and the national government that unites the states (hence the name United States of America). The Constitution authorizes the national, or federal, government to manage both national commerce and foreign policy. Although the granting of those federal powers marked a substantial centralization compared with the earlier Articles of Confederation, the states have retained significant powers, including responsibility for many direct social services (such as health, education, and welfare) and authority over internal commerce.

Over time, however, the national government has managed to increase its influence in many of the areas traditionally subject to state sovereignty. The federal government can review the constitutionality of state legislation, impose federal mandates, and make federal grants to states for such services as education and transportation, contingent upon the states' abiding by federal standards.

This federal structure of national and state authority has allowed states to experiment with a variety of policies in areas such as welfare restructuring, vehicle emissions standards, legalization of marijuana, and educational reforms. But it has also resulted in a lack of standardization in those areas and varying levels of benefits and enforcement across the states.

Political Conflict and Competition

Federalism and the separation of powers have had another important consequence: the multiple levels and branches of elected office in the U.S. political system mean that voters in the United States may go to the polls often and cast dozens of votes in local, state, and national primary and general elections involving hundreds of candidates. In addition, 27 of the 50 states allow citizen-sponsored statewide ballots called *initiatives* and legislature-proposed statewide ballots called *referenda* (the ballots themselves often are called *propositions*) that enable voters to make direct decisions about policy.

THE PARTY SYSTEM

From a comparative perspective, U.S. political parties are fairly weak. Formerly bottom-up organizations linking party members tightly together in purposive grassroots campaigns, political parties in the United States have evolved over time into top-down, candidate-driven national organizations with much looser ties to voters and citizens. American political parties today tend to be weaker and more fragmented than their counterparts in many other countries. This weakness has resulted from the gradual democratization of the candidate nomination process (primary elections are now used to select candidates) and unintended consequences of campaign finance reform (which has restricted spending by political parties, but not by other private groups).

But with much talk recently about the ideological and even geographic polarization of American voters into "red" (Republican) states and "blue" (Democratic) states, it is clear that the U.S. two-party system has certainly endured even as it has evolved. The U.S. plurality system has fostered a two-party system in which the Democratic and Republican parties have won virtually all votes and political offices since their rivalry began over 150 years ago. In the 2016 presidential election, where candidates of the two major parties were very unpopular, those candidates nevertheless together won about 95 percent of the popular vote.

THE DEMOCRATIC PARTY The Democratic Party has its roots in the Democratic-Republican Party, which formed in the 1790s with southern agrarian interests as its base. Andrew Jackson led a splinter group to presidential victory in 1828, calling it the Democratic Party and portraying it as the party of the common man. The Democrats dominated the political scene until 1860 and for most of the years between 1932 and 1968. By the 1930s and with the onset of the Great Depression, the "liberalism" embraced by the Democratic Party had become Franklin Roosevelt's New Deal liberalism, which promoted social welfare, labor unions, and civil rights and was far more concerned with equality than individual freedom.

President Obama confronted myriad groups with significant (and often competing) vested interests in the outcome of the health care reform efforts.

As a coalition party, like its Republican rival, the contemporary Democratic Party is difficult to characterize fully in terms of a set of philosophical principles or even policy preferences. It may be said, however, that the party tends to embrace policies that support minorities, urban dwellers, organized labor, and working women. Democrats in the United States generally perceive state intervention designed to temper the market and enhance equality as both legitimate and necessary. As has been the case with social democratic parties in Britain and elsewhere, however, neoliberal trends since the 1980s have weakened the Democratic coalition, causing conflict over traditional New Deal–type social welfare programs providing such benefits as affirmative action. However, in recent elections healthy majorities of both minority and young voters have consistently favored the Democratic Party. The bitterly contested 2016 Democratic Party presidential primary pitted the more centrist former senator and secretary of state Hillary Clinton against the more leftist Vermont senator Bernie Sanders. Clinton won the nomination with the support of most of the party establishment, but Sanders drew strong support from young Democrats.

THE REPUBLICAN PARTY The Republican Party, nicknamed the Grand Old Party (GOP), is in fact not as old as its rival. It first contested elections in 1856 on an antislavery platform that also appealed to northern commercial interests. With Lincoln's presidential victory in 1860, the party dominated national politics until the 1930s, when the Great Depression brought that era of its supremacy to an end. By the late 1960s, the GOP had regained the presidency, and by the 1990s it regularly obtained congressional majorities as well.

The Republican Party currently brings together a coalition that includes both economic and moral conservatives. It draws support disproportionately from rural dwellers, upper-income voters, evangelical Christians, and voters favoring individual freedom over collective equality, such as libertarians and owners of small businesses.

Although there are fewer registered Republican voters than Democratic voters, registered Republicans have tended to vote more regularly than their rivals. Americans identify themselves with both parties in roughly equal numbers: approximately one-third of adults express a preference for one of the two parties, and most of the remaining one-third identify themselves as some sort of independent or unaffiliated voter. As with Democrats, Republicans are often divided between those who favor greater liberalism in economic and moral issues and those whose cultural or religious preferences call for a greater state role in social issues. These divisions were apparent in the 2016 Republican Party presidential primary, which pitted libertarians who favored free trade and states' rights (like Senator Rand Paul) against social conservatives advocating federal restrictions on abortion and opposing free trade agreements (like Senator Ted Cruz).

The most significant movement within the Republican Party in recent years has been the emergence of the Tea Party. Taking its name from the 1773 protest by colonists against the British imposition of taxes on tea, the modern-day movement emerged in 2009 as a reactionary group within the GOP. Although members of the movement share a strong opposition to any increase in taxation, they are divided between small-government libertarians and social conservatives.[3] Polls regularly indicate that more than 10 percent of Americans consider themselves part of the movement, and more than a fourth of Americans consider themselves supporters.[4] However, since the Tea Party's role in the 2013 government shutdown, unfavorable views of the movement have risen significantly among both Democrats and even many Republicans. Moreover, the Tea Party's embrace of economic nationalism (opposition to free-trade agreements) and white nativism (opposition to immigration) threatens the Republicans' chances of winning the presidency, as the electorate becomes less white and ever more dependent on foreign trade.[5]

The 2016 presidential campaign threatened to destroy the Republican Party, as Donald Trump, a blustery business tycoon and political outsider (with few ties to the Republican Party) easily defeated 16 aspirants competing for the Republican nomination for president. Some of Trump's views, such as his opposition to free trade deals and his stance on immigration, appealed to Tea Party radicals. However, many of his views (especially on foreign policy) clashed with conventional Republican ideas (he was particularly critical of the Iraq War). His views on immigration and his inflammatory statements on race were seen by party leaders as endangering support from the country's increasingly diverse electorate. After Trump won the nomination, some leading Republicans refused to endorse him. His upset victory over Hillary Clinton thus presents new opportunities and challenges for the Republican Party. After the 2016 elections the Republican Party occupied the presidency, had majorities in both houses of Congress, and controlled both the governorship and legislature in half of the states.

THIRD PARTIES If fully one-third of Americans do not regularly identify themselves with either party, is there political space for a third party? In the United States, establishing the kind of presence essential for national viability has proved difficult, if not prohibitive, for smaller parties. Moreover, the dominant parties have all the advantages of incumbency, such as the ability to establish and preserve laws discouraging the financing of third-party candidates and including them on the ballot.

Still, third parties occasionally have emerged on the U.S. political scene as protest voices. In that sense, third parties and their candidates can claim to have had an impact on the political process even if few of them have had any prospect of national electoral success. For example, Ross Perot's populist United We Stand

Party earned nearly 20 percent of the presidential vote in 1992, and Ralph Nader's pro-environment Green Party garnered nearly 3 percent in 2000. In 2016, only about 5 percent of U.S. voters selected a third party, with the Libertarian and Green Party candidates attracting most of those votes.

ELECTIONS

In the United States, in contrast to countries governed by parliamentary systems, terms for all elected offices—and therefore the sequencing of elections—are fixed. Each state determines the conduct of its elections, including the rules for any primary elections (preliminary direct elections held in many states and designed to narrow the field of candidates). Since the 1950s, electioneering in the United States has shifted from campaigning done almost exclusively by party leaders and grassroots party workers to highly centralized and professionalized media campaigns. Election contests today are hugely expensive and marked by media sound bites, talk show interviews, televised debates, targeted tweets, incessant fund-raising, and advertising blitzes, all guided by polls and sophisticated demographic studies.

No campaigns are more illustrative of this American-style electioneering than those for the U.S. presidency. As voters have apparently become less loyal to either party, and in many cases less interested in voting or participating at all, the parties and their candidates have redoubled their efforts (and expenditures) to attract support. In total, the 2016 presidential and congressional candidates spent almost $7 billion, far more than that spent on campaigns in any other country.[6] Campaigns begin early, with an extensive season of primaries, and involve an all-out effort both to promote the candidate and to denigrate the opponents, all in an attempt to mobilize new voters and persuade the undecided.

Levels of voter turnout are on average lower in the United States than in all other advanced democracies considered in this volume. Although voter turnout has actually increased in recent presidential elections—62 percent in 2008, the highest level

Campaigns for the presidency epitomize U.S.-style electioneering. These campaigns cost billions of dollars and include social media outreach strategies to get voters to the polls on Election Day. In his successful presidential campaign, Donald Trump made extensive use of Twitter to communicate directly with his followers.

since 1968, and 58 percent in 2012—only about 40 percent of eligible Americans vote regularly. (The turnout rate was only 36 percent in the 2014 midterm elections, the worst turnout for a general election since 1942.)

CIVIL SOCIETY

Since nineteenth-century French political philosopher Alexis de Tocqueville, observers have marveled at the vibrancy of U.S. civil society and the willingness of its citizens to become civically engaged. Recently, however, analysts have pointed to an apparent weakening of that civic commitment, noting low voter turnout and other signs of growing political apathy among U.S. citizens as evidence of a broader, generational decline in social capital (the web of relationships that connect individuals in society and that can help individual citizens influence political outcomes).[7]

However, precisely because the U.S. policy-making process is so complex and allows so many points of access—including individual officeholders at the national, state, and local level; legislative committees; regulatory agencies; and the initiative process—it has been difficult for individual citizens to influence the political process. As U.S. political parties have grown weaker and less cohesive, various special-interest groups have emerged and expanded their influence. The remarkable proliferation and enormous influence of these groups in the United States set this case apart from that of other democracies.

Interest groups are often organized around a single issue or a cluster of issues (from gun rights to workers' issues) and therefore typically do not officially affiliate with a particular party or candidate. These organized interests can include a single corporation or business association, public interest groups, and even state or local governments. Perhaps most well-known are the political action committees (PACs), political fund-raising organizations that allow corporations and trade unions to support individual candidates. In 2010, the Supreme Court ruled a 2002 campaign finance law unconstitutional in its restrictions on the ability of companies, unions, and other groups to pay directly for political advertisements during election campaigns. This ruling substantially increased special-interest spending.

Spending by PACs, along with all other contributing groups and individuals not directly connected to a candidate's election committee, make up what is called outside money—a segment of campaign finance that has exploded in recent years. These donations totaled over $1 billion in the 2012 election cycle, a tripling from the previous election. During the 2016 elections, super PACs raised almost $1.8 billion. The effects of such outside money on American democracy remain in dispute. In addition to financing political campaigns, these interest groups, along with business corporations and wealthy individuals, exercise their influence through various lobbying techniques to promote the interests of their constituencies.

Society

ETHNIC AND NATIONAL IDENTITY

The first European colonists in America were largely English-speaking Protestants, but early in the country's history the importation of enslaved Africans and a steady stream of emigration from Europe quickly diversified American society. In the mid-nineteenth century, the California gold rush spurred a wave of Asian immigration, and another major migration from southern and eastern Europe began in the 1880s.

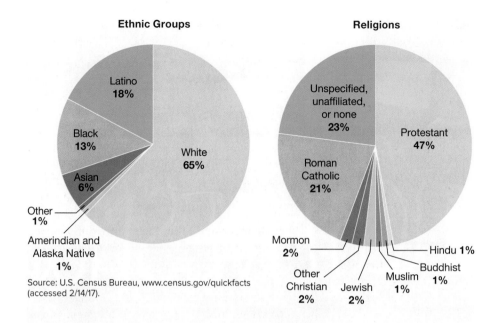

Ethnic Groups

- Latino 18%
- Black 13%
- Asian 6%
- White 65%
- Other 1%
- Amerindian and Alaska Native 1%

Religions

- Unspecified, unaffiliated, or none 23%
- Protestant 47%
- Roman Catholic 21%
- Mormon 2%
- Hindu 1%
- Other Christian 2%
- Jewish 2%
- Muslim 1%
- Buddhist 1%

Source: U.S. Census Bureau, www.census.gov/quickfacts (accessed 2/14/17).

More recently the influx of non-European immigrants, especially **Latinos**, has become an important issue in U.S. politics (see "Immigration, Cultural Diversity, and U.S. National Identity," p. 256). As of 2011, about 13 percent of U.S. citizens were born abroad. (In Canada, the figure is 20 percent.)

IDEOLOGY AND POLITICAL CULTURE

The United States' melting pot image has led to much debate about the distinctiveness of U.S. ideology and political culture. There is broad consensus, however, that American ideology includes six characteristics.

First, although citizens of other industrial democracies are more likely to view freedom as resulting from government policy, Americans typically view their individual freedom in terms of what the state cannot do to them. As a result, whereas many other democracies attempt to specify in their constitutions what the state should provide its citizens, the U.S. Constitution emphasizes citizens' protections from the state. Americans tend to eschew collective or societal goals in favor of personal or individual goals. Consequently, the role of private property in U.S. society is especially important, and taxes, which some citizens view as the state's appropriation of private property, are highly unpopular. This individualism may be one factor that has weakened political parties in the United States and limited their ideological coherence.

Second, an often-observed feature of U.S. political culture is Americans' participation in a plethora of voluntary groups that can be referred to collectively as civil society. Since the nineteenth century, the rich web of civic organizations in the United States exemplified the notion of self-government and political equality and performed a host of tasks that in other societies might be carried out by the state. The large number of protests following the election of Donald Trump might be evidence in support of that view. Clearly, disagreement remains about whether civil society is in danger.

Third, **populism**, the idea that the masses should dominate elites and that the popular will should trump professional expertise, is a key feature of the U.S. creed. As a result, Americans believe in electing public officials at virtually all levels of society, including some law-enforcement officials and judges. Increasingly, Americans are

Black Lives Matter, formed in 2013 to protest institutionalized racism against African Americans, is an example of the plethora of groups that compose the vibrant civil society in the United States.

expressing the desire to "unelect" government officials as well; in recent years, citizens have demanded recall elections for judges in Iowa, a governor in California, and legislators in a number of states. Many states have also seen an explosion of public initiatives giving the electorate a direct say in a growing variety of policy issues. In the 2016 presidential primary campaigns, Donald Trump and Bernie Sanders, candidates from both major parties, embraced populist themes. One growing manifestation of the populist strain in U.S. political culture is the widespread popular disdain for professional politicians. Recent public opinion research found that a growing number of Americans (especially on the political right) would favor a presidential candidate who did not have prior experience in national politics.[8] Despite the fact that Donald Trump is clearly part of the wealthy elite in the United States, his 2016 election is perhaps best explained by a surge in populist rejection of professional politicians.

Fourth, a deep-seated aspect of U.S. political culture, rooted in the frontier mentality of early America, is the belief that all Americans have, and should have, an equal opportunity to become prosperous and successful. In the nineteenth century, Tocqueville observed that the United States had a far more egalitarian class structure than did Europe. Although assessments of economic equality and social mobility were certainly exaggerated even in early America, the notions of equality of opportunity and social mobility have endured as part of a fundamental ethos.

Opinion research confirms that Americans today hold true to the notion of equality of opportunity but place less value on equality of actual economic outcomes. They are likely to believe that success is a function of individual effort. Today disparities of income are greater in the United States than in most of Europe, and they are growing quickly. However, compared with their counterparts in other advanced democracies, Americans tend to oppose state policies aimed at redistributing income to benefit the poor.

Fifth, although the U.S. public has historically viewed its federal state with relatively high levels of trust and pride, a paradoxical, deep-seated liberal distrust of "excessive" central state power is also a prominent feature of the political culture. The American Revolution began as a rebellion against a powerful British state that was seen as abusing its authority through the unjust taxation of its citizens. The United States is unique in that anti-statism became a founding principle of the new regime.

As already discussed, the founders of the U.S. regime consciously sought to embed in the system myriad checks on the power of the central state through the devolution of much power to state and local governments, the establishment of a powerful and independent judiciary, and the separation of powers. As a result, Americans remain skeptical of state efforts to promote social welfare, an outlook that largely explains the relatively small size of the U.S. welfare state. Compared with citizens in other advanced democracies, far fewer Americans hold the state responsible for providing food and housing for every citizen.

Finally, the United States also stands out among advanced democracies in the importance it continues to place on religion. A far higher percentage of its citizens belong to a church or other religious organization than do the citizens of other advanced democracies, and Americans are more likely to believe that clear guidelines differentiate good and evil.

The importance of religion in the United States has been linked to what has been called **utopian moralism**, the tendency of Americans to view the world in terms of good versus evil. At the same time, the "free market" for religion and anti-statism often complicates the quest for moral clarity. On many moral issues, such as abortion, Americans are uncomfortable both with sanctioning behavior they may see as immoral and with restricting personal behavior.

Political Economy

The United States remains the most prosperous and technologically powerful country in the world. With just over 4 percent of the world's population, the United States produces as much of the world's economic output as China, which has nearly 20 percent of the world's population.[9] In the 1990s, while many of the world's economies struggled, the United States enjoyed the longest period of sustained economic growth in its history. For most of the three decades since the 1970s, inflation and unemployment also remained relatively low. However, the global financial crisis and subsequent economic recession that originated with a banking crisis in the United States in 2008 have had long-term negative consequences for the American economy and profoundly influenced its politics as well.

In general, the U.S. state plays a smaller role in the market than do the governments of most other industrialized democracies. The proportion of GDP spent by the state has hovered around 35 percent, less than in most European countries, a figure that has not varied much over time.[10] The United States also has some of the lowest tax rates among the industrialized democracies (see "In Comparison: Taxes as a Percentage of GDP," in this section). However, what the United States does not provide by way of direct state expenditures is often less visible or "submerged," such as various tax breaks for home ownership, children, or student loans and subsidies for employer-provided health care, to name a few. As a result, some observe that the notion of a weak U.S. welfare system is misleading; rather, benefits are often supplied through the private sector and supported by a complicated system of tax breaks targeting specific groups of Americans. Such a system, however, tends to benefit the middle class much more than the poor, who lack the resources to take advantage of tax exemptions and might more easily benefit from public goods, such as nationalized health care.[11]

Although private enterprise is the main engine of the U.S. economy, the state does play a significant role. Starting with the New Deal reforms of the 1930s, the state's role in the economy increased significantly to prevent a market collapse, promote equity, and shield the American political-economic system from fascism on the right and communism on the left. Since the 1980s, governments have attempted at times to scale back the role of the state in the economy. The Reagan administration, for example, deregulated many sectors of the economy (including telecommunications and the airlines) to make them more competitive; under the Clinton administration in the 1990s, reforms also devolved many welfare responsibilities to the states. The 2008 financial crisis once again brought the state into the marketplace on a dramatic scale in the form of fiscal stimuli, corporate bailouts, direct government ownership, and tougher government financial regulations. Over the course of the 2000s, an enormous boom took place in the U.S. housing market, facilitated by low interest rates backed by the Federal Reserve and large inflows of foreign funds seeking to profit from the boom. This easy money made cheap loans available to American consumers and fueled a housing construction frenzy and, ultimately, a housing bubble. Unrestrained by government regulators, financial institutions issued increasingly risky loans to increasingly indebted consumers and then bundled these mortgages together into complex securities and sold them to investors at great profit.

For a season, this bubble kept everyone aloft and happy. Americans were living the American dream of home ownership, jobs were plentiful, and banks were extremely profitable. But when the inflated housing bubble popped and housing prices declined, so too did the value of these mortgage-backed securities. The Wall Street financial institutions that had invested heavily in these securities began to suffer huge losses, prompting investors to flee. As interest rates climbed and property values plummeted, more and more Americans found themselves unable to make mortgage payments and were forced into foreclosure. The federal government stepped in to bail out banks, shore up key businesses, calm troubled financial markets, and jump-start the economy. These steps were designed to increase employment, stimulate investment, lift the economy out of recession, and prevent the kinds of market failures that had led to the crisis in the first place.

Additionally, the U.S. state's intervention in the economy has been aimed at improving the business climate. Over the past 40 years, the tax burden has shifted from corporations to individuals, and the state has granted huge subsidies to agribusiness and given generous tax breaks to corporations. At the same time, in contrast to many European countries, the state has done little to support trade unions. Even during a Republican administration, under George W. Bush, the size of the state grew faster than at any time since the 1970s, though this growth largely involved military and national security spending.[12] State expansion in the form of military spending and recession relief efforts has also raised government debt to dangerous levels, complicating efforts to fund government programs and sharpening political debate, calls for austerity, and pursuit of a balanced budget. In 2011, Standard & Poor's downgraded the U.S. credit rating for the first time in the country's history, citing concern about both the growing debt and the protracted political struggle over raising the debt ceiling.

Despite its wealth and generally impressive record of economic growth, the United States faces numerous political and economic challenges in the twenty-first century. Compounding the problems of the national recession has been the challenge of persistent and growing income inequality. Since the Social Security Act of 1935, the U.S. state has provided a safety net of welfare measures, but the provisions have been less extensive than those of other advanced democracies. The United States spends about 15 percent of its GDP on social expenditures, a lower share than that of almost any other advanced democracy (only Ireland's is lower). Legislation in the 1960s expanded welfare measures to include some health care coverage for the poor and the elderly, but it stopped short of providing universal health care for all citizens. During the Reagan administration, welfare spending per poor recipient fell by one-fifth. Under President Clinton, there was bipartisan support for measures aimed at cutting welfare expenditures, and with some notable exceptions (such as prescription benefits for the elderly), social expenditures remained flat or declined. The economic downturn in 2008 caused a spike in welfare expenditures, which rose to nearly 5 percent of GDP by 2010, nearly double the proportion of just three years previous. As the economy has regained its footing, welfare expenditures have returned to less than 3 percent of GDP in subsequent years.

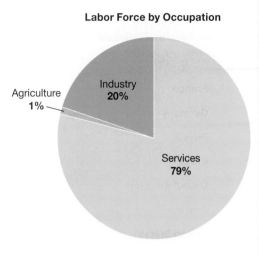

Labor Force by Occupation

Agriculture 1%
Industry 20%
Services 79%

As a result, income inequality in the United States has become a serious and growing problem. While the main measure of inequality, the Gini index, has remained relatively flat in many countries around the world, the United States has seen a dramatic increase over the past two decades. In 1980, the U.S. Gini index stood at 30, where it had been since the late 1960s. Since the 1980s, the U.S. Gini number has risen to 41, similar to that of China and many countries in Africa.[13] The United States has the largest number of millionaires in the world, but it also has a disproportionally large number of poor for a country of its wealth (hence the high degree of inequality). About 15 percent of the country's citizens live below the poverty line, including approximately 22 percent of its children (the highest percentage among the advanced democracies). This poverty is particularly concentrated among African Americans and Latinos, indicating how immigration and racism can compound the likelihood of poverty in the United States. Persistent racial divisions in the United States remain one of the greatest challenges to reducing inequality.

Some scholars believe that growing inequality has a corrosive effect on American society. A recent book by political scientist Robert Putnam illustrates the growing social consequences of economic inequality, which he argues threatens the American Dream of social mobility.[14] Other scholars have argued that the U.S. political system is increasingly dominated by large economic interests, at the expense of the majority of the population.[15] These concerns dovetail with alarm over the role of money in politics and the weakness of U.S. campaign finance laws.

Concern over growing inequality, not usually central to U.S. politics, became a central theme in the 2016 presidential campaign. In the Democratic Party primary campaign, Senator Bernie Sanders mounted a serious challenge to the former senator and secretary of state Hillary Clinton, focused almost entirely on the need to stem the growing economic divide. In the Republican Party primary campaign, real-estate mogul Donald Trump defeated his more mainstream competition by embracing economic nationalism and attacking free-trade deals that he claimed led to the impoverishment of the U.S. working class.

Taxes as a Percentage of GDP

COUNTRY	PERCENTAGE	COUNTRY	PERCENTAGE
France	45.2	South Africa	22.6
Germany	36.1	Mexico	19.7
Russia	35.3	China	18.7
Brazil	32.8	India	16.6
United Kingdom	32.6	Iran	6.4
Japan	30.3	Nigeria	2.8
United States	26.0		

Source: Heritage Foundation Index of Economic Freedom (www.heritage.org). Most recent data available for each country (accessed 8/21/17).

Related to the problems of inequality and poverty is the growing national debt over the past two decades. While U.S. social expenditures are small compared with those of other advanced democracies, the low and declining levels of taxation (see "In Comparison: Taxes as a Percentage of GDP" above), growing numbers of elderly, expanding entitlement programs, inability to control health care expenses, and costs of defense and waging wars in Iraq and Afghanistan have translated into far greater expenses than state revenues can support. This budget deficit has been funded by borrowing. As a result, the United States has an enormous national debt of over $19 trillion; the figure now exceeds the country's annual GDP and has reached a level not seen since World War II. If at some point the United States is no longer able to sustain this debt through borrowing (often from foreign sources such as China), the result could be economic decline and the inability to sustain military commitments and other obligations abroad.

Current Issues in the United States

IMMIGRATION, CULTURAL DIVERSITY, AND U.S. NATIONAL IDENTITY

From the outset, the United States has been a nation of immigrants. Nonetheless, the current wave of immigration has once again proven to be a hot political issue. In recent years, several states have passed increasingly stringent anti-immigration laws, increased penalties for employers who hire undocumented immigrants, required schools to determine the immigration status of students' parents, forbidden illegal immigrants from working or asking for work, and forbidden anyone from renting apartments or even giving rides to illegal immigrants.

Some observers have gone so far as to warn that the volume of immigration, particularly coming from Mexico and elsewhere in Latin America, will undermine the fundamental values of the United States; they claim that this group will resist assimilation because it is so large and distinct.[16] These fears, combined with concerns about cross-border drug trade and violent crime, led to the construction of hundreds of miles of security fences along the U.S.-Mexico border (nearly one-third of the 2,000-mile boundary is fenced). Others are more optimistic about prospects for integration, noting that since the founding of the United States, successive waves of immigrants have been viewed as a threat to American political culture but over time have been assimilated.

Even those observers who agree that the current flow of immigration differs in many important respects from those of the past generally disagree with the assessment that Latin American immigration poses a threat to U.S. society.[17] There is much evidence that Latino immigrants are speaking English and otherwise assimilating into U.S. culture: more than 90 percent of second-generation Latino are either bilingual or mainly English speakers, and many intermarry with non-Latino partners. As one scholar has concluded, "Hispanic immigration is part and parcel of broader American patterns of assimilation and integration. Their story, like that of the Irish, Jews, and Italians before them, is an American story."[18]

Similarly, the broader public reflects these same mixed views regarding immigration. After the September 11, 2001 attacks, support for restricting immigration increased significantly, but this support has steadily declined in recent years.[19] More generally, several scholarly studies indicate that the relatively weak level of social expenditures in the United States has much to do with the country's cultural diversity. In short, citizens may be willing to support immigration, but they also appear much less willing to redistribute wealth to those they feel are not like them.[20] The United States continues to be a melting pot of cultures fed by a steady stream of immigrants, but Americans remain ambivalent and deeply divided about this aspect of their society. If economic difficulties persist over the long term, this situation may increase pressure for restrictions on immigration and make immigrants the flashpoint for anxieties about economic security. At the same time, population analysts are projecting that by 2042, minorities in the United States will in fact become the majority population.

Immigration was front and center in the 2016 presidential campaign. Republican nominee Donald Trump called for a temporary ban on immigration from Muslim countries (as a response to the threat of terrorism), and he proposed to build a wall on the U.S.-Mexico border (to stop illegal immigration). His opponent, Hillary Clinton, attacked those proposals as racist, unfeasible, and counterproductive.

A DYSFUNCTIONAL DEMOCRACY? POLITICAL POLARIZATION IN THE UNITED STATES

Even before the 2008 election of Barack Obama, scholars of U.S. politics pointed to the rapidly growing level of **political polarization**, or degree of political partisanship among members of the two major political parties. Recent presidential elections seemed to highlight a growing divide between "red states" (conservative, religious, and Republican) and "blue states" (more socially liberal, more secular, and Democratic). A number of high-profile events during Obama's first term seemed to underscore this polarization.

Obama took power vowing to end the partisan bickering in Washington, D.C., but soon found his agenda under fierce attack from the Republican opposition. Obama's massive economic stimulus package, introduced in February 2010 in response to the recession, passed without a single Republican vote in the House and with only three Republican votes in the Senate. Not a single Democrat in the Senate and only seven in the House opposed it. Obama's 2010 Affordable Care Act, a centerpiece of his electoral campaign, faced even more partisan opposition: not a single Republican in either the House or the Senate voted for it.

In 2011 and again in 2013, Republicans in the House of Representatives refused to approve an increase in the U.S. debt ceiling, thus effectively limiting the amount of money that the United States could borrow. Failure to raise the debt limit likely would have resulted in the United States defaulting on its debt and easily could have triggered a global economic crisis. In both cases, House Republicans eventually relented. The 2013 partisan brinksmanship resulted in a three-week government shutdown. In 2016 Senate Republicans took the unprecedented step of refusing to consider President Obama's nominee for the Supreme Court, another example of how partisan polarization has threatened the basic operation of the U.S. political system.

A 2014 poll found that 63 percent of likely American voters were very disappointed with the performance of Congress, an improvement from the high of 75 percent negative assessment reported following the 2013 government shutdown.[21] The 2013–14 Congress passed fewer bills and enacted fewer laws than any other Congress in recent history. Not surprisingly, whether this lack of productivity is viewed as a bad thing (governments are elected to take action on behalf of the public) or a good thing (the government that legislates least, governs best, particularly when the president is a Democrat) depends on which party you belong to.

Scholars note that U.S. politics has become increasingly polarized since the 1970s, although earlier historical periods (during the Civil War, for example) have certainly been marked by high levels of polarization. Evidence of this polarization is strongest among political elites.[22] Since the 1970s, strict party-line votes have dramatically increased in Congress. Party unity scores, measuring the percentage of legislators voting with their party majority, have increased from about 70 percent in the 1970s to about 90 percent at present. Measures of the ideology and voting records of members of Congress point to a growing divide between Democratic and Republican legislators. In 1970, moderates constituted 41 percent of senators, but today they account for only 5 percent.[23] In the words of two leading scholars of U.S. politics, "Conservative Democrats and liberal Republicans, who were common in American politics during the 1950s and 1960s, are now extremely rare."[24]

Scholars have pointed to a number of potentially corrosive consequences of this polarization among political elites.[25] They have argued, most obviously, that growing polarization makes it difficult to create legislative coalitions, leading to public policy gridlock. The workings of the federal bureaucracy and the judiciary have been hampered because what were once routine legislative approvals of presidential appointees have become long and drawn-out confirmation battles. One scholar has argued that the polarization has made it harder to pass laws to address economic crises, and that the gridlock in Congress has contributed to growing inequality in the United States because the legislature can't pass measures to protect the poorest Americans.[26] Many observers have lamented that the political discourse among political elites has become less civil.

A lively and ongoing scholarly debate questions whether there has been a similar political polarization among the U.S. public. Some scholars have argued that there is little evidence to suggest that mass polarization has increased with elite polarization.[27] Others contend that mass public opinion increasingly mirrors the polarization of political elites.

Scholars are even more divided about the causes of political polarization in the United States. Some have attributed it to the "democratization" and consequent weakening of U.S. political parties in the 1960s and 1970s (and especially the creation of party primaries to select presidential candidates) that allowed political activists to enter mainstream politics. Others place the blame on lax campaign finance laws and the explosion of special interest groups aimed at mobilizing citizens around single issues. Still others point to laws that give the media access to almost all political deliberations, together with the emergence of commercial media outlets fostering and even amplifying highly partisan positions.[28]

Can polarization be reversed? Many scholars have suggested political reforms aimed at reducing political polarization in the United States. For example, two experts on Latin American politics have suggested that the United States consider adopting a proportional representation electoral system, a feature of most Latin American presidential systems that they argue has fostered compromise among political parties.[29] Others have suggested reforming the rules of Congress and revising political party primaries to better reflect views in the political center.[30] With a political regime intentionally designed to "check" and "balance" political power, these kinds of reforms may not come easily. Looming challenges, however, may compel the kind of cooperation required to bring about the necessary institutional changes.

Key Terms

American Revolution (p. 236)
Articles of Confederation (p. 236)
Bill of Rights (p. 237)
cabinet (p. 242)
civil rights movement (p. 239)
Civil War (p. 238)
Civil War Amendments (p. 238)
Declaration of Independence (p. 236)
federalism (p. 240)
gerrymandering (p. 244)
House of Representatives (p. 241)
Latinos (p. 251)
Mexican-American War (p. 237)

New Deal (p. 239)
Obama, Barack (p. 242)
political polarization (p. 257)
populism (p. 251)
Progressive era (p. 238)
rule of law (p. 240)
Senate (p. 241)
separation of powers (p. 240)
Tea Party (p. 248)
Trump, Donald (p. 245)
utopian moralism (p. 253)
Vietnam War (p. 239)
Washington, George (p. 236)

Soldiers on guard at the Eiffel Tower after a coordinated set of terrorist attacks in Paris killed 130 people and wounded over 350 others. In 2015 and 2016, Islamic terrorists claimed responsibility for the deadliest acts of violence on French soil since World War II. In response, the French government declared a 16-month state of emergency, intended to last through the May 2017 presidential elections.

France

Why Study This Case?

The French case offers a fascinating study of regimes. In little more than two centuries, France has experienced a wide variety of regimes, ranging from authoritarianism (absolute monarchy, revolutionary dictatorship, and empires) to democracy (parliamentary and semi-presidential). During this period, France has been governed by three monarchies, two empires, five republics, a fascist regime, and two provisional governments and has promulgated 15 separate constitutions. The most dramatic transition was, of course, the **French Revolution** (1789–99), in which French citizens overthrew the ancien régime (the European old order of absolute monarchy buttressed by religious authority) and replaced it, albeit briefly, with a democratic republic.

Not until the present **Fifth Republic** (established in 1958) was France able to break this alternating cycle of stern authoritarian rule and chaotic, or at least dysfunctional, democracy. Although revolution is no longer politics as usual and today's French citizens are more centrist, French political life is far from mundane. French citizens remain skeptical, if not cynical, about politics and politicians and vigorously divided on issues such as immigration, unemployment, European integration, and the proper role of the state.

The French case poses two important questions for students of comparative politics. First, French history has given the state a prominent role in its economic development. Today, French citizens enjoy a variety of state-provided benefits and protections that are absent in many other advanced democracies. However, France currently suffers from the highest levels of unemployment since the birth of its current regime in 1958 and is challenged by rapidly escalating public debt. Is France's statist political-economic model compatible with its role in an increasingly globalized society, and can the French government reform that model to protect France's economic competitiveness?

FRANCE

Second, as a legacy of the French Revolution, the French have a powerful sense of citizenship and equality. It has long been a sacrosanct pillar of French political culture that national identity trumps religious or ethnic identity, but over the last few decades, France has become more ethnically diverse and now has a growing Muslim minority. This development has ignited a fierce debate about how the French secular state should deal with this population, and mainstream French politicians have supported policies aimed at limiting the expression of ethnic (as opposed to "French") identity. This debate, and attacks by Islamic terrorists that killed over 230 French citizens (and wounded hundreds more) in Paris and Nice in 2015 and 2016, have shaken up the French political environment and have moved the previously peripheral issues of religion and ethnicity to center stage. Can France protect its commitment to a secular and multiethnic state while integrating its growing Muslim minority?

Historical Development of the State

Whereas French history offers us valuable insights into the study of regimes, this same history is also an essential primer on the rise of the modern nation-state. From Louis XIV's declaration of *L'état, c'est moi* ("I am the state") to Napoleon's establishment of bureaucratic legal codes and the rule of law, the development of the French state offers an archetype for the emergence of a powerful state. Yet it exists alongside a society that views mass demonstrations against authority as an important tool of political change.

ABSOLUTISM AND THE CONSOLIDATION OF THE MODERN FRENCH STATE

In carving out the Holy Roman Empire in the early ninth century, Charlemagne, leader of a Germanic tribe known as the Franks, established a realm encompassing much of western Europe. In doing so, he unified the area we know as France earlier than would occur in any of the other European states. But with Charlemagne's death, Frankish control was reduced to an assortment of small feudal kingdoms and principalities within the confines of what is now France. As with feudal kings elsewhere, the Frankish rulers sought to increase their holdings, stature, and security by squeezing wealth from their subjects. In contrast to the United Kingdom, French feudalism led to absolute monarchs, who centralized authority and developed bureaucracies capable of taxing the subjects and administering the affairs of state.

Absolute monarchy was an important first step in the development of a strong French state, capable of making and executing laws, waging war, and raising money to provide defense. By the fifteenth century, Louis XI had sufficiently centralized his authority such that he could wage expansive wars. In this way, he doubled the size of his kingdom to roughly the current borders of France. He was also able to weaken the influence of the nobility and largely ignore the Church, aristocracy, and commoners. His successors over the next three centuries reinforced these trends, forging a centralized state with a reputation for administrative efficiency that has largely persisted to this day. The pinnacle of this absolutist authority came during the rule of Louis XIV, who dubbed himself the Sun King and famously declared that he alone *was* the state. Although this was an overstatement, the absolutist French state of the seventeenth century was the envy of all Europe. France had a standing professional army, a mercantilist state-run economy, an efficient (though deeply regressive) tax system, and the extravagant palace of Versailles.

Neither war nor court life came cheap, however; the drains on the royal coffers, combined with the system of taxation, had by the eighteenth century reduced the French commoners to famine and bankrupted the state. In response, the French Revolution, which began on July 14, 1789, as a protest over rising bread prices, abolished the monarchy.

THE FRENCH REVOLUTION, DESTRUCTION OF THE ARISTOCRACY, AND EXTENSION OF STATE POWER

The early period of the revolution had many democratic features. A **National Assembly** was created, and that body issued the Declaration of the Rights of Man and of the Citizen, which proclaimed the natural rights of the individual in opposition to the tyranny of monarchy. The revolutionaries concluded that the ancien régime, with its hereditary and religious privileges, must be destroyed and replaced. No longer should birth or faith determine justice, public office, or taxation. "Liberty, Equality, Fraternity!" became the rallying cry of the revolution. But unlike their American counterparts, who feared the tyranny of any centralized authority, French revolutionaries never questioned the need for a powerful centralized state, nor did they fear what might happen were that state to fall into the wrong hands.

In 1791, French moderates wrote a new constitution limiting the monarchy and setting up a representative assembly that in many ways resembled Britain's constitutional monarchy. But this middle-ground effort was undermined both by monarchists on the right (conservative nobles and clerics) and by radical anticlerical republicans on the left. Led by a militant faction known as the Jacobins, the radicals seized power and launched a class war, known as the **Reign of Terror**, in which many who stood in the way of this radical vision of republicanism were executed (including the monarch). As in other, later revolutions, such as in the Soviet Union and China, terror bred turmoil and paranoia such that the very perpetrators of the revolution were themselves devoured by the violence. The Jacobins' ruthless leader, Robespierre, became the guillotine's final victim as the Reign of Terror came to an end in 1794. Although the violence ceased, the ideological and cultural division between two poles—conservative, Catholic, and rural versus progressive, secular, and urban—would resonate in French politics for centuries and in some ways persists today.

In 1799, General Napoleon Bonaparte seized power in a coup d'état that brought the decade of revolutionary turmoil to an end. Unlike the revolution that had swept away the former social and political institutions, Napoleon's coup retained and indeed codified key elements of the revolutionary order. The Napoleonic Code documented the principles that all men are equal before the law; that the people, not a monarch, are sovereign; and that the church and state are separate domains. Further enhancing France's long bureaucratic tradition, Napoleon established a meritocratic civil service that was open to all citizens and a system of elite schools to train these functionaries.[1]

TIMELINE Political Development

800 C.E.	"France" first emerges as an independent power under Charlemagne.
1661–1715	Absolute monarchy culminates in rule of Louis XIV.
1789	French Revolution is launched with storming of the Bastille in Paris.
1799	Napoleon Bonaparte seizes power and brings revolution to an end.
1848, 1871	Popular uprisings lead to the Second and Third Republics.
1940	Third Republic is replaced by Vichy (German puppet) regime.
1946	The weak Fourth Republic is established.
1954	The French leave Vietnam in defeat.
1958	Threat of civil war over Algeria returns Charles de Gaulle to office, leading to the ratification of his presidency and the Fifth Republic by referendum.
1968	The Events of May rioters in Paris demand social and educational reforms.
1969	De Gaulle resigns.
1981	François Mitterrand and the Socialists are elected.
1986	First period of "cohabitation" between Socialist president Mitterrand and neo-Gaullist prime minister Jacques Chirac takes place.
1992	Slim majority of French voters approve Maastricht Treaty, establishing the Economic and Monetary Union (within the European Union) and the euro.
2005	In a referendum, French voters reject proposed European Union constitution.
2017	Emmanuel Macron elected president.

THE RETURN TO ABSOLUTISM IN POSTREVOLUTIONARY FRANCE

Napoleon's strong state became even stronger when he was proclaimed emperor for life in a national referendum in 1804, and the First Republic gave way to the First Empire. Over time, Napoleon's rule increasingly resembled the tyranny of the absolute monarchy that had justified the revolution. He ruled for another 10 years and then abdicated the throne for a year in the wake of a series of military defeats at the hands of the hostile conservative monarchies that surrounded France. After a brief return, he was permanently defeated in 1815 by the British at the Battle of Waterloo.

With military support from the victorious European powers, absolute monarchy, not democracy, replaced Napoleon's empire, and the bitter ideological divisions of the revolutionary era reemerged. The Church and the aristocracy reasserted their privileges until a popular revolt in 1830 forced the Crown to establish a constitutional monarchy and promise to pay more respect to the interests of the rising urban middle class. A third revolution, in 1848, ended monarchical rule, established universal male suffrage, and constituted the short-lived Second Republic. The new republic had a directly elected president—the first such office in Europe. This development reflects the ongoing French preference for a strong executive, albeit one directly chosen by the people; it also reflects an amalgam of monarchical and revolutionary values. In 1848, the people elected as their first president Napoleon's nephew, Louis-Napoleon, who followed in his uncle's footsteps, using a national referendum to proclaim himself emperor. In 1852, Louis-Napoleon (now called Napoleon III) replaced the Second Republic with the Second Empire. He ruled for nearly two decades, presiding over a period of peace and rapid industrial growth.

Both peace and prosperity halted with France's defeat in the Franco-Prussian War of 1870–71, in which Napoleon III was captured, and the Second Empire came to an end. Not surprisingly, the absence of central authority once again led to violent conflict between conservative monarchists and radical republicans. Although conservatives came to dominate the National Assembly, radicals in Paris established a short-lived rival government known as the Paris Commune, until French troops crushed the uprising.

DEMOCRATIZATION AND THE WEAK REGIMES OF THE THIRD AND FOURTH REPUBLICS

From the ashes of the Second Empire emerged France's Third Republic, which survived for 70 years—until the outbreak of World War II. The Third Republic was weakened by the persistent and seemingly irreconcilable splits among various ideological factions, ranging from monarchists to anarchists. These divisions made stable government almost impossible, and successive governments often lasted less than a year. Despite weak government, the powerful bureaucracy remained. And allied with French business interests, it continued to promote economic development.

Political divisions were further polarized by the devastation of World War I, during which more than 1.5 million French people died, and by the economic depression that followed. These crises provided fertile ground for both communism and fascism, as political extremists of the left and the right proffered Stalinist Russia and Nazi Germany, respectively, as preferable alternatives to France's weak and immobilized democratic republic.

This debate was preempted by France's swift defeat at the hands of the overwhelming Nazi military force in the opening weeks of World War II. The Nazi victors collaborated with the French right in setting up the puppet Vichy regime, named after the town in central France where the government was based. Even many French moderates ended up supporting this fascist government, reasoning that the Nazis were better than the threat of a Communist government.[2] Other French citizens, however, including Communists and members of religious groups, resisted the Nazi occupation (both from within France and outside the country). Although the resistance effort was diverse and at best only loosely linked, General Charles de Gaulle, who led French forces in England following his retreat from France in 1940, ultimately came to embody the French anti-Nazi movement.

After World War II, de Gaulle's heroic stature as leader of the resistance effort and his role in France's provisional government positioned him to play an important political role in the new Fourth Republic. However, de Gaulle believed that a major weakness of the previous regime was that too little power had been vested in the presidency—a view not shared by other political leaders. As a result, de Gaulle withdrew from politics. After the war, the new Fourth Republic, based on an electoral system of proportional representation and parliamentary government with a weak prime minister, was frequently as paralyzed as the Third Republic had been. No single party or even a stable coalition of parties was able to form a government for long—20 governments were formed in just 12 years—and thus no political leader was in a position to make difficult choices.

During this period, significant progress took place in such areas as postwar reconstruction and the creation of the European Union. The regime, however, could not effectively deal with France's colonial legacy as independence movements in many colonies grew powerful. The situation was particularly acute in Algeria, a North African and Muslim country that had been under French control for over a century. It was also home to some 1 million French and European settlers. Growing Algerian resistance to French rule had led to significant violence between Algerians, settlers, and the French military. By 1958, French generals in Algeria responded by establishing a provisional government and threatening military action against France itself if Algeria did not remain French. Under these dire circumstances, the government called on de Gaulle to return to politics and seek a way out of the crisis.[3]

THE RECOVERY OF STATE POWER AND DEMOCRATIC STABILITY UNDER THE FIFTH REPUBLIC

As he had a decade earlier, de Gaulle insisted that he would serve only if the French people authorized and accepted a new constitution that established a strong executive and addressed the other ills of the Third and Fourth Republics. The new constitution was put to a referendum and accepted. De Gaulle, who had served briefly as the last **prime minister** of the Fourth Republic, became the first president of the new Fifth Republic, in 1959.

Using his sweeping executive authority, from 1959 to 1968 he granted Algeria independence, established France as an independent nuclear power, withdrew it from the military command structure of the North Atlantic Treaty Organization (NATO), promoted European integration, nationalized a number of key industries and private firms, and established a substantial welfare state.

Although he averted civil war, revitalized the French economy, and restored French national pride, de Gaulle was also criticized (particularly by the left) as an authoritarian demagogue. He failed to command the loyalty of a new generation that had no memories of World War II or de Gaulle's role in it. In 1968, many young Parisians took to the streets in what came to be known as **the Events of May**. Students erected barricades and demanded educational changes, and workers seized factories and called for sweeping social reforms. De Gaulle was able to weather these protests, but in the end he lost his mandate. He turned to the public to galvanize support by presenting a referendum in 1969 on various constitutional reforms. When the referendum failed, he resigned from office.

Political Regime

It might seem that de Gaulle's departure would have signaled the end of the Fifth Republic, so tightly connected was it to de Gaulle himself. But rather than prompting a new round of polarized debate, revolution, and yet another constitution, the regime held, and it remains the current regime of France. Although the French had rejected a leader, they chose not to reject his vision of a republic led by a strong national executive. Since de Gaulle, a series of powerful presidents have each contributed to the image of France as a country with a strong bureaucracy, an independent foreign policy, and an economic system tightly connected to the state.

POLITICAL INSTITUTIONS

THE CONSTITUTION France's current regime, the Fifth Republic (1958–present), is codified in the constitution of 1958. The central goal of de Gaulle's constitution was to eliminate the pure parliamentary system and enhance the power of the executive vis-à-vis France's traditionally powerful and fractious legislature. France thus developed a semi-presidential executive system that was innovative at the time. The Fifth Republic created a system whereby political power is shared by the legislature, a directly elected president, and a prime minister who reports to both the president and the legislature.

The French constitution has proved durable and has seen relatively few significant amendments over the past 50 years. Most notable changes have involved the presidency: in 1962, the constitution was modified to allow direct election of the president; and in 2000, the president's term was reduced from seven to five years to limit divided government.

THE BRANCHES OF GOVERNMENT

THE PRESIDENCY Unlike a presidential system, the French semi-presidential system includes a dual executive: the president is head of state, and the prime minister is head of the government. However, the constitution of 1958 is ambiguous in differentiating the powers of the president and the prime minister. Indeed, the French president has relatively few formal powers, but during the course of the Fifth Republic the president has, by precedent, acquired powers somewhat beyond those specified by the constitution.[4] The ability of French presidents to assume powers that are not explicitly delineated in the constitution was facilitated when, from 1958 to 1981, President de Gaulle (and his political heirs, after 1969) controlled both

---

INFOCUS   **Essential Political Features**

- **Legislative–executive system**: Semi-presidential
- **Legislature**: Parlement
  - **Lower house**: Assemblée nationale (National Assembly)
  - **Upper house**: Sénat (Senate)
- **Unitary or federal division of power**: Unitary
- **Main geographic subunits**: Regions
- **Electoral system for lower house**: Single-member districts with two rounds of balloting
- **Chief judicial body**: Conseil Constitutionnel (Constitutional Council) and the Conseil d'État

the legislature and the presidency. Subsequently, from 1981 to 1986, the Socialists enjoyed the same control of the legislature and the executive.

The constitution envisions the French president as a head of state above the parties. But unlike the United Kingdom's merely symbolic head of state, French presidents hold important political powers—though they are far less explicit powers than those held by their U.S. counterparts. Much of the authority of the French presidents results from the prestige and precedent of de Gaulle and from the fact that the president is the only directly elected political figure with a national mandate.[5] Moreover, French presidents are elected for long terms (five years), although, since 2008, they are limited to two terms in office.

According to the constitution of the Fifth Republic, presidents do not directly govern. Rather, they appoint a prime minister, who must be approved by a majority of the lower house of the legislature. The prime minister is supposed to select a cabinet (called the **Council of Ministers**) and preside over the day-to-day affairs of the government. In practice, when French presidents enjoy a majority in the legislature, they select (and can dismiss) both the prime minister and the members of the cabinet.

The 1958 constitution appears to create a potential conflict between a directly elected president and a legislature dominated by the opposition. This is because the constitution requires the legislature to approve the president's choice of prime minister. However, even when presidents have lacked a majority in the legislature, they have compromised by appointing prime ministers from the opposition. The French have dubbed this situation "cohabitation." What might happen should a president

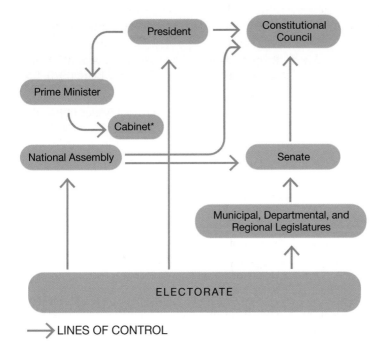

Structure of the Government

*Although the prime minister has the formal authority to select the cabinet, in practice, the president selects both the prime minister and the cabinet.

refuse to compromise is not entirely clear, but to date predictions of a constitutional stalemate have not materialized.

The constitution of the Fifth Republic does give the president some formal tools in addition to those that have become institutionalized over time through precedent. Presidents direct the armed forces. They cannot veto legislation, but they can ask the lower house to reconsider it. They can submit referenda directly to the people. They must sign all laws and decrees. Presidents also have the power to dissolve the legislature and call new elections, a power that has been employed on five occasions, usually to obtain or reinforce legislative majorities to the president's liking. The president also enjoys a powerful staff, whose members help develop and initiate policy and work with the prime minister and the cabinet. The power of the French presidency was underscored in May 2016 when President Hollande used constitutional decree powers to impose a controversial reform of French labor laws, thereby avoiding a vote in the legislature. Opponents of the measure in the lower house failed to pass a censure motion against Hollande's prime minister, Manuel Valls, and the decree stood despite widespread opposition.

Presidents and Prime Ministers of France since 1959

PRESIDENT	DATES IN OFFICE	TERMS	PARTY	PRIME MINISTERS (DATES)
Charles de Gaulle	1959–69 (resigned in second term)	Two	N/A	Michel Debré (1959–62) Georges Pompidou (1962–68) Maurice Couve de Murville (1968–69)
Georges Pompidou	1969–74 (died in office)	One	Gaullist	Jacques Chaban-Delmas (1969–72) Pierre Messmer (1972–74)
Valéry Giscard d'Estaing	1974–81	One	Union for French Democracy	Jacques Chirac (1974–76) Raymond Barre (1976–81)
François Mitterrand	1981–95	Two	French Socialist Party	Pierre Mauroy (1981–84) Laurent Fabius (1984–86) Jacques Chirac (1986–88) Michel Rocard (1988–91) Édith Cresson (1991–92) Pierre Bérégovoy (1992–93) Édouard Balladur (1993–95)
Jacques Chirac	1995–2007	Two	Neo-Gaullist	Alain Juppé (1995–97) Lionel Jospin (1997–2002) Jean-Pierre Raffarin (2002–05) Dominique de Villepin (2005–07)
Nicolas Sarkozy	2007–12	One	Union for a Popular Movement	François Fillon (2007–12)
François Hollande	2012–2017	One	French Socialist Party	Jean-Marc Ayrault (2012–14) Manuel Valls (2014–16) Bernard Cazeneuve (2016–2017)
Emmanuel Macron	2017–present		*La République en Marche!* (Republic Onward!)	Édouard Philippe (2017–present)

Moreover, although the constitution does not specify this authority, presidents have simply asserted the power to remove prime ministers and cabinet members even if those officials have support in the legislature. In short, the prime minister has become a sort of chief aide whose goal is to carry out the president's political agenda. Consequently, the president—not the prime minister—chairs the weekly meetings of the Council of Ministers.

THE PRIME MINISTER French prime ministers are appointed by the president but must have the support of both the president and the legislature. As opposed to many parliamentary systems in which the prime minister is drawn from the members of parliament, Article 23 of the French constitution prevents members of the legislature from serving simultaneously as prime minister. This creates a disconnect between the legislature and the prime minister, and it ties the prime minister more strongly to the president. On paper, the constitution appears to make the prime minister the most powerful politician in France. In practice, though, when presidents enjoy a majority in the legislature, French prime ministers are chiefly responsible for cultivating support for presidential policies from within the legislature rather than setting policy themselves. Prime ministers may be removed with a **motion of censure** (effectively a vote of no confidence), though this requires an absolute majority of the 577 members of the lower house. Though not specified by the constitution, presidents have asserted the right to remove prime ministers even when they are supported by a majority of the legislature (though their replacement must have majority support in the legislature).

When presidents lack a majority in the legislature, which leads to the appointment of a prime minister from an opposing party (**cohabitation**), the prime minister assumes a much greater degree of power, since she or he does not feel bound to subordinate policy matters to a president from another party. Under these conditions, the explicit powers of the prime minister as laid out in the constitution become prominent, effectively creating a parliamentary system with a more ceremonial president.

THE LEGISLATURE France has a bicameral legislature, known as the **parlement**. In fact, it is from France that we get the term *parliament*, which is based on the French word *parler*, meaning "to speak." France's bicameral legislature is composed of the 577-member Assemblée nationale (National Assembly) and a 348-member upper house, the **Sénat** (Senate). Deputies in the National Assembly are elected for five-year renewable terms, and senators are elected for six-year terms. The constitution of the Fifth Republic clearly weakened the legislature vis-à-vis the executive. As a result, the French legislature is weaker than its counterparts in most advanced democracies, but it still plays an important role.[6]

The constitution gives the legislature the right to propose legislation, but most bills (about 80 percent) originate with the executive. The constitution gives the government considerable control over the workings of the legislature, including control of the agenda and the schedule of parliamentary activity. One particularly important instrument that limits the legislature's ability to amend legislation is the **blocked vote**, which forces the legislature to accept bills in their entirety and allows amendments only if they are approved by the government. French legislators also have no power to introduce bills or amendments that affect public spending; only the government may introduce such legislation. Moreover, if the National Assembly does not approve finance bills and the annual budget within 70 days, those items automatically become law.

Another unique feature of the constitution allows governments to submit legislation as motions of confidence. In such cases, the proposed laws are passed unless the legislature can muster a motion of censure against the government. This is not an easy task (it requires an absolute majority), and it may trigger new elections. This feature was used frequently during the 1980s and 1990s as a way of passing important legislation without legislative debate. The constitution's Article 38 also grants the legislature the right to enable the government to legislate via decrees, known as ordinances, though this power has been used sparingly. Finally, the constitution limits the number and power of the legislative committees that once served as powerful legislative tools of previous regimes.

Yet with all of these limitations, the legislature has gradually asserted itself more forcefully. Since the 1970s, it has conducted a weekly questioning of government ministers (though not the president) that is somewhat similar to the British practice known as question time. The French National Assembly now regularly amends legislation, and the executive no longer asserts its right to reject all amendments. In 1995, the legislative session was extended from six months to nine months, and extended special sessions have become fairly common. Legislative committees have become more important in proposing and amending legislation, and motions of censure, while unlikely to pass, are used by the opposition as a way to bring controversial issues to the floor for debate.

A major constitutional reform passed in 2008 has strengthened the National Assembly. This reform made it easier for individual members to introduce legislation, reduced the government's ability to set the legislative agenda, and strengthened the National Assembly's government oversight powers.

The French upper house, the Sénat, is clearly the weaker of the two legislative chambers. It is elected indirectly by an electoral college of local government officials and members of the lower house. This indirect election helps deprive the Sénat of popular legitimacy, and its legislative powers are limited to delaying legislation passed by the lower house. Important legislation has been passed over the objection of the Sénat, most notably during the Socialist governments in power from 1981 to 1986, when the more conservative Sénat opposed much of the legislation enacted by the leftist government. The Sénat's main power resides in its ability to reject constitutional amendments, which require the consent of both houses. In 2016, the Sénat rejected a constitutional amendment proposed by the government that would have stripped French citizenship from dual nationals convicted of committing terrorist acts. Still, the Sénat is widely seen as somewhat obsolete and unrepresentative, composed of elderly conservatives (three-quarters of the representatives are over 65). The French Sénat has been the subject of regular calls for constitutional reform. But since de Gaulle's failed attempt in 1969, the upper house has undergone few constitutional changes.

THE JUDICIARY As in most democracies, the French judiciary is divided into several branches, including civil, criminal, and administrative. The French judicial system is based on continental European code law, in which laws are derived from detailed legal codes rather than from precedent (as in common law used in the United States, Canada, and the United Kingdom). During Napoleon's rule, French laws were systematically codified, and much of that original code remains in place today. The role of judges is simply to interpret and apply those codes. Consequently, judges in France have less discretion and autonomy than those in the common law systems.

The French court system also operates very differently from that in the United States or Canada. Judges play a much greater role in determining whether charges should be brought, and they assume many of the roles of prosecuting attorneys. In France, judges, not lawyers, question and cross-examine witnesses.

Because the 1958 constitution created a semi-presidential system with built-in potential for deadlock of the legislature and the executive, the Fifth Republic also created a **Constitutional Council** to settle constitutional disputes.[7] The Constitutional Council is composed of nine members who are appointed for a single nine-year term by the president and heads of the National Assembly and Sénat. Former presidents of France also serve as lifetime members of the council. The council is empowered to rule on any constitutional matter, so long as there is a request from the government, the president, or at least 60 members of either house of the legislature.

In its early years, the Constitutional Council tended to act rarely, and usually backed presidential actions. Buoyed by very high approval ratings, in recent decades, however, it has shown more independence. For example, in 2008, it rejected legislation that would have allowed for the indefinite imprisonment of dangerous criminals even after their terms had been served. While citizens now have the right to appeal directly to the Constitutional Council to defend their constitutional rights, the vast majority of appeals to the council have come from groups of legislators. One role that the Constitutional Council does not serve is that of a court of last appeal for cases from lower courts; that function is held by other judicial bodies, including the Council of State, France's top administrative court. In 2016, the Council of State struck down laws passed by numerous local governments that would have banned the wearing of the "burkini" (a swimsuit designed to cover virtually the entire body) on beaches (see "Challenges to French National Identity and the Rise of the Nationalist Right," p. 288).

THE ELECTORAL SYSTEM

France's electoral system is majoritarian rather than proportional. Thus, it resembles systems in the United States, Canada, and the United Kingdom more than those in continental Europe. However, the use of a two-round runoff between candidates distinguishes it from the plurality-based system found in those countries. French presidents are directly elected in two rounds of voting every five years. Unless a candidate gets over 50 percent of the vote in the first round (which has never happened in the Fifth Republic), a second round of balloting two weeks later pits the top two candidates against each other.

France also employs a two-round electoral system for its single-member district (SMD) elections of members of the National Assembly. In each district, candidates with over 12.5 percent of the vote face off in a second round of balloting (again, unless a candidate gains over 50 percent of the votes in the first round). During the Socialist administration of François Mitterrand, France experimented with proportional representation for lower house elections, as it had in the Fourth Republic, but then returned to SMDs two years later.[8] Using two rounds of voting does ensure that winning candidates have a majority of the vote in each district, but it still delivers disproportionate outcomes common in SMD elections. In 2017, for example, President

Macron's party won 53 percent of the lower house seats with only 43 percent of the nationwide vote.

By using two rounds of voting for presidential and lower house elections, the French system encourages more parties and candidates than do SMD systems in Canada, the United Kingdom, or the United States. At the same time, the second round of elections still uses a winner-take-all format, and the 12.5 percent threshold for entry into the second round of legislative elections severely limits the number of parties that actually win. The National Front, for example, won nearly 5 percent of the vote in the first round of the 2007 elections, but not a single seat. The complexity of a two-round system can create a rather confusing electoral landscape, because parties and individuals compete for seats while not necessarily expecting that they can win, but rather that a good showing in the first round can translate into leverage to be used against more powerful parties. Small parties, or coalitions, or candidates may throw their support behind a stronger rival as part of a political deal.

REFERENDA

The constitution of the Fifth Republic also allows the president to call national referenda. When de Gaulle lost a 1969 referendum aimed at reforming the upper house of the legislature, he resigned. Since then, referenda have been used less frequently, though often regarding changes to the European Union. Most recently, in 2005, President Chirac submitted a proposed European constitution to a referendum. Voters delivered a resounding rejection of the document despite Chirac's support for it.

LOCAL GOVERNMENT

France is usually considered a prototypical unitary state—all power is concentrated in Paris, the capital and largest city. Furthermore, compared with most of its neighbors, it has experienced relatively little separatism or demands for greater regional autonomy (an independence movement on the island of Corsica is a rare exception). Whereas this is a generally accurate picture, France also has a long history of localism and regionalism that should not be discounted, and three levels of local government—region, department, and commune—that have enjoyed increasing power over time.[9]

France has 18 regions, five of which are overseas. The regions' primary responsibilities are regional planning and economic development. The regions are led by a council that is elected every six years. One level below, 96 departments (plus five overseas territories) have responsibility for such areas as health services and infrastructure. For nearly two centuries, power in the departments resided with a **prefect** appointed by the central government, but a series of reforms in 1982 transferred a great deal of power to directly elected departmental councils, representing over two thousand constituencies called *cantons*. Since 2013, each canton elects a pair of representatives to the department councils, and the pair must consist of a male and female. Finally, at the municipal level there are communes made up of directly elected councils and mayors who handle the main tasks of these communities.

Since the 1982 reforms, local governments have been given some control over taxes and revenues, and as a result their powers have slowly grown. However, their share of the budgetary pie remains very small. A reform passed in 2010 will gradually streamline and reduce the layers and size of French local government. Local governments have decried this project as an attempt to recentralize the country, but the national government has retorted that the current system is too cumbersome and costly.

Local elections in France often serve as a midterm bellwether of sitting governments. The March 2015 local elections, in which the governing Socialists finished third behind the conservatives and the far right, were viewed as a stinging rebuke to President Hollande's government.

Political Conflict and Competition

THE PARTY SYSTEM AND ELECTIONS

By the 1960s, the badly fragmented party system of the Fourth Republic had been replaced by a less fragmented multiparty system that featured a bipolar alternation of coalitions of the center right and the center left. The political bloc of the right was composed mainly of the **Rally for the Republic (RPR)** and the **Union for a Popular Movement (UMP)**. The political bloc of the left was composed mainly of the **French Communist Party (PCF)** and the **French Socialist Party (PS)**. By the late 1970s, each coalition earned about half the vote in French elections. The four major parties together won over 90 percent of the vote. The electoral system helped to ensure this dominance of the two major blocs, because the SMD system, with its two rounds of voting, required coalition building in the second round.

French Presidential Elections, 2017

FIRST ROUND: APRIL 22–23, 2017		
CANDIDATE	PARTY	VOTES (%)
Emmanuel Macron	Republic Onward! (center)	24.0
Marine Le Pen	National Front (right)	21.3
François Fillon	Republicans (center-right)	20.0
Jean-Luc Mélenchon	Indomitable France (left)	19.5
Benoît Hamon	Socialist Party (center-left)	6.4
Nicolas Dupont-Aignan	Republic Arise (center-right)	4.7
Others		4.1
Total		100
SECOND ROUND: MAY 6–7, 2017		
CANDIDATE	PARTY	VOTES (%)
Emmanuel Macron	Republic Onward! (center)	66.1
Marine Le Pen	National Front (right)	33.9
Total		100

Source: French Ministry of the Interior, www.interieur.gouv.fr (accessed 5/8/17).

Since the 1980s, the **four-party, two-bloc system** has been in transition. One important ideological change has been the spectacular demise of the PCF on the left and the emergence of the **National Front (FN)** on the right. The 2017 presidential elections may portend the demise of the two-bloc system that has been in place for almost forty years. Neither of the two finalists for the French presidency represented a major party. **Emmanuel Macron**, a centrist running under the banner of the new centrist *La République en Marche!* (Republic Onward!, REM) party, handily defeated Marine Le Pen, from the far right National Front. The Socialists and the Republicans both performed very poorly. As an additional shock to France's political party system, Macron's REM won an absolute majority in the National Assembly, and France's major parties of the right and left suffered serious losses.

THE FRENCH LEFT Since the 1970s, the Socialist Party (PS) has been the dominant party of the French left, but its dominance was challenged by the presidential elections of 2017.[10] Formed in 1905, the PS was also long divided into social democratic and Marxist camps. In the 1930s, the Socialists were elected to power and led a brief and ill-fated government. After World War II, the Socialist Party reemerged, though it regularly gained fewer votes than the Communists. In the early years of the Fifth Republic, the Socialist Party essentially disappeared until being refounded in 1969 as a much more moderate force. This strategy was vindicated by the 1981 election of François Mitterrand to the presidency; he was the first leftist president of the Fifth Republic. Mitterrand's long presidency (1981–95) was marred by allegations of corruption, by his party's loss of its legislative majority in 1986, and his need to cohabit with a conservative prime minister during most of his two terms in office. The Socialists lost the presidency in 1996, and though they won the legislative election of 1997, they were defeated in the 2002 and 2007 legislative and presidential elections. The 2012 election of President **François Hollande** and the Socialists' absolute majority in the legislature proved to be a short-lived victory. By 2017 the PS had lost the presidency and its majority in the legislature, losing all but 30 of its seats in the lower house in the June legislative elections.

The son of upper-middle-class parents, Hollande was a graduate of the prestigious National Administrative School (ENA) that produces much of the country's bureaucratic and political elite. In the following years, he served in local government, then as a National Assembly deputy, and finally as the leader of the Socialist Party.

Hollande and the PS campaigned on a traditionally leftist platform that included a major tax increase on the wealthy, stricter regulations on the financial sector, reduction of the retirement age that had been raised by his conservative predecessor, and legalization of gay marriage.

Hollande had a difficult presidency.[11] He took office at a time of rising unemployment and growing budget deficits, and he was further damaged by scandals within his cabinet. In March 2014, the Socialists were trounced in local elections and lost control of over 150 localities, including some traditional PS strongholds. Hollande fired his prime minister, Jean-Marc Ayrault, and replaced him with the young and popular Manuel Valls. Valls had been Hollande's interior minister, and was best known for his defense of the 2013 arrest (during a school field trip) and deportation of a 15-year-old Roma girl and her family who were living in France illegally. Valls was criticized by the PS left, but his hard-line stance on immigration was widely popular. Valls was a political centrist who once suggested that the PS should drop the word *socialist* from its label, and he has advocated limits to immigration, the ban on the face veil, and the types of economic reform that are deeply unpopular among the

President Hollande, lamenting his record-low popularity ratings (due largely to France's economic woes), notes that he still has a private life. In fact, widely publicized scandals concerning his private life have also plagued his presidency.

PS left (see "Challenges to French National Identity and the Rise of the Nationalist Right," p. 288).

The terrorist attacks in Paris and Nice in 2015 and 2016 strengthened the conservative and far right opposition to the Socialists. The government's response to those attacks, and a very unpopular reform of French labor laws that was decreed by the government in 2016, further weakened and divided the Socialists. By March 2016, Hollande's approval rating had fallen to 17 percent, the lowest percentage since the start of the Fifth Republic.[12] In late 2016, Hollande announced that he would not seek reelection in 2017, and Prime Minister Valls resigned in order to run for the Socialist Party presidential nomination. In a shocking upset, and a repudiation of Hollande's record in office, Valls lost the primary to Benoît Hamon, representing the far left of the Socialist Party, and was trounced in the first round of elections, winning just over 6 percent of the vote, 22 percent less than Hollande had won in 2012.

The Communist Party (PCF) was the dominant party of the French left after World War II, but in 2012 the Communists won only 10 out of 577 seats in the legislature.

Although other leftist parties exist in France, none of them has much clout. France's environmental party, Europe Ecology—The Greens (EELV), agreed to back the Socialists in the second round in those constituencies where the EELV was eliminated. In exchange, the Socialists committed to a gradual 25 percent reduction in nuclear energy's share of total energy production. The EELV won 5.5 percent of the vote and was awarded two cabinet posts in the Socialist government, but lost ground in 2017, winning only one legislative seat.

THE FRENCH RIGHT The right dominated the politics of the Fifth Republic from 1958 to 1981 under presidents de Gaulle, Pompidou, and Giscard d'Estaing. But since de Gaulle never associated himself with any party, his heirs created various competing parties of the right that were frequently divided by personality and presidential ambitions. The two most important forces were the Rally for the Republic, created by Jacques Chirac, and the **Union for French Democracy (UDF)**, an alliance of five center-right parties founded by Chirac's rival, former president Valéry Giscard d'Estaing. These parties differed in part over the role of the state and their view of the European Union, but over the years, the differences mostly disappeared.

In 2002, President Chirac encouraged most of the center right to cohere as a single party, the Union for a Popular Movement (UMP).[13] The UDF continues to run separately in elections, but its importance has steadily declined (it won less than 3 percent of the vote in 2012). Compared with de Gaulle's eclectic blend of populism and nationalism, the UMP behaves much more like a classical conservative party with its pro-business, pro–free market, and socially conservative outlook.

During the presidency of **Nicolas Sarkozy**, the UMP continued to move in the direction of a free market, though it still supported a relatively strong role for the state.[14] Sarkozy's earliest reforms included a virtual elimination of the inheritance tax and a reduction in taxes on businesses, steps that the president viewed as necessary to stimulate economic growth and employment (but the French left viewed the reforms as favoring the well-off). His administration's proposals to reform the French university and health systems were also controversial and provoked widespread protests. Sarkozy raised the retirement age from 60 to 62, made it easier for firms to employ workers beyond the 35-hour work week, and slashed employment in the public sector. Sarkozy also sought to improve relations with the United States and sent additional French forces to support the U.S.-led war in Afghanistan.

Following Sarkozy's loss in the 2012 presidential election (no president had been turned out of office after one term since 1981), the UMP experienced a period of internal fragmentation. Sarkozy announced his return to politics in 2014 and was elected UMP chairman. Under his leadership, the UMP was renamed the **Republicans**, and his party won a majority of regional offices in the March 2015 elections. In the 2016 Republican presidential primary, François Fillon, a former prime minister under Sarkozy, defeated his former boss and a more moderate former prime minister for the nomination. Fillon won only 20 percent of the vote and failed to make it into the second round of the 2017 elections. The Republicans also fared poorly in the 2017 legislative elections, losing 82 seats, but still remained the largest opposition force in the legislature.

Unity among France's two main conservative parties was partly spurred by the emergence and surprising success of the National Front (FN) on the far right. Until the early 1980s, the FN was a tiny fringe party that never attracted more than 1 percent of the vote. Its emergence as a serious political contender, initially at the local level, was rooted in its advocacy of a reduction in immigration and the expulsion of illegal immigrants. Led by the fiery Jean-Marie Le Pen, it won about 10 percent of the vote in 1986, outpolled the French Communist Party, and won its first seats in the lower house (it won 35 seats). In the 2002 presidential elections, Le Pen benefited from the divided votes among various leftist candidates and made it into a runoff with President Chirac. In the second round, he won less than 20 percent of the vote as voters recoiled from the possibility of a Le Pen presidency. But the factors that make the National Front a success, particularly fears over immigration, remain.

The National Front leadership has been revived with the election of Le Pen's daughter, **Marine Le Pen**, to the top leadership position of the party in 2011. She has reemphasized antiglobalization and Euroskepticism as central values of the party while distancing the FN from the more xenophobic and provocative statements of her less temperate father (see "Challenges to French National Identity and the Rise of the Nationalist Right," p. 288).[15]

Under Marine Le Pen, the FN remains a rightist, nationalist, and socially conservative political party, but she has had some success in moving the party closer to the mainstream of French politics. In the 2012 electoral campaign, she advocated for France to abandon the euro as well as restore the retirement age of 60 (Sarkozy had raised it to 62). At the same time, she pledged to slash legal immigration and deport foreigners convicted of crimes while dramatically beefing up law enforcement (she promised a referendum on instituting the death penalty). In the 2012 presidential elections, Marine Le Pen won about 18 percent of the vote in the first round of elections. It was a historic high for the FN, and in legislative elections the FN established itself as the third largest political force after the PS and the UMP. In May 2014, the unthinkable occurred: the FN won the European elections with 25 percent of the vote, defeating both the UMP and the PS and quadrupling its share of the votes compared with its 2009 European Parliament result.

As part of her plan to make the FN more acceptable to mainstream French voters, Marine Le Pen expelled her father from the party in August 2015 after he made a series of comments that were viewed as racist and xenophobic. This move, and the 2015 and 2016 terrorist attacks, appear to have bolstered popular support for the FN. In the most recent local elections, the FN placed second to the Republicans, handily beating the governing Socialists. Le Pen placed second in the first round of the 2017 presidential elections, winning just over 21 percent of the vote. Facing opposition from most of the parties in the first round, she was able to win just under 34 percent of the vote in the second round. In the 2017 legislative elections, the National Front won only eight seats, a gain of six from the previous election, but an outcome that was far below expectations.

THE FRENCH CENTER By 2017 both the Socialists and mainstream conservatives had been discredited. Hollande's Socialist government was deeply unpopular, and the Socialist Party selected a member of the party's far left as its standard bearer. The candidate for the conservative Republicans was mired in corruption scandals. The election of Emmanuel Macron could portend the emergence of a new political center in France, and perhaps a broader realignment of French politics.

Like most French presidents, Macron was trained as a civil servant at the prestigious National Administrative School and worked in the French Ministry of Economy. After leaving the government to work as an investment banker, he returned to politics to work as an advisor to Socialist President Hollande. In 2014 Hollande appointed him economics minister, and he was responsible for the passage of a series of labor reforms that were bitterly opposed by French trade unions. Macron was briefly a member the Socialist Party, but by 2015 identified himself as an independent. In 2016 Macron quit the government and founded *La République en Marche!* (Republic Onward!, REM) as a centrist political party to support his presidential bid. The party declared itself to be free-market friendly, socially progressive, and pro–European Union.

During the 2017 presidential campaign Macron was attacked by much of the French left as unsympathetic to workers and beholden to the corporate world. Rightists attacked his strong support for the European Union, his advocacy of free trade, and his progressive stance on social positions. At the same time, his campaign attracted support from more centrist Socialists and conservatives. His youth (at 39 he was the youngest French president ever elected), his relative inexperience, and his vague campaign platform make Macron and his REM party unknown quantities in the context of the

The 2017 election of centrist Emmanuel Macron (right) was a shock to the established parties to his right and left. Although Macron had briefly been a member of the Socialist Party, he selected a member of the Conservative opposition, Édouard Philippe (left), to be his prime minister.

French National Assembly Elections, 2012 and 2017

PARTY	2012			2017		
	% VOTE (FIRST ROUND)	# SEATS (SECOND ROUND)	% SEATS (SECOND ROUND)	% VOTE (FIRST ROUND)	# SEATS (SECOND ROUND)	% SEATS (SECOND ROUND)
Republic Onward!	—	—	—	28.2	53.0	306
Socialist Party	29.2	280	48.5	7.4	5.2	30
Republicans (previously Union for Popular Movement)	26.2	194	33.6	15.8	19.4	112
Other parties of the left	9.6	61	10.6	20.9	12.8	45
Other parties of the right	2.4	35	6.1	7.3	1.4	8
National Front	13.8	2	0.4	13.2	1.4	8
Others	18.8	5	0.8	7.2	6.8	68
Total	100	577	100	100	100	577

Source: French Ministry of the Interior, www.interieur.gouv.fr (accessed 6/26/17).

previously stable French political party system. Macron was able to quickly recruit members to run for legislative office, drawing on a core of young supporters. Half of REM's candidates had never run for elective office, and half were women. Despite predictions to the contrary, REM won a majority in the National Assembly, shocking the political establishment.

Macron appointed Édouard Philippe, a member of the conservative Republican Party, as his prime minister. Like Macron, Philippe was trained at France's elite administrative schools, spent time in the business sector, briefly held membership in the Socialist Party, and had relatively little experience in government. Half the members of Macron's first cabinet were women, and the new president appointed members from both the center-right and center-left.

CIVIL SOCIETY

As early as the 1830s, the French scholar Alexis de Tocqueville noted the weakness of French civil associations. Most scholars argue that French interest groups and associations remain weaker than those in most advanced democracies, a function of the powerful state and the emphasis on so-called mass action over organized lobbying. Nevertheless, trade unions and organizations representing private enterprise are two important elements of civil society that are worth discussing in detail.

LABOR UNIONS Observers of French politics, particularly its numerous strikes, commonly speak of how powerful the French labor unions are. This view is misleading. In fact, French labor unions have a long history of being weak and fractious. Less than 8 percent of the French workforce belongs to a union, one of the lowest rates in Europe.[16] And unlike the powerful trade unions found elsewhere on the continent, French labor unions usually have been divided along partisan lines.

Among the most powerful French union confederations is the **General Confederation of Labor (CGT)**, historically linked to the PCF. Its leadership includes many Communist Party members, but many non-Communists are part of the general membership. The CGT was long France's most powerful union, but its power and membership have dwindled, much as the French Communist Party has become a shadow of its former self. Today, the confederation members represent about a quarter of the unionized workforce (and only about 3 percent of all workers are CGT members).

In contrast, the **French Democratic Labor Confederation (CFDT)** and Force Ouvrire (FO) have tended to have more centrist or anticommunist orientations. The CFDT is roughly equal in strength to the CGT, and the FO is slightly smaller. A number of other independent unions exist outside of these larger confederations, and some of them, like the national teachers' union, have waged fierce battles against government reform efforts. In France, more than one trade union can represent workers in French firms, pitting competing unions against each other (in many countries, workers select a single union to represent them).

Paradoxically, the weakness and fragmentation of French unions partially explains the large number of strikes that occur in France. More powerful unions could effectively engage in productive bargaining with employers or the government, but French unions lack this authority. Instead, they resort to public demonstrations and work stoppages as a vital tool to express discontent, a tactic that capitalizes on the French tendency toward mass action and public protest. This was the case in the spring of 2016, when French unions, led by the CGT, staged a wave of strikes to protest the Socialist government's labor law reform, which would make it easier for French firms to fire workers and weaken the power of unions. The CFDT backed the Socialist government and its proposed reforms, highlighting the fragmentation of the French labor movement.

Despite their weakness, unions continue to play a key role in French society and in the management of the country's major welfare organizations (health care, retirement, and social security). French law gives unions the right to represent all workers in firms that employ over 50 employees, whether or not the workers are union members. They are also strongly represented in France's public-sector workforce and are a power to reckon with when any French government attempts to reform welfare benefits.

PRIVATE ENTERPRISE Compared with French labor, the business sector is well organized. Large firms are represented by MEDEF (Movement of French Businesses), and smaller firms are represented by CGPME (General Confederation of Small- and Medium-Size Businesses). Both have tended to support lower taxes on business, more flexible laws to regulate the hiring and firing of workers, and a reduced role for government in the economy. Business has generally supported parties on the right, such as the UMP. Since large numbers of France's business leaders are *énarques*, French business often has privileged access to the state bureaucracy. Not surprisingly, MEDEF

French students demonstrate against the government's proposed labor law reform on March 24, 2016, in Strasbourg, eastern France. Students were at the forefront of protests over the reforms aimed at freeing up the job market and reining in France's high unemployment rate.

has been a strong supporter of economic reforms; CGPME has been less enthusiastic, fearing that deregulation will remove many of the barriers that currently protect small businesses from competition.

ORGANIZED RELIGION Unlike labor unions and private business firms, organized religious institutions have had less of a role in French civil society. France is formally a Catholic nation, and despite minorities of Muslims, Protestants, and Jews, well over half of the French are nominally Catholics. Yet even with the predominance of a single religion, France has long been an anticlerical society. This trait dates back to the revolution, when people saw the church as a tool of monarchical power.[17]

Church and state have been formally separate since 1905 under what is known as *laïcité* (roughly translated as "secularism"). Under *laïcité*, no religion can receive state support, and religious education is restricted. The church continues to play a role in important social rituals (marriages, births, funerals), but not in the daily lives of most French citizens. The church lacks an important or central role in French politics, which has no Christian democratic party as found in other Catholic countries such as Italy or Germany. The church can, however, rally to the defense of its own institutional issues: in the 1980s, church opposition forced the Socialist government to back away from plans to impose stricter government control over religious schools.

As the Catholic Church has waned in power, other religions, particularly Islam, have grown. France has thus seen a rapid growth in mosques and Islamic educational and cultural institutions, something that has made many French citizens nervous. For many of these institutions, the Union of Islamic Organizations acts as an umbrella group. In 2002, the government created the French Council of the Muslim Faith to act as an intermediary between the government and Muslim leaders. This council has had limited success in building state-faith relations, and tensions remain, some of which we discuss next.

Society

ETHNIC AND NATIONAL IDENTITY

In modern times, the French have tended to view themselves as ethnically homogeneous. However, historically this was not the case, and recent trends have challenged that notion. In centuries past, many parts of France maintained distinct ethnic identities that included their own languages and cultures: Gascon, Savoyard, Occitan, Basque, and Breton are just a few. Over time, these unique communities were largely assimilated into a single French identity, though certain ethnic groups, particularly Basques and Corsicans, have retained stronger language and cultural ties.

Assimilation was in part connected to the particular role the French state played in the development of national identity. An important facet of the French Revolution was the idea of a set of universal rights that identified people as citizens rather than subjects of the state. This form of republicanism was unlike that of the American Revolution, where democracy was predicated on an individualism that demanded federalism and a state with lower autonomy and capacity. French revolutionaries believed in the necessity of a powerful state to destroy the institutions of the past (including ethnic identity) and to serve the people's general interests in building the future. A powerful state thus became a key instrument in solidifying and expressing French national identity and patriotism in a way that did not occur in the United States.[18] In contrast to U.S. policy, in France, rivals for public loyalty were eradicated or brought under the control of the state.

This relationship between state and nation is now being challenged by changes in both religious and ethnic identity. In the past, *laïcité* served to subordinate religious identity to the state, and ethnic identities were downgraded through assimilation and nationalism. In fact, French identity is so primary that the national census and opinion surveys cannot, by law, record such basic information as ethnicity and religion (the data on religion and ethnic identity are therefore inexact estimates).

However, ethnic and religious identities are becoming more salient. In the past few decades, France has seen an influx of people from outside Europe, notably from

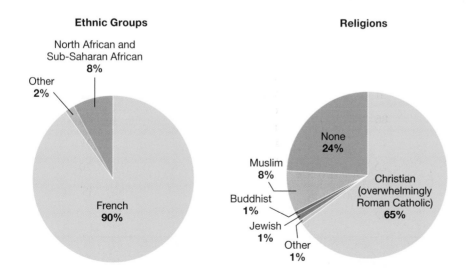

Ethnic Groups

North African and
Sub-Saharan African
8%

Other
2%

French
90%

Religions

None
24%

Muslim
8%

Buddhist
1%

Jewish
1%

Other
1%

Christian
(overwhelmingly
Roman Catholic)
65%

Africa, the Middle East, and Southeast Asia. French citizens of immigrant origin today make up perhaps as much as a fifth to a quarter of the population.[19] As in many countries, immigrants to France and their children often find themselves marginalized due to persistent discrimination, language barriers, and/or a lack of education. French citizens of immigrant origin have virtually no representation in the country's political class, and according to one recent study, France lags far behind its European counterparts in this area.[20] Many immigrants are concentrated in housing projects on the outskirts of Paris and other large cities, where they have poor social services, limited employment opportunities, and little access to transportation. This ghettoization compounds the sense of disconnect from French life and has led to violence. In 2005, France saw a month of heavy rioting across its immigrant suburbs, culminating in a state of emergency and approximately $200 million in damages. A second set of riots, not as large though more violent, occurred in 2007.

In the debate over immigration, the future of the Muslim community takes center stage. Currently, France has the largest Muslim population in Europe outside Turkey; it is estimated at 5 to 6 million people (approximately 10 percent of the population, including foreign born and those born in France). The growth of a large Muslim population has been disconcerting for a country that historically has been overwhelmingly Catholic, if now only nominally so. This situation, not unlike that of other Western countries, is compounded by the particular position of the French state. *Laïcité* means that Muslims are expected to place their faith below that of national and patriotic identity as part of the assimilation process. Yet many Muslims believe that the French state should be more accommodating to their needs, rather than vice versa. Furthermore, in the face of persistent marginalization, many Muslims turn to their faith as a source of identity and meaning.[21]

In the past few years, one prominent example of this conflict has been over the head scarf. Growing expressions of Muslim identity have been a challenge to *laïcité*—in particular, whether girls can wear a head scarf in public schools. Many French on both the left and right have argued that educational institutions, as part of the

IN COMPARISON   Religion and Morality

Is it necessary to believe in God in order to be moral and have good values?
Percentage saying yes:

COUNTRY	PERCENTAGE	COUNTRY	PERCENTAGE
Nigeria	91	Japan	42
Brazil	86	Russia	38
South Africa	75	Germany	33
India	70	United Kingdom	20
United States	53	France	15
Mexico	52		

Note: Data on Iran and China not available.

Source: Pew Center for the People and the Press, 2011 and 2013.

state, cannot allow the wearing of the head scarf without violating the principle of *laïcité*. After a long discussion, France passed a law in 2004 that forbade the wearing of any "conspicuous religious symbol" in schools, whatever the faith. In 2011, the French government went further, banning full-face veils in public and arguing that such coverings promote separatism. While the law generated protest, it has not been much enforced. Whether such steps will help bring minorities into the mainstream or further marginalize them is open to debate. Many French point out that the United Kingdom's much more multicultural approach—for example, female Muslims in the British police force may wear head scarves—has not prevented similar problems of marginalization, and that the Muslim community in the United Kingdom is much more radicalized than it is in France.

How is France resolving these conflicts over immigration and religion? Under President Sarkozy, the government emphasized the need for increased restrictions on immigration, greater emphasis on integrating immigrant populations, and increased emphasis on so-called law and order (which is widely understood to mean a focus on crime committed by immigrants and their offspring and is, to many observers, a not particularly subtle expression of racism). In 2009, Sarkozy proposed a national debate on "what it means to be French." But the debate led to an outpouring of anti-immigrant sentiment, and the government put a stop to the initiative.[22] Sarkozy continued to highlight the challenges of immigration during the 2012 election campaign, partly in an attempt to defend the UMP against the rising National Front. Socialist president Hollande supported the ban on head scarves, and proposed other anti-immigration measures traditionally advocated by the right. The January 2015

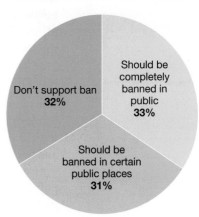

Support for Restricting Public Wearing of the Face Veil in France

Don't support ban **32%**

Should be completely banned in public **33%**

Should be banned in certain public places **31%**

Source: TNS-Sofres Survey, 2010.

A woman wearing a burkini walks in the water August 27, 2016, on a beach in Marseille, France, the day after the country's highest administrative court suspended a ban on full-body burkini swimsuits that has outraged many Muslims.

attacks in Paris by French Islamist terrorists on the satirical weekly Charlie Hebdo, the November 2015 bombings in Paris, and the July 2016 terrorist attack in Nice heightened the tension between the French commitment to *laïcité* and its growing Muslim minority. In response to those attacks, millions of French citizens took to the streets to protest Islamist terrorism.

IDEOLOGY AND POLITICAL CULTURE

The role of the state in shaping French national identity can be seen in the country's ideological landscape and political culture. Ideological divisions in France are much more fragmented than are those in other European countries, where a few coherent and persistent parties tend to dominate the political scene. Divisive historical events, the weakness of civil society, the importance of the state, de Gaulle's hostility toward political parties, the two-round electoral system, and semi-presidentialism have all played a part in creating a system in which individual political leaders, rather than ideological groupings, have been central.

As a result, although we can speak generally of left and right, social democratic or liberal, in fact, the ideological divisions are much more diverse and reflect a range of experiences, such as the battles over the French Revolution and the role of the Catholic Church in French life. In many cases, these values cannot be classified as an ideology at all but rather fall under the term **populism**, or a set of ideas including faith in the common man and suspicion of organized power. From the revolution to Napoleon to de Gaulle, French leaders have often appealed to the masses by seeking to transcend ideology and speak for the people. This populism has helped keep civil society and ideology weak by fostering an ongoing mistrust of such institutions as political parties.

The residual strength of populist ideas explains not only why ideological divisions in France are as much within groups as between them but also why one of the most notable elements of French political culture is the tendency toward mass protests. With civic organizations being too weak to articulate public concerns and with individuals being faithful to the populist notion that the people must struggle against those in power, one of the most common forms of political activity in France is mass protest: marches, demonstrations, and strikes. For example, France regularly averages more than 1,000 workers' strikes per year, compared with fewer than 200 in the United Kingdom. Still, French respondents to political surveys tend to put themselves more on the left of the political spectrum than do those in the United States, the United Kingdom, or Canada.

At the same time, France's populism and faith in the power of mass action is combined with a strong sense of national and patriotic identity and pride in the French state as well as a belief that France is exceptional among countries. This perspective has led to frequent conflict with the United States, a rival with a similar notion of its own exceptionalism but whose ideology of individualism runs counter to the French vision.

Political Economy

Like its continental neighbors, France provides for a strong state role in the political economy. Part of this is a function of modern social democratic policies, whereas other elements can be traced over the course of several centuries.

In the aftermath of World War II, the French government set out to rapidly transform the economy. This took the form of what the French termed **dirigisme**, which can be explained as an emphasis on state authority in economic development—a combination of both social-democratic and mercantilist ideas. Dirigisme involved the nationalization of several sectors of the economy (such as utilities), the promotion of a limited number of "national champion" industries to compete internationally (such as Airbus), the creation of a national planning ministry, and the establishment of the ENA and similar schools to ensure the education of bureaucrats who would be able to direct the economy.

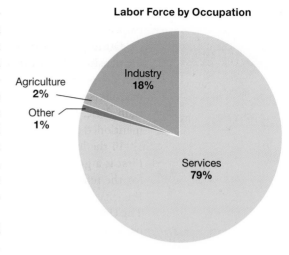

Labor Force by Occupation

Industry 18%

Agriculture 2%

Other 1%

Services 79%

True to its objectives, the dirigiste system helped bring about a transformation of the French economy. Economic wealth grew rapidly, along with increased urbanization. Through the help of economic subsidies from the European Union, France was also able to change its agricultural sector from one of small farms to one of large-scale production. Whereas in the 1950s, France's per capita gross domestic product (GDP) was approximately half that of the United States, within 20 years it had surpassed its historical rivals, the United Kingdom and Germany.[23] Dirigisme, however, came with costs, including a large public sector, an expansive welfare system, and a heavy tax burden.

In an era when most capitalist democracies, including those with social-democratic political economies, are privatizing state-owned firms, the French state has continued to play a very large role in its economy.

As with many other economic systems around the world, in the past 20 years this model has been put to the test. By the mid-1980s, unemployment had risen to over 10 percent, a rate that has persisted and is disproportionately concentrated among the young. Economic growth, which had been double that of the United States from the 1950s to the 1970s, fell to below 2 percent, among the lowest in the European Union. Due to this slow growth, France's per capita GDP has stagnated, again falling below the United Kingdom and Germany and once-poorer countries such as Ireland. France also faces the Europe-wide dilemma of an aging population, compounded by a large public-sector workforce that can retire early with generous benefits. As the French population has grown older, it is thus using an ever-greater share of the welfare system, though fewer young workers are available to fund those expenditures.

The French government has found it difficult to respond to these challenges, in part because of its political culture. As the dirigiste model faces internal stresses, the French economy is also being buffeted by international competition from the United States and Asia as well as within the European Union itself. Increasing globalization presents new opportunities for France's economy, but for many French, globalization is seen as risky economic liberalism extended to the international level. Tellingly, when the French speak of economic liberalization or globalization, they speak of an Anglo-Saxon model, by which they mean the United Kingdom and the United States. Many French thus are worried that domestic economic reforms will essentially Americanize France, undermining their core identity. France is awash in discussions that the country is in decline and must carry out radical change if it is to survive in a changing world. It was Sarkozy's very call for a rupture with the past that helped him win the presidential election.

During his presidency, President Sarkozy proposed a number of changes, including pension reform, expanding the work week, lowering taxes, raising the retirement age, deregulating business, liberalizing the labor market, and cutting government payrolls (see "The Future of the French Welfare State," p. 290). These were easier said than done. Sarkozy faced numerous protests, including the massive 2010 strikes mentioned earlier, and his emphasis on reform no doubt contributed to his defeat.

In the long term, however, some elements may be working in favor of reform. First is a growing consensus that reform is necessary, even if there is less appetite for the reforms themselves. Second is that despite the structural problems of the French economy, in many ways it is highly competitive and thus amenable to reform. The United States may have a higher GDP per capita, for example, but that is partly because Americans work much longer hours than the French. But French workers produce more, per hour of labor, than Germans, British, or Canadians (and only a bit less than Americans).[24] The question is whether France will be able to seize upon the recent EU crisis to turn the country in a new direction.

The return of the Socialist Party to government under François Hollande in 2012 raised new concerns about France's ability to reform its economy. Hollande campaigned on a pledge to raise taxes on the wealthiest French to a 75 percent rate, to rein in the excesses of the financial sector, and to increase social spending. During the first two years of his presidency, the French economy performed very poorly, while other European economies were rebounding. Growth was flat, investment was stagnant, and unemployment remained high. In March 2014, after Hollande's Socialists were drubbed in local elections, the president appointed a new prime minister, Manuel Valls, and a new non-Socialist economy minister, (now President) Emmanuel Macron, who implemented spending cuts and rolled back some tax increases (including the 75 percent tax rate on the wealthiest). In 2016, the Hollande government reformed France's antiquated labor laws that made it difficult to fire workers (and therefore discouraged the creation of full-time jobs), leading to a nationwide wave of strikes and protests. Among other measures, the new law weakens the 35-hour work week, allowing workers to work longer hours in exchange for overtime pay.

Current Issues in France

CHALLENGES TO FRENCH NATIONAL IDENTITY AND THE RISE OF THE NATIONALIST RIGHT

The economic downturn across Europe and the surge of high-profile terrorist attacks in France in 2015 and 2016 have raised fears among many Europeans and outside observers that these difficulties will not just undermine the European Union but also lead to the emergence of populist, nationalist, and xenophobic forces across the continent.

As we have seen in this chapter, support for the rightist National Front is growing. Many French citizens feel threatened by social and economic changes that have accelerated over the last decade. Under the leadership of Marine Le Pen, the National Front has adopted a hostile attitude to the European Union—the FN charges the European Union with being overly bureaucratic, views bureaucracy as a sign of all that is wrong with globalization, and blames it for the wave of immigration. Thus, the FN is calling for France to abandon the euro.

For now, France's electoral system will continue to limit the FN from becoming a major force in the legislature. However, the continued and perhaps growing power of the party will mean that to win elections, the major parties on the left and right will need to contend with their views and even co-opt them. We can already see ample evidence that the FN has changed France's political landscape. During Sarkozy's presidency, legislation was passed banning the wearing of the face veil, the full-face covering worn by some Muslim women (this policy was supported by and continued under President Hollande). In 2016, a number of local governments passed laws banning the "burkini" bathing suit (which covers almost the entire body) on public beaches, until the law was ruled unconstitutional by the courts.

In March 2014, after his Socialist party suffered serious losses to the UMP and FN in local elections, Hollande replaced his prime minister with Manuel Valls, known best for his vigorous enforcement of immigration laws during his stint as Hollande's interior minister. Valls supported the laws passed in 2016 to restrict the public wearing of the burkini swimsuit on French beaches, denouncing that swimsuit as a symbol of "fatal, retrograde Islamism."[25]

After the 2015 and 2016 terrorist attacks in France, most French politicians were careful to point out that the acts were not a representation of mainstream Islam. However, Le Pen, who has compared the Muslim presence in France to the Nazi occupation of the country in the 1940s, stated that the attack was carried out "in the name of radical Islam."

The rise of the FN exposes a deep contradiction in French society. On the one hand are France's republican ideals, rooted in the French Revolution and calling for political freedom, equality of all citizens, a strong national identity, and a strict separation of church and state (*laïcité*). On the other hand is a growing uneasiness about France's growing ethnic diversity, its integration into the European Union, and the need to adapt the "French model" to pressures of globalization. The fact that Marine Le Pen was able to make it to the second round of the 2017 presidential election is

French president of the far right party Front National (FN) and candidate for the 2017 presidential election, Marine Le Pen speaks during her campaign rally on September 3, 2016, in Brachay, France. She won about a third of the vote in the second round of the 2017 presidential elections.

a sign that the FN has tapped into a deep well of discontent in France. But the FN's drubbing in the 2017 legislative elections shows that a strong majority of French voters continue to reject the FN's message.

THE FUTURE OF THE FRENCH WELFARE STATE

What's wrong with France's welfare state? After all, other wealthy European social democracies like Germany, Sweden, and Norway have high taxes and high rates of social spending but have been able to sustain economic growth, high levels of employment, and international competitiveness.[26] France, in contrast, has suffered high unemployment rates (hovering around 10 percent since the 1980s) and has gone from having the world's 8th largest per capita GDP in 1980 down to number 19 by 2008. Private sector growth during that time averaged only 0.8 percent, the second lowest rate among the affluent capitalist democracies that are members of the Organisation for Economic Co-operation and Development (OECD), and the national debt almost tripled. Despite a steady increase in social spending during that period, France faced growing unrest among its poor, immigrant, and under-employed citizens. France's economic stagnation has led to widespread pessimism. In the words of one political scientist, France's "social and economic problems were shared by a handful of other rich European nations, but in no other was the gap between political ideals and social realities so pronounced."[27]

France's European social democratic peers all implemented major reforms of their welfare states in the 1980s and 1990s. They restructured pension and taxation systems, made it easier for employers to hire and fire workers, and trimmed their welfare bureaucracies. Why haven't such reforms prospered in France?

Part of the answer lies in the peculiar nature and rigidity of France's welfare state. Unlike its social democratic counterparts, France has some of the strongest legal protections for its employed workers. These laws make it difficult to lay off workers, in turn making French employers wary of hiring new ones. France's social spending has increased more rapidly than in other social democracies—and, more important, most of that spending went to the already employed middle class. France had one of the world's costliest welfare states that benefited the two-thirds of the population that least needed social benefits. While depriving the poorest French of needed social spending, this system created a solid majority of French citizens who benefit from, and who have opposed any attempt to roll back, France's welfare state.

French political culture became another obstacle to reform. Advocates of implementing the types of welfare reforms that were successful in Scandinavia, Germany, and elsewhere were often portrayed as advocates of globalization and enemies of "the French model." This criticism has come from both the French left and rising French right.

In an attempt to revive France's sclerotic economy, Nicolas Sarkozy campaigned for the presidency in 2007 on a platform of major reform to France's welfare state. He called for a smaller and more efficient public sector, an increase in the retirement age, a reform of French labor laws, and a reduction in taxes. Armed with a strong electoral mandate and a majority in the legislature, Sarkozy might have been expected to implement a significant modernization of France's welfare state. Instead, and despite some relatively minor successes, the reform project stalled. By the end of Sarkozy's term, an additional 1 million people were unemployed, the national debt had skyrocketed, and the poverty rate had increased significantly. What happened?

While it is tempting to blame Sarkozy's failure on the global economic crisis that coincided with his term in office, a better explanation can be found in French politics, the strength of vested interest groups, and the way that French politics reflected French political culture.

In short, the French public supported the *idea* of welfare state reform by electing Sarkozy in 2007, but it vigorously resisted attempts to implement reforms. Although France's welfare state was clearly too costly and inefficient (not to mention insufficiently directed toward France's poor), too many French citizens stood to lose from welfare state reform. Frustrated by societal resistance to his proposed reform, under attack from both the left and the right, and eager to win reelection, Sarkozy soon abandoned much of his reform agenda.

Nevertheless, at some point France will need to undertake a reform of its welfare state. Even François Hollande, who campaigned in 2012 against the Sarkozy reforms and advocated instead a series of tax hikes on the wealthy and an increase in social spending, realized that the current model is unsustainable. And, as we have seen, in May 2016 Hollande's government proposed a major overhaul of the country's restrictive labor laws. President Hollande employed a rarely used decree power to impose the law and avoid a vote in the lower house, provoking outrage from within his own party, and strikes and protests throughout the country. Emmanuel Macron, elected president in May 2017, was an economics minister under President Hollande, and was responsible for designing the law. Macron's appointment of Édouard Philippe, a center-right politician with experience in the private sector, as well as Macron's ability to win a majority in the legislature, suggest that efforts to reform France's welfare state are likely to continue.

Key Terms

absolute monarchy (p. 263)

blocked vote (p. 271)

code law (p. 272)

cohabitation (p. 271)

Constitutional Council (p. 273)

Council of Ministers (p. 269)

dirigisme (p. 287)

the Events of May (p. 267)

Fifth Republic (p. 261)

four-party, two-bloc system (p. 276)

French Communist Party (PCF) (p. 275)

French Democratic Labor Confederation (CFDT) (p. 281)

French Revolution (p. 261)

French Socialist Party (PS) (p. 275)

General Confederation of Labor (CGT) (p. 281)

Hollande, François (p. 276)

laïcité (p. 282)

Le Pen, Marine (p. 278)

Macron, Emmanuel (p. 276)

motion of censure (p. 271)

National Assembly (p. 264)

National Front (FN) (p. 276)

parlement (p. 271)

populism (p. 286)

prefect (p. 274)

prime minister (p. 267)

Rally for the Republic (RPR) (p. 275)

Reign of Terror (p. 264)

Republicans (p. 278)

Sarkozy, Nicolas (p. 278)

semi-presidential (p. 268)

Sénat (p. 271)

Union for a Popular Movement (UMP) (p. 275)

Union for French Democracy (UDF) (p. 278)

A 2013 CDU campaign poster featuring Chancellor Angela Merkel. It reads: "CDU: Successful Together" and "Germany is strong. And shall remain so." After the September 2017 general elections, Merkel was preparing to begin her fourth term as German chancellor.

Germany

Why Study This Case?

Germany commands a prominent position in the world and a pivotal position in Europe. It is Europe's largest and the world's third-largest exporting nation, Europe's biggest economy, the European Union's most populous country, and an integral member of Europe's economic, political, and security organizations. Situated in the heart of the Continent, Germany today in many ways typifies the political, social, and cultural values and institutions of Europe and offers a useful window into the political institutions and public policies shared broadly by many of its European neighbors. By and large, Germans embrace social-democratic political and economic values, champion postmaterialist concerns for the environment, the pursuit of leisure, and human rights, and vigorously promote European integration even as they seek to enhance the competitiveness of Germany's capitalist economy and to strengthen Germany's national security. But in other fundamental ways, Germany sits apart from its European neighbors and poses interesting puzzles for the comparative political scientist.

Germany became a unified state only in the nineteenth century, and perhaps as a result, German nationalism took on powerful and ultimately virulent and destructive force in the twentieth century at the hands of Nazi fascists. The disastrous consequences of this hypernationalism led the allies who defeated Germany to divide the nation in 1945, a division perpetuated for over three decades by the Cold War.

The very successes of German industrialization, democratization after World War II, and peaceful reunification have left the country uncertain about its future. Globalization poses new challenges to Germany's vaunted welfare state. Immigration has raised old questions about race and national identity; the end of the Cold War changed Germany's role as a linchpin of East-West relations; and the expansion of the European Union eastward has weakened the central role that

DENMARK

Baltic Sea

North Sea

Kiel

N

Hamburg

POLAND

Oder R.

THE NETHERLANDS

Hannover

BERLIN

Weser R.

Elbe R.

Essen

Leipzig

Düsseldorf

SAXONY

Dresden

Cologne

Rhine R.

Weimar

Chemnitz

Bonn

LUX.

Frankfurt

CZECH REPUBLIC

Nuremberg

BAVARIA

FRANCE

Danube R.

Stuttgart

BADEN-WÜRTTEMBERG

Munich

Lake Constance

AUSTRIA

SWITZERLAND

the country historically played in that organization. Germany remains a major power, but its role in the post–Cold War international system seems muted, a reflection of a country still troubled by its past and uncertain what future responsibilities it must shoulder.

Historical Development of the State

THE ABSENCE OF A STRONG CENTRAL STATE DURING THE HOLY ROMAN EMPIRE, 800–1806

In 800 C.E., Charlemagne founded in western and central Europe what came to be known as the Holy Roman Empire. By the middle of the ninth century, a collection of German, Austrian, and Czech princes acquired nominal control of this loosely constituted empire, or reich. As a feudal empire, it encompassed an odd assortment of hundreds of principalities, city-states, and other local political entities with varying degrees of autonomy and legitimacy, but there was virtually no allegiance to the center. This weak confederation waxed and waned in size and influence over the next 1,000 years, persisting until the time of Napoleon in the nineteenth century. Whereas comparable feudalism gave way to centralized states in England and France, the Holy Roman Empire remained politically fragmented. The empire took political form with the office of a weak emperor, which rotated among princes, and the imperial Reichstag, or "Congress."

UNIFICATION OF THE GERMAN STATE, THE RISE OF PRUSSIA, AND THE SECOND REICH, 1806–1918

Napoleon's invasion of Germany in 1806 effectively destroyed the empire, inadvertently began the process of German unification, and unleashed the forces of German nationalism that would ultimately lead to the rise of Nazi fascism. Napoleon's offensive wiped out many of the empire's sovereign principalities (there were some 300 at the time) and compelled others to merge with their larger neighbors for protection. Ultimately, only Prussia to the east and Austria to the south were strong enough to resist Napoleon's onslaught and avoid inclusion in the confederation of defeated territories he formed. After Napoleon's defeat in 1815, German allies under Prussian leadership set up a loose confederation of some 40 sovereign mini-states that created for the first time the semblance of a German state.

Over the course of the eighteenth and nineteenth centuries, the kingdom of Prussia in eastern Germany gradually acquired the autonomy, capacity, and legitimacy that allowed it to emerge as a viable core for a modern German state. A series of generally enlightened monarchs established an authoritarian state administered by an efficient and loyal bureaucratic staff, supported by a conservative and wealthy landed aristocracy and defended by a large and well-trained standing army. Just as important as the state's monopoly on violence was its mercantilist promotion of economic growth through the development of national infrastructure, the expansion of education among its subjects, and the enhancement of trade. Prussia established a customs union with neighboring German states that by 1834 included all but Austria.

By the 1860s, Prussia had forceful and capable leadership, a powerful military, and a growing industrial economy. Impressive war victories over Denmark, Austria, and ultimately France drew other German states into the cause and led, in 1871, to the establishment of a national German empire, or what came to be known as the Second Reich. Although the Prussian king was crowned emperor of all Germany, the key figure in the process of expansion and unification was Count Otto von Bismarck, prime minister, or chancellor, of Prussia. A politician, military officer, and member of the landed class, he led a so-called revolution from above in which regime change came not from the lower, disenfranchised classes, but rather from an alliance of "iron and rye"—meaning the industrialists and the landed aristocracy. Through the savvy use of diplomacy, war, and political machinations, the Iron Chancellor, as Bismarck came to be known, dominated German politics for two decades and brought about the first unified modern German state.

Not surprisingly, unified Germany's first national constitution established an authoritarian monarchy with only the trappings of liberal democracy. Sovereignty remained vested in the emperor, or kaiser (derived from the Latin *Caesar*), and political power flowed from him. The Iron Chancellor took no chances that the constitution's nominal democratic allowances would get in the way of his forced-draft modernization drive. Bismarck bullied or circumvented the Reichstag in those few areas where it did have some authority (such as the budget). He encouraged the creation of multiple political parties and then skillfully played them off one another.

But if democracy found infertile ground in modernizing Prussia, catch-up industrialization proved much more successful. In 1890, Bismarck was eased out of office, and Emperor Kaiser Wilhelm II assumed personal control, continuing the policy of rapid industrialization and imperialist expansion. By the early twentieth century, Germany had surpassed Britain in iron production and become a leading industrial power. Society became more complex as both the middle and working classes grew in size and political strength, and the socialist movement captured one-third of German votes by 1912.

German patriotism, however, prevailed over these social divisions and differences. Frustrations associated with Germany's efforts to expand its empire and suspicions about the intentions of its neighbors stoked feelings of nationalism and unfulfilled destiny and contributed to German willingness to bring about World War I (1914–18). But as the war pressed on and took a particularly heavy toll on Germany, the social differences once again rose to the surface. Political liberals, Catholics, and others began to question openly why they had lent their support to an authoritarian government waging war against countries that provided their citizens democratic rights. Workers wondered why they could fight and die but not have an equal vote in the parliament. As the war ground to its bitter conclusion, the emperor made assurances of reform, but these promises offered too little and came too late. German defeat in 1918, combined with urban uprisings, prompted the emperor to abdicate and proclaim Germany a republic.

POLITICAL POLARIZATION AND THE BREAKDOWN OF DEMOCRACY DURING THE WEIMAR REPUBLIC, 1919–33

The political vacuum that followed the collapse of the Second Reich proved to be particularly infertile ground for the establishment of Germany's first republic. No one was prepared for the sudden departure of the emperor, and few had considered

Political Development

800–900 C.E.	Loose confederation of German principalities forms Holy Roman Empire; later known as the First Reich.
1871	Otto von Bismarck unifies Germany; later dubbed Second Reich.
1918	Germany defeated in World War I.
1919	Weimar Republic formed under difficult conditions.
1933	Hitler and Nazis rise to power, establishing the Third Reich.
1945	Hitler and Nazis defeated in World War II.
1945–49	Germany divided among Allies into four occupied zones.
1948	Berlin blockade and airlift takes place.
1949	Federal Republic of Germany (FRG) founded in the west and German Democratic Republic (GDR) in the east.
1952	FRG joins European Coal and Steel Community.
1955	FRG joins NATO, and GDR joins Warsaw Pact.
1957	FRG participates in founding of European Economic Community.
1961	Berlin Wall constructed.
1969	FRG Chancellor Willy Brandt launches policy of *Ostpolitik*.
1989	Berlin Wall falls.
1990	Germany unified as GDR is incorporated into FRG.
1993	Germany becomes a founding member of the European Union.
2005	Angela Merkel elected to first of four terms as chancellor.

how Germany ought to be constituted as a republic with no monarchy. The seeds of cynicism and elitism sown in this era would grow into the extremism and fascist totalitarianism that spelled the republic's doom in less than two decades.

In the face of these and other difficulties, an elected assembly met in the city of Weimar in 1918 to draft a constitution. The **Weimar Republic** featured a remarkably democratic constitution that offered universal suffrage for all adults (ahead of both Britain and the United States), universal health insurance and pensions, and the right to employment or to unemployment compensation. Drafters of the constitution looked to the British parliamentary system as a model, retaining a bicameral parliament with a strong, popularly elected lower house (Reichstag) and a weaker upper chamber (Reichsrat) representing the states. But, in a measure that ultimately doomed the republic, they mistakenly saw the British monarch as the key to that system's stability and replaced the German kaiser with a strong president. This choice resulted in a dual executive, semi-presidential system (similar to the current Russian and French systems) in which the president as head of state was directly and popularly elected, could nominate the chancellor as head of government, and could rule through emergency decree under threatening circumstances.

The Weimar Republic also adopted a proportional representation (PR) electoral system for the Reichstag that specified no minimum threshold of votes and thus fostered a proliferation of parties, many of them small and representing narrow interests. This meant that no party ever won an outright majority in the Reichstag, and increasingly, weak and short-lived coalitions became the norm. Between 1919 and 1933, Germany had more than 20 governments, often functioning as minority coalitions unable to cobble together a majority of seats.

From the start, the Weimar Republic struggled with internal and external challenges that might have doomed even the most stable and resilient regime.[1] These challenges included the humiliation and burden of the Treaty of Versailles concluding World War I, which imposed upon Germany billions of dollars in reparations, military demobilization, the forfeiting of portions of German territory to France, and the loss of Germany's overseas colonies. Moreover, the Weimar Republic faced devastating hyperinflation brought on by war reparations and postwar economic turmoil (the inflation rate at one point in 1923 was 26 billion percent) as well as the consequences of the Great Depression, which caused widespread unemployment in Germany (nearly a third of German workers were unemployed by 1932).

Those opposed to the Weimar regime were able to blame for all these ills the democratic parties that had authored the constitution. A threatened middle class, defeated soldiers, and unemployed workers all proved ripe for recruitment into extreme nationalist and radical Communist movements as the Weimar Republic began to unravel. By 1930, moderate center parties favoring liberal democracy had lost their majority in parliament. Germany's Communist Party, which received only 2 percent of the popular vote in the 1920 Reichstag election, had by 1932 garnered 17 percent. In 1928, the **National Socialist (Nazi) Party**, led by **Adolf Hitler** and running on a platform of militarism and anti-Semitism, commanded less than 3 percent of the vote, but by 1932 it had obtained 37 percent, the highest total for any party during the Weimar period.

Under conditions of increasing instability, German state capacity weakened as violence replaced legislative politics and Communist and Nazi militias fought regularly in the streets. Following the 1932 election, conservative president Paul von Hindenburg and his nationalist supporters faced the difficult choice of forming a coalition government in alliance with moderate parties against the Nazis, declaring martial law and attempting to forcibly shut down the Nazis, or allying with Hitler and the Nazis in an effort to tame them. Hindenburg chose the latter option. In 1933, Hitler used this alliance and mounting disorder first to secure the office of chancellor and then to gain passage of the Enabling Act. The act yielded the Reichstag's powers to the chancellor, effectively dissolving the constitution and bringing the Weimar Republic to an end.

FASCIST TOTALITARIANISM UNDER THE THIRD REICH, 1933–45

Unfettered by constitutional restrictions, Hitler moved swiftly to establish the **Third Reich**, replacing the democratic institutions of the Weimar Republic with those of a Nazi-led fascist totalitarian regime. The Nazis imprisoned political opponents, required a loyalty oath of all civil servants, banned opposition political parties, and placed all social organizations, including clubs and churches, under restrictions or direct party control. Hitler employed state terror and a state-supervised mercantilist economy to achieve the regime's ideological goals of restoring German national power, expanding the German empire, and destroying those political ideologies and ethnic groups that threatened his vision of Aryan supremacy.

In hindsight, it is difficult to understand how a totalitarian political regime with such reprehensible means and ends could be successful, popular, and even legitimate. For many Germans facing social chaos and economic collapse, the stability, order, and national wealth and pride Hitler promised were far more important values than either freedom or equality. Hitler identified and vilified scapegoats for Germany's ills, resurrected the depressed economy, and united the divided country. With extraordinary charisma, he delivered heroically and almost miraculously on his promises to rearm the nation, reclaim lost territories, and restore Germany's pride, power, and prestige. The Nazi propaganda machine effectively used pageantry and propaganda to amplify Hitler's inherent magnetism. As with other totalitarian regimes, such as Stalin's Russia and Mao's China, in Germany Hitler did not hesitate to use terror at the hands of an extensive security apparatus to intimidate opponents and destabilize and atomize society. In increasingly bold and aggressive measures, he rearmed Germany (in violation of the Treaty of Versailles), annexed Austria, occupied Czechoslovakia, and in 1939 invaded Poland, provoking World War II.

But by invading Russia in 1941, Hitler attempted one too many miracles and pushed Nazi aggression, racism, and ultimately genocide beyond the bounds that the world and, increasingly, Germans themselves would tolerate. As with Napoleon before him, Hitler's vaunted war machine proved no match for the harsh Russian winter or the bravery of the Russian people. But before the Nazi machine was ultimately defeated in 1945, it had exterminated some 6 million Jews and millions of other noncombatants on racial and ethnic grounds. The war killed more than 50 million people in Europe alone. Among those casualties was Hitler himself, who committed suicide in a Berlin bunker in 1945, a week before Russian, American, British, and French allies overran and occupied a defeated Germany.

FOREIGN OCCUPATION AND THE DIVISION OF THE GERMAN STATE, 1945–49

In 1945, Germany found itself utterly defeated. Its industry, infrastructure, society, and polity were completely in ruins. The German state surrendered sovereignty to the four Allied powers (Britain, France, Russia, and the United States), each of which occupied a portion of the country. The capital, Berlin, was similarly quartered. Territories that had been seized and annexed by the Nazis were carved off and returned to neighboring countries, and Poland annexed parts of Germany.

Although initial plans called for cooperation among the four occupying forces in moving toward the reestablishment of German sovereignty, the Cold War intervened, leading to a de facto division between the Soviet-occupied eastern zone and the regions in the west occupied by the other three powers. In an obvious step toward establishing a separate West German state, the three Western allies established a common currency for their three zones in 1948. The Soviet Union reacted by blocking land access from the West German sector into West Berlin (located in the eastern sector) that same year. Western allies in turn responded to this blockade with the Berlin Airlift, which delivered vital supplies to West Berlin by air for nearly a year.

The Western allies also ordered the West Germans to convene a separate constitutional assembly, something the Germans were reluctant to do for fear such a move would permanently institutionalize a divided German state. This convention led not to a constitution (deemed too permanent) but to the **Basic Law**, which established the **Federal Republic of Germany (FRG)**—also called West Germany—in 1949 as a democratic and demilitarized state. The Soviets quickly responded by setting up the **German Democratic Republic (GDR)**—also called East Germany—in the same year. "Independence" for both German states did not, however, bring complete sovereignty; each Germany remained beholden to its Cold War patron, exercising what one scholar has labeled semi-sovereignty.[2] Both the United States and the Soviet Union reserved the right to control much of their respective client's foreign policy and even to intervene in domestic matters as deemed necessary, and neither patron fully relinquished that authority until the reunification of the German states in 1990.

In West Germany, as in defeated Japan, Western allies and German reformers took steps to weaken those institutions seen as responsible for Nazi militarism, including sweeping denazification. Reformers also devolved authority from the central state to Germany's federal regions and strengthened democratic institutions. The authors of the Basic Law reformed and broadened the party system to create fewer, larger parties and to encourage coalitions in an effort to prevent the emergence of narrowly defined interests and ideologies. These measures included uniting Catholics and Protestants in separate but like-minded wings of the newly established **Christian Democratic Union (CDU)**, healing a political divide that had persisted since the time of the Reformation in the sixteenth century.

In the context of the Cold War, the United States sought to rebuild the West German economy as an engine of economic revitalization for Western Europe. Like Japan, Germany took up this task of capitalist economic development with seemingly miraculous success, growing rapidly to become one of the wealthiest countries in the world. At the same time, strong democratic leadership brought stable constitutional democracy and a prosperous social democratic political economy to the Federal Republic. Despite political competition among thriving democratic parties, general consensus prevailed across the political spectrum, favoring domestic policies of comprehensive social welfare programs and a state-regulated marketplace as well as a foreign policy that promoted growing European integration and pragmatic measures to ease tensions with East Germany and ultimately embrace unification.

In the GDR, Stalinist totalitarianism replaced fascist totalitarianism. Because the Soviets blamed the capitalist system both in Germany and more globally as responsible for the Third Reich and both world wars, their first step was to eliminate East Germany's capitalist economy and replace it with a new socialist system presided over by a totalitarian Communist Party state. By the end of the 1940s, the eastern portion of Germany possessed political and economic systems almost identical to those of its Soviet mentor. With economic growth rates over the first two postwar decades nearly as impressive as those of its western counterpart, East Germany became the economic showcase of the Communist bloc. But like its Soviet mentor, the East German socialist economy ultimately could not keep pace with the capitalist West. Its failure to do so was demonstrated by the grim reality of life in the GDR. The East German state retained power by force and terror, manifested in its reliance on the *Stasi* ("secret police") to squelch dissent, the construction of the fortified Berlin Wall surrounding West Berlin in 1961, and the summary execution of those caught trying to flee to the West from East Berlin.[3]

Soviet leader Mikhail Gorbachev's efforts to revitalize Communist rule and the economy in the Soviet Union through his 1980s reforms had their more immediate effects not on the Soviet Union but on its central European allies, including East Germany. Gorbachev urged the East German leadership to follow the Soviet reforms, and as public protests in East Germany grew and the pace of the exodus to the West picked up, the economy ground to a halt and the party-state lost its capacity to govern. The East German leaders stepped down and on November 9, 1989, announced the opening of the border between East and West Berlin. Crowds swarmed both sides of the Berlin Wall as the gates were opened, and this tangible and iconic image of the beginning of the end of Germany's division and the collapse of the Iron Curtain was televised across the world.

REUNIFICATION OF THE GERMAN STATE, 1990–PRESENT

The collapse of the East German state and the euphoria shared by all Germans propelled events much more rapidly than anyone could have anticipated. The flood of Germans migrating from East to West prompted hurried negotiations leading to full reunification in 1990, less than one year after the wall fell. In effect, **reunification** meant the incorporation of East Germany into the FRG, the adoption of the West German Basic Law as the constitution of a unified Germany, and the imposition of West Germany's capitalist economic system on East Germany. Although the Basic Law called for a new constitution and national referendum upon reunification, thus far no such action has been taken.

The initial euphoria of national unification gave way to the cold, hard reality of bringing together two sovereign nation-states that shared a language and a pre–World War II history and culture, but little else. The huge inequality in living standards, infrastructure, and income between the western and eastern portions of Germany has been tempered in the decades since unification, but despite huge transfers of wealth, these inequalities are still not resolved.

Political Regime

The founders of Germany's current regime endeavored to prevent the breakdown of democracy that doomed the Weimar Republic. They sought a better balance between local and national power, between the legislature and the executive, between political stability and representative democracy, and between the power of the state and the rights of individuals. They created an innovative political system that also contained some elements of continuity with Germany's institutional past. The German political system has more checks and balances, and is thus less efficient and decisive than the British model, but to date it has proved remarkably stable and effective.[4]

POLITICAL INSTITUTIONS

THE CONSTITUTION Germany's constitution is founded on five principles, designed to avoid both the chaos of the Weimar Republic and the authoritarianism of the Third Reich.[5] First, where Hitler destroyed the power of German states, the Bonn Republic Basic Law created a system of cooperative federalism, in which the federal government and state governments share power. Second, the Basic Law guaranteed an elaborate set of basic political, social, and economic rights. Third,

- **Legislative–executive system**: Parliamentary
- **Legislature**: Parliament
  - **Lower house**: Bundestag (Federal Diet)
  - **Upper house**: Bundesrat (Federal Council)
- **Unitary or federal division of power**: Federal
- **Main geographic subunits**: *Länder* (states)
- **Electoral system for lower house**: Mixed single-member districts and proportional representation
- **Chief judicial body**: Federal Constitutional Court and Federal Court of Justice

to counter the powerful Weimar president, the Bonn Republic established a weak, indirectly elected head of state. Fourth, political power is concentrated in the head of government, the chancellor, elected by and directly responsible to the legislature. Fifth, the Bonn Republic established a powerful and independent judiciary to check the government. Each of these constitutional features will be discussed in more depth in the following sections.

The Basic Law can be amended by a two-thirds majority in both houses. To prevent excessive concentration of state power, however, some constitutional features, such as Germany's federal system and individual rights, cannot be altered.

THE BRANCHES OF GOVERNMENT

THE HEAD OF GOVERNMENT AND THE CABINET German democracy is often referred to as chancellor democracy because the **federal chancellor**, or prime minister, is the most powerful political figure and the chief executive authority in Germany. The office of the chancellor is far more powerful vis-à-vis the head of state to create a stronger, more stable, and more democratic regime than the Weimar Republic.

As is typical in a parliamentary system, the lower house of the legislature (the Bundestag) elects the head of government, who has always been the leader of the largest party in the legislature. As the leader of the largest party or coalition, chancellors expect to see most of their government's policy proposals approved by the legislature. Chancellors appoint and oversee the cabinet, the group of ministers (currently 15) who head government departments. Cabinet ministers need not be members of the legislature (though most are). Chancellors may fire cabinet ministers at any time, although chancellors who preside over coalition governments may threaten the stability of the government when dismissing a cabinet member from a party that is a coalition partner. Indeed, all German cabinets since 1949 have been coalitions of at least two parties, and coalition partners often designate their preferred candidates to occupy the cabinet posts allotted to them.

The actual power of German chancellors has varied over time, depending in part on their ability to dominate their own parties. Two recent German chancellors, Helmut Kohl and Gerhard Schroeder, were especially dominant political figures.

German Chancellors and Their Coalitions, 1949–2017

BUNDESTAG ELECTION YEAR	GOVERNING COALITION	CHANCELLOR (PARTY)
1949	CDU/CSU–FDP, DP	Konrad Adenauer (CDU)
1953	CDU/CSU–FDP, DP	Konrad Adenauer (CDU)
1957	CDU/CSU, DP	Konrad Adenauer (CDU)
1961	CDU/CSU–FDP	Konrad Adenauer (CDU) (to 1963) Ludwig Erhard (CDU)
1965	CDU/CSU–FDP (to 1966) CDU/CSU–SPD (1966–69)	Ludwig Erhard (CDU, 1965–66) Kurt Kiesinger (CDU, 1966–69)
1969	SPD–FDP	Willy Brandt (SPD)
1972	SPD–FDP	Willy Brandt (SPD, to 1974) Helmut Schmidt (SPD, to 1976)
1976	SPD–FDP	Helmut Schmidt (SPD)
1980	SPD–FDP (1980–82) CDU/CSU–FDP (1982–83)	Helmut Schmidt (SPD, 1980–82) Helmut Kohl (CDU)
1983	CDU/CSU–FDP	Helmut Kohl (CDU)
1987	CDU/CSU–FDP	Helmut Kohl (CDU)
1990	CDU/CSU–FDP	Helmut Kohl (CDU)
1994	CDU/CSU–FDP	Helmut Kohl (CDU)
1998	SPD–Greens	Gerhard Schroeder (SPD)
2002	SPD–Greens	Gerhard Schroeder (SPD)
2005	CDU/CSU–SPD	Angela Merkel (CDU)
2009	CDU/CSU–FDP	Angela Merkel (CDU)
2013	CDU/CSU–SPD	Angela Merkel (CDU)

Key to party acronyms:
CDU/CSU: Christian Democratic Union/Christian Social Union
DP: Deutsche Partei, conservatives
FDP: Free Democratic Party
SPD: Social Democratic Party
Note: As this text went to press in September 2017, the composition of Angela Merkel's coalition government was being negotiated.

Kohl was the unquestioned leader of his party, had few powerful rivals, and oversaw German reunification. Schroeder also came to dominate his party and his coalition partner, the Greens.

THE HEAD OF STATE As in most parliamentary systems, in Germany the head of state (the **federal president**) is separate from the head of government. In contrast to the Weimar Republic, in which the substantial powers of a directly elected president were abused to facilitate Hitler's rise to power, the constitution makes the president an indirectly elected and mostly ceremonial figure who performs mainly symbolic tasks. The president may formally sign bills into law, must sign treaties, and can pardon convicted criminals—but usually takes such actions only at the behest of the chancellor. Presidents can, however, refuse to sign laws they believe contravene the constitution. They formally nominate candidates to become chancellor but are expected to select the head of the majority party in the legislature or, absent a majority, the head of the largest party in the legislature. Those candidates, moreover, must receive a majority of votes in the lower house of the legislature. Presidents also decide whether to dissolve the legislature and call new elections when there is no majority.

German presidents are elected for a maximum of two 5-year terms by a special Federal Convention that includes all members of the lower house of the legislature and an equal number of individuals selected by Germany's state legislatures. Presidents are intended to be consensus choices who are highly respected elder statesmen, and they are expected to behave in scrupulously nonpartisan fashion once in office.

THE LEGISLATURE Germany's bicameral legislature, Parliament, is a powerful institution, but the constitution weakened the legislature's power vis-à-vis the chancellor to avoid the problems that had undermined the Weimar Republic. The lower house, the **Bundestag** (Federal Diet), represents the population; the upper house, the **Bundesrat** (Federal Council), represents Germany's 16 states.

The Bundestag is the more powerful of the two houses. It currently has 709 deputies, who are Germany's only directly elected public officials at the federal level. Deputies are elected for a maximum of four years, though elections can occur before the four-year term is complete. The Bundestag's chief power is its capacity to elect the chancellor. Because no German party has ever won a majority of seats in the legislature, members of the lower house select a chancellor (normally the head of the party with the most seats), who can form a majority coalition among the parties in the legislature.

The Bundestag can remove the chancellor, but only through a "constructive" vote of no confidence. During the Weimar Republic, chancellors were often removed from power by the legislature, usually with votes from extreme parties of the right and left who were unable to agree on a new chancellor. The result was a succession of weak chancellors, political paralysis, and the imposition of presidential rule that facilitated the rise of Hitler. As a result, the Basic Law allows the Bundestag to remove a chancellor only if a majority of its members can (constructively) approve a replacement. There have been only two constructive votes of no confidence since 1949, and only one of those was successful. Chancellors may also call for a motion of confidence, and if that motion fails to win a majority, the legislature can be dissolved and new elections can be convened.

While the Bundestag must approve all federal laws, the government (not the legislature) initiates most legislation. The lower house can amend and debate legislation submitted by the government. In addition, the lower house can question members of the government during weekly question hours that are similar to question periods in the United Kingdom. Members submit written questions to ministers ahead of time but can ask supplementary questions during the debate. Much of the work of the Bundestag is performed by powerful legislative committees that have the ability to question government ministers and investigate government activities; they also have the expertise to challenge bills submitted by the government.

The upper house, the Bundesrat, is made up of 69 members who are delegates of the governments of Germany's *Länder* ("states"). Each state appoints between

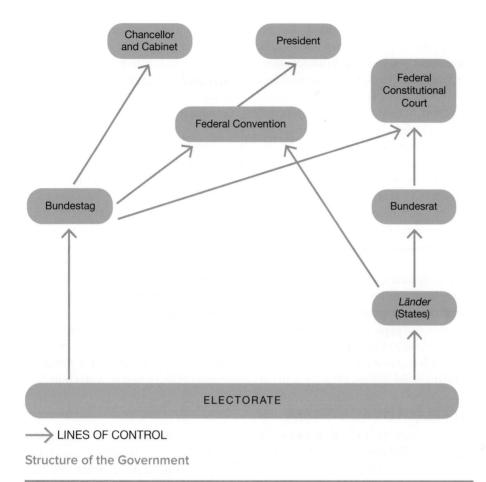

LINES OF CONTROL

Structure of the Government

three and six members, depending on its population, and the minister-president (state prime minister or governor) is usually the head of the state delegation. Within the Bundesrat, delegations of representatives cast their ballots as a bloc, following the instructions of the state government.

All legislation is submitted to the upper house before being sent to the lower house. The Bundesrat must approve all laws that affect the states (including laws that require states to implement policies of the federal government), giving it an effective veto power over about one-third of all legislation. For all other legislation, the Bundesrat's opposition can be overridden by the lower house. When the two houses disagree, joint committees often convene to negotiate a compromise. The Bundesrat must also approve all constitutional amendments.

The Bundesrat has traditionally served as an important check on the federal government because it has very often been controlled by the opposition. Since state elections do not coincide with federal ones, the outcome of state elections can alter the balance of power in the upper house.

THE JUDICIAL SYSTEM In another effort to avoid a repeat of the Weimar Republic, the architects of the Basic Law sought to create an independent judiciary that could safeguard the constitution. The result was the **Federal Constitutional Court**, which serves as the ultimate guardian of the Basic Law. The Constitutional Court settles disputes between states as well as between the federal government and states. It also adjudicates disputes about elections and hears cases when citizens believe their constitutional rights have been violated. The court acts only in response to cases brought before it by either house of the legislature, by lower courts, or by individual citizens. The court has the power of abstract review, meaning that it can review pending legislation on the request of one-third of the members of either house of the legislature.

The Constitutional Court, which is divided into two chambers (called Senates), has 16 members. Each house of the legislature selects half of the members of each chamber, and judges must be approved by a two-thirds majority. Judges are elected to a single 12-year term and must retire by age 68.

The Constitutional Court has been an important, active, and highly respected institution in German politics. It has ruled on some controversial issues, upholding the ban on the Communist and neo-Nazi parties in 1952, approving West Germany's treaty with East Germany in 1973, and making numerous decisions restricting legalized abortion.

The Federal Constitutional Court is entirely independent from the government and from the rest of Germany's legal system that handles criminal and civil matters. For all nonconstitutional issues, Germany employs a system of code law wherein judges interpret and apply complex legal codes rather than relying on precedent or common law. Germany has an elaborate system of courts at the state level and a top tier of courts at the federal level. For all nonconstitutional matters, the Federal Court of Justice of Germany is the highest ordinary court in Germany and the highest appeals court.

THE ELECTORAL SYSTEM

Germany uses an innovative mixed electoral system. Its designers sought a system that would combine the fairness of proportional representation (PR) with the voter-representative link that is a feature of single-member district (SMD) systems. In addition, they envisioned a system that would represent diverse political interests but avoid the legislative fragmentation and instability that characterized the Weimar Republic.

In Germany's lower house, 299 seats are elected using SMDs, where seats are allocated according to first-past-the-post criteria (the candidate with the most votes wins the seat). The remaining seats are awarded to parties from their party lists in each state, according to the proportion of the vote won by each party nationally. Thus, when voting for the Bundestag, Germans vote once for a representative in their district and once for a list of party candidates. The PR seats are subject to a 5 percent threshold; to win seats from PR lists, a party must win at least 5 percent of the vote nationally or win three SMD seats. For decades that threshold successfully limited the number of parties in the Bundestag, including small extremist parties, and has prevented the kind of fragmentation and polarization that plagued the Weimar Republic.

The German electoral system contains one additional feature that is often confusing for German citizens and students of German politics alike. If results from the SMDs produce a Bundestag with a membership that does not accurately reflect each party's national support (as determined by the PR list vote), additional seats must be awarded to parties that are underrepresented by increasing the overall number of seats in the lower house.

The implications of Germany's electoral system are profound. Political parties are strengthened because the national party lists are drawn up by party leaders. Parties are thus directly responsible for selecting at least half of the lower house, and

Seats in the Bundestag after the 2013 and 2017 General Elections

PARTY	2013			2017		
	% VOTE*	% SEATS	# SEATS	% VOTE*	% SEATS	# SEATS
CDU/CSU	41.5	49.2	311	33.0	34.8	246
SPD	25.7	30.5	193	20.5	21.7	153
AfD	4.7	0	0	12.6	13.2	94
FDP	4.8	0	0	10.7	11.2	80
The Left	8.6	10.2	64	9.2	9.7	69
The Greens	8.4	10.0	63	8.9	9.4	67
Others	6.3	0	0	11.3	0	0
Total	100	100	631**	100	100	709**

*Based on the national aggregate of the party list vote.

**Of this total, 299 seats were awarded in single-member constituencies. The remaining seats were awarded via the national party PR list. The extra seats (32 in 2013 and 110 in 2017) were awarded to parties to make their percentage of legislative seats more equivalent to their proportion of the national vote.

Key to party acronyms:

AfD: Alternative for Germany, far right

CDU/CSU: Conservatives

FDP: Free Democratic Party

SPD: Social Democratic Party

Source: Preliminary Results, https://bundeswahlleiter.de/en/bundestagswahlen/2017/ergebnisse/bund-99.html (accessed 9/25/17).

they can more easily enforce internal discipline. PR means that parties (at least those large enough to win 5 percent of the vote or three SMDs) can have a voice in the legislature. The presence of more parties in Germany has also meant that no German political party has ever won a legislative majority. Whether this is a positive or negative feature can be debated. The absence of a clear majority can sometimes lead to prolonged negotiations after elections (as was the case after the 2013 elections, when it took two months to form a new government). The German political system, however, represents a wide range of political views, and the need to form coalitions means that political compromise is a built-in feature. The German electoral system is certainly complex, but it has produced stable and effective governments. Moreover, turnout for elections has been consistently high.

LOCAL GOVERNMENT

Germany's 16 states share power with the federal government, which controls some areas, such as defense and foreign policy; the states have exclusive power over education, administration of justice at the state level, culture, and law enforcement. For all remaining areas not covered by the Basic Law, power is given to the states. German states implement the vast majority of the legislation passed by the federal government. States also have a direct check on the federal government via their representation in the upper house. Unlike U.S. states, German *Länder* and municipal governments have no power to raise taxes, and they are dependent on revenues allocated by the federal government. States are responsible for about two-thirds of German government spending.

Each German state has its own unicameral legislature (elected for four years), which in turn selects a **minister-president** (governor). Minister-presidents are often powerful figures in German politics, and German chancellors have often built their political careers in state politics.

Germany does not allow referenda or initiatives at the national level, but state and local governments have used them and have experimented with other forms of direct democracy.[6] Some states have eliminated the 5 percent threshold for local elections, most localities now directly elect their mayors (rather than having the mayor elected by the council), and some states allow for votes to recall elected officials.

Political Conflict and Competition

THE PARTY SYSTEM

Since 1949, Germany has had a remarkably stable system of political parties, even taking into account reunification and the emergence of new political forces in the 1980s and 1990s.[7] From 1957 to 1983, the party system was dominated by two large forces (the center-right CDU/CSU and the center-left SPD) and one smaller party (the liberal FDP). During that period, those three parties won all the seats in the Bundestag. In the early 1980s, the Greens were able to break into the legislature and occupy political space to the left of the SPD. Reunification in 1990 led to a fifth political force, composed mainly of former East German Communists (currently named the Left).

The two German political parties that have provided every chancellor since 1949 (the CDU/CSU and the SPD) have been characterized as **catchall parties**. Aided by the climate of the Cold War, the dramatic postwar economic recovery, and the advent of television, catchall parties represented a more modern, mass party that appealed more broadly to voters of all types. Such parties therefore presented a more centrist image.

In recent years, Germany's political party system has seen major changes. Chief among them is the decline of Germany's two main parties: in the mid-1970s they captured over 90 percent of the vote, but by 2017 that percentage declined to about 54 percent. Likewise, in the 1970s well over half of Germans reported a strong attachment to a political party, but that figure had dropped to 30 percent by 2009. The emergence of new political parties (the Greens, the Left, and most recently the rightist Alternative for Germany) has shifted Germany from a two-and-a-half party system to a six-party system. An increasing number of Germans (now about a quarter of voters) split their ticket, voting for different parties with their SMD and list ballots. Voter turnout, while still high, has been on the decline (it was 76.2 percent in 2017). In the 2017 general elections, Alternative for Germany won over 12 percent of the vote and over 90 seats in the lower house, the first time a far right party had gained seats since the restoration of democracy after World War II. All these trends explain why political scientists now describe Germany's political system as undergoing a process of "de-alignment."

THE CHRISTIAN DEMOCRATS The notion of a modern catchall party was best illustrated by the creation in 1945 of the Christian Democratic Union (CDU).[8]

Together with its Bavarian component, the Christian Social Union (CSU), the CDU emerged as a pro-business, antisocialist, Christian political party that for the first time in German history appealed to both Catholics and Protestants. The CDU established itself both as a strongly pro-West party with close ties to the United States and as a staunch supporter of a European union.

The CDU/CSU has been led since 2005 by **Angela Merkel**. Merkel has won four consecutive elections. After being elected head of the CDU in 2000, Merkel pushed hard to change the CDU's traditional policy orientation. On the one hand, she moved the party toward the center on such social issues as immigration and the environment. On the other hand, she encouraged the party to adopt free-market policies more similar to those of Britain's Conservatives. Under her leadership, the CDU has promoted tax cuts and reforms to the health care system and has been closer to the United States in foreign policy.

While Merkel is hardly a charismatic leader, as she begins her fourth term as chancellor, she remains Germany's most popular politician. She has maintained a high profile in international affairs, has enacted economic reforms to address Germany's economic challenges, and has promoted policies that seek to improve the lives of women. Germany's central role in the Eurozone economic crisis, and the more recent Syrian refugee crisis, damaged Merkel's popularity, but on the eve of the 2017 general election her approval rating had rebounded to an impressive 74 percent. Nevertheless, her party lost 65 seats in the election.[9]

THE SOCIAL DEMOCRATS The **Social Democratic Party (SPD)** is Germany's oldest party (it was founded in 1863) and was a major actor during the Weimar Republic.[10] The SPD originally had a Marxist orientation and defined itself as a party of the working class, but in the late 1950s it abandoned its radicalism and became a center-left party. In 1969, the SPD finally formed the first coalition government of the left under SPD leader Willy Brandt. Brandt promoted better relations with the Communist bloc and increased worker participation in the management of private enterprise. Although the SPD dominated German politics from the 1970s through 2009, it has not been able to form a government since then. In 2013, it formed a "grand coalition" government with the CDU in exchange for a CDU promise to support a package of reforms (implementation of Germany's first-ever national minimum wage, a reduction in the retirement age, and a reform of Germany's citizenship policy for immigrants). The SPD was awarded some top cabinet positions, including the vice chancellorship and the foreign affairs, justice, labor, and environment ministries. Chancellor Merkel's popularity and her willingness to embrace some SPD policies have posed a severe challenge to the Social Democrats. The party's leader for the 2017 campaign was Martin Schulz, a former president of the European Union. In 2017, the SPD had its worst electoral result since World War II, and after the election announced it would leave the governing coalition and return to the opposition.

THE FREE DEMOCRATS By one measure, the **Free Democratic Party (FDP)** has been Germany's most successful party; it was a member (always as a junior coalition partner) of more post–World War II governments than any other German party. But on another measure, the party has been a colossal failure; it has never led a

After the 2013 general elections, Germany's two major parties formed a "grand coalition." This cartoon portrays the coalition's main leaders (conservative Chancellor Angela Merkel and Social Democratic Party Vice Chancellor Sigmar Gabriel) as odd bedfellows.

German government and currently has no seats in the Bundestag. The FDP has been a staunch defender of free-market economic and civil liberties and has consistently drawn support from professionals and upper-middle-class Germans. Since 1949, support for the FDP has ranged from a low of 4.9 percent (2013) to a high of about 15 percent (2009). Nevertheless, from 1949 to 2008, the FDP was a junior coalition partner in 13 of 18 German governments, making it a crucial "hinge" party that could determine the nature of coalition governments.

In the early years of German democracy, the FDP was a natural ally of the conservatives, given its support of free-market policies. In the late 1960s, the FDP found common cause with the Social Democrats over social reforms and foreign policy. In general, the FDP has been less socially conservative than the CDU/CSU but less supportive of the welfare state than the SPD, and it has consistently supported tax and social spending cuts.

In recent years, the Free Democrats have struggled, failing to surpass the 5 percent threshold in elections. The party's disastrous performance in the 2013 elections, in which its vote dropped 10 percent to just below the 5 percent threshold for receiving legislative seats, eliminated the FDP from the Bundestag for the first time in its history. The FDP staged a political comeback at the national level under its young new leader, Christian Lindner, winning over 10 percent of the votes and 80 seats in the lower house in the 2017 general election.

THE GREENS In the 1970s, some Germans became disenchanted with the three main parties, all of whom shared a broad consensus on promoting rapid industrial growth via the market economy. While coalescing around environmental policies (especially opposition to nuclear energy), **the Greens** represented a host of post-modern issues, such as women's rights, gay rights, pacifism, and grassroots democracy.[11] The Green Party initially viewed itself as an "anti-party party" that would not behave like the established parties and would not compromise its principles in pursuit of power. In a controversial decision, the Greens entered a coalition government as junior partners of the SPD in 1998 and again in 2002, gaining control of three cabinet seats.

By entering government, the Greens gained new respectability and a high profile but also became subject to new political contradictions and pressures. The Greens' traditional pacifism clashed with the SPD–Greens government's policy of German intervention in Kosovo and Afghanistan, leading some members to abandon the party. Even a policy to phase out nuclear power by 2020, spearheaded by a Green environment minister, disappointed radicals within the party, who sought a more immediate end to nuclear power.

The Greens were dealt a minor setback in the 2013 elections, in part due to Chancellor Merkel's decision to abandon nuclear energy. The party's steady rise in votes since 1998 was halted as the Green vote declined by 2 percent, and the party lost five seats in the Bundestag. The Greens have distanced themselves from their more radical beginnings. The party has abandoned its early anticapitalist and even anarchist outlook in favor of a more pragmatic emphasis on sustainability that is more palatable to its mostly affluent, educated, and urban supporters. Nevertheless, the Greens still retain some aspects of their old radicalism, such as the requirement that party lists alternate male and female candidates, and the tradition of having two individuals lead the party (of which one is required to be female). In the 2013 campaign, the Greens proposed income and inheritance tax increases as well as a special wealth tax on incomes over $1.3 million.

THE LEFT The Left (*Die Linke*) was founded in 2007 through a merger of the heirs of the former East German Communists and some leftists who abandoned the SPD.[12] Since 2005 the Left has regularly won about 10 percent of the vote, and in 2017 it won just over 9 percent of the vote and 69 seats in the lower house.

Although the platform of the Left Party is still evolving, it opposes the policies of privatization and tax cuts that recent German governments have pursued, and it has fiercely opposed both the SPD and CDU/CSU foreign policy. The party opposes Germany's membership in NATO (and views the alliance as a tool for U.S. hegemony). In a posture reminiscent of the early Greens, the Left has called itself Germany's only real opposition party (and so was dubbed "the party of no") and vowed not to enter into coalitions with any of the major political parties. However, the Left has entered into coalitions with the SPD at the state level.

OTHER PARTIES Because of Germany's history with totalitarianism, the Basic Law was designed to prevent the emergence of extremist parties on the left or right. Thus Germany has been less tolerant than other European democracies of parties that are deemed to be anti-system. Far-right parties—for example, the National Democratic Party (NPD)—are tolerated in Germany, and they have won seats in state legislatures. But until 2017 they had never surpassed the 5 percent threshold at the federal level. The Constitutional Court banned the Communist left in the 1950s, and until reunification, no party of the extreme left was able to win seats in the legislature.

Frauke Petry, co-leader of the anti-immigration Alternative for Germany party, at the 2016 AfD federal conference. In the September 2017 general elections the AfD won over 12 percent of the vote and was the first German party of the far right to win seats in the lower house since World War II.

Recent efforts, unsuccessful to date, have tried to get the Court to ban the NPD, a party viewed by some as anti-Semitic. The Pirate Party of Germany, which advocates Internet freedom and privacy, has fared poorly in federal elections but was able to gain seats in four state legislatures.

The fastest growing and most alarming newcomer to German politics is the Alternative for Germany (AfD). This right-wing populist party, founded in 2013, ran on a platform calling for Germany to abandon the euro (though not the European Union). In the September 2017 general election it won over 12 percent of the vote and 94 lower house seats.

A wave of anti-immigrant and anti-Muslim marches and protests in response to the Syrian refugee crisis that began in 2015 appears to have strengthened the AfD, which began to call for limits to immigration. Many of those rallies were organized by Patriotic Europeans against the Islamization of the West (PEGIDA), and the AfD has incorporated PEGIDA's platform. At its 2016 Party Congress, the AfD called for a ban of all Islamic symbols, adopting the slogan "Islam Is Not Part of Germany." The party has done remarkably well in state elections over the last few years, and the AfD became the second largest party in Saxony-Anhalt, taking votes away from the major national parties. The AfD placed second and defeated Merkel's party in the September 2016 elections in the chancellor's home state, winning over 20 percent of the vote. At the time, Vice Chancellor Sigmar Gabriel warned that the AfD's rhetoric is dangerously similar to the popular appeal used by the Nazis in the 1920s and 1930s. In April 2016, German authorities arrested some leaders of the anti-immigrant movement, charging them with inciting attacks on refugees.[13] The AfD's surprisingly strong performance in the 2017 general election shocked the German political establishment and led to widespread anti-AfD demonstrations throughout

Germany. The AfD is unlikely to enter a governing coalition in the near future, as all other major parties refuse to work with the far right, but its electoral success may have opened the door for further electoral gains.

ELECTIONS

The 17 German federal elections since 1949 have enjoyed consistently high voter turnout, although numbers have been decreasing since the 1970s. Germany recorded its highest voter turnout in 1972 (91.1 percent) and its lowest in 2009 (70.8 percent). German campaigns have traditionally centered on parties and their platforms, but in recent elections they have become more Americanized—more about personalities and slick advertising.

Owing to the dominance of the CDU and SPD, German campaigns inevitably become a battle between titans. The 2017 campaign was widely criticized as lackluster, as both major parties appeared to agree on most issues, and their leaders were not charismatic campaigners. The CDU and SPD lost votes to smaller parties with younger and more energetic leadership.

CIVIL SOCIETY

We have seen that Germans after 1949 regularly turned out in large numbers to vote and that they overwhelmingly rejected parties on the political extremes. With Germany's spectacular economic recovery, Germans came to support democratic politics, and a democratic German civil society began to germinate. Recent opinion surveys reported that more than half of all Germans were interested in politics, over half had signed a petition, over a third had attended a lawful demonstration, and almost 10 percent had joined in some type of boycott. Survey research has shown that Germany has the second-highest level of protest activity in Western Europe, and the vibrancy of Germany civil society was on display in 2016 as both supporters and opponents of the massive influx of Syrian refugees took to the streets.[14]

LABOR UNIONS AND BUSINESS ORGANIZATIONS Compared with most advanced democracies, trade unions in postwar Germany have been both strong and influential. The Federation of German Labor (DGB) represents most of Germany's trade unions, and during the postwar period about two-thirds of workers were unionized. The DGB has enjoyed a close relationship with the SPD and played a key role in German policy making.

German trade unions, however, have experienced a rapid decline in membership since the 1990s. Between 1991 and 2006, the DGB lost almost half its membership for a variety of reasons, and today only under a quarter of the labor force is unionized. Reunification flooded the labor market, unemployment soared, and economic growth rates declined. Over half of German workers are presently covered by collective bargaining agreements between unions and employers, but that percentage has dropped considerably and rapidly over the past two decades.

German business is also highly organized. The Federal Association of German Employers (BDA) and the Federation of German Industry (BDI) are powerful groups with close ties to the CDU. The BDI is a powerful interest group that often weighs in on major political-economic issues. In 2011, the BDI raised concerns that Angela

Antinuclear protesters outside a German nuclear power plant in March 2011. The protesters created a human chain that was almost 30 miles long.

Merkel's decision to expedite the phasing out of nuclear power could seriously damage Germany's economy by raising energy prices for industry.

OTHER GROUPS As in many Western democracies, German society experienced the growth of a variety of political groups in the 1960s and 1970s. These groups challenged various aspects of the German model of economic growth, including pollution, the status of women, its reliance on nuclear energy, and the dominance of the major political parties. Some of the groups were later integrated into the Greens, thus reflecting the centrality of political parties in the German system; other groups remained autonomous from the party system.

The German women's movement has been particularly influential. Since the founding of the Bonn Republic, women have organized regarding issues of unequal pay, access to legal abortion, and other political rights. In the 1980s, the Greens established a quota for female candidates, thus spurring most other political parties to adopt similar policies.

German churches have also been an important interest group since 1949. Before reunification, over 90 percent of West Germans belonged to either the Catholic or Protestant Church, and the German state provided those churches with generous economic support.

Society

ETHNIC AND NATIONAL IDENTITY

Germany is relatively homogeneous in terms of its ethnic identity. Although unification came late to Germany, a strong shared cultural and even national identity has bound Germans together for a much longer period. Important cultural figures, such as Beethoven, Wagner, and Goethe, helped generate the idea of a single German people, even if what bound these individuals together was not territory, constitutions, or regimes. Opinion research reveals a weak German attachment to the state and state symbols. Such attachments were further weakened by the effects of World War II, wherein nationalism became the fuel for war and genocide. That war also destroyed the Jewish population of Germany, further reducing the country's ethnic and cultural diversity, and large portions of eastern Germany were annexed by Poland.

At the level of national identity, there remain important distinctions across the country, again a reflection of late unification. Recall that Germany can be seen as a fusion of two different systems: the Prussian empire in the north and a series of "free states" and kingdoms in the south. This distinction remains particularly important in the state of Bavaria, which still calls itself a *Freistaat* ("free state"), indicating both its historical role as an independent state before unification and a sense that the region remains separate from (and superior to) much of the rest of Germany.

Bavaria is noted for its high level of economic development and the still-strong role played by Catholicism. In contrast, northern and eastern Germany are overwhelmingly Protestant, though religious affiliation or identity is much weaker there. It may be a stretch to think of Bavarians (or any other German cultural subgroup) as having a distinct ethnic identity, but these groups do identify themselves by custom, dialect, and even particular stereotypes regarding attitudes and behavior.

These distinct, if relatively weak, identities have become more diverse over the past 50 years, through immigration and unification. First, unification with East Germany brought into the country a new population whose historical experiences were quite different. For West Germans, the aftermath of World War II brought denazification, a deep suspicion of national pride, and an emphasis on democratic institutions. In contrast, East Germans did not undergo the type of denazification experienced in the west; the Communist government instead redirected public identity toward the East German state and gave little attention to such events as the Holocaust. At the time of unification, Germany's population in the east embodied an identity that had been shaped by 50 years of socialism—that is, strongly secular and having a complicated relationship to nationalism. Germans as a result often speak of the differences between *Ossi und Wessi* ("east and west"); how distinct these differences are, or will remain, we shall discuss in greater detail later.

Another factor that has transformed national and ethnic identity has been the role of immigration. Germany's postwar economic growth created a demand for labor that the country could not meet; as a result, Germany turned to *Gastarbeiter* ("guest workers") to fill this role. Guest workers from Mediterranean Europe, including especially large numbers from Turkey, were expected to stay only temporarily in Germany and thus were not part of any formal plan for naturalization. Far fewer guest workers returned home than were expected, and eventually entire families and children became part of the German population. By 2010, immigrants constituted about 8 percent of the German population, and about a quarter of these were of Turkish origin.

This growing immigrant population, the largest (in sheer numbers) in Europe, has created significant challenges for the German state and nation. In the past, German identity, including citizenship, centered on notions of race. As such, descendants of ancient German communities in Russia, for example, could gain citizenship, but Turkish children born and raised in Germany were not German citizens. Since 2000, the citizenship laws in Germany have been reformed to recognize and integrate non-German immigrants (though the law forces immigrants to renounce citizenship from their country of origin), but their social integration is far more difficult. Many Germans still have difficulty imagining nonethnic Germans as so-called true Germans, and concerns about political Islam have added a new tension to the situation. Some Germans worry that the country's failure to integrate its Muslim population is leading to the development of a "parallel society" disconnected from democratic institutions and susceptible to fundamentalism (see "Germany's Immigration Dilemma," p. 319).[15]

IDEOLOGY AND POLITICAL CULTURE

German political identity is complicated both by the legacies of late unification and by the rise of fascism. The war and denazification led to a strong undercurrent of national shame and the conclusion that nationalism and even patriotism were values that, at least for Germany, were dangerous and unacceptable. For most of the postwar period, then, the emphasis on democratic institutions was less an expression of national or patriotic identity than a belief that such institutions were a necessary bulwark against extremism and a recurrence of past policies. German political culture emphasized a greater pride in the country's economic achievements than in the state or nation, both of which had taken on negative connotations.

Germans show overwhelming support for democracy, and most Germans express pride in their political institutions and constitution. Indeed, Germans are prouder of their political system than any other aspect of their society, including the economy.[16] Former citizens of East Germany still show lower levels of support for democratic institutions (compared with West Germans) and a weaker awareness that they have particular democratic rights (such as free speech).[17] Some of this behavior is understandably generational, for these differences between Westerners and Easterners are much smaller among people under 25. The concern about a lingering *Mauer im Kopf* ("Berlin Wall of the mind") that still separates the two peoples seems to be fading. Ideologically, there is similarly strong support among Eastern and Western

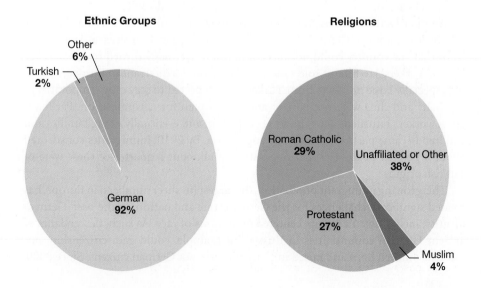

Germans for a political regime that emphasizes collective well-being over individual rights and favors a system that combines capitalism with consensus.

One dramatic shift in Germany's political culture was the rise in post-materialist values (such as political participation, feminism, the environment, and other quality-of-life issues) and a decline in bread-and-butter materialist concerns (such as economic growth, jobs, and order). In 1973, only 13 percent of Germans felt that post-materialist concerns were a priority, but 43 percent took that position in 1995.[18] Post-materialist values have become more pronounced in all advanced democracies, but they are by far the strongest in Germany—which perhaps explains why Germany has had one of the world's most successful Green parties.

Political Economy

Germany can be rightly proud of its economy. Many observers would assert that the *Wirtschaftswunder* ("economic miracle") of the 1950s and 1960s was in part a way for Germany to reinvest national energy and identity around institutions and projects that were removed from the symbols of its fascist past.

The German political-economic structure is manifestly capitalist, but within a social-democratic mold. German political culture strongly emphasizes the importance of collective rights within the context of private property and the marketplace, a view that can be found across both major parties of the left and the right.

Beginning in the 1960s, in an attempt to stimulate economic growth, German governments sought to bring business and labor groups together to negotiate labor agreements and to coordinate economic policy. For decades, the German state regularly coordinated meetings between the main labor and business representatives. Beyond the call for regular meetings, one particularly controversial aspect of Germany's political economy is **codetermination**, a policy advocated by the Social Democrats that requires Germany's largest private firms to give unions half of all seats on their board of directors. A 2014 revision to the codetermination law requires that 30 percent of all board of directors seats be filled by women.

Germany's political-economic model has been credited with fostering rapid growth rates and with limiting conflict between labor and business. However, the model has its critics. German business resisted codetermination and unsuccessfully fought it in the courts. German unions became extremely powerful, often at the expense of other civil society groups that were not part of the system. Critics on the left also argued that codetermination did not really give workers power over major economic decisions.

Since World War II, Germany has developed a sophisticated economy (the fifth largest in the world) and one of the world's most prosperous societies. German industry is famous for its advanced industrial and consumer products, such as automobiles and chemicals, and built much of its economic structure around exports. However, by the 1990s, the economic miracle began to show signs of strain, for several reasons. One problem has been the growing cost of labor. Over time, the German workforce has become less competitive as costs have risen. Second, thanks to globalization,

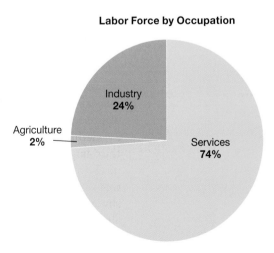

Labor Force by Occupation

Industry 24%

Agriculture 2%

Services 74%

other regional economies have rivaled German exports with their lower costs and increasing technical sophistication. German firms, too, have in many cases chosen to invest outside of Germany, especially in Eastern Europe, where German capital could find an inexpensive yet relatively productive workforce close to home. The expansion of the European Union eastward has only increased this investment, thus raising concerns among Germans. Finally, although Germany has spent enormous amounts of money revitalizing eastern Germany (over $100 billion per year since 1990), productivity, entrepreneurialism, and investment in that region remain much weaker. Assumptions that massive government spending on infrastructure and new technologies would lead to significant private investment and growth in the east have not been borne out.

Growing concerns about the potential decline in German competitiveness in the global economy, a potential shortage of labor that could result from Germany's low birthrate, and rigid rules governing hiring and firing workers have led to reforms, although not without resistance. In 2003, the Social Democratic government proposed what was known as Agenda 2010, a series of measures meant to liberalize the economy. Agenda 2010 met with fierce resistance from labor unions in particular, which limited its implementation. However, changes that did occur included restructuring unemployment benefits, the generosity of which had led to a large number of permanently unemployed recipients. In addition, the increased pressures of the global economy have forced many labor unions to recognize that increased flexibility may be the only way to compete in the global market. What's more, Germany's reputation of having one of the world's most transparent economies was damaged by the discovery that Volkswagen, the country's largest automobile company (and one of its biggest employers), had intentionally designed some of its engines to circumvent emissions testing, and that those cars polluted far more than it claimed.

To be sure, Germany's economy faces myriad challenges, including a graying population and a shortage of skilled labor. But despite recent problems and looming challenges, the German economy continues to be among the world's strongest. In 2010, the economy grew at the fastest rate since unification in 1990, and unemployment dropped to its lowest level since 1992. Today Germany has a budget surplus, low unemployment, and a competitive economy that is growing steadily, if not spectacularly.

Current Issues in Germany

THE POLITICS OF GERMANY'S ENERGY FUTURE

About a quarter of Germany's energy is provided by nuclear power. After the 2011 nuclear disaster in Fukushima, Japan, Chancellor Merkel announced that Germany would completely abandon nuclear power by 2022.

Germany is already a leader in renewable energy production and it is the world's third-largest producer of solar panels.[19] By 2010, Germany got about 17 percent of its electricity from renewable sources (hydro, solar, wind, biomass, and biogas), but that figure is slated to increase to almost 40 percent by 2020. If Germany is going to shy away from nuclear energy in the post-Fukushima era, it will have to accelerate its already impressive pursuit of renewable energy.

Renewable Energy

Renewable energy as a percentage of total energy production:

COUNTRY	PERCENTAGE	COUNTRY	PERCENTAGE
Brazil	84	Russia	17
Germany	33	Mexico	16
China	24	Japan	16
United Kingdom	22	United States	14
Nigeria	21	Iran	6
India	19	South Africa	1
France	17		

Source: "International Energy Statistics," Report, EIA—International Energy Statistics, May 25, 2016, www.eia.gov (accessed 1/25/17).

The political risks of abandoning nuclear power are formidable. German households already pay energy bills that are 40 percent higher than the European Union average, and these costs are likely to rise as nuclear power goes off-line.

GERMANY'S IMMIGRATION DILEMMA

Immigration has become a divisive issue for Germans. A poll taken in September 2010 found that 36 percent of Germans agreed that the country was being "overrun by foreigners," and 58 percent thought that Germany's Muslim population should have their religious practices "seriously curbed."

However, the debate about immigration and the growing resentment of immigrants may hamper Germany's ability to deal with a severe shortage of skilled labor. Since 2005, Germany has enacted legislation that requires immigrants to learn German and make an effort to integrate into German culture. Such policies are politically popular, but they may discourage skilled laborers from immigrating to Germany. Given Germany's low birthrate, a skilled worker shortage threatens to derail the growth of the German economy and drive up labor costs.

Germany's immigrant population has its origins in the wave of *Gastarbeiter* ("guest workers") invited to Germany in the 1950s and 1960s. These people, at first mainly from Southern Europe, were needed to help fuel Germany's rapid postwar economic recovery. Turkish citizens, most of whom are Muslim, soon became the largest group of immigrants, and today Germans of Turkish origin number about 4 million. Initially, most Germans viewed the immigrants as temporary workers and were reluctant to grant them rights as citizens, even when it became apparent that most immigrants wanted to remain in Germany. While the term *Gastarbeiter* is no longer applied, Germans of foreign origin, even those who have lived in Germany for decades, are still often viewed as *Ausländer* ("foreigners"). In the early 1990s, an outbreak of anti-immigrant attacks heightened tensions and caused alarm among

Members of PEGIDA (Patriotic Europeans against the Islamization of the West) protest government immigration policies in Dresden, in November 2016. The banner reads "Islamization, No Thanks."

German politicians.[20] The shocking discovery in 2011 of the National Socialist Underground (NSU), a far-right terrorist group that had murdered immigrants over a 13-year period, led to a parliamentary inquiry, caused the resignation of some top German security officials, and prompted Chancellor Merkel to call for the banning of far-right anti-immigrant parties like the NPD.

Partly in response to such violence, Germany has made some progress in recognizing the need to better integrate immigrants into German society.[21] Legislation passed in 2000 gives children of immigrants the right to gain citizenship, and a recent reform pushed by the Social Democrats within the governing coalition will allow more immigrants to have dual citizenship. A national office of immigration and integration was opened in 2005 and now offers a variety of free courses aimed at providing immigrants with skills that can facilitate their integration into society. Still, German schools have worked poorly for children of immigrants. High school students of Turkish background attend university at far lower rates than the German population at large.

Chancellor Merkel's controversial decision to welcome a large number of refugees from war-torn Syria in 2015 significantly damaged her normally high approval ratings. Over a million refugees settled in Germany in 2015, and another 280,000 arrived in 2016, forcing Germany to impose border controls (usually there are no such controls between EU members). Anti-immigrant violence rose sharply in 2015, especially in eastern Germany. A 2016 survey showed that 81 percent of Germans disapproved of Merkel's handling of the refugee crisis.[22] As a result, in April 2016 Merkel brokered a European Union deal with Turkey aimed at stemming the flow of refugees into Europe. The anti-immigrant AfD Party performed surprisingly well in the 2017 legislative elections, making it the third largest party in the lower house. It is clear that Germany's reputation as a tolerant country with almost no organized far right is being put to the test.

Key Terms

Basic Law (p. 300)
Bundesrat (p. 304)
Bundestag (p. 304)
catchall parties (p. 308)
Christian Democratic Union (CDU) (p. 300)
codetermination (p. 317)
federal chancellor (p. 302)
Federal Constitutional Court (p. 305)
federal president (p. 303)
Federal Republic of Germany (FRG) (p. 300)
Free Democratic Party (FDP) (p. 309)
Gastarbeiter (p. 315)
German Democratic Republic (GDR) (p. 300)
the Greens (p. 311)

Hitler, Adolf (p. 298)
Länder (p. 304)
the Left (p. 311)
Merkel, Angela (p. 309)
minister-president (p. 308)
National Socialist (Nazi) Party (p. 298)
Prussia (p. 295)
reich (p. 295)
reunification (p. 301)
Social Democratic Party (SPD) (p. 309)
Third Reich (p. 298)
Weimar Republic (p. 297)

Japanese demonstrators protest the ruling Liberal Democratic Party government's efforts to reinterpret Japan's pacifist constitution.

Japan

Why Study This Case?

Japan offers an important case for the study of contemporary politics, perhaps foremost to educate a Western audience about what Japan is *not*. Too much of our understanding of Japan is influenced by dangerously misleading stereotypes. For example, Japan is *not*

- *small*. It has a landmass greater than that of Germany or Great Britain; a population larger than that of all non-Asian countries other than the United States, Brazil, Nigeria, and Russia; and an economy fourth only to those of the United States, China, and India.
- *defenseless*. Despite the constitution's famous **Article 9**, which renounces war, Japan possesses a **Self-Defense Force** second only to the U.S. military in technical sophistication, and boasts defense expenditures comparable to or greater than those of all member countries of the North Atlantic Treaty Organization (NATO) except the United States.
- *unique*. In its political stability, state involvement in the economy, cultural conformity, and even ethnic homogeneity, Japan may differ from the United States, but in these and other ways, often the United States is exceptional, not Japan.

If Japan is more "normal" than we might have assumed, it nonetheless remains an intriguing case that defies generalization and begs further investigation.

Politically, an authoritarian vanguard of low-ranking nobles launched a sweeping revolution from above in the latter half of the nineteenth century, modernizing Japan under the mercantilist slogan "**rich country, strong military**." Its militarist successors waged wars of imperialist expansion during the first half of the twentieth century, leading to stunning defeat in 1945. American occupiers then launched a second revolution from above, replacing authoritarian rule

RUSSIA

Sea
of
Okhotsk

Kurile Islands occupied
by the Soviet Union
since 1945, today
administered by Russia,
but southern islands
claimed by Japan

CHINA

Kurile Islands

Sapporo

HOKKAIDO

NORTH
KOREA

Sea
of
Japan

Akita

Takeshima

Sendai
Fukushima

Yellow
Sea

SOUTH
KOREA

HONSHU

TOKYO
Yokohama
Nagoya

Hiroshima
Kobe
Kitakyushu
Osaka
Fukuoka

SHIKOKU

KYUSHU

PACIFIC
OCEAN

East
China
Sea

Ryukyu Islands

Senkaku
Islands
Okinawa

*Bonin
Islands
(Japan)*

*Minami Daito
Jima
(Japan)*

N

Sakishima
Islands

*Iwo Jima
(Japan)*

| 0 | 100 | 200 mi |
| 0 | 100 | 200 km |

Philippine Sea

with a liberal democratic constitution written entirely by the Americans (in just six days) and unamended by the Japanese in more than seven decades.

For nearly six of these past seven decades, the conservative **Liberal Democratic Party (LDP)** governed Japan. Moreover, elected politicians have historically deferred to Japan's nonelected career civil servants, who for much of this period have written most of Japan's laws. Over the past two decades, significant reforms have been implemented, yet political change has not come readily to Japan. This situation raises several important questions: Where does political authority reside in Japan? How has Japan's externally imposed democracy evolved over the years? And does Japanese democracy differ in substantial ways from other advanced industrial democracies?

Economically, under conditions of state-directed industrialization, imperialism, and war, Japan's authoritarian leaders forged a highly centralized economy over the course of the first half of the twentieth century. Concerned about Japan's economic stability in a heightening Cold War, the United States allowed the war-torn nation to retain many aspects of its state-led economic structure. Japan therefore extended into peacetime its wartime mercantilist economy, which linked career bureaucrats, conservative politicians, and big-business elite and was spectacularly successful for several decades.[1] By the 1980s, Japan had achieved and in many cases surpassed the levels of technological prowess, commercial competitiveness, and economic prosperity of the advanced Western industrialized nations.

By the early 1990s, however, this seemingly invincible economy began a dramatic and persistent decline. Japan has experienced nearly three decades of stagnant or slow economic growth and lagging industrial production. For much of this period, banks have been in crisis and unemployment has climbed as the stock market has languished. Japan's workforce is graying even as its population rapidly shrinks. Adding tragic and unprecedented insult to these decades of economic stagnation, in 2011 a devastating 9.0 earthquake and tsunami struck northeast Japan, killing tens of thousands and damaging several nuclear power plants. This catastrophe further hobbled the country's economy, threatened its energy infrastructure, exacerbated political instability, and severely strained state capacity to deal with the humanitarian disaster. Although Japan remains wealthy and most of its citizens relatively prosperous, few countries have faced such a striking peacetime turnaround in economic fortune. How does one account for this dynamic of rapid growth followed by precipitous decline and long-term stagnation? What have been the causes of Japan's economic success and its more recent failures? Must Japan change, and if so, how and when? Only by understanding Japan, its institutions, and where it has come from will we be able to make sense of where it may be headed.

Historical Development of the State

Despite the many cultural oddities that European traders and missionaries discovered when they first arrived in sixteenth-century Japan, they had actually stumbled upon a nation and society whose historical development bore striking similarities to that of their own countries. As in Europe, isolated tribal anarchy had gradually given way to growing national identity and the emergence of a primitive state. Aided by clearly defined natural borders and imperial and bureaucratic institutions borrowed from neighboring China, the Japanese state grew in both capacity and legitimacy. Gradually, a feudal military aristocracy came to *rule* over an increasingly centralized and sophisticated bureaucratic state for many centuries, even as it allowed Japan's emperors to continue to *reign* symbolically.

Whereas in Europe gradually weakening feudalism gave way to powerful modernizing monarchs and ultimately middle-class democracy, Japan's version of centralized feudalism persisted until Western imperialism prompted change in the nineteenth century. Faced with external threats to their nation's sovereignty, authoritarian oligarchs further centralized state power and consciously retained the emperor as a puppet to legitimize their efforts to catch up with the West. During this Meiji era, the oligarchs, borrowing this time not from China but from the institutions of modern European states, established a modern Japanese state that grew in autonomy and capacity as it became a formidable military and industrial power. In further emulating the Western imperial powers, Japan also began to establish its own empire, obtaining colonies in Taiwan (1895) and Korea (1910). In the 1930s, Japan continued its expansion, capturing Manchuria (1931), invading China proper (1937), and sweeping through Southeast Asia at the same time that it launched its attack on Pearl Harbor and the United States (1941). However, this course of imperial expansion and military conquest ended with defeat at the hands of the Americans in 1945, who defanged Japan's militarist state but allowed its mercantilist bureaucracy to remain intact. Before turning to Japan's contemporary political institutions, we first examine the development of the Japanese state.

PREMODERN JAPAN: ADAPTING CHINESE INSTITUTIONS

By the seventh century, Japan's tribal hunters and early rice cultivators came under the powerful cultural influence of Tang dynasty China. Among the most significant and lasting of the dynasty's cultural exports were Buddhism, Confucianism, the Chinese written language, and the trappings of material culture (including modes of dress, architectural styles, and even the use of chopsticks).

Tang China also had a profound influence on political reforms, inspiring the country's leaders to establish an administrative system modeled on the Tang imperial state. To finance this new bureaucracy, the state introduced sweeping land reform, purchasing all land and redistributing it among peasants so that it could be taxed. However, the meritocratic civil bureaucracy soon evolved into a hereditary, self-perpetuating ruling elite supported by a declining tax base. Squeezed mercilessly, the peasants, either for survival or protection, were forced to sell out to local wealthy officials who had managed to arrange tax immunity for their own lands.

From the eighth to the twelfth centuries, political power and wealth steadily shifted from the central government to independent rural landowners, and the urban-centered imperial system gradually disintegrated into a formalistic body

TIMELINE Political Development

645 C.E.	China-inspired Taika political reforms introduced.
1192	Minamoto Yoritomo declared first shogun.
1603	Tokugawa Shogunate established.
1853–54	Japan forcibly opened by U.S. Commodore Matthew C. Perry.
1867–68	Meiji Restoration takes place.
1894–95	First Sino-Japanese War is fought.
1904–05	Russo-Japanese War is fought.
1918–31	Era of Taishō democracy.
1937–45	Second Sino–Japanese War takes place.
1941	Pacific War begins.
1945	Japan is defeated and surrenders in World War II.
1945–52	The United States occupies Japan.
1955	Liberal Democratic Party (LDP) is formed.
1993–94	LDP briefly loses majority in Diet's House of Representatives to an opposition coalition.
2007	LDP loses majority in Diet's House of Councillors.
2009	Democratic Party of Japan (DPJ) gains majority in House of Representatives and forms a coalition government.
2011	Tōhoku earthquake, tsunami, and nuclear disasters take place.
2012	LDP regains a majority in the House of Representatives and forms a coalition government with Shinzō Abe as prime minister.
2014	LDP coalition obtains a supermajority in the House of Representatives.
2016	LDP coalition obtains a supermajority in the House of Councillors.

concerned only with the trappings and rituals of state. In the countryside, territorial nobles or lords, known as *daimyo*, governed the lands they occupied, which were farmed by former peasants, who had become their serfs. The lords and their properties were protected by warrior retainers, or **samurai**.

As their power grew, the landed aristocrats became increasingly dissatisfied with the ineffectual rule of the court. Over the course of the next 400 years, from the thirteenth through the sixteenth centuries, power completely shifted to this military aristocracy. Different clans vied for supremacy, and ascendant clans established a government known as the *bakufu* (literally, "tent government"). This was a period of continual warfare based on attempts at establishing a line of succession and a semblance of unity through military conquest, during which the emperor was largely disregarded. But in Japan, unlike in Europe, the imperial household was neither absolutely empowered nor completely displaced. The emperor had become not so much a person as a reigning symbol; whoever spoke in the name of the imperial chrysanthemum crest spoke with legitimate authority. The emperor became a puppet in the hands of aspiring daimyo, who never destroyed the head of state but forced him to anoint the strongest among them shogun, or dominant lord.

TOKUGAWA SHOGUNATE: CENTRALIZED FEUDALISM

By the end of the sixteenth century, feudal wars had come to a head, and Japan was slowly but surely unified by the Tokugawa shogunate, which imposed an enforced peace for the next two and a half centuries. Successive shoguns from the Tokugawa clan ruled over this feudal hierarchy in the name of the emperor, successfully shoring up the shogunate's authority and keeping the daimyo in check through an effective strategy of divide and rule at home and *sakoku*, or closed-country isolation, abroad.

The power of a local daimyo rested, in turn, on the size and productivity of the hereditary fief or feudal domain he controlled, the peasants who tilled the land, and, most important, the number of samurai the domain could support. The warrior retainers lived with their lords in castle towns that served as the fortresses and administrative centers from which the lords governed their domains. But as the Tokugawa-enforced peace settled over the countryside, the samurai were gradually converted from warriors to civil officials with fiscal, legal, and other administrative responsibilities. These samurai-turned-bureaucrats tackled civilian tasks in the same devoted, selfless manner in which they had been trained to carry out their martial responsibilities. These efficient, skilled, disciplined, and highly respected bureaucrats would come to serve the country well as it faced the challenges of abrupt modernization in the nineteenth and twentieth centuries.

Although Tokugawa Japan's political system was remarkably stable, its social organization and economy developed volatile contradictions. Tokugawa society was strictly hereditary and rigidly hierarchical; individuals were born into a particular station and could neither move between classes nor, for the most part, even advance within their own class. The samurai class was at the top of the hierarchy, but not all samurai were equal. This diverse warrior class ranged from the wealthy and powerful shogun and daimyo to the lowly retainers barely getting by on a subsistence stipend of rice. Next down on the social rung were the peasants, who formed the bulk of the remaining subjects, followed by artisans and craftsmen, and finally, at (or near) the bottom of the social hierarchy, the merchants.[2] As in other Confucian societies, commercial activities, including moneylending, and those people who participated in them were viewed with great disdain. Despite being socially despised, however, by the nineteenth century these merchants had established sophisticated and lucrative trading networks throughout Japan. Moreover, they had established themselves as the financiers of the lifestyles of the upper ranks of the samurai, who over time grew increasingly indebted to the merchants.

When Commodore Matthew C. Perry arrived with his fleet of U.S. warships in 1853 seeking coaling stations and trading opportunities for American ships, he unsuspectingly came upon this system, which was apparently stable but internally ripe for change. The ruling class had status and privilege but was heavily indebted and, in the case of many low-ranking samurai, even impoverished. The merchants were wealthy but socially disdained, lacking both political power and social status. Many Japanese, particularly among the lower ranks of the samurai, had become dissatisfied with what they saw as an increasingly ineffectual Tokugawa government and were ready for revolt. Perry did not cause this revolt, but he certainly facilitated it. This foreign pressure created a crisis of legitimacy for Tokugawa rule, which lacked the military capacity to resist the unfair trade demands of the Americans (and, subsequently, Europeans).

A decade of political chaos ensued, prompting a revolution launched not from below, by restive peasants or even aspiring merchants, but from above, by a handful of junior samurai officials. Much like Germany's nineteenth-century modernizers, this aristocratic vanguard was committed to sweeping change cloaked in traditional trappings. They recognized that the maintenance of Japanese independence required the end of the feudal regime and the swift creation of a modern economic, political, social, and, perhaps most important, military system capable of holding its own against the Western powers. But rather than deposing the symbolic leader of the old regime, the modernizers launched their reforms in the name of the 16-year-old emperor Meiji, ostensibly "restoring" him to his rightful ruling position.

MEIJI RESTORATION: REVOLUTION FROM ABOVE

The group of junior samurai who led the **Meiji Restoration** in 1868 came to be known as the **Meiji oligarchs**. What began as a spontaneous rejection of the Western threat by xenophobic nationalists quickly gave way to regime change led by a handful of low-ranking samurai promoting emulation of and catching up with the West. These oligarchs served as a vanguard in establishing the foundations of the modern Japanese state.

Their first priority was to make Japan a strong and wealthy state capable of renegotiating the unequal treaties the West had imposed on the country. Under the slogan "rich country, strong military," they promoted their mercantilist view of a strong relationship between economic development and industrialization on the one hand, and military and political power in the international arena on the other. They dismantled the feudal state and converted the decentralized feudal domains to centrally controlled political units. They jettisoned the feudal economy, eliminated hereditary fiefs, returned land to the peasants, and introduced a land tax that provided steady revenues to the state. Perhaps most surprisingly, they destroyed their own class, ending samurai privileges.

In 1889, the oligarchs adopted an imperial constitution (patterned after the German constitution) and presented it as a "gift" from the emperor to his subjects. It specified not the rights and liberties of the citizens but the duties and obligations that the subjects owed the emperor and the state. The constitution created some of the formal institutions found in Western democracies, including a bicameral parliament, known as the **Diet**, though its members were chosen by a limited franchise and exercised little real authority. The constitution vested all executive power in the emperor, who appointed the cabinet ministers and retained supreme command over the military. The oligarchs further legitimized this power structure by promoting an emperor-centered form of Shintoism as the mandatory state religion and by inculcating both national patriotism and emperor worship in the education system.

Buttressed by the traditional and charismatic legitimacy of a reigning emperor and the rational-legal legitimacy of an equally symbolic (and largely powerless) parliament, the oligarchs had obtained both the authority and the autonomy to promote painfully rapid development and to create a modern military. These twin goals of developing a rich country and a strong military were carried out by a literate and highly respected bureaucracy, an aggressive and increasingly influential military, and a set of state-supported but privately owned industrial conglomerates known as *zaibatsu*.

By the end of World War I, the Meiji oligarchs had successfully renegotiated the inequitable treaties with the West and established a fragile but rapidly growing economy. However, Japan's foreign policy and economic successes were not matched in the domestic political realm. By the 1920s, Japan was becoming a nation of diverse economic and political interests no longer easily subsumed under a single banner or slogan, and pressure to change the highly authoritarian system was building. The desire for change became increasingly apparent during the reign of the Taishō emperor (1912–26), particularly in the era of Wilsonian democracy after World War I. By that time, the original Meiji oligarchs had passed from the scene, and efforts by their bureaucratic and military successors to maintain the state autonomy of the Meiji political system faced challenges from a middle class demanding democratic rights, laborers organizing for better working conditions, and peasants rioting against onerous taxes.

In an era that came to be known as **Taishō democracy** (1918–31), efforts by these groups and their liberal political proponents to institute democracy were significant but short-lived and ultimately unsuccessful. Different groups increasingly sought to exercise influence in the political realm, and with some success, including the establishment and flourishing of competitive political parties by the early years of the century, election of the first commoner as prime minister in 1918, the alternation of elected governments during the 1920s, and the granting of universal male suffrage by 1925.

THE MILITARIST ERA: IMPERIAL EXPANSION AND DEFEAT

By the end of the 1920s, a number of events had stymied Japan's first genuine but short-lived effort to establish liberal democracy. The Great Depression and the rising global protectionism of the 1930s dealt trade-dependent Japan harsh blows, bringing about increased labor agitation and political unrest as the economy weakened. This domestic instability, combined with anti-Japanese sentiment in China, spurred rising nationalist and fascist sentiments at home and reemerging militarism and adventurism abroad. As in Europe and elsewhere, the emergence of such forces led in the early 1930s to a period of political polarization and increased political violence in which democracy became the chief victim. One Western observer labeled this period an era of "government by assassination."[3]

The era of Taishō democracy ended with the Japanese army's seizure of Manchuria in 1931 and the assassination of the last elected head of government by naval cadets in 1932. Over the next decade, the military steadily expanded its control of the state, ruling in an often uneasy alliance with the bureaucracy and the zaibatsu. Although most historians are not comfortable labeling the Japanese militarist state fascist, the emperor-based system lent itself to the establishment of a near-totalitarian state, one with many similarities to the European fascist states. The state sought to bring under its auspices or otherwise eliminate virtually all pluralist groups and autonomous organizations; that process entailed censoring the press, repressing all forms of political dissent, crushing political parties and other forms of free association, and gaining almost complete control over industrial production.

Also, like its fascist allies in Europe, Japan promoted an ultranationalist ideology and expansionist foreign policy, with the intent of extending its empire. At the height of its power, Japan's so-called Greater East Asian Co-Prosperity Sphere of conquered lands included most of the eastern half of China, Sakhalin and some of the Aleutian Islands, Korea, Taiwan, the Philippines, Indochina, Thailand, Malaya, Burma, Indonesia, and portions of the South Pacific. But as in Europe, Allied forces met, stemmed, and turned back Japanese aggression by 1944. Costly and stunning defeats at sea and on land, followed by the destructive U.S. firebombing of Japanese cities in early 1945 and the atomic bombing of Hiroshima and Nagasaki in August of that year, prompted Japan's unconditional surrender on September 2, 1945.

U.S. OCCUPATION: REINVENTING JAPAN

Japan's defeat and destruction were devastatingly complete: militarily, industrially, even psychologically. Under these conditions, foreign (specifically, American) pressure once again provided the impetus for revolutionary change in Japan. Although the seven-year occupation of Japan was technically an Allied operation, it remained overwhelmingly a U.S. enterprise managed by a single individual: the Supreme Commander of the Allied Powers in Japan, General **Douglas MacArthur**.

Like Commodore Perry's arrival nearly a century earlier, the American occupation of Japan following World War II is significant both for what it changed and for what it did not. The initial plan called for demilitarization to exorcise Japan's militant feudal past and then for democratization to establish American-style democratic values and institutions. Demilitarization proceeded swiftly and included not only the purging of all professional military officers, key wartime politicians, and zaibatsu leaders, but also the disbanding of ultranationalist associations and political parties. These thorough purges destroyed the military class and replaced entrenched politicians with technocrats (in most cases, former bureaucrats) and zaibatsu families with professional managers. Most dramatically, the new "Japanese" constitution (quickly drafted by MacArthur's staff and adopted by the Diet in 1947 almost unaltered) included Article 9, the so-called peace clause. The clause stipulated that Japan would "forever renounce war as a sovereign right" and never maintain "land, sea, and air forces, as well as other war potential."

Changing the status of the emperor—constitutionally and in the eyes of the Japanese citizens—to no longer be a political force was key to MacArthur's democratization efforts. The constitution reduced the emperor's stature from godlike and inviolable to simply symbolic, and it transferred sovereignty to the Japanese people. Other measures of this regime change included extending suffrage to women; clarifying relations among the prime minister, the cabinet, and the two houses of the Diet; guaranteeing civil rights and freedoms; breaking up the zaibatsu and imposing antitrust measures; encouraging labor unions and other interest groups; redistributing land to the peasants; and reforming the education system.

The two-stage approach of demilitarization and democratization remained largely in place for the first two years of the occupation, but the onset of the Cold War (compounded by the Communist victory in China in 1949 and the outbreak of the Korean War in 1950) led to a "reverse course" in occupation policies. The earlier desire to fully demilitarize and democratize Japan gave way to a plan that would make Japan a full, albeit still unarmed, ally of the West. In an effort to rebuild the economy, occupation authorities scaled back the deconcentration of industry

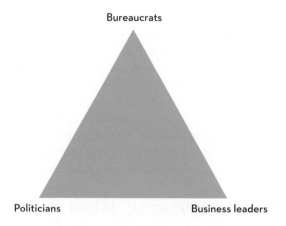

Iron Triangle

Japan's postwar corporatist and elitist state structure is often referred to as an *iron triangle*, and has limited the political influence of Japanese citizens and other pluralist interests.

---

and prohibited labor strikes. They purged and in some cases (re)jailed leftist labor activists even as they released and rehabilitated numerous conservative politicians. Notably, in all the twists and turns of occupation policy, the wartime bureaucracy of technocratic planners was left intact, in part because the American occupiers needed it and in part because the United States saw the bureaucracy simply as civil servants compelled to carry out the orders of the military government.

Today, some occupation reforms are universally considered to have been both successful and beneficial. Others largely failed, whereas still others remain highly controversial and even contradictory. For instance, on paper, Japan has one of the most liberal political systems in the world. But by default and design, its postwar state featured a core elite of experienced bureaucrats closely allied with conservative politicians (many of them former bureaucrats) and big-business executives. Many aspects of this ruling triad, or **iron triangle**, have persisted throughout the past seven decades and have been credited for Japan's remarkable postwar development as well as blamed for its more recent economic troubles. We now turn to an examination of this contemporary political structure.

Political Regime

Is Japan a democracy? The persistent relevance of Japan's ruling triad of bureaucrats, politicians, and business leaders has led to much controversy on this issue. In important ways, Japan's political structures and procedures are democratic. The rights and liberties enshrined in Japan's 1947 constitution certainly exceed those of the U.S. Constitution and are perhaps globally unrivaled. Its citizens are well protected by the rule of law, and its electoral system is probably no more corrupt than that of other advanced liberal democracies. Unlike its American counterpart, Japan's political arena hosts both socialist and Communist parties, arguably resulting in a greater range of political debate and choice than in the United States.

Yet these formal institutions and procedural safeguards of democracy do not tell the whole story. The initial dominance and persistent influence of the postwar

- **Legislative–executive system**: Parliamentary
- **Legislature**: Diet
  - **Lower house**: House of Representatives
  - **Upper house**: House of Councillors
- **Unitary or federal division of power**: Unitary
- **Main geographic subunits**: Prefectures
- **Electoral system for lower house**: Mixed single-member district and proportional representation
- **Chief judicial body**: Supreme Court

bureaucracy and its conservative political and corporate allies have led some analysts to conclude that Japan's democracy is dysfunctional, if not an outright mockery. Long-standing political practices and informal levers and linkages of power have constrained the full functioning of this imported democracy, inviting a closer look at both the formal institutions and substantive practices of Japan's political regime.

POLITICAL INSTITUTIONS

THE CONSTITUTION "We, the Japanese people . . ." The opening phrase of Japan's unamended 1947 constitution reveals what are perhaps the document's two most significant aspects: its American imprint and the transfer of sovereignty from the emperor to the Japanese people. Although America's allies called for the prosecution of Emperor Hirohito as a war criminal, General Douglas MacArthur insisted that the emperor renounce his divinity but be allowed to retain his throne to offer continuity and legitimacy to both the occupation government and the new democratic regime. The constitution reduces the emperor's godlike stature to that of a "symbol of the State and of the unity of the people with whom resides sovereign power." To empower Japanese citizens, the American framers of the Japanese constitution constructed an elaborate system of representative institutions, including universal suffrage, a parliamentary legislature in which the cabinet is responsible to the Diet (rather than to the emperor), and an independent judiciary. The constitution also introduced a greater measure of local autonomy by increasing the role of local elected officials.

Although the constitution has never been amended, a growing number of conservative politicians have advocated rewriting Article 9, the peace clause, in an effort to make Japan, in their words, a "normal" country. And in 2015, the LDP-led coalition government managed to pass legislation that effectively reinterprets the clause, permitting Japan for the first time to engage in "collective defense" with its allies, chiefly the United States. However, this legislation faced widespread opposition, and popular support for the pacifist constitution remains generally strong. Nonetheless, the growing military strength and regional ambitions of neighboring China as well as heightened threats from an unpredictable and nuclear-weapons-capable North Korea are strengthening the resolve of conservatives and softening the resistance of pacifists to formally amend the constitution.

THE BRANCHES OF GOVERNMENT

THE HEAD OF STATE Although invested by the Meiji Constitution with total authority, the imperial institution was always controlled by de facto rulers. The 1947 constitution eliminated even this derivative authority, making the role of the emperor wholly symbolic. Like the British queen, the monarchy symbolizes the unity and continuity of contemporary Japan. The emperor also performs purely ceremonial tasks, such as formally appointing both the prime minister and the chief justice of the Supreme Court, receiving foreign ambassadors, and representing the nation on many important ceremonial occasions at home and abroad.

The Japanese throne is both hereditary and patrilineal; no female heir is permitted to rule in her own right. Emperor Hirohito (who reigned from 1926 to 1989) was succeeded by his eldest son, Akihito, who became Japan's 125th emperor. Although polls show that recent generations of Japanese citizens, like their British counterparts, find themselves increasingly less connected to the throne, significant events, such as the passing of Hirohito and the birth of a prospective heir, generate enormous public interest and a deeper sense of attachment than polls seem to indicate.

THE PRIME MINISTER AND THE CABINET The prime minister serves as head of government and draws from the Diet at least the majority of cabinet members who serve as ministers, or heads, of Japan's 17 bureaucratic ministries and other key agencies. The prime minister is always chosen from the lower house, the House of Representatives, and is elected by the members of that chamber. This has meant that the leader of the majority party in the House of Representatives (or leader of the

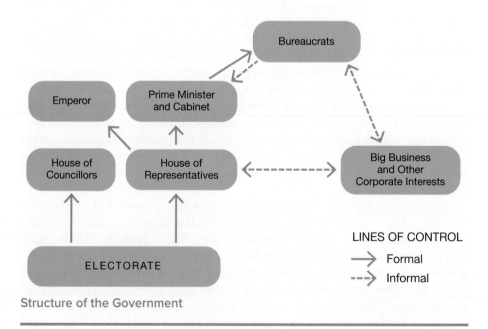

Structure of the Government

dominant party in a ruling coalition) has been elected prime minister. Elections in the lower chamber must be held every four years, but prime ministers serve only as long as they maintain the confidence of the members of the House of Representatives as well as the members of their own party. This process has enhanced the role of internal factional party politics and required that successful candidates to the office of prime minister not just belong to the right party but also curry sufficient favor and rise high enough in a dominant faction within that party.

As the dominant party for nearly six decades since its formation in 1955, the LDP fostered prospective party leaders more concerned with factional ties, personal connections, and backroom bargaining than with promoting a particular ideological or policy agenda. Faction leaders typically brokered this selection process and rotated the office of LDP president (and prime minister) among various factions somewhat frequently. Therefore, although Japanese prime ministers have been experienced and savvy politicians, they tend to be older, have less policy expertise, and, with notable exceptions, serve for far shorter tenures than do their counterparts abroad. The recent exceptions to this rule have been the tenures of LDP Prime Minister **Junichiro Koizumi** (2001–06) and current LDP Prime Minister **Shinzō Abe** (2006–07; 2012–). But during the intervening decade, prime ministers averaged little more than a year in office; overall, a total of 38 heads of government have led the country since 1945 (compared with 14 for the United Kingdom and 9 for Germany). Following Koizumi's departure in 2006, three successive LDP prime ministers came and went in just three years before the LDP lost lower house elections in 2009 to the opposition **Democratic Party of Japan (DPJ)**.

Although elected by a landslide with a mandate to reform politics as usual, the DPJ government followed the same pattern as the LDP. The DPJ put up three prime ministers in three years before losing elections in equally dramatic fashion in 2012 and returning the LDP to government. These short-lived governments were further weakened by what the Japanese call a **twisted Diet**, in which no ruling party or

Serving for only one year in his first term (2006–07), Prime Minister Abe was reelected to lead the LDP ruling coalition in 2012, making him one of Japan's longest-serving heads of government.

coalition controlled both chambers of parliament, from 2007 until 2013. In addition to divided government, scholars also point to disgruntled voters (particularly following the government's handling of the 2011 tsunami, earthquake, and nuclear disaster), weak political leaders, and the rise of new media as possible reasons for the frequent brief tenure of Japan's prime ministers.[4] But whatever the cause, this rapid turnover of elected heads of government has made these political leaders very dependent on the expertise, experience, and connections of the unelected bureaucrats within the ministries over which they ostensibly preside.

THE LEGISLATURE The 1947 constitution establishes Japan's legislature, or Diet (from the Latin *dieta*, meaning "assembly"), as the "highest organ of state power" and claims exclusive law-making authority for the bicameral parliament. The Japanese Diet has two directly elected chambers: the House of Representatives and the House of Councillors.

The **House of Representatives**, the lower house, has 475 members elected for a four-year term. As in other parliamentary systems, the government typically dissolves the lower house before the term has expired to call elections from a position of strength. Alternatively, a vote of no confidence can force dissolution, as it did most recently in 1993. General elections have taken place on average every two to three years since 1947. The upper chamber, the **House of Councillors**, comprises 242 members, elected for fixed six-year terms (staggered so that half the chamber stands for election every three years). Unlike the lower house, the upper house cannot be dissolved. As in other parliamentary systems, Japan's constitution grants the lower house far more power than the upper; the House of Representatives can override any House of Councillors decision on significant legislation with a two-thirds majority vote. However, recent elections in both houses have permitted first the opposition DPJ and then the opposition LDP to use their position in the upper house to obstruct or at least slow the policies and embarrass the leadership of the party in government. Significantly, any effort to amend the constitution's Article 9, the peace clause, would require two-thirds majority support in both chambers in addition to majority support in a national referendum.

Many veteran MPs have established expertise in particular policy areas as well as close ties to bureaucrats and interest groups having jurisdiction over or interest in those policy areas. These legislators are able to exercise a substantial degree of influence over policy formerly reserved for bureaucratic experts and simultaneously weakened party discipline in voting. The importance of pursuing **pork-barrel projects** for home-district constituencies has also weakened allegiance to the government. Therefore, even though the LDP maintained single-party rule for decades and confronted growing demands for change in the face of persistent economic decline, LDP governments hesitated to promote reforms over the objections of these experienced and entrenched politicians bound to networks of bureaucrats, businesses, and local constituencies. Over the years, these institutional relationships have resulted in both LDP and DPJ governments that are hesitant to promote change, despite being elected on platforms promising dramatic reforms to address Japan's economic woes.

THE JUDICIAL SYSTEM The 1947 constitution established for Japan a court system with a high degree of judicial independence from the other branches of government. In practice, however, the LDP over the years has used its political dominance, appointment powers, and other administrative mechanisms to manipulate the courts and ensure judicial decisions in accordance with its political interests. This process was made easier because, unlike the dual system of federal and state courts in the United States, the Japanese system is unitary—all civil, criminal, and administrative matters are under the jurisdiction of a single hierarchy. At the top is the constitutional court, or Supreme Court, whose 15 members are appointed by the cabinet and subject to a retention referendum every ten years.

This combination—of a unitary judicial system dominated for many decades by a single conservative party—has rendered Japan's courts particularly subservient and, like the political party that served as its political patron, distinctly conservative. Even though the Supreme Court is invested with the constitutional power of judicial review, it has seldom used this authority and has been extremely hesitant to declare policies or statutes unconstitutional. Since its creation in 1947, the Court has struck down only nine laws on constitutional grounds and has steadfastly refused to rule on matters relating to what is arguably postwar Japan's most significant constitutional issue: challenges to Japan's military and security activities under Article 9.[5]

THE ELECTORAL SYSTEM

As with other political institutions in Japan, the electoral system is both a cause and consequence of the LDP's long-standing reign. Postwar LDP governments maintained grossly disproportionate voting districts favoring rural, conservative voters who kept the LDP in power and established additional electoral rules that clearly favored the party's interests.[6] Only in recent decades have reforms begun to chip away at these LDP advantages and shift the landscape of electoral institutions and outcomes in Japan.

Representatives in the two chambers of the Diet are elected according to different rules. The 242 members of the upper House of Councillors serve fixed six-year terms, with half of the body facing election every three years. Councillors are elected according to a mixed system of proportional representation in a nationwide election for 96 seats and multimember districts (MMDs) coinciding with Japan's 47 prefectures for the remaining 146 seats. Before 1994, the electoral system used to determine membership in the House of Representatives resembled the MMD system used for the upper house.[7] In 1993, a series of notorious scandals, unpopular tax measures, and precipitous economic decline led numerous LDP members of parliament to defect from the party and form or join opposition parties. These defections brought into government an opposition coalition that lost no time in reforming the rules governing lower house elections. These reforms established a new mixed electoral system in which 300 of the 480 seats were elected from single-member districts (SMD). Further reforms in 2013 reduced the total number of SMD seats from 300 to 295 with the elimination of five rural electoral districts.[8] The remaining 180 seats are chosen by PR from 11 regional constituencies, in which seats are assigned to the parties according to their share of the total bloc-wide votes.

The architects of these reforms sought to shift electoral competition away from local and individual candidate-based campaign organizations known as *koenkai* and highly personalized factional politics within the LDP to national party politics between two dominant parties offering genuine policy alternatives. The 1994 reforms also began a process (still far from complete) of reapportioning districts to reflect demographics more accurately, giving more equitable clout to the much more

A common sight during Japan's election season—a white-gloved campaign worker advocates for her candidate from a loudspeaker-equipped van.

numerous (and typically less conservative) urban voters. Because the government automatically registers voters, virtually all eligible voters in Japan are registered. Accordingly, voter turnout in national elections has been relatively high, usually between 60 and 75 percent. But significantly, even as the system has become more competitive and politicians have increased their clout vis-à-vis the bureaucracy, voter turnout has declined. Although there are a number of reasons for the decline, popular distrust of politicians across the party spectrum as well as disillusionment with the political process and with government's seeming incapacity to bring about genuine reforms are paramount.

LOCAL GOVERNMENT

Japan is divided into 47 administrative divisions, known as prefectures, each with its own elected governor and legislature. Japan is nonetheless a unitary (not a federal) system in which most political power is invested in the central government.

The prefectural governments decide many local issues and are able to raise sufficient taxes to cover about one-third of their expenditures (what the Japanese call 30 percent autonomy). These subnational governments depend on the central government, however, for the remainder of their budget. Central authorities delegate all local authority (at the prefectural and municipal levels) and can, and sometimes do, retract that authority. The national government can override the decision of any local governor and has done so most notably in the case of Okinawa, whose elected local officials have attitudes toward the overwhelming U.S. military presence there that differ significantly from those of national leaders. Okinawans are not alone, however, in wishing for the devolution of more authority and increased local autonomy, and an increasing number of regionally based parties have emerged in recent years.

OTHER INSTITUTIONS

BUREAUCRACY AND THE IRON TRIANGLE Arguably, the Japanese state's most influential—yet entirely extra-constitutional—institution of policy-making authority remains the bureaucracy. As in other liberal democracies, the Japanese bureaucracy staffs the dozen or so ministries comprising the Japanese state, but it is at once smaller in size and greater in influence than any of its Western counterparts.

Ministers appointed to head these ministries are typically elected politicians who obtain their appointments based on political criteria, not policy expertise. Therefore, these ministers rely almost entirely on the career civil servants within their ministries to formulate, facilitate, and ultimately implement and enforce laws and policies. In each ministry, an administrative vice minister with some 30 to 35 years of experience in that particular ministry heads these efforts, presiding over a staff of Japan's brightest, who willingly subject themselves to grueling workweeks for relatively meager compensation.

Enduring linkages among senior bureaucrats, conservative politicians, and corporate executives form what has been referred to as an iron triangle, in which the determination and implementation of policies are often facilitated not by formal negotiations, hearings, or parliamentary votes but by extra-legal directives from government officials to the private sector. Known as **administrative guidance**, these policy directives are often communicated over the phone between former colleagues or during after-work drinking sessions among friends. In the past, ruling bureaucrats traditionally dominated these associations, while reigning LDP governments made sure that the party's most important constituents, including corporations (from which the party received massive campaign funds) and rice farmers (on whose overrepresented vote the party depended), were well taken care of with producer-oriented industrial and financial policies and protectionist trade barriers. Representatives of Japan's large corporations in turn offered firsthand policy advice to the bureaucrats and generally accepted the business-friendly policies and guidance they received in return.

Ties between the bureaucracy and business are further enhanced by an additional practice. Each year, a contingent of retiring but nonetheless highly qualified bureaucrats in their 40s and 50s undergo *amakudari* ("descent from heaven"), either to try their hand in politics or, more commonly, to take senior positions in the very corporations they previously regulated. In turn, the corporations that employ retired civil servants gain not just their skills but also their connections, giving the private sector substantial clout in the policy-making process. At any given time, Japan's policy elite comprise people who not only share a common outlook but also often attended the same prestigious schools and may have worked for decades in the same ministry.

Long credited with leading the postwar economic miracle, Japan's elite bureaucracy is now understandably a logical culprit for the country's more recent decades of economic malaise and growing political dysfunction. The bureaucracy's reputation has been badly tarnished not just by the economy's poor performance but also by a series of scandals and gaffes. These include revelations of kickbacks from politicians and corporations, a variety of costly cover-ups, and the mishandling of natural disaster recovery efforts following the 1995 earthquake in Kobe and the triple tragedy of the **2011 earthquake**, tsunami, and Fukushima nuclear catastrophe. Declining confidence in the bureaucracy and in Japan's iron triangle has led many to conclude that this "well-oiled, conservative machine" is undergoing a "regime shift," in which parliament, interest groups, and even Japanese citizens are gaining political influence. Where, then, does power reside in the Japanese state? It is fair to say that there is no single locus of power in the Japanese state. Even during the era of the bureaucracy's greatest strength, from the 1950s through the 1970s, powerful prime ministers still often held sway over the bureaucracy.[9] And some of Japan's most famous and successful corporations, such as Sony and Honda, achieved their status in part because they defied bureaucratic dictates.

Scholars critical of the Japanese state have described it as headless and susceptible to the kind of uncoordinated drift that led to a quixotic war against the United States in the twentieth century, followed by unsustainable trade surpluses with virtually every industrialized country and an inability to reform sufficiently its twentieth-century mercantilist economy to cope with the challenges of a twenty-first-century globalized economy.[10] Will Japan be able to change, and if so, what will be the impetus? Because elements within the iron triangle have demonstrated little willingness or incentive to change, many observers argue that it is necessary to look beyond this ruling triad and perhaps even beyond Japan to locate the forces and pressures capable of bringing about change.

Political Conflict and Competition

THE PARTY SYSTEM AND ELECTIONS

Like postwar Italy or Sweden, Japan until recent years has offered an example of an advanced industrial democracy governed by a predominant party system. The LDP dominated all other parties from the time of its formation as the merger of conservative parties in 1955 until its defeat at the hands of the DPJ in upper house elections in 2007 and lower house elections in 2009. For most of this period, the Japan Socialist Party (JSP; renamed the Social Democratic Party, or SDP, in 1996), formed as a merger of leftist parties in 1955, served as its perennial loyal opposition. During this period of LDP dominance, several other parties joined the JSP in opposition by taking advantage of Japan's former electoral system to carve out niches in the Japanese electorate among voters who felt excluded by both the larger parties. These included the Japan Communist Party (JCP), which consistently embraced policies to the left of the JSP, and the more moderate Democratic Socialist Party (DSP) and New Komei Party (NKP), which occupied a middle ground between conservative, pro-business LDP politics and the socialist (and pacifist) platform of the JSP.

This remarkably stable one-and-a-half-party system, an important component of the equally stable iron triangle, remained intact for nearly four decades. However, the bursting of Japan's economic bubble in the early 1990s, combined with the LDP government's inept and unpopular efforts to address the structural economic problems that prolonged the economy's slide, led in 1993 to a historic vote of no confidence in LDP rule and the defection of LDP parliamentarians to an opposition coalition. Two successive short-lived opposition coalitions held power long enough (just under a year) to implement electoral reforms that fostered the emergence of the DPJ, a party strong enough to legitimately and consistently challenge LDP rule. To understand the causes and the nature of this revolt and why it was so long in coming, it is necessary to examine both the long-dominant LDP and the DPJ that emerged to challenge this dominance.

THE LIBERAL DEMOCRATIC PARTY Although the LDP no longer has a guaranteed lock on Japan's parliament, the party has managed to control government for nearly six decades since its founding in 1955. The nature of this rule has led some observers to conclude that the LDP has been woefully misnamed: It is conservative, not liberal. Its internal politics have been highly authoritarian, not democratic. And its factional divisions have made it more a collection of mini-parties than a single party.

The LDP can perhaps best be understood as a collection of politicians acting as independent political entrepreneurs bound together in a highly pragmatic electoral machine in which ideological consistency has never taken priority over winning. Over the years, the party established electoral rules and engaged in campaigns and elections with the express purpose of staying in power by maintaining a majority (or at least a healthy plurality) of seats in the parliament. But the LDP became more than just a political machine for members of parliament. The party's persistent control of the government meant that the competition for the LDP presidency was in almost all cases a contest for the office of prime minister.

These contests fostered the emergence of factions, or mini-parties, within the LDP and a clientelist system in which candidates had to vie for the support of patrons within the party who could provide loyal faction members with campaign funds, official party endorsements, appointed positions within the party and the government, and other favors. These faction leaders in turn could count on the support of their faction members in the party's all-important presidential elections. At the local level, to help individual candidates obtain sufficient votes in their home districts, each candidate also constructed a local support group or *koenkai*.

Although factions have become less significant in recent years thanks to electoral reforms that have fostered the emergence of a more competitive two-party system, patron–client relations and informal personal relationships remain important institutions in the LDP and in all of Japan's political parties. Both campaign contributions and votes are secured through expanding circles of co-optation of businesses and other large interest groups as well as through clientelist currying of favor among local communities and individuals by means of pork-barrel projects, favors, and gifts. As in any democracy, projects in the home district, such as bridges and schools,

House of Representatives Election Results by Major Political Party, 2000–2014

	PARTY (IDEOLOGY)					
YEAR	LDP (RIGHT)	DPJ (CENTER)	NKP (CENTER)	SDP (LEFT)	OTHERS	TOTAL SEATS
2000	239	129	29	19	64	480
2003	237	177	34	6	26	480
2005	296	113	31	7	33	480
2009	119	300	21	7	33	480
2012	294	57	31	2	96	480
2014	291	73	35	2	74	475*

*Total seats reduced from 480 to 475 beginning with the 2014 election.

create jobs and deliver votes, and the lucrative contracts and licenses awarded to corporations to build these projects bring campaign donations. Persistent—indeed, mounting—corruption scandals, combined with growing dissatisfaction with LDP governance, prompted the defection of a number of LDP members of parliament to an opposition coalition that wrested power briefly from the LDP in the 1990s. But after a year in exile, the less than popular LDP nonetheless returned to office as part of a series of coalition governments. As Japan entered its second decade of economic malaise, the LDP received a boost in support when voters pinned their hopes for economic recovery and political reform on the promises of maverick politician Junichiro Koizumi, who served as LDP prime minister from 2001 to 2006. He won three consecutive elections with promises to halt Japan's economic malaise and take on the country's conservative bureaucratic and political elite (including his own LDP) and their deeply entrenched constituencies.

Although LDP party rules required the popular prime minister to step down in 2006 after five years as party president, his government managed to implement a number of modest reforms, including the privatization of Japan's postal savings system. But Koizumi's successor, Shinzō Abe, an ardent Japanese nationalist supported by the LDP's more conservative wing, returned Japan to LDP politics as usual, including factional infighting, cozy arrangements with bureaucrats, and corruption scandals. Abe presided over a stunning defeat in the 2007 upper house elections that denied the LDP a majority in the chamber and "twisted" Japan's parliament. The LDP next lost control of the lower house and government in an even more dramatic drubbing in the 2009 House of Representatives election that brought the DPJ to power for the first time. For reasons discussed later, the DPJ also cycled just as quickly through three prime ministers in three years and lost even more dramatically in the 2012 election than had the LDP in 2009. The surprising agent of this LDP turnaround was none other than a rejuvenated Shinzō Abe. Abe led the LDP in an election that more than doubled the LDP's seats in the lower house while promising both to revive the economy through a three-pronged strategy that has come to be known as **Abenomics** and to stand up to China in an increasingly dangerous dispute over islands claimed by both countries (see "Territorial Tempests," p. 351). In a bid to strengthen his party's hand in carrying out controversial reforms, Abe called for elections in 2014, held on to nearly all of the LDP's seats, and, with its coalition partner, maintained the two-thirds majority of seats necessary to override any potential veto in the upper house.

Toning down his personal nationalist sentiments and making genuine progress with his economic revitalization strategy, Abe and the LDP followed the 2009 lower house victory with solid wins in both the 2013 and 2016 upper house elections. With its NKP partner, the governing LDP coalition obtained two-thirds majorities in both chambers of the Diet. This mandate gave the government confidence to push forward with some of the more painful measures of economic reform, including passing a controversial tax increase and negotiating trade deals that threaten the protection of rice farmers.

The string of electoral victories has also given Abe sufficient confidence to act more boldly on the nationalist front. In 2013, he paid a visit to the controversial **Yasukuni Shrine**, which honors Japan's war dead, including those executed as war criminals at the end of World War II. In 2015, in the face of widespread popular protest, his government forced through the Diet divisive legislation reinterpreting Article 9 that authorizes Japanese troops to fight (defensively) overseas for the first

Elected with a mandate to reform Japan's economy, Prime Minister Abe's LDP government has secured supermajorities in both chambers of the Diet. Many believe Abe intends to use this dominant position to push for constitutional reform.

time since 1945. The super majorities in both chambers have also given Abe and his governing coalition the ability to pursue outright revision of the constitution, should they choose to do so. Such a measure would also require ratification by a majority of voters in a national referendum, something polls indicate Japan's citizenry is not yet prepared to do.

DEMOCRATIC PARTY OF JAPAN/DEMOCRATIC PARTY Capitalizing on mounting public frustration with LDP rule during the 1990s and anticipating the intended consequences of the electoral reforms to favor large, organized political parties, the DPJ formed in 1998 as a merger of several reform-minded opposition parties. Capitalizing on voter frustration with the LDP, the DPJ secured upper house electoral victories in 2004 and 2007 and in 2009 obtained a majority of seats in the House of Representatives elections and swept the LDP from power.

Elected into office on a platform of bold promises and with a significant mandate for carrying out political, economic, and social reforms, the DPJ nonetheless struggled both to realize its campaign pledges and to retain the support of voters. The DPJ's first prime minister, **Yukio Hatoyama** (2009–10), came to office vowing to weaken the iron triangle by shifting political authority from bureaucrats to elected politicians and to devolve central political authority to local communities and citizens. The Hatoyama government promised to jump-start the economy, improve relations with China, and reduce the American military footprint in Japan's island prefecture of Okinawa.

But Hatoyama's government failed to deliver on its promises, and the party replaced Hatoyama with Naoto Kan in the hopes of improving the party's prospects in the 2010 upper house elections. But the DPJ and its coalition partners fared poorly in the elections, losing their upper house majority and once again giving Japan a twisted parliament in which the DPJ held a majority in the lower chamber but the LDP-led opposition dominated the upper house. Following that election, Kan and the DPJ

Japanese paying their respects at the controversial Yasukuni Shrine. Yasukuni is revered by Japanese nationalists but criticized by Japan's Asian neighbors, who think the shrine honors the spirit of people who have been convicted of war crimes.

government struggled to keep together its coalition, carry out reforms, or even maintain a consistent policy position. The tragic earthquake, tsunami, and nuclear disaster of 2011 further stalled hope of dramatic progress and prompted Kan's resignation later that year and the party election of Yoshihiko Noda to replace him. An increasingly vocal public and invigorated media voiced strong criticism of the DPJ government's inept handling of the nuclear crisis and cleanup (see "3/11: Japan's Triple Tragedy," p. 350) and its inability to revive Japan's economy. Voters echoed these concerns in the 2012 election that brought the LDP back to government, and the 2014 election that retained LDP rule, sending not so much a message of confidence in the capacity of the LDP as a resounding rejection of this maiden effort of the DPJ to govern effectively. Despite a 2016 merger with another party and a name change, the now "**Democratic Party (DP)**" continues to struggle at the polls.

THE EMERGENCE OF LOCAL PARTIES Japan's unitary political system, the LDP's half-century lock on both party politics and government, and successive electoral systems that favored first a one-party dominant system and now a two-party dominant system have all conspired to restrict the emergence of regional and local political parties in Japan. But the tectonic shifts that permitted the DPJ to unseat the LDP from government in 2009 also began to weaken the grip that national party organizations have held over local politics. In particular, several populist local political leaders have established local political parties in recent years. These local leaders have run campaigns based on platforms reminiscent in some ways of populist movements taking place in the United States and Europe: devolving authority from the national to local levels, promoting nationalism, and in some cases lowering taxes, tightening budgets, and liberalizing trade.[11]

Not surprisingly, both the LDP and DPJ observed the popularity of many of these ideas and brought elements of them into their own party platforms. For Abenomics, the LDP's ambitious economic recovery program, Abe's government explicitly lifted several elements from the local parties' playbooks, including participating in multilateral free-trade negotiations, devolving authority to local "special economic zones," and loosening government regulations that have stifled entrepreneurship. While these efforts of co-optation may weaken the power of local parties, democracy appears to be working. Many objectives of these local political movements may still be realized, even if they are ultimately enacted by the national parties.

CIVIL SOCIETY

Because the reforms that brought about Westernization and democracy were imposed from above (and, in many cases, from *outside*), Japan's political system historically fostered a tradition of "top-down" bureaucratic society rather than a "bottom-up" civil society whose citizens independently organized and participated in political, economic, and social affairs. Like other authoritarian systems, the Meiji and militarist states fostered corporatist and mercantilist institutions to harness Japan's industrial society in the service of modernization and imperialism. Although the U.S. occupiers destroyed many aspects of Japanese authoritarianism and carried out sweeping political, social, and economic reforms, they retained the bureaucracy and, out of fear of communism, squelched many of the nascent civic groups they had initially fostered.

In pursuing economic development and political stability, the postwar Japanese state organized or co-opted interest groups that were important to these goals, such as business and agricultural associations, and formed associations for facilitating their political participation. In exchange for their support, these groups have had their interests well represented (and protected), and they have prospered. During the postwar decades of economic growth, this symbiotic relationship expanded to include many other smaller groups and constituencies in a system of distributional welfare. Independent labor unions, consumer organizations, and other civic groups have been notably absent from these arrangements.

The third point of the iron triangle in addition to politicians and bureaucrats is made up of Japan's large corporations and the large industrial groupings (**keiretsu**) to which they belong. These players have been proponents of and participants in Japan's postwar development. Big business exercises political influence through the Japanese Federation of Economic Organizations, which voices the concerns of large corporations, offers policy recommendations to the government, and provides the lion's share of campaign contributions. Another key pillar of political support has been the agricultural sector, whose highly organized political interests are channeled through local agricultural cooperatives to the national "peak organization" known as Japan Agriculture (JA). Agriculture's key political contribution has been its capacity to provide a dependable and geographically concentrated bloc of votes. In exchange, both LDP and DPJ governments have enacted policies that favor farmers, including price supports, relatively low taxes, and protection from agricultural imports.

Big business and agriculture are not the only interest groups to have offered their campaign contributions and votes in exchange for favorable policies and a share of the benefits of Japan's postwar economic boom. Small and midsize businesses and retailers have been very well organized and have parlayed their electoral support into tax breaks, subsidies, and protection from larger firms. Japan's half-million construction firms are another group worth mentioning, most of which are small, unproductive, and well cared for by an inefficient and corrupt government bidding system for public works.

Japan's faltering economy and growing corruption scandals involving both the LDP and DPJ/DP and their supporters have cast new light on the economic and political costs of the country's corporate welfare system. Critics argue that the LDP's varied and growing host of constituencies led to distributional tyranny, fueled Japan's economic crisis, and stifled political change. Corporatist arrangements have also long excluded interests deemed potentially harmful to the goals of either rapid industrialization or corporate welfare, including trade unions, consumers, environmentalists, and women's groups. As Japan's postindustrial and post-materialist society grows more complex and the political marketplace more competitive, and in the wake of natural disasters such as the Kobe earthquake in 1995 and the 2011 earthquake, tsunami, and nuclear disaster in Fukushima, a host of nongovernmental and nonprofit organizations have emerged and are strengthening Japan's civil society. These civic associations include groups representing pacifists, nationalists, environmentalists, antinuclear advocates, AIDS activists, religious organizations, and many other interests that are broadening and deepening Japan's civil society and enhancing pluralism in this advanced industrial democracy.[12]

Society

ETHNIC AND NATIONAL IDENTITY

Few national populations view themselves as racially and ethnically homogeneous as do the Japanese. Because immigrants constitute only 1 percent of the population and foreign nationals comprise only 2 percent, this perception is grounded in demographic reality. This strong ethnic and national identity has come at the expense of several minority groups, who have been prevented from developing a Japanese identity and enjoying the full privileges of citizenship as Japanese nationals with a separate ethnic heritage. These minorities include the indigenous Ainu in the north and Okinawans in the south; descendants of Koreans, Chinese, and Southeast

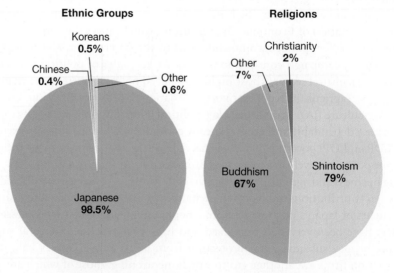

Note: Percentages sum to greater than 100 percent because many Japanese practice both Shintoism and Buddhism.

Asians; and the children of mixed ancestry and foreigners. Although not racially separate, the 2 to 4 million *burakumin* ("social outcasts"), whose ancestors worked in the "unclean" occupations such as grave digging, butchery, and tanning, are also seen as a minority group and have faced intense prejudice. Discrimination in areas such as employment and marriage against these minority groups has been widespread and persistent. Those individuals who have sought to assimilate by taking on Japanese names, mastering the Japanese language, and adopting Japanese cultural mores have generally nonetheless remained socially marginalized and culturally scorned.

However, scholars note that demographic and economic necessity may eventually compel the social integration and mobility that cultural obstacles and state policy have prevented. Japan finds itself at the forefront of a problem confronting many advanced industrial societies: the convergence of an aging population and dwindling fertility rates. The ratio of Japanese senior citizens to the total population was only 12 percent in 1990, but it is expected to climb to nearly 40 percent by 2050. By midcentury, demographers predict, Japan will have 1 million centenarians and 30 percent fewer people overall, and nearly 1 million more people will die each year than are born.

The graying of Japan's population brings economic challenges that other countries certainly face as well, including health and financial care. But the most acute problem Japan faces, far more so than other advanced countries, is that of a declining workforce. Whereas most advanced societies have expanded their labor pools by more fully integrating women and immigrants into the workplace, Japan has been unwilling to embrace either group. And even if Japanese women were fully empowered, economists argue that the only long-term hope for stabilizing Japan's population and workforce is to increase and sustain immigration over many years. Absent this source of workers, consumers, and taxpayers, experts predict that Japan's economy will not just decline but may very well collapse.

IDEOLOGY AND POLITICAL CULTURE

Japan's historical experiences with Shintoism, Buddhism, Confucianism, feudalism, militarism, and bureaucratism have certainly shaped the norms and values that guide Japanese political behavior. So have its experiences with the West, from imposed inequitable treaties and democratic institutions to military defeat and the embrace of Western popular culture. In efforts to attribute political behavior to culture, scholars often point to the group conformity and social hierarchy that pervade most aspects of Japanese life. The basic unit of Japanese society is not the individual but the group, as manifested in such institutions as the family, the company, the political faction, and the nation. Japanese are socialized to defer to the needs of the group and to make decisions through consensus rather than majority vote. Similarly, hierarchy governs most social relationships in Japan, and Japanese are most comfortable in settings where their social standing in relation to that of others is clear. Inferiors yield to their superiors' authority, and superiors are obliged to care for their subordinates' needs. Promotion in firms, bureaucratic ministries, and political party factions is more often based on seniority and personalized patron-client relationships than on merit.

Japan has undergone political and economic modernization, but on its own (not fully Western) terms. Individual freedom and social equality remain less important than being accepted by the group and holding a rightful position in that group's hierarchical division of labor. Perhaps not surprisingly, Japanese are often inclined to accept the political status quo rather than advocate change. In a recent poll, nearly three-fourths of respondents identified themselves as having a political stance ranging from conservative to neutral, whereas less than one-fourth saw themselves as progressive or close to progressive.

Japan's persistently weak economy (combined with the forces of globalization and an ongoing generational change in values) has led to greater income inequality and economic insecurity, and it may lead to greater diversity of political attitudes and perhaps even to a shift in political culture in Japan. The fading of guaranteed permanent employment and rising unemployment among college graduates have led to disillusionment with business and politics as usual and to mounting calls for change, particularly among Japanese youth, who have no memory of wartime hardship or postwar poverty and who place more value on individual fulfillment through leisure diversions and risky entrepreneurial opportunities than through long hours and long years of work for the sake of a company. In short, change may be initiated by a younger generation far more willing and likely to switch both their jobs and their political loyalties.

Political Economy

Japan's sudden and forced introduction to the global political economy in the nineteenth century at the hands of Western imperialists fostered the development of a mercantilist political-economic system concerned with neither liberal freedom nor Communist equality. State-led economic development became not a way of serving the public but rather a means of preserving national sovereignty. Despite the tumultuous change that Japan experienced in the late 1800s and early 1900s, the basic structure of its catch-up mercantilist political economy continued through much of the twentieth century, and key elements persist to the present. Forged under conditions of military rigor, refined during the U.S. occupation, and perfected under the aegis of American military and economic protection, this developmental model propelled Japan from the ashes of devastating military defeat to become the second-largest economy in the world. Not surprisingly, scholars and policy makers alike have sought to understand this developmental "miracle," and the investigation of the model of Japan's **capitalist developmental state** has become an important field of academic study and policy analysis.[13] Japan's political-economic system has permitted a far higher level of state guidance of competitive markets and cooperation with private firms than do the liberal capitalist systems in Britain and the United States. This guidance has included a host of formal and informal economic measures often grouped under the term **industrial policy**. Industrial policies are formulated and implemented by Japan's elite economic bureaucracy after consultation and coordination with the private sector. Measures have included imposing protective tariffs and nontariff barriers on imports, encouraging cooperation and limiting "excessive" competition in strategic export sectors, and offering low-interest loans and tax breaks to firms willing to invest in targeted industries and technologies.

Government guidance has not always worked well or as planned. But for many decades, state-led developmental capitalism kept Japan's economy strong, prosperous, and internationally competitive while keeping its iron triangle of bureaucrats, politicians, and business leaders closely linked. After growing at an average rate of over 10 percent per year during the 1950s and 1960s, Japan's economy still managed to grow over 5 percent per year during the 1970s and 1980s. In fact, from the early 1950s to 1990, Japan's gross domestic product (GDP) grew at twice the rate of those in the other advanced industrial economies. The flagship automotive and consumer electronics companies within Japan's large conglomerates became multinational giants and household names, and the fruits of Japan's rapid growth lifted incomes and opportunities for nearly all Japanese.

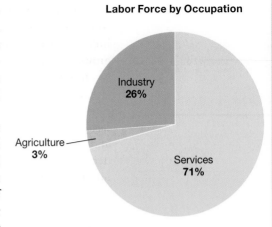

Labor Force by Occupation

Industry
26%

Agriculture
3%

Services
71%

By the 1980s, Japan's very prosperity was masking what now, in hindsight, is much easier to detect as serious structural problems within the model. Even as the international political economy grew ever more integrated and hypercompetitive, the costs of doing business in Japan were mounting. In the face of these competitive pressures, inefficient industries used their influence within the iron triangle to seek protection. They obtained it from a government that had become accustomed to looking after not just economically strategic industries but also politically and socially important ones. This government assistance maintained employment and social stability but also led to waste, overcapacity, and overpricing.

These corporate welfare measures, combined with a rapid jump in the value of Japan's currency, propelled the country's stock and real estate markets skyward in the latter half of the 1980s. Japan was awash in overinflated assets and easy money, which led companies, banks, the Japanese Mafia, and even the government to invest in grossly overpriced assets and risky (even foolish) business ventures. When this asset bubble burst in 1992, the value of stock and property plummeted, growth slowed, and already uncompetitive companies were left with huge debts (and dwindling assets and production with which to repay them). The Japanese labeled these firms **zombies**—essentially dead but propped up by banks and a political system unwilling to force them into bankruptcy and face the social costs of closed businesses and spiraling unemployment.

The government slid deeper into debt as it sustained not just these insolvent firms but also the banks that carried their debts (valued in the trillions of dollars), even as it attempted to stimulate consumer spending. Although a combination of government stimulus measures and liberalizing reforms have breathed some life back into the economy, Japan is now mired in its third consecutive decade of no or slow growth. The economy remains plagued by the three Ds of deflation (declining prices), government debt (more than twice Japan's annual GDP and the largest in the world), and budget deficits (running annually at about 10 percent of GDP).

Over the course of two decades, Japan experienced a reversal of fortune unprecedented in a peacetime economy. While government-business cooperation and a targeted focus on economic development promoted rapid postwar economic growth, this mercantilist political-economic structure proved far less successful once it had caught up and found itself pursuing cutting-edge technologies and competing in unpredictable and rapidly changing global markets. Moreover, as the economy struggled, politicians and bureaucrats boosted the funding of public works and provided generous subsidies to inefficient and uncompetitive firms to prop up employment and preserve voter support. Although these destructive inefficiencies were tolerable during the boom years, they became a significant drag on the Japanese economy and a political albatross for the long-ruling LDP.

Promising to lift Japan's struggling economy, Abe and his LDP government have launched a three-pronged recovery program that came to be labeled Abenomics. The first of the program's three "arrows," as Abe called his economic stimulus measures, sought to increase demand in the economy, and the second took aim at boosting inflation. These fiscal and monetary stimulus policies did spur Japan's economic growth rate and raise prices, but thus far have had less impact on job creation and wage increases.

The third arrow of Abenomics provides for a broad array of structural reforms intended to raise the economy's growth potential and put Japan on track for long-term recovery and growth. But this arrow has proven more difficult to launch, and skeptics fear it may never hit its target. These reforms include proposals for deregulated economic zones, reduced protectionism in agriculture, and more open immigration policies. None of these proposed measures are new, but because each threatens to harm particular interests, both former and present governments have struggled to deliver on these kinds of bold promises of structural reform in the face of conservative bureaucratic, political, and corporate resistance. This resistance has led many observers to conclude that the key to substantial economic liberalization remains political reform.

Current Issues in Japan

3/11: JAPAN'S TRIPLE TRAGEDY

Japan is no stranger to earthquakes or other natural disasters—it has experienced 17 significant earthquakes since 1995 and gave us the word *tsunami*. But this island nation was wholly unprepared for the disastrous Tōhoku earthquake and tsunami that struck the northeast region of Honshu, Japan's largest island, on March 11, 2011. The biggest (of many) tremors registered 9.0 in magnitude on the Richter scale, making it the largest recorded earthquake ever to strike Japan and one of the five most powerful anywhere. With its epicenter 40 miles off the coast and 20 miles under the ocean's surface, the quake generated tidal waves up to 133 feet high that wreaked havoc on the coastline and traveled as far as 6 miles inland. The entire island of Honshu shifted some 8 feet to the east. The earthquake and tsunami caused an estimated 25,000 casualties and hundreds of billions of dollars in damage, and it shaved roughly 5 percent off Japan's annual GDP.

Perhaps, though, a greater long-term danger posed by this disaster has come from the destruction and meltdown of nuclear reactors at the Fukushima Daiichi plant and the associated nuclear accidents and radioactive fallout. Experts have judged this to be the worst nuclear catastrophe since the meltdown in Chernobyl in the former Soviet Union some 25 years earlier. They estimate that the process of cooling and dismantling the three damaged reactors and decontaminating the area could take decades. This ongoing threat of radiation is particularly poignant for Japan, the only country to have experienced widespread radioactive contamination following the atomic bombing at the end of World War II.

The political fallout from the disaster has been significant as well. The crisis initially provided a boost to the flailing DPJ government, but its slow and inadequate response to the disaster prompted growing frustration and activism among Japanese citizens. The iron triangle of Japan, Inc., became a particular target of this popular dissatisfaction when it became apparent that the bureaucratic ministry charged with ensuring the safe operation of the private utility corporation's nuclear plants

Scene of the extensive destruction resulting from Japan's Tōhoku earthquake and tsunami.

had in fact served as its chief promoter. As often happens in these kinds of disasters, the real heroes were its victims. The region experienced virtually no looting or other crimes in the days and weeks following the earthquake and tsunami, and the Japanese people demonstrated a remarkable degree of patience, cooperation, and national purpose. Today, as the government's cleanup efforts fall hopelessly behind schedule and stretch from months to years, and now perhaps decades, this patience has in many cases turned to bitterness and hopelessness.

TERRITORIAL TEMPESTS

An additional thorny challenge lies beyond the shores of Japan's main islands and concerns territorial disputes with each of the country's largest continental neighbors. Although the total landmass of these contested islands could easily fit within the area of metropolitan Tokyo, conflicts with Russia, South Korea, and China over these mostly uninhabited (and in many cases uninhabitable) territories has been rancorous, persistent, and seemingly intractable. Ironically, the conflicts are not so much about the islands themselves, but rather a convergence of bitter historical memories, expressions of national sovereignty, and competition for access to lucrative fisheries and seabed petroleum resources.

The largest of these territories and the source of the most long-standing dispute are what the Russians call the Kurile Islands and the Japanese refer to as the "Northern Territories." Control of this chain of islands stringing northward from Hokkaido (the most northern of Japan's four largest islands) has shifted back and forth between Japan and Russia since the nineteenth century. However, since Japan's defeat in World War II, the entire archipelago has been occupied by the Russians. Because each country forfeited control over the islands as a result of war defeat (Russia in 1905 and Japan in 1945), neither side is willing to legitimize the claims of the other. In fact, this dispute has prevented Japan and Russia from ever concluding a peace treaty ending World War II. Although Japan currently lays claim to only the four southernmost islands in the chain, the two countries appear as far away as ever from resolving this issue that has festered for nearly seven decades.

Moving southward, Japan's island dispute with South Korea concerns two tiny islets whose sizes belie the degree of bitter acrimony between the two countries. The two jagged outcroppings of rock known as the Dokdo (Korea) or Takeshima (Japan) islands are located almost equidistant (just over 100 miles) from both the Korean mainland and Japan's main island of Honshu. Although each country claims sovereignty over the territory, South Korea administers the 46 acres of volcanic rock. South Korea, in particular, remains highly sensitive to this issue since Japan's claim to the territory is founded chiefly on its harsh colonization of Korea in the early twentieth century. When the Japanese prefecture laying claim to the islets launched a "Takeshima Festival" in 2005, an angry Korean mother responded in protest by severing her own finger and that of her son. Another Korean protester set himself on fire.

Likewise, Japan's dispute with China over the Diaoyu Islands (China) or **Senkaku Islands** (Japan) finds its roots in Japan's imperial past. However, rising tensions between these two East Asian powers over the barren outcroppings threaten to escalate this quarrel into outright military conflict. Although each country cites centuries-old historical records to justify its respective claims of sovereignty, Japan formally annexed the five islets in 1895 after its military victory against China that year. The uninhabited outcroppings lie almost equidistant (approximately 200 miles) from the Chinese mainland and Japan's Okinawa.

Although abundant fishing in the area has led to numerous incidents between Chinese fishing boats and Japanese patrol boats (involving at times water cannons, ramming, and even the impounding of boats and personnel), the greater stake in this dispute has been the oil and gas fields discovered in this region. Both countries agreed in 2008 to make the East China Sea a "sea of peace, cooperation and prosperity" and to jointly exploit the seabed petroleum fields; however, bitter accusations and rising nationalist protests on both sides have been common. Nor is it just the seabeds, islands, and fisheries that are being contested. In 2013, the Chinese unilaterally declared an "air defense identification zone" that would require any foreign aircraft flying through the zone to identify itself to Chinese authorities and comply with Chinese regulations. Naturally, the new zone encompassed the islands, and just as predictably, Japanese aircraft have ignored the Chinese requirement (as has the United States, Japan's military ally). Dangerous near misses between Japanese and Chinese military aircraft now compete with sea-based clashes.

These multinational island (and sea and air) disputes are ostensibly foreign policy issues, but they remain salient largely because of conservative nationalist groups in each country. Those groups see any show of flexibility or compromise on the parts of their own governments as a sign of weakness against the imperial designs of their neighbors. This dynamic dangerously demonstrates the compelling power of nationalism and proves in the case of Japan, as illustrated elsewhere in this textbook on comparative politics, that perhaps all politics in the end are domestic politics. But this tempest between Japan and rising China also demonstrates that domestic politics can have profound and potentially deadly international consequences.

Key Terms

Zimbabwean president Robert Mugabe cuts the ribbon at the launch ceremony of a massive hydropower project funded and constructed by China.

Nondemocratic Regimes

Why have some countries failed to establish democracy?

ZIMBABWE IS ONE COUNTRY THAT has failed despite its great potential. As recently as the mid-1980s, Zimbabwe's gross domestic product (GDP) per capita, as well as several other development indicators, were roughly the same as those of Vietnam. But while Vietnam has enjoyed rapid economic development, Zimbabwe has experienced a long period of government mismanagement and economic decline. Vietnam's GDP has grown fourfold, while Zimbabwe's GDP per capita declined by 25 percent. Child mortality rates have similarly grown in Zimbabwe as they declined in Vietnam. In perhaps the most striking example of dysfunction, Zimbabwe now holds the record for the world's highest inflation rate: 231 million percent in 2008. The central bank actually printed a 100-trillion-dollar bill shortly before the currency collapsed.

Still, even though Zimbabwe faced these tremendous hardships, President Robert Mugabe has been able to remain in office since 1980. In the 2013 elections, Mugabe's party, Zimbabwe African National Union-Patriotic Front (ZANU-PF), won two-thirds of the seats in Parliament and has managed to rout the opposition at every turn. In an environment of such economic stress, how is Mugabe able to hold on to power?

One answer lies in natural resources. Many of us are familiar with the notion of "blood" or conflict diamonds. Typically, we are thinking about civil wars and illegal mines that fund arms sales. However, conflict diamonds need not emerge only out of civil war; Zimbabwe's diamonds are also a product of conflict. Unlike in many other African countries, where diamonds have been mined for many decades or longer, Zimbabwe's Marange diamond fields began operation only in 2006, during the depths of the country's economic crisis. Shortly thereafter, the fields were nationalized, providing the potential for hundreds of millions of dollars in sales for the state.

While these resources should have been a lifeline for Zimbabwe, a large share—perhaps the majority—of revenues from diamond sales did not go into the hands of the state. Rather, the diamonds helped fund what the nongovernmental organization (NGO) Global Witness calls a parallel government. Diamond mining rights were extended to firms with clear links to those in power. Significant or majority shares are held by high-ranking members of the Zimbabwean Central Intelligence Organisation (CIO; a secret police force loyal to Mugabe) as well as by individuals in charge of the Ministry of Defense, armed forces, and police.

The implications of this relationship are significant. First, the revenue has given a new lease on life to the ruling ZANU-PF and the security institutions it controls. Funds from diamond sales were directed toward radio-jamming equipment to block broadcasts from stations critical of the government, fleets of vehicles to deploy supporters and attack opposition forces, and direct payments to individuals and tribal leaders to secure their support in elections. Some observers suggest that nearly $1 billion has been spent toward this end. Second, diamond wealth in the hands of ZANU-PF and the security institutions has created a new opportunity for corruption within the state and government. As we discussed in Chapter 6 on democracy, when economic assets are concentrated in the hands of those in power, they create a disincentive to leave office. Zimbabwe has clearly fallen into a "resource trap," where natural resources in fact weaken economic development and strengthen authoritarian rule. It is not surprising, then, that only a fraction of Zimbabwe's diamond wealth has actually wound up in the state treasury.

A final point has to do with the international community. For a number of years, various states and nongovernmental organizations have exerted pressure on Mugabe to step down, deploying such tools as an embargo on military supplies, limits on development aid, and a boycott on diamonds. But Zimbabwe has found a new source of support in China. Unlike the United States or the European Union, China is not concerned about Zimbabwe's authoritarianism or human rights record. China has provided upward of $1 billion in loans and aid to Zimbabwe, and Chinese firms have been active in various development projects, including diamond mining. But this too may have its limits. In 2016, Mugabe canceled the rights of foreign companies to work the diamond fields; this included China, which had the largest investment. Why would the president choose to anger his greatest international backer? The answer may be that as the flow of diamonds declines, those in power seek to retain what resources remain in order to stay in power. A resource trap persists only as long as the resource remains.

LEARNING OBJECTIVES

- Contrast authoritarian and totalitarian regimes.
- Analyze competing theories for the emergence and perseverance of nondemocratic regimes.
- Explain how nondemocratic regimes maintain power.
- Distinguish between personal, monarchical, military, one-party, theocratic, and illiberal regimes.
- Understand the persistence of illiberal regimes despite the trend away from authoritarianism.

"MAN IS BORN FREE, but everywhere he is in chains," wrote Jean-Jacques Rousseau in 1762. Since his time, democracy has emerged and flourished in many places throughout the world. However, according to Freedom House, an American NGO that monitors and promotes democratic institutions around the world, 60 percent of the world's population lives in societies defined as either "partly free," where significant personal liberties and democratic rights exist in theory but are not institutionalized and are subject to restriction, or "not free," where the public has little in the way of civil liberties or opportunity for political participation.[1] In neither case can these regimes be described as democratic.

In this chapter, we will look at the internal dynamics and origins of nondemocratic regimes. After defining these regimes and their relationship to freedom and equality, we will look at their origins, addressing the puzzle of why nondemocratic regimes are the norm in some countries but not in others. Behind this puzzle lies the broader question of the origins of nondemocratic rule, which mirrors our discussion in Chapter 6 on competing explanations for democratization. What variables are associated with nondemocratic rule? This discussion of the possible sources of nondemocratic regimes will lead us into an examination of how nondemocratic rulers maintain their hold on power. Nondemocratic regimes display great diversity; nevertheless, we can identify a number of common features. Finally, we will consider the future of nondemocratic rule. At the end of the Cold War, many assumed that liberal democracy was the wave of the future. In recent years, however, nondemocratic rule has shown an ability to adapt and thrive. The "wave of democracy" may be facing a reverse tide. Whether this is true, and what its implications would be, will be the final consideration of our chapter.

Defining Nondemocratic Rule

One challenge to studying nondemocratic regimes is that they constitute what we could call a residual category—a group of dissimilar things that aren't necessarily the same. Unlike democratic regimes, which can be defined and identified, nondemocratic regimes represent a wide array of systems, many of them bearing little resemblance to one another. This diversity in turn leads to a proliferation of terms that are often used interchangeably and indiscriminately: *autocracy, oligarchy, dictatorship, tyranny.* Even more confusing, in some cases nondemocratic regimes may resemble democracies more closely than they do other nondemocratic regimes. As a result, we tend to speak of nondemocratic regimes in terms of what they deny their citizens: participation, competition, and liberty (the very things that define democracy). We will often use the term **authoritarianism** to cover many of these different forms of nondemocratic rule.

If we want to speak of nondemocratic regimes as more than simply the absence of democracy, however, we need a definition to work with. Scholars define **nondemocratic regimes** as those in which a political regime is controlled by a small group of individuals who exercise power over the state without being constitutionally responsible to the public. In nondemocratic regimes, the public plays no significant role in selecting or removing leaders from office. Political leaders in nondemocratic regimes have much greater leeway to develop policies that they "dictate" to the people (hence the term *dictator*). Not surprisingly, nondemocratic regimes by their nature are built around the restriction of individual freedom. At a minimum, they eliminate people's right to choose their own leaders, and they also restrict to varying degrees other liberties, such as freedom of speech or assembly. The relationship of nondemocratic regimes to equality is less clear. Some nondemocratic regimes, such as communist ones, limit individual freedom in order to produce greater economic equality. Others, such as Mugabe's Zimbabwe, seek to provide neither freedom nor equality, existing only to enhance the power of those in control.[2]

There are various kinds of nondemocratic regimes. Nondemocratic leaders do not necessarily rule in a capricious or an arbitrary manner; indeed, nondemocratic regimes can have a strong institutional underpinning of ideology. As ideologies, fascism and communism, for instance, explicitly reject liberal democracy as an inferior form of social organization, favoring instead a powerful state and restricted individual freedoms. This ideology provided the norms that fascist and communist nondemocratic leaders followed in places like Nazi Germany and the Soviet Union. But other nondemocratic regimes are not ideological and may even be anti-ideological, asserting that the leadership speaks for "the people."

In other cases, few, if any, substantial political ideas are evident among those in power, whose rule is predicated simply on power for power's sake and the benefits it brings. In these cases, it becomes difficult even to speak of a regime, since we are not talking about a set of institutionalized rules and norms for political activity. In

authoritarianism A political system in which a small group of individuals exercises power over the state without being constitutionally responsible to the public

nondemocratic regime A political regime that is controlled by a small group of individuals who exercise power over the state without being constitutionally responsible to the public

---

INFOCUS Nondemocratic Regimes

- A small group of individuals exercise power over the state.
- Government is not constitutionally responsible to the public.
- Public has little or no role in selecting leaders.
- Individual freedom is restricted.
- Nondemocratic regimes may be institutionalized and legitimate.

describing these cases, critics often pejoratively use the term *regime*, coupled with a leader's name (such as the "Fidel Castro regime" in Cuba). This terminology reflects the critics' view that all decisions flow from the ruler, unfettered by political institutions of any sort. The leader, in essence, is the regime.

Totalitarianism and Nondemocratic Rule

Before continuing, we should examine a tricky and often misused term that is applied to a range of nondemocratic regimes: *totalitarianism*. *Totalitarianism*, which should not be confused with *authoritarianism*, connotes violence and terror, and so people often use the word in a partisan way to label a political system that they particularly dislike. This problem of definition goes back to the earlier part of the last century. Many scholars used the term *totalitarianism* to describe Nazi Germany and the Soviet Union and its satellite states. Others countered that when the term was used in a way that equated fascism and communism, it was being applied more for political reasons than for objective classification. Some called for abandoning the term altogether, claiming that it had no real scholarly utility. However, *totalitarianism* remains a valuable term, especially if used consistently and judiciously.

What then is the difference between totalitarianism and other forms of nondemocratic rule? **Totalitarianism** has several important elements. It is a form of nondemocratic rule with a highly centralized state whose regime has a well-defined ideology and seeks to transform and fuse the institutions of state, society, and the economy. The main objective of totalitarianism, unlike those of other nondemocratic regimes, is to use power to transform the total institutional fabric of a country to meet an ideological goal. Finally, due to the ambitious goals of totalitarianism, violence and the resulting terror often become necessary tools to destroy any obstacle to change.[3] Violence and terror not only destroy enemies of the totalitarian ideology, but also, as the political philosopher Hannah Arendt pointed out, they shatter human will, thus eliminating individuals' ability to aspire to, much less create, freedom.[4] Because they achieve these effects, terror and violence are commonly used to break down existing institutions and remake them in the leadership's own image. This is not to say that all violent regimes are totalitarian. The central issue is to what end violence is used. Totalitarianism often emerges when those who have come to power profess a radical or reactionary political attitude that rejects the status quo and sees dramatic, often revolutionary change as indispensable and violence as a necessary or even positive force toward that goal.

totalitarianism A nondemocratic regime that is highly centralized, possessing some form of strong ideology that seeks to transform and absorb fundamental aspects of state, society, and the economy, using a wide array of institutions

TOTALITARIANISM IN THE TWENTIETH CENTURY

The Soviet Union, Germany, and China are all countries that experienced totalitarian regimes during the twentieth century. These three examples illustrate the main features of totalitarianism that we have examined, while also highlighting differences in the way that totalitarian regimes can work in practice.

The Soviet Union under Stalin (1922–53) eliminated the last vestiges of private enterprise and private property, forcibly collectivizing Soviet agriculture and eliminating the land-owning class. Under Stalin's rule, the entire Soviet economy, along

GERMANY

CHINA

with education and culture, came under state control. Soviet citizens were mobilized on a massive scale to modernize the economy. Stalin used systematic terror to carry out his project and to guarantee unwavering loyalty to the Communist Party. He also developed a carefully orchestrated cult of personality (a concept we will discuss later) that in many ways overshadowed the official communist ideology. During the great purges of the late 1930s, millions of Soviet citizens, and much of the Communist Party's top leadership, were imprisoned and executed as Stalin attempted to consolidate his control. Under Stalin's successors, the USSR remained a regime in which the state controlled a great many aspects of its citizens' lives. However, post-Stalin Soviet politics no longer employed systematic state terror to mobilize its citizens, and the Soviet Union was led by a series of uncharismatic party leaders who were unable to develop a cult of personality. Over time, the post-Stalin Soviet Union became less totalitarian and behaved more like a typical authoritarian regime.

The Soviet Union was challenged by the rise of Hitler's Germany, a very different type of totalitarian regime. Hitler's totalitarian regime featured a strong, centralized state, an official fascist ideology, and the use of violence and terror to put that ideology into practice. Hitler attempted to eliminate ethnic groups (most infamously, the Jews) that he viewed as impediments to the construction of an ethnically homogenous society. In the process, many millions of people were killed by the German state. All social organizations, including clubs and churches, were placed under control of Hitler's Nazi Party, and all opposition parties and groups were banned. Like Stalin's Soviet Union, an elaborate cult of personality developed around Hitler. However, Hitler left much of the German economy in private hands, preferring to employ a state-coordinated mercantilist economy to support Germany's expanding empire.

In China, Mao Zedong constructed a totalitarian regime after the victory of the Chinese Communist Party in 1949 that was very much inspired by Stalin's Soviet Union. Like Stalin, Chinese communists placed most elements of society under control of the state, mobilizing the population in an effort to modernize the country and redistribute wealth. Like Stalin, Mao employed systematic terror and violence to consolidate his power and weaken his opponents, and Mao similarly cultivated his image as an infallible and almost godlike ruler. Whereas Stalin's totalitarian regime successfully "crash-modernized" the economy and defended the USSR against Hitler's aggression, Mao's totalitarian regime failed to modernize the country and instead caused economic stagnation and international isolation. Under the leadership of Deng Xiaoping (1978–97), China began to promote the growth of private enterprise and, like the USSR after Stalin's death, gradually moved away from totalitarianism to a more classically authoritarian political system.

As noted earlier in this chapter, today's authoritarian regimes are often labeled totalitarian by their detractors, but totalitarian regimes are rare. Repressive authoritarian regimes in countries like Zimbabwe and Iran do not come close to meeting the definition of totalitarianism, lacking key elements like an official ideology and state control over most of society. The only contemporary case of a totalitarian regime is North Korea, where an elaborate ideology is applied to all aspects of life, and where citizens are routinely mobilized to participate in the totalitarian regime.

Totalitarian Regimes . . .

- Seek to control and transform all aspects of the state, society, and economy.
- Use violence as a tool for remaking institutions.
- Have a strong ideological goal.
- Have arisen relatively rarely.

To sum up, nondemocratic rule is a political regime in which power is exercised by a few, unbound by public or constitutional control. The public lacks not only the right to choose its own leaders but also other personal liberties that those in power may see as a threat, such as freedom of speech or assembly. Totalitarianism is distinguished from other forms of nondemocratic rule by its totalistic ideology, which seeks the fundamental transformation of most domestic institutions and the potential use of violence toward that end.

Origins and Sources of Nondemocratic Rule

Now that we have defined nondemocratic regimes, we might consider their emergence and perseverance. In the last chapter, we spoke about some of the competing explanations regarding why democracy comes about. In a number of these explanations, the discussion was built on the ways in which authoritarian rule can give way to democracy. Let's return to these arguments, with an emphasis on nondemocratic perseverance rather than decline. As always, there is no single or dominant explanation for nondemocratic regimes, and the explanatory power of any theory may be limited by space or time. What may be helpful in explaining authoritarianism in Latin America in the 1970s may be of little use in explaining authoritarianism across the former Soviet Union.

MODERNIZATION AND NONDEMOCRATIC RULE

Recall that a central assertion of the behavioral revolution was that with modernization, societies would become more urban, educated, and politically sophisticated, creating the basic conditions that would catalyze democracy. And indeed, a strong correlation exists between societies that lack modern institutions and nondemocratic rule. Societies that are poor and poorly developed are less likely to have democracy, for a number of reasons that we noted in Chapter 6. One important explanation is the role of the middle class. According to the common political science dictum "no middle class, no democracy," modernization is necessary for the development of an urban, educated middle class with specific political, social, and economic interests that it can articulate and advance, helping to generate demands for democratic rule. The absence of a middle class is more likely to result in polarization between those few in power and a wider population that is weakly organized.

Yet modernization can sometimes lead to nondemocratic rule—even replacing existing democratic regimes. Contrary to our expectations, modernization can be a disruptive and uneven process. Urban areas may experience a sudden transformation of institutions and norms while rural areas lag behind; some people may enjoy technology like telephones and Internet access, as well as infrastructure such as roads and schools, while others lack these benefits. Disruptive shifts in economic institutions (such as from agricultural to industrial) and social institutions (such as changes in gender relations or increased secularism) can generate instability. Modernization can also trend backward, bringing increased inflation or unemployment, weakening economic development, and destabilizing the political order. Where a sufficient number of individuals feel disoriented by change, political movements and leaders may emerge with promises to restore "order" and reconcile the tensions between old institutions and new. Such movements can bring down a democratic regime if it appears unable to resolve these tensions or avoid the pitfalls of modernity. Paradoxically, these nondemocratic movements are often driven by the direct beneficiaries of modernization, such as students and urban intellectuals, who have gained the organizational and ideological tools to articulate a political vision alternative to the status quo.

Nondemocratic regimes run the spectrum of levels of wealth and modernization. We may think of nondemocratic countries as necessarily poor. Yet Singapore and many Persian Gulf states are commonly cited as modern and economically advanced societies where nondemocratic regimes are highly institutionalized (we can also think of countries, like India and South Africa, that are democracies yet relatively poor). Regime type and poverty do not correlate neatly, though it is worth noting that most countries with a per capita GDP at purchasing power parity (PPP) of more than $20,000 are democracies.

ELITES AND NONDEMOCRATIC RULE

In our discussion so far, we've noted that the absence or destabilizing effects of modernization may be a factor in the emergence of authoritarianism. Much of this argument assumes that modernization is strongly correlated with wealth, as agricultural societies become more industrial and developed. However, modernization and wealth do not take into account inequality. As we saw in Chapter 4, countries can vary dramatically in their levels of financial equality, and we can imagine that in highly unequal societies those who monopolize economic power will also monopolize political power.

In particular, elites may be less willing to share power when they fear losing their economic opportunities in the process. In fact, the longevity of nondemocracy may be due precisely to the fact that rivals for power seek control specifically so that they can enrich themselves. The state under these conditions becomes a tool to siphon off resources and maintain control. Regimes that have increased inequality this way may be particularly loath to surrender power, not only because they may be forced to give up their assets but also because they may lose their lives in retribution. The threat of revolution may make these systems particularly unlikely to provide much in the way of participation, competition, or liberty.

resource trap Theory of development in which the existence of natural resources in a given state is a barrier to modernization and democracy

One variant of this argument that we referred to in the case of Zimbabwe is the theory of development known as the **resource trap**. Since natural resources, such as oil, gas, and minerals, might be a source of great wealth, the puzzle is why so many resource-rich countries are undeveloped or nondemocratic. According to this theory, the existence of natural resources is a barrier to modernization and democracy, for several reasons. Resources in the ground give leaders the wealth necessary to run the state without taxation. This means those in power need not bother themselves with the taxation-and-representation trade-off; because they do not need to tax the people, they can effectively ignore their political demands. Even worse, natural resources tend to stunt the development of a modern economy and middle class, since neither is of concern (and may in fact be a threat) to those in power. Finally, since natural resources are not portable, those in power know that should they give up power, they would not be able to take these assets with them. The result is that wealth is highly concentrated in the hands of those in power. Under these conditions, nondemocratic rule can effectively subsidize itself, so long as the resources last and have a market. Oil is the most obvious example of a resource trap, but diamonds, timber, or metals could also serve this function.

SOCIETY AND NONDEMOCRATIC RULE

This discussion returns us to the idea of civil society. Recall that we defined civil society as a fabric of organizations created by people to help define their own interests. These organizations are not necessarily political—in fact, the vast majority of them have no specific political content. Sports teams, groups of collectors and enthusiasts, and religious and other organizations all form civil society. Observers commonly argue that civil society is crucial to democratic life because it allows individuals to organize, articulate their preferences, and form networks that cross economic, social, or political divides. Civil society is thus commonly viewed as a crucible for democratic action, laying the groundwork for democratic institutions.

Conversely, many authoritarian systems are characterized by the absence of civil society. This condition can result from those in power taking steps to absorb, monitor, or destroy any form of independent action not sanctioned by the state. Civil society may also have little precedent in society or be hindered by ethnic or other societal divisions that dissuade people from forming organizations across institutional barriers. The result can be a society that views the state as the primary arena for social organization and therefore focuses more on winning control over the state than on building strong institutions outside it. Interestingly, this emphasis on the state can sometimes go hand in hand with what is known as *populism*. **Populism** is not a specific ideology and in fact draws much of its power from an anti-institutional approach. But generally, populism carries within it the view that elites and established institutions do not fully represent the will of the people and that a new movement, free from ideology and often led by a charismatic leader, can usher in a new order. While populism commonly takes on an antigovernmental, anti-institutional orientation, it often assumes that people need to "take back" the state and set it on the correct path. Populism need not lead to an antidemocratic outcome (the United States has a strong populist tradition but an even stronger belief in democracy). However, we can see how it can destabilize democratic practices and provide a foundation for antidemocratic leaders to come to power.

Finally, civil society may emerge alongside a nondemocratic regime but itself take on nondemocratic tendencies, especially where more democratic forms of civil society have been repressed by the state. Many countries have an array of active organizations with antidemocratic tendencies, such as groups that advocate preferred rights for one ethnic or religious group over another. Anti-Muslim groups in the United States can be seen as a form of civil society, much as we might not

populism A political view that does not have a consistent ideological foundation, but that emphasizes hostility toward elites and established state and economic institutions and favors greater power in the hands of the public

like them. More civil activity can undermine democracy if many nonstate groups view the political process as legitimate only if it meets their specific needs and marginalizes others.

INTERNATIONAL RELATIONS AND NONDEMOCRATIC RULE

International influences can contribute to nondemocratic rule, most obviously through occupation. After World War II, the occupation of Japan and Germany led to democratization, but in Eastern Europe, Soviet control brought an end to democratic movements and eliminated much of civil society. Western imperialism has also contributed to nondemocratic rule. Borders badly drawn by imperial powers, as we discussed in Chapter 3, have created many countries with sharp ethnic and religious divisions that make consensus building difficult and authoritarianism an effective way for one group to monopolize power over others. Imperial institutions can similarly foster authoritarianism by contributing to such things as uneven modernization and weak state autonomy and capacity. Even after the end of Western imperialism, during the Cold War both the Soviet Union and the United States backed authoritarian rulers against democratic forces in order to maintain or expand their influence. The United States played a significant role in overthrowing the democratically elected government in Iran in 1953, fearing that the prime minister was tilting toward the Soviet Union. The Soviet Union crushed revolts in Hungary in 1956 and Czechoslovakia in 1968. China and Russia have more recently become important supporters of nondemocratic regimes in Africa and the Middle East through investment and by building diplomatic support for them in the international community. Iran and Saudi Arabia, too, have sought to use their oil wealth to support like-minded regimes in the region and deepening problems in countries like Iraq and Syria.

CULTURE AND NONDEMOCRATIC RULE

Let us return to the idea of political culture, which argues that the differences in societal institutions—norms and values—shape the landscape of political activity. In previous chapters, we discussed the controversial idea that a culture of democracy or liberty may be a precondition for institutionalized democracy and that certain societies may, for whatever reason, hold these values while others do not. By extension, it could be argued that some societies hold nondemocratic political values. In challenging modernization theory, which essentially equates "Western" with "modern," some scholars argue that culture is much more fixed than modernization theory holds it to be; they believe that modernization will not necessarily cause cultures to Westernize—that is, to adopt such values as secularism, individualism, and liberal democracy. Nondemocratic rule in this view is not the absence of democracy—it is its own set of values.

One common argument in this regard is that democracy is a unique product of interconnected historical experiences in Europe, such as Christianity (particularly Protestantism), the emphasis on individualism and secularism, the development of the nation-state, modern ideologies, early industrialization, and the development of capitalism, among others. These factors, the argument goes, allowed for the creation of democracy as a regime built on liberal values that emphasize freedom—what we typically call Western values.

In contrast, some (both inside and outside the Muslim world) have asserted that Islam views political power and religious power as one and the same. Laws are handed down by God to be observed and defended, and democracy is essentially anathema to the will of God. Cultural arguments can also be found in the debate about Asian values, which we discussed in Chapter 6. As we recall, proponents of the idea of Asian values argue that Asia's cultural and religious traditions stress conformity, hierarchy, and obedience, which are more conducive to a political regime that limits freedom in order to defend social harmony and consensus. The philosophy of Confucianism is frequently cited in this regard, with its emphasis on obedience to hierarchy and its notion of a ruler's "mandate from heaven."

As we have noted, many scholars reject the idea that culture precludes democratic rule. These societies and the peoples within them, it is argued, are far too diverse to represent one set of values. Differences in history, religion, social structure, and other institutions have led to an array of contrasting and overlapping ideas that are in a continuous process of interaction and reinterpretation. Cultural arguments may inform the content of nondemocratic or democratic institutions, but we should be wary of making sweeping arguments about culture and regime type.

There are numerous explanations for nondemocratic rule, and they are contingent on time and space—what might explain one country's regime at one time may be irrelevant at another time or for another country. The lack of modernization or its disruptive nature may reinforce nondemocratic rule. Elite strategies and the fear of sharing power can also help support nondemocratic rule, especially when natural resources are in play. A weak civil society at home and international factors can also play an important role. Finally, culture can be a factor in shaping the contours of nondemocratic institutions, but whether this can explain authoritarianism itself is a much more contentious question. The intersection of these forces can illuminate how and why nondemocratic rule comes to power. Looking at Figure 8.1, we see that authoritarianism remains strong in the Middle East and the former Soviet Union, while in places like Asia and Latin America many authoritarian regimes have given way. There is no simple answer to explain these differences.

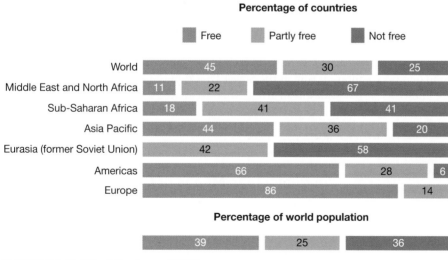

FIGURE 8.1 Political Systems, 2017

Source: Freedom House.

Nondemocratic Regimes and Political Control

We have so far covered some of the main explanations for the establishment of non-democratic regimes. In this section, we consider how these systems stay in power.

In liberal democracies, we take the system of government for granted; so long as participation, competition, and liberty are provided and defended, democracy can continue, often even in the face of significant domestic or international crises. We may assume that nondemocratic regimes are much more precarious, held in place only by fear and vulnerable to revolution at any moment. This is misleading. Nondemocratic regimes vary in their mechanisms of political control, some of which can generate legitimacy like that found in democratic systems. A consideration of the means of nondemocratic rule will give us a sense of this complexity.

COERCION AND SURVEILLANCE

One feature that we initially, and perhaps primarily, associate with nondemocratic regimes and especially with totalitarianism is the use of coercion. Coercion can be defined as compelling individuals by threatening their lives or livelihoods. Compliance with regime goals is often enforced through the threat or use of force against the population, sending a clear signal that those who oppose the regime or government will be dealt with harshly: they will face the loss of their jobs or access to certain resources, arrest, detention without trial, torture, and death. In an extreme example, in the 1970s many nondemocratic regimes in Latin America used "death squads" made up of police or military troops to target individuals suspected of harboring political views opposed to the regime. The death squads abducted and murdered these individuals, frequently after torturing them. In some cases, their bodies were dumped in the open as a warning to others who dared to question the regime. In other cases, the victims simply joined the thousands of "disappeared"—those who were abducted and never seen again. Similar practices can be found in several contemporary authoritarian regimes, including Egypt, Zimbabwe, and Syria both before and during its civil war.

Other regimes have used violence even more indiscriminately. When Stalin consolidated his totalitarian rule in the Soviet Union in the 1930s, he carried out what are known as *purges*—widespread arrests that decimated the ranks of the Communist Party and the state bureaucracy. Former leaders of the 1917 revolution, city mayors

---

INFOCUS   Nondemocratic Means of Control

- Coercion: public obedience is enforced through violence and surveillance.
- Co-optation: members of the public are brought into a beneficial relationship with the state and government, often through corporatism or clientelism.
- Personality cult: the public is encouraged to obey the leader based on his or her extraordinary qualities and compelling ideas.

and local party bosses, high-ranking officers in the army and navy, university professors, scientists, diplomats, and many others were detained, tortured, coerced into confessing during "show trials," forced to implicate others in their supposed crimes, and either sent to forced labor camps or executed. The targets of the purges were not limited to the party or the state; writers, artists, students, farmers, and workers were also among those accused of political sabotage and anti-Soviet views. It is not known how many died in these purges; estimates range from 5 to 20 million. Undoubtedly, in the vast majority of these cases the victims were innocent. Yet innocence was unimportant to Stalin's regime. When everyone was made to fear that they, too, could be arrested, the public could be controlled and even turned against itself since everyone feared being denounced by someone else. Arbitrary arrests, torture, disappearances, and murder continue to be common in many nondemocratic regimes.

Another important means of control is the ability to maintain a close watch over the population. Surveillance allows the government to prevent opposition from organizing and also instills uncertainty among the population—who is being watched? Surveillance may be conducted through the use of an internal security force, or "secret police," charged with monitoring public activity, spying on individuals, and interrogating members of the public suspected of political activity hostile to the regime. In some countries, surveillance has included widespread telephone tapping and the creation of a huge network of public informers, whereby nearly anyone may be the eyes and ears of those in power. With the rise of the Internet and the widespread use of mobile phones, surveillance has become more sophisticated, including the ability to monitor and control many forms of electronic communication, such as e-mail, social networking, and text messages.

CO-OPTATION: CORPORATISM AND CLIENTELISM

The prevalence of coercion and surveillance in some nondemocratic regimes may give the impression that those in power must be ever vigilant against the public to prevent opposition or revolution, which might spring up at any time. But not all nondemocratic regimes need or choose to rely on punishment or surveillance as a central means of control. Another method they may use is co-optation, the process by which individuals outside an organization are brought into a beneficial relationship with it, making them dependent on the regime for certain rewards. Although co-optation is not unique to nondemocratic regimes, it tends to be much more widespread under such regimes than under democratic ones, where people are usually more suspicious of such favoritism and see it as contrary to the democratic process.

CORPORATISM Co-optation can take many forms. The most structured form is **corporatism**, which emerged as a method by which nondemocratic regimes attempted to solidify their control over the public by creating or sanctioning a limited number of organizations to represent the interests of the public and restricting those not set up or approved by the state. These organizations are meant to replace independent organizations with a handful that alone have the right to speak for various sectors of society. For example, under a corporatist regime churches, labor unions, agricultural associations, student groups, neighborhood committees, and the like are all approved, funded, and at least partially controlled by the state. Nonsanctioned, alternative organizations are not allowed.

corporatism A method of co-optation whereby authoritarian systems create or sanction a limited number of organizations to represent the interests of the public and restrict those not set up or approved by the state

Unlike the overlapping memberships, competition, and ever-changing nature of civil society and political parties in a pluralistic society, corporatism arranges society so that each organization is empowered by the state to have a monopoly of representation over a given issue or segment of society (meaning that no other organization may act in that area or speak on that issue). State, society, and the market under corporatism are viewed as a single organic body: each institution cooperates and performs its own specific and limited role and is subordinate to the state and regime.

Corporatism can be an effective form of control, for it gives the public a limited influence (or at least the pretense of influence) in the policy-making process. Farmers or students, for example, may have an official organization with elected officers and resources that are meant to serve their interests. In return, the regime is able to better control the public through these institutions, and civil society is marginalized or eliminated. For the average individual, a state-sanctioned organization is better than none at all, and many willingly participate in the hope that their needs will be met.

Many nondemocratic regimes have used variants of corporatism as a means of control. It is an integral part of totalitarianism, but it also existed in authoritarian Spain and Portugal up to the 1970s. In Spain, for example, a single political party organized most of the business and labor interests into a limited number of "syndicates" that represented both owners and workers in different sectors of the economy. Communist regimes are similarly corporatist. In Cuba, for example, all labor is organized under a single union directly controlled by the state, and independent unions are illegal. Although corporatism differs in form and degree, in all corporatist regimes a limited number of organizations represent and direct societal interests, bringing the public under organized state control.

clientelism A process whereby the state co-opts members of the public by providing specific benefits or favors to a single person or a small group in return for public support

CLIENTELISM A less structured means of co-optation is **clientelism**, whereby the state co-opts members of the public by providing specific benefits to a person in return for public support (such as voting in elections). Unlike corporatism, clientelism relies on individual patronage rather than organizations that serve a large group of people, and it is more ad hoc than corporatism. Clientelism does not require a set of sanctioned and licensed organizations but allows those in power to target and respond to individuals and groups as they see fit, trading benefits for particular forms of support.

In both corporatism and clientelism, the state has a number of perquisites it can use in co-opting individuals. Jobs within the state or in state-run sectors of the economy, business contracts or licenses, public goods such as roads and schools, and kickbacks and bribes are a few of the tools in its arsenal. Such largesse often leads to **rent seeking**, a process in which political leaders essentially use parts of the state to extract income for their supporters, giving them preferred access to public goods that would otherwise be distributed in a nonpolitical manner. For example, leaders might use a nationalized industry for rent seeking, providing supporters with jobs and the ability to siphon off resources from that branch of the state.

rent seeking A process in which political leaders essentially rent out parts of the state to their patrons, who as a result control public goods that would otherwise be distributed in a nonpolitical manner

In general, co-optation is likely to be much more successful than coercion at maintaining nondemocratic regimes, since many in the public may actively support the regime in return for the benefits they derive from it. Political opposition is dealt with not through repression and violence but by incorporating opponents into the system and making them dependent on it or by withholding largesse. Such a regime, however, faces limitations. Corporatist and clientelist regimes can run out of benefits with which to pacify the public, especially if a great deal of the economy is built around state-controlled industries whose major function is to reward the loyal with jobs or opportunities for corrupt practices. Also, in a regime that doles out economic resources for political reasons, problems may emerge as productive resources are siphoned off to secure the acquiescence of the public. At its worst, such a regime can decline into a **kleptocracy** (literally, "rule by theft"), where those in power seek only to drain the state of assets and resources. Russia and Zimbabwe are good examples of such practices. As these assets and resources dry up, co-optation can quickly unravel.

kleptocracy "Rule by theft," where those in power seek only to drain the state of assets and resources

PERSONALITY CULTS

Nondemocratic regimes may also reinforce their rule by emphasizing veneration of the leadership—essentially an emotional appeal to legitimize rule. The most extreme example is what is known as a personality cult. First used to describe Stalin's rule in the Soviet Union, the term *personality cult* refers to promotion of a leader not merely as a political figure but as someone who embodies the spirit of the nation, possesses far more wisdom and strength than the average individual, and is thus portrayed in a quasi-religious manner as all-wise, all-seeing, all-knowing. In other words, personality cults attempt to generate a charismatic form of authority for the political leader from the top down by convincing the public of the leader's admirable qualities.

The media and culture play a vital role in a personality cult: news reports, public rallies, art, music, films, and other means are used to spread flattering imagery of the leader. The country's successes are attributed to the power of the leader, and mistakes are blamed on the mortal flaws of the public or on external enemies. Cults of personality may also be coupled with coercion; the public may not believe the praise, but no one is willing to say so. This is especially the case where charismatic power has faded over time to become little more than a façade, held up only by force. Under these conditions, there is always the chance that the cult will crack, leading to a rapid political decompression. This situation occurred in Romania in 1989, when Nicolae Ceaușescu, the self-styled "conductor" of his country, was shown on national television reacting in a stunned and confused manner when attendees at a public rally he was addressing suddenly grew hostile. Within hours, revolution swept the country; within three days, Ceaușescu and his wife had been executed by firing squad.

Personality cults may also take a weaker but still powerful form. In Iran, the image of Supreme Leader Ayatollah Ali Khamenei adorns shops and billboards around the country and he is portrayed as an embodiment of the 1979 revolution and the country's Shia Muslim faith. Yet in spite of his power, few Iranians would view him as a kind of deity or believe that he has superhuman powers. Russia's Vladimir Putin has built around himself a similar kind of veneration as the embodiment of the state and regime, and some worry that China's President Xi Jinping, in defining himself as the "core leader," is in the process of doing the same.

In looking back over what we have discussed so far, we find that nondemocratic regimes come to power and stay in power in various ways: some of these are "carrots" (rewards for compliance and support); others are "sticks" (threatened or actual punishments). A combination of such carrots and sticks may cause some people, perhaps even a majority, to view the regime as legitimate. They may agree with the regime's ideology, directly benefit from its rule, venerate its leaders, or simply fear political change. The idea of nondemocratic legitimacy may be hard for us to accept. Particularly in Western democracies, there is an assumption that in every nondemocratic regime the people are simply waiting for the chance to install democracy. Yet nondemocratic regimes can be just as institutionalized, stable, and legitimate as any democratic regime. They enjoy some, or even a great deal of, public support, especially if benefits are widespread enough, coercion limited, and political change viewed as fraught with risk. Many, for example, would suggest that the current Chinese regime enjoys widespread public support and that the public has little interest in democratization, which many citizens fear could bring political and economic instability.

Models of Nondemocratic Rule

By now, it should be clear that nondemocratic regimes emerge for different reasons and persist in different ways by using, to different degrees, tools of coercion and co-optation. Political scientists often classify such regimes according to how they use these tools. The most important forms of nondemocratic rule are personal and monarchical, military, one-party, theocratic, and illiberal regimes. Personal and monarchical rule is based on the power of a single strong leader who typically relies on charismatic or traditional authority to maintain power. Under military rule, in contrast, the monopoly of violence that characterizes militaries tends to be the strongest means of control. One-party rule is often corporatist, creating a broad membership as a source of support and oversight. Theocracies derive their power from their claim to rule on behalf of God. Finally, in illiberal regimes the basic structures of democracy exist but are not fully institutionalized and often not respected. Across regimes, we find structures we are familiar with in liberal democracies: heads of state and government, judiciaries, legislatures, and elections. But these are not subject to the rule of law, in the absence of which they reflect the preferences of those in power.

PERSONAL AND MONARCHICAL RULE

Personal and monarchical rule is what usually comes to mind when people think of nondemocratic rule, perhaps because long before modern politics, states, and economies came into being, people were ruled by powerful figures—kings and caesars, emperors and sultans, chiefs and caudillos. Drawing on charismatic or traditional legitimacy, personal and monarchical rule often rests on the claim that one person alone is fit to run the country, with no clear regime or roles to constrain that person's rule. Under this form of rule, the state and society are commonly taken to be possessions of the leader, to be dispensed with as he (or, occasionally, she) sees fit. The ruler is not a subject of the state; rather, the state and society are subjects of the ruler. Ideology may be weak or absent, since rulers justify their control through the logic that they alone are the embodiment of the people and therefore uniquely qualified to act on the people's behalf. This claim may be coupled with a strong personality cult or a reliance on the traditional authority of bloodlines.

In some cases, personal and monarchical rule relies less on charismatic or traditional authority than on a form of co-optation known as **patrimonialism**. Patrimonialism can be seen as a form of clientelism, since a patrimonial leader trades benefits for political support. However, under patrimonialism the benefits are not distributed in an ad hoc way among individuals in society but are instead limited

patrimonialism An arrangement whereby a ruler depends on a collection of supporters within the state who gain direct benefits in return for enforcing the ruler's will

to a small group of regime supporters inside the state itself. This ruling group gains direct benefits in return for enforcing the ruler's will. The state elites swear allegiance to the leadership in return for personal profit. This is a form of co-optation, although under patrimonialism only the ruler's own personal followers benefit. All others in society tend to be held in check by force.

An example of personal rule based on patrimonialism was found in Zaire (now the Democratic Republic of the Congo) under the rule of Mobutu Sese Seko from 1965 until 1997. Although he once commanded a great deal of charismatic legitimacy, over time Mobutu increasingly used patrimonialism as a way to maintain his power. In particular, Mobutu built his patrimonial regime around Zaire's abundant natural resources, such as diamonds, gold, copper, and cobalt. He used these resources not to benefit the country as a whole but to amass his personal fortune; he siphoned off the profits from these resources to enrich himself and his followers. The result was a coterie of supporters who were willing to defend Mobutu in order to maintain their economic privileges.[5] This system of dependence and economic reward helps explain how Mobutu maintained power for more than three decades while Zaire's per capita GDP dropped by two-thirds from the 1970s to the 1990s.

Although monarchies have waned, they remain powerful in parts of the Middle East, such as in Saudi Arabia and across the Persian Gulf. Even when they are not monarchies, regimes with a single ruler attempt to keep power within one family, typically transferring it from father to son. Leaders of such regimes may take on titles such as president, but in essence they function much like traditional monarchs. Personal rule remains common in Africa and is typically coupled to patrimonial regimes that are enriched through control over natural resources or trade. Russia has moved in the direction of patrimonialism as well, with economic and political power held in the hands of a narrow elite around President Vladimir Putin.

MILITARY RULE

A second form of nondemocratic regime is military rule. Once considered relatively unusual, military rule became much more common over the past 50 years, particularly in Latin America, Africa, and parts of Asia. Where governments and states are struggling with legitimacy and stability, often as a result of modernization, and where there is a high level of public unrest or violence, the military has sometimes chosen to intervene directly in politics, seeing itself as the only organized force able to ensure stability. This view is often combined with a sense among military leaders that the current government or regime threatens the military's or the country's interests and should be removed. Military rule may even have widespread public support, especially if people believe that the strong arm of the military can bring an end to corruption or political violence, prevent revolution, and restore stability.

Military rule typically emerges through a coup d'état, in which the armed forces seize control of the state. In some cases, military actors may claim that they have seized control reluctantly, promising to return the state and government to civilian rule once stability has been restored. This was the case in Thailand in 2006 and following Egypt's revolution in 2011. Often, under military rule, political parties and most civil liberties are restricted; civilian political leaders or opponents of military rule are arrested and may be killed. The use of coercion is a common aspect of military rule, since by their nature militaries hold an overwhelming capacity for violence.

IN FOCUS — Types of Nondemocratic Rule

TYPE	DEFINITION	PRIMARY TOOLS OF CONTROL
PERSONAL AND MONARCHICAL RULE	Rule by a single leader with no clear regime or rules constraining that leadership	Patrimonialism: supporters within the state benefit directly from their alliance with the ruler (corruption)
MILITARY RULE	Rule by one or more military officials, often brought to power through a coup d'état	Control of the armed forces, sometimes also allied with business and state elites (bureaucratic authoritarianism)
ONE-PARTY RULE	Rule by one political party that bans or excludes other groups from power	Large party membership helps mobilize support and maintain public control, often in return for political or economic benefits (corporatism, clientelism)
THEOCRACY	"Rule by God"; holy texts serve as foundation for regime and politics	Religious leadership and political leadership fused into single sovereign authority
ILLIBERAL REGIMES	Rule by an elected leadership through procedures of questionable democratic legitimacy	A regime where democratic institutions that rest upon the rule of law are weakly institutionalized and poorly respected

bureaucratic authoritarianism A system in which the state bureaucracy and the military share a belief that a technocratic leadership, focused on rational, objective, and technical expertise, can solve the problems of the country without public participation

This form of government usually lacks both a specific ideology and a charismatic or traditional source of authority. Hence, if the military seeks legitimacy in the eyes of the people, it must often fall back on rational authority. One variant of military rule that reflects this logic is known as **bureaucratic authoritarianism**, a regime in which the state bureaucracy and the military share a belief that a technocratic leadership, focused on rational, objective, and technical expertise, can solve the problems of the country—unlike "emotional" or "irrational" ideologically based party politics. Public participation, in other words, is seen as an obstacle to effective and objective policy making and so is done away with. In the 1960s and 1970s, bureaucratic authoritarian regimes emerged in a number of less-developed countries as rapid modernization and industrialization generated a high degree of political conflict. State and industry, with their plans for rapid economic growth, clashed with the interests of the working class and peasantry, who sought greater political power and a larger share of the wealth. This increasing polarization in politics often led business leaders and the state bureaucracy to advocate military rule as a way to prevent the working class and the peasantry from gaining power over the government.

Over the past 30 years, many bureaucratic authoritarian regimes have transitioned to democracy. However, military rule has not disappeared, and there is no reason to think it may not return in difficult times, as it did in Egypt. Supporters of military rule believe that dispensing with democracy can help facilitate modernization and development. They point to cases like South Korea, Taiwan, and Chile as success stories. But this is a problem of selection bias (see Chapter 1), where people have looked only for cases of economic success. If we concentrate instead on instances of military rule, we can find many more cases that led to poor economic development, such as in much of Latin America.[6]

BACK TO THE BARRACKS? MILITARY RULE IN BRAZIL AND NIGERIA

BRAZIL

NIGERIA

Brazil and Nigeria, though currently governed by democratic regimes, offer comparable examples of military rule that nonetheless yielded different outcomes. Both endured European imperialism and secured their independence (Brazil in 1822 and Nigeria in 1960) without military struggle. Although Brazil has been governed by some form of democracy for nearly half of its two centuries of independence, the Brazilian military intervened to determine each regime change (including seven military coups), from its first republic in 1889 until the emergence of the current democratic regime in 1985. In Nigeria, a military coup in 1965 brought down its first democratic government. Civil war ensued, which also ended with military intervention and the formation of a military government. Between 1965 and the establishment of the current democratic regime in 1999, Nigeria also experienced seven military coups, and unelected military governments have ruled Nigeria for three of its more than five decades of independence.

These military interventions in many cases also share similar causes. The military, and often the public as well, grew weary of weak, divided, and unstable democratic regimes and the economic and social crises they blamed (fairly or unfairly) on weak democracy. The outcomes, however, have varied, as illustrated by the experiences with military rule in both countries since the 1960s. Prior to the 1960s, the Brazilian military typically ventured into the political arena just long enough to initiate regime change before returning to the barracks. But in 1964, military leaders seized the state and held on to it for the next two decades, establishing a bureaucratic authoritarian regime. Military leaders promised political stability and economic progress and initially delivered on their promises, bringing nearly a decade of unprecedented economic growth and prosperity to Brazil. But this technocratic development came with real costs: the generals jettisoned the democratic constitution; banned trade unions; curtailed civil liberties; and silenced opponents with intimidation, torture, and exile. The global energy crisis of the 1970s reversed Brazil's economic gains, bringing a spiral of inflation and indebtedness. Growing dissatisfaction over the next decade brought to Brazil a gradual transition back to democracy.

But while the Nigerian military leaders during this same period likewise promised to create an effective state capable of ending ethnic conflict and promoting economic development, they consistently failed to deliver. Rather than establishing a capable state staffed by technocrats, Nigerian military rule time and again devolved into patrimonialism. While some were less kleptocratic than others, nearly all of the ten military governments that ruled Nigeria from 1965 to 1999 mostly delivered political corruption and economic stagnation.

While both of these cases are examples of military rule ultimately failing to deliver, the Brazilian case was less patrimonial and more successful at fostering development in its early stages. Why the difference? One important explanation has to do with the resource trap. As Africa's largest producer of oil, Nigerian military elites enriched themselves and their supporters while ignoring political and economic demands. In the Brazilian case, oil production took off only after the military left office, limiting patrimonialism. In both cases, modernization proved disruptive, and military rule promised more stability and progress than civilian rule. But lacking accountability, military rule too often replaced one kind of political dysfunction with another as those in power resorted to coercion to subdue civil society.

ONE-PARTY RULE

One-party rule is a regime in which a single political party monopolizes politics and bans other parties or excludes them from power. The ruling party serves several corporatist functions. It helps incorporate the people into the political regime through membership and participation. Typically, the party includes only a small minority of the population—in most communist countries, for instance, party membership has been less than 10 percent—but this still means that hundreds of thousands or millions of people are party members.

Through membership, the party can rely on a large segment of the public that is willing to help develop and support the policies of nondemocratic rule as well as to transmit information back to the leadership on developments in all aspects of society. Single-party regimes are often broken down into smaller units or "cells" that operate at the university, workplace, or neighborhood level. These cells report back to higher levels of the party, help to deal with local problems and concerns, and keep tabs on society as a whole. No area is untouched by the presence of the party, and this helps the party maintain control over the public.

In return for their support, members of the party are often granted privileges that are otherwise denied to the public at large. They may have access to certain resources (better health care or housing, for instance) that nonmembers do not. Positions in government and other important areas of the economy or society are also reserved for party members. One important result of such membership is that a large group of individuals in society directly benefit from the regime and are therefore willing to defend it. This pragmatic membership, however, can backfire: those who embrace party membership only for the personal benefits and not out of any ideological conviction may quickly desert the leadership in a time of crisis.

Finally, the party serves as a mechanism of mobilization. The leadership uses the party as an instrument to deliver propaganda that extols the virtues of the current regime and government; it relies on its rank-and-file members, through demonstrations and mass rallies, to give the appearance of widespread public support and enthusiasm for the leadership. If necessary, it also uses party members to control and harass those who do not support the regime. However, co-optation is the primary mechanism that ensures compliance and support.

One-party regimes are often associated with communism and fascism and have been present in all cases of totalitarianism. However, they can also be found around the world in a variety of nondemocratic regimes. Other parties may exist, but they are typically highly restricted by the government so that they cannot challenge the current regime. For many years, this was the case in Mexico, which was dominated by the Institutional Revolutionary Party, or PRI. Cuba, North Korea, China, Vietnam, and Laos are other examples of one-party regimes, each controlled by a single communist party.

THEOCRACY

Theocratic rule is probably the hardest form of nondemocratic rule to describe and analyze, though it is likely one of the oldest forms of rule. *Theocracy* literally means "rule by God," and a theocratic regime can be founded on any number of faiths and variations within them. A Christian theocracy might look completely unlike a Jewish one, drawing on different beliefs, texts, and traditions. Another obstacle to describing theocracy is the paucity of current examples of such regimes. In fact, some scholars would say there are no remaining theocracies, which would make a discussion of the term in contemporary politics irrelevant. However, we can observe in several countries some elements of theocratic rule, even if such a system does not exist in pure form. In Chapter 3, we noted that one of the recent challenges to ideology has been the rise of fundamentalism, which we defined as the fusion of religion and politics into an ideology that seeks to merge religion and the state. Such a merger, where faith is the sole source of the regime's authority, would render democratic institutions subordinate or in contradiction to the perceived will of God. In the vast majority of cases, such a goal remains hypothetical. Yet we can note cases where theocratic institutions are present and powerful.

Saudi Arabia is one example of a country that combines monarchical and theocratic forms of rule. The ruling family monopolizes politics, and the king acts as the supreme religious leader. Judicial and other matters must conform to Islamic law and are enforced by the Mutawwa'in, or morality police.[7] In Saudi Arabia, conversion from Islam is punishable by death, and other religions and other sects within Islam (Saudi Arabia is majority Sunni) are brought under strict control or banned outright. Afghanistan between 1996 and 2001 could also be described as a theocracy, lacking any constitution and relying instead on local clerics authorized by the Taliban to rule on judicial matters based on their interpretation of Islamic law. Some fear that other countries in the Middle East could become more theocratic following the 2011 uprisings; the clearest example of this would be the Islamic State, which has gained control over large parts of Iraq and Syria. In areas under their control, an extremely harsh interpretation of Islamic law has been imposed, going as far as the introduction of slavery for some non-Muslim peoples and the death penalty for an array of activities viewed as un-Islamic. Theocratic movements have gained power not just in majority Muslim states, but also in places like Buddhist Myanmar, Hindu India, or Jewish Israel. We speak of this in more detail in Chapter 5. However, as with fundamentalism in general, we should not confuse religiosity, or even a wish for religion to play a greater role in politics, with a desire for theocracy.

IRANIAN THEOCRACY: TOTALITARIAN, AUTHORITARIAN, OR ILLIBERAL?

IRAN

When we think of modern theocracy, the most common example that comes to mind is Iran. For much of the twentieth century, Iran's political system was that of a secular monarchy. The monarchy carried out a top-down policy of rapid modernization and secularism and was overtly hostile to religion as a political or cultural force. This backfired; in 1979, a revolution led in part by the charismatic cleric Ayatollah Khomeini swept away the old regime. In the new regime, traditional forms of secular government (executive, legislature, judiciary) were mirrored by unique institutions that were placed under the control of religious leaders.

The post-1979 Iranian constitution states that "all civil, penal, financial, economic, administrative, cultural, military, political, and other laws and regulations must be based on Islamic criteria." A directly elected presidency was given a limited amount of power to direct policy, while Khameini was installed in the more powerful office of the Supreme Leader. Unlike the presidency, this position is held for life and its officeholder chosen by the Assembly of Experts, a body also composed of leading clerics. The Supreme Leader is not a figurehead. Rather, the constitution gives the office a great deal of power over the other branches of government in such areas as appointing the heads of the judiciary and military or dismissing the president. Similarly, an unelected Guardian Council, selected in part by the Supreme Leader, oversees both elections and the work of the parliament. The body can veto legislation on the grounds of being insufficiently Islamic and reject candidates for the legislature, presidency, or local office on the same grounds. The judicial system also draws on the constitutional mandate to enforce religious law, handing down punishments for social or political actions seen in violation of the regime's interpretation of Islamic law. This can range from political opposition to social activity like inappropriate dress or alcohol consumption. Iran is one of the leading countries in its use of the death penalty, topped only by China (which has a much larger population).

The Iranian regime might thus be viewed as totalitarian, and many of its leading opponents do categorize it as such. But even in its most repressive periods, the regime lacked the capacity to completely destroy and remake existing institutions, as totalitarianism requires. Large parts of the clerical establishment remained skeptical of the fusion of faith and state; much of the economy remains in private hands, and civil society and political opposition, while repressed, has never fully disappeared. No single centralized power, like a one-party state, exists. The Supreme Leader's power, while considerable, depends on juggling competing political, economic, and religious factions. The system is far more clientelist than corporatist.

At the other end, it would go too far to describe this as an illiberal democracy, which we will discuss later. There are elections for the presidency, legislature, and the body that chooses the Supreme Leader, but the Guardian Council's regular rejection of candidates makes it hard to view this as true competition. The constitution itself, while allowing for participation, does not support political pluralism even in theory. Perhaps most telling, the fact that women are barred from the position of the Supreme Leader and president indicates that half of the population lacks an important constitutional right. Significant constitutional changes would be necessary before one could speak of Iran as even an illiberal regime.

ILLIBERAL REGIMES

The example of Iran is perhaps the most important for us to consider, since its regime type seems to be growing in prominence around the world. In fact, Figure 8.1 (see p. 365) includes a large group of countries, such as Colombia, Kenya, Lebanon, and Turkey, that are categorized as neither "free" nor "not free" but as "partly free," meaning they fall somewhere between democratic and nondemocratic regimes. These regimes go by a number of names, such as *hybrid*, *electoral authoritarian*, and *semi-democratic*. We will use the term **illiberal regimes**.

What do illiberal regimes have in common? These regimes feature many of the familiar aspects of democracy, though with important qualifications. As a starting

illiberal regime A regime where democratic institutions that rest upon the rule of law are weakly institutionalized and poorly respected

point, while the rule of law may be in place, it is weak. As a result, all the democratic institutions that rest upon the rule of law are weakly institutionalized and poorly respected. Executives, legislatures, and judiciaries have their respective arenas of authority; the public enjoys the right to vote; elections take place regularly; and political parties compete. But these institutions and processes are circumscribed or unpredictable in ways inconsistent with democracy. Executives typically hold an overwhelming degree of power. This power is often concentrated in a presidency that limits the country's ability to remove its president. Moreover, presidents in illiberal systems often rely on referenda to bypass the state and confirm executive power. Legislatures in turn are less able to check the power of the executive, and judicial institutions such as constitutional courts are often packed with the supporters of those in power. In addition, while political competition may exist on paper, parties and groups are restricted or harassed. Government monopolies over print and electronic media are used to deny the opposition a public platform, while the judicial system is used to harass opponents. The military often is not subject to civilian control. Elections are manipulated through changing electoral rules, through vote buying, intimidation, or barring candidates from running.

Illiberal regimes in many ways represent a gray area between nondemocratic and democratic rule. Although these regimes look much like democracies on paper, they are much less so in practice. The big question here is whether illiberal regimes are transitional, in the process of moving from nondemocratic to democratic rule (or vice versa), or are a new form of nondemocracy that uses the trappings of democracy to perpetuate its control. We are increasingly seeing examples of the latter—countries where the transition from authoritarianism to democracy has stalled and government institutions are democratic in name only, so that participation, competition, and liberty are severely curtailed. Equally worrisome is the possibility of developed democracies themselves becoming illiberal over time, something we will explore in Chapter 7.[8]

In Sum: Retreat or Retrenchment for Nondemocratic Regimes?

Although nondemocratic regimes exhibit an amazing diversity and flexibility in maintaining political control, for decades the global trend has been away from this form of rule. In the early part of the last century, democratic countries were few and beleaguered, wracked by economic recession, whereas nondemocratic regimes and totalitarianism in particular, backed by communist and fascist ideologies, seemed to promise radically new ways to restructure state, economic, and societal institutions. The German philosopher Oswald Spengler summarized this view in his 1922 work *The Decline of the West*: "The era of individualism, liberalism and democracy, of humanitarianism and freedom, is nearing its end. The masses will accept with resignation the victory of the Caesars, the strong men, and will obey them. Life will descend to a level of general uniformity, a new kind of primitivism, and the world will be better for it."[9]

Yet the exact opposite has taken place. Figure 8.2 shows that despite the rise of illiberal regimes, the number of countries classified as "not free" and "partly free" has

What Explains the Different Paths of Zimbabwe and South Africa?

In Chapters 2 and 3, we looked at the different paths India and Pakistan took after gaining independence from British rule. Like those two countries, Zimbabwe and South Africa are neighbors whose historical, economic, racial, and political institutions are similar but whose political trajectories over the past three decades could not have been more different. South Africa's democratic transition is well known and regarded as a triumph in the face of tremendous obstacles. In contrast, as we read at the opening of this chapter, Zimbabwe has undergone several decades of political and economic decline. What explains this difference?

For a century, South Africa was controlled by a small white minority that accorded itself political and economic privileges while oppressing the black majority. In response, a resistance movement, the African National Congress (ANC), formed, using peaceful and, later, violent means to bring down the regime. Its leader, Nelson Mandela, served nearly three decades in prison, and yet in spite of this and other repressive government actions, the ANC grew in strength. Faced with international isolation and the growing power of the black majority, the government released Mandela from prison in 1990, conducted negotiations with the ANC and other political parties, and inaugurated full democratic elections in 1994. The result has been a stable liberal democracy for nearly two decades.

What is less well remembered is that South Africa's next-door neighbor Zimbabwe (formerly Rhodesia) confronted a similar set of conditions much earlier. Like South Africa, Rhodesia was controlled by a white minority that dominated the country's economy and politics. Its government was also challenged by a liberation movement, the Zimbabwe African National Union-Patriotic Front (ZANU-PF), which relied on politics, guerrilla warfare, and terrorism to achieve majority rule. To defuse this conflict, the Rhodesian government began negotiations for a transition to democracy in 1978, and the first elections were held in 1980. Yet unlike South Africa, Zimbabwe never became an institutionalized democracy. It functioned as an illiberal regime for 20 years, eroding over time until eventually the country slid into authoritarianism in the early part of this century.

Why did these two countries take such different paths? The answers are unclear and at times seem contradictory. For many, the answer simply lies in leadership. Nelson Mandela's leadership of the ANC, even while in prison, was exceptional. He combined charismatic authority with the organizational skills necessary to keep the movement alive in spite of his detention. His long period in jail only increased his stature at home and abroad, reinforcing the legitimacy of the struggle and helping to intensify international pressure on South Africa. In contrast, the resistance movement in Zimbabwe was led by several different and clashing figures who divided rather than unified the movement. Robert Mugabe, who finally came to power and continues to rule Zimbabwe, was talented politically but more interested in accumulating power than engendering democracy. This argument assumes that political change is essentially a function of individual leadership. Yet other institutional factors set the stage on which such leadership can function.

A farm in Zimbabwe previously owned by a white farmer was appropriated in 2000 by veterans of the war against the previous regime.

In many respects, the paths of Zimbabwe and South Africa differ in degree rather than kind. ZANU-PF was from its inception a highly authoritarian party that allowed for no internal democratic practices and suppressed external opposition. Although the ANC was similarly undemocratic internally, its members worked to include other opposition groups under a common political umbrella. Scholars have also suggested that Zimbabwe's authoritarianism stemmed from ZANU-PF's its close alliance with China and the Soviet Union during the Cold War. This alliance radicalized ZANU-PF's objectives, which came to entail a revolution against colonialism and capitalism. The ANC also benefited from close ties to the Soviet Union, and its founding charter similarly called for the nationalization of industry and land; but unlike ZANU-PF, its political platform did not call for a revolution against capitalism.

An important difference between Zimbabwe's and South Africa's societies also has a bearing on the divergence of their political paths. South Africa is a highly urbanized and relatively industrialized society, especially in comparison with Zimbabwe, whose economy has been largely based on agriculture. South Africa's urbanization, combined with its ethnic, religious, and cultural diversity, contributed to a strong civil society that gave rise to the ANC and helped create and institutionalize that organization's civic and democratic commitments. ZANU-PF could not rely on such foundations, and it became instead a largely rural military movement dominated by one ethnic group.[a]

In part as a result of South Africa's civil institutions, the ANC was careful about how it used violence in its struggle. It consistently emphasized the primacy of politics over violence and the need to minimize the loss of life despite numerous deaths at the hands of the state. The ANC did not directly target white civilians (though a number were killed as a result of attacks on security forces), even though this would have been an easy way to terrorize that minority and mobilize the majority population. In Zimbabwe, by contrast, violence became the primary means toward revolution. When ZANU-PF came to power in 1980, it continued to rely on violence to suppress its opponents. As the party faced growing opposition in the 1990s, it seized agricultural land held by white Zimbabweans, arrested oppositional leaders, and killed or tortured hundreds of people. The result was economic collapse and international isolation.

THINKING CRITICALLY

1. Which country has experienced greater modernization? What role has that played in their differing paths?
2. How might the presence of a vibrant civil society in South Africa have given it an advantage toward democratization over Zimbabwe?
3. Why might Zimbabwe's use of coercion make its regime more vulnerable?

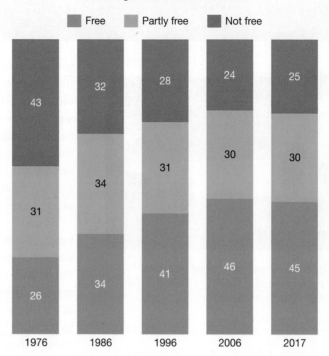

Percentage of countries worldwide

■ Free ■ Partly free ■ Not free

	1976	1986	1996	2006	2017
Not free	43	32	28	24	25
Partly free	31	34	31	30	30
Free	26	34	41	46	45

FIGURE 8.2 Authoritarianism in Decline, 1976–2017

Source: Freedom House.

declined dramatically over just the past four decades. In the 1970s, only a quarter of all countries were democratic; now 45 percent of them are. Why this decline in nondemocratic regimes? We have advanced economic, political, and societal arguments regarding the sources of nondemocratic rule and democratization. One final explanation may be ideological. Nondemocratic rule has lost much of its mobilizing power. Fifty years ago, ideologies predicated on nondemocratic regimes could mobilize people with visions of a world to be transformed. However, in the aftermath of the Cold War there is no longer any strong ideology combining the absence of individual freedom with some broader goal. Leaders may claim that limitations on political rights are necessary for political stability or economic development, but they no longer offer any real alternative vision for politics. It is increasingly difficult to justify nondemocratic regimes through any universal set of ideas.

Does this mean that the days of nondemocratic regimes are numbered? If we look closely at our figure, there are some concerns. According to Freedom House, over the course of the past decade, there has been a steady decline in political rights and civil liberties around the world, with 2016 representing the single largest drop during that period. This marks the 11th year of decline in global democracy. Freedom of expression and the rule of law have been particularly affected, not just in undemocratic and illiberal states, but even in some established democracies. This includes the United States. Over the past twenty years, the number of Americans who approve of having a "strong leader" who "doesn't have to bother" with elections or the legislature has risen to a third of those surveyed—with even higher numbers among those under 29.[10] As we shall discuss in Chapter 7, even the wealthiest and most long-lasting democracies confront economic, social, and political challenges that threaten to delegitimize democratic institutions and democratic practices. This may be providing a new lease on life for authoritarianism with its promise to provide stability in exchange for personal liberty. And such trends may exacerbate political violence, which we considered in Chapter 5.

Key Terms

authoritarianism (p. 358)

bureaucratic authoritarianism (p. 372)

clientelism (p. 368)

corporatism (p. 367)

illiberal regime (p. 376)

kleptocracy (p. 369)

nondemocratic regime (p. 358)

patrimonialism (p. 370)

populism (p. 363)

rent seeking (p. 368)

resource trap (p. 362)

totalitarianism (p. 359)

A pro-Russian separatist stands near pieces of the downed
Malaysia Airlines Flight 17 near Grabovo, Ukraine, in 2014.
Separatists were widely held responsible for firing the antiaircraft
missile that brought down the passenger plane, killing 298 people.

Communism and Postcommunism

Why did communism fail, and what are its legacies?

THE WAR FOR UKRAINE EXEMPLIFIES the complex dynamics of postcommunism. In 1991, the collapse of the Soviet Union led to 15 new sovereign states. Among these was Ukraine, located in the west of the former Soviet Union and second only in size to Russia. With a large agricultural and industrial base and a relatively well-educated population, Ukraine seemed well positioned to integrate into Europe and the global economy. Yet the opposite has happened. Why? Much of the explanation lies in the legacies of communism, and how politics has been conducted since 1991.

Unlike some parts of the former Soviet Union, where ethnic divisions are relatively clear, the distinction between Ukrainians and Russians is not. Western Ukraine was historically part of the Habsburg Empire until 1918. There, a strong Ukrainian nationalism took hold, and the region came under Soviet control only after World War II. In contrast, Eastern Ukraine has been under Russian rule since the end of the eighteenth century and is populated by a mix of Russian and Ukrainian speakers. This division was further compounded by the Soviet Union's ostensible federalism. Though on paper the Soviet Union was made up of 15 autonomous republics, in reality their power was limited. In one important example, in 1954 Soviet General Secretary Nikita Khrushchev transferred control of the region of Crimea from the Russian Republic to the Ukrainian Republic, even though it was historically Russian with no real ties to Ukraine.

With the breakup of the Soviet Union in 1991, these divisions and identities became a central source of conflict. In Ukraine, many nationalists saw the future of the country as part of "Europe," by which they meant the European Union and the Western military alliance, the North Atlantic Treaty Organization (NATO). Others, primarily in the east, lamented their separation from Russia and the loss of the Soviet Union. Ukraine's decision to build a unitary state with a strong presidency, limiting devolution and power sharing, did not help alleviate these tensions.

In 2010, Viktor Yanukovych won the Ukrainian presidential elections. As president, Yanukovych initially seemed to favor Ukraine's realignment westward, though this stance conflicted with Russian president Vladimir Putin's desire to maintain power over the former Soviet republics. Under pressure from Putin, in late 2013 Yanukovych abruptly rejected plans to bring Ukraine into a free-trade agreement with the European Union. In a repeat of events a decade before, thousands began protesting in the capital, Kiev, and Yanukovych responded with force. By February 2014, police had killed nearly a hundred protesters. As unrest spread, Yanukovych fled to Russia. Russia then intervened militarily, taking advantage of the chaos to seize and annex Crimea. Armed militias appeared in Eastern Ukraine as well, some made up of pro-Russian local citizens, while others were clearly Russian troops masquerading as locals. Following heavy fighting that left nearly 10,000 troops and civilians dead, Ukrainian troops withdrew and local leaders proclaimed independence. A 2015 cease-fire agreement ended most hostilities, but provisions for the reintegration of the separatist regions into Ukraine have not been realized, and skirmishes continue. A reignition of the war is a serious threat.

What conclusions can we draw from this conflict that might apply to communist and postcommunist countries? First, in many cases ethnic and national conflict have become potent forces. They can be reactions to the lack of concern for ethnic diversity under communism and thereafter, badly constructed political institutions, and resulting political polarization. Second, such tensions run the risk of spilling across borders, especially where leaders use nationalism as a way to build support. Among postcommunist states burdened by the challenges of economic and political change, authoritarian leaders who promise simple answers, and enemies to blame, can build ample support. Finally, these dynamics threaten not just more authoritarianism but also the risk of conflict that can have global repercussions. Already there are related concerns that China's growing nationalism could follow a similar path of greater ethnic conflict with non-Han Chinese minorities and/or military conflict with a neighboring state. The once widely held view that the end of communism would necessarily pave the way to democracy and capitalism now seems hopelessly naïve.[1]

LEARNING OBJECTIVES

- Understand the foundations of communist ideology.
- Describe how communist systems sought to eliminate inequality.
- Analyze the effects of state control over markets and property.
- Compare how postcommunist states have transformed their economic institutions and political institutions and learn what the outcomes have been.

THE ADVANCED DEMOCRACIES we studied in the last chapter have become the wealthiest and most powerful countries in the world. Yet these wealthy countries continue to struggle with problems of poverty and inequality. Can poverty and inequality be solved? This concern goes to the heart of communist theory and practice, for communism has sought to create a system that limits individual freedoms in order to divide wealth in an equitable manner. This vision of a world without economic distinctions drove the formation of communist regimes around the world, eventually bringing hundreds of millions of people under their banners.

Yet despite the lofty ideals of communist thought, and despite the dramatic emergence of communism as a political regime in the early part of the twentieth century, within less than a century most of the world's communist regimes began to unravel. Why? In this chapter, we look at how communism attempted to reconcile freedom and equality and why communist systems have largely failed at that endeavor. We will begin by looking at the original theories of modern communism, particularly the ideas of Karl Marx. From there, we will investigate how communism progressed from theory into practice as communist regimes were built around the world, most notably in the Soviet Union, Eastern Europe, and China (Table 9.1). How did these systems seek to create equality and bring Marx's ideas to life?

After examining the dynamics of communism in practice, we will study its demise. What were its shortcomings, and why could these limitations not be overcome? Our look at the downfall of communism will take us to our final questions: What comes after communism, and is communism dead? In addressing each of these questions, we will uncover the enormous scope and vision of communist thought, the tremendous challenges of putting it into practice, the serious flaws and limitations that this implementation encountered, and the daunting work of building new political, social, and economic institutions from the rubble of communism's demise.

TABLE 9.1 Communist Regimes in the 1980s

EUROPE	ASIA	AFRICA AND THE MIDDLE EAST	LATIN AMERICA
Albania	Afghanistan	Angola	*Cuba*
Bulgaria	Cambodia	Benin	
Czechoslovakia	*China*	Ethiopia	
East Germany	*Laos*	Mozambique	
Hungary	Mongolia	South Yemen	
Poland	*North Korea*		
Romania	*Vietnam*		
Soviet Union			
Yugoslavia			

Note: Countries still controlled by a communist party as of 2016 are shown in italics.

Communism, Equality, and the Nature of Human Relations

communism (1) A political-economic system in which all wealth and property are shared so as to eliminate exploitation, oppression, and, ultimately, the need for political institutions such as the state; (2) a political ideology that advocates such a system

Communism is a set of ideas that view political, social, and economic institutions in a manner that is fundamentally different from most political thought, challenging much of what we have studied so far. At its most basic level, it is an ideology that seeks to create human equality by eliminating private property and market forces.

Communism as a political theory and ideology can be traced primarily to the German philosopher Karl Marx (1818–83).[2] Marx began with a rather straightforward observation: human beings impart value to the objects they create by investing their own time and labor in them. This value can be greater than the cost of creating the object—for example, a chair maker may spend $50 on materials to build a chair that would sell for $60. The extra $10 reflects the added value of the maker's time and energy. This "surplus value of labor" stays with the object and makes it useful to anyone, not just the maker. This ability to create objects with their own innate value sets humans apart from other animals, but it also inevitably leads to economic injustice, Marx concluded. He argued that as human beings develop their knowledge and technological skills, an opportunity is created for those with political power to extract the surplus value from others, enriching themselves while impoverishing other people. In other words, once human beings learned how to produce things of value, others found that they could gain these things at little cost to themselves simply by using coercion to acquire them. Using the previous example, if the chair maker were employed by a "capitalist," then this employer would benefit from the surplus value of labor and get to keep the extra $10.

Base The economic system of a society, made up of technology (the means of production) and class relations between people (the relations of production).

Bourgeoisie The property-owning class.

Communism According to Marxists, the final stage of history once capitalism is overthrown and the dictatorship of the proletariat destroys its remaining vestiges. In communism, state and politics would disappear, and society and the economy would be based on equality and cooperation.

Dialectical materialism Process of historical change that is not evolutionary but revolutionary. The existing base and superstructure (thesis) would come into conflict with new technological innovations, generating growing opposition to the existing order (antithesis). This would culminate in revolution, overthrowing the old base and superstructure (synthesis).

Dictatorship of the proletariat Temporary period after capitalism has been overthrown during which vestiges of the old base and superstructure are eradicated.

False consciousness Failure to understand the nature of one's exploitation; essentially amounts to "buying into" the superstructure.

Proletariat The working class.

Superstructure All noneconomic institutions in a society (for example, religion, culture, national identity). These ideas and values derive from the base and serve to legitimize the current system of exploitation.

Surplus value of labor The value invested in any human-made good that can be used by another individual. Exploitation results when one person or group extracts the surplus value from another.

Vanguard of the proletariat Lenin's argument that because of false consciousness, an elite communist party would have to carry out revolution; otherwise, historical conditions would not automatically lead to capitalism's demise.

For Marx, then, the world was properly understood in economic terms; all human action flowed from the relations between the haves and the have-nots. Marx believed that structures, rather than people or ideas, made history. Specifically, Marx spoke of human history and human relations as functions of what he termed the base and the superstructure. The **base** is the system of economic production, including the level of technology (what he called the "means of production") and the kind of class relations that exist as a result (the "relations of production"). Resting on the base is the **superstructure**, which represents all human institutions—politics and the state, national identity and culture, religion and gender, and so on. Marx viewed this superstructure as a system of institutions created essentially to justify and perpetuate the existing order. People consequently suffer from "false consciousness," meaning that they believe they understand the true nature of the world around them, but in reality they are deluded by the superstructure imposed by capitalism. Thus Marx and most other communists rejected liberal democracy as a system created to delude the exploited into thinking they have a say in their political destiny when in fact those with wealth actually control politics.

base The economic system of a society, made up of technology (the means of production) and class relations between people (the relations of production)

superstructure All noneconomic institutions in a society (e.g., religion, culture, national identity); these ideas and values derive from the base and serve to legitimize the current system of exploitation

Revolution and the "Triumph" of Communism

Having dissected what he saw as the nature of politics, economics, and society, Marx used this framework to understand historical development and to anticipate the future of capitalism. Marx concluded that human history developed in phases, each driven by a particular kind of exploitation. In each phase, he argued, the form of exploitation was built around the existing level of technology. In early agrarian societies, for example, feudalism was the dominant political and economic order; the rudimentary technology available tied individuals to the land so that their labor could be exploited by the aristocracy. Although such relations may appear stable, technology itself is always dynamic. Marx recognized this and asserted that the inevitable changes in technology would increase tensions between rulers and ruled as these changes empowered new groups who clashed with the base and the superstructure. In the case of feudalism, emerging technology empowered an early capitalist, property-owning middle class, or **bourgeoisie**, whose members sought to gain political power and to remake the economic and social order in a way that better fit capitalist ambitions.

bourgeoisie The property-owning class

Eventually, the tensions resulting from technological advances would lead to revolution; those in power would be overthrown, and a new ruling class would come to power. In each case, change would be sudden and violent and would pave the way for a new economic base and superstructure. Marx called this entire process **dialectical materialism**. *Dialectic* is the term he used to describe history as a struggle between the existing order (the thesis) and the challenge to that order (the antithesis), resulting in historical change (the synthesis). *Materialism* simply refers to the fact that this tension is over material factors, specifically economic ones. Marx believed that revolutions inevitably result from this dialectic process.

dialectical materialism Process of historical change that is not evolutionary but revolutionary; the existing base and superstructure (thesis) would come into conflict with new technological innovations, generating growing opposition to the existing order (antithesis)—this would culminate in revolution, overthrowing the old base and superstructure (synthesis)

proletariat The working class

On the basis of these ideas, Marx concluded that capitalist democracy, which had displaced feudalism, would itself be overthrown by its own internal flaws. As capitalism developed, competition between firms would intensify. The working class, or **proletariat**, would find itself on the losing end of this process as firms introduced more and greater technology to reduce the number of workers and as unprofitable businesses began to go bankrupt in the face of intense competition. The bourgeoisie would grow smaller and smaller as the wealth of society became concentrated in fewer and fewer hands, and large monopolies would come to dominate the economy. The oversupply of labor created by these factors would drive down the wages of the working class and swell the ranks of the unemployed.

Alienated and driven to desperation by these conditions, the proletariat would "gain consciousness" by realizing the true source of their poverty and rise up in rebellion. They would carry out a revolution, seizing control of the state and the economy. Marx saw this process not simply as a national phenomenon but also as an international one. When the conditions were right, he hypothesized, revolution would spread among all the capitalist countries, sweeping away this unjust order.

Once world revolution had taken place, Marx foresaw, there would be a temporary "dictatorship of the proletariat," during which the last vestiges of capitalism, particularly the old remnants of the superstructure, would be swept away. After the institutions of capitalism had been decisively eliminated, the institutions of the

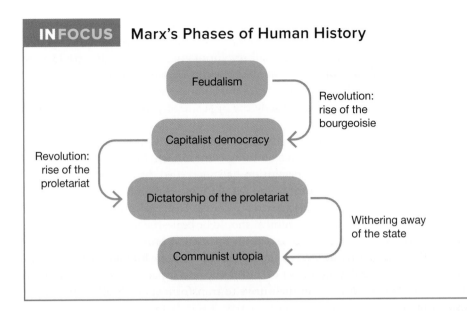

INFOCUS Marx's Phases of Human History

- Feudalism
- Revolution: rise of the bourgeoisie
- Capitalist democracy
- Revolution: rise of the proletariat
- Dictatorship of the proletariat
- Withering away of the state
- Communist utopia

state itself would begin to "wither away." There would be no more need for laws or police, because all people would share equally in the fruits of labor. No longer would there be a need for armies or flags, because people would be united in equality rather than blinded by the false consciousness of nationalism. People would live in a state-less world, and history, which in Marx's view had been driven by exploitation and class struggle, would essentially come to an end. Only then could a person actually speak of "communism"—which is why communist parties would usually describe their own countries as "socialist," since they were still controlled by the state. To further this confusion, in the advanced democracies people often use the word *socialism* interchangeably with *social democracy*. However, most contemporary social democrats view socialism as an end stage, where the state exercises significant but not total control over the economy. For communists, however, socialism is a transitional phase toward a time when private property and the state no longer exist.

Putting Communism into Practice

Communism thus provides an entire worldview, explaining the course of human history and the inevitable ascent into utopia as the products of economic interaction. As we know, such a sweeping theory has proved compelling for many people, especially those who sought to put Marx's ideas into practice.

Two of the most notable followers of Marx's ideas were Vladimir Ilyich Ulyanov, more commonly known as Lenin, and Mao Zedong. Lenin and Mao came to lead communist revolutions in Russia (1917) and China (1949), respectively. Yet although both were inspired by Marx, they departed from his ideas by seeking to carry out revolution in two countries that were weakly industrialized and far from being capitalist. Marx had argued that revolution would occur only where and when capitalism was most advanced and thus most prone to collapse; however, at the end of his life he did hold out the possibility that revolution could occur in less developed Russia,

vanguard of the proletariat Lenin's argument that an elite communist party would have to carry out revolution, because as a result of false consciousness, historical conditions would not automatically lead to capitalism's demise

in contradiction to his own theories.[3] Lenin in particular believed that revolution could be carried out in less advanced countries if leaders constructed a **vanguard of the proletariat**—his term for a small revolutionary movement that could seize power on behalf of the people, who may lack the consciousness necessary to rise up.[4] This approach meant that in reality, communism spread where the level of economic development was relatively low—exactly the opposite of what Marx had originally theorized.

Yet even as the number of communist regimes grew, they faced a common quandary: how exactly to go about building communism. Marx had left no blueprint for what to do once the revolution had succeeded. In many ways, communists assumed that the revolution was the difficult part and that what should occur afterward would unfold as a matter of course. In part because Marx provided no specific outline for how communism should be built, the institutions that were created varied widely. Most were based on forms first built in the Soviet Union after 1917. Because they desired to fundamentally reshape human relations, communist states accrued a high level of autonomy and capacity; their regimes have at times become totalitarian in their drive to transform virtually all basic human institutions.

The task of this transformation was entrusted to the communist elite who came to direct and staff the state.[5] At its apex, political power rested within the Communist Party, a relatively small "vanguard" organization (typically comprising less than 10 percent of the population) whose leading role in the country was typically written directly into the constitution—meaning that there was no constitutional way to remove the party from power. Because the Communist Party embodied what it saw as the "correct" view of human history and future relations, alternative organizations and ideologies making up civil society were seen as hostile to communism and were repressed.

Still, as we discussed in Chapter 8 on nondemocratic regimes, no system of rule can survive through the threat of force alone. Communist parties maintained control over society not only through repression but also by carefully allocating power throughout the country's various political, social, and economic institutions—a thorough form of co-optation. This strategy can be seen clearly in the *nomenklatura*, politically sensitive or influential jobs in the state, society, or economy that were staffed by people chosen or approved by the Communist Party. The *nomenklatura* encompassed a wide range of important positions: the head of a university, the editor of a newspaper, a military officer, a film director. Not surprisingly, party approval often required party membership, making joining the party the easiest way to prove one's loyalty and rise up the career ladder. Party membership could also bring other benefits: better housing, the ability to travel abroad, or access to scarce consumer goods. As a result, party membership was often driven more by opportunism than by idealism; many joined so that they could pursue certain careers or simply gain the benefits that party membership could buy.[6]

nomenklatura Politically sensitive or influential jobs in the state, society, or economy that were staffed by people chosen or approved by the Communist Party

The dominant role played by the Communist Party and the *nomenklatura* created a power relationship different from those in democratic and many other nondemocratic systems. Rather than being centered within the state and government, power rested within the party. For example, when observers referred to the "leader" of a communist country, they were usually referring not to a government official but

Important Figures in Communism

Karl Marx (1818–83) First philosopher to systematically construct a theory explaining why capitalism would fail and be replaced by communism; father of modern communist thought.

Lenin (Vladimir Ilyich Ulyanov) (1870–1924) Applied Marxist thought to Russia, leading a successful revolution in 1917; modified Marxist ideas by arguing that revolution would occur not in most-developed societies but rather in struggling countries such as Russia.

Joseph Stalin (Josef Vissarionovich Dzhugashvili) (1879–1953) Succeeded Lenin as leader of the Soviet Union; embarked on rapid industrialization of the country, modifying Marxism to argue that socialism could be built within just a single country; extended communism to Eastern Europe after World War II; denounced by Nikita Khrushchev in 1956 for his use of a personality cult and terror.

Mao Zedong (1883–1976) Led the Chinese Communist Party and fought against Chinese rivals and Japanese occupiers during World War II; modified communism to focus on the peasantry instead of the working class, given the primarily agrarian nature of China; unleashed the Cultural Revolution in 1966 to weaken the party and increase his own power.

Deng Xiaoping (1905–97) Fought with Mao Zedong against Chinese nationalists and Japanese occupiers during World War II; named general secretary of the Chinese Communist Party in 1956; stripped of all posts during the Cultural Revolution, but emerged as the country's leader after Mao's death; pursued economic liberalization in the 1980s and supported repression of the Tiananmen Square protests.

Fidel Castro (1926–2016) Led the Cuban Revolution in 1959 and defended the communist system against anticommunist forces and U.S. opposition; continued to defend Cuban socialism despite the collapse of the Soviet Union and other communist regimes in Eastern Europe.

Mikhail Gorbachev (1931–) Made general secretary of the Communist Party of the Soviet Union in 1985; initiated the twin policies of perestroika (economic restructuring) and glasnost (political liberalization), which eventually led to increasing discord within the country and a failed coup attempt by hard-line communists who opposed further reform; the resulting dissolution of the Soviet Union left Gorbachev without a country to lead.

to the general secretary of the Communist Party. Indeed, top party leaders often did not hold any important formal position within the state. Though the political systems in communist countries by and large resembled those we see elsewhere in the world, typically with a prime minister or president, a parliament, a judiciary, and local government, all these positions were part of the *nomenklatura* and thus staffed by party members appointed by the party leaders. Although the trappings of democracy, such as parliamentary elections, typically existed, electoral candidates were almost exclusively Communist Party members with no real competition. Moreover, parliaments and other organs of power were little more than "rubber-stamp" institutions, approving decisions sent down the party hierarchy.

As for the party itself, in many ways it intentionally mirrored the state. A general secretary served as chief executive, and a **Politburo** (short for "Political Bureau") and **Central Committee** acted as a kind of cabinet and legislature, respectively, shaping national policy and confirming the decisions of the party leadership. Below the Central Committee, various other bodies extended all the way down to individual places of work or residence, where party members were assigned to basic party organizations called *cells*. These cells were ostensibly intended to represent the interests of the people, but they were primarily mechanisms used by the party to closely monitor the population. Traditionally, the party held a congress every few years. At these meetings, delegates sent from the party cells elected its leadership, but these elections

Politburo The top policy-making and executive body of a communist party

Central Committee The legislature-like body of a communist party

were little more than confirmations of those already in power. Outside the party and state, a limited number of organizations, such as unions, were allowed to function; these were in turn linked to the state and party, completing this highly corporatist structure that included sanctioned organizations for all facets of society.

While the party and its *nomenklatura* controlled key organizations, communist ideology shaped policy and sought to legitimize authoritarian control. Based fundamentally on the theories of Marx as adapted by Lenin and Mao, communist ideology focused on eliminating inequality and promoting economic development. Due to the expansive nature of communist ideology and its promise of a future utopia, it was, perhaps more than the other ideologies we discussed in Chapter 3, a secular "religion." It required unquestioning faith in a set of beliefs and sacrifice for a future reward and boasted its own collection of holy texts, shrines, saints, martyrs, and devils. Adherents venerated charismatic leaders who served as prophets of communism, such as Lenin, Mao, Joseph Stalin, and Fidel Castro. Many charismatic communist leaders reinforced their position through elaborate personality cults, as we discussed earlier.

The quest for and exercise of this monopoly on power, as expressed through the *nomenklatura* and through the party's deep penetration of the state and society, down to the most basic level of home and work, proved to be dangerous and even lethal. In the first decades of communist rule in the Soviet Union, China, and Eastern Europe, the party used terror to eliminate opposition and maintain control. Tens of millions perished, especially in the Soviet Union under Stalin and in China under Mao.

Under Stalin's rule, many people were purged from the Soviet Communist Party and executed for imaginary crimes. These were not cases of mistaken punishment: Stalin used terror and victimized symbolic "criminals" as a way to intimidate the Communist Party and the population as a whole.[7] Similarly, in China, Mao unleashed the Cultural Revolution in the late 1960s, encouraging the public (students, in particular) to attack any institution or individual that was either a remnant of precommunist China or lacked revolutionary zeal. Mao's targets included the **party-state**, which he believed had grown conservative over time and was restricting his power—indeed, his notable slogan was "Bombard the party headquarters." During the next decade, countless Chinese died, books were burned, art was destroyed, and cultural relics were demolished—all for the crime of being "reactionary."[8]

party-state A political system in which power flows directly from the ruling political party (usually a communist party) to the state, bypassing government structures

Communist Political Economy

If the Communist Party's singular quest for power led, in the cases of Stalin and Mao, to its gross abuse, the centralization of economic power similarly created problems that Marxist theory did not anticipate. Communist political-economic systems shared a set of institutions fundamentally different from liberal, mercantilist, or social democratic alternatives, for the state had essentially absorbed both markets and property.[9]

Because the state held the means of production, many of the typical aspects of capitalism that we take for granted—individual profit, unemployment, competition between firms, bankruptcy—were eliminated. Individuals lost their right to control property, including their own labor; the party-state made the decisions about

Communist Political Economy

- Markets and property are wholly absorbed by the state.

- Central planning replaces the market mechanism.

- Individual property rights, individual profit, unemployment, competition between firms, and bankruptcy are all virtually eliminated.

- Most of the nation's means of production are nationalized.

- The economy functions in essence as a single large firm whose sole employees are the public.

- The state provides extensive public goods and social services, including universal systems of public education, health care, and retirement.

- Inequality and poverty are reduced but not eliminated.

how these resources should be used. Communist leaders redirected national wealth toward the goal of collective equality through such mechanisms as industrialization and social expenditures. Several million died in the Soviet Union in the 1930s during the forced collectivization of agriculture. An attempt at rapid industrialization and the collectivization of agriculture during the Great Leap Forward in China (1959-61) led to some 45 million famine deaths. As Mao himself put it, "When there is not enough to eat people starve to death. It is better to let half of the people die so that the other half can eat their fill."[10]

Along with private property, communist systems also eliminated the market forces of supply and demand, believing that these factors were incapable of equitably distributing wealth. Communist countries largely chose to replace the market with the state bureaucracy, which explicitly allocated resources by planning what should be produced and in what amounts, setting the final prices of these goods, and deciding where they should be sold. This system is known as **central planning**.

As might be imagined, planning an entire economy is an extremely difficult task. And communist planners found the task of matching up all the inputs and outputs necessary for producing goods overwhelming. There are simply too many things to plan—in the Soviet Union, for instance, the materials included some 40,000 to 50,000 kinds of physical items—and there are too many unforeseen outcomes, such as a factory failing to deliver its full output or needing to adjust to a change in demand. Because most entities in an economy are interdependent, small problems can have a huge effect on the entire plan. A miscalculation resulting in the underproduction of steel, for example, would have disastrous effects on all those goods dependent on steel, some of which would themselves be components in other finished goods. Central planning, with its emphasis on industrialization, also focused less on consumer goods, leaving things like televisions and cars in short supply.

Another problem encountered in centrally planned economies was the lack of worker incentives. Factories and farms were unconcerned about the quality of their goods, since central planners simply indicated a numerical quota they had to fulfill. Workers did not have to fear losing their jobs or factories going out of business thanks to shoddy work, because under communism employment was guaranteed and firms, being owned by the state, could not go bankrupt. This structure explains in part why all communist countries eventually fell behind economically. In the

central planning A communist economic system in which the state explicitly allocates resources by planning what should be produced and in what amounts, the final prices of goods, and where they should be sold

absence of competition and incentives, innovation and efficiency disappeared, leaving these systems to stagnate.

As we consider these changes, a final question is whether communist institutions eliminated poverty and inequality as they claimed. As we noted in Chapter 4, under communism the Gini index for the Soviet Union and other European communist states was under 30—extremely low, even in comparison with social democracies. Moreover, widespread social expenditures, from roads and electricity to health care and pensions, lifted millions out of severe poverty. At the same time, these benefits were unevenly distributed. Rural areas and regions with ethnic minorities often were far less developed, and poverty never truly disappeared. In addition, members of the *nomenklatura* were able to use their political power to gain access to scarce goods, like better apartments, cars, or foreign travel. The absence of private property did not eliminate corruption. So while communism did create a more equal system, it did so at a high price, and significant elements of inequality remained.

Societal Institutions under Communism

In addition to reengineering politics and economics to eliminate the inequality and exploitation associated with capitalist systems, communist parties also sought to reorder human relations, hoping to sweep away the old superstructure held responsible for generating false consciousness. One aspect of this superstructure viewed with particular hostility was religion.

Marx is known for his oft-cited statement that "religion is the opiate of the masses." Like a drug, religion numbs its practitioners to their pain, in this case by promising them they will be rewarded in the afterlife for enduring their present suffering, thus legitimizing the inequality and poverty perpetuated by the superstructure. As a result, in most communist countries religion was strongly suppressed. In the Soviet Union, most places of worship were closed, converted to other uses, or torn down. In China during the Cultural Revolution, temples and other religious shrines were destroyed. Even where religion was tolerated to a greater extent, it was directly controlled or its practitioners were harassed by the Communist Party.

Marxists also viewed traditional gender relations as a function of capitalism—specifically, as a microcosm of class relations. Men exploit women through the family structure, just as the bourgeoisie exploit the proletariat, and sexual morality serves as a means to perpetuate this gender inequality. Communism envisioned complete economic, social, and political equality between men and women. Even the repressive institution of marriage, like the state, would fade away, replaced by what Marx called "an openly legalized community of free love."[11]

In spite of Marxist ideals, gender relations only partially changed under communist rule. In most communist countries, women were given much greater opportunities than they had experienced previously. To promote industrialization, communist parties encouraged women to enter the workforce and to increase their education. Most countries also enacted liberal divorce and abortion laws and provided social benefits such as state-run child care. Despite these changes, however, women's traditional roles as housekeepers and mothers did not change. The "new socialist woman" was not complemented by a "new socialist man." Traditional patterns of sexism persisted, and women found themselves burdened by the double duty of work inside

IN FOCUS | Societal Institutions under Communism

INSTITUTION	IDEAL	REALITY
RELIGION	Religion, "the opiate of the masses," will disappear.	Religion was suppressed but not eliminated.
GENDER ROLES	Men and women will be economically, socially, and politically equal.	Opportunities for women increased, but women were still expected to fulfill traditional duties in the home.
SEXUALITY	Repressive institutions such as marriage will be replaced by "an openly legalized system of free love."	Many communist countries remained very sexually conservative.
NATIONALISM	Nationalism, exposed as part of the elite's "divide and conquer" strategy, will be eliminated.	Though discouraged from doing so, people clung to old national and ethnic identities.

and outside the home. In addition, while many women worked in important occupations, few rose to positions of any significant political or economic power. Men continued to dominate the top ranks of the party membership, the state, and the economy.[12]

A final aspect of society that communist countries sought to change was national and ethnic identity. As part of the superstructure, nationalism and ethnicity were seen as mechanisms by which the ruling elite pitted the working classes of different countries against one another to divide and rule them. With the advent of the world communist revolution, such divisions were expected to disappear, to be replaced by equality and harmony among all peoples. As a result, communist parties tended to reject any overt expressions of nationalism and ethnicity, though national and ethnic identities often lurked beneath the surface. For example, encompassed within the vast Soviet Union were many ethnic groups, although the Communist Party tended to be dominated by Russians, who made up the single largest ethnic group. Many non-Russians resented this Russian domination. Many Eastern Europeans also viewed communist rule as little more than Russian imperialism; their national identities were therefore sharpened, not erased. This simmering nationalism played an important role in the fall of communism in Eastern Europe and the Soviet Union as well as in the politics thereafter.

The Collapse of Communism

In retrospect, it may seem obvious that communism was bound to fail. And yet on the eve of its collapse in Europe, few expected that it would happen anytime soon. Two factors played an important role in bringing about communism's sudden decline.

The first was the reemergence of Cold War struggles between the Soviet Union and the United States. After the tense decades of the 1950s and 1960s, which were marked by international competition, arms races, and harrowing events such as the

Cuban Missile Crisis, the United States and the Soviet Union settled into a period of détente, in which peaceful coexistence became the main goal. But détente lasted less than a decade. The Soviet Union's invasion of Afghanistan in 1979 to prop up a failing communist regime there and the election of Ronald Reagan as president of the United States in 1980 soured relations between the two countries. Reagan, who viewed the Soviet Union as an "evil empire," embarked on a new policy of military buildup. Growing economic stagnation made it difficult for the Soviet Union to meet this expensive challenge.

At the same time that the United States and the Soviet Union entered a new and costly stage of the Cold War, a new generation of political leaders rose to power in the Soviet Union. Among them was Mikhail Gorbachev, who was chosen as general secretary of the Communist Party in 1985. Unlike his predecessors, Gorbachev recognized the stagnation of the Soviet system and understood the cost of a new arms race. He thus proposed reforming international relations and domestic politics and thereby revitalizing both the Soviet Union and communist thought.

At the domestic level, Gorbachev initiated the twin policies of glasnost (openness) and perestroika (restructuring), with the intention of liberalizing and reforming communism. **Glasnost** encouraged public debate with the hope that a frank discussion of the system's shortcomings would help foster change and increase the legitimacy of the regime. **Perestroika**, or actual institutional reforms in the economy and political system, would flow from this critique. These reforms were expected to include some limited forms of democratic participation and market-based incentives in the economy. Moderate reform, not wholesale transformation, was Gorbachev's goal.

In the international arena, Gorbachev similarly proposed widespread, if moderate, changes. To reduce the Soviet Union's military burdens and improve relations with Western countries, he began to loosen his country's control over Eastern Europe, which had been under the thumb of the Soviet Union since the end of World War II. Gorbachev hoped that some limited liberalization in the region would ease tensions with Europe and the United States, enabling expanded trade and other economic ties.

Nevertheless, as Alexis de Tocqueville famously wrote about the French monarchy, the most dangerous moment for a bad government is usually when it begins to reform itself. Glasnost encouraged public debate, but rather than simply criticize corruption among the *nomenklatura* or the quality or absence of consumer goods, as Gorbachev expected, people began to challenge the very nature of the political system. Ethnic groups within the Soviet Union and citizens of Eastern European states also used glasnost to agitate for greater freedom from Russian domination.

Perestroika had similarly unexpected effects. By seeking political and economic reform, Gorbachev threatened those within the party who had long benefited from the status quo. Political leaders, administrators, factory bosses, and many other *nomenklatura* members resisted reform, taking a stance that led to infighting and instability. This problem was compounded by the uncertainty over how far Gorbachev's reforms would go. Confusion deepened within the party, the state, and society about where communism and the Soviet Union were heading.

Meanwhile, among the Soviet Union's satellite states change was proceeding faster than anyone expected. In 1989, civil society rapidly reasserted itself across

glasnost Literally, openness; the policy of political liberalization implemented in the Soviet Union in the late 1980s

perestroika Literally, restructuring; the policy of political and economic liberalization implemented in the Soviet Union in the late 1980s

TIMELINE Communist History

1848   Karl Marx and Friedrich Engels write *The Communist Manifesto*, a central document in communist thought.

1917   Vladimir Lenin leads the Russian Revolution, creating the Soviet Union as the world's first communist country.

1930s   Josef Stalin begins to arrest and execute Soviet Communist Party members and others to consolidate power.

1945   The Soviet Army occupies Eastern Europe, imposing communist regimes; tensions between the United States and the Soviet Union lead to the Cold War.

1949   The Chinese Communist Party, led by Mao Zedong, gains control over mainland China.

1953   Stalin dies.

1956   Nikita Khrushchev denounces Stalin's use of terror and allows limited open debate; protests in Hungary lead to open revolution against communism; Hungarian revolution put down by the Soviet Army.

1966–76   Mao unleashes the Cultural Revolution in China; the student "Red Guard" attacks symbols of pre-communism and party leaders accused of having grown too conservative.

1976   Mao Zedong dies; China and the United States begin to improve relations; Deng Xiaoping rises to power and starts to enact widespread economic reforms.

1985   Mikhail Gorbachev becomes general secretary of the Soviet Communist Party and begins economic and political reforms.

1989   Student protests for political reform in China's Tiananmen Square are crushed by the military.

1989–90   Eastern Europeans seize on reforms in the Soviet Union to press for dramatic political change; largely peaceful political protests lead to free elections and the elimination of communist rule in Eastern Europe.

1991   Increasing turmoil in the Soviet Union leads communist conservatives to oust Gorbachev and seize power; the coup fails because of weak military support and public demonstrations; the Soviet Union breaks into 15 separate states.

Eastern Europe as people used Gorbachev's new hands-off policy to oppose their countries' communist regimes, demanding open elections and an end to one-party rule. Eastern European Communist Party leaders, realizing that the Soviet Union would no longer intervene militarily to support them, had little choice but to acquiesce. As a result, by 1990 communists had been swept from their monopolies on power across the region. In most cases, this regime change was largely peaceful.

The Soviet Union would not be far behind. By 1991, the country was in deep turmoil: limited reforms had increased the public's appetite for greater change; the end of communism in Eastern Europe further emboldened opposition within the Soviet Union; and ethnic conflict and nationalism were on the rise as various groups sought political power.[13] Communist hard-liners eventually tried to stop the reform process through a coup d'état intended to seize power and detain Gorbachev. However, these leaders lacked the support of important actors, such as the military, and public demonstrations helped bring the poorly planned coup to an end.[14]

Following the failed coup, the individual republics that formed the Soviet Union broke apart. Some of this was the logical result of nationalist, secessionist movements. In addition, communist party elites in many republics saw this as a chance to hang on to power as the leaders of new, sovereign states. Fifteen new independent countries were created, of which Russia is but one. But communism did not collapse everywhere. Although 1989 marked liberalization and the first moves toward democracy in Eastern Europe and the Soviet Union, similar protests in China that year, led by students and encouraged by Gorbachev's example, were met with deadly military force in Tiananmen Square, Beijing. Communist leaders in China did not heed public demands for reform and political liberalization and showed themselves both willing and able to use the army to violently quell peaceful protests. Why did the Soviet Union and China go down such different paths? We will turn to this question at the end of the chapter (see the "Institutions in Action" box, p. 412).

The Transformation of Political Institutions

So far, we have discussed the communist theory regarding the origins of and solutions to inequality, the difficulties in translating theory into reality, and how institutions controlled by the state unraveled across most of the communist world. Yet although the downfall of communism was dramatic, what followed was no less awesome. Postcommunist countries faced, and continue to face, the challenge of building new political, economic, and social institutions to strike a new balance between freedom and equality. Simultaneous transformation of all three areas is unprecedented, and this task has met with varying degrees of success.

REORGANIZING THE STATE AND CONSTRUCTING A DEMOCRATIC REGIME

An underlying task in the transition from communism has been to reorganize the state in terms of its autonomy and capacity. Under communism, the party-state was able to dominate virtually all aspects of human relations without any effective check. But with the collapse of communism, the party was ejected from its leading role in political life. This left many formerly communist countries with a sprawling, if not always powerful or particularly legitimate, postcommunist state that did not embody the rule of law.

Postcommunist countries have also faced the prospect of building democratic regimes where authoritarianism has long been the norm. This project requires numerous tasks: creating a separation of powers between branches of government, choosing between different kinds of executive and legislative institutions, establishing electoral laws and regulating political parties, and doing all of this in a way that generates support among most of the actors in society.

Civil rights and civil liberties have been a final area of concern. As we discussed in Chapter 6, *civil rights* refers to the promotion of equality, whereas *civil liberties* refers to the promotion of freedom, though the two overlap. Civil right and liberties include such things as free speech and equal treatment under the law. Under communism, constitutions typically established an elaborate set of civil liberties, though in reality they were largely ignored by those in power. With the collapse of communism, the challenge has been to expand and protect these once-hollow rights and liberties. This has meant not only strengthening the rule of law so that those once-hollow rights could be enforced but also deciding what kinds of rights and liberties should be enshrined in the constitution and who should be the final arbiter of disputes over them. The role of constitutional courts has been an important issue in countries where traditionally the judiciary had been neither powerful nor independent.

EVALUATING POLITICAL TRANSITIONS

Nearly three decades have passed since communism collapsed in Eastern Europe and the former Soviet Union. How have the postcommunist countries' political transitions fared? The picture is mixed. In Chapter 8, we looked at the data from Freedom House, which ranks countries on a 1-to-100 freedom scale, scoring the most-free countries as 100 and the least free as 0. This ranking is based on such considerations as electoral competition, freedoms of speech and assembly, rule of law, levels of corruption, and protection of human and economic rights.

A number of postcommunist countries have made dramatic strides toward democracy and the rule of law, to such an extent that Freedom House now considers them consolidated democracies—meaning that their democratic regimes have been ranked highly on the Freedom House scale for a decade or so and are therefore stable and largely institutionalized. Most of these democracies can be found in Central Europe (including Poland, the Czech Republic, Slovakia, and Slovenia) and the Baltics (Estonia, Latvia, and Lithuania), areas that share a precommunist history of greater economic development, civil society, democratic institutions, and experience with the rule of law. They also enjoyed more contact with Western Europe and a shorter period of communist rule. All of these factors may help explain why democratic transition in these regions has been more successful and culminated in EU membership. Interestingly, this move to democracy also indicates the power of precommunist institutions despite the best efforts of communist regimes to eradicate them. In contrast, the Balkan countries of Southern Europe (such as Romania, Bulgaria, Croatia, and Serbia) have lagged further behind in the quality of their democratic institutions.

Table 9.2 provides an evaluation of postcommunist countries on a number of political variables, where a rating of 1 represents the most democratic and 7 the least. As noted above, democracy has tended to be stronger in the Central European countries and Baltic countries than in the Balkans. Nevertheless, a critical variable remains the kinds of choices made by elites during the transition process and afterward. Thus the Balkans, after two decades of civil conflict and the persistence of communist elites, lately have seen marked improvement in their democratic practices. Why? One important explanation is the European Union's expansion into this region: Romania

TABLE 9.2 Democratic Progress in Selected Communist and Postcommunist Systems, 2017

COUNTRY	ELECTORAL PROCESS	CIVIL SOCIETY	INDEPENDENT MEDIA	CORRUPTION	DEMOCRACY SCORE*
	1 = MOST DEMOCRATIC; 7 = LEAST DEMOCRATIC				
Estonia	1.50	1.75	1.50	2.50	1.93
Latvia	1.75	1.75	2.00	3.00	2.04
Slovenia	1.50	2.00	2.50	2.50	2.04
Czech Republic	1.25	2.00	2.75	3.50	2.25
Lithuania	2.00	1.75	2.25	3.50	2.32
Poland	1.50	1.75	3.00	3.50	2.57
Slovakia	1.50	2.00	2.75	3.75	2.61
Bulgaria	2.25	2.50	4.25	4.25	3.36
Romania	3.00	2.25	4.25	3.75	3.39
Hungary	3.00	2.75	4.25	4.50	3.54
Croatia	3.00	2.75	4.25	4.25	3.71
Serbia	3.50	2.25	4.50	4.25	3.82
Montenegro	3.50	2.75	4.50	4.75	3.89
Albania	3.75	3.00	4.25	5.25	4.14
Macedonia	4.00	3.25	5.25	4.75	4.43
Bosnia-Herzegovina	3.25	3.50	4.75	5.00	4.54
Georgia	4.50	3.75	4.00	4.50	4.61
Ukraine	3.50	2.50	4.00	5.75	4.61
Moldova	4.00	3.25	5.00	6.00	4.93
Kosovo	4.75	3.75	5.00	5.75	4.96
Armenia	6.00	3.75	5.50	5.25	5.39
Kyrgyzstan	5.50	5.00	6.00	6.25	6.00
Russia	6.75	6.50	6.50	6.75	6.57
Belarus	6.75	6.25	6.75	6.25	6.61
Kazakhstan	6.75	6.50	6.75	6.75	6.64
Tajikistan	6.75	6.50	6.50	6.75	6.64
Azerbaijan	7.00	7.00	7.00	7.00	6.93
Turkmenistan	7.00	7.00	7.00	7.00	6.96
Uzbekistan	7.00	7.00	7.00	7.00	6.96

*"Democracy Score" is a summary score, averaging each country's electoral process, civil society, independent media, and corruption ratings as well as ratings for local democratic governance, national democratic governance, and judicial framework and independence.

Source: https://freedomhouse.org/sites/default/files/NIT2017_booklet_FINAL_0.pdf (accessed 4/14/17).

and Bulgaria joined in 2007, Croatia joined in 2013, and Montenegro and Macedonia are currently negotiating membership. This "EU anchor," as it has been termed, has played an important role in institutionalizing democratic norms as a condition for membership. But we should not overstate the power of the European Union in this regard. Democracy scores have steadily eroded in Hungary, an EU member since 2004 and once considered a leader in postcommunist democratization. Given the recent turmoil in the European Union (see Chapter 7), the extent to which this organization will continue to shape or reinforce democratic norms among and beyond its members is an open question.

As we move eastward from western Europe the situation is less promising. In many of the former Soviet states, including Russia, democracy is illiberal and weakly institutionalized or completely absent. These countries tend to be poorer, and they have little historical experience of democracy due to a long period of Imperial Russian and Soviet control. In many of them, authoritarian leaders, often from the communist *nomenklatura*, have consolidated power in strong presidencies, limiting the possibility for power sharing and democratic accountability. Democratic rights and freedoms are restricted, civil society is weak, and those in power have enriched themselves through corrupt practices. The data in Table 9.2 reveal that the aggregate average scores for Central Europe and the Baltics on a 7-point scale are 2.6 and for the Balkans 4.2; but for the post-Soviet states (excluding the former Soviet republics of the Baltics), the score is 6.1. Support for democracy across the former Soviet Union is often very weak, as we can see from the examples in Table 9.3. Most worrisome, in Central Europe, the Balkans, and the former Soviet Union average democracy scores have declined each year since 2004.[15]

TABLE 9.3 Support for Authoritarianism, 2010–2014

HAVING A STRONG LEADER WHO DOES NOT HAVE TO BOTHER WITH PARLIAMENT AND ELECTIONS IS . . . (PERCENTAGE ANSWERING)		
COUNTRY	VERY/FAIRLY GOOD	BAD/VERY BAD
Poland	22%	78%
Azerbaijan	23	77
Estonia	32	68
Slovenia	32	68
China	42	58
Belarus	47	53
Ukraine	71	29
Romania	75	25
Russia	76	24
Kyrgyzstan	82	18

Source: World Values Survey.

Outside Eastern Europe and the former Soviet Union, democracy has been even slower to spread, and communist regimes in China, Laos, Vietnam, North Korea, and Cuba continue to hold on to power. In some cases, like North Korea and Cuba, opposition to liberalization has helped maintain the status quo, though at the cost of a severely stunted economy. China and Vietnam (and to a lesser extent Laos) have opted instead for economic reform without political change as a way to maintain the communist party's hold on power.

Elsewhere in Asia and in Africa, communist regimes have given way, but such events have often resulted in state collapse and civil war. Most notable of these is Afghanistan. Upon the Soviet Union's withdrawal from that country in 1989, civil war raged until 1996, when the Taliban gained power over most of the country, paving the way for the eventual establishment of Al Qaeda. The legacies of communism and the Cold War in these regions are significant.

GERMANY

GERMAN UNIFICATION AND THE LEGACIES OF DIVISION

For those who are younger, it may seem hard to imagine that for 40 years after World War II, Germany was divided into two independent states. West Germany was constructed out of those areas conquered by UK and U.S. forces, while much smaller East Germany (16 versus 60 million people) was constructed from the area occupied by Soviet forces. Berlin, once the capital of Germany, was itself divided, creating the strange situation where West Berlin was surrounded by East Germany but under West German sovereignty. A wall surrounded the city to keep East Germans from fleeing into West Berlin, and connections between the two countries were limited.

West and East Germany experienced profound institutional changes during the Cold War. West Germany experienced denazification, democratization, and reindustrialization, and became a leading member of what would become the European Union. And although West Germany became a member of the North Atlantic Treaty Organization (NATO), a military alliance, a strong streak of pacifism developed as a legacy of the war. East Germany, meanwhile, came under the control of a communist regime and reindustrialized under a nationalized economy and central planning. The country became part of the Warsaw Pact, the Soviet Union's version of NATO. Still, in spite of these differences, Germans shared in common centuries of history, culture, and other important values and norms. Accordingly, when in 1989 communism began to collapse in Eastern Europe many East Germans saw their future in a reunified Germany, and initial beliefs that East Germany would survive as sovereign democratic state quickly disappeared. Public protests, which began with the chant *wir sind das volk*—"we are the people"—soon changed to *wir sind ein folk*—"we are one people." Within a year, Germany was reunified, far faster than anyone first imagined.

Since 1990, the German government has spent billions of dollars transforming the political, economic, and social fabric of eastern Germany, and in many ways this effort can be viewed as a tremendous success. Yet other, less visible, but more problematic legacies remain. Much of this falls within the category of political culture. East Germany's decades of authoritarian rule, in addition to the Nazi regime and the absence of denazification under communism, resulted in a population whose commitment to democratic values and political tolerance is lower than its compatriots in western

Germany. This has been termed the "Mauer im Kopf"—a wall, like the one that surrounded Berlin, but still in the minds of East Germans separating them from western Germany's political culture.

How much does political culture differ between east and west? A 2014 study indicates that levels of xenophobia are consistently higher (upward of 10 percent) among eastern than western Germans. More surprising is that this difference exists, and is in fact greatest, among those born after 1981 and therefore with the least experience of living under the East German regime. Eastern Germans also show higher support for authoritarianism than western Germans (12 versus 5 percent). These differences may help explain why strong xenophobic movements have emerged of late in eastern Germany, where paradoxically the proportion of foreigners in comparison to the west is relatively low. East Germany's undemocratic past appears to have left institutional legacies far stronger than many expected.[16]

The Transformation of Economic Institutions

In addition to transforming the state and the regime, transitions from communism have confronted the task of reestablishing some separation between the state and the economy. This work involves two processes: privatization, or the transfer of state-held property into private hands, and marketization, or the re-creation of market forces of supply and demand. In both cases, decisions about how to carry out these changes and to what end were influenced by different political-economic alternatives. Let's consider the ways of approaching privatization and marketization before we investigate the different paths postcommunist countries have taken in each area.

PRIVATIZATION AND MARKETIZATION

The transition from communism to capitalism requires a redefinition of property. To generate economic growth and limit the power of the state, the state must reentrust economic resources to the public, placing them back into private hands. But the task of privatization is neither easy nor clear. In fact, before 1989 no country had ever gone from a communist economy to a capitalist one, so no model existed.

Among the many questions and concerns facing the postcommunist countries was how to place prices on the various elements of the economy—factories, shops, land, apartments. To privatize these assets, the state first must determine their value, something difficult in a system where no market has existed. And who should get these assets? Should they be given away? Sold to the highest bidder? Made available to foreign investors? Each option has its own advantages in developing a thriving economy but also risks increasing inequality and generating public resentment.

Privatization was carried out in several different ways, depending on the country and its economic assets. Small businesses, like restaurants or retail shops, were often sold directly to their employees, and some countries also sold many large businesses, like automobile manufacturers, to the highest bidders—often foreign investors. Other countries essentially distributed shares in firms to the public as

Reestablishing Separation of State and Economy

- Privatization: the transfer of state-held property into private hands.
- Marketization: the re-creation of the market forces of supply and demand.

a whole. Scholars debated the benefits of each model; but in the end each form, whether alone or in combination, was shown to work well in some circumstances and badly in others.

No matter what the privatization process, ultimately postcommunist countries included many firms that were overstaffed, outdated, and unable to turn a profit in a market economy. Most problematic were very large industrial firms, such as coal mines and steel plants built in the early years of industrialization; these antiquated behemoths could not compete in the international market. Such firms often needed to be sold or radically downsized, leading to unemployment in a society where employment had previously been guaranteed. Such firms sometimes employed thousands of people and represented the main source of work in a city or region. As a result, in some countries privatization proceeded slowly and unevenly for fear of widespread unemployment and resulting social unrest.

Along with re-creating private property, states needed to re-create a market in which property, labor, goods, and services could all function in a competitive environment that would determine their value. On the surface, marketization appears easier than privatization—a simple matter of eliminating central planning and allowing the market to resurface naturally. But marketization, too, is complicated. One issue of debate concerned how rapidly marketization should take place. Some argued that given the profound nature of the economic transformation in postcommunist states, changes should be gradual to minimize any social disruptions that might undermine these fledgling economies and democracies. In particular, supporters of this "gradualism" feared that sudden marketization would lead to a wild jump in prices as sellers became able to charge whatever they wanted for their goods. Inflation and even hyperinflation could result, undermining confidence in the transition process and generating widespread poverty. Others rejected these arguments, advocating rapid market reforms that would free prices and bring an end to central planning and state subsidies for businesses virtually overnight—a

shock therapy A process of rapid marketization

policy known as **shock therapy**. Such changes would be painful and might initially trigger high rates of inflation, but the pain would end sooner than that accompanying gradualism.

In choosing particular forms of privatization and marketization, postcommunist countries adopted new political-economic models—some gravitating toward the social democratic models of Western Europe, others to the liberalism of the United States and the United Kingdom, and still others to more mercantilist policies.

EVALUATING ECONOMIC TRANSITIONS

How successful have all of these reforms been? The answer again depends on what country we are evaluating. Table 9.4 shows some of the results of over 25 years of transition. A number of countries are now as wealthy as some poorer

TABLE 9.4 Economic Indicators in Selected Communist and Postcommunist Countries, 2016

COUNTRY	PER CAPITA GDP, 2015 (PPP US $)	PER CAPITA GDP, 1989–90 (PPP US $)	TRANSPARENCY INTERNATIONAL CORRUPTION RANKING (1 = LEAST CORRUPT)
Slovenia	32,900	10,400	31
Portugal*	30,600	11,800	29
Poland	27,800	6,000	29
Greece*	26,800	13,200	69
Hungary	26,700	8,500	57
Latvia	26,000	7,800	44
Romania	23,600	5,200	57
Russia	23,200	8,000	131
Cuba	18,900	8,600	60
Azerbaijan	17,300	5,500	123
China	15,500	1,000	79
Albania	11,900	2,700	83
Georgia	10,000	5,200	44
Ukraine	8,300	6,700	131
Moldova	5,300	4,200	123

*Greece and Portugal, non-postcommunist countries, are included for comparison.

Source: World Bank, Transparency International.

noncommunist European states, such as Greece and Portugal. In contrast, many of the former Soviet republics have not done nearly as well. Particularly notable given our opening discussion is Ukraine, which is barely better off than it was upon independence. Why this variation? The countries that have done particularly well have benefited from many of the factors we discussed earlier: shorter periods of Soviet control; more precommunist experience with industrialization, markets, and private property; closer ties with Western Europe; and strong support from the European Union, including membership. Stronger democratic institutions have also led to better judicial structures that can stem corruption and protect property rights.

The countries that have done less well experienced just the opposite. In these countries, freeing up markets often led to uncontrollable inflation and a rapid decline in the standard of living. These problems were compounded by the way privatization was carried out. Many of the most valuable assets fell into the hands of the old *nomenklatura* or a few private individuals, typically supported by corrupt political leaders. Some countries that have done well, such as Russia and Azerbaijan, owe their economic success to natural resources (oil and gas) rather than the development of a private sector, reflecting the problem of the resource trap we spoke of in Chapter 8. A theme running through all these cases is the correlation between economic growth and the rule of law. Where the rule of law is weak, economic transition is much less successful because entrepreneurs (both domestic and international) lack a predictable environment in which to invest, while political leaders and state officials use their positions to siphon off resources for themselves. All of the resource-rich post-Soviet states suffer levels of corruption similar to what we see in the poorer parts of Africa.

Overall, postcommunist countries have seen an increase in inequality, poverty, and unemployment, which is to be expected as markets and private property become central economic forces. Where this process has been balanced by economic prosperity for most of the population, support for change has been stronger. Where a significant part of the population has felt worse off, as in parts of the former Soviet Union, economic change has bred resentment, nostalgia for the old order, and obstacles to democratization. A notable example is Russia, where during the last decade many large industries and natural resources have been renationalized and mercantilist economic policies have been adopted. This nostalgia also ties into Russia's resurgent nationalism and its military involvement in Ukraine.

In general, most postcommunist countries will struggle to maintain the high level of growth necessary to close the gap between themselves and the developed democracies. The rapid growth experienced during the last decade has declined due in part to global economic difficulties, and this has increased skepticism for economic and political reform. It has also increased the appeal of populist and nationalist leaders, thereby undercutting democracy.

Outside of Eastern Europe and the former Soviet Union, the success rate of economic transition has been equally varied. Much attention has focused on China, which is still controlled by a communist party but in many ways can be thought of as "postcommunist" in its economic system. Since the 1970s, China's reforms have included a dramatic expansion of private business and agriculture, all with the support of the Chinese Communist Party. The slogan of this set of economic reforms—"to get rich is glorious"—sounds anything but Marxist, and it is rooted in the practical realization that earlier drives for rapid economic growth led to disaster. Some observers argue that these reforms have succeeded where those in many other communist and postcommunist countries have failed, because the Chinese introduced economic transition while restricting political change so as to better manage the course of reform. Indeed, since 1989 the Chinese economy has grown by leaps and bounds, lifting hundreds of millions out of poverty and dramatically transforming the country, not to mention world trade. As we will discuss in Chapter 11, in many ways the very idea of globalization is strongly tied to China's integration into the world market.

Yet the Chinese model has its own problems. Alongside economic growth and the development of a free market and private property, problems such as inflation, corruption, unemployment, and growing inequality have also surfaced, often exacerbated by the still-powerful presence of the state in the Chinese economy. The weakness of the rule of law only compounds these problems. China's rapid development has been profound; now the question is how strong the country will become. Some see in China a growing economic superpower that will eclipse the economies of much of Asia and perhaps the world. This development is fostering a middle class and civil society that many believe will pave the way for the democratization of one-fifth of the world's population. Indeed, levels of economic development in China now are not much different from those of South Korea and Taiwan when they transitioned to democracy. Others caution, however, that the Chinese "miracle" covers up serious problems like environmental damage. Economic development in China has also slowed, and the country must provide new economic opportunities for an increasingly well-educated population.[17] Domestic and international challenges mean that economic development in China is perhaps more uncertain now than at any time since reforms began in the 1980s.

The Transformation of Societal Institutions

Like political systems and economies, societies, too, have been fundamentally transformed in postcommunist countries. Where once communist control asserted a single unquestionable understanding of human relations and development, people now face a world much more uncertain and unclear. Individuals in postcommunist societies have the freedom to act more independently, but this potential carries with it greater risk. The elimination of an all-encompassing ideology from people's lives has created a social vacuum that must be filled. In all of these countries, the transition from communism has been a wrenching process as people adjust to new realities and seek new individual and collective identities.

CHANGING IDENTITIES

This transformation of society has manifested itself in various ways. Religion, once suppressed by communist parties, has reappeared in many countries. Public opinion research conducted by the World Values Survey (see our discussion of political culture in Chapter 3) indicates that since 1989 religion has increased in prominence in many communist and postcommunist countries. In a 1989–93 survey, they found that nearly 80 percent of Chinese said God was not at all important in their lives; as of 2010–14, that number had dropped to less than a third. Similar shifts can be seen in Russia and many other postcommunist countries. In postcommunist Europe, Christianity has resurfaced as an important force, often as part of nationalism rather than a private profession of faith. Islam has also reemerged in countries with traditionally large Muslim populations, much to the chagrin of leaders who are holdovers from the antireligious Soviet era. In China, too, new and old religious movements are growing. Various Christian movements have gained ground, and Islam has regained its potency among Turkic peoples in far western China. The Communist Party itself has sought to increase its legitimacy by promoting Confucian ideals and practices that were once attacked as symbols of feudal oppression. The re-creation of religious institutions can provide social support during periods of political and economic disruption. It can also increase sectarianism and fundamentalism.

Like religion, ethnic and national identities have also reemerged as potent forms of identification. Levels of national pride have risen across many of those same states surveyed over the same time period. In many postcommunist countries, both leaders and publics have sought to instill national pride and resurrect the values, symbols, and ideas that bind people together. The scope of this task varies among the postcommunist countries. In much of Eastern Europe, a clear sense of ethnic and national identity has existed for many generations. Despite communist rule, many of these social structures not only remained intact but also were reinforced as a form of resistance to communism. In contrast, across the diverse ethnic groups of the former Soviet Union national identity has historically been weaker or divided. Many of these peoples have more limited historical institutions to draw on, and their identities often rely on institutionalizing new symbols and myths. All such identities can be a double-edged sword, of course. Although they can help mobilize the public and provide stability in times of great transition, religious, ethnic, and national identities can also generate division and conflict. This is particularly true when several identities coexist in one country or spill across borders. Ukraine is an example of such a conflict (recall the chapter opening discussion); clashes between ethnic Chinese and the Muslim Turkic Uighur minority in western China are another.

The changes underway in social identities cannot help but affect gender relations as well. Recall our earlier discussion of how communist theory advanced the radical notion of gender equality. Although equality was not realized in practice, women were incorporated into the workforce and provided with social benefits that generated new opportunities for them. With the end of communism, however, many of these policies and institutions have been weakened or challenged. Critics have attacked many communist-era practices such as easy access to abortions, while economic reforms have cut back much of the elaborate social safety net that once benefited women and families. The reemergence of religion has also challenged women's roles in society in some cases. Authoritarianism may also be patriarchal, asserting that women's primary role in society is to be the mothers of the nation.

Finally, there is the question of gender identity itself. Under communism, lesbian, gay, bisexual, and transgender (LGBT) issues were viewed as either a psychological disorder or a result of capitalism's focus on hedonism and individualism. The decline of communism, however, allowed for these identities to enter the public sphere. This change has been met with varying degrees of resistance from some religious institutions and nationalists who view the LGBT community as a danger to the country's moral health.

EVALUATING SOCIETAL TRANSITIONS

Societal transformation among the postcommunist countries has been as varied as political and economic change. An initial, pessimistic take would be that the resurgence of national and religious identities has been a source of destabilization in these countries. There is certainly much evidence to justify this view. In Eastern Europe, the dissolution of Yugoslavia in the 1990s pitted ethnic and religious groups against one another, claiming more than 200,000 lives. Tajikistan, Uzbekistan, Moldova, Azerbaijan, and Armenia as well as the Russian region of Chechnya also saw violent religious and ethnic conflicts as the Soviet Union collapsed, again leading to several hundred thousand dead.

Another related factor is the way in which postcommunist identities have shaped international terrorism. In 1979, the Soviet Union invaded Afghanistan in order to prop up a communist regime on the verge of collapse; this led to a guerrilla movement that drew in support and recruits from around the world, including the Saudi Osama bin Laden, who would found Al Qaeda. Afghanistan would become a crucible for Islamic fundamentalist views that would spread around the world. And just as Afghanistan became a magnet for Middle Eastern fighters in the 1980s, Syria and Iraq have become a magnet for fighters from Russia and postcommunist Central Asia. Some of the strongest supporters of the Islamic State of Iraq and al-Sham (ISIS) have been young Muslims from countries of the former Soviet Union, radicalized by economic difficulties and religious and ethnic marginalization.

Finally, at the state level we see attempts to promote nationalism as a means to legitimize authoritarian rule, especially as ideological legitimacy has waned. In both Russia and China, political leaders stress the unique nature of their societies, which are under threat by outside forces, be that countries or values. This can contribute to ethnic and national conflict both within these countries and between them and their neighbors.

In spite of this, we should not go so far as to say that the legacy of communism is conflict. Ethnic and nationalist violence, while significant after 1989, has largely waned. (Ukraine is an outlier, not the norm.) Moreover, even as surveys document the importance of religion and nationalism, this does not necessarily result in a greater propensity for conflict. Indeed, the World Values Survey shows that publics are less likely to say they are willing to fight for their country now than they were 25 years ago. This is even true in countries like China and Russia, where nationalist values have been a strong component of regime legitimacy. In 1989–93, over 90 percent of Chinese said they were willing to fight for their country; in 2010–14, that number was below 75 percent. In Russia during that same period, willingness to fight declined from 68 percent to 53 percent. This is consistent with responses across the developed democracies, suggesting deeper societal changes in communist and postcommunist countries.

Gender relations in postcommunist countries are equally interesting. The United Nations (UN) uses several indicators to measure the standard of living and differences in that standard between genders. The UN's Gender Inequality Index (Table 9.5) measures inequality between women and men in three areas: health (maternal mortality and adolescent fertility); empowerment (share of parliamentary seats and secondary and higher education levels); and labor (women's participation in the workforce). When we look at the data, we see that many postcommunist countries perform well relative to their level of economic development, ranking higher on the index than the United States or the United Kingdom. This is in part a function of social institutions created under communism, such as mass education and health care.

Such progress does not yet extend into the area of LGBT rights. Several Central European states allow for same-sex partnerships, though neither China nor virtually any of the states from the former Soviet Union do so. Outright discrimination has also grown in a number of places, most notably Russia and Central Asia. There we find increased propaganda that attacks the LGBT community as pedophiles and agents of the West—a view little different from that promoted during the Soviet era. Public opinion surveys indicate a higher degree of homophobia among European postcommunist countries in comparison with

TABLE 9.5 Gender Inequality Index, 2015

COUNTRY	RANK	COUNTRY	RANK
Slovenia	6	**Bulgaria**	45
Germany	9	**Moldova**	46
Canada	18	**Hungary**	49
France	19	**Russia**	52
Japan	21	**Ukraine**	55
Czech Republic	27	**Cuba**	62
United Kingdom	28	**Tajikistan**	65
Poland	30	**Vietnam**	71
Croatia	31	*Mexico*	73
China	37	*South Africa*	90
Slovakia	39	*Brazil*	92
Latvia	41	*Iran*	118
Kazakhstan	42	*India*	125
United States	43	*Afghanistan*	154

Note: The Gender Inequality Index is a composite measure reflecting inequality in health, empowerment (education and participation in legislature), and participation in the workforce. Countries are ranked from 1 to 188; non-postcommunist countries in italics are included for comparison.

Source: UN Development Program.

countries that did not experience communism, and this is true even for most postcommunist states that are now EU members. Yet while homophobia remains high, it has steadily declined in Russia, China, and most other postcommunist states surveyed.

INDIA

COMMUNISM AND DEMOCRACY IN INDIA

Our discussion in this chapter has been almost exclusively about the end, and aftermath, of communism. But is communism finished? Perhaps not. India, a parliamentary democracy with a rapidly growing capitalist economy, would seem an unlikely place to look for insights. This case nonetheless offers some surprising answers and a reminder that communism remains viable as both an ideology and a political economic system, at least in India.

Like many postcolonial countries gaining independence during the twentieth century, India has had a long history with communism. Established in 1925, India's first communist party joined the movement to end British rule in India. Following independence in 1947, a variety of communist parties emerged and participated in local, state, and national politics as part of what came to be known as the Left Front. And even as communist regimes collapsed in Eastern Europe and the Soviet Union and transformed dramatically in China and elsewhere, orthodox Marxist-Leninist parties have regularly won parliamentary majorities in several Indian states. At the same time, a violent communist insurgency threatens revolution across significant swaths of Indian countryside.

Why has communism persisted in India even as it has failed elsewhere? Persistent inequality and grinding poverty, particularly in rural India, provided a ready constituency for communist parties that promised to redistribute wealth through land reform, improve education, and organize labor unions. These parties took root most readily in regions of India less susceptible to the ethnic divisions and conflicts that have otherwise prevented poor Hindus, Muslims, and other so-called backward castes from cooperating politically in many areas. Communist parties have consistently promoted the rights of women and opposed India's caste system, earning them significant support from India's millions of dispossessed.

And at least to some extent, these state-level communist governments, once elected, delivered on their promises to voters, earning them a great deal of loyalty and performance legitimacy. Communist governments in the state of Kerala carried out education reforms in the 1950s and land reform in the 1960s and 1970s, giving the state India's highest literacy and life expectancy rates and lowest fertility and infant mortality rates. Perhaps not surprisingly, India's highest electoral participation rates are also found in those states frequently led by communist governments, indicating that these parties have not just educated their citizens but also brought a higher percentage of them into the democratic process.

But voters can have high expectations, and communist governments have often been thrown out of office in recent years as globalization and India's liberal economic reforms have brought unprecedented wealth to many Indians, promoting private markets and new sources of wealth. India's rising middle class shows little interest in the virtues of communism and sees India's future in the market, not the state. But India's communists have not lost hope, noting that India's recent liberal reforms have exacerbated inequality and will require the kinds of solutions communism can provide. They also warn that the growing threat of communist-armed insurgency in rural India is no coincidence and that a focus on freedom at the expense of equality may come at the cost of revolution, just as Marx predicted. (We will tackle many of these issues in Chapter 10 on developing countries.)

Communism, defined as a set of political institutions first constructed in the Soviet Union a hundred years ago, may now be finished. Yet the motivation that drove the creation of these institutions—the desire to eliminate inequality—remains. And as we have discussed, rising inequality within many countries around the world, both developed and developing, is a pressing concern. As long as inequality and poverty remain, there will be room for ideologies that seek to use politics and the state to solve these problems.

Why Did Reform Fail in the Soviet Union but Succeed in China?

One of the greatest puzzles regarding the collapse of communism has to do with a revolution that did not happen. In 1989, as communism was coming to an end in Eastern Europe and the Soviet Union was on the verge of breaking up, China, too, was experiencing a wave of political protests that threatened to bring down the communist regime. Most notably, student protesters occupied Tiananmen Square in Beijing, the political center of China, calling for liberalization and political reform. At their peak, these protesters numbered in the tens of thousands in Beijing alone, and they spread to other cities throughout the country. Many observers believed that China, like the Soviet Union and Eastern Europe, was at a turning point. The movement expanded from students to professionals and the working class, and the protests were amplified by the widespread presence of the international media, which in turn influenced the actions of the movement.

However, the revolution never occurred. The Chinese leadership declared martial law. Although there were massive public protests to block the approach of the military, army units violently forced their way into Tiananmen Square and dispersed the protesters. Estimates are that several hundred died and thousands were arrested. This outcome is puzzling in comparison with what happened in the Soviet Union and Eastern Europe, where most regimes were overwhelmed by largely nonviolent protests like those in China. What led to such different outcomes?

In Eastern Europe and the Soviet Union, modernization under communism had generated a well-educated class of professionals who were able to articulate their desires for greater political and economic independence. This nascent civil society reacted to a centrally planned economy that was increasingly unable to deliver economic growth or even maintain existing standards of living. Elites in power lost legitimacy—not just in the eyes of society at large but also among themselves. Gorbachev initiated reforms precisely because he faced this crisis of legitimacy and realized that even the ranks of the party no longer had faith in the viability of communism.

As these reforms began to accelerate faster and go further than elites anticipated, international factors amplified this process. Civil society in Eastern Europe looked to the rest of Europe and the EU as a model to emulate. Moreover, Gorbachev's desire to end the Cold War led him to release the Soviet Union's military control over Eastern Europe, emboldening opposition forces there into challenging and toppling those in power. Cultural forces also played a role, for many Eastern European societies viewed their protests as part of a quest to "return to Europe," from which they felt they had been separated while under Soviet rule. At the same time, rival nationalisms within the Soviet Union led to violent clashes, even outright war, between different ethnic groups that helped bring down the country as a whole.

Meanwhile, China in 1989 could not have been more different. Modernization was far behind the levels of the Soviet Union or Eastern Europe. The country remained overwhelmingly agricultural, and while the student protests did contain the seed of civil society, it was small relative to the size of the Chinese public as a whole. Further, while economic reforms in the Soviet Union in the 1980s were a late and limited response to the stagnation of a centrally planned industrial economy, China's reforms had begun earlier and had led to the doubling of its economy over the course of that same decade. Given the chaos and economic disasters that accompanied the Great Leap Forward and the Cultural Revolution, many Chinese could look upon the country in 1989 as finally moving in the right direction. This view in turn bolstered the government's legitimacy both within and outside the regime. Public support for the Communist Party remained strong, and party members and leaders retained a firm conviction that the Tiananmen Square protests would only undermine the country's progress.

With regard to international factors, it is true that the foreign media widely covered the student protests. Still, the Chinese leadership did not need to worry that the use of force would jeopardize the country's future in the same way that Gorbachev believed that the use of force would prevent any integration with Europe or an end to the Cold War. Gorbachev and others argued that communist reforms would mean that Russia and Eastern Europe could "return to Europe" or "rejoin the West." There was no similar sentiment in China, which, if anything, sought recognition as a power unto itself.

This kind of comparative analysis of these differing institutional trends and state trajectories helps make sense of this puzzle, but we should be careful not to assume we can fully explain the outcomes in either of these cases. Chinese liberalization akin to that in the Soviet Union was perhaps closer to occurring than it seems. Documents leaked from the Chinese government suggest that party leader Deng Xiaoping had to push the government and military toward the use of force. In his absence, might Tiananmen Square have become the starting point for political change? If so, what kind of regime and government would we see in China today?

The National Congress of the Communist Party of China convenes every five years in Beijing to make leadership changes within the party.

THINKING CRITICALLY

1. How did the level of modernization in the Soviet Union versus that in China contribute to differences in civil society?
2. How might economic performance explain the difference in the public's view of party elites between the Soviet Union and China?
3. In what way was the "return to Europe" sentiment an international factor in the Soviet Union's path to reform?

In Sum: The Legacy of Communism

According to Marxist thought, capitalism would inevitably lead to great industrialization but also to great injustice, a contradiction that would result in its downfall. On the ruins of capitalism, communism would build a society of total equality. But constructing communism proved to be a daunting task. People in communist systems found little incentive for hard work and innovation and had little freedom to express themselves individually.

For the Soviet Union and Eastern Europe, attempts to solve these problems led to outright collapse. An apt analogy might be the attempts to renovate a dilapidated house that reveal the whole structure to be unsound and that only make the situation worse. At that point, the choice is either to demolish the whole structure or be demolished by it. In 1989, people in a number of Eastern European countries chose to demolish the institutions of communism. Communist structures in the Soviet Union eventually collapsed on the Communist Party and Soviet society. China seems to be in a process of endless (and perhaps precarious) remodeling, while other communist countries, such as North Korea, have yet to carry out any major reforms.

It is not clear what the coming decades will bring to the postcommunist world. All of the world's societies are attempting to grapple again with the challenge of balancing freedom and equality. New political, economic, and social institutions are needed, but in many cases they must be forged out of the rubble of the old order, a situation that is creating unique difficulties and contradictions. Over the past decade, both individual freedom and collective inequality have grown in many countries. Increased civil liberties have arisen alongside poverty, and society has been reborn alongside conflict and hostility.

The results of this diverse process have been dramatically different across the communist and postcommunist world. In some countries, we see the institutionalization of democracy and capitalism; in others, authoritarianism and state-dominated economies remain in place. Moreover, it is apparent that over time these countries will grow increasingly dissimilar. Most Eastern European states have joined the European Union and enjoyed economic growth and democracy, though not without challenges. Within parts of the former Soviet Union, however, economic difficulties, political instability, and nondemocratic rule are more common; those countries more closely resemble developing countries. China and Russia remain question marks. Everywhere, the legacies of communism are likely to last for many generations.

Key Terms

base (p. 387)
bourgeoisie (p. 388)
Central Committee (p. 391)
central planning (p. 393)
communism (p. 386)
dialectical materialism (p. 388)
glasnost (p. 396)
nomenklatura (p. 390)

party-state (p. 392)
perestroika (p. 396)
Politburo (p. 391)
proletariat (p. 388)
shock therapy (p. 404)
superstructure (p. 387)
vanguard of the proletariat (p. 390)

In response to international sanctions, a Russian supporter of Vladimir Putin shows off a T-shirt that reads, "Our nuclear missiles are not afraid of sanctions."

Russia

Why Study This Case?

For decades, Russia stood out from all other countries in the world. Established in 1917, the Soviet Union (which included present-day Russia and many of its neighbors) was the world's first Communist state. The Soviet Union served as a beacon for Communists everywhere, a symbol of how freedom and equality could be transformed if the working class could truly gain power. It provoked equally strong responses among its opponents, who saw it as a violent, dangerous, and power-hungry dictatorship. The rapid growth of Soviet power from the 1930s onward only exacerbated this tension, which eventually culminated in a Cold War between the United States and the Soviet Union following World War II. Armed with thousands of nuclear weapons, these two ideologically hostile states struggled to maintain a balance of power and to avoid a nuclear holocaust. Until the 1980s, many observers believed that humanity would eventually face a final, violent conflict between these two systems.

Yet when the Soviet Union's end finally came, it was not with a bang but with a whimper. In the 1980s, the Soviet Union saw the rise of a new generation of leaders who realized that their system was no longer primed to overtake the West, economically or otherwise. The general secretary of the Soviet Union's Communist Party, Mikhail Gorbachev, attempted to inject limited political and economic reforms into the system. His reforms, however, seemed only to exacerbate domestic problems and polarize the leadership and the public. Gorbachev's actions resulted in the actual dissolution of the Soviet Union and the formation of 15 independent countries, one of which is Russia.

How would Russia be reconstructed from the ruins? Like many of the other postcommunist countries, it had to confront the twin tasks of forging democracy and establishing capitalism in a land that had little historical experience with

Providéniya

Anadyr

*Bering
Sea*

Petropavlovsk-
Kamchatskiy

Magadan

*Sea
of
Okhotsk*

Khabarovsk

*Sea
of
Japan*

JAPAN

Vladivostok

NORTH
KOREA

SOUTH
KOREA

*Yellow
Sea*

S I B E R I A

Lena R.

Yakutsk

*Lake
Baikal*

Irkutsk

MONGOLIA

C H I N A

*ARCTIC
OCEAN*

Norilsk

Krasnoyarsk

Yenisey R.

Novosibirsk

N

Ob R.

Omsk

KAZAKHSTAN

KYRGYZSTAN

TAJIKISTAN

500 mi

500 km

250

250

0

0

*Barents
Sea*

Murmansk

Arkhangelsk

Yekaterinburg

Chelyabinsk

AFGHANISTAN

GREENLAND
(DENMARK)

*Norwegian
Sea*

Petrozavodsk

Vyborg

Nizhniy
Novgorod

Kazan

Volga R.

Volgograd

Astrakhan

UZBEKISTAN

TURKMENISTAN

ICELAND

NORWAY

FINLAND

St. Petersburg

MOSCOW

Caspian Sea

IRAN

SWEDEN

ESTONIA

LATVIA

BELARUS

Rostov

Novorossiysk

CHECHNYA

LITHUANIA

MOLDOVA

Kiev★

UKRAINE

CRIMEA
(controlled
by Russia)

Sochi

*Black
Sea*

GEORGIA

ARMENIA

AZERBAIJAN

TURKEY

GERMANY

POLAND

either process. How does a nation go about creating a market economy after communism? How does it go about building democracy? Russia proves a fascinating study of the quest to build new institutions that reconcile freedom and equality in a manner far different from that of the previous regime. We can learn a lot from Russia's attempt at meeting this awesome challenge.

A quarter century on, the prospects for Russian democracy and development appear to be poor. After an initial decade of incomplete and chaotic political and economic reform, the country began moving away from a liberal economic system and liberal democracy. Under the leadership of President **Vladimir Putin**, Russia has seen the effective end to democratic institutions, as ever-greater authority is concentrated in the hands of the president and those around him. Limitations on federalism, elections, and other changes have all been directed at reducing political power beyond the presidency. Additionally, steps have been taken to restrict civil society: the state has brought the mass media under federal control and increasingly is preventing independent political parties and nongovernmental organizations (NGOs) from functioning. Today, an incipient democratic ideology has been replaced by a focus on Russian nationalism and militarism, reflecting a sense of humiliation that the country has lost its authoritative role in the international system. Russia's seizure of the Crimea from Ukraine in 2014 and accusations of Russian meddling in American and European elections have only further increased hostility. Relations between Russia and the West are now at their worst since the Cold War.

Similarly, the economy, which in the 1990s experienced a drastic and incomplete shift to private property and market forces, has seen both curtailed. Powerful economic leaders whose fortunes rose during that period, the **oligarchs**, have now been largely divested of their wealth, driven from the country, or imprisoned. Assets, particularly natural resources, have been renationalized or transferred to individuals close to Putin. Economic growth has been inconsistent and largely propelled by oil and gas prices. In economics and politics, the country has fallen under the control of the *siloviki* ("men of power"), individuals who, like Putin, have their origins in the security agencies. And yet Putin's consolidation of power and his limitations on democracy and the market have garnered public support. Tired of the chaos of market reforms, cynical about postcommunist politics, and angry about Russia's loss of power in the world, most Russians have appreciated Putin's promise to restore order and Russian pride. To a large extent, he has succeeded.

In 2008, President Putin stepped down from power, having served the two-term limit on the office. His handpicked successor, Dimitri Medvedev, easily won the presidential election and promptly appointed Putin to be his prime minister. Given Medvedev's non-*siloviki* background and the power inherent in the presidential office, some expected that this transfer of power could represent a break with the Putin era. Instead, as prime minister, Putin still called the shots; then he returned to the presidency in 2012, appointing Medvedev as prime minister. Because he is able to serve another two 6-year terms, it appears that Putin will remain in office until 2024. At that point, he will have governed Russia for a quarter of a century.

In many ways, Russia has become as opaque and resistant to change as it was under communism—a worrying sign for that country and the rest of the world. In this chapter, we will look at the past, the promise, and the present of Russian politics and political change, with an eye to where this country may be headed.

Historical Development of the State

RELIGION, FOREIGN INVASION, AND THE EMERGENCE OF A RUSSIAN STATE

Any understanding of present-day Russia and its political struggles must begin with an understanding of how the state developed over time. By the late tenth century, the Kievan state emerged as a major force, stretching from Scandinavia to Central Europe. It had also adopted **Orthodox Christianity**, centered in Constantinople (modern-day Istanbul). Orthodoxy developed distinctly from Roman Catholicism in a number of practical and theological ways, among them the perception of the relationship between church and state. Roman Catholics came to see the pope as the central leader of the faith, separate from the political power of Europe's kings. Orthodoxy, however, did not draw such a line between political and religious authority. This situation, some argue, stunted the idea of a society functioning independently of the state.

Another important development was the Mongol invasion of Russia in the thirteenth century. Some scholars view this occupation as the central event that set Russia on a historical path separate from that of the West—one leading to greater despotism and isolation. Cut off from European intellectual and economic influences, Russia did not participate in the Renaissance, feel the impact of the Protestant Reformation, or develop a strong middle class.

Not all scholars agree with this assessment, however. For some, the move toward despotism had its impetus not in religion or foreign invasion but in domestic leadership. Specifically, they point to the rule of Ivan the Terrible (1547–84), who came to power in the decades following Russia's final independence from Mongol control. Consolidating power in Moscow rather than Kiev, Ivan began to assert Russia's authority over that of foreign rulers and began to destroy any government institutions that obstructed his consolidation of personal power. Though Ivan is viewed in much of Russian history as the unifier of the country, many historians see in him the seeds of repressive and capricious rule.[1] Whatever his legacy, in Ivan's rule we see the emergence of a single Russian emperor, or **tsar** (or *czar*, from the Latin word *Caesar*), who exercised sovereignty over the nation's lands and aristocrats.

TIMELINE Political Development

1552–56	Ivan the Terrible conquers the Tatar khanates of Kazan and Astrakhan; establishes Russian rule over the lower and middle Volga River.
1689–1725	Peter the Great introduces reforms, including the subordination of the church, the creation of a regular conscript army and navy, and new government structures.
1798–1814	Russia intervenes in the French Revolution and the Napoleonic Wars.
1861	Edict of Emancipation ends serfdom.
1917	Monarchy is overthrown and a provisional government established; Bolsheviks in turn overthrow the provisional government.
1918–20	Civil war takes place between the Red Army and the White Russians, or anticommunists.
1938	Joseph Stalin consolidates power; purges begin.
1953	Stalin dies.
1985	Mikhail Gorbachev becomes general secretary and initiates economic and political reforms.
1991	Failed coup against Gorbachev leads to the collapse of the Soviet Union; Boris Yeltsin becomes president of independent Russia.
1993	Yeltsin suspends the parliament and calls for new elections; legislators barricade themselves inside the parliament building, and Yeltsin orders the army to attack parliament; Russians approve a new constitution, which gives the president numerous powers.
1994–96	In a war between Russia and the breakaway republic of Chechnya, Chechnya is invaded, and a cease-fire is declared.
1999	Yeltsin appoints Vladimir Putin prime minister and resigns from office; Putin becomes acting president.
1999	Russia reinvades Chechnya following a series of bomb explosions blamed on Chechen extremists.
2000	Putin is first elected as president.
2008	Medvedev becomes president; Putin becomes prime minister.
2012	Putin returns to presidency.
2014	Russian armed conflict with Ukraine and annexation of Crimea.

Ivan's death left Russia with an identity crisis. Did it belong to Europe, one of numerous rival states with a common history and culture? Or did differences in history, religion, and location mean that Russia was separate from the West? Some rulers, most notably Peter the Great (1689–1725), saw Westernization as a major goal. This view was typified in the relocation of the country's capital from Moscow to St. Petersburg, to place it closer to Europe (it was moved back to Moscow after the Russian Revolution of 1917). Peter consulted with numerous foreign advisers in his quest to modernize the country (particularly the military) and carry out administrative and educational reforms. In contrast, reactionaries such as Nicholas I (1825–55) were hostile to reforms. In Nicholas's case, this hostility was so great that in the last years of his reign even foreign travel was forbidden. Reforms, such as the emancipation of the serfs in 1861, proceeded over time but lagged behind the pace of changes in Europe. Industrialization came late, emerging in the 1880s and relying heavily on state intervention. This inconsistent modernization caused Russia to fall behind its international rivals.

THE SEEDS OF REVOLUTION

The growing disjunction between a largely agrarian and aristocratic society and a highly autonomous state and traditional monarchy would soon foster revolution. As Russia engaged in the great power struggles of the nineteenth and twentieth centuries, it was battered by the cost of war, and national discontent grew. In 1905, Russia experienced a series of domestic shocks in the form of protests by members of the growing working class, who had migrated to the cities during the rapid industrialization of the previous two decades. The Revolution of 1905 forced Nicholas II to institute a series of limited reforms, including the creation of a legislature (the **Duma**). Although these reforms did quell the revolt, they were not revolutionary (the changes themselves were limited), nor did they bring stability to Russia.

World War I was the final straw. The overwhelming financial and human costs of the war exacerbated domestic tensions, weakening rather than strengthening national unity. As the war ground on, Russia faced food shortages, public disturbances, and eventually a widespread military revolt. The tsar was forced to step down in March of 1917, and a noncommunist, republican leadership took control, unwisely choosing to remain in the war. This provisional government had little success asserting its authority. As disorder and public confusion grew, Communist revolutionaries, led by Vladimir Ilyich Lenin (1870–1924), staged a coup d'état. This was no mass rebellion but rather an overthrow of those in power by a small, disciplined force. After a subsequent civil war against anticommunist forces, Lenin began transforming Russia, which was renamed the Soviet Union, the first Communist state in world history.[2]

THE RUSSIAN REVOLUTION UNDER LENIN

In many aspects, Lenin's takeover was a radical, revolutionary event, but in other ways the new Communist government fell back on the conservative institutions of traditional Russian rule. Under Lenin, local revolutionary authority (in the form of **soviets**, or workers' councils) was pushed aside, though it was given superficial recognition in the new name of the country: the Union of Soviet Socialist Republics (USSR). Similarly, although the Communist Party embraced Russia's multinational character by creating a federal system around its major ethnic groups, the new republics had little power. Authority was vested solely in the Communist Party, which controlled all government and state activity. Alternative political parties and private media were banned. A secret-police force, the **Cheka**, was formed to root out opposition; it later became the **KGB**, the body that would control domestic dissent and supervise overseas surveillance. The "commanding heights" of industry were nationalized—seized by the state in the name of the people. Managing all of this new-found power was a growing bureaucratic system composed of the *nomenklatura*—the select list or class of Communist Party members to whom politically influential jobs in the state, society, or economy were given. The Communist state took on the enormous task of managing the basic economic and social life of the country. Such tasks necessitated the state's high degree of capacity and autonomy.

Yet even under Lenin's harsh leadership, the Soviet state did not reach its zenith. For the Soviet leadership, 1917 was intended simply as a first step in a worldwide process. One historian writes evocatively of Soviet telephone operators ready to receive the call that revolution had broken out elsewhere in the world in response to their triumph.[3]

As the years passed without other successful revolutions, the Soviet Union had to confront the possibility that it alone might have to serve as the vanguard of world revolution. Its focus had to shift so that domestic politics, not spreading revolution, would be paramount. Yet many old revolutionaries (those who had taken part in the 1917 events) had little interest in the day-to-day affairs of the party and state. One exception was Joseph Stalin (1879–1953), whose power over the party grew after Lenin died. By appointing loyal followers to positions of power and slowly consolidating his control over party and state institutions through increasingly brutal means, Stalin was able to force out other revolutionary leaders. One by one, those who had fought alongside Lenin in the revolution were removed from power, demoted, exiled, imprisoned, and/or executed.

STALINISM, TERROR, AND THE TOTALITARIAN STATE

By the late 1930s, Stalin had consolidated control over the Soviet party-state and was thus free to construct a totalitarian regime that reached across politics, economics, and society. When a central planning bureaucracy was created to allocate resources and distribute goods, the last vestiges of private property were wiped away.

Power was thus centralized to a degree unknown before Soviet rule.[4] This growing power of the bureaucratic elite was enforced by the secret police, who turned their attention to anyone suspected of opposing Stalin's rule, whether outside the party or within. Estimates are that more than a million people were imprisoned in the 1930s, and nearly 1 million were executed. Stalin's power was solidified through a cult of personality that portrayed him as godlike, incapable of error, and infinitely wise.

STABILITY AND STAGNATION AFTER STALIN

With Stalin's death in 1953, the Soviet leadership moved away from its uses of unbridled terror and centralized power, and Stalin's excesses were publicly criticized to a certain extent. The basic features of the Soviet system, however, remained in place. Power was vested in the **Politburo**, the ruling cabinet of the Communist Party. At its head was the general secretary, the de facto leader of the country. Government positions, such as national legislators, the head of the government, and the head of state, were controlled and staffed by the Communist Party and simply implemented the decisions of the Politburo. The economy also remained under the control of a central planning bureaucracy, and although Russians were no longer terrorized, security forces continued to suppress public dissent through arrest and harassment. All basic aspects of Soviet life were decided by the *nomenklatura*. The party elite became, in essence, a new ruling class.

For a time, this system worked. The state was able to industrialize rapidly by controlling and directing all resources and labor. Moreover, in its infancy, Soviet rule enjoyed a high degree of legitimacy among the public. Even in the darkest years of

Stalin's terror, citizens saw the creation of roads, railways, massive factories, homes, and schools, as well as the installation of electricity, where none had existed before. The Soviet people saw their standard of living increase dramatically.

But by the 1960s, some party leaders had begun to realize that a system so controlled by a central bureaucracy was becoming too institutionalized and conservative to allow for necessary change or innovation. General Secretary Nikita Khrushchev, who took office in 1953 after Stalin's death, made an initial attempt at reform. But Khrushchev was thwarted by the party-state bureaucracy and forced from his position by the Politburo in 1964. He was replaced by Leonid Brezhnev (1964–82), who rejected further reform and placated the *nomenklatura* by assuring them that their power and privileges were protected. Under these conditions, economic growth slowed. In the 1960s, it was still possible to believe that Soviet development might match or even surpass that of the West. But by the 1980s, it was clear that, in many areas, the Soviet Union was in fact stagnating or falling behind.

THE FAILURE OF REFORM AND THE COLLAPSE OF THE SOVIET STATE

Upon Brezhnev's death in 1982, a new generation of political thinkers emerged from the wings seeking to transform the Soviet state. Among its members was Mikhail Gorbachev, who became general secretary in 1985. Unconnected to the Stalinist period, Gorbachev believed that the Soviet state could be revitalized through the dual policies of **glasnost** ("political openness") and **perestroika** ("economic restructuring"). Gorbachev believed that a limited rollback of the state from public life would encourage citizen participation and weaken the *nomenklatura*'s powerful grip. Similarly, it was thought that economic reforms would increase incentives (like better pay) and reduce the role of central planning, thus improving the quality and quantity of goods.

In hindsight, we can see that the attack on state power was disastrous for the Soviet system. Gorbachev unleashed forces he could not control, which led to divisive struggles inside and outside the party. Nationalism grew among the many ethnic groups in the various republics, and some went so far as to demand independence. Critics attacked the corruption and incompetence of the party, calling for greater democracy, and others demanded a greater role for market forces and private property. Still others were disoriented by the changes and upset by the implication that the Soviet past had in fact been a historical dead end.[5]

Party leaders became polarized over the pace and scope of reform. Among them was **Boris Yeltsin** (1931–2007), an early protégé of Gorbachev's who was sidelined as his calls for change grew more radical. Though ejected from the Politburo, Yeltsin was elected president of the Russian Soviet Socialist Republic (the largest republic in the ostensibly federal Soviet system). The moderate Gorbachev was now under attack from two sides: by Yeltsin and other reformers who faulted Gorbachev's unwillingness to embrace radical change, and by conservatives and reactionaries who condemned his betrayal of communism. In August 1991, a group of antireform conservatives sought to stop the disintegration of Soviet institutions by mounting a coup d'état against Gorbachev, hoping that the party-state and the military would join their ranks. After the conspirators placed Gorbachev under arrest, Yeltsin led the resistance, famously denouncing the takeover while standing atop a tank. The army refused to back the coup, and it unraveled within two days.

As the coup collapsed, so did Gorbachev's political authority. Yeltsin seized the opportunity to ban the Communist Party, effectively destroying what remained of Gorbachev's political base. In December 1991, Yeltsin and the leaders of the various Soviet republics dissolved the Soviet Union, and Yeltsin became president of a new, independent Russia. He held this position until 1999, when he named his prime minister, the otherwise unknown Vladimir Putin, acting president. Putin won the presidential elections in 2000 and again in 2004; he stepped down due to term limits in 2008. However, he retained power as prime minister and was reelected as president in 2012.

Political Regime

It is hard to speak of Russia as even an illiberal democracy, since it has few elements of democracy that in fact function to any meaningful degree. Whereas in the 1990s, democratic institutions and civic organizations were weak and poorly institutionalized, in the Putin era they have been effectively stifled. In Russia now, it is difficult to point to any institutions among state or society that are allowed to contribute to democratic activity in a substantive way. As we consider Russia's political regime, therefore, we need to keep in mind the extent to which any of the powers or responsibilities elucidated by the constitution match politics in reality.

POLITICAL INSTITUTIONS

THE CONSTITUTION The Russian constitution is a document born of violent conflict. Independent Russia emerged in the aftermath of a failed coup d'état by opponents of radical reform. This history is different from the recent history of most other Eastern European Communist countries, where Communist leaders were removed from power through public protest and elections. Although the Soviet state was dissolved, many elements of the old regime, including its political leaders, remained

---

INFOCUS **Essential Political Features**

- **Legislative–executive system**: Semi-presidential
- **Legislature**: Federal Assembly
  - **Lower house**: State Duma
  - **Upper house**: Federation Council
- **Unitary or federal division of power**: Federal
- **Main geographic subunits**: Republics, provinces, territories, autonomous districts, federal cities (Moscow and St. Petersburg)
- **Electoral system for lower house**: Proportional representation
- **Electoral system for upper house**: Appointed by local executive and legislature
- **Chief judicial body**: Constitutional Court

intact and in power. Boris Yeltsin thus faced a set of political institutions that were largely unchanged from those of the previous era. This carryover led to conflict. As Yeltsin sought increased reform, the parliament grew so hostile that it sought to block his policies (including constitutional reform) and impeach him. In September 1993, Yeltsin responded by dissolving the parliament. His parliamentary opponents barricaded themselves in their offices, attempted to seize control of the national television station, and called for the army to depose the president. The army sided with Yeltsin, however, containing his opposition and suppressing the uprising with force. This support paved the way for Yeltsin to write a new constitution, which was ratified in 1993. Though the new constitution formally swept away the old legislative order, it could hardly be described as an auspicious beginning for democracy because it facilitated the development of a system that emphasized presidential power.

THE BRANCHES OF GOVERNMENT

THE KREMLIN: THE PRESIDENT AND THE PRIME MINISTER For centuries, Russians have referred to executive power, whether in the form of the tsar or the general secretary, as the Kremlin. Dating back to the eleventh century, the physical structure known as the Kremlin is a fortress in the heart of Moscow that has historically been the seat of state power. Today, much of the Kremlin's power is vested in the hands of the presidency, as elaborated in the 1993 constitution. That constitution created a powerful office through which the president could press for economic and political changes despite parliamentary opposition. Under Yeltsin and Putin, the result has been a semi-presidential system in which the president served as head of state while a prime minister served as head of government. Power is divided between the two offices, but the president has held an overwhelming amount of executive power. Since 2012, the president is directly elected to serve a six-year term (before then, presidential terms were only four years). The president may serve no more than two consecutive terms and can be removed only through impeachment. Vladimir Putin was elected in 2000 after serving as Boris Yeltsin's last prime minister, and he was reelected in 2004 after facing little serious competition for the office. His successor, Dimitri Medvedev, was similarly selected by Putin to run for the office in 2008. Medvedev won easily, since other candidates were effectively barred from running for the office. Putin returned to the presidency in 2012, following an election against a set of weak opposition candidates.

The president's powers are numerous. The president, not parliament, chooses and dismisses the prime minister and other members of the cabinet. The lower house of parliament, the State Duma, may reject the president's nominee, but if it does so three times, the president must dissolve the Duma and call for new elections. The president cannot, however, dissolve the Duma either in the year following parliamentary elections or in the last six months of his term. The president also appoints leaders to eight federal districts that constitute all of Russia, which allows him to oversee the work of local authorities.

The president may propose and veto bills, and, just as important, he can issue decrees—laws that do not require legislative approval, are often not made public, and may not be challenged by citizens in the courts. Putin has often used the power of the decree to directly conduct foreign or domestic policy, such as withdrawing from the International Criminal Court or to reorganize federal districts (both of which occurred in 2016).[6]

Another source of power lies in the president's control of important segments of the state. The president has direct control over the Foreign Ministry, the Defense Ministry, and the Interior Ministry (which handles the police and domestic security), as well as over the armed forces. He also controls the successor to the KGB, the **Federal Security Service (FSB)**, which manages domestic intelligence and is viewed by many as the main political actor in Russia, alongside Putin. Presidential control over these ministries and services allows the office a great deal of influence in foreign affairs and domestic security.

In contrast to that of the president, the prime minister's role is to supervise those ministries not under presidential control and propose legislation to parliament that upholds the president's policy goals. The prime minister also promulgates the national budget. The Russian prime minister and other members of the cabinet, unlike their counterparts in many other parliamentary systems, are not appointed from and need not reflect the relative powers of the various parties in parliament. Because of the president's ability to choose the prime minister and other members of the cabinet, there is less need to form a government that represents the largest parties in parliament.

The appointment of Putin to be prime minister "under" Medvedev raised many questions about the nature of the semi-presidential system in Russia. In advance of the 2008 presidential elections, Putin made it clear that he expected to become prime minister in return for his selection of Medvedev to run for president, and he continued to dominate politics from what was ostensibly the weaker office. This led to a great deal of confusion about where executive power really lay, and Medvedev's decision to step down after one term only reinforced the sense that power is more vested in an individual than any particular office. Putin's personal authority has trumped

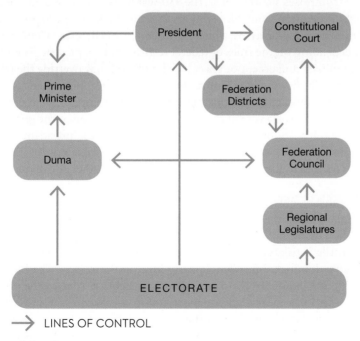

LINES OF CONTROL

Structure of the Government

A 2012 protest by the Communist Party against Putin's reelection. As the banner suggests, Putin (on the left) will hold office another 12 years, when an elderly Medvedev (right) could again return to the presidency until 2030.

institutional authority, rendering problematic our understanding of Russian politics based on formal institutions like the constitution.

THE LEGISLATURE Russia's bicameral parliament is known officially as the Federal Assembly. It comprises a lower house, the 450-seat State Duma, and an upper house, the 170-seat Federation Council. Members of the Duma, the more powerful of the two houses, serve five-year terms, while members of the Federation Council serve varied terms depending on the rules of federal territory they represent. The Duma has the right to initiate and accept or reject legislation and may override the president's veto with a two-thirds vote. The Duma also approves the appointment of the prime minister, though repeated rejections can lead to its dissolution. As in other legislatures, the Duma can call a vote of no confidence in opposition to the prime minister and his government. Should a no-confidence vote pass, the president may simply ignore the decision. If a second such vote passes within three months, however, the president is obliged to dismiss the prime minister and cabinet or call for new Duma elections.

Another area in which the Duma can theoretically wield power is in the drafting of legislation. During the Yeltsin administration, the majority of legislation originated in the Duma, much of it dealing with substantial public issues. However, under Putin the legislature's powers have become increasingly theoretical. As the Duma became dominated by a single party loyal to Putin (see "The Electoral System," p. 429), it has receded from any significant political role, to the point where some view it as little more than a rubber stamp to validate the president's rule. Virtually no legislation submitted by the government is opposed by the Duma, and vice versa. This does not mean that the Duma is inactive, however, as it remains a forum for legislators to lobby for their own preferences and also for the government to provide the appearance of democracy. In fact, the Duma has been described as a "mad printer," for the speed at which it produces legislation, much of which is ambiguous and/or focused on limiting personal freedoms.[7]

As the upper house, the **Federation Council** holds even less power than the Duma. The Federation Council primarily serves to represent local interests and act as a guarantor of the constitution. The body represents all of the 85 federal administrative units, and each unit has two representatives. Since 2002, one representative has been selected by the governor of each region and another by the regional legislature (see the discussion of "Local Government," p. 430). Although the Federation Council does not produce legislation, it must approve bills that deal with certain issues, including taxation and the budget. If the Federation Council rejects legislation (which rarely occurs), the Duma may override the upper house with a two-thirds vote. The Federation Council also theoretically has the ability to impeach the president as well as to approve or reject presidential appointments to the Constitutional Court, declarations of war and martial law, and international treaties. As with the Duma, the Federation Council does not serve as a particularly powerful institution inside the Russian state. Even when legislation goes against the interest of the regions, representatives rarely oppose it.

THE JUDICIARY One of many tasks Russia faces in the coming decades is the establishment of the rule of law. By this, we mean a system in which the law is applied equally and predictably, and no individual is exempt from its strictures. Before Communist rule, Russia did not develop any real traditions of a law-bound state: the tsar acted above the law, viewing the state, society, and economy as his subjects and property. This situation continued into the Soviet era.

At the top of the Russian legal structure lies the **Constitutional Court**. First developed under Mikhail Gorbachev's reforms in the late-Soviet era, the court has 19 members, nominated by the president and confirmed by the Federation Council. As in other countries, the court is empowered to rule on such matters as international treaties, relations between branches of government, violations of civil rights, and impeachment of the president. It has the power of both abstract review (the ability to rule on constitutional issues even when a case has not been brought before it) and concrete review (the ability to rule on specific cases). One role the Constitutional Court does *not* play is that of a court of last appeal for criminal cases; this is the responsibility of the Supreme Court. As in the case of the legislature, the court has not played an activist role. In 2014, following Russia's invasion of the Ukrainian region of Crimea, the court quickly recognized Crimea's annexation. It similarly approved legislation that requires nonprofit organizations that engage in influencing public policy (such as environmental and LGBTQ issues) and receive foreign funding to be registered as "foreign agents."[8] The Rule of Law Index, which looks at such things as constraints on government, regulatory enforcement, and criminal justice, ranked Russia at 92 out of 113 countries surveyed. This is below China (80) and Iran (86).[9]

THE ELECTORAL SYSTEM

Like Russia's other institutions, its electoral structure has changed dramatically over the past 20 years. Candidates for the president must be nominated by a party represented in the Duma. If they are independent candidates, they must collect 2 million signatures in support of their candidacy. This is a formidable task that eliminates many potential contenders. Presidential elections are relatively straightforward: if no candidate wins a majority in the first round, the top two candidates compete against each other in a second round. A president can serve no more than two consecutive terms, though as we've seen in the case of Putin, this can mean simply stepping aside for one term and then running again. In 2000 and 2004, Putin won a majority (over 70 percent in 2004), eliminating the need for a runoff. In 2012, when he returned to office, he won 63 percent of the vote (amid numerous accusations of voter fraud).

The Duma has also held regular elections. Between 1990 and 1993, these were conducted using a plurality system of single-member districts (SMDs), as in the United Kingdom and the United States. With the 1993 constitution, however, Russia adopted a mixed system similar to that found in Japan and Germany. That is, half the seats in the Duma were elected through a plurality system, and the other half were selected in multimember districts (MMDs) using proportional representation (PR), in which the share of the vote given to a party roughly matches the percentage of seats it is allotted.

Under Putin, this system was again changed to consolidate political power. In 2007, Duma elections were held solely under PR to eliminate individual candidates not under party control. Interestingly, 2016 Duma elections returned to a mixed system. Why? Some suggest that a return to single-member districts was intended to provide to the public a greater sense of direct influence over the Duma (though as we noted, it remains a weak body). Perhaps more importantly, reducing PR limits the ability of rival parties to gain a large foothold in the legislature. These explanations suggest that Putin and his ruling party, United Russia, do not take their hold over the Duma for granted.

LOCAL GOVERNMENT

One of the greatest battles within the institutional framework of Russia over the past 15 years has been between the central government and local authorities. Just as tensions between Soviet central power and the republics contributed to the dissolution of the Soviet Union, so, too, centrifugal tendencies have beset Russia since 1991. Like the Soviet Union that preceded it, Russia is a federal system with a bewildering array of more than 80 different regional bodies: 21 republics (22 if we include Crimea, seized from Ukraine in 2014), 46 *oblasts* ("provinces"), 9 *krays* ("territories"), 4 autonomous *okrugs* ("districts"), and the 2 federal cities of Moscow and St. Petersburg (3 if we include Sevastopol, the capital of Crimea).

Each of these bodies has different rights. The 21 republics, for example, represent particular non-Russian ethnic groups and enjoy greater rights, such as to have their own constitution and a state language alongside Russian. This difference is commonly termed **asymmetric federalism**—a system in which power is devolved unequally across the country and its constituent regions, often because of specific laws negotiated between a region and the central government. Each of the territories, regardless of its size or power, has its own governor and local Duma; as described earlier, the governor appoints one representative to the Federation Council, and the Duma appoints the other.

As in other areas, the Putin administration took several steps to reduce regional power and make the territories comply with national laws and legislation. In 2000, the government created federal districts (now eight in total) that encompass all of Russia and its constituent territories. Each district is headed by a presidential appointee, who serves to bring the local authorities more directly under presidential control.

Below the federal districts are governors for the different regional bodies. Since 2012, these have been directly elected, which, as with the electoral reforms for the Duma, were presented as a way for the public to have more direct control over those in power. In reality, as with the Duma the governorships are nominated by the Kremlin and filled by pro-Putin figures who often have little to no connection to the region they rule. The positions can be attractive to candidates, since they provide an opportunity for individuals to enrich themselves, while for the Kremlin they allow the government to maintain greater control over the regions and those it has placed in these offices.

These frequent changes have severely curtailed federalism in Russia, though local offices continue to have power. Many local mayors remain directly elected, and in large cities (such as Moscow and St. Petersburg), they can exercise a great deal of political clout. In 2013, prominent opposition figure Alexei Navalny ran for mayor of Moscow and won nearly 30 percent of the vote (perhaps more, depending on the degree of fraud). Navalny was subsequently arrested on charges of embezzlement and was again briefly detained in March 2017 due to his role in promoting anticorruption protests across the country. Clearly, Putin and his allies realize that local authority could reemerge as a significant threat to those in power. In the end, the role of the Kremlin in directing political elites from the executive down to the local level is indicative of what Putin termed "the power vertical," a centralized, top-down form of political control.[10]

Political Conflict and Competition

THE PARTY SYSTEM AND ELECTIONS

Russia has yet to see the formation of political parties with clear ideologies and political platforms. For most of the past 25 years, multiple parties have risen and disappeared between elections. Given Putin's consolidation of political power, it might be tempting to argue that the country has largely become once again a one-party state, controlled by the pro-Putin United Russia. However, the 2011 Duma elections proved a surprise. Despite United Russia's overwhelming control over the media and state, opposition parties captured nearly half of the seats in the Duma. This result challenges the view that United Russia or any one party is impervious, as well as the idea that Russian society is unable or unwilling to challenge those in power.[11]

THE PARTY OF POWER: UNITED RUSSIA Although so-called **parties of power** have since 1991 consistently represented the largest segment of parties in the Duma, they cannot be described in ideological terms. Russia's parties of power can be defined as those parties created by political elites to support those elites' political aspirations. Typically, these parties are highly personalized, lack specific ideologies or clear organizational qualities, and have been created by political elites during or following their time in office. For example, the Our Home Is Russia Party was created in advance of the 1995 Duma elections as a way to bolster support for Prime Minister Viktor Chernomyrdin and President Yeltsin. Subsequently, in the 1999 elections, Unity was created to bolster Putin's campaign. After Unity beat Fatherland–All Russia handily in the Duma elections, in 2001 the two parties merged to form **United Russia**. Drawing on Putin's popularity and the government's increased control over the electoral process, United Russia swept the 2003 elections and has won a majority of seats ever since (as well as extending its reach over local government). As of the 2016 elections, United Russia holds 344 of 450 Duma seats—a supermajority that gives it the ability to change the constitution without needing the support of any other party.

United Russia boasts a cult of personality around Putin, a youth wing that advances the cause of the party, and party membership as a means for individual access to important jobs in the state and economy. In that sense, Russia resembles a one-party state like Mexico prior to its democratization in the 1990s.[12] United Russia's campaign platforms have emphasized stability and conservatism, economic development (though this has receded as economic difficulties have mounted), and increasingly the restoration of the country as a "great power" in international politics. To contrast the country with what is portrayed as the immorality of the West (such as its support for LGBTQ rights), United Russia has also increasingly positioned itself as the defender of traditional values.

The 2007 Duma elections were widely regarded as evidence that Russia could no longer be considered democratic, even in the most generous definition of the term. The media, largely in the hands of the state, gave overwhelming support to United Russia. Observers concluded that the elections were not fair, did not meet basic standards for democratic procedures, and have become only more fraudulent over time.[13] And yet, in 2011, United Russia suffered a major upset when over half of the popular vote went to several opposition parties (though none represents significant opposition to the Kremlin). In 2016, United Russia managed to reclaim its dominant role in the Duma through a mixture of media control and harassment, but also public disenchantment with elections. Turnout was a record low at less than 50 percent. Whether this reflects the strength or weakness of United Russia is an open question.

COMMUNIST AND LEFTIST PARTIES Before the rise of United Russia, the strongest and most institutionalized party was the **Communist Party of the Russian Federation (CPRF)**, successor of the Soviet-era organization. In the 1995 elections, the CPRF reached its peak, becoming the largest single party in the Duma and raising the fear among many that the country would return to Communist rule. However, since that time, its vote share has declined to less than 15 percent. Even at that small level, it remains the second-largest party in the Duma.

The CPRF differs from most other postcommunist parties in Eastern Europe, many of which broke decisively from their Communist past in the 1990s and successfully recast themselves as social-democratic organizations. In contrast, the CPRF remains close to its Communist ideology and rejects Western capitalism and globalization. It also embraces the Stalinist period and has called for the return of the country to Stalinist ideals. The CPRF criticizes the government but is careful not to attack Putin. As the Russian population ages, the CPRF is losing its traditional base; however, as the second-largest party, it enjoys protest votes from those opposed to United Russia. There are some suggestions that the CPRF may find a new base of support among Russians born after 1991, who have struggled economically. If so, the party could reemerge as a real force in the future. For now, it runs a distant second behind United Russia, with just 13 percent of the vote in 2016 and 42 seats.

A much newer party, **A Just Russia**, can also be placed in the leftist camp. Founded in 2006 as a merger of several smaller parties, A Just Russia defines itself as a social-democratic party along European lines. Its platform emphasizes social justice and reducing inequality, and in general its ideological profile is perhaps clearer than any other party in the Duma. Unlike the CPRF, A Just Russia has been considered by many to be little more than a façade, supported (if not created) by the Kremlin to provide a veneer of multiparty democracy. But again, the 2011 Duma elections confounded many assumptions. A Just Russia came in third, with approximately 13 percent of the vote, and its more confrontational tone suggested that it might become a force in its own right. However, the party quickly resumed its loyalty to the Kremlin, expelling party members who had taken part in public demonstrations against Putin during the 2011 elections. In the 2016 elections, A Just Russia slipped to the smallest party in the Duma, with only 6 percent of the vote and 29 seats.

NATIONALIST PARTIES During the 1990s, one of the most infamous aspects of the Russian party spectrum was the strength of extreme nationalism. That faction is manifested by the ill-named **Liberal Democratic Party of Russia (LDPR)**, headed by Vladimir Zhirinovsky. Neither liberal nor democratic, the LDPR espouses a rhetoric of nationalism, xenophobia, and anti-Semitism, calling for such things as the reconstitution of the Soviet Union (perhaps by force) and exhibiting general hostility toward the West.

In the 1993 elections, many observers were shocked by the LDPR's electoral strength and its gain of 14 percent of the seats in the Duma. Subsequently, the LDPR's fortunes waned to the point where it barely met the 5 percent PR threshold in the 1999 elections. In recent elections, however, it has staged something of a comeback and is now the third-largest party in the Duma, with 39 seats. The survival of the party can be attributed in part to the LDPR's consistent support for Putin and his government; indeed, many observers suspect that the LDPR was created and is supported by the government to serve as a pseudo-opposition that can be controlled.[14]

LIBERAL PARTIES Despite Russia's move toward capitalism, liberalism has made relatively few inroads into political life, and even these have declined of late. During the 1990s, liberalism's standard bearer in Russia was the party **Yabloko**, whose pro-Western and pro-market economy stance drew support from white-collar workers and urban residents in the major cities. Never a major force, Yabloko has seen its electoral fortunes decline to such an extent that in recent Duma elections it has failed to gain a single seat in the legislature. In 2016, the party won less than 2 percent of the vote in the proportional representation portion of the ballot. It currently holds only a few seats in regional legislatures.

Why has liberalism found such rocky soil in Russia? Several factors are at work. First, given the historically statist and collectivist nature of Russian politics, a liberal political ideology is not likely to find a wide range of popular support. A 2011 survey, for example, showed that half of those questioned favored an increased role for government ownership of the economy; such views were not just among older Russians, but also those under age 29 as well as those with a university education (both of whom might be expected to do better in a private economy).[15] Infighting and a lack of strong leadership within liberal parties have not helped. Finally, worsening relations between Russia and the West have also served to tarnish liberalism as a foreign ideology associated with Russian subservience.

CIVIL SOCIETY

As with political parties, civil society in Russia developed in fits and starts. Before the 1917 Russian Revolution, civil society was weak, constrained by authoritarianism, feudalism, and low economic development. With the revolution, what little civil society did exist quickly came under control of the Soviet authorities, who argued that only the party could and should represent the "correct" interests of the population. With the advent of glasnost in the 1980s, however, civil society slowly began to reemerge.

After 1991, civil society grew dramatically in Russia. An array of movements and organizations filled the gaps left in the aftermath of one-party rule. However, during the Putin administration civil society came under state pressure and control, especially those groups that openly criticized the government. Tools to control civil society include the tax code, used to investigate sources of income; the process of registering with authorities, which can be made difficult; and police harassment and arrest on various charges ranging from tax evasion to divulging state secrets. Still, antigovernment protests in Russia in 2011, 2012, and again in 2017 suggested that there remained a current of social activism that could translate into a revived civil society. Not surprisingly, Putin's return to the presidency in 2012 ushered in a new wave of restrictions. All organizations that receive foreign funding must now be registered as "foreign agents," allowing for a high degree of state oversight and control and the possibility of fines and arrest for failing to follow state regulations. A corresponding new law on treason has further intimidated civic organization.[16]

Another notable effect of the restrictions on civil society is in the area of religion. As the Russian government has turned more toward nationalism as a source of legitimacy, it has also emphasized Orthodox Christianity as a central part of what makes Russia unique (and distinct from the West and Western liberalism). In turn, the Russian government has increasingly restricted the ability of many religious groups to proselytize, build seminaries, publish their literature, or run educational programs and has relied on anti-extremism legislation to justify these actions. The return of Orthodox Christianity as a quasi–state religion has been accompanied by attacks on liberal activism, such as the arrest of members of the punk band Pussy Riot, several of whose members were jailed in 2012 for two years on charges of religious hatred.[17]

Civil society has been restricted in Russia not just through direct government control but also through the means of expressing itself—specifically, the media. The collapse of communism saw the emergence of private Russian media that for the first time were able to speak critically on an array of issues. This is not to say that the media were truly independent; the most powerful segments of the media, such as radio and television, remained in the hands of the state or came under the control of wealthy individuals with ties to Yeltsin. Similarly, the media's owners came to support Putin during his consolidation of power, viewing him as the successor to Yeltsin who would preserve their power. Despite this support, Putin soon put strong economic pressure on much of the independent media, employing economic and legal tactics to acquire them and curb their editorial independence.

During the past decade, all of the largest private television stations have come under direct state ownership or have become indirect state-controlled firms. The domestic media have become a consistent purveyor of conspiracy theories that tend to center around the efforts of the United States and the European Union to destroy Russia. Such arguments were especially pronounced during Russia's war with Ukraine. Russia denied the presence of its own troops in Crimea and eastern

Ukraine while arguing that U.S. troops were on the ground. Russia even claimed that the Malaysian Airline flight destroyed over Ukraine had been shot down by the CIA.

Those who continue to openly oppose the government find that their livelihoods and even their lives can be at stake. Alexei Navalny, a lawyer and high-profile leader in 2011 antigovernment protests and candidate for Moscow mayor, was arrested in 2012 on embezzlement charges and held under house arrest for a year. Boris Nemtsov, a former deputy prime minister under Yeltsin and an outspoken critic of Putin, was assassinated near the Kremlin in 2015. Since 1992, more than 50 journalists have been killed in Russia. In terms of press freedom, Russia is ranked 148 out of 180 countries by the organization Reporters without Borders.[18]

Society

ETHNIC AND NATIONAL IDENTITY

Nearly 80 percent of the Russian population is ethnically Russian, and although there are scores of minority groups, none represents more than 4 percent of the population. These minorities include other Slavic peoples, indigenous Siberians who are related to the Inuit of North America, and many others whose communities were absorbed into Russia as part of its imperial expansion over time. And as we mentioned earlier, Russia is historically dominated by a single religious faith, Orthodox Christianity, a branch of Christianity that is separate from the Roman Catholicism and Protestantism that dominate Europe.

NATIONAL IDENTITY AND CITIZENSHIP Russia's relative homogeneity has not helped it avoid ethnic conflict. As in many other countries, some of Russia's ethnic groups have developed nationalist aspirations and seek greater autonomy from the central authorities, even to the point of outright independence. Serious ethnic conflicts have been most prominent among non-Russian populations in the mountainous region known as the Caucasus, in southwestern Russia, near the Black Sea and Turkey. This area is home to a diverse mixture of non-Slavic peoples with distinct languages, customs, and religious faiths. Whereas only about 15 percent of the Russian population is Muslim, Islam is the dominant faith in many parts of the Caucasus.

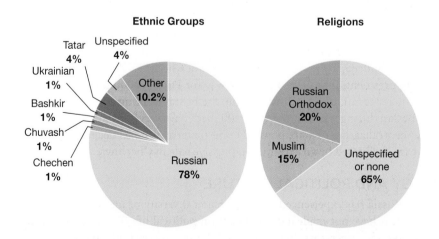

Ethnic Groups

Tatar 4%
Unspecified 4%
Ukrainian 1%
Bashkir 1%
Chuvash 1%
Chechen 1%
Other 10.2%
Russian 78%

Religions

Russian Orthodox 20%
Muslim 15%
Unspecified or none 65%

The Caucasus

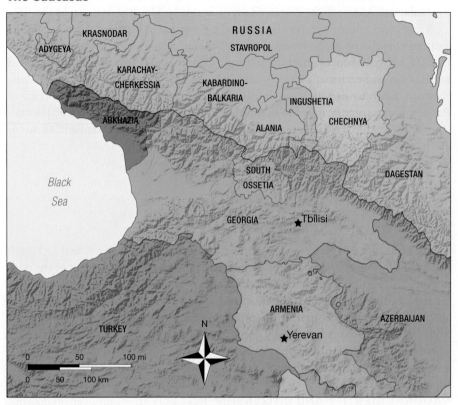

Source: University of Texas Austin, www.lib.utexas.edu/maps/commonwealth/chechnya_rev01.jpg (accessed 1/2/09).

Most notable is the case of **Chechnya**. With the collapse of the Soviet Union in 1991, the various republics broke off to form independent states. Chechnya, however, was not a republic in its own right, but rather part of now-independent Russia. Many Chechens believed that they, too, should have the right of independence and so began to agitate for an independent state. The conflict eventually led to outright war between Russian military forces and Chechen rebels, during which much of the Chechen capital was demolished and tens of thousands of civilians were killed or left homeless. During the mid-1990s, an uneasy peace allowed Chechnya to function as a de facto independent country. In 1999, however, Russian forces reinvaded Chechnya in the aftermath of a series of apartment house bombings in Russia attributed to Chechen rebels. Indeed, it was the second invasion of Chechnya, during Putin's tenure as acting president, that helped pave the way for Putin's 2000 presidential victory. Subsequent terror attacks, most notably the hostage taking at an elementary school in Beslan during which more than 300 died, have served as justification for the further centralization of state power. Domestic terrorism has declined over the past five years, facilitated by an extremely repressive rule in Chechnya.

IDEOLOGY AND POLITICAL CULTURE

Since 1991, Russia has experienced a much greater diversity of ideas, but in many ways those ideas have not made a deep impact on political life. This is particularly true in the case of democratic values. The World Values Survey finds that a majority of citizens are uninterested in politics, would never attend a peaceful demonstration, and show low levels of social trust.

What values, then, can we speak of in Russia today? During the past decade, we have seen the growing importance of nationalism as a central political value in Russia. This is not surprising; in a number of postcommunist countries, the decline of communism has meant that leaders have attempted to recast political legitimacy around the idea of patriotism and nationalism. In Russia, the government has actively promoted this trend by evoking nostalgia for the country's superpower status and by asserting that Russia is not truly Western but somehow different (and thus not subject to such Western notions as pluralism). This sense of restoring a "great Russia" has found an eager audience among many Russians. Most obvious in this regard was Russian involvement in the Ukrainian crisis in 2014, which led to open warfare in the east along the Russia border and the Russian invasion and annexation of Ukrainian Crimea. While international sanctions (because of Russia's role in Ukraine) and other economic challenges have weakened the country's standard of living, support for Putin's domestic and foreign policies remains high. Is this a function of a highly institutionalized political culture, or the government's control over the media? Some suggest it is the latter, rather than the former.[19]

Political Economy

Like other former communist countries, Russia undertook a series of dramatic reforms in the 1990s to privatize state assets and free up market forces. Looking to the lessons of Poland and acting on the advice of Western economic advisers, Russia opted for a course of **shock therapy**, rapidly dismantling central planning and freeing up prices with the hope that these actions would stimulate competition and the creation of new businesses. The immediate result was a wave of hyperinflation: in

The Moscow skyline. In the foreground is the Kremlin. In the background is the Moscow International Business Center, whose growth reflects the influx of oil revenues over the past decades.

1992 alone, the inflation rate was over 2,000 percent. Savings were wiped out, the economy sank into recession, and tensions between President Boris Yeltsin and the parliament deepened, helping to foster the violent clash between the two branches of government in 1993. The gross domestic product (GDP) contracted dramatically; only in the late 1990s did it begin to grow again.

During the late 1990s, Russia began the process of privatization, which was equally problematic. A small number of new businessmen quickly emerged from various ranks of society. Taking advantage of the economic environment to start new businesses and buy old ones, they amassed an enormous amount of wealth in the process. This group of businessmen, who came to be known as the *oligarchs*, were noted for their control of large amounts of the Russian economy (including the media), their close ties to the Yeltsin administration, and the accusations of corruption surrounding their rise to power.

The problem of the oligarchs was compounded in 1996, when the government instituted the loans-for-shares program. Strapped for cash (and fearful of a Communist Party victory in the 1996 presidential elections), the Yeltsin administration chose to borrow funds from the oligarchs in return for shares in those businesses that had not yet been sold off by the state—in particular, the lucrative natural resources industry and the energy sector.

To be fair, Russia's ongoing economic problems are not simply the result of the economic reform policies of the 1990s. Many of these problems are a function and legacy of a Soviet order that had reached a crisis stage, a condition that any set of policies would have had difficulty confronting. Still, the economic reforms of the 1990s left Russia in a tough situation as Putin came to power. The government faced high rates of poverty, a great deal of inequality, the disproportionate power of the oligarchs, widespread corruption and organized crime, and an inefficient state. During the 1990s, the country's GDP declined by around 40 percent.

What has changed in the Russian economy? One of Putin's first steps was to act against the oligarchs and divest them of power. The destruction of the oligarchs was extremely popular among the Russian public, but their elimination did not lead to greater economic transparency. Many assets were renationalized and brought under state control, but in other cases, ownership is murky. A large portion of state firms have been partly or entirely redistributed among the *siloviki* who are close to Putin, forming a new economic elite around the security services. The economic system can be viewed as dominated by a set of factions composed of *siloviki* and other elites who support Putin while competing with one another. If anything, the Russian political economy has become highly patrimonial, and Putin uses his position to provide economic access to his inner circle in return for their loyalty.

When Putin returned to the presidency following his earlier terms as president and his stint as prime minister, he could point to a number of economic successes. The country has enjoyed several years of economic growth after many years of stagnation. As per capita GDP has risen sharply and poverty has declined, Russia has also seen the emergence of a new middle and upper class. Its per capita income at purchasing power parity (PPP) is now similar to Chile's and Argentina's. In short, the economic situation is better than at any time since the collapse of the Soviet Union.

Labor Force by Occupation

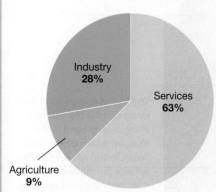

Industry
28%

Services
63%

Agriculture
9%

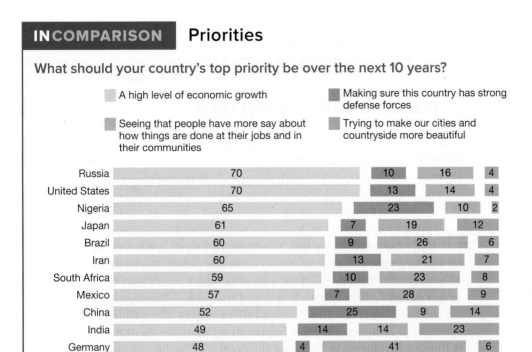

INCOMPARISON · **Priorities**

What should your country's top priority be over the next 10 years?

☐ A high level of economic growth

■ Making sure this country has strong defense forces

☐ Seeing that people have more say about how things are done at their jobs and in their communities

☐ Trying to make our cities and countryside more beautiful

Country				
Russia	70	10	16	4
United States	70	13	14	4
Nigeria	65	23	10	2
Japan	61	7	19	12
Brazil	60	9	26	6
Iran	60	13	21	7
South Africa	59	10	23	8
Mexico	57	7	28	9
China	52	25	9	14
India	49	14	14	23
Germany	48	4	41	6
France	40	7	40	12
United Kingdom	38	12	43	7

Source: Data for Brazil, France, India, Iran, South Africa, and Great Britain from World Values Survey 2005–09. All other data from World Values Survey 2010–14.

However, we should be clear about the sources of this economic progress: most of the country's exports are oil, gas, and metal, all of which benefited from a dramatic growth in the international markets. These resources have provided the overwhelming majority of the country's GDP and government revenues. Many investors, foreign and Russian, are deterred by the high degree of corruption and political intervention in many areas of the economy, and have been further scared off by the war with Ukraine and subsequent international sanctions. Small and medium-size businesses are similarly hindered by bureaucracy and bribery. Finally, the prominence of the *siloviki* in the economy has led to increasing inequality. Russia boasts 112 billionaires, which is particularly striking given the relatively small size of the GDP, both total and per capita. One result of the concentration of wealth and limited opportunities has been a marked emigration of the well educated. According to one account, 350,000 individuals, many of them professionals, left Russia in 2015—a tenfold increase from 2010.[20]

Russia appears to be moving toward a "resource trap" economy like those found in Iran and Saudi Arabia. The argument is that where natural resources are a major part of the economy and owned by the state, they run the risk of giving the state and government too much economic power while stifling other forms of economic development.[21] Declining natural resources or demand for those resources could eventually undermine Russia's economic progress. The danger is not immediate, for the Russian state sits on massive reserves of wealth built up over the past decade. But slower economic growth could prevent Russia from breaking out of a middle-tier level of development. Could this generate a gap between consumer expectations and economic reality and undermine the current regime?

Current Issues In Russia

RUSSIA AND CENTRAL ASIA: A NEW "SILK ROAD" OR THE OLD "GREAT GAME"?

In the early nineteenth century, both Russia and the United Kingdom expanded their power into the Caucasus and Central Asia. The case of the United Kingdom is more familiar to us, because we recall Britain's control over India and its largely unsuccessful attempt to conquer Afghanistan (in which large numbers of British soldiers died). What fewer people (at least non-Russians) recall is Russia's expanding, and relatively late, role in this region during that same period. The contest between these two powers was called in the West, somewhat glibly, the "Great Game." This conflict intensified further as both Russia and the United Kingdom gained direct and indirect control over the fragmenting Persian empire (the ensuing contest would later come to influence the 1979 Iranian Revolution; see the Iran case). Although the Russian Revolution in 1917 and the decline of the British Empire after World War II limited the conflict between these two powers, the notion of a contest between superpowers for this region never really came to an end.

More specifically, the United States usurped Britain's role as a player in the region, and the conflict shifted to one between Russia and the United States. Soviet intervention in Afghanistan in 1979 led to the American arming of anti-Soviet guerrillas and the rise of Al Qaeda. The breakup of the Soviet Union in 1991 fostered conflicts, fueled by ethnic and religious divisions, across the newly independent states in the Caucasus and Central Asia. The September 11, 2001, attacks brought the United States directly into the region through its occupation of Afghanistan and its increased role in Central Asia.

The United States' role in the Great Game, however, is on the wane. Military forces in Afghanistan are drawn down, and the locus of conflict has shifted westward to Iraq and Syria. The constant actor remains Russia, which since 1991 has sought to retain or regain influence over its lost republics in the Caucasus and Central Asia. The new map of the Great Game appears to have moved east, to the countries of Central Asia (such as Kazakhstan, Kyrgyzstan, and Uzbekistan). These countries share a number of similarities. First, they have had little success in democratization since 1991, and power has remained directly in the hands of the Soviet-era leaders. Second, many of them are ethnically diverse, have weak national identities, and have faced serious violent conflict as a result. Most Central Asian states are nominally Islamic, and though religion was suppressed under Soviet rule, Islam—and sometimes, radical variants of it—has surfaced. Finally, the region contains significant deposits of oil and gas.

Now other, new players are entering this game. The first and most important is China, which also shares a border with some of these same Central Asian countries. Since 1991, China has become a major economic actor in the region, in some ways overshadowing the Russian presence. As China has grown, it has looked for energy to fuel this development, and accordingly invested billions of dollars in developing oil, gas, and hydropower across the region, and in transmission and pipelines to carry this energy to China. It has also invested in mining projects to work deposits of gold, uranium, and other metals. Unlike other investors, China has both the industrial and political capacity to operate in uncertain environments—for example, it initiated a major mining project in Afghanistan. Finally, much like other parts of the world, China has become a major exporter of finished goods and consumer products, and Chinese businesses dominate markets in much of Central Asia.

India, too, is showing growing involvement in the region, though at a much lower level than China. India and Pakistan have a long-standing rivalry over Afghanistan, and India has promoted the construction of a network of roads, railways, and pipelines linking Central Asia to its own markets and growing energy needs. India has spoken of this linkage as a "New Silk Road," replacing the metaphor of the Great Game (in which India was a pawn) with the historical analogy of pathways between East and West. This vision would link Central Asia with South Asia, Europe, and the Middle East.

One of the first statements of Putin's new administration articulated Russia's ambitions in the struggle over Central Asia. Putin called for a "Eurasian union" that would remove all barriers to trade, capital, and labor movements among its members. He asserted that this integration was "not about re-creating the USSR," but rather about seeking "a powerful supranational union that can become one of the poles of today's world."[22] The **Eurasian Economic Union (EAEU)** formally came into force in 2015, with Russia joined by Kazakhstan, Belarus, Armenia, and Kyrgyzstan. Ukraine's decision not to join the union in favor of closer ties with the European Union was a central factor in the 2014 war. Given the Ukrainian crisis, the EAEU might seem to be an attempt to project Russian power in competition with Europe. However, its effects may well be felt in Asia instead.

What are the implications of a Russian-led integration, and how might it affect the role of major powers in the region? First, it is not clear that even if the Eurasian Economic Union expands and deepens, it will have the kind of power (or extend

Vladimir Putin (right), Kazakh president Nursultan Nazarbayev (middle), and Belarusian president Alexander Lukashenko (left) shake hands after signing an agreement to establish the Eurasian Economic Union in May 2014.

Russia's authority in the way) we might expect. The Eurasian Economic Union may become a vehicle for greater integration in such areas as trade, but the problems of weak states, ethnic conflict, regional rivalries, and low levels of economic development that plague Central Asia are a formidable barrier to integration. Whether Russia has the ability and leadership to resolve these issues remains to be seen. Nor is it clear how much Russia itself has to offer to the member states of the Eurasian Union beyond access to its own markets.

That said, many Central Asian states are concerned about the rapid expansion of China into the region. China's economic influence over markets and national resources in the region, it is feared, will inevitably turn into Chinese political power, comprising the sovereignty of states in the region. Russia's smaller economy (its total GDP is less than a quarter of China's) may mean that states in the region see Russian influence through the Eurasian Economic Union as less of a threat, and rather as a bulwark against Chinese encroachment. Many Central Asian leaders are concerned that liberalized economic relations with China will lead to Chinese economic control. In contrast, many Central Asians remain tightly connected to Russia through a shared history—though this relationship has its own ethnic concerns, given that countries like Kazakhstan are home to several million ethnic Russians. In the long run, a successful integration could bring Russia and China into more direct competition than at any time since the collapse of the Soviet Union. A new Great Game may define regional dynamics in the decades to come.

RUSSIA'S DEMOGRAPHIC FUTURE

One issue that plagues Russia—and worries its leaders—is the country's demographics. This concern is nothing new—it dates back to the Soviet era and takes several forms.

The first worrisome demographic trend is the general level of Russian health: Russian life expectancy at birth is approximately 70 years: 76 for women and 65 for men. This figure is shockingly low, given the overall level of development of the country. Russia's life expectancy ranks 110th out of 201 countries and territories and is worse than that in much poorer Honduras or Bangladesh. Why? Russia shows an unusually high level of *adult* mortality, especially among men, whose life expectancy is slightly below that of men in India. The primary explanation appears to be a relatively simple one: alcohol. Russian alcohol consumption, particularly among men, is extremely high, by some estimates among the top five in the world. Russia is also by far the highest consumer of hard liquor, and is noteworthy for the prevalance of heavy episodic drinking. This pattern leads to two results: first, a high level of death by circulatory diseases, and second (and perhaps more striking), a very high level of death by accidents, suicides, and homicides—three times higher than in advanced democracies.

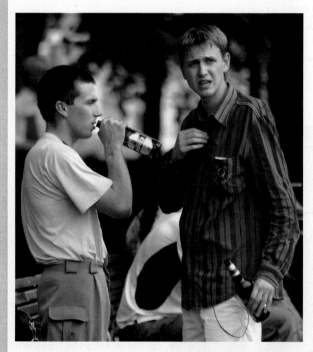
Two young men drinking beer in Moscow. The high level of alcohol consumption in Russia, especially among men, is a major factor in the country's demographic and health concerns.

A second demographic trend worrying Russian leaders is the country's low birth rate. Just as Russia has a low life expectancy rate, it also has an extremely low rate of fertility, even when compared with other European countries where such rates also tend to be low. Again, this issue dates back to the 1960s and is marked by the high rate of abortion, a result of limited access to birth control (Russia's abortion rates are double the European average). The high participation of women in the workforce, as well as economic stresses, creates disincentives to having larger families. When combined with low life expectancy, the result is a shrinking population. In the most extreme scenarios, by 2050 Russia will have lost more than 20 million people. The population will also grow older, reducing the active workforce and increasing pressure on the government to provide services. Ongoing migration from Central Asia may mitigate this decline, but it will also increase the Muslim share of the population, which may increase domestic tensions. An aging, unhealthy population is not a positive sign for the future.[23]

Key Terms

A Just Russia (p. 432)
asymmetric federalism (p. 430)
Caucasus (p. 435)
Chechnya (p. 436)
Cheka (p. 422)
Communist Party of the Russian Federation (CPRF) (p. 432)
Constitutional Court (p. 429)
Duma (p. 422)
Eurasian Economic Union (EAEU) (p. 441)
Federal Security Service (FSB) (p. 427)
Federation Council (p. 429)
glasnost (p. 424)
KGB (p. 422)
Kremlin (p. 426)
Liberal Democratic Party of Russia (LDPR) (p. 433)

nomenklatura (p. 422)
oligarchs (p. 419)
Orthodox Christianity (p. 420)
parties of power (p. 431)
perestroika (p. 424)
Politburo (p. 423)
Putin, Vladimir (p. 419)
shock therapy (p. 437)
siloviki (p. 419)
soviets (p. 422)
tsar (p. 420)
United Russia (p. 431)
Yabloko (p. 433)
Yeltsin, Boris (p. 424)

China's economy has grown at an astonishing pace, epitomized
by the Shanghai skyline. Will that growth continue? And with
what consequences? Will growth keep pace with the increased
demands of an expanding middle class? And as growth outpaces
capacity, how will China cope with increased pollution and pressure on natural resources?

China

Why Study This Case?

Napoleon Bonaparte is said to have described China as a sleeping giant. Centuries later, that description continues to resonate, though with every passing year, it seems less and less appropriate. Today, China is indeed stirring, after centuries of slumber, with repercussions that are transforming the world. But it is not simply these changes that draw our attention; after all, China is neither the first nor the only country to undergo dramatic change. Rather, it is that these changes are taking place in a country that we tend to speak of in superlatives, as having qualities no other country can easily match.

The first of China's superlatives is its history, which extends back at least 4,000 years. Several millennia before most modern nations and states existed in even rudimentary form, China had taken shape as a relatively unified country and people. Civil strife and external invasion tore it apart innumerable times during this process. Yet despite these difficulties, a continuous Chinese civilization has existed for thousands of years and directly shapes and informs modern Chinese society and politics. Second, China is the most populous country in the world with nearly 1.4 billion people. Except for India (whose population also exceeds 1 billion), no other country's population comes close. China has over 175 cities with more than a million inhabitants; the United States has nine.

China's recent and rapid development is a third superlative quality. Beginning in the late 1970s, China's ruling Communist Party introduced more liberal economic policies while maintaining its tight control over political power. Known as reform and opening, these changes launched a period of extended economic growth unmatched in the world. For more than three decades, China's gross domestic product (GDP) grew at an average rate of just under 10 percent a year—double the rate of the other fast-growing "Asian Tigers," such as South Korea and

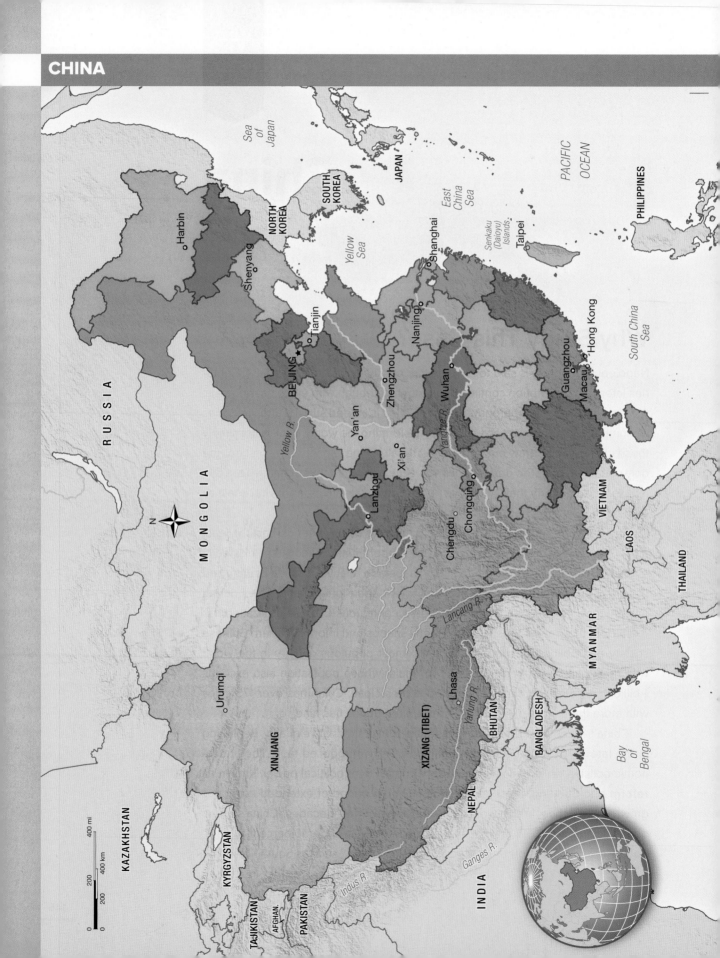

RUSSIA

MONGOLIA

KAZAKHSTAN

KYRGYZSTAN

TAJIKISTAN

AFGHAN.

PAKISTAN

XINJIANG

XIZANG (TIBET)

INDIA

NEPAL

BHUTAN

BANGLADESH

MYANMAR

LAOS

THAILAND

VIETNAM

NORTH KOREA

SOUTH KOREA

JAPAN

PHILIPPINES

Sea of Japan

Yellow Sea

East China Sea

PACIFIC OCEAN

South China Sea

Bay of Bengal

Senkaku (Daioyu) Islands

Harbin

Shenyang

BEIJING

Tianjin

Zhengzhou

Yan'an

Xi'an

Lanzhou

Nanjing

Shanghai

Wuhan

Chengdu

Chongqing

Guangzhou

Macau

Hong Kong

Taipei

Urumqi

Lhasa

Yellow R.

Yangtze R.

Lancang R.

Yarlung R.

Ganges R.

Indus R.

400 mi

200

400 km

200

0

0

Taiwan, and quadruple the average growth rates of the United States, Japan, and the United Kingdom.

The World Bank estimates that reform and opening has raised some 400 million Chinese out of poverty over the past several decades. At the same time, economic reforms have also led to growing income disparities and widespread social disruption. Moreover, growth has slowed in recent years, and observers both in China and abroad are beginning to question the sustainability of this state-led, growth-at-all-costs developmental model. Local governments have run up enormous debts in funding lavish projects, and corruption at all levels of government is widespread. China is thus engaged in a precarious race to reform itself before the shock of these changes overwhelms the country.

Economic modernization is not only transforming the physical and social landscape of the country but also reshaping international finance, trade, politics, and the environment. China, moreover, is becoming a central factor in globalization. Indeed, the flood of cheap Chinese exports into the world market has displaced many workers outside China, heightened concerns in advanced countries about the safety of China's food and toy exports, and substantially lowered rates of global inflation. China's voracious consumption of oil and other raw materials has become a focus of international discussions about global shortages and global climate change. And while China has taken significant steps to address its dangerous levels of air and water pollution, the country faces an environmental crisis of unprecedented proportions that spreads well beyond its borders. Rapid development has also given China increased military might and inspired new confidence to assert territorial claims beyond its traditional borders. These assertions have raised tensions with neighboring countries and prompted concern that a "rising" China may not be a "peaceful" China. Now that the giant is awake, its development and growing international status have profound effects not just internally but also around the world.

Historical Development of the State

CENTRALIZATION AND DYNASTIC RULE

China's first political leaders can be traced to the Shang dynasty (eighteenth to eleventh century B.C.E.), but centralized authority was first established during the Qin dynasty (221–206 B.C.E.). During this period, China first experienced political centralization through the appointment of nonhereditary officials to govern provinces, the minting of currency, the development of standard weights and measures, and the creation of public works, such as roads, canals, and portions of the famous Great Wall. Sovereign power was further centralized and expanded by the Han dynasty (206 B.C.E.–220 C.E.), a reign marked by great cultural flowering and the rise of domestic and international trade, foreign exploration, and conquest. The philosophy of **Confucianism** influenced the imperial leaders with its emphasis on a fixed set of hierarchical roles, meritocracy, and obedience to authority. Confucianism also helped foster the development of the Chinese civil service, a corps of educated men chosen on the basis of a rigorous series of competitive examinations testing their familiarity with Confucian thought. The notion of a meritocratic, professional bureaucracy did not emerge elsewhere in the world for centuries.

The institutionalization of the bureaucracy also promoted the development of a gentry class made up of landowners and their children, who were groomed from birth to join the bureaucracy. This bureaucratic class became the glue that held China together. Subsequent dynasties continued to rely upon the bureaucracy to maintain Chinese unity, even when new dynasties were established by foreign conquerors, as under the Yuan (Mongols) and the Qing (Manchus) dynasties. Such continuity helped foster economic development and innovation, which continued to advance faster than in Europe and other parts of the world.

FOREIGN IMPERIALISM

At the advent of the Ming dynasty (1368–1644), China still led the world in science, economics, communication, technological innovation, and public works. Although such knowledge offered the foundation for Chinese modernization and industrialization, these processes did not take place. Even as Europe experienced the Renaissance, international exploration, and the beginnings of the Industrial Revolution, Chinese innovation and economic development began to stagnate. By the mid-1400s, the Chinese Empire had banned long-distance sea travel and showed little interest in developing many of the technological innovations it had created.

Europe's economic and technological development continued, and its age of exploration and conquest began just as China was closing itself off to the outside world. The Portuguese first reached China by 1514, and during the sixteenth and seventeenth centuries other European traders sought to expand these initial contacts. These remained tightly controlled by the Chinese, however, and attempts to expand connections were futile. But the Chinese Empire was losing its ability to ignore the outside world, and external forces were beginning to test China's power. The First Opium War (1839–42) with Great Britain resulted in a resounding Chinese defeat, forcing China to cede Hong Kong to the British, open other ports for foreign trade, and pay restitution. Various Western powers quickly demanded similar access, and subsequent wars with the French and the Japanese only further weakened China's sovereignty and extended the control of imperial powers over the country. Foreign pressures in turn contributed to growing domestic instability.

THE EROSION OF CENTRAL AUTHORITY: CIVIL WAR AND FOREIGN INVASION

By the beginning of the twentieth century, the centralized authority of the Chinese state, developed over 2,000 years, effectively crumbled. In 1911, a public revolt finally swept away the remnants of the Qing dynasty. China was declared a republic, but it soon fell under the control of regional warlords. In the midst of this chaos, two main political organizations formed to compete for power. The Nationalist Party, or **Kuomintang (KMT)**, slowly grew in strength under the leadership of **Sun Yat-sen**. The party was aided by student protests in 1919 that came to be known as the **May Fourth**

TIMELINE Political Development

1700 B.C.E.	Chinese civilization under Shang dynasty begins.
221 B.C.E.	China unified under Qin dynasty.
1839–42	First Opium War takes place.
1911	Qing dynasty is overthrown.
1919	May Fourth movement takes place.
1921	Chinese Communist Party (CCP) is founded.
1934–35	Long March takes place.
1937–45	Sino-Japanese War is fought.
1949	People's Republic of China (PRC) is founded.
1958–60	Great Leap Forward takes place.
1966–76	Cultural Revolution takes place.
1976	Mao Zedong dies.
1978	Deng Xiaoping comes to power and launches economic reform and opening.
1989	Chinese government cracks down on protesters in Tiananmen Square Massacre.
2001	China joins the World Trade Organization.
2008	China hosts the Beijing Summer Olympics.
2013	Xi Jinping declared president of China.

movement. These nationalist revolts rejected foreign interference in China and called for modernization, radical reform, and a break with traditional values and institutions, including Confucianism.

The second organization was the **Chinese Communist Party (CCP)**, formed in 1921 by leaders of the May Fourth movement. Adhering to the principles of Marx and Lenin, the CCP's founders sought to organize China's nascent working class to resist the exploitation of both foreign imperialists and domestic warlords. Though the KMT's Sun had been educated in the United States, both parties received support from the recently established Soviet Union. In fact, the Soviets saw the KMT as a more likely contender for power than the much smaller CCP and hoped to move the KMT into the Soviet orbit. Following Sun's death in 1925, relations between the KMT and the CCP shortly unraveled. Chiang Kai-shek, head of the KMT's armed forces, took control of the party and expelled or eliminated pro-Soviet and pro-CCP elements. Chiang subdued or co-opted key regional warlords and brutally suppressed the CCP in areas under KMT control. By 1928, the KMT had emerged as the nominal leader of much of the country, while the CCP was pushed out of the cities and into the countryside. The KMT quickly shed any pretense of democracy, growing ever more dictatorial and corrupt.

During the repression of the CCP, power within the party began to pass into the hands of **Mao Zedong** (1893–1976). Deviating from the Marxist convention that revolutions be led by the urban proletariat, Mao believed that a communist revolution could be won by building a revolutionary army out of the far more numerous peasant class. He and the CCP established their own independent communist republic within China, but KMT attacks forced the CCP to flee westward in what came to be known as the **Long March** (1934–35). In this circuitous retreat, the CCP and its loyal followers traveled over 6,000 miles and lost nearly 90 percent of the 100,000 who initially fled by the time the ragtag group arrived at their final destination in Yan'an, located in north-central China. Though heroic, the Long March represented a setback for the CCP. At the same time, it secured Mao's leadership and strengthened his idea that the party should reorient itself toward China's peasant majority. The CCP fostered positive relations with the peasantry during the Long March, engaging in actions that contrasted strongly with the more brutal policies of the KMT. The revolutionary ideology of the CCP and its call for equality drew all classes of Chinese to its ranks.

In 1937, both the KMT and the CCP faced a new threat, as Japan launched a full-scale invasion of the country after several years of smaller incursions. The two parties formed a nominal united front against the invading Japanese, though they continued to battle each other even as they resisted the Japanese advance. While the war weakened KMT power, which was based in the cities, it bolstered the CCP's nationalist credentials and reinforced its ideology of a peasant-oriented communism of the masses. The war also forged a strong communist military, the **People's Liberation Army (PLA)**, trained both to fight the enemy and to win public support. This birth of Chinese communism through peasant guerrilla warfare is quite different from the Soviet experience, in which a small group of urban intellectuals seized control of the state through a coup d'état. In fact, the CCP and PLA comprised a new state and regime in the making.

ESTABLISHMENT AND CONSOLIDATION OF A COMMUNIST REGIME

Japan's defeat at the end of World War II found the CCP much strengthened and the KMT in disarray. The Communists now commanded the support of much of the countryside, while the KMT's traditional urban base of support was shattered by war and weakened by widespread corruption and rampant inflation. Communist attacks quickly routed the KMT, and in 1949 the communist forces entered Beijing unopposed and established the People's Republic of China (PRC). Chiang and the remnants of the KMT fled to the island of Taiwan, declaring *their* Republic of China as the legitimate government of all of China—which the United States recognized (rather than the PRC) until 1979. The island nation continues to claim and maintain its sovereignty, though the PRC has never recognized it and asserts that eventually the province of Taiwan will return to mainland control.

The new communist regime faced the challenge of modernizing a war-ravaged country far behind the West. The CCP's assets, forged during the war, were its organizational strength and a hard-earned reservoir of public legitimacy. Forming a close (if prickly) alliance with the Soviet Union, China began a process of modernization modeled after the Soviet experience: nationalization of industry, collectivization of agriculture, and central planning. At the same time, the CCP began to repress ruthlessly those viewed as hostile to the revolution, including landowners, KMT members and sympathizers, and others suspected of opposing the new order. Several million Chinese were killed.

EXPERIMENTATION AND CHAOS UNDER MAO

Within a few short years, China had diverged from the typical Soviet-style path of communist development. Mao and other Chinese leaders began to see Soviet reforms following Stalin's death as a retreat from communist ideals and revolutionary change, and they upheld China as the true vanguard of world revolution. China's first major break from the Soviet model was the **Great Leap Forward** (1958–60). Rejecting highly centralized planning, Mao reorganized the Chinese people into a series of self-contained communes, which were to serve all basic social and economic functions, from industrial production to health care. Each commune was to set its own policies for economic development within the guidelines of general government policy. In Mao's view, revolutionary change could be achieved by putting responsibility directly into the hands of the masses, moving the country rapidly into communism. State capacity was thus devolved, albeit within an authoritarian system.

Without clear directives and organization, the Great Leap Forward quickly went awry. For example, a campaign to increase steel production led not to the creation of large foundries staffed by skilled employees, as had happened in the Soviet Union, but to the production of a million backyard furnaces built by unskilled communes that consequently produced worthless metal. Overall economic and agricultural production declined, leading to disorder, famine, and the deaths of tens of millions of Chinese. In the face of this debacle, Mao stepped down as head of state in 1959 (though he remained head of the CCP), and China recentralized production and state control. From these events, Mao concluded the problem was not that CCP policies had been too radical, but that they had not been radical enough. Soviet history proved, he reasoned, that without an unwavering commitment to radical change, revolution would quickly deteriorate into bureaucratic conservatism (as Mao now saw occurring in China). He thus sought to place himself back at the center of power and reignite revolutionary fervor by constructing a cult of personality. This effort was first captured in the publication of *Quotations from Chairman Mao Zedong*, the "Little Red Book" of Mao's sayings that became standard reading for the public.[1]

In 1966, the cult took shape as Mao and his supporters accused the CCP itself of having "taken the capitalist road" and encouraged the public (particularly students) to "bomb the headquarters"—meaning, to challenge the party-state bureaucracy at all levels. Schools were closed, and student radicals, called **Red Guards**, took to the streets to act as vanguards of Mao's **Cultural Revolution**. Authority figures (including top party and state leaders, intellectuals, teachers, and even parents) were attacked, imprisoned, tortured, exiled to the countryside, or killed. Historic buildings, writings, and works of art were condemned as "bourgeois" and "reactionary" and then destroyed.

By weakening all social, economic, and political institutions in China, Mao made himself the charismatic center of all authority and wisdom. The result of this new vision was years of chaos and violence as the country slid into near civil war among various factions of the state, society, and the CCP. State capacity and autonomy

Youthful Red Guards gather to read aloud from *Quotations from Chairman Mao Zedong* during the Cultural Revolution.

largely disappeared. The only remaining institution with any authority, the PLA, was finally called upon to restore order. The excesses of the Cultural Revolution were largely curbed by 1968, though factional struggles within the party persisted until Mao's death in 1976 and beyond.

REFORM AND OPENING AFTER MAO

With Mao's death, the incessant campaigns to whip up revolutionary fervor ended. The party gradually came under the control of leaders who had themselves been victims of the Cultural Revolution. Most important was **Deng Xiaoping** (1904–97), a top party leader from the earliest years of the CCP who had been stripped of his post (twice) during the Cultural Revolution. By late 1978, Deng had consolidated his power and set the nation on a very different course.

In contrast to Mao's emphasis on revolutionary action for its own sake, Deng pursued modernization at the expense of communist ideology, in what became known as "reform and opening." The government encouraged the gradual privatization of first agriculture and then business; it also cultivated foreign relations with capitalist countries. Moreover, the government expanded foreign investment and trade while deemphasizing ideology. To quote Deng, "Whether a cat is black or white makes no difference. As long as it catches mice, it is a good cat." China began to embrace the market economy with all its benefits and difficulties.

One reform that did not take place, however, was political. Despite the downgrading of communist ideology, the CCP still maintained complete control over political life, and attempts at public debate in the 1970s were quickly silenced. Although reform and opening lifted hundreds of millions out of poverty, by the 1980s, serious problems had emerged—among them inflation, unemployment, and widespread corruption (particularly within the CCP).

As with the earlier May Fourth movement and the Red Guards of the Cultural Revolution, students once again played a major role in expressing discontent over this situation. In the spring of 1989, an estimated 100,000 students and other citizens—rallying for political reform—marched in the streets of Beijing, and a large group of protesters occupied **Tiananmen Square**. Martial law was declared, but many protesters remained, and on June 4 (now known simply as *liusi*, or "6/4," much as Americans refer to 9/11), the party leadership brought in the military. Although those gathered in the square itself were permitted to leave, hundreds of protesters were killed that day in clashes around Beijing and in other major Chinese cities. Over the next few months, thousands of students and others connected to the protests were arrested, and students throughout China were required to attend communist ideology indoctrination courses.

The regime's swift and violent response to the protest and its vigilant suppression of even hints of political unrest in the decades since Tiananmen have been combined with continued economic reform and opening. Deng Xiaoping and, with his passing in 1997, China's successive CCP leaders have in essence offered an unwritten social contract to their citizens: in exchange for accepting the CCP's monopoly over political power, the Chinese public has been permitted an unprecedented degree of economic freedom and the right to pursue prosperity. Most Chinese have accepted this bargain, resulting in over two additional decades since 1989 of white-hot growth and relative political stability. But as economic growth has slowed in recent years and the challenges associated with this growth-at-all-costs strategy have multiplied, many predict this social contract must change. Can a conservative, authoritarian state continue to preside successfully over a weakening economy and an increasingly vibrant and restive society?

Political Regime

Despite China's four decades of economic reform and global trends of democratization, the country remains stubbornly authoritarian. Certainly China's historical legacy of more than 2,000 years of centralized authoritarian rule (legitimized by Confucian precepts) has buttressed the current regime. But to understand the nature and resilience of China's communist authoritarianism, we must examine the ways in which political control is organized and exercised in a communist party-state.

China's party-state retains the essential organizational structure that the Chinese Communist Party adopted from the Soviet Union at its founding in the 1920s. Though China's reformist leaders have almost fully rejected Marx in their embrace of market freedoms, their decision to retain a closed political system is very much in accord with Lenin's vision of the communist party-state. Lenin contended that for the communist revolution to succeed in Russia, a self-appointed Communist Party elite, enlightened with wisdom and imbued with revolutionary fervor, would need to serve as a vanguard on behalf of the masses. This group alone would have the organizational capacity and resolve to lead the revolution, justifying its political monopoly and role as a "dictatorship of the proletariat."

This ideological and organizational logic has had several consequences for the exercise of political control in China in the period of reform and opening. True to its Leninist heritage, political authority both within the party-state and from the party-state to broader Chinese society still flows largely *from* the party elite *to* those within the party, the state, and society, who are expected to submit to this authority. However, China's rapid economic growth in recent years and its increasingly complex society have compelled the party-state to devolve substantial authority to regional and local officials and to ease its iron grip on society. This strengthening of regional and local authorities has had significant consequences for China's political regime and its state capacity.

POLITICAL INSTITUTIONS

The CCP exercises control over the state, society, and economy through the *nomenklatura* system. Party committees are responsible for the appointment, promotion, transfer, and firing of high-level state, party, and even public-industry personnel (some 10 million positions). The party also maintains direct control over the government and bureaucracy through a political structure by pairing all executive, legislative, and administrative agencies at every level of organization with a corresponding party organ (see the table "Parallel Organization of the Chinese Communist Party and the Chinese Government," p. 455). These CCP bureaus supervise the work of the state agencies and ensure that party interests prevail. This means that although China has a premier, a parliament, and bureaucratic ministries as in democratic regimes, party officials and organizations orchestrate the policy process and direct the votes of the party members who hold elected and appointed government and state offices. The CCP maintains this same organizational control at the regional and local levels of government and also places party "cadre," or officials, in schools, state-owned businesses, and social organizations to supervise—at least theoretically—all aspects of government, economic, and social activity.

In fact, scholars describe ruling communist parties as "greedy institutions" that seek to control all aspects of public and even private life. This was particularly true during the Maoist era of mass campaigns and totalitarian penetration of society. Mao and the party-state ensured control through the *danwei* **(work unit) system**, which gave all urban-dwelling Chinese citizens a lifetime affiliation with a specific industrial or bureaucratic work unit that dictated all aspects of their lives, including family size, housing, daily food rations, health care, and other social benefits. This organizational plan was reinforced by the *hukou* **(household registration) system**, which tied all Chinese to a particular geographic location.

Firmly in place for decades, reform and opening has erased most aspects of these hierarchical structures of state control. Today, the day-to-day choices of most Chinese citizens are governed much less by the party-state and much more by the free market. Among other consequences of the weakening of this social control, China today has a **floating population** of over 250 million itinerant workers who have abandoned their rural *hukou* designation to seek employment in China's cities. Unhindered in leaving the countryside, these rural migrants are in most cases unable to obtain an urban *hukou* designation. They are therefore deprived of the

Parallel Organization of the Chinese Communist Party and the Chinese Government

PARTY OFFICE OR ORGAN	OFFICEHOLDER OR NUMBER OF MEMBERS OR DEPARTMENTS	CORRESPONDING GOVERNMENT OFFICE OR ORGAN	OFFICEHOLDER OR NUMBER OF MEMBERS OR DEPARTMENTS
Chairman	Office abolished in 1982	**President (head of state)**	Xi Jinping
General secretary	Xi Jinping (head of party)	**Premier (head of government)**	Li Keqiang
Politburo Standing Committee (PSC)	7 members	**State Council Standing Committee**	10 members
Politburo	25 members	**State Council**	35 members
Central Committee (CC)	205 members	**National People's Congress Standing Committee**	Approximately 150 members
National Party Congress	2,270 members	**National People's Congress (NPC)**	2,943 members
Central Military Commission (CMC) of the CCP	11 members	**Central Military Commission of the PRC**	11 members (same members as CCP's CMC)
CMC chairman	Xi Jinping	**CMC chairman**	Xi Jinping
Secretariat	Large staff of party officials	**State Council General Office**	Large staff of civil servants
Party departments	Approximately 25 departments	**Bureaucratic ministries**	Approximately 25 ministries, bureaus, and commissions
Central Commission for Discipline Inspection	130 members	**Ministry of Supervision**	Minister and 4 vice ministers

Source: Updated and adapted from Melanie Manion, "Politics in China," in Gabriel Almond et al., *Comparative Politics Today: A World View* (New York: Pearson/Longman, 2004), 428.

public goods, such as public health care and education for their children, that the state still provides for city dwellers.

Still, although market reforms have dramatically increased mobility and altered state-society relations, China's twenty-first-century authoritarian party-state has worked diligently to maintain control over society. The state has drawn on the same technologies that have aided China's rapid development and hastened social mobility to maintain and even enhance its efforts of social control through high-tech surveillance and censorship. We should not, however, overestimate the authoritarian grasp of China's political leaders. Despite Herculean efforts at supervision, the opening of the economy and the growing complexity of Chinese society have inevitably weakened China's authoritarian regime. Economic and financial decentralization have given local authorities and private firms the autonomy to resist central policies and develop greater independence. These changes, combined with the long-standing inefficiency of China's enormous bureaucracy and growing problems of corruption and nepotism at all levels of government (and the sheer size, growing complexity, and persistent backwardness of much of China), also call state capacity into question.

Before exploring the potential consequences of this diminished central authority, we first examine the political institutions of China's authoritarian rule.

THE CONSTITUTION China is ostensibly governed by a constitution that is designated "the fundamental law of the state" and that vests formal authority in both party and state executive and legislative offices. However, under the conditions of authoritarian rule in China, political power remains highly centralized and not fully institutionalized.

Mao and his successors have been little deterred by checks or balances inherent in the formal institutions of either the party or the state. Political leaders have sought in recent years to formalize rules for policy making and succession and have succeeded in imposing mandatory term limits and age limits for appointments at all levels, including the top leadership posts. China's political elites nonetheless continue to rely on their informal sources of power (including personal connections, age, experience, and patronage) as much as or more than formal positions or titles. Although current leaders have agreed to avoid a return to the tyranny of the Maoist era, political rule in post-Mao China has remained largely vested in a single "paramount" leader surrounded by a key group of 25 to 35 highly influential political elites who hold key positions in the party and state.

The personal and particular nature of political rule in China has meant that the *rule of law* has generally not prevailed in China. Legal matters—particularly during the Maoist period, but even beyond—were highly politicized. Most legal institutions have been subject to the ideological priorities of the party-state and the personal motivations of its leaders. But reform and opening has forced the state to seek new means of maintaining control and influence, including increased reliance on legal statutes.

The growing complexity of economic and social life has required the state to adopt new laws governing the environment, contracts, labor relations, trade, and even property. China's reliance on foreign trade, in particular, has had a huge impact on legal reforms as foreign investors, local entrepreneurs, and international bodies such as the World Trade Organization (WTO) have increased pressure on Chinese authorities to abide by contracts and to respect property rights (though not always successfully). This newfound legal adherence is spilling over into other aspects of policy making and portends an even greater role for some of China's other formal political institutions.

COMMUNIST PARTY INSTITUTIONS AND ORGANS

The National Party Congress nominally "elects" its Central Committee (CC), which in turn "selects" the Politburo (short for "political bureau"). But in fact, the seven or so members of the Politburo Standing Committee (PSC) make up the top political leadership of China. The PSC convenes in weekly meetings headed by the general secretary of the party, currently Xi Jinping. The PSC (as the Politburo's dominant senior members) typically determines all key national policy decisions and political appointments. The Politburo effectively serves as China's governing cabinet, and each member is responsible for a particular set of policy areas or issues that roughly correspond to the ministerial portfolios of the government's State Council.

Technically, the Politburo, the PSC, and the general secretary are all "elected" by the CC of the National Party Congress. But in reality, party leaders determine the makeup of these ballots on which all candidates run unopposed. Despite the largely ceremonial role of the CC, its members constitute the pool of China's party officials being groomed for top leadership. The CC, in turn, is elected by the **National Party Congress**, which is somewhat akin to an American political party nominating convention. With well over 2,000 delegates, the National Party Congress is far too unwieldy and meets too infrequently (every five years) to conduct any real policy making. Instead, its "plenary," or full, sessions have been used as venues for announcing changes in policies and leadership and formally endorsing the ideological "line" of the party.

This most recent 18th Party Congress marked the start of General Secretary **Xi Jinping**'s first of what is likely to be two 5-year terms. Once confirmed, Xi—like his predecessors—unveiled a policy vision that would become the hallmark of his tenure: the pursuit of the **Chinese Dream**. Xi defined this vision as "the rejuvenation of the great Chinese nation" and obtaining what he called the "two 100s": China's ascendance to a "moderately well-off society" by 2021 (the centennial of the CCP's founding) and becoming a fully developed nation by 2049 (the hundredth anniversary of the PRC's founding). This vision replaced and built upon the mission statement of the previous decade announced by Xi's predecessor, **Hu Jintao**, at the 17th Party Congress. Hu called for "scientific development and the creation of a **harmonious society**," party-speak for the continuation of economic growth but with more concern for the rising wealth and welfare gaps between urban and rural China.

Delegates to these Party Congress conventions ostensibly represent the more than 88 million members of the CCP, organized at the provincial and local levels.

Several other party organs are worth noting. Like the government, the CCP also staffs its own bureaucracy, known as the Secretariat. The Secretariat oversees the implementation of Politburo decisions and, just as important, the distribution of propaganda in support of these decisions through its propaganda department. Given the important political role of China's military, party leaders have used the Central Military Commission (CMC) to retain tight control over the armed forces. The CMC presides over China's military, reports directly to the Politburo, and has always been chaired by China's paramount leader or his designee. A final party organ, the Central Commission for Discipline Inspection, is charged with maintaining party loyalty

President Xi Jinping (left), China's paramount leader, serves as head of party, state, and military. Premier Li Keqiang (right) functions as a much weaker head of government.

and discipline and rooting out corruption, a particular concern of current leader Xi Jinping. In 2014, Xi also took charge of three new party organizations known as "leading groups" concerned with national security and the Internet.

Each of the institutions just discussed is part of the central party structure located in Beijing. Each province also has a party committee that includes a secretary and a standing committee with departments and commissions following the pattern of the central party apparatus. Below this level, the party is represented by comparable organizations at the county, city, district, township, and village levels. The lower-level party leaders have often exercised a degree of autonomy, which has potentially significant consequences for the devolution of authority and the political liberalization of China.

THE BRANCHES OF GOVERNMENT

Although the national constitution designates China's unicameral legislature, the **National People's Congress (NPC)**—not to be confused with the National *Party* Congress—as the highest organ of the state, all government organizations and bureaucratic ministries remain subservient to party oversight. Nonetheless, day-to-day responsibilities for managing the country's affairs are largely in the hands of the executive State Council's ministries and commissions.

THE HEAD OF STATE The president of the PRC is China's head of state, an entirely titular office. During the reform era, the paramount leader or his designee has always held this office.

Deng Xiaoping, preferring to rule behind the scenes, designated **Jiang Zemin** as head of state in 1993. Jiang held the office of president for two terms until 2003, concurrently with his positions as general secretary of the CCP and head of the CMC. In the early 2000s, Jiang resigned from all three of these positions, handing them one by one to his successor, Hu Jintao. And in a move indicating the increasing

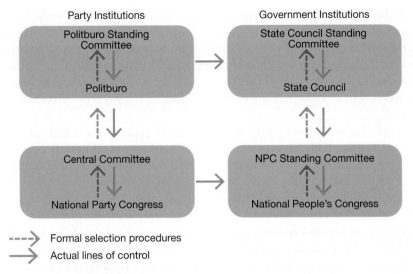

Party Institutions — Government Institutions

Politburo Standing Committee → State Council Standing Committee

Politburo — State Council

Central Committee → NPC Standing Committee

National Party Congress → National People's Congress

- - - → Formal selection procedures
——→ Actual lines of control

Structure of the Government

Governing structures of the CCP are organized according to the party's constitution, which vests formal power in the National Party Congress, but the actual lines of control run opposite to the direction of formal selection. In other words, political clout is inversely proportional to the size and legal standing of the body.

institutionalization of the leadership succession process, Hu Jintao likewise surrendered all three offices to current leader Xi Jinping, culminating in the transfer of the largely ceremonial office of PRC president in 2013. Like his predecessor, it is anticipated that Xi will serve two consecutive terms as president, from 2013 until 2023.

THE STATE COUNCIL The State Council, China's executive branch, is the primary organ of daily government activity and is led by the premier (who serves as head of government). The premier is recommended by the party's Central Committee and then formally elected by the NPC, which has always chosen the recommended candidate.

Li Keqiang was named premier in 2013, when Xi Jinping became PRC president, and will likely serve for two 5-year terms in tandem with President Xi. The premier is typically the second- or third-ranking member of the PSC. With the assistance of several vice premiers, the premier and his cabinet of ministers and commissioners (collectively, the State Council) govern China. The council oversees the work of China's 25 or so bureaucratic ministries and commissions, which manage the country's economy, foreign relations, education, science, technology, and other affairs of state. Under the guidance of its party counterparts, the council's ministries and commissions formulate and implement most of China's laws and regulations.

THE NATIONAL PEOPLE'S CONGRESS The State Council is formally appointed by China's parliament, the National People's Congress (NPC), which serves as China's unicameral legislative branch. NPC elections are held every five years, a schedule observed faithfully only since Mao's death.

The NPC's nearly 3,000 delegates convene annually for about two weeks to "elect" a standing committee of approximately 150 members. The top leader of the NPC must also be a member of the CCP's Politburo Standing Committee, an arrangement that guarantees party control of legislative affairs and demonstrates, once again, the interlocking nature of the party and state. This NPC Standing Committee then meets regularly as a legislative assembly roughly every two months throughout the year.

Despite having the constitutional authority to pass laws and even amend the constitution, the NPC has never had an independent or influential role in policy making. Rather, it has most often served to ratify policies already determined by central leaders. In more recent years, however, as China's economy and society have become more complex, the NPC and its standing committee have gradually become venues for delegates to offer opinions, express dissatisfaction with government policy, and even occasionally cast dissenting votes. As its constituent committees and specialized policy groups have become more knowledgeable and sophisticated, the NPC has started to shape policies of reform. The full NPC is, of course, still far from a democratic parliament. Like its party counterpart, the institution is too large and meets too seldom and too briefly to exert any substantial influence.

THE JUDICIARY Under China's system of authoritarian rule, the law is subject to the leaders, not the other way around. In other words, China's leaders practice rule *by* law, rather than submitting to the rule *of* law more common in constitutional democracies.

In fact, for the most part, the PRC's legal system did not function under Mao, and no criminal code existed before 1978. Legal reforms since that time have established a judicial system, but it remains subservient to the party hierarchy, which routinely protects officials from the law. Party leaders have often applied corruption or abuse-of-office statutes selectively and have fabricated or exaggerated crimes to snare political opponents or hold up one deviant as an example to others.

China has been severely criticized by human rights groups, both for its extensive incarceration of political prisoners and for its eagerness to employ capital punishment for a variety of crimes (including corruption, smuggling, theft, bribery, and rape). Observers estimate that hundreds of thousands of prisoners are being held in labor reeducation camps (ostensibly closed in 2013), "rehabilitation" centers, and other secret jails with no access to the legal system (roughly 10 percent of them are political prisoners). Recent prominent political detainees have included literary critic and human rights activist Liu Xiaobo, who was awarded the 2010 Nobel Peace Prize while serving his fourth prison term, and artist and outspoken government critic Ai Weiwei, who was detained for two months in 2011, ostensibly for tax evasion.

Amnesty International notes that during one of China's periodic "strike hard" campaigns, Chinese authorities executed more criminals (1,781) in three months than did the rest of the world in the previous three years.[2] Scholars estimate that China annually executes more than 2,500 prisoners—half the annual total of just a few years ago, but still more than the rest of the world combined and at a per capita rate roughly comparable to those of Iran and North Korea. Amnesty International also contends that an estimated 50,000 practitioners of the outlawed **Falun Gong** meditation sect and numerous other religious practitioners and ethnic minority activists have been detained as political prisoners. Many of them, as well as other prisoners of conscience, are subjected to torture, inhumane conditions, and even execution.

LOCAL GOVERNMENT

Successive authoritarian regimes, including the current one, have resisted notions of federalism and held to the belief that unity and stability are possible only under strong central leadership. Nonetheless, central control over such a huge and diverse nation has been far from complete, and increased social complexity and the political and financial demands brought on by reform and opening are making their mark on local politics. In recent years, the central party leadership has devolved substantial economic policy-making authority to regional and local officials. These measures have enhanced efficiency and promoted development, but have also greatly expanded opportunities for local corruption and abuse of power.

Local officials are given no authority to tax nor provided with other sources of revenue and have therefore used their control of property and licensing within their jurisdictions to seize lands occupied by local residents, offering only meager compensation in return. These local party-state leaders then sell the property and the right to build factories or other projects at huge profits to developers and factory owners. These local officials then share profits with the developers, leading to the overexpansion of factories and the sprouting of a number of questionable megaprojects across China. Too often, local residents are forced to endure dangerous levels of pollution emitted from these factories or are thrown off the land altogether. Most of the estimated 200,000 annual local protests are related to these kinds of land disputes.

In an effort to address the growing discontent within local communities as well as shore up the legitimacy of communist rule, central political leaders have been experimenting over the past three decades with gradually increasing measures of local democratization. By the early 2000s, some 600,000 villages across China had begun conducting local elections, popularly electing relatively powerless "village committees" and "village heads." But at the same time, increasingly brazen farmers, workers, and entrepreneurs had begun to call for the right to elect their local party secretaries, who are the real locus of power at the village level. Although this last demand has not yet been granted, and political liberalization has not yet "trickled up" in any formal way, its impact on the nearly half of all Chinese still living in villages ought not to be underestimated.[3]

OTHER INSTITUTIONS

THE PEOPLE'S LIBERATION ARMY Chairman Mao famously stated that "political power grows out of the barrel of a gun" and that "the Party commands the gun, and the gun must never be allowed to command the Party."[4] Although the CCP has sought to abide by Mao's admonition, the People's Liberation Army, which comprises China's army, navy, and air force, has played a significant role not just in China's revolutionary history but also in contemporary Chinese politics. Mao used the prestige and heroic stature the PLA garnered in battle before 1949 to add legitimacy to the communist party-state once the PRC was established. The PLA played a key role in economic reconstruction in the 1950s, brought the Red Guard to heel during the chaotic Cultural Revolution, and smashed the protests at Tiananmen Square in 1989. In the reform period, party leaders have sought to narrow both the economic and political roles of the military, but even with its new, "leaner" status, the PLA remains the world's largest military force with a standing army of over two million personnel.

Because of the size and historically important role of the PLA, the CCP established the Central Military Commission, first within the party and later as a second government agency, to guarantee party-state control over the gun. Although this control seems more certain now than perhaps at any other time in PRC history, China's increased security needs and its regional and global interests have enhanced the status of the military and led to growing military assertiveness in shaping China's foreign policy.

Political Conflict and Competition

THE PARTY SYSTEM

Although China's political system includes eight nominally independent political parties, each of these very small parties is entirely subservient to the Chinese Communist Party. The CCP's monopoly of power and the absence of any formal political opposition make China an authoritarian regime led by a one-party state.

THE CHINESE COMMUNIST PARTY Because it offers the primary path not only to political advancement but also to economic and social mobility, membership in the CCP is both sought after and selective. In 2016, the CCP had more than 88 million registered members, making it by far the largest political party in the world. Significantly, over a quarter of current CCP members are under age 35, over a third of them have college degrees, and millions of these card-carrying Communist Party members are capitalists.

While party membership has always been the chief pathway to elite recruitment, over time, different sectors of society have been gradually targeted for inclusion as the needs and priorities of the party-state have evolved. Mao's most significant contribution to communist doctrine was his inclusion of peasants as an integral component of communist revolution. During the 1950s, the CCP sought first to create and then recruit a sector of industrial workers to establish a more orthodox (Marxist) Communist Party. During the Cultural Revolution, the keys to political advancement were ideological purity and a background untainted by either feudal or bourgeois heritage.

Since Mao's death, China's reformist leaders have successively broadened the definition of political correctness in an effort to co-opt into the ranks of the party those deemed important to the reform program. Deng pragmatically emphasized that an "ability to catch mice" (expertise), and not the "color of the cat" (ideological conformity), was the true measure of contribution to China's progress. He welcomed professionals, scholars, and intellectuals into the party. And in 2001, the CCP established a policy known as the **Three Represents** that broadened the identity of the party to include not just workers and peasants but even private entrepreneurs. As of 2011, over 90 percent of China's 1,000 wealthiest individuals were either officials or

China's Paramount Leaders

GENERATION	LEADER AND TENURE	FORMATIVE EXPERIENCE	CAREERS OF POLITICAL ELITE
1st	Mao Zedong (1935–76)	May Fourth movement	Confucian intellectuals and peasants
2nd	Deng Xiaoping (1979–92)	Long March	"Reds": peasants and workers
3rd	Jiang Zemin (1992–2002)	Great Leap Forward	"Experts": engineers and technocrats
4th	Hu Jintao (2002–12)	Cultural Revolution	"Experts": engineers and technocrats
5th	Xi Jinping (2012–22)	Tiananmen Square Massacre	Academics (social science, law) and entrepreneurs

Source: Adapted from Bruce Dickson, "Beijing's Ambivalent Reformers," *Current History* 103 (September 2004): 249–55.

members of the CCP, and over 200 of China's wealthiest individuals were delegates of the National People's Congress in 2015.[5] This convergence of private financial wealth and political influence, combined with the growing income inequality in Chinese society, has led critics to wonder how long a ruling party founded on the principle of destroying the very social class it has now chosen to embrace and reward can endure.

But even as increasing numbers of scholars and other interested observers inside and outside China predict the collapse of CCP rule, this ruling party that is making plans to celebrate the centennial anniversary of its founding in 2021 has managed thus far to resist both external challenges and internal decay.[6] Although the CCP's original heroic stature and revolutionary legitimacy may have little hold on China's younger generations, recent party leaders have effectively employed a mixture of authoritarian controls, patriotic nationalist appeals, and economic benefits to maintain the CCP's virtual monopoly of political power.

THE SUCCESSION AND CIRCULATION OF ELITES One of the greatest challenges to perpetuating the CCP's political dominance has been the issue of political succession. As in most authoritarian systems, China faces the problem of having no institutionalized "vice office" to ease the transition to a successor when the top leader dies.

The passing of Mao in 1976 led to a leadership crisis and rancorous struggle among several elite factions. In an effort to avoid repeating this problem, Deng did not assume formal leadership positions in either the party or the government when he came to power two years later. He retained his position on the PSC until 1987 and chaired the CMC until 1989, but governed largely from behind the scenes, however, serving as the paramount leader of China until his death in 1997.

Deng also sought to institutionalize a succession process that would avoid the uncertainty and instability associated with his own ascendance. As paramount leader, he chose not only his own "third-generation" replacement, Jiang Zemin, but also tapped "fourth-generation" successor Hu Jintao. Just as Jiang and Hu each served a decade as head of state, head of party, and head of military, it is anticipated that current "fifth-generation" leader Xi Jinping will likewise complete 10-year terms as CCP general secretary (2012–22), PRC president (2013–23), and CMC chair (2013–23).

To retain the party's monopoly of power, this core group of party elite has shown its willingness to follow established norms of succession, putting in place term limits and mandatory retirement ages to ensure the circulation of elites. Moreover, the promotion of elites within the party is now based as much on merit as on personal or factional connections.[7] The question remains regarding how long this single-party authoritarian state can balance the co-optation of an increasingly wealthy elite—and the corruption and growing inequality that tend to accompany this co-optation—with the necessary accommodation and repression of a society that is rapidly growing more vocal and varied in its demands.

CIVIL SOCIETY

Because the CCP historically claimed to represent all legitimate social interests, civil society did not officially exist in Mao's China. Any organized interests outside the party-state were considered illegitimate and potentially harmful. Any ethnic, religious, labor, or other forms of organized association not fully controlled by the state were prohibited. Not surprisingly, however, the profound changes associated with reform and opening since Mao's death have not been limited to the economy.

In an effort to confine the social and political impact of economic reform, the party-state has created a number of mass organizations to control society and mobilize social groups to fulfill its own national goals. Awkwardly labeled "government-operated nongovernmental organizations" (GONGOs), these legitimate "mass organizations" formed by the CCP include the Women's Federation, the All-China Federation of Trade Unions, and the Youth Development Foundation. Such groups are led by party officials and assist the party-state in disseminating information and implementing policies.

China's political leaders have watched nervously as the interests and demands of China's citizens have expanded in pace with China's modernization. Although the party-state gradually has begun to open space for civil society by authorizing the work of some half a million legally registered nongovernmental organizations (NGOs), these have largely been restricted to nonpolitical arenas such as providing services to the poor, disabled, and elderly and promoting local environmental protection, typically still with government sponsorship or monitoring. But as rapid urbanization and industrialization have placed increased demands on government at all levels, an estimated 1 to 2 million additional unregistered NGOs have emerged with at least the party-state's tolerance. Many of these organizations offer much-needed services in health care, education, disaster relief, and other areas that local governments are unable or unwilling to provide.

Predictably, a number of these NGOs and social activists have moved from simply providing services to advocating for the groups they serve, including displaced peasants, exploited migrants and factory workers, and those seeking legal redress from corrupt government officials. The party-state has not hesitated to harass, detain, and arrest those groups and individuals who have become too vocal or who stray into controversial areas. In 2016, the government enacted a law further restricting the operation of foreign NGOs in China, requiring them to secure an approved local partner and subjecting them to increased government oversight.

The party's co-optation of private entrepreneurs has given rise to a growing group of **red capitalists**—entrepreneurs who belong to the CCP—who have benefited from economic reform, prefer social stability, and therefore have little reason to challenge

IN COMPARISON | Is the State Too Powerful?

The state controls too much of our daily lives. Percentage of survey respondents who agree:

COUNTRY	PERCENTAGE	COUNTRY	PERCENTAGE
Brazil	76	South Africa	63
Germany	74	Canada	59
India	71	Nigeria	59
Mexico	68	China	39
France	65	Russia	36
United States	65	Japan	34
United Kingdom	64		

Note: Data on Iran not available.
Source: Pew Center for the People and the Press, 2007.

the state or make new demands on the policy agenda.[8] China's Communist Party leaders have recognized that, one way or another, capitalist interests will be heard. However, their determination that such interests be heard from within the party rather than from without may nonetheless have "revolutionary" consequences.

Although this revolutionary potential was perhaps most vividly manifested in the 1989 demonstrations of students and their supporters at Tiananmen Square, a wide variety of social protests have bubbled up outside the official confines of the party-state, both before and since that event. To date, all significant attempts to form unauthorized political or social interest groups have been swiftly repressed, though this repression has not altogether silenced the efforts of many Chinese to give organizational expression to their social interests.

The increasing complexity and openness of China's twenty-first-century society—coupled with the inevitable growing pains of its ongoing economic revolution—almost guarantee that this cycle of subversive rebellion, state repression, and renewed social resistance will repeat itself. Scholars point to a growing variety of increasingly motivated and articulate social groups—out-of-work state employees, displaced farmers, migrant workers, internationally connected environmentalists, members of underground Christian "house" churches, and many others—who are no longer easily subsumed under Mao's one-size-fits-all category of the "masses" and who have stepped up their demands, even in the face of state repression. Peasant protests against illegal land seizures, onerous taxes, local corruption, and environmental hazards as well as urban workers' strikes against layoffs and horrific working conditions are both increasingly common and well organized. Scholars estimate more than 500 such protests take place each day across China. Potentially even more destabilizing is China's floating population of migrant workers, estimated now at over 250 million and growing. These nomadic laborers flock from rural to urban China with little job security, in most cases no legal residency beyond their abandoned villages, and no authorized access to housing, health care, or education. Likewise, China now boasts 700 million "netizens" (active users of the Internet and online communities), 1.2 billion mobile phone subscribers, and more than 300 million bloggers who are increasingly interconnected with one another and the world. These citizens regularly surf and blog, severely testing the regime's capacity to monitor their networking activities and censor their access to politically dangerous resources on the Web.

Party leaders recognize that the country's capacity to compete in the twenty-first century requires embracing the technology of this digital age, and Chinese netizens are happily obliging. While most of these bloggers and surfers are typically connecting with friends, downloading music, or playing online games, this explosion of social media has also given Chinese activists new means to publicize government corruption and abuse, rally support for social causes, and organize protests (both real and virtual).

Predictably, the authoritarian party-state has also taken up its keyboards and filters, in a concerted effort to control social media and restrict its uses. Labeled "Golden Shield" by the government, and more colloquially known as the "Great Firewall of China," the party-state's huge project of social media control has to date been surprisingly successful. By deploying an army of more than 50,000 human monitors, a raft of harsh censorship laws, and a vast, sophisticated network of filtering software, the government has managed to block or quickly remove much of the content it finds politically or morally objectionable.

Can this juxtaposition of an increasingly open economic system and a persistently closed political system endure? Scholars disagree as to whether China's state is "brittle," and therefore unresponsive to societal demands, or "adaptive" and even "consultative" and sufficiently responsive to the country's increasingly complex and vocal civil society to retain its vanguard role.[9] Although these debates persist over whether China's authoritarian political system remains securely intact or is moving toward greater liberalization or inevitable collapse, most observers conclude that this volatile combination is far too contradictory to prevail as is for long.

Society

ETHNIC AND NATIONAL IDENTITY

Though the Chinese commonly view themselves as a homogeneous society, China is not without ethnic diversity. The country is populated mostly by Han Chinese (who make up more than 90 percent of the total population), but it recognizes at least 55 minority nationalities.

Even among Han Chinese, there is tremendous linguistic diversity. For thousands of years, Han Chinese have shared a written language, but Han speakers are divided into eight main language groups and hundreds of dialects. Since the twentieth century, Beijing has imposed Mandarin as the official language of government and education. Despite the persistence of local dialects in many rural areas, education, television, and increased mobility have privileged Mandarin and made it the common tongue, especially among younger Chinese.

Although China's minority nationalities comprise only a small percentage of the population, many reside in strategic "autonomous areas" that make up more

CHINESE POLITICAL FREEDOM

CAN BE SEEN — FROM CYBERSPACE.

TOLES
UNIVERSAL UCLICK
©2012 THE WASHINGTON POST
5·1·12

© Tom Toles/Distributed by Universal Uclick via CartoonStock.com

China's governing party-state has thus far employed its "Great Firewall" to good effect in thwarting the free flow of information. However, it is uncertain how long or how effectively the state will be able to outmaneuver the country's growing population of "netizens."

than 60 percent of China's territory and have a long and often violent history of resistance to the Chinese state (see the map on p. 468). For millennia, China has struggled to maintain sovereignty over its border regions, particularly its western frontiers.

This struggle continues in the twenty-first century as the country faces demands for increased autonomy from the Turkic Uighur minority in the northwestern province of Xinjiang and from Tibetans in the southwest. Advocates for greater autonomy in both regions can point to periods of independence during the first half of the twentieth century and much longer periods of separation from the Chinese empire in the centuries before. But the Chinese communists moved quickly after 1949 to consolidate control over these two sparsely populated regions. They used an uprising in Tibet in 1959 to eliminate opposition to Chinese sovereignty and to force the Tibetan hereditary religious and political leader, the Dalai Lama, into exile in India. Muslim Uighurs and Buddhist Tibetans have long resented Chinese Communist Party control, and proponents of a "Free Tibet" and an "East Turkestan" continue to champion independence or at least greater autonomy. These voices come primarily from outside China's borders, although internal terrorism, violence, and other forms of resistance have been regular occurrences.

Chinese Communist leaders have always viewed sovereign control of both regions as vital and nonnegotiable. The recent discovery, moreover, of extensive fossil fuel reserves in western China and these regions' strategic position as China looks farther

Chinese Ethnolinguistic Groups

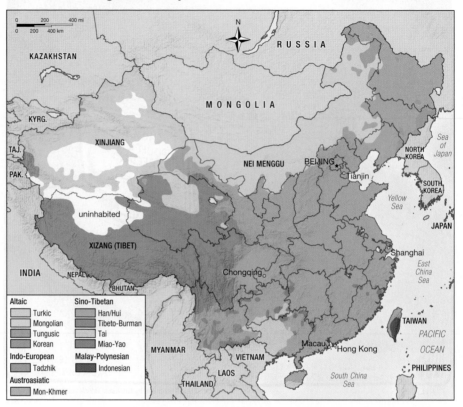

Altaic
- Turkic
- Mongolian
- Tungusic
- Korean

Indo-European
- Tadzhik

Austroasiatic
- Mon-Khmer

Sino-Tibetan
- Han/Hui
- Tibeto-Burman
- Tai
- Miao-Yao

Malay-Polynesian
- Indonesian

westward to Central and South Asia and the Middle East have made full control of these areas even more important to Chinese authorities. In both regions, the regime has countered separatist efforts with an effective pacification strategy that has combined co-optation, assimilation, and repression.

In recent years, the government has pumped billions of dollars into the regions, improving transport and communication infrastructure, including construction of the world's highest-altitude (and most expensive) railway (to Tibet) and citywide broadband in Xinjiang's larger cities. This investment has provided jobs, income, and opportunities for locals, particularly the educated elite. But it has also brought waves of ethnic Han Chinese, who now outnumber the local population in Xinjiang and claim the largest share of new jobs created in both regions. Although the population of the less-accessible Tibet is still over 90 percent ethnic Tibetan, locals in both regions complain that it is only a matter of time before the dominant Han Chinese culture overwhelms their indigenous languages, cultures, and perhaps even faiths.

When resentment and complaints turn violent, as they did in both regions most recently in Tibet in 2008 and Xinjiang in 2009, the regime has not hesitated to react with harsh repression. Harsh repression has not, however, quelled ethnic protest. Since 2009, nearly 150 Tibetans have resorted to self-immolation as a means of protest. China's ethnic Uighurs have targeted Han Chinese with increasingly bold acts of terrorism not just in Xinjiang but also in the cities of Beijing (2013) and Kunming (2014).

IDEOLOGY AND POLITICAL CULTURE

Chinese political culture is in a state of flux, and many of the details will remain unknown until more extensive and reliable public opinion data (banned until very recently) are available. During the rule of Mao Zedong, the party-state attempted to reshape China's traditional political culture through massive propaganda, mobilization, and repression. The importance of communist ideas has waned since the time of Mao's death, especially as a capitalist economy has come to replace state socialism. Communist ideology still has some hold on the countryside, but China's cities reflect a growing diversity of information and ideas. And while Mao violently rejected traditional Confucian cultural norms, China's current leaders have embraced these values as a homegrown source of legitimacy, even as premodern and communist emphasis on the group (whether familial clan or agricultural collective) is giving way to modern cultural values of individualism.

TRADITIONAL CENTRALIZED AUTHORITARIANISM Mao viewed China's "poor and blank" population as ripe for the party-led makeover of political culture, but traditional Chinese political culture was far more resilient than Mao had imagined. Before the communists took power in 1949, China had a long history of centrally imposed authoritarian politics. Mao's communists moved the capital from Nanjing back to Beijing (which had been the imperial capital for centuries), and in doing so directly connected their rule to traditional Chinese authoritarianism.

In many ways, the communist regime replicated elements of the rigid and hierarchical imperial system. For example, China still administers extremely competitive national examinations that determine university admission, and under communist rule, the tradition of respect for one's elders is still reflected in the elevated average age of party leaders. Despite significant efforts by some to improve the status of Chinese women, the male domination of China's communist leadership continues to expose the traditional paternalism of Chinese politics.

CONFUCIANISM One significant influence over the political culture and ideology of the Chinese people has been the teachings of the scholar Confucius (551–479 B.C.E.). Mao launched his 1960s Cultural Revolution with the explicit intent of destroying once and for all the institutional legacies of Confucianism. However, in the moral vacuum resulting from the waning influence of communist ideology in recent decades, the post-Mao Chinese Communist leadership has embraced key elements of Confucian philosophy.

Under the tenets of Confucianism, the role of government is to impose a strict moral code and foster "correct" behavior. Central to the Confucian worldview are the ideas of hierarchy and social harmony. Peace, order, and stability in both the family and the nation flow from the proper actions of benevolent superiors and obedient inferiors who all know their rightful place in society and act accordingly. Not surprisingly, China's authoritarian leaders have found reason to champion these traditional values bolstering central authority, social harmony, and even "small prosperity," a Confucian precept calling for the acceptance of a moderately well off society short of full prosperity.

MAOISM Mao believed that the key to revolutionary success lay in the ability of the Communist Party to create a "new socialist man" and to alter the way people

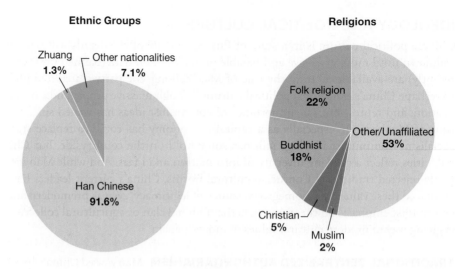

Ethnic Groups

Zhuang 1.3%
Other nationalities 7.1%
Han Chinese 91.6%

Religions

Folk religion 22%
Other/Unaffiliated 53%
Buddhist 18%
Christian 5%
Muslim 2%

think. While building in important ways on traditional Chinese political culture, Mao introduced some radical concepts. For example, instead of rallying to the traditional Confucian notion of harmony, he promoted constant class struggle. On the other hand, Maoism emphasized the collective over the individual, here drawing on traditional Confucian notions. Where traditional Chinese values favored loyalty to the extended family, Mao sought to transfer that loyalty to the larger community, as embodied by the party, the state, and, locally, the *danwei* (work unit). The Communists also claimed to promote egalitarianism, and thus an improvement of the lot of the nation's poor, peasants, and women.

In Mao's view, revolutionary thought (as decreed by the party leadership) could replace Chinese values, and the party could promote these ideas through constant propaganda and slogans, mass campaigns, and the education system, which included intensive sessions of "thought reform" and "self-criticism." Likewise, economic development could be "willed" through massive acts of peasant-driven voluntarism. Mao regularly favored political correctness over technical expertise, often at great cost to China's economy and most infamously during the Great Leap Forward and the Cultural Revolution.

Given the dearth of modern opinion research in Communist China, it is impossible to know whether Maoism has changed Chinese political culture or merely reinforced traditional Chinese characteristics. The ease with which the Chinese people have embraced capitalist reforms and increased individualism as well as tolerated the growth of inequality suggests that Mao's ideas were accepted more out of deference to central authority than out of any deep convictions.

Since Mao's death, the importance of Maoism, and indeed of communism, has waned. China's current leaders neither demand nor desire the type of mass mobilization that was a hallmark of Mao's China. The current leadership instead prefers a largely depoliticized public that is more common in the authoritarian regimes of developing countries, as it was in pre-communist Confucian China.

NATIONALISM Nationalism was a dominant feature of twentieth-century China. It has perhaps become even more important in the twenty-first century, as the nominally communist party-state seeks new sources of legitimacy for retaining its monopoly on political power. The country's long and powerful imperial past (and its humiliation at the hands of foreigners in the nineteenth and twentieth centuries) has bred a strong sense of national pride. Mao's Communists capitalized on this sense of nationalism by melding the struggle for communism with the bitter struggle to expel the Japanese occupiers during World War II.

Fierce nationalism, often manifested as xenophobia, has been a cornerstone of Chinese political culture. Communist leaders frequently use nationalism to maintain support for the political system. China's hostile reaction to the inadvertent U.S. bombing of China's embassy in Yugoslavia in 1999 and the downing of a surveillance plane in 2001, widespread anti-Japanese street protests in 2005, and angry Chinese reactions to foreign protests leading up to the 2008 Summer Olympics are all manifestations of this Chinese nationalism. Indeed, China's successful hosting of the Beijing Olympics both expressed and confirmed the key role of patriotism and nationalism in twenty-first-century China. More recently, China has stirred nationalist sentiment in its territorial disputes with Japan and several Southeast Asian countries over contested islands in the East and South China Seas.

CHALLENGES TO CHINA'S COMMUNIST POLITICAL CULTURE There is growing evidence that the strict party control of Chinese political culture is steadily eroding. The widespread support for the pro-reform student movement in Tiananmen Square in 1989 was the first major sign that the Communist Party no longer had a monopoly on political ideas (even as the party's crushing of the protests demonstrated that the state retained a monopoly of force). Subsequent years have seen steady growth in dissent and protest by China's rural poor, disgruntled industrial workers, and disaffected ethnic minorities. The spiritual success of Falun Gong and China's thousands of illegal Christian "house churches" has frightened the Chinese government, especially these groups' ability to attract and mobilize followers independent of state control. As noted earlier, Internet and social media usage vital to economic growth has exploded in China and created a venue for Chinese social and political activism. For better or worse, booming trade and study and travel abroad have released a flood of Western ideas and values. In sum, it is unclear how long China's leaders can depend on a largely passive and compliant public, especially as rapid economic growth and globalization create new tensions, problems, and opportunities.

Political Economy

From 1949 to 1978, China adopted a Soviet-style communist political-economic model. In choosing this model, Mao Zedong and the CCP leadership consciously opted for equality over freedom. They promised all Chinese an **iron rice bowl** (lifetime employment, health care, and retirement security) and retained state ownership of all property and full control of the economy through central planning. State bureaucrats assigned targets and quotas to producers at all levels of the economy and allocated basic goods to consumers.

As in the Soviet Union, this centrally planned political-economic model favored the development of heavy industry at the expense of consumer goods. It also led to the creation of a massive state economic policy-making bureaucracy not present in capitalist political economies. Between 1949 and 1952, the state gradually nationalized most private industries and mobilized the economy to recover from the eight years of war with Japan and two decades of civil war. By 1952, the communist state had redistributed land to more than 300 million landless peasants. In the mid-1950s, peasants were strongly encouraged to form larger agricultural cooperatives by pooling land, equipment, and labor and sharing profits; such cooperatives gave the state greater political control over the countryside.

Despite the agrarian roots of the Chinese revolution, Mao and the CCP sought to rapidly industrialize China by launching a crash industrialization campaign called the Great Leap Forward (1958–60). Mao believed that China's communist-led masses could be harnessed to carry out rapid industrial growth. To pursue that goal, he favored a policy of **Reds versus experts**—setting politically indoctrinated party cadres (Reds) over those with economic training (experts). Vowing to progress "twenty years in a day" and to catch up with the industrialized West in 15 years, Mao promoted the creation of small-scale, labor-intensive industry (so-called backyard industries) in both cities and the countryside. The Great Leap Forward also collectivized agriculture by creating gigantic communes that became party-controlled providers of education, health care, public works, and industrial production. Ultimately, however, the Great Leap Forward was a colossal failure. The diversion of energy from agriculture to inefficient industry and a drop in food production caused by the forced collectivization of farm production were largely responsible for a three-year famine that killed tens of millions of Chinese people.

By the early 1960s, Mao had been marginalized from the realm of economic policy making, and most of his Great Leap Forward policies had been abandoned. Although agricultural communes remained in place, peasant households were permitted to grow small, private plots. Once they met state production quotas, the peasants were permitted to sell their surplus on the free market. Industries began to emphasize expertise over political correctness and material over moral incentives.

In response to his own marginalization, Mao attacked these new policies as "capitalist." In 1966, he launched the Great Proletarian Cultural Revolution. The persecution unleashed during the next decade targeted those with the most expertise, and the impact on the education system and the economy was devastating. Following several years of utter chaos in which schools were closed and many factories shut down, Mao's disastrous policies were once again shelved.

Labor Force by Occupation

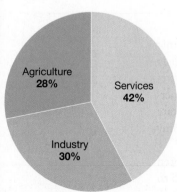

Agriculture 28%

Services 42%

Industry 30%

The chaos of the Cultural Revolution left China a poor and isolated economy. However, things started to improve after the death of Mao in 1976. By late 1978, under the leadership of Deng Xiaoping, economic reform and opening began in fits and starts as the Chinese Communist leadership shifted its focus from the traditional communist goal of equity to creating rapid economic growth.[10] Agricultural communes were disbanded and gradually replaced with the **household responsibility system**—a euphemism for largely private farming. Individual farmers still had to sell a set amount of their produce to the state, but they were free to sell any surplus on the open market. Food production grew dramatically, and the widespread famines that had plagued China for millennia became a thing of the past. Industries were decentralized; in their place, "collective" and "town and village" enterprises were allowed greater economic freedom and encouraged to generate profits. The importance of China's state sector gradually diminished, dropping from about 80 percent in 1980 to under 20 percent by 1996. By the mid-1980s, private industry was permitted (though initially heavily regulated), and the state gradually eliminated price controls. Hoping to end China's economic isolation, the government created **special economic zones** in 1979, offering tax breaks and other incentives to lure foreign investment to a handful of coastal enclaves.

During the 1990s, China's reformers shifted their focus to the urban industrial sector and devolved substantial economic decision-making authority to provincial and local officials and private entrepreneurs. China's socialist command economy had been transformed into what China's communist leaders acknowledged had become a "socialist market economy." These liberal reforms have sparked nearly four decades of astounding economic growth.

Growing at a pace and scope unprecedented in human history, China's economy expanded nearly 10 percent annually for the first three decades of reform and opening, and its GDP has grown some 15-fold. Hundreds of millions of people have been lifted out of poverty, but China remains a poor country. Its per capita GDP at purchasing power parity (PPP) in 2016 was only $14,600; thus China ranked 111th in the world, just ahead of Macedonia but far behind both Mexico (89th at $18,900) and Russia (71st at $26,100).

STATE CAPITALISM AND FOREIGN INVESTMENT

Communist China's twenty-first-century economy is decidedly capitalist. Since the 1990s, party-state reformers have sold off or closed down tens of thousands of inefficient state-owned enterprises (SOEs), putting millions of SOE employees out of work. Since 2002, the private sector's share of industrial output grew from just over half to over three-fourths of total output. But the remaining SOEs are very large, very important, and remain very much favored by China's capitalist system.[11]

In fact, the party-state has tightened its grip on a number of "strategic" industries at the commanding heights of the economy, such as oil and coal, transport, and telecommunication. Of the 98 Chinese firms in the *Fortune* 500 list of the world's largest companies in 2015, the top 12 and all but 22 of them were SOEs. These state firms receive preferential lending, favored market access, and other benefits—privileges that have enhanced their growth and made employment there highly desirable and quite lucrative for Chinese executives. Moreover, the party-state has retained partial or substantial ownership in many of China's ostensibly "private" firms.

Although China's "state capitalism" has permitted the party-state to retain firm control over China's economy and to nurture infant industries in key sectors such as green technology and automobiles, critics note that state-sponsored industrial policies have led to inefficiency, corruption, and surplus labor in the state sector. They have allowed the SOEs to consume the largest share of credit granted by state-owned banks. Despite these drawbacks, China's continued success with its version of state-led capitalism has led some to give this neomercantilist development model the label **Beijing consensus**—an alternative to the long-standing neoliberal free-market developmental model championed by the West and often labeled the "Washington consensus."

In addition, this preferential state treatment for domestic firms has hampered prospects for foreign companies investing or doing business in what has long been coveted as the world's largest potential consumer market. Many observers predicted that China's entry into the World Trade Organization (WTO) in 2001 would spur additional privatization and liberalization. Its WTO membership has required China to take significant market-opening measures, and domestic firms, especially SOEs, face growing competition from foreign enterprises. Still, despite the significant liberalization of the Chinese economy, the country's economic system remains substantially closed. China's economy is freer than Nigeria's and Brazil's but is still more restricted than the economies of Mexico, India, and the South Africa.[12]

CHINA'S GROWTH MODEL BRINGS CHALLENGES

Reform and opening has created rapid growth as well as huge problems. First, as China's enterprises have become more profit oriented, employers are free to lay off unproductive labor. As a result, Mao's iron rice bowl has given way to labor mobility, job uncertainty, and unemployment. The Chinese leadership is betting that China's growing private sector will be able to absorb the unemployed, but the economy must produce at least 25 million jobs a year just to keep up.

Second, after decades of communist emphasis on equality, the reforms of the past four decades have made China much less equal. Inequality has grown between individuals, between urban and rural Chinese, and between regions. China's Gini index (a measure of economic inequality: a score of 0 equals perfect equality, and 100 equals perfect inequality) rose from 16 in 1978 to 39 in 1988. The number peaked at 49 in 2008, and as of 2014 remains at 47. This figure compares with 0.48 in Mexico, 45 in the United States, and 42 in Russia for the same year.

Much of China's inequality is regional. Most of the activity in direct foreign investment and industrialization is concentrated along China's eastern coast, especially in Guangdong Province, Shanghai, Beijing, and Tianjin. Although development is creeping westward and inland megacities such as Chongqing are now full participants in China's explosive economic growth, much of China's poorer hinterland has received far less investment.

Thus China is rapidly urbanizing, but nearly half of its population still lives in the countryside. Early economic reforms largely benefited the rural areas, but more recent reforms have focused primarily on China's cities, and much of rural China remains desperately poor and largely neglected. Prices for agricultural goods are low, taxes are high, school is expensive, health care is poor, and the modern consumer amenities that are increasingly available in urban China are mostly absent in rural areas.

This disparity among regions has pushed hundreds of millions of Chinese to migrate to the cities to escape rural poverty, pulled by the lure of factory jobs and employment in the growing service sector. Although this internal migration is not illegal, most rural Chinese who migrate to cities are unable to secure an urban *hukou*, or residency permit, and therefore are excluded from the relatively more generous urban welfare system. This means that benefits provided to urban *hukou* holders, such as state-provided health care, pensions, unemployment insurance, and education, are for the most part denied to these rural migrants. Even with this discrimination, the state has been unable to stem the tide of migration, despite recent promises to redress the imbalance between urban and rural benefits from reform and opening.

Third, rapid industrial development has created huge resource shortages and environmental damage for China. A fourth of the country is desert, and three-fourths of its forests have disappeared. Its rivers are drying up, and the water and

Prized for their dexterity and docility, single women comprise much of China's increasingly sophisticated assembly-line workforce.

air that remain are filling with harmful chemicals. Half a billion Chinese lack access to safe drinking water, and an equal number breathe dangerously unsafe air—the Chinese are literally "choking on their own success."[13] And increasingly, China's problem has become the world's problem: China surpassed the United States in 2008 as the world's largest emitter of greenhouse gases, and its voracious economy is consuming world resources at an unprecedented rate. Last, China's exports, the engine of its growth, are also causing problems as its trade surplus with its trading partners grows and controversy mounts concerning China's violation of intellectual property rights and the safety and quality of its products.

Add to these growing pains of rapid development a final, potentially far more serious problem: China's economic growth engine is slowing. More than three decades of nearly 10 percent annual GDP growth have given way since 2012 to GDP growth that is averaging closer to 7.5 percent. While this pace is still far more rapid than any of the advanced industrialized economies (or even most developing economies), the prospect of declining growth is particularly troublesome to a government that has staked its legitimacy on the ability to continue delivering prosperity to its populace. Many argue that China's reform process finds itself at a crossroads in which China's leaders will have to make difficult choices while pursuing deep structural changes in the near future.

Disagreement about how to proceed with these reforms has led to the emergence of two broad factions within China's core leadership. One faction, known as **populists**, is led by former paramount leader Hu Jintao and includes current premier Li Keqiang. Leaders in this faction worked their way up through the CCP, often beginning in humble circumstances and serving as local and provincial leaders in poor inland provinces. While recognizing the need for continued reform, the populists favor equality and the need to address China's growing economic disparities, unemployment, and the tattered social safety net.

The other faction, known as **elitists**, is led by Hu Jintao's predecessor, Jiang Zemin, and includes current paramount leader Xi Jinping among others. Leaders in this faction, also known as "princelings," are the offspring of former high-ranking officials. They favor economic freedom and efficiency over equality. Xi Jinping has called for measures to ensure continued economic growth and the strengthening of China's integration into the global economy.

How will this factional struggle play out, and what will it mean for China's twenty-first-century economy? Optimists argue that this "team of rivals" will balance each other out, ensuring that the imperatives of economic freedom and equality will be met. Pessimists caution that if growth continues to slow and economic, social, and environmental conditions continue to worsen, factional compromise may turn to feuding with grave consequences for the world's largest economy.[14]

Current Issues in China

CAN POLLUTED CHINA GO GREEN?

The current state of China's environment is horrific. Air, water, and soil pollution in many areas of the country have reached toxic levels; in recent years, "airpocalypses" in northern Chinese cities have made visibility difficult, breathing dangerous, and respiratory ailments almost inevitable. Water scarcity, desertification, deforestation, the silting of rivers, salinization of soil, and carbon emissions threaten not only China's people and lands but also increasingly China's neighbors and the entire planet. China contains 9 of the 10 most polluted cities in the world, and a 2015 study estimated that air pollution alone led to the premature death of over 1.6 million Chinese in 2014.[15] In recent years, China has become the world's biggest producer of greenhouse gases and the largest consumer of energy. The country showers much of Asia with toxic acid rain; and it discards over 50 billion pairs of disposable chopsticks annually, produced from some 25 million imported trees. Although it is certainly not the first industrializing country to face environmental challenges, China's sheer size and the rapid pace of its development have made the country's pollution problems particularly daunting and their potential consequences dire.

China's acute environmental problems have their roots in the Maoist communist developmental model, which focused on heavy industrialization, wasteful technologies, and pricing policies that undervalued the true cost of inputs such as coal and water and overvalued the economy's industrial outputs.[16] The policies of reform and opening have only exacerbated the environmental crisis. Lacking other sources of legitimacy, China's reformers have pursued growth at all costs in order to boost employment and thereby maintain social and political stability. The party-state has also devolved the bulk of industrial decision-making authority to local officials who have both autonomy and incentive to promote industrialization with little concern for the negative environmental impact of their choices. China has welcomed foreign investment from countries such as Japan, Korea, Taiwan, and the United States. These nations have been happy to export their polluting industries to China rather than retain them in their own backyards.

Finally, China's growing middle class has anxiously pursued the habits and lifestyles of comfort and conspicuous consumption it has seen elsewhere. Everyone in

The "airpocalypse" that has plagued northern China in recent winters offers graphic evidence of the acute environmental problems facing the country.

China aspires to own a car, and many consumers now have the means to attain this dream. China has surpassed the United States as the world's largest auto market, leading critics to warn that China is simply too populated and the world's resources too scarce for its citizens to mimic the lifestyles of the West. If China were to achieve parity with the United States in per capita car ownership, it would possess well over a billion cars—more than the entire global fleet of vehicles in 2011.

What is the solution? Can China "go green"? Although China's environmental situation is bleak, those concerned about pollution point to signs of hope. China's urban middle class has begun to adopt not just modern consumption patterns but also increasingly postmodern and postmaterialist values concerned with health, the environment, and quality of life. More broadly, the swelling numbers of victims of this pollution are becoming increasingly vocal in speaking out and organizing successful protests against local developers and local government officials.

For the first time, the party-state is not only tolerating but also encouraging the efforts of environmental NGOs to address China's many environmental problems. And perhaps most promising, government planners have targeted green energy as a leading growth sector in China's ongoing economic development and have invested heavily in hydroelectric, solar, wind, and clean coal technologies. China has been able to leapfrog to the latest green technologies, using government subsidies and its huge domestic market to obtain a significant share of the global renewable energy market. It has constructed dozens of dams and deployed extensive wind and solar farms domestically. Optimists both inside and outside China argue that the same combination of strong state leadership and entrepreneurial drive that fueled China's remarkable industrialization is now pushing China toward a solution to its huge environmental problems. Time will tell if China can indeed match its industrialization miracle with an environmental one.

CHINA'S DEVELOPMENTAL MODEL AND THE PROBLEM OF CORRUPTION

Environmental pollution poses a very real threat to China's continued development; however, many scholars point to political and economic corruption as an even more insidious challenge to China's economic growth and political stability. All political economies are vulnerable to the abuse of public office for private gain, but authoritarian regimes are particularly susceptible due to the absence of transparency and the rule of law.

Corruption is not just a recent problem in the PRC; the protests a quarter century ago at Tiananmen were motivated by broad dissatisfaction with elite privilege and corrupt practices, not demands for democracy. And while some scholars have argued that China's greater reliance on market competition since then would limit corruption, the combination of increased wealth (more spoils for the taking) and the devolution of decision-making authority to local officials (more public offices for the exploiting) have increased incentives to engage in bribery, kickbacks, rent-seeking, patronage, nepotism, and outright theft.

The costs of corruption to China are significant. Estimates place the outright economic costs of political corruption as high as $100 billion annually, but these corrupt practices exact a far higher toll. They exacerbate inequality, further harm the environment, undermine the legitimacy of the party-state, and feed social frustration with elite privilege. Recognizing this, China's leaders from Mao to the present have launched periodic anticorruption campaigns. But the sweeping effort undertaken by current leader Xi Jinping is impressive both in its breadth and in Xi's willingness to take on top-ranking officials.

Promising to go after both "flies and tigers" (both low- and high-ranking officials), Xi's government announced the arrest and punishment of 182,000 officials for corruption and the abuse of power in 2013. Among those arrested in recent years are wealthy red capitalists, top-ranking military officers, government ministers, and even the high-ranking party cadre. Among the latter is Chongqing party chief **Bo Xilai**, who before his highly publicized arrest and trial in 2013 had been on track to join the PSC as one of China's handful of core party leaders.

Ironically, Xi's anticorruption campaign may cost China's economy even more than the corrupt activities it has ostensibly targeted. Wealthy government officials, business elites, and their families have drastically cut back on the gift giving, parties, and under-the-table deals that have lubricated the "connections" or *guanxi* so important to political and economic transactions in today's China. Economists have estimated that this drop in consumption and the dampening effect of these austerity measures could lead to a loss of over $100 billion in economic activity annually. Others have concluded that this calculation of economic loss is beside the point. They argue that the real purpose of these anticorruption campaigns is to enhance political legitimacy in the eyes of the masses and to eliminate political rivals. In short, the deeply institutionalized corruption of China's authoritarian regime presents a dangerous double-edged sword. As former party elder Chen Yun once stated, "Fight corruption too little and destroy the country; fight it too much and destroy the Party."

Key Terms

Beijing consensus (p. 473)
Bo Xilai (p. 478)
Chinese Communist Party (CCP) (p. 449)
Chinese Dream (p. 457)
Confucianism (p. 447)
Cultural Revolution (p. 451)
danwei (work unit) system (p. 454)
Deng Xiaoping (p. 452)
elitists (p. 476)
Falun Gong (p. 460)
floating population (p. 454)
Great Leap Forward (p. 451)
harmonious society (p. 457)
household responsibility system (p. 472)
Hu Jintao (p. 457)
hukou (household registration) system
   (p. 454)
iron rice bowl (p. 471)
Jiang Zemin (p. 458)

Kuomintang (KMT) (p. 448)
Li Keqiang (p. 459)
Long March (p. 450)
Mao Zedong (p. 450)
May Fourth movement (p. 448)
National Party Congress (NPC) (p. 457)
National People's Congress (NPC) (p. 458)
People's Liberation Army (PLA) (p. 450)
populists (p. 475)
red capitalists (p. 464)
Red Guard (p. 451)
Reds versus experts (p. 472)
reform and opening (p. 445)
special economic zones (p. 473)
Sun Yat-sen (p. 448)
Three Represents (p. 462)
Tiananmen Square (p. 453)
Xi Jinping (p. 457)

Ugandan coffee for export, certified as sustainable by local and international nongovernmental organizations. The attempt to promote "fair trade" between richer and poorer countries is an example of the complexities facing political-economic development in the developing world.

Developing Countries

What are the causes of poverty and wealth?

UP TO THIS POINT, WE HAVE repeatedly considered the role of economic and political institutions in helping (or hindering) development and democracy. These institutions are of particular concern among the poorer or developing countries, where for many a basic standard of living remains far out of reach. How to promote development? And where should those changes begin?

One example that many of us have direct experience with is Fair Trade. At some point, probably everyone reading this has purchased something labeled "Fair Trade" that was produced in the developing world. Most likely it was a cup of coffee with beans originally harvested in Latin America or Africa, but Fair Trade–certified goods run the gamut from coffee and tea to seafood and sugar, from flowers to basketballs. Fair Trade seems like a clear opportunity for producers and consumers to overcome economic and political barriers and create a more beneficial relationship to promote development. Is this the case?

Before we can consider that question, we should understand exactly what Fair Trade means. The idea goes back as far as the 1960s, but a labeling organization was not developed until the late 1980s. The Fair Trade mark would certify that goods met certain standards in several areas. Laborers are to be guaranteed basic working conditions, such as minimum wages and a ban on child labor. Farmers are also organized as cooperatives to pool resources and distribute the premium earned from Fair Trade goods. Environmental standards deal with such practices as the use of pesticides. In return, Fair Trade buyers provide long-term contracts and financing to producers, and agree to a fixed higher price. In 2014, $6 billion in Fair Trade coffee and other foods were sold worldwide. By 2015, over a million and a half individuals in about 70 countries were involved in the production of Fair Trade goods.

As Fair Trade consumption has grown in the developed democracies, so has scrutiny of the system. One argument is that premiums paid through Fair Trade keep inefficient farmers in operation although they would be better off working in some other part of the economy. Others suggest that premiums do not trickle down to the producers but are eaten up by the overhead costs of administering a cooperative. Unfortunately, much of this debate has been driven by ideological preferences or anecdotes.

More recently, a deeper study of Fair Trade raised some significant questions about the impact of the certification system. Researchers in London conducted a four-year study of Fair Trade production of coffee, tea, and flowers in Ethiopia and Uganda. Some of their findings were disturbing. Contrary to assumptions, many of those involved in producing Fair Trade goods are not farm owners but hired workers, including children. These wage laborers often made less than those at typically larger non–Fair Trade farms. Moreover, premiums tended to be gained by a minority of larger farms, meaning the poorest farmers and laborers got far less from the arrangement. Schools, clinics, and other benefits built by cooperatives were often denied to wage laborers.

Do the Ethiopian and Ugandan cases suggest an end to the Fair Trade model? Beyond Africa, Fair Trade has been used extensively in Latin America, where it first began. Studies there do show positive benefits for many farmers, though, as in Africa, wage laborers do not enjoy similar benefits, and cooperatives often suffer from the same kinds of inequality as found in Uganda and Ethiopia. In short, evidence suggests that Fair Trade does provide benefits, but it is not an easy answer to problems of development.

Interestingly, both the African and Latin American cases suggest that profits and other benefits are more equitably distributed when Fair Trade production takes place at a larger scale. This idea may go against our beliefs that large businesses are by nature unjust while small-scale production is more fair and equal. But research suggests that larger firms have greater resources at their disposal, can provide a wider array of benefits, and can be held accountable via unionization and regulation. The image of a family harvesting coffee may have a strong visual and emotional appeal when we buy our latte. But it may distract us from the role of strong institutions as a foundation for large-scale development.[1]

LEARNING OBJECTIVES

- Describe the key characteristics of developing countries.
- Consider how imperialism and colonialism have affected developing countries' state, societal, and economic institutions.
- Compare how post-imperial countries have suffered from ethnic and national division, limited economic growth, and weak states.
- Evaluate and critique (a) societal, economic, and political institutions and policies as pathways to development and democracy; and (b) the role of the international community in fostering or hindering change.

SO FAR, WE HAVE INVESTIGATED two major kinds of countries: the developed democracies and communist and postcommunist countries. But these two categories leave out much of Latin America, Asia, and Africa. Many of the countries in these regions have had neither liberal democratic nor communist regimes. Of these countries, the vast majority have levels of economic industrialization far below those in the developed democracies or the communist and postcommunist world. The traditional labeling of these countries as belonging to a "Third World" unhelpfully grouped together a diverse range of people and political systems according to what they were not, rather than what they were—what we call a residual category. The more recent term *"the Global South"* is vaguely geographic but no more helpful.

How, then, should we understand these countries? Whereas the developed democracies are notable for their early modernization and capitalist development and the communist states for their later, rapid, state-directed modernization and industrialization, the countries discussed in this chapter are characterized by hybrid forms of economic, societal, and political institutions, both foreign-imposed and indigenous.

In this chapter, we develop some ideas and categories to investigate and understand these countries. We will begin by distinguishing among developing countries and examining the relationship between freedom and equality across them. From there, we will look at some of the fundamental experiences and institutions shared by these countries, particularly those associated with imperialism and colonialism. Although imperialism had different effects in different parts of the world, we can generalize about its legacies. Next, we will consider what challenges and obstacles these countries have faced after gaining independence. How does a country reconcile freedom and equality when the conditions may favor neither? And how have some countries managed to enjoy economic and political development while others have stagnated or declined? These topics will lead us into a final discussion of the prospects for political, economic, and societal development in developing countries. What policies might help generate greater democracy, political stability, and economic prosperity in these countries? The difficulties they face are great and the tasks daunting. But out of such challenges can emerge new ideas and innovations with the potential to bring about positive change.

Freedom and Equality in the Developing World

The developing world has often been divided into two groups that indicate important differences in their levels of development. Over the past 50 years, some of these countries, particularly in Asia and parts of Latin America, have experienced dramatic rates of economic growth and democratization, to the point that they now resemble the developed democracies in many ways. These are known as **middle income countries**. In the past three decades, many of these countries have undergone rapid development with a sharp tendency toward democratization and political and social stability. Many of them are also listed in Chapter 7 as within the category of developed democracies, such as Mexico, Brazil, Chile, South Korea, and Taiwan.

In other cases, economic and political structures have remained weak or even grown weaker over the past decades. Some of these countries have slid into greater poverty, violence, and civil conflict. They are often referred to as **lower income countries**, sometimes also known as less-developed countries (LDCs). The World Bank defines lower income countries as those below $4,000 per capita gross domestic product (GDP) at purchasing power parity (PPP), and middle income countries as those between $4,000 and $13,000. We will speak of these lower and middle income countries together as **developing countries** (Table 10.1).

As mentioned in Chapter 8, developing countries, like postcommunist countries, have grown increasingly dissimilar, making organizations like the World Bank even abandon the term of late. However, comparisons can help us understand variations among these countries. Why have some broken out of the trap of underdevelopment and others not? Does it have to do with how states are constructed? Their regimes or political-economic systems? The absence or presence of democracy? Their ethnic, national, or religious institutions? Their culture? Their relationship to developed democracies or other more powerful states? Can we draw lessons from some developing countries and apply these lessons to others?

Before addressing present problems, we should turn to history. Despite differences in their current conditions, developing countries share a legacy of colonialism and imperialism and the experience of belonging to large empires, being possessions of more powerful states. Imperial rule, which lasted for decades or even centuries, dramatically and often rapidly transformed economic, political, and societal institutions in the colonized countries. Although resistance eventually brought down imperial rule, the changes this system wrought could not be easily unmade. To

middle income countries Historically less-developed countries that have experienced significant economic growth and democratization; also known as newly industrializing countries (NICs)

lower income countries Countries that lack significant economic development or political institutionalization or both; also known as less-developed countries (LDCs)

developing countries Lower and middle income countries

TABLE 10.1 Developing Countries, 2017

CENTRAL AND SOUTH AMERICA	ASIA	NORTH AFRICA AND MIDDLE EAST	SUB-SAHARAN AFRICA (CONTINUED)
Antigua & Barbuda	Afghanistan	Algeria	Gambia
Argentina	Bangladesh	Bahrain	Ghana
Belize	Bhutan	Egypt	Guinea
Bolivia	Brunei	Eritrea	Guinea-Bissau
Brazil	Burma (Myanmar)	Ethiopia	Ivory Coast
Chile	Cambodia	Iran	Kenya
Colombia	Cyprus	Iraq	Lesotho
Costa Rica	Fiji	Jordan	Liberia
Dominica	India	Lebanon	Madagascar
Dominican Republic	Indonesia	Libya	Malawi
Ecuador	Kiribati	Morocco	Mali
El Salvador	Korea (South)	Oman	Mauritania
Grenada	Kuwait	Qatar	Mauritius
Guatemala	Laos	Saudi Arabia	Mozambique
Guyana	Malaysia	Syria	Namibia
Haiti	Maldives	United Arab Emirates	Niger
Honduras	Marshall Islands	Yemen	Nigeria
Jamaica	Micronesia		Rwanda
Mexico	Nauru	SUB-SAHARAN AFRICA	São Tomé and Príncipe
Nicaragua	Nepal	Angola	Senegal
Panama	Pakistan	Benin	Seychelles
Paraguay	Palau	Botswana	Sierra Leone
Peru	Papua New Guinea	Burkina Faso	Somalia
St. Kitts & Nevis	Philippines	Burundi	South Africa
St. Lucia	Samoa	Cameroon	South Sudan
St. Vincent & the Grenadines	Singapore	Cape Verde	Sudan
Suriname	Solomon Islands	Central African Republic	Swaziland
Trinidad & Tobago	Sri Lanka	Chad	Tanzania
Uruguay	Taiwan	Comoros	Togo
Venezuela	Thailand	Congo (Democratic Republic of)	Tunisia
	Tonga	Congo (Republic of)	Uganda
EUROPE	Tuvalu	Djibouti	Zambia
Turkey	Vanuatu	Equatorial Guinea	Zimbabwe
	Vietnam	Gabon	

better understand these institutional legacies, it is worth looking at them in some detail, though we should also keep in mind that history is not destiny—imperialism matters, but it is only one factor in explaining the problems of the post-imperial world.

Imperialism and Colonialism

In the first three chapters of this book, we saw that over the past millennium Europe, the Middle East, and Asia embarked on a series of dramatic societal, economic, and political changes that formed the outlines of what are now recognized as the hallmarks of modern society: ethnic and national identity, technological innovation, and political centralization. The growing power of modern societies was soon projected outward to conquer and incorporate new lands and peoples that could contribute to their rapid development. The result was the emergence of **empires**—single political authorities that have under their sovereignty a large number of external regions or territories and different peoples. Although this definition might lead a person to conclude that any large, diverse country is an empire, central to the definition is the idea that lands and peoples that are not seen as an integral part of the country itself are nonetheless under its direct control. The term **imperialism** describes the system whereby a state extends its power to directly control territory, resources, and people beyond its borders. People often use *imperialism* interchangeably with *colonialism*, though these terms are different. **Colonialism** indicates the physical occupation of a foreign territory through military force, businesses, or settlers. Colonialism, then, is often the means for consolidating an empire.

Although imperialist practices began many thousands of years ago, modern imperialism can be dated from the fifteenth century, when technological development in Europe, the Middle East, and Asia—advanced seafaring and military technology in particular—had advanced to such an extent that these countries were able to project their military might far overseas. In Asia, the powerful Chinese empire turned away from this path. Having consolidated power hundreds of years before the states of Europe did, the Chinese state grew conservative and inflexible, interested more in maintaining the status quo than in striking out to acquire new lands. Indeed, at the same time that Europeans were setting out for the Americas, the Chinese were actually retreating from overseas voyages; by 1500, it had become illegal for Chinese subjects to build oceangoing vessels. Similarly, although the powerful Ottoman Empire in the Middle East expanded its power over much of the Arab world and into Asia, North Africa, and parts of Europe, nearly conquering Vienna in 1683, it failed to expand its power farther beyond the Islamic world. Whatever the reasons for this shift in China and the Ottoman Empire, in both cases there existed early state building and imperialism that predated and rivaled Europe. It is thus important to recognize that the peoples who became subject to modern imperialism were not a blank slate, without any of their own institutions. Many of the regions that came under imperial rule already possessed highly developed economic, political, and societal institutions.

Thus, in the 1500s, Europe began a process of imperial expansion that would continue for nearly five centuries. Driven by economic and strategic motives as well as a belief that Christianity and Western culture needed to be brought to the rest of

empire A single political authority that has under its sovereignty a large number of external regions or territories and different peoples

imperialism A system in which a state extends its power to directly control territory, resources, and people beyond its borders

colonialism An imperialist system of physically occupying a foreign territory using military force, businesses, or settlers

TIMELINE Modern Imperialism

1494	Following European discovery, Spain and Portugal partition the Americas between their two empires.
1519–36	Indigenous groups (Aztecs, Incas) are defeated by imperial powers in South America.
1602–52	The Dutch begin to establish control over parts of the Indonesian archipelago and southern Africa. English settlement begins in North America.
1810–25	Wars of independence in Latin America; Spanish and Portuguese rule is brought to an end.
1839–58	United Kingdom expands control into Asia, notably Hong Kong and India.
1884	The Berlin Conference; Africa is rapidly divided among European powers, notably France, Portugal, and Belgium.
1939–45	World War II catalyzes the eventual decolonization of Asia and Africa.
1947	Independence of India; first major decolonization of the twentieth century.
1956–68	Independence of most British, French, and Belgian colonies in Africa after local rebellions against imperial rule.
1975	Independence of most former Portuguese colonies in Africa and Asia.
1997–99	Hong Kong (United Kingdom) and Macau (Portugal) returned to China.

the world, European empires stretched their power around the globe. First, Spain and Portugal gained control over South America, Central America, and large parts of North America. By the seventeenth century, British, French, and other settlers began to arrive in North America, displacing the local populations. In the eighteenth century, Europeans started to assert control over parts of North Africa and the Middle East, shocking Ottoman elites who had long viewed Europeans as technologically and culturally backward. Their shock was shared by the Chinese in the nineteenth and early twentieth centuries as European imperialism rapidly expanded into Asia. Nearly all of Africa, too, was eventually divided up by the European states. This European imperialist expansion was joined briefly by Japan, which in the early twentieth century established its own empire across parts of Asia. In each of these cases,

IN FOCUS Imperialism . . .

- Is a system in which a state extends its power beyond its borders to control other territories and peoples.
- Was propagated by European powers from the sixteenth to the twenty-first centuries.
- Is driven by economic, strategic, and religious motives.
- Often led to colonialism, the physical occupation of foreign territories.

imperial powers possessed well-organized political systems and military structures, technological advances, and economic resources; these advantages were combined with a belief that imperial control was not only possible but also necessary, just, and willed by God.[2]

Institutions of Imperialism

The effect of imperialism on the societies that came under foreign rule differed across time and place, but some common elements resulted from the imposition of modern political, societal, and economic systems onto non-Western societies. As we shall see, this imposition had a dramatic (and often traumatic) effect that continues to the present.[3]

EXPORTING THE STATE

One of the first major effects of imperialism was the transfer of the state to the rest of the world. Recall from Chapter 2 how the modern state that we take for granted today emerged as a result of a long historical process in Europe; before that time, political units tended to have much weaker control over land and their subjects, and territorial sovereignty and the rule of law were tenuous. States, however, eventually succeeded in consolidating power over other forms of political organization, eliminating their rivals, clearly delineating their borders, and establishing sovereignty.

When European empires began to expand around the world, they incorporated new territories into these state structures. Rival states carved up the territories in the quest for economic resources and strategic advantages. The borders drawn by imperial states therefore often reflected the shape of their colonial ambitions rather than existing geographic, religious, or linguistic realities. The borders of 80 percent of African states are drawn according to longitude and latitude, not local geography or population groups. Many of these externally imposed and arbitrary boundaries became the demarcations for independent countries once imperial rule ended. Even countries that were able to resist direct imperial rule, such as Iran, Thailand, and Ethiopia, found themselves under the continuous influence and pressure of these empires.

Having conquered these territories, imperial powers went about establishing state power and authority. In many empires, this meant creating bureaucratic structures similar to those found in the home country in an attempt to "civilize"—to modernize and Westernize—the local population. These institutions commonly included a national language (typically that of the imperial power), police and a military, taxation and legal systems, and basic public goods such as roads, schools, and hospitals. How new institutions were established and new laws enforced differed. Some empires relied on local leaders to enforce their will, whereas others bypassed indigenous elites in favor of their own centralized forms of authority. These differences tended to reflect the degree of state capacity and autonomy found in the imperial country itself. In both cases, few, if any, democratic practices were introduced, even if they were the norm in the home country. Individuals under colonial rule were considered subjects, not citizens, and thus had few political rights.

This imposition of the state had mixed effects. Many subject peoples experienced increased education and the benefits of basic infrastructure that improved communication and transportation. Life expectancies often rose and infant mortality rates declined, although when those trends were combined with traditional family practices they produced a population explosion that in many poor countries continues today. Traditional institutions such as local religions and customs were eroded and replaced by or fused with Western practices and institutions. This transition was incomplete and uneven. Imperial territories remained economically and politically underdeveloped, placing many subject peoples in a kind of institutional limbo, with a hybrid of Western and traditional institutions. The frustration that grew out of this conflicted identity helped fan the flames of anti-imperialism: the desire for freedom from foreign control.

SOCIAL IDENTITIES

The imposition of organizational forms from outside included various new identities that often displaced or were incorporated into existing social institutions. Among these were ethnic and national identities. In much of the world that came under imperial control, people often identified themselves by tribe or religion, by economic position, or by vocation rather than primarily by some ethnic or national identity (institutions that were particularly strong in the West). But just as empires brought their own political institutions with them, they also introduced the concepts of ethnicity and nation. Imperial elites, themselves shaped and defined by national and ethnic identities, took great interest in identifying and classifying different ethnic groups in the regions they came to occupy and structuring their political and economic control around these classifications. Ironically, even as groups were subject to Western classification, they were often divided across imperial borders that had been drawn with little regard for their tribal, religious, or any other identities.

Suddenly, people who had not specially defined themselves by ethnicity found their basic rights being tied to how they were ethnically defined by the empire. In some cases, this ethnic classification was determined by early pseudoscientific notions of race, which held that certain ethnic groups were naturally superior to others. The European and Japanese empires were influenced by the assumption that the colonizing race was superior to the colonized and thus destined to rule them. Different peoples within the empire, too, were subject to hierarchical classification. Certain ethnic groups were promoted to positions of power and economic advantage, while other groups were marginalized. Colonialism often exacerbated these hierarchies as nonindigenous peoples migrated to colonies. Sometimes these migrants were settlers from the home country; in other cases, they were peoples from other parts of the empire or beyond (for example, Indians migrating to Africa or African slaves being brought to Brazil). These foreign presences further sharpened ethnic and racial divisions, especially when such groups were accorded specific economic or political privileges. In short, inequality became tightly interconnected with ethnicity or race.

In addition to ethnicity, imperial powers also introduced the idea of national identity. During the late nineteenth and early twentieth centuries, in particular, national identity grew to be a powerful force in the industrializing world, helping drive competition between the industrial powers and in turn advancing the imperialist cause.

But the peoples brought under imperial control had little or no sense of a strong national identity, little notion of any right to a sovereign state. This combination of nationalism and imperialism proved to be unstable. Empires viewed the peoples living in their overseas possessions as inferior subjects and gave them only limited ability to improve their standing within the empire. Yet the imperial powers' own concept of nationalism provided these subject peoples with the very means to challenge foreign rule. If nationalism meant the right for a people—any people—to live under their own sovereign state, did this not mean that subject peoples had a right to rule themselves? Empires thus provided the ideological ammunition that their subjects would eventually use to overturn imperialism.

Colonialism also affected gender roles in the colonies. It is hard to make generalizations in this area, since in each region existing gender roles differed greatly and each imperial power viewed gender somewhat differently. Some scholars argue that imperialism brought a number of benefits to women, increasing their freedom and equality by improving their access to health care and education. Others reject this argument, asserting that in many cases colonialism restricted women's roles in society. In many non-Western societies, gender roles may have been much less fixed than those found in the modern world, allowing women particular areas of individual freedom, equality, and autonomy. Imperial powers brought with them their own assumptions regarding the status of women, views that were shaped in part by their religious values. These views were imposed through such institutions as education and the legal system. The economic systems imposed by the colonizers often marginalized women.

One example can be found in research on agriculture and gender equality. Some studies suggest that in societies where farming was done through "shifting cultivation" (performed with hoes and hand-weeding rather than plows, which require greater upper-body strength), women more actively participated in the agricultural economy as equals with men. These norms of equal participation extended outward into other areas, such as politics. However, with the advent of imperialism, such practices were transformed by agricultural modernization and industrial development, shifting participatory power away from women and toward men.[4] Even so, given the wide range of imperial practices and non-Western institutions, it is too simplistic to say that imperialism made women's lives worse in all respects. Imperial rule also created new economic opportunities that challenged traditional roles of women within patriarchal family and tribal orders. Women who could get an education, be freed from traditional codes of family and tribal honor, and hold a job outside of the home saw their lives transformed.

INFOCUS   **Political and Social Institutions of Imperialism**

- The state, as a form of political organization, was imposed on much of the world outside of Europe.
- Ethnic and national identities were created where none had existed before colonization.
- Gender roles from the imperial country were often imposed on colonies.

DEPENDENT DEVELOPMENT

Just as imperialism transformed political and social institutions in colonial areas, creating an amalgam of local and Western forms, economic change occurred in a similarly dramatic and uneven way. The first important change in many imperial possessions was the replacement of a traditional agricultural economy with one driven by the needs of the industrializing capitalist home country. Systems that were based largely on subsistence agriculture and barter were transformed into cash economies in which money was used to pay for goods and labor.

Alongside a cash-based economy came the transformation of economic production. Using a mercantilist political-economic system (see Chapter 4), empires sought to extract revenue from their colonies while at the same time using these territories and their people as a captive market for finished goods from the home country. Free trade thus did not exist for the colonies, which were obliged to sell and buy goods within the confines of the empire. Moreover, colonial production was organized to provide goods that were not easily available in the home country. Rather than finished goods, local economies were rebuilt around primary products such as cotton, cocoa, coffee, tea, wood, rubber, and other valuable commodities that could be extracted from the natural environment.

Large businesses were established to oversee these so-called extractive economies, which were often dominated by a single monopoly. For example, in Indonesia the United East India Company, a Dutch firm, gained control over lucrative spice exports while monopolizing the local market for finished goods from Europe, thereby destroying indigenous trade networks that had existed in the region for centuries. Similarly, during the nineteenth century the British East India Company functioned virtually as a state of its own, controlling a large portion of the Indian economy and much of its foreign trade. Export-oriented imperialism also led to the creation of large plantations that could produce vast quantities of rubber, coffee, or tobacco.

This form of economic organization was quite different from that of the home countries and in many respects was ill suited to domestic development. Infrastructure was frequently developed primarily to facilitate effective extraction and export rather than to improve communication or movement for the subject peoples. Jobs were created in the extractive sector, but local industrialization and entrepreneurialism were more limited. The development of agriculture for export instead of for subsistence damaged the ability of these peoples to feed themselves, and the creation of large-scale agricultural production drove many small farmers off the land. Many colonies saw a resulting boom in urbanization, typically in the colonial capital or other cities central to imperial politics and trade. By the late 1500s, for example, the Spanish had established more than 200 cities in Latin America, which to this day remain the central urban areas in the region. Urbanization brought specific benefits, such as improved infrastructure along with new economic opportunities, but it also exacted clear costs. For example, greater population densities meant greater public health problems, such as disease (which the developed countries themselves had experienced earlier).

Let us take a moment to summarize what we have considered so far. By virtue of their organizational strengths, modern states expanded their power around the globe, establishing new political, economic, and social institutions and displacing existing ones. In some cases, these institutions were reflections of the home country;

- Traditional agricultural economies were transformed to suit the needs of the imperialist power.
- Economic organization under imperialism impeded domestic development in the colonies.
- Free trade was often suppressed, as colonies were forced to supply goods only to the imperial country, creating extractive economies in the colonies.

in others, they were designed specifically to consolidate imperial rule. The result was an uneasy mixture of indigenous and foreign structures. New political institutions and new societal identities were introduced or imposed while participation and citizenship were restricted; economic development was encouraged but in a form that would serve the markets of the home country. Imperialism thus generated new identities and conflict by classifying people and distinguishing between them—between rulers and ruled and between subject peoples themselves. At the same time, the contradictions inherent in this inequality and restriction of freedom became increasingly clear to subject peoples as they began to assimilate and develop their own ideas and values. By the early twentieth century, the growing awareness of this system and its inherent contradictions helped foster public resistance to imperialism and paved the way for eventual independence.

The Challenges of Post-Imperialism

Despite the power of empires to extend their control over much of the world, their time eventually came to an end. In Latin America, where European imperialism first emerged, Napoleon's invasion of Spain and Portugal in 1807–8 led to turmoil in the colonies and a series of wars for independence, which freed most of the region by 1826. In Africa and Asia, where imperialism reached its zenith only in the nineteenth century, decolonization came after World War II. Numerous independence movements emerged within the Asian and African colonies, catalyzed by the weakened positions of the imperial powers and promoted by a Western-educated indigenous leadership able to articulate nationalist goals and organize resistance. Some imperial powers resisted bitterly. France fought a brutal war to retain Algeria in the 1960s. Portugal did not fully withdraw from Africa until 1975. Hong Kong was returned to China by the United Kingdom in 1997. For the most part, colonies in Africa and Asia gained independence by the 1960s.

The elimination of imperialism, however, did not bring a sudden end to the problems of the developing world. These countries have continued to struggle with political, social, and economic challenges to development and stability, freedom, and equality. In many cases, these problems are a legacy of imperial rule, although in other cases they stem from particular domestic and international factors that have developed in the years since independence. But herein lies an important puzzle. If we consider the development of successful economic, social, and political institutions over the past 50 years, Asia has fared the best, Africa the worst, and the picture in Latin America is mixed. Even in these regions there is significant variation. What accounts for these differences? Let's first consider some of the more common problems faced across post-imperial countries and then return to this question to see if the answer can provide some strategies for development and democracy.

BUILDING STATE CAPACITY AND AUTONOMY

One central problem that many developing countries have faced in the years after imperialism has been the difficulty in creating effective political institutions. In Chapter 2, we distinguished between weak states and strong states and noted that many scholars look at state power as consisting of state capacity and state autonomy. *Capacity* refers to a state's ability to fulfill basic policy tasks, and *autonomy* refers to its ability to act independently of the public and foreign actors. Both are necessary to carry out policy, and both have been difficult for post-imperial countries to achieve.

In terms of capacity, developing countries are frequently unable to perform many of the basic tasks expected by the public, such as creating infrastructure, providing education and health care, or delivering other public goods. This lack of capacity stretches back to the absence of a professional bureaucracy; the foreigners who ran the imperial bureaucracies in the colonies typically left as soon as the colonies gained independence, precluding an effective transition to a local bureaucracy. These initial problems of capacity were exacerbated by the politicization of the state; in many cases, the bureaucracy has become an important source of jobs, resources, and benefits that political leaders dole out as a way to solidify control. Recall our discussion in Chapter 8 regarding clientelism and rent seeking. Under clientelism, the state co-opts members of the public by providing specific benefits to a person or group in return for public support, like voting in elections. One facet of clientelism, rent seeking, uses parts of the state to extract income for supporters, giving them preferred access to public goods (like jobs) that would otherwise be distributed in a nonpolitical manner. In many developing countries, limited economic development and relatively weak states have fostered a high degree of clientelism and rent seeking, which political leaders have used to gain and hold on to power.[5] Politics thus becomes a question of buying support and understanding how to bypass formal institutions with informal relationships. As we well know, this is not unique to the developing world, but it is most acute among these states.

Autonomy has been equally problematic in the post-imperialist world. On the surface, many of these countries appear to be highly autonomous, able to function without having to respond to public pressure. The prevalence of nondemocratic regimes in much of the developing world seems only to reinforce this impression. However, these states are largely captured by a patrimonial system along the lines of what we see in Zimbabwe (see Chapter 8). The state is not a highly independent actor but is instead penetrated by groups that see it as a resource to be exploited rather than as a tool for achieving national policy. The result of weak capacity and autonomy is high levels of corruption. For example, during military rule in Nigeria in the 1990s, officials stole more than $1 billion from the state treasury. In 2016, the U.S. government seized $1 billion in assets believed to be stolen by individuals close to the Malaysian prime minister. Studies of corruption indicate that the most corrupt countries in the world are developing and postcommunist countries, and there is a clear correlation between the level of development and the degree of corruption (see Table 10.2).

TABLE 10.2 Corruption Index, 2016

COUNTRY	RANK (1 = LEAST CORRUPT)	COUNTRY	RANK (1 = LEAST CORRUPT)
Denmark	1	China	79
Canada	9	India	79
United Kingdom	10	Indonesia	90
United States	18	Pakistan	116
Japan	20	Mexico	123
France	23	Iran	131
Taiwan	31	Russia	131
Botswana	35	Nigeria	136
South Korea	52	Zimbabwe	154
South Africa	64	Venezuela	166
Brazil	79	Somalia	176

Note: The corruption index is based on national surveys regarding the overall extent of corruption (size and frequency of bribes) in the public and political sectors. Rankings: 1–176; some countries share rankings.

Source: Transparency International, http://www.transparency.org/cpi2016 (accessed 5/16/17).

CHINA

MEXICO

NIGERIA

COUNTING THE COSTS OF CORRUPTION

We can illustrate the correlation between development and corruption by taking a closer look at three developing countries studied in this text. As Table 10.2 indicates, China, Mexico, and Nigeria all struggle with relatively high levels of corruption. Each country is located in a different region of the globe, reminding us that corruption challenges developing countries everywhere. All three experienced imperialism, and all have long histories of nondemocratic regimes (though Mexico and Nigeria have both been governed by democratic regimes since 2000). But while all three face developmental challenges compounded by high levels of corruption, levels of development have varied substantially. China now boasts the largest economy in the world, with GDP growth averaging nearly 10 percent annually over the past three decades. During this same period, Mexico grew at an annual rate of just under 3 percent and Nigeria at a rate of just over 4 percent.

Why the discrepancy in growth rates despite similar challenges with corruption? Although many factors are relevant, differences in state autonomy and capacity shed important light on these variations. The resource trap theory discussed in Chapter 8 points to the fact that authoritarian leaders in Mexico and Nigeria controlled vast oil resources, providing them with ample opportunity to enrich themselves. However, democratization in the past fifteen years should have held these public officials accountable to their citizens, thereby curtailing corruption. Unfortunately, in both Mexico and Nigeria, weak but relatively wealthy states simply traded authoritarian patrimonialism for various forms of democratic clientelism—in other words, expanding the circle of corruption rather than eliminating it. Whether authoritarian or democratic, these weak states have lacked both the capacity and the institutions of accountability to prevent government officials—from heads of state to local police officers—from using their access to public resources to pursue private gain.

China is more exceptional. Unlike many developing countries, it has historically benefited from centralized state institutions staffed by a meritocratic bureaucracy. China's one-party system has also been far less accountable to the public than its counterparts in Mexico or Nigeria. Although corruption has worsened in recent decades as economic liberalization has devolved authority to local officials with more opportunity and less constraints to engage in corrupt activities, the central state has remained relatively clean and has sought to fight back against corruption.

But in all three cases, the lack of effective accountability and trust in the rule of law has had a significant impact on development. Corruption has cost Nigeria hundreds of billions of dollars in recent decades and undermined confidence in the regime, exacerbating persistent poverty and ethnic unrest. Corruption costs Mexico an estimated 9 percent of its trillion-dollar GDP each year, facilitates the illicit drug trade, and gravely weakens both local and federal state legitimacy. Even in China, corruption is estimated to cost the economy nearly 100 billion dollars a year and has become so entrenched that the recent anticorruption campaign has put a damper on both legitimate and illegitimate business activity. Clearly, weak political institutions continue to facilitate corruption and threaten development in all three countries.

In addition to compromised capacity and autonomy, states of the developing world are often constrained by international factors. Developing countries are subject to pressure from other, more powerful states and international actors such as the United Nations, the World Bank, multinational corporations, and nongovernmental organizations like Amnesty International and the Red Cross. Frequently wielding much greater economic and political power than the states themselves, these actors can significantly influence the policies of these countries, shaping their military and diplomatic alliances, trade relations, local economies, and domestic laws. Sovereignty is thus compromised.

These constraints on state capacity and autonomy have clear implications for freedom and equality. A state with weak capacity and autonomy is unlikely to be able to establish the rule of law. Laws will not be respected by the public if the state itself is unwilling or unable to enforce and abide by them. Freedom is threatened by conflict and unpredictability, which in turn hinder economic development. A volatile environment and the absence of basic public goods such as roads or education will dissuade long-term investment. Wealth flows primarily into the hands of those who control the state, generating a high degree of inequality. There is no clear regime, and no rules or norms for how politics is to be played.

Unfortunately, where instability is so high often only one institution has a great deal of capacity and autonomy: the military. Where states are weak, military forces often step in and take control of the government themselves, either to stave off disorder or simply to get a turn at draining the state. Military rule has been common in developing countries, and we have seen the military reemerge as an important political force in the Middle East, where political change has been disruptive. Even where military rule has ended, the military often remains a powerful actor with its own political and economic interests, as we saw in the case of Pakistan in Chapter 2.

CREATING NATIONS AND CITIZENS

In the aftermath of colonialism, many developing countries have struggled with the challenge of forging a single nation out of highly diverse societies. Where centralized political authority did not exist before imperialism, identities tended to be quite heterogeneous. Their diversity became problematic when imperial powers began categorizing societal groups and establishing political boundaries and economic and social hierarchies. Migration within empires further complicated relations among these groups. When colonies gained independence, several problems rose to the surface.

First, group divisions often have economic implications, just as they did under colonial rule. Some ethnic or religious groups favored under colonialism continue to monopolize wealth in the post-independence society. For example, in Malaysia and Indonesia ethnic Chinese hold a disproportionate share of national wealth, generating resentment. Similarly, in some African countries Indian immigrants—often brought in by the British as indentured labor—came to control a large portion of the business sector. At the other end of the spectrum, many indigenous populations, such as those in Latin America, are among the poorest in the world, a situation that has sparked ethnically based political movements in several of these countries. Many civil conflicts in developing countries are driven largely by economic concerns that intersect with ethnic or religious differences.

Second, ethnic and religious divisions can similarly complicate politics. In countries where populations are heterogeneous, the battle for political power often falls along ethnic or religious lines as each group seeks to gain control over the state in order to serve its own particular ends (see Chapter 3). Each ethnic or religious group competes for its share of public goods or other benefits from the state. This struggle is central to clientelism and patrimonialism, as each group competes to gain access to resources controlled by the state. At an extreme, this can contribute to authoritarian rule if groups fear losing access to resources if they lose elections.

As a result, where ethnic or religious divisions are strong we often see a form of patrimonialism in which one group dominates the state while effectively freezing other groups out of the political process.[6] In some countries, a majority or plurality may dominate politics, as people of European origin do in Mexico, where the minority indigenous population has little political power. In other cases, a minority may dominate a much larger majority. For example, in Iraq, though most members of the population belong to the Shia sect of Islam, those in power have traditionally been members of the minority Sunni sect. With the overthrow of Saddam Hussein in 2003, conflict emerged between Sunnis and Shias over the future control of the country. A similar dynamic is at work in the Syrian civil war, where individuals from the Alawite sect of Islam have monopolized political power and have been unwilling to relinquish it (see Chapter 5). Economic and political interests thus become entangled with different social identities.

Economic and political difficulties that arise from such social divisions make the creation of a single national identity difficult and weaken the notion of citizenship—that all individuals have a common political relationship to the state. Amid such ethnic and religious diversity, many populations are much less inclined to see the postcolonial state as a true representation of their group's wishes, and states themselves have little beyond the initial struggle for independence on which to build a shared political identity. When ethnic and religious conflicts are extreme, disaffected groups may seek to secede and create their own independent countries. The most recent example of this was the creation in 2011 of South Sudan, which separated from Sudan following a long civil war that pitted a black African south against an Arab north. Under the British Empire, they had been administered as two separate political entities. In advance of their withdrawal in 1956, Britain oversaw the unification of these two areas despite southern Sudanese opposition. South Sudanese independence itself has since led to civil war between leaders from two different ethnic groups.

Gender and family is another important area shaped by the legacies of imperialism. As we noted, gender and family identities and roles have been affected by rapid urbanization and the commercialization of agriculture, which often favored male labor and property rights (such as titles to land). This structure can give women much less leverage in family decisions, such as family size. It also may lead families to view girls as a burden, since they must be married off (often with a dowry) and cannot be expected to take care of their parents in their old age. Thus families may be less willing to invest in their daughters, especially if family sizes are shrinking, placing more pressure on families to have male children. At its most extreme, this favoritism can be deadly, taking the form of female neglect or infanticide. There are estimates that in India some 40 million girls and in China some 60 million girls are "missing" from the expected demographic, having been aborted or having died shortly after birth. Vietnam, Pakistan, and other countries have faced similar issues, either through sex-selective abortions or through neglect of girl babies. Some scholars have already noted that violent conflict and crime in part results when there are a large number of unemployed and unmarried young men—a worrying thought considering that some of the highest gender imbalances are found in the two most populous countries in the world, China and India. In the coming years, the security of women may be a key variable in predicting the security of states.[7]

GENERATING ECONOMIC GROWTH

Economic growth attracts the most focus among those who study developing countries. Indeed, when we think of development, typically economic progress first comes to mind. Because of imperialism, instead of undergoing economic modernization on

---

IN FOCUS Challenges to Building a Unified Nation-State

- Ethnic and religious divisions among different groups in heterogeneous societies (often exacerbated by economic inequality).
- Arbitrary political boundaries imposed by imperial powers.

their own terms, these countries experienced rapid changes directed by the imperial powers to serve their own needs. As a result, upon gaining independence many of these countries found themselves in a continued state of economic dependency on their former empire. But such dependent relationships did not bode well for long-term development, since they often stressed the production of agricultural and other basic commodities in return for finished products. For many developing countries, this unequal relationship was simply a new, indirect form of imperialism, or what some scholars call **neocolonialism**. Breaking this cycle of dependent development was thus the greatest concern for the developing countries following independence.

The former colonies' need to break this cycle resulted in two distinct mercantilist economic policies that were applied throughout the developing world.[8] The first is known as **import substitution**. Under import substitution, countries restrict imports, raising tariff or nontariff barriers to spur demand for local alternatives. To fill this demand, new businesses are built with state funds by creating subsidized or parastatal (partially state-owned) industries. Patents and intellectual property rights are weakly enforced to tap into foreign innovations. Eventually, the hope goes, these firms will develop the productive capacity to compete domestically and internationally. Following World War II, import substitution was commonly used across Latin America and was also taken up in Africa and parts of Asia.

How successful was import substitution? Most observers have concluded that it did not produce the benefits expected, creating instead a kind of "hothouse economy." Insulated from the global economy, the state-supported firms could dominate the local market, but, lacking competition, they were much less innovative or efficient than their international competitors. The idea that these economies would eventually be opened up to the outside world became hard to envision; the harsh climate of the international market, it was thought, would quickly kill off these less competitive firms.

Import substitution thus resulted in economies with large industries reliant on the state for economic support and unable to compete in the international market. Such firms became a drain on state treasuries and a tempting resource for clientelism and rent seeking. This compounded the problem of international debt in these countries, for states had to borrow from other countries to build and subsidize their industries. Uncompetitiveness and debt led to economic stagnation. By and large, these countries also seem to have suffered from what is known as the **middle income trap**. A middle income trap is a situation where countries experience economic growth but are unable to develop at a speed necessary to catch up with developed countries. Thus for every South Korea, there is a Brazil or a South Africa experiencing initially rapid growth that slows down before the country reaches high income status.

Not all postcolonial countries pursued import substitution, however. Several Asian countries eventually discarded import substitution in favor of **export-oriented industrialization**. Countries that pursued an export-oriented strategy sought out technologies and developed industries that focused specifically on exports, capitalizing on what is known as the *product life cycle*. Initially, the innovator of a good produces it for the domestic market and then exports it to the rest of the world. As this product spreads, other countries find ways to make the same good more cheaply or more efficiently and eventually export their own version back to the country that originated the product. Thus, in South Korea, initial exports focused on basic technologies such as textiles and shoes but eventually moved into more complex areas, including automobiles and computers. This policy also had its problems: countries that pursued export-oriented industrialization also relied on high levels of

neocolonialism An indirect form of imperialism in which powerful countries overly influence the economies of less-developed countries

import substitution A mercantilist strategy for economic growth in which a country restricts imports in order to spur demand for locally produced goods

middle income trap A situation where countries experience economic growth but are unable to develop at a speed necessary to catch up with developed countries

export-oriented industrialization A mercantilist strategy for economic growth in which a country seeks out technologies and develops industries focused specifically on the export market

government subsidies and tariff barriers. Yet overall, this strategy has led to levels of economic development much higher than those achieved through import substitution. Some Asian export-oriented countries originally had per capita GDPs far below those of many Latin American and even some African countries. The question of why Latin America pursued a path of import substitution while much of Asia focused on export-led growth is an interesting puzzle, and one that we will turn to at the end of this chapter (see "Institutions in Action," p. 506).

By the 1980s, many developing countries—whether focused on import substitution or still largely focused on agricultural exports, as in Africa—faced deep economic problems, including high levels of government debt. Support from organizations like the World Bank or International Monetary Fund (IMF; see Chapter 11) was conditioned on economic liberalization (see Chapter 4). These policies of liberalization, often known as **neoliberalism**, **structural-adjustment programs**, or the **Washington Consensus**— since they reflect the policy preferences of institutions based in Washington, D.C., such as the World Bank and IMF—typically required countries to privatize state-run firms, end subsidies, reduce tariff barriers, shrink the size of the state, and welcome foreign investment. These reforms have been controversial and their benefits have been mixed. We will discuss this situation in greater detail shortly, when we consider future directions for economic prosperity in the poorer countries.

neoliberalism/structural-adjustment programs/ Washington consensus A policy of economic liberalization adopted in exchange for financial support from liberal international organizations; typically includes privatizing state-run firms, ending subsidies, reducing tariff barriers, shrinking the size of the state, and welcoming foreign investment

INEQUALITY, STATES, AND MARKETS IN SOUTH AFRICA

SOUTH AFRICA

South Africa nicely illustrates the political economic dilemmas faced by developing countries. Under the racial segregationist apartheid regime (1948–94), South Africa's economy adopted mercantilist measures aimed at developing a domestic economy that would elevate Afrikaners (whites of Dutch origin) over both whites of English origin and the black majority. The heavy state presence in the economy, through state-owned enterprises and high levels of tariff protection, was increased as the apartheid regime faced international sanctions and growing isolation in the 1980s.

The electoral victory of the African National Congress (ANC) in 1994 ended apartheid and marked a return to democracy. Many feared that the ANC, which had a socialist ideology and was allied with South Africa's Communist Party, would increase the role of the state in the economy in order to redistribute wealth to the impoverished black majority. There were fears that whites (and their wealth) would leave South Africa in droves.

Yet given its ideological orientation and the extent of inequality and poverty in South Africa, the ANC's political economic approach since 1994 has been quite the opposite. To a large extent, the ANC has pursued the type of Washington Consensus policies we have just discussed. ANC leaders called for an ambitious and much needed plan of state spending to build houses, provide electricity, health care, water, and improve education for the majority of South Africans. At the same time, the ANC leadership was aware that it could not afford those projects unless it attracted foreign investment and unless the South African economy grew rapidly. The 1996 Growth, Employment, and Redistribution program called for the privatization of state-owned enterprises, a reduction of taxes on business, lowering of trade barriers, and relatively conservative macroeconomic policies. The ANC has eschewed radical policies of redistribution of income and wealth so as to preserve a good business climate.

The results have been mixed. On the one hand, South Africa has produced steady (if not always spectacular) economic growth and has attracted foreign investment. ANC governments have dramatically improved the availability of housing, water, electricity, and sanitation to the poor majority. Within Africa, South Africa's economy has often been portrayed as a success story. But at home, the ANC's free-market economic policies have become increasingly unpopular among the black majority. Despite rapid economic growth, unemployment and levels of poverty remain shockingly high, and half of all South Africans remain below the poverty line. South Africa's economic inequality has grown dramatically since the end of apartheid to one of the highest levels in the world. The ANC has made little progress in fulfilling its pledge to redistribute land to blacks (recall our discussion of the different paths of South Africa and Zimbabwe in Chapter 8). Its relatively timid affirmative action programs have enriched a small group of blacks without filtering down to the majority of the population. The ANC's free-market orientation has led to a bitter political break with the usually friendly trade union movement and has splintered the governing party. The leftist Economic Freedom Fighters, created in 2013, has attempted to rally those who are disenchanted with the ANC's political economic orientation.

It remains to be seen whether the ANC's policies will lure enough foreign investment and create enough economic growth to fund increased spending on South Africa's poor majority. And it is equally unclear how long the ANC will be able to withstand domestic political pressure for a major policy shift. Like all developing countries, South Africa's black majority government has struggled to balance the need for economic growth with demands for distribution of wealth.

Puzzles and Prospects for Democracy and Development

We have covered some of the common challenges faced by developing countries in building institutions that will generate economic development and political stability. Our discussion may suggest that much of the developing world faces insurmountable challenges. This is incorrect. Despite ongoing difficulties, much of the developing world has seen dramatic improvements since independence. In 1960, the average life expectancy in India was age 43, and in Brazil, 54; in 2015, these averages increased to ages 68 and 74, respectively. As recently as 1990, the infant mortality rate in Indonesia was 86 per 1,000; in 2015, that rate had dropped to 24.

Of course, we can measure development in many different ways, and different parts of the world have had very different experiences. In general, Asia has done the best. Rapid growth is taking place in many of these countries as well as a trend toward effective states and democratization. Several countries in Latin America have also made great strides, particularly in the last decade, albeit with slower economic growth and high (though shrinking) levels of inequality. Africa remains one of the greatest challenges; it has the lowest rankings on the Human Development Index (HDI) and high levels of civil conflict and corruption. Yet even here, there is progress. For example, between 2005 and 2015 GDP in sub-Saharan Africa rose by more than 50 percent.

What explains variations in development, either between countries or between regions? Scholars increasingly agree on some of the major factors at work, though

Three Paths to Economic Growth

IMPORT SUBSTITUTION	Based on mercantilism. State plays a strong role in the economy. Tariffs or nontariff barriers are used to restrict imports. State actively promotes domestic production, sometimes creating state-owned businesses in developing industries. Criticized for creating "hothouse economies," with large industries reliant on the state for support and unable to compete in the international market.
EXPORT-ORIENTED INDUSTRIALIZATION	Based on mercantilism. State plays a strong role in the economy. Tariff barriers are used to protect domestic industries. Economic production is focused on industries that have a niche in the international market. Seeks to integrate directly into the global economy. Has generally led to a higher level of economic development than import substitution.
STRUCTURAL ADJUSTMENT	Based on liberalism. State involvement is reduced as the economy is opened up. Foreign investment is encouraged. Often follows import substitution. Criticized as a tool of neocolonialism and for its failure in many cases to bring substantial economic development.

their assessments of how to solve the problems differ widely. One important factor we have discussed is the interplay between ethnic divisions and borders (see Chapter 3). Deep ethnic divisions appear to correlate with greater economic and political instability. As we noted earlier, in such cases it may be much more difficult to forge a sense of national identity or national welfare when economic and political institutions are viewed as a means for one group to dominate others rather than as instruments to share power and wealth. This difficulty in forging national identities can be compounded by borders, which may exacerbate conflict by dividing ethnic or religious groups across international boundaries. Such conditions are particularly difficult in Africa.[9]

A second factor is resources. In Chapter 8, we spoke about the resource trap theory of development, which argues that countries with natural resources are hindered from political and economic development because the state or political actors can rely on these resources and effectively ignore public demands or needs. This strategy can further polarize politics when combined with ethnic divisions, since each group will seek to control those assets at the expense of others. Again, while many natural resources are relatively scarce in Asia, they are a central part of African economies, where such things as timber, oil, and diamonds not only lead to conflict but also fuel it, generating revenue for private militias and civil war.

Third, there is the question of governance. This is the hardest factor of the three to get a handle on, though it is perhaps the most important. It is evident to scholars that the obstacles discussed previously, among others, cannot be addressed unless there is an effective state. The state must be able to establish sovereignty and develop public goods and property rights while resisting corruption and allowing for the transfer of power between governments over time. But what is cause and what is effect? Are states weak because of ethnic division and resource traps, or do weak states facilitate these outcomes? This confusion has generated a great deal of controversy in the policy realm. Should reforms be driven by the international community? Centered within developing states? Concentrated at the grassroots societal level? The remainder of this chapter will look at some possible solutions and the debates surrounding them.

MAKING A MORE EFFECTIVE STATE

The view of the state as an aid or obstacle to development in the postcolonial world has shifted over time. In the immediate postwar era, modernization theory focused on the importance of the state in economic and political development, seeing it as the source of industrialization and modern political identities. Aid agencies and developed countries relied on states to be conduits for aid focused on large-scale, top-down development projects like dams or health care. Since 1960, overseas development aid from developed to developing countries has amounted to more than 3 trillion dollars. However, many states failed to live up to expectations because corruption siphoned off resources and many development goals went unrealized. Large but inefficient states, often abetted by foreign funds, were common. As a result, by the 1980s the Washington Consensus took a different tack, encouraging (or pressuring) many developing countries to roll back state power, promote private industry, and limit regulation in the belief that market forces could succeed where states had failed. But while the Washington Consensus viewed states as too big and interventionist, others asserted that the power of these states needed to be redirected rather than reduced. Smaller would not be better if basic public needs still could not be met.[10] Of late, there has been a return to focusing on the state as a vital actor in such areas as delivering public goods. Reducing corruption, improving health care, and increasing economic growth and other basic state responsibilities require greater and more effective state capacity. The question is how we achieve this.

One important place to begin is to remember that there is no one-size-fits-all model, just as there is no homogeneous "developing world." There is tremendous variation in the developing world in terms of pre-imperial, imperial, and post-imperial history, natural resources, ethnic diversity, and other elements. This means that it is difficult to create a common sequence of actions that will improve institutions and create more effective and accountable states. How states can be made more effective depends on the existing institutions one must work with. We will consider some different approaches, understanding that none of these is necessarily the "right" response.

For developing countries that already have a reasonable degree of capacity and autonomy, improving governance may benefit from an emphasis on the rule of law. In Chapter 6, we spoke about this concept, where all individuals and groups are subject to the law irrespective of their power or authority. Much emphasis has been placed on the importance of the rule of law, especially in transitional countries that are moving from nondemocratic to democratic systems. Elected government may increase public participation, but in the absence of the rule of law democratic practices are less likely to become institutionalized. Elections may instead function as a contest to gain control over spoils rather than a system of democratic representation to serve the citizenry as a whole. The puzzle, though, is how to build the rule of law in the first place. Historical models, such as those of the developed democracies where the rule of law emerged over a century or longer, are of limited help. International donors, think tanks, and aid agencies typically argue that building the rule of law requires judicial reform, including stronger constitutional courts (as we discussed in Chapter 6), police, and civil service reform with tougher measures against corruption. The goal is a state that is more predictable and fairer in how it treats its citizens.

However, critics of such reforms argue that policy makers confuse cause and effect. It is not that institutional reforms will create norms regarding the rule of law;

rather, norms must first emerge to generate pressure for institutional change. For example, political elites must demonstrate a commitment to institutional reform. This means not just new rules of the game but also a commitment from political players that they will follow the rules and abide by the outcomes. If individuals with political power are not committed to changes when they work against their immediate interests, rule of law cannot be institutionalized.[11] Equally important is the role of social actors to transmit and promote those values. The Progressive Era in the United States in the late nineteenth century is a good example, where a host of movements and organizations sprang up to fight for such things as labor rights, women's rights, improved health and safety standards, and anticorruption measures. During this era, many powerful civic institutions, such as the League of Women Voters and the American Red Cross, were founded. Similar kinds of groups have emerged in various developing countries, such as the India against Corruption movement, founded in 2011. Fostering social movements and nongovernmental organizations that embody and advance ideas such as the impartiality and universal application of rights may need to go hand in hand with changes in political elites and the institutions they control.

DEVELOPING POLITICAL ENGAGEMENT

We saw earlier that making developing states more effective is connected to institutionalizing the rule of law. Political elites are important in that they must get on board with such changes, and society is central in helping articulate new norms and holding leaders accountable. But this leads us to another puzzle—how do societies get organized in the first place? Recall our discussion in Chapter 6 of civil society, which we defined as organized life outside the state. Civil society can accomplish several important things: it binds people together, creating a web of interests that cuts across class, religion, ethnicity, and other divisions; through activism and organization, it can hold political elites accountable and forms a bulwark against the abuse of state power; and it can inculcate a sense of democratic politics based on interaction, negotiation, consensus, and compromise. But how one can build this is unclear. Discussions of civil society often assume that when a society develops economically people necessarily cultivate a more diverse array of interests, and these inevitably lead to civil society. Even if this is true, it does not provide much guidance for how to consciously build civil society in countries that are less developed.

The lack of clarity around fostering organized political engagement is compounded by the fact that for many development experts this has not been an area of focus, a legacy of the attention paid instead to the state. For example, the World Bank (a major international development organization we will discuss in Chapter 11) has only recently begun to think explicitly about how people mobilize, and to what end. Even this discussion, they note, has tended to emphasize how to "get around" politics rather than improve how politics functions.[12] For example, recall our discussion of Pakistan's electricity problem in Chapter 2. Dealing with electricity theft can be seen as a technical problem to be solved with regulations, meters, and fines. But this ignores the bigger question of how to use civil society as a way to manage a public good and hold citizens, political leaders, and the state accountable to each other. Institutions that work well in developed countries cannot be simply imported into developing countries and expected to work unless the public believes in, trusts, and is part of the process. History is littered with examples of development projects that failed for lack of public legitimacy.

What encourages political engagement and strengthens civil society? Research suggests that accountability is key: that is, monitoring how political leaders and the state are delivering public goods and disseminating information. While there has been a good deal of interest in promoting civil society in developing countries, advocacy groups have often not been focused on institutional reform. Instead, civil society is promoted as a way to manage local issues that have been neglected by the state. This emphasis on the role of local politics is very much consistent with our discussions of devolution in Chapter 7, so it is not surprising that experts from developed democracies would promote the kinds of changes that are under way in their own countries. But to be effective, local engagement needs to hold individuals and institutions accountable all the way up to the national level, influencing parties and national policy. This may seem like a tall order; however, the widespread penetration of mass media and electronic communication (TV, radio, cell phones) across developing countries can allow for effective engagement, increasing the public's political efficacy.[13]

One final caveat: We have discussed civil society as an essential component of democratic participation and state efficacy. These go hand in hand. A state is unlikely to reform without both leadership and pressure from a politically organized and engaged society. But political engagement does not automatically mean better politics. One major challenge is that organized groups are a tempting target for clientelist politics, where political leaders can buy off local groups in return for political support. Civil society can overwhelm a state if it lacks the capacity to meet public demands. Interwar Germany has been cited as an example of a country with a vibrant civil society alongside a weak state, and the Soviet Union can be viewed as another example where growing civil society did not simply bring down the regime but fractured the state as well. Thus, just as we should not look to the state as the sole instrument of development, we should also not conclude that development strategies can be carried by society alone.

PROMOTING ECONOMIC PROSPERITY

Our discussion of states and societies in developing countries has emphasized the critical interaction between organized political engagement and institutional reform. But we have so far not discussed economic development itself, which many people would put front and center. Recall, however, our argument that a primarily economics-based approach, which has dominated development strategies for decades, has in many cases been ineffective due to a failure to focus on political institutions.

One important aspect of this problem lies in the nature of markets and property. Earlier in this chapter, we discussed import substitution versus export-oriented industrialization as methods of industrialization chosen by many developing countries. But these strategies do not account for the majority of workers, who otherwise work in local service, agriculture, or manufacturing. Moreover, these individuals often are part of what is known as the informal economy. The term *informal sector* refers to a segment of the economy that is not regulated, protected, or taxed by the state. Typically, the **informal economy** is dominated by the self-employed or by small enterprises, such as an individual street vendor or a family that makes or repairs goods out of its home. In some cases, the informal economy may represent over

informal economy A segment of the economy that is not regulated or taxed by the state

half of a country's GDP, and women play a large role. According to some research studies, in many developing countries a majority of women working outside the agricultural sector are part of the informal economy. The informal economy can be very flexible, creating opportunities for work where it might otherwise not be available. However, it raises the question of why informal economic activities are so much stronger in developing countries than in more developed ones.

Informal economies are often associated with weak states that are unable to effectively regulate the economy or prevent corruption. Under these conditions, the state may be highly bureaucratic but unable to provide the oversight of property or markets that would be found where the rule of law is strong. In this environment, state and government officials often capitalize on their authority by demanding bribes from business owners to ease their way through regulations. An informal economy also is much more difficult to tax, making it a challenge for states to generate revenue. Finally, because of state weakness in managing markets and property, it is much harder for businesses to scale up into larger firms.

These economic circumstances take us back to the fundamental question of where development efforts should be focused, and can be clearly seen in the debate over one popular development tool, known as *microcredit* or *microfinance*. Though these terms are often used interchangeably, there is a difference. **Microcredit** refers to a system where small loans (often less than $1,000) are made available to small-scale businesses that otherwise lack access to capital. Microfinance covers a much broader spectrum, including credit, savings, insurance, and financial transfers. Microcredit is often funded through nonprofit organizations, and in some cases the borrower is also held accountable to other borrowers in a local association, in that a failure of one individual to repay limits further loans that can be taken out by the members in that association. This system increases the desire for members to vet loans and oversee their use within the association. With globalization, microcredit has expanded; now organizations like the U.S.-based Kiva allow individuals around the world to make loans to people in need. As of 2016, Kiva had over a million and a half lenders and had loaned over $800 billion to over 2 million individuals.[14] Kiva is modeled after Bangladesh's Grameen Bank, whose founder, Muhammad Yunus, won a Nobel Peace Prize in 2006.

microcredit A system in which small loans are channeled to the poor through borrowing groups whose members jointly take responsibility for repayment

While attractive in theory, critics of microcredit and microfinance note that there is scant evidence as to their effectiveness. Studies in India, for example, showed that poor communities that had access to microcredit did not show a drop in poverty or an improvement in outcomes like education, health care, or women's empowerment (the latter of which is a frequent claim made by advocates). There is also no evidence that they are a means for firms to grow and take on employees—a critical step in development and the creation of a middle class. Recalling our discussion of Fair Trade coffee, while the idea of a small business may sound appealing, historically successful development is dependent on a transition to larger firms and an economy where most of the workers are employees rather than entrepreneurs.[15]

If micro-level solutions are not the means to generate economic development, others suggest that focusing on larger scale projects is what is required. The Millennium Villages created in sub-Saharan Africa are the best known—and, like microcredit, controversial—examples. Linked to the United Nations' Millennium Development Goals to improve living standards in the developing world, the Villages' 14 small communities were given targeted interventions to improve the residents' lives, ranging from changes in crop production and improved education to the distribution

Why Did Asia Industrialize Faster than Latin America?

The rise of Asia over the past four decades as a global exporter, producing increasingly sophisticated goods over that time, presents an interesting puzzle, especially when we compare the region's economic development with that of Latin America. In 1970, Brazil's and Argentina's per capita GDP at PPP were between $2,500 and $3,500, higher than South Korea's or Taiwan's. By 2013, while these Latin American countries had GDPs between $11,000 and $18,000, the GDPs of South Korea and Taiwan had soared to between $33,000 and $40,000. How did these Asian countries come from behind and grow so much wealthier than many of their Latin American counterparts within 40 years? A simple explanation—such as a correlation between democracy and speed of economic growth—does not work, since all of these states were authoritarian during most of the last 50 years. What then might be the explanation?

There are several theories regarding Asia's faster growth. According to one argument, which we can describe as geostrategic, the major difference between Latin America and Asia lies in their relationships to the United States and how their political-economic institutions were shaped by these relationships. Latin America's experience of U.S. influence during much of the nineteenth and early twentieth century has been described as neocolonial. In this interpretation, the subordinate relationship of Latin America to the United States effectively prevented the development of industries that could reach an export capacity and be competitive in world markets. Instead, economic development was dominated by foreign (U.S. and European) goods and foreign investments that concentrated on the production of consumer goods for the small upper and middle classes rather than on broader industrialization.

In contrast, following China's 1949 revolution the United States viewed Asia as under direct threat from communism and as a result supported industrialization policies—through preferential trade agreements—that limited foreign direct investment and promoted export-led growth. Whereas Latin American markets were influenced (if not dominated) by Western investments, Asia's drive toward industrialization and export-led growth was fueled by state investments. While this argument can help explain why the regions' economies developed so differently, it doesn't account for a country like Mexico. There, for much of the early twentieth century, foreign investment was limited by the state, and rapid industrial development resembled that of Asia later in the century.

A second argument concentrates on domestic politics and institutions within these regions. One area that has attracted a great deal of attention is land ownership and land reform. In many countries, agriculture is a powerful economic and political force. This is especially the case where agriculture takes the form of large landholdings, which concentrate power in relatively few hands, so that much of the population works land they do not own. Where such landowners are powerful, states may find it difficult to raise funds and build capacity and autonomy. Urbanization and industrialization are held back by the interests of landed elites (who often oppose the rise of both).

In the case of Latin America, economies dominated by large landholders and estates, known as latifundia (*haciendas* in Spanish), developed as part of Spanish and Portuguese colonialism to produce commodities such as sugar and coffee on a large scale for export. Independence from imperialism did not destroy this agricultural system, however, and latifundia economies remained in Latin America as landed elites continued to dominate economic and political institutions. Latin America's economy developed more slowly, therefore, not because it lacked integration with the global economy or exported fewer goods but because the nature of its exports—agriculture and natural resources—did not provide a strong foundation for industrial development.

In Asia as in Latin America, much of the agricultural land was originally concentrated in a small number of estates. However, in places like South Korea and Taiwan one of the first steps the state took after gaining independence was to enact widespread agricultural reform to break the landed elites' monopoly and empower the peasantry. A central motivating factor was the desire to stave off peasant-backed communist revolutions like the ones that happened in China and North Korea, where land reform was a key promise of the Communist Party. This argument in many ways takes us back to the geostrategic issue, though the critical issue here is the role of political elites in Asian countries in bringing the old feudal order to an end. As in the case of our first possible explanation, however, this argument has flaws. The emphasis on the overwhelming power of the latifundia needs to be balanced by a consideration of the fact that Latin America has become an overwhelmingly urban region—over 80 percent of its population now lives in cities. Moreover, as mentioned earlier, many Latin American countries did develop a significant industrial base, even in the absence of land reform.

What, then, is the solution to our puzzle? We cannot draw clear conclusions, though certain factors seem significant. The institutional legacies of imperi-

Workers collect sugar cane on a plantation in the Dominican Republic. A cane cutter earns approximately four U.S. dollars per ton.

alism do appear to be stronger in Latin America than in Asia, although the economic policies in the two regions have been influenced differently by postwar international politics. This intersection of institutions and policies may explain what moved Asia and Latin America down different paths of development that will continue to influence their future.[a]

THINKING CRITICALLY

1. What role did foreign direct investment in Latin America versus state investment in Asia play in the regions' differing paths?
2. How did the legacy of colonialism and its institutions affect Latin America's industrial development?
3. How did concerns about communism influence both the Asian countries' relationship with the United States and their own approach to land reform?

of bed nets to reduce malaria. The idea was that successes could then be tweaked and expanded to new communities. Overall, about $120 million was spent on the project—not a small sum, but far below the trillions that have been spent on global development aid over the past decades.

How have the Millennium Villages fared? The findings are mixed and a source of great debate. One surprising problem goes back to the comparative method that we spoke of in Chapter 1. While scholars could track changes in many of the Millennium Villages, these villages needed to be compared with similar communities that lacked such intervention. For example, one report noted the rapid rise of mobile phone use in the Millennium Villages without noting that this had occurred at the same rate across sub-Saharan Africa as a whole.[16] The absence of reliable data in Millennium and non-Millennium villages meant that researchers had no way to control variables and thus make effective comparisons. As a result, many conclude that it is nearly impossible to evaluate how effective the Millennium Villages have been to date relative to their surrounding communities.

This brings us to a dilemma, one that plagues governments, international actors, and citizens alike. States are necessary to support and protect economic development, but in many developing countries they lack capacity and are one of the biggest obstacles to progress. A common response to this challenge is to effectively bypass the state, whether through grassroots microfunding or attempts to improve conditions village by village. Neither of these approaches fully addresses how to capitalize on any successes they might achieve.

It is easy to draw pessimistic conclusions from our discussions so far. Various attempts to improve institutions in developing countries have produced mixed responses, leaving many to wonder what, if any, progress has been made. However, we can point to steps in the right direction, focused more on methodology than specific policies. As was already mentioned with regard to Fair Trade, microcredit, and the Millennium Villages, one major concern has been that hardly any comparative research has been done in attempting to control variables and look for causal relationships. This may be surprising, but states and international agencies alike have done relatively little comparative research to assess what kinds of policies can work and under what conditions. Now scholars are attempting to more carefully study development strategies before, during, and after they are implemented, comparing these to similar cases where such actions are absent. Only with such comparisons will we be able to draw conclusions about what kinds of development policies actually work.[17]

In Sum: The Challenges of Development

Although they are at different levels of development, almost all developing countries share the legacies of imperial rule. The fusion of local institutions with those of imperial powers created challenges as these countries sought to chart their own independent courses. Weak states; conflicts over ethnicity, nation, religion, and gender; and incomplete and distorted forms of industrialization all contributed to instability, authoritarianism, economic difficulties, and overall low levels of freedom and equality. Some countries have overcome many of these obstacles, but it is unclear whether their strategies and experiences provide lessons that can be easily applied elsewhere in the world.

There is no consensus on how to tackle the most pressing problems of the developing world. Some have advocated ambitious top-down goals and a recommitment of foreign aid toward these outcomes. Others are skeptical that aid interventions are effective. More generally, we have little hard evidence about what does and does not work. This situation suggests that a better bet may be to focus instead on those policies where we can control our variables in order to evaluate what works. Whichever path we choose, globalization, which we will turn to in Chapter 11, will shape future development. Will it take the form of providing new solutions or of creating new barriers to progress?

Key Terms

colonialism (p. 486)
developing countries (p. 484)
empire (p. 486)
export-oriented industrialization (p. 498)
imperialism (p. 486)
import substitution (p. 498)
informal economy (p. 504)
lower income countries (p. 484)

microcredit (p. 505)
middle income countries (p. 484)
middle income trap (p. 498)
neocolonialism (p. 498)
neoliberalism/structural-adjustment
  programs/Washington Consensus (p. 499)

Despite its incredible diversity, persistent ethnic and religious conflicts, and massive levels of poverty, India maintains a thriving democratic system. Here, a man in Amritsar prepares to cast his vote in the 2014 parliamentary elections. Over 550 million votes were cast in this election.

India

Why Study This Case?

India presents a remarkable and instructive case for the study of comparative politics. By 2022, it will eclipse China as the world's most populous country and in 2015 also outpaced China's gross domestic product (GDP) growth. Already it is the world's largest democracy—more people vote in a typical election than the entire population of any other country in the world except China.

Besides being the largest, India is also one of the most improbable of democracies, and herein lies a key puzzle of this case. Scholars most often associate democracy with critical levels of prosperity, mass literacy, urbanization, and national unity. India seemingly disproves this theory with regard to each of these factors. Large, though declining, numbers of the population remain poor and illiterate and are paradoxically three times as likely to vote as the national average.

Most puzzling, perhaps, is how democracy can survive and thrive in a country so dangerously divided by history, language, religion, and **caste**. Today, more than 1.2 billion Indians speak some 325 distinct languages with more than 1,500 dialects.[1] They worship more than 5,000 gods, and six separate religions have at least 50 million adherents each. These ethnic divisions still segregate India socially, economically, and culturally, and have at times erupted into violent conflict and dramatic threats of secession. Given these circumstances, some observers marvel that the country can even stay together, let alone accommodate the cacophony of demands that present themselves.

Others argue that democracy may not be so much the puzzle as the solution. A ponderous but flexible democracy may be the only way of holding this patchwork nation together. Before gaining its independence in 1947, India had already been introduced to—if not allowed to participate in—the liberal practices of its British imperial master. As a sovereign nation, it adopted the political institutions of British democracy, including the parliamentary model. This system has

UZBEK.

TAJIKISTAN

AFGHANISTAN

Claimed by India

Kashmir

Claimed by India

Line of control
with Pakistan

Srinagar

CHINA

Amritsar

Claimed
by China

PAKISTAN

Indus R.

Claimed
by China

NEW
DELHI

NEPAL

BHUTAN

Brahmaputra R.

Agra

Ayodhya

Kanpur

Ganges R.

Imphal

BANGLADESH

Kandla

Bhopal

Ahmadabad

Kolkata
(Calcutta)

MYANMAR

Nagpur

Mumbai
(Bombay)

Arabian
Sea

Hyderabad

Visakhapatnam

Bay
of
Bengal

Panaji

Marmagao

Andaman
Islands

Bangalore

Chennai
(Madras)

Puducherry

Kozhikode

Lakshadweep

Madurai

Kochi

Nicobar
Islands

Tuticorin

SRI
LANKA

N

MALDIVES

INDIAN OCEAN

0   100   200 mi

0   100   200 km

taken root and flourished, but it remains distinctly Indian. India thus offers comparative political scientists a useful petri dish for studying the transferability of democratic institutions to a postcolonial setting in a developing country and the challenges facing such a transplant.

In recent years, the greatest challenge to Indian democracy and political stability has come from persistent religious conflict and increasing fundamentalism. As this case will demonstrate, Sikh and Muslim separatism and Hindu chauvinism have threatened the very democratic system that has sought, so far successfully, to accommodate them. India prevailed in its struggle for colonial independence largely because of one devout Indian's ability to combine the Hindu concept of nonviolence with the liberal notions of tolerance and the separation of religion and state. The charismatic leadership of **Mahatma (Mohandas K.) Gandhi** and the political secularism of his followers successfully united an ethnically diverse colony in the common cause of national independence and democratic nation building.

As has been the case in nearly all other postcolonial countries, modernization has come neither quickly nor easily to India. This huge and still impoverished nation must juggle the maintenance of its notable democracy with the challenges of development and increasing globalization. Although India's urban centers can boast a prosperous and technically savvy elite minority that stands very much in the twenty-first century, the country's rapid economic development over the past two decades has left much of the rest of the population behind. So to the many other divisions threatening India's democracy and political integrity, we must add the inequalities of income and opportunity.

To some extent, India shares with most other less developed and newly industrializing countries the multiple and simultaneous threats of ethnic conflict, political instability, and economic inequality. In that regard, it offers insight into the challenges and opportunities that developing countries face. India is important not just because of its relative ability to manage these challenges democratically but also because its sheer size and growing international prominence guarantee it will have increasing influence in the rest of the world.

Historical Development of the State

Civilization on the Indian subcontinent predates a unified Indian state by several thousand years. Three religious traditions and nearly a thousand years of foreign domination mark the contours of the gradual formation of a sovereign Indian state.

HINDUISM, BUDDHISM, AND ISLAM

The first of India's three main religious traditions emerged over 3,000 years ago in the customs, philosophical ideas, and beliefs associated with **Hinduism**. Like other traditional religions, Hinduism governs not just worship practices but also virtually all aspects of life, including the rituals and norms of birth, death, marriage, eating, and livelihood. For roughly the next 2,000 years, India enjoyed relative freedom from outside influence as Hindu traditions such as polytheism, reincarnation, and the social and political hierarchy of caste infused Indian society.

At the bottom of—technically outside—the hierarchy were the so-called untouchables. High-caste Hindus traditionally considered the touch or even the shadow of these outcastes as polluting.

In independent India, Hindu elites have used these social divisions to establish political patronage networks and to justify and enhance their dominant position in the caste system. Critics of the divisive and exploitative consequences of caste, however, have made efforts to ease the discrimination associated with it and, in particular, its deleterious effects on the untouchables. Calling themselves Dalits ("suppressed groups"), this group now numbers some 170 million people, or about 15 percent of the population.[2]

It was under the auspices of Buddhism—a second religious tradition, originating in India in the sixth century B.C.E.—that rulers commenced India's first efforts at nation building. Spreading Buddhism's message of peace and benevolence to subjects of all ethnic groups and social ranks, dynastic rulers unified much of what is now India by the fourth century B.C.E. and remained in power for several hundred years. However, by the Common Era, Hinduism gradually reemerged as the dominant religion and remained India's prevailing faith. Over 80 percent of Indians identify themselves as Hindu. Today, Hinduism is the world's third-largest religious tradition after Christianity and Islam.

India's 2,000 years of relative isolation gave way to more than a millennium of foreign domination that began with marauding Muslim invaders in the eighth century. The arrival of this third religious tradition at the hands of martial Muslim rulers never fostered the kind of tolerance shared by Hindus and Buddhists. But the introduction of Islam to India gave birth to a new religious tradition, **Sikhism**, which shares beliefs and practices with both the Hindu and Muslim faiths. It also sowed persistent seeds of mutual animosity among India's Hindus, Muslims, and Sikhs. A final wave of Muslim invaders, descendants of Genghis Khan known as **Mughals** (Persian for "Mongol"), ruled a relatively unified India for several hundred years beginning in the sixteenth century. But by the eighteenth century, Mughal rule had weakened at the hands of growing internal Hindu and Sikh dissatisfaction and expanding Western imperialism.

BRITISH COLONIALISM

Beginning with the Portuguese and the Spanish in the sixteenth century and followed by the Dutch and the British by the seventeenth century, the lucrative spice trade beckoned European powers to the Indian Ocean. Lacking a strong centralized state, India was vulnerable to foreign encroachment, and the British in particular made significant commercial inroads. In 1600, the British Crown granted a monopoly charter to the private **East India Company**, which over the years perfected an imperial strategy of commercial exploitation. This private merchant company first cultivated trade, then exploited cheap labor, and ultimately succeeded in controlling whole principalities.

The British introduced both the concept of private property and the English language. With the new language came its science, literature, and—perhaps most

TIMELINE Political Development

1857–58	Sepoy Mutiny is put down, and formal British colonial rule is established.
1885	Indian National Congress is created.
1930	Gandhi leads a boycott of British salt.
1947	India gains independence from Britain; India and Pakistan are created with partition.
1948	Mahatma Gandhi is assassinated.
1947–64	Jawaharlal Nehru serves as prime minister until his death.
1971	India-Pakistan War leads to creation of Bangladesh.
1975–77	Indira Gandhi institutes emergency rule.
1984	Indira Gandhi launches military operations at Amritsar and is assassinated by Sikh bodyguards.
1984–86	Rajiv Gandhi serves as prime minister.
1991	Rajiv Gandhi is assassinated.
1992	Ayodhya mosque is destroyed.
1996	Electoral victory of the Bharatiya Janata Party (BJP) leads to the rise of coalition governments.
1998	Nuclear weapons are tested.
2002	Muslim-Hindu violence breaks out in Gujarat.
2004	Congress-led coalition defeats BJP coalition; Manmohan Singh becomes prime minister.
2005	India and United States begin negotiating controversial nuclear agreement.
2007	Pratibha Patil is elected India's first female president.
2008, 2011	Muslim terrorist bombings in Mumbai and other Indian cities.
2009	Congress-led coalition reelected; Singh continues as prime minister.
2014	BJP-led coalition wins election and Narendra Modi becomes prime minister.

revolutionary—liberal political philosophy. British merchants sought Indian markets for British manufactures, particularly cotton cloth, putting millions of Indian cloth makers out of work. Communication and transportation technology—the telegraph, print media, the postal system, and the railroad (the British laid some 50,000 miles of track)—did much to unify India and give its colonial subjects a shared recognition of their frustrations and aspirations. This was particularly true of those native Indians employed in the colonial military and civil service beginning to develop and articulate a sense of Indian nationalism.

Growing economic frustration, political awareness, and national identity led to the **Sepoy Mutiny** of 1857–58, a revolt backed by the Indian aristocracy and carried out by sepoys (Indian mercenaries employed by the British). In 1858, the British Parliament terminated the East India Company's control of India and placed the territory under direct and far harsher colonial rule. The colony of India became the "brightest jewel in the crown of the British empire."[3]

THE INDEPENDENCE MOVEMENT

By the end of the nineteenth century, calls for self-rule had become louder and more articulate, though still not unified. Two local organizations came to embody the anticolonial movement: the Indian National Congress (INC)—also referred to simply as Congress or the Congress Party—and the Muslim League. But hopes for a gradual transfer of power after World War I were instead met with increased colonial repression, bringing Mahatma (Mohandas K.) Gandhi, a British-trained lawyer, to the leadership of Congress and the broader independence movement. Gandhi, affectionately known by Indians as Mahatma, or "Great Soul," was born in 1869 and came to lead a charismatic nationalist movement embodied in his example of personal simplicity and campaigns for national self-sufficiency.

Gandhi's integrity and example, the charismatic draw of his remarkable strategy of nonviolence, and the increasingly repressive and arbitrary nature of colonial rule swelled the ranks of the independence movement. Among those who joined was a younger generation of well-educated leaders schooled in the modern ideas of socialism and democracy. Chief among them was Jawaharlal Nehru, who succeeded Gandhi as leader of the INC and ultimately became independent India's first prime minister.

Weakened by both economic depression and war, Britain entered into serious negotiations for Indian independence following World War II. The biggest obstacle to independence became not the British but disagreements and divisions among India's many interests, most particularly Hindus and Muslims. Fearful that Muslims, who constituted 25 percent of the population, would be unfairly dominated by the Hindu majority, Muslim leaders demanded a separate Muslim state. Against a background of growing violence, the British opted for partition, creating in 1947 the new state of Pakistan from the two regions of the subcontinent most heavily populated by Muslims: West Pakistan in the northwest and East Pakistan (what would become independent Bangladesh in 1971) in the northeast. From the remaining 80 percent of the colony, the British formed independent India. This declaration led to the uprooting and transmigration (in effect, ethnic cleansing) of more than 12 million refugees—Muslims to Pakistan, Hindus and Sikhs to India—across the hurriedly drawn boundaries. Authorities estimated that as many as 1 million Indians and Pakistanis were killed in the resulting chaos and violence.[4] Among the victims of this sectarian violence was Gandhi himself, assassinated in 1948 by a militant Hindu who saw the leader and his message of religious tolerance as threats to Hindu nationalism. Not surprisingly, the ethnic violence that marked partition and the birth of the Indian nation continues to plague Hindu-Muslim relations in contemporary India as well as India's relations with neighboring Pakistan.

INDEPENDENCE

Like many of the other newly minted countries that would become part of the postwar decolonization movement, independent India faced a host of truly daunting challenges. This included settling some 5 million refugees from East and West Pakistan, resolving outstanding territorial disputes, jump-starting an economy torn asunder by partition in an effort to feed the country's impoverished millions, and creating democratic political institutions from whole cloth. This last task, promised by Nehru and his INC, had to be carried out in the absence of the prosperity, literacy, and liberal traditions that allowed democracy to take hold in advanced democracies and seemed to many an unlikely prospect in India.

Unlike many other postcolonial countries, however, India brought to the endeavor of democratization several distinct advantages. First, its lengthy, gradual, and inclusive independence movement generated a powerful and widespread sense of national identity. Second, although Indians did not control their own destiny under the British raj, the Indian intellectual class was well schooled in both the Western philosophies and the day-to-day practices of liberal democracy. Moreover, independent India inherited not just liberal ideas and traditions but also a sophisticated and generally well-functioning central state apparatus that included an extensive civil service and standing army.

Finally, the long-standing role of the INC as the legitimate embodiment of the independence movement and Nehru as its charismatic and rightful representative gave the new government a powerful mandate. Nehru led the INC to an easy victory in India's first general election in 1951, giving Nehru's government the opportunity to implement his vision of social democracy at home and mercantilist trade policies abroad. The INC would govern India for 45 of its first 50 years of independence and was led for nearly all those years by either Nehru, his daughter, or his grandson.

A NEHRU DYNASTY

Uncle Nehru, as Jawaharlal Nehru was affectionately called, led the INC to two subsequent victories in 1957 and 1962, dying in office in 1964. With his death, the INC began to lose some of its earlier luster and its ability to reach across regional, caste, and religious divisions to garner support. Within two years, Nehru's daughter, Indira Gandhi (no relation to Mahatma), assumed leadership of a more narrowly defined INC and became India's first female prime minister. But when her popularity within the party waned in the 1970s, Gandhi chose in 1975 to suspend the constitution by declaring martial law, or emergency rule.

When Gandhi unexpectedly lifted emergency rule in 1977 and called for new elections, virtually all politicians and the overwhelming majority of voters rallied to the cause of the new Janata (People's) Party in what was seen as an effort to save Indian democracy. This Janata coalition formed the first non-Congress government in India's 30 years of independence. But after two years of factional disputes and indecisive governance, the INC was returned to office—with Gandhi as its leader. Indian voters had spoken, indicating their preference for the order and efficiency of Gandhi's strong hand over the Janata Party's ineptitude.

However, in 1984, Gandhi launched a military operation against Sikh separatists who were demanding an independent Sikh state of Khalistan. Indian troops attacked the Golden Temple in Amritsar, Sikhism's holiest shrine, killing the separatists' firebrand leader and some 1,000 of his militant followers. Vengeance came months later, when Gandhi's Sikh bodyguards assassinated her. In what was to become a motif of communal violence, the assassination sparked violent retribution as angry Hindus murdered thousands of innocent Sikhs throughout India.

Widespread sympathy in the wake of Gandhi's assassination made it natural for the INC to select her son, Rajiv, as its candidate in the 1984 election, giving the Congress Party its largest (and last) outright majority in a general election. Rajiv Gandhi governed for five years, during which he began to shift India's economic focus away from the social-democratic and mercantilist policies of his mother and grandfather. Coming to government in the wake of Thatcher and Reagan's neoliberal economic reforms in the United Kingdom and United States, Rajiv Gandhi used his mandate to promote more liberal market measures that succeeded in boosting the Indian economy and have been expanded in the decades since. Ethnic violence and political divisiveness persisted, however. During a 1991 campaign, two years after Rajiv Gandhi had been turned out of office by a weak opposition coalition, he was assassinated by a Tamil separatist suicide bomber. The Nehru dynasty thus ended, and by the early 1990s coalition governments had become the norm.

COALITION GOVERNMENTS

The decline of the INC's dominance has led to a series of coalition governments typically headed by a national party, such as Congress, but shored up by regional partners. Coalitions of all political stripes have maintained the reforms begun under Rajiv Gandhi and the INC, including economic liberalization and increased political devolution to state governments. The INC's strongest competition has come from the **Bharatiya Janata Party (BJP)**, which by articulating a Hindu nationalist vision very different from that of a secular India promoted by the INC had potential for nationwide scope and appeal. Drawing its strength initially from upper-caste Hindu groups, by the late 1990s the BJP was attracting Hindus of all castes under the banner of Hindu nationalism.

The event that began to galvanize support for the BJP was yet another incident of sectarian violence at a temple site. The Babri Mosque, located in the northern Indian city of **Ayodhya**, had been built by Mughals on a site alleged to be the birthplace of the Hindu god Ram. Muslims and Hindus alike deem the site sacred, and by the 1990s, various Hindu nationalist groups had seized on Ayodhya as both a rallying political issue and a gathering place. In 1992, BJP supporters and other Hindu extremists destroyed the mosque, vowing to rebuild it as a Hindu shrine. This act ignited days of Hindu-Muslim rioting and violence and the killing of many Indians across the country.

In 2002, on the tenth anniversary of the event, Muslims in the state of **Gujarat** set fire to railcars carrying back Hindu activists from a ceremony at Ayodhya, killing 58 people. Hindu retaliatory violence incited by religious militants in the state of Gujarat killed thousands. Sectarian issues continued to simmer as extremist elements in both the Muslim and Hindu camps regularly took aim at each other. The year 2008 proved particularly violent: Muslim terrorists carried out bombings in several of India's large urban centers, and a dramatic assault on Mumbai was led by a Pakistani-based terrorist group that targeted wealthy Indians, Westerners, and Jews.

This communal violence has served to harden positions on both sides and polarize political support. A BJP coalition that came to power in 1998 remained in office until 2004, when it was turned out by a surprisingly resurgent INC and assorted coalition partners. Organizations loosely affiliated with the BJP continue to promote divisive Hindu nationalist rhetoric to garner support and sponsor violence and discrimination against various minority religious and ethnic groups. During its six years in office, however, the BJP coalition governed relatively moderately in an effort to both retain its coalition partners and promote India's national goals of economic growth and stable relations with neighboring countries. Significantly, the president of the INC at the time of its surprise return to office in 2004 and reelection in 2009 was Sonia Gandhi, the Italian-born widow of Rajiv Gandhi. Although she would have been the logical choice to assume the office of prime minister (and extend the Nehru dynasty), the BJP made her foreign birth a divisive campaign issue. Thus she stepped aside and allowed Manmohan Singh to become the country's first Sikh prime minister. Singh's Congress-led coalition governed for two full terms with a great deal of behind-the-scenes influence from Sonia Gandhi.

In an effort to perpetuate both Congress rule and the Nehru dynasty, the family groomed Sonia Gandhi's son and Jawaharlal Nehru's great-grandson, Rahul Gandhi, as the heir apparent. He gained a Congress seat in parliament in 2004 and led the INC's 2014 parliamentary election campaign. But in a sign of both the declining influence of the Nehru dynasty and the maturation of India's democratic regime, a resurgent BJP led by Narendra Modi, the outspoken governor of the state of Gujarat and rising star of the party, swept Congress out of office in the 2014 election. A popular Hindu nationalist, Modi led the BJP to the largest margin of victory and first outright parliamentary majority for any party in three decades. He has formed a government armed with both ardent Hindu sympathies and a strong mandate to carry out bold reforms.

Political Regime

India can easily claim the title of the world's largest democracy. But is it genuine? And does it work? Certainly, it is democratic in form. Its constitution and other political institutions were modeled explicitly on Britain's Westminster parliamentary system, and few changes to the original blueprint have been enacted. Indian democracy nonetheless differs in important ways from that of its colonial mentor and other advanced Western industrialized democracies, and three generations of Indian politicians and citizens from across the ideological spectrum have embraced parliamentary democracy, made it their own, and have made it work. They function and participate in a system that maintains civil parliamentary debate, a politically neutral bureaucracy, an independent judiciary, and firm civilian control over the military.

POLITICAL INSTITUTIONS

THE CONSTITUTION Perhaps befitting India's size and population, its constitution is one of the world's longest, expressing in writing the fundamental principles of Britain's unwritten constitutional order of parliamentary democracy. It establishes India as a federal republic, reserving significant authority for the state governments. The growing reliance on coalition governments has spurred a process of devolution, allowing regional political parties and the states they represent to wrest significant authority from the Center (a term referring to India's national government and its capital in New Delhi). It is too early to tell, but the BJP's decisive electoral victory in 2014 may mark a reversing of this trend of regional devolution and bring more power back to the Center.

Two controversial tenets of the Indian constitution have certainly enhanced the power of the Center. The first of these authorizes the central government to impose "emergency rule" (nationwide martial law), which has been invoked twice during international conflicts with China (1962) and Pakistan (1971). More controversially, Indira Gandhi instituted emergency rule from 1975 to 1977, using it as a blunt (but nonetheless effective) tool against her political opponents, after which the constitution was amended to limit emergency rule to conditions of external aggression or domestic armed rebellion.

Indira Gandhi was not the only prime minister to invoke the second measure, that of presidential rule, which allows the central government to oust a state government and assert direct rule of that state. National governments have employed this measure on more than 100 occasions, when ethnic unrest, local resistance, or simply a political stalemate rendered a state, in the judgment of the Center, ungovernable. Although these measures may seem unusual and have at times been imposed for purposes of political expediency, the violence, disorder, and corruption often associated with regional Indian politics have made presidential rule an important and generally legitimate tool of the central government.[5]

THE BRANCHES OF GOVERNMENT

THE PRESIDENT Because India is a republic, its head of state is a president, not a monarch; as in most other parliamentary systems, the president's role is largely symbolic. The president is authorized to appoint the prime minister, but as with the monarchs of Britain and Japan, this appointment is simply a ceremonial affirmation of the leader of the dominant party or coalition in the parliament.

The constitution does, however, bestow upon the *office* of president several significant responsibilities, even if this authority is largely nominal. Upon the advice of the prime minister and cabinet, the president may declare emergency rule, temporarily suspending constitutional rule in either a state or the entire country. Similarly, the Indian constitution contains a provision authorizing the president (again, upon the advice of the prime minister and cabinet) to enact legislation without the consent or participation of parliament. These "ordinances" (in effect, presidential decrees) may be enacted only under limited conditions but have the same weight and effect as parliamentary legislation. Despite limitations, nearly 20 percent of Indian legislation has originated as a presidential ordinance.[6]

The substantive exception to these symbolic presidential tasks has been the president's role following elections that have produced no majority party (which, until the 2014 election, had been the norm for the past quarter century). Under these circumstances, the president seeks to identify and facilitate the formation of a workable governing coalition. If that is not possible, the president dissolves the parliament and calls new elections. An electoral college, made up of the national and state legislators, elects presidents to five-year renewable terms, though many presidents have in effect been appointed by powerful prime ministers.

The current president, Ram Nath Kovind, was elected in 2017 and serves as India's second Dalit president. Nominated by the BJP government, Kovind most recently served as the governor of the state of Bihar (also a largely ceremonial post). Despite the generally ceremonial nature of the presidency, in recent years several significant measures have been taken through the office. These have included a 2013 presidential ordinance instituting the death penalty for rape, which was enacted in the wake of a particularly brutal gang rape (see "The Politics of Rape," p. 537). In 2014, the previous president, Pranab Mukherjee, declared presidential rule in the state of Andhra Pradesh after the chief minister of the state resigned in protest against the decision to divide the state in half and create the new state of Telangana.

THE PRIME MINISTER AND THE CABINET As in the British system, the Indian prime minister and cabinet constitute the executive branch. The prime minister, as head of the government, manages the day-to-day affairs of government and is the state's most important political figure. The prime minister is typically the leader of the majority party in the lower house of the legislature or a leader from within

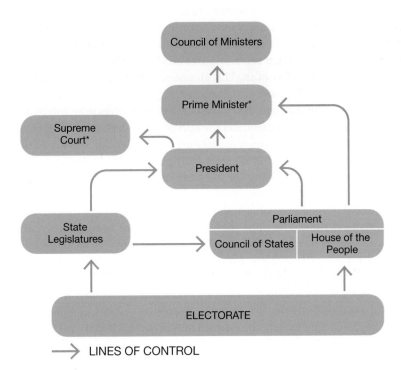

Structure of the Government

*Although the president has the authority to appoint the prime minister and the Supreme Court justices, the de facto power rests with the parliament.

a coalition of parties that can garner sufficient support to constitute a majority, or even a minority, government. As in other parliamentary systems, to remain in office, the prime minister must retain the confidence of the lower house but also has the power to dissolve the lower house and call elections to solidify support for the government.

The prime minister chooses members of the parliament to serve in a Council of Ministers that presides over all government ministries and departments. From this larger council, a smaller and more manageable group of the 20 to 25 most important ministers meets weekly as a cabinet to formulate and coordinate government policy. The current prime minister, Narendra Modi, is also president of the BJP and began his tenure in 2014 following his party's decisive electoral victory.

During the years of Congress Party dominance, the three generations of Nehru prime ministers wielded overwhelming executive power. Although this was most apparent during Indira Gandhi's authoritarian tenure, her father and even her son were also dominant prime ministers who left their personal imprints on the office and on Indian politics. Even during the more recent era of coalition governments in which the prime minister's influence has weakened, the office remains the primary source of policy making and political power. Modi's popularity, the BJP's convincing electoral victory in 2014, and the overwhelming majority its coalition holds in parliament give the prime minister the necessary means to likewise exercise decisive executive power.

THE LEGISLATURE As is true in many parliamentary systems, the lower house, or **House of the People**, dominates India's bicameral legislature. This lower chamber seats 545 members, all but two of whom are elected by voters for terms not to exceed five years. The final two seats are reserved for Anglo-Indians appointed by the president. Despite this chamber's enormous size, India's huge population remains relatively underrepresented. Each representative serves nearly 2 million people—nearly three times that of a member of the U.S. House of Representatives and 20 times that of a member of Britain's House of Commons.

Like the British lower house, the House of the People serves primarily as a chamber of debate between the government and the opposition. It has adopted many of the rituals and institutions of its colonial model, including a neutral Speaker of the House who presides over "question hour." Seen during the era of the INC's dominance as little more than window dressing for the party in power and its prime minister, the lower house has had an increasingly important political role since the emergence of multiparty coalition governments and the strengthening of regional parties.

As its name denotes, the upper house, or **Council of States**, represents India's 29 states and seven territories. All but 12 of its 250 members are indirectly elected by state assemblies (the president appoints the remaining 12) to fixed six-year terms. Although the upper chamber technically possesses most of the same powers as its lower counterpart—including the right to introduce legislation—in practice it has been much weaker. Only the House of the People can introduce bills to raise revenue, and any financial measure the Council of States votes down can be enacted with the majority support of the lower house. Any other deadlocked legislation is put to a majority vote of a joint session, which ensures that the more numerous lower chamber has the upper hand. Most significantly, the prime minister and cabinet are responsible only to the lower house, which can force the prime minister from office by a vote of no confidence.

THE JUDICIARY India has a Supreme Court with a bench of 30 justices (when all vacancies are filled). They are appointed by the president and may serve until age 65. Typically, the most senior judge serves as chief justice.

India's Supreme Court is a constitutional court with the authority of judicial review (the right to rule on the constitutionality of acts of the parliament). This power to interpret the constitution is limited, however, by the comprehensive nature of the Indian constitution. Its power has also been limited by the parliament's ability to reverse court decisions by amending the constitution, as it has done on a number of occasions (the Indian constitution has 98 amendments, making it the longest and most amended in the world). Except during Indira Gandhi's two-year-long emergency rule in the 1970s, when the judiciary was seen as having yielded to the prime minister's political influence both in the appointment of justices and in the suspension of constitutionally guaranteed civil rights, the Supreme Court has enjoyed (and earned) a reputation for fairness and independence.

THE ELECTORAL SYSTEM

As with many of its other political institutions, India's electoral system closely resembles the British model. At the national level, voters use a plurality system to elect representatives to the House of the People, as in Britain and the United States. The country is divided into 543 single-member districts, in which the candidate who earns a plurality of votes on the first ballot is elected. The districts are based primarily on geography and population, but some districts are reserved for the so-called **untouchables** (also called the **Dalits**). The state legislatures elect or otherwise appoint members of the Council of States to staggered six-year fixed terms. The legislature uses a complex single transferable voting system, and seats are apportioned according to each state's population.

Whereas the plurality electoral system in the United States and Britain has favored the emergence of few or only two nationally based large parties and has penalized smaller parties, this is increasingly not the case for India's lower house. The INC certainly used the electoral system to its advantage during its period of dominance. The weakening of the INC's hegemony since the 1990s has splintered the national vote, giving new significance to regional parties based on caste or on linguistic or religious identity.[7]

Recent lower house elections have seated representatives of nearly 40 different political parties, 10 parties with more than 9 seats each. And, until the BJP's decisive win in 2014, no party in recent elections had won a majority of the seats (see "House of the People Election Results, 2004, 2009, and 2014," p. 528).

LOCAL GOVERNMENT

India's extensive regional diversity and the sectarian conflicts troubling the country at the time of its founding led the framers of India's constitution to establish a federal republic that preserved substantial powers for both the various states and the central government. Each of the 29 states has its own elected government consisting of a legislature and a chief minister. The **chief minister** is elected by the state legislature to serve a five-year term and can be removed from office by a vote of no confidence.

State governments in India have a great deal of power, but as in other federal systems, they have limits. The Center's constitutional powers to declare a national emergency or impose presidential rule on a mismanaged or rebellious state are muscular examples of its authority. The federal government is also authorized to challenge any state legislation that contradicts an act of parliament and can even change the boundaries of states as it sees fit. But like their American counterparts, in the day-to-day management of government affairs, Indian states retain a great deal of jealously guarded autonomy. The rise of coalition governments and the growing influence of regional parties in national affairs have only strengthened state power.

India's current division into 29 states and 7 territories reflects several territorial permutations since independence; most recent was the division of the state of Andhra Pradesh in 2014 to form the new state of Telangana. Given India's extensive ethnic diversity, it is perhaps no surprise that 21 additional proposals for new states are now pending with the central government. This growing demand for more states and more devolved authority speaks to an important difference between India's federalism and the American model. State borders in India reflect in most cases linguistic or ethno-religious differences, which pit regional interests against the Center. This conflict has been most pronounced in states such as Punjab, which is dominated by the Punjabi-speaking Sikhs, and Jammu and Kashmir, the only Indian state in which Urdu-speaking Muslims constitute a majority. However, other ethnic groups have also wielded the mechanisms of state authority to assert state interests against the federal government. India is a good example of what political scientists call **asymmetric federalism**, where power is devolved unequally across the country and its constituent regions, often as the result of specific laws negotiated between a given region and the central government.[8]

Significantly, for all of the local conflict and secessionist violence that India has experienced, the Center has held, and the strife has remained localized. With larger populations and religious, linguistic, and territorial disputes sufficient to rival any of those that led to the numerous wars of Europe (and ultimately prompted the formation of the European Union), India has for the most part managed these disputes peacefully and democratically. This is no small feat.

Political Conflict and Competition

Despite occasional heavy-handed government restrictions on civil rights and periodic demonstrations of communitarian intolerance and even violence, Indian politics remains vibrant, open, and generally inclusive. Voter turnout typically averages around 60 percent for parliamentary elections and reached a record of nearly 67 percent in the 2014 election. The nonpartisan Freedom House in 2017 deemed India "free" and gave it a rating of 2 in its political rights and 3 in civil liberties (on a scale of 1 to 7, where 1 is the most free).

In fact, given India's size and diversity, some might argue that political competition has been too inclusive. As one Indian journalist complained, "Everyone in India gets a veto."[9] The competition and conflict—typically, but not always, healthy—reflect the dualism and diversity of India: a prosperous, cosmopolitan, and highly literate minority voting side by side with roughly two-thirds of the electorate who cannot read, have their roots in rural villages or urban slums, and may survive on less than a dollar a day. Both are important components of Indian democracy.

THE PARTY SYSTEM

During the first few decades of independence, India's party system was stable and predictable. Like Japan's Liberal Democratic Party or Mexico's Partido Revolucionario Institucional (Institutional Revolutionary Party), the Indian National Congress presided over a one-party-dominant system that effectively appealed to a broad range of ideological and social groups and co-opted numerous disaffected constituencies, including the poor and minorities. More recently, as national opposition parties and regional and even local interests have gained ground in both state and national elections, this system has become far more fragmented, complex, and unpredictable.

THE CONGRESS PARTY More than just a political party, the Indian National Congress, from its founding in 1885, became the flagship of national independence, commanding widespread appeal and support across the political and even ethnic spectrums. After independence, Jawaharlal Nehru and the INC pursued a slightly left-of-center political ideology of social democracy. This included social policies of "secularism" (more a program of religious equal opportunity than a separation of religion and state) and social reform, continuing the efforts of Gandhi to eliminate caste discrimination.

The party's economic program was marked by democratic socialism, including national five-year plans, state ownership of key economic sectors, and income redistribution through affirmative action programs. These policies earned the support of workers, peasants, and particularly members of the lower castes. At the same time, the INC retained the support of business by respecting private property and supporting domestic industry with mercantilist policies of import substitution. For decades, Congress remained the only party with national appeal.

The INC's dominance began to weaken after Nehru's death, as disagreements grew between Indira Gandhi and party elders in the late 1960s. Gandhi made populist promises to India's poor, vowing to abolish poverty through government programs, but never delivered on those promises. By the 1980s, the INC had begun to move away from its traditional priorities of democratic socialism and religious neutrality. Indira Gandhi began promoting Hindu nationalism, and her son Rajiv launched neoliberal economic reforms. These legacies have outlived their architects and have been embraced even more enthusiastically by other political parties.

By the late 1980s, the INC had surrendered its position of primacy, and the single-party-dominant system gave way to a regionalized multiparty system and coalition governments. Since then, the INC has alternated rule with various permutations of Hindu nationalist coalitions, controlling the government in the first half of the 1990s and then returning to power for a decade from 2004 to 2014. In the 2014 general election, voters expressed their displeasure with the party's growing reputation for political corruption and inaction, handing Congress its worst-ever electoral defeat. The Congress-led coalition government lost nearly three-fourths of its seats, while the INC itself lost nearly 80 percent of its total seats (see "House of the People Election Results, 2004, 2009, and 2014," p. 528). With only 44 seats in the lower house, the INC fell short of the 10 percent of total seats necessary even to be designated a parliamentary party or lead the opposition. This lopsided victory handed the BJP an unprecedented mandate for change.

THE BHARATIYA JANATA PARTY As opposition to the INC grew during Indira Gandhi's 1970s autocratic interlude, a number of contending parties began to emerge or take on new importance. A coalition of some of these opposition parties, under the name Janata (People's) Party, ultimately wrested the government from the INC in the late 1970s. One of the smallest of these coalition partners was Jana Sangh, a Hindu nationalist party that left the Janata coalition in 1980 and changed its name to the Bharatiya Janata Party (BJP), or Indian People's Party.

The BJP's popularity climbed rapidly as support for secularism gave way to increasing sentiment for ethnic and religious parties. The BJP won only two seats in the 1984 House of the People elections, but increasing Hindu nationalist sentiment allowed it to expand its representation to 161 seats by 1996 and form a coalition government. Although the first BJP coalition lasted only 12 days, by 1998 the BJP had become the largest party in the parliament and governed from 1998 until 2004. Although support for the BJP waxed and waned over the next decade, the party returned to government in 2014 after obtaining a majority of seats in the lower house.

From its founding, the BJP has been an outspoken advocate of Hindu national identity. It belongs to a larger constellation of more than 30 loosely tied Hindu nationalist organizations that vary widely in their acceptance of violence and militancy in promoting Hindu nationalism, but all embrace **Hindutva**, or "Hindu-ness," as India's primary national identity and ideal. Similarly, the BJP itself has both moderate and militant elements. Its elected national leaders tend to downplay the party's religious ties, promote it as a more honest alternative to the INC, and emphasize its neoliberal economic policies of privatization, deregulation, and foreign investment. This reputation of honesty and neoliberalism has appealed in particular to India's growing middle class, which is more interested in economic freedom and prosperity than secular equality. The extremist and fundamentalist elements in the BJP are more overtly anti-Muslim. They contend that India's Muslims were forced to convert by foreign invaders and would naturally revert to their native Hinduism in an India permitted to promote its true heritage. They are more prone to violence, praising the assassin of Mahatma Gandhi and the combatants of Ayodhya and Gujarat as heroes and protectors of Indian heritage. Their leaders have been more successful politically at the local and state levels (particularly in the region of India's so-called cow belt, in the Hindu-majority north) but also have been important allies in the BJP's efforts to form national ruling coalitions.

Although criticized both at home and abroad for his long association with Hindu nationalism, Prime Minister Narendra Modi brought his BJP to government in 2014 on promises to promote growth and limit corruption.

The most successful and controversial of these rising regional BJP leaders was current prime minister and former chief minister (governor) of the state of Gujarat, the charismatic and outspoken Narendra Modi. "NaMo" was swept to power as chief minister just before the anti-Muslim violence in Gujarat in 2002 and reelected in 2007, and he has long been viewed as a controversial figure. On the one hand, his policies of fighting corruption and promoting privatization and small and efficient government proved very successful, bringing consistently high economic growth to Gujarat during his tenure. On the other hand, critics charged that Modi and his government did not do enough to prevent the violent attacks against Muslims in the riots of 2002 and in some cases actually condoned and even inflamed the violence. Although Modi was ultimately cleared of all charges against him, he and the BJP recognized that he could not lead the party in a national election contest campaigning on the narrow platform of Hindu nationalism. Instead, the BJP's successful 2014 campaign focused on basic issues that appealed to wide sectors of the population, promising to rein in corruption and inflation, promote education and infrastructure, and boost economic growth. Although Modi's BJP retains a core ideology of Hindu nationalism, both constitutional and electoral constraints have moderated the government's policies.[10]

PARTIES OF THE LEFT India's so-called Left Front consists of a collection of communist and other left-leaning parties whose popularity for many years seemed unaffected by the declining success of communist parties and countries elsewhere in the world. These parties until the 2014 election together managed to garner on average 7 to 10 percent of the national vote and as many as 50 seats in parliament's lower house, giving the communist parties a decisive role in the making and breaking of recent coalitions and therefore a degree of leverage in government policy, despite their minority status.

Like the INC, India's parties of the left did not fare well in the 2014 general election, winning only 11 seats and rendered largely irrelevant to either the ruling BJP-led coalition or the much-diminished opposition INC.

Not all political movements on the left, however, have been willing to work within the democratic system. Chief among these radical groups is the Maoist (or guerrilla communist) insurgency known as **Naxalism**. Named for the region in West Bengal where it originated in the late 1960s, the movement has grown in recent decades, particularly in rural, impoverished areas in more than a dozen states of western India. Naxalite recruits—estimates place the number of armed insurgents at more than 20,000—are drawn primarily from the low castes, outcastes, and tribal natives largely excluded from India's recent and dramatic economic growth.

REGIONAL AND OTHER PARTIES The declining dominance of the INC and the rise of coalition governments gave new prominence to regional and local political parties, which have come to dominate in many states and tip the balance in national elections. Moreover, as INC-supported secularism waned, ethnic, linguistic, and religious identities became increasingly important rallying points for political interests often concentrated by region. For example, states with predominant ethnic or religious identities, such as the Dravidian Tamils in the southern state of Tamil Nadu and the Punjabi Sikhs, have often been led by these regional and state parties. Other parties draw support from lower-caste Indians in several of India's poorer states. Neither the INC nor the BJP holds a majority in a number of India's state parliaments. In addition to ethnic-based regional parties, a single-issue party emerged in 2012 in Delhi, the nation's capital, capitalizing on an anti-graft campaign that began a year earlier. Led by a former tax official, Arvind Kejriwal, the Aam Aadmi ("Common Man's") Party (AAP) performed very well in the 2013 local assembly elections, fared poorly in the 2014 general elections, but retains national ambitions (see "Anti-Graft Campaign and the Common Man's Party," p. 538).

ELECTIONS

Campaigns and elections are essential procedures in any democracy and are often dramatic theatrical events. Certainly this is true of India, where all aspects of an election must be measured in superlatives. In the spring of 2014, nearly 540 million of

House of the People Election Results, 2004, 2009, and 2014

PARTY OR COALITION	2004 SEATS	2009 SEATS	2014 SEATS
UPA			
INC	145	206	44
Other allied parties	72	56	26
NDA			
BJP	138	116	282
Other allied parties	47	43	54
LF	59	24	11
Other Parties	84	100	128
Total	545	545	545

Key to Party Acronyms: BJP: Bharatiya Janata Party; INC: Indian National Congress; LF: Left Front
NDA: National Democratic Alliance; UPA: United Progressive Alliance
UPA and NDA are party coalitions that include the INC and BJP, respectively.

the eligible 815 million voters flocked to the nearly 1 million polling stations to cast votes (a record turnout of nearly 67 percent) using over 1.4 million electronic voting machines. The task was so huge that polling was spread out over more than a month as election officials and their machines migrated across the country harvesting votes.

Perhaps most surprising was the outcome itself, again testament to the authenticity of Indian democracy. Although even the governing Congress Party all but acknowledged in the weeks leading up to the election that its coalition was likely to be turned out of government, few predicted just how thoroughly the BJP would sweep the election. Winning over 30 percent of the popular vote and over 50 percent of the seats, the BJP became the first party other than Congress to win an outright majority of seats and the first party to do so in 30 years (see "House of the People Election Results, 2004, 2009, and 2014" above). This victory and the severe weakening of the opposition gave the charismatic Modi and his party a mandate to carry out promised reforms, heartening his many supporters. His detractors, on the other hand, feared that a victorious Modi would reveal his true stripes—not as a pragmatic economic reformer, but an ardent Hindu nationalist. Despite some troubling signs to the contrary, the BJP government's Hindu nationalist ideology has been tempered by both India's secular constitution and an electorate that remains primarily concerned with the economy.

CIVIL SOCIETY

As the INC's dominance has faded and political authority has become decentralized, more—and more diverse—interests and elements of Indian society have demanded political influence. India has conventional civil organizations representing business, labor, and even peasants, but these groups tend not to be particularly effective in influencing policy. Labor unions are organized by political party and are therefore fragmented and limited in their effectiveness, although they have done much to champion the interests of labor. Business certainly influences both politics and politicians. Corruption is a serious problem among Indian politicians—nearly a third of members of national and state legislatures elected since 2008 face criminal charges—but this influence has been held in check by both traditional Hindu and more modern socialist biases against private business. Peasants are plentiful and at times vocal, but their political demands tend to be episodic and particular.

Communal interests representing ethnic, religious, and caste groups have been far more influential in Indian politics. Hindus, Muslims, and Sikhs all have well-organized groups representing their political interests, as do the Dalits, or untouchables, who have their own political party and constitute one of India's largest mass movements. Although some fear the destabilizing and divisive potential of these religious- and caste-based groups, evidence indicates that their multiple demands have often been addressed substantially (if not fully met) through the political process, thereby defusing civil discord and strengthening the legitimacy of the system.

Less traditional divisions and demands are also taking shape in contemporary Indian civil society, particularly among India's growing middle class. These include significant anticorruption, environmental, and women's movements. A 2011 anti-graft campaign led by social activist Anna Hazare in the nation's capital prompted nationwide protests in support of the effort. Environmental protests include resistance to development projects, such as deforestation and the Narmada Valley Project dam, and advocacy of redress for industrial accidents, such as the 1980s Union Carbide gas-leak disaster in Bhopal. Women's movements bridging class and ethnic divisions have organized to protest so-called dowry deaths, which claim the lives of as many as 25,000 Indian women annually, and more recently the plight of women victims of sexual violence (see "The Politics of Rape," p. 537).

Another important voice of Indian civil society is the media establishment, arguably one of the largest and most active in the world. It comprises 40,000 newspapers and other periodicals, including some 4,000 dailies, all of which enjoy a significant degree of editorial and political freedom and influence. India's extensive radio and television networks are even more important conduits of information and have been subject to more careful government scrutiny and control. This oversight has become increasingly difficult, however, as satellite television has introduced new competition into the market. India's substantial investment in networking the entire country with broadband cable has also expanded avenues for civic communication.

Society

ETHNIC AND NATIONAL IDENTITY

Contemporary India is a complicated jigsaw of astounding ethnic and social diversity pieced together by centuries of imperial conquest.[11] Independent India has sought to create from this patchwork imperial raj a unified and secular nation-state or, more accurately, a "state-nation," recognizing that the country contains multiple ethnic groups with distinct cultural and in many cases political identities.[12] This effort has required of India and its citizens a measure of social tolerance that has not always been available, seemingly leaving the country on the edge of disintegration. Yet for

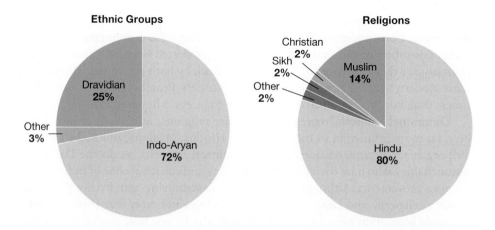

Ethnic Groups

- Dravidian 25%
- Other 3%
- Indo-Aryan 72%

Religions

- Christian 2%
- Sikh 2%
- Other 2%
- Muslim 14%
- Hindu 80%

all the communitarian conflict and threats of secession, national unity has prevailed. Before noting the political culture that has at least to some degree preserved this unity, we turn first to the ethnic and social divisions that threaten it.

When lighter-skinned Indo-Aryans migrated into what is now northern and central India thousands of years ago, they pushed the native, darker-skinned Dravidians southward. Each culture retained separate linguistic and cultural identities that persist to some extent today. Roughly two-thirds of Indians (virtually all in the north) speak some variation of the Sanskrit-based language brought by the Indo-Aryans, which now forms some 10 distinct languages. The most common of these is **Hindi**, one of two official national languages, which is spoken by over one-third of all Indians. Approximately one-fourth of all Indians speak one of the four main Dravidian languages, and another 5 percent claim Urdu as their first language. In all, the constitution recognizes 14 languages, but at least another 30 languages claim over 1 million speakers each. The only other national language is English. Although only some 3 percent of the population speaks English fluently, as in other polyglot former colonies it has become an essential medium for national and international politics and commerce and a significant binding force of Indian unity.

These divisions are at once exacerbated and moderated by religious differences. Although just under 80 percent of Indians share a common faith, regional and linguistic groups practice their Hinduism in different ways. The promotion of Hindu nationalism has brought a degree of unity to these groups, but at the expense of some 14 percent of Indians who are Muslim, 2 percent who are adherents of Sikhism, and a comparable percentage who are Christian. These religious differences have often acquired political significance, leading at times to assassinations and violent pogroms as well as bitter reprisals, secessions, and threats of secession.

The most dramatic flare-ups of sectarian violence have been between Hindus and Muslims. These include the initial partitioning of Muslim Pakistan and Hindu India, their ongoing territorial disputes in **Kashmir**, and the events at Ayodhya in 1992, Gujarat in 2002, and sporadic violence since then. Many Muslims, including most of the political leadership, moved to Pakistan following partition, leaving behind a weakened community in India whose loyalty is still questioned by Hindu nationalists. However, Muslim and Hindu identities are more blurred than we would imagine, especially in villages and at the lower rungs of society, where Muslims incorporate Hindu rituals and Hindus pray at Muslim shrines. Religious and

Pakistan and the Kashmir Dispute

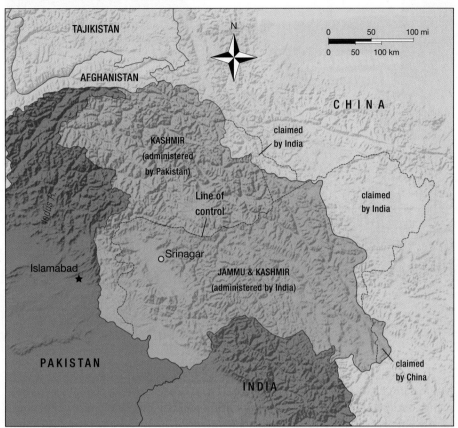

Source: "A Good Vote in the Angry Valley," *Economist*, December 30, 2008, www.economist.com/world/asia/displaystory.cfm?story_id=12868164 (accessed 1/15/09).

other identities in India are often sharper among elites than in the population as a whole—a common result of modernization worldwide.

As if the linguistic and religious differences were not sufficiently divisive, the hierarchical separation of Indian society into castes remains the most significant of India's social divisions. Although industrialization and urbanization have made the caste system today more permeable and flexible than it once was, the system remains socially, politically, and economically important. Neither class identity nor income inequality is as severe in India as in many other developing countries. But those in the lower ranks of India's caste system are typically also the poorest, and the Dalits are the poorest of the poor. In an effort to redress discrimination against these suppressed groups, the government has established affirmative action programs to reserve for them jobs, scholarships, and even seats in the parliament.

IDEOLOGY AND POLITICAL CULTURE

As with many other aspects of Indian politics, India's political culture defies generalization. Nonetheless, two somewhat contradictory values are worth mentioning. On the one hand, Indians tend to identify themselves and their politics locally. Indians are tied most strongly to family, occupational group, and their immediate

Muslims are a relatively small minority in India, but they have played a powerful role in the country's history. Technology links members of the Muslim community to one another and the wider Islamic world.

regional linguistic and religious associates. These ties tend to segment and even fragment politics in India, which promote political identity, awareness, and cooperation locally but also cause political friction and even violence between groups. Although such localization may limit the scope of conflict, it also constrains the kind of mobilization that could address pressing national needs.

On the other hand, despite cultural diversity and contentious politics, Indians continue to identify themselves as Indians and generally support—and see themselves as an important part of—Indian national democracy. So while the bonds of national unity are less powerful than local ties, India's "bewilderingly plural population" nonetheless considers itself as "capable of purposeful collective action."[13] Gandhi and Nehru remain national heroes for most Indians, who take their role as citizens seriously and see Indian democracy as legitimate.

Some find in this combined sense of local power and political efficacy a dangerous tendency toward identity politics. Nehru's secular nationalism has ceded ground to political movements that mobilize supporters in the name of religion or region. Majority Hindus perceive themselves as threatened by minority religions, the prosperous middle class depicts itself as victim of India's poorest outcastes, and Kashmiri Muslims clamor for independence. Globalization has further created a sense that Indian identity as a whole is under threat and must be defended. Yet democracy and unity prevail, which speaks to India's remarkable capacity to adopt and adapt foreign institutions for its own use. An Indian adage claims that "democracy is like cricket—a quintessentially Indian game that just happened to have been invented elsewhere." There is no question that India has made democracy its own.

IN COMPARISON | Fears about Foreign Influence

Our way of life must be protected from foreign influence. Percentage saying yes:

COUNTRY	PERCENTAGE	COUNTRY	PERCENTAGE
India	92	Japan	64
Nigeria	85	Canada	62
South Africa	80	United States	62
Brazil	77	United Kingdom	54
Russia	77	Germany	53
Mexico	75	France	52
China	70		

Note: Data on Iran not available.

Source: Pew Center for the People and the Press, 2007.

Political Economy

By the time India finally obtained its independence from British imperialism, it had seen quite enough of the West's version of liberal free trade. For nearly four decades, successive governments adopted a foreign policy of mercantilist economic nationalism, promoting **import substitution industrialization** and restricting foreign investment and trade. Governments also promoted social-democratic policies domestically to limit the private sector, redistribute wealth, and give the state the leading role in guiding the economy. These policies achieved several significant results. By the late 1970s, chiefly through the gains obtained through the technologically enhanced crops and cropping methods of the 1960s and 1970s **Green Revolution**, India had become one of the largest agricultural producers in the world. For most years since then, it has been a net exporter of food. Import substitution policies established a relatively large—if not broad—middle class and enabled some niches in the economy and some regions of the country to truly prosper.

By the mid-1980s, however, frustration with poverty, corruption, and continued slow growth at home had reached a critical point. Most observers agree that the greatest obstacle to Indian growth has been (and in important ways remains) India's huge bureaucracy with its associated red tape and corruption. Piecemeal efforts during the 1980s to dismantle nearly four decades of this socialist and mercantilist protectionism gave way to substantial liberalization by the early 1990s. Restrictions on foreign investment have been eased, and many state-owned companies have been sold to the private sector.

More significantly, successive governments have sought to weaken India's notorious **license raj**, the bureaucratic red tape requiring licensing and approval processes for operating a business or importing and exporting products. Although some of the most stifling aspects of this highly bureaucratized and politicized system of licenses, permits, and quotas governing virtually all aspects of the economy have been reduced or eliminated, the country continues to suffer from an array of bureaucratic and other barriers to business. Because Indians have found it so difficult to work within this system, most have little choice but to work around it. They do so by paying bribes, which have come to be expected "at almost every point where citizens are governed, at every transaction where they are noted, registered, taxed, stamped, licensed, authorized, or assessed."[14]

Despite the remaining challenges and ongoing resistance to reform in some areas of the economy, the liberalization effort has achieved impressive results. In the decade after launching the reforms, India's economic growth averaged nearly 6 percent per year (twice the rate of the previous 20 years). During the first decade of this century, growth rates averaged over 8 percent a year, in some years nearing the frenzied rates of economic expansion of neighboring China (but with inflation rates to match). Even as the population continued to grow rapidly, the total number of poor Indians declined. Trade and investment grew, and Western **outsourcing** has brought jobs and growth to some segments of the Indian economy. In recent years, however, economic growth has slowed dramatically, declining to barely half the pace of the previous decade. Inflation remains high, bringing "stagflation" to India. Employment and investment have slowed, even as government deficits and bank debts have ballooned.

There is great hope, and some evidence, that Modi's forceful leadership and the sweeping mandate given to the current BJP government will provide the necessary vision and momentum to reignite rapid and sustained growth in the Indian economy. In fact, India's 2015 growth rate outpaced China's, making India the fastest growing large economy in the world. Yet huge economic problems persist. More than one-fourth of Indians live on less than a dollar per day—though the percentage

Despite the sweeping victory of the BJP in the 2014 parliamentary elections, questions remain as to whether the BJP and Prime Minister Narendra Modi will be able to clean up India's many problems.

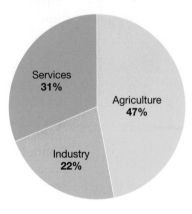

Modern shopping malls have sprung up in cities across India, including this one in Lucknow. Filled with Western and Indian stores, the malls serve the growing middle class but are far beyond the reach of most Indians.

of Indians living in poverty has been cut nearly in half since 1990. Over 40 percent of Indian children are underweight—a number that has not moved significantly for 20 years. The largest number of the world's undernourished people resides in India, even as India consistently ranks among the top two exporters of rice. Corruption and protectionism persist, and the pollution accompanying India's industrial expansion and urban growth threatens to undermine the development success the country has achieved to date. The World Bank predicts that by 2020, India's water, air, and soil resources will be under greater threat than those of any other nation.

Moreover, like many other developing countries that have been drawn into the global economy, India faces an additional problem. Although the economy is growing, it is doing so unevenly. Much has been made of India's recent information technology (IT) boom, and for good reason. Several large Indian computer firms are now globally competitive, and Western companies have flocked to such cities as Bangalore in the south and Hyderabad in the center to take advantage of India's wealth of service workers and English-speaking engineers.

Nevertheless, the IT industry remains largely irrelevant to most Indians. As a whole, it employs little more than 3 million workers out of a labor force of some 500 million and makes up less than 10 percent of India's GDP. Each year, some 12 million Indians enter an economy that produces fewer than 6 million jobs. A handful of India's 29 states receive virtually all of India's foreign investment, and most of the population remains employed in agriculture. This situation has created for India a dual economy that exacerbates both regional and class tensions. An elite, urban, prosperous, and Westernized middle-class minority sits precariously atop a

Labor Force by Occupation

Services 31%

Agriculture 47%

Industry 22%

huge lower class that is largely rural, illiterate, and in many cases unemployed or underemployed.

Scholars and policy makers agree that India must do several things if it is to eliminate or at least address the persistent poverty and inequality and stay ahead of its rapid population growth. Among them are improving conditions for its rural population; improving roads, telecommunication, and other aspects of the infrastructure; increasing foreign investment; and reducing bureaucracy and corruption. Above all, India must provide better education and health care, particularly to Indian girls and women. There is evidence that this can be done. The state of **Kerala**, in southwestern India, boasts female literacy rates of nearly 90 percent and fertility rates and population growth far lower than the national average. These changes are not the result of neoliberal market reforms, but of several decades of socialist state policies in education, health care, and land reform that have generally emphasized equality over freedom and state intervention over free-market policies. These efforts are not the priorities of the Modi government, which has called for greater market competition and smaller government.

In the digital age, smaller government does not have to mean a less capable state. Among other critical tasks, the Indian state must do more to empower the population and weaken the license raj. Starting in 2010, it began to implement a system known as Aadhaar (or "support"), which would give every citizen a unique 12-digit identification number and employ biometrics to identify the population. Teams across the country scan the fingerprints and irises of any individual seeking an identification number and these data are submitted to a growing national database, which will be linked to various state agencies and made accessible by computer, cell phone, and other electronic devices. By 2016, some 93 percent of adult Indians had voluntarily obtained identification numbers.

Although costly to implement, India is reaping the benefits of Aadhaar. Relying on the new identification numbers, government subsidies to the poor can be transferred directly, eliminating corrupt intermediaries and saving the government billions of dollars. Indian banks can connect secure private accounts to smartcards and cellular phones, giving the poor access to banking services (such as government payments and individual deposits) that in the past barely existed. This economic mobility may in turn increase physical mobility, allowing people to move easily and control their economic resources no matter where they are. Aadhaar's proponents argue that by linking all Indians directly to the state and market, this program has become the single most powerful weapon in the ongoing battle to weaken the license raj.[15]

Current Issues in India

When Indians went to the polls in 2014, two issues gained particular prominence: growing outrage at the government's seeming indifference toward violence against women and anger regarding persistent corruption in government. Neither problem is new, but a growing middle class and increasingly vocal civil society are becoming far less tolerant of these and other public policy problems. It remains to be seen if the Indian government and state have either the capacity or the will to tackle these issues and address the demands of an increasingly impatient Indian electorate.

The government's perceived indifference toward rape has angered many Indians. Here, protesters hold a vigil for Nirbhaya, a 23-year-old medical student who died after being attacked on a bus and gang-raped.

THE POLITICS OF RAPE

On a December evening in 2012, a 23-year-old college student and her male friend were abducted on the streets of Delhi by six men in a private bus. The men brutally gang-raped the young woman, who later died from the extensive injuries she incurred in the vicious attack. Tragically, such grisly accounts of sexual assault are all too commonly reported in the Indian press. Numerous reports of sexual violence against women (rape complaints have increased substantially in the past five years even as experts agree that most sexual assaults in India still go unreported) have galvanized India's middle class in protest against both a "culture of complicity" in the discrimination against women and the government's unwillingness or inability to adequately address such violence against women.[16]

Critics argue that while long-standing social attitudes and cultural practices of gender discrimination will not change overnight, much of the problem and therefore the solution rests with the Indian state. They point to India's ponderously slow and overburdened criminal justice system, in which prosecution rates are low, convictions infrequent, and sentences far too lenient. They also note that while India needs a more efficient and effective legal system, the performance of the judges as well as the police is unlikely to improve until elected politicians compel them to do so. Moreover, too many of these officials do not take sexual violence against women seriously. The Mumbai chief of police recently blamed rape on a culture of "promiscuity," and in two separate instances state ministers argued that rape often happens "accidentally" and is "sometimes right, sometimes wrong." The leader of one of India's largest regional parties argued publicly that those convicted of rape are often judged too harshly, concluding that "boys make mistakes."

There is growing awareness among India's citizenry that if politicians are the key to motivating bureaucrats, civil society must in turn hold elected politicians accountable. In the wake of nationwide protests following the rape of the Delhi student in 2012, state and federal governments have passed laws that establish special courts to handle crimes against women; that criminalize voyeurism, stalking, and sexual harassment; and that impose the death penalty for rape attacks leading to the victim's death. The BJP government, after coming to office in 2014, listened to the electorate and pledged "zero tolerance" for violence against women.

Certainly, rape and sexual violence are not exclusively an Indian problem. Three times as many rapes are reported in the United States as in India, although the United States has roughly a fourth of India's population. But no one, least of all India's increasingly agitated and sophisticated citizenry, doubts that India has a rape problem. Or that the government—and the public—must become a larger part of the solution.

ANTI-GRAFT CAMPAIGN AND THE COMMON MAN'S PARTY

Another issue that has stirred anger and frustration among the Indian people is the country's endemic public corruption. Like gender discrimination, political corruption is not a new phenomenon in India. But the recent exposure of a number of particularly egregious political scandals, combined with (and contributing to) a growing public awareness, has spawned a political movement that mobilized Indian civil society, gave birth to a political party, and shook India's political class. Whether the movement will lead to any permanent solutions or lasting political change is yet to be seen.

The decade-long, Congress-led coalition government (2004–14) found itself embroiled in a series of high-profile scandals. The biggest of these involved the auctioning of the 2G wireless spectrum by the government's Telecommunications Ministry in 2008. A subsequent investigation revealed that insider deals involving the issuing of licensing may have cost the government some $40 billion. Delhi's hosting of the Commonwealth Games in 2010 (chaired by a Congress politician) also involved a number of under-the-table, no-bid contracts that resulted in extensive delays and huge cost overruns. A 2012 "Coalgate" scandal concerning the improper distribution of coal resources may have cost taxpayers another $33 billion.[17]

These and other scandals, not to mention the host of petty inconveniences and expenses resulting from the license raj, brought public anger to a boil. The charismatic leader who gave voice and order to this anger was Anna Hazare, a social activist and former Army officer. In 2011, he launched a hunger strike, conducted from a central square of Delhi near the parliament building, which struck a chord not only with India's middle class but also with lower-class workers who felt disenfranchised and ignored by India's political class. Millions rallied to the cause of "Team Anna." Caught off guard, the Congress-led government first ignored, then decried, and after two weeks ultimately capitulated to his demand, agreeing to draft a bill that would set up a powerful new anticorruption body.

By mid-2012, however, little progress had been made on the bill. The situation prompted Arvind Kejriwal, a former civil servant and one of the chief architects of Hazare's political protest, to form a political party. Called the Aam Aadmi (Common Man's) Party (AAP), it sported a broom as its party symbol (for sweeping away corruption). In 2013, Kejriwal and the AAP obtained 30 percent of the vote and 28 of the 70 seats in the Delhi regional parliamentary elections. Although the BJP won 32 seats, the AAP was able to form a minority government with Kejriwal as chief minister.

True to the Common Man image, Kejriwal refused to move into the chief minister's plush residence and even spent one night sleeping on the sidewalk. The AAP government lasted only 49 days, however, before Kejriwal resigned in protest after the Delhi assembly failed to pass the AAP's bill to establish a state ombudsman. The AAP next set its sights on the 2014 national parliamentary elections, hoping to deny a majority of seats to either the BJP or the INC and thereby give the party a strong bargaining position to further promote its anti-graft agenda. Ultimately, the AAP fared poorly in the voting, taking only 4 of the 535 seats. Kejriwal campaigned for a seat from a Varanasi precinct, going head-to-head against the BJP's Modi, and was soundly beaten. Although a watered-down version of the independent watchdog bill was finally passed into law in 2013, it fell far short of the measure advocated by civil activists.

Like others before them, both Hazare and Kejriwal learned the difficulty of turning a single-issue protest movement into a political campaign. On the other hand, the AAP fared better in its national debut than the BJP did in its first national elections in 1984. More significantly, in 2015, the AAP swept Delhi state elections, winning 67 of the 70 seats to the BJP's 3 seats. This stunning victory indicates that the Indian electorate has not forgotten the issue that inspired the movement. The Indian political establishment ignores the issue of political corruption at its peril.

Key Terms

Amritsar (p. 517)
asymmetric federalism (p. 524)
Ayodhya (p. 518)
Bharatiya Janata Party (BJP) (p. 518)
caste (p. 511)
Center (p. 519)
chief minister (p. 523)
Council of States (p. 522)
Dalits (p. 523)
East India Company (p. 514)
emergency rule (p. 517)
Gandhi, Indira (p. 517)
Gandhi, Mahatma (Mohandas K.) (p. 513)
Gandhi, Sonia (p. 519)
Green Revolution (p. 533)
Gujarat (p. 518)
Hindi (p. 530)
Hinduism (p. 513)
Hindutva (p. 526)
House of the People (p. 522)

import substitution industrialization (p. 533)
Indian National Congress (INC) (p. 516)
Kashmir (p. 530)
Kerala (p. 536)
license raj (p. 533)
Modi, Narendra (p. 519)
Mughals (p. 514)
Muslim League (p. 516)
Naxalism (p. 527)
Nehru, Jawaharlal (p. 516)
outsourcing (p. 534)
partition (p. 516)
presidential rule (p. 520)
raj (p. 517)
Sepoy Mutiny (p. 515)
Sikhism (p. 514)
Singh, Manmohan (p. 519)
untouchables (p. 523)

Hassan Rouhani speaks at a campaign rally prior to his successful campaign for president in 2013.

Iran

Why Study This Case?

Like many of the cases in this volume, Iran illustrates important dynamics in comparative politics. Most important, it is associated with what we think of as Islamism, or Islamic fundamentalism. When we speak of fundamentalism, we mean a view of religion as absolute and inerrant that should be legally enforced by making faith the sovereign authority. Faith becomes ideology.

In 1979, the authoritarian, secular Iranian monarchy fell to revolution, an uprising inspired in part by the charisma of the religious leader Ayatollah Ruhollah Khomeini. This Islamic revolution dramatically transformed all aspects of Iranian life, as Khomeini and his followers sought to create a theocracy in which a religious elite dominated the regime. In this "Islamic Republic," law and politics are expected to flow from the Koran, the main spiritual text of Islam. The Iranian Revolution became a source of inspiration for Islamist movements around the world. As numerous countries struggle with reconciling Islam and the state today, the Iranian Revolution remains an important example of the power of Islam as a political vision.

In looking more deeply, however, we find that Iran is atypical and unrepresentative of the politics of Islam or even the politics of the Middle East. Contrary to what many assume, Iran is not an Arab country—the major ethnicity of Iran's population is Persian. Nor do Iranians speak Arabic, the common language of the Middle East; they speak, instead, Farsi, a language closer to English and other European languages. Indeed, Iranians see themselves as a distinct nation; they look upon Arab countries as foreign and often view them with some degree of contempt. Iranians do not necessarily see themselves as part of a broader pan-Islamic or pan-Arabic movement, and that feeling has only intensified since the Arab Spring.

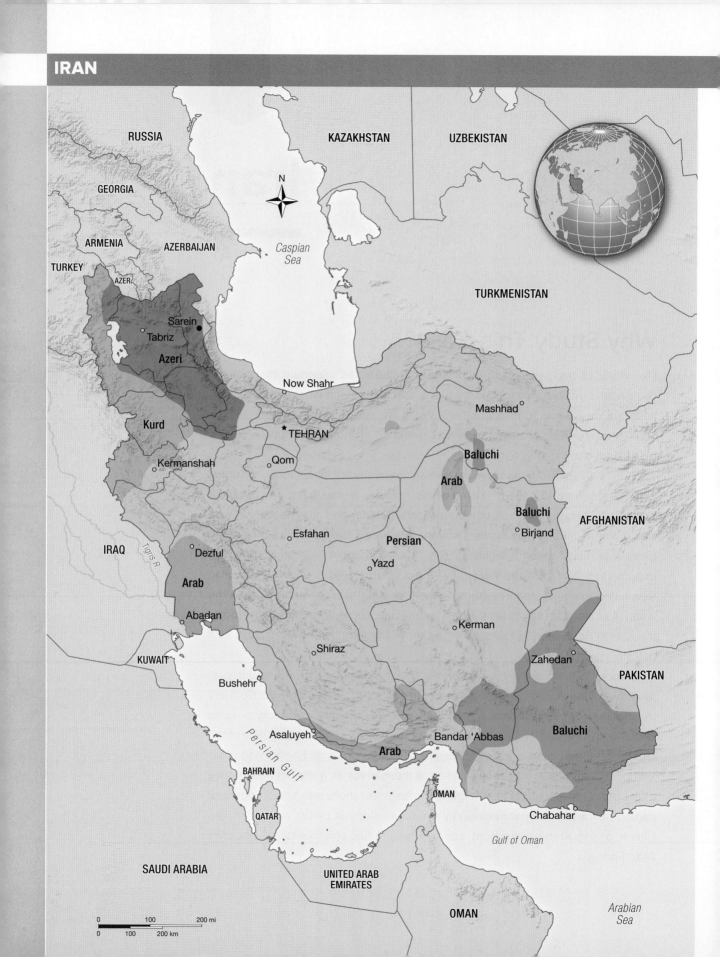

RUSSIA

KAZAKHSTAN

UZBEKISTAN

GEORGIA

N

ARMENIA

AZERBAIJAN

*Caspian
Sea*

TURKMENISTAN

TURKEY

AZER.

Sarein

Tabriz

Azeri

Now Shahr

Mashhad

Kurd

★ TEHRAN

Baluchi

Kermanshah

Qom

Arab

Baluchi

AFGHANISTAN

Esfahan

Persian

Birjand

IRAQ

Dezful

Yazd

Tigris R.

Arab

Abadan

Kerman

Zahedan

PAKISTAN

KUWAIT

Shiraz

Bushehr

Baluchi

Asaluyeh

Persian Gulf

Arab

Bandar 'Abbas

BAHRAIN

OMAN

QATAR

Chabahar

Gulf of Oman

SAUDI ARABIA

UNITED ARAB
EMIRATES

OMAN

*Arabian
Sea*

0   100   200 mi

0   100   200 km

The difference between Iranian ethnicity and Iranian national identity is compounded by religion. Again, at first glance, Iran's revolution might be seen as the first spark in the current wave of Islamist activism and conflict, and there can be no doubt that in its early years the revolution did inspire a new wave of radicalism and political violence across the region. But the international impact of the revolution was tempered because Iranians practice Shiism, a minority form of Islam (practiced by about 10 to 15 percent of the global Muslim population) that differs from the rest of Islam in its belief regarding the rightful heir of the prophet Muhammad. As a result, many followers of Islam around the world reject the Iranian theocracy for avowing a mistaken, even heretical, form of the faith. Despite these divisions, Iran has certainly influenced modern debates on the relationship between politics and Islam, especially among Shiite groups elsewhere in the region (as in Iraq, Afghanistan, and Lebanon). For some, Iran remains an inspiration for political change; for others, it is an example of how religion and politics should not mix. Such conflicting views can be found not only among average Shiites (both inside and outside Iran) but also among Shiism's top clergy.

These complexities help shape Iran's role in the international system. In recent years, Iran has moved toward developing its own nuclear capacity, creating worries among many states that such weapons would make the country a significant regional threat. While an international agreement reached in 2016 has lessened concerns and improved international relations, ongoing tension remains, and there is a significant risk that the agreement could unravel.

In 2013, cleric Hassan Rouhani won a surprising landslide victory, following a campaign in which he promised to advance those social reforms lost under the previous president as well as improve relations with the West. This approach was much like that of former president Mohammad Khatami, who was in office from 1997 to 2005. Like Khatami, Rouhani has found challenging conservative institutions and actors, such as the more powerful Supreme Leader Ayatollah Ali Khamenei, a formidable task. Many of Rouhani's supporters have been disappointed in the limited changes to date. In 2017, Rouhani won a strong mandate in the elections for his second term, but this was less a vote of popular confidence than of opposition to his hard-line opponent. Rouhani has yet to deliver on many of his promises. Can Iran truly reform and become a more liberal, even democratic regime?

Despite its unique institutions, Iran can give us a glimpse into the potential power of Islamic fundamentalism, its limitations, and the sources of resistance to it.

Historical Development of the State

THE PERSIAN LEGACY AND THE ISLAMIC EMPIRE

Iranians trace their national and political origins back thousands of years, at least to the second millennium B.C.E. Around that time, a number of people migrated into the region from Central Asia, and among them was the ethnic group we now know as the Persians. Outside Iran, *Persian* continues to be a common name used to describe the majority population of the country. Until 1935, the country itself was officially known as **Persia**.

During the first millennium B.C.E., the Persians were able to extend their influence throughout the region, subduing other groups and creating the Achaemenid Empire in the process. Under the emperors Cyrus, Darius, and Xerxes, the empire grew vast, stretching from modern-day India across much of the Middle East, and becoming a major foe to the Greek city-states. Although the empire was destroyed by Alexander the Great in 334 B.C.E., the country continued to develop under a series of ruling dynasties. These kings, or shahs, ruled through the sixth century C.E.

The most dramatic transformation of Persia by outside forces occurred in the seventh century with the arrival of Islam, brought by Arabs from the Middle East shortly after the death of the prophet Muhammad in 632 C.E. Although the conquerors adopted many Persian practices and institutions, differences between Persian and Arab culture remained.

The population slowly converted from Zoroastrianism (a native monotheistic faith) to Islam.[1] Up through the eleventh century, Persia was part of several powerful Islamic dynasties that stretched across Central Asia and the Middle East.

DYNASTIC RULE AND THE ADOPTION OF SHIISM

The period from the sixteenth to the early twentieth century saw the rise of two longstanding Iranian dynasties: the Safavids (1502–1736) and the Qajars (1794–1925). Under the Safavids, the country adopted Shiism as the state religion as a way to differentiate the country from its Ottoman rivals, who were Sunni.

Shiism differs from dominant Sunni Islam by arguing that leadership within the Islamic community has been entrusted by God to the family and bloodline of the prophet Muhammad. From Muhammad's son-in-law Ali on down, according to the Shia, the **imams** are the true leaders of the faith, though these descendants have been repeatedly deprived of power by other Muslim leaders. The last of these imams, known as the **Mahdi**, or "guided one," has in fact been concealed by God and is expected by the Shia to reappear at the end of time to restore justice and equality to a corrupted world. In this regard, Shiism resembles Christianity. Moreover, it emphasizes the martyrdom of these descendants of Muhammad, many of whom died at the hands of Sunni rivals.[2]

Another interesting comparison between Shiism and Christianity has been the relationship between faith and state. In Shiism, the particular emphasis on the descendants of Ali returning at the end of time to rule has made worldly politics in some ways secondary to the faith. This view may seem the complete opposite of what we understand about Iran's "Islamic Republic," but it also indicates that for many Shia, an Islamic Republic is a contradiction in terms. We will explore this important perspective later in the chapter.

However, Shiism has long been connected to, if not directly involved in, politics. The Safavids cultivated within Shiism's religious leaders (or *ulema*) a higher clergy, who came to be known as **ayatollahs**. This structure, too, differs from the more decentralized Sunni Islam, and these high-ranking clergy have become a central institution in modern Iranian religion and politics. Yet while Iran's supreme leader has sought to place himself above other clerics, various high-ranking ayatollahs inside and outside Iran have their own followers and issue their own fatwas (religious rulings) independent of any political leaders.

Political Development

1905–6	Constitutional revolution seeks to limit power of the monarchy.
1921	Reza Khan seizes power.
1925	Reza Khan is proclaimed shah and changes his name to Reza Shah Pahlavi.
1941	British and Soviet forces occupy Iran; the shah is forced to abdicate in favor of his son, Mohammad Reza Pahlavi.
1951	Parliament votes to nationalize the oil industry.
1953	Struggle between the shah and Prime Minister Mohammad Mosaddeq culminates in Operation Ajax, in which Mosaddeq is overthrown with U.S. help.
1963	White Revolution begins.
1979	Iranian Revolution takes place: the shah is deposed; Ayatollah Ruhollah Khomeini returns from exile; U.S. embassy is seized and hostages are held for 444 days.
1980	Iraq invades Iran.
1988	Iran-Iraq War ends.
1989	Ayatollah Khomeini dies; Ayatollah Khamenei is elected supreme leader.
1997	Reformer Mohammad Khatami is elected president.
1999	Pro-reform student protests lead to rioting and mass arrests.
2002	Russia begins work on Iran's first nuclear reactor, at Bushehr.
2005	Mahmoud Ahmadinejad is elected president.
2009	Ahmadinejad wins a second presidential term in a disputed election.
2013	Hassan Rouhani is elected president.
2017	Rouhani reelected for a second term.

Although Iran during the Safavid and Qajar eras was able to maintain its power in the face of regional rivals, such as the Ottoman Empire, it inevitably came under pressure from other expanding states. In the early nineteenth century, Russia squeezed Iran from the north, seizing territories, while the United Kingdom conquered neighboring India and attempted to gain control over Afghanistan.

FAILED REFORMS AND THE EROSION OF SOVEREIGNTY

In the last decades of the Qajar dynasty, the monarchy enacted various, albeit half-hearted, reforms. They borrowed these reforms from the West, intending to use them in modernizing the weak state. The monarchy experimented with Western-style economic and political institutions even as it surrendered ever more sovereignty to the British and the Russians. In 1906, religious leaders, intellectuals, and members of the merchant class protested in favor of limitations on the powers of the Qajar monarchy in what came to be known as the **Constitutional Revolution**. The protest resulted in an elected assembly that drew up the country's first constitution and legislative body, known as the **Majlis**. For Iranians, the Constitutional Revolution signifies the country's first attempt at republicanism and democracy, akin to the American Revolution. Unlike other revolutions, however, it lacked a clear ideology or consensus other than weakening or removing the monarchy, and tellingly, secularists came into conflict with some ayatollahs over the future of the regime.

The Constitutional Revolution, while important, did not live up to expectations. Ongoing battles between monarchists and constitutionalists (and between secularists and members of the clergy) opened the way for the United Kingdom and Russia to divide the country into formal spheres of influence in 1907, all but eliminating Persian sovereignty.

The embattled Majlis continued to oppose imperialism, however, rejecting a 1919 agreement that would have granted the United Kingdom significant control over the state and the economy, including Persia's growing oil industry. Amid the ongoing political turmoil in Iran, a relatively obscure military officer came to political power. Born to a poor family, Reza Khan had distinguished himself as a superior military figure, rising rapidly through the ranks. In 1921, he marched into Tehran as part of a wider group of coup plotters, but he quickly outmaneuvered his allies (including the Majlis, who initially gave him their support) and consolidated his rule.

CONSOLIDATION OF POWER UNDER THE PAHLAVI DYNASTY

Reza Shah Pahlavi, as Reza Khan renamed himself, proved to be more than a mere puppet of the British. Upon becoming head of the armed forces, he quickly moved to consolidate his power, removing his fellow conspirators from office and neutralizing threats within and outside Iran. By centralizing the military, he was able to quell several regional rebellions and to limit British and Soviet interference in the country's affairs.

In 1923, the last shah of the Qajar dynasty appointed Reza Khan prime minister and promptly went into exile in Europe; in 1925, the Majlis formally deposed the Qajar dynasty and appointed Reza Khan the new shah. As a monarch with few constraints on his power, the shah pursued a course of dramatic Westernization and state building. That included reforming the bureaucracy, instituting primary and secondary education and a university system, developing road and rail systems, establishing a number of state-owned businesses to develop monopolies in important domestic and export-oriented markets, and abolishing the aristocracy (other than the shah himself).

Iran also exerted greater (if still limited) control over its burgeoning oil industry, which Britain had dominated since its inception. In addition, Reza Shah instituted national conscription as part of his effort to centralize military might and extend state control over what had been a fractious and tribal country. The shah complemented this political centralization with efforts to build a modern national identity by promoting the idea of a single people whose glory extended back thousands of years and drawing on the country's pre-Islamic history.

Finally, as part of his modernization, the shah greatly extended the rights of women, giving them access to education, including at the university level. He

Young women near Tehran University. Although Iranian laws require women to wear the hijab, many do not fully cover their hair as required and otherwise dress in Western clothes.

also sought to root out traditional customs which he believed were holding back their emancipation. Two important symbols were the head scarf (hijab) and cloak (chador), which women wore in public as a sign of modesty and privacy. In 1934, inspired by similar reforms in Turkey, Iran forbade the wearing of the head coverings in schools, a proscription that was later extended to other public facilities. The shah's efforts were part of a broader attack on Shiism and Islamic religious and educational institutions, which were seen as backward and of foreign (that is, Arab) origin.

Modernization came at the expense of democratization as well as traditional practices and religious beliefs. Democratic institutions, such as the press and the Majlis, were curtailed, and religious and political opponents were jailed, exiled, or killed. The power of the clergy was similarly curtailed as the state set its own standards for social norms. By the eve of World War II, Iran had made significant progress in establishing modern political institutions and independence from foreign interference. Yet progress had come at the cost of increased repression of civic life.

World War II again drew the country into international conflict. Reza Shah's friendly relations with Germany raised fears in the United Kingdom and Russia; in 1941, the two countries invaded Iran to open a land corridor between them and to prevent Iran (and its oil) from falling under Axis control. Reza Shah was forced to abdicate in favor of his son, Mohammad Reza Pahlavi, and to go into exile. As World War II gave way to the Cold War, the United States, the United Kingdom, and the Soviet Union all sought to consolidate their power over the country and its oil supplies. Political and religious activity resurfaced in the face of the weakened state and regime.[3]

THE NATIONALIST CHALLENGE UNDER MOSADDEQ AND THE U.S. RESPONSE

In the aftermath of Reza Shah's abdication, republican and religious activity began to reassert itself. The Majlis and the ulema promoted the removal of Western influence over Iran, and many supported nationalization of the oil industry, which was under joint Iranian and British ownership.

Nationalization was advocated in particular by the new prime minister, **Mohammad Mosaddeq**, who represented the **National Front**, a republican party that favored reducing the power of the monarchy or eliminating it altogether. The shah reluctantly conceded to nationalization in 1951, which provoked British anger and led to the withdrawal of Britain's technical support, essentially halting oil production. As the crisis deepened, Mosaddeq relied on political allies such as the Marxist Tudeh Party to reduce the powers of the monarchy.

Mosaddeq's actions were directed toward the goals of national sovereignty and modernization. However, his nationalization of oil generated deep British animosity, while his secularism and republicanism alienated much of the ulema and raised fears within the United States that Iran faced a Communist takeover.

With the shah's support, the United States and the United Kingdom moved to overthrow Mosaddeq through a covert program known as **Operation Ajax**. Several days of conflict between supporters of the prime minister and supporters of the shah, including republicans and the military, finally culminated in a victory for the shah and his backers.

The shah wasted little time in concentrating his power along his father's lines. Reza Shah had expended much of his energy developing an Iran independent of Western power, but his son balanced his quest for sovereignty with a new alliance with the United States. The shah repressed opposition parties and built a powerful secret police (known by its acronym, **SAVAK**); he also marginalized the prime minister and Majlis. The short-lived and turbulent period of democracy thus ended, and its destruction became forever associated with the United States.

AUTHORITARIANISM AND MODERNIZATION DURING THE WHITE REVOLUTION

After bringing the political system under his control, the shah revived the policy of top-down modernization that his father had promoted earlier. Once again, the policy had the effect of marginalizing the ulema. Its reforms, starting in 1963, were known as the **White Revolution**.[4]

The shah's modernization policies included land reform, privatization of state-run industries, a literacy campaign, and the enfranchisement of women. Some reforms, in particular land reform and female enfranchisement, were strongly opposed by religious leaders. In June of 1963, the reforms led to rioting, which the government suppressed violently. A subsequent protest in 1964, over Iran's growing alliance with the United States, was also quickly quelled.

Associated with both protests was Ruhollah Khomeini, an ayatollah based in the holy city of Qom. Khomeini was already known for his writings linking worldly politics to spiritual issues, an interest that extended back to the 1940s and set him apart from most Shia clerics. Khomeini's growing power led the shah to expel him from the country (execution was too dangerous a move). From abroad, he continued to criticize the Iranian regime for its corruption, inequality, and reliance on the United States. Khomeini articulated a vision of an Iran governed by Islam, creating a country that could be a lodestar for revolution across the Middle East.

For the next 15 years, the shah would rule without serious challenge. Rapid, if uneven, modernization continued, fostered by state policy and by rising oil revenues (upward of $20 billion a year by the mid-1970s). Iran built a huge military in response to the shah's desire to project the country as a major regional force and a "great civilization" to be reckoned with on the world stage. Tens of thousands of Americans came to work in Iran, helping to foster rapid social change but also generating resentment thanks to their often patronizing treatment of Iranians. At the same time, the shah's rule became increasingly autocratic as he cracked down on religious institutions and a growing civil society.

All these rapid changes did little to legitimize or support the shah's rule. Billions of dollars in oil revenue flowed into Iran, helping to create a middle class. But much of the money also disappeared into the pockets of those in power, either to build the military or to support the lavish lifestyle of the shah and his family. That so much disruption and misery was tied to oil, and that so much of the oil industry was directed and run by foreigners, helped foster the sentiment that the United States and other Western powers were simply plundering the nation.

OPPOSITION TO THE SHAH AND THE IRANIAN REVOLUTION

The worsening of Iran's economy during the mid-1970s coincided with a growing, highly educated urban youth and increased state repression. Eventually, the situation led to open conflict. In 1977, the new U.S. president, Jimmy Carter, whose administration placed greater emphasis on human rights, began to criticize the shah for his repressive practices. Hoping to pacify his ally, the shah carried out a limited set of reforms, freeing some political prisoners and allowing banned organizations such as the National Front to reorganize.

As U.S. pressure on the shah flagged, Iranians found a second source of external opposition to his repressive rule: the Ayatollah Khomeini. Khomeini had through his works elaborated a vision of an Islamic political system for Iran quite at odds with that of much of the Shia clergy. These ideas culminated in his work *Islamic Government: The Governance of the Jurist*. In this work, he argued that Islamic government should be constructed around the concept of *velayat-e faqih*, or clerical rule; whereas a monarchy was a usurpation of Allah's rule on earth, a system of government by a clergy trained in Islamic jurisprudence would be a continuation of the political system first established by the prophet Muhammad.

The shah, Khomeini, and the United States were now on a collision course. In 1978, the Iranian government attempted a smear campaign against Khomeini, which only increased support for the ayatollah and touched off a series of protests. In September, a massive protest in Tehran in defiance of martial law called for the end of the monarchy and the return of Ayatollah Khomeini. The army fired on the protesters, and some protesters fired back. Scores were killed, and the violence continued to flow with increasingly religious symbolism, including allusions to martyrdom and the coming of the Mahdi.

By late 1978, the shah's power had slipped away. In December, millions of protesters took to the streets of Tehran in defiance of a government ban on such public gatherings. Military units began to defect. The seemingly unshakable Pahlavi dynasty rapidly fell apart, and the shah fled, replaced by a provisional government with a tenuous hold on the country. On February 1, 1979, millions gathered to welcome the Ayatollah Khomeini as he returned to Iran.[5]

THE CONSOLIDATION OF AN ISLAMIC REPUBLIC

The revolution did not automatically mean that Iran would have an Islamic regime. Although most Iranian citizens did call for an "Islamic republic," it is not clear that those supporters agreed with, or even fully grasped, the kind of political system Khomeini was proposing. However, by capitalizing on the political turmoil and drawing on his own charismatic authority, Khomeini was able to undermine the secular provisional government that had replaced the shah. Outflanking the various political and religious factions that had sprung up during the revolution, he gained control of the government and oversaw the drafting of a new constitution that allowed for a faqih (a religious leader with expertise in Islamic law) who would have supreme political authority. Khomeini filled this position until his death in 1989.

The **Islamic Republic of Iran** had a violent birth. The new government suppressed all opposition, including monarchists, members of Marxist and other secular political groups, ethnic minorities, and members of other faiths. From 1979 to 1980, perhaps thousands were executed in the name of "revolutionary justice." The course of Iran's relationship with the international community was also transformed when student radicals seized control of the U.S. embassy and held much of its staff hostage for more than a year.

The convulsions of the revolution were soon compounded by the **Iran-Iraq War**. As the Iranian Revolution unfolded, Iraq's authoritarian leader, Saddam Hussein, perceived these developments as a threat to his own rule over a country in which more than half the population was Shiite. Khomeini himself hoped to spread his Islamic Revolution beyond Iran's borders, and Iraq was the logical next choice. At the same time, Iraq saw in Iran's chaos an opportunity to extend its power in the region and seize Iranian territory that contained many of the country's oil fields. In September 1980, Iraq launched a full-scale invasion of Iran, initiating the Iran-Iraq War, which lasted until 1988, ending in a stalemate. Hundreds of thousands of Iranians and Iraqis were dead. Shortly thereafter, Khomeini himself died, leaving the Islamic Republic without its founder and spiritual guide.

Political Regime

Since 1979, the Islamic Republic of Iran has sought to follow the ideas of Khomeini in creating a political system built around his notion of *velayat-e faqih*, which would replace the sovereignty of men and women with the sovereignty of God as transmitted by the clergy. Yet Khomeini came to power in the wake of a popular revolution driven by the public's demand for a political system that responded to their needs and desires. The new regime would thus have to reconcile the will of the people with what was viewed as the will of God.

How does a nation maintain the ideals and authority of its leader once that leader is gone? How does a revolution remain true to its ideals? In Iran, the result has been a political system quite unlike any other, a mixture of institutions that seek to balance popular rights with the word of God.

POLITICAL INSTITUTIONS

THE CONSTITUTION The Iranian constitution is a product of the 1979 revolution. In its preamble, the constitution lays out the origins of the current regime, which is viewed as a revolt against the "American conspiracy" of the White Revolution.

According to the constitution, the Islamic Republic exists not to serve the individual but to guide the people toward God. The Koran (the holy book of Islam) therefore serves as a spiritual text as well as the foundation for a unified national ideology that is embodied in the political system.

As the constitution itself states, "All civil, penal, financial, economic, administrative, cultural, military, political, and other laws and regulations must be based on Islamic criteria." This concept is consistent with religious fundamentalism in general, which challenges secular notions of statehood and democracy. As such, the Iranian constitution and political institutions are (at least in theory) an attempt to express God's will. At the same time, however, the constitution reflects the fact that the overthrow of the shah was a revolution primarily led by the people, not Khomeini or the ulema. The constitution thus also embodies strongly republican (if not democratic) elements. The result is ongoing political tension between republicanism and theocracy.

THE BRANCHES OF GOVERNMENT

THE SUPREME LEADER AND THE PRESIDENT The particular nature of the Iranian constitution has resulted in a set of political institutions that are quite bewildering to outsiders but consistent with the *velayat-e faqih*. We can see this most clearly in the executive branch of the government. As in many other countries, Iran has a dual executive that divides power between two offices. In most other cases, such

---

INFOCUS **Essential Political Features**

- **Legislative–executive system**: Semi-presidential theocracy
- **Legislature**: Majlis
  - **Lower house**: Majlis
  - **Upper house**: (none)
- **Unitary or federal division of power**: Unitary
- **Main geographic subunits**: *Ostan* (provinces)
- **Electoral system for lower house**: Single-member and multimember district majority
- **Chief judicial body**: Supreme Court

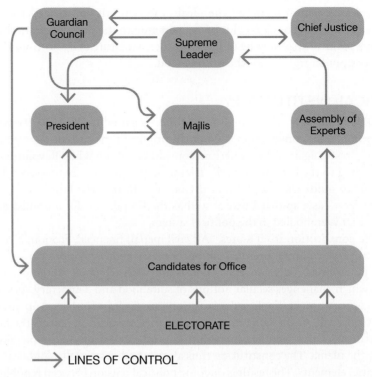

Structure of the Government

divisions fall between the head of state—a monarch or president—and the head of government, usually a prime minister.

Iran's executive does not follow this pattern. The dominant executive is the **supreme leader**, a position created for Khomeini following the revolution as an expression of his charismatic power and political ideology. The supreme leader serves for life, though in theory he can be removed for incompetence or failure to uphold his religious duty.

The supreme leader has numerous, if often indirect, powers. The supreme leader is commander in chief of the armed forces and wields control over the Guardian Council (discussed later). The supreme leader also appoints the chief justice and thus has significant influence over the judicial system. Finally, the supreme leader also maintains control over significant state-owned economic assets.

Since 1989, the supreme leader has been Ali Khamenei, who previously served as the president of the country from 1981 to 1989. He lacks the charismatic or intellectual power of Khomeini or the religious authority of Iran's most senior clerics. Despite this, Khamenei has wrong-footed many of his rivals, slowly consolidating power within the office by allying himself with individuals within the ulema and military.

How is the supreme leader chosen? In theory, the role falls to the **Assembly of Experts**—a body of 88 members, all men and Islamic scholars, who are themselves popularly elected for eight-year terms. According to the constitution, the assembly may also remove the supreme leader if he fails to discharge his constitutional duties, creating at least in theory the capacity for the body to oversee the supreme leader. Since Khamenei has been the only supreme leader to come to power after Khomeini, it is difficult to say how powerful a role this body will play once he passes away.

If the supreme leader functions as a powerful head of state, the **president** is (confusingly) more akin to a head of government. Unlike the supreme leader, the president is directly elected and can serve only two 4-year terms. Within his scope of responsibilities lie drafting the state budget, initiating legislation, and selecting a cabinet of ministers charged with directing various facets of policy. However, he cannot veto legislation, nor may he dissolve the legislature and call for elections—both basic powers among executives. The president is also technically in charge of foreign policy, though given the president's lack of control over the military his powers in this area remain circumscribed. In general, the president is charged with the task of executing the laws, making certain that specific policies are carried out. Since 2013, President Hassan Rouhani, a cleric, has pursued a reformist agenda. This was critical to the success of the 2016 nuclear deal (discussed later) and Rouhani's subsequent reelection to a second term in 2017, but similar attempts at domestic liberalization have been stymied.

THE LEGISLATURE The Islamic Republic retains one political institution from Iran's past. The legislature, or Majlis, is a unicameral body whose members are directly elected on the basis of universal suffrage of men and women over the age of 18. Its 290 members serve four-year terms and must be at least 30 years of age.

As might be suspected, the Majlis, like its predecessors, has a limited amount of authority. Its powers include initiating and passing legislation, overseeing the budget, and approving members of the president's cabinet. Cabinet members may also be removed by a vote of no confidence, though the Majlis's power in this area does not extend to the president or to the supreme leader. The Majlis was dominated by clerics in the early years of the revolution, but their participation has declined while that of members associated with the paramilitary Revolutionary Guard (see "Other Institutions," p. 555) has risen. These are single seats set aside for the Zoroastrian and Jewish communities, and three seats are for Christians. (None of these communities makes up more than 1 percent of the population.) Finally, there are currently 17 women in the Majlis (more than there are clerics).

The inherent supremacy of God's law in the Iranian constitution raises questions about the functioning of the legislature. Since human-made laws are liable to deviate from God's will, the role of the Majlis is technically to legislate in accordance with divine law, and its legislation can be struck down for failing on this account. Despite this limitation, the Majlis is an important actor. While it does not challenge the supreme leader, conflicts between the Majlis and the president over national policy are common, especially with regard to the budget.

The broader limitations of the Majlis are best seen in the presence of two additional bodies, the **Guardian Council** and the **Expediency Council**. The Guardian Council is made up of 12 individuals who serve six-year phased terms: 6 are lawyers nominated by the chief justice and approved by the Majlis; 6 are clerics specializing in religious law and are appointed by the supreme leader. The powers of the Guardian Council are significant; among them is the power to review all legislation that derives from the Majlis, to "ensure its compatibility with the criteria of Islam and the Constitution."[6] It may send legislation back to the Majlis for revision if it finds it incompatible; if the Majlis is unable to revise the legislation to the Guardian Council's satisfaction, a third body, the Expediency Council, mediates.

Members of the Expediency Council are appointed by the supreme leader for five-year terms; until his death in 2017 the council was headed by **Ali Akbar Hashemi Rafsanjani**, a long-standing rival to Khamenei who served as the country's president from 1989 to 1997. The final decision of the Expediency Council cannot be overturned. The Guardian Council (and, to a lesser extent, the Expediency Council) serves as a kind of unelected upper house with substantial powers to restrict the work of the Majlis.

THE JUDICIARY Since 1979, the legal system has been transformed to make it consistent with the objectives of Islamist ideology. At the apex of this branch of government is a **chief justice**, a single figure whose qualifications include an understanding of Sharia (making the appointment of a cleric necessary). The chief justice is appointed by the supreme leader for a five-year term. His role is to manage the judicial institutions and oversee the appointment and removal of judges.

Beneath the chief justice is the Supreme Court, which serves as the highest court of appeal. Like the position of chief justice, this office is entirely staffed by high-ranking clerics chosen for their familiarity with religious law. This role for clerics in the judicial system extends down to the lowest level; only clerics (and, therefore, only men) may serve as judges. As a result of this structure, judges often assert a high degree of independence in interpreting the law, which frequently leads to contradictory opinions across the courts. For this reason, some observers, both inside and outside Iran, view the courts as the most dysfunctional set of institutions in the country.[7] Iran executes the second-highest number of individuals in the world after China—over 500 in 2016, mostly for criminal offenses such as murder and drug smuggling. In comparison, during the same period, the United States executed 20.

THE ELECTORAL SYSTEM

Despite the theocratic limitations, Iran seems to enjoy some elements of democratic participation. In particular, there are direct elections for the Majlis, the Assembly of Experts, and the presidency. Over 70 percent of eligible voters turned out for the 2017 presidential election. This result indicates that even with its restrictions, much of the Iranian republic takes political participation seriously when the people believe they can truly affect politics. Nevertheless, the public is highly constrained in its choices for representation.

The constitution gives the Guardian Council the power to oversee all elections, which as mentioned earlier means that this unelected body may reject any candidate for elected office. In the 2016 Majlis elections, the Guardian Council barred nearly half of candidates for office as "unsuitable" for elections, the highest number since 1979. In the 2017 presidential election, the Guardian Council rejected more 1,000 individuals who applied to run for president. This included all 137 female candidates and even former president Ahmadinejad. Still, the election of President Rouhani indicates that the vetting of candidates does not always prevent reformists from coming to office, and in spite of restrictions the most recent Majlis and Assembly of Experts elections resulted in increased representation by individuals favoring reform.

For the Majlis, Iran uses a combination of single-member and multimember districts. In the single-member districts, the candidate with the largest share of the vote (so long as it is over 25 percent) wins the seat. If no one candidate reaches that threshold, a runoff is held among the top candidates. In multimember districts with more than one seat, voters cast votes for each seat, with similar runoffs if needed. The Assembly of Experts uses a single-member district system, though with no runoff; the candidate who has secured the largest number of votes wins. For the presidency, a simple two-round runoff is held between the top two vote-getters unless one candidate wins a majority outright in the first round (as did Rouhani in both 2013 and 2017).

LOCAL GOVERNMENT

Iran's history, like that of many countries, has been one of a struggle by the state to centralize power. Though the country is currently divided into 31 *ostan*, or provinces, these bodies, like the local institutions below them, have limited authority—a condition that existed long before the current regime. As part of a wave of reforms in 1997, the government passed a law on decentralization that moved power away from the Ministry of the Interior. Before then, the ministry was responsible for local affairs such as appointing regional governors and mayors. After the new law was passed, local councils were created at the village, city, district, and provincial levels to manage local politics and the indirect election of mayors. In a further departure from the past, these councils—more than 100,000 offices in all—were directly elected. Candidates must be approved by the Majlis; while this review is not as onerous as that conducted by the Guardian Council, it remains a barrier. However, in the 2017 local elections (which take place simultaneously with the presidential elections) reformists gained control over the important Tehran city council.

OTHER INSTITUTIONS

THE REVOLUTIONARY GUARD AND THE BASIJ In addition to the institutions discussed earlier, Iran also has several powerful political institutions. Of these, two merit particular mention: the Revolutionary Guard, or Pasdaran, and the Basij, or People's Militia.

The **Revolutionary Guard** is a paramilitary force that emerged from the 1979 revolution. It originally comprised several thousand men from various militias and groups that had sprung up around the revolution and was independent of the armed forces, which Khomeini mistrusted because of their role during the Pahlavi dynasty. Later, during the Iran-Iraq War, the Revolutionary Guard expanded in size to fight on the front lines as a military force. It did this in part by relying on a large people's volunteer militia, known as the **Basij**, which had been formed shortly after the revolution as a grassroots civil defense force. Its members were poorly trained and ill-equipped but imbued with religious and nationalist fervor, and the Basij was known for its "human wave" attacks against the Iraqi front lines.

The end of the war and the consolidation of the revolution undercut the justification for the Revolutionary Guard and the Basij, but both organizations continued to play an influential and growing role in Iranian politics. Though both groups are controlled only by the supreme leader and his allies, the Revolutionary Guard has become an increasingly independent and direct player in Iranian domestic and international affairs as well; its top leaders have taken on important additional roles in the state and government.

The Guard has its own ministry, army, navy, and air force units as well as an unclear role in the development of Iran's nuclear program. It has been active in the region, providing training and some troops in the ongoing conflicts in Iraq and Syria, and has been associated with past acts of terrorism. At home, the Guard has become deeply involved in the Iranian economy. But the Guard leadership is also highly factionalized. Its various elements contend for economic and political power and the support of the supreme leader.

In contrast, the Basij is no longer a significant military force, though it has maintained its importance in other ways. Like the Revolutionary Guard (which has authority over the Basij), the organization has developed substantial economic assets. More disturbing has been its role as a public morality force, often taking responsibility for such things as preventing public displays of affection and seizing illegal satellite dishes. In general, the Guard has become a more active player in politics and is an important tool of the supreme leader in maintaining power. President Rouhani has attempted to limit the Guard's economic power, though so far with little success. This remains a significant obstacle to domestic reform and improved relations with the international community.[8]

Political Conflict and Competition

For many reasons, political competition in Iran is a confusing matter to outside observers (and insiders as well). Iran lacks institutionalized political parties or even a single-party system. This environment is partly a reflection of the regime's populism and its suspicion of traditional party politics. As a result, Iranian politics is frequently described as factionalized and clientelist, dominated by an array of loose political and economic groups that continuously struggle for power.

This factionalization was not an inevitable or a necessary function of Iranian political culture. Following the 1979 revolution, there was an outburst of new political activity. Out of this activity, two dominant parties came into being. The first, the Islamic Republican Party (IRP), was closely allied with Ayatollah Ruhollah Khomeini and his desire to establish a theocracy. Numerous parties stood for the first postrevolutionary elections in 1980, but the electoral system eliminated virtually all groups but the IRP, which gained a majority of seats.

Some independent parliamentarians sought to resist this consolidation of power. Other, more radical groups turned their weapons on the IRP, much of whose leadership was killed in a bombing in 1981. The government responded with increased repression of opposition groups, imprisoning and executing thousands of political activists. In advance of the 1984 elections, all parties other than the IRP were banned. In 1987, even the IRP itself was eliminated.

THE CHALLENGES OF POLITICAL REFORM

After 1987, political debate within the Majlis was limited primarily to economic concerns. Those who favored a more free-market economic approach competed with those who supported more statist policies (see "Society" on p. 559 for a discussion of these different political tendencies). Liberalization was afoot, however, made possible by the death of Khomeini in 1989 and a worsening economy. In 1992, Majlis elections saw a victory for the free-market faction, many of whom in turn supported the

1997 presidential candidacy of the pro-reform Mohammad Khatami. His victory, in which he won over 70 percent of the popular vote, was a surprise to Iranians and outside observers alike.

The reform period of the 1990s saw a dramatic diversification in political views and organizations. Many groups called for improved relations with the outside world, democratic change, and improvement of women's rights (which had been significantly reduced after 1979). In 2000, reform groups went on to win a stunning 189 of the 290 parliamentary seats. In 2001, President Khatami was again overwhelmingly reelected and won over 70 percent of the vote.

But while reformers controlled the Majlis and the presidency, these were relatively weak political institutions. Conservatives still controlled or had the support of the Guardian Council and the Expediency Council, the Revolutionary Guard and Basij, and of course the supreme leader. Soon after the elections, a wave of repression was directed against reformists. In the Majlis, while reformers passed a wide array of legislation to limit state power and increase democratic rights, the bills were mostly vetoed by the Guardian Council. In the 2004 Majlis elections, the Guardian Council banned large numbers of reformist candidates. The 2016 elections saw a return of reformists to the Majlis on the heels of President Rouhani's election, but as in the 1990s their impact has so far been limited.

The other battlefield in the struggle over reform has been the presidency. When Khatami stepped down in 2005, many expected that former president and Khatami backer Ali Akbar Hashemi Rafsanjani would return to power. However, Rafsanjani was trounced by the mayor of Tehran, **Mahmoud Ahmadinejad**. Ahmadinejad benefited from the absence of many pro-reform voters, who had stayed away from the polls because they were dismayed by the conservative counteroffensive in the Majlis. But there was also widespread support for Ahmadinejad, especially among the poor and more conservative, who were attracted by his obvious piety and modesty.

Ahmadinejad's two terms in office were characterized by a more openly confrontational relationship with the United States, an approach abetted by the wars in neighboring Afghanistan and Iraq. He raised the international profile of Iran, frequently traveling and speaking against the United States, Israel, and the inequities of global politics and economic relations. He also made the development of nuclear technology a cornerstone of his policies, though he did not have direct authority over this area. His rising profile eventually put him at odds with the supreme leader.

The 2009 presidential elections pitted Ahmadinejad against several rivals, among them Mir Hossein Mousavi, former prime minister from 1981 to 1989. Long out of power, he campaigned on a strongly pro-reformist agenda, calling for such things as a liberalized press, greater rights for women, and more power for the Majlis. Young people in particular rallied around Mousavi, forming a "Green Wave" movement in favor of his election. It was widely expected that Mousavi and Ahmadinejad would face a runoff; instead, the government announced that, in fact, Ahmadinejad had won over 60 percent of the vote, thus eliminating the need for a second round. This dubious result sparked mass demonstrations around Iran and a ferocious response by the police and Basij, resulting in perhaps 150 dead, more than 1,000 detained, and an unknown number given long sentences or executed. Mousavi came under house arrest, where he remains.

The reelection of Ahmadinejad was both a victory and a loss for conservatives in Iran. After Ahmadinejad, many expected that the next president would be someone close to the supreme leader and unlikely to challenge his views. The supreme leader himself, while not openly supporting any candidate, made it clear from his comments that he supported a close confidant and lead negotiator on Iran's nuclear program.

Yet despite all expectations, the election campaign quickly turned in favor of Hassan Rouhani. Why? Several factors are involved. First, Rouhani ran a much more aggressive campaign than many expected, calling openly for a release of Mousavi and implicitly siding with the Green Wave movement. Second, Rouhani matched these calls with more practical critiques of Iranian politics, such as the economic difficulties that had resulted from international sanctions. Third, Rouhani's earlier experience as a negotiator on the nuclear issue gave credibility to his claim that he could cut a deal with the West that could help improve living conditions at home.

Immediately following Rouhani's elections, expectations were high both inside and outside Iran that a sea change was under way. In September 2013, President Rouhani even spoke directly with President Obama—the first such contact between leaders of the two countries since 1979. Rouhani also stepped away from Ahmadinejad's anti-Israel stance. Moving forward from these gestures, negotiations on the nuclear issue resulted in an international agreement in 2016 that froze Iran's nuclear program in return for an end to sanctions (see "Current Issues in Iran," p. 565). Iran's international economic relations have subsequently improved to some extent, though this has been coupled with numerous arrests of reformers and civil society activists reminiscent of the 1990s. The hope for a new wave of liberalization under Rouhani discounted the power of the supreme leader and those around him, and many of the president's supporters are deeply disappointed in the lack of dramatic change.

CIVIL SOCIETY

As might be expected, civil society in Iran has mirrored the changes and challenges of political competition. After the creation of the Islamic Republic of Iran, the nascent civil society was again stifled, viewed as anathema to the supremacy of religious rule and a threat to national unity during the war with Iraq. Most civic organizations were either absorbed into the state or outlawed. Plurality and autonomy were seen as running counter to religious rule and revolutionary ideals. After Khomeini's death and the end of the war, however, civil society began to reemerge, though it remained marginal and beleaguered. A handful of intellectuals, clerics, and others questioned the current regime and advocated reform, but this activity was frequently met with arrest, torture, and even death.

In the 1990s, President Khatami made the invigoration of Iran's civil society a major plank of his campaign platform, and the media soon took up this cause. New publications rapidly proliferated at all levels of society, from academic journals and independent publishers to magazines and newspapers. Numerous civic organizations also sprang up, dealing with such issues as local government, human rights, the environment, women's rights, and poverty.

The women of this younger generation also made their presence felt. While we assume that since 1979 Iranian women have been deprived of all rights, Iranian women have much higher levels of education than they did under the shah. Most of the college students in Iran are now women. However, political and economic opportunities remain limited, and edicts regarding personal morality (including public dress) strongly affect women's autonomy in the public sphere. Accordingly, the place of women in society remains central to any discussion of liberalization and civic life in Iran.

The flowering of civil society in the 1990s soon came under sustained attack. When a 2000 law restricted the ability of the press to operate, many publications were closed, and journalists were arrested and in some cases killed. Iran's press freedom, according to Reporters without Borders, ranks 165th out of 180 countries.[9] Similar pressure was directed against nongovernmental organizations (NGOs). Many of them were attacked, their offices destroyed, and their members detained. This intensified after the 2009 and 2013 presidential elections.

While the public sphere has come under increased repression in Iran, one area of civic activity that has persevered is electronic communication. Over the past decade, Iran has been an Internet pioneer in the Middle East. Many Internet users have eagerly embraced each new innovation, from blogs to text messaging to social media. Because the government cracked down on traditional media outlets, the Internet has become an important environment for expression of alternative views.

However, it is incorrect to say that the Internet represents some liberated space that the Iranian state cannot control. A number of individuals have been arrested in Iran for Internet activism, or even for posting "immoral" content such as Iranian women not wearing a head scarf. The regime has also taken steps to limit access to important sites like Facebook, YouTube, and Twitter and is filtering various content from non-Iranian websites (and even the sites of Iranian reformists). While President Rouhani, Supreme Leader Khamenei, and other political officials rely on Twitter and Facebook to disseminate their views to the outside world, these applications are actually blocked inside Iran itself. Iranians often get around this restriction by using a virtual private network, but such activity is illegal and the government takes frequent steps to block such tools as they become widespread. Iran's Internet remains among the most restricted, surpassed only by China.

Society

ETHNIC AND NATIONAL IDENTITY

As we noted at the start of this chapter, Iran is distinct from other Islamic states in the Middle East, not only because it embraces the minority Shia branch of Islam but also because the majority population is ethnically Iranian (or Persian) rather than Arab. With their distinct language, history, and culture, ethnic Iranians view themselves as quite separate from people in the Arab states of the Middle East.

At the same time, Iran is not the homogeneous state that its nationalism or distinctive identity might lead us to believe it is. Although Persians make up a majority, much of the population is composed of other ethnic groups. Some of the groups are closely related to the Persian majority; others are not. Among these groups, the two largest are the Azeris and the Kurds. They are particularly important not only because of their size but also because of their connection to ethnic kin outside Iran. In both cases, turmoil and political change in surrounding countries have affected these ethnic minorities and, as a result, the way in which Iran deals with its neighbors.

The largest minority ethnic group in Iran is the Azeri, who comprise around 16 percent of the population (perhaps more) and are concentrated in the north of the country. Like the majority Persians, the Azeris follow Shiism, but they speak a language related to those spoken in Turkey and much of Central Asia.

Historically, the Azeris resided entirely within the Persian Empire, but with the expansion of Russia in the nineteenth century, their region was divided between the two countries. However, an independent Azerbaijan emerged from the collapse of the Soviet Union in 1991. The country's newfound independence helped foster a stronger ethnic identity among Iranian Azeris, and the Azeris in Iran have occasionally protested against discrimination by the Persian majority (though some high-ranking leaders, including Khamenei, are of Azeri descent).

The state's relationship with the Kurds, who comprise 10 percent of the population, is more complicated. The Kurds carried out an armed revolt against the new Islamic Republic of Iran in 1979, gaining some control of parts of northwest Iran. This revolt was ultimately suppressed by military force, though sporadic guerrilla activity continued during the 1980s and 1990s. The rise of a largely autonomous Kurdish region in Iraq following the U.S. invasion raised hopes and fears of a sovereign Kurdish state, something reinforced by the rise of the Islamic State in Iraq and Syria and the de facto emergence of an independent Kurdistan in Iraq. These developments make Iran nervous. In general, the relationship between Kurds and the countries in which they reside generates more tension than that of the Azeris, and ongoing conflicts in Iraq will shape Kurdish activism in Iran.[10]

In addition to Kurds and Azeris, other groups—such as Baluchis along the border with Pakistan and Arabs along the Persian Gulf—have complained of discrimination that has led to protests and sporadic acts of violence. Part of the problem may be that Iran's highly centralized political system has not allowed for a significant devolution of power that would give ethnic and religious minorities greater rights. Non-Persians have few opportunities for education or media in their native language, and Sunnis hold few higher government positions.

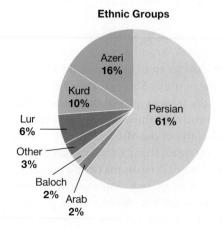

Ethnic Groups

Azeri 16%
Kurd 10%
Lur 6%
Other 3%
Baloch 2%
Arab 2%
Persian 61%

Religions

Muslim (official)* 99.4%
Unspecified 0.3%
Zoroastrian, Jewish, and Christian 0.3%

*From 90 to 95% of the Muslim population is estimated to be Shia; 5 to 10% is estimated to be Sunni.

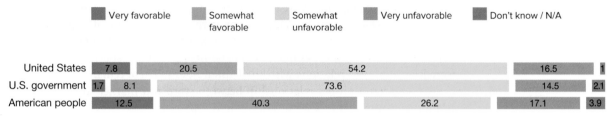

Views of the United States

To what degree do you have a favorable or an unfavorable view of:

■ Very favorable ■ Somewhat favorable ■ Somewhat unfavorable ■ Very unfavorable ■ Don't know / N/A

	Very favorable	Somewhat favorable	Somewhat unfavorable	Very unfavorable	Don't know / N/A
United States	7.8	20.5	54.2	16.5	1
U.S. government	1.7	8.1	73.6	14.5	2.1
American people	12.5	40.3	26.2	17.1	3.9

Source: Iranpoll.com and the Center for International and Security Studies, 2016.

IDEOLOGY AND POLITICAL CULTURE

In the absence of institutionalized political parties and free expression, it is hard to speak of any coherent spectrum of ideologies in Iran. A confusing array of terms is used: *hard-liners, radicals, conservatives, traditionalists, reformers, pragmatists, principalists, technocrats.* This problem is exacerbated by the factionalized and clientelist nature of the system, in which personal relationships are often more important than political ideas. Despite this confusion, we can speak of several loose political attitudes or tendencies, some of them more ideologically coherent than others. As in other countries, the divisions tend to fall along the lines of freedom and equality, though religion exerts an important influence on how both of those values are understood.

One major division is over the relationship between religion and the state. As we might expect, those known as "reformists" in Iran, whose political power rose and fell under the Khatami presidency, call for a reduced or modified role for Islam in politics in favor of the rule of law and democratic reform. This group, whose orientation is more secular, also has unexpected allies among many clerics. For many Shiite religious leaders, the very notion of the *velayat-e faqih* runs counter to the basic tenets of Shiism. Their **quietist** vision, which dominated Iranian Shiism before the revolution, emphasizes that worldly political power cannot be reunited with Islam until the return of the Mahdi. This belief holds that the role of the faith is to act as an intermediary between the state and society in the meantime, influencing spiritual and social values but not getting directly involved in politics.

In contrast, political conservatives ("**principalists**," as they have recently called themselves) support the *velayat-e faqih* and oppose democratization or the return of faith to a primarily social, as opposed to political, role. In their view, faith must be a central institution within the state, guiding politics and society toward God's intent. In some ways, this vision implies that pious rule can hasten the Mahdi's return. Principalists have a significant advantage in their support by the Revolutionary Guard, which makes the prospects for liberalization much more daunting.

The second area of contention is over the relationship between the state and market. At the inception of the Islamic Republic, there was a schism between those who saw the primary role of the revolution as bringing about a moral order and those who

Views of Political Roles for Religious Figures

Percentage of Iranian adults who say religious figures should have ... in political matters

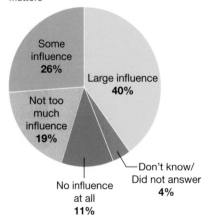

Some influence 26%

Large influence 40%

Not too much influence 19%

Don't know/ Did not answer 4%

No influence at all 11%

Source: Pew Research Center, 2013.

saw the revolution as a means of ensuring economic justice. Just as religion has clashed with politics, so, too, it has led to divisions over the economy. There are those, such as former president Rafsanjani and President Rouhani, who favor economic liberalization and better relations with the international community to increase trade and investment. The supreme leader and many principalists take a more skeptical view of economic reform and liberalization, especially if it is predicated on improved relations with the United States. There remain very real divisions over what a proper relationship between state and market should be in an Islamic society.[11]

Past these debates, we can observe more fixed elements of political culture. Iranian political culture is highly nationalist. In addition, Iranians say that religion remains an important part of their lives, while at the same time the surveys indicate that Iranians express support for more democracy. These views are not contradictory; Iranian religiosity tends more toward the traditional, quietist view that would favor a greater separation between faith and state. Islam remains a central part of Iranian culture and national identity, and political change or democratization would not necessarily mean the secularization of the country along Western lines.

Finally, an enduring part of Iranian political culture is a complicated relationship with the West. Iranian history and consequent national identity are tightly linked to the rise of the West, going back 2,000 years to when Iran, Greece, and,

A banner at Friday prayers, Tehran University, with a quote from Ayatollah Khomeini. Anti-Americanism remains a key facet of the Iranian regime, making diplomatic relations difficult at best.

later, Rome all commanded power and respect. In this way, Iranians may see themselves as equal participants in, and contributors to, Western history in a way other peoples may not. At the same time, the frequent Western (and Arab) interventions in modern Iranian history have created a strong tendency toward viewing international politics in conspiratorial terms, such that every political event is the product of foreign powers with seemingly limitless power. One criticism made of Iranians by outsiders is their tendency for shifting blame to external actors rather than seeing themselves as also responsible for their political destiny. Even so, such views do not mean that average Iranians are opposed to better relations with the United States, even if they view American power with justifiable suspicion.

Political Economy

Iran's economic system reflects the dilemmas of late modernization, authoritarianism, and war. It is also a good example of what is sometimes called the "resource trap," the situation that occurs when a national resource paradoxically makes a country poorer rather than richer.

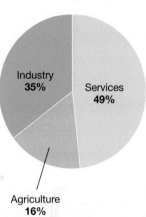

Labor Force by Occupation

Industry 35%
Services 49%
Agriculture 16%

Iran's modern economic development lagged well behind that of the West—it did not begin until the 1920s, under the Pahlavi dynasty. This effort was not a late embrace of liberalism but rather an attempt at top-down industrialization that followed the mercantilist pattern adopted by many countries in the less-developed world. Iran's mercantilist policies helped modernize the country, such that by the 1970s half the population was living in urban areas. At the same time, it led to social dislocation as the country made a rapid jump from an agrarian, isolated, and religiously conservative society in just a few decades.

Top-down mercantilist development led to similar problems in other less-developed countries, though in Iran, the problems were compounded by the discovery of oil. Oil can be more a curse than a blessing, especially when controlled by the state. Rather than directing resources toward the goal of development, leaders give in to a seemingly irresistible temptation, which leads to corruption as they siphon off the wealth to line their own pockets or serve their own policy predilections. Moreover, since the public is eliminated as the major source of state revenue, those in power can effectively ignore the public and repress or co-opt any opposition.

This problem became evident during the time of the White Revolution, when economic development coincided with growing inflation, inequality, and increased repression. Development, built on oil exports and Western imports, also fueled hostility toward Western materialism, or what one critical Iranian scholar of the era called "Westoxication" or "Weststruckness."[12]

As a reflection of the economic factors that helped bring about the 1979 revolution, the new constitution explicitly stated that "the economy is a means, not an end." This position stood in contrast to liberal capitalist systems, in which the quest for wealth and profit becomes "a subversive and corrupting factor in the course of man's development." The oil and other state-owned industries were to remain in the state's hands, and the profits were redirected toward presumably more equitable goals. In addition, numerous private industries were nationalized after their owners fled the revolution.

In many cases, the private industries' assets were turned over to several *bonyads*, or parastatal foundations. The objective of the *bonyads* is ostensibly to help the disadvantaged, such as war veterans and the poor. Over time, however, the *bonyads* have become major economic players and often monopolies, controlling substantial assets and industries (for example, construction, pharmaceuticals, housing, and food) while operating independently of government oversight or taxation.[13] Compared with oil, the *bonyads*, and the state, the private sector is relatively small and dominated by small-scale businesses.

Another important distinction in Iran's economic system is its history of autarky, or economic independence. Just as the 1979 constitution describes profit and wealth as corrupting influences, the postrevolutionary government has had an ambivalent relationship to international economic ties. Oil could be exported to develop the economy, but the government, at least initially, sought a policy of greater self-sufficiency and more state ownership to secure the country from the effects of Westoxication.

During the 1990s, some in the Iranian political leadership took a greater interest in foreign direct investment, particularly to improve the aging technology of the oil sector, but international sanctions have until recently driven away most investment. This may now be changing with an influx of foreign direct investment in the wake of the 2016 nuclear deal, though many investors remain hesitant about investing. Conservatives, including the supreme leader, also continue to emphasize a "resistance economy" independent of the international economy.

The results of the post-1979 economic model have been poor. To be fair, Iran's economy was devastated by the long war with Iraq, which destroyed infrastructure, drained the national treasury, and killed many of the country's young men. By 1988, when the war ended, Iran's per capita gross domestic product (GDP) had fallen to just over half its 1979 level. Oil production, while rising of late, remains only around half of its peak levels of the 1970s.

This Basij banner outside the Iranian Foreign Ministry in Iran links nuclear technology to *national* prestige and autarky.

The official unemployment rate in Iran is around 11 percent (though it may be higher), and the country has long suffered from a high rate of inflation that erodes pensions and savings. Perhaps most striking are the difficult circumstances for Iranian youth, with around 30 percent of those under 24 unemployed. The figures are worse for women and those with higher education, indicating not just high levels of discrimination against women but lack of opportunities in the private sector for young, well-educated Iranians. These difficulties in the labor market have led many young Iranians, especially women, to seek work in the informal (unregulated) economy. And lacking jobs or job security, many educated Iranians have left the country, leading to one of the world's highest rates of "brain drain." Others who have remained are delaying marriage, contributing to one of the lowest birthrates in the region.[14]

Solving Iran's economic problems is not easy. Iran can expect that ongoing revenues from its oil reserves and the development of natural gas will help sustain the state budget, though recent declines in world prices have hurt. Yet even high oil prices will not diversify the economy or provide new sources of employment. President Rouhani has sought better relations with the international community, in part to increase trade and investment, but the supreme leader and many principalists are concerned that a reintegration into the world economy will bring Iran back into a neocolonial relationship. Meanwhile, groups such as the Revolutionary Guard seek to defend their role in the economy. Improving international relations is an important step to economic development, but Iran has critical economic problems and obstacles that only domestic reforms can address.

Current Issues in Iran

THE NUCLEAR PROGRAM

One of the most critical issues confronting the international community at present is Iran's nuclear program. The resolution of this issue will have profound repercussions, and any long-term solution will be complicated by Iranian domestic politics.

Before going any further, we should recall the difference between a nuclear energy program and a nuclear weapons program. In both cases, it is necessary to process, or "enrich," natural uranium, separating the uranium atoms with different numbers of neutrons (isotopes). Natural and low-enriched uranium is made up mostly of U-238 isotopes, and only a small amount is composed of U-235—the fissile isotopes, or those that can sustain a chain reaction. Commercial nuclear programs enrich natural uranium to about 20 percent U-235 in order to create nuclear fuel. Weapons-grade uranium, however, requires enrichment of up to around 90 percent U-235. In other words, while peaceful nuclear programs require enriched uranium, this stockpile can be further enriched to produce a nuclear weapon. Enriching uranium up to weapons grade is a major project that requires a huge number of sophisticated centrifuges operating far beyond what is necessary for nuclear fuel. Once uranium is enriched to weapons grade, the next challenge is turning that uranium into an actual device small enough that it can be fitted onto a missile.

Even before the 1979 revolution, as part of an extensive plan to develop nuclear energy for peaceful purposes, Iran also showed interest in developing a nuclear weapon. This work was mostly halted by the revolution, the Iran-Iraq War, and international sanctions. By the early 1990s, however, Iran sought to actively restart its nuclear program, mining uranium and reaching out to various countries (such as Pakistan and North Korea) for technology and assistance in such areas as centrifuge

Iran's Nuclear Capabilities

Do you approve or disapprove of each of the following?

	APPROVE	DISAPPROVE	DON'T KNOW/REFUSED
Iran developing its own nuclear power capabilities for military use	34%	41%	25%
Iran developing its own nuclear power capabilities for nonmilitary use	56%	21%	24%

Note: Question asked of Iranian adults. Based on surveys conducted May 24–June 6, 2013.

Source: "Iranians Mixed on Nuclear Capabilities," Gallup, October 14, 2013, www.gallup.com/poll/165413/iranians-mixed-nuclear-capabilities.aspx (accessed 9/20/16).

technology. These developments began to raise alarms in the international community, especially given Iran's related development in missile technology.[15]

Over the past decade, both international negotiations and sanctions have attempted to halt Iran's nuclear program. The international community placed increasingly restrictive sanctions on Iran, meant to harm the Iranian economy and deprive the government access to needed technology by limiting trade and other economic opportunities. In addition, international actors have relied on espionage to slow down Iran's nuclear program. The danger of a preemptive military attack by the United States or Israel has been very real, though few believed this would do more than simply delay the nuclear program.

The election of President Rouhani initiated a new round of negotiations seeking an end to the nuclear impasse. In 2013, Iran and members of the international community (United States, United Kingdom, France, Germany, China, and Russia) agreed to temporarily halt enrichment and place Iranian nuclear facilities under the inspection of the International Atomic Energy Agency (IAEA). In return, the international community relaxed sanctions on oil exports and certain imports. A final deal in 2016 stipulated that Iran would reduce its centrifuges and limit uranium enrichment for 15 years, and place the program under IAEA oversight. In return, sanctions would be suspended and funds frozen overseas would be returned.[16]

The deal so far has led to mixed results. The greatest disappointment has been on the Iranian side; in spite of the deal, remaining sanctions over charges of terrorism have limited improvements in such important areas as international banking. Foreign direct investment, while improved, has also been deterred by concerns that businesses will run afoul of remaining American restrictions. Surveys suggest that most Iranians have not felt that their economic situation has yet benefited from the agreement. Finally, there appear no signs that as a result of the agreement diplomatic relations between the United States and Iran will improve. A concern is that barring significant improvement, Iran might pull out of the nuclear agreement. However, the longer the deal remains in place, the greater the likelihood the country will feel the benefit of improved international ties.

ALCOHOL AND DRUGS IN THE ISLAMIC REPUBLIC

Alcohol and drugs have a long history in Iran. Iranian pre-Islamic history is associated with wine production, and Sufi poets such as Rumi draw frequent parallels between love and drunkenness. Many Iranian monarchies, especially the Qajar dynasty of the nineteenth century, are remembered for the drug use of their shahs (and for their prodigious consumption of wine). But such intoxicants are forbidden in Islam.

In 1979, the Islamic Republic reversed the more permissive attitude that had characterized Iran over the past century and ushered in a prohibitive regime, among the strictest in the Middle East. Alcohol was banned, with limited exceptions for the country's non-Muslim minorities, such as Christians

A banner in Sarein, Iran, warning of the dangers of drug addiction.

and Jews. The government also cracked down on opium, heroin, hashish, and other drugs. Penalties for drug and alcohol use were severe, including jail time, lashings, and even execution for drug and alcohol dealers.

Despite this pressure, drug and alcohol use continues in Iran and has perhaps even grown over time. While the total number of Iranians who drink may be small, the World Health Organization reports that Iran is among the top 20 consumers of alcohol in the world—a percentage higher than in Russia, France, Germany, or the United States.[17]

Drug addiction is a far bigger problem. According to the United Nations, Iran has more than a million drug-dependent users and represents one of the most severe addiction problems in the world. As with alcohol, this problem, too, has a regional source: drugs are coming in from Pakistan as well as from Afghanistan, which is the world's biggest producer of opium.

The drug problem in Iran is one of the reasons the country has one of the highest rates of capital punishment in the world; in 2016, the majority of those put to death were convicted on drug charges. This directly counters international law, which restricts capital punishment to crimes involving intentional killing. It is not easy to determine whether the social repression under the Islamic Republic is a main driver of drug addiction in Iran or if this is a more intractable cultural problem that will remain unaffected by any future political changes.[18]

Key Terms

Ahmadinejad, Mahmoud (p. 557)
Assembly of Experts (p. 552)
ayatollah (p. 544)
Basij (p. 555)
bonyads (p. 564)
chief justice (p. 554)
Constitutional Revolution (p. 546)
Expediency Council (p. 553)
Farsi (p. 541)
Guardian Council (p. 553)
imam (p. 544)
Iran-Iraq War (p. 550)
Islamic Republic of Iran (p. 550)
Islamism, or Islamic fundamentalism (p. 541)
Khamenei, Ayatollah Ali (p. 543)
Khatami, Mohammad (p. 543)
Khomeini, Ayatollah Ruhollah (p. 541)
Koran (p. 541)
Mahdi (p. 544)

Majlis (p. 546)
Mosaddeq, Mohammad (p. 548)
Muhammad (p. 543)
National Front (p. 548)
Operation Ajax (p. 548)
Pahlavi, Mohammed Reza (p. 547)
Pahlavi, Reza Shah (p. 546)
Persia (p. 544)
president (p. 553)
principalists (p. 561)
quietist (p. 561)
Rafsanjani, Ali Akbar Hashemi (p. 554)
Revolutionary Guard (p. 555)
Rouhani, Hassan (p. 543)
SAVAK (p. 548)
Shiism (p. 543)
supreme leader (p. 552)
theocracy (p. 541)
velayat-e faqih (p. 549)
White Revolution (p. 548)

Javier Duarte, former governor of the Mexican state of Veracruz, after his arrest in Guatemala in April 2017. Duarte was charged with embezzling funds and involvement in organized crime. At least six former Mexican governors are being investigated on corruption charges, an example of the endemic corruption that plagues Mexican politics.

Mexico

Why Study This Case?

Mexico offers a fascinating case study of three challenges to a young democracy that are of particular interest to students of comparative politics: the need for the state to establish political order, the need to implement the most effective and fair strategy for economic development, and the need to establish political transparency and the rule of law.

The first challenge has been the need to achieve political order and to avoid the violence and disruption associated with a lack of order. Mexico's first spurt of economic development took place under Porfirio Díaz's brutal authoritarian regime in the late nineteenth and early twentieth centuries. That regime was displaced by the Mexican Revolution (1910–17), an extended period of cataclysmic mass violence and political anarchy. The chaos was finally ended by a unique and remarkably flexible semi-authoritarian regime governed by a dominant political party, the **Partido Revolucionario Institucional (PRI)**. Mexico's post-1917 politics was relatively peaceful: after 1920, power was transferred between leaders through regular elections, and after the late 1930s, the military was thoroughly subordinate to civilians. Since 2000, Mexico has been governed by its first democratic regime but has struggled to impose order. Mexico's first two democratic presidents waged a war against Mexico's increasingly powerful drug cartels and unleashed the most serious wave of violence the country has seen since the Mexican Revolution. The violence has traumatized Mexican society, raised serious questions about the capacity and autonomy of the Mexican state, and led some domestic and foreign observers to wonder whether Mexico could become a failed state. A second challenge facing Mexico is determining the appropriate role for the state in economic development. Modern Mexican history has seen radical shifts between free-market political-economic systems

UNITED STATES

Gulf of Mexico

PACIFIC
OCEAN

Gulf of California

Baja California

BAJA
CALIFORNIA

BAJA
CALIFORNIA
SUR

Guadalupe
Island

Tijuana

Colorado R.

Ciudad
Juárez

Sierra Madre Mountains

Torreón

Monterrey

Rio Grande
Rio Bravo del Norte

San Luis
Potosí

León

R. Lerma

Guadalajara

Rio Grande
de Santiago

MICHOACÁN

Cuernavaca

MORELOS

GUERRERO

Acapulco

MEXICO
CITY

Puebla

Oaxaca

OAXACA

Veracruz

CHIAPAS

Mérida

BELIZE

GUATEMALA

HONDURAS

EL SALVADOR

Revillagigedo Islands

N

200 mi
100
0

200 km
100
100
0
0

and a more statist political economy. Today Mexico is one of Latin America's most open economies. Its embrace of neoliberal economics since the 1990s has made Mexico a middle-class society that is far more affluent than it was during the decades of statist economics, and it has experienced an export boom. But the dislocations caused by Mexico's opening to the global economy worsened inequality, devastated its most vulnerable citizens, and fueled a massive wave of immigration to the United States.

A final challenge facing Mexico is the struggle between the rule of law and transparency on the one hand and the endemic corruption cultivated by decades of one-party rule on the other. Those who believed that Mexico's embrace of democracy and a more open economy would reduce corruption and improve accountability have been sorely disappointed to date. Decades of authoritarian rule weakened the rule of law and left Mexico with a police force and judiciary with low capacity, little accountability, and vulnerability to corruption. The inability of the Mexican state to defend its citizens from the violence unleashed by drug cartels has raised doubts about the competence of its corruption-riddled security apparatus and judiciary.

The return to power of the PRI in 2012 has renewed both hope and skepticism about each of these three dilemmas. President **Enrique Peña Nieto** pledged to strengthen democracy through a series of political reforms and to further open Mexico's economy as a way of stimulating economic growth, increasing oil revenue, and modernizing the economy. Since taking office, he has enacted some ambitious and controversial reforms of the oil sector, and he has pledged to break up powerful monopolies that dominate much of the economy. Can Peña Nieto shepherd these reforms through the Mexican political system, and can he improve Mexico's sluggish and unequal economy?

Peña Nieto's success with these first two challenges will likely depend largely on his ability to improve transparency, empower Mexico's feeble judiciary, strengthen the rule of law, and reduce systemic corruption. Can he distance himself and his party from the PRI's reputation as a bastion of patronage, corruption, and opacity?

Historical Development of the State

The history of the modern Mexican state can be viewed as a struggle between political order, which has almost always been achieved by authoritarian rulers, and periodic outbursts of violence and political anarchy.[1]

When the Spanish conquistador **Hernán Cortés** arrived in Mexico in 1519, he encountered well-established and highly sophisticated indigenous civilizations. The country had long been home to such peoples as the Maya, Aztecs, and Toltecs, who had relatively prosperous economies, impressive architecture, sophisticated agricultural methods, and powerful militaries. Within three years of their arrival, the

Spanish conquerors had defeated the last Aztec leader, destroyed the impressive Aztec capital, and decimated the indigenous population. The surviving indigenous peoples of Mexico, concentrated in the central and southern parts of the country, became a permanent underclass of virtual slaves and landless peasants.

The Aztec Empire was replaced by the equally hierarchical, authoritarian, and militaristic Spanish Empire, which created a legacy very different from that imparted to the United States by British colonialism. Mexico was the richest of Spain's colonial possessions (indeed, it was far richer at the time than Britain's territories to the north), and Spain ruled the distant colony with an iron fist, sending a new viceroy to the colony every four years. Colonial viceroys were absolute dictators: armed with the terror of the Spanish Inquisition, they were able to stamp out most political dissent. Without any civilian oversight, rampant corruption thrived in the colonial administration.

INDEPENDENCE AND INSTABILITY: THE SEARCH FOR ORDER

The struggle for independence can be viewed as a conflict over control of the state between the aristocracy loyal to Spain and the increasingly powerful and wealthy **criollos** (Mexican-born descendants of the Spanish colonists). When Spain adopted a progressive-liberal constitution in 1812, conservative Mexican elites accepted independence as the only means to preserve order and the status quo. The leading rebels and political conservatives agreed that an independent Mexico, declared in 1821, would preserve the role of the Catholic Church and implement a constitutional monarchy with a European at the head. **Mexico's War of Independence** lasted 11 years and cost over half a million lives.

Because Mexico's independence was dominated by political conservatives who sought to preserve the economic and social status quo, it did nothing to alleviate the poverty of Mexico's indigenous people and its large **mestizo** population. The power of the large landholders grew with independence, and the newly independent Mexico became more unequal and politically unstable. Much of the turmoil and political chaos that plagued Mexico over the next half-century was caused by a dispute between conservatives who wanted to maintain a monarchy and liberals who wanted a U.S.-style democracy. After independence, Mexico was dominated by local military strongmen, and Mexico's weak central state could not impose its authority.

Due to the weakness of its state, Mexico could not prevent the secession of Texas in 1836. The impotence of a fragmented Mexico became even more apparent in the 1840s, when a rising imperial power, the United States, defeated the country in the **Mexican-American War** (1846–48) and claimed half of Mexico's territory (present-day Arizona, California, Colorado, Nevada, New Mexico, Texas, and Utah).

THE PORFIRIATO: ECONOMIC LIBERALISM AND POLITICAL AUTHORITARIANISM

From 1876 to 1910, Mexican politics was dominated by **Porfirio Díaz**, who had himself reelected for much of the period. He imposed a brutal authoritarian regime (known as the *Porfiriato*) and gave Mexico its first taste of stability since independence. Díaz was also responsible for Mexico's first real economic development and was the first Mexican ruler to impose the power of the state on remote areas.

TIMELINE Political Development

1810–21	War of Independence fought against Spain.
1846–48	One-half of Mexico's territory lost in war with the United States.
1910–17	Mexican Revolution takes place.
1917	Revolutionary constitution adopted.
1929	Official revolutionary party created, later becoming the PRI.
1934–40	Presidency of Lázaro Cárdenas, during which land reform is promoted, the oil industry is nationalized, and the state is given a larger role in the economy.
1939	The PAN formed as a conservative opposition to the revolution.
1968	Student protest movement against the Mexican government violently repressed.
1981–82	Economic collapse caused by sudden drop in oil prices and Mexico's inability to pay its foreign debt.
1988	President Carlos Salinas de Gortari assumes power after elections widely viewed as fraudulent.
1994	NAFTA put into effect.
	Zapatistas, indigenous peasants in the southern state of Chiapas, rebel.
	PRI presidential candidate Luis Donaldo Colosio assassinated while campaigning; replaced by Ernesto Zedillo.
2000	PAN candidate Vicente Fox elected, marking the first defeat of the PRI in 71 years.
2006	Felipe Calderón, of the PAN, is elected president and escalates the war against Mexico's drug cartels.
2012	Enrique Peña Nieto begins a six-year term as president, marking the return to power of the PRI.

THE REVOLUTION

The **Mexican Revolution** (1910–17) can be viewed as a struggle between two groups attempting to seize control of the state. The first included middle-class Mexicans resisting the dictatorship of Díaz, who sought a more democratic political system with a capitalist economy. The second included radical social reformers who proposed, among other things, agrarian reform. Both groups sought to weaken the role of the Catholic Church.

In the first phase of the revolution, middle-class political reformers, led by the landowner **Francisco Madero**, defeated the Díaz dictatorship. The second phase of the revolution involved a struggle between these moderate political reformers and advocates of radical socioeconomic change. The most famous revolutionary advocate of the poor was **Emiliano Zapata**, a young mestizo peasant leader. Zapata organized a peasant army in Morelos, south of Mexico City, to push for agrarian reform. In the north of Mexico, **Francisco (Pancho) Villa** organized an army of peasants and small farmers.

During the revolution, Mexico descended into political chaos—armed bands led by regional warlords, known as *caciques*, fought one another over a period of 10 years. About 1.5 million Mexicans (about 7 percent of the total population) died in or as a result of the conflict, and thousands more fled north to the United States. Order was restored only in 1917, under the leadership of a northern governor, **Venustiano Carranza**. He defeated not only those who wanted a return to a dictatorship but also Zapata and Villa, the more radical voices of the revolution.

The **Constitution of 1917** called for regular elections as well as harsh measures to weaken the Catholic Church. The constitution sought to prevent the reemergence of a dictatorship by devolving political power to Mexico's states, adopting federalism, and barring presidents, governors, mayors, and federal legislators from reelection. It provided elaborate protection for indigenous communal lands and called for land reform. It was also a nationalist document, prohibiting foreign ownership of Mexican land and mineral rights.

During the presidencies of Álvaro Obregón (1920–24) and Plutarco Elías Calles (1924–28), Mexico ended the political bloodshed and developed a political system capable of maintaining order. Obregón promoted trade unions but brought them under state control. He also promoted land reform while tolerating the presence of large landed estates. He managed to gain the support and recognition of the United States, which had feared the revolution as a socialist experiment. Most significantly, he purged the army and weakened the revolutionary generals who had continued to meddle in politics. President Calles consolidated state power by imposing the first income tax and investing in education and infrastructure. He vigorously enforced the constitution's limit on the power of the Catholic Church.

After Calles left power, he created, in 1929, his most enduring legacy: the Partido Nacional Revolucionario, later renamed the Partido Revolucionario Institucional (PRI). From the outset, the PRI was conceived as a party of power and a party of the state. Its colors (red, white, and green) are the colors of the Mexican flag. Its goal was to encompass all those who had supported the revolution, and its members thus ranged from socialists to liberals. Moreover, it was designed to incorporate and co-opt the most important organizations and interest groups in Mexican society, starting with the army. The PRI's main purpose was to end political violence by controlling the political system and the process of presidential succession. After decades of instability and violence, the revolution's leaders brought Mexico an unprecedented period of political peace.

STABILITY ACHIEVED: THE PRI IN POWER, 1929–2000

For decades, the PRI provided Mexico with the much-desired political stability that its founders had sought. Under the PRI, Mexico held presidential elections every six years, and presidents assumed office without violence or military intervention. The PRI regime featured a strong president, directly elected for a single six-year term. Though not stipulated in the 1917 constitution, PRI presidents claimed the power to name their successors by officially designating the PRI candidate for the presidency; for more than 80 years, no official PRI candidate lost a presidential election. During most of the PRI's tenure in office, the Mexican president enjoyed the reverence and aloofness of monarchical heads of state while possessing far more power than the typical democratic president. Most important, until 2000, Mexican presidents controlled the vast machinery of the PRI and used the state to dispense patronage.

Unlike U.S. presidents, they faced no effective check on their power from the legislature, judiciary, or state governments, all of which were controlled by the PRI.

Under the PRI, regular elections were held for national, state, and local offices, and opposition parties actively contested these elections. During most of this period, there was no formal censorship of the press, and Mexicans were free to voice their opinions and criticize the government. Mexicans were also free to live where they wanted, and according to their constitution, they were living in a democratic state.

But under its surface, the Mexican regime had clear authoritarian tendencies. The PRI held an inordinate amount of power. Between 1929 and 2000, the PRI controlled the presidency and the vast majority of seats in the legislature and at the state and local level. The PRI dominated major trade unions and peasant organizations. Through its control of the state, the PRI controlled major pieces of the economy, including Mexico's vast oil wealth. The PRI became expert at co-opting possible sources of opposition, including the press and the weak opposition parties. Unlike many authoritarian regimes, the PRI did not often need to revert to harsh measures of repression; when necessary, however, the regime used a variety of tactics to stifle the opposition. Most notorious were the massacre of peaceful student demonstrators in Mexico City in 1968 and the increasing use of electoral fraud to preserve its political dominance.

Just as Mexico's political system contained a mixture of democratic and authoritarian features, its political-economic model was also contradictory. Some goals of the more radical supporters of the revolution, like land reform and the nationalization of oil and mineral wealth, were promoted during the presidency of Lázaro Cárdenas (1934–40). But his successors were far more willing to accommodate the Mexican elite that the revolution had left largely intact.

THE SLOW EROSION OF PRI POWER, 1980–2000

By the early 1980s, the vaunted stability of the Mexican regime was called into question by a series of interrelated economic and political challenges to PRI rule. The economic crises of the 1980s (due mainly to Mexico's massive foreign debt) and mid-1990s (caused by a sudden devaluation of Mexico's currency, the peso) unleashed numerous challenges to the party's political hegemony. The conservative opposition in northern Mexico, long an advocate of free-market economic policies, began to seriously contest and occasionally win local and state elections. The PRI was then forced to revert to ever-increasing and ever-more-overt electoral fraud to deny power to the opposition.

The 1988 election of PRI president Carlos Salinas de Gortari was possible only through electoral fraud, and the popular outrage that resulted led to reforms of the electoral system that would eventually benefit the opposition. Salinas continued the PRI's gradual adoption of a neoliberal economic program by signing the **North American Free Trade Agreement (NAFTA)** with the United States and Canada, and by eliminating the last remnants of the revolution's more radical agenda (such as Mexico's commitment to land reform). Mexico's economy was opened to foreign investment, and the political system began a process of liberalization. As a result of the economic crisis, and due in part to the electoral reforms enacted under Salinas, the watershed election of July 2000 ended the PRI's 71-year control of the presidency. **Vicente Fox**, candidate of the conservative **Partido Acción Nacional (PAN)**, handily defeated **Francisco Labastida** of the PRI, despite an expensive and elaborate PRI campaign.

Since 2000, Mexico has operated under the same constitution adopted after the Mexican Revolution. President Fox and his PAN successor, Felipe Calderón, were Mexico's first two democratically elected presidents, and they operated in a much more pluralistic and competitive political system. The election of Enrique Peña Nieto in 2012 marked the PRI's return to power at the national level (it had maintained considerable power at the state and local level).

Political Regime

POLITICAL INSTITUTIONS

Political scientists describe Mexico as democratic after 2000 because that is when the PRI, and its vast network of patronage and clientelism, was first dislodged from the presidency. The democratic political regime—initially established by the Mexican Revolution and subsequently manipulated by the PRI's authoritarian regime—remains in place today.

THE CONSTITUTION On paper, the Mexican regime does not differ markedly from that of the United States. The Constitution of 1917 calls for a presidential legislative–executive system; a separation of judicial, legislative, and executive power; and a system of federalism that at least formally gives Mexico's states considerable power. During the 71-year domination of the PRI, Mexican presidents enjoyed near-dictatorial powers with few checks on their authority, and incumbent presidents designated their successors.

How, then, did the opposition manage to win local and state elections in the 1980s? And how did the opposition unseat the PRI in the 2000 presidential election? Part of the answer to these questions lies in the growing illegitimacy of the regime during the 1970s, when Mexico's economy began to deteriorate. But the erosion of PRI legitimacy was also the result of widespread outrage at the PRI's blatant and unabashed disregard for the rule of law in the 1980s and 1990s. As opposition to the PRI grew, and as the PRI resorted more openly and more regularly to widespread

---

INFOCUS   **Essential Political Features**

- **Legislative–executive system**: Presidential

- **Legislature**: Congreso de la Unión (National Congress)

  - **Lower house**: Cámara de Diputados (Federal Chamber of Deputies)

  - **Upper house**: Cámara de Senadores (Senate)

- **Unitary or federal division of power**: Federal

- **Main geographic subunits**: *Estados* (states)

- **Electoral system for lower house**: Mixed single-member district and proportional representation

- **Chief judicial body**: Suprema Corte de Justicia de la Nación (National Supreme Court of Justice)

electoral fraud, sectors of the party pushed for democratization. Seeking to polish its image, the PRI passed a number of reforms that favored the opposition.

One important set of reforms, passed in 1977, changed the electoral law to guarantee the presence of the opposition in the legislature. Other reforms gave the legislature control over judicial appointments and imposed electoral safeguards that greatly reduced the ability of a government to steal an election.

THE BRANCHES OF GOVERNMENT

THE PRESIDENT Mexican presidents were viewed as elected monarchs. However, on paper, the 1917 constitution created a president with powers similar to those of the president of the United States. The perception that Mexico had an "imperial presidency" had more to do with the 71-year dominance of the PRI than with the provisions of the constitution. A Mexican president can issue executive decrees that have the force of law in a few areas (including international trade agreements). The president can directly introduce legislation in Congress and can veto legislation initiated by Congress. Until 1994, Mexican presidents had extensive power to appoint and remove judges. As recently as 1982, President **José López Portillo** essentially decreed the nationalization of Mexico's banking system. However, Mexican presidents serve a single six-year term, meaning that all of them are lame ducks. Mexican presidents no longer select their successors and now have far less power over the economy than they had during the 1917–2000 period.

Mexican presidents appoint and preside over a large cabinet of ministers, who oversee the various government departments. In recent decades, the **secretary of government**, which controls internal political affairs, and the **secretary of the treasury**, which oversees the economy, have been the highest-profile cabinet posts and have often been stepping-stones to the presidency. Since 2000, the Mexican cabinet has included 19 cabinet secretaries, in addition to seven policy coordinators whose job is to ease communication among ministries. Since Vicente Fox's historic victory in 2000, Mexico's presidents have lacked a majority in Congress. As a result, some of the constitutional checks on presidential power that were long absent in the Mexican system have become more effective. Presidents Fox, Calderón, and Peña Nieto have had to contend with a fragmented and increasingly assertive legislature and have thus been forced to bargain with the two major opposition parties in order to pass legislation. In recognition of this new reality, in 2013 President Peña Nieto approved the Pact for Mexico, a formal agreement with the two major opposition parties on many proposed political and economic reforms.

THE LEGISLATURE Mexico has a bicameral legislature, called the **National Congress**, which is composed of a lower house (the **Chamber of Deputies**) and an upper house (the **Senate**).[2] The 500-member Chamber of Deputies has the power to pass laws (with a simple majority for most laws), levy taxes, and verify the outcome of elections. Mexico's upper house is composed of 128 members: 3 senators from each state and the Federal District of Mexico City, and an additional 32 senators selected from a national list on the basis of proportional representation. The upper house has fewer powers than the lower house, but it does have the power to confirm the president's appointments to the Supreme Court, approve treaties, and approve federal intervention in state matters.

Both houses have a committee system that on paper looks much like the U.S. system. In practice, however, Mexican legislators and the legislative committees lack the

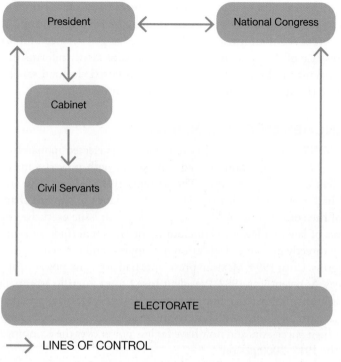

LINES OF CONTROL

Structure of the Government

teeth of their northern counterparts because of one key difference: Mexican legislators cannot be reelected to consecutive terms. As a result, most Mexican deputies enter the lower house without any legislative experience, effectively depriving Mexico of the kind of senior lawmakers who dominate the U.S. system.

Even after the PRI's loss of the presidency in 2000, single-term legislators were reluctant to disobey their party leadership if they hoped to be nominated for another post in local or state government. Since returning to power in 2012, the PRI has formally proposed amending the constitution to allow legislators to be reelected, but only with the approval of their parties. If enacted, this reform may increase the experience and prestige of legislators, but it may not make them any more willing to vote independently from their parties.

The Mexican legislature is currently in transition. Until 1988, the PRI regularly won over 90 percent of lower house seats and never lost a Senate seat. Between 1970 and 2003, it averaged 66.9 percent of the seats in the lower house, dwarfing the presence of its nearest rival, the PAN (National Action Party), which averaged about 17 percent during that period.[3] In 1997, the two main opposition parties were able to form a coalition and take control of the lower house.

Before 1997, the lower house approved about 98 percent of the legislation submitted by the executive, but that percentage has fallen steadily since then. Moreover, the number of laws originating in the legislature (instead of in the president's office) has increased dramatically. Since 2000, the lower house has successfully resisted pieces of legislation proposed by Fox, Calderón, and Peña Nieto. Because Mexican parties in the legislature have been extraordinarily well disciplined (Mexican legislators almost always vote according to the wishes of the party leadership), it has been almost impossible for presidents to poach votes from opposition legislators.

In recent years, Congress blocked some legislation and radically altered other measures. Since the return of democracy in 2000, Mexican presidents have achieved legislative victories only by negotiating with the opposition-controlled legislature. For example, upon taking office President Peña negotiated a legislative agreement called the *Pacto por México* (Pact for Mexico) to gain a majority in the legislature in support of over 90 key reforms.

THE JUDICIARY Mexico's judiciary is structured according to the U.S. model. Like the United States, Mexico has a **National Supreme Court of Justice** as well as courts at the local and state levels. The 11 Supreme Court justices are appointed by the president and are confirmed by a two-thirds vote of the Senate. However, unlike the United States, in Mexico these justices are limited to 15-year terms.

The Mexican judiciary has important formal powers, but during the authoritarian period the Supreme Court never overturned any law, and it tended to view its jurisdiction in very limited terms. In the 1980s, dramatic changes were introduced to give the Supreme Court far greater jurisdiction and power.[4] The Supreme Court can now determine the constitutionality of legislation upon the request of one-third of the lower house, but it can strike down a law only if a supermajority of 8 out of 11 justices agrees. The reforms have increased the independence of the judiciary by creating a seven-member Federal Judicial Council to oversee the administration of justice.

Mexico's judicial system is severely hampered by a widespread perception that judges, especially at the local level, are corrupt. Since 2000, Mexican presidents have made it a priority to enhance the prestige and power of the beleaguered judiciary. An even more serious problem is the overall weakness of the rule of law in Mexico. According to one prominent political scientist, "Mexico is already, up to a point, a democracy, a middle-class society, and an open economy, but is nowhere near to becoming a nation of laws."[5]

Like the legislature, Mexico's judicial system is currently in transition. A number of constitutional amendments since the mid-1990s have led to significant reforms. A 2008 amendment required all state and federal judicial systems to move from a European-style inquisitorial system to an oral-based jury model by 2016. The reform's implementation is behind schedule, and by late 2016 only 23 of Mexico's states and the Federal District of Mexico City had begun to implement the reforms. Mexico will have to retrain its lawyers and judges, but once implemented, the reforms will hopefully lead to a more transparent and effective legal system.[6] The new system will place greater emphasis on due process rights for those accused of crimes and will impose the presumption of innocence. A 2010 reform gave Mexicans the ability to use class action lawsuits to permit groups of citizens to sue in defense of their rights. Given the lack of resources and training, many government officials came to believe that the new reforms were too often letting criminals go free. In 2017, the Peña Nieto administration supported a new law that would roll back many of the earlier reforms, giving more power to the police and military, allowing the use of torture to gain confessions, and placing the burden of proving innocence on the accused.

THE ELECTORAL SYSTEM

Due to a long history of electoral fraud, the PRI agreed in 1996 to create a truly independent **Federal Electoral Institute** and a Federal Electoral Tribunal to adjudicate all electoral disputes. Mexico now has a sophisticated and transparent electoral system featuring a national electoral register and voter identification cards, public funding for electoral campaigns, and strict limits on private contributions. Nevertheless, the bitterly contested presidential elections of 2006 raised new concerns about Mexico's electoral system and generated calls for further reform.

Mexican presidents are directly elected, and as in the United States there are no provisions for a second round of voting if a candidate fails to win a majority of the popular vote. In the context of Mexico's political party system, in which three main parties have each won about a third of the vote, this has meant that all recent elections have produced presidents with a relatively small plurality of the vote, and with a legislature dominated by the opposition. Indeed, each of the last three Mexican presidents won successively smaller percentages of the popular vote, and Calderón won the disputed 2006 election with only about 36 percent of the vote. President Calderón introduced legislation in December 2009 to create a two-round voting system, but it failed to gain legislative support.

Mexico now uses a mixed electoral system for the lower house, which includes 300 single-member districts and 200 proportional representation seats. Deputies in the lower house serve three-year terms. Mexico's electoral system for the upper house is unique. Senators serve six-year terms, and three are elected from each state and the federal district. The party with the most votes wins two Senate seats, and the party finishing second is automatically awarded the third seat. An additional 32 seats are allocated according to PR. Elections to the Senate take place at the same time as the presidential elections. Parties must get at least 2 percent of the national vote in order to win seats from the PR lists.

Mexico's electoral law also has provisions that make it difficult for a party to win a majority of the seats in either house of the legislature. A party's total number of seats in the lower house cannot exceed the percentage of the party's PR vote by more than 8 percent. In effect, this means that to gain a legislative majority, a party would need to get at least 42 percent of the PR vote and then win a large number of single-member contests to push the total number of seats over 50 percent. In Mexico's system of three major political parties, legislative majorities have, to date, been elusive. This means that, in stark contrast to the 1917–2000 period of PRI dominance, divided government is likely to be the rule in the future.

President Peña Nieto, with the support of the conservative PAN, has recently reformed the Federal Electoral Institute. It now has power over local elections, where fraud has been more widespread, as well as the power to annul the results in close elections where candidates have overspent the legal limits.

LOCAL GOVERNMENT

Despite being formally federal, Mexico operated very much like a unitary political system during authoritarianism. Excessive localism and a history of instability and political violence caused by the absence of a weak central authority favored the PRI's centralizing tendencies, despite the federalist constitutional rhetoric. Federal authorities controlled local elections, local budgets, local police forces, and so forth. Until 1997, the mayor of Mexico City was a cabinet member appointed directly by the president.

Mexico currently has 31 states and a Federal District of Mexico City, each with its own constitution and unicameral legislature.[7] States are subdivided into *municipios* (similar in some ways to county governments in the United States). State governors, county councils, and county presidents are now elected directly. Until 1988, all governors were from the PRI, although in the 1980s only widespread electoral fraud prevented opposition victories. Indeed, some of the first serious opposition to PRI hegemony came at the local level, especially in Mexico's prosperous north, where unpopular PRI local leaders and state governors were successfully defeated by opposition candidates. The PRI's use of electoral fraud at the local level helped ignite regional opposition to the party's heavy-handed centralist policies. The first opposition governor took power in 1989, in the state of Baja California. In the 1990s, the PRI began to accept opposition victories in numerous local elections, and by the end of that decade opposition parties controlled seven governorships.

Mexican states have important powers, but their sovereignty is far more circumscribed by federal authorities, especially the federal bureaucracy, than is state sovereignty in other federal systems such as Brazil, Germany, and the United States. The federal government collects about 90 percent of all tax revenue. Since the return to democracy an increasing portion of government spending—currently about half of the total—has been delegated to state and local governments, often as the result of horse trading between presidents and the opposition majority in the legislature.

In the 1980s and 1990s, state and local politics provided the first opportunities for Mexico's anti-PRI opposition, although some local and state offices (especially in rural areas) remained PRI strongholds long after the party lost the presidency in 2000. A good example is the rural west coast state of Guerrero, where the PRI retained a lock on state government until being ousted by the leftist **Partido de la Revolución Democrática (PRD)** in the gubernatorial elections of 2005. Another example is the southern state of Oaxaca, where a PRI governor was accused of repression and corruption, and where the PRI lost power only in 2010, when the two main opposition parties joined forces.

Following the U.S. model, Mexican states and localities have their own police forces, but these forces have been widely viewed as bastions of corruption. Since 2006, local police have been replaced in some areas by federal forces to root out corruption. The investigation surrounding the shocking disappearance of 43 university students at a rural teacher's college in September 2014 revealed that the local government, the local police, and drug traffickers had worked together to kidnap the students. Still, Mexicans have more confidence in their local governments than in the federal government (see "Confidence in Mexican Institutions, 2015," p. 591).

Political Conflict and Competition

THE PARTY SYSTEM

During Mexico's long authoritarian period following the Mexican Revolution, opposition parties were mostly tolerated; some were even encouraged to exist, to give superficial legitimacy to the PRI-dominated system. The PRI skillfully cultivated and selectively co-opted all the opposition parties, which were generally weak and divided until the 1980s. Mexico's major parties thus predate the transition to democracy after 2000.

THE PARTIDO REVOLUCIONARIO INSTITUCIONAL The PRI was founded in 1929 as a way of ending Mexico's often-violent struggle for political power. From the start, the PRI was viewed as a party representing the interests of the Mexican state.

During its long rule, the PRI became increasingly indistinguishable from the state, and the immense power of Mexico's presidents resulted from their effective control over both the party and the state.

A key element of the PRI's exercise of power was the use of **patron-client relationships**, in which powerful government officials delivered state services and access to power in exchange for the delivery of political support.

Even with its historic defeat in the July 2000 presidential elections, the PRI continued to wield enormous power at the state and local level, where its old-style political machines were most effective and where allegations of old-style PRI corruption were commonplace. Even before the PRI's return to the presidency in July 2012, the PRI governed 20 of Mexico's 31 states.

After losing the presidency in 2000, the PRI was rudderless. As a party designed to serve sitting presidents, it no longer had a clear leader. The official party leadership, the PRI legislative delegation, and PRI governors all wielded considerable power and produced what one observer has called "a hydra-headed behemoth."[8] Recent changes in the PRI structure, however, have led to the direct election of a party president, and by 2011 the PRI seemed poised for a political comeback. The failure of the Fox and Calderón administrations to enact badly needed reform (largely due to the stubborn opposition of the PRI) and the inconclusive drug war, combined with the internal rancor within the leftist PRD after its narrow loss in the 2006 elections, created a political opening for the PRI. Mexico governor Enrique Peña Nieto, a young and charismatic PRI leader, completed the party's remarkable political comeback with his victory in the 2012 presidential elections. Ironically, Peña Nieto attempted to identify the "new" PRI with an ambitious agenda to reform the very system the party had created in the early twentieth century.

The PRI remains an enigmatic political party whose ideology is hard to define. Currently, it is best viewed as being located on the center-right in the Mexican party system. In 2012, about half of voters who define themselves as being on the right or in the center supported the PRI, while less than a quarter of self-defined leftists backed the PRI. Peña Nieto has tried to portray the PRI as a modern, centrist, democratic party, but the bases of the PRI's power at the state and local level are still controlled by old-style PRI machine politicians associated with corruption, co-optation, and electoral fraud.

Peña Nieto has had a mixed record in office. He has been able to negotiate a series of important economic reforms, most prominently a constitutional amendment that will allow private investment in the energy sector. He was able to pass a major reform of Mexico's educational system, and a law that would break up its telecommunications monopolies. But Peña Nieto's term in office has also been marked by a number of serious problems, most important being his failure to stem corruption, impunity, and violence. The 2014 disappearance and murder of 43 students in Guerrero state revealed a local government and police force that were deeply penetrated by drug cartels. The government proved unable to conduct a credible investigation, and international investigators blasted the government's handling of the crisis. In 2015, the dramatic escape from a high-security prison of Mexico's most notorious drug lord further damaged the president's reputation.

THE MEXICAN LEFT A serious leftist political force emerged only in the 1980s, when a leftist faction within the PRI, led by Michoacán governor Cuauhtémoc Cárdenas, bolted from the party in protest over the PRI's embrace of neoliberal economic reforms.[9] Cárdenas, the son of the former president most famous for promoting land reform and nationalizing Mexico's oil, then led the newly formed Partido de la Revolución Democrática (PRD) in a coalition of four opposition parties in the 1988 elections.

Bolstered by the high-profile leadership of Cárdenas and boosted by the PRI's loss of popularity, the PRD performed extremely well in the 1988 elections. Many observers believe that had there not been significant electoral fraud, the PRD would have won those elections. Despite this auspicious start, the PRD struggled as a leftist opposition party. It has been plagued by internal fighting and has been unable to capture enough voters outside its strongholds in Mexico City and the south.

The PRD clearly stands to the left of the PRI and the PAN. During the 1980s and 1990s, it attacked the PRI's neoliberal reforms and neglect of poor Mexicans. It advocated more nationalist and protectionist policies than had been pursued by the PRI since the 1940s. Some PRD candidates at the state and local level have had considerable success, and the PRD has controlled Mexico City's government since 1997.

The former PRD mayor of Mexico City, **Andrés Manuel López Obrador**, a charismatic populist, emerged as the front-runner in the 2006 presidential election but saw his lead slip away as the conservative opposition portrayed him as a dangerous radical who would threaten Mexico's prosperity and harm relations with the United States. Long after his defeat, López Obrador continued to claim that his razor-thin loss in the 2006 election was the result of fraud and

Andrés Manuel López Obrador, of the leftist PRD, having himself sworn in as "legitimate president" after narrowly losing the 2006 presidential election.

illegal government action, despite a ruling to the contrary by Mexico's Federal Electoral Tribunal. His defiant stand, his refusal to recognize the government of Felipe Calderón, seemed to cast doubt on his and his party's commitment to democracy and served only to frighten middle-class Mexicans.[10] Partly as a result, the PRD lost support in subsequent elections.

In the 2012 presidential campaign, López Obrador toned down his leftist rhetoric and performed better than expected, but he came in second with about 32 percent of the vote. He once again unsuccessfully challenged the legitimacy of the electoral process in Mexico, claiming that the PRI had bought votes and illegally funded its campaign. The PRD proved less popular in legislative elections than its presidential candidate. It received less than 20 percent of the vote for the legislature, coming in third behind the PRI and the PAN. Shortly after the elections, López Obrador resigned from the PRD. He launched a new political movement, called **MORENA (National Regeneration Movement)**, thus further dividing Mexico's left and opening the door for new leadership within the PRD. MORENA won 8 percent of the vote and 21 seats in the 2015 lower house elections, seriously weakening the PRD, and positioning López Obrador for a third presidential run in 2018.

THE MEXICAN RIGHT The Partido Acción Nacional (PAN) was founded in 1939 by defectors from the PRI. The PAN became the only opposition party to develop a strong organizational presence, especially in its strongholds in northern Mexico and the state of Yucatán. The party emerged as a conservative response to the leftist policies of the PRI during the late 1930s and early 1940s. It advocated Christian-democratic ideas, opposing the PRI's anticlericalism and supporting pro-business policies. Since its base of power was state politics, the PAN became an early advocate of states' rights and opposed the centralization of power that was a feature of Mexican politics under the PRI.

Like many conservative parties, the PAN has been divided historically between Catholic social conservatives and more free-market-oriented business interests. The more pro-business wing has dominated the party since the late 1980s, but the PRI's adoption of neoliberal economic strategies during that decade threatened to steal the PAN's thunder. The PAN continues to be plagued by internal division, and PAN legislators have been less willing to follow their own leadership than have legislators from the PRI or PRD.

PAN candidate Vicente Fox won the 2000 presidential election, but he was not a prototypical PAN leader and did not share much of the social conservatism that is typical of many PAN leaders. His roots were in business, and his charisma and his personal support network allowed him to overcome much opposition within his own party and helped expand the PAN's appeal to new voters. In the 2000 presidential campaign, Fox created his own campaign organization. That organization did not depend on the official PAN hierarchy, which was dominated by Fox's political rivals. Once in office, Fox formed a cabinet that included no members of the PAN's more conservative "traditionalist" wing, and his closest advisers were non-PAN members. He had stormy relations with the traditionalist wing of the PAN, which dominates the legislature and the party hierarchy.

Fox's successor, Felipe Calderón, had been involved in conservative politics his entire adult life. His father was a founder of the PAN, and Calderón became leader of its youth wing in his twenties. He held a variety of elected political positions and twice served as a federal deputy. He served as party president in the 1990s, when the PAN first began to mount a serious challenge to the PRI. Vicente Fox appointed him secretary of energy, an important cabinet post in oil-rich Mexico. Calderón narrowly defeated the leftist Andrés Manuel López Obrador in the bitterly contested 2006 presidential election. In office, Calderón generally proved to be a social conservative and a supporter of free-market policies. His campaign to defeat Mexico's drug cartels delivered mixed results. The ensuing violence tarnished Calderón's previously high approval ratings in opinion polls.

For the 2012 presidential election, the PAN selected Mexico's first-ever woman presidential candidate, Josefina Vázquez Mota. Partly because of Calderón's poor image and popular frustration with the two previous PAN presidencies, and partly because she was less well known than her two competitors, Vázquez Mota did poorly in the election, winning just over a quarter of the vote.

Since the watershed 2000 election and the transition to democracy, the Mexican party system has been in flux. Beginning in the 1990s, there was a significant partisan "dealignment," in which many voters abandoned the PRI. Not all those voters have realigned themselves with other parties, however, and a large segment of the Mexican electorate remains "fluid."

Mexico's current party system is extremely competitive. There are four major parties, but in most of the country, two parties contend for power.[11] In Mexico's more

Seats in the Chamber of Deputies and Senate after the Two Most Recent Elections

PARTY	CHAMBER OF DEPUTIES SEATS (2015)		CHAMBER OF DEPUTIES SEATS (2012)		SENATE SEATS (2012)		SENATE SEATS (2006)	
	NUMBER	%	NUMBER	%	NUMBER	%	NUMBER	%
PRI*	250	50	240	48	61	48	39	30
PRD**	88	18	136	27	28	22	36	28
PAN	108	22	114	23	38	29	52	41
MORENA	21	4						
Others	33	6	10	2	1	1	1	1
Total	500	100	500	100	128	100	128	100

*The PRI includes seats for the Mexican Green Party, allied with PRI.
**The PRD includes seats for the Mexican Labor Party and the Citizens Movement, allied with PRD.
Key to Party Acronyms:
PAN: National Action Party (Conservative)
PRD: Party of the Democratic Revolution (Leftist)
PRI: Institutional Revolutionary Party
MORENA: National Regeneration Movement (Leftist)
Source: http://electionresources.org (accessed 6/24/17).

prosperous north and west, the PAN and the PRI fight for votes, while in poorer southern Mexico the PRD (and MORENA) and the PRI are chief rivals. Only in Mexico City and the surrounding areas do all three parties truly compete on an equal footing. The PRI remains the only party with support in all regions, while the PRD and the PAN have more regionally concentrated bases of support. About 70 percent of Mexicans identify with parties of the left, center, or right, and 30 percent claim to be independent.[12]

A variety of smaller parties compete for, and regularly win, seats in the Mexican legislature. The most important of these is the Mexican Green Party (PVEM), a mislabeled and entirely opportunistic party that has almost nothing in common with its environmentally oriented European counterparts. The PVEM was allied with the leftist PRD in the 1997 elections and then backed the conservative PAN in 2000. Since then, the PVEM has run in an electoral alliance with the PRI. In the 2015 lower house elections, smaller parties, including the new leftist party MORENA, gained seats at the expense of the three major parties.

ELECTIONS

During most of the PRI's long authoritarian rule, elections were more national celebrations of PRI power than competitive electoral campaigns. Every six years, the country was decked out in the PRI's colors, patronage was dispensed on a massive scale, and the PRI nominees (in effect, the presumed winners) toured their constituencies and made speeches.

The 2000 presidential campaign broke with this tradition. It was the first to be governed by new electoral finance rules, which not only sharply limited private contributions but also provided candidates with public financing. Access to the media by all political parties was far more equitable than ever before. While PRI candidates still enjoyed an advantage, the playing field was more level than it had been in past elections. The first truly fair and competitive election was also the first national campaign in which U.S.-style mudslinging was widespread. The PRI portrayed Fox as a U.S. lackey; for his part, Fox questioned Labastida's "macho" credentials. Some of the most negative campaigning took place between the two PRI contestants for the nomination. The 2000 campaign was also the first truly modern campaign in Mexican history. Television took on a pivotal role. The campaign culminated in two televised presidential debates, which the charismatic and engaging Fox won handily.

The 2006 presidential campaign was Mexico's first "normal" presidential contest.[13] In 2000, the main issue had been democratization and the defeat of the PRI's semi-authoritarian regime. In 2006, Mexicans faced their first real choice between parties of the right and left. The early front-runner, Andrés Manuel López Obrador (of the leftist PRD) ran a campaign aimed at improving the plight of Mexico's poor. His main opponent, the PAN's Felipe Calderón, advocated a pro-business set of policies aimed at increasing employment. Calderón chipped away at López Obrador's initial lead by questioning his commitment to democracy and portraying him as a dangerous leftist who would threaten Mexico's economic stability. The campaign was characterized by an unprecedented level of impassioned and negative attack ads. The outcome of the 2006 election revealed a polarized and divided electorate; Calderón and López Obrador each won just over 35 percent of the vote, and Calderón won by a mere one-half of a percentage point.

The 2012 campaign was the first to take place under electoral reforms adopted in 2007 and 2008, and that reduced allowable private campaign funding by almost half. The campaign featured two lackluster debates between the main presidential candidates.[14] In some ways, each of the three major candidates had to defend their questionable records. Peña Nieto had to try to distance himself from the PRI's association with authoritarian rule while fending off attacks involving his record as governor of the state of Mexico. Peña Nieto proposed policies that largely continued the PAN's agenda of fighting organized crime and liberalizing the economy while at the same time calling for increased social spending. Josefina Vázquez Mota had the unenviable task of defending the PAN's association with the bloody war against drug cartels as well as Mexico's sluggish economic growth under two previous PAN administrations, and she was saddled by outgoing President Calderón's low popularity ratings. The leftist López Obrador sought to distance himself from what many Mexicans viewed as his irresponsible behavior in the aftermath of the 2006 presidential elections. He was the only major candidate to call for an end to Mexico's war against drug cartels, and the only one to oppose reforming Mexico's energy sector. Peña Nieto won the election with 38.2 percent of the vote (López Obrador won 31.6 percent, and Vázquez Mota of the PAN won 25.4 percent). Although the PRI won the presidency, the party lost its majority in the legislature, forcing President Peña Nieto to negotiate with the opposition in order to pass legislation.

CIVIL SOCIETY

During authoritarianism, Mexican groups and associations were often incorporated into the state in a system known as *corporatism*. The paternalistic PRI would then mediate among different groups while making sure that no one group challenged

Mexican citizens, like these members of vigilante groups in the southeastern state of Guerrero in 2014, have organized to combat violence by drug gangs.

government power. The PRI was formally divided into three sectors (labor, peasants, and the "popular" middle class), each dominated by PRI-controlled mass organizations. It would be a mistake, however, to assume that the Mexican state could control all autonomous groups in society. Indeed, a variety of autonomous civil society organizations emerged in the 1980s and 1990s, mainly in response to economic crises, predating the PRI's ouster from power in 2000.[15]

Given its level of economic development, Mexican civil society remains weak compared with many other Latin American countries.[16] Eighty-five percent of Mexicans report that they belong to no civil society organization, and a similar percentage say they have never worked formally or informally with others to resolve community problems.[17] A long history of a strong and paternalistic state, and a deep-seated distrust of others, which according to opinion research far exceeds the Latin American norm, may be responsible. In the words of a former Mexican foreign minister, "It should not be altogether surprising that after nearly five hundred years of a strong state, civil society should be weak. From this perspective, Mexicans are disorganized . . . because an all-powerful state has crowded them out."[18]

Mexican civil society may be weak in comparative perspective, but in recent years increasing numbers of Mexicans have become frustrated by their government's inability to protect them against organized crime. The willingness of Mexicans to organize to defend their communities from violence may be an encouraging example of Mexican civil society in action, but it can also have potentially dangerous consequences, and it threatens to create yet another set of armed groups beyond state control. After 43 college student protesters disappeared in September 2014, demonstrations took place throughout Mexico demanding that the federal government take action against corrupt local governments.

BUSINESS Although the PRI successfully co-opted Mexico's private sector for decades, it can be argued that business groups later emerged as the most powerful source of opposition to authoritarian rule. During authoritarianism, most private-sector interests were channeled into a variety of semi-official organizations, including the National Chamber of Industries and the National Chamber of Commerce. Until 1996, private-sector membership in these organizations was mandatory. Even though the PRI never gave business organizations formal representation within the governing party, business interests wielded power through more informal organizations and channels. The secretive Business Coordinating Council (CCE), which represents some of Mexico's wealthiest capitalists, had close ties to the Fox government.

In the PRI-led authoritarian regime, the relationship between the business sector and the PRI was complex and often contradictory. The PRI's policies generally favored the private sector, especially big business. At the same time, business leaders bitterly opposed attempts by some PRI presidents to enact the social agenda of the Mexican Revolution. In the 1970s, presidents Luis Echeverría Álvarez and José López Portillo sought to expand the role of the state in the economy, and their policies damaged business-government relations. Although those policies were short-lived, they served to garner opposition to the PRI among northern business interests. Moreover, they were an important factor in the business sector's early support for the conservative PAN in the last decades of PRI authoritarianism and after the return of democracy in 2000. The prospect of a PRD victory in 2006 clearly alarmed much of the business sector, which feared that the election of the leftist López Obrador would damage Mexico's business climate. Their situation encouraged many business leaders to rally behind PAN candidate Felipe Calderón.

Since returning to power in 2012, the PRI relationship with big business has been strained. President Peña Nieto has actively sought to weaken the power of monopolies that dominate key areas of the Mexican economy, like the media, telecommunications, and the banking sectors. These reforms are popular with Mexican citizens, who are tired of paying higher prices that result from the monopolies, but the business sector attacked the reforms as an attempt by the PRI government to strengthen state regulation of the private sector. The Peña Nieto government passed reforms making it harder for businesses to block government regulation in the courts. The business community opposed his plans to raise sales taxes.

LABOR After the Mexican Revolution, the PRI actively supported the unionization of Mexican workers. However, the unions were thoroughly integrated into and controlled by the governing party. They received massive subsidies from the state, which made them politically pliant. They enjoyed privileged treatment under the PRI, in part because they were never able to incorporate much of the workforce (about 16 percent, at their peak) and because one-third of their members were government employees. The labor movement in Mexico was highly centralized. The dominant labor organization, the **Confederation of Mexican Workers (CTM)**, was created by the PRI and became one of the main supporters of the governing party. Until his death in 1997, Fidel Velázquez Sánchez served as a pillar of PRI authoritarianism and dominated the CTM for more than 50 years.

Unions independent of the PRI are a relatively new phenomenon. In 1997, Mexico's independent unions formed the National Union of Workers (UNT) to compete with the CTM. Since the mid-1990s, a series of laws and court decisions have weakened the grip of the formerly official unions. Neoliberal economic policies that have been implemented over the last three decades have created challenges for the CTM. Its membership has clearly suffered from the economic reforms, and its leadership no longer benefits from government patronage. On the one hand, democratic reforms are likely to give labor unions more autonomy and a greater ability to contest government policy. On the other hand, the recent reforms passed by the Calderón and Peña Nieto governments were aimed at weakening the power of important unions. For example, in 2013 the legislature passed a reform of Mexico's education system that broke the control of the powerful teacher's union over the hiring and evaluation of teachers.

THE MEDIA The PRI-dominated authoritarian regime maintained a political lock on the media through co-optation more than coercion. Rather than imposing censorship, the government courted the favor of Mexico's media by purchasing advertisements in pro-PRI media outlets, giving supportive media voices cheap access to infrastructure, and bribing reporters outright. Mexico's largest media conglomerate, Televisa, was extremely close to the PRI.

By the early 1990s, the PRI had loosened its control over the media somewhat. The government stopped bribing reporters, and the wave of privatizations created a more competitive media environment, allowing for criticism of the PRI. Since the return of democracy in 2000, Mexico has had a more vibrant media that is often critical of the government. Still, the power of Mexico's two main television networks, which are historical bastions of PRI support, was left largely intact. In the 2012 elections, these networks were criticized for coverage that favored the PRI. The leftist candidate Andrés Manuel López Obrador, backed by a social media protest movement, claimed that the Mexican media had unfairly favored its old patron, the PRI. However, as we have seen, since taking office the Peña Nieto administration has enacted reforms to weaken conglomerates like Televisa.

While Mexico's media has flourished in the democratic era, Mexico's journalists have often been targeted by drug cartels after reporting on the violence that has plagued Mexico.[19] At least 16 journalists were murdered over the last decade, and the Committee to Protect Journalists ranked Mexico as the seventh most dangerous country for journalists. Much of the Mexican media are still heavily dependent on government advertising and

INCOMPARISON	Internet Access

Do you use the Internet, at least occasionally? Percentage saying yes:

COUNTRY	PERCENTAGE	COUNTRY	PERCENTAGE
United Kingdom	85	Russia	58
Germany	80	China	50
United States	79	Brazil	49
France	75	Mexico	37
Japan	66	India	7

Note: Data for Iran, Nigeria, and South Africa not available.
Source: Pew Center for the People and the Press, 2012.

access to information. In some cases, these factors have led to the return of the type of self-censorship that was common during the decades of authoritarian rule.

One positive trend has been the growing importance of social media in Mexico. During the 2012 electoral campaign, a student movement, called #YoSoy132, used Twitter and Facebook to call attention to what the protesters viewed as uncritical media coverage of the PRI's candidate Peña Nieto, eventually persuading the major networks to televise the second presidential electoral debate. However, the impact of social media may be limited by the very low levels of Internet access; in 2013, only 18 percent of Mexicans reported using the Internet daily, and only 37 percent said they used the Internet at least occasionally (see "In Comparison: Internet Access," p. 589).[20]

Society

ETHNIC AND NATIONAL IDENTITY

The journalist Alan Riding has described Mexico as a nation proud of its indigenous past but ashamed of its indigenous present.[21] After the Mexican Revolution, the PRI glorified and embraced its indigenous ancestry and inculcated pride in the *mestizaje*, or "blending of cultures," produced by the Spanish Conquest. Indigenous peoples who have not assimilated into mestizo Mexico have been politically marginalized and become victims of Mexico's worst poverty, whereas Mexico's wealthy elite have tended to be lighter skinned and of European origin.

The PRI's success in perpetuating the myth of *mestizaje* may help explain how it avoided the kind of ethnically based violence that has plagued other ethnically diverse nations. But that myth was violently shattered on January 1, 1994, when a rebel army made up mostly of ethnic Mayans, the **Zapatista Army of National Liberation (EZLN)**, occupied several towns in Mexico's southernmost state of Chiapas.[22]

Many viewed the EZLN as solely an indigenous group seeking greater autonomy for Mexico's long-neglected native population. It soon became clear, however, that the EZLN included among its demands the democratization of the Mexican political system and an end to the neoliberal reforms that had ravaged the indigenous poor. The EZLN was reacting to the devastation caused by neoliberal trade policies that had exposed the inefficient peasant farmers to competition from cheaper foreign imports. The call for democratization was partly a response to the political lock that the PRI maintained on some of Mexico's poorest and most heavily indigenous regions.

The Zapatista uprising was surprisingly popular within Mexico and, together with the economic crisis, helped erode PRI political dominance and accelerate electoral reforms. In 1996, the Zedillo government signed the **San Andrés Peace Accords** with the EZLN, promising protection of indigenous languages and granting indigenous communities political autonomy. These provisions were never implemented, and as of 2017, the standoff between the government and the Zapatistas continues; the EZLN is controlling some remote communities, and its demands remain largely unmet.

IDEOLOGY AND POLITICAL CULTURE

Perhaps the most important aspect of Mexican political culture is a profound distrust of the state and the government. Opinion research demonstrates that Mexicans have a far more negative view of their political system and state than do their

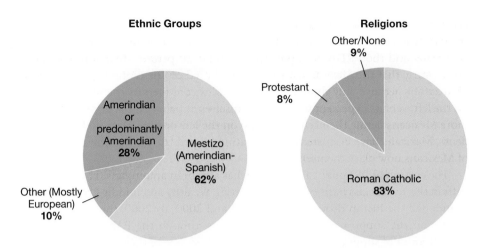

Ethnic Groups

- Amerindian or predominantly Amerindian **28%**
- Mestizo (Amerindian-Spanish) **62%**
- Other (Mostly European) **10%**

Religions

- Other/None **9%**
- Protestant **8%**
- Roman Catholic **83%**

counterparts in Europe, the United States, and even Latin America. A 2015 poll showed that only about a fifth of Mexicans were very or somewhat satisfied with the way democracy works; it was the lowest assessment of any of the 18 Latin American countries polled.[23]

Decades of authoritarian rule and poor performance of governments since 2000 may explain why over 70 percent of Mexicans express little or no interest in politics, notwithstanding a temporary surge of interest during the historic 2000 presidential elections.[24] Unlike communist regimes, which actively promote political mobilization, Mexican authoritarianism sought to contain and limit popular participation in politics through a variety of methods, notably co-optation. Mexico's political culture continues to show the effects of decades of authoritarian rule: the country has very low levels of participation in politics, party membership, and political activism. Although there is some evidence of a steady increase in popular political activity since the 1980s, declining voter turnout is still a concern. Turnout declined to 59 percent in 2006, but rebounded to 65 percent in 2013. In midterm legislative elections, turnout has hovered around 50 percent.

During authoritarianism, most Mexicans professed sympathy for no political party. The erosion of PRI hegemony in the 1980s and 1990s and the increasing

Confidence in Mexican Institutions, 2015

	A LOT	SOME	A LITTLE	NONE	DON'T KNOW/N/A
Church	36.5	25.7	21.6	15.2	1.0
Armed forces	25.9	32.8	27.7	12.3	1.1
Police	5.0	19.0	34.7	40.8	0.5
Judiciary	4.7	19.2	35.8	38.0	2.3
Congress	4.4	19.9	34.6	36.8	4.4
Federal government	3.9	17.1	35.2	42.4	1.3
Political parties	2.0	13.8	34.2	48.8	1.2

Source: www.latinobarometro.org (accessed 6/24/17).

competitiveness of elections led far more Mexicans to identify with a political party. By 2000, the PRI and the PAN each enjoyed the support of about one-third of the electorate, and the PRD was supported by about 10 percent. Opinion data show quite clearly that the Mexican electorate is anchored on the center right. The leftist PRD suffers because only about 20 percent of Mexicans identify themselves as being on the left, versus 23 percent who view themselves as being on the right.[25] Although more Mexicans define themselves as being on the left or right than do U.S. respondents, Mexicans have been steadily gravitating toward the center, where 41 percent of Mexicans now place themselves.

The erosion of PRI political hegemony has also been accompanied by a dramatic shift in the social class basis of Mexico's parties. Wealthy and middle-class Mexicans abandoned the PRI in droves between 1989 and 2000. By 2000, the PRI depended mostly on the support of lower-class Mexicans, though the PAN had nearly the same amount of support among poor voters. Indeed, one of the remarkable changes between 1989 and 2000 was the PAN's ability to garner support from all classes. In the 2006 election, the leftist PRD did best among poorer voters, while the PAN was clearly favored by wealthier and more educated voters. But region more than any other factor best explains party support in Mexico.

In 2011, political scientist (and former Mexican foreign minister) Jorge Castañeda published a controversial book in which he argued that Mexico's political culture was ill-suited to the conditions of democratic politics, a middle-class society, and an increasingly globalized economy.[26] Castañeda identifies excessive individualism, an exaggerated aversion to any form of conflict, disdain for the rule of law, and a xenophobic attitude toward the United States as signal features of Mexican culture that are likely to hamper its future development. He argues that these cultural traits have a long history, and he views the authoritarian regime of the PRI as a reflection of Mexican culture rather than a cause for it. For Castañeda, this deep-seated culture helps explain a plethora of ills afflicting Mexican society, including a weak civil society, the widespread lack of respect for political institutions, and Mexico's endemic corruption. His critics attacked the book as overly simplistic, filled with stereotypes, and reflective of the values of a wealthy Mexican who spent much of his life outside of Mexico.

Opinion research reveals that most Mexicans favor democracy over authoritarianism, but their levels of support for democratic rule are below average for Latin America. In 2015, about 47 percent stated that democracy was preferable to any other kind of government, among the lowest levels of support in Latin America.[27] If there is positive news, it is that only 15 percent said that authoritarian rule might be preferable in some circumstances. This figure has dropped from a high of 43 percent in 2000 and has remained fairly constant even as the public's attachment to democracy has eroded.

Political Economy

Between 1917 and 1980, leaders of the PRI agreed on some main features of the Mexican economy. First, Mexico's industrialization would be encouraged through **import substitution industrialization (ISI)** policies, which employed high tariffs to protect Mexican industries and agriculture. Government policies provided Mexican entrepreneurs with subsidized credit and energy and very low taxes. The PRI's ability to control labor, and therefore labor costs, also benefited Mexico's entrepreneurs. Second, Mexico was to have a capitalist economy, but the Mexican state played an important role in key sectors of the economy, though far less than in socialist economies.

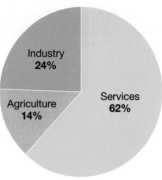

Labor Force by Occupation

Despite this general consensus, economic policies of the PRI presidents between 1917 and 2000 fluctuated a great deal. The nationalists, usually associated with the left wing of the PRI, placed more emphasis on redistribution of income, plenty of state social spending, and a strong state presence in the economy. Their economic policies tended to be strongly nationalistic, and they sought greater economic independence from the United States.

President Lázaro Cárdenas, who served from 1934 to 1940, was the most important advocate of economic nationalism. He used the PRI to organize and mobilize Mexico's workers and peasants, and he was the first president to implement the land reform called for in the Constitution of 1917. He integrated peasants and workers into state-controlled unions, and he strengthened the Mexican state by nationalizing the foreign-dominated oil industry and creating a state oil monopoly (**PEMEX**). His policies won the PRI the enduring political loyalty of Mexico's workers and peasants. Future Mexican presidents never addressed the socioeconomic aspirations of the Mexican constitution as much as Cárdenas did, but the presidencies of Adolfo López Mateos (1958–64) and Luis Echeverría Álvarez (1970–76) followed policies that mirrored the views of the PRI nationalist left.

The economic liberals—including Miguel Alemán Valdés (1946–52), Gustavo Díaz Ordaz (1964–70), Miguel de la Madrid Hurtado (1982–88), and Carlos Salinas de Gortari (1988–94)—favored economic growth over redistribution. They tended to favor freer trade, increased foreign investment in the Mexican economy, and better relations with the United States. Presidents de la Madrid and Salinas undertook a major change in Mexico's political economic policies by liberalizing its statist, ISI-oriented economy, abandoning long-entrenched social commitments (such as land reform), and entering the General Agreement on Tariffs and Trade (GATT) in 1986 and NAFTA, with the United States and Canada, in 1994. Since 2000, presidents Fox, Calderón, and Peña Nieto have continued these neoliberal economic policies.

DIMENSIONS OF THE ECONOMY

In aggregate wealth, Mexico is a prosperous developing country, and compared with other developing countries, it is fairly industrialized. Industry accounts for about one-quarter of its gross domestic product (GDP), and agriculture now accounts for around 14 percent. The country is also rich in natural resources, especially oil, which is its chief economic asset. Since the presidency of Lázaro Cárdenas, Mexican oil has been controlled by the state monopoly, PEMEX.

From the 1940s to about 1980, the Mexican economy, bolstered by the peace and stability of the authoritarian regime, and benefiting from increased U.S. investment, grew spectacularly. Mexico became more industrialized, urban, and educated. Its economy also became more heavily dependent on the United States.

ECONOMIC CRISES IN THE TWILIGHT OF PRI AUTHORITARIANISM

In the 1970s, Mexican presidents used the country's vast oil wealth to support massive government spending in an attempt to alleviate chronic inequality and poverty. The spending fueled inflation and began to erode the value of the peso. Mexico incurred vast debts from foreign lenders, who viewed the oil-rich country as a trustworthy borrower. By the 1980s, oil accounted for over two-thirds of the value of Mexico's exports. A major drop in world oil prices in 1981 exposed the shaky foundation of Mexico's economy, and the country came close to defaulting on its international debt in August 1982.

The response by presidents de la Madrid and Salinas was to abandon the decades-old model of protectionism and state interventionism and embrace neoliberal economics, thus beginning a reversal of the country's political economy. By terminating the constitution's promise of land reform and opening up Mexico to a flood of cheap agricultural imports, the government in effect devastated many of Mexico's poorest peasants. The country's steady economic recovery in the late 1980s and early 1990s was upset in 1994 and 1995 by its most severe economic depression since the 1930s. In December 1994, the value of the Mexican peso collapsed, and the Mexican economy was saved only by the International Monetary Fund's largest bailout ever. Between 1994 and 1996, real wages dropped 27 percent, and an estimated 70 percent of Mexicans fell below the official poverty line.[28] Mexico had abandoned ISI policies and embraced free trade and globalization as a response to the economic crisis of the early 1980s, but this response had made it even more vulnerable to economic instability.

NAFTA AND GLOBALIZATION

NAFTA has drastically reduced most tariffs on agricultural goods traded among Mexico, Canada, and the United States. Between 1993 and 2012, trade between the United States and Mexico increased by over 500 percent. As a result, Mexico has been flooded by U.S. products (such as corn and pork) that cost one-fifth as much to produce as similar Mexican products. NAFTA has doubled the amount of food Mexico imports from the United States, thereby lowering food prices for consumers but creating a massive crisis for millions of Mexico's farmers. About one-fifth of Mexicans work in agriculture, the vast majority poor subsistence farmers who have been hurt the most by NAFTA competition. As a result, Mexico has eliminated millions of jobs in agriculture. NAFTA has also exacerbated the gap between the wealthy north and the impoverished south.[29]

In many other ways, however, NAFTA benefits Mexico. Manufacturing exports to the United States have skyrocketed, growing at an average rate of 75 percent annually since the agreement went into effect.[30] Overall, Mexican exports rose sevenfold between 1994 and 2011. Greater access to U.S. markets has also been a boon to Mexico's fruit and vegetable producers, who now supply much of the U.S. winter market, although exports of agricultural goods have grown very modestly compared with those of manufactured goods. Cheaper imports have benefited a wide variety of Mexican producers and consumers.

Mexico's embrace of NAFTA clearly created a more diversified economy. In the 1980s, oil made up about two-thirds of the country's exports. Mexico now exports a wider variety of goods, but it remains extremely dependent on the U.S. market, to which it sends over 80 percent of all its exports.

Mexico's entry into NAFTA has attracted more direct U.S. investment in Mexico. Much of that investment has gravitated toward **maquiladoras**, factories that import materials or parts to make goods that are then exported. These factories, concentrated along the Mexico-U.S. border, account for about half of all Mexico's exports. They now generate more foreign exchange for Mexico than does any other sector, including oil. The maquiladoras have added half a million jobs to Mexico's north, but some critics argue that the operations add relatively little to the Mexican economy because most materials and technology are imported. Average maquiladora wages are above Mexico's minimum wage but far below the average wage in the manufacturing sector. The concentration of maquiladoras in Mexico's wealthier north has exacerbated the country's severe north-south income gap.

Whether NAFTA has created more winners than losers is a hot topic of debate within Mexico. One result of the new pressures created by NAFTA has been the increased flow of Mexicans to the United States in search of employment. It is clear, however, that NAFTA has dislocated millions of Mexicans and will create new political and economic challenges for future Mexican administrations.

ECONOMIC POLICIES AND ISSUES

Despite the commitment to greater equality brought about by the Mexican Revolution and the efforts of some reformist presidents to help the poor, Mexico was and is a country of massive inequality. The pre-1980s statist policies were unable to address the persistence of massive poverty in Mexico, and the more recent shift to neoliberal policies has only increased the gap between rich and poor.

Poverty continues to be a serious problem for Mexico, despite significant improvements in the last two decades. Between 1992 and 2008, extreme poverty declined from about 21 percent to about 18 percent of the population, and the overall poverty rate dropped from 53 percent to 47 percent.[31] Poverty in Mexico is most pronounced in rural areas, still home to some 23 million people. Despite the legacy of land reform, most rural Mexicans cannot support themselves on their tiny plots of land, and many are forced to seek work as migrant laborers. Millions have migrated to already overcrowded urban areas, seeking employment and a better life, and millions more have immigrated to the United States for the same reasons.

Mexico's wealth is also geographically unequal. Northern Mexico is far wealthier than the central and southern regions. While the north is characterized by large-scale export agriculture (benefiting from proximity to the U.S. market), land use is much more fragmented in the south. Southern Mexico has a far poorer infrastructure, lower levels of education, and more poverty.

Another indicator of the degree of inequality in Mexico is the tremendous size and importance of the **informal sector**. It is estimated that well over one-quarter of the labor force is employed in the underground economy as informal vendors of goods and services, producing about 13 percent of Mexico's GDP. Mexican cities are full of *ambulantes* (street vendors), which local governments have fought unsuccessfully to regulate. These workers pay no taxes on their earnings but enjoy few protections or benefits.

Despite these problems Mexico has been able to decrease its levels of poverty since democratization in 2000 due to steady increases in social spending as a percentage of GDP. But efforts to increase social spending even further have been hampered by Mexico's inability to collect taxes, especially when compared with wealthier industrialized countries. Attempts to raise taxes meet with widespread skepticism, in part because Mexico's traditionally corrupt state is simply not trusted. President Peña Nieto signed a law in 2013 to increase the income tax on the wealthiest Mexicans, impose a tax on stock market profits, and reduce a whole host of tax breaks.

Despite the myriad problems facing Mexico's economy, we would be remiss if we failed to point out the biggest change in Mexico's political economy over the last two decades. Since its recovery from the economic crisis of the mid-1990s, and under the presidencies of Zedillo, Fox, Calderón, and Peña Nieto, about half of Mexico's population has entered the middle class. Several factors are responsible for this dramatic shift.[32] First, economic stability since the mid-1990s, and especially the containment of inflation, has benefited the middle class. Second, government antipoverty programs have kept many Mexicans from falling out of the middle class. The conditional cash transfer program called Oportunidades (Opportunities) gives payment to about a quarter of all Mexican families in exchange for pledges that their children remain in school and get preventive medical care. Finally, Mexico's entry into NAFTA has created a more competitive economy, lowering prices of food and consumer goods for Mexicans.

THE BATTLE OVER OIL

State ownership of oil and President Lázaro Cárdenas' slogan "The oil is ours!" became important symbols of the Mexican Revolution and Mexico's independence from foreign domination of its economy. PEMEX, the state oil company founded by Cárdenas in 1938, has played an enormous role in Mexico's economy. It is Mexico's biggest company and its biggest source of tax revenue (in 2013, taxes on its revenue funded a third of the federal budget). But PEMEX has been losing money (in 2016, it lost about $14 billion), in part because it lacks the capital and expertise to explore deep-water oil reserves in the Gulf of Mexico. As a result, oil production has steadily declined.

In 2013, President Peña Nieto signed into law a bitterly contested constitutional reform that would permit foreign and private investment in the Mexican gas and oil sector for the first time in over 70 years. In March 2014, he called the energy reform "the most important economic change in Mexico in 50 years."[33] PEMEX lost its monopoly over the sale of gasoline but now pays lower taxes to the government. The powerful National Union of Mexican Oil Workers, whose strict control over labor has hampered PEMEX's ability to hire skilled labor, no longer has seats on the PEMEX governing board. A company that for decades was run as a government agency (it was chaired by the energy minister) now has a more independent board of directors.

Current Issues in Mexico

MEXICO'S DRUG WAR: CAN THE MEXICAN STATE CONTAIN ORGANIZED CRIME?

The Mexican Revolution successfully strengthened state power and autonomy and ended endemic violence in Mexico. Yet the long domination of the PRI, its dependence on patron-client relations, its co-optation, and its electoral fraud all helped perpetuate a culture of corruption and lawlessness that now increasingly threatens the state and its capacity, autonomy, and legitimacy.

Over the past two decades, Mexico has seen an alarming rise in drug trafficking, driven by the growing market for illegal drugs north of the border and facilitated by a Mexican legal system that is both weak and corrupt. Mexico has experienced a dramatic growth of drug-related violence and a steady stream of corruption scandals involving drug money. The drug cartels are well funded, heavily armed, and often protected by local police forces and state governments. They intimidate local governments and have brutally executed politicians, police, and journalists who stand in their way. A series of investigations in 2008 implicated federal antidrug officials in the drug trade and further damaged the government's image.

Shortly after his inauguration, President Calderón called on the army to combat the cartels, and in 2009 he sent troops to replace corrupt local police forces in some cities along the U.S. border. The military response only emboldened the drug cartels, which initiated a campaign of assassination aimed at the police and antidrug authorities.

By 2017, the drug war had claimed at least an estimated 80,000 lives. Almost 90 percent of those deaths have been execution-style killings. In some areas, the rise in violent deaths has been dramatic. For example, Ciudad Juárez, on the U.S. border, had a 2010 murder rate of 229 per 100,000 inhabitants, making it more dangerous than Kandahar (Afghanistan) or Baghdad (Iraq).[34]

The Calderón and Peña Nieto administrations can boast of apprehending a number of top drug cartel leaders, but there is a vigorous debate in Mexico about whether the drug war is being or ever can be won.[35] Opinion polling in 2014 revealed strong

Mexico's Drug Cartels

A map of the areas controlled by Mexico's drug cartels. Much of Mexico is plagued by drug crime.

Source: "A Glimmer of Hope," *Economist*, November 24, 2012, www.economist.com/news/special-report/21566774-after-five-years-soaring-murder-rates-killings-have-last-begun-level/print (accessed 6/6/14).

The disappearance of 43 students in September 2014 shocked Mexican society. Their disappearance and murder appear to have been the result of collaboration between local government, police, and drug gangs, highlighting the problem of corruption and impunity in Mexico.

public support for the military campaign against drug traffickers but also showed a decline in the percentage of Mexicans who think that the campaign is making progress (only 37 percent of Mexicans now share this view).

The drug war is also compromising human rights. Although most attention in Mexico has focused on the battle between the Mexican state and drug traffickers, concern is growing about the impact of that conflict on human rights. When the mayor of a rural community cooperated with drug traffickers in the kidnapping (and presumed murder) of 43 college students in September 2014, even the most jaded observers of Mexican politics were alarmed by organized crime's penetration of local politics and law enforcement. Mexico has never had a professional, reliable police force, and corruption is particularly rampant at the state and local level.[36] As a result, presidents Calderón and López Peña have relied on the armed forces to carry out their war against drug gangs.

However, with the increased reliance on the military have come thousands of allegations of human rights abuses against civilians. According to a 2015 Human Rights Watch report, "Mexico's security forces have participated in widespread enforced disappearances since former president Calderón launched a 'war on drugs.' Members of all security forces continue to carry out disappearances during the Peña Nieto administration, in some cases, collaborating directly with criminal groups."[37]

MIGRATION

Mexicans have a long history of emigrating across the 2,000-mile border between Mexico and the United States. Mexicans have argued that the United States depends on Mexican immigrants and that the latter's right to work in the United States should be guaranteed through bilateral agreements. But many Americans have focused on the negative effects of Mexican immigration to the United States.

Why has there been such a steady flow of Mexicans into the United States? Most of them are seeking the higher standard of living in the United States, although the first wave of immigrants in the early twentieth century were also fleeing the violence of the Mexican Revolution. During the severe labor shortages of World War II, the United States established the Bracero Program, which allowed more than 4 million Mexicans to work temporarily in the United States between 1942 and 1964. Today, almost 11 million Mexicans live in the United States (about 10 percent of Mexico's total population and 4 percent of the U.S. population).

From 1965 to 1986, an estimated 5.7 million Mexicans immigrated to the United States, 81 percent of them undocumented.[38] The United States operated a de facto guest-worker program whereby border enforcement was tough enough to prevent a flood of immigration but not so strict as to prevent a steady flow of cheap and undocumented labor. The costs of illegal immigration were raised just enough that only about one in three undocumented Mexicans could be caught and returned. Most immigrants who tried to enter the United States succeeded, although not on the first try. The U.S. attempt to enforce border control was largely symbolic, and it never threatened the availability of cheap labor. The dramatic growth of undocumented Mexican immigrants, especially after the economic crisis in Mexico during the early 1980s, became a political crisis in the United States during the 1980s and 1990s. The result was the 1986 U.S. **Immigration Reform and Control Act (IRCA)**, which imposed sanctions on employers of undocumented immigrants and toughened the enforcement of immigration laws. At the same time, it provided amnesty for long-time undocumented workers and legalized about 2.3 million Mexican immigrants. In the late 1990s, however, illegal immigration continued to skyrocket. In 2006, the U.S. administration of George W. Bush proposed tougher border controls as well as measures aimed at giving legal status to more Mexicans living in the United States.

It is a near certainty that immigration will continue to be a point of contention between the United States and Mexico for years to come. Proposals by U.S. president Donald Trump to build a wall along the U.S.-Mexico border, and to force Mexico to pay for it (with a tax on Mexican exports to the United States), raised the ire of Mexican leaders. Mexico's treasury secretary, Luis Videgaray, retorted, "to build a wall between Mexico and the United States is a terrible idea. It is an idea based on ignorance, that has no basis in the reality of North American integration."[39] In January 2016, President Peña Nieto canceled a trip to Washington in protest of Trump's proposals.

Key Terms

Bracero Program (p. 598)

Calderón, Felipe (p. 576)

Carranza, Venustiano (p. 574)

Chamber of Deputies (p. 577)

Confederation of Mexican Workers (CTM) (p. 588)

Constitution of 1917 (p. 574)

Cortés, Hernán (p. 571)

criollos (p. 572)

Díaz, Porfirio (p. 572)

Federal Electoral Institute (p. 579)

Fox, Vicente (p. 575)

Immigration Reform and Control Act (IRCA) (p. 599)

import substitution industrialization (ISI) (p. 592)

informal sector (p. 595)

Labastida, Francisco (p. 575)

López Obrador, Andrés Manuel (p. 583)

López Portillo, José (p. 577)

Madero, Francisco (p. 573)

maquiladoras (p. 594)

mestizo (p. 572)

Mexican-American War (p. 572)

Mexican Revolution (p. 573)

Mexico's War of Independence (p. 572)

MORENA (National Regeneration Movement) (p. 583)

municipios (p. 580)

National Congress (p. 577)

National Supreme Court of Justice (p. 579)

North American Free Trade Agreement (NAFTA) (p. 575)

Partido Acción Nacional (PAN) (p. 575)

Partido de la Revolución Democrática (PRD) (p. 581)

Partido Revolucionario Institucional (PRI) (p. 569)

patron-client relationships (p. 582)

PEMEX (p. 593)

Peña Nieto, Enrique (p. 571)

San Andrés Peace Accords (p. 590)

secretary of government (p. 577)

secretary of the treasury (p. 577)

Senate (p. 577)

Televisa (p. 589)

Villa, Francisco (Pancho) (p. 573)

Zapata, Emiliano (p. 573)

Zapatista Army of National Liberation (EZLN) (p. 590)

Though its economy has grown significantly in recent years, Brazil continues to face extreme economic inequality. In São Paulo, Parque Real, a favela (or slum), sits next to the upscale Morumbi neighborhood.

Brazil

Why Study This Case?

What a difference five years can make! In 2011, Brazil was being hailed as a model for Latin American development. Its economy was booming, driven by commodity exports and the promise of newly discovered oil reserves. Its two-term president, Luiz Inácio Lula da Silva, of the leftist Workers' Party (PT), could boast real progress in reducing poverty and inequality due to a series of market-friendly welfare measures. Between 2002 and 2009, over 20 million Brazilians were lifted out of poverty. Brazil appeared to have weathered the 2008 global financial crisis better than most countries. Da Silva's success and popularity allowed him to anoint his protégée Dilma Rousseff as his successor, and she was elected Brazil's first female president in 2010. Brazilians were proud of the country's progress and confident about its future. Brazil became an important leader of the developing world, and its global profile was enhanced when it was announced that Brazil would host the 2014 World Cup and the 2016 Summer Olympic games.[1]

By 2016, all of that progress was called into question. Brazil's economy began to stumble due to a major drop in global commodity prices and economic mismanagement, and it was mired in its most serious economic recession since the return of democracy in the 1980s. A series of corruption scandals and protests over government spending on the World Cup and Olympic Games rocked the Rousseff government. Rousseff narrowly won reelection in 2014, but her government soon floundered amid new charges of massive corruption, massive protests, and continued economic decline. By the spring of 2016, Rousseff's approval ratings had dropped below 10 percent. In August 2016, she was impeached by Brazil's legislature on charges of manipulating government finances in order to win reelection, and she was replaced by Brazil's conservative vice president, Michel Temer, who has also been dogged by corruption allegations. To make

BRAZIL

TRINIDAD AND TOBAGO

VENEZUELA

COLOMBIA

GUYANA

SURINAME

FRENCH GUIANA

ATLANTIC OCEAN

Orinoco R.

Negro R.

Amazon R.

Manaus

Belo Monte Hydroelectric Project

Belém

Represa de Tucuruí

Fortaleza

Madeira R.

Amazon River Basin

Teresina

Recife

Xingu R.

Tocantins R.

Represa de Sobradinho

Rio Branco

PERU

Guaporé R.

BAHIA

São Francisco R.

Salvador

BOLIVIA

Brasília

MINAS GERAIS

Belo Horizonte

Paraná R.

SÃO PAULO

RIO DE JANEIRO

PARAGUAY

São Paulo

Rio de Janeiro

Curitiba

CHILE

PACIFIC OCEAN

RIO GRANDE DO SUL

Porto Alegre

ATLANTIC OCEAN

ARGENTINA

URUGUAY

N

0   200   400 mi

0   200   400 km

matters worse, Brazil's image as host of the Summer Olympic Games was threatened by construction delays, budget constraints, and the outbreak of the Zika virus.

Indeed, Brazil is a country full of paradoxes and surprises. It is the seventh-largest economy in the world and has a dynamic industrial sector. It has strikingly modern cities, such as São Paulo and Rio de Janeiro. According to the International Monetary Fund (IMF), Brazil will soon have a larger economy than the United Kingdom and is poised to become the sixth-largest economy in the world.[2] But Brazil is also plagued by some of the worst poverty, inequality, and indebtedness on the planet, and its cities are burdened by sprawling slums and violence. One Brazilian economist dubbed Brazil **Belindia** to denote this odd combination of Belgium's modernity and India's underdevelopment.[3]

Given Brazil's history of extreme inequality and endemic poverty, it might have been expected to experience a mass revolution along the lines of those in Russia, Mexico, and China. At the very least, we might have assumed a history of political violence similar to that of South Africa during apartheid. But while violence has punctuated its history, Brazil has avoided cataclysmic revolutions or civil war. For over 150 years following its independence from Portugal in 1822, Brazil alternated between weak democratic regimes dominated by economic elites and authoritarian rule, usually presided over by the military.

From 1964 to 1985, a military dictatorship quashed a growing mass movement and suspended most political freedoms. Nevertheless, Brazil experienced a gradual and remarkably peaceful transition to a more effective democracy in the mid-1980s, and today it is the world's fourth-largest democracy. Brazilian democracy is characterized by regular elections and broad civil liberties and has enabled a peaceful succession of power.

Despite this admirable political record, serious questions remain about the long-term viability of Brazilian democracy. Can a democratic regime persist amid extraordinarily high levels of economic inequality? Will the growing wave of crime and lawlessness erode confidence in democracy and the rule of law? Will Brazil's legacy of statism, clientelism, corruption, and political deadlock prevent democratic reforms?

Endowed with a gigantic and geographically insulated country and blessed with formidable natural resources, Brazilians have a strong sense of national identity that makes Brazil unlike many of its Latin American neighbors. Few would have predicted the widespread and occasionally violent movement that swept Brazil in the summer of 2013, on the eve of the World Cup. Demonstrators decried the poor quality of public services and the widespread corruption, and protested massive government spending to prepare for these international events amid continuing poverty and inequality. By 2016, that disaffection had led to the removal of the president, casting doubt about a future that once seemed so promising.

Historical Development of the State

THE RELUCTANT COLONY

Pedro Álvares Cabral first arrived in Brazil in 1500, when he was blown off course on his way to India. He claimed the territory for the Portuguese Crown, but Portugal initially paid little attention to it. Unlike the Spaniards, who encountered sophisticated empires and vast mineral wealth in their Latin American colonies, the Portuguese found the land sparsely populated (by between 1 million and 6 million indigenous Americans), and it offered no apparent mineral resources. While the Spaniards focused much of their energy on populating and exploiting their new-found territories, the Portuguese Crown continued to focus on the lucrative spice trade with the East, and it built few permanent colonies.

Despite this neglect, the Portuguese established trading posts along their new territory's coast. The early explorers discovered a hardwood that produced a valuable red dye; its Latin name was *Brasile*, for which the new territory was named. In response to incursions by the French in the 1530s, the Portuguese Crown attempted to take more permanent control of Brazil. The government doled out massive territories (often larger than Portugal itself) to *donatários* (nobles) who were willing to settle the remote land and defend it from foreigners. Brazil's first capital was established in 1549 in the northeastern coastal town of Salvador, also called Bahia.

The Portuguese Crown's decision to cultivate sugar in Brazil first transformed the colony from a backwater into a more vital part of the Portuguese Empire. Brazil had unlimited rich land on which to cultivate sugar, but it lacked the necessary labor pool. Initial attempts to enslave the indigenous population backfired: the relatively small population was quickly decimated by European-borne disease, war, and harsh treatment, and the survivors fled deep into Brazil's interior.

By the late sixteenth century, the Portuguese had come to depend on African slaves to maintain the sugar economy. From 1550 to 1850, between 3 million and 4 million African slaves were shipped to Brazil, and at that time, Brazil's African population was far larger than its tiny white minority. Almost half of all Brazilians today have some African ancestry.

Unlike the United States, Brazil soon developed a large **mulatto** population (Brazilians of a mixed white and black ancestry). Portuguese settlers also mixed with indigenous people in the interior, which resulted in a smaller but still significant *caboclo* population.

The institution of slavery turned Brazil into the world's first great plantation export economy. The slave-based sugar economy generated massive wealth for the white minority and established a pattern that persists today: a tiny (mostly white) elite controls the vast majority of wealth, while much of the population lives in poverty.

By the mid-seventeenth century, Brazil's sugar economy had begun a steady decline, caused in part by fierce competition from Spanish, French, and Dutch colonies in the Caribbean. The presence of the Portuguese Crown was relatively small and concentrated largely in the sugar-producing areas of the northeast coast.

THE GOLD AND DIAMOND BOOM AND THE RISE OF BRAZIL

The discovery of gold in the 1690s and diamonds in the 1720s forever changed the fate of Brazil. Mineral wealth was concentrated in the southeast and led to a demographic shift southward that has continued to this day; the central interior region,

TIMELINE Political Development

1500	Portuguese arrive in Brazil.
1690s	Gold is discovered.
1763	Capital transferred from Salvador to Rio de Janeiro.
1822	Pedro I declares Brazilian independence from Portugal.
1822–89	Pedro I establishes a semi-authoritarian monarchical regime.
1888	Slavery is abolished.
1889–1930	First Republic, a quasi-democratic regime, is established.
1930	Military overthrows the republic and establishes authoritarian rule.
1937–45	Rule of Getúlio Vargas's Estado Nôvo (New State), an authoritarian regime.
1945–64	Second Republic, a democratic regime, is established.
1960	The capital is transferred from Rio de Janeiro to Brasília.
1964–85	Authoritarian military regime rules Brazil.
1985	New Republic, a democratic regime, is established.
2003	Luiz Inácio Lula da Silva assumes presidency.
2011	Dilma Rousseff assumes presidency.
2016	Rousseff impeached and replaced by Vice President Michel Temer.

called Minas Gerais ("General Mines"), became the country's most populous area. The Portuguese began to establish settlements in the interior, and in 1763 the capital was moved south from Salvador to Rio de Janeiro. The eighteenth-century gold boom generated massive wealth, but much of Brazil's gold ended up in Europe.

By the end of the eighteenth century, the Portuguese Empire had weakened in the face of growing British, French, and Dutch power. The Portuguese Crown reacted by attempting to tighten its control of its Brazilian colony, imposing unpopular taxes on the colonists. These measures provoked a rebellion in the gold-mining capital of Vila Rica in 1789, but unlike the outcome of U.S. rebellion against Britain, in Brazil the Portuguese quickly crushed the uprising. Moreover, the colonial elites, frightened by Haiti's slave rebellion in 1791, were too fearful of the Afro-Brazilian majority to push for outright independence.

THE PEACEFUL CREATION OF AN INDEPENDENT BRAZILIAN STATE

Although Brazilian colonial elites did not advocate independence, the economic development spurred by mineral wealth created demands for increased autonomy and helped establish a distinct Brazilian identity. Furthermore, the colonial elites in the huge territory developed strong regional identities. Ironically, events in Europe more than colonial dissatisfaction paved the way for independence.

Napoleon Bonaparte's invasion of the Iberian Peninsula (Spain and Portugal) in 1807 was the catalyst for independence movements in Spanish America. Portugal's monarchy fled the invading French and moved the royal court to Brazil, a de facto recognition that Brazil had become the center of the Portuguese Empire. The arrival of the Portuguese monarch entailed transplanting the Portuguese state bureaucracy to Brazil, and Rio de Janeiro soon became a modern, cosmopolitan capital. Recognizing the importance of its colony, King João VI designated Brazil a kingdom, coequal with Portugal. The king returned to Portugal in 1821 after the end of the Napoleonic Wars, but he left his son Pedro on the Brazilian throne with instructions to support independence.

In this unusual manner, Pedro I became the leader of Brazil's transition to independence and spared the country the kind of bloody wars experienced by much of Spanish America. Pedro I declared Brazil's independence on September 7, 1822, and Portugal offered little resistance. Without its own armed forces, and facing the prospect of rebellion by powerful regional elites, Brazil depended heavily on the British, who quickly became its major trading partner.

Emperor Pedro I promulgated a constitution in 1824 and did not behave as an absolutist monarch. Nevertheless, the constitution was essentially authoritarian with a very strong executive. In 1826, Pedro I inherited the Portuguese throne from his father, and shortly thereafter he returned to Portugal, leaving his own son, Pedro II, on the Brazilian throne. Pedro I's official abdication in 1830 greatly weakened the power of the central state and further enhanced the power of regional elites. Pedro II formally assumed the throne in 1840 from a caretaker regency when he was only 14 years old, and he ruled Brazil until 1889.

Brazil's peaceful independence movement and the presence of reasonably enlightened monarchs during the nineteenth century were crucial for solidifying the Brazilian national identity and, most important, stemming the countless regional rebellions that plagued the country during its first half-century of statehood. Under the empire (1822–89), the foundations were laid for a strong central state dominated by the monarch. Brazil was also fortunate to find a new export product to replace sugar and minerals: coffee cultivation began in the 1820s in central and southern Brazil, further drawing economic development southward toward the coffee capital of São Paulo. Bolstered by the importation of slaves (which continued until the British banned the slave trade in 1850), Brazil quickly became the world's leading coffee producer.

Although the emperor opposed slavery, the Brazilian state did little to end it, largely because the economy depended so heavily on slave labor. When the monarchy finally decreed the abolition of slavery in 1888, the conservative Brazilian rural elite begrudgingly accepted the new reality rather than risk a U.S.-style civil war. Slave labor was partly replaced by a massive influx of immigration from Europe.

REPUBLICANISM AND THE CONTINUATION OF OLIGARCHIC DEMOCRACY

Brazil's military overthrew the monarchy, established the First Republic (1889–1930), and turned the republic over to civilian political elites (oligarchs). Although the monarchy was abolished and a constitutional democracy was established, political power continued to be held tightly by a somewhat expanded political elite. At the state level, the governorships were controlled by economic oligarchs and their network of local bosses. Presidents selected their successors and then used a vast web of patronage and clientelism to deliver the vote.

During the First Republic, the state governments—particularly the most important states of São Paulo, Minas Gerais, Rio de Janeiro, and Rio Grande do Sul—became more powerful at the expense of the federal government. The weak federal government and the decentralization of power suited Brazil's powerful economic interests. The elitist nature of the republic alienated people in the growing urban middle class, who sought increased participation; the nascent industrial working class in São Paulo, who sought the creation of a welfare state; and immigrants, who were inspired by radical European ideologies. Demands for political and economic reform were met with harsh repression. New forces of opposition weakened the First Republic, but the increased infighting among regional leaders was the root cause of the regime's failure.

GETÚLIO VARGAS AND THE NEW STATE

In October 1930, the military once again intervened in politics, this time to end the First Republic. Military leaders installed **Getúlio Vargas**, an elite politician from Rio Grande do Sul who had been a losing candidate for the presidency. Vargas acted quickly to enhance the power of the federal government, replacing elected governors with his appointees. In 1933, a new constitution reduced the autonomy of individual states while maintaining the elected president and Congress. Vargas broke his pledge to hold democratic elections and, in 1937, created a new dictatorial regime he called the **Estado Nôvo** (New State).

The Estado Nôvo was clearly inspired by fascist Italy and Germany, whose regimes featured a strong, authoritarian central state, and by Franklin Roosevelt's New Deal policies. But Vargas is best viewed more as a typical Latin American than as a fascist or social democrat. Unlike both the monarchy and the First Republic, which largely catered to the agricultural elite, Vargas's bases of support included the urban industrialists, middle-class professionals, workers, and sectors of the military.

The authoritarian Estado Nôvo was responsible for some of the first protections and welfare benefits for Brazil's urban workers, and Vargas's regime mobilized labor and raised wages. Vargas established state firms to promote industrialization in key sectors, such as steel, and imposed protectionist policies to shield Brazilian industry from foreign competition (such as import substitution industrialization, or ISI). As a result, Brazil experienced an industrial boom after 1930. Vargas also modernized and professionalized the Brazilian military.

After 1945, pressure mounted for Vargas to convene free elections. In the aftermath of World War II, during which Brazil had sent troops to help defeat fascism in Europe, dictatorships fell out of favor. In October 1945, Brazil's military, emboldened by its enhanced role in the dictatorship and its successful contribution to the Allied war effort, deposed Vargas and convened elections.

THE DEMOCRATIC EXPERIMENT: MASS POLITICS IN THE SECOND REPUBLIC

During the Second Republic (1945–64), Brazilians had their first real taste of democracy, and for the first time there was real competition for control of the state. The Brazilian masses, mobilized by Vargas during the Estado Nôvo, had become a force to be reckoned with. Suffrage was expanded dramatically (though only about one-fifth of the electorate participated during elections), and new national parties, including the Communist Party of Brazil, attempted to appeal to voters.

In 1950, Vargas, the former dictator, was elected to the presidency in a deeply polarized election. He attempted to continue the populist policies of the Estado Nôvo, but a vigorous opposition that controlled the legislature and the press stymied his policy proposals. In 1954, Vargas broke the deadlock by resigning, and shortly thereafter stunned the nation by committing suicide.

In the aftermath of Vargas's death, one of his followers, Juscelino Kubitschek, was elected president. Often considered Brazil's greatest president, Kubitschek was responsible for a number of grandiose public works, including the moving of Brazil's capital from Rio de Janeiro, on the coast, to Brasília, deep in the interior.

BREAKDOWN OF DEMOCRACY AND MILITARIZATION OF THE STATE

Following Vargas's dictatorship, democracy was established but never consolidated. Brazil's democracy was deeply polarized between supporters and opponents of Vargas's populist policies. Opponents of Vargas and his successors called on the military to end democracy to prevent a return to populism; they also sought to reduce the role of the state in the economy. Supporters of Vargas and his successors viewed Brazil's democracy as weak, ineffective, and beholden to the country's wealthy elite. They increasingly advocated leftist policies that called for a growth in the state's role in the economy through a wave of nationalizations.

This political polarization crystallized during the presidency of **João Goulart** (1961–64), a minister of labor under Vargas. In the context of the Cold War, the military and many on the right viewed Goulart as a dangerous leftist and a potential dictator who reminded them too much of Vargas. His term began inauspiciously, for the military insisted that the Brazilian legislature curtail the president's power before allowing him to take office. But Goulart spent much of his first years in power, and a great deal of political capital, in passing a national referendum that restored his full powers and deeply alarmed his opponents. A severe economic crisis caused by rampant inflation and growing debt exacerbated political tensions. In 1964, after Goulart attempted to rally workers and peasants to his defense and after he clumsily alienated the military by backing some mutinous officers, the Brazilian military, with U.S. support, once again seized power.

The military had intervened in Brazilian politics six times since 1889, but in each instance, soldiers had quickly retreated to their barracks, leaving politics to civilian leaders. By 1964, the Brazilian military believed it was time to take control of the state and hold onto it. Encouraged by the United States and politicians on the right, Brazilian military leaders thought they possessed the leadership skills to preserve political order, the power to prevent a feared Communist revolution, and the technical skills to run the economy.

Brazilian military leaders presided over a regime that has often been described as **bureaucratic authoritarian**.[4] Military leaders suspended the constitution and then decreed a new authoritarian one, banned existing parties and replaced them with two official ones to contest local and congressional elections (eliminating direct

History of Brazilian Regimes

REGIME	YEARS	TYPE	OUTCOME
Empire	1822–89	Quasi-democratic constitutional monarchy	Military coup
First Republic	1889–1930	Quasi-democratic republic	Military coup
Provisional government	1930–37	Authoritarian republic	Getúlio Vargas seizes power with military backing
Estado Nôvo	1937–45	Authoritarian republic	Military coup
Second Republic	1945–64	Democratic republic	Military coup
Military regime	1964–85	Military dictatorship	Controlled, negotiated transition
New Republic	1985–present	Democratic republic	

elections for governors and the president), took control of trade unions, and severely restricted civil liberties. They sought to erase for good the populist legacy of Vargas. The office of the president, a post held by a series of military leaders, issued numerous decrees that gradually stripped the political system of its democratic features. Torture, disappearances, and exile became commonplace.

Although it initially attempted to reduce the role of the state in the economy, the Brazilian military eventually adopted policies of state-led industrialization that were in many ways a continuation of Vargas's statism. The state spent lavishly on major infrastructure projects, including hydroelectric dams, a paved highway to penetrate the Amazon rain forest, and even a nuclear power program. Military rule coincided with a period of sustained spectacular economic growth (1968–74) that averaged over 10 percent growth annually—a period known as the "economic miracle."

GRADUAL DEMOCRATIZATION AND THE MILITARY'S RETURN TO THE BARRACKS

The period immediately following the economic miracle, however, featured an economic crisis and growing domestic opposition. In response, the military slowly began to loosen its political grip on the country while maintaining ultimate control. This process coincided with the global energy crisis that hit Brazil particularly hard, raising its already high level of international debt. Inflation skyrocketed to levels that exceeded those under Goulart. The "official" opposition party tolerated by the regime became more vigorous in its call for regime change and more successful in legislative elections.

The military's carefully laid plans for controlling the transition unraveled in 1984, when members of the pro-military party in the legislature unexpectedly backed a civilian democratic reform candidate, Tancredo Neves. He died shortly after his election and was replaced by the more conservative José Sarney, but the momentum of political reform could not be stopped. In 1987, a constituent assembly was elected to write a new democratic constitution that was formally adopted in 1988.

Political Regime

POLITICAL INSTITUTIONS

Brazil has been a democracy since the adoption of its current constitution in 1988. The constitution was written in the waning days of the country's authoritarian regime and made important compromises in a number of areas.

THE CONSTITUTION In many ways, the current constitution is similar to that of the Second Republic. However, in reacting to the long period of authoritarian rule, the constitution's framers established a set of rights that could not be amended or curtailed—for example, the principles of federalism, the separation of powers, and certain individual rights. Compared with previous documents, the current constitution imposes very strict limits and controls on the government's ability to declare a state of siege and thus limit civil liberties during wartime. Constitutional amendments are possible and can be initiated by the legislature (if one-third of the members of either house agree), the state legislatures (if a majority agrees), or the president. Such amendments can pass only with the support of separate two-thirds-majority votes in both houses of the legislature.

THE BRANCHES OF GOVERNMENT

THE PRESIDENT Brazilian presidents act as both head of government and head of state. The president and a vice president are elected for four-year terms and may serve a second term.[5] The Brazilian president has the power of line-item vetoes, allowing for rejection of select aspects of legislation. The president has the power to initiate and push legislation through the legislature (about 80 percent of all legislation is initiated by the president) and is the only individual capable of initiating budgetary legislation. While presidents may veto legislation, these vetoes can be overridden by

---

INFOCUS **Essential Political Features**

- **Legislative–executive system**: Presidential
- **Legislature**: Congresso Nacional (National Congress)
  - **Lower house**: Câmara dos Deputados (Chamber of Deputies)
  - **Upper house**: Senado Federal (Federal Senate)
- **Unitary or federal division of power**: Federal
- **Main geographic subunits**: Estados (states)
- **Electoral system for lower house**: Proportional representation
- **Chief judicial body**: Supremo Tribunal Federal (Federal Supreme Court), Tribunal Superior Eleitoral (Supreme Electoral Court), and the Superior de Justiça (Supreme Court of Justice)

Former president Dilma Rousseff (on the right) was impeached in 2016, when the legislature ruled that she had illegally concealed Brazil's budget deficits. She was replaced by her conservative vice-president Michel Temer (left), who almost immediately became the target of corruption investigations.

a simple majority in both houses of the legislature. Presidents may issue decrees, but the legislature can overturn them; decrees become law for only 30 days unless adopted by the legislature.

However, the formal power of Brazilian presidents has to date been weakened by fragmentation of the legislature. Brazilian heads of government need to patch together legislative majorities from fractious and poorly disciplined political parties. Faced with the lack of legislative majorities, Brazilian presidents have often resorted to legislating by emergency decree, thereby circumventing the legislature altogether.[6]

Perhaps the greatest power of Brazilian presidents comes from their ability to make appointments to the cabinet and top levels of Brazil's vast bureaucracy. Brazilian presidents have used this power to build legislative coalitions, but it has also helped to reinforce Brazil's long tradition of patrimonialism and corruption. The massive corruption scandals implicating much of Brazil's political system, and the impeachment of Rousseff in 2016, seem to fall in line with this tradition.

THE LEGISLATURE Brazil's legislature, the **National Congress (Congresso Nacional)**, is composed of two houses with equal power. The 513-member **Chamber of Deputies (Câmara dos Deputados)** is the lower house (whose members are elected to four-year terms), and the 81-member **Federal Senate (Senado Federal)** is the upper house (whose members are elected for eight-year terms). There are no term limits for members of either house.

Both houses must approve all legislation before it is sent to the president; when the houses disagree on legislation, they convene joint committees to iron out differences. The legislature can override presidential vetoes with a majority vote of both houses and can, with a two-thirds vote in both houses, amend the constitution with the agreement of the president. As in the United States, the Senate has the power to

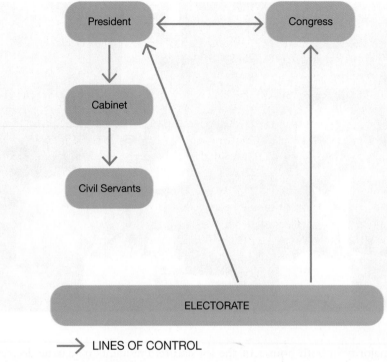

LINES OF CONTROL

Structure of the Government

---

try a president or cabinet members for impeachable offenses and must approve top presidential appointments.

The actual power of the Brazilian legislature is a complex matter. On the one hand, legislators do not play a key role in most policy making. This situation exists for many reasons, including the dominance of the president, the weakness of the political parties, the individualism of legislators, and the relatively weak committee system. A persistent problem limiting the effectiveness of the legislature has been an inability to reach a quorum on key matters. Legislators often view their jobs as stepping-stones to more prestigious and lucrative occupations, such as state governorships or top bureaucratic posts.

On the other hand, the constitution allocates significant power to Congress, and Brazil's legislature has played an important if not leading role from time to time.[7] Several high-profile congressional hearings (called *parliamentary commissions of investigation*) have exposed fraud and corruption, even at the highest level of government. In 1992, Congress impeached President Fernando Collor de Mello on corruption charges, forcing his resignation. In 2010 and 2011, Congress conducted several high-profile investigations of government behavior.[8] Most recently, the Chamber of Deputies voted for impeachment hearings against President Dilma Rousseff, and the Senate convicted her by a 61–20 vote.

THE JUDICIARY Along with the legislature and executive branches, the judiciary is the third branch of government in Brazil. At the highest level is the **Federal Supreme Court (Supremo Tribunal Federal)**, whose 11 justices are appointed by the president and approved by a majority vote in the Senate for a term not to exceed 30 years. This court has the final say on all constitutional questions. The 30 judges of the Supreme Court of Justice, Brazil's highest criminal court, are similarly appointed and approved, and they also serve no more than 30 years.

The Federal Supreme Court has gained a reputation for independence since the return of democracy, but it has also been swamped by a huge caseload. (Recent reforms have attempted to ameliorate this problem by limiting the scope of cases that the Federal Supreme Court can consider.) The president, state governors, and the leadership of the legislature, among others, can petition the Federal Supreme Court to rule on the constitutionality of laws, further adding to the backlog of cases.

Brazil's federal judicial structure is replicated at the state and local levels. The court system also features a Supreme Electoral Court (Tribunal Superior Eleitoral), an increasingly common institution in developing countries, designed to prevent fraud. Most observers agree that elections in Brazil have been remarkably transparent and fair, largely because of the Electoral Court. The Court has become increasingly active, and has on numerous occasions removed state governors accused of using their official powers to win reelection.

Historically, the Brazilian judiciary has enjoyed less power than its U.S. counterpart, and the Federal Supreme Court has been reluctant to challenge the ongoing use of presidential emergency decrees. However, during his first term, President da Silva enacted a series of measures that gave the higher courts more power, especially the provision that made their decisions binding on lower-level courts. Brazil's judiciary has taken the lead in the investigation and prosecution of those involved in the massive corruption scandal at the state oil company, Petrobras. At the lower levels, the Brazilian legal system is regularly criticized as beholden to economic elites and riddled with corruption. Many poor citizens feel that they cannot be fairly represented within the system, and most Brazilians think there is little or no equality before the law.[9] One survey reported that about 40 percent of Brazilians believe it is possible to bribe a judge.[10] Brazil's judiciary is overworked and underfunded, and it has been estimated that two-fifths of prison inmates are awaiting trial.[11]

THE ELECTORAL SYSTEM

Brazil's electoral system is largely to blame for the multiplicity of relatively weak and loosely disciplined parties that make governing the country so difficult. For senate races, the three candidates with the most votes win seats. But the electoral system used for Brazil's lower house (and for all state legislatures) is unusual and controversial. It uses a system, called **open-list proportional representation (PR)**, in which citizens vote for a specific individual on a party list (rather than simply for the entire party list, as is done in normal closed-list PR systems). Votes for each party (and for candidates associated with each party) are then tallied, and seats are allocated to each party proportionally. However, the determination of how seats are allocated to individual party members is based on the number of votes those members receive. Candidates must therefore campaign under their own names (not just their party labels) and have an incentive to promote their own candidacies at the expense of their party colleagues.

The open-list PR system weakens the power of political parties and the ability of those parties to enforce internal discipline. The parties are further fragmented because state-level parties, not the federal party hierarchy, determine the composition of party lists. The tendency has been for individual candidates to seek the backing of powerful state-level politicians, further enhancing Brazil's tradition of clientelism and pork-barrel politics. Moreover, unlike many systems that employ PR, Brazil has no threshold for gaining seats, which means that even the smallest political parties can easily gain representation in the legislature. Indeed, according to measures of the numbers of parties and their relative size, Brazil has the world's most fragmented party system.[12]

While Brazil's electoral system for the legislature makes it hard to form legislative majorities, its system of electing presidents guarantees that presidents enjoy majority support. If no candidate wins a majority of the vote in the first round (which has been the norm since 1985), a second round of balloting takes place between the top two first-round contenders.

Districts for both houses of the legislature are the 26 states plus the federal district. For the lower house, the number of legislators per district is determined roughly according to population and ranges from a low of 8 to a maximum of 70. This minimum allocation has overrepresented the least populated (and most conservative) sectors of Brazil and has underrepresented urban Brazil, but attempts to change the allocation have been blocked by representatives of all parties from the overrepresented regions.[13] Because each Brazilian state also sends three senators to Congress, this system has, as in the United States, added to the overrepresentation of sparsely populated, rural, and generally more conservative states.

LOCAL GOVERNMENT

Brazil is a large and diverse country, and since colonial times there has been tension between control by the federal government and the desire for regional autonomy. Brazil's new democracy has firmly reestablished the principle of **robust federalism**, and Brazilian federalism devolves more power to the states than most other federal systems.[14]

Each of Brazil's 26 states (plus the federal district) has an elected governor and a unicameral legislature. Since 1997, governors can be reelected to a second term. Brazilian states are further divided into more than 5,000 *municípios* ("municipalities"), similar to U.S. counties, that are governed by elected mayors and elected councils. Brazilian states have historically owned their own banks and have even run some industries. The constitution allocates to state and local governments a huge chunk of all federal tax revenue. State governors have been largely free to spend as they please, and many states have run up huge debts with the federal government. Brazil differs from most other federal systems in that the constitution of 1988 does not spell out specific spending responsibilities in areas such as health and education.

Over time, the federal government has gradually reasserted itself vis-à-vis the states, intervening in (and in some cases privatizing) the state banking systems. The federal government forced some states to sell state-owned utilities and rein in state spending. During the two terms of President Cardoso, states and municipalities were forced to assume a greater portion of welfare spending. Nevertheless, much of Brazilian politics can still be seen as the politics of the governors; Brazilian presidents must negotiate with powerful state governors, much as they must bargain with Brazil's fractious legislature.

OTHER INSTITUTIONS

THE MILITARY AND THE POLICE We have seen that Brazil's military played an important role in its domestic politics. From the late nineteenth century until 1964, the military acted mainly as an arbiter, intervening in politics to depose leaders it found unacceptable and then returning to the barracks, handing power over to the civilians.

Indeed, Brazil's democratic transition in the 1970s was led mostly by the military, which after two decades of rule was eager to leave economic problems to the civilians to solve. Because military leaders controlled the transition to democracy, there were no attempts to bring Brazilian military officials to justice for destroying democracy or for engaging in widespread human rights abuses. The military was able to pressure the transitional government to pass a widespread amnesty for members of the armed forces.[15]

As a result, Brazil's military continues to be a powerful arm of the state and has far more autonomy than the military in most other advanced democracies. Article 142 of the constitution calls on the military to guarantee law and order. At the same time, democratic governments, beginning with that of President Collor de Mello, have cut military budgets, purged military leaders most closely connected to the authoritarian regime, redeployed troops away from population centers, and removed the military from cabinet and top bureaucratic posts. Some Brazilians who were victims of the military's human rights abuses have received compensation, and the resulting publicity has further eroded the image of the military.

After decades of military resistance, President Dilma Rousseff, who was jailed and tortured during the military regime, swore in a seven-member Truth Commission in 2011. In December 2014, the Commission produced a final report documenting 434 political murders and thousands more cases of torture and other abuses. It recommended that 100 military perpetrators still living be tried for human rights violations, but these recommendations have not been acted upon, and the Brazilian military refuses to apologize for its behavior during the military dictatorship.

Brazil's police forces, however, have continued to be a subject of concern among human rights experts, who have noted the high levels of "state violence" perpetrated against Brazil's poorest citizens. State governments control their own civil police forces (which mainly investigate crimes) and military police forces (which are uniformed and armed). The military police, like the military itself, are governed by their own judicial system, which has in practice allowed the police to act outside the law. Off-duty officers are often hired by business owners to kill homeless street dwellers, and many of the dead have been children. The large number of such killings has exceeded the number of deaths caused by the military during the two decades of authoritarian rule, leading one observer to call Brazil an "ugly democracy."[16]

Political Conflict and Competition

THE PARTY SYSTEM AND ELECTIONS

Brazil's party system has perhaps been the most vilified aspect of the country's democratic regime. Brazil has a fragmented multiparty system with weak and fickle political parties, due largely to the electoral laws described earlier.[17] Twenty-eight parties currently hold seats in the lower house of the legislature, and seven gained over 5 percent of the vote in the 2014 election. Opinion research consistently shows extremely low levels of party identification and low public confidence in parties.[18] The weakness of political parties complicates presidents' attempts to find a majority to support their legislative proposals. Before she was forced to step down in 2016, President Rousseff presided over an informal coalition of nine parties. Presidents' need to bargain regularly with a number of parties has only increased the pork-barrel aspects of the Brazilian political system and has often made it hard to implement tough decisions, such as reductions in state spending. It has also contributed to the numerous corruption scandals that have plagued the legislature. Since her party had so few seats in the legislature, when Rousseff lost the support of her major coalition partners, she was easily impeached.

Historically, Brazil's parties have been highly personalistic—based on the leadership of a powerful or charismatic individual instead of on an ideology. Today, the weakness of those parties' ideological components is evident in the large number of party members who, after being elected, change affiliation or leave to create new parties.[19] This activity has occurred most often after the election of a president from another party, prompting legislators to switch to the governing party to ensure their access to patronage.

Another serious problem is the sheer number of political parties and their lack of internal discipline. In 2014, the biggest party, President Rousseff's Workers' Party (PT), was in fact quite small: it won only 14 percent of the vote and about the same percentage of seats in the Chamber of Deputies. Legislators respond far more to local barons, government incentives, and pork-barrel opportunities than to their party leadership. Since Brazilian electoral laws allow candidates to run as members of a party without approval of the party leadership (in Brazil, any elected member of the legislature is guaranteed a place on the ballot in the following election), there is little incentive for party loyalty. Moreover, Brazil's powerful federalism further weakens party cohesion: it is common for legislators to vote across party lines with members of their state delegations to support legislation of local interest.

Given the large number of political parties, it is not surprising that Brazilian parties run the gamut from right to left.

THE BRAZILIAN LEFT The Workers' Party (PT) is Latin America's most important party of the left and has been the most important Brazilian political party since the election of da Silva in 2002.[20] It was founded in 1980 mainly among unionized industrial workers but has grown to incorporate landless workers, rural unions, and other disaffected Brazilians. It has also attracted significant support from educated middle-class Brazilians. It claims to represent Brazil's poor, and it advocates social democracy. Compared with most of Brazil's parties, the PT has practiced a high degree of internal democracy and has had fewer defections and splits, although the

Composition of the Brazilian Legislature after the 2014 Elections

PARTY	CHAMBER OF DEPUTIES		SENATE	
	# OF SEATS	% OF SEATS	# OF SEATS	% OF SEATS
PT*	70	13.6	12	14.8
PMDB*	66	12.8	18	22.2
PSDB	54	10.5	10	12.3
PSD*	37	7.2	3	3.7
PP*	36	7.0	5	6.1
PR*	34	6.6	4	4.9
PSB	34	6.6	7	8.6
DEM	22	4.2	5	6.1
Others	160	31.5	17	21.3
Total	513	100	81	100

*Parties that supported the government of President Dilma Rousseff until her impeachment.

Key to Party Acronyms:

DEM: Democrats

PMDB: Party of the Brazilian Democratic Movement

PP: Progressive Party

PR: Party of the Republic

PSB: Brazilian Socialist Party

PSD: Social Democratic Party

PSDB: Brazilian Social Democracy Party

PT: Workers' Party

Sources: www2.camara.leg.br/camaranoticias/noticias/POLITICA/475427-PT-E-PMDB-ELEGEM-NOVAMENTE
-AS-MAIORES-BANCADAS.html and http://g1.globo.com/politica/eleicoes/2014/blog/eleicao-em-numeros/post
/pt-e-pmdb-encolhem-mas-mantem-maiores-bancadas-no-congresso-psdb-cresce-na-camara.html (accessed
12/3/14).

party has always had radical and more moderate factions. Da Silva was elected in 2002 partly on the PT's reputation for honesty and clean government. That reputation was badly tarnished, however, by a series of corruption scandals in 2005 and 2006. A large number of corruption scandals, discontent over public spending to support Brazil's hosting of the World Cup and Olympic Games, and a slowing economy led voters to punish the PT in 2014. Not only did the party lose votes and seats in elections to both houses of Congress, but President Rousseff also won reelection by a very narrow margin over her center-right opponent. The future of the PT is very much in doubt since Rousseff was impeached and her predecessor, da Silva, was convicted on charges of corruption in 2017.

Despite its roots as a radical working-class party, the PT has clearly established itself in government as a moderate center-left force. Given the fragmentation of the Brazilian party system, Presidents da Silva and Rousseff were forced to ally with parties to the right of the PT, and this helped pull the PT to the political center.

Brazil has numerous other leftist parties, and only some have supported the PT. For example, the Democratic Labor Party (PDT) was founded late in the

Brazilian military dictatorship by the brother-in-law of João Goulart, the leftist president deposed by the military in 1964, and it has been a steady ally of the PT.

THE BRAZILIAN CENTER The two main centrist parties are the Party of the Brazilian Democratic Movement (PMDB) and the Brazilian Social Democracy Party (PSDB). Both parties include a mix of free-market conservatives and social democrats, and neither has a clear ideological orientation. The PMDB was the most important pro-democracy opposition party in the years of the transition and played a critical role in the move toward direct elections and a new constitution. Today, the PMDB is a classical "catchall" political party, best viewed as a pragmatic coalition of regional party bosses. More than any Brazilian party, it is a party based on clientelism. It is currently the biggest party in the legislature; it has almost twice as many members as the PT; and it controls the largest number of governorships, state legislatures, and local governments. The PMDB has had cabinet positions in most governments since the return of democracy and was an important, though ultimately unreliable, ally of presidents da Silva and Rousseff. Under Rousseff, the vice president and the heads of both houses of Congress were PMDB members. Vice President Michel Temer became president in April 2016, when Rousseff was impeached, due in large part to PMDB votes against her. Despite the tremendous political clout of the PMDB, Temer is the first PMDB member to become president since 1985. However, like the PT, the PMDB has been dogged by allegations of corruption. In July 2016, the PMDB's Eduardo Cunha was forced to resign as speaker of the lower house over allegations that he had accepted millions of dollars in bribes (he was sentenced to 15 years in prison in 2017), and numerous other party members, including President Temer, have been accused of corruption. Since taking office, Temer has had some success passing economic austerity measures, but he has also been accused of being out of touch with Brazilian society, and his cabinet included no women or Afro-Brazilians. By June 2017 his approval rating had plummeted to 7 percent, lower than any approval rating given to his predecessor, Dilma Rousseff.

The PSDB is the party of former two-term president **Fernando Henrique Cardoso**. Cardoso and other prominent PMDB members bolted to form the PSDB in protest over the PMDB's patron-client politics. The PSDB initially distinguished itself as a social-democratic alternative to the PMDB, but since Cardoso's two terms in office, it has been more closely associated with free-market reforms. Its presidential candidates in the 2010 and 2014 presidential election lost to Dilma Rousseff in the second round of voting. The PSDB is the third biggest party in the legislature, and it controls five governorships. Together with the DEM, discussed next, the PSDB has become a mainstay of the opposition.

THE BRAZILIAN RIGHT The most important party of the right, the Democrats (DEM; called the Liberal Front Party until 2007) grew out of the two "official" parties tolerated during the military regime. The DEM is a free-market, pro-business party, differing from parties of the center mainly in its opposition to land reform and its conservative stand on social issues. The DEM is currently the fourth-largest party in the legislature and in recent years has been in opposition, allied with centrist parties. It has been one of the strongest critics of the center-left governments of the PT.

In 2011, a faction of the party broke away to form the Social Democratic Party (PSD), and while it is a center-right party like the DEM, since its creation it has formed part of the government's legislative majority. A number of smaller parties of the right regularly win seats in the legislature. The Progressive Party (PP) has its roots among the supporters of Brazil's military regime and is a free-market, pro-business party. Nevertheless, like the PSD, the PP has been a willing legislative ally of the current leftist government. The Party of the Republic (PR) has drawn a lot of support from Brazilian evangelicals.

OTHER PARTIES Many citizens of advanced democracies think about Brazil mainly because of concern about its large Amazon rain forest. However, environmentalism has yet to become a strong movement in Brazil. The Green Party (PV), led by Marina Silva, won under 4 percent of the vote and 15 deputies in the lower house in 2010. Silva is a well-known environmental activist who was President da Silva's minister of the environment from 2003 to 2008, when she resigned in protest over the PT's weak commitment to environmental issues. More recently, Silva joined the center-left Brazilian Socialist Party (PSB) and agreed to run for vice president in 2014 on the PSB ticket. When the PSB's presidential candidate died in a plane crash, she took his place and won almost a quarter of the vote in the first round of elections. The Green Party suffered from Silva's defection, winning only 2 percent of the vote and losing almost half its lower house seats in the 2014 legislative elections.

CIVIL SOCIETY

After the return to democracy, activism in urban and rural trade unions grew quickly. The growth of decentralized Protestant religious groups, many with a conservative political agenda, helped to reinvigorate civil society. A host of environmental, human rights, and women's groups emerged as well. Opinion research shows that well over half of Brazilians say they belong to some sort of civil society organization.[21] In short, Brazil has a vibrant civil society.

Former president Rousseff laments that widespread protests in the summer of 2013 hurt Brazil's image as it prepared to host the 2014 World Cup.

Brazil's largest social movement is the Landless Workers Movement (MST), a peasant organization that has fought for land reform. It has advocated legal change but has often supported and even organized peasant seizure of uncultivated, privately owned land.[22] This activism has been opposed, often violently, by Brazil's powerful landlords, often with the support of the police forces and the tacit tolerance of the rural courts. Hundreds of MST workers have been killed for trying to address Brazil's extremely unequal landholding patterns. Still, MST pressure has resulted in a major redistribution of land to peasants.

Despite centuries of church support for the most conservative elements of Brazilian society, the Roman Catholic Church in Brazil played an essential role in mobilizing civil society to protest the military regime. Spurred by changes in Rome, especially the Second Vatican Council (1962-65), much of the Brazilian Catholic Church, including some of the hierarchy, embraced a new interpretation of the role of religion. Liberation theology, which developed in the 1960s among a group of Catholic intellectuals that included numerous Brazilians, held that the church should use its power and prestige to teach the poor how to improve their lives immediately, in both physical and spiritual terms.

Society

ETHNIC AND NATIONAL IDENTITY

Brazil has an extremely diverse population that has emerged from a blending of Native Americans, African slaves, and Europeans. Unlike much of Spanish America and the United States during their colonial periods, a significant amount of intermarriage took place among racial groups in Brazil. Today, around 40 percent of Brazilians consider themselves to be of mixed race, and 80 percent claim some African ancestry.

Brazilians have a complex vocabulary to describe the rainbow of skin colors, ranging from *preto* ("black") to *mulato claro* ("light brown"). Despite the Brazilian myth of racial democracy, there is an extremely strong association between skin color and wealth. Wealthy Brazilians tend to be lighter skinned, and blacks are

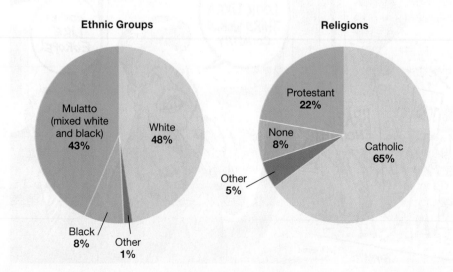

Ethnic Groups

Mulatto (mixed white and black)
43%

White
48%

Black
8%

Other
1%

Religions

Protestant
22%

None
8%

Other
5%

Catholic
65%

disproportionately present among Brazil's poor.[23] Relatively few blacks are found at the highest level of business or government. Blacks or mixed-race Brazilians are twice as likely to be unemployed, and whites earn on average 57 percent more than do Brazilians of color.[24]

Race was not a prominent political topic in Brazil until President Fernando Henrique Cardoso brought it to the national agenda in the 1990s. He began a national dialogue on affirmative action before and during his administration. Cardoso enacted measures to redress the problem, including quotas for Afro-Brazilians in some government ministries and the diplomatic corps. The most controversial aspect of affirmative action in Brazil has been the imposition of admissions quotas for Afro-Brazilians at some public universities.[25] Racially based admissions quotas were first attempted in 2001, when the state of Rio de Janeiro adopted a 40 percent quota for state universities. A federal Law of Social Quotas passed in 2012 required all federal universities to reserve spots for students of African descent. Today, over 70 percent of public universities have some sort of affirmative action policy.

Racial quotas have provoked fierce debate within Brazil. Critics say it is virtually impossible to know who is black in a country where 80 percent of Brazilians have some African ancestry. They believe that affirmative action policies would be more widely accepted and more effective if they were more flexible and targeted poor Brazilians regardless of race. Defenders of quotas point to the dramatic increase in blacks at universities that formerly were mostly white. They argue that the debate about racial discrimination is healthy and long overdue.

Brazil has also become a religiously diverse country after centuries of domination by the Roman Catholic Church. While the vast majority of Brazilians claim to be Catholic, Brazil has seen an extraordinary explosion of Protestants, especially from Pentecostal movements, over the past two decades. In addition, many Brazilians (even white Brazilians) practice one of several Afro-Brazilian religions, such as Macumba, Candomblé, or Umbanda, often in addition to Catholicism.

IDEOLOGY AND POLITICAL CULTURE

In the early years after Brazil's return to democracy, surprisingly large percentages of Brazilians expressed support for authoritarian rule, but the economic growth and redistribution over the last decade has changed the way Brazilians view democracy. In 2015, despite massive corruption scandals and widespread protests against the government, 69 percent of Brazilians reported that democracy was preferable to any other system; this figure has increased from only 30 percent in 2001.

Brazilians have fluctuated in their overall satisfaction with democracy. In 2001, only 20 percent were very or somewhat satisfied with democracy in Brazil, but that figure rose to 50 percent in 2010.[26] More recently, however, satisfaction with democracy has plummeted—in 2015, only 21 percent of Brazilians surveyed expressed satisfaction. Since then, numerous corruption scandals and the impeachment of Rousseff have led to even more dissatisfaction with Brazil's democracy.

Despite massive inequalities, Brazil's citizens are not deeply polarized in terms of their ideology. Relatively few Brazilians identify themselves as being on the far left or right, and the vast majority of Brazilians locate their ideology as being center, center-right, or center-left.[27]

Labor Force by Occupation

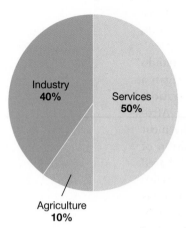

Industry
40%

Services
50%

Agriculture
10%

Political Economy

Over the years, Brazil's state, through the implementation of import substitution industrialization policies, has played a major role in the economy by limiting imports, regulating credit and wages, controlling the currency, and even owning and operating sectors of the economy. Statist policies have often resulted in spectacular economic growth, as was the case during the so-called economic miracle (1967–73), when annual growth rates averaged 11 percent. But statist policies have also been blamed for a number of problems that have long plagued the Brazilian economy.

Perhaps the most serious problem is inflation. An inflation rate of 90 percent was a major reason for the breakdown of democracy in 1964. The military regime was initially successful at reducing the inflation rate, but inflation still averaged 20 percent during the military period. The rate began to skyrocket in the 1970s due to a rise in oil prices, high interest rates, and heavy state spending. Inflation eroded wages and hurt Brazil's poorest disproportionately.

Another serious problem has been foreign indebtedness. However, in recent years Brazil's export-led rapid growth has reduced its indebtedness significantly. President da Silva paid off Brazil's debt to the IMF early, saving the country almost a billion dollars in interest payments. In 2008, international credit rating agencies judged Brazil's debt to be "investment grade" for the first time in the country's history, a sign that Brazil was moving rapidly toward financial stability.

Finally, there is the problem of unemployment. Brazil's rapid economic growth has reduced unemployment in Brazil, but a large sector of the population remains jobless. And that joblessness is a chief cause of the country's endemic poverty and inequality. As a result, a large portion of Brazil's population (perhaps as much as two-thirds of the active workforce) makes its living in the informal sector.[28]

Reducing Inequality and Poverty in Brazil, 1990–2016

	1990	2000	2016
Average number of years of schooling	3.8	5.6	7.7
GDP growth rate	−4.4	4.3	−3.8
Gini index	61	59	52
Infant mortality rate per 1,000 live births	51.4	28.9	12.3
Life expectancy	66.3	70.2	75.5
Literacy rate	74.6	90.0	92.6
Percentage of population below international poverty line	16.2	10.2	3.8
Poverty rate	41.9	35.2	21.4
Unemployment rate	3.7	9.3	7.5

Note: Data provided are for the year indicated or the closest year for which data are available.

Sources: United Nations Development Indicators, http://hdr.undp.org (accessed 6/29/2016); CIA World Factbook; http://ipeadata.gov.br (accessed 5/24/17).

Though the Brazilian state still has a relatively large presence in the economy, democratic governments have gradually reduced that role. And democratization has addressed some, but certainly not all, of Brazil's economic problems.

By 2013, after a decade of steady growth and low inflation, the Brazilian economy had begun to stagnate, inflation began to increase, and Brazil's public debt began to grow. By 2016, Brazil's inflation rate was over 12 percent, its gross domestic product (GDP) had shrunk for two consecutive years, and the unemployment rate approached 7 percent.

Despite impressive records of aggregate growth since the return of democracy, the most troublesome feature of Brazil's economy is its endemic poverty and persistently high levels of inequality. In recent years, Brazilian governments have enacted policies that have slowly but steadily reduced Brazil's infamous inequality, but Brazil is still among the world's most unequal countries. Brazil's ranking in the 2016 UN Human Development Index now stands at 79th, below Iran (69th), Mexico (77th), and Russia (49th).

The 2002 election of President da Silva raised hopes for a fundamental resetting of economic priorities. Da Silva campaigned on a pledge to end hunger in Brazil. In office, he steered a more cautious course. He rejected further tax increases, though his administration improved tax collection, and his ability to increase social spending was constrained by Brazil's huge debt burden, commitments to state and local governments, and his inability and reluctance to reduce the state bureaucracy.

Despite these obstacles, Da Silva's policies to reduce poverty clearly had dramatic success. Between 2003 and 2010, the percentage of Brazilians living in extreme poverty dropped from 15 percent to 7 percent, and 20 million Brazilians were lifted out of poverty.[29] Most important in this regard was the establishment of the **Bolsa Família (Family Fund)**, a conditional cash transfer program.[30] In 2003, da Silva merged several antipoverty programs into the Bolsa Família, which pays monthly small cash stipends to Brazil's poorest families on the condition that recipients' children attend school and receive medical attention. The federal government makes payments directly to a family debit card that is usually held by the mother of the family. By the end of 2013, the program had reached almost 14 million families (a quarter of Brazil's population) and is currently the largest targeted welfare program in the world. Together with other policies such as a 50 percent increase in the minimum wage, the result was a dramatic drop in poverty and a steady reduction in inequality.

When the conservative Michel Temer became president in 2016, after Rousseff's impeachment, he moved quickly to address Brazil's worsening economic crisis. Temer proposed a package of austerity measures, including a dramatic cut in public spending and a major pension reform.

Brazil's poorest citizens use a government-issued ATM card to collect the monthly stipend that is part of the Bolsa Família program.

Current Issues in Brazil

ECONOMIC INEQUALITY AND CRIME

Despite its many advances, Brazilian democracy faces a litany of challenges. First among them is the inequality and poverty that persist even as Brazil has taken enormous economic strides. It remains to be seen whether Brazil's state, especially under the conservative president Temer, can continue to redirect its energy to improve the lot of its poor majority.

A related challenge is the epidemic of crime, which Brazilians regularly name as one of the country's most serious problems. Brazil's murder rate has doubled since democratization, and Brazil now has one of the highest rates of homicide by guns in the world (about 40,000 Brazilians die from gun violence each year). To a considerable extent, crime is a symptom of Brazil's endemic poverty, persistent inequality, and stubborn unemployment. Much crime in Brazil can be linked to the drug trade that has infested Brazil's favelas. For decades, Brazil's police have generally retreated from the favelas, where they are outnumbered and often outgunned. In recent years, however, the government has successfully reasserted control over some of the most notorious favelas.

In November 2010, 2,700 members of the Brazilian police and military entered Complexo do Alemão, a group of 12 favelas in Rio de Janeiro that were controlled by drug gangs. The security forces dislodged the traffickers, arrested top leaders, and established "pacifying police units" to patrol the favelas. The murder rate has plummeted in favelas where the police have reasserted control, though concern remains that criminals are just being shunted to other communities.

Brazilian security forces occupy the Morro do Alemão favela in Rio de Janeiro in November 2010 after battling with heavily armed drug traffickers.

POLITICAL CORRUPTION

Even in the context of Latin America, where political corruption is commonplace, Brazilian democracy has been plagued by a nonstop series of high-profile corruption scandals.[31]

When da Silva assumed the presidency in 2003, however, there were high hopes that the era of political corruption was over, since his PT enjoyed a reputation as a party of "clean government." Those hopes were soon dashed as the minority PT scrambled to achieve legislative support for the president's agenda. In the notorious *mensalão* ("monthly stipend") scandal of 2005 and 2006, the governing party was found to have paid opposition legislators to vote for the PT agenda, using funds from state-owned enterprises. President da Silva's chief of staff, communications director, and the entire top leadership of the PT were forced to resign (and in 2013 were finally sentenced to prison), but da Silva emerged unscathed and won reelection (though his party lost seats in the legislature). Corruption charges continued into da Silva's second term. In December 2007, the president of the Senate, a close ally of the president, was forced to give up his leadership post because of corruption charges. In 2008, a scandal erupted over misuse by top government officials of government-issued credit cards.

President Rousseff took power in 2011, vowing to attack government corruption. But in her first year in office, seven of her cabinet ministers were forced to resign over allegations of corruption; they included her ministers of the presidency (her chief of staff), defense, and labor. A new wave of corruption allegations emerged from the massive infrastructural expenditures for Brazil's hosting of the 2014 World Cup and the 2016 Olympic Games. In the aftermath of her narrow reelection in October 2014, important members of Rousseff's PT were implicated in a corruption investigation of the state-owned oil firm, Petrobras. In February 2015, the top leadership of Petrobras was forced to resign over allegations that the oil company and much of the Brazilian political class had received bribes from Brazil's largest construction conglomerate, Odebrecht, in exchange for state construction contracts. The scandal hit very near the presidency, since at the time of the alleged bribes Rousseff was head of Petrobras. Ironically, Rousseff was impeached in 2016 not because of corruption, but rather because she illegally covered up the presence of budget deficits that might have hurt her 2014 reelection chances. Odebrecht claims that it made large, illegal donations to Rousseff's 2014 presidential campaign. Michel Temer, her replacement as president, was formally charged in June 2017 with accepting bribes in exchange for political favors, leading to calls for his impeachment. By 2017, a third of Temer's cabinet and almost a third of the members of Brazil's national congress were under investigation for corruption.[32] Even the highly popular former president da Silva, leading the polls in the run-up to the 2018 presidential elections, was convicted on corruption charges. With President Temer and virtually the entire political class under investigation for accepting illegal campaign contributions from Brazilian businesses (a crime that can lead to prison terms), legislators proposed in 2017 to grant themselves amnesty from charges of campaign finance violations. A former Brazilian Supreme Court chief justice called the proposal "a denial of the rule of law."[33] By 2017, it was clear that the endemic nature of political corruption poses a major threat to Brazilian democracy.

There are many possible explanations for the persistence of corruption in Brazilian politics, but many scholars blame the Brazilian electoral system, which favors a proliferation of weak parties in the legislature and a low level of accountability for individual legislators. In early 2014, Brazil adopted a tough new anticorruption law aimed at addressing the growing public anger over political corruption. It is too early to tell whether the law will have real teeth, because it depends on notoriously corrupt local authorities to enforce its provisions.

A March 2016 demonstration against political corruption. The banner reads "Corrupt Congress."

Key Terms

Belindia (p. 603)

Bolsa Família (Family Fund) (p. 623)

bureaucratic authoritarian (p. 608)

caboclo (p. 604)

Cardoso, Fernando Henrique (p. 618)

Chamber of Deputies (Câmara dos Deputados) (p. 611)

da Silva, Luiz Inácio Lula (p. 601)

Estado Nôvo (p. 607)

Federal Senate (Senado Federal) (p. 611)

Federal Supreme Court (Supremo Tribunal Federal) (p. 612)

Goulart, João (p. 608)

Landless Workers Movement (MST) (p. 620)

liberation theology (p. 620)

mulatto (p. 604)

National Congress (Congresso Nacional) (p. 611)

open-list proportional representation (PR) (p. 613)

robust federalism (p. 614)

Rousseff, Dilma (p. 601)

Temer, Michel (p. 601)

Vargas, Getúlio (p. 607)

Workers' Party (PT) (p. 616)

Nelson Mandela's death in December 2013 led to a nationwide outpouring of appreciation for democratic South Africa's founding father. While his funeral was a time to celebrate his legacy, it was also an opportunity for some South Africans to reflect on the failures to implement some of Mandela's vision for a rainbow nation. During his eulogy for Mandela, President Jacob Zuma, who was mired in corruption scandals and faced with charges that his government was neglecting South Africa's impoverished majority, was booed by some audience members.

South Africa

Why Study This Case?

True to its remarkable modern history of tragedy and triumph, South Africa is a nation of paradoxes. The contradictions that constitute South African history and the remarkable capacity of South Africans to face and resolve them make this an intriguing case to study.

South Africa is fascinating for several other reasons as well. Like Russia, it presents two cases in one. Before the early 1990s, South Africa's politics, society, and economy were dominated by the racist authoritarian system known as apartheid, or "separateness." From 1948 to 1994, that systematically segregated races and privileged white South Africans. But with the collapse of the apartheid regime, the "new" South Africa of the past two decades has been a fascinating petri dish of unfolding multicultural democracy.

South Africa's remarkable and relatively peaceful transition from oppressive minority rule to a broad-based democracy is an even more compelling reason to study this case. Refuting the mid-1990s doomsday predictions of incendiary race wars, the overwhelming majority of South African citizens chose reconciliation over revolution, opting for ballots over bullets as a means of resolving seemingly intractable political differences.

South Africa has taken noteworthy strides since its return to democracy in 1994. Politically, its democratically elected legislature approved a constitution with broad political rights and civil liberties, and its government has convened regular nationwide elections. Socially, South Africans vanquished the world's most elaborate and overtly racist authoritarian regime and forged a common nation from its ashes. Economically, the government confounded its critics by avoiding the "easy" path of populist redistribution, instead cutting government expenditures and debt while delivering impressive gains in access to basic necessities for the country's poorest citizens.

MOZAMBIQUE

ZIMBABWE

Limpopo R.

Messina

Polokwane

SWAZILAND

Richards Bay

Durban

Ladysmith

KWAZULU-NATAL

PRETORIA
(TSHWANE)

Johannesburg

Marikana

LESOTHO

Orange R.

East London

BLOEMFONTEIN

Vaal R.

Port Elizabeth

Kimberley

De Aar

BOTSWANA

N

Orange R.

Upington

Mossel Bay

WESTERN CAPE

NAMIBIA

Saldanha

CAPE TOWN

ATLANTIC
OCEAN

INDIAN
OCEAN

100 mi
50
0
100 km
50
0

Make no mistake, however; this tale of two South Africas cannot yet boast a fairy-tale ending. The decades of political violence, social partition, and economic deprivation that victimized over 80 percent of the population left some horrible and lasting scars. Compounding the legacies of racism and authoritarianism is a host of pernicious social problems, such as rampant violent crime, brooding racial tension, endemic corruption, and the pandemic of HIV/AIDS. As if these challenges were not enough, the remarkable regime change created unmet expectations for rapid economic change and social equality, and there are concerns that democracy has been successful only because post-apartheid governments have faced no serious opposition.

How can a democratic government fare under such challenging circumstances? As one editorial asked, "How can a . . . revolutionary movement, forged by 40 years of struggle against white supremacy, transform itself into a multiracial ruling party, to run a sophisticated industrial economy? How can a new generation of leaders, without the aura of struggle, restrain the pressures towards populism and maintain a tolerant democracy when so many African governments have so noticeably failed?"[1] This case seeks to address these questions and the historical puzzle of why apartheid, enforced by such a small minority, managed to persist so successfully for so long and how its collapse and replacement came about under relatively peaceful circumstances.

Twenty years after South Africa's transition to a multiracial democracy, there are growing concerns about the lack of political alternation. In May 2014, the African National Congress (ANC) party won its fifth consecutive majority in the legislature, and South Africa's democratic opposition remains relatively weak and fragmented. Can South Africa avoid the negative consequences of single-party political domination (corruption, lack of accountability, and an unequal political playing field) that have plagued other "dominant-party" systems examined in this text (for example, Japan, Mexico, Russia, and China)?

Historical Development of the State

The Dutch East India Company officials who first established a fort in what is today Cape Town encountered tribes of Khoisans, whom they soon enslaved. When these native Africans died of disease and slavery, the Dutch settlers imported slaves, mostly from Southeast Asia.[2] In the interior of South Africa, a variety of Bantu-speaking tribes were ending their centuries-long migration southward from central Africa, integrating with the hunters and herders who had long inhabited the region. Among the largest of these tribes were the Zulu, the Sotho, and the Swazi kingdoms.

DUTCH RULE

While most of the colonial "scramble for Africa" took place in the nineteenth century, European domination of South Africa began almost two centuries earlier.

Cape Town was initially settled by the Dutch East India Company to resupply ships heading to and from Dutch colonies in Indonesia. The early Dutch settlers, known as **Boers** (or "farmers"), and later **Afrikaners**, quickly seized the fertile land of the Cape of Good Hope. The European residents of the cape developed their own culture, based on their conservative Protestant **Dutch Reformed Church** and their unique language, called **Afrikaans**. The small and isolated Cape Colony was fairly prosperous until it was seized by the British Empire in 1795. The Dutch ceded formal control of the region to the British in 1814.

BOER MIGRATION

As Britain quickly began to integrate this new colony into its burgeoning empire, the arrival of waves of British settlers was seen as a threat to Boer society. Bristling under British rule, many Cape Colony Boers (and their slaves) undertook a migration into the interior of southern Africa after the British banned slavery. That migration, the **Great Trek** of 1835, would later gain the status of heroic myth. Beginning in 1835 and over the following decade, thousands of **Voortrekkers** (Afrikaans for "pioneers") drove their wagons northeast to regain their autonomy and preserve their way of life. They met strong initial resistance from the Xhosa and other Bantu kingdoms, though whites had important technological advantages in these conflicts and were able to exploit the numerous divisions among the indigenous tribes. By the early 1840s, Afrikaners were firmly ensconced in the interior of South Africa. The Boers created two states, known as the Boer republics, in which slavery, strict segregation of races, the Afrikaans language, and the Dutch Reformed Church were protected by law.

Initially, the British grudgingly tolerated the interior Boer republics. However, the discovery there of massive deposits of diamonds (in 1870) and gold (in 1886) changed everything. English speakers flooded into the interior, and the city of Johannesburg quickly became an English-speaking enclave in the Boer-controlled state of Transvaal. Transvaal president Paul Kruger attempted to limit the influence of the English by denying them the vote. In 1895, English diamond magnate Cecil Rhodes used the pretense of Boer discrimination against English settlers and the presence of slavery in the Boer republics to incite a rebellion among the English. President Kruger declared war on England in 1899.

DEFEAT OF THE AFRIKANERS IN THE BOER WARS

Though outnumbered five to one, the Boers fought tenaciously to defend their independence during the **Boer Wars** of 1880–81 and 1899–1902. By 1902, the British had defeated the Boers, and the Boer republics had become self-governing British colonies. In exchange for signing a peace treaty, the Boers were promised full political rights, protections for their language and culture, and the ability to deny blacks the vote in the former Boer republics. In 1910, these agreements were formalized in the **Union of South Africa**.

THE RENAISSANCE OF AFRIKANER POWER

English and Afrikaners worked together to create a single British colony, and the first prime minister of the Union of South Africa was a former Afrikaner military leader. The Native Land Act of 1913 prevented blacks from owning land except

1652	The Dutch arrive at the Cape of Good Hope.
1795	Cape Town captured from the Dutch by the British.
1880–81; 1899–1902	Boer Wars fought between the Afrikaners and the British.
1910	The Union of South Africa formed, dominated by English-speaking South Africans.
1948	Afrikaner National Party elected and apartheid begins.
1960	African National Congress banned.
1964	Nelson Mandela imprisoned.
1990	Mandela released from prison.
1990–93	Transition made to democracy as the result of negotiations between Mandela and President F. W. de Klerk.
1994	After historic multiracial elections, ANC majority government established under Nelson Mandela.
1996	Democratic constitution approved.
1999	Legislative elections won by ANC; Thabo Mbeki named president.
2008	Thabo Mbeki replaced as president by Kgalema Motlanthe.
2009	Jacob Zuma becomes president.
2014	Jacob Zuma reelected after the ANC wins its fifth consecutive election.

in designated "reserves" (less than 10 percent of the total land of South Africa). Discrimination against blacks continued in the former Boer republics. Only in the largely English Cape Colony were mixed-race individuals (referred to as "**coloreds**" in South Africa) and a small number of blacks allowed to vote. Nowhere in South Africa were rights for the black majority granted, and racial discrimination was the rule even in English-governed areas. In the face of this institutionalized racial oppression, the **African National Congress (ANC)** was founded in 1912 as a non-violent advocate for multiracial democracy.

The first elections in the united country brought to power the South African Party (SAP), which included both English speakers and Afrikaners. But many Afrikaners, especially those in the former Boer republics, continued to resent the English deeply. The Afrikaners enjoyed full political rights, but the English controlled most of the country's wealth, especially its mineral profits and budding industry.

As has so often been the case throughout their history, the Afrikaners resisted being marginalized, but this time they did so within the political system. The formation of the **National Party (NP)** in 1914 was the most important step in their attempt to organize and mobilize the Afrikaner population. The NP demanded that Afrikaans be recognized alongside English, and it called for South Africa to secede from the British Empire.

In the mid-1930s, NP leader Daniel Malan articulated the policies of white supremacy that later became the hallmark of apartheid. At the same time, Malan called for Afrikaner control of the state so that wealth held by the English could be redistributed to Afrikaners. Malan's goals appealed to the mass of poor white Afrikaner workers, who felt threatened by the better-off English and by the growing number of even poorer black workers (who vied for their jobs). The NP realized that if Afrikaners could be unified, they could not be denied power. In 1948, the NP was elected to office.

THE APARTHEID ERA

The apartheid era is distinguished by the NP's two goals: consolidating Afrikaner power and eliminating all vestiges of black participation in South African politics. To a considerable degree, apartheid simply codified and intensified the racial segregation that existed in the mid-twentieth century. During an era when racial discrimination was being challenged in virtually every other country, Afrikaner leaders sought to construct elaborate legal justifications for it. According to Hendrik Verwoerd, the leading ideologue of apartheid (and prime minister from 1958 to 1966), South Africa was composed of four distinct "racial groups" (white, African, colored, and Indian). He argued that whites, as the "most civilized" of the four groups, should have absolute control of the state.

The Population Registration Act of 1950 divided South Africa into these four racial categories and placed every South African into one of those categories. Once Africans were divided into races, the apartheid architects argued that blacks (about three-quarters of the population) were not citizens of South Africa. Blacks were deemed to be citizens of 10 remote "tribal homelands" (dubbed **Bantustans**) whose boundaries and leaders were decreed by the government. The Bantustans, somewhat akin to Native American reservations, constituted only around 13 percent of South Africa's territory and were usually made up of noncontiguous parcels of infertile land separated by white-owned farms. The NP chose black leaders (often tribal chiefs) loyal to the party goals to head the Bantustan governments. All blacks in South Africa, therefore, were in effect "guests" and did not enjoy any of the rights of citizenship. The 1971 Bantu Homelands Citizenship Act allowed the government to grant "independence" to any Bantustan, and though government propagandists defended the measure as an act of "decolonization," in reality it had little impact. Over the next decade, many Bantustans became "independent," though no foreign government would recognize them as sovereign states.

Racial segregation in the rest of South Africa went even further. Members of each of the four racial groups were required to reside in areas determined by the government. The vast majority of blacks who lived and worked in white areas were required to carry internal visas at all times. Each year, failure to carry such a pass resulted in hundreds of thousands of deportations to a "homeland" that, more often than not, the deportee had never before set foot in. The apartheid authorities created new racial categories and designed separate residential areas for South Africans of Asian descent, or of mixed race, often forcibly relocating them. Other infamous laws reinforced racial segregation. The Prohibition of Mixed Marriages Act (1950) banned relations across racial lines, and the Reservation of Separate Amenities Act (1953) provided the legal basis for segregating places as diverse as beaches and restrooms.[3]

The apartheid system retained many of the trappings of a parliamentary democracy. Apartheid South Africa had regular elections, a fairly vigorous press, and a seemingly independent judiciary. The vast majority of South Africans, however, were disenfranchised and utterly powerless. The regime tolerated mild opposition on some issues but ruthlessly quashed individuals and groups who actively opposed apartheid itself.

THE BUILDING OF APARTHEID AND THE STRUGGLE AGAINST IT

Among the pillars of South African apartheid was the 1950 **Group Areas Act**, which prohibited South Africans of different races from living in the same neighborhoods. The practical implications were immediate and devastating: nonwhites were forcibly relocated to areas outside South African cities.

The apartheid regime met resistance from its very inception. The most important organization resisting racial discrimination was the African National Congress (ANC), a largely black organization that sought suffrage for blacks. The ANC was initially nonviolent and politically moderate in its calls for multiracial democracy. Under the leadership of **Nelson Mandela**, it led a series of nonviolent civil disobedience campaigns against apartheid laws.[4]

Fierce repression of this protest by the apartheid regime had two major consequences. First, some blacks, tiring of the nonviolent, gradualist approach of the ANC, advocated a more confrontational opposition to apartheid. The growing repression persuaded the ANC to ally with the South African Communist Party and to initiate military action against the apartheid regime. Second, the apartheid leaders, alarmed by the growing resistance, banned the ANC and other anti-apartheid groups. The government countered by arresting Nelson Mandela and other top ANC leaders in 1963 and sentencing them to life in prison. The ongoing repression led to the incarceration and murder of thousands of South Africans who actively resisted apartheid.

Although not all whites supported the apartheid system, the NP skillfully retained the majority's allegiance. For Afrikaners, the NP dramatically improved their political and economic status, making them dependent on the perpetuation of the status quo. The NP played on English-speaking whites' fears of black rule. Moderate white critics of apartheid were mostly tolerated because they generally held little sway among the white population at large.

Though the NP subdued most domestic resistance to apartheid, the system faced growing hostility from abroad. The end of colonialism created independent African states that supported the ANC, and the United Nations condemned apartheid as early as 1952 and imposed an arms embargo on South Africa in 1977. Nevertheless, in the context of the Cold War, South Africa was able to gain support (from the United States, in particular) by portraying its fight against the ANC as a struggle against communism. Moreover, the world's major capitalist powers had lucrative investments in South Africa and were ambivalent about promoting black rule.

TRANSITION TO DEMOCRACY

There was nothing inevitable about South Africa's peaceful transition from apartheid to majority rule, and there were five major reasons that explain this fortunate outcome.

First, the growth of opposition to apartheid had at its core a demographic component. The black population was growing more quickly, and it was increasingly concentrated in urban areas, which were more subject to political mobilization. Most of these newly urban blacks lived in squalid conditions in South Africa's townships, which doubled in population between 1950 and 1980. These demographic trends meant that despite largely successful efforts to deny blacks political power, their economic power and significance were rapidly expanding. The creation of the United Democratic Front (UDF) in 1983 effectively united trade unions and the major black and white anti-apartheid groups. The number of protests, strikes, boycotts, and slowdowns grew, requiring ever-greater levels of repression by the apartheid regime. The ANC, whose leadership was either in prison or in exile, waged a guerrilla war against the apartheid regime. That struggle was never able to dislodge the heavily armed white regime, but neither could the regime destroy the ANC or stop the escalating violence.

Second, by the 1980s, the deficiencies in the apartheid economic model had become increasingly apparent. During this decade, South Africa's economy was among the most stagnant in the developing world, growing at an average annual rate of only about 1 percent. The apartheid economic system had raised the standard of living for South Africa's whites, especially Afrikaners, but it had also led to serious distortions and inefficiencies that were by now beginning to take a toll.

Third, by the mid-1970s, even leading Afrikaner politicians were convinced that apartheid was an anachronistic system that needed reform if it was to survive. The reforms that followed paved the way for a future transition to democracy. President F. W. de Klerk (1989–94) repealed much of the most egregious apartheid legislation. He also legalized black political parties, including the ANC and the PAC, and freed their leaders. The crisis of apartheid served to split the traditionally unified Afrikaner leadership, opening the window to even greater reform.

Fourth, during the 1980s, many countries imposed embargoes on South Africa, limiting trade and foreign investment, though powerful nations such as the United States and the United Kingdom continued to trade with the regime into the 1990s. Of greater importance was the winding down of the Cold War in the 1980s. On the one hand, it deprived the South African regime of a key source of international legitimacy: the decline of communism weakened its claim that it was facing a communist insurgency. On the other hand, the collapse of the Soviet Union and the Soviet bloc weakened the ANC sectors that promoted communist revolution in South Africa.

Finally, South Africa's transition to democracy likely would not have occurred (or at the very least would not have been as peaceful or successful) without skilled leaders. F. W. de Klerk's role in forcing Prime Minister P. W. Botha's resignation and his courageous decisions in 1990 to free Mandela and legalize the ANC were essential to the peaceful regime change. De Klerk used his unblemished credentials as an NP stalwart to persuade NP die-hards to accept democratic reform and convince most Afrikaners that their interests would be safeguarded under majority rule.

Likewise, Nelson Mandela risked a great deal by negotiating the terms of the transition with the NP government. Mandela and the ANC leadership agreed to power sharing and numerous guarantees to assuage white fears, and they were able to restrain radicalized blacks who wanted quick redress for decades of abuse under apartheid. Negotiations between the black leadership and the NP were protracted and difficult. De Klerk and Mandela faced serious opposition from radical sectors

Nelson Mandela greets supporters after his release from prison in February 1990. Upon being released, he immediately became the representative of the black majority in negotiating for a democratic transition. Mandela received the Nobel Peace Prize in 1993. In 1994, his ANC won a landslide victory in the country's first multiracial elections and Mandela became South Africa's first black president. He died in late 2013.

of their own camps. Nevertheless, an interim constitution was approved in 1993, paving the way for democratic elections and majority rule in 1994. In recognition of their important role in the South African transition, de Klerk and Mandela were awarded the 1993 Nobel Peace Prize.

Political Regime

POLITICAL INSTITUTIONS

During the apartheid regime, South African whites enjoyed relatively democratic institutions. Nonwhites had much more limited political rights, or none whatsoever. As a result, few considered the country to be democratic. After the political transition in 1994, however, political rights were extended to the population as a whole, regardless of race. South Africa is now a democracy with broad political rights and civil liberties commensurate with those found in advanced democracies. South Africa's long tradition of democratic institutions, albeit highly restrictive ones, helped smooth the transition to multiracial democracy. The architects of the 1994 transition did not need to create an entirely new democratic system from scratch but merely reformed existing democratic institutions and extended them to the entire population.

THE CONSTITUTION The new democratic regime is fundamentally enshrined in the South African constitution, approved in 1996. The constitution attempts to balance majority and minority concerns carefully, affirming the basic values of human rights regardless of "race, gender, sex, pregnancy, religion, conscience, belief, culture, language and birth," a list far more detailed than that of most democratic constitutions. Eleven official languages are recognized. The constitution also upholds citizens' rights to housing, health care, food, water, social security, and even a healthy environment. Reacting to decades of apartheid authoritarianism, the constitution includes unusually detailed provisions limiting the powers of the state to arrest, detain, and prosecute individuals. Finally, it enshrines the principle of affirmative action, stating that to achieve greater equality, laws and other measures can be used to promote or advance individuals who have been discriminated against.

The constitution also firmly protects the rights of private property, a provision added to assure the white population that their property would not be seized by a black-majority government. Perhaps most important, the constitution defines itself as the supreme law of the land: parliament must act within its confines, and a Constitutional Court can now strike down unconstitutional behavior. This is a departure from the past, when the parliament and the government reigned supreme.

THE BRANCHES OF GOVERNMENT

Since 1994, the South African system has been transformed into one similar to those in many other democracies—a bicameral parliament and a Constitutional Court. Interestingly, because of historic compromises between Afrikaner and English-speaking whites, South Africa has three capitals. The seat of government is located in Pretoria, the traditional heart of Afrikaner power and the center of the former Boer republics. Cape Town, where English influence was historically strongest, is the legislative capital. South Africa's judicial capital is located in Bloemfontein.

THE PRESIDENT The chief executive of South Africa is the president. This title is rather confusing, however. Like a typical prime minister, the president is chosen from, and by, members of the National Assembly—the lower house of the legislature—and can be removed by a vote of no confidence. But unlike in most parliamentary systems, the South African president serves as both head of state and head of government. Like most prime ministers, the president chooses a cabinet of

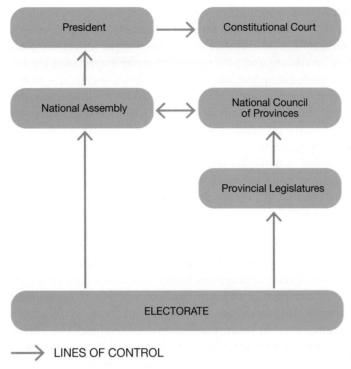

Structure of the Government

---

ministers, signs or vetoes legislation presented by the National Assembly, and can refer legislation to the Constitutional Court as necessary. The president may also call national referenda, dissolve the National Assembly, and (in some situations) call new elections. If the president wishes to dissolve the National Assembly, a majority of the lower house must support the dissolution and three years must have passed since it was first elected. The president is unable to call snap elections as in most other parliamentary systems.

The president is stronger than a typical prime minister. As head of state and head of government, the president not only exerts authority over the cabinet (which he or she selects and which he or she can dismiss) and government policy (like a typical head of government) but also speaks on behalf of the nation and represents the country on the world stage (as a head of state does). As is common in parliamentary systems, motions of no confidence require the support of a majority of the members of the National Assembly, and if successful require that the president and entire cabinet resign. President Jacob Zuma faced six unsuccessful motions of no confidence between 2009 and 2017, easily defeating the first five motions. In August 2017 a motion of no confidence against Zuma was narrowly defeated, as some legislators from the president's party voted against him. As in all parliamentary systems, South Africa's head of government serves at the behest of his or her political party and can be replaced by the party at any time. After the surprisingly close result of the August 2017 motion, there was speculation that the ANC might decide to remove its increasingly unpopular leader before the next election.

THE LEGISLATURE South Africa has a bicameral parliament. The lower and more powerful of its two houses, the National Assembly, currently has 400 members. Members serve for five-year terms, and they are charged with electing and removing the president, preparing and passing legislation, and approving the national budget. As in the United Kingdom, the lower house has a weekly "question time," when members can question members of the cabinet (and very infrequently, the president). For a variety of reasons, the National Assembly has not often demonstrated its independence vis-à-vis the president. The dominance of the ANC and the rules enforcing strict party discipline have limited the independence of parliament members.[5]

The upper house is the National Council of Provinces, and it is considerably weaker than the lower house. Its 90 members are indirectly elected by the nine provincial legislatures and include the premier of each province. Each province, regardless of its size or population, sends 10 delegates, who cast their votes as a bloc. The power of the National Council depends on the type of legislation under consideration. When the National Assembly is dealing with national policy (such as foreign affairs or defense), the National Council has relatively little influence. When proposed legislation affects the provinces, however, the National Council can amend or reject measures, forcing the two houses to form a mediation committee to hammer out a compromise. Ultimately, the National Assembly can override the upper house with a two-thirds vote. In short, the National Council exists to ensure that local interests are heard at the national level, which is especially important when the provinces are distinguished by ethnicity, language, and culture.

THE JUDICIARY Another important component of the transition to democratic multiracial rule in South Africa is the Constitutional Court. This body hears cases regarding constitutional issues. Its 11 members serve 12-year terms and are appointed by the president on the basis of the recommendations of a judicial commission. The commission is made up of government and nongovernment appointees who evaluate candidates' qualifications and take racial and gender diversity into account.

To date, the court has shown a tendency for activism and independence. Most recently, in April 2016 the Constitutional Court ordered President Jacob Zuma to pay back public money that he had spent to remodel his private home. At a time of growing concern about the ruling party's monopoly of political power, the South African judiciary has proven to be a crucial check on the government. In contrast to the legislature, and the presidency, a majority of South Africans continue to express trust in the judiciary (see "The Evolution of Levels of Trust in South Africa, 2006–2015," p. 652).

THE ELECTORAL SYSTEM

The current electoral rules in South Africa mark a significant departure from the past. Under apartheid, the country used the British single-member district, or plurality, system. As part of the transition to democracy, South Africa had to decide what election method would best represent the needs of a diverse public and help consolidate democratic legitimacy by creating an inclusive system. The result was the creation of an electoral system based on pure proportional representation (PR).

Voters now cast their votes not for individual candidates, but for a party that is designated on the ballot by name, electoral symbol, and a picture of the head of the party (so that illiterate voters are not excluded). To ensure the greatest possible proportionality, representatives are elected from a single nationwide constituency, and there is no minimum threshold for receiving seats in the legislature. The number of seats a party wins is divided proportionally to reflect the percentage of the total vote it receives. At elections, voters are given two ballots: one for the national legislature and one for their provincial legislature.

Overall, the electoral system in South Africa has successfully created an inclusive political atmosphere and has averted conflict and violence. Electoral turnout has been very high; in the 2014 elections, turnout was over 73 percent of registered voters (about 80 percent of eligible voters registered).

Some critics have argued that the use of PR has created a disconnect between the National Assembly and the citizens. Because members of parliament are tied to their party instead of their constituency, they are not accountable to local communities. Political parties, most notably the governing ANC, have stifled internal dissent and limited the independence of legislators by threatening to remove them from the party electoral list if they stray too far from the party's wishes. Critics inside South Africa have suggested that the country consider adopting a mixed electoral system, in which some percentage of the seats are filled by plurality while the remaining are filled by PR. This would give voters a local representative with whom they could identify as well as the ability to cast their vote for a particular party. However, after some discussion on electoral reform in recent years, such suggestions have faded and the current system has become institutionalized. The ANC, in particular, has been unwilling to change an electoral system that has so far delivered it a huge majority.

LOCAL GOVERNMENT

Below the national level, South Africa is divided into nine provinces, each with its own elected assembly. Members are elected for a term of five years, and elections for the national and provincial legislatures occur simultaneously. In turn, the members of each assembly elect a premier to serve as the province's chief executive. The provincial assemblies have their own constitutions, pass legislation, and send delegates to the National Council of Provinces.

It is difficult to call South Africa a federal state, however, and the concept itself is a politically charged issue. During the transition to democracy, the ANC in particular was skeptical of federalism. At that time, the NP, the architects of apartheid, favored federalism as a way to limit the ANC's power. Meanwhile, some Afrikaners hoped that a federal right to self-determination could pave the way for outright secession. The 1996 constitution reflects these concerns by supporting regional and ethnic diversity. Still, the constitution gives the central government the ability to overturn local legislation relatively easily, and any powers not delimited by the constitution reside with the central, not the local, government. Provinces also have limited power to levy taxes, giving them little financial autonomy.[6]

Since democratization, municipal governments have become increasingly important. The ANC has suffered its most important defeats at the local level, where complaints about the delivery of services have boosted the fortunes of the opposition. In the 2009 provincial elections, the ANC lost control of Western Cape Province, and **Democratic Alliance (DA)** leader Helen Zille became premier. An increasing number of protests against ineffective local governments, some of which turned violent, set the stage for a major increase in the DA vote in the May 2011 municipal elections. In addition to retaining control of the Western Cape Province, the party won almost a quarter of the national vote and made its first inroads into areas that had previously been bastions of ANC support. A public opinion study conducted by the country's Independent Electoral Commission showed that South Africans held local governments in lower esteem than any other level of government, and other studies show that over half of South Africans view local governments as corrupt.[7]

Political Conflict and Competition

THE PARTY SYSTEM AND ELECTIONS

During apartheid, few political parties existed, and the NP dominated politics from 1948 until 1994. The main opposition was the weak Progressive Federal Party (PFP), which peacefully opposed apartheid laws and favored multiracial democracy within a federal framework. The enfranchisement of the nonwhite population has dramatically changed the political spectrum, though as in the past it remains dominated by one major party.

THE AFRICAN NATIONAL CONGRESS (ANC) The dominant party since 1994 has been the African National Congress (ANC), which led the struggle against white rule starting in 1912.[8] During the ANC's long period underground and in exile, it developed an ideology strongly influenced by Marxism, favoring the nationalization of land and industry. Economic equality was seen as a necessary mechanism for overcoming racial discrimination. The ANC cultivated relations with communist countries, such as the Soviet Union and China, and at home formed an alliance with the much smaller South African Communist Party, the SACP (which still operates within the framework of the ANC).

Many white South Africans, including some opponents of apartheid, were troubled by the ANC's demands for radical political and economic change. Since winning power in 1994, the ANC has stood for racial and gender equality and a strong state role in the expansion of economic opportunities for nonwhites. But it has also embraced property rights that it views as essential for economic growth and a prerequisite for the provision of jobs, education, and social services to the poor black majority. As such, its ideology is unclear and often contradictory, encompassing a mixture of social-democratic and liberal views, a lingering radicalism, and an emphasis on unity. The ANC increased its share of the vote in each of the first three democratic elections and has won a large majority of the vote in each of the five elections since 1994, but its share of the vote dropped in 1999 and 2014.

The preponderance of ANC power raises concerns. Some observers fear that the party so easily embraced democracy after its long struggle in part because it has done so well in a democratic system. Were the ANC to face losing power, it might not look upon the democratic process so favorably. These concerns were heightened in particular by **Thabo Mbeki**'s tenure in office (1999–2008), when his rhetoric and that of the ANC grew increasingly intolerant of those who challenged it. ANC leaders, including current president Jacob Zuma, have at times made statements that portray the ANC as the only truly patriotic political party and that envision the ANC as the only party capable of governing.[9]

In general, however, the ANC's record in office has been positively evaluated by most South Africans, who give it high scores for managing the economy, improving health care, and promoting racial equality. South Africans have been most critical of the ANC's record on creating jobs, reducing crime, narrowing the gap between the rich and poor, and fighting corruption.

Over the past decade, the ANC has increasingly suffered from internal political discord. A political schism emerged in late 2007 between ANC "populists," led by trade unions and the party rank and file, and the more technocratic wing, dominated by former president Mbeki. The populist challenge within the party helped propel Jacob Zuma's victory over Mbeki in the bitterly contested party leadership election of December 2007. After winning the ANC leadership, Zuma began to replace Mbeki loyalists with his own supporters in key party posts. Although Zuma was able to force Mbeki to resign in September 2008, Zuma could not become president because he was not a member of the legislature. The ANC appointed Kgalema Motlanthe, an ally of Zuma, as a caretaker president to serve until the 2009 general elections.

South Africa's current president is a striking contrast from his aloof, intellectual predecessor, Thabo Mbeki. Jacob Zuma is the ANC's most prominent Zulu politician. Unlike the scholarly Mbeki (or Nelson Mandela, who was a lawyer), Zuma grew up poor and received no formal education. He became involved in the ANC in the 1960s and was sentenced to 10 years in prison in 1963. (He served time at Robben Island prison with Nelson Mandela.) After his release, he became a top ANC leader in exile. After the return of democracy, Zuma quickly rose within the ANC hierarchy, an ascent

President Jacob Zuma is portrayed here as a leader plagued by corruption charges.

that culminated in his 1997 appointment as executive deputy president (Mbeki's number two). While often portraying himself as the victim of the ANC power elite, Zuma is the consummate ANC insider.

Zuma's rise to power within the ANC was clouded in controversy. In 2005, he was charged with raping a young woman in his home. He admitted to having unprotected sex with the woman, whom he knew to be HIV-positive, but claimed the relationship was consensual. Zuma was acquitted of the charges, but his statement under oath that he had showered after the intercourse to reduce his risk of contracting HIV infuriated many South Africans.

In 2005, Zuma was fired from his position as deputy president after being accused of corruption and racketeering in a government arms-procurement scandal. Charges were brought against him in 2007, but they were dropped in April 2009, shortly before the general election. Zuma has claimed that the corruption charges were politically motivated. He rose to power with strong support from South Africa's labor unions, those frustrated with the pace of change under Mandela and Mbeki. Some feared that Zuma might become an economic populist who could reverse the pro-business and pro-growth economic policies long pursued by the ANC. In December 2007, Zuma easily defeated Thabo Mbeki in elections for the ANC presidency, which virtually guaranteed that he would become president after the April 2009 general election.

Zuma's personal life continues to be a source of contention. He is a polygamist who married his fifth wife in 2010. After taking office, he apologized for fathering a child with a woman to whom he was not married. In short, Zuma's less-polished image appears to be a dramatic departure from those of Mandela and Mbeki, and has helped South Africa's poor majority relate to him. But appearances can be deceiving. Below the surface there is considerable continuity between Zuma's policies and those of his two more circumspect predecessors.

In the run-up to the 2014 election, controversy continued to dog Zuma. In 2013, opposition parties in the legislature alleged that the president had used public funds for improvements to his personal residence, charges that were upheld in a 2016 Constitutional Court ruling. In December 2013, Zuma was heckled during his eulogy for Nelson Mandela. Nevertheless, a public opinion survey carried out in late 2011 gave Zuma a 66 percent approval rating, and the ANC won a resounding victory in the 2014 elections, assuring this controversial leader a second term in office. By 2016, however, President Zuma's approval rating had dropped from a high of 64 percent to 36 percent, damaged by continuing allegations of corruption and a stagnant economy.[10]

President Zuma's 2017 firing of his well-respected finance minister, who was known for his opposition to corruption, threatened to further divide the governing party. Zuma's deputy president, the head of the ANC, and quite a few ANC members of parliament blasted the decision. The ANC's growing internal divisions were highlighted in 2017 when Zuma narrowly survived a motion of no confidence despite the ANC's large majority in the legislature.

OTHER PARTIES Zuma's rise to the leadership of the ANC, and his ability to force Mbeki's resignation, prompted the creation of the Congress of the People (COPE). This breakaway party, led by Mosiuoa Lekota, a former defense minister under Mbeki, had the potential to become the first genuine black opposition party to the ANC. Despite internal divisions, a flawed political campaign, and lack of funds leading up to the 2009 elections, COPE was able to win more than 7 percent of the vote and 30 seats in the legislature, making it South Africa's third-largest political party. However, COPE suffered a stunning setback in the 2011 municipal elections, when it won under 3 percent of the vote, and in the 2014 general elections it won under 1 percent of the vote and only three seats in the legislature.

A second party to break away from the ANC was Agang South Africa. It was formed in 2013 by Mamphela Ramphele, a black female physician and scholar who was a former managing director of the World Bank. Ramphele's new party sought to attract black voters frustrated over corruption and cronyism within the ANC. Despite a promising start, the new party made a series of strategic errors and won only two seats in the 2014 elections.

The most interesting new party to emerge from the ANC is the **Economic Freedom Fighters (EFF)**, led by the young and radical firebrand Julius Malema. Malema, the former head of the ANC youth organization, was expelled from the ANC for making radical and incendiary statements that contradicted ANC policy. Malema and the EFF represent the radical and Marxist left of the ANC, fostered during decades of anti-apartheid armed struggle. Since its inception in 2013, the EFF has been a fierce critic of what it views as the overly pro-business and excessively free-market orientation of the ANC. Most controversially, it calls for

Legislators from the Economic Freedom Fighters Party protest during President Zuma's state of the nation address in February 2016.

expropriation of white-owned land and the nationalization of South Africa's banks and mines. The new party's base is overwhelmingly made up of young and black South Africans. The party won just over 6 percent of the vote, and 25 seats, in the 2014 elections, making it South Africa's third largest political force, but for the moment, it has failed to provide a real challenge to the ANC from the left.

To date, the most important opposition party in South Africa is the Democratic Alliance (DA). The DA is the successor to the pre-1994 white anti-apartheid party, the Progressive Federal Party (PFP). In the early years of the transition to democracy, the DA entered into alliance with the remnants of the now defunct National Party (most former National Party members now support the DA). It is primarily a liberal party that favors a small state, individual freedoms, privatization of state-run firms, and greater devolution of power to local governments. In the 2004 elections, the DA won 12 percent of the votes and 50 seats. In the 2006 local elections, it beat the ANC in Cape Town (at the time, the only local municipal council not controlled by the ANC), and won about 15 percent of the vote nationally.

Helen Zille, a liberal journalist during apartheid and the white mayor of Cape Town, became DA leader in 2007. Under her leadership, the DA has been an increasingly outspoken opponent of the ANC. Public support for the DA has grown since the 1994 elections, but its primary base of support remains the white, colored, and Indian population. In 2008, just under 8 percent of South Africans said they identified with the DA. In the 2009 elections, the DA increased its vote share to over 16 percent and won control of Western Cape Province (the only province not controlled by the ANC). The DA performed well in the 2011 municipal elections. In the 2014 general elections, it won just over 22 percent of the vote and 89 seats, solidifying its role as the leading party of the opposition.

However, to become a serious challenger to the ANC, the DA will have to broaden its appeal to black voters (it won only 22 percent of black voters in 2014), and it will need to change the perception that it is the party of whites. Survey data show that South Africans who identify with the DA tend to be Afrikaans speakers, wealthy, white, highly educated, and older.[11] In May 2015, **Mmusi Maimane** became the DA's first black leader, and he is currently South Africa's leader of the opposition in the National Assembly. Maimane would appear to be well positioned to attract more black voters to the DA. In his mid-30s, he grew up poor in the black township of Soweto and has a white wife and mixed-race children.

South Africa's fourth largest party, the **Inkatha Freedom Party (IFP)**, played an ambiguous role in apartheid and post-apartheid politics. The IFP, founded in 1975 by Zulu chief Mangosuthu Buthelezi, challenged apartheid institutions but also participated in local government in the KwaZulu "homeland," one of the remote areas created to remove blacks from desirable areas and deprive them of basic citizenship.

During the 1980s, animosity grew between the IFP and the ANC: the ANC saw the IFP as having been co-opted by the government, while the IFP viewed the ANC as dominated by ethnic Xhosas who did not represent Zulu interests. The animosity soon erupted into violence that was abetted by the apartheid regime as a way to weaken both sides. After the first democratic elections, however, the ANC was careful to bring members of the IFP into the government cabinet, which helped to diffuse much of the tension between the two parties.

The IFP was embarrassed in 2004 after failing to do well even in the elections for KwaZulu's provincial legislature, and the party left the national government. Fears that the IFP could threaten the stability of the country have disappeared. The long-term viability of a Zulu political party is doubtful since Jacob Zuma, a Zulu, became president in 2009. Since then, the IFP has steadily declined. In the 2014 general elections, it was hurt by internal divisions and thus won only 2.4 percent of the vote and 10 seats.

Aided by South Africa's proportional representation election system, a number of small parties regularly win seats in the legislature. But the dominance of the ANC, which has never held less than 60 percent of the seats in the legislature, dwarfs the opposition. However, in recent general elections the steady growth of the opposition, and especially the gains made by parties to the right and left of the ANC (the DA and the new EFF), have deprived the ANC of a two-thirds majority in the lower house. As a result, the ANC will need to work with the opposition if it wants to amend the constitution and pass certain types of legislation.

We have seen that despite its slow and steady decline in electoral support, the ANC has retained a large majority of the electorate since 1994, and South Africa remains a dominant-party system. Does the continued dominance of a single party threaten democracy in South Africa, as has been argued by some scholars?[12] Other democracies, such as Japan, have been dominated by a single political party. Nevertheless, the dominance of a single party may threaten democracy in the long run by encouraging corruption, contributing to political apathy, and insulating the governing party from public criticism. Moreover, some observers have argued that the ANC's internal structure is particularly centralized and hierarchical, and they point out that many in the ANC view its opposition as unpatriotic and disloyal.[13]

National elections are held at least every five years, and according to survey data from 2008, about 68 percent of South Africans identify with a political party. Since

South African National Assembly Elections, 2004, 2009, and 2014

PARTY	2004		2009		2014	
	% VOTE	# SEATS	% VOTE	# SEATS	% VOTE	# SEATS
ANC	70	279	66	264	62	249
DA	12	50	17	67	22	89
EFF	—	—	—	—	6	25
IFP	7	28	5	18	2	10
COPE	—	—	7	30	1	3
NNP	2	36	—	—	—	—
Others	9	7	5	21	7	24
Total	100	400	100	400	100	400

Key to Party Acronyms: ANC: African National Congress; COPE: Congress of the People; DA: Democratic Alliance; EFF: Economic Freedom Fighters; IFP: Inkatha Freedom Party; NNP: New National Party

Source: Electoral Commission of South Africa, www.elections.org.za (accessed 6/1/14).

1994, South African political parties have been heavily influenced by race. In the words of one leading scholar, "Post-apartheid South African elections bear an unmistakable racial imprint: Africans vote for one set of parties, whites support a different set of parties, and, with few exceptions, there is no cross-over voting between these groups."[14] In the 1999 elections, for example, 95 percent of blacks voted for the ANC, IFP, or other predominantly black parties, while 81 percent of whites supported the DA or other mostly white parties. Only colored and Indian voters more evenly split their votes among black and white parties (40 percent of coloreds and 34 percent of Indians backed white parties).[15]

CIVIL SOCIETY

The exclusionary nature of the apartheid regime was built upon the policy of destroying black opposition, which it carried out by weakening any form of organized resistance. Black civil society in South Africa was crushed to an extent not seen elsewhere in colonial Africa: traditional institutions were undermined, co-opted, and repressed wherever possible. Yet even with such pressure, anti-apartheid nongovernmental organizations (NGOs) continued to form and were vital in organizing the resistance that would help bring about democracy.

Since democratization, South Africa has developed a civil society that one scholar describes as "vigorous, effective, and shallow."[16] After 1994, the ANC attempted to co-opt many civil society groups, bringing them under its direction. Nevertheless, a whole host of groups has formed to pressure ANC-led governments on a gamut of issues, from providing basic services to protecting minority groups. Perhaps the best example of an effective civil society group is the Treatment Action Campaign (TAC), which successfully pressured the government into an about-face in its HIV/AIDS policies. Founded in 1998 by HIV-positive activists, the TAC used a variety of tactics, ranging from legal action to civil disobedience.

Despite the proliferation of civil society groups, some see South African civil society as shallow because engagement is still restricted to the relatively well-off minority. Moreover, from a comparative perspective, and with the exception of political protest, other forms of public activism (including membership in pressure groups) remain low in South Africa. A 2010 study of 20 African countries showed that South Africans' civic and political participation was among the lowest in the region.[17]

One major actor in civil society is organized labor—in particular, the **Congress of South African Trade Unions (COSATU)**, formed in 1985 to promote workers' rights and oppose apartheid. In post-apartheid South Africa, COSATU remains powerful in defending labor interests.[18] Like many other organizations that were involved in the battle against apartheid, COSATU is strongly tied to the ANC through what is known as the Triple Alliance, which links COSATU, the ANC, and the SACP.

Despite this alliance, COSATU has been openly hostile to the ANC's liberal economic policies, and this hostility has generated friction. COSATU has complained about the consistently high rate of unemployment that has weakened the union movement. (Only a small minority of South Africa's workforce is unionized.) It has also been vocal in opposing the government's weak criticism of the Mugabe regime in neighboring Zimbabwe. COSATU has considered severing its ties to the ANC, but like other civic actors, it fears that doing so will result in its political marginalization. While COSATU backed Jacob Zuma's challenge to Thabo Mbeki, relations between Zuma and COSATU soon soured. A wave of COSATU-led strikes in 2010, mainly over demands for higher wages, crippled South Africa's economy. COSATU eventually compromised over the issue, sensitive to criticisms that excessive wage demands might worsen South Africa's very high unemployment rate. Another wave of strikes in South Africa's mines in 2012 turned violent, leading some top COSATU leaders to call for nationalization of the mines. In 2014, COSATU expelled its largest member union, the National Union of Metalworkers of South Africa (NUMSA), after NUMSA's leadership called on COSATU to end its alliance with the ANC. NUMSA members made up about 15 percent of COSATU membership, and other COSATU unions left the organization in support of the metal workers.

A second important element of civil society is the media. Since 1994, electronic and print media have expanded substantially, making for a relatively well-informed public. South Africans place a high degree of trust in the media, more so than they place in any of the state institutions, perhaps due in part to the ethnic integration of television and other outlets. In 2008, concerns were raised when individuals close to the ANC leadership purchased one of South Africa's four main media groups, and in 2010, the ANC introduced and passed proposals aimed at countering what it viewed as an excessively critical media. Some of those measures were interpreted as attempts to muzzle South Africa's vibrant and independent media. Over the next year, the bill was heavily amended. The version approved in November 2011, called the Protection of State Information bill, limited the ability to classify documents to police, security, and intelligence services, and it significantly reduced prison sentences for most illegal disclosures of information. But the ANC rejected calls to include an exception protecting the release of information that could be shown to be in the public interest.

After decades of apartheid authoritarianism, South Africans are sensitive to any perceived erosion of their hard-won civil liberties. The Protection of State

Information bill and the ANC's plan to create a special tribunal to adjudicate complaints about unfair media coverage are signs of the governing party's increasingly defensive posture vis-à-vis South Africa's media. But the controversy also reveals a number of strengths in South Africa's democracy. The government was forced to heavily amend the legislation. Public protest and debate were vigorous and indicated that South African civil society is not easily intimidated by the government. President Zuma, yielding to public protest, refused to sign the bill and sent it back to the legislature for more deliberation. Finally, opponents have vowed to challenge the new law in South Africa's Constitutional Court, if Zuma were to sign the bill. That body has shown its willingness to overturn legislation.

Society

Given the ethnic diversity of South Africa's inhabitants and the colonial and national policies of systematic racial discrimination, it is no surprise that South African society has been (and in many ways remains) significantly divided along racial and ethnic lines. In fact, one of the most tragic effects of apartheid was that the social policy of racial segregation was compounded—indeed, reinforced—by political persecution and economic discrimination.

What is surprising is the extent to which both groups and individuals in contemporary South Africa identify with the South African nation and express patriotism toward the state. A recent public opinion survey found that 83 percent of respondents express pride in being South African, and about half of South Africans claim a primary identification as South African, versus about 10 percent of South Africans who identify primarily with an ethnic group. Unfortunately, this shared national identity has not easily been translated into domestic peace or tolerance among the country's various groups. Despite South Africa's ability to avoid much of the ethnic violence and civil war that plagues other portions of the continent, there is much truth to former president Thabo Mbeki's indictment that South Africa remains in many ways two nations: one is wealthy and largely white; the other, poor and largely black. And, alarmingly, the percentage of South Africans who express confidence that South Africa can achieve racial harmony, though still a majority, has been declining.

RACISM IN THE RAINBOW NATION

Race relations have come a long way since Nelson Mandela issued his famous call for a multiethnic "rainbow nation." Public opinion research demonstrates that in the first decade of democracy, most South Africans thought that race relations had improved. However, since democratization a number of highly publicized incidents have challenged the idea of a rainbow nation.

In 2008, after the administration of the formerly all-white Afrikaner University of the Free State decided to integrate dormitories, angry white students produced a video of a mock initiation in which black students (portrayed by black staff members) were humiliated. A discovery of a whites-only restroom in a police station, a shooting rampage by a racist youth gang (in which four blacks were killed), and a number of anti-Afrikaner slogans employed by Julius Malema, the former leader of the ANC Youth League, have all been disturbing examples of the fact that racism and racial tensions have not been eradicated. Malema, who was closely associated with President Jacob Zuma, made a series of statements that appeared to incite violence against Afrikaners leading to his 2010 conviction on charges of issuing hate speech and his expulsion from the ANC in 2012.

ETHNIC AND NATIONAL IDENTITY

As we have discussed, South Africa is truly a multiracial and multiethnic society. Under apartheid, the government not only enforced policies of separate racial development but also used its "homelands" policy to divide and conquer the country's many ethnic and tribal groups. Although Bantustans (homelands) were legally dissolved in 1994, many citizens (particularly urban blacks) had never identified with or even visited their alleged homeland. Nonetheless, black Africans, particularly rural blacks, retain strong ethnic identities.

Like black South Africans, the white population has a long history of ethnic division, stemming from the colonial-era conflict between the Afrikaners and the British. Apartheid allowed Afrikaners to separate the minority whites from the majority blacks and to culturally dominate the white English subculture.

But whereas ethnic groups were fastidiously segregated under apartheid, language has rendered the multiethnic fabric of South Africa far more complex. Indeed, linguistic differences have brought groups together and pushed them apart. Nine languages spoken exclusively by blacks are now enshrined in the constitution. Though violently resisted by blacks during apartheid, Afrikaans remains the preferred tongue of Afrikaners as well as most colored South Africans. As is true in many polyglot former colonies, the English language unifies the country's citizens somewhat. However, because most blacks do not speak English as their first language, the more dominant it becomes in South Africa, the greater the disadvantage blacks will have vis-à-vis the white minority.

Similarly, religion has both unified and divided South African society. From a comparative perspective, South Africa remains a religious society. More than two-thirds of all South Africans, including most whites and coloreds and nearly two-thirds of blacks, identify themselves as Christian. Over 70 percent report that religion is very important to them, and 64 percent consider themselves religious.[19] However, the percentage of South Africans who claim to be religious dropped 19 percent from 2005 to 2012, and the 2011 census was the first to omit questions about religiosity.[20] The Dutch Reformed Church (sometimes called "the National Party in prayer") had a particularly important role in unifying Afrikaners (first against the British, then against black Africans) and providing divine justification (at least in the eyes of its members) for their separate and superior status.

As with racial discrimination in the United States, the dismantling of legal racism in South Africa and the national strides taken toward reconciliation have not fully eliminated racial prejudice or distrust. Levels of black-on-white violence and even black-on-black violence climbed during the 1990s, particularly in the townships. Murder rates in South Africa are now nearly nine times higher than those in the United States.

Despite persistent racial tensions, South Africans enjoy a remarkably high level of national identity and patriotism. And while the apartheid state essentially excluded all nonwhites from political life, citizenship is now universally shared. However, the legacies of division and exclusion, combined with the perceived inability of the ANC

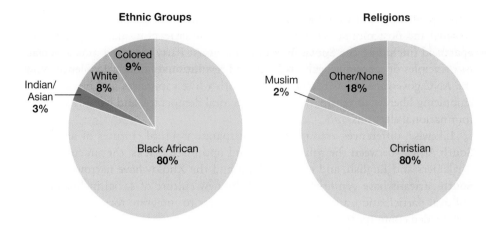

Ethnic Groups

Colored 9%
White 8%
Indian/Asian 3%
Black African 80%

Religions

Muslim 2%
Other/None 18%
Christian 80%

government to deliver socioeconomic benefits, have dampened citizen participation and increased levels of political apathy since apartheid ended. Recent polls show that support for democracy remains very strong in South Africa, but trust in government and satisfaction with government policy have declined in recent years.

EDUCATION AS A SOURCE OF INEQUALITY

Perhaps the most enduring legacy of apartheid can be found in South Africa's woefully inadequate education system.[21] Although its schools are formally integrated, de facto segregation by race remains the norm. Since the end of apartheid, the percentage of black South Africans receiving no schooling whatsoever has dropped from 24 percent to 10 percent, but that figure is still much higher than for whites, coloreds, or Asians.

Most schools serving blacks lack basic amenities such as textbooks, libraries, and science laboratories, while schools serving mostly white students have vastly superior facilities. Half of all students in South Africa drop out of high school before taking their "metric" exam, which is required for graduation. Only about half of blacks pass their metric exams, but 99 percent of whites, 92 percent of Indians, and 76 percent of coloreds get passing grades. According to the 2011 census, 8.3 percent of blacks received some sort of higher education—over double the percentage in 1996, two years after apartheid ended—but the percentage for white South Africans was over 36 percent. In 2015, nationwide protests on college campuses throughout South Africa called attention to the fact that blacks make up only a very small percentage of the total university population, and most university faculty members are white. This massive education deficit has created a major shortage of skilled black labor and is a serious impediment to the ANC's goal of integrating blacks into South Africa's business elite.

IDEOLOGY AND POLITICAL CULTURE

Although it may be troubling for the future of South African democracy, a relative decline in levels of political interest since the tumultuous early 1990s should not be surprising. Since the fall of apartheid, political ideologies have also become less pronounced and more pragmatic. In the old South Africa, Afrikaner politicians and intellectuals combined and refined political and theological ideas to form an ideology of racist authoritarianism. Like many other movements of resistance in colonial and postcolonial settings, the ANC and other revolutionary opponents of apartheid (including the South African Communist Party) adopted radical socialist principles of economic egalitarianism and revolutionary political violence. Now the ANC government has reached out to both white capitalists and black voters, embracing liberal capitalism, promoting electoral democracy, and handily winning four national elections.

Likewise, differences among the very disparate political cultures of apartheid South Africa—between the ruling whites and oppressed blacks, the subcultures of Afrikaners and English, and even the Zulu and the Xhosa—have narrowed. Many South Africans have genuinely embraced the new culture of social inclusion and political participation and have supported efforts to integrate former adversaries and divided communities.

Certainly the highest-profile effort of bridge building was the **Truth and Reconciliation Commission**. Convened in 1995 and led by **Archbishop Desmond Tutu**, the commission was charged with two goals: first, establishing the "truth" of crimes committed (on all sides) from the time of the 1960 Sharpeville Massacre through the outlawing of apartheid in 1994; and second, using that truth as the essential foundation for healing the deep wounds of the era. The commission was given the authority to hear confessions, grant amnesty to those who were deemed to have told the complete truth, and provide recommendations for promoting long-term reconciliation (including reparation payments). While the commission uncovered a great deal of horrific "truth," much controversy surrounded the final report (some alleged it was too critical of apartheid; others suggested it was too quick to condemn actions by the ANC). Though it is not surprising, given the enormity of the crimes, genuine reconciliation has remained elusive. In February 2015, the Justice Ministry ordered the release of former police colonel Eugene de Kock, a self-confessed apartheid-era death squad leader responsible for over 100 acts of torture and murder. His release rekindled the debate over reconciliation. De Kock, whose nickname was "Prime Evil," had confessed his horrific crimes to the Truth and Reconciliation Commission and had received amnesty for many of them. South African courts nevertheless sentenced him to multiple life sentences until

The Evolution of Levels of Trust in South Africa, 2006–2015

Percentage expressing a lot or some trust in:

	2006	2011	2015
Courts	68	56	57
Electoral agency	57	62	56
Police	48	49	45
Ruling party	61	61	41
Parliament	55	66	39
President	69	69	32

Source: www.afrobarometer.org (accessed 8/19/16).

the ANC government decided to release him "in the interest of nation building and reconciliation."

Nonetheless, many observers remain optimistic that ANC-governed South Africa can overcome the tragedies of the country's history and its current social and economic woes, including endemic crime and violence. They argue that both the South African people and political culture have shown a remarkable capacity to avoid conflict even in the face of serious economic and social problems. Scholars note "countervailing sources of stability" in South Africa's political culture, including a pervasive tradition of collective decision making (known as *ubuntu*), the ANC's proven pragmatism and political discipline, and the "prudential caution" of whites and blacks that was forged during the period of transition. Perhaps most important, with the rise of a new black capitalist class, the country has seen the gradual emergence of a multiracial elite.

South Africa's political culture shows many signs of supporting democracy. According to a 2011 public opinion study, about 60 percent of South Africans are satisfied with how democracy works (down from about 65 percent in 2006), and most of them think democracy is preferable to all other systems.[22] South Africans express strong support for the protection of civil liberties and minority rights, and a large majority of South Africans reject the notion of one-party rule. South Africans are split fairly evenly between those who believe that the government is responsible for improving the well-being of the population and those who believe that individuals are primarily responsible for themselves.

Political Economy

The political and social challenges confronting South Africa today cannot be separated from its economic challenges. Having vanquished the demon of apartheid, South Africa faces massive unemployment, growing income inequality, and persistent poverty among its poorest citizens.[23]

The challenge facing the ANC government has been to adopt policies that can ameliorate these problems without alienating its broad and disparate constituencies as well as to preserve South Africa's nascent democracy and civil liberties. Moreover, successful democratic political transition has not guaranteed the social and economic transformation of South Africa. In fact, it has in some ways made it more problematic, as issues of equality—delayed in the name of promoting political freedom—have taken on more significance.

To its credit, for two decades ANC governments were able to improve the economy by curtailing debt, reversing inflation, and expanding exports. They also improved employment opportunities and income for the growing black middle class; for South Africa's poor, they greatly expanded access to basic necessities, such as water, electricity, and housing (see "What Difference Did Democracy Make?," p. 655). By African standards, the South African economy is highly developed, and its companies have become major investors elsewhere in the region. South Africa's economy is also highly diversified although still fairly dependent on the country's large mineral resources, particularly gold and diamonds.

Historically, both British- and Afrikaner-controlled governments sponsored political-economic systems that favored their own ethnic

Labor Force by Occupation

- Industry 23%
- Agriculture 5%
- Services 72%

constituents. In the early twentieth century, government policy facilitated English ownership and control of mines and other industries, even in Afrikaner-dominated regions of the country. Squeezed by wealthier and more highly skilled English workers from above and by cheaper black labor from below, Afrikaners sought political power largely to redress what they saw as economic oppression.

With this power, the NP government promoted essentially mercantilist policies of import substitution to promote local and, more specifically, Afrikaner industry. Though those policies were initially adopted to nurture an Afrikaner capitalist class, by the 1970s the international economic sanctions imposed on South Africa gave the state little option but to substitute local production and markets for those lost abroad. During its tenure, the NP government intervened extensively in the marketplace, imposing high tariffs and other trade barriers on imports; bestowing lucrative government contracts on favored firms; establishing state-owned enterprises (SOEs) in such key industries as weapons, steel, and energy production; and using oligopolistic profits from industries ranging from gold and diamond exports to fuel industrialization.

Throughout the 1970s, the South African economy thrived and Afrikaners prospered. At the same time, the absence of economic opportunity for black Africans and the prohibition against the formation of black trade unions kept black labor costs artificially low, encouraging foreign investors eager to take advantage of the cheap labor and relative stability that authoritarian South Africa promised. During the 1980s, however, foreign firms and countries faced growing moral and legal pressures to divest their South African interests. At that time, too, multiracial trade unions (including COSATU) were legalized and began demanding higher wages. Finally, the government began to face a shortage of skilled labor. Limiting access to education for blacks meant that the economy could not depend on a large pool of educated workers. These pressures dealt severe—and some would say ultimately fatal—economic blows to the apartheid regime.

Given the history of policies benefiting the English and the Afrikaners, many observers expected the victorious ANC to adopt statist policies to redress the discrimination and exclusion that blacks had experienced for generations. Not only would such policies have promised to be popular with the ANC's majority black constituency, but this kind of progressive state intervention, designed to redistribute wealth and promote greater equality, would also have been in harmony with the long-standing socialist ideological heritage of the ANC and its allies. White property owners feared that a great share of their economic assets would simply be seized by the state. This, then, would be state manipulation of the market by the left rather than the right—but state intervention all the same.

The ANC's approach to the economy was much less radical than expected, and in many ways the ANC ultimately pursued a liberal political-economic model. In 1994, Nelson Mandela announced the Reconstruction and Development Programme (RDP), which focused on meeting the basic needs of South Africans living in poverty. The ANC argued that housing, electricity, jobs, safe drinking water, affordable health care, and a safe environment had to take precedence over economic growth.

Within two years, however, the ANC government had recognized that the huge costs of the RDP were unsustainable in the absence of substantially more foreign investment and greater, rapid economic growth. In addition, the failure of communism in Eastern Europe and the Soviet Union and the increasing popularity

What Difference Did Democracy Make?

% HOUSEHOLDS WITH	BLACK AFRICAN			COLORED			WHITE		
	1996	2001	2011	1996	2001	2011	1996	2001	2011
Formal dwelling	54	60	73	89	89	90	99	99	99
Tap water	74	80	89	95	97	98	97	99	99
Electricity	45	41	81	84	82	94	99	97	99
Flush toilets	78	78	90	88	89	92	99	99	99

Source: Statistics South Africa, based on national census data, www.statssa.gov.za/census/census_2011/census_products/Census_2011_Fact_sheet.pdf (accessed 7/10/17).

of neoliberal market solutions within international development circles helped turn the ANC leadership away from its socialist roots. In 1996, the government adopted a plan of liberal macroeconomic structural adjustment known as **Growth, Employment, and Redistribution (GEAR)**. GEAR called for opening trade, privatizing SOEs, and otherwise limiting the state's role in the marketplace in an effort to stimulate growth and attract foreign investment. These policies have paid dividends: growth rates under the ANC have been steady, if not spectacular, and are a vast improvement over apartheid-era governments.

Not surprisingly, this dramatic shift in redistributive priorities and interventionist policies has angered the ANC's longtime allies on the left, COSATU and the SACP. In labor protests against GEAR, COSATU leaders have called the GEAR privatization of the SOEs "born-again apartheid" and predicted devastating consequences for South Africa's working poor. The government has found itself in the position of being praised by the International Monetary Fund for promoting GEAR privatization and delivering steady rates of economic growth and at the same time being attacked by its erstwhile anti-apartheid allies. The 2013 creation of the Economic Freedom Fighters (EFF) Party by former ANC youth leader Julius Malema created a new electoral rival to the ANC's left. The EFF called for a dramatic increase in redistribution of South Africa's wealth and nationalization of some of the private sector.

In facing this catch-22, the government is trying to please all sides. The ANC remains committed to land reform and basic health care, and it funds programs to provide water, electricity, phones, and housing to the poor. It also continues to woo foreign investment by cutting inflation, lowering taxes, and keeping a lid on its spending to promote economic growth. It has targeted key industries and manufacturing sectors, offering low-interest loans and other incentives for investment. As in other developing economies, the government has promoted microcredit, or small-loan, initiatives designed to assist the very poorest in starting businesses. So far, GEAR and related policies have borne some fruit in the form of increased growth rates that, it is hoped, will help reduce unemployment over the coming decade. But there are still serious obstacles to be overcome.

Chief among these is persistent income inequality (see "In Comparison: Gini Index of Economic Inequality," p. 657). Despite the ANC government's affirmative action efforts and the emergence of a small but growing black middle and upper class, the white minority still dominates the economy. South Africa has one of the highest levels of income inequality in the world. Moreover, while the rising income of some blacks and the government's redistribution efforts have led to a decline in inequality among races, overall inequality among all South Africans continues to increase. The danger is that a white economic elite will simply be replaced by a black one, and income redistribution will be no better (and perhaps worse) than before apartheid.

The ANC has been especially unsuccessful in redistributing land, which remains overwhelmingly concentrated in the hands of the white minority. By 2016, less than 10 percent of land had been redistributed to blacks—a figure far short of the goal of 30 percent initially established by the ANC.[24] Until recently the ANC has supported a system of voluntary land reform, in which the state purchased land for redistribution from willing sellers. In 2016, the ANC passed an Expropriation Bill, which allows the state to expropriate land from private owners as long as it pays fair market value for the property.

South Africa continues to suffer from extremely high rates of unemployment. By 2016, unemployment had risen to 26 percent, and the rate was much higher for young and black South Africans. Some have blamed South Africa's rigid labor laws, but COSATU and others have questioned the government's commitment to job creation. South Africa's growth rate has simply not been high enough to generate enough employment. The persistence of massive levels of poverty is an equally vexing problem facing South Africa. About half of all South Africans are below the official poverty level. When asked to identify the greatest problem facing South Africa, the largest percentage of survey respondents cited unemployment.[25]

The ANC's main approach to affirmative action has been its policy of **Broad-Based Black Economic Empowerment (BEE)**. The goal of BEE is to increase the presence of disadvantaged South Africans (including coloreds and Asians) in a number of areas of the economy, including ownership of business, access to corporate management and training, and access to government procurement. Beginning in 2007, the government adopted a number of codes creating targets for each of these areas. State organizations and enterprises, and private-sector firms that wish to do business with the state, must show progress on meeting some combination of these goals. New state agencies have been developed to rate organizations and enterprises, using "scorecards" that award points for meeting individual targets.

To date, BEE results have been mixed. A small group of blacks with close ties to the ANC have benefited enormously from the policy, but their success has only increased the gap between wealthy and poor blacks. Critics of the policy claim that inequality in the educational system and massive unemployment are the root causes of inequality in South Africa. Others fear the system will become cumbersome and a burden on the private sector.

A final challenge worth noting is the loss of human resources through the emigration of skilled workers. This brain drain is sometimes called "white flight," because a high proportion of those leaving South Africa are young white professionals who are increasingly skeptical of their prospects in their native country. The brain drain is particularly noticeable in the English-speaking population, whose ties to the country are not as old as those of the Afrikaners. It is estimated that nearly 20 percent of whites have emigrated from South Africa since the early 1990s.[26] To develop and

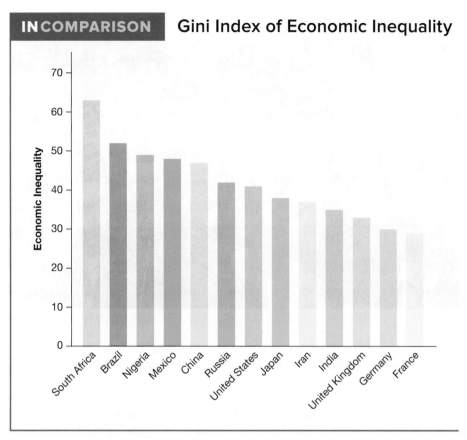

IN COMPARISON Gini Index of Economic Inequality

Economic Inequality

South Africa, Brazil, Nigeria, Mexico, China, Russia, United States, Japan, Iran, India, United Kingdom, Germany, France

Note: Graph reflects data for most recent year available. The Gini index measures inequality (100 = complete inequality; 0 = complete equality).

Source: The World Bank, http://data.worldbank.org/indicator/SI.POV.GINI (accessed 7/28/17); CIA World Factbook, https://www.cia/gov/library/publications/the-world-factbook (accessed 5/20/14).

diversify its economy, South Africa needs to create as well as retain its most skilled workers, both black and white.

Democratic governments have reoriented the South African economy since the days of apartheid. But in the face of the enormous challenges that remain, there is a growing disillusionment with the state of South Africa's economy. According to a recent public opinion study, a steadily growing number of South Africans feel that the government's economic policies have "hurt most people and benefited only a few."[27] One sign of the growing frustration over the state of the South African economy was the wave of violent strikes that shook South Africa's mining sector in the summer of 2012. A strike at a large platinum mine in Marikana, in the North West Province, resulted in 45 deaths when striking miners confronted police. Strikes quickly spread to other mines, where workers demanded higher wages and better working conditions.

By 2016, South Africa's economy was experiencing its worst economic crisis in decades. Growth was anemic and had declined for four consecutive years, South Africa's public debt increased dramatically, and its credit rating was lowered. Much of the downturn was caused by a sharp decline in prices for key export commodities. But President Zuma's inability to stem government spending

South African workers protest the deaths of 45 miners during clashes with police in 2012. The workers were striking for better pay, and the violence, which the press described as a massacre, increased tensions between the ANC government and South Africa's powerful National Union of Mineworkers.

and corruption, and his sometimes erratic governing style, have also contributed to the crisis. In March 2017, Zuma fired his finance minister, Pravin Gordhan, who had a reputation as a fierce anticorruption advocate. Gordhan was replaced by a Zuma loyalist with little economic expertise. The firing raised fears that Zuma might embrace a more populist political-economic orientation, and South Africa's international bond rating was downgraded to junk status as a result.

Current Issues in South Africa

CRIME AND CORRUPTION

South Africans regularly cite crime as among the most serious problems facing the country. Crime rates skyrocketed after the transition to democracy but have steadily dropped after peaking in 2003. The rate of violent crime in South Africa, including murder, rape, and carjacking, is extremely high. Nearly 15,000 South Africans are murdered each year, a rate nine times greater than the U.S. average. Carjacking, often resulting in death or serious injury, is commonplace and has increased dramatically since 1994. Pernicious inequality, unemployment, and poverty, particularly in the townships, and corruption in the police force have exacerbated the serious crime problem. Crime not only undermines the social fabric but also deters domestic and international investment and diverts security resources that could be spent elsewhere.

South Africa also faces a serious problem of deep-seated government corruption. According to South Africa's auditor general, graft and cronyism have led to massive waste and have hampered the government's ability to deliver services and reduce inequality.[28] Public opinion research has shown a steady growth in public concern about corruption since 1994, fueled in part by a number of high-profile corruption scandals that affected the governing ANC. By 2011, a quarter of South African respondents told researchers that corruption was one of the most important problems facing the country; this figure was double the one in 2002.[29] The data show that provincial local governments in particular are viewed as corrupt (over half of respondents view them as corrupt), while about 40 percent of respondents view the president and legislators as corrupt.

Faced with growing public concern over corruption, in 1999 President Mbeki established an elite crime-fighting unit: the Directorate of Special Operations, popularly known as the Scorpions. The unit, whose motto was "loved by the people, feared by the criminals," was well funded, highly trained, and had its own staff of investigators and prosecutors. It quickly became a popular and highly effective unit, achieving conviction rates much higher than those of the regular police force. The Scorpions ran into trouble, however, when the force began to investigate corruption within the ANC government. When they brought corruption charges against then former deputy president Jacob Zuma that led to his firing, Zuma's supporters claimed that the Scorpions were merely attempting to limit opposition within the ANC. A bitter political rivalry and turf war broke out between the police and the Scorpions. Despite widespread public opposition in 2008, Zuma's supporters passed legislation that reintegrated the Scorpions into the police force, effectively disbanding the unit.

Once in office, Zuma pledged to crack down on corruption by creating a performance, monitoring, and evaluation cabinet post within the government. Nevertheless, in recent years the ANC has been rocked by numerous scandals that call into question Zuma's commitment to fighting corruption. Zuma has attempted to weaken the power of the National Prosecuting Authority, the government prosecution office that has raised over 700 charges of corruption, fraud and tax evasion. Allegations that the president is corrupt and a 2016 court ruling that he used public

Demonstrators protest the perceived corruption of President Jacob Zuma in April 2017.

funds to remodel his personal residence have contributed to the concern about a growing lack of transparency. Zuma's 2017 firing of a well-respected anticorruption finance minister led to nationwide protests against the perceived corruption of the ANC.

THE DEVASTATION OF HIV/AIDS

South Africa is believed to have the highest number of HIV-positive citizens in the world (estimated in 2015 at about 7 million people, or 18 percent of the population), and at the height of the epidemic 1,000 South Africans died of AIDS every day.[30] Despite increased access to affordable drugs, most of those infected will die of the disease. Besides being a human and social tragedy, this situation will have, and already has had, huge consequences for the economy. The HIV/AIDS pandemic has damaged South Africa's economy, and South Africans' life expectancy has dropped from age 60 to age 50 in the past two decades. The health care system is underfunded and grossly inadequate, and corporations are increasingly wary of investing in personnel, given the mortality odds their employees face.

Compounding this problem is a high degree of stigma attached to those with HIV/AIDS, not to mention the questionable handling of the issue by Thabo Mbeki and other ANC politicians. They cast doubt on the causal link between HIV and AIDS and resisted conventional drugs and drug protocols prescribed in the West, citing scientifically dubious theories and charging the West with racist views of African sexuality. Pressure from international and domestic activist groups and from Nelson Mandela (whose son died of AIDS) is slowly raising awareness and the level of treatment, but treatment remains limited in the face of this devastating epidemic.

Under President Zuma, South Africa is beginning to make gains in the fight against HIV/AIDS. His government has initiated the world's largest HIV testing and treatment program. (Zuma publicly announced that he had been tested.) There is now evidence that the rate of HIV/AIDS infections has leveled off, but attempts to stem the tide are hampered by the reluctance of South African men to use condoms as well as the alarmingly high rate of rape. Rumors that President Zuma favors Nkosazana Dlamini-Zuma to be his successor has alarmed some public health advocates. She is a former wife of Zuma, and current chair of the African Union, who, as South Africa's health minister from 1994 to 1999, rejected advice from the scientific community about the best way to treat HIV/AIDS.

Key Terms

Nigeria's vast oil resources have been a source of great wealth, but this "resource curse" has also fostered endemic corruption and violence, exacerbated income inequality, and caused untold environmental damage.

Nigeria

Why Study This Case?

Nigeria stands out in ways both impressive and disheartening. First, this "giant of Africa" is noteworthy for its sheer size: it is the largest country in Africa in terms of population and is predicted by midcentury to trail only India and China as the world's third most populous nation. Second, in 2014, Nigeria passed South Africa as the continent's largest economy. And third, unlike many other African countries, Nigeria is blessed with enormous natural wealth, from oil to agriculture. Following independence from British rule in 1960, these assets were expected to make Nigeria a major regional, if not global, actor.

Yet exactly the opposite happened. Nigeria has become renowned for all that can go wrong with political misrule, social unrest, economic inequality, and environmental degradation. For much of the time since independence, the country has been under military rule. These long periods of military dictatorship have coincided with widespread corruption, and substantial portions of the country's oil revenues and other resources have been channeled to those in power. Even as Nigeria earns billions of dollars in oil exports each year, it has become one of the poorest and least-developed countries in the world. Nigeria offers an excellent example of a country whose natural resources have been used by those in power to buy supporters and repress the public.

However, the long era of military rule may now be at an end. In 1999, Nigeria returned to civilian rule, and since then a fragile democratic system has taken hold. Still, much remains to be done. Nigeria lacks effective rule of law and continues to be recognized as one of the most corrupt countries in the world. The state lacks the capacity to carry out many basic tasks and also has questionable control over the monopoly of violence, in terms of both civilian authority over the military and the ability to contain the country's widespread political and criminal violence. The standard of living for the average Nigerian remains very low—more than

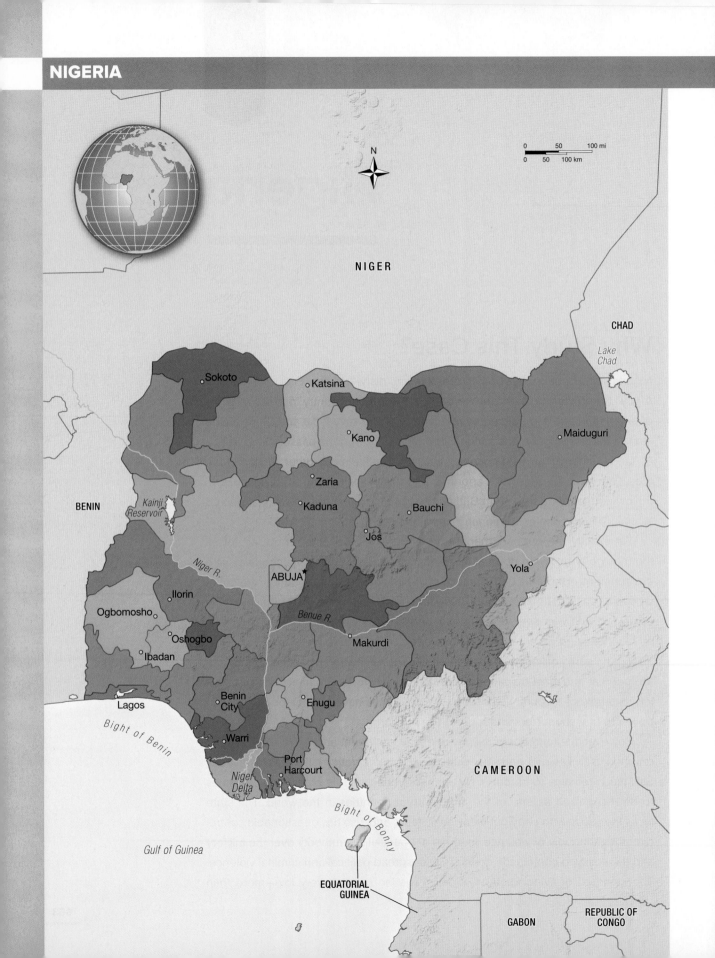

N

0   50   100 mi
0   50   100 km

NIGER

CHAD

Lake
Chad

Sokoto

Katsina

Kano

Maiduguri

BENIN

Kainji
Reservoir

Zaria

Kaduna

Bauchi

Jos

Niger R.

ABUJA

Yola

Benue R.

Ilorin

Ogbomosho

Oshogbo

Ibadan

Makurdi

Benin
City

Enugu

Lagos

Warri

Port
Harcourt

CAMEROON

Bight of Benin

Niger
Delta

Bight of Bonny

Gulf of Guinea

EQUATORIAL
GUINEA

GABON

REPUBLIC OF
CONGO

three-fourths of the population survives on less than two dollars per day, far below what the country's wealth should ensure. And despite the return of democratic governance, levels of corruption, economic underdevelopment, income inequality, political violence, and environmental damage have increased rather than declined.

These legacies of political misrule may seem challenging enough for Nigeria, but the country's sheer size and diversity are another concern. Nigeria contains more than 250 ethnic groups, whose local interests and differences have been sharpened by a perniciously corrupt form of federalism. Although nearly three decades of military rule kept this fractiousness in check, democratic rule has allowed tensions and violence to surface. Most disturbing are the growing ethnic rifts between the Muslim north and the Christian and animist south as well as the rise of an Islamic insurgency associated with the terrorist organization Boko Haram. The prospect of increasing tension among faiths in Nigeria leads some observers to worry that in the long run, the country will be ungovernable and will return to authoritarianism, civil war, or both. Is Nigeria doomed to be a failed or even partitioned state?

Nigeria provides a fascinating, if daunting, example of the possibilities and potential limits of state power and democracy under conditions of postcolonialism and a vast wealth of natural resources. Can the most recent transition from military rule to democracy help bring stability and prosperity to Nigeria? Or are the problems of state capacity and autonomy such that democracy cannot help improve them—and might even make them worse?

Historical Development of the State

Like many other developing countries, Nigeria's history progressed from local political organization to imperial control to more recent independence and instability. Contrary to common assumptions, precolonial Nigeria was neither undeveloped nor poorly organized. Rather, the region contained varying degrees and kinds of political and social organizations, some of which were highly complex and wide ranging.

Nigeria was the setting for several early kingdoms. As the roots of today's dominant ethnic groups began to take shape, new forms of political organization emerged. Around 1200 C.E., the Hausa to the north established a series of powerful city-states that served as conduits of north–south trade. In the southwest, the Yoruba kingdom of Oyo extended its power beyond the borders of modern-day Nigeria into present-day Togo. This kingdom grew wealthy through trade and the exploitation of natural resources, facilitated by its location along the coast. In the southeast, the Igbo (or, Ibo) maintained less-centralized political power, though they too had a precedent of earlier kingdoms and would come to play a central role in modern Nigerian politics.

ISLAM AND THE NIGERIAN NORTH

The fortunes of these three dominant ethnic groups (the Hausa, Yoruba, and Igbo) and other peoples in what is now Nigeria changed dramatically as contact with peoples, politics, and ideas from outside West Africa increased. The first important impact came not from Europe, however, but from the Middle East, with the spread of Islam.

By the eleventh century, Islam had found its way into the Hausa region of northern Nigeria, carried along trade routes linking the region to North Africa and beyond. By the fifteenth century, Islam had brought literacy and scholarship to the region through the Arabic language, though its influences remained largely confined to the Hausa elite. By the late eighteenth century, however, expanding contact with Islamic regions led to increasing conversions to the faith. The religion's growing influence was solidified by the leadership of Usman dan Fodio (1754–1817).

A religious scholar, Usman played an important role in spreading Islam among the Hausa and Fulani. He found widespread support among the peasantry, who felt oppressed under the city-states' warring monarchies and who saw in Islam's message a promise of greater social equality. Their embrace of Islam in turn alarmed those in power, eventually precipitating a conflict between the city-states and Usman. Following an initial conflict, Usman declared jihad against the Hausa city-states in 1804 and by 1808 had overthrown the ruling monarchs, establishing what became known as the Sokoto Caliphate. The Sokoto Caliphate became the largest empire in Africa at the time, providing a uniform government to a region previously wracked by war. Islam would now play a central role in western Africa and in the eventual establishment of an independent Nigerian state.

EUROPEAN IMPERIALISM

As Islam and centralized political organization spread across the north, the south experienced similarly dramatic effects with the arrival of the European powers. Europeans had begun arriving along Nigeria's coast by the late fifteenth century, purchasing from indigenous traders agricultural products and slaves (often captives from local wars). From the seventeenth to the nineteenth century, Europeans established several coastal ports to support the burgeoning slave trade, and the United Kingdom became the major trading power. During that time, more than 3 million slaves were shipped from Nigeria to the Americas.

In 1807, the United Kingdom banned the slave trade and established a naval presence off Nigeria's coast for enforcement, though illegal trade continued for another half century. The precipitous decline in the region's major export contributed to the collapse of the Yoruba's Oyo Empire and to divisions and warfare among its people. This disunity in turn paved the way for an expanded British presence in the interior. This colonial presence further expanded as British industrialization generated ever-greater demand for resources, such as palm oil, cocoa, and timber. At the same time, British missionaries began to proselytize in the coastal and southern regions, converting large numbers of Igbo and Yoruba to Christianity.

By 1861, the British had established a colony at Lagos. By the time of the 1884–85 Berlin Conference, other European powers had recognized the United Kingdom's "sphere of influence" along the coast. Fearing French and German encroachment in the interior, the United Kingdom quickly joined the European powers' scramble for Africa by asserting its authority far inland. Through a combination of diplomacy, co-optation, and force, Britain established control over both the north and the south.

In many areas, the British relied upon a policy of indirect rule. For example, as the Sokoto Caliphate was brought under British control, local leaders were simply absorbed into the new state bureaucracy. Furthermore, the British colonial administration respected Sharia—Islamic law—in noncriminal matters and prohibited Christian proselytizing in the northern region. Such policies helped limit local resistance but increased the power of some ethnic groups over others, giving them greater authority within the imperial administration. In areas where indirect rule was less successful, as among the Igbo, resistance was much more significant. In 1914, the various protectorates in the area under British control were unified under the name *Nigeria*. However, as a reflection and reinforcement of its distinct regional differences, the country remained highly decentralized administratively.

Following unification, Nigeria experienced dramatic change under British imperial rule. The British developed a modern infrastructure including ports, roads, and railways to facilitate economic development and extraction. Agricultural production continued to play an important role in exports. Within Nigerian society, development meant establishing Western educational policies and institutions, especially in regions where Christian missionaries were active. In general, indirect rule meant the development of a new local elite group more Westernized and more conscious of the complexities of imperialism. The creation of a colonial legislative council, with local elections for some of the seats, introduced the idea of democratic representative institutions, no matter how limited.

As in other British colonies such as India, exposure to Western ideas served as the foundation for resistance as Nigerians embraced what had once been alien concepts of nationalism, sovereignty, and self-rule. Such ideas, however, were not easily planted in Nigeria's complex political and cultural terrain. As economic development, urbanization, and state centralization increased the integration of Nigeria as a whole, however, the tentative notion of a Nigerian nation and state that could be independent from colonial rule began to emerge.

Following World War II, Nigeria saw the rapid expansion of various civil society organizations, ranging from political parties and ethnic movements to labor unions and business movements. Among the numerous political leaders who emerged during that time was Benjamin Nnamdi Azikiwe (1904–96). Born in northern Nigeria, Azikiwe studied and taught in the United States before returning to Nigeria in 1938. He established a daily newspaper and in 1944 helped found what later came to be known as the National Council of Nigerian Citizens (NCNC), which advocated national unity and self-government. While the NCNC sought to appeal to all Nigerians, it drew heavily from the Igbo. Other political parties, such as the Northern People's Congress (NPC) and the Action Group Party (AGP), were backed by Hausa Muslims and the Yoruba, respectively.

The British government attempted to deal with the rising tide of Nigerian activism, strikes, and competing demands by reforming the local constitution, creating regional assemblies, and formalizing the decentralized nature of imperial rule through a system of federalism. Executive power remained in the hands of a British governor, but increasingly authority devolved to the local level. Thus, while Nigerian nationalism became a potent force among some political elites, at the same time the devolution of power reinforced regional tendencies.

By the late 1950s, a great wave of independence was sweeping across Africa. The British government took measures to move Nigeria toward full independence. The British legislated an array of constitutional reforms that effectively created autonomous regions in the north, west, and east with the goal of ensuring the country's eventual national independence while remaining within the British Commonwealth. The new federal political structure consisted of three regions (Northern, Western, and Eastern), a directly elected House of Representatives, a Senate whose members were indirectly elected by the regional assemblies, a prime minister, and a governor-general who served as the representative of the British monarchy. Azikiwe was appointed governor-general.

On October 1, 1960, Nigeria formally gained its independence, creating what is known as the **First Republic**. Without much of the violence and destruction that plagued decolonization elsewhere, Azikiwe was named the first head of the new government. The new nation also enjoyed ongoing industrialization, strong exports, and the promise of oil revenues whose potential was just beginning to be explored.

INDEPENDENCE, CONFLICT, AND CIVIL WAR

The relative peace and the promises of an independent Nigeria quickly experienced rougher waters, however. Fragile coalition governments battled over some of the most essential questions regarding Nigerian statehood, including the scope of central versus local powers and national versus regional identity. Internal infighting and electoral setbacks weakened the major parties, and various groups across Nigeria made demands that the federal system be further decentralized to make way for additional states. Meanwhile other groups and leaders opposed such tactics, fearing these actions would undermine their own territorial authority or even lead to the breakup of the country. Sharply contested elections and electoral alliances were marked by ethnic tensions and electoral discrepancies. Economic disparities sharpened the ethnic conflict, and each group viewed the state as a means to siphon off wealth for its own people.

In the violent aftermath of the contentious 1965 regional assembly elections in the Western Region, 2,000 people died. Amid the increasing disorder, a group of army officers, primarily Igbos, staged a coup d'état, assassinating the prime minister, the leaders of several political parties, and a number of military officials from the north. The coup leaders suspended the constitution, banned political parties, and called for a unitary government and the end to northern domination. But the coup failed to impose order, setting off civil war instead. Conflict erupted between northern and Igbo troops; the coup leaders were in turn overthrown, and many of them were killed. Many Igbo living in the north were also massacred, and Igbo leaders who had supported the coup and an end to federalism as a way to weaken northern power now believed that their people and region had no future in a multiethnic Nigeria.

In May 1967, the Igbo-dominated Eastern Region seceded from Nigeria, declaring itself the **Republic of Biafra**. Although outnumbered and outgunned, the Biafrans held off the Nigerian military for three years, aided in part by international supporters who believed the Nigerian government was conducting a genocidal war against the Igbo. Azikiwe, who had been dismissed from his post by the military government and was himself an ethnic Igbo, became a prominent supporter of Biafran independence. In 1970, Biafra was defeated. Although the defeat did not lead to the Igbo extermination that many had feared, the war itself exacted huge costs in military and civilian life: estimates range from 500,000 to 3 million fatalities.[1]

THE MILITARY ERA

The armed forces ended the Nigerian Civil War, but their role in the politics of Nigeria was just beginning. The 1966 countercoup in response to the takeover by Igbo army officers established the Federal Military Government (FMG), which

Political Development

1100s	Hausa kingdom is formed in the north; Oyo kingdom is formed in the southwest.
1472	Portuguese navigators reach the Nigerian coast.
1500s–1800s	Slave trade develops and flourishes.
1809	Sokoto Caliphate is founded.
1861–1914	Britain acquires Lagos and establishes a series of Nigerian protectorates.
1960	Nigeria achieves independence and creates the First Republic.
1967–70	In Nigerian Civil War, Biafra fails to win independence.
1976	Olusegun Obasanjo comes to power, initiating transition to civilian rule.
1979	Elections bring Shehu Shagari to power, establishing the Second Republic.
1983–93	Military rulers again seize power.
1993	Transition to civilian rule (the Third Republic) fails; Sani Abacha seizes power.
1995	Activist Ken Saro-Wiwa is executed.
1998	Abacha dies; Abdulsalami Abubakar succeeds him as the military head of government.
1999	Military rule ends and the Fourth Republic is established; Obasanjo is elected president.
2000	Sharia criminal law is adopted by 12 northern states.
2007	Obasanjo steps down; Umaru Yar'Adua comes to power in a fraudulent election, marking Nigeria's first civilian transfer of power.
2009	Yar'Adua negotiates an amnesty with Niger Delta militants, and Boko Haram launches its Islamic insurgency in the north.
2010	Yar'Adua dies in office, and Vice President Goodluck Jonathan is named president.
2011	Jonathan is elected president in a relatively clean democratic election.
2015	Former military ruler Muhammadu Buhari is elected, marking the first democratic transfer of power between civilians from different parties.

initially claimed that it would soon return power to civilian control. The FMG argued that in advance of any such transition, Nigeria needed to undergo dramatic political and economic reform. The FMG broke Nigeria into a number of federal states, hoping to weaken regional and ethnic power. The government also sought to move the country away from its reliance upon agriculture, a shift made possible in part by the emergence of oil as a major source of revenue. By the 1970s, Nigeria had become one of the top 10 oil-producing countries in the world. The result was rapid if uneven development of the country in numerous areas.

The FMG came to power with a certain degree of public support, given its call for an end to divisive ethnic-based politics and the creation of an effective state. Yet military rule simply replaced one form of patronage with another, tapping oil revenues as a way to enrich those in power and their supporters—a theme that would recur again and again with subsequent regime changes, both military and civilian. Widespread corruption, crime, and stagnating economic development led to another coup in 1975 led by General Murtala Muhammed. Muhammed cracked down on corruption and took the long-delayed steps necessary for the return of civilian rule, thereby earning widespread popular support. But within a year, he was assassinated in a failed coup attempt, which brought to power General **Olusegun Obasanjo**, who nonetheless continued Muhammed's plans for the restoration of civilian rule.

A new constitution enacted in 1979 ushered in the **Second Republic**, which replaced the old parliamentary system with a presidential system in hopes of strengthening central authority and preventing a breakdown like the one that had occurred a decade earlier. Democratic elections were held in 1979, and Obasanjo willingly retired from political and military life, making him one of the most popular Nigerians and favoring his return to politics.

The 1979 presidential elections resulted in a victory for the northerner Shehu Shagari, whose civilian government faced numerous obstacles, including ongoing ethnic factionalism and declining state revenues as a result of dropping oil prices. The resultant economic recession fostered unrest, which the government sought to quell with increased public spending and corrupt payments to potential detractors. Inflation and foreign debt increased, and capital fled. When the Shagari government sought to stay in power in 1983 by rigging elections, the military once again seized power, led by a young general, **Muhammadu Buhari**.

After 1983, Nigeria experienced another decade and a half of military rule, a period dominated by two men: General **Ibrahim Babangida** and General **Sani Abacha**. Babangida, an ethnic Gwari and a Muslim, had the unenviable task of dealing with Nigeria's mounting economic crisis. Backed by the International Monetary Fund and the World Bank, he implemented a neoliberal structural-adjustment program that made drastic cuts in public spending and dramatically worsened the lives of average Nigerians. In politics, too, while Babangida asserted that he would restore civilian rule, he increased tension by packing the military government with northerners, deepening regional and ethnic resentments. In the late 1980s, he sought to initiate a civilian transition under his control, even to the point of creating new political parties and platforms. Under growing public pressure, presidential elections for this **Third Republic** were held in 1993, but Babangida quickly annulled the results. That action set off a wave of public protests, strikes, and the fear of a new civil war. Babangida stepped down in the face of the unrest, installing a caretaker civilian government. Within three months, his second-in-command, Sani Abacha, a northerner, had taken the reins of power for himself in yet another military coup.

Abacha's government lacked many of the skills that had allowed Babangida to remain in power for such a long time. While Babangida sought to co-opt his opponents as much as possible, using force only as a last resort, Abacha regularly employed violence as a means of public control. Political leaders and activists involved in the 1993 elections and ensuing crisis were arrested, and Abacha's government repressed and murdered critics of the regime. In 1995, a number of civilian and military officials were imprisoned for allegedly plotting against Abacha, among them former President Obasanjo. The writer and environmentalist **Ken Saro-Wiwa**, a critic of the regime and of the Shell Oil Company's role in Nigeria, was also arrested, and later executed, for his opposition to the regime.

Saro-Wiwa's execution led to Nigeria's expulsion from the Commonwealth of Nations and the imposing of sanctions by the United States and the European Union. Not only did Abacha repress the Nigerian people, he also stole an estimated $6 billion from the state. This dark period ended suddenly in 1998, when he died of a heart attack. Perhaps realizing the dangers of military rule, General Abubakar, who succeeded him, rapidly carried out a democratic transition and released all political prisoners. In 1999, free presidential elections were held, bringing Obasanjo to power again as the first head of state in the current **Fourth Republic**.

Political Regime

Nigeria offers a sober lesson in the challenges facing postcolonial countries struggling to institutionalize capable states and stable governments. Nigeria has experimented with an assortment of political regimes and experienced more than its share of political turmoil in its nearly six decades of independence. The country has vacillated between authoritarian military regimes and democratic civilian republics (both parliamentary and presidential) and has had a variety of federal, state, and local political arrangements.

Independent Nigeria's most prominent form of government has been **patrimonialism**, in which personal rule by both authoritarian and democratic leaders has been shored up by the economic privileges those leaders bestow upon a coterie of loyal followers. Not surprisingly, the divisiveness, corruption, and illegitimacy of patrimonialism have meant that bullets, not ballots, have more frequently determined Nigerian regime shifts and changes in government. These changes have shared at least two features: each has promised improved governance, and each has largely failed to deliver on its promise. Whether military or civilian, no regime has worked particularly well in Nigeria.

On a brighter note, the current Fourth Republic, ushered in with the transition back to civilian democracy in 1999, has successfully sponsored five elections, kept the military in its barracks, and survived longer than any of its democratic predecessors. Significantly, the most recent presidential election in 2015 yielded Nigeria's first electoral defeat of an incumbent and transition to an opposition candidate.

IN FOCUS | Essential Political Features

- **Legislative–executive system**: Presidential
- **Legislature**: National Assembly
  - **Lower house**: House of Representatives
  - **Upper house**: Senate
- **Unitary or federal division of power**: Federal
- **Main geographic subunits**: States
- **Electoral system for lower house**: Single-member district plurality
- **Chief judicial body**: Supreme Court

Perhaps most important, Nigerians seem willing to keep trying. As one observer noted, "Although they have badly botched it up when they achieve democratic rule, Nigerians refuse to settle for anything less."[2]

Over the years, Nigerians have developed a number of important components of successful democracy, including diverse and vigorous media, an educated and often critical elite, outspoken human rights organizations, a growing middle class, and a respected legal profession and judiciary. In short, Nigerians have sought to establish the rules and procedures of an effective political regime, but political instability, ethnic disunity, and political and bureaucratic corruption persist.

If this current democratic regime is unable to deliver on its promises and devolves into corruption and chaos, history has shown that authoritarian rule will likely replace it. Nigerians may dislike military rule, but their patience for bad democracy also has its limits.

POLITICAL INSTITUTIONS

THE CONSTITUTION Since independence, Nigeria has been governed by six constitutions. While successive military juntas simply dispensed with the rule of law, democratic regimes have not fared much better, discarding and rewriting the rules of government on average every four years. Not to be outdone, the government recently announced plans to hold a national convention to rewrite the most recent 1999 constitution, arguing that the current document was hurriedly drafted by the last military junta. With some justification, critics complain that the problem for Nigerian political leaders has not been coming up with rules of good governance, but rather abiding by them.[3] Well-meaning leaders have oftentimes sought in good faith to revise legal norms to better accommodate both the developmental and the democratic aspirations of the Nigerian people and the realities of their ethnic and religious differences. Too often, however, neither military rulers nor civilian elites (nor foreign corporations or domestic insurgents, for that matter) have felt bound by those rules.

Nigeria's first national constitution, promulgated in 1960, reflected its colonial heritage in at least two ways. First, like all former British colonies, independent Nigeria established itself as a constitutional monarchy with a Westminster-style parliamentary democracy: the British monarch remained the head of state, legislative authority was placed in the hands of a bicameral parliament, and executive power was vested in a prime minister and cabinet. Second, the colonial pattern of "divide and rule" governance was further institutionalized with the codification of the regional division of Nigeria into the Hausa- and Fulani-dominated north, the Igbo-dominated east, and the Yoruba-dominated west.

In 1963, after only three years of independence, Nigeria reconstituted itself as a republic, replacing the queen of England as head of state with its own elected but largely ceremonial president. The revised parliamentary system ostensibly remained in place over the next decade and a half, though military rule for most of that period precluded its functioning. When the military finally acceded to civilian rule in 1979, the constitution of the Second Republic established an American-style presidential system with a directly elected president (as both head of state and head of government), a bicameral legislature, and a separate constitutional court. Subsequent constitutions (of 1989, 1995, and 1999) have retained the presidential system. Nigeria's current Fourth Republic, established in 1999, is thus a federal democratic republic with a presidential executive and a bicameral legislature.

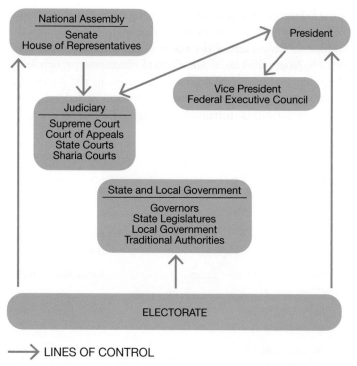

Structure of the Government

LINES OF CONTROL

THE BRANCHES OF GOVERNMENT

THE EXECUTIVE Nigeria's frequent leadership changes are largely a consequence of the substantial social, economic, and political challenges facing this postcolonial country. Those changes and challenges have in turn fostered the personal rule of authoritarian leaders and hampered efforts to institutionalize more legitimate executive rule. As the table "Nigerian Heads of Government" (see p. 674) indicates, in its nearly six decades of independence, Nigeria has been ruled for fully half of this time by patrimonial strongmen.

Nigeria's current president, Muhammadu Buhari, is only the sixth democratically elected executive to govern Nigeria and the first to defeat an incumbent in a democratic election. A former general and northern Hausa Muslim, Buhari first came to power in a military coup in 1983 and ruled Nigeria with an iron fist before being ousted in another coup in 1985. During his 20-month rule, Buhari arrested hundreds of corrupt officials and businessmen, executed drug dealers, and expelled thousands of illegal immigrants. He was elected president in 2015 as a self-avowed democrat, having competed unsuccessfully in three previous presidential elections. He replaced **Goodluck Jonathan**, an ethnic Ijaw Christian from southern Nigeria, who first assumed the presidency in 2010 after President Umaru Yar'Adua died in office. The president of Nigeria is directly elected by the people and nominates his or her own running mate, who automatically becomes vice president if the president is elected. The president also appoints ministers to the Federal Executive Council, or cabinet, which is charged with initiating and implementing the policies and programs of the federal government. In a nod to Nigeria's ethnic challenges and in an effort to avoid favoritism (if not clientelism), the constitution requires the president to appoint ministers from each of the states of the Nigerian republic. This quota system, which Nigerians refer to as the **federal character principle**, is also used with federal appointments and civil service positions in the government bureaucracy.[4] Each ethnic group is allotted a certain portion of federal positions based on its regional population. Unfortunately, though the federal character principle

Nigerian Heads of Government

NAME (TENURE)	ETHNICITY (RELIGION)	OFFICE	PATH TO POWER	REGIME TYPE
Abubakar Tafawa Balewa (1960–66)	Hausa-Fulani (Muslim)	Prime minister	Elected (indirectly)	Parliamentary democracy (First Republic)
Johnson T. U. Aguiyi-Ironsi (1966)	Igbo (Christian)	Military head of government	Coup	Authoritarian military rule
Yakubu Gowon (1966–75)	Tiv (Christian)	Military head of government	Coup	Authoritarian military rule
Murtala Muhammed (1975–76)	Hausa-Fulani (Muslim)	Military head of government	Coup	Authoritarian military rule
Olusegun Obasanjo (1976–79)	Yoruba (Christian)	Military head of government	Coup	Authoritarian military rule
Shehu Shagari (1979–83)	Hausa (Muslim)	President	Elected (directly)	Presidential democracy (Second Republic)
Muhammadu Buhari (1983–85)	Hausa (Muslim)	Military head of government	Coup	Authoritarian military rule
Ibrahim Babangida (1985–93)	Gwari (Muslim)	Military head of government	Coup	Authoritarian military rule
Ernest Shonekan (1993)	Yoruba (Christian)	Interim head of government	Appointed	Civilian puppet rule (proposed Third Republic)
Sani Abacha (1993–98)	Kanuri (Muslim)	Military head of government	Coup	Authoritarian military rule
Abdulsalami Abubakar (1998–99)	Gwari (Muslim)	Military head of government	Assumed power	Authoritarian military rule
Olusegun Obasanjo (1999–2007)	Yoruba (Christian)	President	Elected (directly)	Presidential democracy (Fourth Republic)
Umaru Yar'Adua (2007–10)	Fulani (Muslim)	President	Elected (directly)	Presidential democracy (died in office)
Goodluck Jonathan (2010–15)	Ijaw (Christian)	President	Appointed/Elected (directly)	Presidential democracy
Muhammadu Buhari (2015–)	Hausa (Muslim)	President	Elected (directly)	Presidential democracy

may have eased ethnic rivalries by spreading the spoils of office among the various groups, it has exacerbated corruption. Bribery, waste, and corrupt ties between political patrons and clients in the private sector remain the norm in Nigeria's largely dysfunctional civil service, which "absorbs most of the budget but delivers little in the way of service."[5]

THE LEGISLATURE Although in practice, the president and his or her cabinet initiate budgetary legislation and most other important bills, the constitution designates the National Assembly, Nigeria's federal legislature, as the highest lawmaking body. This bicameral legislature consists of a lower House of Representatives and an upper Senate, in which both representatives and senators serve four-year renewable terms.

The **House of Representatives** contains 360 seats, and each member represents an individual district. The 109 seats in the Senate are divided among Nigeria's 36 states (three seats each) and the federal district of Abuja (one seat). Despite their appointed constitutional roles, both chambers of the National Assembly have served as little more than rubber stamps for the executive branch, even during periods of democratic rule. This results in part from the same party controlling both branches of government for most of Nigeria's democratic history, but is also due to the legislature's lack of experience, expertise, and staff support. In recent years, however, the National Assembly has demonstrated less compliance in passing budgetary bills and has become more vocal in expressing the demands of regional and even local interests.

These regional disagreements speak to the huge political challenge an increasingly democratic Nigeria faces in overcoming its seemingly intractable ethnic divisions. Some critics have argued that a parliamentary system might better address Nigeria's challenges of cultural pluralism by reducing conflict between the executive and legislative branches. Others have called for a unicameral legislature or even the distribution and rotation of key executive posts among the dominant ethnic groups, as is done with civil service appointments (and, informally, with presidential candidates; see "The Electoral System," p. 676).

THE JUDICIARY Nigeria inherited a colonial legal system that combined British common law with an assortment of traditional or customary laws that the colonial government had permitted to handle local matters (including Sharia, which predominated in the Northern Region). This legacy fostered a court system and rule of law that historically, even during periods of military rule, retained a degree of independence and legitimacy. However, military dictatorships regularly flouted this independence, routinely ignoring legal checks and using an intimidated judiciary to silence and even eliminate political opponents. The most infamous case of "judicial terrorism" was the 1994 Abacha military tribunal that resulted in the aforementioned execution of the noted playwright and activist Ken Saro-Wiwa.[6]

With the return to democratic rule, an effort has been made to reestablish the legitimacy and independence of the judiciary. The 1999 constitution established a Supreme Court, a Federal Court of Appeals, and a single unified court system at the national and state levels. The rule of law has been further strengthened with successive governments launching anticorruption campaigns, most recently with President Buhari's pledges to launch an "anticorruption war." But although the courts have had some success in prosecuting former state officials for enriching themselves while in office and addressing electoral fraud, these anticorruption efforts have typically faltered as they have drawn closer to those who are still in office or remain politically influential.

Nigeria's federal constitution also permits individual states to authorize traditional subsidiary courts, giving these customary legal systems significant judicial clout. The most controversial of the traditional systems have been the Islamic Sharia courts, which now function in 12 of the predominantly Muslim northern states.[7] As discussed later in this case, Nigerians have debated heatedly and, in some cases, violently over the role and jurisdiction of the Sharia courts.

THE ELECTORAL SYSTEM

Like other presidential systems, Nigerians directly elect their president and separately elect members of both chambers of the National Assembly. But unlike the U.S. system, in Nigeria, presidents, senators, and representatives all serve four-year terms, with elections for all three offices held in the same year. In an effort to ensure that the president serves with a national mandate, the winning presidential candidate must obtain both an overall majority of votes nationwide and at least 25 percent of the ballots cast in at least two-thirds of the states.[8] If no candidate succeeds in winning a majority of total votes and obtaining the two-thirds threshold in the first round, a second round of voting takes place a week later, pitting the top two candidates against each other in a runoff.

Nigeria's dominant **People's Democratic Party (PDP)** put in place another informal arrangement designed to enhance the legitimacy of presidential elections when the country returned to democracy in 1999. Christian politicians from the south feared that democracy would always favor the more numerous Muslim population in the north and that southern candidates would thereby be shut out of power. As reassurance, PDP leaders established an informal system of presidential rotation known as **zoning**, in which the party would alternate every two terms nominating candidates from the north and the south. While this agreement facilitated support for reestablishing democratic rule, it limited the pool of qualified presidential candidates and exacerbated ethnic divisions by framing issues and policy priorities in terms of alternating regions and religions. Moreover, this plan also ran into problems when President Yar'Adua (a northern Muslim who succeeded a southern Christian) died in office in 2010. As directed by the constitution, he was succeeded by the vice president, Goodluck Jonathan, who happened to be a Christian from the south. Jonathan's successful bid for a full second term in 2011 angered many northern politicians, who saw it as a violation of the zoning system, which should have given a northern president a full two terms. Jonathan's election prompted substantial protest and violence in the north, and anticipation that he would seek reelection led to the 2013 merger of the three largest opposition parties into the **All Progressives Congress (APC)** Party and the defection of a sizable number of northern PDP politicians to the APC. This strengthened opposition agreed upon Buhari, a northern Muslim, as its candidate in the 2015 contest and elected him to office, thus preserving the informal zoning rotation.

All 360 seats in the House of Representatives are contested in single-member districts (SMDs) apportioned roughly equally by population. The 109 members of the Senate are also elected from single-member districts, with each of 36 states divided

Former military ruler Muhammadu Buhari casts his vote in the 2015 presidential election that brought him to power, marking Nigeria's first electoral contest in which an opposition candidate defeated an incumbent.

into three districts. The federal district, or "capital territory," of Abuja elects one senator in a single-seat constituency for the 109th seat. These winner-take-all, single-member districts historically favored the dominant PDP and one or two smaller opposition parties, allowing them to dominate both chambers of the National Assembly. However, Buhari's commanding win in the 2015 presidential election carried many APC legislative candidates in on his coattails, giving the APC a majority in both chambers. Several other smaller parties have managed on occasion to win seats in the House, reflecting the geographic concentration of ethnic groups willing to vote in blocs large enough to win a plurality of votes.

LOCAL GOVERNMENT

Constitutionally, Nigeria is a federal republic with national, state, and local levels of governance. In 1970, the Federal Military Government divided the republic into 12 states following the Nigerian Civil War, which nearly split the country permanently. The number of states grew to 19 in 1976, 30 by 1991, and 36 by 1996, plus the Federal Capital Territory. The number of local government units has vacillated dramatically over time, reflecting the uncertainty of how federalism should be constituted in Nigeria and the temptations to govern by clientelism. Patronage appointments of local officials guarantee both the longevity and the loyalty of local government in delivering votes for state and national party organizations.

Nigeria faces countervailing demands of centralization and devolution. On the one hand, the national government's control of the bulk of oil revenues provides the patrimonial glue that keeps the local regions dependent upon the center. But as increasingly diverse and articulate voices have entered a progressively democratic political arena, the calls for enhanced state and local autonomy have grown louder. Those demands range from expanded state control over the budget (and, for the oil-rich **Niger Delta**, local control over its oil revenues), to a separate military for each region, to full-fledged dismemberment of Nigeria.

To date, local and even state governments have enjoyed little autonomy from the national government and have no means of generating revenue. Put simply, the central government controls the purse strings, and the Nigerian purse depends almost completely upon oil revenues. (The non-oil sector makes up just 4 percent of the private sector.) Not surprisingly, as oil revenues have expanded, so has the public sector at all levels, as have the degrees of corruption associated with that patronage. At the same time, the expansion of oil revenues has led to increased disputes over the national distribution of these funds—known as the **derivation formula**—and the percentage of revenues that should accrue to the oil-producing localities.[9]

OTHER INSTITUTIONS

THE MILITARY Although the Fourth Republic has managed to sponsor five successive and relatively peaceful democratic elections, independent Nigeria's tumultuous history cautions us not to become too confident that the military will remain in its barracks. Nigeria's nearly three decades of experience with military rule (1966–79 and 1983–99) left a deep impression on Nigerian politics. It is not a coincidence that most of Nigeria's most powerful leaders (including former coup leaders and recent and current elected presidents Obasanjo and Buhari) boast a military background. As elsewhere in postcolonial Africa and in much of the developing world, the military has served as one of the few stable avenues of meritocratic social mobility and has long been able to attract many of Nigeria's best, brightest, and most ambitious. This avenue has been particularly important for the ethnic Muslims of northern Nigeria, who have been educationally and economically disadvantaged compared with southern Nigerians. Although the south is the source of Nigeria's oil, for many years the north controlled the army and used that control, in the form of military dictatorships, to redistribute oil wealth.

Scholars have offered a number of explanations for the military's nonintervention in Nigeria's Fourth Republic.[10] They point to President Obasanjo's legislation in the early 2000s requiring the retirement of all military officers who previously held political offices during the period of military rule. They also note the government's seizure of senior military officers' corruptly acquired money and properties and the growing professionalization of the younger cohorts of officers. The military's dismal performance in its fight against Boko Haram insurgents in the north and efforts to curtail widespread oil theft in the south have also tarnished its image. That said, a military coup plot was preempted in 2004, and persistent corruption and the inefficacy of civilian rule, combined with the vast spoils of office, remain tempting justifications for the military once again to try to usurp control. Only time will tell if Nigeria's military is prepared to make its recent withdrawal from public life permanent.

Political Conflict and Competition

THE PARTY SYSTEM

Politics in oil-rich, patrimonial Nigeria has been described as a "contest of self-enrichment."[11] Whether fought with ballots or bullets, the stakes have indeed been high, the competition fierce, and corruption and violence all too common. Not surprisingly, political parties and the party system have fared best under democratic regimes and have withered during periods of military rule. Although the names have changed over time, Nigerian political parties have continued to reflect the ethnic divisions of identity politics, despite efforts of democratic and even some military regimes to establish cross-ethnic national parties.

Because of this, we can discuss Nigeria's parties in terms of their ethnic identity and, therefore, their geographic location rather than place them on a left–right political continuum. This regional party identity has exacerbated ethnic tensions and complicated efforts to establish democratic institutions and legitimize national party politics. Moreover, most state and local contests have been dominated by the region's leading party, typically permitting that party to control the governor's office, the state assembly, and local councils. This control, in turn, allows the party to marshal sufficient votes to capture the seats in the national Senate and House of Representatives as well. This reminds us that in Nigeria, all politics are in the first instance local, and that in these local communities, ethnicity and clientelist networks have been very important.

Although recent democratic elections under Nigeria's Fourth Republic have offered some hope for the establishment of cross-ethnic parties with national appeal, strengthened democracy has also given stronger voice to persistent sectarian and even local separatist demands.

ELECTIONS

Colonial-era parties survived through the First Republic (1960–66), but were banned from the onset of military rule until Olusegun Obasanjo came to power in 1976. Obasanjo legalized the establishment of political parties in 1978, and some 150 parties were formed in that year alone. Subsequent democratic and military governments sought to impose order on this political cacophony by compelling the formation of nationwide parties and the establishment of a two-party system. With the return to democracy in 1999, the Fourth Republic attempted to foster political parties with a national, or "federal," character by permitting only those parties that maintained well-established national organizations to participate in elections that year. Three parties qualified, and not surprisingly, each reflected its regional base in one of the country's main ethnic groups: the People's Democratic Party, representing the northern Hausa; the All People's Party (APP), representing the eastern Igbo; and the Alliance for Democracy (AD), representing the western Yoruba.

The subsequent four elections have followed this trend of growing democracy and even a gradually declining regional basis for party affiliation, but have continued patterns of electoral corruption and (until the most recent election) PDP dominance. The 2003 election, the first sponsored by a civilian government in 20 years, returned Obasanjo to office. In 2007, he stepped down as required by the constitution, marking the first ever succession of democratically elected executives in Nigerian history. Umaru Yar'Adua, Obasanjo's handpicked candidate, succeeded him, winning a landslide victory with purportedly 70 percent of the vote. The victory was marred, however, by opposition and foreign observer charges of widespread corruption and fraud in electoral contests at all levels. Coming to office thanks to what was arguably Nigeria's most corrupt election, Yar'Adua in many ways redeemed himself in the eyes of the electorate. He battled political corruption and negotiated a ceasefire in the Niger River Delta, but fell ill and died in his third year in office. His vice president, Goodluck Jonathan, assumed the presidency and the right to finish out

Yar'Adua's four-year term. As a southern Christian, Jonathan was initially seen as simply a caretaker until the 2011 election would permit the PDP's northern political bosses to resume their "turn" in the rotating "zoning" system. But he lost no time in pursuing his predecessor's reform agenda and promising to tackle three of Nigeria's biggest problems: rigged elections, woefully inadequate electricity, and the insurgency in his native Niger Delta. Significantly, Jonathan sacked the powerful but corrupt head of the Nigerian election commission and replaced him with an impeccably honest academic, who oversaw Nigeria's cleanest elections in both 2011 and 2015.

In the run-up to the 2015 election, as it became clear that Jonathan would again flout the PDP's zoning arrangement and pursue reelection, the three largest opposition parties (with a faction from a fourth party) put aside their differences and in 2013 merged to form a broad coalition party, the All Progressives Congress (APC). Later that same year, a group of prominent national PDP leaders and state governors, dissatisfied with Jonathan's reelection plans and the poor performance (and declining popularity) of the Jonathan government, defected from the PDP and ultimately combined their forces with the opposition APC. As a southern Christian facing a united opposition, with little positive to show for his five years in office, Jonathan was handily defeated by the APC's candidate, popular northern former military leader Buhari (see the table "Results of Recent Nigerian National Elections," p. 682). This APC victory, the first peaceful passing of power from one elected political party to another, marks a significant watershed in Nigeria's efforts to consolidate a two-party democratic electoral system that can offer a legitimate choice to Nigerian voters.

Even after this apparent step forward and five consecutive affirmations of the democratic electoral process, Nigerians' patience for democratic rule continues to be tested by endemic government corruption, political and gangster violence, and persistent economic misery. Much of the half-trillion dollars in oil revenues earned during the PDP's quarter-century control of government was neither invested nor distributed. Rather, it found its way into the hands of both regional and national political elites, despite the professed and at times genuine efforts of top leaders to stem this corruption. Oil has generated immense wealth in their country, but over three-fourths of Nigerians still live on less than two dollars a day, and critics of the former ruling PDP labeled it the "Poverty Development Party."

Nigeria's ethnic and religious fault lines also remain starkly apparent; in the 2015 election, Buhari earned nearly 54 percent of the popular vote, but won only 5 of the 17 southernmost states. Jonathan won nearly 45 percent of the vote, but captured only 3 of the northernmost states. When asked in 2015 how satisfied they were with how democracy works in Nigeria, nearly 70 percent of respondents indicated they were not very or not at all satisfied, compared with 63 percent of respondents in 2008 and only 14 percent in 2000.[12]

Not surprisingly, oil revenues have been the primary lubricant in making democracy "work" in this postcolonial state comprising some 250 highly diverse ethnic groups. National political leaders have co-opted regional and local elites with promises of cash and political appointments in exchange for delivering votes. This clientelist system has given a great electoral advantage to the incumbent party, which has had control of the "excess crude account," a giant slush fund of surplus oil revenues.

But things are improving. In 2010, President Jonathan sacked the corrupt director of Nigeria's election commission, who was largely responsible for rigging past elections, and replaced him with a highly respected academic who pledged to clean up Nigeria's electoral politics. In the run-up to the 2011 elections, the newly led

Despite a succession of democratic elections, political violence—among other problems— threatens Nigerian democracy.

commission fingerprinted all 73.5 million eligible voters, required that all ballots be printed abroad, and established an "open secret ballot system" in which voters' fingerprints were scanned at the polls and voters were asked to remain at the polling stations until all votes were tallied locally. In addition, the government established the Nigerian Sovereign Investment Authority in 2011. This trust is designed to insulate oil revenues from the hands and pockets of politicians, instead directing the funds toward economic development. Addressing Nigeria's poverty, inequality, and unemployment will likely do more to consolidate democracy than any other measures.

If Nigeria's elections are becoming more transparent, sadly, they remain quite violent. In the weeks leading up to the 2011 election, several politicians arranged to have their opponents murdered, while others hired gangs to intimidate rivals' campaigns. On election day, groups threw hand grenades to dissuade would-be voters, and others stole ballot boxes or snatched tally sheets.[13] The period immediately following the election was even worse, as dissatisfied voters, in many cases stirred up (or even paid) by losing candidates, went on looting and killing sprees. Some 800 Nigerians died in just the first week after the elections, as simmering ethnic and religious tensions merged with electoral disappointment and economic deprivation. The greatest violence occurred (and persists) in Nigeria's Muslim north, where incomes and literacy rates are a fraction of those in the south and where poverty drives young men into the arms of criminal gangs and militant Islamic groups.[14]

Encouragingly, the 2015 elections improved in these regards, with far fewer casualties than in previous elections. Observers attribute much of this relatively peaceful outcome to outgoing President Jonathan's quick and gracious concession of defeat. On the day the results were announced, Jonathan urged his supporters to reject violence, stating "nobody's ambition is worth the blood of any Nigerian." But more must be done. As with corruption, solving electoral and ethnic violence and

An election worker marks the finger of a Nigerian voter. Observers judged the 2015 presidential election Nigeria's cleanest polling to date.

promoting democracy will require in the first instance alleviating Nigerian poverty. Perhaps Nigerians are patient enough to wait for this. When asked about the corruption and violence that accompanied a recent election, one voter concluded, "We have anger, but we have even more hope."

CIVIL SOCIETY

Neither the British colonial government nor the series of post-independence military authoritarian regimes was able to squelch Nigeria's rich tradition of activism and dissent. In Nigeria's relatively short postcolonial history, a wide variety of formal interest groups and informal voluntary associations have emerged and persisted. Under the relaxed environment of the Fourth Republic, these groups and organizations have proliferated and strengthened. Some of them, particularly professional associations and other NGOs, have risen above Nigerians' identity politics, drawn their support from across Nigeria's cultural spectrum, and functioned in ways that promote national integration. Others, particularly those based on ethnic and religious identities, are among the most resilient of groups and in some cases serve to fragment Nigerian society.

Formal and informal ethnic and religious associations have always played an important role in Nigerian society, often promoting the economic or other local interests of a particular minority group. Among the most important of these issue-based minority associations were those that emerged in the Niger Delta to protect the interests of ethnic and other groups in the region. The **Movement for the Survival of the Ogoni People (MOSOP)**, established by Ken Saro-Wiwa in the 1990s to defend the interests of the Ogoni, employed a variety of legal and extralegal political tactics to secure more financial benefits with fewer environmental costs from foreign-operated oil interests in the Niger Delta. As conditions in the region have

Results of Recent Nigerian National Elections

PARTY:	PDP	APP/ANPP/CPC*	AD/ACN[†]	OTHER PARTIES	TOTAL
ELECTION YEAR		PRESIDENTIAL VOTE (%)			
1999	62.8	37.2	No candidate	—	100
2003	61.9	32.2	No candidate	5.9	100
2007	69.8	18.7	7.5	4.0	100
2011	58.9	31.9	5.4	3.8	100
2015	45.0	APC[‡] 54.0	—	1.0	100
		SENATE SEATS			
1999	65	24	20	0	109
2003	73	28	6	0	107[§]
2007	87	14	6	2	109
2011	71	14	18	6	109
2015	49	APC[‡] 60	—	0	109
		HOUSE SEATS			
1999	212	79	69	0	360
2003	213	95	31	7	346[§]
2007	260	61	31	4	356[§]
2011	199	64	69	22	354[§]
2015	125	APC[‡] 225	—	10	360

*The APP renamed itself the All Nigeria People's Party (ANPP) after a merger with a smaller independent party in 2003. The Congress for Progressive Change (CPC) formed in 2009 to support Buhari's candidacy and drew most of its supporters from the ANPP, though the latter has continued as a separate party.

[†]The Action Congress of Nigeria (ACN) is the result of the 2006 merger of the Alliance for Democracy and several smaller parties.

[‡]The All Progressives Congress (APC) is a merger of the ACN, ANPP, CPC, and defectors from the PDP.

[§]Contested returns from some districts reduced the total number of candidates seated in some Senate and House elections.

worsened and more and broader constituencies feel they have a right to a portion of the oil revenues, groups in the Niger Delta have more readily turned to violence.

Many of these militant groups are more or less loosely connected to the **Movement for the Emancipation of the Niger Delta (MEND)**, an umbrella organization that claims to act on behalf of the Delta's oppressed peoples and exploited environment. Numerous militant subgroups have engaged in "bunkering" (illegally siphoning off) oil, kidnapping foreign oil workers and sailors, ransoming captured ships, and even launching daylight attacks on oil pipelines and facilities in the region. Former president Yar'Adua negotiated a 2009 truce and amnesty that his successor Jonathan, who came from the Delta region, continued. While this truce, unlike previous efforts, brought a significant drop in violence in the region, President Buhari, a northerner, has been less sympathetic to the regional concerns, and rebel and criminal violence has increased since 2015. The lines dividing ethnic and environmental political associations, insurgent separatist movements, youth fraternities (or cults), and common criminal gangs are blurring in this complex and troubled region.

Tragically, growing political violence in the Niger Delta has been eclipsed by rising terrorism in Nigeria's northern interior and ongoing sectarian and ethnic conflict elsewhere in this patchwork country. The radical Islamist sect known as Boko Haram (loosely translated from the Hausa as "Western education is forbidden") has waged a seven-year insurgency designed to root out Christian and Western influence and establish an Islamic Caliphate. This group has presented the single largest threat to peace in Nigeria, claiming responsibility for hundreds of terrorist attacks and the deaths of tens of thousands of Nigerians, particularly in the northeast. These assaults included a series of bombings and shootings during Christian religious services in the region, brutal attacks on government buildings and schools, and in 2014, the kidnapping of hundreds of schoolgirls. A single attack in 2015 left as many as 2000 dead, and in the same year, Boko Haram pledged its allegiance to the Islamic State, raising fears about the group's ties to organized terrorist organizations outside of Nigeria (for more details, see "Boko Haram," p. 689). In addition, Muslims and Christians frequently engage in riots in several northern and central states and farmers and herders regularly clash in the same areas.

Modern civic associations such as trade unions and professional organizations played a prominent role in the anticolonial struggle and have been relatively active in promoting their particular, and at times more collective, interests since the time of independence. Unions representing workers in the all-important petroleum industry— for example, the National Union of Petroleum and Natural Gas Workers (NUPENG)— have used their strategic position to exert influence on the political process. Formal associations such as those representing legal, medical, and journalism professionals have also begun to articulate the political interests of Nigeria's growing professional class. Particularly since the end of military rule and the establishment of the Fourth Republic, NGOs promoting issues such as development, democracy, and civil rights have exerted more influence in Nigerian politics. Most active among these latter groups have been those organizations engaged in monitoring Nigeria's elections.

IN COMPARISON Choosing between a Good Democracy and a Strong Economy

If you had to choose between a good democracy or a strong economy, which would you say is more important?

	GOOD DEMOCRACY (PERCENTAGE)	STRONG ECONOMY (PERCENTAGE)
Nigeria	59	40
India	56	41
Mexico	53	41
China	50	44
Brazil	50	46
South Africa	40	58
Russia	15	74

Source: Pew Center for the People and the Press, 2007.

Society

ETHNIC AND NATIONAL IDENTITY

As this chapter has demonstrated, group identity is a powerful force in Nigerian politics, with deep-seated rivalry among the Yoruba, Igbo, Hausa, and Fulani peoples. In addition, nearly a third of the population belongs to none of these groups, further complicating the ethnic map. Nigeria can claim more than 250 separate ethnic groupings with many more languages.

This diversity has created significant problems for the consolidation of democracy, because each group has temptations to see politics in zero-sum terms. An electoral victory by a Hausa candidate, for example, is viewed as a blow to the interests of the Yoruba, and vice versa. Such ethnic divisions were largely responsible for the collapse of civilian government in 1966 and of course for the Nigerian Civil War. Subsequent military leaders often sought to play on fears of ethnic conflict as a justification for authoritarianism, arguing that democracy only exacerbated the fault lines between regions and peoples. Changes in the federal structure (creating more territorial divisions), the executive system (replacing a parliamentary system with a presidential one), and the party system (the effort to ban ethnic parties) similarly reflected the desire to weaken local authority and shift more power to the center. In 1991, even the capital was moved—it went from Lagos to Abuja, a city built from scratch in the center of the country.

How has the transition to democracy affected ethnic relations? Since the end of military rule, communal violence has risen. The state is no longer able to suppress the public as it pleases, and the struggle for control over the state has returned to the populace. Since the return to civilian rule in 1999, ethnic conflicts have taken thousands of lives and displaced millions of Nigerians. This violence, which often has economic motives, originates in conflicts over access to state funds, oil revenues, jobs, and other resources. Incomes in the country's northeast are half those in the south, and fewer than 5 percent of women in some northeast states are able to read and write. And with the return to democracy, political elites often capitalize on these conflicts as a way to build their local bases of support, even to the point of inciting conflict by paying supporters to attack rival groups.

As we have noted, the conflicts also have a religious component, with deepening fissures separating the Muslims concentrated in the north and the Christians and animists concentrated in the south. This sectarian division has been exacerbated by the growing influence of Sharia law in the northern states. Shortly after the 1999 elections, a dozen northern states made Sharia the primary law, extending it to criminal and other matters. The imposition of Sharia touched off some of the worst violence under civilian rule, and the seeming incompatibility between secular national law and an expansive regional use of Sharia remains a serious and potentially destabilizing issue.

IDEOLOGY AND POLITICAL CULTURE

Could the conflicts between north and south, Christian and Muslim, lead to civil war, another military coup, or the dissolution of the country itself? Perhaps. As we have seen, political parties in Nigeria tend to be built around individual leaders and ethnic groups. In this case, ideology plays a limited role compared with more narrow communal concerns. Similarly, it is commonly asserted that Nigerians have a low sense of patriotism or pride in their state, presumably a result of their stronger local

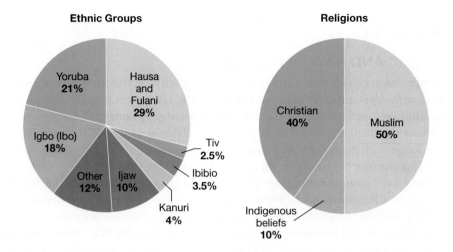

Ethnic Groups

- Yoruba 21%
- Hausa and Fulani 29%
- Igbo (Ibo) 18%
- Tiv 2.5%
- Ibibio 3.5%
- Other 12%
- Ijaw 10%
- Kanuri 4%

Religions

- Christian 40%
- Muslim 50%
- Indigenous beliefs 10%

identity and the legacy of military rule. The Nigerian novelist and political activist Chinua Achebe once described Nigerians as "among the world's most unpatriotic people," which, he argued, was a serious impediment to prosperity and democracy.[15]

Despite these concerns, however, some aspects of Nigerian political culture continue to lend support to the state and the democratic regime. A 2012 survey of Nigerians showed that even with the tensions and disappointments that have followed the return of civilian rule, 69 percent continue to support democracy and reject military rule (though this figure is down from 72 percent in 2008 and a high of 84 percent in 2000). Nigerians also strongly oppose a political system dominated by a single party or leader, an attitude quite different from that in many other African democracies, where such domination is common. Over time, Nigerians have come to base their support for democracy less on economic performance and more on trustworthy leaders and similar factors—quite the opposite of what is expected in less-developed countries with weakly institutionalized democracy.[16] Moreover, while Achebe may be right to assert that Nigerians do not express great patriotism (political pride in the Nigerian state), surveys nonetheless show that Nigerians exhibit a high degree of pride in a national identity (pride in their people) broader than a particular ethnic group. Those views, if sustained, may help limit communal tension and build ties across ethnic and religious divisions.

Political Economy

The misfortune of the Nigerian economy has been a constant theme throughout our discussion. The economic difficulties Nigeria has faced since independence are not unusual among less-developed countries, but they are particularly egregious given Nigeria's position as one of the world's largest oil producers, earning some $30 to $40 billion each year in oil export revenues. However, its economic difficulties exist not so much in *spite* of its oil resources but largely *because* of them.

Nigeria's predicament is an excellent example of what scholars sometimes refer to as the **resource curse**. Abundant natural resources under state-control often support nondemocratic rule. Rather than reliance on a public whom it depends upon for tax revenues, these ruling regimes can employ state-controlled resources to buy off key stakeholders and pay for the repression of others. In fact, much of Nigeria's state machinery functions to siphon off this oil wealth.

Political corruption, as one observer has noted, is not a flaw in Nigeria's political economic system; rather, it *is* the system.[17] And oil revenue is at the heart of what may be called a "70 percent system." In a country where over 70 percent of the population lives on less than $2 per day and where oil accounts for over 70 percent of the government's revenue, more than 70 percent of Nigeria's overall wealth is held by less than 1 percent of the population. And nearly this entire "top million" who count themselves among the wealthy elite are more or less closely connected to the Nigerian state or government.

Nigerian politicians are among the highest paid in the world. As recently as 2012, members of the Nigerian legislature received over $1 million in salary and allowances each year. In addition, conservative estimates place the amount of stolen or "missing" oil revenues since the discovery of oil in the 1970s at over $400 billion. In the year leading up to the 2011 presidential and legislative elections, it is estimated the central government and ruling PDP distributed up to $10 billion under the table to national, regional, and local political elites. The Buhari government's anti-corruption investigation concluded in 2016 that some $7 billion was stolen from government coffers between 2006 and 2013.

Furthermore, this preoccupation with natural resource wealth tends to distort the economy by diverting it from other forms of development. Until the 1970s, Nigeria led the world in peanut and palm oil exports, and agriculture is still Nigeria's largest employer. But Nigeria is now the world's largest importer of rice, and although the country each day produces over 2 million barrels of oil and exports hundreds of thousands of barrels of oil, it imports nearly all of its gasoline. It is estimated that nearly half a million barrels of oil are stolen each day.

Each of these factors is evident in the development of Nigeria's political-economic system. Like other less-developed countries, in the years following independence Nigeria opted for a system of import substitution, creating tariff barriers and parastatal industries with the objective of rapidly industrializing the country. This ambitious program was made possible by oil sales, which during the 1970s benefited from high prices. However, these programs suffered from policies directing resources toward certain industries for political reasons without a clear understanding of whether the investments would be profitable. For example, $8 billion was spent in the attempt to create a domestic steel industry that in the end produced barely any steel.[18] The decline in oil prices in the 1980s and the consequent economic crisis and spiraling foreign debt led Nigeria to initiate a policy of structural adjustment that moved the country away from import substitution, although the economy remained highly regulated and closed to trade.

The limited reforms also did not address the fact that Nigeria remained highly dependent upon oil exports and that the revenues from those exports were in the hands of military rulers. While the public suffered from the effects of structural adjustment, such as unemployment and inflation, authoritarian governments used their financial resources to co-opt some opponents while repressing others. Economic reforms only facilitated this clientelism, because newly liberalized markets and privatized state assets could be doled out in return for political support.

By the 1990s, corruption had reached such heights as to be described by one scholar as outright "predation" under an "avaricious dictatorship."[19] The Nigerian economy not only suffered from the outright theft of state funds but also became a center for illicit activity, including narcotics trafficking, human trafficking, money laundering, and, perhaps best known, the so-called 419, or advance-fee, scams. One might argue

Labor Force by Occupation

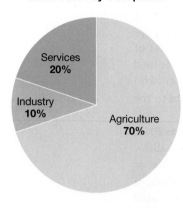

Services 20%

Industry 10%

Agriculture 70%

that corruption should not be a central concern if it has helped provide funds for economic development, but the reality is that far too little of this wealth has ever been reinvested in the country. Nigeria ranks 152nd out of 188 countries in the Human Development Index. In Nigeria, great oil wealth and endemic corruption, inequality, and poverty are intimately and tragically interrelated.

In fairness, successive elected governments under the current Fourth Republic have taken steps to break with the corrupt practices of the previous regimes and improve Nigeria's prospects for economic development. These steps included the development of a wide-ranging reform program launched in 2003 called the **National Economic Empowerment and Development Strategy (NEEDS)**. Among other measures, the NEEDS program increased the transparency of government finances and created an Economic and Financial Crimes Commission to pursue theft and money laundering. This commission took some impressive steps to tackle Nigeria's endemic corruption, seizing hundreds of millions of dollars in stolen assets and arresting former government officials for the misappropriation of funds.[20] NEEDS also focused on the country's inadequate infrastructure, seeking to boost electricity production, improve transportation, increase telecommunications, and expand access to sanitation and clean drinking water. The NEEDS program, which ran through 2007, made some significant headway in addressing some of Nigeria's thorniest development challenges.

Although pledging to continue these efforts, the Jonathan government struggled to maintain this momentum in either stemming corruption or promoting development. His government did restructure Nigeria's foreign debt, modernize its heavily indebted banking system, privatize electrical production, and begin to address the country's dismally inadequate economic infrastructure in areas such as power generation and transportation. The Jonathan government also attracted more foreign direct investment than any previous (or subsequent) government and more than any other African country (owing in part to high oil prices). Nigeria today boasts nearly 150 million mobile phone subscribers and has a growing service sector, including a prosperous "Nollywood" entertainment industry. And yet, Africa's largest economy still produces only one-tenth of South Africa's electrical output with three times the population.

The Buhari government came to power with a mandate to root out Nigeria's endemic corruption and invest reclaimed revenues in fighting terrorism and creating jobs. President Buhari's war on corruption has made significant strides with the arrest of a number of former government officials (predictably all from the opposition party) and the recovery of nearly $1.5 billion during his first year in office. President Buhari and his vice president have both taken a 50 percent pay cut and are taking measures to further expose illicit ties between the oil industry and political leaders.

Of course, the long-term success of any developmental efforts will hinge on the critical factor of oil. Increased tampering with oil facilities by insurgents in the Niger Delta combined with plummeting oil prices in recent years have cut both oil production and government revenues. These blows to the Nigerian economy have been cushioned somewhat by the launching in 2012 of the Nigerian Sovereign Investment Authority (NSIA). Designed largely to insulate oil revenues from the grasp of national and regional politicians, the fund channels profits from crude oil sales to the independent NSIA, which invests these monies in funds designed to enhance infrastructure, aid development, and manage fluctuations in oil prices. Since 2013, significant investments have been made in all three areas, providing key support during a time of economic hardship. Still, huge problems remain, reflecting the enormous impact that the oil industry will continue to have on the Nigerian political economy.

Current Issues in Nigeria

BOKO HARAM

Although only a tiny fraction of the roughly 100 million Nigerian Muslims embrace the extremism of radical Islam, Nigeria now confronts a violent group of Islamic insurgents that seems to be gaining strength in recent years even as its terrorist activities have become more violent and indiscriminate. The group's formal name translates as "People committed to the propagation of the prophet's teachings and jihad," but it is known as Boko Haram ("Western education is forbidden").

The movement began as a peaceful Islamic splinter group in 2002 based in Nigeria's northeastern state of Borno. But when its charismatic leader was captured by the military in 2009 and publicly executed on the spot, he was replaced by a far more radicalized leader, Abubakar Shekau. Since 2009, Shekau has led increasingly frequent, deadly, and coordinated terrorist attacks with the vague goal of rooting out Western influences, destabilizing and overthrowing the government, and establishing an Islamic caliphate in northern Nigeria.

Boko Haram initially targeted primarily state institutions such as police stations, government buildings, and military installations, but its targets have become increasingly "soft," including Christian churches, bus stations, schools, refugee camps, and even mosques. Of the more than 20,000 casualties linked to this violence since 2009, most have been Muslims. Moreover, nearly half of these casualties have come at the hands of the military and police, whose use of force has in many cases been as indiscriminate as that of the terrorists. The state's inability to curb the terrorist acts as well as its resort to extrajudicial killings and other human rights violations have angered local citizens and driven recruits into the terrorists' ranks. In addition, while the overwhelming majority of Nigerians have little sympathy for Boko Haram, the growing economic disparity between the Christian south and Muslim north and the generally ineffectual and corrupt performance of the federal government have strengthened the social welfare role of Islam and increased popular support for the enforcement of Sharia law as an attractive alternative to the state's inability to impose the rule of law or maintain a monopoly of violence.

Nearly three-fourths of northerners live on less than $200 a year. The literacy rate in the state of Borno—where Boko Haram is based—is barely 15 percent, compared to over 90 percent in Lagos, the southern commercial capital. Northerners also have felt politically marginalized since the transition to democracy. During periods of military rule, northerners dominated the state and ensured that significant portions of the south's oil wealth were redistributed to the north. For well over half of the nearly two decades since the transition to democracy, southerners have held the office of president.

As is the case with unrest in the Niger Delta to the south, any long-term solution to the northern insurgency will require carrots as well as sticks. Boko Haram, like the dominant militant group MEND in the Niger Delta, has become more of an umbrella organization that has split over time into factions and attracted assorted criminals and other opportunists, some not even Muslim, who have taken advantage of the franchise name and reputation. Beginning in 2014, there has been talk of

The insurgent Islamist group Boko Haram has been the source of much controversy in Nigeria. Here in Baga Village, a poster advertises the search for Boko Haram leader Abubakar Shekau.

negotiating with at least some of these factions and offering amnesty, counseling, education, and organized sports programs for those willing to renounce violence and their affiliation with Boko Haram. Critics argue that while this kind of "hearts and minds" campaign is admirable, it may be too little, too late.

OIL AND THE NIGER DELTA

It is fitting to conclude this chapter with a final discussion of oil. And nowhere do Nigeria's multitude of complex political, social, economic, and environmental problems and prospects converge more acutely than in the oil-producing Niger Delta. Home to some 31 million Nigerians comprising more than 40 distinct ethnic groups and speaking more than 250 dialects, this region also typically produces over 2 million barrels of crude oil a day and has the potential to produce up to 3 million barrels. Tragically, as much as half a million barrels a day are stolen by local militias and gangsters, who also kidnap oil workers, pirate tankers, and wreck production facilities. Corrupt national and local politicians steal or squander the lion's share of revenues from the oil that is not stolen.

Meanwhile, millions of gallons of oil and other effluents contaminate the Niger's delicate tropical ecosystem. A 2013 report estimated that drinking water in certain areas of the Delta contains some 900 times the amount of benzene (a carcinogen) deemed safe by the World Health Organization and further predicted that cleaning the crude oil residue in the area will take decades and billions of dollars. The illegal "flaring," or burning off, of natural gas alone is by some estimates the world's single largest contributor of greenhouse gas and wastes $500 million in potential gas revenues each year.

Although the region has been troubled for many decades, in recent years its impoverished communities have become increasingly angry, organized, and restive. With the reestablishment of democracy in 1999, politicians began to arm local gangs to rig elections for them. International oil producers who operate in Nigeria have worsened matters by providing regular payments to local leaders as tribute for operating in their communities. This practice has increased conflict and competition among ethnic groups in the Delta and between community leaders and unemployed youth, as each group vies for a share of the funds. Armed militias—frequently linked to political parties—have sprung up, battling, often violently, over oil. The militant group MEND has become the largest and best organized of these groups, launching frequent and increasingly brazen attacks since 2006.

Both authoritarian and elected governments have tried a variety of schemes to calm the region, including military operations and offers of amnesty. Most successful of these was a truce negotiated in 2009 in which thousands of militants surrendered in exchange for unconditional pardon, a monthly stipend, and the promise of retraining and education. The government also promised to adjust the derivation formula, allocating more oil revenues directly to Delta communities. However, the promised retraining was slow to materialize, and violence in the region has once again been on the rise with the electoral defeat of Jonathan, an Ijaw—the largest ethnic group in the Delta—who grew up in the region and had made broad promises of rehabilitation and redress. As violence increased and as oil prices and government revenues have fallen, Jonathan's successor Buhari—a northern Hausa—slashed the budget for the program by 70 percent, practically ensuring increased violence and declining oil production. A lasting solution to this conflict will not be easy; it will require more effective policing, local governance, central control over the actions of foreign oil producers, and acknowledgment of the economic and environmental demands of the local population most directly affected and deeply harmed by these activities. As this chapter has shown, for all the potential benefits this resource windfall could offer to the country and its people, the curse of Nigerian oil expresses itself in myriad ways and will not be easily lifted.

Key Terms

Abacha, Sani (p. 670)
All Progressives Congress (APC) (p. 676)
Azikiwe, Benjamin Nnamdi (p. 667)
Babangida, Ibrahim (p. 670)
Boko Haram (p. 665)
Buhari, Muhammadu (p. 670)
derivation formula (p. 678)
federal character principle (p. 674)
First Republic (p. 668)
Fourth Republic (p. 671)
Fulani (p. 666)
Hausa (p. 666)
House of Representatives (p. 675)
Igbo (Ibo) (p. 665)
Jonathan, Goodluck (p. 673)
Movement for the Emancipation of the Niger Delta (MEND) (p. 683)
Movement for the Survival of the Ogoni People (MOSOP) (p. 682)

National Economic Empowerment and Development Strategy (NEEDS) (p. 688)
Niger Delta (p. 677)
Obasanjo, Olusegun (p. 670)
patrimonialism (p. 671)
People's Democratic Party (PDP) (p. 676)
Republic of Biafra (p. 668)
resource curse (p. 686)
Saro-Wiwa, Ken (p. 670)
scramble for Africa (p. 666)
Second Republic (p. 670)
Sharia (p. 667)
Sokoto Caliphate (p. 666)
Third Republic (p. 670)
Yoruba (p. 665)
zoning (p. 676)

Crowds of people queue up in front of a new Apple Store in Chongqing, China. China is Apple's largest market, ahead of the United States and Europe.

Globalization and the Future of Comparative Politics

How do global forces shape local communities?

THE MIDDLE OF THIS DECADE represented a turning point in history. When calculated at purchasing power parity (PPP), China has overtaken the United States as the world's largest economy. By this measure, America's domination of the global economy, which emerged in the mid-nineteenth century by surpassing the United Kingdom, has come to an end. China's economy is expected to continue growth at a faster pace than that of the United States, further increasing the gap between them. By 2025, China could surpass the U.S. gross domestic product (GDP) in total market terms, not just in PPP.

Several questions prompted by these circumstances have been the source of heated debate around the globe, and they inevitably revolve around questions of globalization. The first is one of cause and effect. Did globalization lead to the rise of China, or did China lead to the rise of globalization? Most observers assume the former, that the rise of globalization—the spread of new forms of communication like the Internet, the end of the Cold War, and the expansion of liberal economic ideas over communism—meant that China, long isolated from the rest of the world, could finally partake in and benefit from a global order. In this view, globalization has been an inexorable force that has drawn in China just as it has other countries and parts of the world. Others, however, make a convincing case that it is China that has driven globalization. Domestic economic reforms in China starting in the 1980s focused on export-driven growth. This in turn transformed economies worldwide. Local industries have disappeared worldwide in the face of Chinese competition, while commodities like copper and oil are exported to feed China's development. Even the decline of global poverty that we discussed in Chapter 10 has been driven largely by China's economic growth.

These developments lead to a second set of questions. What will the rise of China mean to political globalization—the spread and deepening of shared political ideologies and values? We tend to see two diametrically opposed views.[1] The first posits that China's deepening international ties are transforming the country's domestic politics. This is essentially a liberal view, asserting that globalization leads to the global spread of democratic ideas alongside the emergence of a middle class. Combined, these changes will eventually sweep the Communist Party away. No authoritarian system can block this process.

Others are more skeptical. In their view, China is the country driving global political change, not the one being changed by it. Reforms in domestic economic institutions have allowed China to capitalize on and expand globalization, but these reforms serve only to reinforce authoritarian legitimacy at home by promising prosperity in exchange for acquiescence. Moreover, growing economic power means that China increasingly has the ability to reshape the global order to its liking. This power includes pressuring its Asian neighbors to accede to Chinese demands as well as growing influence via trade and investment from Latin America to Africa (recall our discussion of Zimbabwe in Chapter 8). All of these changes are undercutting the West's promotion of liberal values. The world may continue to globalize, as this argument goes, but it will be on China's authoritarian terms.

We are thus presented with two fairly stark alternatives, each based on a very different view of the causes and effects of globalization. Is globalization changing and transforming China in a way that will bring it to democracy? Or is China the engine of globalization, shaping the international system in a way that serves its authoritarian regime? Interestingly, despite their very different conclusions, these arguments share an emphasis on globalization that diminishes the role of domestic institutions that has been central to this book. Both arguments rest on the assumption that China is inexorably rising to the position of a dominant world actor and tend to ignore domestic factors within China.

As comparativists, we should scrutinize these arguments more closely. For example, although China's GDP has leaped forward, in per capita terms it is still far poorer than the developed democracies (about 15 percent of the U.S. GDP). And the belief that it will soon catch up to the developed democracies is not so certain, either. China may face the kind of "middle income trap" that we spoke of in the last chapter. Slowing economic growth, an aging population, extensive environmental damage, increased corruption, deepening inequality, and growing public protests are all domestic factors that may limit China's rise to prominence and even undermine globalization itself. Who knows? A generation ago, scholars and pundits spoke of "Japan as Number One," as one famous book was titled.[2] Perhaps China, like globalization itself, will not change the world in ways we expect.

LEARNING OBJECTIVES

- Define globalization.
- Describe how political globalization challenges sovereignty.
- Compare how economic globalization can transform markets and property within and between countries.
- Analyze how societal globalization may undermine old identities and create new ones.
- Evaluate whether globalization is new, exaggerated, or inevitable.

THE CENTRAL THEME OF THIS TEXTBOOK has been the struggle to balance freedom and equality. When societies clash over how to reconcile these two values, states must confront the resulting problems by using their capacity to generate and enforce policy. Democratic institutions presume that freedom and equality are best reconciled through public participation, whereas nondemocratic regimes significantly restrict such rights. The variety of institutional tools available has led to a diverse political world, where freedom and equality are combined and balanced in many different ways.

Over the past two decades or more, this dynamic has become more international in scope. Of course, domestic politics has always been shaped by international forces, such as war and trade, empires and colonies, migration and the spread of ideas. But to some observers, linkages between states, societies, and economies appear to be intensifying, and at an increasingly rapid pace they are challenging long-standing institutions, assumptions, and norms. This process is commonly known as **globalization**, a term that fills some with a sense of optimism and others with dread. Although the extent of globalization and its long-term impact remain unclear, behind it lies the sense that the battle over freedom and equality is an international one, no longer a concern to be solved by each country in its own way.

globalization The process of expanding and intensifying linkages between states, societies, and economies

What does this mean for comparative politics? At the end of Chapter 1, we discussed how comparative politics (and political science) remains hindered by problems of data and theory that are often unable to predict, much less explain, human behavior. Comparative politics has suffered in the past from scholars understanding too few cases, thus making comparisons difficult. But if globalization is transforming domestic politics, the very idea of comparative politics could be open to question. To play devil's advocate, wouldn't studying Brazil's energy-export sector be more valuable than investigating the internal workings of its legislature? Wouldn't a study of Internet traffic in the European Union yield better puzzles and answers than a study of German political culture? Wouldn't comparativists learn more from studying transnational crime networks than judicial politics in South Africa?

Of course, we can argue that "globalized" questions need not come at the expense of comparative politics, but the question remains whether scholars of political science are missing the big questions that lie in the space between comparative politics (the study of politics within countries) and international relations (the study of politics between them). The questions just listed present a false dilemma, because we needn't choose between these areas of research. However, such questions help us consider the issue that comparative politics as it is structured now may not be focused on important global puzzles and institutions. In summary, is there even such a thing as domestic politics any longer? Is everything that we've read in this book up to this point becoming obsolete or irrelevant? And if so, how are we to study politics in a globalized world?

In this chapter, we look at the concept of globalization and its potential impact on both comparative politics and the ongoing struggle over the balance of freedom and equality. We will begin by defining globalization and determining how we might measure it. Next, we will consider some possible effects of globalization, including how it may change political, economic, and societal institutions at the domestic level. We will also ask some questions about the progress of globalization—whether it is in fact something fundamentally new, profound, and inevitable. We will then conclude with a discussion of how the old dilemma of balancing freedom and equality may change in a globalized world.

What Is Globalization?

We could argue that we have lived in a globalized world for millennia. Even as early humans dispersed around the world tens of thousands of years ago, they maintained and developed long-distance connections with one another through migration and trade. Such contacts helped spur development through the dissemination of knowledge and innovations. For example, it is speculated that the technology of written language was created independently only three or four times in human history: in the Americas, in Asia, and in the Middle East. All other written languages were essentially modeled after these innovations as the idea of writing things down spread to other communities.[3] Thousands of years ago, empires stretched from Asia to Europe and people moved between these areas, exchanging goods and ideas. Trade routes forged even more far-flung connections between people who were only dimly aware of each other's existence. For example, in the first century c.e. the Romans treasured silk imported from distant China, although they did not fully understand how it was made or where it came from. Were these, then, "globalized" societies?

When we speak about globalization, we don't simply mean international contacts and interaction, which have existed for tens of thousands of years. According to the political scientists Robert O. Keohane and Joseph S. Nye Jr., one important distinction between globalization and these earlier ties is that many of these past relationships were relatively "thin," involving a small number of individuals. Although such connections may have been extensive across a vast region, these connections did not directly affect large numbers of individuals. In contrast, globalization can be viewed as a process by which global connections grow increasingly "thick," creating an extensive and intensive web of relationships between many people across vast distances. In the twenty-first century, people are not distantly connected by overland routes plied by traders, diplomats, and missionaries; they are directly participating in a vast and complex international network through travel, communication, business, and education. Globalization is a system in which human beings are no longer part of isolated communities that are linked through narrow channels of diplomatic relations or trade. Entire societies are now directly connected to global affairs. Thus globalization represents a change in human organization and interconnection.[4]

Globalization has a number of potential implications for comparative politics. First, due to the thickening of connections between people across countries, globalization breaks down the distinction between international relations and domestic politics, making many aspects of domestic politics subject to global forces. Debates over environmental policy become linked to climate change; struggles over inequality are framed by concerns about trade, offshore outsourcing, and immigration; health care is influenced by the threat of pandemics. As a result, political isolation becomes difficult or even impossible.

Second, globalization can also work in the other direction, essentially "internationalizing" domestic issues and events. Given that globalization deepens and widens international connections, local events, even small ones, can have ripple effects throughout the world. These interconnections across space are further amplified by the speed of today's world. Whereas technological change once took years or centuries to spread from region to region, today a new piece of software or video can be downloaded or viewed at the same time everywhere. The Internet allows the rapid dissemination of news and information from every corner of the globe, no matter how remote. The world seems to live increasingly in the same moment—what happens to someone in one place immediately affects others around the world.

In short, globalization is a process that creates intensive and extensive international connections, changing traditional relationships of time and space. Is globalization overturning or transforming the very foundations of politics? Would such a change make the world a better place—more prosperous, stable, and democratic—or just the opposite? And finally, is any of this inevitable? These are big questions of profound significance that have found little consensus. Let us first consider how we can think about the nature of institutions in a globalizing world.

Institutions and Globalization

We have spoken of globalization as a process, one that creates more extensive and intensive connections across the globe. These changes can, in turn, change the institutions of economics, politics, and society. At the start of this textbook, we spoke of institutions as being a key reference point for modern life. Institutions are organizations or patterns of activity that are self-perpetuating and valued for their own sake. The modern world is codified by them. Institutions such as states, culture, property, and markets establish borders, set boundaries for activity and behavior, and allocate authority, norms, rights, and responsibilities. Moreover, by doing so they establish local identity and control—a particular state, religion, or set of cultural values holds sway over the land and people here but not there. Space and time are thus understood and measured through institutions.

The question we now ask is whether this will still be true in the future. It may be that before long, domestic institutions will not be the most important actors in people's lives. Long-standing institutions like states, cultures, national identities, and political-economic systems now face a range of international forces and organizations that transform, challenge, or threaten their traditional roles. Let's look at some of the reasons this might be the case.

To begin, globalization is associated with the growing power of a host of nonstate or supra-state entities. Most can be grouped into three categories that we touched on in previous chapters: **multinational corporations (MNCs)**, **nongovernmental organizations (NGOs)**, and **intergovernmental organizations (IGOs)**. All three organizational forms are decades, if not centuries, old, but their role and impact are rapidly expanding as they benefit from and contribute to globalization. MNCs are firms that produce, distribute, and market goods and services in more than one country. They wield assets and profits far larger than the GDPs of most countries in the world and are able to influence politics, economic developments, and social relations through the goods and services they produce and the wealth at their disposal. NGOs are national and international groups that are independent of any state and pursue policy objectives and foster public participation. Some, such as Greenpeace and Amnesty International, can shape domestic and international politics by mobilizing public support across the globe. IGOs, groups created by states to serve particular policy ends, include the United Nations, the World Trade Organization (WTO), the European Union, and the Organization of American States.

In some cases, these forms of organizations are part of a broader **international regime**. The use of this term in the study of international relations is similar to our use of *regime* in comparative politics. Recall from Chapter 2 that in comparative politics, regimes are defined as the fundamental rules and norms of politics, a set of institutions that empower and constrain states and governments. International regimes function in the same way, but they link states together through rules and norms that shape their relationships to one another, usually regarding some specific issue (such as greenhouse gases or trade).

In addition to MNCs, NGOs, and IGOs, technology-driven forms of organization also play a role in globalization. This is not new. All earlier waves of human interconnection were dependent on technological changes, such as the domestication of plants and animals, the invention of writing, advances in seafaring, and the invention of the telegraph. Technology is not inherently globalizing or globalized, though in many cases technology and globalization can reinforce each other.

In the last 40 years, one of the most important examples of such reinforcement has been the development of the Internet. Originally created by the U.S. government as a way to decentralize communications in the event of a nuclear war, the Internet has grown far beyond this initial limited objective to become a means for people to exchange goods and information, much of it beyond the control of any one state or regulatory authority. As bandwidth has increased and more information has been digitized, the Internet has transformed from a tool into an entity in its own right, holding a tremendous amount of content. Unlike MNCs, NGOs, or IGOs, the Internet has no single "location" to speak of—indeed, we hardly even speak of "the Internet" any longer, so ubiquitous is its presence. The Internet is also unlike a typical regime: it has technical standards, but it does not have norms that link states together to address a specific issue or meet a specific goal; it is not the means toward

multinational corporation (MNC) Firm that produces, distributes, and markets its goods or services in more than one country

nongovernmental organization (NGO) A national or international group, independent of any state, that pursues policy objectives and fosters public participation

intergovernmental organization (IGO) Group created by states to serve certain policy ends

international regime The fundamental rules and norms that link states together and shape their relationships to one another, usually regarding some specific issues (such as greenhouse gases or trade)

Nonstate Organizations and Globalization

ORGANIZATION	DEFINITION	EXAMPLE
MULTINATIONAL CORPORATIONS (MNCs)	Firms that produce, distribute, and market their goods or services in more than one country	Apple, General Electric
NONGOVERNMENTAL ORGANIZATIONS (NGOs)	National and international groups, independent of any state, that pursue policy objectives and foster public participation	Greenpeace, Red Cross
INTERGOVERNMENTAL ORGANIZATIONS (IGOs)	Groups created by states to serve particular policy ends	United Nations, European Union

any one end. Discussions of authority, sovereignty, and control become problematic. But as technological change facilitates the growing reach of nonstate or supra-state actors, these actors in turn tend to foster further technological change.

Are these organizations, whether the United Nations or the Internet, indeed institutions? This is an important question, for as we have noted, institutionalization carries with it authority and legitimacy. Many MNCs, IGOs, and NGOs are legitimate and highly valued—seemingly indispensable parts of the global system. The same could be said of the Internet or other forms of technology, such as satellite television or the global positioning system (GPS). As institutions, then, they can call on a degree of influence and power. This influence may augment and improve the workings of domestic institutions; it may also conflict with or undermine them. Let us consider this idea further through the familiar categories of states, economies, and societies.

Political Globalization

In Chapter 2, we noted that in historical terms the state is relatively new, a form of political organization that emerged only in the past few centuries. Because of their unique organization, states were able to spread quickly across the globe, supplanting all other forms of political organization. Yet we also noted that if states have not always been present, there may come a time when they will no longer be the dominant political actor on the face of the earth. States may at some time cease to exist. Some see globalization as the force that will bring about this dramatic political change, but whether such a change is to be welcomed or feared is uncertain.

At the core of this debate is the fact that globalization and globalized institutions complicate the ability of states to maintain sovereignty. In some cases, states may give up sovereignty intentionally—giving authority to IGOs, for instance, to gain some benefit or alleviate some existing problem. The European Union is an excellent example of this—though, as we have seen, even under these conditions sovereignty is often given up reluctantly or rejected outright. The United Kingdom's decision to leave the European Union reminds us how sovereignty and integration can clash and that the former does not easily give way to the latter. In other cases, the loss of sovereignty may be unintentional. The growth of the Internet, for example, has had important implications for states regarding legal authority in many traditional areas, since it does not readily conform to international boundaries or rules. It can circumvent legal restrictions on certain forms of speech in a way that traditional newspapers or television cannot, through e-mail, websites, and social networks. Developments such as electronic currency may further erode the powers of states by undercutting their ability to print money, levy taxes, or regulate financial transactions—all critical elements of sovereignty.

What do these changes mean for state autonomy and capacity? One possible scenario is that states will become bound to numerous international institutions that will take on many of the tasks that states normally conduct. In this scenario, a web of organizations, public and private, domestic and international, would shape politics and policy, set standards, and enforce rules on a wide range of issues where states lack effective authority. The rule of law would become a preserve less of individual states than of a set of global institutions created for and enforced by a variety of actors.

With this diffusion of responsibility, sovereignty would decline. States would be "hollowed out," constrained by their reliance on the globalized world. This would affect their use of force. People cannot arrest computer viruses or enact sanctions against global warming, and despite the United States' call for a "war on drugs" and a "war on terror," we cannot declare war on such threats in the conventional sense. For globalized states, then, war may become largely ineffective and too risky, for it may undermine vital international connections. This narrowing of state sovereignty as a result of globalization is what the *New York Times* columnist Thomas Friedman famously referred to as a "golden straitjacket."[5] In this view, political globalization may bring about a more peaceful world order, constraining states' tendencies toward violent conflict by dispersing sovereignty among numerous actors and diminishing the capacity and autonomy of states.

It has been argued in addition that globalization will change not only the utility of force but also the nature of public participation and democracy. The increasing interconnection between domestic and international institutions makes it more difficult for sovereign actors to function without oversight from other organizations and to hide their actions from others. An example here is the development of the International Criminal Court, which has been charged with holding state leaders accountable for human rights violations in Libya, Sudan, and the former Yugoslavia. NGOs, such as Human Rights Watch or Transparency International (an anticorruption NGO), can play a similarly powerful watchdog role. Globalization will thus make politics less opaque and more open to scrutiny by domestic and international communities.

In contrast to these optimistic views, others see political globalization not as a pathway to peace and participation but as a source of dangerous fragmentation and weakened democracy. First, in their view, violence will not lose its utility in the international system as optimists hope; it will simply change form, much as it did when states themselves first appeared. According to this argument, globalization can empower violent international actors and movements that in many ways are the exact opposite of the modern state. These groups are decentralized and flexible, hold no territory, exercise no sovereignty, and are able to draw financial and other support from across the globe. In many ways, then, they are like other nonstate actors. Yet unlike NGOs and MNCs, these groups seek to achieve their objectives by acquiring and using force, applying it in ways that may be difficult for states or other international actors to counter.

Globalized criminal organizations and terrorist groups are perfect examples of this new threat. These are decentralized groups empowered by globalized technology, such as cell phones, encrypted e-mail, web sites, social media, and satellite television, which allows them to communicate, disseminate propaganda, access money, and recruit new members. Indeed, many argue that such groups look more like a social network than any formal nonstate actor.[6] Although states may at times be able to use conventional force against such groups where they have a physical presence, there is often no central location to attack or any easy way to keep individuals and information from simply dispersing and regrouping elsewhere. States, whose military capacity is geared toward fighting other states, may be ill equipped to battle small groups and "dark networks" that can take advantage of globalization to attack and undermine existing institutions.

Second, many question how a more globalized political system can be more democratic. Although deeper international connections may increase transparency, this does not necessarily lay out a mechanism that enables individuals to act on available information. As we noted in Chapter 6, modern liberal democracy is based on republicanism, the ability of people to choose their representatives through a competitive process. But who votes for international organizations? These bodies may be indirectly elected or appointed from the member states—or they may not be directly accountable to anyone at all. Thus, while a person may laud the work of Greenpeace or the World Wildlife Fund, it is instructive to note that these organizations are neither subject to popular democratic control nor necessarily more transparent than states themselves. A "democratic deficit" becomes a concern, an idea first raised with regard to the European Union. If power moves to global institutions, representation and democratic control may grow weaker since citizens lack the ability to control these bodies, which then grow distant from the citizenry and their preferences. At an extreme, this process could lead to a new form of global illiberalism such as we discussed in Chapter 8, whereby representative institutions exist but have been hollowed out by the loss of sovereignty and by the power of global technocratic institutions and elites.[7]

These are two starkly different visions of politics in a globalized world, and they reflect our opening discussion of China. In both scenarios, states and state functions become more diffused as power shifts to the global level. For optimists, international cooperation follows; these developments undermine the logic of war and increase transparency. For pessimists, deepening international connections facilitate new violent organizations and weaken democratic ties between the people and their representatives. Some combination of both scenarios is also possible.

Economic Globalization

Politics is not the only realm in which globalization is taking place. In fact, when many people think about globalization economics comes to mind, and this is the area that tends to generate the most controversy and debate. Economic globalization entails several distinct but interrelated elements that we should take into consideration. While the development of political globalization may be thought of as piecemeal or incremental, scholars tend to point to a set of specific institutions and regimes as vital components of economic globalization.

Bretton Woods system An economic regime that manages international economic relations; this includes the International Monetary Fund (IMF), the World Bank, and the World Trade Organization (WTO)

The **Bretton Woods system** is a global economic regime created in 1944 to manage international economic relations, whose instability was commonly cited as a driving force behind the Great Depression and World War II. Three important institutions emerged from the Bretton Woods system: the International Monetary Fund (IMF), the World Bank, and the General Agreements on Tariffs and Trade (GATT), later replaced by the World Trade Organization (WTO). The objectives of these three institutions were to expand and manage economic relations between countries. The IMF helps manage exchange rates between countries and provides loans to states in financial difficulty (recall our discussion of Greece in Chapter 7, which had to turn to the IMF for loans when it faced economic crisis). The World Bank provides loans and technical assistance to advance development in developing countries, something we discussed in the previous chapter. The WTO oversees trade agreements between the member states to lower tariffs and remove other nontariff barriers. For the past 70 years, these organizations have been at the center of a global liberal-economic regime. The Bretton Woods system also helped facilitate the policies of the Washington Consensus, which we mentioned in our discussion of structural adjustment in Chapter 10. The Washington Consensus emphasized rolling back the state's control over the market through privatization, deregulation, trade, and financial liberalization. Many assert that the deepening of economic globalization over the past two decades was enabled by the Bretton Woods system and catalyzed by the policies of the Washington Consensus.

Observers point to several important facets of economic globalization that are directly or partially related to the emergence of the Bretton Woods system and the Washington Consensus. First, and perhaps most obvious, is the globalization of international trade. National economies have grown deeply integrated as the production and marketing of goods has become more mobile—goods can be made by workers, and sold to consumers, in many more places around the world. Some of this is due to technological changes, but much can be traced back to the creation of a global liberal-economic regime that has encouraged trade between countries. Alongside trade globalization is the integration of capital and financial markets—markets for money—around the world. Banking and credit, stocks, and investment abroad all fall under this category. Money, too, is more mobile—investments and loans can be made from, and to, many more places around the world. Globalization deepens the connections between workers, goods, and wealth.

foreign direct investment (FDI) The purchase of assets in a country by a foreign firm

Some examples can offer perspective on the growth of economic globalization. In 1992, world exports in merchandise came to approximately $3 trillion; by 2015, the total was over $19 trillion. **Foreign direct investment (FDI)** (the purchase of assets in a country by a foreign firm) was under $200 billion in 1992; by 2007, it had reached approximately $2 trillion (though it had fallen back to just over $1.75 trillion in 2015—see Figure 11.1).[8] As mentioned earlier, economic globalization is also associated with the emergence of a number of MNCs that dominate global markets. Assisted by more-open markets and reduced transportation costs, large firms can make profits that rival the GDPs of many countries. For example, Apple's total profits in 2016 were over $200 billion, close to Finland and New Zealand's GDP at purchasing power parity. Another commonly noted example of financial

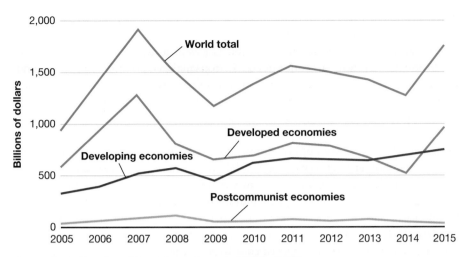

FIGURE 11.1 Foreign Direct Investment, 2005–2015

This graph shows the dramatic increase in foreign direct investment over the past decade, particularly within the developed world. Developing and postcommunist countries have seen more modest investment.

Source: World Investment Report, 2016, http://unctad.org/en/PublicationsLibrary/wir2016_en.pdf (accessed 8/11/16).

globalization is through financing; around one-third of the United States' $19 trillion in state debt is held internationally, with the biggest owners being China and Japan.

These economic developments are amplified by expanding global communication, which we spoke of earlier, which has transformed the way that markets, firms, and individuals interact. Technological innovations, alongside economic liberalization, have reduced many traditional economic barriers. People are able to buy goods and services from around the world using fewer or no intermediaries. As a result, markets are more open and firms and workers face greater competition. In the area of investment, too, changes have allowed firms, states, and individuals to move their money internationally and rapidly, jumping in and out of markets as they see fit. Many people liken these changes to the creation of railroads and the telegraph in the nineteenth century, which helped transform the way economies were networked.

Perhaps the best-known example of this intersection among globalized labor, technology, and markets is **offshore outsourcing**. Outsourcing has long existed: it is simply one process a firm uses to move some of its work to a secondary business that can do the work more efficiently or cheaply. However, in the past much of this outsourcing was done inside domestic or regional economies. The rise of a postindustrial and information-based economy, however, has meant that many jobs can now be moved a great distance away to wherever a cost advantage can be found. Examples include call centers, data processing, animation, and software programming. In 2002, offshore outsourcing accounted for around $1.3 billion in economic activity; by some estimates, the current figure is around $500 billion. India is often

offshore outsourcing A process by which a firm moves some of its work to a secondary business outside the home country that can do the work more efficiently or cheaply

noted as a major provider of outsourced labor, but Eastern Europe, Latin America, and Africa have been active as well.

For optimists, economic globalization is a vehicle for global prosperity. The expansion of international economic connections makes it possible to allocate goods and services, labor, and finance through a broader market, one unfettered by tariff barriers and other obstacles that states might erect. Countries are able to export what they produce best, encouraging innovation, specialization, and lower costs. Jobs are also created as capital flows and transnational corporations take advantage of new markets and new opportunities. In the end, wealth is diffused more effectively through open markets for goods, labor, and capital and so raises standards of living worldwide. Globalization is thus viewed as a positive, liberalizing trend, a global division of labor that is lifting billions out of poverty and generating greater prosperity by allowing more people to be a part of an international marketplace for goods and labor. And in fact, globalization is associated with the decline in extreme poverty, especially in export-oriented countries in Asia.

Others view economic globalization with more suspicion. To return to our discussion of political economy in Chapter 7, while optimists emphasize how globalization has increased overall wealth, critics would instead point to rising inequality. While it is true that increased wealth has reduced inequality between many developing and developed countries, inequality within many countries has at the same time grown dramatically. More globalized trade has lowered prices and increased the variety and quality of goods. It has also contributed to the loss of jobs when firms have been able to move overseas to take advantage of cheaper labor or lower levels of regulation. More generally, critics say that the globalization of firms, markets, and labor means that businesses are able to avoid government taxation, oversight, and public accountability. In this view, as economic globalization weakens state capacity and autonomy, it is replaced not with a global rule of law but rather a global economy that lacks any sovereign control. Freedom and equality are thus compromised.

USA

CANADA

MEXICO

North American Free Trade Agreement (NAFTA) An agreement between Canada, Mexico, and the United States that liberalizes trade between the three countries

NAFTA, THE TRANS-PACIFIC PARTNERSHIP, AND THE FUTURE OF FREE TRADE

The case of the 1994 **North American Free Trade Agreement (NAFTA)** between the United States, Canada, and Mexico does a good job of illustrating our earlier discussion. NAFTA drastically reduced tariffs on agricultural goods traded among Mexico, Canada, and the United States such that between 1993 and 2012, trade between the United States and Mexico increased by over 500 percent. Many Americans looked at NAFTA only in terms of whether it was costing American jobs, unaware of how it affected the Mexican economy. For example, U.S. products such as corn and pork cost one-fifth as much to produce as similar Mexican products. NAFTA doubled the amount of food Mexico imports from the United States, thereby lowering food prices for consumers but creating a massive crisis for millions of Mexico's farmers. About one-fifth of Mexicans work in agriculture, the vast majority poor subsistence farmers who have been hurt the most by NAFTA competition. As a result, Mexico has eliminated millions of jobs in agriculture. NAFTA has also exacerbated the gap between the wealthy north and the impoverished south.

In many other ways, however, NAFTA benefits Mexico. Manufacturing exports to the United States have skyrocketed, growing at an average rate of 75 percent annually since the agreement went into effect. Overall, Mexican exports rose sevenfold between 1994 and 2011. Greater access to U.S. markets has also been a boon to Mexico's fruit and vegetable producers, who now supply much of the U.S. winter market. Cheaper imports have benefited a wide variety of Mexican producers and consumers.

Whether NAFTA has created more winners than losers is a hot topic of debate within Mexico and the United States. One result of the new pressures created by NAFTA has been an increased flow of displaced Mexicans to the United States in search of employment. Because NAFTA, unlike the free trade agreements that created the European Union, did not allow for the free movement of people across borders, much of that immigration to the United States has been illegal. It is also clear that free trade agreements create "winners" and "losers" in all countries, such as those who lose their jobs as firms move from one country to another. This explains why some people in those countries often oppose the agreements.

In 2015, Mexico, Japan, and the United States along with nine other countries sought to form the **Trans-Pacific Partnership (TPP)**. The TPP proposed to enhance free trade by lowering trade barriers among a group of countries situated along the Pacific Rim, while setting standards for environmental and intellectual property protection. As with any free trade deal, the TPP was opposed by a diverse set of groups in many of the countries slated to become members. In the United States, for example, labor, environmental groups, and members of Congress from both major political parties expressed opposition to the TPP, criticizing its potentially detrimental impact on the environment, wages, and domestic industry, and criticizing the secrecy with which the deal was negotiated. Upon election President Donald Trump made good on his promise to abandon the deal and has demanded a renegotiation of NAFTA. Some suggest that these actions will spur a new set of trade agreements across Latin America and Asia, led not by the United States but rather by China.

Trans-Pacific Partnership (TPP) Proposed agreement among twelve countries to liberalize trade though reduced tariffs and common regulations; abandoned by the United States in 2017

Societal Globalization

Whether globalization and the political and economic transformations it brings become instruments of greater cooperation and prosperity or sources of conflict and hardship may depend on how societies themselves are transformed by globalization.

We have explored how political globalization may challenge state sovereignty and power and how economic globalization changes markets for goods, labor, and capital. The idea of societal globalization views a similar process, in which traditional societal institutions are weakened, possibly creating new identities that do not belong to any one community or nation. As we know from previous chapters, in the premodern world people's identities were rather limited and narrow, focused on such things as family, tribe, village, and religion. Only with the rise of the state did national identities begin to emerge. Individuals began to see themselves tied to a much larger community of thousands, or millions, of strangers bound together by complex myths and symbols including flags, legends, and anthems. This transformation coincided with the development of sovereignty, whereby borders and citizenship reinforced the notion of national identity—one people, one state.

Some argue that as globalization proceeds, these central aspects of individual and collective identity are giving way. Just as the state and domestic economic institutions are being challenged, so, too, are traditional identities. One factor is demographic—specifically, the increasing mobility of humans, fleeing conflict but also seeking better economic opportunities elsewhere in the world. In 2015, nearly a quarter of a billion people—3 percent of the world's population—moved across international borders. These are figures not seen for at least a century.[9] As we spoke of in Chapter 7, migration flows have the potential to change the cultural and political landscapes of many countries as they deal with questions of integration, multiculturalism, and citizenship.

As increasing numbers of people move around the globe, technological innovations like the Internet and cell phones also expand the capacity of individuals to become interconnected. Cell phone penetration is now high even among developing countries, and broadband is rapidly expanding across the globe (Figure 11.2). As electronic communications continue to grow, people find ways to link up with one another across time and space, building and deepening connections. Text messaging, websites, and social networks are all examples of virtual interconnections that have become integral to, or perhaps have even displaced, physical spaces and relationships.

How might this process shape societal institutions and identities? We can point to two possible trajectories. The first is that societal globalization engenders global multiculturalism. Different cultures will link and combine to a greater extent thanks to connections that are not bound by traditional barriers of time and space. This means not only that a globalized society will draw from many sources but also that the interconnection of domestic institutions at the global level will create new values, identities, and culture—a process of "creative destruction" or "hybridity" that will enrich all cultures.[10] One result of this outcome could be a global *cosmopolitanism*—

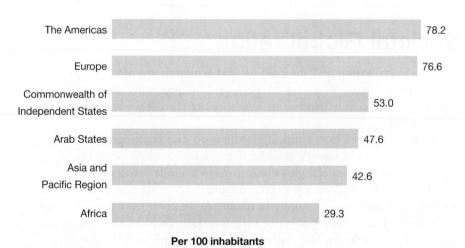

Per 100 inhabitants

FIGURE 11.2 Mobile Broadband Subscriptions by Region, 2016

Note: Mobile broadband subscribers are those who access the Internet on their mobile devices via cellular networks.

Source: ITU World Telecommunication/ICT Indicators database (accessed 4/17/17).

a term that comes from the Greek *kosmos*, or "universe," and *polis*, or "state." Cosmopolitanism is thus a universal, global, or "worldly" political order that draws its identity and values from everywhere. Historically, the cosmopolis was the physical space where disparate ideas usually came together—notably, the city. A globalized world, however, holds the potential for an international cosmopolitanism that binds people together irrespective of where they are.

Parallel to global cosmopolitanism is the idea of globalized democracy. We have already spoken of how globalization might shape political institutions at the domestic and international levels, though we focused largely on the development of nonstate and supra-state organizations as rivals to the state. When we focus on societal globalization and its effects on democracy, however, we return to our notion of civil society. The argument here is that growing international connections at the societal level would generate not only a form of cosmopolitanism but also a civic identity that stretches beyond traditional barriers and borders. This global civil society—organized life stretching beyond and above the state—can take shape in formal organizations like NGOs as well as in such informal manifestations as social movements or more basic grassroots connections between people drawn together by shared interests and values. This global civil society could in turn shape politics by creating new opportunities for concerted public action and new ways of thinking about politics and participation at the domestic and international levels.[11] Finally, this development of global cosmopolitanism and civil society could help facilitate democratic change across countries by informing and amplifying local political action.

As you might expect, there are critics of such views, skeptical of the notion that increased globalization will benefit social progress. Their criticisms are twofold. First, some contend that globalization overwhelms people with innumerable choices, values, ideas, and information that they are unable to understand, evaluate, or escape—especially people who are not part of the globalized elite. Confusion, alienation, and public backlash can emerge as people seek to hold on to their identities in the face of these changes. Nationalism and fundamentalism can be viewed as reactions to a globalized society that people find alien and hostile to their own way of life. A possible result of societal globalization is atomization or a retreat into old identities, rather than the creation of some kind of widespread global cosmopolitanism or civil society. Of course, much of this argument assumes that national identities are inherently problematic. An alternative view asserts that national identities are worth preserving and such things as mass immigration should be limited to preserve these institutions.

Along those lines, a second criticism emphasizes not the reaction to societal globalization but rather its eventual outcome. Even in the absence of a backlash against globalization, the critics contend, societal globalization will not generate a richer global culture and cosmopolitanism. Rather, it will trigger cultural and intellectual decline. Societies will trade their own cultures, institutions, and ideas for a common global society shaped not by values or worldliness but by speed and consumption. The things that make each society unique—languages, food, music, history, customs, values, and norms—will be absorbed, rationalized, and packaged for mass consumption everywhere. Such critics would note that it is no accident that after the U.S. and Chinese militaries, the third- and fourth-largest employers in the world (and the largest private employers) are Walmart and McDonald's. This view of globalization sees a process whereby what is unique in each society is repackaged and sold to the rest of the planet, while those things that lack mass appeal are thrown away or driven out, replaced by what satisfies the widest public and the lowest common denominator. This process can be thought of as a disenchantment of the world, what one scholar calls "the globalization of nothing."[12]

Taking Stock of Globalization

Globalization, like many processes of change, conjures up utopian and dystopian visions of the future. Perhaps a better way to look at globalization is to think about it as a set of choices that involve difficult trade-offs. The economist Dani Rodrik has spoken of globalization creating a "trilemma" involving global economic integration, the nation-state, and democracy. For Rodrik, these three elements are difficult to reconcile; it is possible to have any two of the three, but all three is not possible. Whatever framework we use, any discussion of globalization rests on the assumption that it is an unprecedented and inevitable turning point in history. But what is the evidence for this? Our task now is to match evidence against argument and consider what impact globalization has had on the world to date and whether, as is often assumed, this is truly something new that lacks historical analogy.

IS GLOBALIZATION NEW?

We can begin by questioning the assumption that globalization is a fundamentally new development in human history. As we noted earlier, for thousands of years humanity was linked across great distances, spreading people, goods, and ideas around the world. Scholars, however, have noted that such connections were often extensive but not intensive. But we should not underestimate how deep many of these connections were for their time. Medieval Europe was tightly interconnected through political, economic, and societal institutions, while a thousand years earlier the Persian Empire bound together people from Europe to North Africa and as far as India, shaping cultural values and human development. In many of these cases, war was an important component, disrupting old institutions and propelling change.

Let us look at a more recent phenomenon: the development of modern imperialism. The spread of European power into Latin America, Africa, the Middle East, and Asia profoundly reshaped domestic and international relations as Western political, economic, and social systems were transplanted into these parts of the world. Imperialism and the declining costs of transportation also helped facilitate the migration of millions of Europeans to these regions. By comparison, the current world of passports, visas, and immigration in some ways constrains human mobility far more than other factors did just a century ago.

The late nineteenth century saw the rise of the first NGOs and IGOs, such as the Red Cross, founded in 1863, and the International Telegraph Union (ITU), in 1865. And those who marvel at the advent of Internet communication forget that the first transatlantic cable connected Europe and North America by telegraph in 1866, spurring a global system of rapid communication and trade. In his famous work *The Economic Consequences of the Peace*, the economist John Maynard Keynes wrote of the dramatic impact of such changes:

> The inhabitant of London could order by telephone, sipping his morning tea in bed, the various products of the whole earth, in such quantity as he might see fit, and reasonably expect their early delivery upon his

doorstep; he could at the same moment and by the same means adventure his wealth in the natural resources and new enterprises of any quarter of the world, and share, without exertion or even trouble, in their prospective fruits and advantages; or he could decide to couple the security of his fortunes with the good faith of the townspeople of any substantial municipality in any continent that fancy or information might recommend.[13]

This may sound like the current global economy, but Keynes was actually writing about the period before World War I. Indeed, the rise of electronic commerce, often heralded as a central piece of globalization, would not be possible without the previous establishment of such institutions as the telephone, national postal services, passable roads, ports, and commercial shipping—all things that far predate globalization.

At that time, many observers believed that globalization would lead to the abolition of war and the spread of international law and world government. For others, however, these rapid changes also brought with them concerns and dangers not unlike those discussed today. Migration and trade triggered not only fears of cultural destruction but also violent resistance, including nationalism and fascism. Marxist and anarchist ideas also attracted followers around the world, some of whom sought revolution and engaged in terrorism. In these confusing and often violent developments, some predicted the decline and collapse of Western society, not unlike some of the gloomier prognostications we hear today.

These examples suggest that it may be shortsighted of us to think that today's global interconnections are more dramatic than any that came before or that they portend changes that are beyond our power to control. History may help us better understand the present; we should not assume that what is occurring now is unique and that the past has nothing to teach us.

IS GLOBALIZATION EXAGGERATED?

Earlier in this chapter we considered globalization's impact on political, economic, and societal institutions and whether globalization is making the world better or worse. Is its impact as great as many of its supporters or critics assert? In light of the recent global recession, it may seem obvious that globalization is real and can be dangerous. But given the different ways we can think about globalization, the situation is more complicated.

As is often the case, the data present a mixed picture. Let us begin with political globalization. Some have suggested it would lead to greater transparency and global democratic institutions, while others have worried that the result would be an important loss of democratic participation and the rise of rival nonstate and nondemocratic actors. In both of these cases, the assumption is essentially that globalization means the eclipse of the state, yet there is still not a great deal of evidence showing that either scenario is taking place. At the most basic level, even as globalization has spread, so, too, have the number of states; sovereignty has remained a critical demand of people around the world, from Kurdistan to South Sudan. While observers of globalization have long pointed to the European Union as evidence that globalization is reducing state sovereignty, 50 years after the European Union was created no other part of the world has shown a desire or ability to replicate this model. The European Union itself now faces unprecedented difficulties.

Indeed, over the past decade sovereign authority has reasserted itself in many areas. For instance, while many have assumed that the stateless, almost anarchic nature of the Internet and electronic communications would virtually displace the state, governments have found ways to regulate content and limit access. Chinese censorship of websites and social media like Facebook and the European Internet privacy laws are good examples. There is little comprehensive evidence that states are becoming more transparent or hollowed out under globalization; rather, it seems that the nature of their capacity and autonomy is changing to meet new challenges. At the same time, the idea that stateless actors such as terrorists are beyond the reach of states seems exaggerated, as new technologies can weaken or empower states and nonstate actors alike. Terrorist groups may have a global reach, but often they are—or aspire to be—more centralized than globalization suggests. The very name of the Islamic State fighting in Syria and in Iraq shows its aspirations—not to function as a borderless political community, but to form a military, conquer land, and build a modern empire. For now, at least, states and the aspiration to statehood still matter.

If the picture of states and globalization is not clear, it may seem that in the area of economic globalization, our evidence could be more comprehensive. Although people may not agree on the effects of economic globalization, even the limited data we have regarding trade and foreign direct investment do indicate a profound change over the last two decades. For example, developing countries now make up half of world GDP when measured by purchasing power parity, and much of this growth is driven by international trade and investment.

But here, too, caveats are in order. For example, despite impressive growth, the total levels of international trade represent only about a quarter of global GDP. Ninety percent of all fixed investment (investment in physical assets) in the world is still domestic; investors buy relatively few foreign stocks; and in contrast to our notion of the agglomeration of far-flung businesses, the merger of firms continues to be heavily driven by such factors as physical proximity and cultural connections. There is a reason that Silicon Valley exists as a physical place near a strong research university (Stanford) and in a network of personal connections. The "home bias" in economic activity continues to be strong, much more so than we expect.[14] Like states, distance itself still matters.

What about prosperity and poverty? Has globalization made a difference? In Chapter 4, we noted that since the 1980s extreme poverty has fallen dramatically as a percentage of the world population. Much of this change has been driven primarily by domestic reforms in one very large country—China—and China's subsequent integration into the global market. In other words, what we see as a uniform and inexorable process of globalization may be more effectively viewed through the lens of traditional comparative politics: changes in the domestic political and economic institutions first in China and, more recently, in India.

Finally, we should note that many of the economic changes that have occurred during the period of globalization don't have anything to do specifically with international relations. Economies have been transformed less by the Internet than by the expansion of computer technology and robotics that have replaced unskilled and some skilled labor. The applications of these innovations, both at home and abroad, are critical to explaining rising inequality.[15]

So far, we've found no unequivocal evidence regarding political or economic globalization. What about at the level of society? Here, too, we confront the limitations of our data. Both supporters and opponents of societal globalization often start from the proposition that national and local identities are giving way in the face of broader global forces, whether as part of some growing hybridity, cosmopolitanism, or homogenization. Whether this will be a peaceful process or a positive outcome tends to be the basis of their disagreement. But again we must ask, is this process actually taking place? Are more people identifying themselves as global citizens than in the past? Starting with the 2005–9 World Values Survey, surveyors began to ask people whether they saw themselves as world citizens. Among 31 countries surveyed, respondents agreed strongly with this proposition, with the most positive responses among those under age 29. This figure increased slightly between the survey period of 2005–9 and those surveys taken in the period 2010–14. This increase would seem to be consistent with increasing societal globalization.

Yet when we look at other related questions, we get a different view. When those same respondents are asked whether they trust individuals of another nationality, the response is quite negative. Even more interesting is that these levels of mistrust are higher among young people than among older generations. Of respondents under age 29, 63 percent said they did not trust people of another nationality, compared with 58 percent for those over age 50. Nor does the level of mistrust correlate easily with levels of globalization of a given country. Let's compare our findings with the Index of Globalization developed by the Swiss Federal Institute of Technology (see Table 11.1, p. 712). We can see that countries with the lowest levels of youth mistrust are also highly globalized, such as Sweden and Australia, supporting our hypothesis regarding societal globalization and cosmopolitanism. But we also find highly globalized countries like Cyprus, Malaysia, and Slovenia that exhibit high levels of mistrust. Not only does the world's most globalized country in the Index of Globalization, the Netherlands, show high youth mistrust—those levels are nearly 15 percent higher for people under 29 than those over 50—Sweden, the United States, Australia, and Germany also show higher levels of mistrust among the youth than older generations. Rather than younger and presumably more globalized generations feeling a greater sense of trust of other nationalities, they in fact feel more mistrustful. This raises the possibility that as countries become more globalized, younger generations come to feel themselves more globally connected, but also wary of those connections.

GLOBALIZATION AND THE FUTURE OF IRAN

IRAN

Iran's relationship to globalization captures many of the points we've raised earlier. The Swiss Federal Institute of Technology regularly produces an Index of Globalization that ranks countries in terms of their economic, social, and political globalization, using such variables as FDI, international information flows, and membership in international organizations (we'll return to this index shortly). In 2016, the index placed Iran at 154 of 192 countries. There are several reasons that can explain this. Several decades of strained international ties and economic sanctions have weakened links between Iran and the rest of the world, limiting an array of contacts and interactions. Domestic politics are more important, however. As we discussed in Chapter 8, Iran's regime is authoritarian and theocratic, having come to power in 1979 on a wave of public hostility to U.S. involvement in domestic affairs. As a result, the new regime was built in part on values critical of globalization, which was seen as tantamount

TABLE 11.1 Globalization and Trust among Young People

COUNTRY	DO NOT TRUST PEOPLE OF ANOTHER NATIONALITY VERY MUCH OR AT ALL (%)	INDEX OF GLOBALIZATION 100 = HIGHLY GLOBALIZED
Peru	87.8	66.27
Malaysia	85.5	78.14
Egypt	82.5	63.20
China	81.7	62.02
Romania	79.6	76.51
Thailand	79.0	70.76
Morocco	78.1	65.95
Japan	77.8	72.26
Colombia	77.7	60.34
Mexico	76.8	62.29
Iraq	75.1	43.66
Ghana	72.8	54.17
Cyprus	70.6	85.00
Rwanda	69.8	45.56
Slovenia	69.6	76.91
South Korea	68.7	67.03
Brazil	67.1	61.40
Netherlands	66.9	92.84
Jordan	64.1	69.19
Russia	63.4	68.25

to Western imperialism. The regime limited contact with the outside world through steps such as censorship and restrictions on foreign investment. It saw limiting connections with the outside world as a way to defend the revolution against hostile forces, much in the same way similar arguments were used by the Soviet Union.

In spite of these restrictions, however, many observers point to new pressures that may be inevitably globalizing Iran. Much of this discussion tends to focus on the young, since Iran's median age is 27 (ten years lower than that of the United States). The rise of the Internet and satellite television has had a profound effect on the consumption of international information. Though satellite dishes are illegal, they can be found everywhere on rooftops across the country. And although the regime has deployed firewalls and a "cyberarmy" to control the Internet, many rely on virtual private networks to get around these obstacles. Young Iranians are well versed on Western movies, music and pop culture, and technology, fostering a lively, underground community of rockers, rappers, skaters, and other forms of counterculture. Many see

COUNTRY	DO NOT TRUST PEOPLE OF ANOTHER NATIONALITY VERY MUCH OR AT ALL (%)	INDEX OF GLOBALIZATION 100 = HIGHLY GLOBALIZED
Turkey	61.3	71.33
India	59.1	52.38
Chile	58.9	72.23
Uruguay	56.1	66.63
Ukraine	54.6	70.24
Taiwan	54.3	n/a
Trinidad and Tobago	53.8	62.79
Georgia	49.6	64.13
South Africa	49.5	66.72
Argentina	47.4	58.54
Spain	45.7	84.56
Germany	45.6	84.57
Poland	44.4	81.32
Hong Kong	44.1	n/a
United States	41.4	79.73
Australia	36.6	82.97
Sweden	25.2	87.96

Note: Answers are for individuals under age 29.

Sources: 2010–14 World Values Survey, www.worldvaluessurvey.org/wvs.jsp (accessed 8/11/16); 2017 KOF Index of Globalization, http://globalization.kof.ethz.ch (accessed 5/9/17).

this as evidence of social change that will inevitably sweep away the current regime. After all, even the government leadership relies on Twitter to reach the international community—in spite of the fact that Twitter remains banned at home.

As we've discussed in this section, the presence of a globalized counterculture is not evidence of political change or inevitable democratization, however. Increased international contact in Russia after 1991 was followed by less democracy, not more, and globalization in China has not led to political liberalization. In 2009, massive demonstrations in Iran (known as the Green Wave) spearheaded by youth over a fraudulent election relied on video, cell phones, and Twitter to mobilize the public and attract international attention. But this had no impact on the regime, which was able to use violence to silence the opposition. Subsequent research suggests that part of the failure of the Green Wave had to do with its inability or unwillingness to build connections beyond its own demographic. Globalization may have helped foster a more connected youth, but the domestic politics of democratization will turn on a wide array of populations and existing institutions. Revolutions cannot be won by sharing content; they must be led.

Did Globalization Cause Economic Recession?

The global economic recession that struck in 2008 continues to reverberate worldwide; global GDP growth is expected to remain below recession levels at least until 2020, if not beyond. In Chapter 8, we talked about the ongoing Greek economic crisis, emphasizing how political institutions shaped their predicament. But the case of Greece is also deeply tied to global economic developments. This raises a question: Is globalization in general to blame for the current economic challenges? If so, what does this mean for the future of globalization and global economic growth? A few pages (or a few hundred) can't fully cover this dramatic event. Nevertheless, we can examine the institutions of domestic and international finance to begin answering these questions.

In considering the relationship between globalization and economic recession, we need to look at how the current difficulties unfolded. To begin with, we should consider what we mean when we say that globalization "caused" the current recession. It is not enough to simply say that this recession was linked to global economic forces; if that were the case, then any major economic downturn—such as the one beginning in 1929—could be seen as a product of globalization because then, as now, forces like trade and international finance were involved. If we believe that globalization is a causal factor, we need to determine which global relationships, intensified over the past decades, created conditions that contributed to the eventual downturns in the United States, Europe, and elsewhere.

What exactly happened? Most observers trace the crisis to the United States (and, to a lesser extent, Europe) and its real estate market. This housing boom—a rapid increase in housing prices and housing stock—can be seen as a market "bubble." Market bubbles can occur in any area of an economy where prices rise rapidly and higher than their traditionally understood values. Prices rise dramatically because the public begins to see a particular market as generating almost limitless growth and profits. This can occur in virtually any market, from housing to stocks; most famously, in Holland in the 1600s a bubble formed in the market for tulips. While such bubbles can have global factors (the tulip bubble was fueled in part by trade), psychological factors are more important, since they drive mass expectations of profits, the rapid inflation of prices, and the eventual bursting of the bubble and resulting panic. To return to our discussion in Chapter 1, an understanding of cognitive, often seemingly irrational factors may tell us more in this regard than any consideration of global forces.

But it would be too simple to conclude that the psychology of the masses—the foolishness of crowds, if you will—can alone explain major economic declines. While a bubble in housing prices was a catalyst for the current recession, this does not take into consideration what led to the rise in housing prices or stocks to begin with or why the impact spread so far. To account for the broader causes and effects of the housing bubble and its collapse, many would point to the international liberalization of finance (in other words, the global movement of money) over the past few decades.

We noted earlier in this chapter the rise of IGOs like the IMF and the World Bank, and the role that the Bretton Woods system played in the process of economic liberalization. These institutions originated immediately after World War II, but it was primarily after the Cold War that restrictions on capital began to be eased, allowing finance to move unimpeded around the world. Money could go where it wanted, investing in stocks or providing loans worldwide to people, firms, and countries. But easy movement in could also mean easy movement out. It was already clear two decades ago that liberalized finance could lead to "capital flight" if international investors grew jittery about a country's economic or political situation. In the late 1990s, investors fled from many East Asian markets following the collapse of a market bubble in the region. But even then global liberalization expanded, increasing the possibility that, as the system of global finance grew, a problem in one part of the world would radiate across countries and markets. Thus, as the housing bubble in the United States began to deflate, it affected not only American but also European banks that had invested in this area. And as American and European banks began to wobble, investors began to withdraw from stock markets around the world. Shrinking values of real estate and stocks eliminated wealth, dried up credit, decreased demand, and increased unemployment in the advanced democracies and beyond. Countries whose exposure to global finance was more limited, like China and India, suffered much less. Still, these same countries rely on foreign markets for exports, meaning that the continued economic weakness of richer countries affects developing countries as well. China was able to stave off the recession in part by increasing debt, though this now appears to be finally weakening economic growth.

In short, we could conclude that while economic recession is not itself a function of globalization,

Unfinished apartment buildings sit at an abandoned construction site in Spain following the collapse of the country's real estate bubble in 2008.

the globalization of finance created a much riskier world economy. It is possible that in the future global finance will become more regulated in order to prevent similar bubbles and panics. But does this mean less globalization? Is it possible to have a more globalized, more integrated, and at the same time more regulated world? Perhaps if globalization continues to expand, it will do so under the guidance of restrengthened states and international institutions. This chapter is yet to be written.

THINKING CRITICALLY

1. How has the increasingly unrestricted flow of money made economies more vulnerable to "capital flight"?
2. Why did the deflation of the housing bubble in the United States also affect European banks?
3. In what sense does economic globalization come at the expense of strong state autonomy?

IS GLOBALIZATION INEVITABLE?

For the sake of argument let us reject all of the qualifiers just raised and assume that globalization is a fundamentally new phenomenon whose effects are profound, whether for good or ill. For those who make this assumption, it often follows that globalization is a juggernaut that people, groups, societies, and states cannot stop. Is this true? To illustrate this point, let us return to history, and to Keynes. After noting the profound economic changes that occurred before World War I, he remarked that, above all, the average individual regarded these changes as "normal, certain, and permanent, except in the direction of further improvement, and any deviation from it as aberrant, scandalous, and avoidable."[16]

Yet this state of affairs was not permanent. International trade was disrupted by the onset of World War I, whose effects were further compounded by a subsequent world depression. Keynes himself came to play a role in the Bretton Woods system precisely because he noted that global economic development was fragile and required the active role of states. History suggests, then, that globalization is not unstoppable; deglobalization can occur as well, as it has in the past.

Globalization can be limited or reversed in a number of ways. One is through economic crisis. The heady period of economic development a hundred years ago was finally undermined by financial collapse in the 1930s. In its immediate aftermath, trade, investment, and immigration across the globe declined, often as a result of new national barriers that reflected increased isolationism, protectionism, and nationalism. To take one example, between 1901 and 1910 the United States accepted nearly 1 million immigrants a year; it would not reach even half that level again until the 1970s. Ongoing global economic difficulties could continue to work against globalization, reducing economic ties, migration, or other forms of globalization.

Indeed, recent global economic challenges have pointed to this very possibility. As we noted in previous chapters, much of what has developed in comparative politics over the past decade has taken place in the context of rapid global economic growth. The rise of China as a major exporting power, Russia and Brazil as suppliers of energy and other natural commodities, and India as a hub for outsourcing, as well as the integration of global markets for investment, are a few examples of this rapid economic growth that have had important political implications. Today, a good portion of this development has been blunted by significant economic difficulties. Global GDP growth now is a quarter below where it stood in the first half of the 2000s, and the same is true of foreign direct investment. Exporters have faced weakened overseas markets and the threat of increased trade barriers. These changes portend a weakening of the web of interconnections that define globalization.

Ongoing difficulties may also increase public opposition to globalization. Many people's concerns about how globalization might affect such things as the environment, labor standards, immigration, and democratic practices are being translated into antiglobalization activism. Opposition to more liberalized global trade already emerged in the late 1990s. The TPP has been abandoned by the United States and tensions have arisen surrounding NAFTA. We find such opposition to increased integration and globalization across the political spectrum and around the world, though it is particularly pronounced in the developed democracies. Recent surveys show that in countries such as the United States, Japan, Germany, and Mexico, fewer than half the public believes that trade creates jobs, and this has become a central focus of political campaigns in many countries.[17] Such opposition may help pave the way for greater international coordination of globalization, or countries may choose to resolve the "trilemma" of economic integration, democracy, and the nation-state by choosing the latter two over the former.

Whatever the outcome, it seems premature to declare that either a world of states or an age of globalization has come to an end. Certainly, it is more provocative to claim that a new era is upon us, whether it is a utopia of prosperity and peace or a dystopia of inequality and conflict. As we saw in Chapter 1, politics is one arena where new activities emerge, are institutionalized, and come to define our lives. But the resulting institutions can become ossified and break down, leading to turmoil. New institutions emerge to take their place—some of which produce more human happiness, and some less. Wherever we find ourselves now, it is not certain that we face major changes in our political institutions. And even if we do, it is not clear whether such changes will be a pathway to progress or a setback for humanity. So long as domestic political institutions matter, the study of comparative politics remains a critical endeavor. And you, too, are now a participant in that important work.

In Sum: The Future of Freedom and Equality

Our world may now be undergoing a profound change in institutions, though this idea is subject to debate. One result of this transformation could be an evolution of the struggle over freedom and equality. Both values can be measured not just within states but also between them. Does one country's freedom or equality come at the expense of another's? How can freedom or equality be balanced globally in the absence of any single sovereign power or dominant regime? The very meanings of freedom and equality may evolve as new ways of thinking about individual choice and collective aspirations emerge. These changes could lead to greater stability, peace, and prosperity for humanity or to greater conflict and misery. Whatever the path, states and nations, regimes, ideologies, and culture continue to play the dominant role in driving domestic politics, and domestic politics in driving world affairs. Comparative politics gives us the power to analyze the present, glimpse the future, and play a role in shaping the course of human progress.

Key Terms

Bretton Woods system (p. 702)
foreign direct investment (FDI) (p. 702)
globalization (p. 695)
intergovernmental organization (IGO) (p. 698)
international regime (p. 698)
multinational corporation (MNC) (p. 698)

nongovernmental organization (NGO) (p. 698)
North American Free Trade Agreement (NAFTA) (p. 704)
offshore outsourcing (p. 703)
Trans-Pacific Partnership (TPP) (p. 705)

Notes

CHAPTER 1: INTRODUCTION

1. Gary King, Robert O. Keohane, and Sidney Verba, *Designing Social Inquiry: Scientific Inference in Qualitative Research* (Princeton, NJ: Princeton University Press, 1994).
2. Gerardo Munck and Richard Snyder, "Debating the Direction of Comparative Politics: An Analysis of Leading Journals," *Comparative Political Studies* 40 (January 2007): 10. See also Jason P. Abbott and Kevin Fahey, "The State and Direction of Asian Comparative Politics: Who, What, Where, How?" *Journal of East Asian Studies* 14 (2014): 109–34.
3. Adam Przeworski, "Is a Science of Comparative Politics Possible?" and Robert J. Franzese, Jr., "Multicausality, Context-Conditionality, and Endogeneity," in *The Oxford Handbook of Comparative Politics*, ed. Charles Boix and Susan Stokes (Oxford: Oxford University Press, 2009).
4. Aristotle, *The Politics*, trans. T. A. Sinclair (New York: Viking, 1992).
5. Niccolò Machiavelli, *The Prince*, trans. W. K. Marriott (New York: Knopf, 1992).
6. For more on the behavioral revolution, see Robert A. Dahl, "The Behavioral Approach in Political Science: Epitaph for a Monument to a Successful Protest," *American Political Science Review* 55 (December 1961): 763–72.
7. James D. Fearon and David D. Laitin, "Integrating Qualitative and Quantitative Methods," in *The Oxford Handbook of Political Methodology*, ed. Janet M. Box-Steffensmeier, Henry E. Brady, and David Collier (Oxford: Oxford University Press, 2008); Amel Ahmed and Rudra Sil, "When Multi-Method Research Subverts Methodological Pluralism—or, Why We Still Need Single-Method Research," *Perspectives on Politics* 10 (December 2012): 935–53.
8. Nicholas Kristof, "Professors, We Need You!" *New York Times*, February 15, 2014.

INSTITUTIONS IN ACTION

a. Daniel Kahneman, *Thinking, Fast and Slow* (New York: Farrar, Straus and Giroux, 2013).
b. Philip E. Tetlock and Dan Gardner, *Superforecasting: The Art and Science of Prediction* (New York: Crown Publishers, 2015).

CHAPTER 2: STATES

1. U.S. history explains why *state* has different connotations for Americans. During the period of revolutionary struggle and the creation of a federal system, the former British colonies in America viewed themselves as independent political units—that is, as states. With the creation of a federal system of government, however, their individual powers were subordinated to a central authority. The United States of America, in other words, eventually became a system of national government, and the term *state* was left as a remnant of the brief period when these units acted largely as independent entities.
2. Max Weber, "Politics as a Vocation," in *From Max Weber: Essays in Sociology*, ed. and trans. H. H. Gerth and C. Wright Mills (New York: Oxford University Press, 1958), 77–128.

3. This idea has been developed by Charles Tilly, "War Making and State Making as Organized Crime," in *Bringing the State Back In*, ed. Peter Evans, Dietrich Rueschemeyer, and T. Skocpol (New York: Cambridge University Press, 1985), 169–91.

4. Azar Gat, *War in Human Civilization* (New York: Oxford University Press, 2006); Lawrence Keeley, *War before Civilization: The Myth of the Peaceful Savage* (New York: Oxford University Press, 1997).

5. Angus Maddison, *Contours of the World Economy, 1–2030 AD* (New York: Oxford University Press, 2007).

6. Charles Tilly, *Coercion, Capital, and European States: 990–1990* (Oxford: Blackwell, 1990).

7. Francis Fukuyama, *The Origins of Political Order: From Prehuman Times to the French Revolution* (New York: Farrar, Straus and Giroux, 2011).

8. Mancur Olson, "Democracy, Dictatorship, and Development," *American Political Science Review* 87 (September 1993): 567–76; Margaret Levy, "The State of the Study of the State," in *Political Science: The State of the Discipline*, ed. Ira Katznelson (New York: Norton, 2002), 40–43.

9. For the cultural explanation, see David Landes, *The Wealth and Poverty of Nations: Why Some Are So Rich and Some So Poor* (New York: Norton, 1999), as well as Fukuyama, *The Origins of Political Order*, and Ricardo Duchesne, *The Uniqueness of Western Civilization*, vol. 28 (Leiden and Boston: Brill, 2011).

10. Stephen D. Krasner, "The Case for Shared Sovereignty," *Journal of Democracy* 16 (2005): 69–83.

11. Bruce Gilley, *The Right to Rule: How States Win and Lose Legitimacy* (New York: Columbia University Press, 2009), 4.

12. Weber, "Politics as a Vocation."

13. Robert I. Rotberg, ed., *When States Fail: Causes and Consequences* (Princeton, NJ: Princeton University Press, 2003).

14. Olaf J. de Groot and Anja Shortland, "Gov-aargh-nance—'Even Criminals Need Law and Order,'" CEDI Discussion Paper Series, Center for Economic Development and Institutions (February 2011), www.cedi.org.uk (accessed 2/6/12); World Bank, United Nations Office on Drugs and Crime, and Interpol, *Pirate Trails: Tracking the Illicit Financial Flows from Pirate Activities off the Horn of Africa* (Washington, DC: World Bank, 2013), https://openknowledge.worldbank.org/handle/10986/16196 (accessed 2/12/15), License: CC BY 3.0 IGO.

15. Graham Denyer Willis, *The Killing Consensus: Police, Organized Crime, and the Regulation of Life and Death in Urban Brazil* (Berkeley: University of California Press, 2015).

INSTITUTIONS IN ACTION

a. Christophe Jafferlot, "India and Pakistan: Interpreting the Divergence of Two Political Trajectories," *Cambridge Review of International Affairs* 15 (July 2002): 253–67; Philip Oldenburg, *India, Pakistan and Democracy: Solving the Puzzle of Divergent Paths* (New York: Routledge, 2010).

CHAPTER 3: NATIONS AND SOCIETY

1. See, for example, J. Philippe Rushton, "Ethnic Nationalism, Evolutionary Psychology and Genetic Similarity Theory," *Nations and Nationalism* 11 (2005): 489–507.

2. Edward L. Glaeser, "Inequality," KSG Working Paper no. RWP05-056 (October 2005), SSRN: http://ssrn.com/abstract=832653 (accessed 7/12/16); see also Marc Hooge, Tim Reeskens, and Ann Trappers, "Ethnic Diversity and Generalized Trust in Europe: A Cross-National Multilevel Study," *Comparative Political Studies* 42 (February 2009): 198–223.

3. *Évolution du Climat Politique au Québec*, https://sondage.crop.ca/survey/start/cawi /Rapport%20politique%20-%20F%C3%A9v%202016.pdf (accessed 7/12/16).

4. Charles Tilly, ed., *The Formation of National States in Western Europe* (Princeton, NJ: Princeton University Press, 1975); see also Reinhard Bendix, *Nation-Building and Citizenship* (Berkeley: University of California Press, 1964); Douglass C. North and R. P. Thomas, *Rise of the Western World: A New Economic History* (New York: Cambridge University Press, 1976).

5. Stathis Kalyvas, "Civil Wars," in *The Oxford Handbook of Comparative Politics*, ed. Carles Boix and Susan C. Stokes (New York: Oxford University Press, 2007); James D. Fearon and David D. Laitin, "Ethnicity, Insurgency, and Civil War," *American Political Science Review* 97 (February 2003): 75–90.

6. Stefan Wolff, "Building Democratic States after Conflict: Institutional Design Revisited," *International Studies Review* 12 (March 2010): 128–41.

7. Destutt de Tracy, Antoine Louis Claude, *A Treatise on Political Economy* (New York: Kelley, 1970).

8. Thomas Jefferson, *Notes on the State of Virginia: Query XVII: Religion*, http://teachingamericanhistory.org/library/index.asp?document=291 (accessed 7/12/16).

9. Quoted in George Plechanoff, *Anarchism and Socialism* (Chicago: Kerr, 1909), 80.

10. Bruce Lawrence, *Defenders of God: The Fundamentalist Revolt against the Modern Age* (New York: Harper and Row, 1989), 78.

11. For an excellent discussion of fundamentalism in Christianity, Islam, and Judaism, see Karen Armstrong, *The Battle for God* (New York: Ballantine, 2001).

12. Gilles Kepel, *Revenge of God: The Resurgence of Islam, Christianity and Judaism in the Modern World*, trans. Alan Brayley (University Park: Pennsylvania State University Press, 1994); see also Daniel Philpott, "Has the Study of Global Politics Found Religion?" *Annual Review of Political Science* 12 (2009): 183–202.

13. Samuel P. Huntington, *The Clash of Civilizations and the Remaking of World Order* (New York: Simon & Schuster, 1996).

14. Ronald Inglehart and Christian Welzel, "How Development," *Foreign Affairs* 88 (March–April 2009): 33–48.

INSTITUTIONS IN ACTION

a. Alfred Stepan, Juan J. Linz, and Yogendra Yadav, *Crafting State-Nations: India and Other Multinational Democracies* (Baltimore, MD: Johns Hopkins University Press, 2011).

CHAPTER 4: POLITICAL ECONOMY

1. For a discussion of the difficulties inherent in providing public goods, see Mancur Olson, *The Logic of Collective Action: Public Goods and the Theory of Groups* (Cambridge, MA: Harvard University Press, 1965).

2. On deflation, see Nouriel Roubini and Stephen Mihm, *Crisis Economics: A Crash Course in the Future of Finance* (New York: Penguin, 2010).

3. Clyde E. Dankert, ed., *Adam Smith, Man of Letters and Economist* (Hicksville, NY: Exposition Press, 1974), 218.

4. Eduard Bernstein, *Evolutionary Socialism: A Criticism and Affirmation* (New York: Schocken, 1961).

5. OECD Tax Database, available at www.oecd.org/ctp/taxdatabase (accessed 7/12/16).

6. For more on the variation within social democratic systems, see Gosta Esping-Anderson, *The Three Worlds of Welfare Capitalism* (Princeton, NJ: Princeton University Press, 1990).

7. For a discussion of communist political economies, see Robert W. Campbell, *The Socialist Economies in Transition: A Primer on Semi-Reformed Systems* (Bloomington: Indiana University Press, 1991).

8. The classic work on mercantilism is Friedrich List, *The National System of Political Economy* (New York: Kelley, 1966).

9. For a defense of mercantilism, see Ha-Joon Chang, *Bad Samaritans: The Myth of Free Trade and the Secret History of Capitalism* (New York: Bloomsbury, 2007); on Trump, see Binyamin Appelbaum, "On Trade, Donald Trump Breaks with 200 Years of Economic Orthodoxy," *New York Times*, March 10, 2016.

10. Charles I. Jones and Peter Klenow, "Beyond GDP? Welfare across Countries and Time," NBER Working Paper no. 16352 (September 2010).

11. For calculation of global Gini index, see Branko Milanovic, *The Haves and the Have-Nots: A Brief and Idiosyncratic History of Global Inequality* (New York: Basic Books, 2011); on poverty, see Xavier Salai-i-Martin and Maxim Pinkovskiy, "Parametric Estimations of the World Distribution of Income," NBER Working Paper no. 15433 (October 2009).

12. The United Nations Human Development Indicators are available at http://hdr.undp .org (accessed 7/12/16).

13. Milanovic, *The Haves and the Have-Nots*, 87–97.

14. Richard A. Easterlin, *Happiness, Growth, and the Life Cycle* (New York: Oxford University Press, 2011).

15. On Latin America in particular, see *Beyond Facts: Understanding Quality of Life* (Washington, DC: Inter-American Development Bank, 2008).

16. Fraser Institute, *Economic Freedom of the World Annual Report 2015*, available at www .freetheworld.com (accessed 7/12/16).

INSTITUTIONS IN ACTION

a. United Nations Development Programme, Regional Human Development Report for Latin America and the Caribbean (New York: United Nations Development Programme, 2016), www.latinamerica.undp.org/content/rblac/en/home/library/human _development/informe-regional-sobre-desarrollo-humano-para-america-latina-y-e (accessed 7/16/16); see also World Bank, "A Slowdown in Social Gains," LAC Poverty and Inequality Monitoring (Washington, DC: World Bank Group, 2016), http://documents.worldbank.org/curated/en/2016/04/26211205/slowdown -social-gains (accessed 7/12/16).

CHAPTER 5: POLITICAL VIOLENCE

1. William McCants, *The ISIS Apocalypse: The History, Strategy, and Doomsday Vision of the Islamic State* (New York: Macmillan, 2015).

2. For the opposing views, see Max Abrahms, "What Terrorists Really Want," *International Security* 32 (Spring 2008): 78–105, and Robert Pape, *Dying to Win: The Strategic Logic of Suicide Terrorism* (New York: Random House, 2005).

3. Theda Skocpol, *States and Social Revolutions: A Comparative Analysis of France, Russia, and China* (Cambridge: Cambridge University Press, 1979).

4. Timur Kuran, "Now Out of Never: The Element of Surprise in the East European Revolution of 1989," *World Politics* 44, no. 1 (October 1991): 7–48. See also Bruce Bueno de Mesquita and Alastair Smith, "Political Succession: A Model of Coups, Revolution, Purges, and Everyday Politics," *Journal of Conflict Resolution* 61, no. 4: 707–43.

5. Tim Krieger and Daniel Meierrieks, "Does Income Inequality Lead to Terrorism?" CESifo Working Paper Series No. 5821, March 23, 2016, http://ssrn.com /abstract=2766910 (accessed 7/12/16).

6. Max Abrahms, "The Political Effectiveness of Terrorism Revisited," *Comparative Political Studies* 45, no. 3 (2012): 366–93.

7. Subhayu Bandyopadhyay, Todd Sandler, and Javed Younas, "The Toll of Terrorism," *Finance and Development*, 52, no. 2 (June 2015): 26–28.

8. Maximilien Robespierre, *On the Moral and Political Principles of Domestic Policy*, 1794, http://legacy.fordham.edu/halsall/mod/robespierre-terror.asp (accessed 7/23/16).

9. Orin Starn, "Maoism in the Andes: The Communist Party of Peru—Shining Path and the Refusal of History," *Journal of Latin American Studies* 27, no. 2 (1995): 399–421.

10. Mohammed M. Hafez, "Armed Islamist Movements and Political Violence in Algeria," *Middle East Journal* 54 (Autumn 2000): 572–91.

11. Mark Juergensmeyer, *Terror in the Mind of God: The Global Rise of Religious Violence* (Berkeley: University of California Press, 2003). See also David Livingstone Smith, *Less than Human: Why We Demean, Enslave, and Exterminate Others* (New York: St. Martin's Press, 2011).

12. Alexis de Tocqueville, *The Old Regime and the Revolution* (New York: Harper and Brothers, 1856), 27.

13. William Pierce, "The Morality of Survival," May 2001, https://archive.org/details /TheDr.WilliamL.PierceCollectionaudio (accessed 07/21/16). See also Brad Whitsel, "*The Turner Diaries* and Cosmotheism: William Pierce's Theology," *Nova Religio* 1 (April 1998): 183–97.

14. J.M Berger, "The Turner Legacy: The Storied Origins and Enduring Impact of White Nationalism's Deadly Bible," The International Centre for Counter-Terrorism, September 2016, https://icct.nl/wp-content/uploads/2016/09/ICCT-Berger-The -Turner-Legacy-September2016-2.pdf (accessed 3/1/17).

15. Matthew J. Walton, and Susan Hayward, "Contesting Buddhist Narratives: Democratization, Nationalism, and Communal Violence in Myanmar." *Policy Studies* 71 (2014): 1–81.

16. Shane Harris, *The Watchers: The Rise of America's Surveillance State* (New York: Penguin, 2010).

17. *An Historical Review of the Constitution and Government of Pennsylvania* (London, 1759), i.

INSTITUTIONS IN ACTION

a. Lin Noueihed, "Peddler's Martyrdom Launched Tunisia's Revolution," Reuters Africa, January 19, 2011, http://www.reuters.com/article/tunisia-protests-bouazizi -idAFLE70G18J20110119 (accessed 1/31/12).

CHAPTER 6: DEMOCRATIC REGIMES

1. C. B. MacPherson, *The Life and Times of Liberal Democracy* (New York: Oxford University Press, 1977).

2. Christopher Blackwell, ed., *Demos: Classical Athenian Democracy*, www.stoa.org/projects /demos/home (accessed 7/12/16).

3. For details, see Charles Tilly, "War Making and State Making as Organized Crime," in *Bringing the State Back In*, ed. Peter B. Evans, Dietrich Rueschemeyer, and Theda Skocpol (New York: Cambridge University Press, 1985), 165–91; see also Francis Fukuyama, *The Origins of Political Order* (New York: Farrar, Straus and Giroux, 2011).

4. Adam Przeworski and Fernando Limongi, "Modernization: Theories and Facts," *World Politics* 49, no. 2 (1997): 155–83.

5. Daron Acemoglu and James A. Robinson, *Economic Origins of Dictatorship and Democracy* (New York: Cambridge University Press, 2007).

6. Alexis de Tocqueville, *Democracy in America*, vol. 2, trans. Henry Reeve (New York: Henry G. Langley, 1845), 125, Google Books.

7. Vladimir Tismaneanu, *In Search of Civil Society: Independent Peace Movements in the Soviet Bloc* (London: Routledge, 1990).

8. David S. Law and Mila Versteeg, "The Evolution and Ideology of Global Constitutionalism," Legal Studies Research Paper Series, Paper no. 10-10-01, October 4, 2010.

9. Philip B. Kurland and Ralph Lerner, eds., *The Founders' Constitution*, University of Chicago Press, http://press-pubs.uchicago.edu/founders/documents/v1ch15s50.html (accessed 3/13/17).

10. An exhaustive discussion of the different forms of electoral systems and other facets of voting and elections can be found at the ACE Electoral Knowledge Network website, www.aceproject.org (accessed 7/12/16).

11. Maurice Duverger, *Political Parties: Their Organization and Activity in the Modern State* (New York: Wiley, 1964).

12. Advocates for majority SMDs in the United States can be found at the Center for Voting and Democracy website, www.fairvote.org (accessed 7/12/16).

13. For more on this debate, see the ACE Electoral Knowledge Network website, www .aceproject.org (accessed 7/12/2016), as well as *Electoral System Design: The New International IDEA Handbook* (Stockholm: International Institute for Democracy and Electoral Assistance, 2005).

14. Matt Qvortrup, "Europe Has a Referendum Addiction," *Foreign Policy*, June 21, 2016; David Butler and Austin Ranney, *Referendums around the World: The Growing Use of Direct Democracy* (Washington, DC: American Enterprise Institute, 1994).

INSTITUTIONS IN ACTION

a. Minxin Pei, "5 Ways China Could Become a Democracy," *Diplomat* (February 13, 2013).

CHAPTER 7: DEVELOPED DEMOCRACIES

1. T. R. Reid, *The United States of Europe: The New Superpower and the End of American Supremacy* (New York: Penguin, 2005).

2. See the discussion of the 2016 edition of World Development Indicators at http:// blogs.worldbank.org/opendata/2016-edition-world-development-indicators-out-three -features-you-won-t-want-miss (accessed 7/14/16).

3. "More Mexicans Leaving Than Coming to the U.S.," Pew Research Center, November 19, 2015, www.pewhispanic.org/2015/11/19/more-mexicans-leaving-than-coming-to -the-u-s (accessed 7/14/16).

4. Desmond Dinan, *Europe Recast: A History of the European Union* (Boulder, CO: Lynne Rienner Publishers, 2014).

5. See the website of the EU: http://europa.eu/about-eu (accessed 7/12/16).

6. Martin Feldstein, "The Failure of the Euro: The Little Currency That Couldn't," *Foreign Affairs* 91, no. 1 (January/February 2012): 105–16.

7. Jean-Paul Faguet, "Decentralization and Governance," *World Development* 53 (January 2014): 2–13.

8. Anne Power, *Cities for a Small Continent* (Bristol, UK: Policy Press, 2016).

9. Ronald Inglehart, "Globalization and Postmodern Values," *Washington Quarterly* 23, no. 1 (Winter 2000): 215–28.

10. United States Census Bureau, "Projections of the Size and Composition of the U.S. Population: 2014 to 2060 Population Estimates and Projections," www.census.gov/ content/dam/Census/library/publications/2015/demo/p25-1143.pdf (accessed 7/14/16).

11. OECD Publishing (2015), "Education at a Glance 2015: Highlights," www.oecd -ilibrary.org/education/education-at-a-glance-2015_eag-2015-en (accessed 7/14/16).

12. OECD Publishing (2011), "An Overview of Growing Income Inequalities in OECD Countries: Main Findings," www.oecd.org/els/soc/49499779.pdf (accessed 7/14/16).

13. Kenneth M. Johnson, Layton M. Field, and Dudley L. Poston, "More Deaths Than Births: Subnational Natural Decrease in Europe and the United States," *Population and Development Review* 41, no. 4 (December 2015): 651–80.

14. Ibid.

INSTITUTIONS IN ACTION

a. Aris Trantidis, *Clientelism and Economic Policy: Greece and the Crisis* (New York: Routledge, 2016).

UNITED KINGDOM

1. R. C. van Caenegem, *The Birth of the English Common Law* (Cambridge: Cambridge University Press, 1989).

2. Jeremy Black, *Walpole in Power* (Straud, UK: Sutton, 2001).

3. For a discussion of the link between economic and democratic development, see Barrington Moore Jr., *Social Origins of Dictatorship and Democracy* (Boston: Beacon Press, 1966).

4. For a discussion of Thatcherism and its effects, see Earl Reitan, *The Thatcher Revolution: Margaret Thatcher, John Major, and Tony Blair, 1979–2001* (Lanham, MD: Rowman & Littlefield, 2003); for her own perspective, see Margaret Thatcher, *The Downing Street Years* (New York: HarperCollins, 1993).

5. For a discussion of the constitution in practice, see Peter Hennessy, *The Hidden Wiring: Unearthing the British Constitution* (London: Victor Gollancz, 1995).

6. Roger Mortimore, "Monarchy as Popular as Ever Ahead of Queen's 90th Birthday Celebrations," *Ipsos MORI*, April 15, 2016. www.ipsos-mori.com/researchpublications /researcharchive/3720/Monarchy-popular-as-ever-ahead-of-Queens-90th-Birthday -celebrations.aspx (accessed 7/27/16). For a useful discussion of the value of the British monarchy to political life, see Vernon Bogdanor, *The Monarchy and the Constitution* (Oxford: Clarendon Press, 1996).

7. British question time can be seen regularly on the public affairs channel C-SPAN and can be accessed online at www.cspan.org.

8. Meg Russell, *The Contemporary House of Lords: Westminster Bicameralism Revived* (Oxford: Oxford University Press, 2014).

9. "Breaking the Old Place Up," *Economist*, November 4, 1999.

10. Anthony Giddens, *The Third Way: The Renewal of Social Democracy* (Malden, MA: Blackwell, 1998).

11. Mark Garnett and Philip Lynch, *The Conservatives in Crisis* (Manchester, UK: Manchester University Press, 2003).

12. Philip Lynch and Robert Garner, "The Changing Party System," *Parliamentary Affairs* 58, no. 3 (June 2005): 533–54.

13. An interesting discussion of the changing nature of class and civil society in Britain can be found in Peter A. Hall, "Great Britain: The Role of Government and the Distribution of Social Capital," in Robert D. Putnam, ed., *Democracies in Flux: The Evolution of Social Change in Contemporary Society* (New York: Oxford University Press, 2002), pp. 21–57.

14. Martin Durham, "Abortion, Gay Rights, and Politics in Britain and America," *Parliamentary Affairs* 58, no. 1 (January 2005): 89–103.

15. For further discussion, see James Ball, "How British Are the British," *Guardian*, October 6, 2011.

16. John Locke, *Two Treatises on Government: Of Civil Government Book II*, ch. 7 (1689; Online Library of Liberty, 2014), http://oll.libertyfund.org/titles/222 (accessed 11/14/14).

17. John Cassidy, "By George, Britain's Austerity Program Didn't Work," *New Yorker*, December 5, 2013.

18. David Baker and Philippa Sherrington, "Britain and Europe: The Dog That Didn't Bark," *Parliamentary Affairs* 58, no. 2 (April 2005): 303–17.

19. James Bennett, "After the Brexit," *New Criterion* 32:5 (January 2014): 40–46.

20. Matthijs Matthias, "David Cameron's Dangerous Game: The Folly of Flirting with an EU Exit," *Foreign Affairs* 92 (September/October 2013): 10–16.

UNITED STATES

1. Francis Fukuyama, "American Political Decay or Renewal? The Meaning of the 2016 Election," *Foreign Affairs,* July/August 2016, pp. 58–68.

2. David R. Mayhew, *Divided We Govern: Party Control, Lawmaking, and Investigations, 1946–2002,* 2nd ed. (New Haven, CT: Yale University Press, 2005).

3. On the Tea Party movement, see Vanessa Williamson, Theda Skocpol, and John Coggin, "The Tea Party and the Remaking of Republican Conservatism," *Perspectives on Politics* 9 (March 2011): 25–43.

4. NORC Center for Public Affairs Research, "The People's Agenda: America's Priorities and Outlook for 2014," *AP/GfK Polls,* January 2, 2014, http://surveys.ap.org/data/ NORC /AP_NORC_2014_PeoplesAgenda_Poll_Topline_Final.pdf (accessed 8/9/14). For a survey of recent polls, see Karlyn Bowman and Jennifer Marsico, "As the Tea Party Turns Five, It Looks a Lot Like the Conservative Base," *Forbes,* February 24, 2014, www .forbes.com/sites/realspin/2014/02/24/as-the-tea-party-turns-five-it-looks-a-lot-like -the-conservative-base (accessed 8/11/14).

5. Peter Beinart, "The White Strategy," *Atlantic,* July/August 2016, pp. 81–86.

6. As reported by the Center for Responsive Politics, www.opensecrets.org/overview/cost .php?display=T&infl=Y (accessed 1/14/17).

7. Robert Putnam, *Bowling Alone: The Collapse and Revival of American Community* (New York: Simon and Schuster, 2000).

8. Jonathan Rauch, "What's Ailing American Politics?" *Atlantic,* July/August 2016, pp. 51–63.

9. See CIA, The World Factbook, 2014, www.cia.gov/library/publications/the-world -factbook (accessed 8/11/14).

10. Graham K. Wilson, *Only in America? The Politics of the United States in Comparative Perspective* (Chatham, NJ: Chatham House, 1998), p. 61.

11. See Sven Steinmo, *The Evolution of Modern States: Sweden, Japan, and the United States* (New York: Cambridge University Press, 2010). For the "submerged state," see Suzanne Mettler, *The Submerged State: How Invisible Government Policies Undermine American Democracy* (Chicago: University of Chicago Press, 2011).

12. Richard Kogan, "Federal Spending, 2001 through 2008," Center on Budget and Policy Priorities, March 2008, www.cbpp.org/3-5-08bud.htm (accessed 8/2/08).

13. For details, see the CIA, The World Factbook, www.cia.gov/library/publications /the-world-factbook (accessed 11/18/14).

14. Robert Putnam, *Our Kids: The American Dream in Crisis* (New York: Simon and Schuster, 2015).

15. See Martin Gilens and Benjamin Page, "Testing Theories of American Politics: Elites, Interest Groups, and Average Citizens," in *Perspectives on Politics* 12, no. 3 (September 2014): 564–81.

16. Samuel P. Huntington, *Who Are We? The Challenges to America's National Identity* (New York: Simon and Schuster, 2004).

17. Tamar Jacoby, ed., *Reinventing the Melting Pot: The New Immigrants and What It Means to Be American* (New York: Basic Books, 2004).

18. Robert A. Levine, "Assimilation, Past and Present," *Public Interest* (Spring 2005): 108.

19. "Fewer Americans Favor Cutting Back Immigration," Gallup, July 10, 2008, www.gallup.com (accessed 2/19/09).

20. Alberto Alesina and Edward Glaeser, *Fighting Poverty in the US and Europe: A World of Difference* (Oxford: Oxford University Press, 2006).

21. "Congressional Performance," *Rasmussen Reports*, www.rasmussenreports.com/public_content/politics/mood_of_america/congressional_performance (accessed 8/13/14).

22. A good overview of this evidence can be found in Robin Stryker, National Institute of Civil Discourse Research Brief 6: "Political Polarization," University of Arizona, prepared September 1, 2011, http://nicd.arizona.edu/sites/default/files/research_briefs/NICD_research_brief6.pdf (accessed 11/18/14).

23. Richard H. Pildes, "Why the Center Does Not Hold: The Causes of Hyperpolarized Democracy in America," *California Law Review* 99, no. 2 (April 2011): 203. Available from http://scholarship.law.berkeley.edu/cgi/viewcontent.cgi?article=1039&context=californialawreview (accessed 10/18/14).

24. Alan Abramovitz and Kyle Saunders, "Is Polarization a Myth?" www.csupomona.edu/~smemerson/business318/AbramCulWarMythVSFIORINA.pdf (accessed 11/18/14).

25. See, for example, Ronald Brownstein, *The Second Civil War: How Extreme Partisanship Has Paralyzed Washington and Polarized America* (New York: Penguin Press, 2007), and Nolan McCarty, Keith Poole, and Howard Rosenthal, *Polarized America: The Dance of Ideology and Unequal Riches* (Cambridge, MA: MIT Press, 2006).

26. Nolan McCarty, "The Policy Consequences of Partisan Polarization in the United States," http://bcep.haas.berkeley.edu/papers/McCarty.doc (accessed 1/2/11).

27. See, for example, Morris P. Fiorina and Samuel J. Abrams, "Political Polarization in the American Public," *Annual Review of Political Science* 11 (2008): 563–88.

28. An excellent discussion of the causes of political dysfunction in the United States is Jonathan Rauch, "What's Ailing American Politics?" *Atlantic*, July/August 2016, pp. 51–63. On the fragmentation and politicization of the U.S. media, see Susan Glasser, "Covering Politics in a Post-Truth America," Brookings Institution, www.brookings.edu/essay/covering-politics-in-a-post-truth-america/?utm_medium=partner&utm_source=politico&utm_campaign=essay17 (accessed 12/7/16).

29. Carlos Pereira and Carlos Aramayo, "Political Polarization: What the U.S. Can Learn from Latin America," www.brookings.edu/opinions/2011/0301_polarization_pereira_aramayo.aspx (accessed 1/3/12).

30. See, for example, R. Pildes, "Why the Center Does Not Hold," pp. 273–333.

FRANCE

1. Malcolm Crook and John Dunne, "Napoléon's France: History and Heritage," *Modern and Contemporary France* 8 (2000): 429–31.

2. John Hellman, "Memory, History, and National Identity in Vichy France," *Modern and Contemporary France* 9 (2001): 37–42.

3. For more, see Serge Bernstein, *The Republic of de Gaulle, 1958–1969* (Cambridge, UK: Cambridge University Press, 1993).

4. Robert Elgie, "The French Presidency," in *Developments in French Politics*, 5th ed., ed. Alistair Cole, Sophie Meunier, and Vincent Tiberj (London: Palgrave MacMillan, 2013), 19–34.

5. From 1958 to 1962, presidents were indirectly elected by an electoral college composed of elected officials. De Gaulle sought direct election of the presidency to enhance both his power and that of the institution of the presidency.

6. On the French legislature, see Sylvain Brouard, Olivier Costa, and Eric Kerrouche, "The 'New' French Parliament: Changes and Continuities," in Cole et al., *Developments in French Politics*, 35–52.

7. Alec Stone, *The Birth of Judicial Politics in France* (New York: Oxford University Press, 1992).

8. Ironically, one reason France returned to single-member districts was that proportional representation gave the far right National Front its first representation in the legislature, a result that dismayed the mainstream parties.

9. On French local government, see Alistair Cole and Romain Pasquier, "Local and Regional Governance," in Cole et al., *Developments in French Politics*, 69–87.

10. An excellent overview of the PS is by Frédéric Sawicki, "Political Parties: The Socialists and the Left," in Cole et al., *Developments in French Politics*, 104–19.

11. Raymond Kuhn, "Mister Unpopular: François Hollande and the Exercise of Presidential Leadership, 2012–2014," *Modern and Contemporary France* 22, no. 4 (2014): 435–57.

12. James McAuley, "France's Hollande Is So Unpopular That His Own Party May Not Support Him," *Washington Post*, April 16, 2016, www.washingtonpost.com/world/europe /frances-hollande-so-unpopular-that-maybe-his-own-party-wont-support-him/2016 /04/15/264bcf66-018d-11e6-8bb1-f124a43f84dc_story.html (accessed 5/30/16).

13. On the UMP, see Florence Haegel, "Political Parties: The UMP and the Right," in Cole et al., *Developments in French Politics*, 88–103.

14. On Sarkozy's presidency, see Andrew Knapp, "A Paradoxical Presidency: Nicolas Sarkozy, 2007–2012," *Parliamentary Affairs* 66 (2013): 33–51.

15. Aurelien Mondon, "The National Front in the Twenty-First Century: From Pariah to Republican Contender?" *Modern and Contemporary France* 22, no. 3 (2014): 301–320.

16. At http://stats.oecd.org/Index.aspx?DataSetCode=UN_DEN (accessed 6/27/14). For some comparative perspective, the figures for Germany and the United Kingdom are 18 percent and 26 percent, respectively.

17. A good overview of church–state relations in France is Herman Salton, "Unholy Union: History, Politics and the Relationship between Church and State in Modern France," *Review of European Studies* 4, no. 5 (2012): 135–47.

18. For a discussion of the differences between the United States and France, see Robert A. Levine, "Assimilating Immigrants: Why America Can and France Cannot," Rand Occasional Paper (Santa Monica, CA: Rand Corporation, 2004).

19. Michèle Tribalat, "An Estimation of the Foreign-Origin Population of France in 1999," *Population* 59, no. 1 (2004): 49–79.

20. Vincent Tiberj and Laure Michon, "Two-tier Pluralism in 'Colour-blind' France," *West European Politics* 36, no. 3 (2013): 580–96.

21. Rahsaan Maxwell and Erik Bleich, "What Makes Muslims Feel French?" *Social Forces* 93, no. 1 (September 2015): 155–79.

22. Robert Marquand, "France President Sarkozy Drops National Identity Debate," *Christian Science Monitor*, February 9, 2010, www.csmonitor.com/World/Europe/2010/0209 /France-President-Sarkozy-drops-national-identity-debate (accessed 6/27/14).

23. Angus Maddison, *The World Economy: A Millennial Perspective* (Paris: OECD, 2001), 132, 185.

24. *International Comparisons of GDP per Capita and per Employed Person, 17 Countries, 1960–2008*, report prepared by Division of International Labor Comparisons, U.S. Bureau of Labor Statistics, July 28, 2009, www.bls.gov/fls/flsgdp.pdf (accessed 11/17/11).

25. At www.apnewsarchive.com/2016/National-Front-leader-Marine-Le-Pen-says-the -overturning-of-a-ban-on-burkinis-in-a-French-Mediterranean-town-is-not-surprising -but-the-battle-is-not-over/id-dd465614837349caa0686ea0a0065f6c (accessed 8/27/16).

26. This discussion draws heavily on the analysis of Timothy B. Smith, "France in Crisis? Economic and Welfare Policy Reform," in Cole et al., *Developments in French Politics*, 186–202.

27. Smith, "Welfare Policy Reform," 186.

GERMANY

1. On the Weimar Republic, see M. Rainer Lepsius, "From Fragmented Party Democracy to Government by Emergency Decree and National Socialist Takeover: Germany," in Juan Linz and Alfred Stepan, eds., *The Breakdown of Democratic Regimes: Europe* (Baltimore, MD: Johns Hopkins University Press, 1978), 34–79.

2. See Peter Katzenstein's discussion of West Germany's "semi-sovereignty," in Peter Katzenstein, *Policy and Politics in West Germany: The Growth of a Semi-Sovereign State* (Philadelphia: Temple University Press, 1987).

3. For an excellent discussion of the Stasi, see Timothy Garton Ash, *The File* (New York: Vintage, 1998).

4. Dan Hough and Emil Kirchner, "Germany at 60: Stability and Success, Problems and Challenges," *German Politics* 19, no. 1 (March 2010): 1–8.

5. Adapted from M. Donald Hancock and Henry Krish, *Politics in Germany* (Washington, DC: CQ Press, 2009), 80–103.

6. Brigitte Geissel, "How to Improve the Quality of Democracy? Experiences with Participatory Innovations at the Local Level in Germany," *German Politics and Society* 27, no. 4 (Winter 2009): 51–71.

7. On the German party system, see Steven Weldon and Andrea Nusser, "Bundestag Election 2009: Solidifying the Five Party System," in *Between Left and Right: The 2009 Bundestag Elections and the Transformation of the German Party System,* ed. Eric Langenbacher (New York: Berghahn Books, 2010), 69–85.

8. A good historical treatment of the CDU is Ulrich Lappenküper, "Between Concentration Movement and People's Party: The Christian Democratic Union in Germany," in *Christian Democracy in Europe Since 1945*, vol. 2, eds. Michael Gehler and Wolfram Kaiser (New York: Routledge, 2004), 25–37. An excellent analysis of recent changes in the party is Clayton Marc Clemens, "Beyond Christian Democracy? Welfare State Politics and Policy in a Changing CDU," *German Politics* 22, nos. 1–2 (2013): 191–211.

9. "Germany's Social Democrats pick Martin Shulz as leader," *The Economist*, January 28, 2017, www.economist.com/news/europe/21715589-they-will-probably-still-lose -angela-merkel-germanys-social-democrats-pick-martin-schulz (accessed 2/8/17).

10. On the SPD, see Jonathan Olsen, "Past Imperfect, Future Tense: The SPD before and after the 2013 Federal Election," *German Politics and Society* 32, no. 3 (Autumn 2014), 46–58.

11. Wolfgang Rüdig, "The Perennial Success of the German Greens," *Environmental Politics* 21, no. 1 (2012): 108–30.

12. On the Left Party, see Dan Hough and Michael Kob, "Populism Personified or Reinvigorated Reformers? The German Left Party in 2009 and Beyond," *German Politics and Society* 27, no. 2 (Summer 2009): 77–91.

13. On the AfD, see Thomas Meaney, "Germany's New Nationalists," *New Yorker*, October 3, 2016, 54–62.

14. Taehyun Nam, "Rough Days in Democracies: Comparing Protests in Democracies," *European Journal of Political Research* 46, no. 1 (January 2007): 97–120.

15. "Paving the Way for a Muslim Parallel Society," *Der Speigel*, March 29, 2007.

16. David Conradt, *The German Polity*, 9th ed. (New York: Houghton Mifflin Harcourt, 2009), 77.

17. See, for example, the World Values Survey 1981–1999, "Views of a Changing World 2003," Pew Center for the People and the Press, www.people-press.org/2003/06/03 /views-of-a-changing-world-2003 (accessed 3/8/17).

18. Russell J. Dalton, *Citizen Politics* (New York: Chatham House, 2002), p. 84.

19. "Renewable Energy Policy in Germany: An Overview and Assessment," Joint Global Change Research Institute, 2009, www.globalchange.umd.edu/energytrends /germany/6 (accessed 3/8/17); and "German Lessons," *Economist*, April 3, 2008, www.economist.com/node/10961890?story_id=10961890 (accessed 3/8/17).

20. J. Mushaben, "From Ausländer to Inlander: The Changing Faces of Citizenship in Post-Wall Germany," *German Politics & Society* [serial online] 28, no. 1 (March 30, 2010): 141–64. Available from Academic Search Premier, Ipswich, MA (accessed 2/8/17).

21. Marc Morjé Howard, "Germany's Citizenship Policy in Comparative Perspective," in *German Politics and Society* 30, no. 1 (Spring 2012): 39–51.

22. Anna Sauerbrev, "The End of the Merkel Era," *New York Times*, February 10, 2016, www.nytimes.com/2016/02/11/opinion/the-end-of-the-merkel-era.html (accessed 5/12/16).

JAPAN

1. T. J. Pempel and Keiichi Tsunekawa, "Corporatism without Labor: The Japanese Anomaly," in *Trends toward Corporatist Intermediation*, eds. Philippe Schmitter and Gerhard Lehmbruch (New York: Sage, 1990).

2. There was also an underclass or outcast segment of society known as the *eta* or *burakumin*, who were discriminated against for their work in the ritually impure trades, such as tanning and butchering.

3. Hugh Byas, *Government by Assassination* (New York: Alfred A. Knopf, 1942).

4. "Experts Ponder Reasons for Japan's Rash of Short-Term Prime Ministers," *Japan Times*, January 1, 2012.

5. David S. Law, "The Anatomy of a Conservative Court: Judicial Review in Japan," *Texas Law Review* 87 (June 2009): 1545–93.

6. Although the population of voting districts was relatively balanced when districts were originally set up after the war, the LDP never reapportioned them even as the countryside became depopulated. In exchange for their voting loyalty, farmers were assured high prices for their rice and were given voting clout as much as five times greater than that of urban voters, who were less likely to vote for the LDP. In the 1990 lower house elections, for example, opposition parties won nearly 54 percent of the popular vote but garnered only 44 percent of the seats. Likewise, even though the DPJ outpolled the LDP in the 2010 upper house elections, it garnered fewer seats.

7. Under the old system, all representatives were elected from multimember districts (MMDs) in which voters had a single nontransferable vote (SNTV), which they cast for a specific candidate instead of a party list. This unusual MMD/SNTV system created a variety of incentives and consequences both for the LDP, which benefited immensely from the rules, and for opposition parties struggling to compete.

8. Under 2013 changes to the electoral law designed to reduce malapportionment, district boundaries in 17 prefectures have been redrawn and five districts have been eliminated without replacement (one each in Fukui, Yamanashi, Tokushima, Kōchi, and Saga). The number of first-past-the-post seats has reduced to 295, and the total number of seats decreased to 475.

9. Kakuei Tanaka, who served as prime minister during the early 1970s, was the consummate Japanese politician and likely Japan's most influential. He presided over a powerful LDP faction but was forced to resign and ultimately was convicted of financial misdeeds involving huge sums of money.

10. See, for example, Karel van Wolferen, *The Enigma of Japanese Power* (New York: Alfred A. Knopf, 1989).

11. Ken Victor Leonard Hijino, "Delinking National and Local Party Systems: New Parties in Japanese Local Elections," *Journal of East Asian Studies* 13 (2013): 107–35.

12. See Simon Andrew Avenell, "Civil Society and the New Civic Movements in Contemporary Japan: Convergence, Collaboration and Transformation," *Journal of Japanese Studies* 25 (2009): 247–83.

13. The seminal study in this field is Chalmers Johnson, *MITI and the Japanese Miracle: The Growth of Industrial Policy, 1925–1975* (Stanford, CA: Stanford University Press, 1982).

CHAPTER 8: NONDEMOCRATIC REGIMES

1. See the Freedom House website, www.freedomhouse.org (accessed 7/12/16).

2. For an excellent discussion of the bewildering varieties of nondemocratic rule, see Juan J. Linz, *Totalitarian and Authoritarian Regimes* (Boulder, CO: Lynne Rienner, 2000).

3. Linz, *Totalitarian and Authoritarian Regimes*.

4. Hannah Arendt, *Totalitarianism* (New York: Harcourt, Brace and World, 1951).

5. Michael Bratton and Nicholas Van de Walle provide details of Mobutu's rule in "Neopatrimonial Regimes and Political Transitions in Africa," *World Politics* 46, no. 4 (1994): 453–89.

6. See Guillermo O'Donnell, *Modernization and Bureaucratic Non-democratic Regimes: Studies in South American Politics* (Berkeley, CA: Institute of International Studies, 1973); see also Hristos Doucouliagos and Mehmet Ali Ulubaşoğlu, "Democracy and Economic Growth: A Meta-Analysis," *American Journal of Political Science* 52, no. 1 (2008): 61–83.

7. Muhammad Al-Atawneh, "Is Saudi Arabia a Theocracy? Religion and Governance in Contemporary Saudi Arabia," *Middle Eastern Studies* 45, no. 5 (2009): 721–37.

8. Martin R. Rupiya, ed. *Zimbabwe's Military: Examining Its Veto Power in the Transition to Democracy, 2008–2013* (Pretoria: African Public Policy & Research Institute, 2013).

9. Oswald Spengler, *The Decline of the West* (New York: Knopf, 1928), 347.

10. See the World Values Survey Wave 6 findings at www.worldvaluessurvey.org (accessed 7/12/16).

INSTITUTIONS IN ACTION

a. Jan-Werner Müller, "Defending Democracy within the EU." *Journal of Democracy* 24, no. 2 (2013): 138–49.

CHAPTER 9: COMMUNISM AND POSTCOMMUNISM

1. Taras Kuzio, "Competing Nationalisms, Euromaidan, and the Russian–Ukrainian Conflict." *Studies in Ethnicity and Nationalism* 15, no. 1 (April 2015): 157–69.

2. For a good overview of communist theory, see Alfred Meyer, *Communism* (New York: Random House, 1984).

3. See Marx's 1882 preface to the Russian translation of the *Communist Manifesto*, www.marxists.org (accessed 7/16/16).

4. See V. I. Lenin, *What Is to Be Done? Burning Questions of Our Movement*, trans. Joe Fineberg and George Hanna (New York: International Publishers, 1969).

5. For a comparative discussion of different communist systems, see Stephen White et al., *Communist and Post-Communist Political Systems* (New York: St. Martin's Press, 1990).

6. See Michael Voslensky, *Nomenklatura: Anatomy of the Soviet Ruling Class* (Garden City, NY: Doubleday, 1984).

7. See Robert Conquest, *The Great Terror: A Reassessment* (New York: Oxford University Press, 1990).

8. See Lowell Dittmer, *China's Continuous Revolution: The Post-Liberation Epoch, 1949–1981* (Berkeley: University of California Press, 1987).

9. Robert W. Campbell, *The Socialist Economies in Transition: A Primer on Semi-Reformed Systems* (Bloomington: Indiana University Press, 1991).

10. Quoted in Frank Dikotter, *Mao's Great Famine: The History of China's Most Devastating Catastrophe, 1958–62* (New York: Bloomsbury, 2010), 88.

11. Karl Marx and Friedrich Engels, *Manifesto of the Communist Party*, www.marxists.org/archive/marx/works/1848/communist-manifesto (accessed 7/16/2016).

12. Joni Lovenduski and Jean Woodall, *Politics and Society in Eastern Europe* (Bloomington: Indiana University Press, 1987), 158.

13. The best retrospective studies of the collapse of communism in Eastern Europe and its effects in the Soviet Union can be found in Mark Kramer, "The Collapse of East European Communism and the Repercussions within the Soviet Union," parts 1–3, *Journal of Cold War Studies* (Fall 2003, Fall 2004, and Spring 2005).

14. On the collapse of communism in Eastern Europe, see Timothy Garton Ash, *The Magic Lantern: The Revolution of 1989 Witnessed in Warsaw, Budapest, Berlin and Prague* (New York: Random House, 1990); on the collapse of communism in the Soviet Union, see David Remnick, *Lenin's Tomb: The Last Days of the Soviet Empire* (New York: Random House, 1993).

15. Freedom House, *Nations in Transit 2017* (Washington, DC: Freedom House, 2017), https://freedomhouse.org/sites/default/files/NIT2017_booklet_FINAL_0.pdf (accessed 4/14/17).

16. Oliver Decker, Johannes Kiess, and Elmar Brähler, "Die Stabilisierte Mitte Rechtsextreme Einstellung in Deutschland 2014," Kompetenzzentrum für Rechtsextremismus- und Demokratieforschung, Leipzig University, 2014, http://research.uni-leipzig.de/kredo/Mitte_Leipzig_Internet.pdf (accessed 7/16/16).

17. Robert J. Barro, *Economic Growth and Convergence, Applied Especially to China*. No. w21872. National Bureau of Economic Research, 2016, http://www.nber.org/papers/w21872 (accessed 7/16/16). See also David Shambaugh, *China's Future* (New York: John Wiley & Sons, 2016).

RUSSIA

1. For a fascinating Soviet-era interpretation of Ivan's leadership, see the Sergei Eisenstein film *Ivan the Terrible* (1945).

2. For a discussion of this period, see Richard Pipes, *Three "Whys" of the Russian Revolution* (New York: Vintage, 1995).

3. Mary McAuley, *Soviet Politics: 1917–1991* (New York: Oxford University Press, 1992), 26–27.

4. See Robert Conquest, *The Great Terror: A Reassessment* (New York: Oxford University Press, 1991); Anne Applebaum, *Gulag: A History* (New York: Doubleday, 2003).

5. For a discussion of the last days of Soviet rule, see David Remnick, *Lenin's Tomb: The Last Days of the Soviet Empire* (New York: Random House, 1993).

6. Thomas Remington, *Presidential Decrees in Russia: A Comparative Perspective* (New York: Cambridge University Press, 2014).

7. Alexander Podrabinek, "Useless Parliament," Institute for Modern Russia, May 20, 2014, https://imrussia.org/en/politics/747-useless-parliament (accessed 3/16/17).

8. "Russia: Government vs. Rights Groups," *Human Rights Watch*, January 9, 2017, https://www.hrw.org/russia-government-against-rights-groups-battle-chronicle (accessed 1/10/17).

9. World Justice Project, Rule of Law Index 2016, http://data.worldjusticeproject.org (accessed 1/8/17).

10. Elizabeth Teague, "Russia's Return to the Direct Election of Governors: Re-Shaping the Power Vertical?" *Region: Regional Studies of Russia, Eastern Europe, and Central Asia* 3, no. 1 (2014): 37–57.

11. Richard Sakwa, *Putin Redux: Power and Contradiction in Contemporary Russia* (New York: Routledge, 2014).

12. Andrew Konitzer and Stephen Wegren, "Federalism and Political Recentralization in the Russian Federation: United Russia as the Party of Power," *Publius* 36, no. 4 (2006): 503–22.

13. Mikhail Myagkov, Peter Ordeshook, and Dimitri Shakin, *The Forensics of Election Fraud: Russia and Ukraine* (Cambridge, UK: Cambridge University Press, 2009).

14. Sakwa, *Putin Redux*; Luke March, "Managing Opposition in a Hybrid Regime: Just Russia and Parastatal Opposition," *Slavic Review* 68, no. 3 (Fall 2009): 504–27.

15. World Values Survey, Wave 6, http://www.worldvaluessurvey.org (accessed 1/9/17).

16. "Laws of Attrition: Crackdown on Russia's Civil Society after Putin's Return to the Presidency," *Human Rights Watch,* April 24, 2013, www.hrw.org/reports/2013/04/24/laws-attrition (accessed 10/30/14).

17. Masha Gessen, *Words Will Break Cement: The Passion of Pussy Riot* (New York: Riverhead, 2014).

18. Reporters without Borders, *Press Freedom Index 2016*, http://en.rsf.org (accessed 1/10/17).

19. Sergei M. Guriev and Daniel Treisman, "What Makes Governments Popular," https://ssrn.com/abstract=2882915 or http://dx.doi.org/10.2139/ssrn.2882915 (accessed 1/10/17).

20. "Russia Facing Biggest Brain Drain in Two Decades," *Moscow Times*, June 10, 2016, https://themoscowtimes.com/articles/russia-facing-biggest-brain-drain-in-two-decades-53254 (accessed 3/16/17).

21. Some emphasize that "resource traps" are much more complicated than simply asserting that resources lead to authoritarianism or poorly functioning state institutions. See Pauline Jones Luong and Erika Weinthal, *Oil Is Not a Curse: Ownership Structure and Institutions in Soviet Successor States* (Cambridge: Cambridge University Press, 2010).

22. Vladimir Putin, "A New Integration Project for Eurasia: The Future in the Making," *Oriental Review,* October 11, 2011, http://orientalreview.org/2011/10/11/new-integration-project-for-eurasia-making-the-future-today (accessed 3/16/17).

23. Kazuhiro Kumo, *Mortality Trends in Russia Revisited: A Survey*, Institute of Economic Research, Hitotsubashi University, 2012, https://ideas.repec.org/p/hst/ghsdps/gd12-239.html (accessed 9/14/14); Sergey Aleksashenko, "The Russian Economy in 2050: Heading for Labor-Based Stagnation," Brookings Institute, 2015, https://www.brookings.edu/blog/up-front/2015/04/02/the-russian-economy-in-2050-heading-for-labor-based-stagnation (accessed 1/11/17).

CHINA

1. For a list of quotations, see Mao Zedong, *Quotations from Chairman Mao Tse Tung,* Mao Tse Tung Internet Archive, 2000, www.marxists.org/reference/archive/mao/works/red-book (accessed 5/18/17).

2. See Amnesty International, "China: 'Strike Hard' Anti-Crime Campaign Intensifies," press release, July 23, 2002, web.amnesty.org/library/Index/engASA170292002?Open (accessed 11/17/03).

3. Salvatore Babones, "A Rural Incubator for China's Political Reforms?" *Foreign Affairs* (October 14, 2015), www.foreignaffairs.com/articles/china/2015-10-14/country-lessons (accessed 6/22/16).

4. Mao Zedong, "Problems of War and Strategy," in *Selected Works,* vol. 2 (Beijing: Foreign Language Press, 1965), 225.

5. See *Hurun Report*, September 22, 2011, www.hurun.net/usen/NewsShow.aspx?nid=154 (accessed 11/9/11), and October 14, 2015, www.hurun.net/en/ArticleShow.aspx?nid=14678 (accessed 6/22/16).

6. See, for example, Richard McGregor, *The Party: The Secret World of China's Communist Rulers* (New York: HarperCollins, 2010).

7. Francis Fukuyama, "China and East Asian Democracy: Patterns of History," *Journal of Democracy* 23 (January 2012): 14–26.

8. Bruce Dickson, *Red Capitalists in China: The Party, Private Entrepreneurs and Prospects for Political Change* (Cambridge: Cambridge University Press, 2003).

9. See, for example, George Gilboy and Eric Heginbotham, "China's Coming Transformation," *Foreign Affairs* (July/August 2001): 26–39, and Jessica Teets, "Let Many Civil

Societies Bloom: The Rise of Consultative Authoritarianism in China," *China Quarterly* 213 (March 2013): 19–38.

10. Gordon White, *Riding the Tiger: The Politics of Economic Reform in Post-Mao China* (Palo Alto, CA: Stanford University Press, 1993).

11. Nicholas Lardy, *Markets over Mao: The Rise of Private Business in China*, Washington, DC: Peterson Institute for International Economics, 2014.

12. James Gwartney, et al., "Economic Freedom of the World: 2016 Annual Report, "The Fraser Institute (2016), www.fraserinstitute.org/sites/default/files/economic-freedom-of-the-world-2016.pdf (accessed 5/18/17).

13. Joseph Kahn and Jim Yardley, "As China Roars, Pollution Reaches Deadly Extremes," *New York Times*, August 26, 2007.

14. Cheng Li, "China's Team of Rivals," *Foreign Policy* (March/April 2009): 88–93.

15. Dan Levin, "Study Links Polluted Air in China to 1.6 Million Deaths a Year," *New York Times*, August 13, 2015, www.nytimes.com/2015/08/14/world/asia/study-links-polluted-air-in-china-to-1-6-million-deaths-a-year.html (accessed 6/23/16).

16. Kenneth Lieberthal, *Governing China: From Revolution through Reform* (New York: W. W. Norton, 2004), 277–79.

CHAPTER 10: DEVELOPING COUNTRIES

1. Christopher Cramer, Deborah Johnston, Carlos Oya, and John Sender, "Fairtrade and Labour Markets in Ethiopia and Uganda," *Journal of Development Studies*; 53, no. 6 (2017): 841–56. Raluca Dragusanu, Daniele Giovannucci, and Nathan Nunn, "The Economics of Fair Trade," *Journal of Economic Perspectives* 28, no. 3 (Summer 2014): 217–36.

2. For two excellent studies of imperialism in practice, see L. H. Gann and Peter Duignan, eds., *Imperialism in Africa, 1870–1960* (Cambridge, UK: Cambridge University Press, 1969–75); and Nicolas Tarling, ed., *The Cambridge History of Southeast Asia* (Cambridge, UK: Cambridge University Press, 1992).

3. A general discussion of the impact of imperialism can be found in Philip D. Curtin, *The World and the West: The European Challenge and the Overseas Response in the Age of Empire* (Cambridge, UK: Cambridge University Press, 2000).

4. Alberto F. Alesina, Paola Giuliano, and Nathan Nunn, "On the Origins of Gender Roles: Women and the Plough," *Quarterly Journal of Economics*. 2013; vol. 128, no. 2 (May 2013): 469–530. Elizabeth Schmidt, *Peasants, Traders and Wives: Shona Women in the History of Zimbabwe, 1870–1939* (New York: Heinemann, 1992).

5. See Joel S. Migdal, *Strong Societies and Weak States: State-Society Relations and State Capabilities in the Third World* (Princeton, NJ: Princeton University Press, 1988).

6. For a discussion of these issues, see Stuti Khemani et al., *Making Politics Work for Development: Harnessing Transparency and Citizen Engagement* (Washington DC: World Bank, 2016).

7. Valerie M. Hudson, Mary Caprioli, Bonnie Ballif-Spanvill, Rose McDermott, and Chad F. Emmett, "The Heart of the Matter: The Security of Women and the Security of States," *International Security* 33 (Winter 2009): 7–45; John Bongaarts and Christophe Z. Guilmoto, "How Many More Missing Women? Excess Female Mortality and Prenatal Sex Selection, 1970–2050," *Population and Development Review* 41, no. 2 (2015): 241–69.

8. For a discussion of different paths of industrialization, see Stephan Haggard, *Pathways from the Periphery: The Politics of Growth in Newly Industrializing Countries* (Ithaca, NY: Cornell University Press, 1990).

9. Raphael Franck and Ilia Rainer, "Does the Leader's Ethnicity Matter? Ethnic Favoritism, Education, and Health in Sub-Saharan Africa," *American Political Science Review* 106, no. 2 (May 2012): 294–325.

10. Francis Fukuyama, *State Building: Governance and World Order in the 21st Century* (Ithaca, NY: Cornell University Press, 2004).

11. Anna Persson, Bo Rothstein, and Jan Teorell, "Why Anticorruption Reforms Fail—Systemic Corruption as a Collective Action Problem," *Governance* 26, no. 3 (July 2013): 449–71.

12. *Making Politics Work for Development*, 213.

13. Claudio Ferraz and Frederico Finan, "Exposing Corrupt Politicians: The Effects of Brazil's Publicly Released Audits on Electoral Outcomes," *Quarterly Journal of Economics* 123, no. 2 (May 2008): 703–45.

14. See www.kiva.org (accessed 8/2/16).

15. Abhijit V. Banerjee, Esther Duflo, Rachel Glennerster, and Cynthia Kinnan, "The Miracle of Microfinance? Evidence from a Randomized Evaluation (April 10, 2013)," MIT Department of Economics Working Paper No. 13-09, http://ssrn.com/abstract =2250500 (accessed 8/2/16); see also Daniel Altman, "Please Do Not Teach This Woman to Fish," *Foreign Policy* (June 9, 2014), http://foreignpolicy.com/2014/06/10 /please-do-not-teach-this-woman-to-fish (accessed 04/21/17).

16. Michael Clemens and Gabriel Demombynes, "The New Transparency in Development Economics: Lessons from the Millennium Villages Controversy," Center for Global Development Working Paper No. 342 (2013).

17. Abhijit Banerjee and Esther Duflo, *Poor Economics: A Radical Rethinking of the Way to Fight Global Poverty* (New York: PublicAffairs, 2011).

INSTITUTIONS IN ACTION

a. Atul Kohli, *State Directed Development: Political Power and Industrialization in the Global Periphery* (New York: Cambridge University Press, 2004).

INDIA

1. The Indian Constitution identifies 18 official or "scheduled" languages.

2. For a careful and thorough discussion of the caste system, its origins, evolution, and social and political consequences for India, see Susan Bayly, *The New Cambridge History of India: Caste, Society, and Politics in India from the Eighteenth Century to the Modern Age* (Cambridge, UK: Cambridge University Press, 1999).

3. Stanley Wolpert, *India* (Berkeley: University of California Press, 1991), 55.

4. Yasmin Khan, *The Great Partition* (New Haven, CT: Yale University Press, 2007).

5. Bhagwan D. Dua, "Presidential Rule in India: A Study in Crisis Politics," *Asian Survey* 19 (June 1979): 611–26.

6. The limiting conditions for the "promulgation" of a presidential ordinance include (1) at least one of the chambers of parliament must not be in session; (2) the circumstances must necessitate immediate action; and (3) the ordinances must ultimately be approved by parliament or repromulgated. See Shubhankar Dam, "An Institutional Alchemy: India's Two Parliaments in Comparative Context," *Brooklyn Journal of International Law* 39, no. 2 (2014): 613–55.

7. Pradeep Chhibber and Ken Kollman, "Party Aggregation and the Number of Parties in India and the United States," *American Political Science Review* 92 (June 1998): 329–42.

8. See Alfred Stepan, Juan J. Linz, and Yogendra Yadav, "The Rise of 'State-Nations,'" *Journal of Democracy* 21 (July 2010): 50–68.

9. Arun Shourie, "Two Concepts of Liberty," *Economist*, March 3, 2005.

10. Ashutosh Varshney, "Hindu Nationalism in Power," *Journal of Democracy* 25 (October 2014): 34–45.

11. Mukul Kesavan, "India's Embattled Secularism," *Wilson Quarterly* 27 (Winter 2003): 61.

12. Stepan et al., "The Rise of 'State-Nations.'"

13. Kesavan, "India's Embattled Secularism," 63.

14. Edward Luce, *In Spite of the Gods* (New York: Anchor Books, 2007), 78.

15. Unique Identification Authority of India, http://uidai.gov.in (accessed 5/25/17).

16. Beina Xu, "Governance in India: Women's Rights," *Council on Foreign Relations Backgrounder*, June 10, 2014, www.cfr.org/india/governance-india-womens-rights/p30041 (accessed 8/6/14).

17. Sumit Ganguly, "India and Its Neighbors," *Journal of Democracy* 25 (April 2014): 93–104.

IRAN

1. Michael Axworthy, *A History of Iran: Empire of the Mind* (New York: Basic Books, 2008).

2. For a discussion of Shiism in Iran and elsewhere, see Heinz Halm, *Shi'ism* (New York: Columbia University Press, 2004), and Moojan Momen, *An Introduction to Shia Islam* (New Haven, CT: Yale University Press, 1985).

3. For a discussion of this period and the increasing U.S. influence in Iranian politics, see Kenneth M. Pollack, *The Persian Puzzle: The Conflict between Iran and America* (New York: Random House, 2004).

4. Ali M. Ansari, "The Myth of the White Revolution: Mohammad Reza Shah, 'Modernization,' and the Consolidation of Power," *Middle Eastern Studies* 37, no. 3 (July 2001): 1–24.

5. For an analysis of these events, see Charles Kurzman, *The Unthinkable Revolution in Iran* (Cambridge, MA: Harvard University Press, 2004).

6. From *International Constitutional Law*, www.servat.unibe.ch/icl/ir__indx.html (accessed 10/20/14).

7. Hadi Ghaemi, "The Islamic Judiciary," *The Iran Primer*, U.S. Institute of Peace, http://iranprimer.usip.org/resource/islamic-judiciary (accessed 9/20/16).

8. Frederic Wehrey, Jerrold D. Green, Brian Nichiporuk, Alireza Nader, Lydia Hansell, Rasool Nafisi, and S. R. Bohandy, *The Rise of the Pasdaran: Assessing the Domestic Roles of Iran's Islamic Revolutionary Guards Corps* (Santa Monica, CA: RAND Corporation, 2009), www.rand.org/pubs/monographs/MG821 (accessed 9/20/16).

9. Reporters without Borders Press, Freedom Index 2016, https://rsf.org/en/ranking (accessed 9/20/16).

10. "Iran: Human Rights Abuses against the Kurdish Minority," London: Amnesty International Publications, 2008; see also Rasmus Christian Elling, *Minorities in Iran: Nationalism and Ethnicity after Khomeini* (New York: Palgrave Macmillan, 2013).

11. A good discussion of different political values and positions in Iran can be found in Ray Takeyh, *Guardians of the Revolution: Iran and the World in the Age of the Ayatollahs* (New York: Oxford University Press, 2009).

12. Jalal Al Ahmad, *Weststruckness*, trans. John Green and Ahmad Alizadeh (Costa Mesa, CA: Mazda, 1997).

13. David E. Thaler, Alireza Nader, Shahram Chubin, and Jerrold D. Green, *Mullahs, Guards, and Bonyads: An Exploration of Iranian Leadership Dynamics* (Santa Monica CA: Rand Corporation, 2010), www.rand.org/content/dam/rand/pubs/monographs/2009/RAND_MG878.pdf (accessed 5/1/17).

14. Djavad Salehi-Isfahani and Daniel Egel, *Iranian Youth in Times of Crisis*, Working Paper, Belfer Center for Science and International Affairs, Harvard Kennedy School, September 2010, http://belfercenter.ksg.harvard.edu/files/Salehi-Isfahani_DI-Working-Paper-3_Iran-Youth-Crisis.pdf (accessed 09/20/16); see also Bijan Khajehpour, "Can Rouhani Reverse Iran's Brain Drain?" *Al Monitor*, January 12, 2014.

15. J. Reardon, *Containing Iran: Strategies for Addressing the Iranian Nuclear Challenge* (Santa Monica, CA: RAND Corporation, 2012).

16. Joint Comprehensive Plan of Action, U.S. Department of State, http://www.state.gov/e/eb/tfs/spi/iran/jcpoa (accessed 9/20/2016).

17. World Health Organization, *Global Status Report on Alcohol and Health*, 2014, www.who .int/substance_abuse/publications/global_alcohol_report/en (accessed 9/20/16).

18. "Iran's 'Staggering' Execution Spree: Nearly 700 Put to Death in Just Over Six Months," Amnesty International, July 23, 2015, https://www.amnesty.org/en/latest /news/2015/07/irans-staggering-execution-spree (accessed 9/20/2016).

MEXICO

1. For a good overview of the development of the Mexican state, see Alan Knight, "The Weight of the State in Modern Mexico," in *Studies in the Formation of the Nation State in Latin America*, ed. James Dunkerley (London: Institute of Latin American Studies, 2002), 212–52.

2. For the best English-language overview, see Luis Carlos Ugalde, *The Mexican Congress: Old Player, New Power* (Washington, DC: Center for Strategic and International Studies, 2000).

3. Ugalde, *The Mexican Congress*, 146.

4. Jodi Finkel, "Judicial Reform as Insurance Policy: Mexico in the 1990s," *Latin American Politics and Society* 47, no. 1 (Spring 2005): 87–111.

5. Jorge Castañeda, *Mañana Forever? Mexico and the Mexicans* (New York: Alfred A. Knopf, 2011), xvi.

6. José Antonio Caballero, "Judiciary: The Courts in Mexico," *Americas Quarterly*, Spring 2013, www.americasquarterly.org/judiciary-courts-mexico (accessed 5/27/13).

7. Wayne Cornelius, Todd Eisenstadt, and Jane Hindley, eds., *Subnational Politics and Democratization in Mexico* (San Diego, CA: Center for U.S.-Mexican Studies, 1999); R. Andrew Nickson, *Local Government in Latin America* (Boulder, CO: Lynne Reinner, 1995), 199–209.

8. Pamela Starr, "Fox's Mexico: Same as It Ever Was?" *Current History*, February 2002, 62.

9. Kathleen Bruhn, *Taking on Goliath: Mexico's Party of the Democratic Revolution* (University Park: Pennsylvania State University Press, 1997).

10. Kathleen Bruhn, "López Obrador, Calderón, and the 2006 Electoral Campaign," in *Consolidating Mexico's Democracy*, eds. Jorge Domínguez, Chappell Lawson, and Alejandro Moreno (Baltimore, MD: Johns Hopkins University Press, 2009), 169–88.

11. Joseph Klesner, "Electoral Competition and the New Party System in Mexico," paper presented at the annual meeting of the Latin American Studies Association, Washington, DC, September 6–8, 2001; and Joseph Klesner, "A Sociological Analysis of the 2006 Elections," in Domínguez, Lawson, and Moreno, eds., *Consolidating Mexico's Democracy*, 50–70.

12. D. Xavier Medina Vida, Antonio Uges, Shaun Bowler, and Jonathan Hisker, "Partisan Attachment and Democracy in Mexico: Some Cautionary Observations," in *Latin American Politics and Society* 52, no. 1 (January 2010): 66–87.

13. An outstanding edited volume on the 2006 presidential elections is Domínguez et al., eds., *Consolidating Mexico's Democracy*.

14. An excellent treatment of the 2012 elections is Gustavo Flores-Macías, "Mexico's 2012 Elections: The Return of the PRI," *Journal of Democracy* 24, no. 1 (January 2013): 128–41. For a translated video of the second Mexican presidential candidate debate, see www.c-span.org/video/?192963-1/mexican-presidential-debate (accessed 11/22/14).

15. Joseph L. Klesner, "Who Participates? Determinants of Political Action in Mexico," *Latin American Politics and Society* 51, no. 2 (Summer 2009): 59–90.

16. Alberto J. Olvera, "The Elusive Democracy: Political Parties, Democratic Institutions, and Civil Society in Mexico," *Latin American Research Review* (Special Issue, 2010): 79–107.

17. Castañeda, *Mañana Forever?*, 9.

18. Castañeda, *Mañana Forever?*, 12.

19. The Committee to Protect Journalists has information about violence against Mexican journalists, available at http://cpj.org/americas/mexico/2014/?page=1 (accessed 6/4/14).

20. Data from the 2013 Latinobarómetro Survey, available at www.latinobarometro.org (accessed 6/5/14).

21. Alan Riding, *Distant Neighbors* (New York: Vintage, 1989), 199.

22. Three excellent overviews are Tom Hayden, ed., *The Zapatista Reader* (New York: Thunder's Mouth Press, 2002); Lynn Stephen, *Zapata Lives: Histories and Cultural Politics in Southern Mexico* (Berkeley: University of California Press, 2002); and Chris Gilbreth and Gerardo Otero, "Democratization in Mexico: The Zapatista Uprising and Civil Society," *Latin American Perspectives* 28, no. 4 (July 2001): 7–29.

23. See latinobarometro.org (accessed 6/5/16).

24. In 2009, 72 percent of Mexicans expressed little or no interest in politics, according to the Latinobarómetro Survey, at www.latinobarometro.org (accessed 7/6/11).

25. From the 2015 Latinobarómetro Survey. See www.latinobarometro.org (accessed 6/5/16).

26. Castañeda, *Mañana Forever?*

27. See www.latinobarometro.org (accessed 6/5/16).

28. Paul Cooney, "The Mexican Crisis and the Maquiladora Boom: A Paradox of Development or the Logic of Neoliberalism?" *Latin American Perspectives* 28, no. 3 (May 2001): 55–83.

29. Rafael Tamayo-Flores, "Mexico in the Context of the North American Integration: Major Regional Trends and Performance of Backward Regions," *Journal of Latin American Studies* 33 (2001): 377–407.

30. Tamayo-Flores, "Mexico in the Context of the North American Integration," 377–407.

31. Castañeda, *Mañana Forever?*, 34.

32. See the discussion in Castañeda, *Mañana Forever?*, 61–62.

33. Quoted in Andrew Williams, "Pemex, Mexico's State Oil Giant, Braces for the Country's New Energy Landscape," *Washington Post*, June 6, 2014, www.washingtonpost.com/business/pemex-mexicos-state-oil-giant-braces-for-a-the-countrys-new-energy-landscape/2014/06/04/07d171d6-ea69-11e3-93d2-edd4be1f5d9e_story.html (accessed 6/6/14).

34. Howard Campbell, "No End in Sight: Violence in Ciudad Juárez," in *NACLA Report on the Americas* 44, no. 2 (May/June 2011): 19–24.

35. A very critical view of the drug war is from Jorge Castañeda, "What's Spanish for Quagmire?" *Foreign Policy* 177 (January/February 2010): 76–81.

36. See an interview with George Grayson, December 23, 2011, www.coha.org/professor-grayson-on-mexico's-drug-war (accessed 6/24/17).

37. Human Rights Watch, "World Report 2015: Mexico," www.hrw.org/world-report/2015/country-chapters/mexico (accessed 6/5/15).

38. Douglas Massey, Jorge Durand, and Nolan Malone, *Beyond Smoke and Mirrors: Mexican Immigration in an Era of Economic Integration* (New York: Russell Sage Foundation, 2002), 45.

39. See http://ktla.com/2016/03/03/no-scenario-where-mexico-will-pay-for-donald-trumps-wall-treasury-secretary-says (accessed 6/5/16).

BRAZIL

1. Two recent overviews of Brazilian politics and society that emphasize Brazil's accomplishments and challenges are Alfred Montero, *Brazil: Reversal of Fortune* (Cambridge, UK: Polity Press, 2014), and Michael Reid, *Brazil: The Troubled Rise of a Global Power* (New Haven, CT: Yale University Press, 2014).

2. "Brazilian Economy Overtakes UK's, Says CEBR," www.bbc.co.uk/news/business-16332115 (accessed 7/5/17).

3. Marshall Eakin, *Brazil: The Once and Future Country* (New York: St. Martin's Press, 1998), 1.

4. For an excellent overview, see Alfred Stepan, ed., *Authoritarian Brazil* (New Haven, CT: Yale University Press, 1973).

5. In 1997, President Fernando Henrique Cardoso was able to push a constitutional amendment through the legislature that allows presidents and state governors to run for a second term. Cardoso became the first president to avail himself of that opportunity and was reelected in 1998.

6. Scott Mainwaring, "Multipartism, Robust Federalism, and Presidentialism in Brazil," in *Presidentialism and Democracy in Latin America*, eds. Scott Mainwaring and Matthew Soberg Shugart (New York: Cambridge University Press, 1997), 55–109.

7. Angelina Cheibub Figueiredo and Fernando Limongi, "Congress and Decision-Making in Democratic Brazil," in *Brazil since 1985: Economy, Polity, and Society*, eds. Maria D'Alva Kinzo and James Dunkerley (London: Institute of Latin American Studies, 2003), 62–83.

8. Juan Linz and Alfred Stepan, "Crises of Efficacy, Legitimacy, and Democratic State Presence: Brazil," in *Problems of Democratic Transition and Consolidation*, eds. Juan Linz and Alfred Stepan (Baltimore, MD: Johns Hopkins University Press, 1996), 166–89.

9. Latínobarómetro, online data analysis available at www.latinobarometro.org/latino/LATAnalizeQuestion.jsp (accessed 6/24/11). On the Brazilian judiciary, see Fiona Macaulay, "Democratization and the Judiciary: Competing Reform Agendas," in Kinzo and Dunkerley, eds., *Brazil since 1985: Economy, Polity, and Society*, 93–96.

10. Latínobarómetro, online data analysis available at www.latinobarometro.org/latino/LATAnalizeQuestion.jsp (accessed 6/24/11).

11. *Economist,* "Weird Justice," www.economist.com/node/21679861/print (accessed 7/1/16).

12. Michael Reid, *Brazil: The Troubled Rise of a Global Power* (New Haven, CT: Yale University Press, 2014), 267.

13. In 1989, the vote of one citizen of Roraima, a poor northern state, was the equivalent of 33 votes in São Paulo, Brazil's largest state. Timothy Power, "Political Institutions in Democratic Brazil," in *Democratic Brazil: Actors, Institutions, and Processes*, eds. Peter Kingstone and Timothy Power (Pittsburgh, PA: University of Pittsburgh Press, 2000), 27.

14. Scott Mainwaring, "Multipartism, Robust Federalism, and Presidentialism in Brazil," in Mainwaring and Shugart, eds., *Presidentialism and Democracy in Latin America*, 55–109.

15. Wendy Hunter, *Eroding Military Influence in Brazil: Politicians against Soldiers* (Chapel Hill: University of North Carolina Press, 1997), 42–71.

16. Anthony Pereira, "An Ugly Democracy? State Violence and the Rule of Law in Postauthoritarian Brazil," in Kingstone and Power, eds., *Democratic Brazil: Actors, Institutions, and Processes*, 217–35.

17. Scott Mainwaring and Timothy Scully, "Introduction: Party Systems in Latin America," in *Building Democratic Institutions: Parties and Party Systems in Latin America*, eds. Scott Mainwaring and Timothy Scully (Stanford, CA: Stanford University Press, 1995), 1–35.

18. A comparative survey in 1997 found that Brazil had the lowest level of party identification in Latin America. See J. Mark Payne, Daniel Zovatto, Fernando Cavillo-Flórez, and Andrés Allamand Zavala, *Democracies in Development: Politics and Reform in Latin America* (Washington, DC: Inter-American Development Bank, 2002), 136.

19. Scott Mainwaring, *Rethinking Party Systems in the Third Wave of Democratization: The Case of Brazil* (Stanford, CA: Stanford University Press, 1999), 140–45.

20. On the Workers' Party, see William Nylen, "The Making of a Loyal Opposition: The Worker's Party (PT) and the Consolidation of Democracy in Brazil," in Kingstone and Power, eds., *Democratic Brazil: Actors, Institutions, and Processes*, 126–43.

21. Latínobarómetro online data analysis, based on a 2008 survey, www.latinobarometro.org/latino/LATAnalizeQuestion.jsp (accessed 6/24/11).

22. On the MST, see Miguel Carter, "The Landless Rural Workers Movement and Democracy in Brazil," *Latin America Research Review* 45 (Special Issue 2010): 186–217.

23. A good overview of race relations is Bernd Reiter and Gladys Mitchell, eds., *Brazil's New Racial Politics* (Boulder, CO: Lynne Rienner, 2010).

24. Jon Jeter, "Affirmative Action Debate Forces Brazil to Take Look in the Mirror," *Washington Post*, June 16, 2003, A1.

25. João Feres Júnior, Verônica Toste Daflon, and Luiz Augusto Campos, "Lula's Approach to Affirmative Action and Race," *NACLA Report on the Americas* 44, no. 2 (March/April 2011): 34–35.

26. As reported in *Economist*, December 2, 2010, www.economist.com/node/17627929 (accessed 7/5/17).

27. Based on 2008 survey data from Latinobarómetro, www.latinobarometro.org/latino/LATAnalizeQuestion.jsp (accessed 6/24/11).

28. Timothy Power and J. Timmons Roberts, "The Changing Demographic in Context," in Kingstone and Power, eds., *Democratic Brazil: Actors, Institutions, and Processes*, 246.

29. Data on extreme poverty were downloaded from the Instituto de Pesquisa Econômica at www.ipeadata.gov.br (accessed 11/24/14). Data on overall poverty reduction appear in Aaron Ansell, "Brazil's Social Safety Net under Lula," *NACLA Report on the Americas* 44, no. 2 (March/April 2011): 23–26.

30. For an excellent overview, see Fábio Veras Soares, Rafael Perez Ribas, and Rafael Guerreiro Osório, "Evaluating the Impact of Brazil's *Bolsa Família*: Cash Transfer Programs in Comparative Perspective," *Latin American Research Review* 45, no. 2 (2010): 173–90.

31. On corruption in Brazil, see Matthew M. Taylor, "Brazil: Corruption as Harmless *Jeitinho* or Threat to Democracy?" in *Corruption and Politics in Latin America*, eds. Stephen D. Harris and Charles Blake (Boulder, CO: Lynne Reiner, 2010), 89–111.

32. For an overview of the corruption charges, see "Disillusionment Grows as Graft Probe Deepens," *Latin American Weekly Report*, April 20, 2017, 8.

33. Simon Romero, "Brazil's Leaders See Way Out of Scandal: Amnesty," *New York Times*, March 15, 2017, www.nytimes.com/2017/03/15/world/americas/brazil-congress-amnesty.html?smprod=nytcore-ipad&smid=nytcore-ipad-share&_r=0 (accessed 3/16/17).

SOUTH AFRICA

1. Anthony Sampson, "Men of the Renaissance," *Guardian* (London), January 3, 1998, 19.

2. For a discussion of South African history, see Leonard Thompson, *The History of South Africa* (New Haven, CT: Yale University Press, 2001).

3. "Apartheid Legislation 1850s–1970s," *South African History Online*, www.sahistory.org.za/article/apartheid-legislation-1850s-1970s (accessed 7/12/17); contains a detailed explanation of the apartheid legislative acts.

4. For more on the emergence of the struggle against apartheid and Mandela's role in it, see Nelson Mandela, *Long Walk to Freedom: The Autobiography of Nelson Mandela* (Boston: Little, Brown, 1996).

5. Pierre de Vos, "Key Institutions Affecting Democracy in South Africa," in *Testing Democracy: Which Way Is South Africa Going?*, eds. Neeta Misra-Dexter and Judith February (Cape Town: ABC Press, IDASA, 2010), 94–116.

6. Vinothan Naidoo, "The Provincial Government Reform Process in South Africa: Policy Discretion and Developmental Relevance," *Politikon* 36, no. 2 (August 2009): 259–74.

7. Celia Dugger, "South Africa Exults Abroad but Frets at Home," *New York Times*, April 19, 2011, 4; and Iris Wielders, "Perceptions and Realities of Corruption in South Africa." Afrobarometer Briefing Paper 110, January 2013, www.afrobarometer.org (accessed 5/20/13).

8. On the ANC, see Roger Southall, "From Liberation Movement to Party Machine? The ANC in South Africa," *Journal of Contemporary African Studies* 32, no. 3 (2014): 331–48.

9. For one account, see Andrew Feinstein, *After the Party: A Personal and Political Journey through the ANC* (Johannesburg: Jonathan Ball Publishers, 2007).

10. Paul Graham and Carmen Alpin, "Public Attitudes towards the President of the Republic of South Africa, Jacob Zuma," Afrobarometer Briefing Paper 104, October 2012, www.afrobarometer.org (accessed 5/26/14).

11. Paul Graham, "Party Identification in South Africa: Profiles for the ANC and the DA," Afrobarometer Briefing Paper 108, December 2012, www.afrobarometer.org (accessed 6/6/17).

12. See, for example, Alex Boraine, *What's Gone Wrong? South Africa on the Brink of Failed Statehood* (New York: NYU Press, 2014).

13. Kebapetse Lotshwao, "The Lack of Internal Party Democracy in the African National Congress: A Threat to the Consolidation of Democracy in South Africa," *Journal of African Studies* 35, no. 4 (December 2009): 901–14.

14. Karen E. Ferree, "Framing the Race in South Africa: The Political Origins of Racial-Census Elections (New York: Cambridge University Press, 2011), 1.

15. The data are taken from Karen Ferree, "The Microfoundations of Ethnic Voting, Evidence from South Africa," Afrobarometer Working Paper 40, June 2004, www.afrobarometer.org (accessed 12/17/11).

16. Steven Friedman, "Beneath the Surface: Civil Society and Democracy after Polokwane," in Misra-Dexter and February, eds., *Testing Democracy*, 117.

17. Ann-Sofie Isaksson, "Political Participation in Africa: Participatory Inequalities and the Role of Resources," Afrobarometer Working Paper 121, September 2010, www.afrobarometer.org (accessed 6/3/11).

18. On COSATU, see Sakhela Buhlungu, "Gaining Influence but Losing Power? COSATU Members and the Democratic Transformation of South Africa," *Social Movement Studies* 7, no. 1 (May 2008), 31–42.

19. Misra-Dexter and February, eds., *Testing Democracy*, 153.

20. Gallup International, Global Index of Religiosity and Atheism, 2012, www.wingia.com/web/files/news/14/file/14.pdf (accessed 5/23/14).

21. *Economist,* "South African Schools: Desegregation and Investment Have Yet to Boost Black Schoolchildren," January 13, 2011, www.economist.com/node/17913496 (accessed 7/10/17).

22. "Summary of Results," 2006 and 2011, www.afrobarometer.org (accessed 5/21/14).

23. An excellent overview is Charles Simkins, "South African Disparities," *Journal of Democracy* 22, no. 3 (July 2011): 105–19.

24. *Economist*, "Land Reform in South Africa," December 3, 2009, www.economist.com/node/15022632 (accessed 7/10/17).

25. Afrobarometer data, www.afrobarometer.org (accessed 5/21/14).

26. Dominic Griffiths and Maria L. C. Prozesky, "The Politics of Dwelling: Being White in South Africa," *Africa Today* 56, no. 4 (summer 2010): 28.

27. Misra-Dexter and February, eds., *Testing Democracy*, 162.

28. Lydia Polgreen, "South Africans Suffer as Graft Saps Provinces," *New York Times*, February 18, 2012, www.nytimes.com/2012/02/19/world/africa/south-africans-suffer-as-graft-saps-social-services.html?ref=southafrica&pagewanted=print (accessed 5/22/14).

29. Iris Wielders, "Perceptions and Realities of Corruption in South Africa," Afrobarometer Briefing Paper 110, January 2013, www.afrobarometer.org (accessed 5/20/14).

30. Estimate by the United Nations AIDS Organization, http://www.unaids.org/en/regionscountries/countries/southafrica (accessed 6/6/17).

NIGERIA

1. Charles R. Nixon, "Self-Determination: The Nigeria/Biafra Case," *World Politics* 24, no. 4 (July 1972): 473–97.

2. Blaine Harden, *Africa: Dispatches from a Fragile Continent* (Boston: Houghton Mifflin, 1990), 247.

3. For a useful discussion of the Nigerian constitutional process, see Julius O. Ihonvbere, "How to Make an Undemocratic Constitution: The Nigerian Example," *Third World Quarterly* 21 (2000): 343–66.

4. The 1999 constitution states that the "composition of the Government of the Federation or any of its agencies and the conduct of its affairs shall be carried out in such a manner as to reflect the federal character of Nigeria and the need to promote national unity, and also to command national loyalty thereby ensuring that there shall be no pre-dominance of persons from a few states or from a few ethnic or other sectional groups in that government or in any of its agencies." See E. Ike Udogu, "Review of Rotimi T. Suberu's *Federalism and Ethnic Conflict in Nigeria*," *Journal of Third World Studies* (Spring 2004): 296–300.

5. "A Reporter's Tale," *Economist*, February 26, 2004.

6. For the term *judicial terrorism*, see Shu'aibu Musa, "Shades of Injustice: Travails of Muslim Activists in Nigeria in the Hands of Successive Regimes," paper presented at the International Conference of Prisoners of Faith, London, February 17, 2002 (London: Islamic Human Rights Commission, 2002), www.ihrc.org.uk/attachments/7668_02feb17drmusaSHADES%20OF%20INJUSTICE.pdf (accessed 7/20/17).

7. For a useful discussion of Sharia and asymmetrical federalism, see M.H.A. Bolaji, "Shari'ah in Northern Nigeria in the Light of Asymmetrical Federalism," *Journal of Federalism* 40, no. 1 (2009): 114–35.

8. Matthijs Bogaards, "Ethnic Party Bans and Institutional Engineering in Nigeria," *Democratization* 17 (August 2010): 730–49.

9. Udogu, "Review of Rotimi T. Suberu's *Federalism and Ethnic Conflict in Nigeria*."

10. William Ehwarieme, "The Military Factor in Nigeria's Democratic Stability, 1999–2009," *Armed Forces & Society* 37 (2011): 494–511.

11. Howard French, *A Continent for the Taking* (New York: Alfred A. Knopf, 2004), 27.

12. Michael Bratton and Richard Houessou, "Demand for Democracy Is Rising in Africa, but Most Political Leaders Fail to Deliver," *Afrobarometer Policy Paper* 11 (April 23, 2014): 10; "Summary of Results for Nigeria, 2015," *Afrobarometer Round 6* (Practical Sampling International, 2015), http://afrobarometer.org/sites/default/files/publications/Summary%20of%20results/nig_r6_sor_en.pdf (accessed 7/16/16).

13. "Ballots and Bullets: Political Violence Reaches New Heights," *Economist*, April 14, 2011.

14. Brandon Kendhammer, "Talking Ethnic but Hearing Multi-Ethnic: The PDP in Nigeria and Durable Multi-Ethnic Parties in the Midst of Violence," *Commonwealth & Comparative Politics* 48 (February 2010): 48–71.

15. Chinua Achebe, *The Trouble with Nigeria* (London: Heinemann, 1983), p. 15.

16. Bratton and Houessou, "Demand for Democracy Is Rising in Africa," 10; Michael Bratton and Peter Lewis, "The Durability of Political Goods? Evidence from Nigeria's New Democracy," *Afrobarometer Working Paper* 48 (April 2005), 1–43 (accessed 6/20/17).

17. Adam Nossiter, "In Nigeria, Where Graft Is the System," *New York Times*, February 5, 2014.

18. "A Tale of Two Giants," *Economist*, January 13, 2000.

19. Peter Lewis, "From Prebendalism to Predation: The Political Economy of Decline in Nigeria," *Journal of Modern African Studies* 34, no. 1 (March 1996): 79–103.

20. International Monetary Fund, "Nigeria: 2005 Article IV Consultation, Concluding Statement," International Monetary Fund, March 25, 2005, www.imf.org/external/np/ms/2005/032505.htm (accessed 7/20/17).

CHAPTER 11: GLOBALIZATION AND THE FUTURE OF COMPARATIVE POLITICS

1. Jeffrey Wasserstrom, "China & Globalization," *Daedalus* 143, no. 2 (2014): 157–69.

2. Ezra F. Vogel, *Japan as Number One: Lessons for America* (Cambridge, MA: Harvard University Press, 1979).

3. Jared Diamond, *Guns, Germs, and Steel: The Fate of Human Societies* (New York: Norton, 1997).

4. See Robert O. Keohane and Joseph S. Nye Jr., "Introduction," in *Governance in a Globalizing World*, eds. Joseph S. Nye and John D. Donahue (Washington, DC: Brookings Institution Press, 2000), 1–41.

5. Thomas Friedman, *The Lexus and the Olive Tree* (New York: Farrar, Straus, and Giroux, 2000).

6. Daniel Cunningham, Sean Everton, and Philip Murphy, *Understanding Dark Networks: A Strategic Framework for the Use of Social Network Analysis* (New York: Rowman & Littlefield, 2016).

7. Charles Kupchan, "The Democratic Malaise: Globalization and the Threat to the West," *Foreign Affairs* 91 no. 1 (January/February 2012): 62–7.

8. *World Investment Report 2016*, www.unctad.org (accessed 8/11/16).

9. See the United Nations Department of Economic and Social Affairs Population Division, www.un.org/en/development/desa/population/migration/data/estimates2/estimates15.shtml (accessed 8/11/16).

10. Tyler Cowen, *Creative Destruction: How Globalization Is Changing the World's Cultures* (Princeton, NJ: Princeton University Press, 2004); Jan Nederveen Pieterse, *Globalization and Culture: Global Mélange* (New York: Rowman & Littlefield, 2015).

11. John S. Dryzek, "Global Civil Society: The Progress of Post-Westphalian Politics," *Annual Review of Political Science* 15 (2012): 101–19.

12. George Ritzer, *The Globalization of Nothing* (Thousand Oaks, CA: Pine Forge Press, 2007), and *Enchanting and Disenchanted World: Continuity and Change in the Cathedrals of Consumption* (Thousand Oaks, CA: Pine Forge Press, 2009).

13. John Maynard Keynes, *The Economic Consequences of the Peace* (New York: Harcourt, Brace, and Howe, 1920), 11–12.

14. Eelke De Jong, *Culture and Economics: On Values, Economics and International Business* (New York: Routledge, 2009).

15. Martin Ford, *Rise of the Robots: Technology and the Threat of a Jobless Future* (New York: Basic Books, 2015).

16. Keynes, *The Economic Consequences of the Peace*, 12.

17. "Faith and Skepticism about Trade, Foreign Investment" (Washington, DC: Pew Research Center Global Attitudes Project, September 16, 2014).

Glossary / Index

Page numbers in **boldface** refer to key terms as they are called out in the text. Page numbers in *italics* refer to figures and tables.

2011 earthquake, 339: Disastrous 9.0 earthquake that struck the northeast region of Honshu, Japan's largest island, causing a destructive tsunami that resulted in the meltdown of several nuclear reactors

Aadhaar system, 536

Aam Aadmi, 527, 538–539

Abacha, Sani, 670, 670–671, 674, 675: Oppressive Nigerian military dictator from 1993 to 1998 who came to power in a military coup

Abe, Shinzō, 327, **335,** *335,* 342–343, *343*: Conservative nationalist Liberal Democratic Party politician and two-time prime minister of Japan (2006–07; 2012–)
    economic policies of, 342, 344–345, 349–350

Abenomics, 342, 344–345, 349–350: In Japan, Prime Minister Shinzō Abe's three-pronged plan for economic recovery, including monetary easing (raising inflation), fiscal stimulus (budget increases), and structural reform

abortion, 182
    in communist countries, 394, 408
    in Germany, 306, 314
    in Russia, 443
    sex-selective, 497
    in United Kingdom, 220, 224, 226
    in United States, 244, 248, 253

absolute monarchy, 206, 261, **263,** 263–266: The stage in the evolutionary development of Europe between the more decentralized feudal monarchies of the Middle Ages and the constitutional governments of the modern era

abstract review, 154, 182, 429: Judicial review that allows the constitutional court to rule on questions that do not arise from actual legal disputes

Abubakar, Abdulsalami, 671, *674*
Abuja district, 675, 677, 685
accountability, and political engagement in developing countries, 504
Achaemenid Empire, 544
Achebe, Chinua, 686
Action Congress of Nigeria (ACN), *683*

Action Group Party (AGP), 667
Act of Union (1707), 211, 228
Adenauer, Konrad, *303*

administrative guidance (in Japan), 339: Extra-legal policy directives from government officials to the private sector

advance-fee (419) scams, 687
affirmative action
    in Brazil, 621
    in India, 525, 531
    in South Africa, 500, 638, 655–656
    in United States, 247
Affordable Care Act, 258
Afghanistan, 44, *46–47,* 151, 557
    and China, 441
    drug production in, 567
    ethnic conflicts in, 63
    and France, 278
    gender equality in, *410*
    and Germany, 311
    Islam in, 375, 409, 543
    and Pakistan, 48, 441
    and Russia, 440
    and Soviet Union, 396, 402, 408–409, 440
    terrorism in, 131
    theocracy in, 375
    and United Kingdom, 440, 545
    and United States, 440
Africa. *See also specific countries.*
    communist regimes in, *386,* 402
    developing countries in, 483, *485,* 500, 501
    ethnic and national identity in, 64, 501
    ethnolinguistic diversity in, *65*
    Fair Trade in goods from, 481, 482
    happiness in, *108*
    immigration from, 284
    imperialism and colonialism in, 64, 486, 487, 488, 492, 708
        British, 208, 224, 496
        French, 267
    import substitution in, 498
    Indian immigrants in, 489, 496
    military rule in, 371
    Millennium Villages in, 505, 508

Al Qaeda, *49,* 118, 134, 402, 409, 440
Alternative for Germany (AfD), 312, *312,* 320
alternative runoff voting, 164

***amakudari,* 339**: Literally "descent from heaven," in which retiring Japanese senior bureaucrats take up positions in corporations or run for political office

ambulantes, 595
American Red Cross, 503

American Revolution, 63–64, **236,** 253, 283: The conflict between Britain and the American colonists that resulted in U.S. independence (1775–83)

Amnesty International, 460, 495, 698

Amritsar, *510,* **517**: Northern Indian city and location of the Golden Temple, Sikhism's holiest shrine

analytical concepts in comparative politics, 5

anarchism, 71, 71–72, *72,* 74: A political ideology that stresses the elimination of the state and private property as a way to achieve both freedom and equality for all

ancien régime, 261, 264
Andhra Pradesh state of India, 54, 521, 524
Angles, 205
Anglican Church, 206
animist faiths, 665, 685
Antifederalists, 240
anti-Semitism, 298, 312, 433
anti-statism, 253

apartheid in South Africa, 30, 57–58, 60, 124, **629,** 634–635: The policy of segregation put in place by the Afrikaner-dominated racist authoritarian regime in South Africa that was in power from 1948 to 1994
    civil society in, 647
    economic policies in, 499, 654
    electoral system in, 640
    ideology and political culture in, 652
    political parties in, 642
    society in, 649, 650, 651
    and transition to democracy, 124, 635–637

Apple, *692,* 702
April 6 Youth Movement, 139
Aquino, Corazon, 171
Arabs, 541, 544, 559, 560
Arab Spring, 3–4, 6, 15, 20–21, *21,* 138–139, 541
    Bouazizi as inspiration for, *2,* 3, 20, 139
    in Egypt, 4, *21,* 118, 138–139, *139*
    political violence in, *116,* 117–118
    as revolution, 118, 125, 138

area studies, 9: A regional focus when studying political science, rather than studying parts of the world where similar variables are clustered

Arendt, Hannah, 359
Argentina, 182
    electoral system in, 162
    gross domestic product of, 506
    happiness in, 109
    societal globalization and trust in, *713*
    and United Kingdom, 208
aristocracy
    in France, 264, 265
    in India, 515
    in Iran, 546
    in Mexico, 572
    in United Kingdom, 209, 215, 226
Aristotle, 10–11, *12*
Arizona, 237, 572
Armed Islamic Group (GIA), 132
Armenia, *400,* 408, 441

Article 9, 323, 331, 336, 337, 342–343, *343*: The clause in Japan's postwar constitution that requires Japan to renounce the right to wage war; also known as the *peace clause*

Articles of Confederation, 236, 240, 245: In the United States, the weak confederal regime that governed the colonies after 1781; it was replaced by the U.S. Constitution after 1790

Aryans, 299, 530
ascription of ethnic identity, 56
Asia. *See also specific countries.*
    agricultural reform in, 507
    area studies of, 9
    communist regimes in, *386,* 402
    cultural values in, 170
    democratization in, 3, 151, 170–171
    developed democracies in, *179*
    developing countries in, 483, *485,* 500
    economic growth in, 484, 500, 506–507
    export-oriented industrialization in, 499
    happiness in, *108,* 109
    immigration from, 193, 194
    imperialism and colonialism in, 486, 487, 492, 708
    import substitution in, 498
    and Latin America compared, 506–507
    mercantilism in, 99, 101–102
    middle income countries in, 484
    military rule in, 371
    mobile broadband subscriptions in, *706*
    post-imperialism in, 492, 498
    rise of modern state in, 38
    semi-presidential systems in, 158
Asian South Africans, 57, 651, 656
al-Assad, Bashar, 4, 117
al-Assad, Hafez, 117

Assembly of Experts, 376, **552,** 552–553, 554, 555: In Iran, the elected body that chooses the supreme leader

assimilation, 193, 283, 347

asymmetric federalism, 42, 44, **430, 524**: A system where power is devolved unequally across the country and its constituent regions, often the result of specific laws negotiated between the region and the central government; for example, some regions are given greater power over taxation or language rights than others—a more likely outcome in a country with significant ethnic divisions

    in India, 78, 524

    in Russia, 42, 430

Athens, 62, 147

attitudes, political. *See* political attitudes

Aung San Suu Kyi, 171

Australia

    as developed democracy, *179,* 182

    electoral system in, 164, 182

    happiness in, *108*

    immigrant population in, 192, 193

    judiciary in, 154, 244

    liberalism in, 96

    parliamentary system in, 156

    societal globalization and trust in, 711, *713*

    wealth measures in, 104, 106

Austria, 295, 296, 299

autarky in Iran, 564

authoritarianism, 358: A political system in which a small group of individuals exercises power over the state without being constitutionally responsible to the public

    in Brazil, 603, 607, 608–609, 610

    bureaucratic, **372, 608**

    in China, 39, *401,* 453, 455, 460, 461, 469, 694

    and coercion path of political organization, 34

    corporatism in, 368

    in France, 261

    gender roles in, 408

    in Germany, 295, 296, 403

    in Indonesia, 143

    international relations in, 364

    in Iran, 548–549, 563

    in Japan, 323, 325, 326, 345

    in Mexico, 571, 572, 575

        and civil society, 586, 588, 589, 590

        and corruption, 494

        under Díaz, 569, 572

        and local government, 580

        and political culture, 591, 592

        and political parties, 581, 591

        under PRI, 575, 576, 585, 586, 588, 589

        and rule of law, 571

    in Middle East, 3, 138

    and nationalism, 7

    in Nigeria, 494, 671, 673

    political control in, 366, 368

    postcommunist, *401*

    in South Africa, 629, 631

    in Syria, 117

    terrorism risk in, 140

    totalitarianism compared to, 359, 360

    worldwide trends in, 365, *380,* 381

    in Zimbabwe, 378, 379

autocracy, 358

autonomy, 44–50, **45**: The ability of the state to wield its power independently of the public

    in developing countries, 493–496, 502

    in globalization, 700, 704

    in imperialism, 488

    in origins of democracy, 148

    in political-economic systems, 95, 98, 99, 100

    and political ideologies, 70, 71

    in post-imperialism, 493–496

Axis powers in World War II, 547

ayatollah, 544: In Shiite Islam, a title in the religious hierarchy achieved by scholars who have demonstrated highly advanced knowledge of Islamic law and religion

Ayodhya, 518, 526, 530: North-central Indian city where the Babri Mosque was destroyed in 1992

Ayrault, Jean-Marc, 276

Azerbaijan, *400, 401,* 405, *405,* 408, 560

Azeris, 559–560

Azikiwe, Benjamin Nnamdi, 667, 668: Nigerian nationalist and independent Nigeria's first head of state (1960–66)

Aztecs, 571–572

Babangida, Ibrahim, 670, *674*: Military ruler of Nigeria from 1985 to 1993 who sought to establish the failed Third Republic

Babri Mosque, 518

baby boomer generation, 200

backbenchers, 213, 214, 215

Baghdad, 597

Bahrain, 96

Baja California, 581

bakufu, 327

Bakunin, Mikhail, 71

Balewa, Abubakar Tafawa, *674*

Balkan states, 399, 401

Baltic states, 399, 401

Baluchis, 560

Bangalore, 535

Bangladesh, 505, 516

banking system

    in Brazil, 614

    central banks in, **91,** 91–92, 93

    globalization of, 702, 715

    in Mexico, 577

Bantu, 632

Bantu Homelands Citizenship Act (1971), 634

Brazilian Social Democracy Party (PSDB), *617,* 618
Brazilian Socialist Party (PSB), *617,* 619

Bretton Woods system, 702, 715, 716: An economic regime that manages international economic relations; this includes the International Monetary Fund (IMF), the World Bank, and the World Trade Organization (WTO)

Brexit, 169, 175–177, *202,* **203,** 225, 227–228, 229–231: British exit from the European Union realized in a 2016 referendum
    and Cameron, 210, 214, 220, 230–231
    challenges in, *210*
    and Farage, *174,* 221
    and May, 210, 220, 222
    and nationalism, 59
    prediction of, 21

Brezhnev, Leonid, 424
British Commonwealth, **208,** 668
British East India Company, 224, 491, **514,** 515
British Empire, 37, 208, 440, 492, 496, 605
    American colonies of, 235–236, 253
    in India, 224, 440, 491, 496, 511, 514–516
    mercantilism in, 99
    in Nigeria, 666–668, 672
    in South Africa, 632–633
    in Sudan, 497

Broad-Based Black Economic Empowerment (BEE), 656: South Africa's affirmative action program that aims to create a new class of black owners and management through a series of quotas and targets

Brown, Gordon, 219
Buddhism, 135, 326, 375, 514

Buhari, Muhammadu, 670, 673, *674,* 678: Former military ruler and current democratically elected president of Nigeria (2015–)
    anti-corruption efforts of, 675, 687, 688
    economic policies of, 688
    election of (2015), *674,* 676, 677, 680
    and Niger Delta conflicts, 683, 691

Bulgaria, *108, 109,* 399, *400,* 401, *410*

Bundesrat, 304, 304–305: The upper house of Germany's legislature

Bundestag, 302, **304,** 306, *307,* 310, 311: The lower house of Germany's legislature

burakumin, 347
bureaucracy
    in Brazil, 606, 608, 611, 612, 623
    in China, 448, 455, 471–472, 495
    in France, 264, 266
    in imperialism, 488
    in India, 519, 533–534
    in Japan, 328, 332, 336, 339–340, 343, 345

    in military rule, 372
    in Nigeria, 667, 672, 674
    in post-imperialism, 493
    in Russia, 439
    in Soviet Union, 423
    in United States, 242

bureaucratic authoritarianism, 372, 608: (1) A system in which the state bureaucracy and the military share a belief that a technocratic leadership, focused on rational, objective, and technical expertise, can solve the problems of the country without public participation; (2) A form of authoritarian rule, common in Latin America during the 1960s and 1970s (in Brazil, in 1964–85), in which military leaders and civilian technocrats presided over conservative anticommunist regimes

burkini swimsuits in France, 273, *285,* 289
Burma, 135, 331
Burundi, *46–47*
Bush, George W., 245, *245,* 254, 599
Business Coordinating Council (CCE), 588
business organizations
    in France, 281–282
    in Germany, 313–314
    in Japan, 345
    in Mexico, 587–588
    in United Kingdom, 223
Buthelezi, Mangosuthu, 646

cabinet, 152, 155, 156: The appointed officials who serve the executive in overseeing the various state bureaucracies
    in Brazil, 611, 618, 624
    in France, 269, 271
    in Germany, 302
    in India, 520, 521–522
    in Iran, 553
    in Japan, 334
    in Mexico, 577
    in Nigeria, 675
    in South Africa, 639, 640
    in United Kingdom, **207,** 207–208, 212, 213–214
    in United States, **242**

caboclo, **604**: Brazilian of mixed European and indigenous ancestry

Cabral, Pedro Álvares, 604
caciques, 574

Calderón, Felipe, 576, 577, 583: Mexico's conservative president from 2006 to 2012; he was responsible for waging a war against drug cartels that led to a major increase in violence
    antidrug policies of, 584, 597–598
    economic policies of, 586, 588, 593, 596
    election of, 580, 584, 586
    labor policies of, 589
    legislature under, 578, 582
    and PAN, 584

California, 237, 572
Calles, Plutarco Elías, 574
Câmara dos Deputados, **611,** 611–612
Cambridge University, 224

Cameron, David, 205, 210, 220, *220*: Conservative prime minister of the United Kingdom from 2010 to 2016; resigned following the Brexit referendum, which he campaigned against
    and Brexit vote, 210, 214, 220, 230–231
    economic policies of, 220
    and independence movement in Scotland, 210

campaign financing, 182
    in Brazil, 625
    in Japan, 339
    in Mexico, 583, 585, 586
    in United States, 246, 250, 259

Canada, 29
    corruption in, *494*
    as developed democracy, *180,* 182, 183, *183*
    devolution in, 190
    economic liberalization in, *110*
    education in, *105,* 195
    electoral system in, 162, 163, 164, 182
    ethnic and national identity in, 59
    fear about foreign influence in, *533*
    federalism in, 42
    gender equality in, *105,* 106, *410*
    gross domestic product of, *91, 103, 180,* 183, *183*
    happiness in, *108*
    health care in, 88
    immigrant population in, 192, 193
    judiciary in, 154, 244
    liberalism in, 96, 104
    in NAFTA, 181, 189, 575, 593, 594, 704
    patriotism in, 61
    political attitudes in, 68
    political culture in, 80
    public debt in, 196
    referenda and initiatives in, 168
    state capacity and autonomy in, 45
    state control in, *465*
    state power in, 44, 45
    taxation in, *91, 183*
    trade regulations in, 94
    wealth measures in, *103,* 104, *105,* 106
cantons, 274

capacity, 44, 44–50: The ability of the state to wield power to carry out basic tasks, such as defending territory, making and enforcing rules, collecting taxes, and managing the economy
    in developing countries, 493–496, 502, 504
    in globalization, 700, 704
    in imperialism, 488
    in origins of democracy, 148

    in political-economic systems, 95, 98, 99, 100
    and political ideologies, 70, 71
    in post-imperialism, 493–496

Cape Town, 631, 632, 638, 645

capitalism, 95: A system of production based on private property and free markets
    in China, 464–465, 469, 473–474
    and communism compared, 392–393, 394
    in developed democracies, 183
    in Germany, 300, 317
    in Japan, 348
    in liberalism, 95, 96
    Marxist theory on, 386, 387, 388, 389, 414
    in mercantilism, 100, 102
    in Mexico, 592
    in modernization theory, 12
    in Russia, 433
    in social democracy, 96, 97
    in South Africa, 652, 653
    in United Kingdom, 219
    in United States, 233, 238, 239

capitalist developmental state (Japan as), 348: Japan's modern neomercantilist state, which has embraced both private property and state economic intervention

capital punishment
    in China, 376
    in India, 521, 538
    in Indonesia, 145
    in Iran, 376, 554, 567
    in United Kingdom, 226
    in United States, 554
Capriles, Henrique, 84
captured states, 45, 64
Cárdenas, Cuauhtémoc, 582–583
Cárdenas, Lázaro, 575, 593, 596

Cardoso, Fernando Henrique, 614–615, **618,** 621: Brazil's president from 1995 to 2002; he was responsible for significant economic and political reform

Caribbean region, *108,* 208, 604

Carranza, Venustiano, 574: Mexican revolutionary leader who eventually restored political order, ended the revolution's violence, and defeated the more radical challenges of Emiliano Zapata and Francisco (Pancho) Villa

Carter, Jimmy, 549
case study method, 7–10, 13, 14, 15
Castañeda, Jorge, 592

caste (system in India), 411, **511,** 514, 518, 523, 525, 527, 529, 531: Hindu hereditary social grouping

Castro, Fidel, 391, 392

civil war
  in China, 448–450
  in England, **206**
  in Nigeria, 668, 677, 685
  in Spain, 72
  in Syria, 4, 5, 496–497
  in United States, **238,** 258

civil war (United States), 238, 258: In the United States, the conflict between the southern, slaveholding states and the North, or the Union; the victory of the North preserved the unity of the United States and resulted in the abolition of slavery

Civil War Amendments, 238: In the United States, the constitutional amendments that abolished slavery (Thirteenth Amendment), guaranteed all citizens due process and equal protection under the law (Fourteenth Amendment), and prohibited race-based voter discrimination (Fifteenth Amendment)

The Clash of Civilizations and the Remaking of World Order (Huntington), 77
class. *See also* middle class
  in India, 529
  in United Kingdom, 215, 219, 223–224
Clegg, Nick, 221
clerical rule in Iran, 549, 550

clientelism, 368, 368–369: A process whereby the state co-opts members of the public by providing specific benefits or favors to a single person or a small group in return for public support
  in Brazil, 607, 614, 618
  in developing countries, 493, 496, 498, 504
  in Greece, 198, 199
  in Iran, 556, 561
  in Japan, 341
  in Mexico, 576
  in Nigeria, 677, 680, 687

Clinton, Bill, 254, 255
Clinton, Hillary, 247, 248, 255, 257
clothing and dress of Muslims
  in France, 273, 284–285, *285,* 289
  in Iran, 547, *547*
coalition governments, 155, 157, 158, 161, 168
  in Brazil, 160
  in Germany, *310*
    chancellors in, 302–303, *303*
    Free Democratic Party in, 308, 309, 310
    Green Party in, 311
    Merkel in, 308
    Nazi Party in, 298
    in post–World War II reforms, 300
    Social Democratic Party in, 309, *310,* 311
    in Weimar Republic, 298
  in India, 518–519
    corruption in, 538

local power in, 524
party system in, 525, 526, 527, *528*
president in, 521
prime minister in, 522
  in Japan, 333, 335, 336, 340, 342
  in United Kingdom, 205, 213, 214, 220
    Cameron in, 210
    Conservatives and Liberal Democrats in, 220–221, 227, *228*
coal resources in India, 538
cocoa, 491

code law, 272, 272–273: Law derived from detailed legal codes rather than from precedent

codetermination, 317: The system requiring that unions occupy half of all seats on the boards of directors of Germany's largest private firms

coercion
  and legitimacy of state, 39, 42
  in nondemocratic regimes, 366–367
  and origin of political organization, 33, 34
coffee, 491, 507
  in Brazil, 606
  Fair Trade in, *480,* 481–483, 505

cohabitation, 269, 271, 276: In France, an arrangement in which presidents lacking a majority of legislative power appoint an opposition prime minister who can gain a majority of support in the legislature

Cold War era, 12, 77, 125, 178, 198
  Brazil in, 608
  Germany in, 293, 299, 300, 308, 402
  Iran in, 547
  Japan in, 325, 331
  nondemocratic rule in, 364, 380
  South Africa in, 635, 636
  Soviet Union in, 12, 364, 395–396, 412, 417
  United States in, 12, 364, 395–396
  Zimbabwe in, 379

collective responsibility, 214: In the United Kingdom, tradition that requires all members of the cabinet either to support government policy or to resign

collectivist consensus, 209, 219: Postwar consensus between the United Kingdom's major parties to build and sustain a welfare state

collectivization of agriculture, 393
Collor de Mello, Fernando, 160, 612, 615
Colombia, 376, *712*

colonialism, 483, 484, **486,** 486–488: An imperialist system of physically occupying a foreign territory using military force, businesses, or settlers
  in Brazil, 603, 604–606
  of British Empire. *See* British Empire

developed democracy, 175–201, 483: A country with institutionalized democracy and a high level of economic development

    contemporary challenges for, 184
    definition of, **177,** 178–179
    demographic changes in, 197, 200
    devolution in, 177, 185, 189–191, 200
    economic institutions in, 194–200
    in European Union, 174, 175–177, 185–189
    freedom and equality in, 177, 181–184
    Germany as, 197, 200
    Greece as, 198–199
    gross domestic product of, 178, *180,* 183, *183,* 196, 198
    immigration in, 176, 181, 188, 192–194, 196–197
    income redistribution in, 183, *183*
    Japan as, 179, *180,* 182, *183,* 197
    list of, *179, 180*
    Mexico as, *180,* 180–181, 182
    political diversity in, 184
    political institutions in, 177, 185–191
    postindustrialism in, 177, 194–195
    postmodern values in, 191–194
    social expenditures in, 183, 190, 195–197
    societal institutions in, 177, 191–194
    sovereignty in, 185–191
    in transition, 184, 200–201
    United Kingdom as, *174,* 175–177, *180,* 182, *183*
    United States as, 179, *180,* 182, 183, *183,* 200

developing countries, 178, 481–509, **484:** Lower and middle income countries

    civil society in, 503–504
    corruption in, 493, 494–495, 502
    creating nations and citizens in, 496–497
    democracy and development in, 481, 500–508
    economic growth in, 497–501, 504–508
    ethnic and national identity in, 496–497, 501
    Fair Trade with, *480,* 481–483
    freedom and equality in, 483, 484–486
    gross domestic product of, 484, 500, 710
    imperialism and colonialism in, 483, 484, **486,** 486–492
    increasing state effectiveness in, 501–503
    informal economy in, 504–505
    list of, *485*
    microcredit and microfinance in, 505
    political engagement in, 503–504
    post-imperialism in, 492–500
    religious violence in, 133
    social identities in, 489–490
    state capacity and autonomy in, 493–496

devolution, 43, 44, 143: A process in which political power is "sent down" to lower levels of state and government

    in developed democracies, 177, 185, 189–191, 200
    in India, 518, 519
    in Japan, 338
    in Nigeria, 667, 677

    in United Kingdom, 43, 44, 190, 191, 210, 217, 218, 225, 226, 228
    in United States, 190, 253

dialectical materialism, 387, **388:** Process of historical change that is not evolutionary but revolutionary; the existing base and superstructure (thesis) would come into conflict with new technological innovations, generating growing opposition to the existing order (antithesis)—this would culminate in revolution, overthrowing the old base and superstructure (synthesis)

diamonds
    in Brazil, 604–605
    in South Africa, 632, 653, 654
    in Zimbabwe, 355–356
Diaoyu Islands, 352

Díaz, Porfirio, 569, **572,** 573: Mexican dictator who ruled from 1876 to 1910 and was deposed by the Mexican Revolution

Díaz Ordaz, Gustavo, 593
Dickens, Charles, 224
dictatorship, 358
    of proletariat, 387, 388, 454

Diet (Japan), 329, 333, 334, 336: Japan's bicameral parliament
    electoral system for, 337–338
    twisted, **335,** 335–336, 342

direct democracy, 148, 169

dirigisme, 287: In France, an emphasis on state authority in economic development; a combination of social-democratic and mercantilist ideas

Dlamini-Zuma, Nkosazana, 660
Dokdo islands, 352
Dominican Republic, *507*
donatários, 604
dowry deaths in India, 529
Dravidians, 527, 530
drug addiction in Iran, 567
drug trafficking and violence
    in Brazil, 624, *625*
    in Mexico, 569, 571, 582, 584, 586, *587,* 596–598
Duarte, Javier, *568*

Duma, 422, 426, 428–429: Lower house of the Russian legislature
    election to, 430, 431–433
    in local government, 430, 431
    party system in, 431–433

Dupont-Aignan, Nicolas, *275*
Dutch colonizers, 37, 514, 604, 605
    in Brazil, 604
    in future United States, 235
    in India, 514

in Indonesia, 143, 491, 632
in South Africa, 499, 631–632
Dutch East India Company, 491, 631, 632

Dutch Reformed Church, 632, 650: In South Africa, conservative Protestant Church that has historically been central to Afrikaner culture

Dzhugashvili, Josef Vissarionovich, 391. *See also* Stalin, Joseph

earthquake damage in Japan
    in Kobe (1995), 339, 346
    and tsunami (2011), 325, 336, **339,** 344, 346, 350–351, *351*
Easterlin, Richard A., 108
Easterlin paradox, 108, 109
Eastern Europe
    civil society in, 151, 364
    communism in, 124, 125, 385, 392, 395, 396, 397
        collapse of, 3, 124, 138, 188, 397–398, 402, 412, 414
    democratization in, 151, 171
    ethnic and national identity in, 395, 408
    in European Union, 188
    German investment in, 318
    happiness in, *108*
    immigration from, 250
    nondemocratic rule in, 364
    outsourcing to, 704
    political transitions in, postcommunist, 399–402
    "return to Europe" view in, 412, 413
    revolutions in, 124, 125
    societal transitions in, postcommunist, 408
East Germany, 300, 301, 315, 316, 402–403

East India Company (British), 224, 491, **514,** 515: A firm created to develop trade between the United Kingdom and India

East India Company (Dutch), 491, 631, 632
East Pakistan, 516
Echeverría Álvarez, Luis, 588, 593
Economic and Financial Crimes Commission, 688
The Economic Consequences of the Peace (Keynes), 708–709

Economic Freedom Fighters (EFF), 500, **644,** 644–645, *645,* 646: In South Africa, a leftist political party that broke away from the African National Congress (ANC) in 2013; it is led by the former head of the ANC youth, Julius Malema
    economic policies of, 655
    in National Assembly, *647*

economic globalization, 701–705, 716–717. *See also* globalization
economic inequality, 19
    in Brazil, *600,* 601, 603, 604, 620–621, 622–623, *623*
        and crime, 624
        Gini index on, *103, 623, 657*
    in China, *103,* 255, 406, 447, 474, *657,* 695
    in communist theory, 385, 386–387, 394
    in developed democracies, 183, *183,* 195, 196

in France, *103, 183, 657*
in Germany, *103, 183,* 301, *657*
Gini index as measure of, **104.** *See also* Gini index
in globalization, 111, *111,* 114, 704
and happiness, 109
in India, 411, 513, 535–536, *657*
in Iran, *103,* 563–564, *657*
in Japan, *103, 183,* 348, *657*
in Latin America, 112–113
measures of, 102–109
in Mexico, *103,* 181, 474, 590, 593, 594, 595, *657*
in Nigeria, *103, 657, 662,* 663, 665, 680, 681
and nondemocratic rule, 362–363
as obstacle to democracy, 150
political ideologies on, 70, 71, 73
in postcommunist countries, 406
and poverty, 104, 106–107, 112–113
in Russia, *103,* 106–107, 439, 474, *657*
social expenditures in, 89–90, 183, 196
in South Africa, *103,* 499–500, 634, 649, 653, 655–656, *657*
in Soviet Union, 106–107
terrorism in, 130
in United Kingdom, *103, 183,* 223–224, 227, *657*
in United States, 19, 73, 195, 233, 252, 255–256, 474
    Gini index on, *103, 183, 657*
in Venezuela, 84

economic liberalization, 84, **110,** 110–111, 499: Changes consistent with liberalism that aim to limit the power of the state and increase the power of the market and private property in an economy
    in China, *110,* 495
    comparison in different countries, *110*
    in France, *110,* 287
    global, 714–715
    in India, *110,* 518
    in Iran, *110,* 562
    in Japan, *110,* 350
    in Latin America, 112

economic recession (2008), 220, 227
    in Brazil, 601
    globalization as factor in, 714–715
    in United States, 199, 253, 254, 255, 714, 715
economy
    central planning of, **393,** 412, 413
    components of, 86–94
    in developed democracies, 178–179, *180,* 181–182, 194–200
    in developing countries, 497–501, 502, 504–508
    extractive, 491
    freedom and equality in, 85
    globalization of, 701–705, 716–717. *See also* globalization
    gross domestic product of. *See* gross domestic product
    growth of, 91–93, 94
    in imperialism and colonialism, 491–492, 497–498

economy (*continued*)

    inequality in. *See* economic inequality

    informal, **504, 595**. *See also* informal economy

    information-based, 195, 200

    institutions in, 85, 94, 120

        in postcommunist countries, 403–407

    liberalization of, **110**. *See also* economic liberalization

    middle income trap in, **498**

    money supply in, 91–93

    political. *See* political economy

    in postcommunist countries, 403–407, 419

    in post-imperialism, 497–499

    postindustrial, 194–195

    regulation of, 87, **93**

    in rise of modern state, 36

    and wealth measurements, 102–109

education

    in Brazil, 58, *105,* 614, 621, *623*

    in China, *105,* 455, 459, 464, 466, 470, 472, 474

    conditional cash transfers for, 113, 596, 623

    and democracy in modernization, 148, 170

    in developed democracies, 195, 196

    in France, *105,* 264, 278, 282, 284

    in Germany, *105,* 295, 307

    in Human Development Index, 105, *105,* 106, 138

    in imperialism and colonialism, 489, 490

    in India, *105,* 411, 524, 536

    in Iran, *105,* 546–547, 559

    in Japan, *105,* 329, 331

    in Mexico, *105,* 574, 589, 595

    in Nigeria, *105,* 667, 672, 681, 689, 691

    in post-imperialism, 493

    as public good, 88, 107

    as right, 172

    in Russia, *105,* 421, 433, 434

    social expenditures on, 90, 196

    in South Africa, 58, *105,* 642, 649, 651, 656

    in United Kingdom, *105,* 224

    in United States, *105,* 195, 245, 246

Egypt, 4

    Arab Spring in, 4, *21,* 118, 138–139, *139*

    happiness in, *108,* 109

    military rule in, 371, 372

    nondemocratic regime in, 366

    revolution in, 124, 127, 371

    societal globalization and trust in, *712*

elections, 17, 41

    in Brazil, 613, 616–619

    in developing countries, 502

    electoral systems in, 162–168

    to European Parliament, 166, 176, 186, 199, 221, 279

    in France, *275,* 276, *280*

        to European Parliament, 279

        to local government, 275

        party system in, *275,* 275–280

    in Germany, *303,* 304, *307,* 313

        party system in, 308–313

    in Greece, 199

    in India, 53–54, 518–519, 520–521, 527–528, *528*

        to legislature, 53, *510,* 523, 525, 528, *528,* 538, 539

        party system in, 525–527

    in Indonesia, *142,* 143–144

    in Iran, 554–555, 556–558, 559

    in Japan, *338,* 340–345, *341*

    in Mexico, 569, 579–580, 585–586

        and campaign financing, 583, 585, 586

        fraud in, *575,* 577, 579, 580, 581, 583

        to legislature, 578, 580

        media coverage of, 586, 589, 590

        party system in, 574–575, 578, 581–585

    in Nigeria, 670, 679–682

        corruption and fraud in, 676, 679, 680–681

        presidential, 670, 671, 673, *674,* 676, *677,* 679–682

        and violence, 681

        voter identification in, 681

    in Pakistan, 25, 26

    in Russia, 429–430

        party system in, 431–433

    in South Africa, 164, 165, *165,* 639, 642–647

    in United Kingdom, 205, 210, 213, 222

        to European Parliament, 166

        to House of Commons, 163–164, 166–167, 214, 216–217, 221

        party system in, *163,* 163–164, *217,* 218–222

        results of, *163, 217*

    in United States, 244–245, 249–250, 257

        cost of, 249, 250

        electoral college results in, 245

        immigration policy issues in, 257

        party system in, *245,* 246–249, 252, 255

        and political culture and ideology, 73

        populism in, 252

    in Venezuela, 83, 84

    voter turnout in. *See* voter turnout

    winner-take-all, 120, 163, 167, 244, 245, 274, 677

electoral authoritarian regime, 376

electoral college

    in France, 272

    in India, 521

    in United States, 244–245

electoral system, 17, **162,** 162–168: A set of rules that decide how votes are cast, counted, and translated into seats in a legislature

    in Brazil, 166, 613–614, 626

    in communist and postcommunist countries, *400*

    in developed democracies, 182

    in France, 273–274

    in Germany, 166, 168, 182, 306–307

    in India, 411, 523

    in Iran, 554–555

    in Japan, 337–338

    in Mexico, 168, 182, 575, 579–580

    mixed type, 167–168

elitists, 476: Faction of Chinese Communist Party officials who are the offspring of former high-ranking cadre and who favor economic growth and market liberalization

emergency rule, 517, 519–520, 523, 524: Law invoked by Indian national government to suspend the constitution by declaring martial law

empire, 486: A single political authority that has under its sovereignty a large number of external regions or territories and different peoples

endogeneity, 10, 80: The issue that cause and effect are not often clear, in that variables may be both cause and effect in relationship to one another

English Civil War, 206: Seventeenth-century conflict between Parliament and the monarch that temporarily eliminated and permanently weakened the monarchy

equality, 19: A shared material standard of individuals within a community, society, or country

Estado Nôvo, 607, 608, *609*: The populist authoritarian regime of Getúlio Vargas in Brazil between 1937 and 1945

ethnic conflict, 63: A conflict in which different ethnic groups struggle to achieve certain political or economic goals at each other's expense

ethnic identity/ethnicity, 56: Specific attributes and societal institutions that make one group of people culturally different from others

Eurasian Economic Union (EAEU), 441, *441*, 441–442: Economic and political union among several former Soviet states

executive, 152, 152–153: The branch of government that carries out the laws and policies of a state
    in China, 459
    in developed democracies, 182

Free Democratic Party (FDP), *307,* 308, **309,** 309–310: In Germany, a small centrist party that has often formed part of governing coalitions

freedom, 19: The ability of an individual to act independently, without fear of restriction or punishment by the state or other individuals or groups in society

French Communist Party (PCF), 266, **275,** 276, 277, 281: One of the dominant parties of the French left since the end of World War II

French Council of the Muslim Faith, 282

French Democratic Labor Confederation (CFDT), 281: A smaller confederation backed by the Socialist Party

gerrymandering, 244: In the United States, the process of apportioning electoral districts to favor one political party or marginalize certain groups

Gini index, 104, 104–105, 106, 107: A statistical formula that measures the amount of inequality in a society; its scale ranges from 0 to 100, where 0 corresponds to perfect equality and 100 to perfect inequality

glasnost, 396, 424, 434: Literally, "openness"; the policy of political liberalization implemented in the Soviet Union in the late 1980s

globalization, 4, 693–717: The process of expanding and intensifying linkages between states, societies, and economies

Good Friday Agreement, 218, 224: Historic 1998 accord between Protestants and Catholics in Northern Ireland that ended decades of violence

goods
    private ownership of, 87, 88
    public, **88**. *See also* public goods
Gorbachev, Mikhail, 31, 391, 396–397, 398, 412, 413, 417, 424–425
    and East Germany, 301
    glasnost and perestroika policies of, **396,** 424
    judiciary under, 429

Gordhan, Pravin, 658
Gore, Al, 245

Goulart, João, 608, 609, 618: The Brazilian leftist president (1961–64) whose removal by the military began a long period of authoritarian rule

government, 31, 32, *32,* 50: The leadership or elite in charge of running the state
    executive branch of, **152**. *See also* executive branch
    head of, **152**. *See also* head of government
    judicial branch of, 154–155. *See also* judiciary
    legislatures in, **153**. *See also* legislatures

government-operated nongovernmental organizations, 464

Gowon, Yakubu, *674*
Grameen Bank, 505
Grand Old Party (GOP), 247
Great Britain, 228, 448
    in United Kingdom, **205**. *See also* United Kingdom
Great Depression era, 73, 702, 716
        Germany in, 298
        Japan in, 330
        United States in, 239, 246, 247
Greater East Asian Co-Prosperity Sphere, 331
Greater London Assembly, 218
Greater London Council, 43
Great Firewall of China, 466, *467*
Great Game in Central Asia, 440, 441

Great Leap Forward, 393, 413, **451,** 470, 472: Mao Zedong's disastrous 1958–60 effort to modernize China through localized industrial production and agricultural communes

Great Trek (1835), 632: The epic migration of Afrikaners (Voortrekkers) into the interior of South Africa in 1835 to escape British colonization

Great Wall of China, 447
Greece
    corruption in, 198–199, *405*
    as developed democracy, 182
    economy of, 188, 702, 714
        crisis in, 198–199, *199*
        indicators on, 405, *405*
    in European Union, 188, 199
    in globalization, 714
    International Monetary Fund in, 702
    origins of democracy in, 147

origins of political organization in, 34
political ideology in, 71
Green Party (Brazil), 619
Green Party (Germany), 168, *307,* 308, 310–311, **311,** 314, 317
Green Party (Mexico), 585
Green Party (United Kingdom), *163,* 166, 221, *222*
Green Party (United States), 249
Greenpeace, 698, 701

Green Revolution (India), 533: Period during the 1960s and 1970s when technologically enhanced crops and cropping methods dramatically improved food production in India

Green Wave movement (Iran), 557, 558, 713

gross domestic product (GDP), 90, 102–104, 106: The total market value of all goods and services produced by a country over a period of one year
    of Asia and Latin America compared, 506
    of Brazil, *103, 180, 256,* 506, 622, *623*
    of China, *103, 180, 256,* 405, 445, 473, 475, 693, 694
    of communist and postcommunist countries compared, *405*
    and democracy, *180,* 362
    of developed democracies, 178, *180,* 183, *183,* 196, 198
    of developing countries, 484, 500, 710
    of European Union, 188
    of France, *91, 103, 180, 183, 256,* 287, 290
    of Germany, *91, 103, 180, 183, 256*
    and globalization, 710, 714, 716
    and happiness, 108, 109
    and Human Development Index, 106, *180*
    of India, *103, 180, 256,* 511
    of Iran, *103, 180, 256,* 564
    of Japan, *91, 103, 180, 183, 256,* 349
    of lower income countries, 484
    of Mexico, *91, 103, 180, 256,* 473
    of middle income countries, 484
    of Nigeria, *103, 180, 256*
    of Russia, *103, 256,* 405, 438, 439
    of South Africa, *103, 180, 256*
    of South Korea, *91, 103, 180,* 506
    and taxation, 90, *91,* 196
    of United Kingdom, *91, 103, 180, 183,* 226–227, *256*
    of United States, *91, 103, 180,* 183, *183,* 253, 255, *256,* 693, 694
    of Venezuela, 112

Group Areas Act (1950), 635: The centerpiece of apartheid legislation that divided South Africans into four racial categories and required strict segregation of housing along racial lines

Growth, Employment, and Redistribution (GEAR), 499, **655**: In South Africa, the 1996 liberal macroeconomic structural adjustment plan that moved the African National Congress toward a more market-friendly political policy

historical development of state *(continued)*
    in France, 263–267
    in Germany, 295–301
    and globalization, 696–697, 698, 699, 708–709, 716
    in India, 513–519
    in Iran, 543–550
    in Japan, 326–332
    in Mexico, 571–576
    in Nigeria, 665–671
    in Russia, 420–425
    in South Africa, 631–637
    in United Kingdom, 205–210
    in United States, 235–240

Hitler, Adolf, 40, **298,** 298–299, 360: The Nazi leader during the Third Reich who led Germany to defeat in World War II

HIV/AIDS in South Africa, 631, 643, 647–648, 660
Hobbes, Thomas, 11, *12,* 33

Hollande, François, *270, * **276,** 289: Socialist president of France from 2012 to 2017
    anti-immigration proposals of, 285
    approval ratings of, 277, *277,* 279
    economic policies of, 270, 288, 291
    election of (2012), 276
    labor reforms of, 279, 291
    local elections under, 275

Holy Roman Empire, 263, 295
homelands policy in South Africa, 60, 634, 646, 650
Home Office, 214
homicide rate
    in Brazil, 624
    in South Africa, 650, 658
homophobia, 409–410
homosexuality, 226, 409–410
    and LGBTQ issues, 408, 409–410, 429, 432
    rights associated with, 172, 220, 224, 409
    and same-sex marriage/partnerships, 192, 226, 409
Honda Motor Company, 340
Hong Kong, 208, 448, 492, *713*
household registration system, **454,** 474

household responsibility system, 472: In China, Deng Xiaoping's highly successful 1980s rural reform program that lowered production quotas and allowed the sale of surplus agricultural produce on the free market

House of Commons, 209, 212, 213, 214–215, 522: Lower house of the UK legislature
    election to, *163,* 163–164, 166–167, 214, 216–217, *217,* 221, 222
    party system in, *163, 217, 222*

House of Councillors, 336, 337: The upper and weaker chamber of Japan's parliament

House of Lords, 209, 213, 214, 215, 216: Upper house of the UK legislature, whose reform is currently being debated

House of Representatives (Japan), 334–335, **336**: The lower and more powerful chamber of Japan's parliament
    electoral system for, 337
    party system in, 342, 343

House of Representatives (Nigeria), 668, **675**: Lower house of Nigerian parliament
    election to, 676–677, *683*
    party system in, 679

House of Representatives (United States), 241, 242–243, 522: The lower house of the U.S. Congress (legislature)
    election to, 244, *245*
    political polarization in, 257–259

House of the People, 522: Lower and more powerful house of Indian parliament
    election to, 523, 525, 528, *528*

housing
    and economic recession (2008), 254, 714, 715
    in France, 284
    in United Kingdom, 227

Hu Jintao, 457, 458–459, 463, *463,* 475: China's paramount leader from 2002 to 2012

hukou **(household registration) system, 454,** 474: Maoist program that tied all Chinese to a particular geographic location

Human Development Index (HDI), 105, 105–106: A statistical tool that attempts to evaluate the overall wealth, health, and knowledge of a country's people
    and Arab Spring, 138
    in Brazil, *105,* 623
    comparison in different countries, *105, 180*
    and democratization, 171
    in developed democracies, 178, 179, *180*
    in developing countries, 500
    and happiness, 109
    in Mexico, *105,* 623
    in Nigeria, *105,* 688

human rights concerns
    in Brazil, 615, 619
    in China, 460–461
    in International Criminal Court, 700
    in Iran, 549
    in Mexico, 598
    in Nigeria, 672, 689
    in United Kingdom, 211, 216
Human Rights Watch, 598, 700
Hungary, 364
    as developed democracy, 182
    economic indicators in, *405*
    electoral system in, 168, 182
    gender equality in, *410*
    political ideology in, 71
    political transitions in, postcommunist, *400,* 401

hung parliament, 210, 220, 221: In the United Kingdom, an election result in which no party wins a majority of parliamentary seats, such as the 2010 and 2017 parliamentary elections

Huntington, Samuel P., 77
Hussein, Saddam, 31, 496, 550
Hutus, 57
hybrid or illiberal regimes, 376
Hyderabad, 54, 535

hyperinflation, 92: Inflation of more than 50 percent a month for more than two months in a row
    in Germany, 298
    in Russia, 437–438

hypothesis, 7, 9
Hyundai vehicles, *171*

ideational, 120: Having to do with ideas

ideational factors in political violence, **120,** 120–121, 122, 137
    in Arab Spring, 139
    in religious violence, 133
    in revolutions, 125
    in terrorism, 130
identity
    citizenship in, 60
    ethnic and national. *See* ethnic and national identity
    in globalization, 705–707
    religious, 75
    social
        in imperialism, 489–490
        in postcommunist countries, 407–408
    as social construction, 55–56
ideology
    in fundamentalism, **75,** 75–76, 133
    political, **69.** *See also* political ideology

Igbo (Ibo), 665, 666, *674*: Predominantly Christian ethnic group concentrated in southeast Nigeria
    under British rule, 667
    coup staged by, 668
    ethnic identity of, 685
    in Federal Military Government, 668
    political party of, 679
    regional division of, 672
    in Republic of Biafra, 668

illiberal regime, 370, 372, **376,** 376–377: A regime where democratic institutions that rest upon the rule of law are weakly institutionalized and poorly respected
    in globalization, 701
    terrorism risk in, 140
    Zimbabwe as, 378

imams, 544: Descendants of the prophet Muhammad, considered by Shia to be true political and religious leaders of Islam

immigration
    to Brazil, 606
    to developed democracies, 176, 181, 188, 192–194, 196–197
    in European Union, 176, 188, 192, 193, 320, 705
    to France, 192, 276–277, 279, 283–285, 288
    to Germany, 192, 200, 293, 312, 315–316, 319–320
    and globalization, 706, 707, 708, 709, 716
    from India, 489, 496
    from Iran, 564
    to Japan, 193, 197, 346, 347
    from Mexico, 181, 193, 256–257, 571, 595, 598–599, 705
    from South Africa, 656
    of Syrian refugees, 4, 312, 313–314, 320
    to United Kingdom, 192, 221, 224–225, 226, 230
    to United States, 192–193, 194, 200, 233, 250–251, 256–257, 716
        from Mexico, 181, 193, 256–257, 571, 595, 598–599, 705

Immigration Reform and Control Act (IRCA), 599: U.S. immigration legislation (1986) that toughened American immigration laws while granting amnesty to many longtime undocumented workers

imperialism, 483, 484, **486,** 486–492: A system in which a state extends its power to directly control territory, resources, and people beyond its borders
    compared to colonialism, 486
    dependent development in, 491–492, 498
    and globalization, 708
    historical timeline on, *487*
    institutions of, 488–492
    in Iran, 546
    in Nigeria, 666–668
    nondemocratic rule in, 364
    and post-imperialism, 492–500
    social identity in, 489–490
    state authority and power in, 488

import substitution, 498, 499, 501, 504: A mercantilist strategy for economic growth in which a country restricts imports in order to spur demand for locally produced goods
    in Brazil, 607, 622
    in India, 525, 533
    in Mexico, **592,** 593, 594
    in Nigeria, 687
    in South Africa, 654

import substitution industrialization, 592: In Mexico, the political-economic model followed during the authoritarian regime of the PRI, in which the domestic economy was protected by high tariffs in order to promote industrial growth

Independent Unionist Party, *222*
Index of Globalization, 711, *712–713*

elections in, *142,* 143–144
happiness in, *108*
imperialism and colonialism in, 143, 491, 632
infant mortality rate in, 500
post-imperialism in, 496

inductive reasoning, 7, 14, 15: Research that works from case studies in order to generate hypotheses

industrial policy (in Japan), 348: In Japan, government measures designed to promote economic and industrial development

Industrial Revolution, 38, 77, 178, 203, 226
industrial sector
    in Asia and Latin America compared, 506–507
    in Brazil, 607, 609
    in China, 471–472, 473, 474–475, 476–477, 506
    in developed democracies, 178, 179, *180,* 194, 195
    in export-oriented industrialization, 498–499, 501, 504
    in France, 287
    in Germany, 293, 296, 317, 318
    in globalization, 694
    in India, 525, 531, 533, 535
    in Iran, 563, 564
    in Japan, 325, 345, 348, 349
        and bureaucracy, 339
        and civil society, 345, 346
        historical development of, 326, 329, 330
        post-World War II, 331
    in Mexico, 592, 593, 594
    in Nigeria, 687
    in post-imperialism, 498–499
    in Russia, 422, 423, 438
    in South Africa, 379, 654, 655
    in United Kingdom, 203, 208, 209, 226, 227
    in United States, 238
infant mortality rate, 489, 500, *623*

inflation, 92: An outstripping of supply by demand, resulting in an increase in the general price level of goods and services and the resulting loss of value in a country's currency
    in Brazil, 608, 609, 622
    in China, 406
    and deflation, **92,** 92–93, 349
    in Germany, 298
    and hyperinflation, **92,** 298, 437–438
    in India, 534
    in Iran, 563, 564
    in Japan, 349
    in Mexico, 593
    in Nigeria, 670, 687
    in Russia, 437–438
    in South Africa, 653, 655
    in United States, 253
    in Venezuela, 84–85, 92
    in Zimbabwe, 355

informal economy/sector, 198, **504,** 504–505: A segment of the economy that is not regulated or taxed by the state
    in Brazil, 622
    in Iran, 564
    in Mexico, **595**

informal institutions, 17: Institutions with unwritten and unofficial rules

information-based economy, 195, 200, 703
information technology in India, 535
Inglehart World Values Survey, 77, 80, *80*

initiative, 169: A national vote called by members of the public to address a specific proposal
    in Germany, 308
    in United States, 246, 252

Inkatha Freedom Party (IFP), 646, 647, *647*: The small Zulu political party in South Africa that is currently a party in opposition to the African National Congress

instant-runoff voting, 164
institutional factors in political violence, 120, 121–122, 137
    in Arab Spring, 138
    in religious violence, 133
    in revolutions, 124–125
    in terrorism, 130
Institutional Revolutionary Party, 374

institution, 5, 16–17: An organization or activity that is self-perpetuating and valued for its own sake
    in democratic state, 152–155
    in developed democracies, 177, 183–184, 185–200
    in developing countries, 488–492, 502–503
    economic, 85, 94, 120
        in postcommunist countries, 403–407
    in ethnic identity, 56
    formal and informal, **17**
    in globalization, 697–699
    in imperialism, 488–492
    political. *See* political institutions
    in postcommunist countries, 398–410
    societal, 120, 407–410
    in states, 28–29, 31, *32*

intellectual property, 87, 498
interest rates, 92, 94

intergovernmental organization (IGO), 698, 699, 708, 714: Group created by states to serve certain policy ends

intergovernmental system, 186: A system in which two or more countries cooperate on issues

International Atomic Energy Agency (IAEA), 566
International Criminal Court, 426, 700
International Monetary Fund (IMF), 594, 603, 655
    in developing countries, 499
    in economic globalization, 702, 714
    in Greece, 702
    in Nigeria, 670

international regime, 698: The fundamental rules and norms that link states together and shape their relationships to one another, usually regarding some specific issues (such as greenhouse gases or trade)

international relations, 5: A field in political science that concentrates on relations between countries, such as foreign policy, war, trade, and foreign aid
    and democratization, 151, 171
    in globalization, 697
    and nondemocratic rule, 364

International Telegraph Union (ITU), 708
Internet
    access in different countries, *589*
    and Arab Spring, 139
    in China, 466, *467*, 471, 559, 710
    in economic globalization, 114
    in globalization, 697, 698–699, 700, 701, 706, 710
    intellectual property on, 87
    in Iran, 559, 712–713
    in Mexico, 589, *589,* 590
    surveillance on, 367
Inter-Services Intelligence agency, *49*
Interstate Commerce Commission, 239
Inuit, 190, 435
Iran, 541–567
    alcohol and drug use in, 566–567
    branches of government in, 551–554
    civil society in, 549, 558–559
    Constitutional Revolution in (1906), **546**
    constitution of, 550, 551, 554, 563, 564
    corruption in, *494*, 563, *626*
    economic inequality in, *103*, 563–564, *657*
    economic liberalization in, *110*, 562
    elections in, 554–555, 556–558, 559
    electoral system in, 554–555
    essential political features in, 551
    ethnic and national identity in, 541–543, 546, 559–560, *560*, 562–563
    fundamentalism in, 541, 551
    gender equality in, *105, 410*, 557, 558–559
    Gini index on, *103, 657*
    in globalization, 711–713
    gross domestic product of, *103, 180, 256,* 564
    happiness in, *108*
    historical development of state, 543–550
    Human Development Index on, *105, 623*
    ideology and political culture in, 561–563
    imperialism in, 488
    and Iraq, 550, 555, 556, 558, 564, 565
    Islamic Republic of, 541, 544, **550**
    judiciary in, 552, 554
    labor force in, *563*
    legislature in, 553–554
        election to, 554–555, 557
    local government in, 555
    map of, *542*

    modernization of, 546–550, 563
    national priorities in, *439*
    nondemocratic regime in, 360, 364
    nuclear technology in, 543, 557, 558, 564, *565,* 565–566
    oil in. *See* oil, in Iran
    personality cult in, 369
    political conflict and competition in, 556–559
    political economy in, 563–565
    political institutions in, 547, 551
    political parties in, 556
    political reform in, 545–546, 555, 556–558
    political regime in, 550–556
    presidents in, 553
        election of, 554, 555, 557–558, 559
    prime ministers in, 548
    religion in. *See* religion, in Iran
    renewable energy in, *319*
    Revolutionary Guard in, 553, **555,** 555–556, 561, 565
    revolution of 1979 in, 124, 127, 375–376, 440, 541, 543, 565
        and constitution, 550, 551, 563
        and Khomeini, 549–550
        and political culture, 562
        and political economy, 563–564
        and political parties, 556
    and Russia, 545, 546, 547, 566
    society in, 559–563
    structure of government in, *552*
    supreme leader of, 376, **552,** 552–553, 554, 556, 557, 558
    taxation in, *256*
    theocracy in, 375–376
    timeline of political development in, *545*
    totalitarianism in, 376
    and United States, 364, 547, 563, 711
        in Ahmadinejad presidency, 557
        economic policies in, 562
        Iranian views of, *561, 562*
        in Khomeini rule, 549, 550
        in Mosaddeq overthrow, 548
        nuclear technology concerns in, 566
        in White Revolution, 551
    voter turnout in, 554
    wealth measures in, *103, 105*
    White Revolution in, **548,** 551, 563

Iran-Iraq War, 550, 555, 558, 564, 565: The 1980–1988 conflict between the two countries, started by Iraq

Iraq, 31, 364, 557
    civil war in, 5
    devolution process in, 43
    as fragile state, *46–47*
    international relations of, 151
    invasion of, 122, 138
    and Iran, 550, 555, 556, 558, 564, 565
    Islamic State in, 710
    Islam in, 118, 122, 375, 409, 496, 543, 710

Kurdistan, 560, 709
Kurds, 559, 560
Kurile Islands, 351–352
KwaZulu, 646
Kyrgyzstan, *400, 401,* 440, 441

Labastida, Francisco, 575, 586: In Mexico, the first-ever PRI candidate to lose a presidential election; he was defeated in 2000 by Vicente Fox of the PAN

labor force
    in Brazil, *622*
    in China, *472,* 474
        floating population in, **454,** 454–455, 465
    in Fair Trade policies, 481–482
    in France, 281, *287,* 288, 290
    in Germany, 313, 315, 317, *317,* 318, 319
    in globalization, 703–704
    in India, *535,* 535–536
    in Iran, *563*
    in Japan, 347, *349*
    in Mexico, 588, 592, 593, *593,* 595
    in Nigeria, *688*
    in Russia, *438*
    in South Africa, 648, *653,* 654
    in United Kingdom, *227*
    in United States, *255*
labor strikes in France, 281, 286, 288, 291
labor unions, 73
    in Brazil, 619
    in France, 279, 280, 281
    in Germany, 313–314, 317, 318
    in India, 528–529
    in Mexico, 574, 575, 588–589
    in Nigeria, 667, 684
    in South Africa, 500, 636, 643, 648, 654
    in United Kingdom, 209, 223
    in United States, 254

Labour Party, 205, 209, 210, 221: One of the United Kingdom's two largest parties; since 2010, it has been the party in opposition
    and Blair, 205, 213, 219, 220
    and Brexit vote, 231
    and civil society, 223
    economic policies of, 226, 227
    in electoral system, 216, 217, *217*
    in House of Commons, 163, *163,* 166, 167, 221, *222*
    ideology of, 219
    and local governments, 43, 217–218, 228
    and party system, 218, 219
    and trade unions, 209, 223

Lagos, 666, 685, 689

laïcité, **282,** 283, 284–286, 289: In France, the subordination of religious identity to state and national identity—state over church

laissez-faire, 95: The principle that the economy should be "allowed to do" what it wishes; a liberal system of minimal state interference in the economy

Länder, **304,** 304–305: German states

Landless Workers Movement (MST), 620: The large Brazilian social movement that has fought for land reform

land reform, 506–507
    in Brazil, 620
    in India, 536
    in Iran, 548
    in Japan, 326
    in Mexico, 574, 575, 583, 593, 594, 595
    in South Africa, 500, 655, 656
language
    in China, 466, *468*
    diversity in Africa, *65*
    in ethnic and national identity, 30, 56–57, 61, 62
    in France, 283, 284
    in Germany, 319
    in globalization, 696, 707
    in imperialism, 488
    in India, 44, 48, 54, 78, 511, 514, 524, 527, 530
    in Iran, 541, 559, 560
    in Japan, 326, 347
    in Mexico, 590
    in Nigeria, 666, 685
    as research challenge, 8, 9
    in rise of modern state, 37, 38
    in Russia, 430, 435
    in South Africa, 30, 632, 633, 638, 640, 650
    state power over, 42
    in United Kingdom, 205, 223, 224
Laos, 374, 402
latifundia, 507
Latin America. *See also specific countries.*
    and Asia compared, 506–507
    civil society in, 587
    communist regimes in, *386*
    culture in, 151
    democracy in, 3, 148, 149, 171, 592
    developing countries in, 483, 500
    economy in, 84, 112–113, 484, 500, 506–507
    Fair Trade in goods from, 481, 482
    happiness in, *108*
    immigration from, 193, 194, 256–257
    imperialism and colonialism in, 491, 492, 507, 708
    import substitution in, 498, 499
    middle income countries in, 484
    military rule in, 371, 373
    nondemocratic regimes in, 361, 366
    outsourcing to, 704
    political corruption in, 624
    political culture in, 80
    post-imperialism in, 492, 493, 496, 498

in France, 270, 271–272, 273–274
in Germany, 297, 302, 304, 305, 306
in India, 53, 521, 522, 523, 525
in Japan, 334–335, 336, 337, 340, 342
in Mexico, 577, 578, 579, 580
in mixed electoral systems, 167
in Nigeria, 675
in parliamentary systems, 155, 156, 302
in Russia, 426, 428
in South Africa, 638, 640
in United Kingdom, 209, 211, 213
in United States, 241

lower income countries, 484: Countries that lack significant economic development or political institutionalization or both; also known as less-developed countries (LDCs)

Lukashenko, Alexander, *441*

Maastricht Treaty, 169

MacArthur, Douglas, 331: The U.S. general who presided over the seven-year occupation of Japan (1945–52)

Macedonia, *400*, 401, 473
Machiavelli, Niccolò, 11, *12*
macro-level studies, 20

Macron, Emmanuel, 176, *270*, 274, **276**, 279–280: A young and relatively inexperienced centrist economist, elected president of France in 2017
    economic policies of, 288, 291
    election of (2017), *275*, *276*, 279, *279*

Madero, Francisco, 573: An initial leader of the Mexican Revolution and a landowner who sought moderate democratic reform

Madison, James, 161

Maduro, Nicolás, 84–85

Magna Carta, 147, **206**, 211: The 1215 document signed by King John of England that set the precedent for limited monarchical powers

Mahdi, 544, 549, 561: In Shiism, a term for the "hidden imam," the descendant of Muhammad who will return to earth to usher in a new age

Maimane, Mmusi, 646: The current leader of South Africa's Democratic Alliance and leader of the opposition in the National Assembly; he is the party's first black leader

Majlis, 546, 547, 548, 553–554, 555, 556–557: Legislature of Iran

majoritarian (system), 162, 164, 166, 167, **211**: Term describing the virtually unchecked power of a parliamentary majority in the UK political system
    in France, 273
    in United Kingdom, **211**, 218

Malan, Daniel, 634
malaria, 508
Malaya, 331
Malaysia, 170
    corruption in, 493
    post-imperialism in, 496
    societal globalization and trust in, 711, *712*
Malaysia Airlines Flight 17, downing of, *382*, 435
Malema, Julius, 644, 649, 650, 655
Mali, 158
Manchuria, 326, 330
Mandarin language, 466

Mandela, Nelson, 41, 378, **635**, 643, 644: The long-imprisoned leader of the African National Congress who became South Africa's first post-apartheid president
    arrest of, 635
    call for rainbow nation, 649
    death of, *637*
    economic policies of, 654
    HIV/AIDS policies of, 660
    and transition to democracy, 636–637, *637*
    Zuma eulogy for, *628*, 644

Maoism, 469–470

Mao Zedong, 389, 391, 392, 393, **450**, 451–452, *463*: Leader of the Chinese Communist revolution who dominated Chinese politics from the founding of the PRC until his death in 1976
    anticorruption campaign of, 478
    charismatic leadership of, 126
    civil society under, 464
    consolidation of state under, 38
    Cultural Revolution of, 392, 394, 413, **451**, 452, *452*, 462, 469, 470, 472
    danwei system of, **454**, 470
    death of, 452, 459, 462, 463, 470, 472
    economic policies of, 471–472, 474
    Great Leap Forward of, 393, 413, **451**, 470, 472
    inclusion of peasants in CCP, 462
    judiciary under, 460
    People's Liberation Army under, 461
    political culture under, 469–470
    Reds versus experts policy of, **472**
    totalitarian regime of, 360

maquiladoras, 594, 594–595: In Mexico, factories that import goods or parts to manufacture goods that are then exported

Marbury v. Madison, 243
marijuana, legalization of, 43, 44
marketization in postcommunist countries, 403, 404

market, 86, 86–87, 94: The interaction between the forces of supply and demand that allocates resources
    in communism, 98, 99, 393
    in economic recession (2008), 714
    and free market policies. *See* free market policies

market (*continued*)
    globalization of, 703, 714, 715
    housing bubble in, 254, 714
    in liberalism, 95, 96, 98
    in mercantilism, 98, 100
    in postcommunist countries, 403, 404
    in social democracy, 96, 98
    state regulation of, 87, 93
    supply and demand in, 86, 87

Marx, Karl, 11, 96, 101
    on class identity, 224
    and communism, 97–98, 101, 385, 386–389, 391, 392, 414
    on economic development and inequality, 12, 101
    on gender relations, 394
    on phases of human history, 388–389
    on religion, 394
    on revolution, 388–390
    terms in theory of, 387
Marxism, 387, 642
Mary II, Queen of England, 207
Mateen, Omar, 136–137
materialism, dialectical, 387, **388**
Mauer im Kopf, 316, 403

May, Theresa, 205, 210, 220, *220,* 221–222, 227, 228, 230: Leader of the Conservatives in the United Kingdom; prime minister and head of government since 2016

Maya, 571, 590

May Fourth movement, 448, 448–449: In China, a student-led anti-imperialist cultural and political movement growing out of student demonstrations in Beijing on May 4, 1919

Mbeki, Thabo, 642, 643, 644, 648, 649, 659, 660: South Africa's former two-term president who was forced to resign in 2008 when he failed to win the election as the African National Congress leader

McDonald's, 707
McKinley, William, 136
McVeigh, Timothy, 135, 137
means of production, 387, 392
media
    censorship of. *See* censorship
    in China, 412, 413
    in communist and postcommunist countries, *400*
    in developing countries, 504
    in illiberal regimes, 377
    in India, 529
    in Iran, 559, 712–713
    in Japan, 336, 344
    in Mexico, 575, 586, 589–590
    in Nigeria, 672
    in personality cult, 369
    in Russia, 434–435
    social media. *See* social media

    in South Africa, 30, 648–649
    in United States, 249, 259
Medvedev, Dimitri, 419–420, 426, 427, *428*

Meiji oligarchs, 326, 329, 329–330: The vanguard of junior samurai who led Japan's nineteenth-century modernization drive

Meiji Restoration, 329, 329–330: Japan's 1867–68 "revolution from above," which launched Japan's modernization in the name of the Meiji emperor
    constitution in, 329, 334

Mélenchon, Jean-Luc, *275*
melting pot, 200, 251, 257

Member of Parliament (MP), 213, 214, 215, 222–223: In the United Kingdom, an individual legislator in the House of Commons

mensalão scandal, 624
Menzies, Robert, 156

mercantilism, 99, 109, 112, 146: A political-economic system in which national economic power is paramount and the domestic economy is viewed as an instrument that exists primarily to serve the needs of the state
    in China, 473
    in developed democracy, 182, *183*
    export-oriented industrialization in, 498–499, 501
    in France, 264, 287
    in Germany, 295, 299
    Gini index in, 104
    in imperialism and colonialism, 491
    import substitution in, 498, 501
    in India, 518, 525, 533
    in Iran, 563
    in Japan, 100, 101–102, 323, 325, 329, 345, 348, 349
    in Mexico, 180
    political-economic system in, 95, 98, *101*
    in post-imperialism, 498
    in Russia, 406
    in South Africa, 499, 654

Merkel, Angela, *292, 303,* **309,** 313–314: Germany's current conservative chancellor, as of 2017
    coalition government of, 308, *310*
    and Eurozone economic crisis, 309, 313
    foreign policies of, 309
    immigration policies of, 320
    nuclear energy policy of, 311, 314, 318

mestizaje, 590

mestizos, 572, 590: Mexicans of mixed European and indigenous blood, who make up the vast majority of Mexico's population

Mexican-American War, 237, 237–238, **572**: The conflict between Mexico and the United States (1846–48) that resulted in U.S. acquisition of half of Mexico's territory, much of the current Southwest of the United States

Andrés Manuel López Obrador, a two-time presidential candidate for the PRD

Morocco, *712*

Mosaddeq, Mohammad, 548: Prime minister of Iran; deposed in 1953 by Operation Ajax

Moscow, 420, 421, 426
    local government in, 430, 431, 435
    skyline of, *437*

motion of censure, 271, 272: In France, an act of legislature against the government, requiring new elections when proposed legislation submitted as matters of confidence are not passed

motion of confidence, 272, 304
Motlanthe, Kgalema, 643
Mousavi, Mir Hossein, 557, 558

Movement for the Emancipation of the Niger Delta (MEND), 683, 689, 691: In Nigeria, militant separatist group from the Niger Delta

Movement for the Survival of the Ogoni People (MOSOP), 682: In Nigeria, ethnic association founded by Ken Saro-Wiwa to promote interests of ethnic Ogoni in the Niger Delta

Movement of French Businesses (MEDEF), 281–282
Mubarak, Hosni, 4, *21,* 139
Mugabe, Robert, *354,* 355–357, 358, 378, 648

Mughals, 514: Muslim invaders who ruled India for several hundred years beginning in the sixteenth century

Muhammad (prophet), 40, **541,** 544, 549: Main prophet of Islam

Muhammed, Murtala, 670, *674*
Mukherjee, Pranab, 521

mulatto (population in Brazil), 604: A Brazilian of mixed white and black ancestry

multicausality, 8, 80: When variables are interconnected and interact together to produce particular outcomes

multiculturalism, 193, 706

multimember district, 164, 165: An electoral district with more than one seat
    in Iran, 555
    in Japan, 337
    in Russia, 430

multinational corporation (MNC), 698, 699, 701, 702: Firm that produces, distributes, and markets its goods or services in more than one country

Mumbai, 518
municípios (Brazil), 614

municipios **(Mexico), 580**: County-level governments in Mexican states

murder rate
    in Brazil, 624
    in South Africa, 650, 658
Muslim Brotherhood, 139

Muslim League, 25, 49, **516**: Indian Muslim independence organization

Muslims. *See* Islam
Myanmar, 135, 170, 171, 375

Nader, Ralph, 249
NAFTA, 181, 189, **575,** 593, 594–595, 596, **704,** 704–705, 716
Nagasaki bombing, 331
Napoleon I, Emperor of France (Napoleon Bonaparte), 264
    on China, 445
    and Holy Roman Empire, 295
    invasion of Germany, 295
    invasion of Spain and Portugal, 492, 606
    legal code of, 263, 264, 272–273
    nationalism under, 62–63
    populism of, 286
    referenda of, 169, 265
    rise and fall of, 30, 265
Napoleon III, Emperor of France, 266
Napoleonic Code, 264, 272–273
Napoleonic Wars, 606
Narmada Valley Project dam, 529

nation, 58: A group that desires self-government through an independent state

National Administrative School, 276, 279, 287
National Alliance, 135

National Assembly (France), 264, 266, 271–272, 273, 280: Lower house of the French parliament
    election to, 273–274, 276, *280*

National Assembly (Nigeria), 675, 676

National Assembly (South Africa), 638, 639, **640**: South Africa's legislature
    election to, 164, *165, 641, 647*

National Chamber of Commerce, 588
National Chamber of Industries, 588

national conflict, 63, 63–64, 79: A conflict in which one or more groups within a country develop clear aspirations for political independence, clashing with others as a result

National Congress (Brazil), 611, 611–612: Brazil's legislature

National Congress (Mexico), 577, 577–579: Mexico's bicameral legislature

National Council of Nigerian Citizens (NCNC), 667
National Council of Provinces, 640, 641

Navalny, Alexei, 431, 435

Naxalism, 527: Radical Maoist (or guerrilla communist) insurgency in India

Nazarbayev, Nursultan, *441*
Nazi Germany, 71, 266, 293, **298,** 298–299, 300
    as nondemocratic regime, 358, 359, 360

Nehru, Jawaharlal, 516, 517, 525, 532: India's first prime minister (1947–64) and successor to Mahatma Gandhi as leader of the INC

Nemtsov, Boris, 435

neocolonialism, 498, 506: An indirect form of imperialism in which powerful countries overly influence the economies of less-developed countries

neocorporatism, 223

neoliberalism/structural-adjustment programs/ Washington consensus, 499: A policy of economic liberalization adopted in exchange for financial support from liberal international organizations; typically includes privatizing state-run firms, ending subsidies, reducing tariff barriers, shrinking the size of the state, and welcoming foreign investment
    in India, 525, 526
    in Mexico, 571, 575, 582–583, 584, 588, 590, 594, 595
    in Nigeria, 670
    in South Africa, 655
    in United Kingdom, **205,** 209, 219, 226, 227, 518
    in United States, 518

neo-Nazi parties, 306
Nepal, 43
Netherlands, 187, 711, *712*
netizens in China, 466, *467*
Nevada, 237, 572
Neves, Tancredo, 609

New Deal, 239, 246: A set of policies implemented in the United States between 1933 and 1938 that used state intervention to stimulate the economy and counter the effects of the Great Depression

New Delhi, 519
New Komei Party (NKP), 340, *341,* 342
New Labour Party, 210
New Mexico, 237, 572
New National Party (NNP), *647*
New Silk Road, 441
New York, 235
New Zealand, 702
    economic liberalization in, *110*
    happiness in, *108*
    immigrant population in, 193
    liberalism in, 96
    referenda in, 168
Nice, terrorist attack in, 263, 277, 286

Nicholas I of Russia, 421–422
Nicholas II of Russia, 422
Niger, *46–47,* 106

Niger Delta, 677, 679, 680, 688, 689: World's third-largest wetland and source of Nigerian oil and economic and ethnic conflict
    Movement for the Emancipation of the Niger Delta, **683,** 689, 691
    oil and environmental concerns in, 682–684, 690–691

Nigeria, 663–691
    branches of government in, 673–676
    civil society in, 667, 682–684
    Civil War in, 668, 677, 685
    colonial rule of, 38, 666–668, 672
    constitution of. *See* constitution, of Nigeria
    corruption in. *See* corruption, in Nigeria
    economic growth in, 494
    economic inequality in, *103, 657, 662,* 663, 665, 680, 681
    economic liberalization in, *110*
    elections in, 670, 679–682
        corruption and fraud in, 676, 679, 680–681
        presidential, 670, 671, 673, *674,* 676, *677,* 679–682
    electoral system in, 162, 676–677
    environmental issues in, *662,* 665, 682–684, 690, 691
    essential political features in, 671
    ethnic and national identity in. *See* ethnic and national identity, in Nigeria
    fear about foreign influence in, *533*
    First Republic of, **668,** 679
    Fourth Republic of. *See* Fourth Republic (Nigeria)
    as fragile state, *46–47*
    Gini index on, *103, 657*
    gross domestic product of, *103, 180, 256*
    happiness in, *108*
    historical development of state, 665–671
    Human Development Index on, *105,* 688
    ideology and political culture in, 685–686
    importance of democracy and economy in, *684*
    independence of, 667–668, 672
    judiciary in, 675–676
    labor force in, *688*
    legislature in, 668, 672, 675
        election to, 676–677, *683*
        political parties in, 679
        salary in, 687
    local government in, 677–678, 679
    map of, *664*
    military rule in, 373–374, 663, 665, 668–671, 672, 678, 679, 689
    morality in, *284*
    national priorities in, *439*
    natural resources of, *662,* 663, 666, 686
    oil in. *See* oil, in Nigeria
    patrimonialism in, 373, **671**
    political conflict and competition in, 678–684
    political economy of, 474, 686–689

nihilism, 130: A belief that all institutions and values are essentially meaningless and that the only redeeming value is violence

***nomenklatura* (of Communist Party), 390,** 390–391, 392, **422**: Politically sensitive or influential jobs in the state, society, or economy that were staffed by people chosen or approved by the Communist Party

nondemocratic regime, 29, 355–381: A political regime that is controlled by a small group of individuals who exercise power over the state without being constitutionally responsible to the public

nongovernmental organization (NGO), 698: A national or international group, independent of any state, that pursues policy objectives and fosters public participation

nontariff regulatory barriers, 94, 100, 102: Policies and regulations used to limit imports through methods other than taxation

North American Free Trade Agreement (NAFTA), 181, 189, **575,** 593, 594–595, 596, **704,** 704–705, 716: An agreement between Canada, Mexico, and the United States that liberalizes trade between the three countries

Northern Ireland, 43, 163, 166, 190, 191, **224**: Northeastern portion of Ireland that is part of the United Kingdom; also known as Ulster

pacifism
in Germany, 311, 402
in Japan, *322*
Pact for Mexico (2013), 577, 579

Pahlavi, Mohammad Reza, 547, 547–550: Monarch of Iran from 1941 to 1979

Pahlavi, Reza Shah, 546, 546–548: Monarch of Iran from 1925 to 1941

Pahlavi dynasty, 546–548, 563
Pakistan, 560
and Afghanistan, 48, 441
British colonialism in, 224
corruption in, *494*
drug production in, 567
election of 2013 in, 25, 26
energy problems in, *24,* 25–26, 39, 48, 503
as failing state, 48–49, 78
as fragile state, *46–47*
gender imbalance in population of, 497
happiness in, *108*
and India, 48–49, 78, 441, 516, 519, 530, *531*
as irrational state, 48
Islam in, 25, 48, 516, 530
military rule in, 495
nuclear technology in, 26, 39, 48, *49,* 565
state capacity and autonomy in, 48
terrorism based in, 48, 128, 518
Pakistan Muslim League, 25
Palestinians, 60, 61, *108*
Pan Africanist Congress (PAC), 636
Panhellenic Socialist Movement, 198

parastatal, 99: Industry partially owned by the state

Paris, 266, 274, 284
terrorist attack in, 140, *260, 263,* 277, 286
Paris Commune, 266

parlement, 271, 271–272: France's bicameral legislature

parliamentary commissions of investigation, 612

parliamentary system, 155, 155–156: A political system in which the roles of head of state and head of government are assigned to separate executive offices
benefits and drawbacks of, 158, 159
executive powers in, 157
in France, 261
in Germany, 302, 303, 304–305
in India, 519, 520, 522
in Japan, 329, 336
in Nigeria, 672
political parties in, 155, 161
proportional representation in, 166, 168
in Russia, 426, 428–429
single-member districts in, 163–164, 166–167, 168
in South Africa, 638–640
in United Kingdom, 206, 211–217

Parliament (United Kingdom), 206, 207, 208, 212, 214–215: Name of the UK legislature
democratization of, 209
in hung parliament, **210,** 220, 221
immigration policies of, 225
majority in, 211
prime minister as member of, 213

Partido Acción Nacional (PAN), 575, 576, 580, 583, 584–585, 586: Conservative Catholic Mexican political party that until 2000 was the main opposition to the PRI
election results, 578, *585*
and political culture, 592

Partido de la Revolución Democrática (PRD), 581, 583, 585: Mexico's main party of the left
economic policies of, 588
election results, 582, 583, *585*
and political culture, 592

Partido Nacional Revolucionario, 574

Partido Revolucionario Institucional (PRI), 525, 569, 571, 574–577, 581–582: Political party that emerged from the Mexican Revolution to preside over an authoritarian regime that lasted until 2000
and civil society, 586–590
economic policies of, 583, 588, 592–593
election results, 575, 578, 580, 582, *585*
and electoral fraud, 575, 577, 581, 596
erosion of power (1980–2000), 575–576, 591–592
and ethnic identity, 590
in legislature, 575, 578, 582
in local government, 580–581, 582
opposition to, 581, 584
and PAN, 584–585
in party system, 581–585
and political culture, 591–592
in presidency, 574–575, 582, 585–586

parties of power (in Russia), 431, 431–432: Russian parties created by political elites to support their political aspirations; typically lacking any ideological orientation

partition (of India and Pakistan), 48–49, 78, **516,** 530: Creation of the new states of Pakistan and India from the South Asian British colony of India in 1947

Party of the Brazilian Democratic Movement (PMDB), *617,* 618
Party of the Republic (PR), *617,* 619

party-state, 392, 398: A political system in which power flows directly from the ruling political party (usually a communist party) to the state, bypassing government structures
in China, 453, 454, 455, 461, 464, 466, 469, 473, 477

party system. *See* political parties
path dependence, 18

patrimonialism, 138, **370,** 370–371, 493, 496: An arrangement whereby a ruler depends on a collection of supporters within the state who gain direct benefits in return for enforcing the ruler's will
    in Brazil, 611
    in Nigeria, 373, **671**
    in Syria, 117–118, 138

PATRIOT Act (2001), 137
Patriotic Europeans against the Islamization of the West (PEGIDA), 312, *320*

patriotism, 55, **61:** Pride in one's state
    in France, 283, 284, 286
    in Germany, 296, 316
    in Nigeria, 685–686
    in Russia, 437
    in South Africa, 649, 650

patron-client relationships, 582: Relationships in which powerful government officials deliver state services and access to power in exchange for the delivery of political support
    in Brazil, 618
    in Mexico, **582,** 596

Paul, Rand, 248
Pearl Harbor attack, 326
Pedro I, Emperor of Brazil, 606
Pedro II, Emperor of Brazil, 606

PEMEX, 593, 596: Mexico's powerful state-owned oil monopoly

Peña Nieto, Enrique, 571, 577, 599: Mexico's current president and the first PRI member to be elected president since the return of democracy in 2000
    antidrug policies of, 597–598
    economic policies of, 571, 582, 588, 593, 595, 596
    election of (2012), 576, 582, 586
    electoral reforms of, 580
    judicial system under, 579
    labor policies of, 589
    legislature under, 578, 579
    media under, 589, 590

Pennsylvania, 235
Pentagon, terrorist attack on, 17
Pentecostal movement in Brazil, 621

People's Democratic Party (PDP), 676, 677, 679, 680, *683*: Political party that has dominated Nigerian politics since its formation in 1998; its base was originally the Hausa Muslim ethnic group of northern Nigeria

People's Liberation Army (PLA), 450, 452, 461–462: China's military

People's Militia, 555, 556
People's Republic of China, 450

perestroika, 396, 424: Literally, "restructuring"; the policy of political and economic liberalization implemented in the Soviet Union in the late 1980s

Perot, Ross, 248–249
Perry, Matthew C., 328–329

Persia, 544, 546: Name for Iran before 1935

Persian Empire, 560, 708
Persian Gulf, 362, 371, 560
Persians in Iran, 541, 543–544, 559, 560
personality cult, 41, 360, 369–370
    of Putin, 369, 432
    of Stalin, 360, 369, 423
personal rule, 370–371, 372
Peru, 59–60, 131, 132, *712*
Peter the Great (of Russia), 421
Petrobras, 160, 613, 625
Petry, Frauke, *312*
Philippe, Édouard, *279,* 280, 291
Philippines, 170, 171, 331
philosophy in study of politics, 11, 22, 33
Pierce, William, 135
piracy, 44
Pirate Party, 312
Plaid Cymru, 163, *163,* 221, *222*
plurality systems, 155, 162–163, 182
    in Canada, 162, 163
    in Germany, 168
    in India, 162, 523
    majority-based systems compared to, 164
    in mixed electoral system, 167
    in Nigeria, 162
    proportional representation compared to, 164, 165, 166
    in Russia, 430
    in South Africa, 640, 641
    in United Kingdom, 162, 163, *163,* 216, 217, 220
    in United States, 162, 163, 242, 244, 245, 246
Poland
    corruption in, *400, 405*
    as developed democracy, 179, *180,* 182
    economic indicators in, *180, 405*
    in European Union, 188
    gender equality in, *410*
    and Germany relations, 299, 315
    gross domestic product of, *180, 405*
    political transitions in, postcommunist, 399, *400, 401*
    societal globalization and trust in, *713*
police
    in Brazil, 615, 620, 624
    in imperialism, 488
    as institution, 17
    in Mexico, 571, 581, 582
        confidence in, *591*
        and drug trafficking, 596, 597, 598
    in power of state, 28
    in South Africa, *652,* 658, 659
    in surveillance, 367

Politburo (of Communist Party), 391: The top policy-making and executive body of a communist party
    in China, *455,* 456, 460
    in Soviet Union, **423,** 424

political action committees, 250

political attitude, 55, **66,** 66–69, 81: Description of one's views regarding the speed and methods with which political changes should take place in a given society
    in fundamentalism, 75–76
    and ideologies, 74
    on political violence, 66, 67, 120–121
    spectrum of, 66–68, *68*

political conflict and competition, 161, 182, 184
    in Brazil, 616–620
    in China, 462–466
    in France, 275–282
    in Germany, 308–314
    in India, 524–529
    in Iran, 556–559
    in Japan, 340–346
    in Mexico, 581–590
    in Nigeria, 678–684
    in Russia, 431–435
    in South Africa, 642–649
    in United Kingdom, 218–223
    in United States, 246–250
political control in nondemocratic regimes, 366–370

political culture, 76, 76–81, 151: The basic norms for political activity in a society
    in Brazil, 621
    in China, 469–471
    in democracy, 364
    in France, 263, 286, 287, 290
    in Germany, 316–317, 403
    in India, 530, 531–532
    in Iran, 556, 561–563
    in Japan, 347–348
    in Mexico, 590–592
    in Nigeria, 685–686
    in nondemocratic rule, 364–365
    in Russia, 436–437
    in South Africa, 651–653
    in United Kingdom, 225–226
    in United States, 251–253

political-economic system, 94, 94–114: The relationship between political and economic institutions in a particular country and the policies and outcomes they create
    in communism, 95, 97–99, 386, 392–394
    comparison of, 102–109
    in developed democracies, 181–182
    happiness in, 107–109, *108*
    Human Development Index on, 105–106
    inequality and poverty in, 104–105
    in liberalism, 95–96, 98, 109–114

    in mercantilism, 95, 98, 99–102
    in social democracy, 95, 96–97, 98, 101, 146
    wealth in, 102–109

political economy, *82,* 83–115: The study of the interaction between states and markets
    in Brazil, 474, 609, 622–623
    in China, 471–476
    communist, 392–394
    components of, 86–94
    definition of, **85**
    in developed democracies, 181–182
    in developing countries, 498–499, 502
    in France, *183,* 261, 286–288, 290–291
    in Germany, *183,* 317–318
    in globalization, 704
    in India, 410–411, 474, 533–536
    in Iran, 563–565
    in Japan, *183,* 348–350
    markets and property in, 86–87, 403–404
    in Mexico, 474, 569, 571, 575, 592–596
    money, inflation, and economic growth in, 90–93
    in Nigeria, 474, 686–689
    in postcommunist countries, 403–407
    in post-imperialism, 498–499
    public goods in, 88–89
    regulation of, 87, 93
    in Russia, 437–440
    social expenditures in, 89–90
    in South Africa, 474, 499–500, 653–658
    in Soviet Union, 19, 106–107, 423
    taxation in, 90
    trade in, 93–94
    in United Kingdom, *183,* 226–228
    in United States, *183,* 253–256
    in Venezuela, *82,* 83–85, 112, 113
political engagement in developing countries, 503–504
political globalization, 694, 699–701, 709–710

political ideology, 55, 66, **69,** 69–73, 81: The basic values held by an individual about the fundamental goals of politics or the ideal balance of freedom and equality
    and attitudes, 74
    in Brazil, 621
    in China, 469–471
    in France, 286
    on freedom and equality, 72, *72*
    in Germany, 316–317
    in globalization, 694
    in India, 531–532
    in Iran, 561–563
    in Japan, 347–348
    in Mexico, 590–592
    in Nigeria, 685–686
    of political parties, 161
    in Russia, 436–437
    in South Africa, 651–653
    in totalitarianism, 261, 359, 360

state control that is politically motivated (*continued*)
  in globalization, 137
  and hate crimes, 136–137
  ideational factors in, **120,** 120–121. *See also* ideational
      factors in political violence
  in India, 78
  individual factors in, 121. *See also* individual factors in
      political violence
  institutional factors in, 120. *See also* institutional factors
      in political violence
  in Iran, 543
  in Japan, 330
  in Mexico, 574, 580
  in Nigeria, 665, *681,* 684
  in nondemocratic regimes, 359, 366–367, 371
  origin of political organization in, 33–34
  in Pakistan, 26
  political attitudes on, 66, 67, 120–121
  and political culture, 77
  religion as motivation in, 76, 121, 130, 132, 133–136,
      137
  in revolutions, 122–127
  in South Africa, 129, 379, 603, 631, 652
  in Syria, *116,* 117–118
  in terrorism, 122–123, 127–133
  in totalitarianism, 359, 360, 366–367
  in United States, 134, 135, 136–137
  in Zimbabwe, 379

politics, 6: The struggle in any group for power that will
give one or more persons the ability to make decisions for
the larger group
  globalization of, 694, 699–701, 709–710
  need for study of, 22
  philosophical approach to study of, 11, 22, 33
  science of, 20–21. *See also* political science

pollution. *See also* environmental issues
  in China, *444,* 447, 461, 475, 476–477, *477*
  in Germany, 314
  modern and postmodern values on, 192
  state regulations on, 93
Pompidou, Georges, *270, 277*
Popper, Karl, 20
population
  aging of. *See* aging population
  of China, 445, 663
      gender imbalance in, 497
  of India, 445, 511, 514, 522, 536, 663
      gender imbalance in, 497
  of United States, 200, 253
Population Registration Act (1950), 634

populism, 363: A political view that does not have a consistent
ideological foundation, but that emphasizes hostility toward
elites and established state and economic institutions and
favors greater power in the hands of the public
  in Brazil, 608, 609
  in China, **475**

in devolution, 191
in France, 278, **286,** 288
in Germany, 312
in Greece, 199
in Japan, 344
in South Africa, 629, 631, 643, 658
in United Kingdom, 176, 221
in United States, 248, **251,** 251–252, 363

populism (in the United States), 251: A key feature
of U.S. ideology; the idea that the masses should dominate
elites and that the popular will should trump those with
professional expertise

populists (in China), 475: Faction of Chinese Communist
Party officials who have risen from relatively humble
backgrounds and who favor decreasing inequality

Porfiriato, 572

pork-barrel projects, 336: Government appropriation or
other policy supplying funds for local improvements to
ingratiate legislators with their constituents
  in Brazil, 614, 616
  in Japan, **336,** 341

Portugal
  and China, 448
  corporatism in, 368
  culture in, 151
  economic indicators in, 405, *405*
  imperialism and colonialism of, 37, 112, 487, 492, 507, 514
      in Brazil, 603, 604–606
      in India, 514
  invasion by Napoleon, 492, 606
postal savings system in Japan, 342
postcommunism, 178, 384, 398–414
  economic institutions in, 403–407, 419
  political institutions in, 398–402
  in Russia, 417–443
  societal institutions in, 407–410
  in Ukraine, 383–384
post-imperialism, 492–500
  corruption in, 493, 494–495
  creating nations and citizens in, 496–497
  economic growth in, 497–499
  in India, 513
  state capacity and autonomy in, 493–496
postindustrialism, 703
  in developed democracies, 177, 194–195
post-materialist values in Germany, 317

postmodern, 184: Characterized by a set of values that
center on "quality of life" considerations and give less
attention to material gain
  values in, 191–194, 200, 477

poverty, 104
  in Brazil, 45–46, 601, 603, 622–623, *623,* 624
  in China, 102

party system under, 428, 431, 432, 433
and patrimonialism in Russia, 371
personality cult of, 369, 432
reelection as president (2012), 420, 425, 426, *428,* 430, 434, 438
semi-presidential system under, 426
term limits on, 425, 426, 430
and Ukraine, 384

Putnam, Robert, 255

Qajar dynasty, 544–546, 566
Qin dynasty, 38, 447
Qing dynasty, 126, 448

qualitative method, 14, 15: Study through an in-depth investigation of a limited number of cases

quangos, 223: In the United Kingdom, quasi-autonomous nongovernmental organizations that assist the government in making policy

quantitative method, 14, 15: Study through statistical data from many cases

Québec, 59
question time
in France, 272
in India, 522
in South Africa, 640
in United Kingdom, 213, 214

quietists, 561, 562: Description of view within Shiism that rejects theocracy and the direct role of religion in the state

quota (in trade), 94: A nontariff barrier that limits the quantity of a good that may be imported into a country

quota system (in Brazil), 58, 621
Quotations from Chairman Mao Zedong, 451, *452*

racial issues, 57–58
in Brazil, 57, 58, 620–621
in France, 285
in Germany, 299
in imperialism and colonialism, 489
in South Africa, 30, 57–58, 60, 629, 631, 633, 649–650
in United States, *252,* 255
racial quota systems in Brazil, 58, 621

radicals, 66: Those with a political attitude that favors dramatic, often revolutionary change
political attitudes of, 66, 67, 68, *68,* 69, 74, 75
and totalitarianism, 359

Rafsanjani, Ali Akbar Hashemi, 554, 557, 562: President of Iran from 1989 to 1997; current head of the Expediency Council

rainbow nation, 58, 649–650

raj, 517, 529: Hindu word for "rule"
license raj, **533,** 536, 538

Rally for the Republic (RPR), 275, 277–278: Party formed by Jacques Chirac as the more nationalist, socially conservative, Euroskeptic force of the French right

Ramphele, Mamphela, 644
rape
in India, 521, 529, 537–538
in South Africa, 658
in United States, 538

rational choice, 14, 14–15: Approach that assumes that individuals weigh the costs and benefits and make choices to maximize their benefits

rational-legal legitimacy, 40, 40–41, 42: Legitimacy based on a system of laws and procedures that are highly institutionalized

rational states, 48

reactionaries, 67: Those who seek to restore the institutions of a real or an imagined earlier order
political attitudes of, 67–68, *68,* 69, 74, 75
and totalitarianism, 359

Reagan, Ronald, 254, 255, 396, 518
reasoning
deductive, **7,** 9
inductive, **7**
Reconstruction and Development Programme (RDP), 654

red capitalists, 464, 464–465: In China, Private entrepreneurs who are also members of the Chinese Communist Party and whose interests generally align with those of the party-state

Red Cross, 495, 503, 708

Red Guard, 451, *452,* 462: In China, radicalized youth who served as Mao Zedong's shock troops during the Cultural Revolution

Reds versus experts, 472: In China, term describing Mao Zedong's policy favoring politically indoctrinated party cadres (Reds) over those people who had economic training (experts)

referendum, 168, 168–169: A national vote called by a government to address a specific proposal, often a change to the constitution
in France, 169, 270, 274
in Germany, 308
in South Africa, 639
in United States, 168, 246

Reform Act (1832), 209

reform and opening (of China), 445, 447, 452–453, 454, 474, 476: In China, Deng Xiaoping's economic liberalization policy, starting in the late 1970s

Reformasi movement, 143–144
refugees, Syrian, 4, 312, 313–314, 320

regime, 29, 32, *32,* 50, 359, 698. *See also* political regimes. The fundamental rules and norms of politics, embodying long-term goals regarding individual freedom and collective equality, where power should reside, and the use of that power

regulation, 93: A rule or an order that sets the boundaries of a given procedure
  economic, 93
  in liberalism, 95, 96
  social, 93
  in social democracy, 97
  on trade, 93–94
    nontariff, **94,** 100, 102

reich, 295: The German term for "empire"
  Second Reich, 296
  Third Reich, **298,** 298–299, 300

Reichsrat, 297
Reichstag, 296, 297, 298

Reign of Terror, 127, **264**: Seizure of power and class war launched by radical Jacobins in revolutionary France (1793–94)

relations of production, 387

relative deprivation model, 124, 126, 130: Model that predicts revolution when public expectations outpace the rate of domestic change

religion, 74–76. *See also specific religions.*
  in Brazil, *284,* 619, 620, *620,* 621
  and charismatic legitimacy, 40
  in China, 394, 407, 467, 469, *470*
  in communist countries, 394, 395, 407
  and democratization, 151, 152
  and ethnic identity, 56–57
  in France, 282, *283,* 283–286
    compared to other countries, *284*
    Islam, 263, 273, 282, 284–286, *285,* 289
  fundamentalism in, **75,** 75–76, 375
  in Germany, 300, 314, 315, *316*
    compared to other countries, *284*
    Islam, 312, 316, 319, *320*
    and political parties, 308–309
  of immigrant population, 193–194, 257
  in imperialism, 486, 489
  in India, 78–79, 411, 511, 513–514, 518, 525, *530,* 530–531
    and civil society, 529
    and communism, 411
    compared to other countries, *284*
    Hindu. *See* Hindus in India
    Islam. *See* Islam, in India
    and local governments, 524
    and parliamentary elections, 53
  in Iran, 541, 543, 550, *560*
    and alcohol and drug use, 566–567
    and civil society, 558–559
    and ideology, 561, 562
    Islam. *See* Islam, in Iran
  in Japan, *284,* 329, *346,* 347
  in Mexico, *284,* 574, *591*
  and morality, *284*
  in Nigeria, 665–666, *686*
    Christianity. *See* Christianity, in Nigeria
    in civil society, 682–684
    compared to other countries, *284*
    of heads of government, *674*
    Islam. *See* Islam, in Nigeria
    and regional divisions, 685
    and violence, 685
    and zoning system, 676
  in Pakistan, 25, 48, 516, 530
  and political culture, 76–77
  in postcommunist countries, 407, 408, 409
  in post-imperialism, 496–497
  and postmodern values, 192
  privatization of, 74
  reemergence in politics, 15, 75
  and rise of modern state, 35, 37
  in Russia and Soviet Union, *284,* 394, 420, 434, 435, *435*
  in South Africa, *284,* 632, 650, *651*
  in theocracy, 372, 375
  in United Kingdom, 206, 218, 223, 224, *225,* 284
    Islam in, 218, 224, 225, 285
  in United States, 233, *251,* 253, *284*
  and violence, 76, 121, 130, 132, 133–136, 137
renewable energy, *319*
  in China, *319,* 477
  in Germany, 318, *319*

rent seeking, 368, 493, 498: A process in which political leaders essentially rent out parts of the state to their patrons, who as a result control public goods that would otherwise be distributed in a nonpolitical manner

Reporters without Borders, 435, 559

republicanism, 147, 701: Indirect democracy that emphasizes the separation of powers within a state and the representation of the public through elected officials
  in Brazil, 606–607
  in France, 283
  in Iran, 546, 548, 551

Republican Party (France), *275,* 276, **278,** 279, *280*: The main party of the French right, and a renaming of the Union for a Popular Movement

Republican Party (United States), 246, 247–248, 255
  in Civil War era, 238
  election results, *245*
  and political polarization, 257–258

Republic of Biafra, 668: Igbo-dominated Eastern Region that tried, and failed, to secede from Nigeria in 1967

separation of powers, 147, 148, 158: The clear division of power among different branches of government and the provision that specific branches may check the power of other branches
    in Brazil, 610
    in postcommunist countries, 398
    in presidential systems, 157, 159
    in United States, **240,** 240–241, 253

Sepoy Mutiny, 515: Failed 1857–58 revolt against the British in India, sponsored by the Indian aristocracy and carried out by sepoys, who were Indian soldiers employed by the British

September 11, 2001, terrorism attacks, 17, 134, 136, 257, 440
Serbia, 399, *400*
serfs in Russia, emancipation of, 422
service sector
    in China, 474
    in developed democracies, 178, 179, *180,* 195
    in Nigeria, 688
    in United Kingdom, 227
sexuality, in communism, 395
sexual orientation, 226, 409–410
    and LGBTQ issues, 408, 409–410, 429, 432
    rights associated with, 172, 220, 224, 409
    and same-sex marriage/partnerships, 192, 226, 409
sexual violence
    in India, 521, 529, 537–538
    in South Africa, 658
    in United States, 538
Shagari, Shehu, 670, *674*
Shang dynasty, 447
Shanghai, *444,* 474

Sharia, 667: System of Islamic law
    in Iran, 554
    in Nigeria, **667,** 675, 676, 685, 689

Sharif, Nawaz, 25, 26
Sharpeville Massacre (1960), 652
Shekau, Abubakar, 689, *690*
Shell Oil Company, 670

Shiism, 369, 496, **543**: Minority sect of Islam that differs from Sunnism over the rightful heir and proper descendants of the prophet Muhammad
    Christianity compared to, 544
    in Iran, **543,** 544, 547, 549, 559, 560, 561
    in Iraq, 550
    Sunni Islam compared to, 544

Shining Path, 132
Shintoism, 329

shock therapy, 404, 437: A process of rapid marketization

shogun, 328: A dominant lord in feudal Japan

Shonekan, Ernest, *674*
Siberia, 435

Sikhism, 514: Indian religious tradition combining elements of Hindu and Muslim beliefs

Sikhs in India, 78, 513, 514, 517, 519, 524, 527, 529

siloviki, **419,** 438, 439: In Russia, "men of power" who have their origins in the security agencies and are close to President Vladimir Putin

Silva, Marina, 619
Singapore, 96, 170, 362

Singh, Manmohan, 519: Indian National Congress prime minister of India, 2004–14

single-member district (SMD), 162, 162–164, 166–168, 182: An electoral district with one seat
    in France, 273–274
    in Germany, 306, 307
    in India, 523
    in Iran, 554–555
    in Japan, 337
    in Mexico, 580
    in Nigeria, 676–677
    in Russia, 430
    in United Kingdom, 216, 217
    in United States, 244

single-transferable vote in Northern Ireland, 217
Sinn Féin, 163, *163,* 221, *222,* 231
Skocpol, Theda, 124–125
slavery
    in Brazil, 57, 489, 604, 606
    Nigeria as source of slaves in, 666
    in South Africa, 631, 632
    in United States, 235, 238
Slavic peoples, 435
Slovakia, 399, *400, 410*
Slovenia
    economic indicators in, *405*
    gender equality in, *410*
    political transitions in, postcommunist, 399, *400, 401*
    societal globalization and trust in, 711, *712*
Smith, Adam, 95–96, 101
snap elections
    in South Africa, 639
    in United Kingdom, 210, 220
social contract, 12, 33

social democracy (socialism), 70, 73, 389: (1) A political-economic system in which freedom and equality are balanced through the state's management of the economy and the provision of social expenditures; (2) a political ideology that advocates such a system
    in Bolivarian socialism, 83–85
    in Brazil, 616, 618
    in developed democracies, 182, 183, *183*
    in France, 276, 286–287, 290
    in Germany, 97, 293, 300, 317
    Gini index in, 104, 394

Sotho, 631
South Africa, 629–661
   apartheid in. *See* apartheid in South Africa
   branches of government in, 638–640
   charismatic leadership in, 41
   citizenship in, 60, 634, 646, 650
   civil rights and liberties in, 30, 172, 633, 634, 637–638,
      648–649, 653
   civil society in, 379, 647–649
   constitution of, 637–638, 640, 641, 650
   corruption in, *494, 626,* 631, 658–660
      under Zuma, *628,* 643, *643,* 644, 658, *659,* 659–660
   crime in, 658–660
   Dutch in, 499, 631–632
   economic decline in, 657–658
   economic growth in, 498, 636, 655
   economic inequality in, *103,* 499–500, 634, 649, 653,
      655–656, *657*
   economic liberalization in, *110*
   elections in, 164, 165, *165,* 639, 642–647
   electoral system in, 164, 165, *165,* 640–641, *652*
   essential political features in, 638
   ethnic and national identity in, 59–60, 649, 650–651,
      651
   fear about foreign influence in, *533*
   gender equality in, *105, 410,* 642
   Gini index on, *103,* 657
   gross domestic product of, *103, 180, 256*
   happiness in, *108*
   historical development of state, 631–637
   HIV/AIDS in, 631, 643, 647–648, 660
   homelands policy in, 60, 634, 646, 650
   ideology and political culture in, 651–653
   immigration from, 656
   importance of democracy and economy in, *684*
   judiciary in, 640, *652*
   labor force in, 648, *653,* 654
   legislature in, 629, 638, 639, 640
      election to, 164, *165,* 640–641, 644, 645, 646, *647*
      trust in, *652*
   local government in, 641–642, 644, 645
   map of, *630*
   miner protests in, 657, *658*
   morality in, *284*
   national priorities in, *439*
   natural resources of, 632, 653, 654
   political conflict and competition in, 642–649
   political economy of, 474, 499–500, 653–658
   political institutions in, 637–638, 640, 651, *652*
   political parties in, 636, 639, 642–647, *647*
      in electoral system, 164, *165,* 640–641
      in local government, 641–642, 644, 645
      trust in, *652*
   political regime in, 30–31, 124, 637–642
   political violence in, 129, 379, 603, 631, 652
   president of, 638–639, *652*
   regime change in, 30–31, 124

religion in, *284,* 632, 650, *651*
renewable energy in, *319*
revolution in, 124
societal globalization and trust in, *713*
society in, 649–653
state control in, *465*
structure of government in, *639*
taxation in, *256,* 641, 655
timeline of political development in, *633*
wealth measures in, *103,* 104, *105*
and Zimbabwe compared, 129, 148, 378–379, 500
South African Communist Party, 499, 635, 636, 642, 648,
   652, 655
South African Party (SAP), 633
South America. *See also specific countries.*
   developed democracies in, *179*
   developing countries in, *485*
   imperialism and colonialism in, 487
   origins of political organization in, 34
   rise of modern state in, 38
Southeast Asia, 208, 284
South Korea
   agriculture in, *180,* 507
   challenges in comparative research on, 9
   corruption in, *494*
   economic growth in, 484, 498
   economic liberalization in, *110*
   export-oriented industrialization in, 498
   gross domestic product of, *91, 103, 180,* 506
   happiness in, *108,* 109
   and Japan relations, 352
   mercantilism in, 100
   military rule in, 372
   societal globalization and trust in, *712*
   taxation in, *91*
   wealth measures in, *103, 105,* 106
South Sudan, *46–47,* 63, 497, 709

sovereignty, 27, 27–28: The ability of a state to carry out
actions or policies within a territory independently from
external actors or internal rivals
   and autonomy, 45
   in developed democracies, 177, 185–191, 200
   in developing countries, 486, 488, 490, 495, 501
   in globalization, 699–700, 701, 705, 709–710
   in mercantilism, 99
   and national identity, 59, 61, 63, 64
   of nation-states, 63
   and political violence, 119

soviets, 422: In Russia, name given to workers' councils
that sprang up in 1917

Soviet Union, 422–425
   and Afghanistan, 396, 402, 408–409, 440
   authoritarianism in, 360
   central planning in, 393, 423
   and China compared, 412–413

special economic zones, 473: Enclaves established since 1980 by the Chinese government that have offered tax breaks and other incentives to lure foreign investment

state, 25–51: (1) The organization that maintains a monopoly of force over a given territory; (2) a set of political institutions to generate and execute policy regarding freedom and equality

state-sponsored terrorism, 48, **128,** *129*: Terrorism supported directly by a state as an instrument of foreign policy

Tea Party, 248: A reactionary, but diffuse, group within the U.S. Republican Party that emerged in 2009; its adherents generally favor low taxes, small government, and socially conservative policies

Televisa, 589: Mexico's largest media conglomerate, which for decades enjoyed a close relationship with the PRI

Temer, Michel, 601, *611,* 618: Brazil's conservative president, and vice-president under Dilma Rousseff, who ascended to the presidency after the impeachment of Rousseff

terrorism, 15, 117, 118, 122–123, 127–133, 191: The use of violence by nonstate actors against civilians in order to achieve a political goal

Thatcher, Margaret, 43, **205,** 209–210: Conservative prime minister of the United Kingdom from 1979 to 1990

the Events of May, 267: Parisian riots of 1968 in which students and workers called for educational and social reforms in France

the Greens, 311: Germany's environmental party

the Left, 311: The party farthest to the left of all Germany's major parties; an alliance of leftist Social Democrats and remnants of former East German Communists

theocracy, 75, 118, 370, 372, 375–376, **541**: Rule by religion or religious leaders

theory, 10, 14–15: An integrated set of hypotheses, assumptions, and facts

The Troubles, 224: Name given to the three decades of extreme ethnic conflict (late 1960s to late 1990s) between Northern Ireland's nationalists or republicans, who are mostly Catholic, and unionists or loyalists, who are mostly Protestant

Third Reich, 298, 298–299, 300: The name Adolf Hitler gave to his fascist totalitarian regime (1933–45)

Third Republic (France), 266

Third Republic (Nigeria), 670: In Nigeria, democratic regime proposed by General Ibrahim Babangida in 1993; precluded by General Sani Abacha's military coup in the same year, following annulled elections

Third Way, 205, 219, 226: In the United Kingdom, term describing recent policies of the Labour Party that embrace the free market

Third World, 178, 179, 483
Thirty Years' War, 37

Three Represents, 462: Jiang Zemin's 2001 policy co-opting private entrepreneurs into the Chinese Communist Party

Tiananmen Square, 69, 398, 412, 413, **453,** 462, 465, 471, 478: Historic plaza in Beijing where the Chinese party-state crushed the 1989 pro-reform demonstration

Tibet, 467, 468
Tilly, Charles, 35
tobacco, 491
Tocqueville, Alexis de, 134, 150, 250, 252, 280, 396
Togo, *108*
Tōhoku earthquake in Japan (2011), 350–351, *351*

Tokugawa, 328, 328–329: The military clan that unified and ruled Japan from the seventeenth to the nineteenth centuries

Tokyo, 351
Toltecs, 571
Tories, **205**. *See also* Conservative Party

totalitarianism, 359, 359–361: A nondemocratic regime that is highly centralized, possessing some form of strong ideology that seeks to transform and absorb fundamental aspects of state, society, and the economy, using a wide array of institutions
    authoritarianism compared to, 359, 360
    in China, 360
    in Germany, 298–299, 360
    in Iran, 376
    one-party rule in, 374
    political control in, 366, 368
    in Soviet Union, 359–360, 366–367, 423

trade, 93–94
    of Asia and Latin America compared, 506–507
    of Brazil, 604, 606, 607, 622
    of China, 441, 447, 456, 475, 506, 694
    in communism, 99
    comparative advantage in, **94**
    in export-oriented imperialism, 491
    in export-oriented industrialization, 498–499, 501, 504
    in Fair Trade, *480,* 481–483, 505, 508

    of France, 279
    GATT on, 593, 702
    of Germany, 318
    globalization of, 114, 696–697, 702–705, 709, 710, 716
    in imperialism and colonialism, 491
    in import substitution, 498, 499, 501. *See also* import substitution
    of India, 514, 515, 525, 533
    of Iran, 546, 566
    of Japan, 330, 348–349
    of Latin America, 112, 481, 482, 498, 499, 506, 507
    in mercantilism, 99–102
    of Mexico, 180–181, 590, 592, 593, 594–595, 704–705
    NAFTA on, 181, 189, 575, 593, 594–595, 596, 704–705, 716
    of Nigeria, 663, 666, 667, 687
    oil and gas exports in, 88–89
    and origins of political organization, 34
    in post-imperialism, 498–499
    and rise of modern state, 35, 37
    of Russia, 439
    of South Africa, 499, 653, 654, 655, 657
        embargoes in, 635, 636
    tariffs in. *See* tariffs
    Trans-Pacific Partnership (TPP) in, **705,** 716
    of United Kingdom, 230
    of United States, 94, 236, 704–705, 716

Trades Union Congress (TUC), 223: The United Kingdom's largest trade union confederation

trade unions. *See* labor unions

traditional legitimacy, 40, 41, 42: Legitimacy that accepts aspects of politics because they have been institutionalized over a long period of time

traditional values, 77, 80, *80*

Trans-Pacific Partnership (TPP), 705, 716: Proposed agreement among twelve countries to liberalize trade though reduced tariffs and common regulations; abandoned by the United States in 2017

Transparency International, 198, 700
transportation systems
    as public good, 88, 90
    in rise of modern state, 34
    social expenditures on, 90
    state regulation of, 93
Transvaal, 632
Treatment Action Campaign (TAC), 647–648
Tribunal Superior Electoral (Brazil), 613
Trinidad and Tobago, *713*
Triple Alliance, 648

Trump, Donald, 21: The current president of the United States, elected in 2016
    economic policies of, 100, 255, 705
    election of, 245, *245,* 248, *249,* 251, 252, 255

immigration policy of, 257
wall proposal of, 599

trust of other nationalities, societal globalization affecting, 711, *712–713*

Truth and Reconciliation Commission (South Africa), 652, 652-653: The post-apartheid body established in South Africa to document apartheid-era human rights abuses and to give reparations to victims and amnesty to perpetrators who confessed to crimes

Truth Commission (Brazil), 615

tsar, 420, 426: Russian word for emperor (also *czar*, from Latin *Caesar*)

tsunami and earthquake damage in Japan (2011), 325, 336, **339,** 344, 346, 350–351, *351*
Tudeh Party, 548
tulip bubble, 714
Tunisia, 4, 20, 118
   Arab Spring in, 138, 139
Turkey, 560
   illiberal regime in, 376
   immigrants in Germany from, 315, 319, 320
   societal globalization and trust in, *713*
   taxation and GDP in, *91*
Turkmenistan, *400*
The Turner Diaries (Pierce), 135
Tutsi, 57

Tutu, Archbishop Desmond, 652: The anti-apartheid activist and leader of South Africa's Anglican Church who chaired the Truth and Reconciliation Commission

twisted Diet, 335, 335–336, 342: Situation in which no party or coalition of parties controls both chambers of the Japanese parliament; common since 2007

Twitter, *249,* 559, 590, 713
two-and-a-half party system, 219
tyranny, 358

ubuntu, 653
Uganda, *480,* 482
Uighurs, 467, 468
Ukraine
   downing Malaysia Airlines Flight 17 in, *382,* 435
   economic transitions in, postcommunist, 405, *405*
   ethnic divisions in, 408, 409
   and Eurasian Economic Union, 441
   and Europe, 384
   and European Union, 441
   gender equality in, *410*
   political culture in, 77
   political transitions in, postcommunist, *400, 401*
   and Russia, *382,* 383–384, 406, 419, 429, 437
      media reports on, 434–435
   societal globalization and trust in, *713*
   societal transitions in, postcommunist, 408, 409

ulema, 544, 548, 551, 552
Ulster, 224
Ulyanov, Vladimir Ilyich, 391. *See also* Lenin
unemployment
   in Brazil, 621, 622, *623,* 624
   in China, 406, 474
   in France, 261, 276, *282, 287,* 288, 290
   in Germany, 318
   in Greece, 198
   in India, 536
   in Iran, 564
   in Japan, 325, 348
   Marxist theory on, 388
   in Nigeria, 681, 687
   in South Africa, 500, 648, 653, 655, 656, 658
   in United Kingdom, 227

unicameral system, 153, 182: A political system in which the legislature comprises one house
   in Brazil, 614
   in China, 458, 459–460
   in Germany, 308
   in Iran, 553–554
   in Mexico, 580
   in United States, 236

Union Carbide, 529

Union for a Popular Movement (UMP), 275, 278, *280*: A single cohesive party of the French center right formed in 2002 with Jacques Chirac's encouragement, which has since been renamed the Republicans

Union for French Democracy (UDF), 278: An alliance of five French center-right parties founded in 1978 by Jacques Chirac's rival and former president Valéry Giscard d'Estaing as a more neoliberal force of the French right

Union of South Africa, 632: The 1910 name given to the British colony that integrated British and Afrikaner colonists after the Boer Wars

Union of Soviet Socialist Republics (USSR), 422. *See also* Soviet Union

unitary state, 42, 42–43: A state in which most political power exists at the national level, with limited local authority
   China as, 42
   France as, 42, 274
   Japan as, 42
   Ukraine as, 384
   United Kingdom as, 43, 217

United Arab Emirates, 96

United Democratic Front (UDF), 636: The unified anti-apartheid coalition in South Africa created in 1983 from the major black and white opposition groups

United East India Company, 491
United Kingdom, 203–231
    and Afghanistan, 440, 545
    branches of government in, 212–216
    Celtic fringe of, **205**
    in Central Asia, 440
    centralization of power in, 43
    civil society in, 222–223
    class identity in, 223–224
    coalition governments in, 205, 210, 213, 214, 220–221, 227, *228*
    corruption in, *494, 626*
    counterterrorism measures in, 137, 140
    currency in, 188
    democratization in, 203, 209
    as developed democracy, *174,* 175–177, *180,* 182, *183*
    devolution in, 43, 44, 190, 191, 210, 217, 218, 225, 226, 228
    economic inequality in, *103, 183,* 223–224, 227, *657*
    economic liberalization in, *110*
    elections in. *See* elections, in United Kingdom
    electoral system in, 162, *163,* 163–164, 166–167, 182, 216–217, *217,* 222
    essential political features in, 211
    ethnic and national identity in, 59, 210, 223, 224–225, *225*
    in European Union, 205, 211, 219, 227–228, *229,* 699
        Brexit vote on. *See* Brexit
    fear about foreign influence in, *533*
    and France relations, 265
    gender equality in, *105,* 106, *409, 410*
    and Germany relations, 299
    Gini index on, *103, 183, 657*
    gross domestic product of, *91, 103, 180, 183,* 226–227, *256*
    happiness in, *108*
    historical development of state, 205–210
    ideology and political culture in, 225–226
    immigration to, 192, 224–225, 226, 230
    and India, 545
    industrialization of, 203
    Internet use in, *589*
    and Iran, 545, 546, 547, 548, 566
    in Iraq War, 213, 214
    judiciary in, 215–216
    labor force in, *227*
    legislature in, 153, 206, 214–215
    liberalism in, 73, 96, 99
    local and regional government in, 43, 217–218, 225, 228
    map of, *204*
    monarchy in, 41, 203, 205, 206–208, 211, 212, 213
    morality in, *284*
    national priorities in, *439*
    official name of, **205**
    oil industry in, 88, 89
    parliamentary system in, 206, 211–217
    political conflict and competition in, 218–223

    political economy of, *183,* 226–228
    political ideologies in, 73
    political institutions in, 211–212
    political parties in, 209, 212, 214, 218–222
        and civil society, 222–223
        in electoral system, 216–217, *217,* 222
        in House of Commons, *163,* 222
    political regime in, 211–218
    prime ministers in, **208,** 212–213, 214
    public debt in, 196
    religion in, 206, 218, 223, 224, *225*
        compared to other countries, *284*
        Islam in, 218, 224, 225, 285
    renewable energy in, *319*
    Scottish bid for independence from, 59, 203, 210, 216, 218, 225, 228–229, *230,* 231
    society in, 223–226
    and South Africa relations, 636
    state control in, *465*
    structure of government in, *215*
    taxation in, *91, 183,* 209, 218, *256*
    timeline of political development in, *207*
    as unitary state, 43, 217
    unwritten constitution of, 203, 211–212
    wealth measures in, *103, 105,* 106

United Kingdom Independence Party (UKIP), 164, **216,** 219, 220, 221: Populist and Euroskeptic political party favoring British exit from the European Union
    and Brexit vote, *174,* 176, 231
    Farage as leader of, *174,* 176, 221
    in House of Commons, *163,* 166, 167, 221
    immigration concerns of, 194, 221, 225

United Kingdom of Great Britain and Northern Ireland, 205: Official name of the British state

United Nations, 567
    condemning apartheid, 635
    in developing countries, 495
    Development Program, 105–106, 112
    Gender Inequality Index, 409–410, *410*
    and globalization, 698, 699
    Human Development Index, **105,** 178. *See also* Human Development Index
    as intergovernmental system, 186
    Millennium Development Goals, 505
United Progressive Alliance (UPA), *528*

United Russia, 431, 431–432: Main political party in Russia and supporter of Vladimir Putin

United States, 11–12, 233–259
    and Afghanistan, 440
    aging population in, 200
    alcohol consumption in, 567
    American Revolution in, 63–64, **236,** 253, 283
    border with Mexico, 257, 597, 598, 599
    branches of government in, 241–244

work unit system, **454,** 470
World Bank, 104, 178, 447, 484, 644
  in developing countries, 495, 499, 503
  in economic globalization, 702, 714
  in Nigeria, 670
World Cup, Brazil hosting, 601, 603, 617, *619,* 625
World Health Organization, 567, 690
World Trade Center, terrorist attack on, 17
World Trade Organization (WTO), 456, 473–474, 698, 702
World Values Survey, 77, 80, 192, 711
  Inglehart map of, *80*
  in postcommunist countries, 407, 409
  in Russia, 436–437
World War I
  and France, 266
  and Germany, 296, 298
  and Japan, 330
  and Russia, 126
  and United Kingdom, 208, 209
  and United States, 239
World War II, 30, 95
  and Brazil, 607
  and Bretton Woods system, 702
  and European Union, 185
  and France, 266
  and Germany, 39, 151, 266, 293, 299–301, 315, 317, 364, 402
  and Greece, 198
  and import substitution policies, 498
  and India, 516
  and Iran, 547
  and Japan, 100, 101, 151, 323, 325, 331–332, 342, 350, 351–352, 364
  and Mexico, 598
  and Nigeria, 667
  and post-imperialism, 492
  and reactionary, 68
  and Syria, 117
  and Ukraine, 383
  and United Kingdom, 203, 208, 209, 218, 226
  and United States, 331–332, 598
World Wildlife Fund, 701
Wyoming, 237

xenophobia, 68, 193
  in China, 471
  in France, 278, 279
  in Germany, 403
  in Japan, 329
  in Mexico, 592
  in Russia, 433
  in United Kingdom, 225
Xhosa, 632, 646, 652

Xi Jinping, 456, **457,** 458, *458,* 459, 463, *463*: China's paramount leader, serving simultaneously as head of the party (Chinese Communist Party general secretary), head of

the state (president of the People's Republic of China), and head of the military (Central Military Commission chair)
  anticorruption campaign of, 478
  and Chinese Dream, 457
  as elitist, 476
  personality cult of, 369

Xinjiang province of China, 467, 468

Yabloko, 433: Small party in Russia that advocates democracy and a liberal political economic system

Yanukovych, Viktor, 384
Yar'Adua, Umaru, 673, *674,* 676, 679–680, 683

Yasukuni Shrine, 342, *344*: The controversial Shinto shrine honoring Japan's war dead

Yeltsin, Boris, 424, 424–425: President of Russia from 1991 to 1999
  civil society under, 434, 435
  constitution under, 426
  economic policies of, 438
  legislature under, 426, 428
  media controlled by, 434
  party system under, 431
  semi-presidential system under, 426

Yemen, *2, 46–47*

Yoruba, 665, 666, *674*: Ethnic group largely confined to southwest Nigeria whose members are divided among Christian, Muslim, and local animist faiths
  ethnic and national identity of, 685
  political party of, 667, 679
  regional division of, 672

Youth Development Foundation, 464
YouTube, 139, 559
Yuan dynasty, 448
Yucatán, 584
Yudhoyono, Susilo Bambang, 144
Yugoslavia, 64, 408, 700
Yunus, Muhammad, 505

zaibatsu, 330, 331
Zaire, 371

Zapata, Emiliano, 573, 573–574: Southern Mexican peasant leader of the revolution most associated with radical land reform

Zapatista Army of National Liberation (EZLN), 590: Largely Mayan rebel group that staged an uprising in Mexico in 1994, demanding political reform and greater rights for Mexico's indigenous people

Zedillo, Ernesto, 590, 596
Zhirinovsky, Vladimir, 433
Zika virus, 603
Zille, Helen, 641, 645

Web Links

UNITED KINGDOM

- BritainUSA, website of the British government in the United States (www.gov.uk /government/world/usa)
- British Broadcasting Corporation (www.bbc.com)
- British Politics Group (http://britishpoliticsgroup.blogspot.com)
- British Prime Minister (www.gov.uk/government/organisations/prime-ministers-office -10-downing-street)
- Conflict Archive on the Internet, on conflict and politics in Northern Ireland, 1968 to the present (www.cain.ulst.ac.uk)
- Foreign and Commonwealth Office (www.fco.gov.uk)
- London University, on constitutional reform (www.ucl.ac.uk/constitution-unit)
- Parliament (www.parliament.uk)
- Scottish Parliament (www.scottish.parliament.uk)
- Welsh Assembly (www.wales.gov.uk)

UNITED STATES

- C-SPAN, public-service media outlet focused on U.S. politics (www.c-span.org)
- Library of Congress (www.loc.gov)
- National Archives, repository for government documents (www.archives.gov)
- Project Vote Smart, website on elections, elected officials, and candidates (www.votesmart.org)
- Real Clear Politics, an aggregator of political news and blogs (www.realclearpolitics.com)
- Roll Call, website focused on Congress (www.rollcall.com)

FRANCE

- Assemblée nationale (www.assemblee-nat.fr)
- Constitutional Council (www.conseil-constitutionnel.fr)
- *Le Monde diplomatique* (www.mondediplo.com)
- Ministry of Foreign Affairs (www.diplomatie.gouv.fr/en)
- President's website (www.elysee.fr/)
- Prime minister's website (premier-ministre.gouv.fr/en)

GERMANY

- Germany's Basic Law, online version (www.constitution.org/cons/germany.txt)
- Germany's Christian Democratic Party (www.cducsu.de)
- Germany's Free Democratic Party (www.fdp-fraktion.de)
- Germany's Green Party (www.gruene-bundestag.de)
- Germany's Left Party (www.linksfraktion.de)
- Germany's legislature (www.bundestag.de)
- Germany's Social Democratic Party (www.spd.de/)
- Information about Germany, a one-stop portal (www.deutschland.de/)
- Spiegel Online International (www.spiegel.de/international/)

JAPAN

- Japanese constitution (http://japan.kantei.go.jp/constitution_and_government_of_japan/constitution_e.html)
- Japanese prime minister and cabinet (http://japan.kantei.go.jp/index.html)
- Japanese Statistical Data; provides regularly updated statistical information in 19 different categories, including demographic, geographic, and economic data (http://www.stat.go.jp/english/)
- National Diet of Japan; links to House of Councillors and House of Representatives that provide extensive information on membership, relative strength of parties, and electoral and legislative procedures (http://www.sangiin.go.jp/eng/; http://www.shugiin.go.jp/internet/index.nsf/html/index_e.htm)

RUSSIA

- Carnegie Endowment for International Peace, Russian and Eurasian Program (www.carnegieendowment.org)
- *Moscow Times* (www.moscowtimes.ru)
- Radio Free Europe/Radio Liberty (www.rferl.org)
- Russia Today (http://rt.com/)
- Transitions Online (www.tol.org)

CHINA

- China general information: an unofficial site offering useful general information (www.chinatoday.com/general/a.htm)
- China's political system: this official government site describes the political structure, fundamental laws, rules, regulations, and practices of China since its founding (www.china.org.cn/english/Political/25060.htm).
- A Country Study, China: this Library of Congress Country Studies Series presents a description and analysis of the historical setting and the social, economic, political, and national security systems of China (lcweb2.loc.gov/frd/cs/cntoc.html).

INDIA

- GOI directory of Indian government websites (http://goidirectory.nic.in)
- Government and politics of South Asia, South and Southeast Asian Studies, Columbia University Libraries (www.columbia.edu/cu/lweb/indiv/southasia/cuvl/govt.html)
- *Outlook*, a popular weekly newsmagazine (http://outlookindia.com)
- Parliament (http://parliamentofindia.nic.in)
- *Times of India* (http://timesofindia.indiatimes.com)

IRAN

- The Iran Primer (http://iranprimer.usip.org/)
- Islamic Republic News Agency (www.irna.com/en)
- Ministry of Foreign Affairs, Islamic Republic of Iran (www.mfa.gov.ir)
- Press TV (www.presstv.ir/)
- Website of President Hassan Rouhani (president.ir)
- Website of the Supreme Leader Ayatollah Khamenei (www.leader.ir)

MEXICO

- *El Universal*, a Mexican daily newspaper (www.eluniversal.com.mx/english)
- *La Jornada*, a Mexican daily newspaper (www.jornada.unam.mx)
- Latin American Network Information Center, Mexico, an encyclopedic collection of links maintained by the University of Texas, Austin (www.lanic.utexas.edu/la/mexico)
- Mexican government offices and agencies (www.mexonline.com/mexagncy.htm)
- *Reforma*, a Mexican daily newspaper (www.reforma.com)

BRAZIL

- IESP-UERJ—Instituto de Estudos Sociais e Politicos, Instituto Universitário de Pesquisas do Rio de Janeiro—an excellent source of online data (http://www.iesp.uerj.br/welcome -to-iesp-uerj/)
- Landless Workers Movement (www.mst.org.br)
- Latin American Network Information Center, an encyclopedic collection of links maintained by the University of Texas, Austin (lanic.utexas.edu/la/brazil)
- Links to major Brazilian periodicals (newslink.org/sabra.html)
- The Workers' Party (www.pt.org.br)

SOUTH AFRICA

- African National Congress (www.anc.org.za)
- African Studies Internet Resources: South Africa, Columbia University Libraries (www.columbia.edu/cu/lweb/indiv/africa/cuvl/SAfr.html)
- Afrobarometer (www.afrobarometer.org)
- Democratic Alliance (www.da.org.za)
- Inkatha Freedom Party (www.ifp.org.za)
- *Mail and Guardian* (www.mg.co.za)
- South African Broadcasting Corporation (www.sabcnews.co.za/portal/site/SABCNews/)
- South African government (www.gov.za)

NIGERIA

- African Studies Internet Resources: Columbia University Libraries (http://library.columbia.edu/locations/global/africa.html)
- Economic and Financial Crimes Commission (www.efccnigeria.org)
- *Guardian* (Nigeria) (www.ngrguardiannews.com)
- *IRIN* News.org, a service of the UN Office for the Coordination of Humanitarian Affairs (www.irinnews.org)
- Niger Delta Development Commission (http://nddc.gov.ng/)
- Nigeria Direct: Official Government Gateway (www.nigeria.gov.ng)

For Further Reading

CHAPTER 1

Aristotle. *The Politics*, trans. T. A. Sinclair (New York: Viking, 1992).

Brady, Henry, and David Collier, eds. *Rethinking Social Inquiry: Diverse Tools, Shared Standards*, 2nd ed. (Lanham, MD: Rowman & Littlefield, 2010).

Goodin, Robert E., ed. *The Oxford Handbook of Political Science* (Oxford: Oxford University Press, 2009).

Kahneman, Daniel. *Thinking, Fast and Slow* (New York: Farrar, Straus and Giroux, 2013).

King, Gary, Robert O. Keohane, and Sidney Verba. *Designing Social Inquiry: Scientific Inference in Qualitative Research* (Princeton, NJ: Princeton University Press, 1994).

Machiavelli, Niccolò. *The Prince*, trans. W. K. Marriott (New York: Knopf, 1992).

Munck, Gerardo L., and Richard Snyder. *Passion, Craft and Method in Comparative Politics* (Baltimore, MD: Johns Hopkins University Press, 2007).

Tetlock, Philip E., and Dan Gardner. *Superforecasting: The Art and Science of Prediction* (New York: Crown, 2015).

CHAPTER 2

Brown, Archie. *The Myth of the Strong Leader: Political Leadership in the Modern Age* (New York: Basic Books, 2014).

Fukuyama, Francis. *The Origins of Political Order: From Prehuman Times to the French Revolution* (New York: Farrar, Straus and Giroux, 2011).

Gat, Azar. *War in Human Civilization* (New York: Oxford University Press, 2006).

Gilley, Bruce. *The Right to Rule: How States Win and Lose Legitimacy* (New York: Columbia University Press, 2009).

Landes, David. *The Wealth and Poverty of Nations: Why Some Are So Rich and Some So Poor* (New York: W. W. Norton, 1999).

Maddison, Angus. *Contours of the World Economy, 1–2030 AD* (New York: Oxford University Press, 2007).

Tilly, Charles. *Coercion, Capital, and European States: 990–1990* (Oxford, UK: Blackwell, 1990).

Weber, Max. "Politics as a Vocation." *Max Weber: Essays in Sociology*. H. H. Garth and C. Wright Mills, eds. and trans. (New York: Oxford University Press, 1958).

CHAPTER 3

Baldwin, Kate, and John D. Huber. "Economic vs. Cultural Differences: Forms of Ethnic Diversity and Public Goods Provision." *American Political Science Review* 104, no. 4 (2010).

Dalton, Russell J., and Christian Welzel, eds. *The Civic Culture Transformed: From Allegiant to Assertive Citizens*. (Cambridge: Cambridge University Press, 2014).

Fearon, James D., and David D. Laitin. "Ethnicity, Insurgency, and Civil War." *American Political Science Review* 97, no. 1 (2003): 75-90.

Harrison, Lawrence, and Evgeny Yasin. *Culture Matters in Russia—and Everywhere: Backdrop for the Russia–Ukraine Conflict* (Lanham, MD: Lexington Press, 2015).

Huntington, Samuel P. *The Clash of Civilizations and the Remaking of World Order* (New York: Simon & Schuster, 1996).

Lawrence, Bruce. *Defenders of God: The Fundamentalist Revolt against the Modern Age* (New York: Harper and Row, 1989).

Lipset, Seymour Martin, and Gary Marks. *It Didn't Happen Here: Why Socialism Failed in the United States* (New York: W. W. Norton, 2001).

Norris, Pippa, and Ronald Inglehart. *Sacred and Secular: Religion and Politics Worldwide* (New York: Cambridge University Press, 2004).

Stepan, Alfred, Juan Linz, and Yogendra Yadav. *Crafting State-Nations: India and Other Multinational Democracies* (Baltimore, MD: Johns Hopkins University Press, 2011).

Welzel, Christian. *Freedom Rising: Human Empowerment and the Quest for Emancipation* (Cambridge: Cambridge University Press, 2013).

CHAPTER 4

Bernstein, Eduard. *Evolutionary Socialism: A Criticism and Affirmation* (New York: Schocken, 1961).

Easterlin, Richard A. *Happiness, Growth, and the Life Cycle* (New York: Oxford University Press, 2011).

List, Friedrich. *The National System of Political Economy* (New York: Kelley, 1966).

Milanovic, Branko. *Global Inequality: A New Approach for the Age of Globalization* (Cambridge: Harvard University Press, 2016).

Milanovic, Branko. *The Haves and the Have-Nots: A Brief and Idiosyncratic History of Global Inequality* (New York: Basic Books, 2011).

Olson, Mancur. *The Logic of Collective Action: Public Goods and the Theory of Groups* (Cambridge, MA: Harvard University Press, 1965).

Piketty, Thomas. *Capital in the Twenty-First Century* (New York: Belknap Press, 2014).

Smith, Adam. *An Inquiry into the Nature and Causes of the Wealth of Nations*. Edwin Cannan, ed. (Chicago: Chicago University Press, 1976).

CHAPTER 5

Abrahms, Max. "The Political Effectiveness of Terrorism Revisited." *Comparative Political Studies* 45, no. 3 (2012): 366–93.

Boot, Max. *Invisible Armies: An Epic History of Guerrilla Warfare from Ancient Times to the Present* (New York: Norton, 2013).

Crenshaw, Martha. "The Causes of Terrorism." *Comparative Politics* 13, no. 4 (July 1981): 379–399.

Goldstone, Jack A. *Revolutions: A Very Short Introduction* (Oxford: Oxford University Press, 2014).

Juergensmeyer, Mark. *Terror in the Mind of God: The Global Rise of Religious Violence* (Berkeley: University of California Press, 2003).

Kuran, Timur. "Now Out of Never: The Element of Surprise in the East European Revolution of 1989." *World Politics* 44, no. 1 (October 1991): 7–48.

Skocpol, Theda. "France, Russia, China: A Structural Analysis of Social Revolutions." *Comparative Studies in Society and History* 18, no. 2 (April 1976): 175–210.

Tilly, Charles, and Sidney Tarrow. *Contentious Politics* (Boulder, CO: Paradigm Publishers, 2007).

Walt, Stephen M. *Revolution and War* (Ithaca, NY: Cornell University Press, 1996).

CHAPTER 6

Acemoglu, Daron, and James A. Robinson. *Economic Origins of Dictatorship and Democracy* (New York: Cambridge University Press, 2007).

Dalton, Russell J. *Citizen Politics: Public Opinion and Political Parties in Advanced Industrial Democracies* (Washington, DC: CQ Press, 2013).

de Tocqueville, Alexis. *Democracy in America*, vol. 2, Henry Reeve, trans. (New York: Henry G. Langley, 1845).

Diamond, Larry, and Marc F. Plattner. *Electoral Systems and Democracy* (Baltimore, MD: Johns Hopkins University Press, 2006).

Duverger, Maurice. *Political Parties: Their Organization and Activity in the Modern State* (New York: Wiley, 1964).

MacPherson, C. B. *The Life and Times of Liberal Democracy* (New York: Oxford University Press, 1977).

Nathan, Andrew J., Mark F. Plattner, and Larry Diamond, eds. *Will China Democratize?* (Baltimore, MD: Johns Hopkins University Press, 2013).

Schmitter, Philippe C., and Terry Lynn Karl. "What Democracy Is ... and Is Not" *Journal of Democracy* 2, no. 3 (1991): 75-88.

CHAPTER 7

Brym, Robert. "After Postmaterialism: An Essay on China, Russia and the United States." *Canadian Journal of Sociology* 41, no. 2 (2016): 1–18.

Crepaz, Markus. *Trust beyond Borders: Immigration, the Welfare State, and Identity in Modern Societies (*Ann Arbor: University of Michigan Press, 2007).

Dinan, Desmond. *Europe Recast: A History of the European Union* (Boulder, CO: Lynne Rienner Publishers, 2014).

Hemerijck, Anton. *Changing Welfare States* (Oxford: Oxford University Press, 2013).

Howard, Marc Morjé. *The Politics of Citizenship in Europe (*New York: Cambridge University Press, 2009).

Inglehart, Ronald. "After Postmaterialism: An Essay on China, Russia and the United States: A Comment." *Canadian Journal of Sociology* 41, no. 2 (2016): 213–22.

Mudde, Cas, and Cristóbal Rovira Kaltwasser. *Populism in Europe and the Americas: Threat or Corrective for Democracy?* (Cambridge, UK: Cambridge University Press, 2012).

Putnam, Robert D. "E Pluribus Unum: Diversity and Community in the Twenty-first Century." *Scandinavian Political Studies* 30, no. 2 (2007): 137–74.

Steinmo, Sven. *The Evolution of Modern States: Sweden, Japan and the United States.* (Cambridge, UK: Cambridge University Press, 2010).

CHAPTER 8

Arendt, Hannah. *Totalitarianism* (New York: Harcourt, Brace and World, 1951).

Diamond, Larry, Marc F. Plattner, and Christopher Walker, eds. *Authoritarianism Goes Global: The Challenge to Democracy* (Baltimore, MD: Johns Hopkins University Press, 2016).

Hamid, Shadi. *Temptations of Power: Islamists and Illiberal Democracy in a New Middle East* (New York: Oxford University Press, 2014).

Levitsky, Steven, and Lucan A. Way. "The Rise of Competitive Authoritarianism." *Journal of Democracy* 13, no. 2 (April 2002): 51-65.

Linz, Juan. *Totalitarian and Authoritarian Regimes* (Boulder, CO: Lynne Rienner, 2000).

Linz, Juan J., and Alfred Stepan. *Problems of Democratic Transition and Consolidation: Southern Europe, South America, and Post-Communist Europe* (Baltimore, MD: Johns Hopkins University Press, 1996).

Moffitt, Benjamin. *The Global Rise of Populism: Performance, Political Style, and Representation* (Stanford, CA: Stanford University Press, 2016).

Weinthal, Erika, and Pauline Jones Luong. "Combating the Resource Curse: An Alternative Solution to Managing Mineral Wealth." *Perspectives on Politics* 4, no. 1 (March 2008): 35–53.

CHAPTER 9

Bunce, Valerie, and Sharon Wolchik. *Defeating Authoritarian Leaders in Postcommunist Countries* (New York: Cambridge University Press, 2011).

Darden, Keith, and Anna Grzymala-Busse. "The Great Divide: Literacy, Nationalism, and the Communist Collapse." *World Politics* 59, no. 1 (October 2006): 83-115

Krastev, Ivan. "Paradoxes of the New Authoritarianism." *Journal of Democracy* 22, no. 2 (April 2011): 5-16

Lampton, David. *Following the Leader: Ruling China, from Deng Xiaoping to Xi Jinping* (Berkeley: University of California Press, 2014).

Marx, Karl, and Friedrich Engels. "Manifesto of the Communist Party." *Selected Works in Three Volumes*, vol. 1 (Moscow: Progress Publishers, 1969).

McAuley, Mary. *Soviet Politics 1917–1991* (New York: Oxford University Press, 1992).

Shambaugh, David. *China's Future* (New York: John Wiley & Sons, 2016).

Zimmerman, William. *Ruling Russia: Authoritarianism from the Revolution to Putin* (Princeton, NJ: Princeton University Press, 2014).

CHAPTER 10

Banerjee, Abhijit, and Esther Duflo. *Poor Economics: A Radical Rethinking of the Way to Fight Global Poverty* (New York: PublicAffairs, 2011).

Collier, Paul, and Jan Willem Gunning. "Why Has Africa Grown Slowly?" *Journal of Economic Perspectives* 13, no. 3 (Summer 1999).

Deaton, Angus. *The Great Escape: Health, Wealth, and the Origins of Inequality* (Princeton, NJ: Princeton University Press, 2013).

Easterly, William. *The Tyranny of Experts: Economists, Dictators, and the Forgotten Rights of the Poor* (New York: Basic Books, 2015).

Fukuyama, Francis. *State Building: Governance and World Order in the 21st Century* (Ithaca, NY: Cornell University Press, 2004).

Gann, L. H., and Peter Duignan, eds. *Imperialism in Africa, 1870–1960* (Cambridge, UK: Cambridge University Press, 1969-75).

Haggard, Stephan. *Pathways from the Periphery: The Politics of Growth in Newly Industrializing Countries* (Ithaca, NY: Cornell University Press, 1990).

Kohli, Atul. *State Directed Development: Political Power and Industrialization in the Global Periphery* (New York: Cambridge University Press, 2004).

CHAPTER 11

Bhagwati, Jagdish. *In Defense of Globalization* (Oxford, UK: Oxford University Press, 2007).

Collier, Paul. *Exodus: How Migration Is Changing Our World* (Oxford, UK: Oxford University Press, 2013).

Dryzek, John S. "Global Civil Society: The Progress of Post-Westphalian Politics." *Annual Review of Political Science* 15 (2012): 101-19.

Findlay, Ronald, and Kevin H. O'Rourke. *Power and Plenty: Trade, War, and the World Economy in the Second Millennium* (Princeton, NJ: Princeton University Press, 2007).

Ford, Martin. *Rise of the Robots: Technology and the Threat of a Jobless Future* (New York: Basic Books, 2015).

Keynes, John Maynard. *The Economic Consequences of the Peace* (New York: Harcourt, Brace and Howe, 1920).

Pieterse, Jan Nederveen. *Globalization and Culture: Global Mélange* (New York: Rowman & Littlefield, 2015).

Rodrik, Dani. *The Globalization Paradox: Democracy and the Future of the World Economy* (New York: Norton, 2011).

Credits